Japan

**Sapporo &
Hokkaidō**
p571

**Northern
Honshū
(Tōhoku)**
p501

**The Japan Alps &
Central Honshū**
p212

Kyoto
p297

**Hiroshima &
Western Honshū**
p434

**Mt Fuji &
Around Tokyo**
p156

Tokyo
p70

Kansai
p358

Shikoku
p641

Kyūshū
p695

**Okinawa & the
Southwest Islands**
p768

Rebecca Milner,
Ray Bartlett, Andrew Bender, Craig McLachlan, Kate Morgan,
Simon Richmond, Tom Spurling, Phillip Tang, Benedict Walker,
Wendy Yanagihara

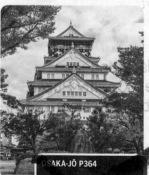

OSAKA-JŌ P364

NISHIKI MARKET, KYOTO
P304

Contents

ON THE ROAD

NATIONAL ART CENTER
TOKYO P84

Contents

Welcome to Japan

Japan is truly timeless, a place where ancient traditions are fused with modern life as if it were the most natural thing in the world.

Traditional Culture

On the surface, Japan appears exceedingly modern, but travelling around it offers numerous opportunities to connect with the country's traditional culture. Spend the night in a ryokan (traditional Japanese inn), sleeping on futons and tatami mats, and padding through well-worn wooden halls to the bathhouse (or go one step further and sleep in an old farmhouse). Chant with monks or learn how to whisk bitter *matcha* (powdered green tea) into a froth. From the splendour of a Kyoto geisha dance to the spare beauty of a Zen rock garden, Japan has the power to enthral even the most jaded traveller.

Spectacular Outdoors

Japan is a long and slender, highly volcanic archipelago. It's over two-thirds mountains, with bubbling hot springs at every turn. In the warmer months there is excellent hiking, through cedar groves and fields of wildflowers, up to soaring peaks and ancient shrines (the latter founded by wandering ascetics). In the winter, all this is covered with snow and the skiing is world class. (And if you've never paired hiking or skiing with soaking in onsen, you don't know what you've been missing.) Meanwhile in the southern reaches, there are tropical beaches for sunning, snorkelling, diving and surfing.

Exquisite Food

Wherever you are in Japan, it seems, you're never more than 500m from a great meal. Restaurants often specialise in just one dish – perhaps having spent generations perfecting it – and pay close attention to every stage, from sourcing fresh, local ingredients to assembling the dish. Moreover, you don't have to travel far to discover that Japanese cuisine is deeply varied. The hearty hotpots of the mountains are, for example, dramatically different from the delicate sushi for which the coast is famous. It's also intensely seasonal, meaning you can visit again at a different time and experience totally new tastes.

Dynamic Cities

The neon-lit streetscapes of Japan's cities look like sci-fi film sets, even though many of them are decades old. Meanwhile, cities like Tokyo and Osaka have been adding new architectural wonders that redefine what buildings – and cities – should look like. There's an indelible buzz to these urban centres, with their vibrant street life, 24-hour drinking and dining scenes, and creative hubs that turn out fashion and pop culture trends consumed the world over. Travel is always smooth and efficient, whether you're using the subway to get around or the *shinkansen* (bullet trains) to go from one city to the next.

Why I Love Japan

By Rebecca Milner, Writer

I've lived in Tokyo for 15 years now and am continuously surprised – sometimes on a daily basis – by something new. Such is the joy of living in a place that prides itself on constant renewal and reinvention; it seriously never gets old. Over the years I have had many opportunities to introduce visiting family and friends to Japan. Seeing the awe and enchantment on their faces when first seeing Kyoto's Golden Temple or experiencing the kindness of complete strangers never fails to take me back to the moment I first arrived and was instantly smitten.

For more about our writers, see p928

Above: Osaka (p359)

Japan

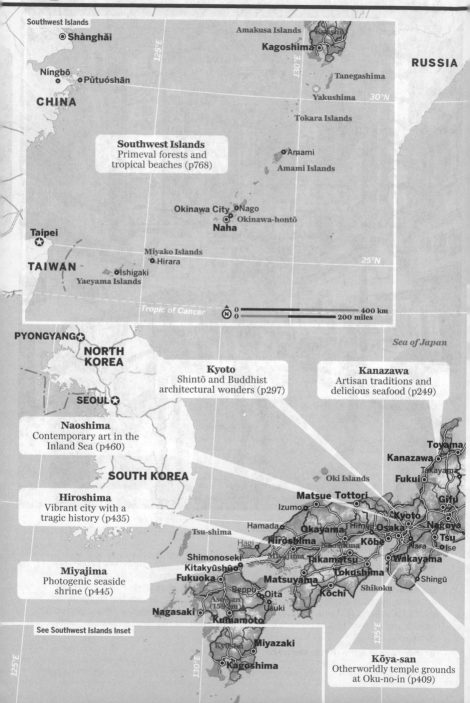

Southwest Islands

● Shànghǎi

CHINA

Níngbō ○   ○ Pǔtuóshān

RUSSIA

Amakusa Islands   Kyūshū

Kagoshima ○

Tanegashima

Yakushima   30°N

Tokara Islands

Southwest Islands
Primeval forests and
tropical beaches (p768)

○ Amami

Amami Islands

Okinawa City ○ Nago
○ Okinawa-hontō
Naha

Taipei ✪

TAIWAN   Miyako Islands
○ Hirara   25°N

○ Ishigaki
Yaeyama Islands

Tropic of Cancer   Ⓝ 0 ——— 400 km
0 ——— 200 miles

PYONGYANG ✪

**NORTH
KOREA**   *Sea of Japan*

Kyoto
Shintō and Buddhist
architectural wonders (p297)

Kanazawa
Artisan traditions and
delicious seafood (p249)

SEOUL ✪

Naoshima
Contemporary art in the
Inland Sea (p460)

Toyama
Kanazawa ○
Takayama

SOUTH KOREA

○ Oki Islands   **Fukui**   **Gifu**

Matsue Tottori
Izumo ○

Hiroshima
Vibrant city with a
tragic history (p435)

Hamada ○   **Kyoto** ○
Okayama Himeji **Osaka**   **Nagoya**
Tsu-shima   **Hiroshima**   **Kōbe**   **Tsu**
Hagi   Miyajima   Nara   ○ Ise
Takamatsu   **Wakayama**

Shimonoseki
Kitakyūshū ○   **Tokushima**
Fukuoka ○   **Matsuyama**   **Kōchi**   ○ Shingū
Beppu ○   Shikoku

Miyajima
Photogenic seaside
shrine (p445)

Aso-san ○ Oita
(1592m) ○ Usuki
Nagasaki ○   **Kumamoto**

See Southwest Islands Inset

Kyūshū   **Miyazaki**

Kagoshima

Kōya-san
Otherworldly temple grounds
at Oku-no-in (p409)

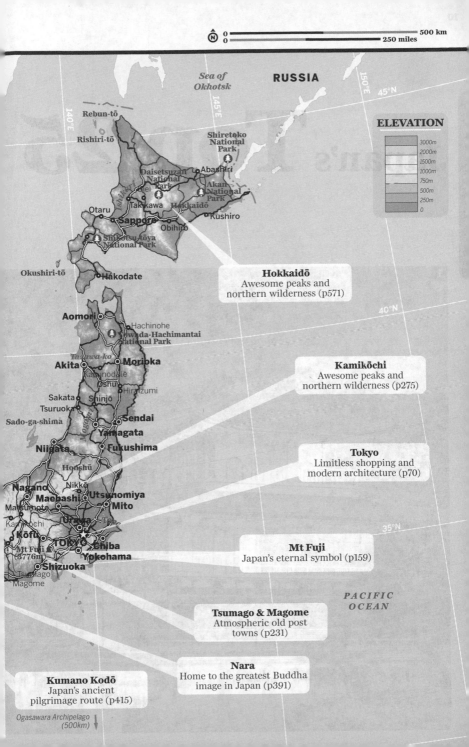

0 500 km

0 250 miles

Sea of Okhotsk

RUSSIA

Rebun-tō

Rishiri-tō

Shiretoko National Park

Abashiri

Daisetsuzan National Park

Akan National Park

Otaru

Takikawa

Hokkaidō

Sapporo

Obihiro

Kushiro

Shikotsu-Tōya National Park

Okushiri-tō

Hakodate

ELEVATION

3000m
2000m
1500m
1000m
750m
500m
250m
0

Aomori

Hachinohe

Towada-Hachimantai National Park

Towada-ko

Akita

Morioka

Kakunodate

Ōshū

Hiraizumi

Sakata

Shinjō

Tsuruoka

Sendai

Sado-ga-shima

Yamagata

Niigata

Fukushima

Honshū

Nagano

Nikkō

Matsumoto

Maebashi

Utsunomiya

Kamikōchi

Urawa

Mito

Kōfu

TOKYO

Chiba

Mt Fuji 3776m

Yokohama

Shizuoka

Tsumago

Magome

Hokkaidō
Awesome peaks and
northern wilderness (p571)

Kamikōchi
Awesome peaks and
northern wilderness (p275)

Tokyo
Limitless shopping and
modern architecture (p70)

Mt Fuji
Japan's eternal symbol (p159)

Tsumago & Magome
Atmospheric old post
towns (p231)

Nara
Home to the greatest Buddha
image in Japan (p391)

Kumano Kodō
Japan's ancient
pilgrimage route (p415)

*Ogasawara Archipelago
(500km)*

*PACIFIC
OCEAN*

Japan's **Top 25**

Kyoto's Temples & Gardens

1 Kyoto (p297), Japan's imperial capital for a thousand years, is home to more than a thousand temples. Some are monumental: Kinkaku-ji is an exquisite pavilion sheathed entirely in gold leaf. Some are more subtle: the simple beauty of Shōren-in, made of unadorned wood, reveals itself while you sip *matcha* at the teahouse. Others are more meditative still, particularly Ryōan-ji, with its stark Zen rock garden. While famous temples draw crowds, the majority see few visitors – meaning there are myriad ways to find moments of peace among tranquil surrounds. Kinkaku-ji, Kyoto (p321)

Soaking in Onsen

2 Highly volcanic Japan bubbles with onsen (hot springs; p63). The Japanese have turned the simple act of bathing into a folk religion and the country is dotted with temples and shrines to this most relaxing of faiths. Not convinced? Wait until you give it a try (and feel years of stress melt away). There are baths literally everywhere, but Kyūshū and Tōhoku (Northern Honshū) are particularly famous for their springs. Two worth-a-detour towns include Kurokawa Onsen and Nyūtō Onsen, both hidden away in the mountains.

Japanese Cuisine

3 One of the joys of travelling in Japan is experiencing the true breadth of the country's cuisine (p54). Sushi (raw fish on vinegar-seasoned rice) may be synonymous with Japan, but head to the mountains, for example, and you'll discover a hearty cuisine that draws from the land. It's hard not to eat well in Japan: such is the care and thought put into ingredients and presentation. What's more, you can have a superlative meal on any budget: even (and often especially) a humble bowl of noodles can be sublime.

Cherry-Blossom Viewing (Hanami)

4 Come spring, cherry trees burst into white and pink flowers. That's the cue for locals to gather in parks and along river banks for sake-fuelled cherry-blossom-viewing parties called *hanami*. More elaborate bacchanals – complete with barbecues and turntables – carry on long past dark for *yozakura* (night-time cherry blossoms). The best places to see the blossoms is a hot debate, but two favourites include Kyoto's Maruyama-kōen (p313; pictured above right), with its dramatic weeping cherry tree, and Tokyo's Yoyogi-kōen, where the grassy lawns become one week-long party scene.

Staying in a Ryokan

5 Ryokan simply means 'inn', but in this modern age of hotels, the word has come to mean an inn with a particular aesthetic and attitude towards service that feels more traditionally Japanese. Most ryokan (p867) have tatami (woven reed mat) floors where guests sleep on futons (quilted mattresses) rather than beds. They're usually low-slung buildings with winding corridors of highly polished wood. In better ones, staff wear kimonos and are highly attuned to guests' needs. These will also serve exquisite meals of local, seasonal ingredients – a truly memorable experience.

Tokyo's Modern Architecture

6 Tokyo (p70) is forever reaching into the future, pushing the boundaries of what's possible on densely populated, earthquake-prone land, adding ever taller, sleeker structures. Edgy designer boutiques from Japan's award-winning architects line Omote-sandō; mega-malls redefine the urban landscape; and the world's tallest free-standing tower – Tokyo Sky Tree – is a twisting spire that draws on ancient building techniques. Tokyo has long been a source of inspiration for designers; perhaps it will be for you, too. Omote-sandō (p91)

Oku-no-in at Kōya-san

7 Riding the funicular up to the sacred Buddhist monastic complex of Kōya-san feels like ascending to another world. There are over a hundred temples here, the highlight of which is Oku-no-in (p410), where paths weave their way among towering cryptomeria trees and time-worn stone stupas covered in moss and lichen. Other temples offer a different experience: the chance to spend the night, dine on traditional vegetarian Buddhist cuisine and wake up early for (optional) morning meditation with the resident monks.

6

MATT MUNRO/LONELY PLANET ©

Tsumago & Magome

8 Tsumago and Magome are two post towns along the old Nakasendō (p230), one of five foot highways (used by lords and messengers alike) that connected Tokyo and Kyoto during the feudal era. The old path remains, paved with large stones, and it is possible to hike 7.8km between the two towns, through sleepy alpine hamlets and cedar forests, past waterwheels and rice paddies. The towns themselves are a treat too, with narrow lanes and low-slung dark wooden buildings that serve as inns, noodle restaurants and craft shops. Tsumago

Daibutsu (Great Buddha) of Nara

9 Nara's 15m-tall gilt-bronze Buddha statue was first cast in the 8th century, at the dawn of the Japanese empire. It's among the largest gilt-bronze effigies in the world and the temple that houses it, Tōdai-ji (p394), is among the world's largest wooden structures. It's hard to describe the Great Buddha without using superlatives; it's simply awesome. It's also just one of many things to see in the pleasing grassy expanse that is Nara-kōen (Nara Park). Nearby Nara National Museum, for example, has fascinating relics on display.

Hiroshima

10 Hiroshima (p435) today is a forward-thinking city with attractive, leafy boulevards. It's not until you visit the Peace Memorial Museum that the true extent of human tragedy wreaked by the atomic bomb becomes vividly clear. A visit here is a heartbreaking, important history lesson and the park around the museum, much of which was designed by modernist Tange Kenzō, offers many opportunities for reflection. The city's spirit of determination – as well as its food – will ensure that you'll have good memories to take with you.

Sumo

11 The purifying salt sails into the air. The two giants leap up and crash into each other. A flurry of slapping and heaving ensues. Who will shove the other out of the sacred ring and move up in the ranks? From the ancient rituals to the thrill of the quick bouts, sumo is a fascinating spectacle. Tournaments take place several times a year (in Tokyo (p144), Nagoya, Osaka and Fukuoka); outside of tournament season you can catch an early morning practice session at one of the stables where wrestlers live and train.

Mt Fuji

12 Even from a distance Mt Fuji (p159) will take your breath away. Close up, the perfectly symmetrical cone of Japan's highest peak is just awesome. Dawn from the summit? Pure magic. Fuji-san is among Japan's most revered and timeless attractions. Hundreds of thousands of people climb it every year, continuing a centuries-old tradition of pilgrimages up the sacred volcano. Those who'd rather search for perfect views from the less-daunting peaks nearby can follow in the steps of Japan's most famous painters and poets.

Art on Naoshima

13 Naoshima (p460) is one of Japan's great success stories: a rural island about to become a ghost town, now a world-class centre for contemporary art. Many of Japan's most lauded architects have contributed structures, including museums, a boutique hotel and even a bathhouse – all designed to enhance the island's natural beauty and complement existing settlements. The resulting blend of avant-garde and rural Japan is captivating. It has also inspired some Japanese to relocate here to open cafes and inns. Yayoi Kusuma's *Pumpkin*

Skiing

14 Come winter, copious dumps of dry, powdery snow turn the mountains of Japan into peaks of meringue. In recent decades, Niseko (p589) has emerged as Asia's top ski resort and a global destination, backed up by a thriving, cosmopolitan après-ski scene. If first tracks and an evening hot-spring soak are all you desire, there are hundreds of smaller resorts around the country that see fewer visitors (reminiscent of the days when Japan's excellent snow was still a well-kept secret). For thrill-seekers, there are backcountry opportunities, too. Gala Yuzawa (p563)

Hiking Ancient Pilgrimage Trails

15 For centuries Japan's remote mountains were crossed by mountain ascetics seeking enlightenment in what must have felt like the ends of the earth. Less self-punishing pilgrims still follow their paths. Deep in southern Kansai, the Kumano Kodō (p416) network of trails links three Shintō shrines. On the island of Shikoku, the 88 Temple Route is Japan's most famous Buddhist pilgrimage. Dewa Sanzan, in Northern Honshū, covers three sacred peaks. Modern transport means you can sample trails like these in a day. Kumano Kodō (p415)

Kanazawa

16 Kanazawa (p249), an old feudal-era capital on the Sea of Japan coast, has long flown under the radar, perhaps because it wasn't easy to get to (that's changed since the 2015 opening of the Hokuriku Shinkansen linking Tokyo to Kanazawa). Those in the know have long held the city in esteem for its local cuisine, which draws heavily on fresh seafood from the nearby coast, and its artisan tradition, still strong today. Kanazawa's signature crafts include lacquerware, kimono-dyeing and gold-leaf decoration. Kenroku-en (p252)

Castles

17 Japan's castles are evocative of its feudal past, peopled with sword-wielding samurai, whisper-footed ninja and all-powerful shoguns. The curving roofs of the castle keeps, often stacked storeys high, are emblematic of traditional architecture. The castles are made of wood, but may sit atop foundations of enormous stones. Few originals survive; the must-sees are the 'White Egret Castle' Himeji-jō (p389), newly reopened after extensive restoration, and its natural foil, Matsumoto-jō, the fearsome black 'Crow Castle'. Matsumoto-jō (p267)

Wild Hokkaidō

18 Hokkaidō (p571) is Japan's last frontier, a largely untamed, highly volcanic landscape of massive mountains startlingly pock-marked with crystal-blue caldera lakes and opalescent, sulphur-rich hot springs. Its flora and fauna is more closely related to Sakhalin, Russia, than the rest of Japan. Hikers, cyclists and road trippers are drawn to the big skies, open spaces and dramatic topography. With a new bullet-train connection to Tokyo, Japan's northernmost island has never been more accessible. Jigoku-dani (p598)

Beaches & Forests of the Southwest Islands

19 The string of islands known as the Nansei-shotō (Southwest Islands; p768) extends some 1000km southwest of Kyūshū towards Taiwan. The climate is balmy, tropical even, most of the year. Some of the islands, like Ishigaki and the Kerama Islands, are known for palm-fringed beaches of white sand and turquoise waters. Others, like Yakushima and remote Iriomote-jima, are covered in primeval forest – some of the last virgin forest left in Japan. Kabira-wan, Ishigaki-jima (p803)

City Nightscapes

20 Something magical happens when the sun sets in the Land of the Rising Sun: the grey city streets turn into crackling canyons of neon. Nowhere is this light show more dramatic than along Osaka's Dōtombori (p365) canal and in Tokyo's Kabukichō district (though any sizeable city will have a colourful entertainment district). And don't miss the opportunity to ascend a city skyscraper, to an observatory or hotel bar: at night, Japan's metropolises appear truly beautiful, as if the sky were inverted, with the glittering stars below. Kabukichō (p94)

Kyoto's Geisha Culture

21 Geisha are one of the most enduring icons of traditional Japanese culture, an embodiment of the aesthetics of an older world. Their legacy is strongest in Kyoto. A few times a year, usually in spring, the city's geisha perform dances for the public (a rare treat). Year-round you can stroll through Kyoto's historic geisha districts, such as Gion (p315), lined with exclusive teahouses; lantern-lit, their windows screened by bamboo shades, these beautiful wooden structures are where geisha continue to entertain elite audiences to this day.

PIUS LEE/SHUTTERSTOCK ©

Kamikōchi

22 One of the most stunning natural vistas in Japan, Kamikōchi (p275) is a highland river valley enveloped by the soaring peaks of the Northern Japan Alps. Easy day hikes are possible along the pristine Azusa-gawa through tranquil forests of willow, larch and elm trees. The birthplace of Japanese alpinism, Kamikōchi is also the gateway for more challenging treks up some of the country's tallest mountains, such as Yariga-take (3180m). Private cars are banned from Kamikōchi, which lessens the impact of the crowds.

Miyajima

23 The *torii* – the vermilion gate marking the entrance to a Shintō shrine – that floats in the sea at Miyajima (p445) is among Japan's most photogenic and enchanting scenes. You'll want to visit at high tide, when the waters lap up against the World Heritage–listed shrine, Itsukushima-jinja, built right at the water's edge like a pier. Most visitors come for a day trip from Hiroshima, but you can stay the night here in a ryokan and have the island (mostly) to yourself before the first ferry pulls in.

Traditional Festivals

24 Catching a *matsuri* (traditional festival) is like stepping back in time: men and women wear colourful cotton kimono – and sometimes the men just wear short coats and *fundoshi* (the loincloths worn by sumo wrestlers). Some see parades of portable shrines or floats go through the streets; others involve dancing, bonfires or drumming. The celebrations have their roots in Shintō and Buddhist traditions but they also serve to renew age-old community bonds. August sees the lion's share of festivals, but they happen year-round.

Shopping in Tokyo

25 Tokyo is one of the world's great shopping cities, with grand old department stores, avant-garde boutiques, vintage shops and style mavens who set global trends. Harajuku (p147) is the gathering point for Tokyo's eccentric fashion tribes – as much a destination for shopping as for people-watching; Ginza, meanwhile, is the city's classic shopping district, recently revamped. Tokyoites shop – economy be damned – with an infectious enthusiasm. Join them in the hunt for the cutest fashions, the latest gadgets or the perfect teacup.

PERATI KOMSON/SHUTTERSTOCK ©

Need to Know

For more information, see Survival Guide (p879)

Currency
Yen (¥)

Language
Japanese

Visas
Visas are issued on arrival for most nation-alities for stays of up to 90 days.

Money
Post offices and some convenience stores have international ATMs. Most hotels and depart-ment stores, but only some restaurants and ryokan, accept credit cards.

Mobile Phones
Purchase prepaid data-only SIM cards (for unlocked smartphones only) online, at airport kiosks or at electronics stores. For voice calls, rent a pay-as-you-go mobile.

Time
Japan Standard Time (GMT/UTC plus nine hours)

When to Go

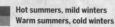

Hot summers, mild winters
Warm summers, cold winters

Sapporo
GO Apr–Oct

Takayama
GO Apr–Oct

Tokyo
GO any time

Kyoto
GO Mar–May or Sep–Nov

Naha
GO Mar–Nov

High Season
(Apr & May, Aug)

➡ Weather in April and May is generally fantastic; August is hot and humid but the season for festivals.

➡ Accommodation is pricey and hard to find during cherry-blossom season (late March to early April), Golden Week (early May) and O-Bon (mid-August).

Shoulder
(Jun & Jul, Sep–Dec)

➡ June and July is rainy season (except Hokkaidō); typhoons roll through in September.

➡ Prices and crowds increase in resort areas during autumn foliage season (November).

Low Season
(Jan–Mar)

➡ Cold days and snowy mountains make this peak ski season, but affordable and uncrowded elsewhere.

➡ Many businesses close over the New Year period (end December and early January).

Useful Websites

Lonely Planet (www.lonely-planet.com/japan) Destination information, hotel bookings, traveller forum and more.

Japan National Tourism Organization (www.jnto.go.jp) Official tourist site with planning tools and events calendar.

HyperDia (www.hyperdia.com) Comprehensive train schedules and fares.

Japan Meteorological Agency Tropical Cyclone Page (www.jma.go.jp/en/typh) Up-to-date weather satellite images (good for checking on typhoons).

Bento (http://bento.com) English-language restaurant guide for major cities in Japan.

Tokyo Cheapo (https://tokyo-cheapo.com) Budget saving tips for Tokyo and travel in Japan.

Important Numbers

Drop the 0 in the area code when dialling from abroad.

Ambulance & fire	119
Police	110
Country code	81
International access code	010
International operator	0051

Exchange Rates

Australia	A$1	¥84
Canada	C$1	¥85
Europe	€1	¥120
New Zealand	NZ$1	¥80
UK	£1	¥141
US	US$1	¥114

For current exchange rates, see www.xe.com.

Daily Costs

**Budget:
Less than ¥8000**

➡ Dorm bed: ¥3000

➡ Bowl of noodles: ¥750

➡ Happy hour beer: ¥500

➡ One-day subway pass: ¥600

➡ One temple or museum entry: ¥500

**Midrange:
¥8000–20,000**

➡ Double room at a business hotel: ¥10,000

➡ Dinner for two at an *izakaya* (Japanese pub-eatery): ¥6000

➡ Half-day cycling tour or cooking class: ¥5000

➡ Temple and museum entries: ¥1500

**Top End:
More than ¥20,000**

➡ Double room in a nice hotel: from ¥25,000

➡ Dinner for two at a good sushi restaurant: from ¥15,000

➡ Taxi ride between city sights: ¥2500

Opening Hours

Note that some outdoor attractions (such as gardens) may close earlier in the winter. Standard opening hours:

Banks 9am to 3pm (some to 5pm) Monday to Friday

Bars from around 6pm to late

Department stores 10am to 8pm

Museums 9am to 5pm, last entry 4.30pm; often closed Monday (if Monday is a national holiday, the museum will close on Tuesday)

Post offices 9am to 5pm Monday to Friday; larger ones have longer hours and open Saturday

Restaurants lunch 11.30am to 2pm; dinner 6pm to 10pm; last orders half an hour before closing

Arriving in Japan

Narita Airport (p891) Express trains and buses run often to central Tokyo (around ¥3000; one to two hours) between 6am and 10.30pm. Taxis start at ¥20,000.

Haneda Airport (p891) Trains and buses (¥400 to ¥1200, 30 to 45 minutes) to central Tokyo run often from 5.30am to midnight; times and costs depend on your stop in the city. There aren't many night buses. For a taxi budget between ¥5000 and ¥8000.

Kansai International Airport (p891) Express trains run frequently to Kyoto (from ¥2850, 75 minutes) and Osaka (¥1430, 35 minutes). Buses cost ¥1050 to ¥1550 to central Osaka (50 minutes), ¥2550 to Kyoto (90 minutes). Trains and buses stop running close to midnight. A shared taxi service to Kyoto costs ¥3600; a standard taxi to Osaka starts at ¥14,500.

Getting Around

Train Trains are fast, efficient, reliable and can get you just about anywhere; discount rail passes make train travel very affordable.

Ferry Good for getting to distant islands or for fans of slow travel.

Bus The cheapest way to make long-haul journeys and the only way to get to some mountain and rural destinations.

Car Rental cars are widely available, roads are great, driving is safe, and a car will give you plenty of freedom. Especially recommended in Hokkaidō, Kyūshū and Okinawa. Drive on the left.

Air A large network of domestic flights and an increased presence of budget carriers makes this a good option for long distances or time-pressed itineraries.

For much more on
getting around,
see p891

First Time Japan

For more information, see Survival Guide (p879)

Checklist

➡ Purchase a Japan Rail Pass.

➡ Get an international licence if you plan to rent a car.

➡ Book tickets online for sumo or national theatre performances (to score good seats) and for Tokyo's Ghibli Museum, if you plan to visit.

➡ Check online for local events that might be appealing (or might make finding accommodation tricky).

What to Pack

➡ Slip-on shoes, as you'll be taking off your shoes a lot.

➡ Any medications you might want, as finding local equivalents may be challenging.

➡ As little as possible! Hotel rooms are small and trains can get crowded. You can buy most things you'll need.

Top Tips for Your Trip

➡ If you want to cover a lot of ground, get a Japan Rail Pass, which offers unlimited use of the extensive and efficient Japan Rail system; if your trip focuses on a limited area, look into cheaper regional passes.

➡ Stay at least one night in a ryokan (traditional Japanese inn) and visit at least one onsen (hot spring bath).

➡ Splurge at lunch. Many restaurants offer meals that cost half of what you'd find at dinner, often for a meal that's not much smaller.

➡ Rent a pocket wi-fi device. Japan has some free wi-fi networks but they can be clunky. Constant wi-fi means you can use navigation apps.

➡ Learn a couple of basic Japanese phrases. The locals will love you for trying.

What to Wear

Dressing in layers is ideal as weather can fluctuate by the day (or when you step off a hot street into an air-conditioned cafe). Keep in mind that you may be taking your shoes off and sitting on the floor, so you might want to pack socks even during sandal season (and second-guess that short skirt).

Casual clothes are fine in the cities, but you'll feel out of place if you're dressed as if heading to the gym. Some high-end restaurants and bars do have a dress code, but this usually just means no sleeveless shirts or sandals on men.

Sleeping

Advance booking is highly recommended, especially in major tourist destinations.

➡ **Hotels** Midrange and luxury, domestic and international chains, and a few boutique properties can be found in all major cities.

➡ **Business Hotels** Compact, rooms clustered around train stations.

➡ **Ryokan** Traditional Japanese inns, found usually in countryside and resort areas.

➡ **Hostels & Guesthouses** Affordable and plentiful in tourist destinations, often with English-speaking staff; most have dorm and double rooms.

Cash

Be warned that there are still many places in Japan – particularly outside the cities – that don't accept credit cards. Ryokan and smaller restaurants and shops are common cash-only places. It's wise to assume you'll need to pay cash; stock up when you're in a town with an ATM.

Bargaining

Bargaining is not common practice in Japan; flea markets are an exception.

Tipping

Tipping is not customary in Japan (leaving money on the table in a restaurant will usually result in the waiter chasing you down the street to give it back). High-end restaurants and hotels will usually add a 10% service fee to the bill.

Language

The level of English ability in Japan is generally low – or random at best (fluent English speakers can appear in the most unlikely situations); it's easier to get around the bigger cities, which are well signposted in English. English is studied in school, so slow, simple queries can usually be addressed, and with the recent uptick of tourism, more establishments are specifically hiring clerks and servers with English ability. Most Japanese are more comfortable with written than spoken English, so whenever possible, email is often the best means of communicating.

Phrases to Learn Before You Go

 Is there a Western-/Japanese-style room?
洋室/和室はありますか?
yō·shi·tsu/wa·shi·tsu wa a·ri·mas ka

Some lodgings have only Japanese-style rooms, or a mix of Western and Japanese – ask if you have a preference.

 Please bring a (spoon/knife/fork).
(スプーン/ナイフ/フォーク)をください。
(spūn/nai·fu/fō·ku) o ku·da·sai

If you haven't quite mastered the art of eating with chopsticks, don't be afraid to ask for cutlery at a restaurant.

3 **How do I get to ...?**
…へはどう行けばいいですか?
... e wa dō i·ke·ba ī des ka

Finding a place from its address can be difficult in Japan. Addresses usually give an area (not a street) and numbers aren't always consecutive. Practise asking for directions.

 I'd like a nonsmoking seat, please.
禁煙席をお願いします。
kin·en·se·ki o o·ne·gai shi·mas

There are smoking seats in many restaurants and on bullet trains so be sure to specify if you want to be smoke-free.

5 **What's the local speciality?**
地元料理は何がありますか?
ji·mo·to·ryō·ri wa na·ni ga a·ri·mas ka

Throughout Japan most areas have a speciality dish and locals usually love to talk food.

Etiquette

Japan is famous for its etiquette, though it's not as strict as you might think (and foreign visitors are usually given a pass).

➡ **Greetings** Japanese typically greet each other with a slight bow, but may greet foreigners with a handshake; hugging and cheek kissing is considered alarming.

➡ **Queueing** The Japanese are famous queuers, forming neat lines in front of subway doors, ramen shops etc.

➡ **Eating & Drinking** Eating and drinking on streets and subway cars is generally frowned upon; beverages in resealable containers are an exception.

➡ **Shoes Off** Many lodgings and restaurants (and even some museums!) request you leave your shoes at the door. Just take a quick look around – for a sign or slippers in the foyer – to see if this rule applies. Never wear shoes on tatami mats.

➡ **Religious Sites** There is no dress code for visiting a shrine or temple but it's polite to keep your voice down.

What's New

Olympics 2020

The biggest news is that the country is ramping up its tourist infrastructure for 2020. Car-rental agencies have cars with English-language GPS; Kyoto is experimenting with tourist-friendly facilities. Changes aren't across the board, but in general, there's more English on the ground.

New Shinkansen Lines

The Hokkaidō Shinkansen (bullet train) opened in 2016, linking Tokyo with the southernmost city on Hokkaidō, Hakodate. In 2015, the Hokuriku Shinkansen opened, connecting Tokyo and Kanazawa via Nagano. New rail passes were also introduced.

Narita Airport Terminal 3

In 2015 Narita opened a third terminal just for budget carriers, which have an increased presence in Japan. Flying is now a realistic money-saving strategy.

Northern Honshū's 'Joyful' Trains

Several new tourist trains – some with sake bars or foot baths – have started running on scenic routes that cut through mountains or wend along the coast. (p512)

Better Wi-fi Coverage

More and more tourist sights, cities and prefectures are offering free wi-fi to travellers. It's not seamless, but it's much better than it used to be. Wi-fi is now common in most lodgings.

Sanriku Kaigan Reborn

Heavily damaged by the 2011 tsunami, this coastal region in Northern Honshū is getting creative about how to rebuild and re-invent itself. The result (a work in progress) includes a dynamic new food scene. (p522)

Hands-Free Travel

Japan's baggage courier services have made it easier for foreign travellers to ship their bags ahead, to the airport or their next hotel. (p893)

New Museums

Tokyo got a stylish new museum devoted to the *ukiyo-e* (woodblock print) artist Hokusai (p105); Kyoto debuted the Kyoto Railway Museum (p302).

Tsukiji Market in Limbo

The fate of Tokyo's famed fish market remains up in the air, with the decision to relocate to be revisited in late 2017. Either way, the lively Outer Market will remain. (p79)

Tokyo Bay

Tennōzu Isle on Tokyo Bay has several new artsy attractions, including the excellent Archi-Depot – a museum for architecture models. (p107)

Naoshima Evolving

The contemporary art showcase on the islands of the Seto Inland Sea continues to add new installations, most recently on Teshima (in 2016). (p465)

Discount Bus Passes

The new Shōryūdō Highway Bus pass offers unlimited bus travel around key destinations in the Japan Alps (which are tricky to do by train). (p234)

For more recommendations and reviews, see lonelyplanet.com/japan

If You Like...

Temples & Shrines

Kinkaku-ji Kyoto's iconic golden temple. (p321)

Tōdai-ji Ancient wooden home of Nara's famous Daibutsu (Great Buddha) statue. (p394)

Sensō-ji Tokyo's most famous Buddhist temple and a pilgrimage site for more than a millennium. (p104)

Tōshō-gū Ornate mausoleum for Japan's legendary shogun, Tokugawa Ieyasu. (p200)

Oku-no-in Other-worldly collection of temples and moss-covered stupas in the forest. (p410)

Ise-jingū Japan's spiritual centre, dedicated to the Sun Goddess. (p422)

Zenkō-ji Grand old Nagano temple with fascinating secret passages and stories. (p280)

Fushimi Inari-Taisha Photogenic procession of *torii* (gates) up a Kyoto hillside. (p303)

Gardens

Kenroku-en Kanazawa's strolling garden is considered a masterpiece of the form. (p252)

Ryōan-ji Kyoto's famous Zen rock garden. (p322)

Ritsurin-kōen Seventeenth-century landscape garden in Takamatsu, once the playground of lords. (p685)

Katsura Rikyū Former imperial villa with gardens that unfold in stunning vistas. (p326)

Byōdō-in Rare surviving example of a Heian-era 'Pure Land' garden. (p320)

Saihō-ji Kyoto's 'Koke-dera' (moss temple) has enchanting, velvety grounds. (p325)

Adachi Museum of Art The picturesque landscape garden at this Matsue museum complements the paintings inside. (p476)

Kōraku-en Sprawling strolling garden with ponds and teahouses in Okayama. (p455)

Museums

Tokyo National Museum Home to the world's largest collection of Japanese art. (p97)

Kyoto National Museum Kyoto's top museum with classical artworks, historical artefacts and temple treasures. (p310)

Gasshō-zukuri Folk Village Open-air museum of traditional rural architecture. (p246)

National Museum of Ethnology Interactive showcase of the world's cultures, past and present. (p370)

Edo-Tokyo Museum The story of how a fishing village evolved into a sprawling, modern metropolis. (p105)

Hiroshima Peace Memorial Museum Evocative (and often heartbreaking) account of the atomic bomb and its aftermath. (p439)

Japan Folk Crafts Museum Exhibitions highlighting the beauty of everyday objects. (p89)

Okinawa Prefectural Museum & Art Museum Deep dive into Okinawa's history, way of life and ecosystem. (p787)

Castles

Himeji-jō The grande dame of Japanese castles, freshly restored. (p389)

Matsumoto-jō Japan's oldest surviving wooden castle, in the mountains of Nagano. (p267)

Matsue-jō Excellent views from atop the original wooden keep and boat rides around the moat. (p474)

Matsuyama-jō Among Japan's finest original castles, lording over Matsuyama on the island of Shikoku. (p671)

Hikone Castle This 17th-century stunner has a rare, intact keep. (p426)

Inuyama-jō Japan's oldest standing castle began life as a fort in 1440. (p225)

Nijō-jō Kyoto's castle is known for its 'nightingale' floors that creak when you walk on them. (p305)

Shuri-jō The seat of power of the former Ryūkyū Empire, painstakingly reconstructed from historical records. (p789)

Osaka-jō Reconstruction of Osaka's famously flamboyant castle. (p364)

Modern Architecture

Naoshima An island of contemporary art museums, including several designed by Japanese architect Andō Tadao. (p460)

Omote-sandō Boutique-lined boulevard that doubles as a walk-through showcase for contemporary Japanese design. (p91)

DT Suzuki Museum Meditative monument to Zen scholar DT Suzuki by Taniguchi Yoshio. (p252)

Tokyo Metropolitan Government Building Tokyo's city hall, by pre-eminent modernist Tange Kenzō, is inspired by Europe's cathedrals. (p92)

Miho Museum IM Pei–designed museum of ancient artefacts sunk into a mountain. (p428)

21st Century Museum of Contemporary Art Lithesome, light-filled space by award-winning duo SANAA. (p252)

Umeda Sky Building Forty-storey, space-age Arc de Triomphe by Hara Hiroshi in Osaka. (p359)

Archi-Depot Tokyo repository for architecture models by famous names. (p109)

Shopping

Harajuku Tokyo fashion central. Brand names on the main drags; avant-garde boutiques on the backstreets. (p147)

BLBAIXAI/SHUTTERSTOCK ©

Top: Umeda Sky Building
Bottom: Ameya-yokochō

Downtown Kyoto Department stores, famed retailers of traditional crafts, tea shops and more. (p352)

Kanazawa A city with a well-preserved artisan culture; it's especially known for lacquerware and gold leaf. (p256)

Minami Osaka's streetwise shopping district has plenty of high-street brands and second-hand shops. (p379)

Morioka The place in Japan to buy tea kettles and other wares made of cast iron. (p516)

Tsuboya Pottery Street Folksy Okinawan pottery in Naha. (p787)

Markets

Tsukiji Outer Market Shop where the pros go for kitchen tools and ingredients. (p79)

Nishiki Market Kyoto's central food market, with plenty of souvenir packaged items – like rice crackers and sake. (p304)

Daichi Makishi Kōsetsu Ichiba Naha's central market brims with island specialities. (p787)

Hirome Ichiba Bustling market in Kōchi (Shikoku) with dozens of restaurants and food stalls. (p665)

Dōguya-suji Arcade Covered arcade for myriad kitchenware items in Osaka. (p379)

Ameya-yokochō Tokyo's last open-air market dates to the tumultuous days after WWII. (p150)

Beaches

Nishibama Beach This stretch of Aka-jima is possibly the best of several white-sand stunners in Okinawa's Kerama Islands. (p794)

Sunayama Beach Postcard-perfect beach with a rock arch on Miyako-jima. (p798)

Habushi-ura This long sandy stretch on Nii-jima is a favourite spot for Tokyo surfers. (p186)

Kominato Kaigan Quintessential tropical scene 1000km from the mainland, on Chichi-jima. (p209)

Shirara-hama Kansai's most popular beach has white sands and plenty of local beach culture. (p421)

Ikumi Beach Laid-back hub of Shikoku's nascent surfing community. (p655)

Train Journeys

Kurobe Gorge Railway Thrill ride along bridges suspended over the Kurobe Gorge. (p266)

Resort Shirakami Sightseeing train on the Gonō line, which hugs the rugged northern coast between Akita and Aomori. (p512)

Sunrise Seto/Izumo Japan's last, old-school sleeper train travels from Tokyo to Takamatsu and Izumo. (p899)

JR Senmō Line Tiny two-car train running along Hokkaidō's northern coast, past antique wooden stations. (p635)

Enoden Beloved streetcar that winds through the coastal communities between Kamakura and Enoshima. (p187)

Scenic Views

Miyajima See the island's famous floating *torii* (gate) at high tide. (p445)

Matsushima Look over the bay towards the hundreds of tiny windswept islands, spiked with wispy pines. (p510)

Kamikōchi Admire the snowcapped peaks of the Japan Alps from this idyllic river valley. (p275)

Kussharo-ko Crystal-blue caldera lake in Hokkaidō, best viewed from the mountains above. (p631)

Sakurajima See Kagoshima's smoking volcano lording over the city's skyline. (p757)

Iya Valley Head to Oku-Iya ('deep Iya') to see the vine bridges suspended over the gorge. (p656)

Hakone Catch a glimpse of Mt Fuji reflected in Ashi-ko on a clear winter morning. (p167)

Oki Islands Rugged coastal cliffs on remote, barely developed islands. (p478)

Pop Culture

Akihabara Tokyo's famous hot spot for fans of anime, manga and video games. (p95)

Ghibli Museum Enchanting museum designed by Japan's leading animator, Miyazaki Hayao (the king of Japanese anime). (p110)

Harajuku Where Tokyo fashion trends grow legs. (p89)

Kyoto International Manga Museum Galleries of manga, plus special exhibitions and workshops. (p305)

Mizuki Shigeru Museum Pilgrimage spot in Western Honshū for fans of Mizuki's other-worldly characters. (p479)

Amerika-Mura Colourful Osaka warren of streetwear and secondhand shops. (p365)

Maricar Cosplay (costume play) go-karting through the streets of Tokyo. (p112)

Month by Month

January

Japan comes to life again after the lull of the New Year holiday. Winter grips the country in the mountains and in the north, ushering in ski season (take care when driving in snow country).

⚜ Shōgatsu (New Year)

Families come together to eat and drink to health and happiness. The holiday is officially 1 to 3 January, but many businesses and attractions close the whole first week, and transport is busy. *Hatsu-mōde* is the ritual first shrine visit of the new year.

☆ Coming-of-Age Day

The second Monday of January is Seijin-no-hi (Coming-of-Age Day), the collective birthday for all who have turned 20 (the age of majority) in the past year. Young women don gorgeous kimonos for ceremonies at Shintō shrines.

February

February is the coldest month and the peak of Japan's ski season.

⚜ Setsubun Matsuri

The first day of spring is 3 February in the traditional lunar calendar, a shift once believed to bode evil. As a precaution, people visit Buddhist temples, toss roasted beans and shout 'Oni wa soto! Fuku wa uchi!' ('Devil out! Fortune in!').

⚜ Yuki Matsuri

Two million visitors head to Sapporo's annual snow festival in early February. Highlights include the international snow sculpture contest, ice slides and mazes for kids and plenty of drunken revelry. Book accommodation very early. (p582)

☉ Plum-Blossom Viewing

Plum *(ume)* blossoms, which appear towards the end of the month, are the first sign that winter is ending. Kairaku-en in Mito is the most famous viewing spot but parks and gardens all over Japan have plum trees.

March

Spring begins in fits and starts. The Japanese have a saying: *sankan-shion* – three days cold, four days warm.

☉ Hina Matsuri

On and around 3 March (also known as Girls' Day), public spaces and homes are decorated with *o-hina-sama* (princess) dolls in traditional royal dress.

⚜ AnimeJapan

Formerly known as the Tokyo International Anime Fair, AnimeJapan (www.anime-japan.jp) is the world's largest anime (Japanese animation) fair, held in Tokyo in late March. There are events and exhibitions for industry insiders and fans alike.

April

Warmer weather and blooming cherry trees make this a fantastic month to be in Japan, though places like Kyoto can get very crowded.

💿 Cherry-Blossom Viewing

When the cherry blossoms burst into bloom, the Japanese hold rollicking *hanami* (blossom viewing) parties. The blossoms are fickle and hard to time: on average, they hit their peak in Tokyo or Kyoto between 25 March and 7 April.

🎎 Takayama Spring Matsuri

On 14 and 15 April the mountain town of Takayama hosts the spring instalment of its famous festival. This is the more elaborate of the two (the other is in October), with parades of spectacular floats lit with lanterns and a lion dance. Book accommodation well in advance. (p237)

May

May is one of the best months to visit: it's warm and sunny in most places and the fresh green in the mountains is stunning. Be wary of the travel crush during the Golden Week holiday.

🎎 Sanja Matsuri

The grandest Tokyo festival of all, this three-day event, held over the third weekend of May, attracts around 1.5 million spectators to Asakusa. The highlight is the rowdy parade of *mikoshi* (portable shrines) carried by men and women in traditional dress. (p115)

Most Japanese are on holiday from 29 April to 5 May, when a series of national holidays coincide (called 'Golden Week'). This is one of the busiest times for domestic travel, so be prepared for crowded transport and accommodation. Many businesses close for a week in mid-August, as Japanese return to their home towns for O-Bon festivities (or go on holiday instead). Restaurants and shops start shutting down from 29 December for the New Year holiday, which ends on 3 January (though many places close until 6 January). During this time, transport runs and accommodation remains open (although it's pricey).

June

Early June is lovely, though by the end of the month *tsuyu* (the rainy season) sets in. As mountain snow melts, hiking season begins in the Japan Alps (though double-check for higher elevations).

July

When the rainy season passes, suddenly it's summer – the season for festivals and *hanabi taikai* (fireworks shows). It does get very hot and humid; head to Hokkaidō or the Japan Alps to escape the heat.

🗻 Mt Fuji Climbing Season

Mt Fuji officially opens to climbing on 1 July, and the months of July and August are ideal for climbing the peak. (p159)

🎎 Gion Matsuri

The most vaunted festival in Japan is held on 17 and 24 July in Kyoto, when huge, elaborate floats are pulled through the streets.

Three evenings prior, locals stroll through street markets dressed in beautiful *yukata* (light cotton kimonos). Accommodation is expensive and difficult to find. (p332)

🎎 Tenjin Matsuri

Held in Osaka on 24 and 25 July, this is one of the country's biggest festivals. On the second day, processions of *mikoshi* (portable shrines) and people in traditional attire parade through the streets, ending up in hundreds of boats on the river. (p371)

🎎 Fuji Rock Festival

Japan's biggest music festival takes place over one long (and often wildly muddy and fun) weekend at a mountain resort in late July. Big-name acts on the large stages; indie bands on the smaller ones. (p564)

August

Hot, humid weather and festivals continuing apace. School holidays mean beaches and cooler mountain areas get crowded. Many Japanese return to their home towns (or take a holiday) around O-Bon, so transit is hectic and shops may close.

✿ Summer Fireworks Festivals

Towns across Japan hold spectacular summer fireworks festivals in late July and early August. Among the best: Sumida-gawa Fireworks festival (p115; Tokyo, late July), Lake Biwa Fireworks festival (near Kyoto, early August) and the Naniwa Yodogawa Fireworks festival (Osaka, early August).

✿ World Cosplay Summit

Some 30 countries compete in early August (or late July) in Nagoya to see who has the best *cosplayers* (manga and anime fans who dress up as their fave characters). (p220)

✿ Sendai Tanabata Matsuri

Sendai's biggest event celebrates a Chinese legend about the stars Vega and Altair, stand-ins for two star-crossed lovers who meet once a year on 7 July (on the old lunar calendar, early August on the modern one). Downtown is decorated with coloured streamers. (p506)

✿ Nebuta Matsuri

Over several days in early August, enormous, illuminated floats are paraded through the streets of Aomori in Northern Honshū accompanied by thousands of rowdy, chanting dancers. A famous festival; book accommodation early. (p526)

✿ Peace Memorial Ceremony

On 6 August, a memorial service is held in Hiroshima for victims of the WWII atomic bombing of the city. Thousands of paper lanterns are floated down the river. (p441)

✿ Matsumoto Bonbon

Matsumoto's biggest event takes place on the first Saturday in August, when hordes of people perform the city's signature 'bonbon' dance through the streets. (p269)

✿ O-Bon (Festival of the Dead)

Three days in mid-August are set aside to honour the dead, when their spirits are said to return to the earth. Graves are swept, offerings are made and lanterns are floated down rivers, lakes or the sea to help guide spirits on their journey.

✿ Awa-odori Matsuri

The city of Tokushima, on the southern island of Shikoku, comes alive from 12 to 15 August for the nation's largest and most famous *bon* dance. These dances, part of O-Bon celebrations, are performed to welcome the souls of the departed back to this world. (p647)

✿ Rōsoku Matsuri

Kōya-san's already deeply atmospheric Oku-no-in is lit with some 100,000 candles on 13 August for Rōsoku Matsuri during O-Bon. (p413)

✿ Daimon-ji Gozan Okuribi

Huge fires in the shape of Chinese characters and other symbols are set alight in the hills around Kyoto during this festival, which forms part of the O-Bon rites. It's one of Japan's most impressive spectacles. (p332)

✿ Earth Celebration

Sado-ga-shima island, off the coast of Northern Honshū, is the scene of this internationally famous festival of dance, art and music, held in late August. Highlights include *taiko* (drum) performances and workshops. (p561)

September

Days are still warm, hot even, though less humid. Though the odd typhoon rolls through this time of year, this is generally a great time to travel in Japan.

✿ Kishiwada Danjiri Matsuri

Osaka's wildest festival, held over the third weekend in September, is a kind of running of the bulls except with *danjiri* (festival floats), many weighing more than 3000kg – take care and stand back. Most of the action takes place on the second day. (p372)

☉ Moon Viewing

Full moons in September and October call for *tsukimi*, moon-viewing gatherings. People eat *tsukimi dango* – *mochi* (pounded rice) dumplings, round like the moon.

October

Pleasantly warm days and cool evenings make this an excellent time to be in Tokyo. The autumn foliage peaks in the Japan Alps at this time.

🎎 Asama Onsen Taimatsu Matsuri

In early October, Asama Onsen in Matsumoto holds this spectacular fire festival, which sees groups of men, women and children parade burning bales of hay through narrow streets en route to an enormous bonfire. (p269)

🎎 Kurama-no-hi Matsuri

On 22 October, huge flaming torches are carried through the streets of the tiny hamlet of Kurama in the mountains north of Kyoto. This is one of Japan's more primeval festivals. (p332)

🎎 Matsue Suitōro

Held on Saturdays, Sundays and holidays throughout October in the Western Honshū city of Matsue, this festival of light and water takes place around the city's scenic castle. Lanterns are floated in the moat and rival drumming groups compete on the banks. (p476)

👁 Roppongi Art Night

Held in mid- to late October, this weekend-long (literally, as venues stay open all night) arts event (www.roppongiartnight. com) sees large-scale installations and performances taking over the streets of Roppongi in Tokyo.

🎎 Kyoto Experiment

Kyoto's international performing arts festival (http://kyoto-ex.jp) is held in late October or early November.

🎎 Halloween

Japan has taken to Halloween in a big way. Tokyo's Shibuya draws thousands of costumed revellers on 31 October. Osaka's Amerikamura becomes one big street party. (p365)

November

Crisp and cool days with snow starting to fall in the mountains. Autumn foliage peaks in and around Tokyo and Kyoto, which can draw crowds.

🎎 Shichi-Go-San (7-5-3 Festival)

This adorable festival in mid-November sees parents dress girls aged seven (shichi) and three (san) and boys aged five (go) in wee kimonos and head to Shintō shrines for blessings.

December

December is cold across most of Japan. Year-end parties fill city bars and restaurants; commercial strips are decorated with seasonal illuminations. Many businesses shut down from 29 or 30 December to between 3 and 6 January.

👁 Luminarie

Kōbe streets are lined with elaborate, illuminated arches every year for this event in early December, in memory of the victims of the 1995 Great Hanshin Earthquake. (p386)

🍴 Toshikoshi Soba

Eating buckwheat noodles on New Year's Eve, a tradition called toshikoshi soba, is said to bring luck and longevity – the latter symbolised by the length of the noodles.

☆ Joya-no-kane

Temple bells around Japan ring 108 times at midnight on 31 December, a purifying ritual.

Plan Your Trip
Itineraries

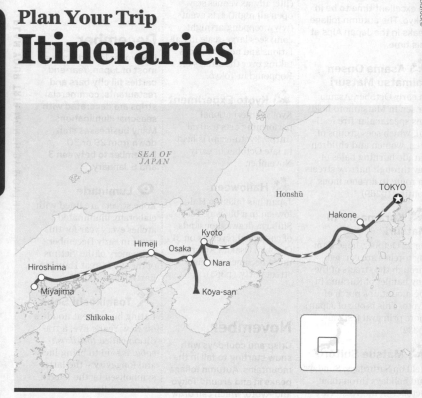

SEA OF JAPAN

Honshū

TOKYO

Hakone

Kyoto

Himeji

Osaka

Nara

Hiroshima

Miyajima

Kōya-san

Shikoku

2 WEEKS Tokyo, Kyoto & Hiroshima

This is a classic route for first-time visitors. It hits many star attractions, can be done year-round and takes advantage of the excellent value and seamless travel offered by a Japan Rail Pass.

Start with a couple of days in **Tokyo**, getting your bearings and a taste of big-city Japan – the skyscrapers, the bustle and all that neon. Then hop on the bullet train for **Kyoto**.

You'll need two or three days (minimum) to sample the best of Kyoto's temples and gardens. From here you can make side trips to **Nara**, home of the Daibutsu (Great

Buddha), and **Osaka**, famous for its vivid nightscape and street food.

Take a one-night detour to the mystical mountain monastery **Kōya-san** (where you can spend the night in a Buddhist temple). Then head west on to **Himeji** to see Japan's best castle, Himeji-jō.

Next stop is **Hiroshima**, for the moving Peace Memorial Park. Further down the coast is **Miyajima**, with its photogenic floating shrine. You can spend the night in a ryokan (traditional inn) here before taking the train back to Tokyo. On your way back there, drop into the mountain hot-spring resort of **Hakone** to get your onsen fix.

Shibuya Crossing, Tokyo (p87)

Atomic Bomb Dome, Hiroshima (p435)

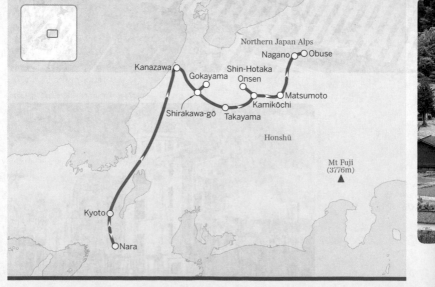

Northern Japan Alps

Nagano ○—○ Obuse

Kanazawa ○   Shin-Hotaka
          Gokayama   Onsen
                              ○ Matsumoto
Shirakawa-gō   Kamikōchi
          Takayama

Honshū

Mt Fuji
(3776m)
▲

Kyoto ○

○ Nara

2 WEEKS Kyoto, Kanazawa & the Japan Alps

This route highlights Japan's traditional culture and its natural beauty. Spend several days exploring Kyoto and Kanazawa, known for their culinary and artistic traditions, and a week driving through the Japan Alps, the setting for charming rural hamlets and hidden onsen (hot spring) villages.

Spend the first few days in **Kyoto**, exploring the city's famous temples, shrines and gardens. Be sure to budget time for the less-famous ones too, which are more peaceful, and for a day trip to **Nara**. Kyoto and Nara have excellent national museums with classical art and artefacts. In the evenings, stroll Kyoto's historic geisha district.

Next take the train to **Kanazawa**, a city that, in its heyday, rivalled Kyoto in its contributions to the arts. As befitting its location near the Sea of Japan, Kanazawa is known for great seafood, but also for its lasting artisan tradition and its strolling garden, Kenroku-en. Kyoto and Kanazawa are excellent places to shop for traditional crafts.

Get a car and head for the mountains of Hida. The villages of **Shirakawa-gō** and **Gokayama** are famed for farmhouses with dramatically angled thatched roofs. In the World Heritage–listed Ainokura village, you can spend the night in one.

Continue to **Takayama**, a charming old post town with well-preserved wooden buildings (now housing galleries, sake breweries and craft shops) and narrow streets. For beautiful alpine scenery and hiking, head to **Kamikōchi**; then, for rustic onsen (hot springs), to **Shin-Hotaka Onsen**.

You'll eat well in the mountains: local specialities include soba (buckwheat noodles), beef, *hoba-miso* (sweet miso paste grilled on a magnolia leaf) and foraged mushrooms and shoots.

From here drive east to the town of **Matsumoto**, home to one of Japan's best original castles, Matsumoto-jō. Near Nagano, pretty **Obuse**, another well-preserved mountain town, is home to the Hokusai Museum. End your trip in **Nagano** with a visit to the impressive Zenkō-ji temple.

Nagano has a *shinkansen* (bullet train) station so you can catch a train onward, or drive straight on to Narita Airport.

As snow can close mountain passes in winter, this route is best in spring, summer or autumn.

Top: Kasuga Taisha, Nara (p395)
Bottom: Shirakawa-gō (p245)

Tokyo, Mt Fuji & Around

1 WEEK

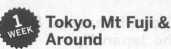

Japan often feels like a destination that requires a long trip and lots of advanced planning, but it needn't be. Between Tokyo and the towns in its orbit, on the coast and in the mountains, you can cover a lot of varied terrain, taking in both contemporary and traditional Japan.

Basing yourself in **Tokyo** has several advantages: you won't have to haul bags around while you travel and you can make plans on the fly, according to weather and mood. Though if you do back-to-back day trips, the JR Tokyo Wide Pass, which can be purchased in Japan, can save money.

For good transit connections, dining and entertainment options, Shinjuku is the best base, though other neighbourhoods, like Asakusa and Ueno on the east side, have cheaper digs.

In a few days, you can take in many of Tokyo's highlights, such as the bright lights and 24-hour buzz of Shinjuku and Shibuya; Harajuku's shrine, Meiji-jingū; the contemporary architecture along Omote-sandō; the seafood at Tsukiji Outer Market; and the charming old town of Yanesen. You can also just take it easy, hanging out in one of the city's fun, bohemian haunts, like Shimo-Kitazawa.

Summer is the season for climbing **Mt Fuji**, which is a two-hour train ride west of Tokyo. You can do it as one long overnight climb – to hit the summit for sunrise – or stay a night in a mountain hut. Year-round you can visit the Fuji Five Lake region, to see Mt Fuji reflected in the lakes.

For shrines and temples head north to **Nikkō**, home of the grand World Heritage–listed Tōshō-gū, the 17th-century shrine for shogun Tokugawa Ieyasu. There are hiking and onsen opportunities up this way, too. An hour south of Tokyo are more subdued Zen temples, founded centuries earlier, in the one-time medieval capital **Kamakura**. Kamakura, on the Pacific coast, has evolved into a hip beach community with cafes and surf shops.

Round off your trip with a visit to **Hakone**, a hot-spring resort town in the mountains southwest of the city, about two hours away by train. There are spa complexes here for day trippers, or you can splurge on a night in a ryokan (traditional Japanese inn).

Top: Mt Fuji
Bottom: View from Tokyo City View (p81)

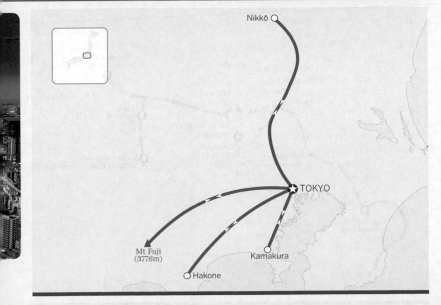

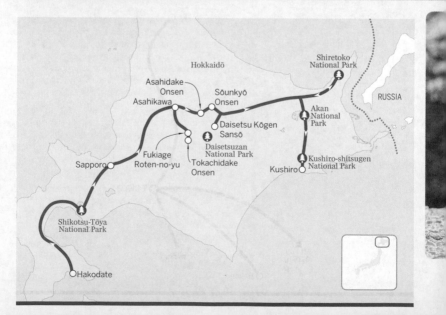

MIKE LYVERS/GETTY IMAGES ©

2 WEEKS The Wilds of Hokkaidō

Japan's northernmost island, Hokkaidō, has much of what you want out of Japan: steaming onsen and rugged, volcanic peaks, city lights and foodie cred, as well as something you wouldn't expect – the opportunity for an epic road trip. Snow falls early in Hokkaidō, so this is a summer trip.

Start in **Hakodate**, Hokkaidō's southernmost port, which has a charming 19th-century city centre. You can arrive via the new *shinkansen* (bullet train) line that opened in 2016, connecting Hakodate with Tokyo in four hours.

After a fresh seafood breakfast at Hakodate's fish market, drive to **Shikotsu-Toya National Park**, home to caldera lakes and an active volcano. Budget time to soak in the springs of Noboribetsu Onsen inside the park.

Next stop: **Sapporo**, Hokkaidō's capital city (and Japan's fifth largest). Get your city fix here, among the neon lights of the dining and drinking district Susukino. Then head to Hokkaidō's second city, **Asahikawa**; like Sapporo, Asahikawa is a famous ramen town. It's also the gateway for Daisetsuzan National Park, Japan's largest national park and a mostly untouched wilderness of dense forest, high in the mountains.

There are three villages on the perimeter of the park: **Tokachidake Onsen**, **Asahidake Onsen** and **Sōunkyō Onsen**. All have hot springs, lodging and good day treks. Don't miss **Fukiage Roten-no-yu**, near Tokachidake Onsen, one of Japan's best in-the-wild onsen. It's also worth spending a night at **Daisetsu Kōgen Sansō**, a truly remote mountain lodge.

Continue east to the World Heritage–listed **Shiretoko National Park**, land that Hokkaidō's indigenous people, the Ainu, referred to as 'the end of the world'. There are hikes here, through primeval woods, and more hidden hot springs.

Akan National Park is most famous for its startlingly clear and blue caldera lakes, Kussharo-ko and Mashu-ko. This is also the best place on Hokkaidō to learn about the Ainu; there are some (touristy) Ainu villages here, such as Akan Kotan.

Finally wend down to **Kushiro-shitsugen National Park**, home to the endangered Japanese red-crowned crane. From Kushiro it's easy to get to New Chitose Airport, south of Sapporo.

PICHIT TONGMA/SHUTTERSTOCK ©

Top: Akan National Park (p627)
Bottom: *Tanchō-zuru* (red-crested white crane), Kushiro-shitsugen National Park (p635)

2 WEEKS Kyūshū & Okinawa

PLAN YOUR TRIP ITINERARIES

Considered off the beaten track, Kyūshū really delivers: it's got a fantastic city in Fukuoka, riveting history in Nagasaki, excellent onsen and smoking volcanoes. Heading south, the Satsuma Peninsula dissolves into a chain of semi-tropical islands, including Okinawa, stretching into the Pacific. If you want to see something totally different, this trip is for you.

Fly into **Fukuoka** from Tokyo and spend a day exploring this hip city, known for its outdoor food stalls and rich, pork-bone ramen. You can tour Kyūshū easily by train – there's a rail pass just for the island – but it helps to have a car. It'll come in handy for working your way down the coast via the pottery town of **Karatsu** to **Hirado**, a small island that punches above its size history-wise. After visiting Hirado, **Arita** is another pottery town worth a stop on your way to **Nagasaki**.

History, of course, weighs heavily on Nagasaki, the second Japanese city destroyed by an atomic bomb. But Nagasaki also has a colourful cosmopolitan legacy that lives on today in its food and architecture. From Nagasaki cut into the heartland to **Kurokawa Onsen**, one of Japan's best onsen towns, where you can stay in a ryokan.

Next head south, past the active volcano **Aso-san** and the castle town **Kumamoto** (still recovering from a 2016 earthquake) to **Kagoshima**. The city at the tip of the Shimabara Peninsula is known for *tonkatsu* (breaded and fried pork cutlets), *shōchū* (strong distilled liquor) and Sakura-jima – the smoking volcano that lords over the skyline. South of Kagoshima are the hot sand baths of **Ibusuki**.

Return the car and catch a speedboat from Kagoshima to **Yakushima**, an island with primeval, moss-strewn forests and seaside onsen. Spend the night (or longer for serious hiking).

Back in Kagoshima, take the slow ferry for an epic overnight ride to Okinawa-hontō, the largest of the Okinawa Islands. Spend a day or two exploring the capital city **Naha**, the former seat of the Ryūkyū Empire, sipping fresh juice from the market and enjoying island delicacies. From Naha, it's a one-hour jet-foil ride to the idyllic, palm-fringed **Kerama Islands** – where you can get your beach fix. Then catch a flight back to Tokyo from Naha.

Top: Shuri-jō, Naha (p789)
Bottom: Yakushima (p771)

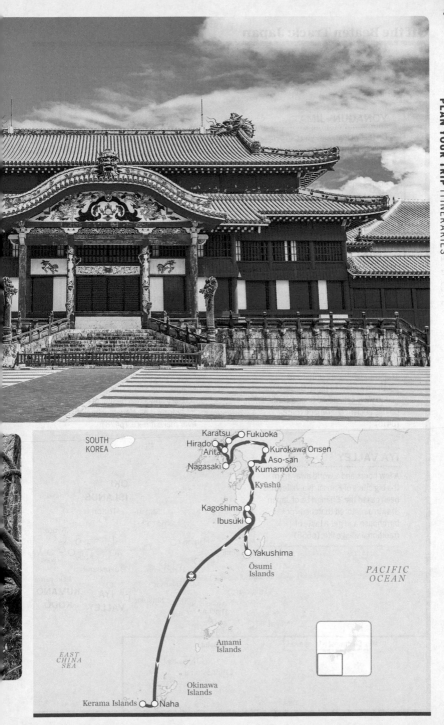

SOUTH KOREA

Karatsu   Fukuoka
Hirado   Kurokawa Onsen
Arita   Aso-san
Nagasaki   Kumamoto
                Kyūshū

Kagoshima
Ibusuki

                Yakushima
                Ōsumi
                Islands   PACIFIC
                                            OCEAN

EAST
CHINA
SEA   Amami
                    Islands

                    Okinawa
                    Islands
Kerama Islands   Naha

Off the Beaten Track: Japan

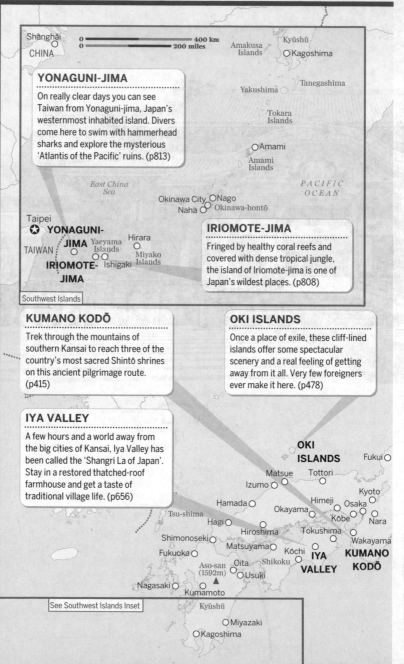

Shànghǎi
CHINA

0 — 400 km
0 — 200 miles

Amakusa Islands

Kyūshū
○ Kagoshima

YONAGUNI-JIMA

On really clear days you can see Taiwan from Yonaguni-jima, Japan's westernmost inhabited island. Divers come here to swim with hammerhead sharks and explore the mysterious 'Atlantis of the Pacific' ruins. (p813)

Yakushima ○
Tanegashima

Tokara Islands

○Amami
Amami Islands

PACIFIC OCEAN

East China Sea

Okinawa City ○Nago
Naha ○ Okinawa-hontō

Taipei
✪ YONAGUNI-
JIMA
TAIWAN
Yaeyama Islands
Hirara
○
Miyako Islands
IRIOMOTE- Ishigaki
JIMA

IRIOMOTE-JIMA

Fringed by healthy coral reefs and covered with dense tropical jungle, the island of Iriomote-jima is one of Japan's wildest places. (p808)

Southwest Islands

KUMANO KODŌ

Trek through the mountains of southern Kansai to reach three of the country's most sacred Shintō shrines on this ancient pilgrimage route. (p415)

OKI ISLANDS

Once a place of exile, these cliff-lined islands offer some spectacular scenery and a real feeling of getting away from it all. Very few foreigners ever make it here. (p478)

IYA VALLEY

A few hours and a world away from the big cities of Kansai, Iya Valley has been called the 'Shangri La of Japan'. Stay in a restored thatched-roof farmhouse and get a taste of traditional village life. (p656)

OKI
ISLANDS
Fukui ○

Matsue Tottori
Izumo ○ ○

Kyoto
Himeji ○Osaka
Hamada ○ Okayama ○ ○○ Kōbe Nara
Tsu-shima Hagi ○
Hiroshima ○ Tokushima Wakayama
Shimonoseki ○ Matsuyama ○ Kōchi IYA KUMANO
Fukuoka ○ Shikoku VALLEY KODŌ
Aso-san Ōita Shikoku
(1592m) ○Usuki
Nagasaki ○ ▲
Kumamoto

See Southwest Islands Inset

Kyūshū

○Miyazaki
○Kagoshima

0 500 km
0 250 miles

RUSSIA

Sea of Okhotsk   RUSSIA

RISHIRI-TŌ & REBUN-TŌ

SHIRETOKO NATIONAL PARK

Abashiri

Daisetsuzan National Park

Takikawa   Biei   Akan National Park

Otaru   Sapporo   Hokkaidō   Kushiro

Shikotsu-tōya National Park   Obihiro

Okushiri-tō   Hakodate

Aomori

Towada-Hachimantai National Park   Hachinohe

Sea of Japan

Akita   Morioka
Kakunodate

Sakata   Oshu
Tsuruoka   Shinjō
DEWA SANZAN
Sendai
Yamagata
SADO GA-SHIMA   Fukushima
Niigata

Noto Peninsula

Toyama   Nikkō
Nagano   Utsunomiya
Kanazawa   Mito
Honshū   Maebashi
Kōfu   Urawa   **TOKYO**
Gifu   Chiba
Nagoya   Yokohama
Mt Fuji (3776m)
Tsu   Shizuoka   *PACIFIC OCEAN*
Ise

SHIRETOKO NATIONAL PARK

With no sealed roads and a healthy population of brown bears, Shiretoko earns the title of Japan's last true wilderness. The rewards for tackling the tough trails here are long soaks in hot springs. (p623)

RISHIRI-TŌ & REBUN-TŌ

Almost as far north as you can go in Japan, these two islands burst into riotous blooms of wildflowers each year from May to August. They're a true delight for hikers and photographers. (p618 & p617)

DEWA SANZAN

Complete the three-mountain hike that makes up this trail through the wilds of Yamagata, a favourite pilgrimage for the *yamabushi* (mountain priests). (p551)

OGASAWARA ARCHIPELAGO

This is as far off the beaten track as you can get in Japan. A full 25½-hour ferry ride from Tokyo, these semitropical islands – complete with whales, sharks and dolphins – feel like a different world. (p208)

SADO-GA-SHIMA

A wild outpost of rugged mountains and coastline, each August this island rocks to the sound of the famous Kodō Drummers during the fabulous Earth Celebration. (p557)

Ogasawara Archipelago (500km)

Plan Your Trip
Skiing in Japan

With its 500 ski resorts, Japan is not the skiing and snowboarding world's best-kept secret anymore. Those in the know come from around the globe to make the most of regular snowfall, stunning mountain vistas, reasonable costs, friendly locals and great variety of après-ski options.

Need to Know

The Season

Usually kicks off in December, though conditions are highly variable. January and February are peak months across the country. Things begin to warm up in March, heralding the close of the season in April.

The Snow

Basically, more snow falls on the Sea of Japan side of the mountains, with more snow the further north you go. Hokkaidō's Niseko ski area receives a whopping 15m of snow every year!

What to Bring

Almost everything you'll need is available in Japan. If you have large feet (longer than 30cm), bring your own boots. If you're on the big side, bring your own clothing and gloves, too.

Costs

Japan is a surprisingly reasonable place to ski or snowboard. Lift tickets and accommodation are competitively priced as the number of domestic skiers has been in decline for years.

Resources

An excellent website for checking out the Japan ski scene is www.snowjapan.com (in English).

Where to Ski

Japan's best-known ski resorts are found in the Japan Alps and on the northern island of Hokkaidō. The former lays claim to the highest mountains, while the latter boasts the deepest and most regular snowfall in the country.

While the ski resorts of Northern Honshū have seen tough times since the Great East Japan Earthquake, they offer up some wonderful options. And don't forget the Niigata mountains, easily accessed by *shinkansen* (bullet train) from Tokyo.

There are some 500 ski areas in Japan – do you homework before you go to find the right place for you. Here is our pick of the best:

Niseko As far as most foreign skiers are concerned, Niseko (p589) is how you say 'powder' in Japanese. This is understandable, as Niseko receives an average snowfall of 15m annually. Located on Hokkaidō, Niseko is actually four interconnected ski areas: Niseko Annupuri, Niseko Village (also known as Higashiyama), Grand Hirafu and Hanazono.

Furano More or less in the centre of Hokkaidō (the town also hosts a belly-button festival, Heso Matsuri, to celebrate being in the middle!), Furano (p605) shot to world fame after hosting FIS World Ski and Snowboarding Cup events. Relatively undiscovered in comparison to Niseko, Furano rewards savvy powder fiends with polished runs through pristine birch forests.

Sapporo Teine It's so close to Sapporo, Hokkaidō's capital, that buses run from downtown hotels to

Skiing in Japan

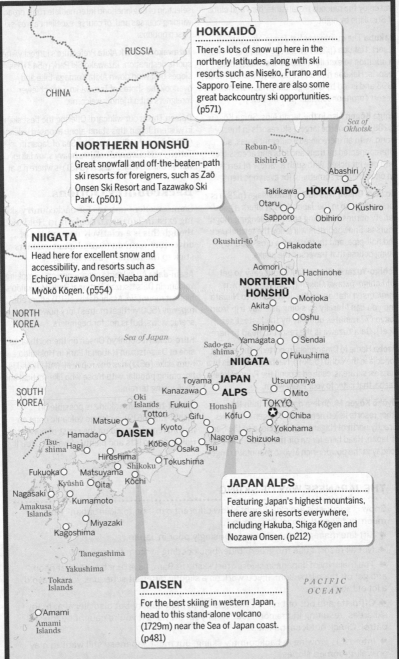

0 — 400 km
0 — 200 miles

RUSSIA

CHINA

NORTH KOREA

SOUTH KOREA

Sea of Japan

Sea of Okhotsk

Sea of Japan

PACIFIC OCEAN

HOKKAIDŌ

There's lots of snow up here in the northerly latitudes, along with ski resorts such as Niseko, Furano and Sapporo Teine. There are also some great backcountry ski opportunities. (p571)

NORTHERN HONSHŪ

Great snowfall and off-the-beaten-path ski resorts for foreigners, such as Zaō Onsen Ski Resort and Tazawako Ski Park. (p501)

NIIGATA

Head here for excellent snow and accessibility, and resorts such as Echigo-Yuzawa Onsen, Naeba and Myōkō Kōgen. (p554)

JAPAN ALPS

Featuring Japan's highest mountains, there are ski resorts everywhere, including Hakuba, Shiga Kōgen and Nozawa Onsen. (p212)

DAISEN

For the best skiing in western Japan, head to this stand-alone volcano (1729m) near the Sea of Japan coast. (p481)

Rebun-tō
Rishiri-tō
Abashiri
Takikawa **HOKKAIDŌ**
Otaru Kushiro
Sapporo Obihiro
Okushiri-tō Hakodate
Aomori Hachinohe
NORTHERN HONSHŪ
Akita Morioka
Oshu
Shinjō
Sado-ga-shima Yamagata Sendai
NIIGATA Fukushima
Toyama **JAPAN** Utsunomiya
Kanazawa **ALPS** Mito
Oki Islands Fukui Honshū **TOKYO**
Tottori Gifu Kōfu Chiba
Matsue Kyoto Yokohama
Hamada **DAISEN** Nagoya Shizuoka
Tsu-shima Hagi Kōbe Osaka Tsu
Hiroshima Shikoku Tokushima
Fukuoka Matsuyama Kōchi
Kyūshū Oita
Nagasaki Kumamoto
Amakusa Islands
Miyazaki
Kagoshima
Tanegashima
Yakushima
Tokara Islands
Amami
Amami Islands

Sapporo Teine (p582). You can swish down slopes used in the 1972 Sapporo Winter Olympics by day and enjoy the raucous restaurants, bars and clubs of Susukino by night.

Hakuba The quintessential Japan Alps ski resort, Hakuba (p277) offers eye-popping views in addition to excellent and varied skiing in six resorts. Hakuba hosted Winter Olympic events in 1998 and is led by the legendary Happō-One Ski Resort (pronounced 'hah-poh-oh-neh').

Shiga Kōgen Also in the Japan Alps, Shiga Kōgen (p288) is one of the largest ski resorts in the world, with an incredible 19 different areas, all interconnected by trails and lifts and accessible with one lift ticket. With such a variety of terrain on offer, there is something for everyone here.

Nozawa Onsen This quaint little village (p287) is tucked high up in the Japan Alps. It offers a good variety of runs, including some challenging mogul courses. Snowboarders will enjoy the terrain park and half-pipe, and there's even a cross-country skiing course that traverses the peaks.

Echigo-Yuzawa Onsen Talk about easy to get to! Echigo-Yuzawa Onsen (p563) has its own *shinkansen* station on the Jōetsu line to Niigata and you can literally go skiing as a day trip from Tokyo (77 minutes one way by the fastest service!). Gala Yuzawa is the resort to head to here.

Naeba Home to Dragondola, reportedly the longest gondola in the world (5.5km), Naeba (p564) has two massive ski areas, centred around the Prince Hotel Naeba, that cater to your every whim.

Myōkō Kōgen Much less developed than the other resorts listed here, Myōkō Kōgen (p565) is directly north of Nagano city and close to the Sea of Japan. Head here for an off-the-beaten-path ski holiday in the powder-rich Myōkō mountain range.

Zaō Onsen Ski Resort Arguably the top ski slopes in Northern Honshū, Zaō (p548) has a huge selection of beginner and intermediate runs, broad winding courses and, of course, excellent après-ski onsen options.

Tazawako Ski Park Akita Prefecture's largest winter sports destination, Tazawako Ski Park (p543) has slopes that wind down Akita Komaga-take and overlook the shores of Tazawa-ko. Expect fewer foreigners but a friendly welcome.

Daisen This is our wildcard! Offering the best skiing in western Japan, this stand-alone exposed volcano (1729m) is only 10km from the Sea of Japan in Tottori Prefecture and catches heavy snowfall in winter. Daisen White Resort (p481) is where it's at.

Backcountry Options

Some excellent options for backcountry skiing exist in Japan, particularly in Hokkaidō, though this is a relatively new sphere of adventure tourism (most Japanese skiers stick to the mainstream places).

Asahi-dake An extreme experience on a smoking volcano in Daisetsuzan National Park. Hokkaidō's highest mountain, Asahi-dake (p610) offers one ropeway (500 vertical metres), dry powder and scenic views, but is not for beginners.

Kuro-dake At Sōunkyō Onsen on the northeastern side of Daisetsuzan National Park in Hokkaidō, Kuro-dake (p611) has one ropeway and lift and is becoming popular with those who like vertical and challenging terrain.

Rishiri-tō Extreme skiing is possible on Rishiri-zan (p619), a classic volcanic cone on its own remote island off the coast of northern Hokkaidō. No lifts and plenty of walking. You'll

---

THE JAPANESE WAY OF SKIING

Snow is snow, skis are skis – right? How different can it be to ski in Japan? Not very much, but keep the following in mind:

➤ Lift-line management can be surprisingly poor in Japan.

➤ Not all resorts use the green/blue/black coding system for difficulty.

➤ The majority of Japanese skiers start skiing at 9am, have lunch exactly at noon, and get off the hill by 3pm. If you work on a slightly different schedule, you will avoid a lot of the crowds.

➤ Off-piste and out-of-bounds skiing is often high quality but also illegal at many ski areas, resulting in the confiscation of your lift pass if you're caught by the ski patrol. Check out local policies.

➤ Interest is growing in backcountry skiing, but most Japanese still want to play on well-groomed slopes.

need a guide from Rishiri Nature Guide Service (p619). Book early!

Costs

Many people unfamiliar with skiing in Japan often assume that it will cost an arm and a leg to ski here. But, even after factoring in the international air ticket, it might actually be cheaper to ski for a week in Japan than in your home country. Are we mad? Let's check the numbers.

Lift Tickets & Equipment Rental A full-day lift ticket at most ski areas in Japan still costs between ¥4000 and ¥6000, although Niseko is up to ¥7400. This is significantly less than a full day at large resorts in North America or Europe. Full equipment rental is typically no more than ¥5000 per day (both ski and snowboard sets are available). The Japanese tend to be connoisseurs of quality, which means that you need not worry about getting stuck with shabby and/or outdated gear.

Accommodation You can find plenty of decent accommodation in the ¥6500 to ¥10,000 range at major ski areas in Japan, and this price will often include one or two meals. This is well under what you'd expect to pay for similar accommodation in North America or Europe. The budget traveller will find a variety of backpacker-type hostels near most resorts, and families will be glad to know that young children (under six years of age) can usually stay for free or at a significant discount.

Food On-slope meals mostly top out at around ¥1000, cheaper than what you'd pay in North America or Europe. The restaurant selection anywhere you go is also varied, including the likes of ramen (egg noodles), udon (wheat noodles), karē-raisu (curry rice) and gyūdon (sliced beef on rice), as well as more familiar fast-food options including sandwiches, pizza, burgers and kebabs.

Transport Airport-to-resort transport in Japan costs no more than in other countries, and is

MICHAEL H/GETTY IMAGES ©

usually faster and more efficient (and, unlike in North America, you don't need to rent a car).

Can You Say 'Ski' in Japanese?

That's right: it's 'ski' (all right, it's pronounced more like 'sukee'), but the point is that communication won't be much of a problem on your Japan ski trip.

Tackling the language barrier has never been easier: most of the better-known resorts employ a number of English-speaking foreigners and Japanese who have spent time overseas. They work the lifts and in the cafeterias, and often find employment in the hotels or guesthouses that are most popular with foreign guests.

All major signs and maps are translated into English, and provided you have some experience of large resorts back home, you'll find the layout and organisation of Japanese resorts to be pretty intuitive.

The information counter at the base of the mountain always has helpful and polite staff available to answer questions.

DID YOU KNOW?
- ➡ The first Winter Olympics held outside Europe or North America was at Sapporo in 1972.
- ➡ Snowboarding first debuted as an Olympic sport at the 1998 Nagano Winter Olympics.

Plan Your Trip

Travel with Children

Safe, clean and full of mod cons, Japan is a great place to travel with kids. The downside is that many cultural sights (shrines, temples and museums) may bore them; you'll want to work in plenty of activities to keep things fresh. Teens will love the pop culture and neon streetscapes.

Best Regions for Kids

Tokyo

Pop culture galore: stay in a hotel with a giant Godzilla statue, explore the world of Japan's top animator, Miyazaki Hayao, at the Ghibli Museum, take in an amusement park or shop for character goods. Teens will love neighbourhoods like Harajuku (p89) and Shibuya (p87).

Okinawa & the Southwest Islands

Work in a little beach time in subtropical Okinawa – a popular destination for local families. Off-the-beaten-track island Taketomi is great for kids: there are no cars (only bicycles!) and great, low-key beaches.

Central Honshū

Hiking and skiing in the Alps, cycling past rice fields and exploring old farm villages outside Takayama and a fantastic castle in Matsumoto.

Sapporo & Hokkaidō

Great skiing, snowboarding, hiking and camping opportunities for outdoorsy families.

Eating

Supermarkets, bakeries, fast-food restaurants and convenience stores stock sandwiches and other familiar foods; supermarkets carry baby food.

If your child has allergies, get someone to write them down in Japanese. Chain restaurants often have common allergens marked on the menus with icons.

If you plan to stay at a ryokan with a meal plan, discuss any menu modifications when you book (places that regularly get foreign tourists should be accommodating); you can also book a stay without meals.

Local families take a lot of meals at 'family restaurants' (ファミレス; famiresu), chains like Gusto, Jonathan's, Saizeriya and Royal Host, that have kids' meals, high chairs, big booths and nonsmoking sections. High chairs are not as common as in the West.

Sleeping

Most hotels can provide a cot for an extra fee (providing there's enough room for one). Some hotels have triple rooms, but quads or rooms with two queen-sized beds are rare.

Local families often stay in traditional accommodation (ryokan and minshuku) with large tatami rooms that can hold up to five futons, laid out in a row.

Hostels often have family rooms (or at worst, a four-person dorm room that you can book out). These also often have kitchen facilities.

International hotels in Tokyo partner with local childcare agencies that have English-speaking staff.

Infants

Nappies (diapers), bottles, wipes and medications are available at large pharmacies.

Department stores, shopping malls and larger train stations usually have nappy-changing facilities.

Breastfeeding is generally not done in public, though some mums do (find a quiet corner and use a shawl and likely no one will notice).

Getting Around

Trains have priority seating for pregnant passengers and those with small children. It's best to avoid trains during morning rush hour (7am to 9.30am). If you must, children under 12 can ride with mums in the less-crowded women-only carriages. Children between the ages of six and 11 ride for half-price on trains (including bullet trains); under-6s ride for free.

Train stations and buildings in larger cities usually have lifts; many attractions, such as temples and shrines, do not have ramps (and prams do not get the same access to special elevators and back passages for visitors in wheelchairs). Beware that side streets often lack pavements.

Travelling by car (outside major cities) is often a good strategy for families, as it makes child and luggage-wrangling easier. Child seats in taxis are generally not available, but most car-rental agencies will provide one if you ask in advance.

Children's Highlights
Amusement Parks

➡ **Tokyo Disney Resort, Tokyo** (p113) See Disney Sea park (and classic Disney attractions).

➡ **Universal Studios Japan, Osaka** (p370) The Japanese version of the American theme park.

➡ **Fuji-Q Highland, Fuji-Yoshida** (p163) Best known for its thrill rides.

➡ **Tokyo Dome City, Tokyo** (p113) Kiddie rides and a roller coaster in the heart of Tokyo.

Trains

➡ **Kyoto Railway Museum, Kyoto** (p302) The history of Japanese trains, from steam engines to shinkansen (bullet trains).

➡ **JR SCMAGLEV & Railway Park, Nagoya** (p219) See an actual maglev (the world's fastest train) and test-ride a *shinkansen* simulator.

Baseball

See the crowds go wild for Japan's favourite sport. All major cities have a local team.

➡ **Tokyo Dome, Tokyo** (p144)

➡ **Mazda Zoom Zoom Stadium, Hiroshima** (p444)

➡ **Fukuoka Yafuoku! Dome, Fukuoka** (p702)

➡ **Sapporo Dome, Sapporo** (p586)

➡ **Kyōcera Dome, Osaka** (p378)

Cycling Tours

➡ **Satoyama Experience, Hida-Furukawa** (p242) Views of rice fields and farmhouses.

Skiing & Snowboarding

➡ **Niseko United, Niseko** (p589) One of Japan's biggest resorts, with English-speaking instructors and children's ski camps.

PLANNING

Very little special planning is necessary for travellers with children heading to Japan, but do bring any medicines that your child takes regularly (or may need), as Japanese pharmacies don't sell foreign medications (though similar ones can be found). The *shinkansen* (bullet train) is very smooth and few travellers report feeling motion sickness, but you might consider preventative measures; winding mountain roads are as nausea-inducing as anywhere. The only other thing you might want to pack are small plastic forks and spoons, as not all restaurants have these on hand.

Tuna sashimi with sea grape and wasabi

Plan Your Trip
Eat & Drink
Like a Local

As visitors to Japan quickly discover, the people here are
absolutely obsessed with food. You'll find that every island and
region of Japan has its own meibutsu (local speciality) that is a
point of pride.

The Year in Food

At finer restaurants, not only does the menu change with the seasons but so does the crockery and the garnishes (which are often seasonal flowers, sprigs or leaves).

Spring (Mar–May)

The new growth of spring finds its way onto tables in the form of *takenoko* (bamboo shoots) and *sansai* (mountain vegetables). Especially good if you're in the mountains.

Summer (Jun–Aug)

The season for cooling dishes like *reimen* (cold ramen) and *zaru soba* (cold buck-wheat noodles served on a bamboo tray). And nothing says summer like *kaki-gōri* (shaved ice topped with sweet syrup).

Autumn (Sep–Nov)

The first sign of autumn is silvery *sanma* (Pacific saury) on menus. Other delicacies: matsutake mushrooms, ginkgo nuts, candied chestnuts and *shinmai*, the first rice of the harvest season.

Winter (Dec–Feb)

Friends come together for steaming *nabe* (hotpot) dishes; this is also the season for *fugu* (pufferfish) and oysters.

Food Experiences

Must-Dos

➜ Getting a breakfast of fresh seafood at a morning market, such as Tokyo's Tsukiji Outer Market (p79) or Hokkaidō's Hakodate Morning Market (p636).

➜ Gazing upon (and sampling) all the glorious delights to be found in a department store food hall.

➜ Basking in the full sensory culinary experience that is *kaiseki* (Japan's haute cuisine), best eaten at one of Kyoto or Kanazawa's superlative restaurants.

➜ Grabbing late-night noodles after a rousing round of karaoke in one of Japan's famous nightlife districts.

➜ Splurging on a chef's tasting menu at a top-class sushi restaurant, such as those found in Tokyo's Ginza district.

➜ Raising a glass of sake with the locals in a classic *izakaya* (Japanese pub-eatery).

Cheap Eats

➜ **Tachigui Noodles** *Tachigui* means 'stand and eat' and is shorthand for budget shops, often found in or around train stations, where for a few hundred yen you can stand at the counter and slurp down a bowl of hot soba or udon.

➜ **Onigiri** These are triangles or discs of sticky rice, often wrapped in seaweed and stuffed with the likes of salmon, cod roe or pickled plum. Convenience stores and vendors at larger train stations sell them. Cost: ¥100 to ¥200.

➜ **Curry Rice** This student favourite is Japan's take on curry: it's thick, brown, often more sweet than spicy, and belly-filling, served over sticky rice and rarely more than ¥1000. Curry shops, both fast-food chains and independent ones, are ubiquitous.

➜ **Festival Food** Japanese festivals, traditional and contemporary, always have food stalls selling all sorts of hot, cheap treats on a stick (like squid) or fresh off the griddle (like *yaki-soba*, stir-fried noodles).

➜ **Bakeries** In addition to rather conventional sandwiches and Danishes, Japanese bakeries sell snacks subtly spiked with Japanese flavours such as *mentaiko* (spicy cod roe) and *anko* (sweetened red-bean paste).

Dare to Try

➜ **Nattō** These partially fermented soybeans with the scent of ammonia are the litmus test by which Japanese judge a foreigner's sense of culinary adventure (don't be surprised if someone asks you: 'Can you eat *nattō*?').

➜ **Uni** With the flavour of a distilled tidal pool, the appearance of a small orange brain and the texture of custard, *uni* (sea urchin) is the holy grail for many sushi fans but an acquired taste. Season: summer.

➜ **Shiokara** Chunks of seafood fermented in their own heavily salted viscera. *Shiokara* is a classic grandpa bar snack, washed down with sake at old-school *izakaya*.

➡ **Inago no Tsukudani** Grasshoppers braised in soy sauce and sugar is a speciality in the mountains of Central Honshū.

➡ **Shirako** Known as *shirako*, milt (the sperm sac) from cod or *fugu* is a winter delicacy. It can be found in sushi restaurants around Japan, usually poached and served in a light, citrusy soy sauce.

Local Specialities

Tokyo

➡ **Sushi** With the country's leading fish market, Tokyo gets first dibs on the best catch of the day.

➡ **Creative Cooking** Tokyo diners have a big appetite for novelty, and chefs and restaurateurs are happy to oblige. This might mean a new twist on ramen that sparks a national craze or an innovative way of blending Japanese haute cuisine and modern French that lands a local restaurant on a world's best list.

The Japan Alps & Central Honshū

➡ **Mountain Cuisine** The rugged Alps are far from the sea and fertile plains. Here the staples include soba (buckwheat noodles) and potatoes; foraged mushrooms and shoots; game, like deer; and river fish, like *ayu* (sweetfish). Food is often charcoal-grilled or served in hotpots.

➡ **Sea of Japan Coast** The Sea of Japan's cold waters produce excellent seafood. The most prized catch is *kan-buri* (winter-fattened yellowtail). Fresh seafood turns up in abundance in Kanazawa's brand of *kaiseki* (haute cuisine).

Kyoto

➡ **Kaiseki** Japan's haute cuisine developed in the old imperial capital. Kyoto has the most highly regarded *kaiseki* restaurants in the country (including some for diners on more modest budgets).

➡ **Tea & Sweets** The home of the tea ceremony is naturally the best place to sample green tea and the *wagashi* (Japanese sweets) served with it. Nearby Uji is Japan's most famous tea-producing region.

Kansai

➡ **Osaka** Japan's third-largest city has a lively dining scene. Two can't-miss local dishes are

Preparation for tea ceremony

tako-yaki (grilled octopus dumplings), usually sold at street stalls, and *okonomiyaki* (a grill-it-yourself savoury pancake).

➡ **Kōbe** The cosmopolitan port city is famous for its bakeries and high-end beef.

➡ **Vegetarian Temple Food** The temple complex Koya-san (p409) is an excellent place to sample *shōjin-ryōri*, the vegetarian cuisine of Buddhist monks.

Hiroshima & Western Honshū

➡ **Hiroshima-yaki** You can't visit Hiroshima without sampling the city's distinctive style of *okonomiyaki* (a savoury pancake), topped with noodles and a fried egg.

➡ **Oysters** In winter, oyster lovers from across Japan seek out the bivalves harvested from the Inland Sea near Hiroshima. Temporary *kaki-goya* ('oyster houses') with makeshift grills appear in town on the coast.

Northern Honshū (Tōhoku)

➡ **Hotpots** Hotpot dishes are common in the remote and rugged deep north of Japan's mainland. Each area has its own style: in

Okonomiyaki

Yamagata it's made with taro; in Akita it's made with *kiritanpo* – kneaded rice grilled on bamboo spits.

➡ **Gyūtan** Sendai's local speciality is thinly sliced, surprisingly tender beef tongue grilled over charcoal.

➡ **Sake** Niigata is known for its distinctive style of crisp, dry sake (called *tanrei karakuchi*).

Sapporo & Hokkaidō

➡ **Shellfish** Hokkaidō's cold waters are fertile breeding grounds for flavourful crab, scallops and surf clams in winter and shrimp and sea urchin in summer.

➡ **Miso Ramen** Sapporoites keep warm in winter with ramen spiked with pungent miso and topped with vegetables stir-fried with garlic.

➡ **Lamb BBQ** Hokkaidō locals love lamb grilled over hot coals (a dish called *jingisukan*) paired with copious mugs of draught beer.

Shikoku

Largely rural Shikoku excels in simple pleasures, such as udon (in Kagawa) and *katsuo-tataki* (seared bonito; in Kōchi).

Kyūshū

➡ **Hakata Ramen** Fukuoka is Japan's top ramen pilgrimage spot. Here the signature style is thin noodles served in an intensely rich *tonkotsu* (pork bone broth). Eat it at one of the city's many *yatai* (open-air food stalls).

➡ **Nagasaki Fusion** While the rest of Japan was closed to the outside world from the 17th to mid-19th century, Nagasaki was permitted a small foreign community, consisting mainly of Chinese, Portuguese and Dutch. *Shippoku-ryōri*, the city's curiously fusion haute cuisine, is coloured by these influences. Also try *castella*, a sponge cake based on the recipe of a 16th-century Portuguese missionary.

Okinawa & the Southwest Islands

Okinawa, which was its own kingdom until the mid-19th century, has a food culture all its own. Local dishes to try include *mimigā* (sliced pigs' ears marinated in vinegar) and *gōyā champurū* (stir-fry containing bitter melon, an Okinawan vegetable). *Awamori* is Okinawa's firewater, brewed from rice.

JUNICHI MIYAZAKI/LONELY PLANET ©

Yakitori

How to Eat & Drink

When to Eat

➡ **Breakfast** The traditional Japanese breakfast consists of rice, miso soup and a few side dishes such as a small piece of cooked fish and *nattō* (partially fermented beans); this is what is served at a ryokan (traditional inn). Head to cafes for baked goods and coffee.

➡ **Lunch** Eaten between 11.30am and 1pm, lunch is often a set meal – which includes a nice balance of protein, carbs (usually rice) and vegetables – typically consumed perfunctorily.

➡ **Dinner** Unless they're urbanites doing overtime, most Japanese eat dinner fairly early, around 6pm. Like lunch, the aim is balance. When eaten out, dinner is often an accompaniment for booze, becoming a drawn-out affair with a variety of small dishes ordered a few at a time.

Where to Eat

➡ **In the City** Japan's larger cities have a good spread of cuisines, so you can take your pick from restaurants specialising in different Japanese dishes or Chinese, Thai, French, Italian and more. Look to food courts in department stores and train stations for easy options.

➡ **In the Country** Resort towns will have clusters of eateries but note that many small restaurants will either close between lunch and dinner or not serve dinner at all – as most Japanese guests prefer to book meals at their accommodation. Indeed, in rural areas, the top foodie meals are often served at ryokan (traditional inns), where the dishes make ample use of local ingredients.

Menu Decoder

➡ **Setto** (セット) Set menu/course

➡ **Morning setto** (モーニングセット) Cafe breakfast set, usually of egg, toast and coffee

➡ **Party plan** (パーティプラン; *pāti puran*) Course of several dishes and an hour or two of all-you-can-drink, which can often be ordered at an *izakaya* (Japanese pub-eatery)

➡ **Teishoku** (定食) Set menu/course

➡ **Tabe-hōdai** (食べ放題) All-you-can-eat (often a set time in which you can order an unlimited number of plates)

➡ **Viking** (バイキング; *baikingu*) All-you-can-eat buffet

➡ **Nomi-hōdai** (飲み放題) All-you-can-drink

➡ **Ippin ryōri** (一品料理) À la carte

➡ **Nomimono** (飲み物) Drinks

Plan Your Trip
Japan on a Budget

Japan has a reputation as an expensive place to travel to, but it's an image that doesn't hold up on the ground. With a little strategy, it can be very reasonable – budget-friendly, even. Many of the country's top sights, for example, cost nothing and free festivals take place year-round.

Budget Accommodation

➡ **Business Hotels** These economical (and to be honest, rather utilitarian) hotels are the best deals for couples: book early online and get a double room for roughly ¥8000 (US$65); singles cost about ¥6000 (US$50). They are often clustered around train stations and outdo each other with perks like free breakfast and wi-fi.

➡ **Guesthouses & Hostels** Japanese cities (and some rural areas) are seeing an influx of boutique-style guesthouses – often more stylish than hotels that cost twice the price (though bathrooms will be shared). A double or single room is comparative to a business hotel; dorm beds cost around ¥3000 (US$25). Often such lodgings are staffed by travellers, who speak English and can give good local tips on where to eat well and cheaply.

➡ **Capsule Hotels** A capsule berth costs slightly more than a dorm bed in a hostel (maybe ¥4000 per night), but you get more privacy. You probably wouldn't want to stay every night in a capsule, but they're good for saving money in cities where hotels are pricier.

➡ **Manga Kissa** All-night *manga kissa* (cafes for reading comic books) double as ultra-discount lodgings: sign up for a 'night pack' (around ¥1500 for eight hours) in a private cubicle. The cafes know what's up: many have showers and rent blankets.

Top Free Sights

Fushimi Inari-Taisha
Kyoto's most photogenic shrine (p303), with hundreds of vermilion *torii* (gates).

Dōtombori
Osaka's famous neon strip (p365) with lots of snack vendors.

Nara-kōen
Green expanse with temples and a herd of semi-wild deer in Kansai (p398).

Hiroshima Peace Park
Moving memorial (p439) to this city's tragic history.

Shibuya Crossing
Tokyo's famous intersection (p87), abuzz with youthful urban energy and lit by giant video screens.

Sapporo Beer Museum
The history of beer in Japan, in the original Sapporo factory (p579).

21st Century Museum of Contemporary Art
Kanazawa museum (p252) with outdoor public art installations (the building is cool too!).

Arashiyama Bamboo Grove
Enchanting tunnel of bamboo (p323) in Kyoto.

Transport Deals

➡ **Japan Rail Pass** (p901) Like the famous Eurail Pass, this is one of the world's great travel bargains and is the best way to see a lot of Japan on a budget. It allows unlimited travel on Japan's brilliant nationwide rail system, including the lightning-fast *shinkansen* (bullet train).

➡ **Seishun Jūhachi Kippu** (p903) Another steal, if you time it right (and don't mind long train rides): for ¥11,850 (US$100), you get five one-day tickets good for travel on any regular Japan Railways train (meaning not the *shinkansen* or any high-speed express trains). This deal is only available a few weeks a year.

➡ **Local Travel Passes** Most cities and regions offer some kind of discount pass scheme. Check in with the nearest TIC for the latest deals, which will often be advertised in English on flyers.

➡ **Car Hire** (p896) While highway tolls aren't cheap, renting a car can be economical if you're travelling as a family or are plotting an itinerary that takes you away from major rail hubs.

➡ **Bus** (p894) Long-distance buses are the cheapest way to get around and longer routes have night buses, which save a night on accommodation.

➡ **Discount Flights** (p893) Japan has several new budget carriers that offer bus-like pricing on some routes – just be sure to factor in the time and cost of going to/from the airport.

Free Attractions

➡ **Shrines & Temples** The vast majority of Shintō shrines in Japan cost nothing to enter. Likewise, the grounds of many temples can be toured for free (often, you only have to pay to enter the halls or a walled garden).

➡ **Traditional Festivals** Throughout the year festivals take place at shrines and temples and through city streets. They're free, an excellent way to see traditional culture come alive and are well attended by cheap food vendors. For a calendar, see JNTO's festivals page (www.jnto. go.jp/eng/location/festivals).

➡ **Parks** Parks are generally free to enter (and some gardens are, too); pack a picnic and settle in for an afternoon of people watching.

➡ **Contemporary Architecture** Japan's cities, especially Tokyo, have some fantastic buildings designed by big names in Japanese architecture.

➡ **Markets & Shopping Arcades** Many seaside towns have fish markets and some cities still have old-fashioned open-air markets; cities without markets will at least have covered shopping arcades full of sundry shops that offer a peek into local life.

➡ **Art Galleries** Take the pulse of Japan's art scene in free galleries, mostly in Tokyo, Kyoto and Osaka. For info on exhibitions and events see Tokyo Art Beat (www.tokyoartbeat.com) and Kansai Art Beat (www.kansaiartbeat.com).

➡ **Strolling** It costs nothing to walk around the city or village where you are staying, and this can be one of the most rewarding, relaxing and fascinating parts of your trip.

Eating on the Cheap

➡ **Shokudō** You can get a good meal in these all-round Japanese eateries for under ¥1000 (US$8.50). The tea is free and there's no tipping.

➡ **Bentō** These 'boxed meals', which include a variety of dishes, can be picked up for under ¥1000 at supermarkets. Department store food halls sell gourmet ones for a little bit more; visit just before closing to buy them on markdown.

➡ **Noodles** You can get a steaming bowl of tasty ramen for as little as ¥600 (US$5). *Tachigui* (stand-and-eat counter joints) sell soba (buckwheat noodles) and udon (thick white wheat noodles) for even less – starting as low as ¥350 per bowl.

➡ **Convenience Stores** The best friend to all budget travellers, convenience stores stock sandwiches, rice balls, hot dishes and beer, all of which you can assemble into a very affordable (if not exactly healthy) meal.

Money Saving Tips

➡ **¥100 Stores** Stock up on sundry goods – even food and souvenirs – at these budget emporiums where everything costs only ¥100. Every city has one; look for the colourful '¥100' signs.

➡ **Flea Markets** Secondhand kimonos can be picked up at flea markets for ¥1000 to ¥2000; other finds include pretty sake cups and tea sets. Shrines often host flea markets.

➡ **Daytime Karaoke** Get your karaoke in during daytime hours (usually before 6pm) and you'll pay less than half what you would during peak hours.

Plan Your Trip
Hiking in Japan

Blessed with a geography that is more than two-thirds mountain terrain, Japan offers outdoors enthusiasts the most diverse climate in all of Asia. From the rugged shores and wind-weathered peaks of Hokkaidō in the north, to the tropical island jungles of Okinawa in the south, this country has it all.

Where to Hike

Mt Fuji & Around Tokyo

Mt Fuji Japan's best-known and highest mountain (p159) at 3776m. A gruelling climb that more than 300,000 people make each summer, many hiking overnight to be at the peak at sunrise.

Oku-Tama Region One of Tokyo's top hiking getaway spots (p199), with mountains, waterfalls, woodlands and walking trails. Head to Mitake-san for the day.

Kamakura The 3km Daibutsu hiking course (p190) winds past ancient temples and shrines in Japan's medieval capital to the giant Buddha statue at Hase.

The Japan Alps & Central Honshū

Home to the North, Central and South Alps, central Honshū is a hiking hot spot for Japan.

North Alps Excellent high-mountain trails. From Kamikōchi (p276), climb Yariga-take (3180m) and Oku-Hotaka-dake (3190m). From Murodō on the Tateyama-Kurobe Alpine Route (p270), climb Tateyama (3015m) and Tsurugi-dake (2999m). From Hakuba (p277), take the gondola and chairlifts to climb Karamatsu-dake (2695m).

Hakusan A sacred peak in Hakusan National Park, (p253) the 'white mountain' is criss-crossed with great hiking trails.

Nakasendō Walk the 8km hike (p230) from Magome to Tsumago in the historic and attractive Kiso Valley.

Need to Know

The Land
Japan is on the Pacific 'Rim of Fire' and is one of the most geologically active areas in the world. Think high mountains, volcanoes, earthquakes and hot springs. Fuji-san is 3776m tall and 21 other peaks top 3000m.

The Season
Lower latitude and lower altitude hikes can be walked year-round. With heavy winter snowfalls, higher peaks such as the North, Central and South Alps and those in Hokkaidō have a July-to-October season. The official season for climbing Mt Fuji is 1 July to mid-September.

What to Bring
Almost everything you'll need is available in Japan. If you have large feet, bring your own hiking boots.

Multiday Hikes
Mountain hut rates can include meals and bedding, so week-long hikes can be done with minimal gear. There are plenty of camping areas, but you'll need to carry everything.

Resources
For more on hikes throughout Japan, check out http://hikinginjapan.com.

Kyoto

Kyoto may be known for its temples and shrines, but it is also surrounded by mountains.

Kurama & Kibune Only 30 minutes north of Kyoto, these two tranquil valleys (p328) are linked by a trail over the ridge between them. A peaceful escape from the city.

Daimonji-yama There is no finer walk in the city than the 30-minute climb to the viewpoint above Ginkaku-ji in Northern Higashiyama.

Kansai

Kumano Kodō Walk on ancient pilgrimage routes in the wilds of the Kii Peninsula (p416). Or go the whole way and walk the 500km 33 Sacred Temples of the Kannon Pilgrimage.

Hiroshima & Western Honshū

Daisen A five-hour return climb of this 1729m stand-alone volcano affords excellent views of the San-in region (p481).

Kuniga Coast The coastal romp from Matengai Cliff to Kuniga Beach offers jaw-dropping scenery on the sleepy island of Nishino-shima (p480), in the Oki Islands Geopark.

Northern Honshū (Tōhoku)

Dewa Sanzan The collective name for three sacred peaks (p551) – Haguro-san, Gas-san and Yudono-san – which represent birth, death and rebirth respectively. The climb up Gas-san (1984m) is a good challenge.

Hakkōda-san Wildflower-filled marshes, a ridge trail and peaks in Aomori Prefecture (p534).

BEST...
....
➡ **Iconic hike:** Mt Fuji (p159)

➡ **Remote volcano:** Rishiri-dake (p619), Hokkaidō

➡ **Island hike:** Miyanoura-dake (p771), Yakushima

➡ **Base for hiking:** Kamikōchi (p275), North Alps

➡ **Pilgrimage:** 88 Temple (p654) walk, Shikoku

➡ **Scenery:** Tateyama-Kurobe Alpine Route (p270), North Alps

---

Sapporo & Hokkaidō

There's so much hiking here that you could spend weeks in the northern wilds.

Daisetsuzan National Park Pick your walks in this massive park (p610) in the centre of Hokkaidō, with day trips to a week-long challenge the length of the park.

Shiretoko National Park This World Heritage Site (p623) offers day walks of up to three days, plenty of hot springs and *higuma* (brown bears!).

Akan National Park Brilliant day-trip options including Me-Akan-dake (p629; 1499m) and O-Akan-dake (p630; 1371m).

Rishiri-zan A standalone volcano (p619; 1721m) on its own island off the northern coast of Hokkaidō.

Shikoku

Ishizuchi-san At 1982m, the highest peak (p679) in western Japan. Great day and overnight hikes in Ehime Prefecture.

Tsurugi-san Shikoku's second-highest peak (p661; 1955m) provides both easy walks and multiday hiking opportunities.

88 Temple Pilgrimage 2015 was the 1200th birthday of Kōbō Daishi's legendary 1400km 88-temple pilgrimage (p654) around Shikoku.

Kyūshū

Kirishima-Yaku National Park Excellent options including climbing Karakuni-dake (1700m), Kirishima's highest peak (p761).

Kaimon-dake This beautifully symmetrical 924m cone (p758) on the Satsuma Peninsula is a brilliant day walk.

Kujyū-san Knock off Kyūshū's highest peak (1791m), known for its spectacular pink azaleas in spring.

Okinawa & the Southwest Islands

Yakushima Lots of hiking options on this World Heritage–listed island (p771). Climb Miyanoura-dake (1935m) or hike on myriad tracks that criss-cross the island.

Iriomote-jima A Japanese jungle hike (p809) on one of Okinawa Prefecture's westernmost islands.

Plan Your Trip
Visiting an Onsen

With thousands of onsen (hot springs) scattered across the archipelago, the Japanese have been taking the plunge for centuries. The blissful relaxation that follows a good long soak can turn a sceptic into a convert and is likely to make you an onsen fanatic.

Japan's Bathing Culture

Some locals will tell you that the only distinctively Japanese aspect of their culture – that is, the only thing that didn't ultimately originate in mainland Asia – is the bath. There are accounts of onsen bathing in Japan's earliest historical records, and over the millennia the Japanese have turned the simple act of bathing in an onsen into something like a religion.

Onsen water comes naturally heated from a hot spring and often contains a number of different minerals. Onsen are reputed to makes one's skin *sube-sube* (smooth), while the chemical composition of particular waters are believed by some to help cure ailments such as high blood pressure, indigestion or poor circulation. At the very least, you will sleep very, very well after a soak.

Konyoku (mixed bathing) was the norm in Japan until the Meiji Restoration, when the country sought to align itself with more 'civilised' Western ideas and outlawed the practice. It's rare to encounter *konyoku* in Japan's urban centres, but in the countryside and on smaller islands the practice is more common. Unless stated otherwise, it's okay for a woman to enter rural, unattended baths in a swimsuit or with a 'modesty' towel.

Shy bathers take heart: many *onsen ryokan* (traditional hot-spring inns) offer what they call 'family baths' (家族風呂;

Need to Know

Onsen Lingo

男湯 *(otoko-yu)* male bath

女湯 *(onna-yu)* female bath

露天風呂 *(rotemburo)* outdoor bath

水風呂 *(mizuburo)* cold water bath – beware!

足湯 *(ashi-yu)* foot bath

Costs

Some of Japan's rural onsen are free; day spas with many baths cost about ¥2500. Most onsen fall in the middle, around ¥1000 (US$8.50).

Before You Get In

➡ Double-check the door curtains – some inns switch the male/female signs overnight to give guests a different bathing experience.

➡ Go slow: the hot water can cause blood pressure changes.

➡ Sulphur springs can discolour jewellery, especially silver.

kazoku-buro) or 'private baths' (貸切風呂; *kashikiri-buro*), small baths that can be used privately (solo, as a couple or as a family) for an hour. This may be free of charge or cost a few thousand yen. High-end inns might offer rooms with private hot-spring baths – the ultimate in luxury.

Onsen Etiquette

Bathing isn't just a pastime, it's a ritual – one so embedded in Japanese culture that everyone knows exactly what to do. This can be intimidating to the novice, but really all you need to know to avoid causing alarm is to wash yourself before getting into the bath. It's also a good idea to memorise the characters for men (男) and women (女), which will be marked on the *noren* (curtains) hanging in front of the respective baths.

Upon entering an onsen or *sentō* (public bath), the first thing you'll encounter is a row of lockers for your shoes. After you pay your admission and head to the correct changing room, you'll find either more lockers or baskets for your clothes. Take everything off here and enter the bathing room with only the small towel.

That little towel performs a variety of functions: you can use it to wash (but make sure to give it a good rinse afterwards) or to cover yourself as you walk around. It is not supposed to touch the water though, so leave it on the side of the bath or – as the locals do – folded on top of your head.

Park yourself on a stool in front of one of the taps and give yourself a thorough wash. Make sure you rinse off all the suds. When you're done, it's polite to rinse off the stool for the next person. At more humble bathhouses you might have little more than a ladle to work with; in that case, crouch low and use it to scoop out water from the bath and pour over your body – taking care not to splash water into the tub – and scrub a bit with the towel.

In the baths, keep your head above the water and your splashing to a minimum. Whether or not you want to rinse off depends on you and the nature of the waters: some people want to keep the minerals on their skin; others prefer to wash.

Before heading back to the changing room, wipe yourself down with the towel to avoid dripping on the floor.

Where to Soak

Onsen Ryokan A night in a ryokan (traditional inn) with its own bathhouse is the best way to relax traditional Japanese-style. Check in early to maximise bath time.

Onsen Resorts These clusters of baths and inns, often along a river, are the ultimate onsen getaway. Guests wear *yukata* (light cotton kimonos) and *geta* (wooden sandals) as they wander the town hopping from bath to bath. Some towns encourage bath hopping with discount passes.

Onsen in the Wild Hidden in the mountains or along undeveloped coasts, these humble baths may be no more than a pool in a riverbed blocked off with stones or a tidal basin beside crashing waves. Bathing is open-air, co-ed and usually free.

Best Onsen By Region

No matter where your itinerary takes you, there's an excellent onsen experience nearby.

TATTOO WARNING

Many onsen, larger bathhouses with leisure facilities (called 'super *sentō*') and saunas refuse entry to people with tattoos because of the association of tattoos with the *yakuza* (Japanese mafia). Those with strict policies will have signs posted that make their stance clear. If there are no explicit signs prohibiting tattoos and yours is fairly inconspicuous it's unlikely anyone will make a fuss, but do keep it covered at reception; you can also try covering it with medical tape. *Sentō*, which are public bathhouses for the local community, often have no policy against tattoos.

PUBLIC BATHHOUSES

Known as *hadaka no tsukiai* (naked friendship), communal bathing has long been seen in Japan as a great social leveller. As little as 50 years ago, many private homes in Japan did not have baths, so in the evenings people headed off to the neighbourhood *sentō* (銭湯; public bath). More than just a place to wash oneself, the *sentō* served as a kind of community meeting hall, where news and gossip were traded and social ties strengthened.

Unlike onsen, the water in *sentō* is more often plain tap water; still, *sentō* are hard to beat for local experience. Some look as though they haven't changed in decades. Others – sometimes called 'super *sentō*' (スーパー銭湯) – have evolved with the times, adding saunas, jet baths and more. Admission rarely costs more than ¥500 (a super *sentō* will cost more). You're expected to bring your own towel and toiletries; however, you can show up empty handed and rent a towel and purchase soap, shampoo etc for a small price. Most bathhouses are open from around 3pm to midnight.

Sento Guide (www.sentoguide.info) is the English-language resource about bathhouses around Japan.

Tokyo Yes, even ultra-urban Tokyo has onsen! These vary from small *sentō* (fortunate enough to be situated on real springs) to elaborate bathing leisure complexes. The latter is an experience unto its own; try Ōedo Onsen Monogatari (p111) on Tokyo Bay.

Around Tokyo Hakone (p167), made up of seven small onsen resorts in the mountains southwest of Tokyo, is the capital's favourite escape. There are many gorgeous inns here with baths. For onsen in the wild, venture to the Izu Islands (p185).

The Japan Alps & Central Honshū There are numerous onsen towns tucked atmospherically in the mountains here (meaning some lovely vistas from the outdoor baths). Some favourites include Shin-Hotaka Onsen (p244), Minakami Onsen (p293) and Nakabusa Onsen (p274).

Kyoto Funaoka Onsen (p331) is a beautiful old bathhouse in the heart of the city; up in the hills to the north of the city, Kurama Onsen (p331) is a great getaway spot.

Kansai Kinosaki (p431) is the quintessential onsen town, with seven public baths, dozens of *onsen ryokan* and a long history. Ryūjin Onsen (p414) is all but hidden in the mountainous Kii Peninsula to the south of the region.

Western Honshū & the Inland Sea While not an onsen (it uses just ordinary water), Naoshima Bath – I Heart Yū (p461) is Japan's coolest *sentō*, with an interior created by contemporary artist Ōtake Shinrō.

Northern Honshū The deep north is famous for its rustic wooden bathhouses and milky, mineral-rich waters. Remote Nyūtō Onsen (p544) is somewhere many Japanese would like to visit once in their lives.

Hokkaidō Japan's northernmost island is highly volcanic, so it has lots of onsen. There are onsen towns, like the popular resort Noboribetsu Onsen (p598), and onsen in the wild, like Fukiage Roten-no-yu (p613), which is just an untended pool deep in the mountains.

Shikoku Matsuyama is home to Dōgo Onsen (p678), one of Japan's most storied onsen (literally: it famously appears in Natsume Sōseki's classic novel *Botchan*). Founded during 'the age of the gods', it's currently housed in a castle-style building from 1894.

Kyūshū Several of Japan's most popular onsen resorts are here, including the rather commercial but fun Beppu (p741), more highbrow Yufuin (p738) and secluded Kurokawa Onsen (p737). All the way in the south, at Ibusuki (p759), you can sit neck-deep in hot sand instead.

Okinawa & the Southwest Islands The Ōsumi Islands (p771) specialise in seaside onsen, some surrounded by upmarket facilities, others just pools of rocks by the sea – like Yakushima's Hirauchi Kaichū Onsen (p774).

Regions at a Glance

Tokyo

Food
Culture
Shopping

Sushi & More

Not only does Tokyo have more restaurants than any other city in the world, it also has more great ones. Whether it's a top-flight sushi-tasting course in Ginza or a late-night bowl of ramen, you will eat well – very well – here.

Past, Present & Future

Tokyo is famous for its pop culture – its eccentric street fashion, lurid anime and *kawaii* (cute) characters. But there's so much more to the city: visit its excellent museums and look to the future on those giant video screens. Tokyo is a city always in flux, which is one of its enduring charms.

Shop, Shop, Shop

Didn't think you were getting out of here empty-handed, did you? Tokyo is a shopper's paradise, offering everything from traditional crafts to the latest lifestyle gadgets and fashion boutiques galore.

p70

Mt Fuji & Around Tokyo

Onsen
Outdoors
Temples

Hot Spring Getaways

Some of Japan's most beloved onsen towns are just a few hours from Tokyo. Each has its own flavour – mountain hideaways to the north, lakeside resorts to the west and laid-back coastal villages to the south.

Mountains & Sea

In addition to climbing Mt Fuji, outdoor activities include hiking among cedar groves, strolling along bluffs, surfing and sea kayaking. Options range from Tokyo day trips to island excursions.

Temples for the Ages

The cultural legacies of different historical eras come to life in the vibrant 17th-century shrines and temples of Nikkō and the more austere ones of medieval Kamakura.

p156

The Japan Alps & Central Honshū

Onsen
Villages
Skiing

Mountain Hot Springs

The mountainous heart of Japan bubbles over with exquisite hot springs and fantastic inns in which to enjoy them – you're spoiled for choice here. There's nothing like gazing up at snowy peaks while steam rises from your body.

Thatched Roofs

Travel to the remote village of Shirakawa-gō (or, even remoter, Ainokura) and fall asleep to the sound of chirping frogs in a centuries-old thatched-roof farmhouse.

Powder Peaks

Ski some of Asia's best slopes, with breathtaking views of the northern Japan Alps. Après-ski soaking in hot springs is a must (there's nightlife in some ski towns, too).

p212

Kyoto

Temples
Culture
Food

Shintō & Buddhist Masterpieces

With over 1000 Buddhist temples and more than 400 Shintō shrines, Kyoto is the place to savour Japanese religious architecture and garden design. Find a quiet temple to call your own or join the throngs at a popular shrine.

Japan's Cultural Storehouse

Japan's cultural capital for over a millennium has it all: historic geisha districts and teahouses, classical theatre performances and crafts like lacquerware and *washi* (Japanese paper).

Traditional Cuisine

Kyoto is the spiritual home of *kaiseki* (Japanese haute cuisine); you can also sample humbler tastes in the local market or try a cooking class.

p297

Kansai

Cities
Temples
History

Urban Pleasures

Get your city fix in one of Kansai's urban centres, like the bold and brash commercial hub Osaka or the cosmopolitan port city Kōbe. Both have vibrant dining scenes, nightlife and shopping districts.

Pilgrimage Sites

See the remains of Japan's earliest temples – and the Great Buddha – in Nara and Horyū-ji, visit mystical monasteries and walk ancient pilgrimage routes further south.

Castles & Tombs

There aren't many original castles left in Japan but two of the best are here: the 'White Egret Castle' of Himeji and Hikone-jō. The town of Asuka is home to burial mounds from the early days of Japanese history.

p358

Hiroshima & Western Honshū

Culture
History
Outdoors

Artsy Islands

Naoshima (and the islands in its orbit) in the Inland Sea have become synonymous in Japan with contemporary art and architecture. Come see works from international artists inside buildings that enhance the natural scenery.

Momentous Events

Hiroshima is a moving place to reflect on the history of the last century and the way forward. Other areas of Western Honshū were key players in Japan's 19th-century modernisation.

Slow Excursions

Cycle over bridges linking the tiny islands of the Inland Sea, rent a car and drive through the bucolic rural scenery of Yamaguchi, or head to Tottori's forlorn sand dunes.

p434

Northern Honshū (Tōhoku)

Outdoors
Onsen
Culture

Parks & Peaks

Northern Honshū is blessed with some spectacular mountains. Temperate summers lure hikers, while snowy winters attract powder fiends and snow bunnies.

Rustic Escapes

That image you have of milky white waters and stars overhead or the steamy wooden bathhouse all by its lonesome in the mountains – that's Tōhoku.

Festivals & Ancient Rites

Nobody in Japan does festivals like they do up here. Ancient customs and beliefs live on in Tōhoku, preserved by centuries of isolation. Sample food prepared the way it has been for generations, or follow in the footsteps of mountain ascetics.

p501

Sapporo & Hokkaidō

Outdoors
Food
Culture

Pristine Wilderness

This is big mountain country and big snow country, where skiers carve snow drifts reaching several metres in depth and where hikes through old-growth forests can last for days. There's much to explore on foot, by bicycle or by car.

Seafood & Ramen

The northern waters produce excellent seafood up here, including delicacies like *uni* (sea urchin) and crab. Capital city Sapporo's specialities are *miso-rāmen* and its namesake beer.

Ainu Legacy

The culture of Hokkaidō's indigenous Ainu people is represented in museums, on stages where traditional songs are sung, and in shops, restaurants and inns run by Ainu descendants.

p571

Shikoku

Nature
Temples
Outdoors

Japan's Shangri La Valley

A short drive from the mainland madness, Iya Valley has dramatic gorges, ancient vine bridges and a hint of sustainable living. Raft or hike along the pristine Yoshino-gawa.

Good Buddha

The 88-temple pilgrimage is a rite of passage for many Japanese who, dressed in white and armed with a walking stick, lower the pulse, raise the gaze and seek to honour the great Buddhist saint, Kōbō Daishi.

Surfin' Shikoku!

There's good surfing, especially at Shishikui in Tokushima and Ikumi Beach in Kōchi; the crowd-free swells at Ōkinohama should be legendary. There's also a slow-life, beach-bum vibe to match.

p641

Kyūshū

History
Nature
Onsen

Saints & Samurai

Christian rebellions led to over two centuries of seclusion, during which Nagasaki's Dejima Island was Japan's window to the world. Visit the city to learn about this fascinating chapter of Japanese history.

Mountains of Fire

Kyūshū is home to two of Japan's most famous – and famously active – volcanoes: always smoking Sakurajima, which lords over the skyline of the city of Kagoshima, and Aso-san, a hulking giant in the middle of the island.

In Hot Water – and Hot Sand

Soak away riverside in intimate Kurokawa Onsen or in one of Beppu's onsen, or get buried in a sand bath in Ibusuki. Even Kyūshū's biggest city, Fukuoka, has natural onsen.

p695

Okinawa & the Southwest Islands

Beaches
Hiking
Food

Sun-Soaked

Splash out on the gorgeous golden beaches of the Kerama or Ishigaki Islands, where you can whale-watch in winter and have the sand all to yourself.

Super Cedars

Climb into the green, pulsing heart of Yakushima, where ancient cedar trees grow really, really tall. Looking more like a *Star Wars* set than Earth, this is the closest we've come to an otherworldly experience.

Island Cuisine

Tuck into a plateful of *gōyā champurū,* Okinawa's signature stir-fry with bitter melon. Add some *awamori,* the local firewater, and you'll be ready to grab the *sanshin* (banjo) and party.

p768

On the Road

Sapporo &
Hokkaidō
p571

Northern
Honshū
(Tōhoku)
p501

The Japan Alps &
Central Honshū
p212

Kyoto
p297

Mt Fuji &
Around Tokyo
p156

Hiroshima &
Western Honshū
p434

Kansai
p358

Tokyo
p70

Shikoku
p641

Kyūshū
p695

Okinawa & the
Southwest Islands
p768

Tokyo

POP 13,415,350 / 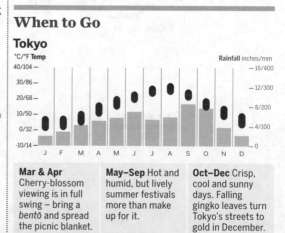 03

Best Places to Eat

➜ Kyūbey (p125)
➜ Shinsuke (p133)
➜ Tonki (p128)
➜ Tensuke (p135)
➜ Kagari (p124)

Best Places to Sleep

➜ Sawanoya Ryokan (p121)
➜ Hoshinoya Tokyo (p116)
➜ Claska (p118)
➜ Nui (p121)
➜ Hanare (p120)

Why Go?

Tokyo (東京) is a city forever reaching into the future, resulting in sci-fi streetscapes of crackling neon and soaring towers. It is constantly reinventing itself – most recently as a culinary and pop-culture mecca (and a must-visit for anyone interested in either). Yet it is also a city steeped in history, and you can find traces of the shogun's capital on the kabuki stage or under the cherry blossoms in Ueno Park.

There are excellent museums here, along with everything else you could ask of Japan – grand temples, atmospheric shrines, fascinating contemporary architecture, elegant gardens and, yes, even hot springs. Tokyo, however, is also a place where sightseeing can take a backseat. To get to know the city is to enjoy it as the locals do: by splurging on sushi in Ginza, scouting new looks in Harajuku or just wandering the lanes of one of the city's more atmospheric quarters, such as Yanesen or Kagurazaka. And don't forget the varied and often outrageous nightlife – more proof of Tokyo's indefatigable spirit.

When to Go

Tokyo

°C/°F Temp | Rainfall inches/mm

40/104 — | — 16/400
30/86 — | — 12/300
20/68 — | — 8/200
10/50 — | — 4/100
0/32 — |
-10/14 — | — 0

J F M A M J J A S O N D

Mar & Apr Cherry-blossom viewing is in full swing – bring a *bentō* and spread the picnic blanket.

May–Sep Hot and humid, but lively summer festivals more than make up for it.

Oct–Dec Crisp, cool and sunny days. Falling gingko leaves turn Tokyo's streets to gold in December.

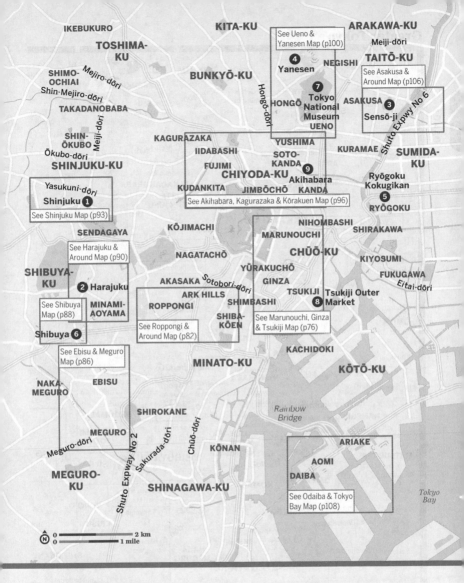

Tokyo Highlights

1 Shinjuku (p139) Raising a glass in this colourful nightlife district.

2 Harajuku (p147) Joining the city's eccentric fashion tribes as they shop.

3 Sensō-ji (p104) Soaking up the atmosphere at Asakusa's centuries-old temple.

4 Yanesen (p97) Losing yourself in the vestiges of the old city.

5 Ryōgoku Kokugikan (p144) Catching the salt-slinging, belly-slapping ritual of sumo.

6 Shibuya (p87) Getting swept up in the crowds and neon lights of this buzzing spot.

7 Tokyo National Museum (p97) Seeing the world's largest collection of Japanese art.

8 Tsukiji Outer Market (p79) Snacking and shopping for foodstuffs.

9 Akihabara (p95) Venturing into the belly of the pop culture beast.

Greater Tokyo

TOKYO

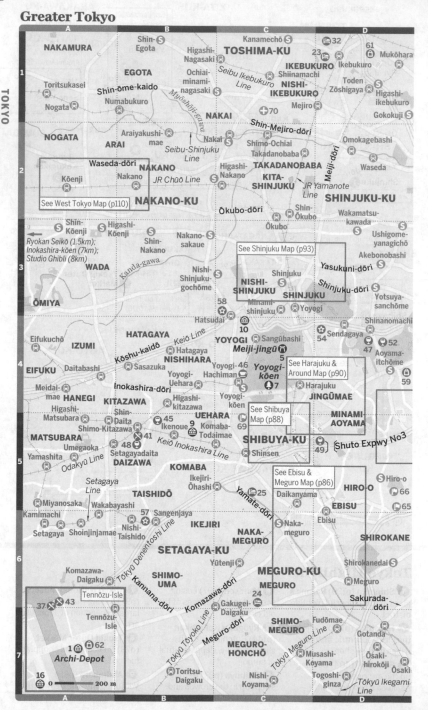

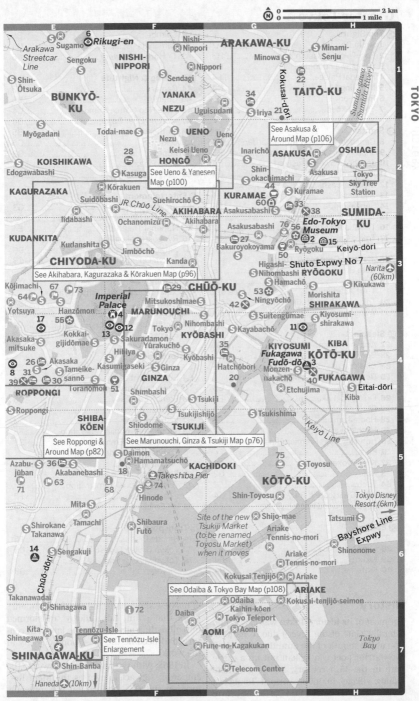

Greater Tokyo

History

For most of its history, Tokyo was called Edo (literally 'Gate of the River') due to its location at the mouth of the Sumida-gawa. Until the warrior poet Ōta Dōkan put up a castle here in the 15th century, it was a remote fishing village. In 1603, warlord Tokugawa Ieyasu decided to make Edo Castle the centre of his new shogunate (military government). From that point, Edo quickly transformed into a bustling city and, by the late 18th century, had become the most populous city in the world.

In 1868, with the reversion of power to the emperor – an act known as the Meiji Restoration (p830) – the capital was officially moved from Kyoto to Edo, which was then renamed Tokyo, meaning Eastern Capital. At the same time, Japan ended its 250 years of self-prescribed isolation and began to welcome foreign influence with open arms. Western fashions and ideas were adopted as Tokyo eagerly sought to take its place among the pantheon of the world's great cities.

In 1923 the Great Kantō Earthquake and ensuing fires levelled much of the city; Tokyo was all but destroyed once more during the devastating Allied air raids in the final years of WWII. The city remade itself – and then some – in the decades after the US occupation. A soaring economic crescendo followed, culminating in the giddy heights of the 1980s 'bubble economy'. The humbling 'burst' in the '90s led to a recession that still continues today. Yet Tokyo remains the beating heart of its island nation, never ceasing to reinvent itself.

◉ Sights

Tokyo can feel more like a collection of cities than one cohesive one. In Edo times, the city was divided into Yamanote ('uptown' or 'high city') and Shitamachi ('downtown' or 'low city'). On the elevated plain west of the castle (now the Imperial Palace), Yamanote was where the feudal elite built their estates. In the east, along the banks of the Sumida-gawa, Shitamachi was home to the working classes, merchants and artisans.

Even today, remnants of this distinction exist: the east side of the city is still a tangle of alleys and tightly packed quarters. Neighbourhoods such as Asakusa and Ueno retain a down-to-earth vibe, more traditional architecture and an artisan tradition – the closest approximation to old Edo that remains.

Yamanote developed into the moneyed commercial and business districts of today. Further west, newer neighbourhoods such as Shinjuku and Shibuya developed after the Great Kantō Earthquake and WWII – this is the hypermodern Tokyo of riotous neon and giant video screens.

On and around Tokyo Bay is the city that is still being built: islands of reclaimed land that host leisure and entertainment facilities and soon many venues for the upcoming 2020 Summer Olympics.

◉ Marunouchi & Nihombashi

Marunouchi is a high-powered business district. Its top draw is the Imperial Palace, Tokyo's symbolic centre. Neighbouring

---

❶ MUSEUM DISCOUNT PASS

Grutto Pass (¥2000; www.rekibun.or.jp/grutto) gives you free or discounted admission to 79 attractions around town within two months. If you plan on visiting more than a few museums, it's excellent value. All participating venues sell them.

Nihombashi is the city's geographic centre, a historic neighbourhood with shops and restaurants that date to the era of the shogun.

★ Imperial Palace
PALACE

(皇居; Kōkyo; Map p72; ☏ 03-5223-8071; http://sankan.kunaicho.go.jp/english/guide/koukyo.html; 1 Chiyoda, Chiyoda-ku; tours usually 10am & 1.30pm Tue-Sat; Ⓢ Chiyoda line to Ōtemachi, exits C13b & C10) **FREE** The Imperial Palace occupies the site of the original Edo-jō, the Tokugawa shogunate's castle. In its heyday this was the largest fortress in the world, though little remains of it today apart from the moat and stone walls. Most of the 3.4-sq-km complex is off-limits, as this is the emperor's home, but you can join one of the free tours organised by the Imperial Household Agency to see a small part of the inner compound.

Tours (lasting around 1¼ hours) run at 10am and 1.30pm usually on Tuesday through to Saturday, but not on public holidays or afternoons from late July through to the end of August. They're also not held at all from 28 December to 4 January or when Imperial Court functions are scheduled.

Reservations are taken – via the website, phone or by post – up to a month in advance. Alternatively, show up at least 30 minutes before the tour at the tour office at the **Kikyō-mon** (桔梗門) – if there is space you'll be able to register and take part. Bring photo ID.

The tour will take you past the present palace (Kyūden), a modest low-rise building completed in 1968 that replaced the one built in 1888, which was largely destroyed during WWII.

If you're not on the tour, head to the southwest corner of **Imperial Palace Plaza** (Map p76) to view two bridges – the iron **Nijū-bashi** (Map p72) and the stone **Meg-ane-bashi** (Map p72; 1 Chiyoda, Chiyoda-ku; Ⓢ Hibiya line to Hibiya, exit B6). Behind the bridges rises the Edo-era **Fushimi-yagura** watchtower.

The main park of the palace grounds is the **Imperial Palace East Garden** (東御苑;

Marunouchi, Ginza & Tsukiji

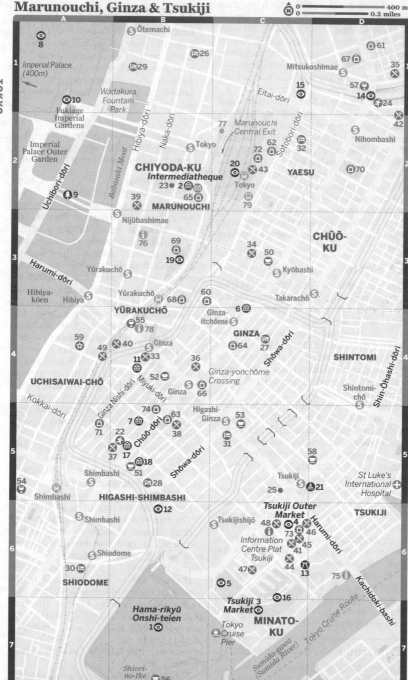

Marunouchi, Ginza & Tsukiji

Map p76; ⊙9am-4pm Nov-Feb, to 4.30pm Mar–mid-Apr, Sep & Oct, to 5pm mid-Apr–Aug, closed Mon & Fri year-round) **FREE**, which is open to the public without reservations. You must take a token upon arrival and return it at the end of your visit.

★**National Museum
of Modern Art (MOMAT)** MUSEUM
(国立近代美術館; Kokuritsu Kindai Bijutsukan; Map p96; ☑03-5777-8600; www.momat.go.jp/english; 3-1 Kitanomaru-kōen, Chiyoda-ku; adult/student ¥430/130, extra for special exhibitions; ⊙10am-5pm

Tue-Thu, Sat & Sun, to 8pm Fri; S Tōzai line to Takebashi, exit 1b) Regularly changing displays from the museum's superb collection of more than 12,000 works, by both local and international artists, are shown over floors four to two; special exhibitions are mounted on the ground floor. All pieces date from the Meiji period onward and impart a sense of how modern Japan has developed through portraits, photography, contemporary sculptures and video works. Don't miss the 'Room with a View' for a panorama of the Imperial Palace East Garden (p75).

Crafts Gallery   MUSEUM
(東京国立近代美術館 工芸館; Map p96; www.momat.go.jp/english; 1 Kitanomaru-kōen, Chiyoda-ku; adult/child ¥210/70, 1st Sun of month free; ☺10am-5pm Tue-Sun; S Tōzai line to Takebashi, exit 1b) Housed in a vintage red-brick building, this annexe of MOMAT (p77) stages excellent changing exhibitions of *mingei* (folk crafts): ceramics, lacquerware, bamboo, textiles, dolls and much more. Artists range from living national treasures to contemporary artisans. The building was once the headquarters of the imperial guards, and was rebuilt after its destruction in WWII.

Pasona   LANDMARK
(パソナ; Map p76; ☑03-6734-1260; 2-6-4 Ōtemachi, Chiyoda-ku; ☺9am-5.30pm Mon-Fri; S Tōzai line to Ōtemachi, exit B6) FREE The exterior of the nine-storey office of local recruitment firm Pasona is clad in plants, while inside around 200 species of fruits, vegetables, rice and herbs make up its urban farm. Staff take meetings beneath trellises from which tomato plants and grape vines dangle, sitting on benches under which bean sprouts germinate. The company canteen, surrounded by a rice paddy and flowers, hosts classical-music miniconcerts each day at noon that are open to the public.

Tokyo Station   LANDMARK
(東京駅; Map p76; www.tokyostationcity.com/en; 1-9 Marunouchi, Chiyoda-ku; ℝ JR lines to Tokyo Station) Tokyo Station celebrated its centenary in 2014 with a major renovation and expansion. Kingo Tatsuno's original elegant brick building on the Marunouchi side has been expertly restored to include domes faithful to the original design, decorated inside with relief sculptures. It's best viewed straight on from the plaza on Miyuki-dōri, the rooftop garden of the KITTE (Map p76; https://jptower-kitte.jp/en; 2-7-2 Marunouchi, Chiyoda-ku; ☺11am-9pm Mon-Sat, to 8pm Sun; ℝ JR lines to Tokyo, Marunouchi south exit) shopping mall, or the terrace on the 7th floor of the Shin-Maru Building.

★ Intermediatheque   MUSEUM
(Map p76; ☑03-5777-8600; www.intermediatheque.jp; 2nd & 3rd fl, JP Tower, 2-7-2 Marunouchi, Chiyoda-ku; ☺11am-6pm Sun & Tue-Thu, to 8pm Fri & Sat; ℝ JR Yamanote line to Tokyo, Marunouchi exit) FREE Dedicated to interdisciplinary experimentation, Intermediatheque cherry picks from the vast collection of the University of Tokyo (Tōdai) to craft a fascinating, contemporary museum experience. Go from viewing the best ornithological taxidermy collection in Japan to a giant pop-art print or the beautifully encased skeleton of a dinosaur. A handsome Tōdai lecture hall is reconstituted as a forum for events, including the playing of 1920s jazz recordings on a gramophone or old movie screenings.

WHAT'S NEW IN TOKYO

➡ Shibuya is right now undergoing a massive redevelopment. By the time you read this, Shibuya Station South District (projected completion: 2018) and East Tower (projected completion: 2019) might already be open. The 11th-floor 'Sky Lobby' of Shibuya Hikarie (p147) has a scale model of what Shibuya will look like when everything is completed in 2027 (there are good views from here, too).

➡ Ginza, too, is getting a reboot: in spring 2017, the neighbourhood welcomed its newest shopping centre, Ginza Six (p145), following the recent opening of malls Tōkyū Plaza Ginza and Ginza Place.

➡ The fate of Tsukiji Market (p79) is up in the air again, moving at the earliest (if at all) in 2017. The new structure, called Toyosu Market (豊洲市場), is slated to open on a reclaimed island on Tokyo Bay. Either way, the fantastic Outer Market (p79) will remain.

➡ Other new openings include the Sumida Hokusai Museum (p105) and the art galleries on Tennōzu Isle (p109).

Tokyo International Forum ARCHITECTURE
(東京国際フォーラム; Map p76; ☎03-5221-9000; www.t-i-forum.co.jp; 3-5-1 Marunouchi, Chiyoda-ku; 🚉JR Yamanote line to Yūrakuchō, central exit) [FREE] This architectural marvel designed by Rafael Viñoly houses a convention and arts centre, with eight auditoriums and a spacious courtyard in which concerts and events are held. The eastern wing looks like a glass ship plying the urban waters; take the lift to the 7th floor and look down on the tiny people below. Also look out for the statue of Ōta Dōkan, the samurai who first built the Edo Castle in 1457.

Also visit for the twice-monthly **Ōedo Antique Market** (大江戸骨董市; Map p76; ☎03-6407-6011; www.antique-market.jp; ⏲9am-4pm 1st & 3rd Sun of month) and food trucks serving bargain meals and drinks to local office workers at lunch Monday to Friday.

Nihombashi (Nihonbashi) BRIDGE
(日本橋; Map p76; www.nihonbashi-tokyo.jp; 1 Nihombashi, Chūō-ku; [S] Ginza line to Mitsukoshimae, exits B5 & B6) Guarded by bronze lions and dragons, this handsome 1911-vintage granite bridge over Nihombashi-gawa is partly obscured by the overhead expressway. It's notable as the point from which all distances were measured during the Edo period and as the beginning of the great trunk roads (the Tōkaidō, the Nikkō Kaidō etc) that took *daimyō* (feudal lords) between Edo and their home provinces.

⊙ Ginza & Tsukiji 銀座・築地

Ginza is Tokyo's most polished neighbourhood, a luxury fashion centre resplendent with department stores, art galleries and exclusive restaurants; the city's principal kabuki theatre, Kabuki-za, is here, too. A short walk away is a commercial centre of a different kind: the Tsukiji Market area, with all that you need to eat and make a great meal.

★**Tsukiji Market** MARKET
(東京都中央卸売市場, Tokyo Metropolitan Central Wholesale Produce; Map p76; ☎03-3261-8326; www.tsukiji-market.or.jp; 5-2-1 Tsukiji, Chūō-ku; ⏲5am-1pm, closed Sun, most Wed & all public holidays; [S] Hibiya line to Tsukiji, exit 1) [FREE] Fruit, vegetables, flowers and meat are sold here, but it's seafood – around 2000 tonnes of it traded daily – that Tsukiji is most famous for. The frenetic **inner market** *(jōnai-shijō)* is slated to move to Toyosu in 2017 or possibly later; the equally fascinating outer market, comprising hundreds of food stalls and restaurants, will stay put.

Before coming here, check the market's online calendar to make sure it's open, and for instructions on attending the **tuna auctions**, which start around 5am.

Tsukiji's star attraction is *maguro* (bluefin tuna) as big as submarine torpedoes and weighing up to 300kg: the sight (and sound) of these flash-frozen whoppers being auctioned is a classic Tokyo experience, worth getting up early (or staying up late) for.

Visitors begin pitching up for one of the 120 allotted places for viewing the auctions from around 3.30am at the **Fish Information Center** (おさかな普及センター; Osakana Fukyū Senta; Map p76; Kachidoki Gate, 6-20-5 Tsukiji, Chūō-ku; ⏲1am-1pm) in the northwest corner of the market. It's on a first-come, first-served basis. The first batch of 60 visitors go in to see the auctions between 5.25am and 5.50am; the second batch is from 5.50am to 6.15am. As public transport does not start running until around 5am, you will either need to walk or take a taxi to the market this early in the morning.

If you show up later, there's still plenty to see. The intermediate wholesalers' area (p80) is open to visitors at 10am. Shops in the **Uogashi-yokochō** (魚がし横町; Map p76; ⏲5am-2pm) – a cluster of tiny restaurants, and food and souvenir stalls within the *jōnai-shijō* – and the outer market are open even earlier and don't shut until around 2pm.

Exercise caution and respect when visiting Tsukiji so as not to spoil the opportunity for future visitors. Large groups, babies and young children are prohibited from the inner market.

When the market does move, public access to the new market will change.

➡ **Fruit & Vegetable Auctions**
(Map p76; ☎03-3261-8326; www.tsukiji-market.or.jp; 5-2-1 Tsukiji, Chūō-ku; ⏲8am market days; [S] Ōedo line to Tsukijishijomae, exit A1) Attending the vegetable and fruit auctions in that section of Tsukiji Market is far less fuss than the tuna auction; just turn up from around 7am. The incredibly perfect and pricey melons you see in department stores go on sale around 8am.

➡ ★**Tsukiji Outer Market**
(場外市場; Jōgai Shijō; Map p76; 6-chōme Tsukiji, Chūō-ku; ⏲5am-2pm; [S] Hibiya line to Tsukiji, exit 1) Here, tightly packed rows of vendors hawk market and culinary-related goods, such as dried fish, seaweed, kitchen knives, rubber boots and crockery. It's also a fantas-

tic place to eat, with great street food and a huge concentration of small restaurants and cafes, most specialising in seafood. Some of the wholesalers and shops formerly in Tsukiji (p79) inner market can now be found in **Tsukiji Uogashi** (築地魚河岸; Map p76; www.tsukiji-market.or.jp) here.

The area can get very crowded – avoid the narrow lanes if you're pushing a stroller or pulling luggage. Come early as most shops in the Outer Market close by 2pm.

Seafood Intermediate Wholesalers' Area MARKET
(水産仲卸業者売場; Map p76; ☎03-3261-8326; www.tsukiji-market.or.jp; 5-2-1 Tsukiji, Chūō-ku; 🕐10-11am; [S] Hibiya line to Tsukiji, exit 1) This area of the Tsukiji Market (p79), which opens to the public from 10am, is where you can see all manner of sea creatures lain out in boxes and styrofoam crates. It's a photographer's paradise, but you need to exercise caution to avoid getting in the way. Handcarts, forklifts and motorised vehicles perform a perfect high-speed choreography – not accounting for tourists.

Don't come in large groups, with small children or in nice shoes. By 11am the crowds have dwindled and the sprinkler trucks plough through to prep the empty market for tomorrow's sale.

Namiyoke-jinja SHINTO SHRINE
(波除神社; Map p76; ☎03-3541-8451; www.namiyoke.or.jp; 6-20-37 Tsukiji, Chūō-ku; [S] Hibiya line to Tsukiji, exit 1) Giant lion masks used in the area's annual festival flank the entrance to the 'avoid the waves' Shintō shrine where Tsukiji's workers and residents come to pray. Also look for the dragon-shaped taps over the purification basins.

Tsukiji Hongwan-ji BUDDHIST TEMPLE
(築地本願寺; Map p76; ☎03-3541-1131; www.tsukijihongwanji.jp; 3-15-1 Tsukiji, Chūō-ku; 🕐6am-5pm; [S] Hibiya line to Tsukiji, exit 1) [FREE] When this impressive branch of the mother temple in Kyoto fell victim to the Great Kantō Earthquake of 1923, it was rebuilt in a classical Indian style, making it one of the most distinctive Buddhist places of worship in Tokyo.

Talks in English about dharma are usually held on the last Saturday of the month from 5.30pm. See the temple website for more information.

★ **Hama-rikyū Onshi-teien** GARDENS
(浜離宮恩賜庭園; Detached Palace Garden; Map p76; www.tokyo-park.or.jp/park/format/index028.html; 1-1 Hama-rikyū-teien, Chūō-ku; adult/child ¥300/free; 🕐9am-5pm; [S] Ōedo line to Shiodome, exit A1) This beautiful garden, one of Tokyo's finest, is all that remains of a shogunal palace that once extended into the area now occupied by Tsukiji Market (p79). The main features are a large duck pond with an island that's home to a charming tea pavilion, **Nakajima no Ochaya** (中島の御茶屋; Map p76; www.tokyo-park.or.jp/park/format/restaurant028.html; tea set ¥500; 🕐9am-4.30pm), as well as some wonderfully manicured trees (black pine, Japanese apricot, hydrangeas etc), some of which are hundreds of years old.

GINZA'S GALLERIES

There are plenty of free shows to view at Ginza's galleries:

Gallery Koyanagi (ギャラリー小柳; Map p76; ☎03-3561-1896; www.gallerykoyanagi.com; 8th fl, 1-7-5 Ginza, Chūō-ku; 🕐11am-7pm Tue-Sat; [S] Ginza line to Ginza, exit A9) Exhibits notable local and international artists.

Ginza Graphic Gallery (ギンザ・グラフィック・ギャラリー; Map p76; ☎03-3571-5206; www.dnp.co.jp/gallery/ggg; 7-7-2 Ginza, Chūō-ku; 🕐11am-7pm Tue-Fri, to 6pm Sat; [S] Ginza line to Ginza, exit A2) Focuses on advertising and poster art.

METoA Ginza (Map p76; ☎03-5537-7411; www.metoa.jp/en; Tōkyū Plaza Ginza, 5-2-1 Ginza, Chūō-ku; 🕐11am-9pm; [S] Ginza line to Ginza, exit C2) Showcases some of Mitsubishi Electric's latest technologies in inventive collaborations with artists.

Shiseido Gallery (資生堂ギャラリー; Map p76; ☎03-3572-3901; www.shiseido.co.jp/e/gallery/html; basement fl, 8-8-3 Ginza, Chūō-ku; 🕐11am-7pm Tue-Sat, to 6pm Sun; [S] Ginza line to Shimbashi, exit 1 or 3) Specialises in experimental art.

Tokyo Gallery + BTAP (東京画廊; Map p76; ☎03-3571-1808; www.tokyo-gallery.com; 7th fl, 8-10-5 Ginza, Chūō-ku; 🕐11am-7pm Tue-Fri, to 5pm Sat; [S] Ginza line to Shimbashi, exit 1 or 3) Shows challenging, often political works by Japanese and Chinese artists.

TOKYO IN...

Two Days

Start with a pilgrimage to **Meiji-jingū** (p89) in Harajuku, followed by a stroll along **Omote-sandō** (p91), to check out the jaw-dropping contemporary architecture (and occasionally outre fashion). Then walk down to Shibuya to see **Shibuya Crossing** (p87) all lit up. After dark, head to Shinjuku for *yakitori* in **Omoide-yokochō** (p131) and a drink in one of the bohemian watering holes of Golden Gai (p140).

The following day, skip breakfast and head to **Tsukiji Outer Market** (p79), where you can cobble together a morning meal from the food vendors. Visit the landscape garden **Hama-rikyū Onshi-teien** (p80) then continue up to Ginza, home to department stores and art galleries. Catch an act of kabuki at **Kabuki-za** (p143).

Four Days

On day three, visit the old side of town for some sightseeing in Asakusa and Ueno, finishing with an afternoon amble through the atmospheric Yanesen neighbourhood (p103) and dinner at **Shinsuke** (p133).

The next day take the west to the magical **Ghibli Museum** (p110), followed by a stroll through **Inokashira-kōen** (p110). Spend the afternoon exploring one of Tokyo's more off-beat neighbourhoods, such as bohemian Shimo-Kitazawa (p92) or anime-mad Akihabara (p95). In the evening, head to Roppongi. The excellent **Mori Art Museum** (p81) stays open until 10pm, after which you can head out into the wilds of the neighbourhood's infamous nightlife.

Besides visiting the park as a side trip from Ginza or Tsukiji, consider travelling by boat (p155) to or from Asakusa via the Sumida-gawa (Sumida River).

Nakagin Capsule Tower ARCHITECTURE
(中銀カプセルタワー; Map p76; 8-16-10 Ginza, Chūō ku; [S] Ōedo line to Tsukijishijō, exit A3) A Facebook campaign has been started by some residents and fans to save Kurokawa Kishō's early-1970s building, which is a seminal work of Metabolist architecture. The tower's self-contained pods, which can be removed whole from a central core and replaced elsewhere, are in various states of decay and the building is swathed in netting, but it's still a very impressive design.

Roppongi, Akasaka & Around

Legendary for its nightlife, Roppongi has reinvented itself in the last decade via architecture, with the addition of the chic Roppongi Hills and Tokyo Midtown complexes and with the establishment of several excellent art museums. A short walk northeast is Akasaka; the proximity of Japan's parliament in Nagatachō and numerous embassies has long given this district an upmarket cachet.

★ **Roppongi Hills** LANDMARK
(六本木ヒルズ; Map p82; www.roppongihills.com/en; 6-chōme Roppongi, Minato-ku; 🕒 11am-11pm; [S] Hibiya line to Roppongi, exit 1) Roppongi Hills set the standard for 21st-century real-estate developments in Tokyo. The centrepiece of the office, shopping, dining and entertainment complex is the 54-storey Mori Tower, home to the Mori Art Museum and Tokyo City View observatory. Scattered around it is plenty of public art, such as Louise Bourgeois' giant, spiny **Maman spider sculpture** (Map p82) and the benches-cum-sculptures along Keyakizaka-dōri, as well as the recreated Edo-style **Mohri Garden** (Map p82).

Mori Art Museum MUSEUM
(森美術館; Map p82; www.mori.art.museum; 52nd fl, Mori Tower, Roppongi Hills, 6-10-1 Roppongi, Minato-ku; adult/child/student ¥1600/600/1100; 🕒 10am-10pm Wed-Mon, to 5pm Tue, inside Sky Deck 10am-10pm; [S] Hibiya line to Roppongi, exit 1) Atop Mori Tower this gigantic gallery space sports high ceilings, broad views and thematic programs that continue to live up to all the hype associated with Roppongi Hills. Contemporary exhibits are beautifully presented and include superstars of the art world from both Japan and abroad.

Admission is shared with **Tokyo City View** (東京シティビュー; Map p82; ☎ 03-6406-6652; www.roppongihills.com/tcv/en; 52nd fl, Mori Tower, Roppongi Hills, 6-10-1 Roppongi, Minato-ku; adult/child/student ¥1800/600/1200;

Roppongi & Around

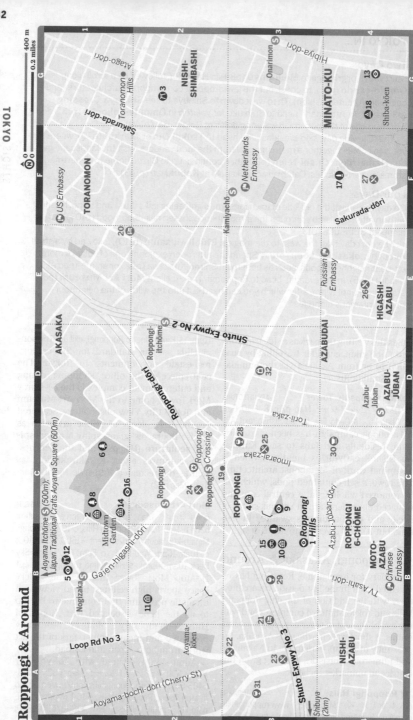

Roppongi & Around

TOKYO SIGHTS

⊙10am-11pm Mon-Thu & Sun, to 1am Fri & Sat), which wraps itself around the 52nd floor. From this 250m-high vantage point you can see 360-degree views of the seemingly never-ending city. Weather permitting you can also pop out to the external rooftop Sky Deck (additional adult/child ¥500/300; 11am to 8pm) for alfresco views.

Complex 665   GALLERY
(Map p82; 6-5-24 Roppongi, Minato-ku; ⊙11am-7pm Tue-Sat; Ⓢ Hibiya line to Roppongi, exit 1) Opened in October 2016, this new three-storey building tucked on a backstreet is the location of three major commercial art galleries: **Taka Ishii, ShugoArts** and **Tomio Koyama Gallery.** The free shows gather up an eclectic selection of Japanese contemporary works and are generally worth a look.

Tokyo Midtown   LANDMARK
(東京ミッドタウン; Map p82; www.tokyo-mid-town.com/en; 9-7 Akasaka, Minato-ku; ⊙11am-11pm; Ⓢ Ōedo line to Roppongi, exit 8) This sleek complex, the yin to nearby Roppongi Hills' (p81) yang, brims with sophisticated bars, restaurants, shops, art galleries, a hotel and leafy public spaces. Escalators ascend alongside human-made waterfalls of rock and glass, bridges in the air are lined with backlit *washi* (Japanese handmade paper), and planters full of soaring bamboo draw your eyes through

skylights to the lofty heights of the towers above.

Behind the complex is **Hinokichō-kōen** (檜町公園; Map p82; Ⓢ Hibiya line to Roppongi, exit 7). Formerly a private garden attached to an Edo-period villa, Hinokichō was reopened as a public park. The adjacent **Midtown Garden** (Map p82; Ⓢ Hibiya line to Roppongi, exit 7) is a cherry-tree-lined grassy space that makes a perfect spot for a picnic.

21_21 Design Sight   MUSEUM
(21_21デザインサイト; Map p82; ☎03-3475-2121; www.2121designsight.jp; Tokyo Midtown, 9-7-6 Akasaka, Minato-ku; admission varies; ⊙11am-8pm Wed-Mon; Ⓢ Ōedo line to Roppongi, exit 8) An exhibition and discussion space dedicated to all forms of design, the 21_21 Design Sight acts as a beacon for local art enthusiasts, whether they be designers themselves or simply onlookers. The striking concrete and glass building, bursting out of the ground at sharp angles, was designed by Pritzker Prize–winning architect Andō Tadao.

Suntory Museum of Art   MUSEUM
(サントリー美術館; Map p82; ☎03-3479-8600; www.suntory.com/sma; 4th fl, Tokyo Midtown, 9-7-4 Akasaka, Minato-ku; admission varies, child free; ⊙10am-6pm Sun-Wed, to 8pm Fri & Sat; Ⓢ Ōedo line to Roppongi, exit 8) Since its original 1961 opening, the Suntory Museum of Art has subscribed to an underlying philosophy of

[i] ROPPONGI ART TRIANGLE

Keep your ticket stub for **Mori Art Museum** (p81), **Suntory Museum of Art** (p83) or the **National Art Center Tokyo** (p84), and when you visit one of the other two galleries you'll be entitled to a discount on admission. At any of these venues, pick up the *Art Triangle Roppongi* walking map, which lists dozens of smaller galleries in the area.

lifestyle art. Rotating exhibitions focus on the beauty of useful things: Japanese ceramics, lacquerware, glass, dyeing, weaving and such. Its current Tokyo Midtown (p83) digs, designed by architect Kuma Kengō, are both understated and breathtaking.

National Art Center Tokyo MUSEUM
(国立新美術館; Map p82; ☎03-5777-8600; www.nact.jp; 7-22-1 Roppongi, Minato-ku; admission varies by exhibition; ⏲10am-6pm Wed, Thu & Sat-Mon, to 8pm Fri; [S] Chiyoda line to Nogizaka, exit 6) Designed by Kurokawa Kishō, this architectural beauty has no permanent collection, but boasts the country's largest exhibition space for visiting shows, which have included titans such as Renoir and Modigliani. Apart from exhibitions, a visit here is recommended to admire the building's awesome undulating glass facade, its cafes atop giant inverted cones and the great gift shop **Souvenir from Tokyo** (スーベニアフロムトーキョー; Map p82; ☎03-6812 9933; www.souvenirfromtokyo.jp; ⏲10am-6pm Sat-Mon, Wed & Thu, to 8pm Fri).

Nogi-jinja SHINTO SHRINE
(乃木神社; Map p82; ☎03-3478-3001; www.nogijinja.or.jp; 8-11-27 Akasaka, Minato-ku; ⏲9am-5pm; [S] Chiyoda line to Nogizaka, exit 1) This shrine honours General Nogi Maresuke, a famed commander in the Russo-Japanese War. Hours after Emperor Meiji's funerary procession in 1912, Nogi and his faithful wife committed ritual suicide, following their master into death. An **antiques flea market** is held on the shrine grounds on the fourth Sunday of each month (9am to 4pm).

General Nogi's Residence (旧乃木邸; Map p82; ⏲9am-4pm) [FREE] is up the hill from the shrine. This is where Nogi disembowelled himself and his wife slit her throat; it's open to the public only on 12 and 13 September, although you can peek through the windows the rest of the year.

Canadian Embassy Stone Garden GARDENS
(Map p72; www.canadainternational.gc.ca/japan-japon/index.aspx?lang=eng; 7-3-38 Akasaka, Minato-ko; ⏲garden 10am-5.30pm Mon-Fri; [S] Ginza line to Aoyama-itchōme, exit 4) [FREE] Bring photo ID, sign in and take the escalator up to the entrance to the Canadian Embassy, which is fronted by this stark and brilliant stone sculpture garden. Designed by the Zen priest Shunmyō Masuno, natural and cut stones from the Hiroshima region are used to represent Canada's geological character. Over the balcony, the trees of the Akasaka Palace and the distant skyscrapers provide *shakkei*, the 'borrowed scenery' that's a key principle of Japanese garden design.

Tokyo Tower TOWER
(東京タワー; Map p82; www.tokyotower.co.jp/english; 4-2-8 Shiba-kōen, Minato-ku; adult/child/student main deck ¥900/400/500, incl special deck ¥1600/800/1000; ⏲observation deck 9am-10pm; [S] Ōedo line to Akabanebashi, Akabanebashi exit) Something of a shameless tourist trap, this 1958-vintage tower remains a beloved symbol of the city's post-WWII rebirth. At 333m it's 13m taller than the Eiffel Tower, which was the inspiration for its design. It's also painted bright orange and white in order to comply with international aviation safety regulations.

The main observation deck is at 145m (there's another 'special' deck at 250m). There are loftier views at the more expensive Tokyo Sky Tree (p105).

Zōjō-ji BUDDHIST TEMPLE
(増上寺; Map p82; ☎03-3432-1431; www.zojoji.or.jp/en/index.html; 4-7-35 Shiba-kōen, Minato-ku; ⏲dawn-dusk; [S] Ōedo line to Daimon, exit A3) [FREE] One of the most important temples of the Jōdō (Pure Land) sect of Buddhism, Zōjō-ji dates from 1393 and was the funerary temple of the Tokugawa regime. It's an impressive sight, particularly the main gate, **Sangedatsumon** (解脱門), constructed in 1605, with its three sections designed to symbolise the three stages one must pass through to achieve nirvana. The **Daibonsho** (Big Bell; 1673) is a 15-tonne whopper considered one of the great three bells of the Edo period.

Atago-jinja SHINTO SHRINE
(愛宕神社; Map p82; ☎03-3431-0327; www.atago-jinja.com; 1-5-3 Shiba, Minato-ku; ⏲dawn-dusk; [S] Hibiya line to Kamiyachō, exit 3) Climbing the 85 stone steps up to this rustically attractive shrine will give you a workout. They are known as *shussei-no-ishiden* (stone stair-

case of success) after a legend that a samurai managed to climb them on horseback to deliver plum blossoms to Tokugawa Ieyasu. The 1603-vintage shrine occupied the highest point in Edo, 26m abovc sea level.

Tokyo Garden Terrace LANDMARK

(Map p72; www.tgt-kioicho.jp.e.yu.hp.transer.com; 1-2 Kioi-chō, Chiyoda-ku; [S] Namboku line to Nagatachō, exit 9A) This new mixed-use development is best visited for its pleasant surrounding gardens and public art, including *White Deer* by Nawa Kōhei and the giant metallic flowers of Ōmaki Shinji. Opened in 2016, on the former site of the Akasaka Grand Prince Hotel, the only piece remaining of the old complex is the restored Kitashirakawa Palace. Originally built in 1930 for the Korean Crown Prince Yi Un, this baronial-style mansion is now a restaurant and bar.

Ebisu, Meguro & Around

This broad collection of hip neighbourhoods, which includes Daikanyama and Naka-Meguro, has excellent art and crafts museums, fashionable boutiques, (relatively) quiet streets and few tourists by day.

TOP Museum MUSEUM

(東京都写真美術館; Tokyo Photographic Arts Museum; Map p86; ☎03-3280-0099; http://topmuseum.jp; 1-13-3 Mita, Meguro-ku; ¥500-1000; 🕑10am-6pm Tue, Wed, Sat & Sun, to 8pm Thu & Fri; 🚆JR Yamanote line to Ebisu, east exit) Tokyo's principal photography museum reopened in 2016 after a two-year overhaul. In addition to drawing on its extensive collection, the museum also hosts travelling exhibitions. In the fall, it curates a show of up-and-coming Japanese photographers. Usually several exhibitions happen simultaneously; ticket prices depend on how many you see.

The museum is at the far end of Yebisu Garden Place, on the right side of the complex if you're coming from Ebisu Station.

Yamatane Museum of Art MUSEUM

(山種美術館; Map p86; ☎03-5777-8600; www.yamatane-museum.or.jp; 3-12-36 Hiroo, Shibuya-ku; adult/student/child ¥1000/800/free, special exhibits extra; 🕑10am-5pm Tue-Sun; 🚆JR Yamanote line to Ebisu, west exit) When Western ideas entered Japan following the Meiji Restoration (1868), many artists set out to master oil and canvas. Others poured new energy into *nihonga* – Japanese-style painting, usually done with mineral pigments on silk or paper – and the masters of this latter movement are represented here. From the collection of 1800 works, a small number are displayed in thematic exhibitions.

Beer Museum Yebisu MUSEUM

(エビスビール記念館; Map p86; ☎03-5423-7255; www.sapporoholdings.jp/english/guide/yebisu; 4-20-1 Ebisu, Shibuya-ku; 🕑11am-7pm Tue-Sun; 🚆JR Yamanote line to Ebisu, east exit) [FREE] Photos, vintage bottles and posters document the rise of Yebisu, and beer in general, in Japan at this small museum located where the actual Yebisu brewery stood until 1988. At the 'tasting salon' you can sample four kinds of Yebisu beer (¥400 each). It's behind the Mitsukoshi department store at Yebisu Garden Place.

Meguro-gawa RIVER

(目黒川; Map p86; [S] Hibiya line to Naka-Meguro) Lined with cherry trees and a walking path, the Meguro-gawa (not so much a river as a canal) is what gives the neighbourhood

TOKYO FOR CHILDREN

A popular destination for local families is **Odaiba**. Here, kids can meet ASIMO the humanoid robot at the **National Museum of Emerging Science & Innovation** (p109) and run loose at virtual-reality arcade **Tokyo Joypolis** (p113).

With its **zoo** (p102) and **National Museum of Nature & Science** (p102), Ueno is another good bet. The **Tokyo National Museum** (p97) has samurai swords, as does the **Japanese Sword Museum** (p94) in Shinjuku.

The magical **Ghibli Museum** (p110) honours Japan's own animation genius, Miyazaki Hayao *(Princess Mononoke, Spirited Away)* and is part of a larger park, **Inokashira-kōen** (p110). If your kids have caught the Japanese character bug, reward good behaviour with a trip to toy emporium **KiddyLand** (p148).

Japanese kids are wild about trains – chances are yours will be, too. The southern terrace at **Shinjuku Station** overlooks the multiple tracks that feed the world's busiest train station. Another treat is a ride on the driverless **Yurikamome Line** that weaves in between skyscrapers.

Ebisu & Meguro

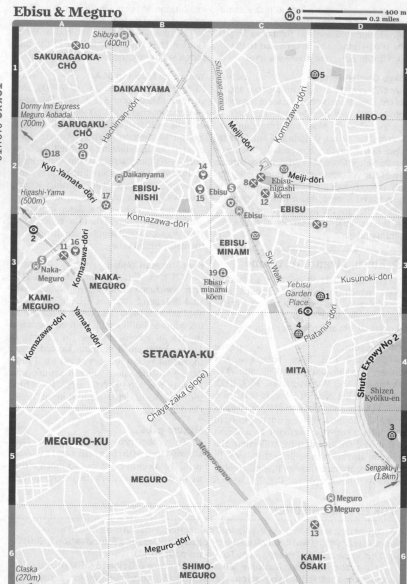

Naka-Meguro its unlikely village vibe. On either side you'll find boutiques and a handful of eating and drinking spots.

Tokyo Metropolitan Teien Art Museum

MUSEUM

(東京都庭園美術館; Map p86; www.teien-art-museum.ne.jp; 5-21-9 Shirokanedai, Minato-ku; adult/child ¥1100/800; ⊗10am-6pm, closed 2nd

Ebisu & Meguro

👁 Sights

- 1 Beer Museum Yebisu D3
- 2 Meguro-gawa A3
- 3 Tokyo Metropolitan Teien Art Museum D5
- 4 TOP Museum C4
- 5 Yamatane Museum of Art D1
- 6 Yebisu Garden Place C3

🍴 Eating

- 7 Afuri C2
- 8 Ebisu-yokochō C2
- 9 Ippo D3
- 10 Nagi Shokudō A1
- 11 Ōtaru A3
- 12 Ouca C2
- 13 Tonki D6

🍸 Drinking & Nightlife

- 14 Bar Trench B2
- 15 Buri B2
- 16 Nakame Takkyū Lounge A3

★ Entertainment

- 17 Unit A2

🛍 Shopping

- 18 Daikanyama T-Site A2
- 19 Kapital C3
- 20 Okura A2

& 4th Wed each month; 🚆 JR Yamanote line to Meguro, east exit) Although the Teien museum hosts regular art exhibitions – usually of decorative arts – its appeal lies principally in the building itself: it's an art-deco structure, a former princely estate built in 1933, designed by French architect Henri Rapin. A lengthy renovation (in 2014) saw the addition of a modern annexe designed by artist Sugimoto Hiroshi.

Tip: budget time to lounge around on the perfectly manicured lawn.

Sengaku-ji BUDDHIST TEMPLE
(泉岳寺; Map p72; www.sengakuji.or.jp; 2-11-1 Takanawa, Minato-ku; 🕒 7am-6pm Apr-Sep, to 5pm Oct-Mar; [S] Asakusa line to Sengaku-ji, exit A2) The story of the 47 *rōnin* (masterless samurai) who avenged their master, Lord Asano – put to death after being tricked into pulling a sword on a rival – is legend in Japan. They were condemned to commit *seppuku* (ritual disembowelment) and their remains were buried at this temple. It's a sombre place, with fresh incense rising from the tombs, placed there by visitors moved by the loyalty of the samurai.

👁 Shibuya

Shibuya is the heart of Tokyo's youth culture and hits you over the head with its sheer presence: the continuous flow of people, the glowing video screens and the tangible buzz.

★ Shibuya Crossing STREET
(渋谷スクランブル交差点; Shibuya Scramble; Map p88; 🚆 JR Yamanote line to Shibuya, Hachikō exit) Rumoured to be the busiest intersection in the world (and definitely in Japan), Shibuya Crossing, is like a giant beating heart, sending people in all directions with every pulsing light change. Perhaps nowhere else says 'Welcome to Tokyo' better than this. Hundreds of people – and at peak times said to be over 1000 people – cross at a time, coming from all directions at once yet still managing to dodge each other with a practised, nonchalant agility.

Hachikō Statue STATUE
(ハチ公像; Map p88; Hachikō Plaza; 🚆 JR Yamanote line to Shibuya, Hachikō exit) Come meet Tokyo's most famous pooch, Hachikō. This Akita dog came to Shibuya Station everyday to meet his master, a professor, returning from work. The professor died in 1925, but Hachikō kept coming to the station until his own death 10 years later. The story became legend and a small statue was erected in the dog's memory in front of Shibuya Station. The surrounding plaza is Tokyo's most popular rendezvous point and is always abuzz.

Myth of Tomorrow PUBLIC ART
(明日の神話; Asu no Shinwa; Map p88; 🚆 JR Yamanote line to Shibuya, Hachikō exit) Okamoto Tarō's mural, *Myth of Tomorrow* (1967), was commissioned by a Mexican luxury hotel but went missing two years later. It finally turned up in 2003 and, in 2008, the haunting 30m-long work, which depicts the atomic bomb exploding over Hiroshima, was installed inside Shibuya Station. It's on the 2nd floor, on the way to the Inokashira line.

★ Shibuya Center-gai AREA
(渋谷センター街; Shibuya Sentā-gai; Map p88; 🚆 JR Yamanote line to Shibuya, Hachikō exit) Shibuya's main drag is closed to cars and chock-a-block with fast-food joints and high-street fashion shops. At night, lit bright as day, with a dozen competing soundtracks (coming from who knows where), wares spilling onto the streets, touts in sunglasses, and strutting teens, it feels like a block party – or Tokyo's version of a classic Asian night market.

Shibuya

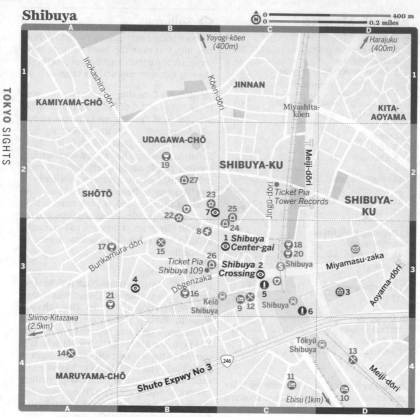

Shibuya

Spain-zaka
AREA

(スペイン坂; Map p88; ⬚ JR Yamanote line to Shibuya, Hachikō exit) Shibuya's most atmospheric little alley is typical Tokyo bricolage, with a Mediterranean flavour, a mismatch of architectural styles, cutesy clothing stores and a melting pot of restaurants all along a narrow, winding brick lane.

Dōgenzaka
AREA

(道玄坂; Love Hotel Hill; Map p88; ⬚ JR Yamanote line to Shibuya, Hachikō exit) Dōgenzaka, named for a 13th-century highway robber, is a maze of narrow streets. Home to one of Tokyo's largest clusters of love hotels (hotels for amorous encounters), it's also known as Love Hotel Hill. It's more than a little seedy, but some of the older hotels have fantastical (if not a bit chipped and crumbling) facades.

d47 Museum
MUSEUM

(Map p88; www.hikarie8.com/d47museum; 8th fl, Hikarie bldg, 2-21-1 Shibuya, Shibuya-ku; ⊙11am-8pm; ⬚ JR Yamanote line to Shibuya, east exit) **FREE** Lifestyle brand D&Department combs the country for the platonic ideals of the utterly ordinary: the perfect broom, bottle opener, or salt shaker (to name a few examples). See rotating exhibitions of its latest finds from all 47 prefectures at this one-room museum. The excellent d47 Design Travel shop is next door.

Japan Folk Crafts Museum
MUSEUM

(日本民藝館; Mingeikan; Map p72; http://min geikan.x0.com; 4-3-33 Komaba, Meguro-ku; adult/student/child ¥1100/600/200; ⊙10am-4.30pm Tue-Sun; ⬚ Keiō Inokashira line to Komaba-Todaimae, west exit) The *mingei* (folk crafts) movement was launched in the early 20th century to promote handmade objects over mass-produced ones. The leaders of the cause founded this museum to house some 17,000 examples of exquisite craftwork from around Japan. From Komaba-Tōdaima Station, walk with the train tracks on your left; when the road turns right (after about five minutes), the museum will be on your right. Note that the museum closes between exhibitions.

⊙ Harajuku & Aoyama

Harajuku is one of Tokyo's biggest draws, thanks to its grand shrine, Meiji-jingū, outré street fashion, impressive contemporary architecture and art museums. Neighbouring Aoyama is a shopping and dining district for the city's fashionable elite.

LOCAL KNOWLEDGE

'PURIKURA' PHOTO BOOTHS

It's easy to see why teens get sucked into the cult of *purikura* ('print club', aka photo booths): the digitally enhanced photos automatically airbrush away blemishes and add doe eyes and long lashes for good measure (so you come out looking like an anime version of yourself). After primping and posing, decorate the images on screen with touch pens. The resulting photo stickers make the perfect Tokyo souvenir.

While you'll find *purikura* booths in most arcades, **Purikura no Mecca** (プリクラのメッカ; Map p88; 3rd fl, 29-1 Udagawa-chō, Shibuya-ku; purikura ¥400; ⊙24hr; ⬚ JR Yamanote line to Shibuya, Hachikō exit) has nothing but – and numerous options to choose from. Note that all-guy groups aren't allowed in.

★ Meiji-jingū
SHINTO SHRINE

(明治神宮; Map p72; www.meijijingu.or.jp; 1-1 Yoyogi Kamizono-chō, Shibuya-ku; ⊙dawn-dusk; ⬚ JR Yamanote line to Harajuku, Omote-sandō exit) **FREE** Tokyo's grandest Shintō shrine is dedicated to the Emperor Meiji and Empress Shōken. Constructed in 1920, the shrine was destroyed in WWII air raids and rebuilt in 1958; however, unlike so many of Japan's postwar reconstructions, Meiji-jingū has an authentic feel. The towering 12m wooden *torii* gate that marks the entrance was created from a 1500-year-old Taiwanese cyprus. Note that Meiji-jingū is currently undergoing renovations bit by bit in preparation for its 100th anniversary, but will remain open.

Meiji-jingū Gyoen
GARDENS

(明治神宮御苑; Inner Garden; Map p90; ¥500; ⊙9am-4.30pm, to 4pm Nov-Feb; ⬚ JR Yamanote line to Harajuku, Omote-Sandō exit) On the grounds of Meiji-jingū (accessed via the shrine's main approach) is the strolling garden, Meiji-jingū Gyoen. It was once a feudal estate; after it came under imperial control, the Meiji Emperor himself designed the iris garden as a gift to the Empress Shōken. There are peaceful walks, a good dose of privacy at weekdays, and spectacular irises in June.

★ Yoyogi-kōen
PARK

(代々木公園; Map p72; www.yoyogipark.info; ⬚ JR Yamanote line to Harajuku, Omote-sandō exit) If it's a sunny and warm weekend afternoon,

Harajuku & Around

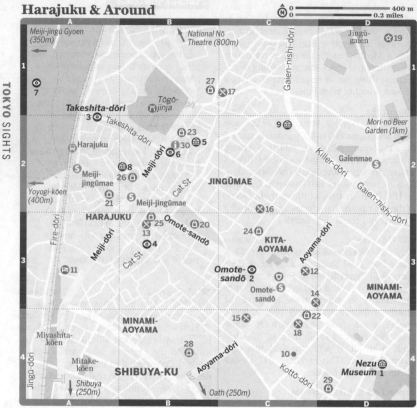

you can count on there being a crowd lazing around the large grassy expanse that is Yoyogi-kōen. You can also usually find revellers and noisemakers of all stripes, from hula-hoopers to African drum circles to a group of retro greasers dancing around a boom box. It's an excellent place for a picnic and probably the only place in the city where you can reasonably toss a frisbee without fear of hitting someone.

During the warmer months, festivals take place on the plaza across from the park (see website, in Japanese, for a schedule). Cherry blossoms draw huge crowds and parties that go late into the night.

★**Takeshita-dōri**   AREA
(竹下通り; Map p90; ᴙ JR Yamanote line to Harajuku, Takeshita exit) This is Tokyo's famously outré fashion bazaar, where trendy duds sit alongside the trappings of decades of fashion subcultures (plaid and safety pins for

the punks; colourful tutus for the *decora;* Victorian dresses for the Gothic Lolitas). Be warned: this pedestrian alley is a pilgrimage site for teens from all over Japan, which means it can get packed.

Kawaii Monster Cafe   NOTABLE BUILDING
(Map p90; ☎ 03-5413-6142; http://kawaii monster.jp/pc/; 4th fl, YM Bldg, 4-31-10 Jingūmae, Shibuya-ku; cover charge ¥500, drinks from ¥800; ◷ 11.30am-4.30pm, 6-10.30pm Mon-Sat, 11am-8pm Sun; ᴙ JR Yamanote line to Harajuku, Omote-sandō exit) Lurid colours, surrealist installations and out-of-this world costumes – this is the vision of Sebastian Masuda, stylist to pop star Kyary Pamyu Pamyu, who designed this new cafe. It's an embodiment of the now-reigning aesthetic of *guro-kawaii* (somewhat grotesque cuteness). Food and drink (not what you're here for, but you have to order something) are coloured to match the decor.

Harajuku & Around

TOKYO SIGHTS

Omote-sandō
AREA

(表参道; Map p90; Ⓢ Ginza line to Omote-sando, exits A3 & B4, Ⓡ JR Yamanote line to Harajuku, Omote-sandō exit) This regal boulevard was originally designed as the official approach to Meiji-jingū. Now it's a fashionable strip lined with high-end boutiques. Those designer shops come in designer buildings, which means Omote-sandō is among the best places in the city to see contemporary architecture.

Highlights include the Dior boutique by SANAA (Nishizawa Ryue and Sejima Kazuyo), and the Tod's boutique by Itō Toyō – both Pritzker Prize–winning Japanese architects.

Cat Street
AREA

(キャットストリート; Map p90; Ⓡ JR Yamanote line to Harajuku, Omote-sandō exit) Had enough of crowded Harajuku? Exit, stage right, for Cat Street, a windy road lined with a mishmash of boutiques and more room to move. The retail architecture is also quite a spectacle, as this is where smaller brands strike their monuments to consumerism if they can't afford to do so on the main drag.

Design Festa
GALLERY

(デザインフェスタ; Map p90; ☎ 03-3479-1442; www.designfestagallery.com; 3-20-2 Jingūmae, Shibuya-ku; ⊙ 11am-8pm; Ⓡ JR Yamanote line to Harajuku, Takeshita exit) **FREE** Design Festa has been a leader in Tokyo's DIY art scene for nearly two decades. The madhouse building itself is worth a visit; it's always evolving. Inside there are dozens of small galleries rented by the day. More often than not, the artists themselves are hanging around, too.

Ukiyo-e Ōta Memorial Museum of Art
MUSEUM

(浮世絵太田記念美術館; Map p90; ☎ 03-5777-8600; www.ukiyoe-ota-muse.jp; 1-10-10 Jingūmae, Shibuya-ku; adult ¥700-1000, child free; ⊙ 10.30am-5.30pm Tue-Sun; Ⓡ JR Yamanote line to Harajuku, Omote-sandō exit) Change into slippers to enter the peaceful, hushed museum that houses the excellent *ukiyo-e* (woodblock prints) collection of Ōta Seizo, the former head of the Toho Life Insurance Company. Seasonal, thematic exhibitions are easily digested in an hour and usually include a few works by masters such as Hokusai and Hiroshige. It's often closed the last few days of the month.

WORTH A TRIP

SHIMO-KITAZAWA

The narrow streets of Shimo-Kitazawa (下北沢) are barely passable by cars, meaning a streetscape like a dollhouse version of Tokyo. It's been a favourite haunt of generations of students, musicians and artists and there's a lively street scene all afternoon and evening, especially on weekends. If hippies – not bureaucrats – ran Tokyo, the city would look a lot more like Shimo-Kitazawa.

Numerous cafes and secondhand clothing shops can be found on the north side of the train station. Come dusk, the scene shifts to the south side, where restaurants and bars are clustered, and 'Shimokita' makes for a fun evening out. Some favourite haunts include *izakaya* (Japanese pub-eatery) **Shirube** (汁べゑ; Map p72; ☎ 03-3413-3785; 2-18-2 Kitazawa, Setagaya-ku; dishes ¥730-1060; ⊗ 5.30pm-midnight; 🗷 🅑) – you'll need a reservation on weekends; tiny dive bar **Ghetto** (月灯; Map p72; 1-45-16 Daizawa, Setagaya-ku; ⊗ 8.30pm-late); and cave-like rock-and-roll bar **Mother** (マザー; Map p72; ☎ 03-3421-9519; www.rock-mother.com; 5-36-14 Daizawa, Setagaya-ku; ⊗ 5pm-2am Sun-Thu, 5pm-5am Fri & Sat).

Shimo-Kitazawa can be reached in less than 10 minutes from Shinjuku, via the Oda-kyū line, or from Shibuya, via the Keiō Inokashira line.

The shop in the basement sells beautifully printed *tenugui* (traditional hand-dyed thin cotton towels).

Watari Museum of Contemporary Art MUSEUM
(ワタリウム美術館; Watari-Um; Map p90; ☎ 03-3402-3001; www.watarium.co.jp; 3-7-6 Jingūmae, Shibuya-ku; adult/student ¥1000/800; ⊗ 11am-7pm Tue & Thu-Sun, to 9pm Wed; Ⓢ Ginza line to Gaienmae, exit 3) This progressive and often provocative museum was built in 1990 to a design by Swiss architect Mario Botta. Exhibits range from retrospectives of established art-world figures (such as Yayoi Kusama and Nam June Paik) to graffiti and landscape artists – with some exhibitions spilling onto the surrounding streets. 'Pair' tickets cost ¥1600 for two.

There's an excellent art bookshop, **On Sundays** (Map p90; ⊗ 11am-8pm), in the basement.

★ **Nezu Museum** MUSEUM
(根津美術館; Map p90; ☎ 03-3400-2536; www.nezu-muse.or.jp; 6-5-1 Minami-Aoyama, Minato-ku; adult/student/child ¥1100/800/free, special exhibitions extra ¥200; ⊗ 10am-5pm Tue-Sun; Ⓢ Ginza line to Omote-sandō, exit A5) Nezu Museum offers a striking blend of old and new: a renowned collection of Japanese, Chinese and Korean antiquities in a gallery space designed by contemporary architect Kuma Kengo. Select items from the extensive collection are displayed in seasonal exhibitions. The English explanations are usually pretty good. Behind the galleries is a woodsy strolling garden laced with stone paths and studded with teahouses and sculptures.

There's a glass-walled cafe (also designed by Kuma), too.

⊙ Shinjuku

Shinjuku is a whole city within the city. Its breadth and scale are simply awesome – more than three million people a day pass through the train station alone. To the west is Nishi-Shinjuku, a planned district of soaring skyscrapers; to the east, the city's largest entertainment district.

★ **Tokyo Metropolitan Government Building** NOTABLE BUILDING
(東京都庁; Tokyo Tochō; Map p93; http://www.metro.tokyo.jp/english/offices/observat.htm; 2-8-1 Nishi-Shinjuku, Shinjuku-ku; ⊗ observatories 9.30am-11pm; Ⓢ Ōedo line to Tochōmae, exit A4) **FREE** Tokyo's seat of power, designed by Tange Kenzō and completed in 1991, looms large and looks somewhat like a pixelated cathedral (or the lair of an animated villain). Take an elevator from the ground floor of Building 1 to one of the twin 202m-high observatories for panoramic views over the never-ending cityscape (the views are virtually the same from either tower). On a clear day (morning is best), you may catch a glimpse of Mt Fuji to the west.

Shinjuku I-Land PUBLIC ART
(新宿アイランド; Map p93; 6-5-1 Nishi-Shinjuku, Shinjuku-ku; Ⓢ Marunouchi line to Nishi-Shinjuku) An otherwise ordinary office complex, Shinjuku I-Land (completed in 1995 but conceived before the bursting of the economic bubble) is home to more than a dozen public artworks, including one of Robert Indiana's *Love* sculptures and two *Tokyo Brushstroke* sculptures

Shinjuku

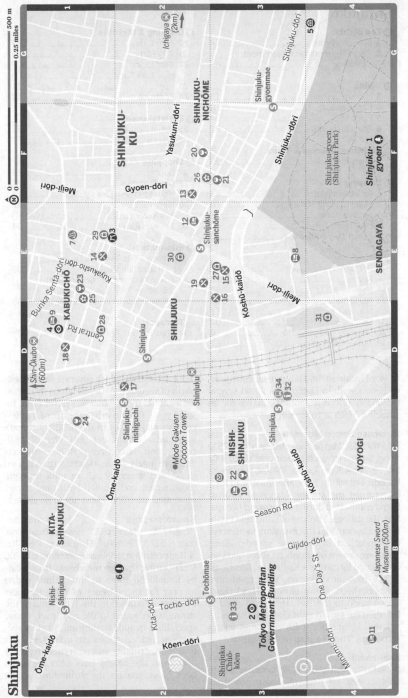

Shinjuku

by Roy Liechtenstein. The open-air courtyard, with stonework by Giulio Paolini and several reasonably priced restaurants, makes for an attractive lunch or coffee stop.

Japanese Sword Museum   MUSEUM
(刀剣博物館; Map p72; www.touken.or.jp; 4-25-10 Yoyogi, Shibuya-ku; adult/student/child ¥600/300/ free; ☺9am-4.30pm Tue-Sun; ☒Keiō New line to Hatsudai, east exit) In 1948, after American forces returned the *katana* (Japanese swords) they'd confiscated during the postwar occupation, the national Ministry of Education established a society, and this museum, to preserve the feudal art of Japanese sword-making. There are dozens of swords on show here, accompanied by excellent English explanations.

The museum's location, in a residential neighbourhood, is not obvious. Head down Kōshū-kaidō to the Park Hyatt and make a left, then the second right under the highway, followed by another quick right and left in succession. There's a map on the website.

Kabukichō   AREA
(歌舞伎町; Map p93; ☒JR Yamanote line to Shinjuku, east exit) Tokyo's most notorious red-light district, which covers several blocks north of Yasukuni-dōri, was famously named for a kabuki theatre that was never built. Instead you'll find an urban theatre of a different sort playing out in the neighbourhood's soaplands (bathhouses just shy of anti-prostitution laws), peep shows, cabarets and love hotels. It's less sketchy than it used to be, and generally safe to walk through, though men and women both may attract unwanted attention – best not to go alone.

Hanazono-jinja   SHINTO SHRINE
(花園神社; Map p93; www.hanazono-jinja. or.jp; 5-17-3 Shinjuku, Shinjuku-ku; ☺24hr; ⓢMarunouchi line to Shinjuku-sanchōme, exits B10 & E2) During the day, merchants from nearby Kabukichō come to this Shintō shrine to pray for the solvency of their business ventures. (Founded in the 17th century, the shrine is dedicated to the god Inari, whose specialities include fertility and worldly success). At night, despite signs asking revellers to refrain, drinking and merrymaking carry over from the nearby bars onto the stairs here. Most Sundays, the shrine hosts a **flea**

market (青空骨董市; Aozora Kottō-ichi; Map p93; http://kottou-ichi.jp; 🕐 dawn-dusk Sun).

★ Shinjuku-gyoen PARK

(新宿御苑; Map p93; ☎ 03-3350-0151; www.env.go.jp/garden/shinjukugyoen; 11 Naito-chō, Shinjuku-ku; adult/child ¥200/50; 🕐 9am-4.30pm Tue-Sun; [S] Marunouchi line to Shinjuku-gyoenmae, exit 1) Though Shinjuku-gyoen was designed as an imperial retreat (completed 1906), it's now definitively a park for everyone. The wide lawns make it a favourite for urbanites in need of a quick escape from the hurly-burly of city life. Don't miss the greenhouse, with its giant lily pads and perfectly formed orchids, and the cherry blossoms in spring.

Place M GALLERY

(Map p93; www.placem.com; 3rd fl, 1-2-11 Shinjuku, Shinjuku-ku; 🕐 noon-7pm; [S] Marunouchi line to Shinjuku-gyoenmae, exit 2) [FREE] Run by four veteran photographers (including pioneering street photographer Moriyama Daido), this gallery is a key player in the local scene, hosting exhibitions as well as workshops to nurture new photographers; it also runs a press. There are a few other small photography galleries in the neighbourhood – you'll find tons of flyers by the door.

👁 Akihabara, Kagurazaka & Kōrakuen

This swathe of central Tokyo runs alongside Soto-bōri, the former outer moat of Edo Castle, and the Kanda-gawa. From west to east there's the charming old geisha district of Kagurazaka; Korakuen, home to one of the city's best traditional gardens and the sports and leisure complex Tokyo Dome; and finally Akihabara, the centre of the *otaku* (geek) universe. Pick up an English map of Akihabara at **Akiba Info** (Map p96; ☎ 080-3413-4800; www.animecenter.jp; 2nd fl, Akihabara UDX Bldg, 4-14-1 Soto-Kanda, Chiyoda-ku; 🕐 11am-5.30pm Tue, Wed & Fri-Sun; 📶; 🚉 JR Yamanote line to Akihabara, Electric Town exit); the helpful staff there speak English.

★ Koishikawa Kōrakuen GARDENS

(小石川後楽園; Map p96; ☎ 03-3811-3015; http://teien.tokyo-park.or.jp/en/koishikawa; 1-6-6 Kōraku, Bunkyō-ku; adult/child ¥300/free; 🕐 9am-5pm; 🚉 Ōedo line to Iidabashi, exit C3) Established in the mid-17th century as the property of the Tokugawa clan, this formal strolling garden incorporates elements of Chinese and Japanese landscaping. It's among Tokyo's most attractive gardens, although nowadays the *shakkei* (borrowed scenery) also includes the other-worldly Tokyo Dome (p144).

Don't miss the **Engetsu-kyō** (Full-Moon Bridge), which dates from the early Edo period (the name will make sense when you see it), and the beautiful vermilion wooden bridge **Tsuten-kyō**. The garden is particularly well known for its plum blossoms in February, irises in June and autumn leaves.

Yasukuni-jinja SHINTO SHRINE

(靖国神社; Map p96; ☎ 03-3261-8326; www.yasukuni.or.jp; 3-1-1 Kudan-kita, Chiyoda-ku; 🕐 6am-5pm; [S] Hanzōmon line to Kudanshita, exit 1) Literally 'For the Peace of the Country Shrine', Yasukuni is the memorial shrine to Japan's war dead, around 2.5 million souls. First built in 1869, it is also incredibly controversial: in 1979, 14 class-A war criminals, including WWII general Hideki Tōjō, were enshrined here.

The main approach is fronted by a 25m-tall *torii* (entrance gate) made of steel and bronze; behind the main shrine, seek out the serene grove of mossy trees and the ornamental pond.

For politicians, a visit to Yasukuni, particularly on 15 August, the anniversary of Japan's defeat in WWII, is considered a political statement. It's a move that pleases hawkish constituents but also one that draws a strong rebuke from Japan's Asian neighbours, who suffered greatly in Japan's wars of expansion during the 20th century.

Akagi-jinja SHINTO SHRINE

(赤城神社; Map p96; ☎ 03-3260-5071; www.akagi-jinja.jp; 1-10 Akagi-Motomachi, Shinjuku-ku; [S] Tōzai line to Kagurazaka, exit 1) Kagurazaka's signature shrine only bares a passing resemblance to the traditional ones around the city. In 2010 the shrine, which can trace its history back centuries, was completely remodelled by Kengo Kuma, one of Japan's most prominent contemporary architects. The result is a sleek glass box for the main shrine building.

Origami Kaikan GALLERY

(おりがみ会館; Map p96; ☎ 03-3811-4025; www.origamikaikan.co.jp; 1-7-14 Yushima, Bunkyō-ku; 🕐 shop 9am-6pm, gallery 10am-5.30pm Mon-Sat; 👪; 🚉 JR Chūō or Sōbu lines to Ochanomizu, Hijiri-bashi exit) [FREE] This exhibition centre and workshop is dedicated to the quintessential Japanese art of origami, which you can learn to do yourself in classes here. There's a shop-gallery on the 1st floor, a gallery on the 2nd, and a workshop on the 4th where you can watch the process of making, dyeing and decorating origami paper.

Akihabara, Kagurazaka & Kōrakuen

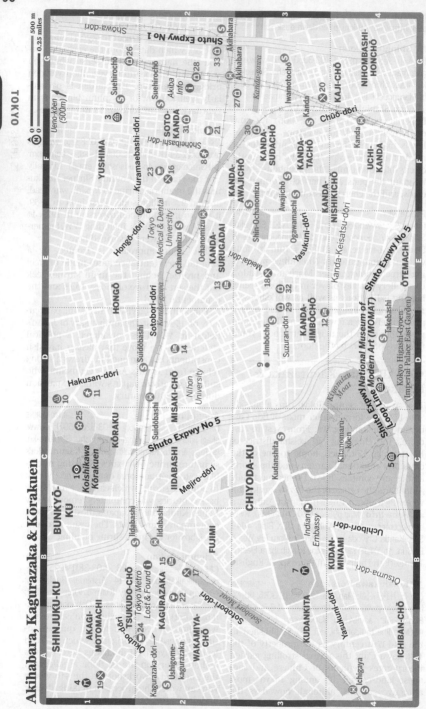

0 — 500 m
0 — 0.25 miles

Shōwa-dōri

Shuto Expwy No 1

Akihabara

Ueno-kōen (500m)

Suehirochō
Suehirochō
Akiba Info

YUSHIMA

Kuramaebashi-dōri

SOTO-KANDA

Iwamotochō

KAJI-CHŌ

NIHOMBASHI-HONCHŌ

Akihabara

Kanda-gawa

Kanda

Chūō-dōri

Kanda

Shohei-bashi-dōri

KANDA-SUDACHŌ

KANDA-TACHŌ

UCHI-KANDA

Hongō-dōri

Tokyo Medical & Dental University

Ochanomizu

Ochanomizu

KANDA-SURUGADAI

Shin-Ochanomizu

KANDA-AWAJICHŌ

Awajichō

Awajichō

Ogawamachi

Yasukuni-dōri

KANDA-NISHIKICHŌ

Kanda-Keisatsu-dōri

HONGŌ

Sotobori-dōri

Kanda-gawa

Suidōbashi

Meidai-dōri

Kanda-Keisatsu-dōri

Shuto Expwy No 5

ŌTEMACHI

Kiyomizu-Moat

Kōkyo Higashi-Gyoen (Imperial Palace East Garden)

National Museum of Modern Art (MOMAT)

Takebashi

Kitanomaru-kōen

Hakusan-dōri

KŌRAKU

Suidōbashi

MISAKI-CHŌ

Nihon University

Suidōbashi

Jimbōchō

Suzuran-dōri

KANDA-JIMBŌCHŌ

Shuto Expwy No 5
Loop Line

Kudanshita

CHIYODA-KU

Koishikawa Kōrakuen

BUNKYŌ-KU

IIDABASHI

Mejiro-dōri

FUJIMI

Indian Embassy

Uchibori-dōri

KUDAN-MINAMI

SHINJUKU-KU

AKAGI-MOTOMACHI

Ōkubo-dōri

TSUKUDO-CHŌ

Tokyo Metro Lost & Found

Iidabashi

Iidabashi

Sotobori-dōri

Sotobori-Moat

KUDANKITA

Yasukuni-dōri

Ōtsuma-dōri

ICHIBAN-CHŌ

KAGURAZAKA

Kagurazaka-dōri

Ushigome-kagurazaka

WAKAMIYA-CHŌ

Ichigaya

Akihabara, Kagurazaka & Kōrakuen

3331 Arts Chiyoda   GALLERY
(Map p96; ☑03-6803 2441; www.3331.jp/en; 6-11-14 Soto-Kanda, Chiyoda-ku; ⊙noon-7pm Wed-Mon; 🚻; 🚇Ginza line to Suehirochō, exit 4) FREE A major exhibition space, smaller art galleries and creative studios now occupy this former high school, which has morphed into a forward-thinking arts hub for Akiba. It's a fascinating place to explore. There's a good cafe and shop selling cute design items, as well as a play area for kids stocked with recycled toys and colourful giant dinosaurs made of old plastic toys.

◉ Ueno & Yanesen

Ueno is the cultural heart of Tokyo. Its central park, Ueno-kōen, has the city's highest concentration of museums, including the Tokyo National Museum. The neighbouring areas of Yanaka, Nezu and Sendagi are collectively known as Yanesen. It's a charming part of Tokyo that feels like time stopped several decades ago.

★ **Tokyo National Museum**   MUSEUM
(東京国立博物館, Tokyo Kokuritsu Hakubutsukan; Map p100; ☑03-3822-1111; www.tnm.jp; 13-9 Ueno-kōen, Taitō-ku; adult/child & senior/student ¥620/free/410; ⊙9.30am-5pm Tue-Sun

year-round, to 8pm Fri Mar-Dec, to 6pm Sat & Sun Mar-Aug; 🚉JR lines to Ueno, Ueno-kōen exit) If you visit only one museum in Tokyo, make it the Tokyo National Museum. Here you'll find the world's largest collection of Japanese art, including ancient pottery, Buddhist sculptures, samurai swords, colourful *uki-yo-e* (woodblock prints), gorgeous kimonos and much, much more. Visitors with only a couple of hours to spare should focus on the **Honkan** (Japanese Gallery) and the enchanting **Gallery of Hōryū-ji Treasures** (法隆寺宝物館), which displays masks, scrolls and gilt Buddhas from Hōryū-ji (in Nara Prefecture, dating from 607).

With more time, you can explore the three-storied **Tōyōkan** (Gallery of Asian Art), with its collection of Buddhist sculpture from around Asia and delicate Chinese ceramics. The **Heiseikan** (平成館), accessed via a passage on the 1st floor of the Honkan, houses the **Japanese Archaeological Gallery**, full of pottery, talismans and articles of daily life from Japan's prehistoric periods.

Check whether it's possible to access the usually off-limits garden, which includes several vintage teahouses; it opens to the public from mid-March to mid-April and from late October to early December.

Tokyo National Museum

HISTORIC HIGHLIGHTS

It would be a challenge to take in everything the sprawling Tokyo National Museum has to offer in a day. Fortunately, the Honkan (Japanese Gallery) is designed to give visitors a crash course in Japanese art history from the Jōmon era (13,000–300 BC) to the Edo era (AD 1603–1868). The works on display here are rotated regularly, to protect fragile ones and to create seasonal exhibitions – you're always guaranteed to see something new.

Buy your ticket from outside the main gate then head straight to the Honkan with its sloping tile roof. Stow your coat in a locker and take the central staircase up to the 2nd floor, where the exhibitions are arranged chronologically. Allow two hours for this tour of the highlights.

The first room on your right starts from the beginning with **ancient Japanese art ❶**. Be sure to pick up a copy of the brochure Highlights of Japanese Art at the entrance.

Continue to the **National Treasure Gallery ❷**. 'National Treasure' is the highest distinction awarded to a work of art in Japan. Keep an eye out for more National Treasures, labelled in red, on display in other rooms throughout the museum.

Moving on, stop to admire the **courtly art gallery ❸**, the **samurai armour and swords ❹** and the **ukiyo-e and kimono ❺**.

Next, take the stairs down to the 1st floor, where each room is dedicated to a different decorative art, such as lacquerware or ceramics. Don't miss the excellent examples of **religious sculpture ❻** and **folk art ❼**.

Finish your visit with a look inside the enchanting **Gallery of Hōryū-ji Treasures ❽**.

ALEX SEGRE/ALAMY STOCK PHOTO ©

Ukiyo-e & Kimono (Room 10)
Chic silken kimono and lushly coloured *ukiyo-e* (woodblock prints) are two icons of the Edo era (AD 1603–1868) *ukiyo* – the 'floating world', or world of fleeting beauty and pleasure.

Japanese Sculpture (Room 11)
Many of Japan's most famous sculptures, religious in nature, are locked away in temple reliquaries. This is a rare chance to see them up close.

MUSEUM GARDEN

Don't miss the garden if you visit during the few weeks it's open to the public in spring and autumn.

Heiseikan & Japanese Archaeology Gallery

Research & Information Centre

8

Hyōkeikan

Kuro-mon

Main Gate

Gallery of Hōryū-ji Treasures
Surround yourself with miniature gilt Buddhas from Hōryū-ji, said to be one of Japan's oldest Buddhist temples, founded in 607. Don't miss the graceful Pitcher with Dragon Head, a National Treasure.

GREG ELMS/GETTY IMAGES ©

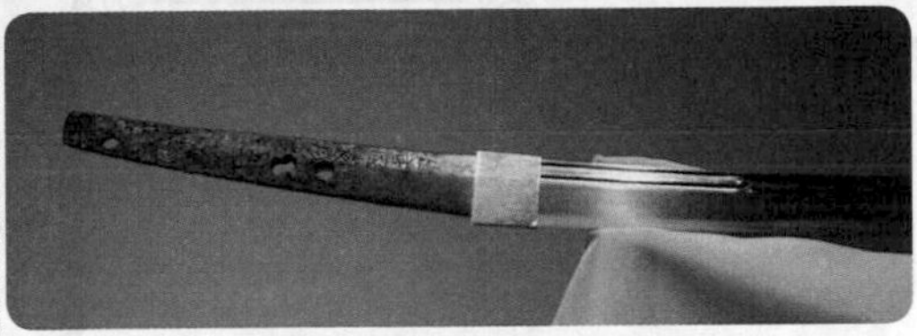

Courtly Art (Room 3-2)
Literature works, calligraphy and narrative picture scrolls are displayed alongside decorative art objects, which allude to the life of elegance led by courtesans a thousand years ago.

Samurai Armour & Swords (Rooms 5 & 6)
Glistening swords, finely stitched armour and imposing helmets bring to life the samurai, those iconic warriors of Japan's medieval age.

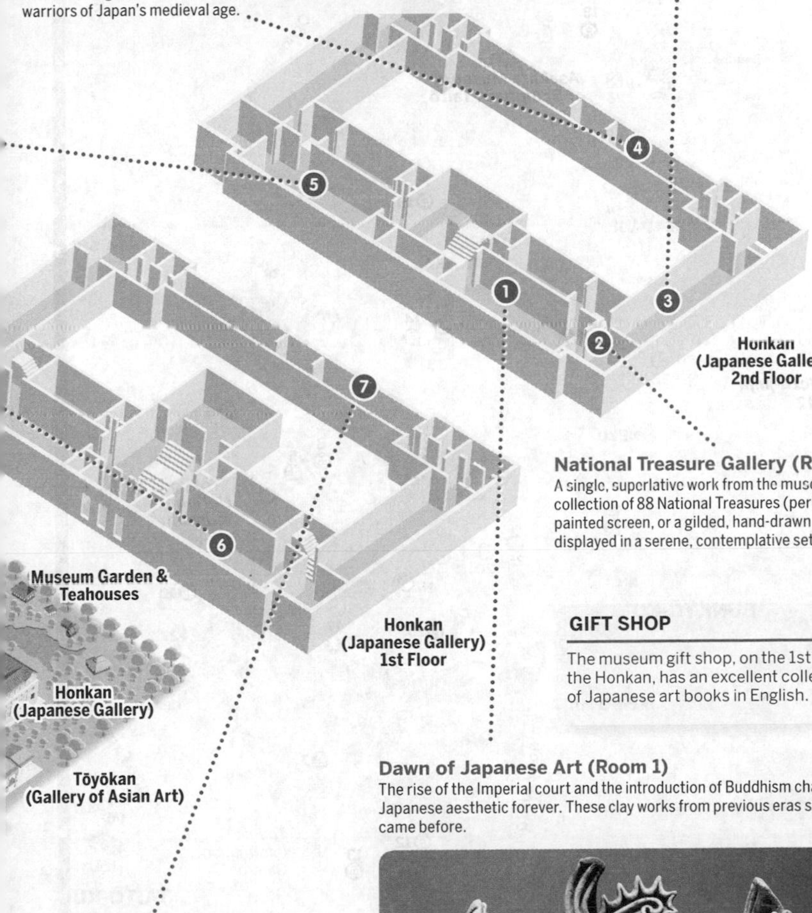
1
2
3
4
5
6
7
Honkan
(Japanese Gallery)
2nd Floor
Honkan
(Japanese Gallery)
1st Floor
Museum Garden &
Teahouses
Honkan
(Japanese Gallery)
Tōyōkan
(Gallery of Asian Art)

National Treasure Gallery (Room 2)
A single, superlative work from the museum's collection of 88 National Treasures (perhaps a painted screen, or a gilded, hand-drawn sutra) is displayed in a serene, contemplative setting.

GIFT SHOP
The museum gift shop, on the 1st floor of the Honkan, has an excellent collection of Japanese art books in English.

Dawn of Japanese Art (Room 1)
The rise of the Imperial court and the introduction of Buddhism changed the Japanese aesthetic forever. These clay works from previous eras show what came before.

Folk Culture (Room 15)
See artefacts from Japan's historical minorities – the indigenous Ainu of Hokkaidō and the former Ryūkyū Empire, now Okinawa.

Ueno & Yanesen

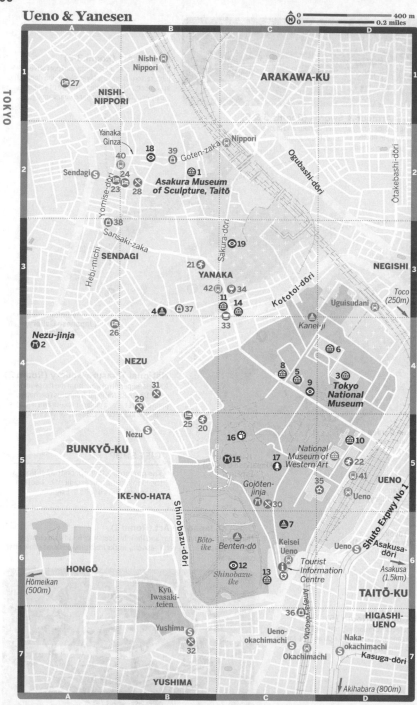

Ueno & Yanesen

TOKYO SIGHTS

The museum regularly hosts temporary exhibitions (which cost extra); these can be fantastic, but sometimes lack the English signage found throughout the rest of the museum.

Kuro-mon GATE
(Map p100; www.tnm.jp; Tokyo National Museum, 13-9 Ueno-kōen, Taitō-ku; ℝ JR lines to Ueno, Ueno-kōen exit) West of the main gate to Tokyo National Museum (p97) is the Kuro-mon (Black Gate), transported from the Edo-era mansion of a feudal lord. You can view the facade from outside the museum. On weekends, from 10am to 4pm, the gate is opened for visitors inside the museum to pass through.

Kuroda Memorial Hall GALLERY
(黒田記念室; Map p100; ☑03-5777-8600; www.tobunken.go.jp/kuroda/index_e.html; 13-9 Ueno-kōen, Taitō-ku; ⊙9.30am-5pm Tue-Sun; ℝ JR lines to Ueno, Ueno-kōen exit) FREE Kuroda Seiki (1866–1924) is considered the father of modern Western-style painting in Japan. In this 1928-vintage hall, an annexe to Tokyo National Museum (p97), some of his works are displayed, including key pieces such as *Maiko Girl* and *Wisdom, Impression and Sentiment*, a striking triptych of three nude women on canvases coated with ground gold.

Ueno-kōen PARK
(上野公園; Map p100; http://ueno-bunka.jp; Ueno-kōen, Taitō-ku; ℝ JR lines to Ueno, Ueno-kōen & Shinobazu exits) Best known for its profusion of cherry trees that burst into blossom in spring (making this one of Tokyo's top *hanami* – blossom viewing – spots), sprawling Ueno-kōen is also the location of the city's highest concentration of museums. At the southern tip is the large scenic pond, **Shinobazu-ike** (不忍池; Map p100), choked with lotus flowers.

Ueno Tōshō-gū SHINTO SHRINE
(上野東照宮; Map p100; ☑03-3822-3455; www.uenotoshogu.com; 9-88 Ueno-kōen, Taitō-ku; ¥500; ⊙9am-5.30pm Mar-Sep, to 4.30pm Oct-Feb; ℝ JR lines to Ueno, Shinobazu exit) This shrine inside Ueno-kōen was built in honour of Tokugawa Ieyasu, the warlord who unified Japan. Resplendent in gold leaf and ornate details, it dates from 1651 (though it has had recent touch-ups). You can get a pretty good look

❶ GETTING AROUND UENO & YANESEN

Ueno-kōen (p101) and Yanesen are great places to stroll; they're also great places to cycle. Hipster bicycle manufacturer **Tokyobike Rental Services** (Map p100; ☎03-3827-4819; www.tokyobike.com/rental; 6-3-12 Yanaka, Taitō-ku; per day ¥2500; ☺10am-7pm Wed-Sun; 🚇JR Yamanote line to Nippori, west exit) in Yanaka rents seven-speed city bikes. Reserve one in advance by sending an email with your name, desired day and height.

Meanwhile, the 'tōzai' (東西; east–west) route of the **Megurin** (めぐりん; www.city.taito.lg.jp/index/kurashi/kotsu/megurin; ☺single ride/day pass ¥100/300) community bus does a helpful loop around the area. Useful stops include **No 2** (Map p100), across from the Ueno Park exit at Ueno Station, **No 9** (Map p100) in front of Yanaka Cemetery (Yanaka Rei-en Iriguchi) and **No 12** (Map p100) for Yanaka Ginza (Yanaka Ginza Yomise-dōri). Stops are announced on the bus, which runs approximately every 15 minutes from 7am to 7pm.

from outside the gate, if you want to skip the admission fee.

Kiyōmizu Kannon-dō
BUDDHIST TEMPLE

(清水観音堂; Map p100; ☎03-3821-4749; 1-29 Ueno-kōen, Taitō-ku; ☺9am-4pm; 🚇JR lines to Ueno, Shinobazu exit) Ueno-kōen's (p101) Kiyōmizu Kannon-dō is one of Tokyo's oldest structures: established in 1631 and in its present position since 1698, it has survived every disaster that has come its way. It's a miniature of the famous Kiyomizu-dera in Kyoto and is a pilgrimage site for women hoping to conceive as it enshrines Kosodate Kannon, the protector of childbearing and child-raising.

Ueno Zoo
ZOO

(上野動物園, Ueno Dōbutsu-en; Map p100; ☎03-3828-5171; www.tokyo-zoo.net; 9-83 Ueno-kōen, Taitō-ku; adult/child ¥600/free; ☺9.30am-5pm Tue-Sun; 🚇JR lines to Ueno, Ueno-kōen exit) Japan's oldest zoo, established in 1882, is home to animals from around the globe, but the biggest attractions are two giant pandas that arrived from China in 2011 – Rī Rī and Shin Shin. There's also a whole area devoted to lemurs, which makes sense given Tokyoites' love of all things cute.

National Museum of Nature & Science
MUSEUM

(国立科学博物館; Map p100; ☎03-5777-8600; www.kahaku.go.jp/english; 7-20 Ueno-kōen, Taitō-ku; adult/child ¥600/free; ☺9am-5pm Tue-Thu, Sat & Sun, to 8pm Fri; 🚇JR lines to Ueno, Ueno-kōen exit) The **Japan Gallery** here showcases the rich and varied wildlife of the Japanese archipelago, from the bears of Hokkaidō to the giant beetles of Okinawa. Elsewhere in the museum: a rocket launcher, a giant squid, an Edo-era mummy, and a digital seismograph that charts earthquakes in real time. There's English signage throughout, plus an English-language audio guide (¥300).

Shitamachi Museum
MUSEUM

(下町風俗資料館; Map p100; ☎03-3823-7451; www.taitocity.net/taito/shitamachi; 2-1 Ueno-kōen, Taitō-ku; adult/child ¥300/100; ☺9.30am-4.30pm Tue-Sun; 🚇JR lines to Ueno, Shinobazu exit) This small museum recreates life in the plebeian quarters of Tokyo during the Meiji and Taishō periods (1868–1926), before the city was twice destroyed by the Great Kantō Earthquake and WWII. There are old tenement houses and shops that you can enter.

Yanaka Ginza
AREA

(谷中銀座; Map p100; 🚇JR Yamanote line to Nippori, north exit) Yanaka Ginza is pure, vintage mid-20th-century Tokyo, a pedestrian street lined with butcher shops, vegetable vendors and the like. Most Tokyo neighbourhoods once had stretches like these (until supermarkets took over). It's popular with Tokyoites from all over the city, who come to soak up the nostalgic atmosphere, plus the locals who shop here.

★ Asakura Museum of Sculpture, Taitō
MUSEUM

(朝倉彫塑館; Map p100; www.taitocity.net/taito/asakura; 7-16-10 Yanaka, Taitō-ku; adult/student ¥500/250; ☺9.30am-4.30pm Tue, Wed & Fri-Sun; 🚇JR Yamanote line to Nippori, north exit) Sculptor Asakura Fumio (artist name Chōso; 1883–1964) designed this atmospheric house himself. It combined his original Japanese home and garden with a large studio that incorporated vaulted ceilings, a 'sunrise room' and a rooftop garden with wonderful neighbourhood views. It's now a reverential museum with many of the artist's signature realist works, mostly of people and cats, on display.

Yanaka-reien
CEMETERY

(谷中霊園; Map p100; 7-5-24 Yanaka, Taitō-ku; 🚇JR Yamanote line to Nippori, west exit) One of Tokyo's

City Walk
A Ramble Through Yanesen

START TOKYO NATIONAL MUSEUM
END SENDAGI STATION
LENGTH 3KM; TWO HOURS

If you have time, visit the **1 Tokyo National Museum** (p97) before you start exploring Yanaka, with its temples, galleries and old wooden buildings. If not, simply follow the road northwest out of **2 Ueno-kōen** (p101) until you hit Kototoi-dōri. At the corner is the **3 Shitamachi Museum Annex**, actually a preserved, century-old liquor store. Across the street is **4 Kayaba Coffee** (p141), if you need a pick-me-up.

From here, it's a short walk to **5 SCAI the Bathhouse** (p104), a classic old public bathhouse turned contemporary art gallery. It's a worthwhile detour to continue down to **6 E-dokoro** (p150), the studio of painter Allan West, and to see the ancient, thick-trunked **7 Himalayan cedar tree** on the corner. In and around here, you'll pass many temples, including **8 Enju-ji**, where Nichika-sama, the 'god of strong legs' is enshrined; it's pop-

ular with runners. Feel free to stop in any of the temples; just be respectful and keep your voice low.

Now double back towards the entrance of **9 Yanaka-reien** (p102), one of Tokyo's most atmospheric and prestigious cemeteries (also a favourite sunning spot of the neighbourhood's many stray cats). When you exit the cemetery, continue with the train tracks on your right, climbing until you reach the bridge, which overlooks the tracks (a favourite destination for trainspotters).

Head left and look for the sign pointing towards the **10 Asakura Museum of Sculpture, Taitō** (p102), the home studio of an early-20th-century sculptor and now an attractive museum. Back on the main drag, continue down the **11 Yūyake Dandan** – literally the 'Sunset Stairs' – to the classic mid-20th-century shopping street, **12 Yanaka Ginza** (p102). Pick up some snacks from the vendors here, then hunker down on a milk crate on the side of the road with the locals and wash it all down with a beer. Walk west and you can pick up the subway at Sendagi Station.

WORTH A TRIP

RIKUGI-EN

A strong contender for Tokyo's most beautiful garden, **Rikugi-en** (六義園; Map p72; ☑ 03-3941-2222; http://teien.tokyo-park.or.jp/en/rikugien; 6-16-3 Hon-Komagome, Bunkyō-ku; adult/child ¥300/free; ⊗ 9am-5pm; ☒ JR Yamanote line to Komagome, south exit) was designed to reflect the aesthetic of traditional Waka poetry. Built by a feudal lord in 1702, it has walkways that pass over hills and stone bridges, and by trickling streams and scenes inspired by famous poems. There's a teahouse where you can drink *matcha* (powdered green tea; ¥510) alfresco while overlooking the garden's central pond.

There is almost always something in bloom at Rikugi-en, though the garden is most famous for its maple leaves in late autumn. Usually during late November and early December, the park stays open until 9pm and the trees are illuminated after sunset; expect crowds.

largest graveyards, Yanaka-reien is the final resting place of more than 7000 souls, many of whom were quite well known in their day. It's also where you'll find the tomb of Yoshinobu Tokugawa (徳川慶喜の墓), the last shogun. Come spring it is one of Tokyo's main cherry-blossom-viewing spots.

SCAI the Bathhouse GALLERY

(スカイザバスハウス; Map p100; ☑ 03-3821-1144; www.scaithebathhouse.com; 6-1-23 Yanaka, Taitō-ku; ⊗ noon-6pm Tue-Sat; ☒ Chiyoda line to Nezu, exit 1) FREE This 200-year-old bathhouse has for several decades been an avant-garde gallery space, showcasing Japanese and international artists in its austere vaulted space.

★Nezu-jinja SHINTO SHRINE

(根津神社; Map p100; ☑ 03-3822-0753; www.nedujinja.or.jp; 1-28-9 Nezu, Bunkyō-ku; ⊗ 24hr; ☒ Chiyoda line to Nezu, exit 1) Not only is this one of Japan's oldest shrines, it is also easily the most beautiful in a district packed with attractive religious buildings. The opulently decorated structure, which dates from the early 18th century, is one of the city's miraculous survivors and is offset by a long corridor of small red *torii* (gates) that makes for great photos.

◉ Asakusa & Sumida River
浅草・隅田川

Tokyo's eastern neighbourhoods, on the banks of the Sumida-gawa, have an old-Tokyo (*shitamachi*) feel, with venerable temples and shrines, lovely gardens, traditional restaurants and artisan shops. Zone in on Asakusa's atmospheric Buddhist temple complex Sensō-ji and the sumo hot spot of Ryōgoku, home to the ancient sport's Tokyo stadium and a top-class history museum.

★Sensō-ji BUDDHIST TEMPLE

(浅草寺; Map p106; ☑ 03-3842-0181; www.senso-ji.jp; 2-3-1 Asakusa, Taitō-ku; ⊗ 24hr; ☒ Ginza line to Asakusa, exit 1) FREE Tokyo's most sacred temple enshrines a golden image of Kannon (the Buddhist Goddess of Mercy), which, according to legend, was miraculously pulled out of the nearby Sumida-gawa by two fishermen in AD 628. The image has remained on the spot ever since but is never on public display. The present structure dates from 1958. Entrance to the temple complex is via the fantastic, red **Kaminari-mon** (雷門; Thunder Gate; Map p106) and busy shopping street **Nakamise-dōri**.

Before passing through the gate, look to either side to see statues of Fūjin (the god of wind) and Raijin (the god of thunder), and under the giant red lantern to see a beautiful carved dragon.

Stalls along Nakamise-dōri sell everything from tourist trinkets to genuine Edo-style crafts. At the end of Nakamise-dōri is the temple itself, and to your left you'll spot the 55m-high **Five-Storey Pagoda** (五重塔; Map p106). It's a 1973 reconstruction of a pagoda built by Tokugawa Iemitsu.

It's a mystery as to whether or not the ancient image of Kannon actually exists, as it's not on public display. This doesn't stop a steady stream of worshippers from visiting. In front of the temple is a large **incense cauldron**: the smoke is said to bestow health and you'll see people rubbing it into their bodies through their clothes.

At the eastern edge of the temple complex is **Asakusa-jinja** (浅草神社; Map p106; ☑ 03-3844-1575; www.asakusajinja.jp/english; ⊗ 9am-4.30pm), a shrine built in honour of the brothers who discovered the Kannon statue that inspired the construction of Sensō-ji. (Historically, Japan's two religions, Buddhism and Shintō were intertwined and it was not uncommon for temples to include shrines and vice versa.) The current building, painted a deep shade of red, dates to 1649 and is a rare example of early Edo architecture. It's also the epicentre of one of Tokyo's most important festivals, May's Sanja Matsuri (p115).

The entire temple complex is always busy, particularly so at weekends; consider visiting at night to see it with fewer people and the buildings beautifully illuminated.

Super Dry Hall ARCHITECTURE

(フラムドール; Flamme d'Or; Map p106; www.asahibeer.co.jp/aboutus/summary/#headQuarter; 1-23-1 Azuma-bashi, Sumida-ku; [S] Ginza line to Asakusa, exit 4) Also known as Asahi Beer Hall, the headquarters of the brewery was designed by Philippe Starck and completed in 1989 and remains one of the city's most distinctive buildings. The tower, with its golden glass facade and white top floors, is supposed to evoke a giant mug of beer, while the golden blob atop the lower jet-black building is the flame (locals, however, refer to it as the 'golden turd').

Tokyo Sky Tree TOWER

(東京スカイツリー; Map p106; www.tokyo-skytree.jp; 1-1-2 Oshiage, Sumida-ku; 350m/450m observation decks ¥2060/3090; ⏲8am-10pm; [S] Hanzōmon line to Oshiage, Sky Tree exit) Tokyo Sky Tree opened in May 2012 as the world's tallest 'free-standing tower' at 634m. Its silvery exterior of steel mesh morphs from a triangle at the base to a circle at 300m. There are two observation decks, at 350m and 450m. You can see more of the city during daylight hours – at peak visibility you can see up to 100km away, all the way to Mt Fuji – but it is at night that Tokyo appears truly beautiful.

★ **Edo-Tokyo Museum** MUSEUM

(江戸東京博物館; Map p72; ☎03-3626-9974; www.edo-tokyo-museum.or.jp; 1-4-1 Yokoami, Sumida-ku; adult/child ¥600/free; ⏲9.30am-5.30pm, to 7.30pm Sat, closed Mon; [R] JR Sōbu line to Ryōgoku, west exit) This history museum, in a cavernous building, does an excellent job laying out Tokyo's miraculous transformation from feudal city to modern capital, through city models, miniatures of real buildings, reproductions of old maps and *ukiyo-e* (woodblock prints). It starts with a bang as you cross the life-sized partial replica of the original Nihombashi bridge and gaze down on facades of a kabuki theatre and Meiji-era bank. There is English signage throughout and a free audio guide available (¥1000 deposit).

Sumida Hokusai Museum MUSEUM

(すみだ北斎美術館; Map p72; ☎03-6658-8931; http://hokusai-museum.jp; 2-7-2 Kamezawa, Sumida-ku; adult/child/student ¥1200/400/900; ⏲9.30am-5.30pm Tue-Sun; [S] Oedo line to Ryōgoku, exit A4) The artist Katsushika Hokusai was born and died close to the location of this new museum, opened in 2016. The striking aluminium-clad building is designed by Pritzker Prize–winning architect Kazuyo Sejima. The museum's collection numbers more than 1500 pieces and includes some of the master's most famous images, such as *The Great Wave off Kanagawa* from his series *Thirty-six Views of Mount Fuji*.

★ **Fukagawa Fudō-dō** BUDDHIST TEMPLE

(深川不動尊; Map p72; ☎03-3630-7020; www.fukagawafudou.gr.jp; 1-17-13 Tomioka, Kōtō-ku; ⏲8am-6pm, to 8pm on festival days; [S] Ōedo line to Monzen-Nakachō, exit 1) Belonging to the esoteric Shingon sect, this is very much an active temple where you can attend one of the city's most spectacular religious rituals. *Goma* (fire rituals) take place daily in an auditorium in the Hondō (Main Hall) at 9am, 11am, 1pm, 3pm and 5pm, plus 7pm on festival days (1st, 15th and 28th of each month). Sutras are chanted, giant *taiko* drums are pounded and flames are raised on the main altar as an offering to the deity.

At the end of the 30-minute ceremony, people line up to have their bags and other

ℹ ASAKUSA TOURIST INFORMATION CENTER

The roof terrace of the **Asakusa Culture Tourist Information Center** (浅草文化観光センター; Map p106; ☎03-3842-5566; http://taitonavi.jp; 2-18-9 Kaminarimon, Taitō-ku; ⏲9am-8pm; 📶; [S] Ginza line to Asakusa, exit 2) has fantastic views of **Tokyo Sky Tree** (p105) and the Nakamise-dōri approach to **Sensō-ji** (p104). Free guided tours of Asakusa depart from the centre on Saturdays and Sundays at 11am and 1.15pm. Also check to see if its program of **geisha entertainment** is running: it usually happens in April, June, July, October and November on Saturday at 1pm and 2.30pm with free tickets being issued at the centre from 10am.

Asakusa & Around

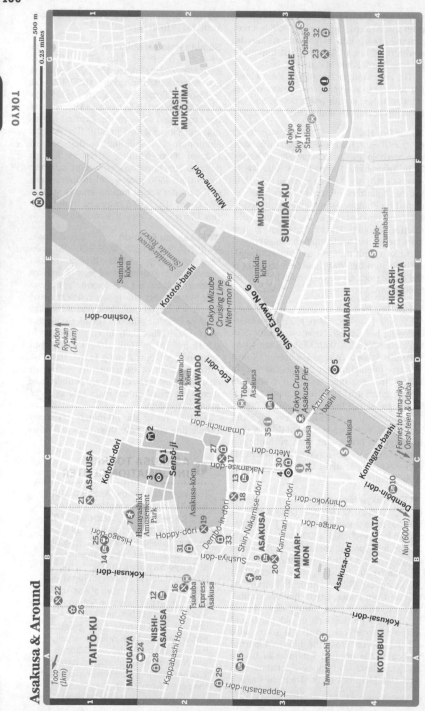

Toco (1km)

Andon Ryokan (1.4km)

Nui (600m)

Ferries to Hama-rikyū Onshi-teien & Odaiba

TAITŌ-KU

MATSUGAYA

NISHI-ASAKUSA

ASAKUSA

HANAKAWADO

HIGASHI-MUKŌJIMA

MUKŌJIMA

SUMIDA-KU

OSHIAGE

NARIHIRA

AZUMABASHI

HIGASHI-KOMAGATA

KOMAGATA

KAMINARI-MON

KOTOBUKI

Senso-ji

Tokyo Sky Tree Station

Sumida-kōen

Sumida-gawa (Sumida River)

Tokyo Mizube Cruising Line Niten-mon Pier

Tokyo Cruise Asakusa Pier

Hanayashiki Amusement Park

Hanakawado-kōen

Asakusa-kōen

Kappabashi Hon-dōri

Tsukuba Express Asakusa

Oshiage

Honjo-azumabashi

Tawaramachi

Azuma-bashi

Komagata-bashi

Kototoi-bashi

Shuto Expwy No 6

Kototoi-dōri

Kototoi-dōri

Yoshino-dōri

Mitsume-dōri

Edo-dōri

Umamichi-dōri

Nakamise-dōri

Shin-Nakamise-dōri

Dembō-in-dōri

Dembō-in-dōri

Hoppy-dōri

Sushiya-dōri

Hisago-dōri

Chinyoko-dōri

Kaminari-mon-dōri

Orange-dōri

Asakusa-dōri

Metro-dōri

Kokusai-dōri

Kokusai-dōri

Kappabashi-dōri

Tōbu Asakusa

Asakusa & Around

Top Sights
1 Sensō-ji C2

Sights
2 Asakusa-jinja C2
3 Five-Storey Pagoda C2
4 Kaminari-mon C3
5 Super Dry Hall D4
6 Tokyo Sky Tree G3

Activities, Courses & Tours
7 Hanayashiki B1
8 Jakotsu-yu B3
Mokuhankan .... (see 33)

Sleeping
9 Bunka Hostel Tokyo B3
10 Hatago C4
11 Japonica Lodge D3
12 Khaosan World B2
13 Ryokan Shigetsu C3
14 Sukeroku No Yado Sadachiyo B1
15 Tokyo Ryokan A3

Eating
16 Asakusa Imahan B2
17 Chōchin Monaka C2
18 Daikokuya C3
19 Hoppy-dōri B2
20 Iriyama Sembei B3
21 Onigiri Yadoroku C1
22 Otafuku B1
23 Rokurinsha G3

Drinking & Nightlife
24 Café Otonova A2
25 'Cuzn Homeground B1

Entertainment
26 Oiwake A1

Shopping
27 Fujiya C2
28 Ganso Shokuhin Sample-ya A2
29 Kappabashi-dōri A2
30 Kurodaya C3
31 Marugoto Nippon B2
32 Sumida City Point G3
33 Tokyo Hotarudo B2

Information
34 Asakusa Culture Tourist Information Center C3
35 Tōbu Sightseeing Service Center C3

possessions passed over the dying flames as a blessing.

While here, don't miss the trippy **prayer corridor** with 9500 miniature Fudōmyō (a fierce-looking representation of Buddha's determination) crystal statues. Upstairs is also a beautifully decorated gallery (open until 4pm) depicting all 88 temples of the 1400km pilgrimage route on the island of Shikoku; it is said that offering a prayer at each alcove has the same effect as visiting each temple.

Kiyosumi-teien GARDENS
(清澄庭園; Map p72; http://teien.tokyo-park.or.jp/en/kiyosumi/index.html; 3-3-9 Kiyosumi, Kōtō-ku; adult/child ¥150/free; 🕒 9am-5pm; [S] Ōedo line to Kiyosumi-Shirakawa, exit A3) One of Tokyo's most picturesque retreats, Kiyosumi-teien started out in 1721 as the villa of a *daimyō* (domain lord; regional lord under the shoguns). After the villa was destroyed in the 1923 earthquake, Iwasaki Yatarō, founder of the Mitsubishi Corporation, purchased the property. He used company ships to transport prize stones here from all over Japan, which are set around a pond ringed with Japanese black pine, hydrangeas and Taiwanese cherry trees.

Odaiba & Tokyo Bay
お台場・東京湾

This collection of artificial islands on Tokyo Bay was developed as a family-oriented entertainment district, with malls, arcades and the onsen theme-park Ōedo Onsen Monogatari. More grown-up attractions include the art galleries of Tennōzu Isle (p109) and pleasure-boat cruises (p112) on the bay. Toyosu is the planned site for the new fish market (should the relocation from Tsukiji go ahead).

The automated (driverless) **Yurikamome line** monorail runs around Odaiba, connecting the artificial islands to 'mainland' Tokyo. While principally a means of getting around, the ride itself is a treat: from Shimbashi (the central Tokyo terminus) the elevated tracks wend in-between skyscrapers before doing a loop to reach Rainbow Bridge, which it then takes over the waters to Odaiba. Fares are from ¥190 to ¥360; a one-day pass costs ¥820/¥410 per adult/child.

Odaiba Kaihin-kōen PARK
(お台場海浜公園; Odaiba Marine Park; Map p108; http://www.tptc.co.jp/en/c_park/01_02; 1-4-1 Daiba, Minato-ku; 🕒 24hr; [R] Yurikamome line to

Odaiba & Tokyo Bay

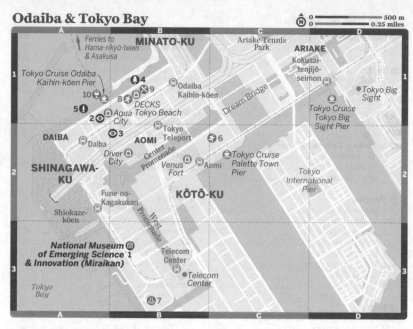

Odaiba & Tokyo Bay

◎ **Top Sights**
1 National Museum of Emerging
Science & Innovation
(Miraikan) B3

◎ **Sights**
2 ChihiraJunco A1
3 Fuji TV Building B2
4 Odaiba Kaihin-kōen B1
5 Statue of Liberty A1

◎ **Activities, Courses & Tours**
6 Dai-kanransha......................................C2
7 Ōedo Onsen Monogatari.....................B3
8 Tokyo Joypolis B1

⊗ **Eating**
9 Bills..B1
Hibiki...(see 2)

◎ **Drinking & Nightlife**
10 Jicoo the Floating Bar A1

Odaiba Kaihin-kōen) One of the best views of
Tokyo is from this park's promenades and
elevated walkways – especially at night
when old-fashioned *yakatabune* (low-slung
wooden pleasure boats), decorated with lanterns, traverse the bay. Also here you'll find

an 800m-long artificial **beach** and an 11m
replica of the **Statue of Liberty** (Map p108),
plus plenty of teens and students kicking
around.

ChihiraJunco   ROBOT
(地平ジュンこ; Map p108; 3rd fl, Aqua City, 1-7-
1 Daiba, Minato-ku; ⊙11am-9pm; ℝYurikamome
line to Odaiba Kaihin-kōen) **FREE** The future
is here. Maybe. ChihiraJunco is a demure
lady android created by Toshiba who has
her own information counter adjacent to
the people-staffed information counter at
the Aqua City shopping mall. At the time
of research, she was not (yet?) able to answer spoken questions; however, she does
answer questions entered into the touch
panel – in Japanese, English or Chinese.

Fuji TV Building   ARCHITECTURE
(フジテレビ; Map p108; ☎0180-993-188; 2-4-8
Daiba, Minato-ku; adult/child ¥550/300; ⊙Tue-
Sun 10am-6pm; ℝYurikamome line to Daiba) Designed by the late, great Kenzō Tange, the
Fuji TV headquarters building is easily recognisable by the 1200-tonne orb suspended
from the scaffolding-like structure. It's free
to take the escalators up to the 7th floor;
admission is for the observatories inside
the orb.

WORTH A TRIP

TENNŌZU ISLE

Tennōzu Isle, one of Tokyo Bay's artificial islands, spent the 20th century as a warehouse district. It still is – just now some of those warehouses contain breweries and galleries. **TY Harbor Brewery** (Map p72; ☑ 03-5479-4555; www.tyharborbrewing.co.jp; 2-1-3 Higashi-Shinagawa, Shinagawa-ku; lunch set ¥1200-1700, dinner mains from ¥1700; ⏱ 11.30am-2pm & 5.30-10pm; 🚇 🅿) was the first to move in; beers brewed on the premises here are served in a canalside restaurant (along with yummy hamburgers and salads). Next to the brewery is the bakery **Breadworks** (Map p72; ☑ 03-5479-3666; www.tyharborbrewing.co.jp; 2-1-6 Higashi-Shinagawa, Shinagawa-ku; breads & pasteries from ¥200; ⏱ 8am-8pm), which uses brewer's yeast in its breads.

New on the block is **Archi-Depot** (建築倉庫; Kenchiku Sōko; Map p72; ☑ 03-5769-2133; http://archi-depot.com; Warehouse Terrada, 2-6-10 Higashi-Shinagawa, Shinagawa-ku; adult/child ¥1000/500; ⏱ 11am-9pm Tue-Sun), a fascinating museum for miniature models – the kind architects make to conceptualise buildings. Many of the big names of Japanese architecture are represented here (Ban Shigeru, Kuma Kengo). Next door is the art supply store **Pigment** (Map p72; ☑ 03-5781-9550; https://pigment.tokyo; Terrada Harbor One Bldg., 2-5-5 Higashi-Shinagawa, Shinagawa-ku; ⏱ 11am-8pm, closed Mon & Thu), which runs workshops on calligraphy, traditional Japanese painting (and more) through **T-Art Academy** (Map p72; https://pigment.tokyo/academy; Terrada Harbor One Bldg., 2-5-5 Higashi-Shinagawa, Shinagawa-ku; per person from ¥4000). Across the canal, in another warehouse, is the collection of five contemporary galleries that make up the **Terrada Art Complex** (Map p72; http://art.terrada.co.jp; 3rd fl, 1-33-10 Higashi-Shinagawa, Shinagawa-ku; ⏱ 11am-6pm Tue-Thu & Sat, to 8pm Fri).

While you're walking around, you'll see large, brilliantly coloured murals from the internationally active collective Pow! Wow!. The district also holds pop-up events; for information, see www.terrada.co.jp.

Tennōzu Isle is connected to Odaiba (Tokyo Teleport Station) and Osaki (on the JR Yamanote line) via the Rinkai line.

⭐ **National Museum of Emerging Science & Innovation (Miraikan)** MUSEUM
(未来館; Map p108; www.miraikan.jst.go.jp; 2-3-6 Aomi, Kōtō-ku; adult/child ¥620/210; ⏱ 10am-5pm Wed-Mon; 🚆 Yurikamome line to Telecom Center) *Miraikan* means 'hall of the future', and exhibits here present the science and technology that will (possibly!) shape the years to come. Lots of hands-on displays make this a great place for kids, while a new multilingual smartphone app makes a game out of visiting. Don't miss the demonstrations of humanoid robot ASIMO and the lifelike android Otonaroid. The Gaia dome theatre/planetarium (adult/child ¥300/100) has an English audio option and is popular; book online one week in advance.

⊙ West Tokyo

Tokyo's western suburbs, linked by the iconic JR Chūō line, are anything but dull. Neighbourhoods such as Nakano, Kōenji, Ogikubo and Kichijōji are popular with locals, who appreciate the vintage mid-20th-century look and bohemian spirit that set this area apart from downtown.

⭐ **Nakano Broadway** NOTABLE BUILDING
(中野ブロードウェイ; Map p110; www.nbw.jp; 5-25-15 Nakano, Nakano-ku; ⏱ varies by shop; 🚆 JR Sōbu-Chūō line to Nakano, north exit) This vintage 1960s shopping mall – at the end of the equally vintage **Nakano Sun Mall** (中野サンモール; Map p110; 5-64 Nakano, Nakano-ku) covered arcade – helped cement Nakano's reputation as an underground Akihabara. It's filled with small shops aimed at collectors of all sorts; many sell manga (Japanese comics) and vintage toys, but there are also those specialising in antique watches, darts...you name it.

Harmonica-yokochō MARKET
(ハーモニカ横丁; http://hamoyoko.com; 1-2 Kichijōji-Honchō, Musashino-shi; 🚆 JR Sōbu-Chūō line to Kichijōji, north exit) This covered market, with low ceilings and red paper *chōchin* (lanterns), originated as a black market after WWII. Some of the vendors – the fishmongers, for example – have been around for decades, but there are some trendy new boutiques and bars here too. There's a morning market every third Sunday (7am to 10am).

West Tokyo

West Tokyo

★ **Inokashira-kōen**   PARK
(井の頭公園; www.kensetsu.metro.tokyo.jp/sei
buk/inokashira/index.html; 1-18-31 Gotenyama,
Musashino-shi; 🚃 JR Sōbu-Chūō line to Kichijōji, Kōen
exit) One of the city's best parks, Inokashira-
kōen has a big pond in the middle flanked
by woodsy strolling paths. You can rent row
boats and swan-shaped pedal boats to take
out onto the water (¥700 per hour). On weekends performance artists and craft vendors
gather here (along with lots of Tokyoites of
all ages). Don't miss the ancient **shrine** (井の
頭弁財天; Inokashira-kōen, Musashino-shi; ⏱ 7am-
4.30pm) FREE to the sea goddess Benzaiten.

To reach the park, walk straight from the
Kōen exit of Kichijōji Station, cross at the light

and veer right at Marui ('0101') department
store; the park is at the end of the lane. Along
the way, you'll pass shops selling takeaway
items such as *yakitori* (grilled chicken skewers) and hot dogs.

★ **Ghibli Museum**   MUSEUM
(ジブリ美術館; www.ghibli-museum.jp; 1-1-
83 Shimo-Renjaku, Mitaka-shi; adult ¥1000,
child ¥100-700; ⏱ 10am-6pm, closed Tue; 🚃 JR
Sōbu-Chūō line to Mitaka, south exit) Master
animator Miyazaki Hayao, whose Studio
Ghibli produced *Princess Mononoke* and
Spirited Away, designed this museum.
Fans will enjoy the original sketches; kids,
even if they're not familiar with the movies,
will fall in love with the fairy-tale atmosphere (and the big cat bus). Don't miss the
original 20-minute animated short playing
on the 1st floor.

Tickets must be purchased in advance, and
you must choose the exact time and date you
plan to visit.

Get tickets through a travel agent before
you arrive in Japan or from a kiosk at any
Lawson convenience store in Tokyo (this is
trickier, as it will require some Japanese-
language skills to navigate the ticket machine). Both options are explained in detail on
the website, where you will also find a useful
map. Tickets are non-transferable; you may
be asked to show an ID.

Getting to Ghibli (pronounced 'jiburi') is
all part of the adventure. A minibus (round
trip/one way ¥320/210) leaves for the museum every 20 minutes from Mitaka Station
(bus stop 9). The museum is on the western
edge of Inokashira-kōen, so you can also

walk there through the park from Kichijōji Station in about 30 minutes.

Reversible Destiny Lofts
ARCHITECTURE

(天命反転住宅; Tenmei Hanten Jūtaku; ☑ 0422-26-4966; www.rdloftsmitaka.com/english; 2-2-8 Ōsawa, Mitaka-shi; adult/child ¥2700/1000; ♿; ☒ JR Sōbu-Chūō line to Mitaka, south exit) Designed by husband and wife Arakawa Shūsaku (1936–2010) and Madeleine Gins (1941–2014) and completed in 2005, this housing complex certainly strikes against the mould: Created 'in memory of Helen Keller' the nine units have undulating, ridged floors, spherical dens and ceiling hooks for hammocks and swings. All this is meant to create a sensory experience beyond the visual (though the building is plenty colourful). Inside access is by tour only (check the website); the guides can speak some English.

Some units are occupied by residents, but others are available for short-term stays (p122).

From JR Mitaka Station, take bus 51 or 52 (¥220, 15 minutes, every 10 to 15 minutes) from bus stop 2 on the station's south side and get off at Ōsawa Jūjiro (大沢十字路); you can see the building from the bus stop. Not all buses go this far, so show the driver where you want to go. Bus 1 (¥220, 25 minutes, every 10 to 15 minutes) goes here from Kichijōji Station (south exit, bus stop 3), alongside Inokashira-kōen.

🏃 Activities

Onsen

★ Ōedo Onsen Monogatari
ONSEN

(大江戸温泉物語; Map p108; www.ooedoonsen.jp; 2-6-3 Aomi, Kōtō-ku; adult/child ¥2280/980, surcharge Sat & Sun ¥200; ⊗ 11am-9am, last entry 7am; ☒ Yurikamome line to Telecom Center, Rinkai line to Tokyo Teleport with free shuttle bus) Just to experience the truly Japanese phenomenon that is an amusement park centred on bathing is reason enough to visit. The baths here, which include gender-divided indoor tubs and outdoor *rotemburo* (outdoor baths), are filled with real hot-spring water, pumped from 1400m below Tokyo Bay. Come after 6pm for a ¥500 discount. Visitors with tattoos will be denied admission.

Upon entering, visitors change their clothes for a choice of colourful *yukata* (light cotton kimonos) to wear while they stroll around the complex, which is a lantern-lit re-creation of

WORTH A TRIP

EDO-TOKYO OPEN AIR MUSEUM

The fantastic, yet little-known **Edo-Tokyo Open Air Architecture Museum** (江戸東京たてもの園; www.tatemonoen.jp/english; 3-7-1 Sakura-chō, Koganei-shi; adult/child ¥400/free; ⊗ 9.30am-5.30pm Tue-Sun Apr-Sep, to 4.30pm Oct-Mar; ♿; ☒ JR Chūō line to Musashi-Koganei) has a collection of historic buildings rescued from Tokyo's modernising zeal. Among them are an Edo-era farmhouse, a modernist villa and a whole strip of early-20th-century shops, all of which you can enter. Take the Chūō line west to Musashi-Koganei (four stops past Kichijōji); from the station's north exit, take bus 2 or 3 for Koganei-kōen Nishi-guchi. It's a short walk through Koganei-kōen (Tokyo's second-largest park) to the museum.

an old Tokyo downtown area, with food stalls and carnival games.

There's a huge variety of baths here, including jet baths, pools of natural rock and, on the ladies' side, personal bucket-shaped baths made of cedar. These are segregated by gender, but there's also a communal outdoor foot bath, set in a garden, where mixed groups and families can hang out together (the town area is also communal).

You can also crash here overnight, sleeping on reclining chairs in the lounge, bathing at whim if you want to dig deep into the onsen experience; there's a surcharge of ¥2000 per person if you stay between 2am and 5am.

★ Spa LaQua
ONSEN

(スパ ラクーア; Map p96; ☑ 03-5800-9999; www.laqua.jp; 5th-9th fl, Tokyo Dome City, 1-1-1 Kasuga, Bunkyō-ku; weekday/weekend ¥2635/2960; ⊗ 11am-9am; Ⓢ Marunouchi line to Kōrakuen, exit 2) One of Tokyo's few true onsen, this chic spa complex relies on natural hot-spring water from 1700m below ground. There are indoor and outdoor baths, saunas and a bunch of add-on options, such as *akasuri* (Korean-style whole-body exfoliation). It's a fascinating introduction to Japanese health and beauty rituals.

★ Rokuryu Kōsen
BATHHOUSE

(六龍鉱泉; Map p100; ☑ 03-3821-3826; 3-4-20 Ikenohata, Taitō-ku; ¥460; ⊗ 3.30-11pm Tue-Sun; Ⓢ Chiyoda line to Nezu, exit 2) Dating from 1931, this

DON'T MISS

CITY STREET GO-KARTING

We're not sure how this is legal (and Nintendo has had words to say about copyright infringement), but at least at the time of writing it still is: go-karting on the streets of Tokyo dressed as your favourite Mario Kart character. It brings the idea of Tokyo as a real-life video game experience to a whole new level.

There are a few operators, of which **Maricar** (マリカー; Map p72; ☑ 0120-81-9999, 080-9999-2525; http://maricar.jp; 1-23-15 Kita-Shinagawa, Shinagawa-ku; per person from ¥3500; ⓡ Keikyū line to Kita-Shinagawa) is the most established and foreigner-friendly. The operation feels a little slap-dash and there's no practising on the go-karts, which can be tricky at first, before you're on the road with trucks and buses, so absolutely speak up if you're not comfortable; one of the English-speaking guides will hang back with you, or re-route the course.

While daytime is best for snapping photos, the night course over the Rainbow Bridge across Tokyo Bay to Odaiba wins for sheer thrill.

If you're keen to ride through the streets of Akihabara, local operator **Akiba Kart** (アキバカート; Map p96; ☑ 03-6206-4752; http://akibanavi.net; 2-4-6 Soto-kanda, Chiyoda-ku; 1hr from ¥2700; ⊗ 10am-8pm; ⓡ JR Yamanote line to Akihabara, Electric Town exit) is another (slightly cheaper) option.

In either case, you absolutely must have a valid international (or Japanese) driving licence to participate.

gem of a neighbourhood *sentō* (public bath) has a beautiful mural of the wooden arched bridge Kintai-kyo in Iwasaki on the bathhouse wall. The amber-hued water is packed with minerals that are reputed to be excellent for your skin, if you can stand the water temperature – a scalding-hot 45°C in the cooler of the two pools!

The bathhouse is located down a small lane next to a shop with a green awning.

Thermae-yu   ONSEN

(テルマー湯; Map p93; ☑ 03-5285-1726; www. thermae-yu.jp; 1-1-2 Kabukichō, Shinjuku-ku; weekdays/weekends & holidays ¥2360/2690; ⊗ 11am-9am; ⓡ JR Yamanote line to Shinjuku, east exit) The best (and most literal) example to date that red-light district Kabukichō is cleaning up its act: the 2016 opening of this gleaming onsen complex. The tubs, which include several indoor and outdoor ones (sex-segregated), are filled with honest-to-goodness natural hot-spring water. There are several saunas, including a hot-stone sauna (*ganbanyoku*, ¥810 extra). Sorry, no tattoos allowed.

Komparu-yu   BATHHOUSE

(金春湯; Map p76; ☑ 03-3571-5469; www002.upp. so-net.ne.jp/konparu; 8-7-5 Ginza, Chūō-ku; ¥460; ⊗ 2-10pm Mon-Sat; ⓡ Ginza line to Shimbashi, exit 1 or 3) Join women and salarymen freshening up at this simple bathhouse without stand-up showers that's been located here since 1863. Tile art includes old-school koi (carp) and the traditional Mt Fuji motifs.

Jakotsu-yu   BATHHOUSE

(蛇骨湯; Map p106; ☑ 03-3841-8645; www.jakotsuyu.co.jp; 1-11-11 Asakusa, Taitō-ku; adult/child ¥460/180; ⊗ 1pm-midnight Wed-Mon; ⓢ Ginza line to Tawaramachi, exit 3) Unlike most *sentō* (public baths), the tubs here are filled with pure hot-spring water, naturally the colour of weak tea. Another treat is the lovely, lantern-lit, rock-framed *rotemburo* (outdoor bath). Jakotsu-yu is a welcoming place; it has English signage and doesn't have a policy against tattoos. It's an extra ¥200 for the sauna, ¥140 for a small towel.

Cruises

Tsukishima Monja Yakatabune   CRUISE

(月島もんじゃ屋形船; ☑ 03-3533-6699; www. 4900yen.com; 2-6-3 Shin-Kiba, Kōtō-ku; per person from ¥5000; ⓢ Yūrakuchō line to Shin-Kiba, main exit) Two-hour (day and night) cruises around Tokyo Bay on a *yakatabune* (traditional pleasure boat), with free-flowing beer and all-you-can eat *monja-yaki* (a savoury, scrambled batter-style dish and Tokyo speciality): this is the cheapest *yakatabune* package around, and the only one that regularly lets you book for as few as two people. Reservations essential; you'll need a Japanese speaker to help book.

The drawback is that their departure point is Shin-Kiba pier; free shuttles from Shin-Kiba Station to the pier depart every 10 minutes, 45 to 15 minutes prior to the boat's embarkation.

Tokyo Bay Cruise CRUISE

(Map p76; ☎03-5679-7311; www.ss3.jp; 1 Nihombashi, Chūō-ku; 45/60min cruises ¥1500/2000; [S] Ginza line to Mitsukoshimae, exit B5 or B6) For a unique perspective on Tokyo, hop aboard one of these daily river cruises. Lasting either 45 minutes or an hour, they proceed along the Nihombashi-gawa towards the Sumida-gawa, or make a loop around Nihombashi-gawa to Kanda-gawa. The landing stage is next to Nihombashi.

You'll get to see beneath many historic bridges as well as the expressway built above the river.

Amusement Parks

Tokyo Disney Resort AMUSEMENT PARK

(東京ディズニーリゾート; ☎domestic calls 0570-00-8632, from overseas +81-45-330-5211; www.tokyodisneyresort.co.jp; 1-1 Maihama, Urayasu-shi, Chiba-ken; 1-day ticket for 1 park adult/child ¥7400/4800, after 6pm ¥4200; 🕐varies by season; 🚉JR Keiyō line to Maihama) Here you'll find not only Tokyo Disneyland, modelled after the one in California, but also Tokyo DisneySea, an original theme park with seven 'ports' evoking locales real and imagined (the Mediterranean and 'Mermaid Lagoon', for example). DisneySea targets a more grown-up crowd, but still has many attractions for kids. Both resorts get extremely crowded, especially on weekends and during summer holidays; you'll have to be strategic with your fast passes. Book admission tickets online to save time.

Tokyo Joypolis AMUSEMENT PARK

(東京ジョイポリス; Map p108; http://tokyo-joypolis.com; 3rd-5th fl, DECKS Tokyo Beach, 1-6-1 Daiba, Minato-ku; adult/child ¥800/300, all-rides passport ¥4300/3300, passport after 5pm ¥3300/2300; 🕐10am-10pm; 🚉Yurikamome line to Odaiba Kaihin-kōen) This indoor amusement park is stacked with virtual-reality attractions and adult thrill rides, such as the video-enhanced Halfpipe Canyon; there are rides for little ones, too. Separate admission and individual ride tickets (¥500 to ¥800) are available, but if you plan to go on more than half a dozen attractions, the unlimited 'passport' makes sense.

Tokyo Dome City Attractions AMUSEMENT PARK

(東京ドームシティアトラクションズ; Map p96; ☎03-3817-6001; www.tokyo-dome.co.jp/e/attractions; 1-3-61 Kōraku, Bunkyō-ku; day pass adult/child/teenager ¥3900/2100/3400; 🕐10am-9pm; 👪; 🚉JR Chūō line to Suidōbashi, west exit) The top attraction at this amusement park next to Tokyo Dome (p144) is the 'Thunder Dolphin' (¥1030), a roller coaster that cuts a heart-in-your-throat course in and around the tightly packed buildings of downtown. There are plenty of low-key, child-friendly rides as well. You can buy individual-ride tickets, day passes, night passes (valid from 5pm) and a five-ride pass (¥2600).

Hanayashiki AMUSEMENT PARK

(花やしき; Map p106; ☎03-3842-8780; www.hanayashiki.net/index.html; 2-28-1 Asakusa, Taitō-ku; adult/child ¥1000/500; 🕐10am-6pm; [S] Ginza line to Asakusa, exit 1) Japan's oldest amusement park has creaky old carnival rides and heaps of vintage charm. Once you're inside, you can buy tickets for rides (which cost a few hundred yen each). A haunted-house attraction here allegedly housed a real ghost that is said to still appear on the grounds.

Dai-kanransha FERRIS WHEEL

(大観覧車; Map p108; www.daikanransha.com; 1-3-10 Aomi, Kōtō-ku; ¥920; 🕐10am-10pm Sun-Thu, to 11pm Fri & Sat; 🚉Yurikamome line to Aomi) The world's tallest Ferris wheel when it opened in 1999 (it lost that title in 2000), this Odaiba landmark offers glorious views over the city and the bay. It's also great eye-candy when illuminated at night in a rainbow of colours.

☞ Tours

Bus tours are convenient for travellers who want to cover a lot of ground in one day (or want some respite from navigating). Walking tours offer insight into the history and culture of particular districts.

Bus Tours

Gray Line BUS

(☎03-3595-5948; www.jgl.co.jp/inbound/index.htm; per person ¥4000-13,000) Offers half-day and full-day tours with stops, covering key downtown sights and also day trips to Mt Fuji and Hakone. Pick-up service from major hotels is available, otherwise most tours

> **ℹ RICKSHAW RIDES**
>
> Hang around the entrance to **Sensō-ji** (p104) long enough and you're bound to get approached by a scantily clad, strapping young man offering you…a ride in his *jinrikisha* (rickshaw). Rides start at ¥4000 per 10 minutes for two people (¥3000 for one person).

leave from in front of the Dai-Ichi Hotel in Shimbashi (near Ginza).

Hato Bus Tours BUS

(Map p72; ☎ 03-3435-6081; www.hatobus.com; per person ¥1500-12,000; ⓇJR Yamanote line to Hamamatsuchō, south exit) Tokyo's most well-known bus-tour company offers hour-long, half-day and full-day bus tours of the city. Shorter tours cruise by the sights in an open-air double-decker bus; longer ones make stops. Tours leave from Hato Bus terminals in the annexe of the World Trade Centre in Hamamatsuchō, and Shinjuku and Tokyo train stations.

SkyBus BUS

(Map p76; ☎ 03-3215-0008; www.skybus.jp; 2-5-2 Marunouchi, Chiyoda-ku; tours adult/child from ¥1600/700, Sky Hop Bus ¥2500/1200; ⏱ ticket office 9am-6pm; ⓇJR Yamanote line to Tokyo, Marunouchi south exit) Open-top double-decker buses cruise through different neighbourhoods of the city (for roughly 50 to 80 minutes); most have English-language audio guidance aboard. The Sky Hop Bus plan allows you to hop on and off buses on any of the three routes.

Walking Tours

Tsukiji Market Information Centre WALKING

(Map p76; ☎ 03-3541-6521; www.tsukijitour.jp; 4-7-5 Tsukiji, Chūō-ku; tour per person from ¥8800; ⏱ 9am-3pm market days; Ⓢ Hibiya line to Tsukiji, exit 2) This popular 2½-hour tour of Tsukiji Market (p79) for a minimum of two people starts with a video and finishes up with a sushi lunch in the area. When the market moves, it will continue tours in the Outer Market (p79) area and likely include a sushi-making class at a local restaurant.

Haunted Tokyo Tours TOURS

(www.hauntedtokyotours.com; hauntedtokyotours@ hotmail.com; per person from ¥4500) Fun and friendly English-speaking guides take amblers to the scenes of some of the city's most notorious ghost haunts and urban legends. You'll never look at Tokyo the same way again.

Meeting points are explained on the website; contact is via email only.

Ueno Free Walking Tour WALKING

(Map p100; https://tokyosgg.jp/guide.html; 7-47 Ueno-kōen, Taitō-ku; ⓇJR lines to Ueno, Ueno-kōen exit) FREE Free tours of Ueno, conducted in English by volunteer guides, leave from in front of the Green Salon (グリーンサロン) cafe every Sunday, Wednesday and Friday at 10.30am and 1pm. No sign-up is necessary.

Imperial Palace East Garden Walking Tour WALKING

(Map p76; ☎ 03-6280-6710; JNTO Tourist Information Center, 3-3-1 Marunouchi, Chiyoda-ku; Ⓢ Chiyoda line to Nijūbashimae, exit 1) FREE Two-hour guided walking tours of the Imperial Palace East Garden (p75) are available every Wednesday, Saturday and Sunday; meet at the JNTO Tourist Information Center (p152) before 1pm.

➷ Courses

Cooking

★ Buddha Bellies COOKING

(Map p96; http://buddhabelliestokyo.jimdo.com; 2nd fl, Uekuri Bldg, 22-4-3 Kanda-Jimbōchō, Chiyoda-ku; courses from ¥7500; Ⓢ Shinjuku line to Jimbōchō, exit A2) Professional sushi chef and sake sommelier Ayuko leads small hands-on classes in sushi, *bentō* (boxed lunch) and udon making. Prices start at ¥7500 per person for a 2½-hour course.

Tokyo Cooking Studio COOKING

(東京クッキングスタジオ; Map p72; http://tokyo.cookingstudio.org; Hins Minato #004, 3-18-14 Minato, Chūō-ku; classes for up to 3 people starting from ¥30,000; Ⓢ Yūrakuchō line to Shintomichō, exit 7) Genial English-speaking chef Inoue Akira is a master of soba – noodles made from nutty buckwheat flour. He's taught how to make and eat this classic Tokyo dish to chefs who have gone on to win Michelin stars for their cooking. Classes are held in a compact kitchen overlooking the Sumida River.

Tokyo Cook COOKING

(Map p82; ☎ 03-5414-2727; www.tokyo-cook.com; 3rd fl, Roppongi Green Bldg, 6-1-8 Roppongi, Minato-ku; classes from ¥8640; Ⓢ Hibiya line to Roppongi, exit 3) Among the several types of cooking classes on offer here in English are ones focusing on making vegetarian dishes, the temple food *shojin-ryori* and soba noodles. It's held inside the restaurant Sougo (p125).

Tokyo Sushi Academy COOKING

(Map p76; ☎ 03-3362-2789; http://sushimaking. tokyo; 2nd fl, Tsukiji KY Bldg, 4-7-5 Tsukiji, Chūō-ku; per person ¥5400; ⏱ 9am-3pm Sat; Ⓢ Hibiya line to Tsukiji, exit 1) English-speaking sushi chefs will give you a 30-minute crash course in making the vinegared rice speciality, after which you'll have an hour in which to make (and eat) as much of your favourite type of sushi as you like. Classes are held on Saturday (and sometimes Sunday) in a modern kitchen a stone's throw from the Tsukiji Outer Market (p79).

Arts & Crafts

★ Wanariya
TRADITIONAL CRAFT

(和なり屋; Map p72; ☎03-5603-9169; www.wanariya.jp; 1-8-10 Senzoku, Taitō-ku; indigo dyeing/weaving from ¥1920/1980; ⏰10am-5pm Thu-Tue; Ⓢ Hibiya line to Iriya, exit 1) A team of young and friendly Japanese runs this indigo dyeing and traditional hand-loom-weaving workshop where you can learn the crafts and have a go yourself in under an hour or so. It's a great way to make your own unique souvenir, with a range of items you can dye, from *tenugui* (thin cotton towels) to canvas sneakers.

★ Mokuhankan
TRADITIONAL CRAFT

(木版館; Map p106; ☎070-5011-1418; http://mokuhankan.com/parties; 2nd fl, 1-41-8 Asakusa, Taitō-ku; per person ¥2000; ⏰10am-5.30pm Wed-Mon; Ⓡ Tsukuba Express to Asakusa, exit 5) Try your hand at making *ukiyo-e* (woodblock prints) at this studio run by expat David Bull. Hour-long 'print parties' are great fun and take place daily; sign up online. There's a shop here too, where you can see Bull's and Jed Henry's humorous *Ukiyo-e Heroes* series – prints featuring video-game characters in traditional settings.

Ohara School of Ikebana
IKEBANA

(小原流いけばな; Map p90; ☎03-5774-5097; www.ohararyu.or.jp; 5-7-17 Minami-Aoyama, Minato-ku; per class ¥4000; Ⓢ Ginza line to Omote-sandō, exit B1) Every Thursday, from 10.30am to 12.30pm, this well-regarded, modern ikebana school teaches introductory flower-arrangement classes in English. Sign up via email by 3pm the Tuesday before.

🎎 Festivals & Events

Hanami
CULTURAL

(花見) Cherry-blossom-viewing obsession takes over as locals flock to the city's parks and cemeteries from late March to mid-April for parties under the trees.

Kōenji Awa Odori
CULTURAL

(高円寺阿波おどり; www.koenji-awaodori.com) The most famous of Tokyo's *awa odori* (dance festivals for O-Bon) sees 12,000 participants in traditional costumes dancing their way through the streets of Kōenji over the last weekend of August.

ⓘ ADVANCE PLANNING

➜ The best workshops and courses are designed for small groups, so sign up in advance (usually possible online).

➜ If you want to try go-karting, get an international driving licence in your home country.

➜ Book tickets for sumo, kabuki and Giants baseball games online to lock in good seats. Tickets usually go on sale one month to two months prior.

➜ Tickets for the **Ghibli Museum** (p110) go on sale three months in advance; reserve yours asap.

➜ Other attractions that require advanced reservations include the **Imperial Palace** (p75), if you want to tour the grounds, and **Reversible Destiny Lofts** (p111).

Sanja Matsuri
PARADE

(三社祭) Arguably the grandest Tokyo *matsuri* (festival) of all, this three-day festival, held over the third weekend of May, attracts around 1.5 million spectators to Asakusa-jinja (p104). The highlight is the rowdy parade of *mikoshi* (portable shrines) carried by men and women in traditional dress.

Anime Japan
FAIR

(www.anime-japan.jp) Events and exhibitions for industry insiders and fans alike in late March at Tokyo Big Sight.

Tokyo Game Show
FAIR

(東京ゲームショウ; http://tgs.cesa.or.jp) Get your geek on when the Computer Entertainment Suppliers Association hosts Tokyo Game Show, a massive expo at Makuhari Messe in late September.

Sumida-gawa Fireworks
FIREWORKS

(隅田川花火大会, Sumida-gawa Hanabi Taikai) Held the last Saturday of July, the largest of the summer fireworks shows sees 20,000 pyrotechnic wonders explode over Asakusa.

Tokyo Filmex
FILM

(東京フィルメックス; http://filmex.net) This film festival in late November focuses on emerging directors in Asia and screens many films with English subtitles.

Design Festa
ART

(デザインフェスタ; www.designfesta.com) In mid-May a wide showcase of work from budding designers and artists is displayed at Tokyo Big Sight. A second showing takes place in November.

🛏 Sleeping

Central neigbouhoods like Marunouchi (convenient for *shinkansen* hub Tokyo Station) and Ginza are typically pricey: this is where many of Tokyo's finest luxury hotels can be found. Roppongi and Shibuya, which both have solid midrange options, are good for night owls (otherwise give them a pass): both are nightlife centres.

The busy western hub of Shinjuku is a traveller favourite, thanks to its many rail links and dining and drinking options. Note that many budget hotels in Shinjuku that target foreign travellers are in the red-light district, Kabukichō; while it's highly unlikely you'd encounter any real danger, some might find it unpleasant to walk past shady characters night after night. The neighbourhoods north of Shinjuku – Ikebukuro in particular – are good for hostels and budget ryokan (traditional inns).

Ueno and Yanesen abound with ryokan and good budget options, though these hoods can be sleepy at night. Asakusa, in the northeastern corner of Tokyo, is backpacker central with the best selection of hostels; on the downside, staying here can mean long train rides to other parts of the city.

Marunouchi (Tokyo Station), Shinjuku, Shibuya and Ikebukuro all have direct access to Narita Airport on the Narita Express; Ueno has its own direct line to Narita, the Skyliner.

🛏 Marunouchi & Nihombashi

★ Wise Owl Hostels Tokyo HOSTEL ¥
(Map p72; ☑03-5541-2960; www.wiseowlhostels. com; 3-22-9 Hatchōbori, Chūō-ku; dm/d from ¥3600/9000; ❂✳🖧) This industrial-looking hostel ticks all the right boxes, starting with a super-convenient location above the subway and a relatively short walk or taxi ride from Marunouchi and Ginza. A clever configuration of wooden-cubicle bunks makes up the dorms. There's friendly service, a third-wave coffee stand in the lobby, DJ bar in the basement and attached *izakaya* for food.

Grids Akihabara HOSTEL ¥
(Map p72; ☑03-5822-6236; www.grids-hostel. com; 2-8-16 Higashi-kanda, Chiyoda-ku; dm/s/d from ¥3300/3500/7200; ❂✳🖧; Ⓢ Shinjuku line to Iwamotochō, exit A4) Following what is

becoming a common hostel format in Tokyo (conversions of older office buildings with a cafe-bar on the ground floor), Grids adds to the mix by throwing in four Japanese-style tatami-mat rooms (sleeping up to four; ¥20,000), as well as more private rooms with en-suite bathrooms. The dorms offer sturdy metal-frame bunks with good mattresses.

It's around a 10-minute walk to Akihabara across the Kanda-gawa. If this hostel is full, it runs a very similar one around 1km south in Higashi-nihombashi.

Yaesu Terminal Hotel BUSINESS HOTEL ¥¥
(八重洲ターミナルホテル; Map p76; ☑03-3281-3771; www.yth.jp; 1-5-14 Yaesu, Chūō-ku; s/d ¥11,500/16,500; ✳@🖧; 🚃 JR lines to Tokyo, Yaesu north exit) This sleek little business hotel on cherry-tree-lined Sakura-dōri has contemporary lines and a minimalist look. Rooms are the usual compact business-hotel size, but they're decently priced for this neighbourhood and each showcases intriguing contemporary artworks by radiographic artist Steven Meyers.

★ Hoshinoya Tokyo RYOKAN ¥¥¥
(星のや東京; Map p72; ☑050-3786-1144; http:// hoshinoyatokyo.com/en; 1-9-1 Ōtemachi, Chiyoda-ku; r from ¥72,000; Ⓢ Marunouchi line to Ōtemachi, exit A1) In creating its brand-new contemporary ryokan in the heart of Tokyo, Hoshinoya has barely put a foot wrong. Overcoming a location boxed in by office towers, this ryokan is all about insulating yourself from the city in a building that incorporates timeless craftsmanship and the best of traditional Japanese design and service.

★ Aman Tokyo DESIGN HOTEL ¥¥¥
(Map p76; ☑03-5224-3333; www.aman.com/resorts/aman-tokyo; 1-5-6 Ōtemachi, Chiyoda-ku; r from ¥90,750; ❂✳@🖧✉; Ⓢ Marunouchi line to Ōtemachi, exit A5) Overlooking the Imperial Palace (p75) from atop Ōtemachi Tower, the Aman incorporates natural materials – including dark stone walls, blonde wood and white *washi* (rice paper) – into its elegant, minimalist design. Enormous rooms all have baths with stunning city views – something you also get from the giant stone bath filled with onsen water in the spa. It's outstanding.

★ Palace Hotel Tokyo HOTEL ¥¥¥
(パレスホテル東京; Map p76; ☑03-3211-5211; www.palacehoteltokyo.com; 1-1-1 Marunouchi, Chiyoda-ku; r from ¥62,000; ❂✳@🖧✉; Ⓢ Chiyoda line to Ōtemachi, exit C13b) With its prestigious address, the gorgeously renovated Palace

Hotel offers the refinement and elegance that its name suggests. Sniff the botanically perfumed air as you stride its plush corridors. Request a room with a balcony – they're a bit more expensive but worth it for the chance to soak up private alfresco views of the city.

Ginza & Tsukiji 銀座・築地

★Prime Pod Ginza Tokyo CAPSULE HOTEL ¥

(Map p76; ☎03-5550-0147; http://theprimepod.jp; 13th fl, Duplex Tower 5/13 Bldg, 5-13-19 Ginza, Chūō-ku; capsules from ¥5200; [S] Hibiya line to Higashi-Ginza, exit 3) You're unlikely to find a cheaper place to sleep in chic Ginza than this capsule hotel, which is suitably contemporary in its stylings. For a bit more headroom than in your average capsule, request one of the corner pods when you book (rates are also cheaper online).

There are separate male and female floors. The lobby is on the 13th floor next to a cafe-bar with great views of the area.

Daiwa Roynet Hotel Ginza BUSINESS HOTEL ¥¥

(ダイワロイネットホテル銀座; Map p76; ☎03-5159-1380; www.daiwaroynet.jp/english/ginza; 1-13-15 Ginza, Chūō-ku; s/d & tw from ¥16,500/22,000; 🚭❄@📶; [S] Yūrakuchō line to Ginza-itchōme, exit A10) You can take your pick from various drinks and amenities kits at the reception of this very centrally located business hotel. Rooms are well designed, with larger than usual bathrooms for this type of set-up. There's also a women-only floor.

★Park Hotel Tokyo DESIGN HOTEL ¥¥¥

(Map p76; ☎03-6252-1111; http://en.parkhoteltokyo.com; Shiodome Media Tower, 1-7-1 Higashi-Shimbashi, Minato-ku; s/d from ¥29,000/35,000, art rooms from ¥35,000/40,000; 🚭❄@📶; [S] Ōedo line to Shimbashi, exit 7) Kudos to the Park Hotel for commissioning 31 artists to decorate 31 of its 31st-floor rooms. The results are very impressive with all-Japanese themes ranging from sumo and Zen to *yokai* (monsters) and geisha. See the various themes online and book well in advance for popular rooms such as the cherry-blossom one.

★Mitsui Garden Hotel Ginza Premier HOTEL ¥¥¥

(三井ガーデンホテル銀座プレミア; Map p76; ☎03-3543-1131; www.gardenhotels.co.jp; 8-13-1 Ginza, Chūō-ku; r from ¥38,000; 🚭❄@📶; [S] Ginza line to Shimbashi, exit 1) If you book ahead and online, rooms at this upmarket business hotel are a steal – as low as ¥17,300. It has a great location, pleasantly decorated rooms, and a high-rise lobby with killer Shiodome and Tokyo Tower (p84) views.

Roppongi, Akasaka & Around

★Zabutton Good Hostel HOSTEL ¥

(Map p72; ☎03-6277-6499; www.zabutton.jp; 1-29-20 Higashi-Azabu, Minato-ku; dm/d & tw ¥3780/8640; 🚭❄📶; [S] Ōedo line to Akabanebashi) This combined cafe-bar and hostel on a delightful shopping street is really good news. The dorms have nicely designed wooden-box bunks, there's one tatami (reed mat) room that's the double, a kitchen/common room and a roof deck with a partial view of Tokyo Tower (p84). Staff are super-friendly.

★Kaisu HOSTEL ¥

(Map p72; ☎03-5797-7711; www.kaisu.jp; 6-13-5 Akasaka, Minato-ku; dm/r with shared bathroom from ¥3900/10,500; 🚭❄📶; [S] Chiyoda line to Akasaka, exit 7) Occupying a former *ryōtei* (geisha house), Kaisu is a flashpacker hostel with mid-century-modern and surfer-chic stylings. Dorms offer wooden bunks with the gorgeous old building's exposed beams on show. English-speaking staff are very friendly and there's a great cafe-bar where you can mingle with locals.

First Cabin Akasaka CASPULE HOTEL ¥

(Map p72; ☎03-3583-1143; http://first-cabin.jp; 3-13-7 Akasaka, Minato-ku; capsule from ¥4500; 🚭❄📶; [S] Chiyoda line to Akasaka, exit 2) This slick and modern capsule-hotel chain offers 2.5-sq-metre cabins with decent headroom and floor space filled with a comfy mattress. Upgrade to 4.4-sq-metre 1st-class cabins for more room to stand up beside the bed and a side table. There's a large communal bath to soak in, and separate floors for men and women.

★Hotel S BOUTIQUE HOTEL ¥¥

(ホテル S; Map p82; ☎03-5771-2469; http://hr-roppongi.jp; 1-11-6 Nishi-Azabu, Minato-ku; r from ¥17,000, apt per month from ¥216,000; 🚭❄@📶; [S] Hibiya line to Roppongi, exit 2) The various styles of room at this boutique property capture the arty design spirit of Roppongi. Some of the more expensive duplex-type rooms have Japanese design elements such as tatami (in charcoal) and circular *hinoki* (wooden baths). The entry-level rooms are also a cut above the usual.

ℹ AIRPORT ACCOMMODATIONS

For late-night arrivals and early-morning departures, sleeping at the airport is an economical option.

9 Hours (📞 0476-33-5109; http://ninehours.co.jp/en/narita; Narita International Airport Terminal 2; capsule ¥4900; ❄❋🛜) This slick capsule hotel inside Narita Airport has roomy, space-age pods and separate sleeping and shower rooms for men and women. It's possible to stay for only a few hours, too (¥1500 for the first hour, plus ¥500 per additional hour).

Royal Park Hotel the Haneda (ロイヤルパークホテル ザ 羽田; 📞 03-6830-1111; www.rph-the.co.jp/haneda/en; Haneda Airport International Terminal; s/d from ¥15,300/19,400; ❄❋@🛜) Haneda Airport's transit hotel is good value if you factor in the cost of not having to take a taxi for late-night arrivals. It's relatively new; rooms have modern decor and are stocked with amenities.

For more on staying in Narita, or tips for spending a long layover there, see p208.

Hotel Mystays
Premier Akasaka   BUSINESS HOTEL ¥¥
(Map p72; 📞 03-6229 3280; www.mystays.com/mystays-p-akasaka; 2-17-54 Akasaka, Minato-ku; r from ¥7500; ❄❋🛜; 🚇 Chiyoda line to Akasaka, exit 5a or 5b) This slick new business hotel is a superb deal if you manage to bag one of its relatively spacious rooms at their low occupancy rate. When busy, the room rates increase to ¥16,000, which is still not bad for this ritzy district. Pluses include a coin laundry and small gym.

★ Hotel Ōkura   HOTEL ¥¥¥
(ホテルオークラ東京; Map p82; 📞 03-3582-0111; www.okura.com; 2-10-4 Toranomon, Minato-ku; s/d from ¥48,500/54,800; ❄❋@🛜🏊; 🚇 Hibiya line to Kamiyachō, exit 4B) While the beloved original 1962 hotel, a design classic, has been demolished to make way for a new building (set to open in 2019), the Ōkura's elegant South Wing remains intact – and long may it do so! Rooms are bright, large and have tasteful Japanese design touches. The public areas ooze retro glamour and service is courteous to a fault.

🛏 Ebisu, Meguro & Around

Dormy Inn Express
Meguro Aobadai   BUSINESS HOTEL ¥¥
(ドーミーインエクスプレス目黒青葉台; Map p72; 📞 03-6894-5489; www.hotespa.net/hotels/meguro; 3-21-8 Aobadai, Meguro-ku; s/d from ¥14,000/20,000; ❄❋@🛜; 🚇 Hibiya line to Naka-Meguro) If you prefer to base yourself somewhere less hectic – but no less fun – try this business hotel along the canal in hip Naka-Meguro. This chain sets itself apart with its large communal bath (the

rooms have showers, too), evening ramen service and free bicycles. Rooms are fresh and modern thanks to being spruced up in 2015.

★ Claska   BOUTIQUE HOTEL ¥¥¥
(クラスカ; Map p72; 📞 03-3719-8121; www.claska.com/en/hotel; 1-3-18 Chūō-chō, Meguro-ku; s/d from ¥15,400/28,500; ❄❋🛜; 🚌 No 1, 2, or 7 from Meguro Station to Shimizu, 🚉 Tōkyū Tōyoko line to Gakugei Daigaku, east exit) The Claska is hands-down Tokyo's most stylish hotel, though you might not know it from the retro business-hotel facade. No two rooms are alike: some have tatami and floor cushions; others have spacious terraces and glass-walled bathrooms. Its 20 rooms fill up fast. The only drawback is the out-of-the-way location, about 2km west of Meguro Station.

The easiest way to get here is by taxi from Meguro Station (about ¥1000, 10 minutes); there's also a bus stop very near the hotel. Free bicycles (up to three hours) allow guests to explore the surrounding neighbourhood, a residential enclave known for its interior-design shops.

🛏 Shibuya & Shimo-Kitazawa

★ Shibuya Granbell Hotel BOUTIQUE HOTEL ¥¥
(渋谷グランベルホテル; Map p88; 📞 03-5457-2681; www.granbellhotel.jp; 15-17 Sakuragaoka-chō, Shibuya-ku; s/d from ¥14,000/23,000; ❄❋@🛜; 🚉 JR Yamanote line to Shibuya, south exit) Though priced about the same as a business hotel, the Granbell is far more stylish. Some rooms have glass-enclosed bathrooms, Simmons beds and pop-art curtains. The hotel is on the quieter side of Shibuya, towards Daikanyama; still, it's just a few minutes' walk from the station.

Hotel Mets Shibuya BUSINESS HOTEL ¥¥¥
(ホテルメッツ渋谷; Map p88; ☎03-3409-0011; www.hotelmets.jp/shibuya; 3-29-17 Shibuya, Shibuya-ku; s/d incl breakfast from ¥15,500/25,000; 🚭❄@📶; 🚉JR Yamanote line to Shibuya, new south exit) Super-convenient and comfortable, the Hotel Mets is part of Shibuya Station's quiet south side. For a business hotel it's fairly stylish and the double beds clock in at a roomy 160cm. Bonus: breakfast is included, either a buffet spread or toast and eggs at the in-house cafe. Reception is on the 4th floor.

Excel Hotel Tōkyū HOTEL ¥¥¥
(エクセルホテル東急; Map p88; ☎03-5457-0109; www.tokyuhotelsjapan.com/en/te/te_shibu/index.html; 1-12-2 Dōgenzaka, Shibuya-ku; s/d from ¥28,500/34,500; 🚭❄@📶; 🚉JR Yamanote line to Shibuya, Mark City exit) This hotel is right on top of Shibuya Station, a location you'll be grateful for after a long day. Rooms are spacious though ordinary. Prices rise along with the floor numbers, but you can get a pretty good view with a simple upgrade for ¥2000 per night to a 'city view' room. The hotel is part of the Mark City complex.

Harajuku & Aoyama

Dormy Inn Premium Shibuya Jingūmae BUSINESS HOTEL ¥¥
(ドーミーインプレミアム渋谷神宮前; Map p90; ☎03-5774-5489; www.hotespa.net/hotels/shibuya; 6-24-4 Jingūmae, Shibuya-ku; s/d from ¥11,490/15,990; 🚭❄📶; 🚉JR Yamanote line to Harajuku, Omote-sandō exit) Dormy is a popular chain of business hotels, thanks to its free nightly ramen service (9.30pm to 11pm) and traditional communal baths (rooms have private showers, too). Other perks include bicycle rentals and a free morning shuttle service to Shibuya Station. Rooms are typically small with double beds (140cm).

Shinjuku & Northwest Tokyo

Book and Bed HOSTEL ¥
(Map p72; ☎03-6914-2914; http://bookandbedtokyo.com; 7th fl, 1-17-7 Nishi-Ikebukuro, Toshima-ku; dm from ¥3780; 🚭❄@📶; 🚉JR Yamanote line to Ikebukuro) Tokyo's newest headline-generating hostel invites guests to curl up in cubbyholes tucked inside a bookshelf. 'Compact' bunks have 80cm-wide beds; standard ones (¥4860) have 120cm-wide beds and lockers. Naturally, all come with reading lights. Of the 2000 or so books on display, about 200 are in English, including many travel guides.

Note that the 'bookshelf' room is also the common area (though bunks have curtains); the 'bunk' room has more privacy. The hostel is above the Kirin City pub. Staff speak English.

Kimi Ryokan RYOKAN ¥
(貴美旅館; Map p72; ☎03-3971-3766; www.kimi-ryokan.jp; 2-36-8 Ikebukuro, Toshima-ku; s/d from ¥4860/6590; 🚭❄@📶; 🚉JR Yamanote line to Ikebukuro, west exit) Easily one of the best budget ryokan in Tokyo, Kimi has been welcoming overseas guests for decades. There are tatami rooms of various sizes and a Japanese-style lounge area that's conducive to meeting other travellers. Clean showers and toilets are shared, and there's a lovely Japanese cypress bath. Book well in advance.

Apartment Hotel BOUTIQUE HOTEL ¥¥
(アパートメントホテル新宿; Map p93; ☎03-6273-0991; http://ap-shinjuku.com; 4-4-10 Shinjuku, Shinjuku-ku; s/d ¥10,000/12,000; 🚭❄📶; 🚉JR Yamanote line to Shinjuku, south exit) No joke – the rooms here are tiny, but you won't find a hotel in Shinjuku (and this close to the station!) with more creative panache. Apartment Hotel moonlights (daylights?) as an antique shop and the rooms, each different, are furnished with in-house stock. It's in a vintage, low-slung apartment building, with a little bar on the roof. Book well ahead.

Tōkyū Stay Shinjuku HOTEL ¥¥
(東急ステイ新宿; Map p93; ☎03-3353-0109; 3-7-1 Shinjuku, Shinjuku-ku; s/d ¥15,600/30,000; 🚭❄@📶; [S]Marunouchi line to Shinjuku-sanchōme, exit C3) This new property is nestled among the *izakaya* and bars of Shinjuku-sanchōme. Rooms are stark to the point of having zero personality, but everything is crisp and clean. All rooms have washing machines; doubles have kitchenettes and 160cm-wide beds. Smaller, cheaper 'semi-double' rooms have 140cm beds (and no kitchen; ¥22,000). Prices drop slightly if you stay a week.

Kadoya Hotel HOTEL ¥¥
(かどやホテル; Map p93; ☎03-3346-2561; www.kadoya-hotel.co.jp; 1-23-1 Nishi-Shinjuku, Shinjuku-ku; s/d from ¥9980/15,800; 🚭❄@📶; 🚉JR Yamanote line to Shinjuku, west exit) Kadoya has been welcoming foreign tourists for decades and is above all friendly and accommodating. The standard rooms show their age, but are clean, comfortable and a steal for Nishi-Shinjuku. The more recently updated 'comfort' rooms (single/double from ¥12,200/17,800) have

more space, Japanese-style bath-tubs and more stylish decor. There's also a coin laundry.

Hotel Gracery Shinjuku

HOTEL ¥¥

(ホテルグレイスリー新宿; Map p93; ☎03-6833-2489; http://shinjuku.gracery.com/; 1-19-1 Kabukichō, Shinjuku-ku; s/d from ¥16,000/22,000; ☀❀@⊛; ☒ JR Yamanote line to Shinjuku, east exit) The big draw of this huge (970 rooms!) new hotel in the new Todo Building complex is the enormous Godzilla statue that seems to be taking a bite out of it (you'll have no trouble finding it). Everything here is fresh and modern, though the lobby can be noisy and chaotic. Also, it's smack in the middle of Kabukichō, the red-light district.

★ Park Hyatt Tokyo

LUXURY HOTEL ¥¥¥

(パークハイアット東京; Map p93; ☎03-53 22-1234; http://tokyo.park.hyatt.com; 3-7-1-2 Nishi-Shinjuku, Shinjuku-ku; d from ¥60,000; ☀❀@⊛ ☒; ☒ Ōedo line to Tochōmae, exit A4) This eyrie atop a Tange Kenzō–designed skyscraper in west Shinjuku looks no less tasteful and elegant than when it opened 20 years ago, and it remains a popular spot for visiting celebrities. The hotel starts on the 41st floor, meaning even the entry-level rooms have fantastic views; 'Park Deluxe' rooms look out towards Mt Fuji. Perks include morning yoga classes.

🛏 Akihabara, Kagurazaka & Kōrakuen

Tokyo Central Youth Hostel

HOSTEL ¥

(東京セントラルユースホステル; Map p96; ☎03-3235-1107; www.jyh.gr.jp/tcyh; 18th fl, 1-1 Kagurakashi, Shinjuku-ku; dm ¥4050, with YHA discount ¥3450; ☀❀@⊛; ☒ JR Sōbu line to Iidabashi, west exit) Sitting right on top of well-connected Iidabashi Station, this clean, well-managed hostel has fantastic transport access. It also has luxury-hotel-worthy night views. The drawbacks: a utilitarian atmosphere and an 11pm curfew. Sleeping is on basic wooden bunks in gender-segregated four-bed dorms. There's a breakfast buffet (¥600) and laundry machines.

There's little signage out front, but it's in the big office building in front of Iidabashi Station; take the elevator to the 18th floor.

★ Hotel Niwa Tokyo

HOTEL ¥¥

(庭のホテル; Map p96; ☎03-3293-0028; www.hotelniwatokyo.com; 1-1-6 Misaki-chō, Chiyoda-ku; s/d from ¥14,600/17,400; ❀@⊛; ☒ JR Sōbu line to Suidōbashi, east exit) A traditional Japanese design with a contemporary spin in the public

areas and the reasonably spacious rooms of the Niwa put it well ahead of the usual bland midrangers. We like the rock garden and bamboo grove out front and the *shōji* (traditional paper screens) across the windows in the rooms.

Gakushikaikan

HOTEL ¥¥

(学士会館; Map p96; ☎03-3292-5938; www.gakushikaikan.co.jp; 3-28 Kandanishiki-cho, Chiyoda-ku; s/tw incl breakfast from ¥9940/14,365; ❀⊛; ☒ Hanzōmon line to Jimbōchō, exit A9) An academic air hangs over this retro hotel that's owned by seven major Japanese universities. It's a quirky place but the rooms are great value given the location and the complimentary breakfast. It has way more style and atmosphere than a comparable business hotel.

★ Hilltop Hotel

HISTORIC HOTEL ¥¥¥

(山の上ホテル; Map p96; ☎03-3293-2311; www.yamanoue-hotel.co.jp; 1-1 Kanda-Surugadai, Chiyoda-ku; s/d from ¥20,100/28,320; ❀@⊛; ☒ JR Chūō or Sōbu lines to Ochanomizu, Ochanomizu exit) This art-deco gem from the 1930s exudes personality and charm, with antique wooden furniture and a wood-panelled lounge. Mishima Yukio wrote his last few novels here. The older rooms in the main building come with antique writing desks and leather chairs.

🛏 Ueno & Yanesen

★ Toco

HOSTEL ¥

(トコ; Map p72; ☎03-6458-1686; http://backpackersjapan.co.jp; 2-13-21 Shitaya, Taitō-ku; dm/r from ¥2800/6800; ☀❀@⊛; ☒ Hibiya line to Iriya, exit 4) A group of friends renovated this old wooden building (which dates to 1920 and was once frequented by geisha) and turned it into one of Tokyo's most attractive hostels. Private tatami rooms and dorms with wooden bunks surround a small garden. The hostel is hidden behind a trendy bar-lounge (open 7pm to 11.30pm) in a modern building at the front.

★ Hanare

GUESTHOUSE ¥¥

(Map p100; ☎03-5834-7301; http://hanare.hagiso.jp; 3-10-25 Yanaka, Taitō-ku; r incl breakfast from ¥12,960; ☒ Chiyoda line to Sendagi, exit 2) A project of Tokyo University of the Arts, Hanare offers five immaculate tatami rooms in an old dormitory house, which has been tastefully upgraded to retain original features such as wooden beams. There's a shared bathroom, but you'll be given tickets to the local *sentō* (public bath), as the concept is to use Yanaka as an extension of the guesthouse.

Reception is in the nearby cafe-gallery Hagiso (p133), where you'll be served a traditional breakfast.

★ Hōmeikan   RYOKAN ¥¥
(鳳明館; Map p72; ☏03-3811-1181; www.homeikan.com; 5-10-5 Hongō, Bunkyō-ku; s/d from ¥8100/14,040; ❄☎; Ⓢ Ōedo line to Kasuga, exit A6) Although it's a little out of the way in a residential neighbourhood, this beautifully crafted wooden ryokan is an old-world oasis in the middle of Tokyo. The main Honkan wing dates from the Meiji era and is registered as an important cultural property, though we prefer the annexe, Daimachi Bekkan, with its winding corridors and garden.

★ Sawanoya Ryokan   RYOKAN ¥¥
(旅館澤の屋; Map p100; ☏03-3822-2251; www.sawanoya.com; 2-3-11 Yanaka, Taitō-ku; s/d from ¥5400/10,152; ❄@☎; Ⓢ Chiyoda line to Nezu, exit 1) Sawanoya is a gem in quiet Yanaka, run by a very friendly family and with all the traditional hospitality you would expect of a ryokan. The shared cypress and earthenware baths are the perfect balm after a long day (some rooms have their own bath, too). The lobby overflows with information about travel options in Japan.

Bicycles are also available for rent, and lion-dance performances are occasionally held for guests.

Hotel Graphy   BOUTIQUE HOTEL ¥¥
(Map p100; ☏03-3828-7377; www.hotel-graphy.com; 4-5-10 Ikenohata, Taitō-ku; r from ¥9500, dm/s with shared bathroom from ¥2900/7500; ❄@☎; Ⓢ Chiyoda line to Nezu, exit 2) Hotel Graphy falls somewhere between a boutique hotel and a hostel. It has a hip, modern vibe with a spacious lounge, kitchen, roof terrace – even a yoga room. Rooms are minimalist (read: fairly spartan) with retro furniture. Dorms and the cheapest singles have shared bathrooms.

Rates drop significantly for weekly and monthly stays.

TokHouse   RENTAL HOUSE ¥¥
(Map p100; ☏090-9674-4198; www.tokhouse.com; 3-52-9 Sendagi, Bunkyō-ku; s/d/q from ¥8000/10,000/13,000; ❄☎; ☒ JR Yamanote line to Nishi-Nippori, west exit) For the price of a room in a business hotel you can get your own apartment, with a fully equipped kitchen, close to Yanaka and Sendagi. There's a two-night minimum stay and a ¥5000 to ¥6000 cleaning fee; ask about discounts for families with children. Richard, the American owner and a long-time

Tokyo resident, has lots of tips for exploring the area.

Annex Katsutarō Ryokan   RYOKAN ¥¥
(アネックス勝太郎旅館; Map p100; ☏03-3828-2500; www.katsutaro.com; 3-8-4 Yanaka, Taitō-ku; s/d from ¥6600/12,000; ❄@☎; Ⓢ Chiyoda line to Sendagi, exit 2) More like a modern hotel than a traditional ryokan, the family-run Annex Katsutarō has spotless, thoughtfully arranged tatami rooms with attached bathrooms. It's ideal for exploring the old Yanaka district. Breakfast (from ¥430) and bicycles (a bargain ¥300 a day) are also available.

🛏 Asakusa & Sumida River
浅草・隅田川

★ Nui   HOSTEL ¥
(ヌイ; Map p72; ☏03-6240-9854; http://backpackersjapan.co.jp/nui_en; 2-14-13 Kuramae, Taitō-ku; dm/d from ¥3000/8000; ❄@☎; Ⓢ Ōedo line to Kuramae, exit A7) In a former warehouse, this hostel has raised the bar for stylish budget digs in Tokyo. High ceilings mean bunks you can comfortably sit up in and there is an enormous shared kitchen and work space. Best of all is the ground-floor cafe-bar and lounge (open 8am to 1am), with furniture made from salvaged timber; it's a popular local hang-out.

★ Bunka Hostel Tokyo   HOSTEL ¥
(Map p106; ☏03-5806-3444; http://bunkahostel.jp; 1-13-5 Asakusa, Taitō-ku; dm/f from ¥3000/16,800; ☒ Tsukuba Express to Asakusa, exit 4) This is one of the most stylish of the new crop of hostels popping up across town, which combine a cafe or bar open to the public in the foyer with a hostel above. Bunka offers capsule-style bunks; roomier versions where you can stand up go for ¥5000 a bed.

The family room sleeping up to four offers great views across the area.

★ Andon Ryokan   RYOKAN ¥
(行燈旅館; Map p72; ☏03-3873-8611; www.andon.co.jp; 2-34-10 Nihonzutsumi, Taitō-ku; s/d from ¥6500/7560; ❄@☎; Ⓢ Hibiya line to Minowa, exit 3) About 2km north of Asakusa, the contemporary Andon Ryokan is fabulously designed in form and function. It has tiny but immaculate tatami rooms and a spectacular upper-floor spa with a manga-style mural, which can be used privately. Toshiko, the friendly owner, collects antiques, which are displayed around the ryokan, and will serve you breakfast on dishes worth more than your stay.

Andon also has a full program of cultural events, bike rentals and laundry facilities. It's a five-minute walk from the subway.

Japonica Lodge   HOSTEL ¥

(ジャポニカロッジ; Map p106; ☑03-6802-7495; www.japonica-lodge.com; 1-3-3 Hanakawado; tent from ¥2500; ❸❋☎; ⓢGinza line to Asakusa, exit 5) This is far from a conventional hostel. Japonica Lodge is an outdoor goods shop (also selling traditional crafts and running a green-tea cafe) that allows guests to road test their tents, sleeping mats and bags for the night. The shop is open from 11.30am to 8pm, but you can slip into your tent after 6pm.

For those planning an outdoor adventure trip, this place is a dream, with a knowledgeable English-speaking owner and lots of information on hiking and climbing routes.

Khaosan World   HOSTEL ¥

(Map p106; ☑03-3843-0153; http://khaosan-tokyo.com/en/world; 3-15-1 Nishi-Asakusa, Taitō-ku; dm/d from ¥2800/9000; ❸❋@☎; ⓡTsukuba Express to Asakusa, exit A2) One of Tokyo's most oddball hostels, Khaosan World has taken over an ageing love hotel and left much of the design elements intact – things like mirrored ceilings and glittering brocade wallpaper (don't worry: it's clean). There's a wide variety of rooms to choose from, including ones with tatami floors and capsule-style bunks. There are cooking and laundry facilities, too.

Tokyo Ryokan   RYOKAN ¥

(東京旅館; Map p106; ☑090-8879-3599; www.tokyoryokan.com; 2-4-8 Nishi-Asakusa, Taitō-ku; r from ¥7000; ❸❋☎; ⓢGinza line to Tawaramachi, exit 3) This tidy little inn has only three small tatami rooms and no en-suite bathrooms but tons of charm. There are touches of calligraphy, attractive woodwork and sliding screens. Kenichi, the owner, is an avid traveller, speaks fluent English and is super-knowledgeable about Asakusa.

★Sukeroku No Yado Sadachiyo   RYOKAN ¥¥

(助六の宿貞千代; Map p106; ☑03-3842-6431; www.sadachiyo.co.jp; 2-20-1 Asakusa, Taitō-ku; d with/without half-board from ¥33,600/19,600; ❸❋@☎; ⓢGinza line to Asakusa, exit 1) This stunning ryokan virtually transports its guests to old Edo. Gorgeously maintained tatami rooms are spacious for two people, and all come with modern, Western-style bathrooms. Splurge on an exquisite meal here, and make time for the *o-furo* (traditional Japanese baths), one made of fragrant

Japanese cypress and the other of black granite. Look for the rickshaw parked outside.

Hatago   BUSINESS HOTEL ¥¥

(旅籠; Map p106; ☑03-6802-7277; http://asakusa hotel.org; 2-6-8 Komagata, Taitō-ku; s/tw from ¥8000/12,000; ❸❋@☎; ⓢGinza line to Asakusa, exit 4) If you're looking for a hotel in this part of town, the Hatago is a good bet. Rooms are typically small but come with tatami floors (even though you sleep on beds) and other Japanese touches. Breakfast is included and staff speak English. Rates go up on weekends.

Ryokan Shigetsu   RYOKAN ¥¥

(旅館指月; Map p106; ☑03-3843-2345; www.shigetsu.com; 1-31-11 Asakusa, Taitō-ku; s/d from ¥8000/16,950; ❸❋@☎; ⓢGinza line to Asakusa, exit 1) South of Sensō-ji (p104), this spotless and atmospheric ryokan has Japanese-style rooms with *shōji* (sliding rice-paper screen) doors and windows. There's a shared *o-furo* (traditional Japanese bath) made of cedar, with views of Tokyo Sky Tree (p105).

🛏 West Tokyo

★Reversible Destiny Lofts   APARTMENT ¥¥

(天命反転住宅; Tenmei Hanten Jūtaku; ☑0422-26-4966; www.rdloftsmitaka.com/english; 2-2-8 Ōsawa, Mitaka-shi; s/d/q from ¥17,300/20,300/29,300; ❸❋☎; ⓡJR Sōbu-Chūō line to Mitaka, south exit) This is a rare opportunity to sleep within one of Tokyo's most eccentric architectural landmarks. The two apartments – one has one bedroom, the other has two (sleeping up to two or four, respectively) – were designed for maximum wonderment, with contrasting colours and textures and oddly shaped rooms. Both have washing machines, kitchens and hammocks. You need to book a minimum of four nights.

The drawback is that the units are rather out of the way. From JR Mitaka Station, take bus 51 or 52 (¥220, 15 minutes, every 10 to 15 minutes) from bus stop 2 on the station's south side and get off at Ōsawa Jūjiro (大沢十字路); you can see the building from the bus stop. Not all buses go this far, so show the driver where you want to go. Bus 1 (¥220, 25 minutes, every 10 to 15 minutes) goes here from Kichijōji Station (south exit, bus stop 3), alongside Inokashira-kōen.

★Ryokan Seikō   RYOKAN ¥¥

(旅館西郊; ☑03-3391-0606; www.ryokan.or.jp/english/yado/main/28600; 3-38-9 Ogikubo, Suginami-ku; s/d from ¥6000/12,000; ❋☎; ⓡJR

Sōbu-Chūō line to Ogikubo) Maximise your Japan experience by shacking up at this rambling traditional lodge in an 80-year-old building. Rooms have tatami floors, sliding paper doors and futons; bathrooms are shared. The halls are of highly polished wood; the lobby looks like a slightly cluttered living room. The downside: curfew is 11pm (midnight at the absolute latest).

BnA Hotel
BOUTIQUE HOTEL ¥¥

(Map p110; www.bna-hotel.com; 2-4-7 Kōenji-kita, Suginami-ku; tw from ¥20,000; ❄❀🛜; 🚊 JR Sōbu line to Kōenji, north exit) There's a lot to love about new Kōenji hotel BnA: it's in a fun neighbourhood, just a minute's walk from the train station, the rooms were decorated by two Tokyo artists and the lobby doubles as a bar and event space. There's just not a lot of space: so far just two small rooms, though there are plans to expand.

Nakano Sun Plaza Hotel
HOTEL ¥¥

(中野サンプラザホテル; Map p110; 📞03-3388-1177; www.sunplaza.jp; 4-1-1 Nakano, Nakano-ku; s/d from ¥13,900/16,200; ❄❀🛜; 🚊 JR Sobu-Chūō line to Nakano, north exit) As far as midrange hotels go, this one has a few advantages: it's one block from the train station; rooms are a little bigger than average; and, best of all, double rooms look out towards the Shinjuku skyline. It's not stylish, but is clean and comfortable and, surprisingly, not a chain. Reception is on the 16th floor.

🍴 Eating

As visitors to Tokyo quickly discover, the people here are absolutely obsessed with food. The city has a vibrant and cosmopolitan dining scene and a strong culture of eating out – popular restaurants are packed most nights of the week. Best of all, you can get superlative meals on any budget.

🍴 Marunouchi & Nihombashi

★Dhaba India
SOUTH INDIAN ¥

(ダバ インディア; Map p76; 📞03-3272-7160; http://dhabaindia.com/dhaba/index.html; 2-7-9 Yaesu, Chūō-ku; lunch from ¥850, mains from ¥1370; ⊗11.15am-3pm & 5-11pm Mon-Fri, noon-3pm & 5-10pm Sat & Sun; 📶; 🚇 Ginza line to Kyōbashi, exit 5) Indian meals in Tokyo don't come much better than those served at this long-established restaurant with deep-indigo plaster walls. The food is very authentic, particularly the curries served with basmati

TOP TOKYO DINING EXPERIENCES

➡ Noshing on *yakitori* (chicken skewers) and knocking back beers with Tokyo's workday warriors under the train tracks in Yūrakuchō.

➡ Gazing upon (and sampling) all the glorious delights to be found in a department-store food hall.

➡ Making a pilgrimmage to Tsukiji's Outer Market (p79) for street food (such as grilled oysters) and professional tools (such as chef's knives).

➡ Visiting a traditional festival and getting *yaki-soba* (fried noodles) or *okonomiyaki* (savoury pancakes) hot off the grill.

➡ Grabbing late-night noodles after a rousing round of karaoke.

➡ Splurging on an *omakase* (chef's tasting menu) at a top-class sushi restaurant.

rice, naan or crispy *dosa* (giant lentil-flour pancakes). Set lunches are spectacularly good value.

★Taimeiken
JAPANESE ¥

(たいめいけん; Map p76; 📞03-3271-2464; www.taimeiken.co.jp; 1-12-10 Nihombashi, Chūō-ku; lunch from ¥800, omelette ¥1950; ⊗11am-8.30pm Mon-Sat, to 8pm Sun; 📶; 🚇 Ginza line to Nihombashi, exit C5) *Yoshoku*, Western cuisine adapted to Japanese tastes, has been the draw here since 1931, in particular its borscht and coleslaw (a bargain ¥50 each). For the food movie *Tampopo* (1985), directed by Itami Jūzō, it created *Tampopo omuraisu* (an omelette wrapped around tomato-flavoured rice) and it's been a signature dish ever since.

★Hōnen Manpuku
JAPANESE ¥

(豊年萬福; Map p76; 📞03-3277-3330; www.hounenmanpuku.jp; 1-8-16 Nihombashi-Muromachi, Chūō-ku; mains ¥1280-1850; ⊗11.30am-2.30pm & 5-11pm Mon-Sat, 5-10pm Sun; 📶; 🚇 Ginza line to Mitsukoshimae, exit A1) Hōnen Manpuku's interior is dominated by giant *washi* (Japanese handmade paper) lanterns, beneath which patrons tuck into bargain-priced beef or pork sukiyaki and other traditional dishes. Ingredients are sourced from gourmet retailers in Nihombashi. Lunchtime set menus are great value, and there's a riverside terrace in the warmer months.

Rose Bakery Marunouchi
BAKERY ¥

(ローズベーカリー 丸の内; Map p76; 03-3212-1715; http://rosebakery.jp; Meiji-Yasada Bldg, 2-1-1 Marunouchi, Chiyoda-ku; cakes & quiches from ¥410, lunch set ¥1250; 11am-7pm; ; Chiyoda line to Nijūbashimae, exit 3) Tokyo has taken to Paris' Rose Bakery style of dining. Branches of this delicious organic cafe have popped up here in the Comme des Garçons boutique as well as at the same fashion company's Dover Street Market (p146) in Ginza and Isetan (p148) in Shinjuku. Vegetarians are well served here, as are those with a sweet tooth.

Tokyo Rāmen Street
RAMEN ¥

(東京ラーメンストリート; Map p76; www.tokyoeki-1bangai.co.jp/ramenstreet; B1 First Avenue Tokyo Station, 1-9-1 Marunouchi, Chiyoda-ku; ramen from ¥800; 7.30am-10.30pm; JR lines to Tokyo Station, Yaesu south exit) Eight hand-picked *rāmen-ya* operate branches in this basement arcade on the Yaesu side of Tokyo Station (p78). All the major styles are covered – from *shōyu* (soy-sauce base) to *tsukemen* (cold noodles served on the side). Long lines form outside the most popular shops, but they tend to move quickly.

★ Tamahide
JAPANESE ¥¥¥

(Map p72; 03-3668-7651; www.tamahide.co.jp; 1-17-1 Nihombashi-Ningyōchō, Chūō-ku; oyakodon from ¥1500, dinner set-course menu from ¥6800; 11.30am-1pm daily, 5-10pm Mon-Fri, 4-10pm Sat & Sun; Hibiya line to Ningyōchō, exit A1) For generations people have been lining up outside this restaurant to try its signature dish *oyakodon* – a sweet-savoury mix of chicken, soy broth and egg, served over a bowl of rice. It also has dishes using minced chicken or duck and they're all delicious and filling. Pay before you sit down at lunch.

✕ Ginza & Tsukiji 銀座・築地

★ Kagari
RAMEN ¥

(篝; Map p76; 4-4-1 Ginza; small/large ramen ¥950/1050; 11am-3.30pm & 5.30-10.30pm; Ginza line to Ginza, exit A10 or B1) Don't get confused – even though the English sign outside Kagari says 'Soba', this stands for *chūka soba*, meaning Chinese noodles, ie ramen. Kagari's luscious, flavoursome chicken broth makes all the difference here and has earned the shop a cult following; there's sure to be a long queue trailing from its tucked-away location on a Ginza alley.

A word to the wise: outside of the busy lunch period you can avoid lining up too long by heading to Kagari's branch in the underground arcade between the C1 and C2 exits of the Marunouchi line at Ginza. Look for it behind the Gano Delicatessen Bar.

★ Tsukugon
JAPANESE ¥

(つくごん; Map p76; www.tsukugon.co.jp; 4-12-5 Tsukiji, Chūō-ku; snacks from ¥210; 6.30am-2pm Tue-Sun; Hibiya line to Tsukiji, exit 1) For five generations the same family has been making seafood-paste products here, including *kamaboko* (steamed fish paste) and *date-maki* (rolled omelette with fish paste). Try their delicious speciality *chiyoda* (a bacon-wrapped onion with fish paste) warm from the pan.

Yamachō
JAPANESE ¥

(山長; Map p76; 03-3248-6002; 4-16-1 Tsukiji; omlette slices ¥100; 6am-3.30pm; Hibiya line to Tsukiji, exit 1) Don't miss the delicious oblongs of sunshine-yellow egg on sticks sold at this venerable purveyor of *tamago-yaki* (Japanese rolled-egg omelettes). They come in a variety of flavours and you can watch them being expertly made as you line up to buy.

Shimanto-gawa
IZAKAYA ¥

(四万十川; Map p76; 03-3591-5202; http://diamond-dining-shops.jp/shimantogawa/yurakucho; 2-1-21 Yūrakuchō, Chiyoda-ku; cover charge per person ¥380, dishes from ¥1000; 4-11.30pm; ; Ginza line to Hibiya, exit A4) This beneath-the-train-tracks *izakaya* takes its theme literally by creating a dining area of wooden booths built beside and over a flowing stream – the Shimanto-gawa is a river in Shikoku – and serving up *Tosa-ryōri* (the specialist cuisine of Shikoku's Kōchi Prefecture). Try the seared bonito grilled on straw-fed fires.

★ Apollo
GREEK ¥¥

(Map p76; 03-6264-5220; www.theapollo.jp; 11th fl, Tōkyū Plaza Ginza, 5-2-1 Ginza, Chūō-ku; mains ¥1800-5800; 11.30am-10pm; Ginza line to Ginza, exits C2 & C3) Ginza's glittering lights are the dazzling backdrop to this ace import from Sydney with its tasty take on modern Greek cuisine. The Mediterranean flavours come through strongly in dishes such as grilled octopus and fennel salad, taramasalata, and Kefalograviera cheese fried in a saganaki pan with honey, oregano and lemon juice. Portions are large and meant for sharing.

★ Trattoria Tsukiji Paradiso!
ITALIAN ¥¥

(Map p76; 03-3545-5550; www.tsukiji-paradiso.com; 6-27-3 Tsukiji, Chūō-ku; mains ¥1500-3600; 11am-2pm & 6-10pm; Hibiya line to Tsukiji, exit 2) A paradise for food lovers, indeed. This charming, aqua-painted trattoria serves seafood pasta dishes that will make you want to lick the plate clean. Its signature linguine is packed with shellfish in a scrumptious tomato, chilli and garlic sauce. Lunch (from ¥980) is a bargain, but you may well need to wait in line; book for dinner.

Sushikuni JAPANESE ¥¥
(鮨國; Map p76; ☎03-3545-8234; 4-14-15 Tsukiji, Chūō-ku; seafood rice bowls from ¥3000; ⏲10am-3pm & 5-9pm Thu-Tue; 📋; [S] Hibiya line to Tsukiji, exit 1) Specialising in bowls of sushi rice topped with seafood, this low-key spot is the place to indulge in the freshest of melt-in-the-mouth *uni* (sea urchin) and the salty pop of *ikura* (salmon roe) straight from the market. It's also open in the evenings.

Yūrakuchō Sanchoku Inshokugai JAPANESE ¥¥
(有楽町産直飲食街; Map p76; www.sanchoku-inshokugai.com/yurakucho; International Arcade, 2-1-1 Yūrakuchō, Chiyoda-ku; cover charge per person ¥400, dishes from ¥500; ⏲24hr; 🚆JR Yamanote line to Yūrakuchō, Yūrakuchō exit) Stalls dishing up *yakitori* (charcoal-grilled meat or vegetable skewers) have long huddled under the tracks here. This red-lantern-lit alleyway is a modern collective, which sticks to the cheap, cheerful and smoky formula, but uses quality ingredients sourced direct from producers around the country. Sample steak from Hokkaidō and seafood from Shizuoka.

Maru JAPANESE ¥¥
(銀座圓; Map p76; ☎03-5537-7420; www.maru-mayfont.jp/ginza; 2nd fl, Ichigo Ginza 612 Bldg, 6-12-15 Ginza, Chūō-ku; lunch/dinner from ¥1100/4800; ⏲11.30am-2pm & 5.30-9pm Mon-Sat; 📋; [S] Ginza line to Ginza, exit A3) Maru offers a contemporary take on *kaiseki* (Japanese haute cuisine) fine dining. The chefs are young and inventive and the appealing space is dominated by a long, wooden, open kitchen counter across which you can watch them work. Its good-value lunches offer a choice of mainly fish dishes.

★ **Kyūbey** SUSHI ¥¥¥
(久兵衛; Map p76; ☎03-3571-6523; www.kyubey.jp; 8-7-6 Ginza, Chūō-ku; lunch/dinner from ¥4000/10,000; ⏲11.30am-2pm & 5-10pm Mon-Sat; 📋; [S] Ginza line to Shimbashi, exit 3) Since 1936, Kyūbey's quality and presentation has won it a moneyed and celebrity clientele. Even so, this is a supremely foreigner-friendly and relaxed restaurant. Friendly owner Imada-san speaks excellent English as do some of his team of talented chefs, who will make and serve your sushi, piece by piece.

🍴 Roppongi, Akasaka & Around

★ **Gogyō** RAMEN ¥
(五行; Map p82; ☎03-5775-5566; www.ramendining-gogyo.com; 1-4-36 Nish-Azabu, Minato-ku; ramen from ¥1290; ⏲11.30am-4pm & 5pm-3am, to midnight Sun; [S] Hibiya line to Roppongi, exit 2) Keep an eye on the open kitchen: no, that's not your dinner going up in flames but the cooking of *kogashi* (burnt) ramen, which this dark and stylish *izakaya* (Japanese pub-eatery) specialises in. It's the burnt lard that gives the broth its dark and intense flavour. There are plenty of other dishes on the menu, and a good range of drinks too.

Mornington Cresent BAKERY ¥
(Map p82; http://mornington crescent.co.jp; 1-14-3 Higashi-Azabu, Minato-ku; cakes from ¥380; ⏲11am until sold out occasional Sat; [S] Ōedo line to Akabane-bashi) British baker Stacey Ward has caused a sensation with her authentic marzipan Battenburg cake and Victoria sponges – so much so that fans line up for anything up to an hour to purchase these and other sweet treats at her Saturday bake sales. Check the website for exact dates and for details of baking classes also held here.

Gonpachi IZAKAYA ¥
(権八; Map p82; ☎03-5771-0170; www.gonpachi.jp/nishiazabu; 1-13-11 Nishi-Azabu, Minato-ku; skewers ¥190-1500, set lunch weekday/weekend from ¥900/2200; ⏲11.30am-3.30am; 🚭📋; [S] Hibiya line to Roppongi, exit 2) This cavernous old Edo-style space (said to have inspired a memorable set in Quentin Tarantino's *Kill Bill*) is a Tokyo dining institution, with other less-memorable branches scattered around the city. *Kushiyaki* (charcoal-grilled skewers) are served here alongside noodles, tempura and sushi.

★ **Sougo** VEGETARIAN ¥¥
(宗胡; Map p82; ☎03-5414-1133; www.sougo.tokyo; 3rd fl, Roppongi Green Bldg, 6-1-8 Roppongi, Minato-ku; mains ¥600-2000, set lunch/dinner from ¥1500/5000; 🌿📋; [S] Hibiya line to Roppongi, exit 3) Sit at the long counter beside the open kitchen or in booths and watch the expert chefs prepare delicious and beautifully presented *shōjin-ryōri* (vegetarian cuisine as served at Buddhist temples). Reserve at least one day in advance if you want them to prepare a vegan meal. Look for it in the building opposite the APA Hotel.

LAURIE NOBLE/GETTY IMAGES ©

GREG ELMS/GETTY IMAGES ©

1. Akihabara (p149)
Shops specialising in electronics, manga and anime are a drawcard of this Tokyo neighbourhood.

2. Fortune teller, Tokyo
Traditional culture still thrives in Japan – even in one of its most futuristic cities.

3. Tokyo National Museum (p97)
Samurai armour, Japanese art and detailed kimonos are on display at this showstopping museum.

4. Sensō-ji (p104)
Asakusa's atmospheric, centuries-old Buddhist temple is also Tokyo's most-visited.

COWARD_LION/GETTY IMAGES ©

Also here is Tokyo Cook (p114), offering a variety of Japanese cooking classes in English.

★ Honmura-An
SOBA ¥¥

(本むら庵; Map p82; ☎03-5772-6657; www.honmuraantokyo.com; 7-14-18 Roppongi, Minato-ku; soba from ¥900, set lunch/dinner ¥1600/7400; ◎noon-2.30pm & 5.30-10pm Tue-Sun, closed 1st & 3rd Tue of month; ⊗ 🔊 🎧; 🅂Hibiya line to Roppongi, exit 4) This fabled soba shop, once located in Manhattan, now serves its handmade buckwheat noodles at this rustically contemporary noodle shop on a Roppongi side street. The delicate flavour of these noodles is best appreciated when served on a bamboo mat, with tempura or with dainty slices of *kamo* (duck).

Jōmon
IZAKAYA ¥¥

(ジョウモン; Map p82; ☎03-3405-2585; http://teyandei.com/?page_id=18; 5-9-17 Roppongi, Minato-ku; skewers ¥300-1000; ◎6pm-5am; 🎧🎧; 🅂Hibiya line to Roppongi, exit 3) This wonderfully cosy kitchen has bar seating, rows of ornate *shochu* (liquor) jugs lining the wall and hundreds of freshly prepared skewers splayed in front of the patrons – don't miss the heavenly *zabuton* beef stick. It's almost directly across from the Family Mart – look for the name in Japanese on the door.

★ Kikunoi
KAISEKI ¥¥¥

(菊乃井; Map p72; ☎03-3568-6055; http://kikunoi.jp; 6-13-8 Akasaka, Minato-ku; lunch/dinner from ¥5940/17,820; ◎noon-1pm Tue-Sat, 5-8pm Mon-Sat; 🅂Chiyoda line to Akasaka, exit 7) Exquisitely prepared seasonal dishes are as beautiful as they are delicious at this Michelin–starred Tokyo outpost of a three-generation-old Kyoto-based *kaiseki* (Japanese haute cuisine) restaurant. Kikunoi's chef Murata has written a book translated into English on *kaiseki* that the staff helpfully use to explain the dishes you are served, if you don't speak Japanese. Reservations are necessary.

★ Tofuya-Ukai
KAISEKI ¥¥¥

(とうふ屋うかい; Map p82; ☎03-3436-1028; www.ukai.co.jp/english/shiba; 4-4-13 Shiba-kōen, Minato-ku; lunch/dinner set menu from ¥5500/8400; ◎11am-10pm, last order 8pm; 🎧🎧; 🅂Ōedo line to Akabanebashi, exit 8) One of Tokyo's most gracious restaurants is located in a former sake brewery (moved from northern Japan), with an exquisite traditional garden, in the shadow of Tokyo Tower (p84). Seasonal preparations of tofu and accompanying dishes are served in the refined *kaiseki* style. Make reservations well in advance.

✖ Ebisu, Meguro & Around

★ Afuri
RAMEN ¥

(あふり; Map p86; 1-1-7 Ebisu, Shibuya-ku; noodles from ¥880; ◎11am-5am; ⊗🎧; 🅁JR Yamanote line to Ebisu, east exit) Hardly your typical, surly *rāmen-ya*, Afuri has upbeat young cooks and a hip industrial interior. The unorthodox menu might draw eye-rolls from purists, but house specialities such as *yuzu-shio* (a light, salty broth flavoured with yuzu, a type of citrus) draw lines at lunchtime. Order from the vending machine.

★ Tonki
TONKATSU ¥

(とんき; Map p86; 1-2-1 Shimo-Meguro, Meguro-ku; meals ¥1900; ◎4-10.45pm Wed-Mon, closed 3rd Mon of month; ⊗🎧; 🅁JR Yamanote line to Meguro, west exit) Tonki is a Tokyo *tonkatsu* (crumbed pork cutlet) legend, deep-frying pork cutlets, recipe unchanged, for nearly 80 years. The seats at the counter – where you can watch the perfectly choreographed chefs – are the most coveted, though there is usually a queue. There are tables upstairs.

From the station, walk down Meguro-dōri, take a left at the first alley and look for a white sign and *noren* (doorway curtains) across the sliding doors.

Ouca
ICE CREAM ¥

(櫻花; Map p86; www.ice-ouca.com; 1-6-6 Ebisu, Shibuya-ku; ice cream from ¥400; ◎11am-11.30pm Mar-Oct, noon-11pm Nov-Feb; 🅁JR Yamanote line to Ebisu, east exit) Green tea isn't the only flavour Japan has contributed to the ice-cream playbook; other delicious innovations available (seasonally) at Ouca include *kuro-goma* (black sesame), *kinako kurosato* (roasted soy-bean flour and black sugar) and *beni imo* (purple sweet potato).

Ōtaru
IZAKAYA ¥

(おおたる; Map p86; ☎03-3710-7439; 1-5-15 Naka-Meguro, Meguro-ku; dishes ¥330-600; ◎11.30am-2am) Ōtaru isn't winning any Michelin stars, but we're giving it three stars of our own for atmosphere. In increasingly redeveloped Naka-Meguro, this *izakaya* (Japanese pub-eatery), in an old wooden building festooned with lanterns, stands out. The food is standard *izakaya* fare – sashimi, grilled fish, fried chicken – and exceedingly reasonable. Ōtaru is right on the Meguro-gawa, open through the afternoon. Table charge ¥400.

Ippo　　　　　　　　　　　　IZAKAYA ¥¥

(一歩; Map p86; ☎03-3445-8418; 2nd fl, 1-22-10 Ebisu, Shibuya-ku; dishes ¥500-1500; ⏱6pm-3am; ⬜; Ⓡ JR Yamanote line to Ebisu, east exit) This mellow little *izakaya* (Japanese pub-eatery) specialises in simple pleasures: fish and sake (there's an English sign out front that says just that). The friendly chefs speak some English and can help you decide what to have grilled, steamed, simmered or fried (or if you can't decide, the ¥2500 set menu is great value). The entrance is up the wooden stairs.

Ebisu-yokochō　　　　　　STREET FOOD ¥¥

(恵比寿横町; Map p86; www.ebisu-yokocho.com; 1-7-4 Ebisu, Shibuya-ku; dishes ¥500-1500; ⏱5pm-late; Ⓡ JR Yamanote line to Ebisu, east exit) Locals love this retro arcade chock-a-block with food stalls dishing up everything from humble *yaki soba* (fried buckwheat noodles) to decadent *hotate-yaki* (grilled scallops). Seating is on stools, while tables are fashioned from various items such as repurposed beer crates. It's a loud, lively (and smoky) place, especially on a Friday night; go early to get a table.

You won't find English menus, but the adventurous can get away with pointing at their fellow diners' dishes (you'll be sitting cheek-to-jowl with them). Even if you don't stop to eat, it's worth strolling through. The entrance is marked with a rainbow-coloured sign.

🍴 Shibuya

★ **d47 Shokudō**　　　　　　JAPANESE ¥

(d47食堂; Map p88; www.hikarie8.com/d47shokudo/about.shtml; 8th fl, Shibuya Hikarie, 2-21-1 Shibuya, Shibuya-ku; meals ¥1200-1780; ⏱11am-2.30pm & 6-10.30pm; ⬜⬜; Ⓡ JR Yamanote line to Shibuya, east exit) There are 47 prefectures in Japan and d47 serves a changing line-up of *teishoku* (set meals) that evoke the specialities of each, from the fermented tofu of Okinawa to the stuffed squid of Hokkaido. A larger menu of small plates is available in the evening. Picture windows offer bird's-eye views over the trains coming and going at Shibuya Station.

Gyūkatsu Motomura　　　　TONKATSU ¥

(牛かつ もと村; Map p88; 03-3797-3735; basement fl, 3-18-10 Shibuya, Shibuya-ku; set meal ¥1200; ⏱10.30am-10.30pm Mon-Sat, 10.30am-8.30pm Sun; ⬜⬜; Ⓡ JR Yamanote line to Shibuya, east exit) You know *tonkatsu*, the deep-fried breaded pork cutlet that is a Japanese staple; meet *gyūkatsu*, the deep-fried breaded beef cutlet that is Tokyo's latest food-craze. At Motomura, the beef is super-crisp on the outside and still very rare on the inside; diners get a small individual grill to finish the job to their liking. Set meals include cabbage, rice and soup.

Motomura is exceeding popular, with long queues common. It has since opened other shops in Shibuya and around Tokyo to handle the overflow; check inside for other locations.

Sagatani　　　　　　　　　SOBA ¥

(嵯峨谷; Map p88; 2-25-7 Dōgenzaka, Shibuya-ku; noodles from ¥290; ⏱24hr; ⬜⬜; Ⓡ JR Yamanote line to Shibuya, Hachikō exit) Proving that Tokyo is only expensive to those who don't know better, this all-night joint serves up bamboo steamers of delicious noodles for just ¥290. You won't regret 'splurging' on the ごまだれそば (*goma-dare soba;* buckwheat noodles with sesame dipping sauce) for ¥390. Look for the stone mill in the window and order from the vending machine.

Food Show　　　　　　SUPERMARKET ¥

(フードショー; Map p88; basement fl, 2-24-1 Shibuya, Shibuya-ku; ⏱10am-9pm; ⬜; Ⓡ JR Yamanote line to Shibuya, Hachikō exit) This takeaway paradise in the basement of Shibuya Station has steamers of dumplings, crisp *karaage* (Japanese-style fried chicken), artfully arranged *bentō* (boxed meals), sushi sets, heaps of salads and cakes almost too pretty to eat. It's also home of the ¥10,000 melons. A green sign pointing downstairs marks the entrance at Hachikō Plaza.

Nagi Shokudō　　　　　　VEGAN ¥

(なぎ食堂; Map p86; http://nagishokudo.com; 15-10 Uguisudani-chō, Shibuya-ku; lunch/dinner set menu ¥1050/1550; ⏱noon-4pm, 6-11pm Mon-Sat, to 4pm Sun; ⬜⬜⬜; Ⓡ JR Yamanote line to Shibuya, west exit) A vegan haven in fast-food laced Shibuya, Nagi serves up dishes such as falafel and coconut curry. The most popular thing on the menu is a set meal with three small dishes, miso soup and rice. It's a low-key, homey place with mismatched furniture, cater-corner from a post office (and hidden behind a concrete wall; look for the red sign).

Kaikaya　　　　　　　　SEAFOOD ¥¥

(開花屋; Map p88; ☎03-3770-0878; www.kaikaya.com; 23-7 Maruyama-chō, Shibuya-ku; lunch from ¥850, dishes ¥850-2300; ⏱11.30am-2pm & 5.30-10.30pm Mon-Fri, 5.30-10.30pm Sat & Sun; ⬜⬜; Ⓡ JR Yamanote line to Shibuya, Hachikō exit) 🌿 Traveller favourite Kaikaya is one chef's attempt to bring the beach to Shibuya. Surfboards hang on the walls and much of what's on the menu is caught in nearby Sagami Bay. Seafood is served both Japanese- and Western-style. One must-try is the *maguro no kama* (tuna collar; ¥1200). Reservations recommended; there's a table charge of ¥400 per person.

From Dōgenzaka, turn right after the police box and the restaurant, with a red awning, will be on your right.

✗ Harajuku & Aoyama

★ Harajuku Gyōza-rō　　　DUMPLINGS ¥
(原宿餃子楼; Map p90; 6-4-2 Jingūmae, Shibuya-ku; 6 gyōza ¥290; ⏱11.30am-4.30am; 🚇; 🚊JR Yamanote line to Harajuku, Omote-sandō exit) *Gyōza* (dumplings) are the only thing on the menu here, but you won't hear any complaints from the regulars who queue up to get their fix. Have them *sui* (boiled) or *yaki* (pan-fried), with or without *niniku* (garlic) or *nira* (chives) – they're all delicious. Expect to wait on weekends, but the line moves quickly.

★ Maisen　　　TONKATSU ¥
(まい泉; Map p90; http://mai-sen.com; 4-8-5 Jingūmae, Shibuya-ku; lunch/dinner from ¥995/1680; ⏱11am-10pm; 🌐🚇; 🚊Ginza line to Omote-sandō, exit A2) You could order something else (maybe fried shrimp), but everyone else will be ordering the famous *tonkatsu* (breaded, deep-fried pork cutlets). There are different grades of pork on the menu, including prized *kurobuta*

AOYAMA'S MARKETS

On weekends a **farmers' market** (Map p90; www.farmersmarkets.jp; 5-53-7 Jingū-mae, Shibuya-ku; ⏱10am-4pm Sat & Sun; 🚊Ginza line to Omote-sandō, exit B2), with colourful produce and a dozen food trucks, sets up on the plaza in front of the United Nations University on Aoyama-dōri. It's as much a social event as a shopping stop. Events pop up, too, including the hipster flea market **Raw Tokyo** (Map p90; www.rawtokyo.jp; ⏱11am-6pm, 1st Sat & Sun of the month) – with DJs and live painting. For a festival atmosphere any day of the week, check out the food vendors at **Commune 246** (Map p90; http://commune246.com/; 3-13 Minami-Aoyama, Minato-ku; ⏱11am-10pm; 🌐🚇🚇; 🚊Ginza line to Omote-sandō, exit A4).

(black pig), but even the cheapest is melt-in-your-mouth divine. The restaurant is housed in an old public bathhouse. A take-away window serves delicious *tonkatsu sando* (sandwich).

Higashiya Man　　　SWEETS ¥
(ひがしや まん; Map p90; 📞03-5414-3881; www.higashiya.com/shop/man/; 3-17-14 Minami-Aoyama, Minato-ku; sweets ¥300; ⏱11am-7pm; 🚇; 🚊Ginza line to Omote-sandō, exit A4) *Manjū* (まんじゅう) – that's where the shop's name comes from; it's not just for men! – are hot buns stuffed with sweetened red-bean paste. They're steamed fresh at this take-away counter, a popular pit-stop for Aoyama shoppers. Inside the tiny shop, there's a greater selection of traditional Japanese sweets, many packaged beautifully for gifts.

Sakura-tei　　　OKONOMIYAKI ¥
(さくら亭; Map p90; 📞03-3479-0039; www.sakuratei.co.jp; 3-20-1 Jingūmae, Shibuya-ku; okonomiyaki ¥950-1500; ⏱11am-midnight; 🌐📶 📶🚇; 🚊JR Yamanote line to Harajuku, Takeshita exit) Grill your own *okonomiyaki* (savoury pancakes) at this funky place inside the gallery Design Festa (p91). In addition to classic options (with pork, squid and cabbage), there are some wacky innovations (like taco or carbonara *okonomiyaki*). There's also a great value 90-minute all-you-can-eat plan (lunch/dinner ¥1250/2100).

Kinokuniya International Supermarket　SUPERMARKET ¥
(紀ノ国屋　インターナショナル; Map p90; www.super-kinokuniya.jp/store/international; basement fl, AO bldg, 3-11-7 Kita-Aoyama, Minato-ku; ⏱9.30am-9pm; 🚇; 🚊Ginza line to Omote-sandō, exit B2) Kinokuniya carries expat lifesavers such as Marmite and peanut butter; crusty, wholegrain bread; and cheeses galore (at a price of course).

Mominoki House　　　JAPANESE ¥¥
(もみの木ハウス; Map p90; www.mominoki-house.net; 2-18-5 Jingūmae, Shibuya-ku; lunch/dinner set menu from ¥980/2500; ⏱11am-3pm & 5-11pm; 🌐📶🚇; 🚊JR Yamanote line to Harajuku, Takeshita exit) 🍴 Boho Tokyoites have been coming here for tasty macrobiotic fare since 1976. The casual dining room, which looks like a grown-up (indoor) tree fort and features several cosy, semi-private booths, has seen some famous visitors too, such as Paul McCartney. Chef Yamada's menu is heavily vegan, but also includes free-range chicken and *Ezo shika* (Hokkaidō venison, ¥4800).

Yanmo SEAFOOD ¥¥¥

(やんも; Map p90; ☎03-5466-0636; www.yanmo.co.jp/aoyama/index.html; basement fl, T Place bldg, 5-5-25 Minami-Aoyama, Minato-ku; lunch/dinner set menu from ¥1100/7560; 🕐11.30am-2pm & 6-10.30pm Mon-Sat; 🚭; [S] Ginza line to Omote-sandō, exit A5) Freshly caught seafood from the nearby Izu Peninsula is the speciality at this upscale, yet unpretentious restaurant. If you're looking to splash out on a seafood dinner, this is a great place to do so. The reasonably priced set menus include sashimi and steamed and grilled fish. Reservations are essential for dinner. Lunch is a bargain, but you might have to queue.

🍴 Shinjuku

★Nagi RAMEN ¥

(凪; Map p93; www.n-nagi.com; 2nd fl, Golden Gai G2, 1-1-10 Kabukichō, Shinjuku-ku; ramen from ¥850; 🕐24hr; 📄; 🚆 JR Yamanote line to Shinjuku, east exit) Nagi, once an upstart, has done well and now has branches around the city – and around Asia. This tiny shop, one of the originals, up a treacherous stairway in Golden Gai, is still our favourite. (It's many people's favourite and often has a line.) The house speciality is *niboshi* ramen (egg noodles in a broth flavoured with dried sardines).

Look for the sign with a red circle.

Nakajima KAISEKI ¥

(中嶋; Map p93; ☎03-3356-4534; www.shinjyuku-nakajima.com; basement fl, 3-32-5 Shinjuku, Shinjuku-ku; lunch/dinner from ¥800/8640; 🕐11.30am-2pm & 5.30-10pm Mon-Sat; 🚭📄; [S] Marunouchi line to Shinjuku-sanchōme, exit A1) In the evening, this Michelin-starred restaurant serves exquisite *kaiseki* (Japanese haute cuisine) dinners. On weekdays, it also serves a set lunch of humble *iwashi* (sardines) for one-tenth the price; in the hands of Nakajima's chefs they're divine. The line for lunch starts to form shortly before the restaurant opens at 11.30am. Look for the white sign at the top of the stairs.

Numazukō SUSHI ¥

(沼津港; Map p93; 3-34-16 Shinjuku, Shinjuku-ku; plates ¥100-550; 🕐11am-10.30pm; 🚭📶📄; 🚆 JR Yamanote line to Shinjuku, east exit) Shinjuku's best *kaiten-sushi* (conveyor-belt sushi) restaurant is pricier than many, but the quality is worth it. It's popularity means that few plates make it around the long, snaking belt without getting snatched up (you can also order off the menu, if you don't see what you want). This is a good choice if you don't want a full meal.

Omoide-yokochō YAKITORI ¥

(思い出横丁; Map p93; Nishi-Shinjuku 1-chōme, Shinjuku-ku; skewers from ¥150; 🕐noon-midnight, vary by shop; 📄; 🚆 JR Yamanote line to Shinjuku, west exit) Since the postwar days, smoke has been billowing night and day from the rickety, wooden *yakitori* stalls that line this alley by the train tracks, literally translated as 'Memory Lane' (and less politely known as Shonben-yokochō, or 'Piss Alley'). Several stalls have English menus. See if you can't spot the one that has appeared on the cover of Lonely Planet's Tokyo guide.

Shinjuku Asia-yokochō ASIAN ¥

(新宿アジア横丁; Map p93; ☎03-3207-7218; rooftop, 2nd Toa Hall bldg, 1-21-1 Kabukichō, Shinjuku-ku; dishes ¥450-1250; 🕐5pm-midnight Tue-Thu & Sun, 5pm-5am Fri & Sat; 📄; 🚆 JR Yamanote line to Shinjuku, east exit) A rooftop night market that spans the Asian continent, Asia-yokochō has vendors dishing out everything from Korean *bibimbap* to Vietnamese *pho*. It's noisy, a bit chaotic and particularly fun in a group.

★Donjaca IZAKAYA ¥¥

(呑者家; Map p93; ☎03-3341-2497; 3-9-10 Shinjuku, Shinjuku-ku; dishes ¥350-850; 🕐5pm-7am; 📄; [S] Marunouchi line to Shinjuku-sanchōme, exit C6) The platonic ideal of a Shōwa-era (1926–89) *izakaya*, Donjaca, in business since 1979, has red pleather stools, paper-lantern lighting and hand-written menus on the wall. The food is equal parts classic (grilled fish and fried chicken) and inventive: house specialities include *natto gyoza* (dumplings stuffed with fermented soy beans) and *mochi* gratin. Excellent sake is served in convenient tasting sets.

If it's full, staff will likely direct you around the corner to the larger annexe.

Tsunahachi TEMPURA ¥¥

(つな八; Map p93; ☎03-3352-1012; www.tunahachi.co.jp; 3-31-8 Shinjuku, Shinjuku-ku; lunch/dinner from ¥1512/2484; 🕐11am-10.30pm; 🚭📄; 🚆 JR Yamanote line to Shinjuku, east exit) Tsunahachi has been expertly frying prawns and vegies for more than 90 years and is an excellent place to get initiated in the art of tempura (foreign tourists get a handy cheat sheet on the different condiments). Set menus (except for the cheaper ones at lunch) are served piece by piece, so everything comes hot and crisp. Indigo *noren* (curtains) mark the entrance.

Kozue JAPANESE ¥¥¥

(梢; Map p93; ☎03-5323-3460; http://tokyo.park.hyatt.jp/en/hotel/dining/Kozue.html; 40th fl, Park Hyatt, 3-7-1-2 Nishi-Shinjuku, Shinjuku-ku; lunch set menu ¥2850-12,400, dinner set menu ¥12,400-27,300; ⊙11.30am-2.30pm & 5.30-9.30pm; ⊜⊙; Ⓢ Ōedo line to Tochōmae, exit A4) It's hard to beat Kozue's combination of well-executed, seasonal Japanese cuisine, artisan crockery and soaring views over Shinjuku from the floor-to-ceiling windows. As the (kimono-clad) staff speak English and the restaurant caters well to allergies and personal preferences, this is a good splurge spot for diners who don't want to give up complete control. Reservations are essential.

✖ Akihabara, Kagurazaka & Kōrakuen

★ Ethiopia
JAPANESE ¥

(エチオピア; Map p96; ☎03-3295-4310; 3-10-6 Kanda-ogawamachi, Chiyoda-ku; curry from ¥900; ⊙11am-10pm Mon-Fri, to 8.30pm Sat & Sun; ⊙; Ⓢ Hanzōmon line to Jimbōchō, exit A5) In studenty Jimbōchō, Japanese curry cafes are 10 a penny and fiercely competitive. Ethiopia is a seasoned champ, offering jumbo serves and curries packed with meat and vegetables. The spice level goes from zero to a nuclear-thermal 70! Pay at the machine as you enter the wonderfully retro shop.

Komaki Shokudō
VEGAN ¥

(こまきしょくどう; Map p96; ☎03-5577-5358; http://konnichiha.net/fushikian; Chabara, 8-2 Kanda Neribei-chō, Chiyoda-ku; set meals from ¥980; ⊙11am-7.30pm; ⊙; Ⓡ JR Yamanote line to Akihabara, Electric Town exit) A Kamakura cooking school specialising in shōjin-ryōri (Buddhist-style vegan cuisine) runs this cafe within the Chabara (p149) food market. Its nonmeat dishes are very tasty and it sells some of the ingredients used. Round off your meal with great coffee from Yanaka Coffee opposite.

Amanoya
DESSERTS ¥

(天野屋; Map p96; www.amanoya.jp; 2-8-15 Soto-Kanda, Chiyoda-ku; desserts from ¥500; ⊙10am-6pm Mon-Sat, to 5pm Sun; ⊙; Ⓡ JR Chūō or Sōbu lines to Ochanomizu, Hijiri-bashi exit) The owner of this charming dessert cafe is a bit of a collector, as you'll discover from the eclectic bits and bobs on display ranging from model trains to carved masks. Motherly women dole out sweet treats, such as mochi rice cakes, as well amazake, a mildly alcoholic milky sake beverage that's long been a house speciality.

Kikanbō
RAMEN ¥

(鬼金棒; Map p96; http://karashibi.com; 2-10-8 Kaji-chō, Chiyoda-ku; ramen from ¥800; ⊙11am-9.30pm Mon-Sat, to 4pm Sun; Ⓡ JR Yamanote line to Kanda, north exit) The karashibi (カラシビ) spicy miso ramen here has a cult following. Choose your level of kara (spice) and shibi (a strange mouth-numbing sensation created by Japanese sanshō pepper). We recommend futsu-futsu (regular for both) for first-timers; oni (devil) level costs an extra ¥100. Look for the red door curtains and buy an order ticket from the vending machine.

There are two branches next to each other here – one serving ramen in a soup, the other (on the corner) serving the noodles separately for dipping in the stock.

Kado
JAPANESE ¥¥

(カド; Map p96; ☎03-3268-2410; http://kagurazaka-kado.com; 1-32 Akagi-Motomachi, Shinjuku-ku; lunch/dinner set menus from ¥800/3150; ⊙11.30am-2.30pm & 5-11pm; ⊜⊙; Ⓡ Tōzai line to Kagurazaka, exit 1) Set in an old wooden house with a white lantern out front, Kado specialises in katei-ryōri (home-cooking). Dinner is a set course of seasonal dishes (such as grilled quail or crab soup). At lunch there's no English menu, so your best bet is the カド定食 (kado teishoku), the daily house special. Bookings are required for dinner.

Canal Cafe
ITALIAN ¥¥

(カナルカフェ; Map p96; ☎03-3260-8068; www.canalcafe.jp; 1-9 Kagurazaka, Shinjuku-ku; lunch from ¥1600, dinner mains ¥1500-2800; ⊙11.30am-11pm Tue-Sat, to 9.30pm Sun; ⊜✎⊙; Ⓡ JR Sōbu line to Iidabashi, west exit) Along the languid moat that forms the edge of Kitanomaru-kōen, this is one of Tokyo's best alfresco dining spots. The restaurant serves tasty wood-fired pizzas, seafood pastas and grilled meats, while over on the self-service 'deck side' you can settle in with a sandwich, muffin or just a cup of coffee.

✖ Ueno & Yanesen

★ Kamachiku
UDON ¥

(釜竹; Map p100; ☎03-5815-4675; http://kamachiku.com/top_en; 2-14-18 Nezu, Bunkyō-ku; noodles from ¥850, small dishes ¥350-850; ⊙11.30am-2pm Tue-Sun, 5.30-9pm Tue-Sat; ⊙; Ⓢ Chiyoda line to Nezu, exit 1) Udon (thick wheat noodles) made fresh daily is the speciality at this popular restaurant, in a beautifully restored brick warehouse from 1910 with a view onto a garden. In addition to noodles, the menu includes lots of izakaya-style small dishes (such as grilled fish and vegies). Expect to queue on weekends.

Hagiso

JAPANESE ¥

(Map p100; [☎] 03-5832-9808; http://hanare.hagiso. jp; 3-10-25 Yanaka, Taitō-ku; mains ¥815-1300; ⊙8-10.30am & noon-9pm; [S] Chiyoda line to Sendagi, exit 2) This attractive new cafe and gallery, run by students from Tokyo University of the Arts (Geidai), is a good all-rounder for meals, drinks and sweets in the heart of Yanaka. Its Japanese-style breakfast is a great deal at ¥325, while lunch set menus may include a hearty vegetable curry or Japanese-style hamburger steak. Expect to wait on weekends as it's popular.

★Innsyoutei

JAPANESE ¥¥

(韻松亭; Map p100; [☎] 03-3821-8126; www.inn-syoutei.jp; 4-59 Ueno-kōen, Taitō-ku; lunch/dinner from ¥1680/5500; ⊙restaurant 11am-3pm & 5-9.30pm, tearoom 11am-5pm; [⊠]; [R] JR lines to Ueno, Ueno-kōen exit) In a gorgeous wooden building dating back to 1875, Innsyoutei (pronounced 'inshotei' and meaning 'rhyme of the pine cottage') has long been a favourite spot for fancy *kaiseki*-style meals while visiting Ueno-kōen (p101). Without a booking (essential for dinner) you'll have a long wait but it's worth it. Lunchtime *bentō* (boxed meals) offer beautifully presented morsels and are great value.

There's an attached rustic teahouse serving *matcha* (powdered green tea) and traditional desserts from ¥600.

★Shinsuke

IZAKAYA ¥¥

(シンスケ; Map p100; [☎] 03-3832-0469; 3-31-5 Yushima, Bunkyō-ku; ⊙5-9.30pm Mon-Fri, to 9pm Sat; [⊝][⊠]; [S] Chiyoda line to Yushima, exit 3) In business since 1925, Shinsuke has honed the concept of an ideal *izakaya* to perfection: long cedar counter, 'master' in *happi* (traditional short coat) and *hachimaki* (traditional headband), and smooth-as-silk *dai-ginjo* (premium-grade sake). The food – contemporary updates of classics – is fantastic. Don't miss the *kitsune raclette* – deep-fried tofu stuffed with raclette cheese.

Also, unlike other storied *izakaya* that can be intimidating to foreigners, the staff here are friendly and go out of their way to explain the menu in English.

★Hantei

JAPANESE ¥¥

(はん亭; Map p100; [☎] 03-3828-1440; http://hantei. co.jp; 2-12-15 Nezu, Bunkyō-ku; meals from ¥3000; ⊙noon-3pm & 5-10pm Tue-Sun; [⊠]; [S] Chiyoda line to Nezu, exit 2) Housed in a beautifully maintained, century-old traditional wooden building, Hantei is a local landmark. Delectable

skewers of seasonal *kushiage* (fried meat, fish and vegetables) are served with small, refreshing side dishes. Lunch includes eight or 12 sticks and dinner starts with six, after which you'll continue to receive additional rounds (¥210 per skewer) until you say stop.

✗ Asakusa & Sumida River
浅草・隅田川

★Onigiri Yadoroku

JAPANESE ¥

(おにぎり 浅草 宿六; Map p106; [☎] 03-3874-1615; http://onigiriyadoroku.com; 3-9-10 Asakusa, Taitō-ku; set lunch ¥660 & ¥900, onigiri ¥200-600; ⊙11.30am-5pm Mon-Sat, 6pm-2am Thu-Tue; [⊠]; [R] Tsukuba Express to Asakusa, exit 1) *Onigiri* (rice-ball snacks), usually wrapped in crispy sheets of *nori* (seaweed) are a great Japanese culinary invention and this humbly decorated and friendly place specialises in them. The set lunches, including a choice of two or three *onigiri*, are a great deal. At night there's a large range of flavours to choose from along with alcohol.

Kintame

JAPANESE ¥

(近為; Map p72; [☎] 03-3641-2740; www.kintame. co.jp; 1-14-5 Tomioka, Kōtō-ku; meals from ¥1390; ⊙11am-5pm Tue-Sun; [S] Ōedo line to Monzen-Nakachō, exit 1) This branch of the famous Kyoto-based pickle shop provides tastings of its traditional preserves done in a variety of ways, including with salt, vinegar miso and soy sauce. At a communal table you can also try its filling and good-value meals of fish marinated in sake lees (the deposits produced during the alcohol's fermentation).

At the end of the shopping street leading to Fukagawa Fudō-dō (p105), it's a good place for lunch when visiting the temple.

Rokurinsha

RAMEN ¥

(六厘舎; Map p106; www.rokurinsha.com; 6th fl, Solamachi, 1-1-2 Oshiage, Sumida-ku; ramen from ¥850; ⊙10.30am-11pm; [⊝][⊠]; [S] Hanzōmon line to Oshiage, exit B3) Rokurinsha's speciality is *tsukemen* – ramen noodles served on the side with a bowl of concentrated soup for dipping. The noodles are thick and perfectly al dente and the soup has a rich *tonkotsu* (pork bone) base. It's an addictive combination that draws lines to this outpost in Tokyo Sky Tree Town.

Daikokuya

TEMPURA ¥

(大黒家; Map p106; [☎] 03-3844-1111; www.tem-pura.co.jp/english/index.html; 1-38-10 Asakusa, Taitō-ku; meals ¥1550-2100; ⊙11am-8.30pm Sun-Fri, to 9pm Sat; [⊠]; [S] Ginza line to Asakusa, exit 1)

DON'T MISS

ASAKUSA STREET FOOD

Asakusa is great for street food. Here are some local favourites:

Iriyama Sembei (入山煎餅; Map p106; 1-13-4 Asakusa, Taitō-ku; sembei from ¥130; ⏰10am-6pm Fri-Wed; 🚇Tsukuba Express to Asakusa, exit 4) At this century-old shop you can watch *sembei* (flavoured rice crackers) being hand-toasted on charcoal grills. Get them hot as takeaway or packaged as souvenirs.

Hoppy-dōri (ホッピー通り; Map p106; 2-5 Asakusa, Taitō-ku; skewers from ¥120; 🚇Tsukuba Express to Asakusa, exit 4) Along either side of the street popularly known as Hoppy-dōri – 'hoppy' is a cheap malt beverage – food vendors set out stools and tables for customers to nosh on cheap *yakitori* (skewers of grilled meat or vegetables) from noon until late.

Chōchin Monaka (ちょうちんもなか; Map p106; 2-3-1 Asakusa, Taitō-ku; ice cream ¥330; ⏰10am-5pm; 📷; 🚇Ginza line to Asakusa, exit 1) Traditionally, *monaka* are wafers filled with sweet bean jam. At this little stand on Nakamise-dōri, they're filled with ice cream instead – in flavours such as *matcha* (powdered green tea) and *kuro-goma* (black sesame).

Near Nakamise-dōri, this is the place to get old-fashioned tempura fried in pure sesame oil, an Asakusa speciality. It's in a white building with a tile roof. If there's a queue (and there often is), you can try your luck at the annexe one block over, where they also serve set-course meals.

★Otafuku   JAPANESE ¥¥
(大多福; Map p106; ☎03-3871-2521; www.otafuku. ne.jp; 1-6-2 Senzoku, Taitō-ku; oden ¥110-550; ⏰5-11pm Tue-Sat, to 10pm Sun; 📷; 🚇Tsukuba Express to Asakusa, exit 1) Over a century old, Otafuku specialises in *oden* (a classic Japanese stew). It's simmered at the counter and diners pick what they want from the pot. You can dine cheaply on radishes and kelp, or splash out on scallops and tuna or a full-course menu for ¥5400. Whichever way you go, you get to soak up Otafuku's convivial, old-time atmosphere.

Look for a shack-like entrance and lantern on the northern side of Kototoi-dōri.

★Kappō Yoshiba   JAPANESE ¥¥
(割烹吉葉; Map p72; ☎03-3623-4480; www.ka-pou-yoshiba.jp/english/index.html; 2-14-5 Yokoami, Sumida-ku; dishes ¥600-6600; ⏰11.30am-2pm & 5-10pm Mon-Sat; 📷; 🚇Ōedo line to Ryōgoku Station, exit 1) The former Miyagino sumo stable is the location for this one-of-a-kind restaurant that has preserved the *dōyo* (practice ring) as its centrepiece. Playing up to its sumo roots, you can order the protein-packed stew *chanko-nabe* (for two people from ¥4600), but Yoshi-ba's real strength is its sushi, which is freshly prepared in jumbo portions.

The lunch *nigiri* set menu (¥1000) is a bargain, but you'll probably want to come in the evening when the *dōyo* becomes a stage for traditional live music performances.

At 7.30pm on Monday, Wednesday, Friday and Saturday, former wrestlers sing *sumo jinku* (a type of folk song) for 15 minutes, while at 7pm on Tuesday and Thursday the female duo Kitamura Shimai play a short concert on *Tsugaru shamisen* (Japanese lutes). This is followed at 8pm by a pianist tinkling the ivories on the grand piano by the sushi counter (and stained-glass window of a sumo wrestler!).

★Asakusa Imahan   JAPANESE ¥¥¥
(浅草今半; Map p106; ☎03-3841-1114; www. asakusaimahan.co.jp; 3-1-12 Nishi-Asakusa, Taitō-ku; lunch/dinner set menu from ¥3800/10,000; ⏰11.30am-9.30pm; 😊📷; 🚇Tsukuba Express to Asakusa, exit 4) For a meal to remember, swing by this famous beef restaurant, in business since 1895. Choose between courses of suki-yaki (sauteed beef dipped in raw egg) and *shabu-shabu* (beef blanched in broth); prices rise according to the grade of meat. For diners on a budget, Imahan sells a limited number of cheaper lunch sets (from ¥1500).

🍴 Odaiba & Tokyo Bay
お台場・東京湾

Bills   INTERNATIONAL ¥
(ビルズ; Map p108; www.bills-jp.net; 3rd fl, Sea-side Mall, DECKS Tokyo Beach, 1-6-1 Daiba, Mina-to-ku; mains from ¥1400; ⏰9am-10pm Mon-Fri, 8am-10pm Sat & Sun; 😊📶📷👶; 🚇Yurikamome line to Odaiba Kaihin-kōen) Australian chef Bill Granger has had a big hit with his restau-rant chain in Japan – unsurprising given how inviting and spacious a place this is. The menu includes his classics such as ricot-ta hotcakes, and lunch and dinner mains

such as *wagyū* burgers. The terrace also has great bay views.

Hibiki
JAPANESE ¥¥

(響; Map p108; ☑ 03-3599-5500; www.dynac-japan.com/hibiki; 6th fl, Aqua City, 1-7-1 Daiba, Minato-ku; lunch set menu ¥1000-2000, dishes ¥650-2700; ⊙ 11am-3pm & 5-11pm; 📶; 🚇 Yurikamome line to Daiba, south exit) Hibiki has glittering views across the bay, and a menu featuring seasonal dishes, hearty grilled meats and fresh tofu, along with sake and *shōchū* (strong distilled alcohol often made from potatoes). The lunch set is a good deal and includes a small salad bar; choose your main dish from the samples out the front. There's a ¥550 seating charge at dinner.

✖ West Tokyo

★ Tensuke
TEMPURA ¥

(天すけ; Map p110; ☑ 03-3223-8505; 3-22-7 Kōenji-kita, Suginami-ku; lunch/dinner from ¥1100/1600; ⊙ noon-2.15pm & 6-10pm Tue-Fri, 11.30am-3pm & 6-10pm Sat & Sun; ⊝; 🚇 JR Sōbu line to Kōenji, north exit) An entirely legitimate candidate for eighth wonder of the modern world is Tensuke's *tamago* (egg) tempura. We don't know how the chef (who is quite a showman) does it, but the egg comes out batter-crisp on the outside and runny in the middle. It's served on rice with seafood and vegetable tempura as part of the *tamago tempura teishoku* (玉子天ぷら定食).

There's a blue and orange sign out front; expect to queue.

Daily Chiko
ICE CREAM ¥

(デイリーチコ; Map p110; basement fl, Nakano Broadway, Nakano-ku; cone from ¥280; ⊙ 10am-8pm; 🚇 JR Sōbu-Chūō line to Nakano, north exit) A Nakano legend and one of Nakano Broadway's few original shops, this ice-cream counter features eight flavours of soft-serve – and you can get them all in one towering cone (¥490). Or just two or three, if you believe in moderation. The only-in-Japan *yuzu* (柚子; a kind of citrus) and *ramune* (ラムネ; cider) flavours are delicious.

Tetchan
YAKITORI ¥

(てっちゃん; 1-1-2 Kichijōji-Honchō, Musashino-shi; skewers from ¥110; ⊙ 4-11pm; 🚇 JR Sōbu-Chūō line to Kichijōji, north exit) Located inside the labyrinthine covered market Harmonica-yokochō, Tetchan has been drawing locals for years. But it's now become something of a tourist destination too, thanks to its new interior of acrylic 'ice' by architect Kuma Kengo (known for his more establishment works). There's no English menu, but safe bets include *tsukune* (chicken meatballs), *buta bara* (pork belly) and *motsu-ni* (stewed offal).

★ Okajōki
IZAKAYA ¥¥

(陸蒸気; Map p110; ☑ 03-3228-1230; www.nakano-okajoki.com; 5-59-3 Nakano, Nakano-ku; lunch/dinner set menu ¥900/3980; ⊙ 11.30am-3pm & 4-10pm Mon-Fri, 4-10pm Sat & Sun; 🚇 JR Sōbu-Chūō line to Nakano, north exit) The *yaki-zakana* (焼き魚; grilled fish) lunch here is legendary. The fish are roasted around a large central hearth, and are served as a set with rice, miso soup and pickles. There's no English menu, but some common fish are *shake* (しゃけ; salmon), *nishin* (にしん; Pacific herring) and *saba* (さば; mackerel). Order at the kiosk at the entrance and expect a line.

For dinner, a set menu, which includes sashimi and grilled fish, makes ordering easy. Reservations recommended for dinner.

🍷 Drinking & Nightlife

Roppongi certainly has the lion's share of foreigner-friendly bars, while Shinjuku offers the retro warren Golden Gai (p140) and the gay-bar district Ni-chōme (p136).

Other top party districts include youthful Shibuya and Harajuku; Shimbashi and Yūrakuchō, which teem with salarymen; and Ebisu and nearby Daikanyama, both of which have some excellent bars. Asakusa's Hoppy-dōri (p134) is a fun, retro-style hangout.

If you've never tried a karaoke box (a small room rented by you and a few of your friends), it's definitely less embarrassing than singing in a bar in front of strangers. With booze and food brought directly to your room, it can easily become a guilty pleasure; rooms generally cost around ¥700 per person per hour. Look for neon signs that say カラオケ (karaoke) in any entertainment district.

Tokyo holds its own with London and New York when it comes to top dance venues. Top international DJs and domestic artists do regular sets at venues with body-shaking sound systems. Most clubs don't get going until after midnight (and can keep going past dawn). You'll need to show a photo ID to enter.

Fridays and Saturdays are the big nights out, though you'll find people in bars most nights of the week.

🍷 Marunouchi & Nihombashi

★ Nihombashi Toyama   BAR
(日本橋とやま館; Map p76; ☑ 03-6262-2723;
http://toyamakan.jp; 1-2-6 Nihombashi-muromachi,
Chūō-ku; ⏰ 11am-9pm; Ⓢ Ginza line to Mitsukoshimae, exit B5) Scattered around central Tokyo
you'll find many places like this that promote
the products of a region of Japan. At this
slickly designed outlet, there's a a great bar
offering a selection of Toyama's best sakes
from 17 different breweries. A set of three
30mL cups costs a bargain ¥700 (90mL cups
from ¥600 each). English tasting notes are
available.

100% Chocolate Cafe   CAFE
(Map p76; ☑ 03-3273-3184; www.meiji.co.jp/sweets/
choco-cafe; 2-4-16 Kyōbashi, Chūō-ku; ⏰ 8am-
8pm Mon-Fri, 11am-7pm Sat & Sun; Ⓢ Ginza line
to Kyōbashi, exit 5) Meiji is one of Japan's top
confectionery companies and this cafe, at its
Tokyo headquarters, showcases the brand's
range of chocolate. Fittingly the interior
sports a ceiling that mimics a slab of chocolate. Sample three types of drinking chocolate
for ¥500, then peruse the scores of different
flavoured bars that you can take away.

Manpuku Shokudō   PUB
(まんぷく食堂; Map p76; ☑ 03-3211-6001; www.
manpukushokudo.com; 2-4-1 Yūrakuchō, Chiyoda-
ku; cover charge ¥300; ⏰ 24hr; Ⓡ JR Yamanote line
to Yūrakuchō, central exit) Down your beer or sake
as trains rattle overhead on the tracks that
span Harumi-dōri at Yūrakuchō. This convivial *izakaya* (Japanese pub-eatery), plastered

with old movie posters, is open round the
clock and has bags of atmosphere.

Happy hour, when beers are ¥280, runs
from 11am to 8pm Monday to Friday and 3pm
to 8pm Saturday.

🍷 Ginza & Tsukiji 銀座・築地

★ Turret Coffee   CAFE
(Map p76; http://ja-jp.facebook.com/turretcoffee;
2-12-6 Tsukiji, Chūō-ku; ⏰ 7am-6pm Mon-Sat, noon-
6pm Sun; Ⓢ Hibiya line to Tsukiji, exit 2) Kawasaki
Kiyoshi set up his plucky indie coffee shop
next to Starbucks. It takes its name from
the three-wheeled delivery trucks that beetle
around Tsukiji Market (p79) – there's one on
site. Ideal for an early-morning espresso en
route to or from the outer market area.

★ Cafe de l'Ambre   CAFE
(カフェ・ド・ランブル; Map p76; ☑ 03-3571-
1551; www.h6.dion.ne.jp/~lambre; 8-10-15 Ginza,
Chūō-ku; coffee from ¥650; ⏰ noon-10pm Mon-Sat,
to 7pm Sun; Ⓡ Ginza line to Ginza, exit A4) The sign
over the door here reads 'Coffee Only' but,
oh, what a selection. Sekiguchi Ichiro started
the business in 1948 and – remarkably at the
age of 100 – still runs it himself, sourcing and
roasting aged beans from all over the world.
It's dark, retro and classic Ginza.

★ Cha Ginza   TEAHOUSE
(茶・銀座; Map p76; ☑ 03-3571-1211; www.
uogashi-meicha.co.jp/shop/ginza; 5-5-6 Ginza, Chūō-
ku; ⏰ 11am-5pm, shop to 6pm Tue-Sun; Ⓢ Ginza
line to Ginza, exit B3) At this slick contemporary
tea room, it costs ¥800 for either a cup of
perfectly prepared *matcha* (green tea) and a

GAY & LESBIAN TOKYO

Tokyo has a small but very lively gay quarter, Shinjuku-nichōme. However, outside this and
a handful of other places, the gay scene is all but invisible. Some favourite spots include:

Aiiro Cafe (アイイロ カフェ; Map p93; http://aliving.net/aiirocafe/; 2-18-1 Shinjuku, Shinjuku-ku; ⏰ 6pm-2am Mon-Thu, 6pm-5am Fri & Sat, 6pm to midnight Sun; Ⓢ Marunouchi line to
Shinjuku-sanchōme, exit C8) Occupying the former spot of Ni-chome institution Advocates
(and many old-time regulars still call it that), Aiiro is the best place to start any night out
in the neighbourhood (thanks to the all-you-can-drink beer for ¥1000 happy-hour special). The bar itself is teeny-tiny; the action happens on the street corner outside, which
swells to block-party proportions in the summer.

Arty Farty (アーティファーティ; Map p93; www.arty-farty.net; 2nd fl, 2-11-7 Shinjuku, Shinjuku-ku; ⏰ 6pm-1am; Ⓢ Marunouchi line to Shinjuku-sanchōme, exit C8) A fixture on Tokyo's gay
scene for many a moon, Arty Farty welcomes all in the community to come shake a tail
feather on the dance floor here. It usually gets going later in the evening.

Tokyo's annual **pride parade** (http://tokyorainbowpride.com) takes place in May. For
more advice on travelling in Tokyo, have a look at Utopia Asia (www.utopia-asia.com).

small cake or two, or for a choice of *sencha* (premium green tea). Buy your token for tea at the shop on the ground floor, which sells top-quality teas from various growing regions in Japan.

Jugetsudo
TEAHOUSE
(寿月堂; Map p76; ☑03-6278-7626; www.jug-estudo.fr; 5th fl, Kabuki-za Tower, 4-12-15 Ginza, Chūō-ku; ⊗10am-5.30pm; ⓢHibiya line to Higashi-Ginza, exit 3) This venerable tea seller's main branch is closer to Tsukiji, but this classy outlet in the Kabuki-za Tower has a Kengo Kuma–designed cafe where you can sample the various Japanese green teas, including *matcha*, along with food. Book for its tea-tasting experience (¥4000), which covers four different types of tea and runs from 10am to noon.

Kagaya
PUB
(加賀屋; Map p76; ☑03-3591-2347; http://ka-gayayy.sakura.ne.jp); B1 fl, Hanasada Bldg, 2-15-12 Shimbashi, Minato-ku; ⊗7pm-midnight Mon-Sat; ⓡJR Yamanote line to Shimbashi, Shimbashi exit) It is safe to say that there is no other bar owner in Tokyo who can match Mark Kagaya for brilliant lunacy. His side-splitting antics are this humble *izakaya*'s star attraction although his mum's nourishing home cooking also hits the spot. Bookings are essential.

🍷 Roppongi, Akasaka & Around

★ Brewdog
CRAFT BEER
(Map p82; ☑03-6447-4160; www.brewdog.com/bars/worldwide/roppongi; 5-3-2 Roppongi, Minato-ku; ⊗5pm-midnight Mon-Fri, 3pm-midnight Sat & Sun; 🛜; ⓢHibiya line to Roppongi, exit 3) This Scottish craft brewery's Tokyo outpost is nestled off the main drag. Apart from its own brews, there's a great selection of other beers, including Japanese ones on tap, mostly all served in small, regular or large (a full pint) portions. Tasty food and computer and board games to while away the evening round out a class operation.

★ The Garden
CAFE
(Map p82; ☑03-3470-4611; www.i-house.or.jp/eng/facilities/tealounge; International House of Japan, 5-11-16 Roppongi, Minato-ku; ⊗7am-10pm; 🛜; ⓢŌedo line to Azabu-Jūban, exit 7) Stare out from this serene tea lounge across the beautiful late-16th-century garden, hidden behind International House of Japan. There are plenty of tempting pastries and cakes, as well as more substantial meals should you wish to linger – and who could blame you!

LOCAL KNOWLEDGE

MISSED THE LAST TRAIN?

You're not alone – or stuck for options. Nightlife districts such as Roppongi, Shinjuku and Shibuya have plenty of 24-hour options for night crawlers who were lured out late by the neighbourhood's charms but who'd rather not fork over the yen for a taxi ride home. In addition to love hotels and *manga kissa* (cafes where you pay by the hour to read manga, Japanese comic books, in a private booth that can double as a teeny sleeping cubicle), consider waiting for the first train at a karaoke parlour; most offer discounted all-night packages from midnight to 5am.

★ These
LOUNGE
(テーゼ; Map p82; ☑03-5466-7331; www.these-jp.com; 2-15-12 Nishi-Azabu, Minato-ku; cover charge ¥500; ⊗7pm-4am, to 2am Sun; ⓢHibiya line to Roppongi, exit 3) Pronounced *teh*-zeh, this delightfully quirky, nook-ridden 'library lounge' overflows with armchairs, sofas, and books on the shelves and on the bar. Imbibe champagne by the glass, whiskies or seasonal-fruit cocktails. Bites include escargot garlic toast, which goes down very nicely with a drink in the secret room on the 2nd floor. Look for the flaming torches outside.

★ Sake Plaza
SAKE
(日本酒造会館; Map p72; www.japansake.or.jp; 1-6-15 Nishi-Shimbashi, Minato-ku; ⊗10am-6pm Mon-Fri; ⓢGinza line to Toranomon, exit 9) Sake Plaza isn't a bar, but who cares when you can get 30mL thimbles of regionally brewed sake (some 36 types) or *shōchū* (16 types) for as little as ¥100 a shot. There are four tasting sets of three glasses from ¥200 to ¥500. This showroom and tasting space is an ideal place to learn about the national drink.

It's on the ground floor at the back of the Japan Sake Brewers Association Building (日本酒造会館).

★ SuperDeluxe
CLUB
(スーパー・デラックス; Map p82; ☑03-5412-0515; www.super-deluxe.com; B1 fl, 3-1-25 Nishi-Azabu, Minato-ku; admission varies; ⓢHibiya line to Roppongi, exit 1B) This groovy basement performance space, also a cocktail lounge and club of sorts, stages everything from electronic music to literary evenings and creative presentations in the 20 x 20 PechaKucha (20 slides

x 20 seconds) format. Check the website for event details. It's in a brown-brick building by a shoe-repair shop.

🍷 Ebisu, Meguro & Around

Ebisu has a lively bar scene frequented by young professionals. Most places are small – often just a counter – and it's fun to bounce from one to the next.

★ Nakame Takkyū Lounge LOUNGE
(中目卓球ラウンジ; Map p86; 2nd fl, Lion House Naka-Meguro, 1-3-13 Kami-Meguro, Meguro-ku; cover before/after 10pm ¥500/800; ⏰6pm-2am Mon-Sat; 🚇Hibiya line to Naka-Meguro) *Takkyū* means table tennis and it's a serious sport in Japan. This hilarious bar looks like a university table-tennis clubhouse – right down to the tatty furniture and posters of star players on the wall. It's in an apartment building next to a parking garage (go all the way down the corridor past the bikes); ring the doorbell for entry.

Bar Trench COCKTAIL BAR
(バートレンチ; Map p86; 📞03-3780-5291; http://small-axe.net/bar-trench/; 1-5-8 Ebisu-Nishi, Shibuya-ku; cover charge ¥500; ⏰7pm-2am Mon-Sat, 6pm-1am Sun; 🚉JR Yamanote line to Ebisu, west exit) One of the pioneers in Tokyo's new cocktail scene, Trench (named for the trench-like alley in which it is nestled) is a tiny place with the air of old-world bohemianism. It has a short but sweet menu of original tipples. Highlights include the 'Shady Samurai' (green-tea-infused gin with elderflower liquor, egg white and lime; ¥1620).

Buri BAR
(ぶり; Map p86; 📞03-3496-7744; 1-14-1 Ebisu-nishi, Shibuya-ku; ⏰5pm-3am; 🚉JR Yamanote line to Ebisu, west exit) Buri – the name means 'super' in Hiroshima dialect – is one of Ebisu's most popular *tachinomi-ya* (standing bars). On almost any night you can find a lively crowd packed in around the horseshoe-shaped counter here. Generous quantities of sake (more than 40 varieties; ¥770) are served semifrozen, like slushies in colourful jars.

🍷 Shibuya

★ Good Beer Faucets CRAFT BEER
(グッドビアフォウセッツ; Map p88; http://shibuya.goodbeerfaucets.jp; 2nd fl, 1-29-1 Shōtō, Shibuya-ku; pints from ¥800; ⏰5pm-midnight Mon-Thu & Sat, to 3am Fri, 4-11pm Sun; 😊🛜; 🚉JR Yamanote line to Shibuya, Hachikō exit) With 40 shiny taps, Good Beer Faucets has one of the city's best selections of Japanese craft brews and regularly draws a full house of locals and expats. The interior is chrome and concrete (and not at all grungy). Come for happy hour (5pm to 8pm Monday to Thursday, 1pm to 7pm Sunday) and get ¥200 off any pint.

Contact CLUB
(コンタクト; Map p88; 📞03-6427-8107; www.contacttokyo.com; basement, 2-10-12 Dōgenzaka, Shibuya-ku; ¥2000-3500; 😊; 🚉JR Yamanote line to Shibuya, Hachikō exit) This is Tokyo's newest hot spot, a stylish underground club that's keen on keeping up with the times (even if that means it's a little heavy on rules): the dance floor is no smoking and no photos (so you can dance with abandon). Weekends see big international names and a young, fashionable crowd. Under-23s get in for ¥2000. ID required.

Currently the club is 'members only', so to get in you have to sign up on the website. Look for the entrance in the back of a parking lot.

Rhythm Cafe BAR
(リズムカフェ; Map p88; 📞03-3770-0244; http://rhythmcafe.jp; 11-1 Udagawa-chō, Shibuya-ku; ⏰6pm-2am; 🚉JR Yamanote line to Shibuya, Hachikō exit) Run by a record label, fun and funky Rhythm Cafe often draws more customers than it can fit, meaning the party spills into the street. It's known for having off-beat event nights (such as the retro Japanese pop night on the fourth Thursday of the month). Drinks start at ¥700; when DJs spin, the cover is around ¥1000.

Nonbei-yokochō BAR
(のんべえ横丁; Map p88; www.nonbei.tokyo; Shibuya 1-chōme, Shibuya-ku; 🚉JR Yamanote line to Shibuya, Hachikō exit) Nonbei-yokochō is one of Tokyo's anomalous – and endangered – strips of old wooden shanty bars, here in the shadow of the elevated JR tracks. There's a wonderfully eclectic assortment of teeny-tiny bars, though note that some have cover charges (usually ¥500 to ¥1000). **Tight** (タイト; Map p88; 2nd fl, 1-25-10 Shibuya, Shibuya-ku; ⏰6pm-2am Mon-Sat, to midnight Sun) is one that doesn't.

Womb CLUB
(ウーム; Map p88; 📞03-5459-0039; www.womb.co.jp; 2-16 Maruyama-chō, Shibuya-ku; cover ¥1500-4000; ⏰11pm-late Fri & Sat, 4-10pm Sun; 🚉JR Yamanote line to Shibuya, Hachikō exit) A long-time (in club years, at least) club-scene fixture, Womb gets a lot of big-name international DJs playing mostly house and techno on Friday and Saturday nights. Frenetic lasers and

strobes splash across the heaving crowds, which usually jam all four floors. Weekdays are quieter, with local DJs playing EDM mix and ladies getting free entry (with flyer).

🍷 Harajuku & Aoyama

Little Nap Coffee Stand　CAFE
(リトルナップコーヒースタンド; Map p72; www.littlenap.jp; 5-65-4 Yoyogi, Shibuya-ku; ⊙9am-7pm Tue-Sun; ⓢ Chiyoda line to Yoyogi-kōen, exit 3) Few people enter Yoyogi-kōen from the entrance near the subway stop of the same name, except those who live nearby. Odds are, on their way, they've stopped by Little Nap for a well-crafted latte (¥400). On Sundays, there's always a crowd loitering out front.

Oath　BAR
(Map p72; http://bar-oath.com; 4-5-9 Shibuya, Shibuya-ku; ⊙9pm-5am Mon-Thu, to 8am Fri & Sat, 5-11pm Sun; ⓢ Ginza line to Omote-sandō, exit B1) A tiny space along a somewhat forlorn strip of highway, Oath is a favourite after-hours destination for clubbers – helped no doubt by the ¥500 drinks and lack of cover charge. Underground DJs spin here sometimes, too.

Two Rooms　BAR
(トゥールームス; Map p90; ☎03-3498-0002; www.tworooms.jp; 5th fl, AO bldg, 3-11-7 Kita-Aoyama, Minato-ku; ⊙11.30am-2am Mon-Sat, to 10pm Sun; ⓢ Ginza line to Omote-sandō, exit B2) Expect a crowd dressed like they don't care that wine by the glass starts at ¥1600. You can eat here too, but the real scene is at night by the bar. Call ahead (staff speak English) on Friday or Saturday night to reserve a table on the terrace, which has sweeping views towards the Shinjuku skyline.

Montoak　CAFE
(モントーク; Map p90; 6-1-9 Jingūmae, Shibuya-ku; ⊙11am-3am; ⊜; ⓡ JR Yamanote line to Harajuku, Omote-sandō exit) This stylish, tinted-glass cube is a calm, dimly lit retreat from the busy streets. It's perfect for holing up with a pot of tea or carafe of wine and watching the crowds go by. Or, if the weather is nice, score a seat on the terrace. Drinks from ¥700.

🍷 Shinjuku

★BenFiddich　COCKTAIL BAR
(ベンフィディック; Map p93; ☎03-6279-4223; 9th fl, 1-13-7 Nishi-Shinjuku, Shinjuku-ku; ⊙6pm-

MEIJI-JINGŪ GAIEN BEER GARDENS

Summer beer gardens are a Tokyo tradition (typically running late May to early September). Two of the city's best are within Meiji-jingū Gaien (the 'Outer Garden' of Meiji-jingū). **Mori-no Beer Garden** (森のビアガーデン; Map p72; www.rkfs.co.jp/brand/beer_garden_detail.html; 1-7-5 Kita-Aoyama, Minato-ku; ⊙5-10pm Mon-Fri, 3-10pm Sat & Sun; ⓡ JR Sōbu line to Shinanomachi) hosts up to 1000 revellers for all-you-can-eat-and-drink spreads of beer and barbecue under a century-old tree.

At the more patrician **Sekirei** (鶺鴒; Map p72; ☎03-3746-7723; www.meijikinenkan.gr.jp/restaurant/company/sekirei; Meiji Kinenkan, 2-2-23 Moto-Akasaka, Minato-ku; cover charge ¥500; ⊙5-10.30pm; ⓡ JR Sōbu line to Shinanomachi), you can quaff beer on the neatly clipped lawn of the stately Meiji Kinenkan (a hall used for weddings); traditional Japanese dance is performed nightly around 8pm.

3am Mon-Sat; ⓡ JR Yamanote line to Shinjuku, west exit) Step into the magical space that is BenFiddich. It's dark, it's tiny, and vials of infusions line the shelves, while herbs hang drying from the ceiling. Classical music simmers and soars. The barman, Kayama Hiroyasu, in a white suit, moves like a magician. There's no menu, but cocktails run about ¥1500; service charge is 10%.

★Zoetrope　BAR
(ゾートロープ; Map p93; http://homepage2.nifty.com/zoetrope; 3rd fl, 7-10-14 Nishi-Shinjuku, Shinjuku-ku; cover charge ¥1000; ⊙7pm-4am Mon-Sat; ⓡ JR Yamanote line to Shinjuku, west exit) A must-visit for whisky fans, Zoetrope has some 300 varieties of Japanese whisky behind its small counter – including hard-to-find bottles from cult favourite Chichibu Distillery. The owner speaks English and can help you pick from the daunting menu. Whisky by the glass from ¥400 to ¥19,000, though most are reasonable.

New York Bar　BAR
(ニューヨークバー; Map p93; ☎03-5323-3458; http://tokyo.park.hyatt.com; 52nd fl, Park Hyatt, 3-7-1-2 Nishi-Shinjuku, Shinjuku-ku; ⊙5pm-midnight Sun-Wed, to 1am Thu-Sat; ⓡ Ōedo line to Tochōmae, exit A4) Head to the Park Hyatt's 52nd floor to

swoon over the sweeping nightscape from the floor-to-ceiling windows at this bar (of *Lost in Translation* fame). There's a cover charge of ¥2400 if you visit or stay past 8pm (7pm Sunday); go earlier and watch the sky fade to black. Cocktails start at ¥2000. Note: dress code enforced and 20% service charge levied.

On the 41st floor, the Peak Bar offers views that are arguably just as good. There's no cover here and you can take advantage of the generous 'Twilight Time' all-you-can-drink deal (5pm to 8pm; ¥5000, unlimited canapes included).

Akihabara, Kagurazaka & Kōrakuen

★ Imasa
CAFE

(井政; Map p96; ☑03-3255-3565; www.kanda-imasa.co.jp; 2-16 Soto-Kanda, Chiyoda-ku; drinks ¥600; ⊙11am-4pm Mon-Fri; ⓡ JR Chūō or Sōbu lines to Ochanomizu, Hijiri-bashi exit) It's not every day that you get to sip your coffee or tea in a cultural property. Imasa is the real deal, an old timber merchant's shophouse dating from 1927 but with Edo-era design and detail, and a few pieces of contemporary furniture. Very few houses like this exist in Tokyo or are open to the public.

★ Craft Beer Server Land
CRAFT BEER

(Map p96; ☑03-6228-1891; Okawa Bldg B1F, 2-9 Kagurazaka, Shinjuku-ku; service charge ¥380; ⊙5pm-midnight Mon-Fri, noon-midnight Sat & Sun; ⓢ; ⓡ JR Sōbu line to Iidabashi, west exit) With some 14 Japanese craft beers on tap, going for a reasonable ¥500/840 a glass/pint, plus good food (the fish and chips is excellent), this

brightly lit basement bar with wooden furniture and a slight Scandi feel is a winner.

Look for the English sign as you head up the slope.

★ Mugimaru 2
CAFE

(ムギマル2; Map p96; ☑03-5228-6393; www.mugimaru2.com; 5-20 Kagurazaka, Shinjuku-ku; coffee ¥550; ⊙noon-8pm Thu-Tue; ⓢ Tozai line to Kagurazaka, exit 1) This old house, completely covered in ivy, is a charmer with a welcoming owner and a couple of cats. Seating is on floor cushions; warm, squishy *manjū* (steamed buns) are the house speciality.

It's located in a tangle of alleys just off Ōkubo-dōri – look for a sign with a cat and potted plants out front.

N3331
CAFE

(Map p96; ☑03-5295-2788; http://n3331.com; 2nd fl, mAAch ecute, 1-25-4 Kanda-Sudachō, Chiyoda-ku; ⊙11am-10.30pm Mon-Sat, to 8.30pm Sun; ⓡ JR Yamamote line to Akihabara, Electric Town exit) Climb the original white-tile-clad stairs to the former platform of Mansei-bashi Station to find this ultimate trainspotters' cafe. Through floor-to-ceiling windows, watch commuter trains stream by while you sip on coffee, craft beer or sake and enjoy snacks.

@Home Cafe
CAFE

(@ほぉ〜むカフェ; Map p96; www.cafe-athome.com; 4th-7th fl, 1-11-4 Soto-Kanda, Chiyoda-ku; drinks from ¥500; ⊙11.30am-10pm Mon-Fri, 10.30am-10pm Sat & Sun; ⓡ JR Yamanote line to Akihabara, Electric Town exit) 'Maid cafes' with *kawaii* (cute) waitresses, dressed as saucy French or prim Victorian maids, are a stock in trade of Akiba. @ Home is one of the more 'wholesome' of them.

GOLDEN GAI

Golden Gai, a warren of tiny alleys and narrow, two-storey wooden buildings, began as a black market following WWII. It later functioned as a licensed quarter, until prostitution was outlawed in 1958. Now those same buildings are filled with more than a hundred closet-sized bars. Each is as unique and eccentric as the 'master' or 'mama' who runs it. That Golden Gai – prime real estate – has so far resisted the kind of development seen elsewhere in Shinjuku is a credit to these stubbornly bohemian characters.

The best way to experience Golden Gai is to stroll the lanes and pick a place that suits your mood. Bars here usually have a theme – from punk rock to photography – and draw customers with matching expertise and obsessions (many of whom work in the media and entertainment industries). Since regular customers are their bread and butter, some establishments are likely to give tourists a cool reception. Don't take it personally. Japanese visitors unaccompanied by a regular get the same treatment; this is Golden Gai's peculiar, invisible velvet rope. However, there are also an increasing number of bars that expressly welcome tourists (with English signs posted on their doors). Note that many bars have a cover charge (usually ¥500 to ¥1500).

You'll be welcomed as *go-shujinsama* (master) or *o-jōsama* (miss) the minute you enter. The maids serve drinks and dishes, such as curried rice, topped with smiley faces.

They'll also play games with patrons, such as *moe moe jankan* (rock, paper, scissors).

It's a little titillating, perhaps, but this is no sex joint – just (more or less) innocent fun for Akiba's *otaku* (geeks).

★ Ueno & Yanesen

★ Yanaka Beer Hall   CRAFT BEER
(Map p100; ☑ 03-5834-2381; www.facebook.com/ yanakabeerhall; 2-15-6 Ueno-sakuragi, Taitō-ku; ⊙ noon-8.30pm Tue-Fri, 11am-8.30pm Sat & Sun; 🐾; Ⓢ Chiyoda line to Nezu, exit 1) Exploring Yanesen can be thirsty work so thank heavens for this craft-beer bar, a cosy place with some outdoor seating. It's part of a charming complex of old wooden buildings that also house a bakery-cafe, bistro and events space. It has several brews on tap, including a Yanaka lager that's only available here.

Kayaba Coffee   CAFE
(カヤバ珈琲; Map p100; ☑ 03-3823-3545; http:// kayaba-coffee.com; 6-1-29 Yanaka, Taitō-ku; drinks from ¥450; ⊙ 8am-11pm Mon-Sat, to 6pm Sun; Ⓢ Chiyoda line to Nezu, exit 1) This vintage 1930s coffee shop (the building is actually from the '20s) in Yanaka is a hang-out for local students and artists. Come early for the 'morning set' (coffee and a sandwich for ¥800). In the evenings, Kayaba morphs into a bar.

★ Asakusa & Sumida River
浅草・隅田川

★ Café Otonova   CAFE
(カフェ・オトノヴァ; Map p106; ☑ 03-5830-7663; www.cafeotonova.net/#3eme; 3-10-4 Nishi-Asakusa; ⊙ noon-11pm, to 9pm Sun; Ⓢ) Tucked firmly away on an alley running parallel to Kappabashi-dōri (p150), this charming cafe occupies an old house. Exposed beams are whitewashed and an atrium has been created, with cosy booths upstairs and a big communal table downstairs in front of the DJ booth. It's a stylish cafe by day and a romantic bolthole for drinks at night, with no table charge.

★ Camera   CAFE
(Map p72; ☑ 03-5825-4170; http://camera1010. tokyo; 4-21-8 Kuramae, Taitō-ku; ⊙ 11am-6pm Tue-Sun; Ⓢ Asakusa line to Kuramae, exit A3) English-speaking pastry cook Yamada Miwako runs this delightful cafe that's combined with a boutique selling the quality leathergoods of Tamura Kosuke. There's good coffee and smoothies to go with some unusual items, such as *onigiri* (rice-ball snacks) topped with spam. The take-out sandwiches and salads are excellent, too.

★ Popeye   PUB
(ポパイ; Map p72; ☑ 03-3633-2120; www.40beers ontap.com; 2-18-7 Ryōgoku, Sumida-ku; ⊙ 11.30am-4pm & 5-11pm Mon-Sat; 🐾; ⑱ JR Sōbu line to Ryōgoku, west exit) Popeye boasts an astounding 70 beers on tap, including the world's largest selection of Japanese beers – from Echigo Weizen to Hitachino Nest Espresso Stout. The happy-hour deal (5pm to 8pm) offers select brews with free plates of pizza, sausages and other munchables. It's extremely popular and fills up fast; get here early to grab a seat.

From the station's west exit, take a left on the main road and pass under the tracks; take the second left and look for Popeye on the right.

'Cuzn Homeground   BAR
(Map p106; www.homeground.jpn.com; 2-17-9 Asakusa, Taitō-ku; beer ¥800; ⊙ 11am-6am; 🐾; Ⓢ Ginza line to Tawaramachi, exit 3) Run by a wild gang of local hippies, 'Cuzn is the kind of bar where anything can happen: a barbecue, a jam session or all-night karaoke, for example.

★ Odaiba & Tokyo Bay
お台場・東京湾

Jicoo the Floating Bar   COCKTAIL BAR
(ジークザフローティングバー; Map p108; ☑ 0120-049-490; www.jicoofloatingbar.com; cover from ¥2600; ⊙ 8-10.30pm Thu-Sat; ⑱ Yurikamome line to Hinode or Odaiba Kaihin-kōen) For a few nights a week, the futuristic cruise-boat Himiko, designed by manga and anime artist Leiji Matsumoto, morphs into this floating bar. Board on the hour at Hinode pier and the half-hour at Odaiba Kaihin-kōen. The evening-long 'floating pass' usually includes some sort of live music; check the schedule online as sometimes events drive up the price.

Ageha   CLUB
(アゲハ; www.ageha.com; 2-2-10 Shin-Kiba, Kōtō-ku; cover ¥2500-4000; ⊙ 11pm-5am Fri & Sat; Ⓢ Yūrakuchō line to Shin-Kiba, main exit) This gigantic waterside club, the largest in Tokyo, rivals any you'd find in LA or Ibiza. Top international and Japanese DJs appear here. Free buses run between the club and a bus stop on the east

side of Shibuya Station (on Roppongi-dōri) all night. Events vary widely; check the website for details and bring photo ID.

🍷 West Tokyo

★Cocktail Shobō
BAR

(コクテイル書房; Map p110; 3-8-13 Kōenji-kita, Suginami-ku; ⏲11.30am-3pm Wed-Sun, 5pm-midnight Mon-Sun; 🚆 JR Sōbu line to Kōenji, north exit) At this bar-bookstore mash-up, the wooden counter doubles as a bookshelf and the local crowd comes as much to sip cocktails (from ¥450) as it does to flip through the selection of worn paperbacks. It's a cosy place, and like most bars in Kōenji, a labour of love. During lunch hours, curry and coffee are served.

Blue Sky Coffee
CAFE

(ブルースカイコーヒー;4-12Inokashira,Mitaka-shi; coffee from ¥250; ⏲1-5pm; 🚆 Keiō Inokashira line to Inokashira-kōen) This tiny cafe looks like it could be the work of Studio Ghibli: a wooden cottage secreted in the woodsy perimeter of Inokashira-kōen concealing a shiny, state-of-the-art coffee roaster. The coffee is made with care, and is the cheapest around.

☆ Entertainment

Live Music

★Unit
LIVE MUSIC

(ユニット; Map p86; ☎03-5459-8630; www.unit-tokyo.com; 1-34-17 Ebisu-nishi, Shibuya-ku; ¥2500-5000; 🚆 Tōkyū Tōyoko line to Daikanyama) On weekends, this subterranean club has two shows: live music in the evening and a DJ-hosted event that gets started around midnight. The solid line-up includes Japanese indie bands, veterans playing to a smaller crowd and overseas artists making their Japan debut. Unit is less grungy than other Tokyo live houses and, with high ceilings, doesn't get as smoky.

★WWW
LIVE MUSIC

(Map p88; www-shibuya.jp/index.html; 13-17 Udagawa-chō, Shibuya-ku; tickets ¥2000-5000; 🚆 JR Yamanote line to Shibuya, Hachikō exit) In a former arthouse cinema (with the tell-tale tiered floor still intact), this is one of those rare venues where you could turn up just about any night and hear something good. The line-up varies from indie pop to punk to electronica. Upstairs is the new WWW X, with more space.

Shinjuku Pit Inn
JAZZ

(新宿ピットイン; Map p93; ☎03-3354-2024; www.pit-inn.com; basement, 2-12-4 Shinjuku, Shinjuku-ku; from ¥3000; ⏲matinee 2.30pm, evening show 7.30pm; [S] Marunouchi line to Shinjuku-sanchōme, exit C5) This is not the kind of place you come to talk over the music. It's the kind of place you come to sit in thrall of Japan's best jazz performers (as Tokyoites have been doing for half a century now). Weekday matinees feature up-and-coming artists and cost only ¥1300.

Tokyo Opera City Concert Hall
CLASSICAL MUSIC

(東京オペラシティコンサートホール; Map p72; ☎03-5353-9999; www.operacity.jp; 3rd fl, Tokyo Opera City, 3-20-2 Nishi-Shinjuku, Shinjuku-ku; ¥3000-5000; 🚆 Keiō New line to Hatsudai) This beautiful, oak-panelled, A-frame concert hall, with legendary acoustics, hosts the Tokyo Philharmonic Orchestra among other well-regarded ensembles, including the occasional *bugaku* (classical Japanese music) group. Free lunchtime organ performances take place monthly, usually on Fridays. Information and tickets can be acquired at the box office next to the entrance to the Tokyo Opera City Art Gallery.

Club Quattro
LIVE MUSIC

(クラブクアトロ; Map p88; ☎03-3477-8750; www.club-quattro.com; 32-13-4 Udagawa-chō, Shibuya-ku; tickets ¥3000-4000; 🚆 JR Yamanote line to Shibuya, Hachikō exit) This small, intimate venue has the feel of a slick nightclub and attracts a more grown-up, artsy crowd than the club's location – near Center-gai – might lead you to expect. Though there's no explicit musical focus, emphasis is on rock and world music, with many an indie darling passing through.

Tokyo Bunka Kaikan
CLASSICAL MUSIC

(東京文化会館; Map p100; www.t-bunka.jp/en; 5-45 Ueno-kōen, Taitō-ku; ⏲library 1-8pm Tue-Sat, to 5pm Sun; 🚆 JR lines to Ueno, Ueno-kōen exit) The Tokyo Metropolitan Symphony Orchestra and the Tokyo Ballet both make regular appearances at this concrete bunker of a building designed by Maekawa Kunio, an apprentice of Le Corbusier. Prices vary wildly; look out for monthly morning classical-music performances that cost only ¥500. The gorgeously decorated auditorium has superb acoustics.

Oiwake
TRADITIONAL MUSIC

(追分; Map p106; ☎03-3844-6283; www.oiwake.info; 3-28-11 Nishi-Asakusa, Taitō-ku; admission

¥2000; food/drink from ¥700; ⌚5.30pm-midnight; 🚉Tsukuba Express to Asakusa, exit 1) Oiwake is one of Tokyo's few *minyō izakaya,* pubs where traditional folk music is performed. It's a homey place, where the waitstaff and the musicians – who play *tsugaru-jamisen* (a banjo-like instrument), hand drums and bamboo flute – are one and the same. Sets start at 7pm and 9pm; children are welcome for the early show. Seating is on tatami.

Performing Arts

★ Kabuki-za THEATRE

(歌舞伎座; Map p76; ☎03-3545-6800; www.kabuki-bito.jp/eng; 4-12-15 Ginza, Chūō-ku; tickets ¥4000-21,000, single-act tickets ¥800-2000; 🚉Hibiya line to Higashi-Ginza, exit 3) The flamboyant facade of this venerable theatre, which was completely reconstructed in 2013 to incorporate a tower block, makes a strong impression. It is a good indication of the extravagant dramatic flourishes that are integral to the traditional performing art of kabuki. Check the website for performance details and to book tickets; you'll also find an explanation about cheaper one-act, day seats.

A full kabuki performance comprises three or four acts (usually from different plays) over an afternoon or an evening (typically 11am to 3.30pm or 4.30pm to 9pm), with long intervals between the acts. Make sure to rent a headset (single act ¥500) for blow-by-blow explanations in English, and pick up a *bentō* (boxed meal) to snack on during the intervals.

If four-plus hours sounds too long, 90 sitting and 60 standing tickets are sold on the day for each single act. You'll be at the back of the auditorium but the views are still good. Some acts tend to be more popular than others, so ask ahead as to which to catch, and arrive at least 1½ hours before the start of the performance.

Setagaya Public Theatre PERFORMING ARTS

(世田谷パブリックシアター; Map p72; ☎03-5432-1526; www.setagaya-pt.jp; 4-1-1 Taishidō, Setagaya-ku; tickets ¥3500-7500; 🚉Tōkyū Den-en-toshi line to Sangenjaya, Carrot Tower exit) The best of the city's public theatres, Setagaya Public Theatre puts on contemporary dramas as well as modern *nō* (a stylised Japanese dance-drama, performed on a bare stage) and sometimes *butoh* (an avant-garde form of dance). The smaller **Theatre Tram** shows more experimental works. Both are located inside the Carrot Tower building connected to Sangenjaya Station, a five-minute train ride from Shibuya.

ℹ GETTING TICKETS

The easiest way to get tickets for many live shows and events is at one of the **Ticket Pia** (チケットぴあ; ☎0570-02-9111; http://t.pia.jp; ⌚10am-8pm) kiosks scattered across Tokyo. Its online booking site is in Japanese only.

National Nō Theatre THEATRE

(国立能楽堂; Kokuritsu Nō-gakudō; Map p72; ☎03-3230-3000; www.ntj.jac.go.jp/english; 4-18-1 Sendagaya, Shibuya-ku; adult ¥2600-4900, student ¥1900-2200; 🚉JR Sōbu line to Sendagaya) The traditional music, poetry and dances that *nō* is famous for unfold here on an elegant cypress stage. Each seat has a small screen displaying an English translation of the dialogue. Shows take place only a few times a month and can sell out fast; purchase tickets one month in advance through the Japan Arts Council website.

The theatre is 400m from Sendagaya Station; from the exit, walk right along the main road and turn left at the traffic light.

National Theatre THEATRE

(国立劇場, Kokuritsu Gekijō; Map p72, ☎03-3265-7411; www.ntj.jac.go.jp/english; 4-1 Hayabusa-chō, Chiyoda-ku; tickets from ¥1500; [S]Hanzōmon line to Hanzōmon, exit 1) This is the capital's premier venue for traditional performing arts with a 1600-seat and a 590-seat auditorium. Performances include kabuki, *gagaku* (music of the imperial court) and *bunraku* (classic puppet theatre). Earphones with English translation are available for hire (¥650 plus ¥1000 deposit). Check the website for performance schedules.

Tokyo Takarazuka Theatre THEATRE

(宝塚劇場; Map p76; ☎03-5251-2001; http://kageki.hankyu.co.jp/english/index.html; 1-1-3 Yūrakuchō, Chiyoda-ku; tickets ¥3500-12,000; [S]Hibiya line to Hibiya, exits A5 & A13) If you love camp, this is for you. The all-female Takarazuka revue, going back to 1914, stages highly stylised musicals in Japanese (English synopses are available) where a mostly female audience swoons over actresses, some of whom are in drag.

It's massively popular so shows often sell out. Fear not: there are 49 standing tickets (¥1500) sold daily for each show.

Robot Restaurant CABARET
(ロボットレストラン; Map p93; ☎03-3200-5500; www.shinjuku-robot.com; 1-7-1 Kabukichō, Shinjuku-ku; tickets ¥8000; 🕒shows at 4pm, 5.55pm, 7.50pm & 9.45pm; 🚉JR Yamanote line to Shinjuku, east exit) This Kabukichō spectacle is wacky Japan at its finest, with giant robots operated by bikini-clad women and enough neon to light all of Shinjuku – though it's become more family-friendly in recent years. Reservations aren't necessary but are recommended: the show's popularity is evinced by the ever-creeping ticket price. Look for discount tickets at hotels around town.

If the price makes you think twice, you can still swing by for a photo-op with two of the robots parked outside. You can also grab a drink (and a taste of Robot Restaurant's signature gilded plastic, game-show-set aesthetic) at new sister bar **Ren** (蓮; Map p93; 1-10-10 Kabukichō, Shinjuku-ku; 🕒6pm-6am) around the corner.

P.A.R.M.S LIVE PERFORMANCE
(☎012-075-9835; www.pasela.co.jp; 7th fl, Pasela Resorts Akihabara-Denkigai, 1-13-2 Soto-kanda, Chiyoda-ku; admission incl 1 drink Mon-Fri ¥1500, Sat & Sun ¥3500; 🕒shows 5.30pm & 8.15pm Mon-Fri, 10.30am Sat & Sun; 🚉JR Yamanote line to Akihabara, Electric Town exit) Shows by the girl group Kamen Joshi – singing and dancing young women wearing cute outfits and hockey masks – are all the rage at this live-music show in the Pasela Resort's karaoke emporium. It's a chance to swing around a light sabre (handed out to audience members) in a thoroughly Akiba night out.

DON'T MISS

SUMO PRACTICE

Not in town for a sumo tournament? You can still catch an early-morning practice session at a 'stable' – where the wrestlers live and practise. Overseas visitors are welcome at **Arashio Stable** (荒汐部屋, Arashio-beya; Map p72; ☎03-3666-7646; www.arashio.net/tour_e.html; 2-47-2 Hama-chō, Nihombashi, Chūō-ku; [S] Toei Shinjuku line to Hamachō, exit A2) [FREE], so long as they mind the rules (check the website). Visit between 7.30am and 10am – you can watch through the window or on a bench outside the door. There is no practice during tournament weeks.

When Joanna Lumley made her travel documentary about Japan, she joined in the crazy dance routine here; if it's good enough for *Ab Fab's* Patsy, it's good enough for us!

Spectator Sports

★Ryōgoku Kokugikan SPECTATOR SPORT
(両国国技館, Ryōgoku Sumo Stadium; Map p72; ☎03-3623-5111; www.sumo.or.jp; 1-3-28 Yokoami, Sumida-ku; ¥2200-14,800; 🚉JR Sōbu line to Ryōgoku, west exit) If you're in town when a tournament is on – for 15 days each January, May and September – catch the big boys in action at Japan's largest sumo stadium. Doors open at 8am, but the action doesn't heat up until the senior wrestlers hit the ring around 2pm. Tickets can be bought online one month before the start of the tournament.

Around 200 general-admission tickets are sold on the day of the match from the box office in front of the stadium. You'll have to line up very early (say 6am) on the last couple of days of the tournament to snag one.

If you get there in the morning when the stadium is still pretty empty, you can usually sneak down to the box seats. You can rent a radio (¥100 fee, plus ¥2000 deposit) to listen to commentary in English. Stop by the basement banquet hall to sample *chanko-nabe* (the protein-rich stew eaten by the wrestlers) for just ¥300 a bowl.

★Tokyo Dome BASEBALL
(東京ドーム; Map p96; www.tokyo-dome.co.jp/e; 1-3 Kōraku, Bunkyō-ku; tickets ¥2200-6100; 🚉JR Chūō line to Suidōbashi, west exit) Tokyo Dome (aka 'Big Egg') is home to the Yomiuri Giants. Love 'em or hate 'em, they're the most consistently successful team in Japanese baseball. If you're looking to see the Giants in action, the baseball season runs from the end of March to the end of October. Tickets sell out in advance; get them early at www.giants.jp/en.

If you'd rather root for the underdog (whoever is playing the Giants), you can drown your sorrows in the beer served by the *uriko,* young women with kegs strapped to their backs, who work the aisles with tireless cheer.

Tokyo Dome is also used for pop concerts by major Japanese and visiting singers and groups.

Jingū Baseball Stadium BASEBALL
(神宮球場; Jingū Kyūjo; Map p90; ☎0180-993-589; www.jingu-stadium.com; 3-1 Kasumigaoka-machi, Shinjuku-ku; tickets ¥1600-4600; [S] Ginza line to Gaienmae, exit 3) Jingū Baseball Stadium, built in 1926, is home to the Yakult Swallows,

Tokyo's number-two team (but number-one when it comes to fan loyalty). Night games start at 6pm; weekend games start around 2pm. Pick up tickets from the booth next to Gate 9, which is open 11am to 5pm (or until 20 minutes after the game starts).

Same-day outfield tickets cost just ¥1600 to ¥1900 (¥500 for children) and are usually available – unless the Swallows are playing crosstown rivals, the Yomiuri Giants.

LOCAL KNOWLEDGE

FOOD TO GO

Heading off on the *shinkansen*? The basement of department store **Daimaru** (Map p76; ☎03-3212-8011; www.daimaru.co.jp/tokyo; 1-9-1 Marunouchi, Chiyoda-ku; ⏲10am-9pm, restaurants 11am-11pm; 🚆JR lines to Tokyo Station, Yaesu exit), on the eastern Yaesu side of Tokyo Station, is the best place to pick up *bentō* (boxed meals) for the journey.

Shopping

Marunouchi & Nihombashi

Tokyo's grandest and oldest department stores, **Mitsukoshi** (三越; Map p76; ☎03-3241-3311; www.mitsukoshi.co.jp; 1-4-1 Nihombashi-Muromachi, Chūō-ku; ⏲10am-7pm; [S]Ginza line to Mitsukoshimae, exit A2) and **Takashimaya** (高島屋; Map p76; www.takashimaya.co.jp/tokyo/store_information; 2-4-1 Nihombashi, Chūō-ku; ⏲10am-8pm; [S]Ginza line to Nihombashi, Takashimaya exit), politely stand off against each other on either side of Nihombashi. These temples to consumerism have been challenged in recent years by contemporary-styled shopping malls such as **Coredo Muromachi** (コレド室町; Map p76; http://31urban.jp/lng/eng/muromachi.html; 2-2-1 Nihonbashi-Muromachi, Chūō-ku; ⏲most shops 11am-7pm; [S]Ginza line to Mitsukoshimae, exit A4) and KITTE (p78), which stock up on trending brands and designer arts and crafts in one handy location. Marunouchi's Naka-dōri is a super pleasant strip of high-class boutiques.

★Muji HOMEWARES

(無印良品; Map p76; ☎03-5208-8241; www.muji.com; 3-8-3 Marunouchi, Chiyoda-ku; ⏲10am-9pm; 🚆JR Yamanote line to Yūrakuchō, Kyōbashi exit) The flagship store of the famously understated brand sells elegant, simple clothing, accessories and homewares. There are scores of other outlets across Tokyo, including a good one in Tokyo Midtown, but the Yūrakuchō store is the largest with the biggest range. It also offers tax-free shopping, bicycle rental (¥1080 a day from 10am to 8pm) and a great cafeteria.

Tokyo Character Street TOYS

(東京キャラクターストリート; Map p76; www.tokyoeki-1bangai.co.jp; B1 First Avenue Tokyo Station, 1-9-1 Marunouchi, Chiyoda-ku; ⏲10am-8.30pm; 🚆JR lines to Tokyo Station, Yaesu exit) From Doraemon to Hello Kitty and Ultraman, Japan knows *kawaii* (cute) and how to merchandise it. In the basement on the Yaesu side of Tokyo Station (p78), some 15 Japanese TV networks and toy manufacturers operate stalls selling official plush toys, sweets, accessories and the all-important miniature character to dangle from your mobile phone.

Ginza & Tsukiji 銀座・築地

Start your power-shopping trip in the heart of Ginza at Ginza Yon-chōme Crossing, the intersection of Harumi-dōri and Chūō-dōri (aka Ginza-dōri), right in front of the Wako and **Mitsukoshi** (三越; Map p76; www.mitsukoshi.co.jp; 4-6-16 Ginza, Chūō-ku; ⏲10am-8pm; [S]Ginza line to Ginza, exits A7 & A11) department stores and on top of Ginza Station on the Ginza line. Each weekend Chūō-dōri becomes a pedestrian paradise when it's blocked to traffic from noon to 5pm – along it you'll find some of the area's finest shops, including the new **Ginza Six** (Map p76; http://ginza6.tokyo; 6-10 Ginza, Chūō-ku; ⏲10am-10pm; [S]Ginza line to Ginza, exit A2) mall.

★Itōya ARTS & CRAFTS

(伊東屋; Map p76; www.ito-ya.co.jp; 2-7-15 Ginza, Chūō-ku; ⏲10.30am-8pm Mon-Sat, to 7pm Sun; [S]Ginza line to Ginza, exit A13) Nine floors (plus several more in the nearby annexe) of stationery-shop love await visual-art professionals and seekers of office accessories with both everyday items and luxury such as fountain pens and Italian leather agendas. You'll also find *washi* (fine Japanese handmade paper), *tenugui* (beautifully hand-dyed thin cotton towels) and *furoshiki* (wrapping cloths).

★Takumi ARTS & CRAFTS

(たくみ; Map p76; ☎03-3571-2017; www.ginza-takumi.co.jp; 8-4-2 Ginza, Chūō-ku; ⏲11am-7pm Mon-Sat; [S]Ginza line to Shimbashi, exit 5) You're unlikely to find a more elegant selection of traditional folk crafts, including toys, textiles and ceramics from around the country. Ever thoughtful, this shop also encloses

DON'T MISS

TOP TOKYO SHOPPING EXPERIENCES

➡ Strolling the boutique-lined backstreets of Ura-Hara (p147).

➡ Window-shopping and people-watching on **Chūō-dōri**, fashionable Ginza's main drag.

➡ Making a trip to the original **Mandarake** (p151) in Nakano.

➡ Stocking up on the basics at **Uniqlo**.

➡ Visiting one of Tokyo's grand old *depāto* (department stores), such as **Mitsukoshi** (p145).

➡ Browsing the secondhand shops in Kōenji.

➡ Taking the pulse of youth fashion in Shibuya.

➡ Shopping for traditional crafts on Asakusa's side streets.

information detailing the origin and background of the pieces if you make a purchase.

★Akomeya FOOD
(Map p76; ☎03-6758-0271; www.akomeya.jp; 2-2-6 Ginza, Chūō-ku; 🕙shop 11am-9pm, restaurant 11.30am-10pm; [S] Yūrakuchō line to Ginza-itchōme, exit 4) Rice is at the core of Japanese cuisine and drink. This stylish store sells not only many types of the grain but also products made from it (such as sake), a vast range of quality cooking ingredients and a choice collection of kitchen, home and bath items.

★Dover Street Market Ginza FASHION & ACCESSORIES
(DSM; Map p76; ☎03-6228-5080; http://ginza.doverstreetmarket.com; 6-9-5 Ginza, Chūō-ku; 🕙11am-8pm; [S] Ginza line to Ginza, exit A2) A department store as envisioned by Kawakubo Rei (of Comme des Garçons), DSM has seven floors of avant-garde brands, including several Japanese labels and everything in the Comme des Garçons line-up. The quirky art installations alone make it worth the visit.

Tsukiji Hitachiya HOMEWARES
(つきじ常陸屋; Map p76; 4-14-18 Tsukiji, Chūō-ku; 🕙8am-3pm Mon-Sat, 10am-2pm Sun; [S] Hibiya line to Tsukiji, exit 1) Tokyo chefs and cooks seek out Hitachiya for hand-forged knives, sturdy bamboo baskets and other great kitchen and cooking tools.

Uniqlo FASHION & ACCESSORIES
(ユニクロ; Map p76; www.uniqlo.com; 5-7-7 Ginza, Chūō-ku; 🕙11am-9pm; [S] Ginza line to Ginza, exit A2) This now-global brand has made its name by sticking to the basics and tweaking them with style. Offering inexpensive, quality clothing, this is the Tokyo flagship store with 11 floors and items you won't find elsewhere.

🛍 Roppongi, Akasaka & Around

Top Japanese and international fashion boutiques, and craft and design shops can be found in and around Roppongi Hills (p81) and Tokyo Midtown (p83). Head down into the basement of the National Art Center Tokyo (p84) for a great gift shop or over to **Axis Design** (アクシスビル; Map p82; www.axisinc.co.jp; 5-17-1 Roppongi, Minato-ku; 🕙11am-7pm; [S] Hibiya line to Roppongi, exit 3) in Roppongi for an eclectic range of design-focused outlets.

★Japan Traditional Crafts Aoyama Square ARTS & CRAFTS
(伝統工芸　青山スクエア; Map p72; ☎03-5785-1301; http://kougeihin.jp/home.shtml; 8-1-22 Akasaka, Minato-ku; 🕙11am-7pm; [S] Ginza line to Aoyama-itchōme, exit 4) Supported by the Japanese Ministry of Economy, Trade and Industry, this is as much a showroom as a shop exhibiting a broad range of traditional crafts, including lacquerwork boxes, woodwork, cut glass, paper, textiles and earthy pottery. The emphasis is on high-end pieces, but you can find beautiful things in all price ranges here.

🛍 Ebisu & Around

★Okura FASHION & ACCESSORIES
(オクラ; Map p86; www.hrm.co.jp/okura; 20-11 Sarugaku-chō, Shibuya-ku; 🕙11.30am-8pm Mon-Fri, 11am-8.30pm Sat & Sun; [R] Tōkyū Tōyoko line to Daikanyama) Almost everything in this enchanting shop is dyed a deep indigo blue – from contemporary tees and sweatshirts to classic work shirts. There are some beautiful, original items (though unfortunately most aren't cheap). The shop itself looks like a rural house, with worn, wooden floorboards and whitewashed walls. Note: there's no sign out the front, but the building stands out.

Kapital FASHION & ACCESSORIES

(キャピタル; Map p86; ☎03-5725-3923; http://kapital.jp; 2-20-2 Ebisu, Shibuya-ku; ⏰11am-8pm; 🚉JR Yamanote line to Ebisu, west exit) Cult brand Kapital is hard to pin down, but perhaps a deconstructed mash-up of the American West and the centuries-old Japanese aesthetic of *boro* (tatty) chic comes close. Almost no two items are alike; most are unisex. The shop itself is like an art installation. The staff, not snobby at all, can point you towards the other two shops nearby.

Daikanyama T-Site BOOKS

(代官山T-SITE; Map p86; http://tsite.jp/daikanyama; 17-5 Sarugaku-chō, Shibuya-ku; ⏰7am-2am; 🚉Tōkyū Tōyoko line to Daikanyama) Locals love this stylish shrine to the printed word, which has a fantastic collection of books on travel, art, design and food (and some of them in English). The best part is that you can sit at the in-house Starbucks and read all afternoon – if you can get a seat that is.

The building, designed by Tokyo firm KDa, is cool too: it looks woven.

🛍 Shibuya

★Tokyu Hands DEPARTMENT STORE

(東急ハンズ; Map p88; http://shibuya.tokyu-hands.co.jp; 12-18 Udagawa-chō, Shibuya-ku; ⏰10am-8.30pm; 🚉JR Yamanote line to Shibuya, Hachikō exit) This DIY and *zakka* (miscellaneous goods) store has eight fascinating floors of everything you didn't know you needed. Like reflexology slippers, bee-venom face masks and cartoon-character-shaped rice-ball moulds. Most stuff is inexpensive, making it perfect for souvenir- and gift-hunting. Warning: you could lose hours in here.

There's another branch inside in **Shinjuku** (Map p93; Takashimaya Times Sq, 5-24-2 Sendagaya, Shibuya-ku; ⏰10am-8.30pm; 🚉JR Yamanote line to Shinjuku, new south exit).

Fake Tokyo FASHION & ACCESSORIES

(Map p88; ☎03-5456-9892; www.faketokyo.com; 18-4 Udagawa-chō, Shibuya-ku; ⏰noon-10pm; 🚉JR Yamanote line to Shibuya, Hachikō exit) This is one of the best places in the city to discover hot underground Japanese designers. It's actually two shops in one: downstairs is Candy, full of brash, unisex streetwear; upstairs is Sister, which specialises in more ladylike items, both new and vintage. Look for the 'Fake Tokyo' banners out front.

Shibuya 109 FASHION & ACCESSORIES

(渋谷109; Ichimarukyū; Map p88; www.shibuya109.jp/en/top; 2-29-1 Dōgenzaka, Shibuya-ku; ⏰10am-9pm; 🚉JR Yamanote line to Shibuya, Hachikō exit) See all those dolled-up teens in Shibuya? This is where they shop. Nicknamed *marukyū,* this cylindrical tower houses dozens of small boutiques, each with its own carefully styled look (and competing soundtrack). Even if you don't buy anything, you can't understand Shibuya without making a stop here.

Loft DEPARTMENT STORE

(ロフト; Map p88; ☎03-3462-3807; www.loft.co.jp; 18-2 Udagawa-chō, Shibuya-ku; ⏰10am-9pm; 🚉JR Yamanote line to Shibuya, Hachikō exit) This emporium of homewares, stationery and accessories specialises in all that is cute and covetable. The 1st floor, which stocks seasonal stuff and gifts, is particularly ripe for souvenir-hunting.

Shibuya Hikarie MALL

(渋谷ヒカリエ; Map p88; www.hikarie.jp; 2-21-1 Shibuya, Shibuya-ku; ⏰10am-9pm; 🚉JR Yamanote line to Shibuya, east exit) The first five floors of this glass skyscraper are filled with the latest trendy boutiques. In the basement levels are dozens of gourmet take-away counters.

🛍 Harajuku & Aoyama

Harajuku is trend-central. Malls and department stores on the main drags here carry international fast-fashion brands alongside home-grown ones. For edgier wares, head to the backstreets, an area know as 'Ura-Hara' (deep Harajuku). Aoyama is where many of the top names in Japanese fashion design, such as Issey Miyake, **Comme Des Garcons** (コム・デ・ギャルソン; Map p90; www.comme-des-garcons.com; 5-2-1 Minami-Aoyama, Minato-ku; ⏰11am-8pm; [S]Ginza line to Omote-sandō, exit A5) and Yohji Yamamoto, have their flagship boutiques.

★Sou-Sou FASHION & ACCESSORIES

(そうそう; Map p90; ☎03-3407-7877; http://sousounetshop.jp; 5-3-10 Minami-Aoyama, Minato-ku; ⏰11am-8pm; [S]Ginza line to Omote-sandō, exit A5) Kyoto brand Sou-Sou gives traditional Japanese clothing items – such as split-toed *tabi* socks and *haori* (coats with kimono-like sleeves) – a contemporary spin. Sou-Sou is best known for producing the steel-toed, rubber-soled *tabi* shoes worn by Japanese construction workers in fun, playful designs, but it also carries bags, tees and super-adorable children's clothing.

★ Dog
FASHION, VINTAGE

(ドッグ; Map p90; www.dog-hjk.com/index.html; basement fl, 3-23-3 Jingūmae, Shibuya-ku; ⏰noon-8pm; 🚉JR Yamanote line to Harajuku, Takeshita exit) Club kids and stylists love the showpiece items at legendary Ura-Hara boutique Dog. The store itself, which is decorated to look like a derelict carnival funhouse, is much of the appeal: it looks like an art installation.

It's a tiny place, though, and it has taken to charging admission for tour groups, but ordinary browsers are welcome. Look for graffiti over the entrance and head down the stairs.

★ Musubi
ARTS & CRAFTS

(むす美; Map p90; http://kyoto-musubi.com; 2-31-8 Jingūmae, Shibuya-ku; ⏰11am-7pm Thu-Tue; 🚉JR Yamanote line to Harajuku, Takeshita exit) *Furoshiki* are versatile squares of cloth that can be folded and knotted to make shopping bags and gift wrap. This shop sells pretty ones in both traditional and contemporary patterns. There is usually an English-speaking clerk who can show you how to tie them, or pick up one of the English-language books sold here.

★ Laforet
FASHION & ACCESSORIES

(ラフォーレ; Map p90; www.laforet.ne.jp; 1-11-6 Jingūmae, Shibuya-ku; ⏰11am-8pm; 🚉JR Yamanote line to Harajuku, Omote-sandō exit) Laforet has been a beacon of cutting-edge Harajuku style for decades and lots of quirky, cult favourite brands still cut their teeth here (you'll find some examples at the ground floor boutique, Wall). A range of looks are represented here from *ame-kaji* (American casual) to gothic (in the basement).

Bedrock
FASHION & ACCESSORIES

(ベッドロック; Map p90; 4-12-10 Jingūmae, Shibuya-ku; ⏰11am-9pm, to 8pm Sun; Ⓢ Ginza line to Omote-sandō, exit A2) Walking into Bedrock is like stepping into Keith Richards' boudoir, or the costume closet for *Pirates of the Caribbean* – all leather, feathers and lace. Enter through a secret staircase in the back of the Forbidden Fruit juice bar.

Gallery Kawano
CLOTHING

(ギャラリー川野; Map p90; www.gallery-kawano.com; 4-4-9 Jingūmae, Shibuya-ku; ⏰11am-6pm; 🚉Ginza line to Omote-sandō, exit A2) This store has a good selection of vintage kimonos in decent shape, priced reasonably (about ¥5000 to ¥15,000). The knowledgeable staff will help you try them on and pick

out a matching *obi* (sash); they're less excited about helping customers who try things on but don't intend to buy.

KiddyLand
TOYS

(キデイランド; Map p90; www.kiddyland.co.jp/en/index.html; 6-1-9 Jingūmae, Shibuya-ku; ⏰10am-9pm; 🚉JR Yamanote line to Harajuku, Omote-sandō exit) This multistorey toy emporium is packed to the rafters with character goods, including all your Studio Ghibli, Sanrio and Disney faves. It's not just for kids either; you'll spot plenty of adults on a nostalgia trip down the Hello Kitty aisle.

Chicago Thrift Store
VINTAGE

(シカゴ; Map p90; 6-31-21 Jingūmae, Shibuya-ku; ⏰10am-8pm; 🚉JR Yamanote line to Harajuku, Omote-sandō exit) Chicago is crammed with all sorts of vintage clothing, but best of all is the extensive collection of used kimonos and *yukata*, priced very low, in the back.

🏢 Shinjuku

Shinjuku is a major shopping hub, with several malls and department stores attached to the station and big electronics stores nearby.

Beams
FASHION & ACCESSORIES

(ビームス; Map p93; www.beams.co.jp; 3-32-6 Shinjuku, Shinjuku-ku; ⏰11am-8pm; 🚉JR Yamanote line to Shinjuku, east exit) Beams, a national chain of boutiques, is a cultural force in Japan. This multistorey Shinjuku shop is particularly good for the latest Japanese streetwear labels and work from designers giving traditional looks a modern twist (including men, women and unisex fashions). Also sometimes available: crafts, housewares and original artwork (the line-up is always changing).

Isetan
DEPARTMENT STORE

(伊勢丹; Map p93; www.isetan.co.jp; 3-14-1 Shinjuku, Shinjuku-ku; ⏰10am-8pm; Ⓢ Marunouchi line to Shinjuku-sanchōme, exits B3, B4 & B5) Most department stores play to conservative tastes, but this one doesn't. For an always changing line-up of up-and-coming Japanese womenswear designers, check out the Tokyo Closet (2nd floor) and Re-Style (3rd floor) boutiques. Men get a whole building of their own (connected by a passageway). Don't miss the basement food hall, featuring famous purveyors of sweet and savoury goodies.

Don Quijote
GIFTS & SOUVENIRS

(ドン・キホーテ; Map p93; ☎03-5291-9211; www.donki.com; 1-16-5 Kabukichō, Shinjuku-ku; ⏰24hr; 🚉JR Yamanote line to Shinjuku, east exit)

This fluorescent-lit bargain castle is filled to the brink with weird loot. Chaotic piles of electronics and designer goods sit alongside sex toys, fetish costumes and packaged foods. Though it's now a national chain, it started as a rare (at the time) 24-hour store for the city's night workers.

Kinokuniya BOOKS
(紀伊國屋書店; Map p93; www.kinokuniya.co.jp; Takashimaya Times Sq, 5-24-2 Sendagaya, Shibuya-ku; ⊙10am-8pm; ᴙ JR Yamanote line to Shinjuku, south exit) The 6th floor here has a broad selection of foreign-language books and magazines, including many titles on Japan and English-teaching texts. Note that the rest of the store is currently closed for renovation.

🏯 Akihabara

Akihabara is the place to geek out on goods related to anime, manga, J-Pop and gaming. It's also known as the electronics district, though these days deals are hard to find. (Check prices in your home country online before buying big-ticket items here.) Surprisingly, Akihabara can also be a great place to shop for locally made souvenirs, thanks to the creative malls under the JR railway tracks heading north towards Ueno.

★ 2k540 Aki-Oka Artisan ARTS & CRAFTS
(アキオカアルチザン; Map p96; www.jrtk.jp/2k540; 5-9-23 Ueno, Taitō-ku; ⊙11am-7pm Thu-Tue; ᴙ Ginza line to Suehirochō, exit 2) This ace arcade located under the JR tracks (its name refers to the distance from Tokyo Station) offers an eclectic range of stores selling Japanese-made goods – everything from pottery and leatherwork to cute aliens, a nod to Akihabara from a mall that is more akin to Kyoto than Electric Town. The best for colourful crafts is **Nippon Hyakkuten** (日本百貨店; http://nippon-dept.jp).

★ Mandarake Complex MANGA, ANIME
(まんだらけコンプレックス; Map p96; www.mandarake.co.jp; 3-11-2 Soto-Kanda, Chiyoda-ku; ⊙noon-8pm; ᴙ JR Yamanote line to Akihabara, Electric Town exit) When *otaku* (geeks) dream of heaven, it probably looks like this giant go-to store for manga and anime. Eight storeys are piled high with comic books and DVDs, action figures and cell art just for starters. The 5th floor is devoted to women's comics, while the 4th floor is for men.

Chabara FOOD
(ちゃばら; Map p96; www.jrtk.jp/chabara; 8-2 Kanda Neribei-chō, Chiyoda-ku; ⊙11am-8pm; ᴙ JR

JIMBŌCHŌ

The neighbourhood **Jimbōchō** (Map p96; Kanda-Jimbōchō, Chiyoda-ku; Ⓢ Hanzōmon line to Jimbōchō, exits A1, A6 or A7) has more than 170 new and secondhand booksellers – proof that the printed word is alive and well in Tokyo. Amid tottering stacks of volumes, you'll find everything from antique guidebooks of the Yoshiwara pleasure district to obscure sheet music from your favourite symphony.

Recommended stores to target are **Ohya Shobō** (大屋書房; Map p96; ☎03-3291-0062; www.ohya-shobo.com; 1-1 Kanda-Jimbōchō, Chiyoda-ku; ⊙10am-6pm Mon-Sat; ᴙ Hanzōmon line to Jimbōchō, exit A7), purveyor of antique books, maps and original *ukiyo-e* prints, and **Komiyama Shoten** (小宮山書店; Map p96; ☎03-3291-0495; www.book-komiyama.co.jp; 1-7 Kanda-Jimbōchō, Chiyoda-ku; ⊙11am-6.30pm Mon-Sat, to 5.30pm Sun; Ⓢ Hanzōmon line to Jimbōchō, exit A7) for art books, prints and posters.

Yamanote line to Akihabara, Electric Town exit) This under-the-train-tracks shopping mall focuses on artisan food and drinks from across Japan, including premium sake, soy sauce, sweets, teas and crackers – all great souvenirs and presents.

mAAch ecute MALL
(Map p96; ☎03-3257-8910; www.maach-ecute.jp; 1-25-4 Kanda-Sudachō, Chiyoda-ku; ⊙11am-9pm Mon-Sat, to 8pm Sun; ᴙ Chūō or Sōbu lines to Akihabara, Electric Town exit) JR has another shopping and dining hit on its hands with this complex crafted from the old station and red-brick railway arches at Mansei-bashi. Crafts, homewares, fashions and food from across Japan are sold here; look for craft beers from **Hitachino Brewing Lab** and freshly roasted beans from **Obscura Coffee Roasters**.

Yodobashi Akiba ELECTRONICS
(ヨドバシカメラAkiba; Map p96; www.yodobashi-akiba.com; 1-1 Kanda Hanaoka-chō, Chiyoda-ku; ⊙9.30am-10pm; ᴙ JR Yamanote line to Akihabara, Shōwa-tōriguchi exit) This is the big branch of Yodobashi Camera where locals shop. It has eight floors of electronics, cameras, toys, appliances, CDs and DVDs on the 7th-floor branch of Tower Records, and even restaurants. Ask about export models and VAT-free purchases.

WORTH A TRIP

KAPPABASHI KITCHENWARE TOWN

Kappabashi-dōri (合羽橋通り; Map p106; Ⓢ Ginza line to Tawaramachi, exit 3) is the country's largest wholesale restaurant-supply and kitchenware district. Gourmet accessories include bamboo steamer baskets, lacquer trays, neon signs and *chōchin* (paper lanterns). It's also where restaurants get their freakishly realistic plastic food models.
Ganso Shokuhin Sample-ya (元祖食品サンプル屋; Map p106; ☎ 0120-17-1839; www.ganso-sample.com; 3-7-6 Nishi-Asakusa, Taitō-ku; ⊗ 10am-5.30pm; Ⓢ Ginza line to Tawaramachi, exit 3) has a showroom of tongue-in-cheek ones, plus key chains and kits to make your own.

Akihabara Radio Kaikan   MANGA, ANIME
(秋葉原ラジオ会館; Map p96; http://akihabara-radiokaikan.co.jp; 1-15-6 Soto-kanda, Chiyoda-ku; ⊗ 11am-8pm; Ⓡ JR Yamanote line to Akihabara, Electronic Town exit) Despite its name, Radio Kaikan has nothing to do with radios and everything to do with Japanese pop culture. It was completely rebuilt in 2014 to include nine floors of shops selling manga, anime, collectables such as models and figurines, fanzines, costumes and gear. Shops include **Volks** for dolls, **K-Books** (Kブックス; Map p96; www.k-books.co.jp) and **Kaiyōdō Hobby Lobby** (海洋堂ホビーロビー; Map p96; ☎ 03-3253-1951; www.kaiyodo.co.jp; ⊗ 11am-8pm Thu-Tue).

Ueno & Yanesen

★ **Ameya-yokochō**   MARKET
(アメヤ横町; Map p100; www.ameyoko.net; 4 Ueno, Taitō-ku; ⊗ 10am-7pm, some shops close Wed; Ⓡ JR lines to Okachimachi, north exit) Step into this partially open-air market paralleling and beneath the JR line tracks, and ritzy, glitzy Tokyo feels like a distant memory. It got its start as a black market, post-WWII, when American goods were sold here. Today, it's packed with vendors selling everything from fresh seafood and exotic cooking spices to jeans, sneakers and elaborately embroidered bomber jackets.

★ **Yanaka Matsunoya**   HOMEWARES
(谷中松野屋; Map p100; www.yanakamatsunoya.jp; 3-14-14 Nishi-Nippori, Arakawa-ku; ⊗ 11am-7pm Mon & Wed-Fri, 10am-7pm Sat & Sun; Ⓡ JR Yamanote line to Nippori, west exit) At the top of Yanaka Ginza (p102), Matsunoya sells household goods – baskets, brooms and canvas totes, for example – simple in beauty and form, and handmade by local artisans.

Edokoro Allan West   ART
(繪処アランウエスト; Map p100; ☎ 03-3827-1907; www.allanwest.jp; 1-6-17 Yanaka, Taitō-ku; ⊗ 1-5pm, from 3pm Sun, closed irregularly; Ⓢ Chiyoda line to Nezu, exit 1) **FREE** In this masterfully converted garage, long-time Yanaka resident Allan West paints gorgeous screens and scrolls in the traditional Japanese style, making his paints from scratch just as local artists have done for centuries. Smaller votive-shaped paintings start at ¥5000; the screens clock in at a cool ¥6 million.

Shokichi   ARTS & CRAFTS
(Map p100; ☎ 03-3821-1837; http://shokichi.main.jp; 3-2-6 Yanaka, Bunkyō-ku; ⊗ 10am-6pm Wed-Sun; Ⓢ Chiyoda line to Sendagi, exit 1) Mitsuaki Tsuyuki makes and sells his incredible hand puppets here – look out for lifelike renditions of Japanese celebs and, natch, Elvis. He can hand-make a portrait puppet from a photograph (¥40,000). Far more affordable are the quick portraits he draws via one of his hand puppets (¥1000).

Asakusa & Sumida River
浅草・隅田川

★ **Kakimori**   STATIONERY
(カキモリ; Map p72; ☎ 03-3864-3898; www.kakimori.com; 4-20-12 Kuramae, Taitō-ku; Ⓢ Asakusa line to Kuramae, exit 3) Stationery lovers flock from far and wide to this shop that allows you to custom build your own notebooks (from around ¥1000), choosing the paper, covers, binding and other bits and pieces to make a unique keepsake. It also stocks pens, pencils and 24 colours of ink by Japanese brand Pilot.

★ **Marugoto Nippon**   FOOD & DRINKS
(まるごとにっぽん; Map p106; ☎ 03-3845-0510; www.marugotonippon.com; 2-6-7 Asakusa, Taitō-ku; ⊗ 10am-8pm; Ⓢ Ginza line to Tawaramachi, exit 3) Think of this as a modern mini department store, showcasing the best of Japan's best in terms of speciality food and drink (ground floor) and arts and crafts (2nd floor). There are also plenty of tasting samples, and cafes and restaurants on the 3rd and 4th floors if you want something more substantial.

★ Tokyo Hotarudo
VINTAGE

(東京蛍堂; Map p106; ☑03-3845-7563; http://tokyohotarudo.com; 1-41-8 Asakusa, Taitō-ku; ⊙11am-8pm Wed-Sun; ⛟Tsukuba Express to Asakusa, exit 5) This curio shop is run by an eccentric young man who prefers to dress as if the 20th century hasn't come and gone already. If you think that sounds marvellous, then you'll want to check out his collection of vintage dresses and bags, antique lamps, watches and decorative *objet*.

The entrance is tricky: look for a vertical black sign with a pointing finger.

Kurodaya
STATIONERY

(黒田屋; Map p106; ☑03-3844-7511; 1-2-5 Asakusa, Taitō-ku; ⊙10am-6pm; ⛟Ginza line to Asakusa, exit 3) Since 1856, Kurodaya has been specialising in *washi* (traditional Japanese paper) and products made from paper such as cards, kites and papier-mâché folk-art figures. It sells its own designs and many others from across Japan.

Sumida City Point
ARTS & CRAFTS

(Map p106; ☑03-6796-6341; http://machidokoro.com; 5F Tokyo Skytree Town Solamachi, 1-1-2 Oshiage, Sumida-ku; ⊙10am-9pm; ⛟Hanzōmon line to Oshiage, exit B3) Promoting the many artisans and craft businesses of the Sumida ward area, this showroom sells locally made items, from cosmetics and fashion to soy sauce. There's a cafe where you can sample food specialities, watch craftspeople providing demonstrations, and ask the experts on hand to guide you to specific shops outside of the gravitational pull of the Sky Tree (p105).

Fujiya
ARTS & CRAFTS

(ふじ屋; Map p106; ☑03-3841-2283; www.asakusa-noren.ne.jp/tenugui-fujiya/sp.html; 2-2-15 Asakusa, Taitō-ku; ⊙10am-6pm Wed-Mon; ⛟Ginza line to Asakusa, exit 1) Fujiya specialises in *tenugui*: dyed cloths of thin cotton that can be used as tea towels, handkerchiefs, gift wrapping (the list goes on – they're surprisingly versatile). Here they come in traditional designs and humorous modern ones.

⌂ West Tokyo

Mandarake Complex
ANIME, MANGA

(まんだらけ; Map p110; www.mandarake.co.jp; 5-52-15 Nakano, Nakano-ku; ⊙noon-8pm; ⛟JR Sōbu-Chūō line to Nakano, north exit) This is the original Mandarake – the go-to store for all things manga and anime – and the origin of Nakano Broadway's transformation into a geek's paradise. Once a small, secondhand comic-book store, Mandarake now has 25 shops just inside Nakano Broadway. Each specialises in something different, be it books, cell art or figurines.

Kita-Kore Building
FASHION & ACCESSORIES

(キタコレビル; Map p110; 3-4-11 Kōenji-kita, Suginami-ku; ⊙1-8pm; ⛟JR Sōbu line to Kōenji, north exit) A must-see in Kōenji, the Kita-Kore Building is a dilapidated shack of a structure housing a handful of seriously outré shops. Really, it's more art installation than shopping destination, though we do know of at least one person who's actually bought stuff here – Lady Gaga.

ⓘ Orientation

Officially, central Tokyo is made up of 23 *ku* (wards). Unofficially, central Tokyo is whatever falls within the JR Yamanote line, the elevated rail loop that circles the city. Many of the stations on the Yamanote line are transit hubs and, as a result, are the most developed. A good many of the city's sights, accommodation, bars and restaurants lie in neighbourhoods on the loop, which include Marunouchi (Tokyo Station), Ebisu, Shibuya, Harajuku, Shinjuku, Akihabara and Ueno.

The Imperial Palace grounds form the city's incongruously verdant core. No roads pass through here, and no subways pass under, meaning that navigating the very centre of the city is necessarily a circuitous affair.

Tokyo is the antithesis of the neat grid, which can make it difficult to connect the dots without a map (smartphones are a lifesaver and fortunately Tokyo has more and more free wi-fi). Only major boulevards have names, though these sometimes change when the road bends or joins with another. Central neighbourhoods with significant tourist spots often have maps and street signs in English.

ⓘ Information

DANGERS & ANNOYANCES

The biggest threat to travellers in Tokyo is the city's general aura of safety. It's wise to keep up the same level of caution and common sense that you would back home. Of special note are reports that drink-spiking continues to be a problem in Roppongi (resulting in robbery, extortion and, in extreme cases, physical assault). Be wary of following touts into bars there and in Kabukichō; men are also likely to be solicited in both neighbourhoods. Women, especially those alone, walking through Kabukichō and Dōgenzaka (both are red-light districts) risk being harassed.

Twenty-four-hour staffed *kōban* (police boxes) are located near most major train stations.

INTERNET ACCESS

Tokyo now has more free wi-fi hot spots than it used to have, though the system still feels clunky. To avoid frustration, heavy users might consider renting a pocket internet device.

MEDICAL SERVICES

Seibo International Catholic Hospital (聖母病院; Map p72; ☑ 03-3951-1111; www.seibokai.or.jp; 2-5-1 Nakaochiai, Shinjuku-ku; ᴿ JR Yamanote line to Mejiro, main exit) and **St Luke's International Hospital** (聖路加国際病院; Seiroka Kokusai Byōin; Map p76; ☑ 03-3541-5151; http://hospital.luke.ac.jp; 9-1 Akashi-chō, Chūō-ku; ⓢ Hibiya line to Tsukiji, exits 3 & 4) both have some English-speaking doctors.

MONEY

It's easy to find cash in Tokyo: convenience stores and post offices with international ATMs are everywhere. While credit cards are widely accepted here, it's still a good idea to carry some cash on.

TELEPHONE

Data SIMs for unlocked smartphones can be purchased at kiosks in the arrivals terminals at both Narita and Haneda airports and also from major electronics stores, such as Bic Camera and Yodobashi Camera, in town.

TOURIST INFORMATION

Tokyo Metropolitan Government Building Tourist Information Center (Map p93; ☑ 03-5321-3077; 1st fl, Tokyo Metropolitan Government bldg 1, 2-8-1 Nishi-Shinjuku, Shinjuku-ku; ⊙ 9.30am-6.30pm; ⓢ Ōedo line to Tochōmae, exit A4) has English-language information and publications. Additional branches in Keisei

---

ⓘ LOST & FOUND

Larger train and subway stations have dedicated lost-and-found windows (labelled in English); otherwise lost items are left with the station attendant. Items not claimed on the same day will be handed over to the operator's lost-and-found centre. Items not claimed after several days are turned over to the police.

JR East Infoline (☑ in English 050-2016-1603; ⊙ 10am-6pm)

Toei Transportation Lost & Found (☑ 03-3816-5700; ⊙ 9am-8pm)

Tokyo Metro Lost & Found (Map p96; ☑ 03-5227-5741; www.tokyometro.jp/en/support/lost/index.html; ⊙ 9am-8pm) Office located inside Iidabashi Station on the Namboku line.

Ueno Station, Haneda Airport and Shinjuku Bus Terminal.

Note that Tourist Information Centers (TICs) cannot make accommodation bookings.

Asakusa Culture Tourist Information Center (p105) This ward-run TIC has lots of info on Asakusa and Ueno, and a Pia ticket counter (for purchasing tickets to concerts and shows), near the entrance to Sensō-ji.

Japan Guide Association (☑ 03-3863-2895; www.jga21c.or.jp) Can put you in contact with licensed, professional tour guides.

JNTO Tourist Information Center (Map p76; ☑ 03-3201-3331; www.jnto.go.jp; 1st fl, Shin-Tokyo Bldg, 3-3-1 Marunouchi, Chiyoda-ku; ⊙ 9am-5pm; ☎; ⓢ Chiyoda line to Nijūbashi-mae, exit 1) Run by the Japan National Tourism Organisation, this TIC has information on Tokyo and beyond. There are also branches in Narita Airport terminals 1 and 2.

JR East Travel Service Center (JR東日本訪日旅行センター; Map p76; www.jreast.co.jp/e/customer_support/service_center_tokyo.html; Tokyo Station, 1-9-1 Marunouchi, Chiyoda-ku; ⊙ 7.30am-8.30pm; ☎; ᴿ JR Yamanote line to Tokyo, Marunouchi north exit) Tourist information, money exchange, and bookings for ski and onsen getaways. There are branches in the two airports, too.

Moshi Moshi Box Harajuku Information Center (もしもしインフォメーションスペース; Map p90; 3-235 Jingūmae, Shibuya-ku; ☎; ᴿ JR Yamanote line to Harajuku, Omote-sandō) Area maps, luggage forwarding and travel help in English.

Tōbu Sightseeing Service Center (Map p106; ☑ 03-3841-2871; www.tobu.co.jp/foreign; Tōbu Asakusa Station, 1-4-1 Hanakawado, Taitō-ku; ⊙ 7.20am-7pm) Sells passes for Tōbu rail transport from Asakusa to Nikkō and unlimited hop-on, hop-off bus services around Nikkō.

Tokyo Tourist Information Center (Map p76; ☑ 03-3287-2955; 2-4-10 Yūrakuchō, Chiyoda-ku; ⊙ 11am-7.30pm Mon-Fri, 10am-7pm Sat & Sun; ☎; ᴿ JR Yamanote line to Yūrakuchō, Hibiya exit) Booking counters for tours, money exchange machines, wi-fi and a shop with a range of souvenirs.

USEFUL WEBSITES

Go Tokyo (www.gotokyo.org) The city's official website includes information on sights, events and suggested itineraries.

Lonely Planet (www.lonelyplanet.com/tokyo) Destination information, hotel bookings, traveller forum and more.

Time Out Tokyo (www.timeout.jp) Arts and entertainment listings.

Tokyo Food Page (www.bento.com) City-wide restaurant coverage.

Tokyo Cheapo (https://tokyocheapo.com) Hints on how to do Tokyo on the cheap.

ℹ Getting There & Away

AIR

Haneda Airport

Closer to central Tokyo, **Haneda Airport** (p891) has two domestic terminals and one international terminal. Note that some international flights arrive at awkward night-time hours, between midnight and 5am, when trains, buses and the monorail to central Tokyo will not be running. Keep in mind the price of a taxi (or the hours spent camped at the airport) when you book your ticket.

There's a **Tourist Information Center** (☎ 03-6428-0653; ⊙24hr; 🖥) in the international terminal, on the 2nd floor of the arrivals lobby.

Narita Airport

The excellent, modern **Narita Airport** (p891) is inconveniently located 66km east of Tokyo. There are three terminals (the new Terminal 3 handles low-cost carriers). Note that only terminals 1 and 2 have train stations. Free shuttle buses run between all the terminals every 15 to 30 minutes (from 7am to 9.30pm). Another free shuttle runs between Terminal 2 and Terminal 3 every five to 12 minutes (4.30am to 11.20pm); otherwise it is a 15-minute walk between the two terminals. All terminals have tourist information desks.

BUS

The easiest port of entry for travellers coming by bus from other parts of Japan is the new **Shinjuku Bus Terminal** (バスタ新宿; Busuta Shinjuku; Map p93; ☎ 03-6380-4794; http://shinjuku-busterminal.co.jp; 5-24-55 Sendagaya, Shibuya-ku; 🖥; 🚉 JR Yamanote line to Shinjuku, new south exit), part of the JR Shinjuku train station complex. There's a tourist information centre on the 3rd floor and direct access to JR rail lines on the 2nd floor.

CAR & MOTORCYCLE

Driving on the *shutokō*, the convoluted Tokyo city expressway, is not for the faint of heart. If you're arriving by rental car from other parts of Japan, it's advisable to return it on the outskirts of the city and take the train in the rest of the way.

TRAIN

Tokyo Station (p78) is the main point of entry for travellers coming via *shinkansen* (bullet train) from other parts of Japan. From Tokyo Station you can transfer to the JR Chūō and JR Yamanote lines as well as the Marunouchi subway line.

Coming from points west, if you're staying on the west side of the city, you can choose to get off one stop early, at Shinagawa, where you can connect to the JR Yamanote line. From points east, and if you're staying on the east side of the city, you can choose to get off one stop early, at Ueno; from Ueno you can transfer to the JR Yamanote line and the Ginza and Hibiya subway lines.

ℹ Getting Around

TO/FROM THE AIRPORT

Haneda Airport

Bus

Purchase tickets at the kiosks at the arrivals hall. In Tokyo, there's a ticket counter inside the **Shinjuku Bus Terminal** (p153).

Friendly Airport Limousine (www.limousine-bus.co.jp/en) Coaches connect Haneda with major train stations and hotels in Shibuya (¥1030), Shinjuku (¥1230), Roppongi (¥1130), Ginza (¥930) and others; fares double between midnight and 5am. Travel times vary wildly, taking anywhere from 30 to 90 minutes depending on traffic. Night buses depart for Shibuya Station at 12.15am, 12.50am and 2.20am and Shinjuku Bus Terminal at 12.20am and 1am; for Haneda, there is a bus from Shibuya Station at 3.30am and one from Shinjuku Bus Terminal at 4am. Regular service resumes at 5am.

Haneda Airport Express (http://hnd-bus.com) Though more useful for suburban destinations than downtown ones, coaches do travel to handy places such as Shibuya Station (¥1030) and Tokyo Station (¥930) in about an hour, depending on traffic, from 5am to midnight. Night buses depart for Shibuya Station (¥2600) via Roppongi Hills at 12.50am and 2.20am.

Monorail

Tokyo Monorail (www.tokyo-monorail.co.jp/english) leaves about every 10 minutes (5am to midnight) for Hamamatsuchō Station (¥490, 15 minutes), which is on the JR Yamanote line. Good if you're staying near Ginza or Roppongi.

Taxi

Fixed fares include Ginza (¥5600), Shibuya (¥6400), Shinjuku (¥6800), Ikebukuro (¥8500) and Asakusa (¥6900). There's a 20% surcharge between 10pm and 5am. Credit cards accepted.

Train

Keikyū Airport Express (www.haneda-tokyo-access.com/en) trains depart several times an hour (5.30am to midnight) for Shinagawa (¥410, 12 minutes), where you can connect to the JR Yamanote line. From Shinagawa, some trains continue along the Asakusa subway line, which serves Higashi-Ginza, Nihombashi and Asakusa stations.

Note that the international and domestic terminals have their own stations; when traveling to the airport, the international terminal is the second to last stop.

Narita Airport

Bus

Purchase tickets from kiosks in the arrivals hall (no advance reservations necessary). From Tokyo, there's a ticket counter inside the **Shin-juku Bus Terminal** (p153).

Friendly Airport Limousine (www.lim-ousinebus.co.jp/en) Scheduled, direct, reserved-seat buses (¥3100) depart from all Narita Airport terminals for major hotels and train stations in Tokyo. The journey takes 1½ to two hours depending on traffic. At the time of research, discount round-trip 'Welcome to Tokyo Limousine Bus Return Voucher' tickets (¥4500) were available for foreign tourists; ask at the ticket counter at the airport.

Keisei Tokyo Shuttle (www.keiseibus.co.jp) Discount buses connect all Narita Airport terminals and Tokyo Station (¥1000, approximately 90 minutes, every 20 minutes from 6am to 11pm). There are less frequent departures from Tokyo Station for Narita Airport terminals 2 and 3 between 11pm and 6am (¥2000), which are handy for budget flights at odd hours.

Train

Both Japan Railways (JR) and the independent Keisei line run between central Tokyo and Narita Airport terminals 1 and 2. For Terminal 3, take a train to Terminal 2 and then walk or take the free shuttle bus to Terminal 3 (and budget an extra 15 minutes). Tickets can be purchased in the basement of either terminal, where the entrances to the train stations are located.

Keisei Skyliner (www.keisei.co.jp/keisei/tetudou/skyliner/us) The quickest service into Tokyo runs nonstop to Nippori (¥2470, 36 minutes) and Ueno (¥2470, 41 minutes) stations, on the city's northeast side, where you can connect to the JR Yamanote line or the subway (Ueno Station only). Trains run twice an hour, 8am to 10pm. Foreign nationals can purchase advanced tickets online for slightly less (¥2200). The Skyliner & Tokyo Subway Ticket, which combines a one-way or round-trip ticket on the Skyliner and a one-, two- or three-day subway pass, is a good deal.

Keisei Main Line Limited-express trains (*kaisoku kyūkō*; ¥1030, 71 minutes to Ueno) follow the same route as the Skyliner but make stops. This is a good budget option. Trains run every 20 minutes during peak hours.

Narita Express (www.jreast.co.jp/e/nex) A swift and smooth option, especially if you're staying on the Tokyo's west side, N'EX trains depart Narita approximately every half-hour between 7am and 10pm for Tokyo Station (¥3020, 53 minutes) and Shinjuku (¥3190, 80 minutes); the latter also stops at Shibuya (¥3190; 75 minutes). Additional trains run to Shinagawa (¥3190, 65 minutes) and Ikebukuro (¥3190, 85 minutes). At the time of research, foreign tourists could purchase return N'EX tickets for ¥4000 (valid for 14 days; ¥2000 for under 12s). Check online or enquire at the JR East Travel Service centres at Narita Airport for the latest deals. Long-haul JR passes are valid on N'EX trains, but you must obtain a seat reservation (no extra charge) from a JR ticket office.

Taxi

Fixed-fare taxis run ¥20,000 to ¥22,000 for most stops in central Tokyo. There's a 20% surcharge between 10pm and 5am. Credit cards accepted.

BICYCLE

Tokyo is not a bicycle-friendly city. Bike lanes are almost nonexistent and you'll see no-parking signs for bikes everywhere (ignore these at your peril: your bike could get impounded, requiring a half-day excursion to the pound and a ¥3000 fee). Still,

---

❶ TOKYO TRANSPORT PASSES

Prepaid re-chargeable Suica and Pasmo cards work on all city trains, subways and buses. With either (they're essentially the same), you'll be able to breeze through the ticket gates of any station without having to work out fares or transfer tickets. Fares for pass users are also slightly less (a few yen per journey) than for paper-ticket holders.

The only reason not to get a Suica or Pasmo is to take advantage of Tokyo Metro's 24-hour unlimited ride pass (adult/child ¥600/300). Note that it is only good on the nine subway lines operated by Tokyo Metro. There are other (more expensive) passes that include rides on Toei subway and Tokyo-area JR lines, but the Tokyo Metro pass is the best deal.

Suica or Pasmo cards can be purchased from any touch-screen ticket-vending machines in Tokyo (including those at Haneda and Narita airports). Suica (available at JR stations) requires a minimum initial charge of ¥2000 (which includes a ¥500 deposit). Pasmo (available at subway and commuter line stations) requires a minimum initial charge of ¥1000 (which includes a ¥500 deposit). The deposit (along with any remaining charge) is refunded when you return the pass to any ticket window.

Both passes can be topped-up at any touch-screen ticket-vending machine (not just, for example, at JR stations for Suica passes) in increments of ¥1000. Ticket-vending machines have an English option so all of this is actually quite easy.

you'll see people cycling everywhere and it can be a fun way to get around. Some hostels and ryokan have bikes to lend. See **Rentabike** (http://rent-abike.jp) for places around town that rent bikes.

Cogi Cogi (http://cogicogi.jp; 24hr ¥2400) is a bike-sharing system with a growing number of ports around the city. There are instructions in English, but it's a little complicated to use and requires that you sign up in advance online and have wi-fi connection to sync with the ports.

BOAT

Tokyo Cruise (水上バス, Suijō Bus; ☎ 0120-977-311; http://suijobus.co.jp) water buses run up and down the Sumida-gawa (Sumida River), roughly twice an hour between 10am and 6pm, connecting Asakusa with Hama-rikyū Onshi-teien (¥980, 35 minutes) and Odaiba (¥1260, 70 minutes). Tickets can be purchased immediately before departure, if available, at any pier.

Tokyo Mizube Cruising Line (東京水辺ライン; ☎ 03-5608-8869; www.tokyo-park.or.jp/water-bus) water buses head down the Sumida-gawa from Asakusa to Ryōgoku (¥310), Hama-rikyū Onshi-teien (¥620) and Odaiba (¥1130), and then back up again. Schedules are seasonal, and infrequent in winter. Tickets can be purchased just before departure.

BUS

Toei (www.kotsu.metro.tokyo.jp/eng/services/bus.html) runs an extensive bus network, though in most cases it's easier to get around by subway.
➜ Fares are ¥210/110 per adult/child; there are no transfer tickets. Deposit your fare into the box as you enter the bus; there's a change machine at the front of the bus that accepts ¥1000 notes.
➜ Most buses have digital signage that switches between Japanese and English. A recording announces the name of the stops, so listen up and press the button when your stop is announced.

SUBWAY

Tokyo has 13 subway lines, nine of which are operated by **Tokyo Metro** (www.tokyometro.jp/en) and four by **Toei** (www.kotsu.metro.tokyo.jp/eng). The lines are colour-coded, making navigation fairly simple. Unfortunately a transfer ticket is required to change between the two; a Pasmo or Suica card makes this process seamless, but either way a journey involving more than one operator comes out costing more. Rides on Tokyo Metro cost ¥170 to ¥240 (¥90 to ¥120 for children) and on Toei ¥180 to ¥320 (¥90 to ¥160 for children), depending on how far you travel.

TRAIN

Tokyo's extensive rail network includes JR lines, a subway system and private commuter lines that depart in every direction for the suburbs, like spokes on a wheel. Trains arrive and depart precisely on time. Journeys that require transfers

ⓘ TOKYO NAVIGATION TIPS

➜ Figure out the best route to your destination with the Japan Travel app (https://navitimejapan.com); you can download routes to be used offline, too.

➜ Most train and subway stations have several different exits. Try to get your bearings and decide where to exit while still on the platform; look for the yellow signs that indicate which stairs lead to which exits.

➜ If you're not sure which exit to take, look for street maps of the area usually posted near the ticket gates, which show the locations of the exits.

between lines run by different operators cost more than journeys that use only one operator's lines. Major transit hubs include Tokyo, Shinagawa, Shibuya, Shinjuku, Ikebukuro and Ueno stations.

JR lines

The JR network covers the whole country and includes the *shinkansen* (bullet train). In Tokyo, the above-ground Yamanote (loop) and the Chūō–Sōbu (central) lines are most useful. Tickets start at ¥133 and go up depending on how far you travel.

Private lines

Private commuter lines service some of the hipper residential neighbourhoods. Useful trains:

Keiō Inokashira line (from Shibuya for Shimo-Kitazawa and Kichijōji)

Odakyū line (from Shinjuku for Shimo-Kitazawa)

Tōkyū-Tōyoko line (from Shibuya for Daikan-yama and Naka-Meguro)

The commuter lines run *tokkyū* (特急; limited-express services), *kyūkō* (急行; express) and *futsū* (普通; local) trains; when in doubt, take a local.

TAXI

Taxis in Tokyo feature white-gloved drivers, seats covered with lace doilies and doors that magically open and close – an experience in itself. They rarely make economic sense though, unless you have a group of four.
➜ Fares start at ¥730 for the first 2km, then rise by ¥90 for every 280m you travel (or for every 105 seconds spent in traffic).
➜ There's a surcharge of 20% between 10pm and 5am.
➜ Drivers rarely speak English, though fortunately most taxis now have navigation systems. It's a good idea to have your destination written down in Japanese, or better yet, a business card with an address.
➜ Most (but not all) taxis take credit cards.

Mt Fuji & Around Tokyo

Best Places to Eat

➡ Bonzō (p191)

➡ Araiya (p197)

➡ Gyōshintei (p205)

➡ Kawatoyo Honten (p208)

Best Places to Sleep

➡ K's House Itō Onsen (p177)

➡ Arai Ryokan (p184)

➡ KAI Hakone (p171)

Why Go?

With ancient sanctuaries, hot springs, mountains and beaches, the region surrounding Tokyo is a natural foil for the dizzying capital. Really, you couldn't design it any better if you tried.

Authentic country ryokan, regional cuisines and cedar-lined trails are all within two hours of central Tokyo, as well as the symbol of Japan itself, alluring Mt Fuji. There's history here too, including a medieval capital and ports that were among the first to open to the West. These are, for better or for worse, well-visited places and you'll find transport and communication to be a comparative breeze.

Ferries and flights also provide easy access to the Izu Islands, but if you're really looking to get away, then set sail for the World Heritage–listed Ogasawara Archipelago, some 1000km south from Tokyo, where you can spot whales, swim with dolphins and snorkel alongside green turtles and a rainbow of tropical fish.

When to Go
Kawaguchi-ko

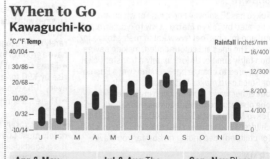

Apr & May Experience the flush of spring in the mountains north and west of Tokyo.

Jul & Aug The official season for Mt Fuji climbing and beach hopping around the Izu Peninsula.

Sep–Nov Pleasant temperatures and fewer crowds, save when the autumn leaves blaze red.

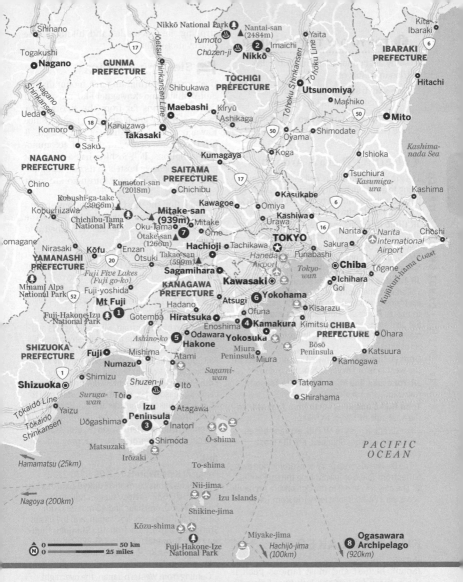

Mt Fuji & Around Tokyo Highlights

1 **Mt Fuji** (p159) Watching the sunrise from the majestic summit of Japan's highest mountain and national symbol.

2 **Nikkō** (p200) Taking in the grandeur of old Edo at the dazzling shrines and temple.

3 **Izu Peninsula** (p175) Flip-flopping between sandy beaches and hot springs.

4 **Kamakura** (p187) Resetting your senses in the Zen temples of Japan's medieval capital.

5 **Hakone** (p167) Hopping between onsen, art museums and hiking trails while enjoying gorgeous scenery.

6 **Yokohama** (p192) Sampling craft beer, contemporary art and jazz tunes in this port city.

7 **Mitake** (p199) Hiking at Mitake-san, on the mountainous and forested western edge of Tokyo.

8 **Ogasawara Archipelago** (p208) Getting back to nature on this pristine, subtropical island chain.

ⓘ TOKYO DAY TRIP PLANNER

Many destinations make possible day trips from Tokyo:

One-way travel up to an hour Yokohama, Kamakura, Mt Takao, Oku-Tama

One-way travel up to two hours Fuji Five Lakes, Hakone, Nikkō, Atami, Itō

ⓘ Getting There & Around

The greater Tokyo area is well served by trains going to and from the city; it's not as easy to get between places without having to double back to a transit hub. Useful train lines:

JR Chūō line Runs west from Tokyo; transfer at various stations for connecting trains to Takao-san, Oku-Tama and Fuji Five Lakes. The Chūō line continues to destinations in Nagano prefecture, but it's a long ride.

JR Tokaidō main line Runs south from Tokyo to Yokohama, then southwest to Odawara (transfer for trains to Hakone) and Atami, the gateway to the Izu Peninsula. Both Odawara and Atami are also stops on the Tokaidō *shinkansen* (bullet train), which continues west to Kyoto, Osaka and Hiroshima.

Odakyu line Runs southwest from Shinjuku, on the west side of Tokyo, to Hakone.

JR Yokosuka line Runs south from Tokyo to Kamakura via Yokohama.

Tobu Nikkō line Runs north from Asakusa, on the east side of Tokyo, to Nikkō.

For direct access to Mt Fuji, express buses, which depart from Shinjuku, are the most convenient.

The Izu Islands are a ferry or hydrofoil ride away, either from Tokyo or towns along the Izu Peninsula. The only way to get to the Ogasawara Archipelago is via a 24-hour-long ferry trip from Tokyo.

FUJI FIVE LAKES 富士五湖

☑ 0555

Japan's highest and most famous peak is the natural draw of the Fuji Five Lakes region, but even if you don't intend to climb Fuji-san, it's still worth coming to enjoy the visual and natural delights around the volcano's northern foothills; the five lakes here act as natural reflecting pools for the mountain's perfect cone.

Yamanaka-ko is the easternmost lake, followed by Kawaguchi-ko, Sai-ko, Shōji-ko and Motosu-ko. Particularly during the autumn *kōyō* (foliage) season, the lakes make a good overnight trip out of Tokyo for leisurely strolling, lake activities and hiking in the nearby mountains.

🛏 Sleeping & Eating

If you're not overnighting in a mountain hut, Fuji-Yoshida and Kawaguchi-ko make good bases. Most inns far from the station offer free pick-up if given advance notice. Since Kawaguchi-ko is the hub of the region, it has the greatest concentration of accommodation options. Fuji-Yoshida has a couple of great, inexpensive hostels in its old-fashioned little alleys. Sai-ko and Motosu-ko are great for camping.

You'll find the most dining options around Kawaguchi-ko and Fuji-Yoshida, while the lake areas are blessedly less developed and thus have fewer options.

Campers will want to bring their own provisions, picked up from Kawaguchi-ko or Fuji-Yoshida, or brought from Tokyo.

ⓘ Getting There & Away

The Fuji Five Lakes area is most easily reached from Tokyo by bus or train, with Fuji-Yoshida and Kawaguchi-ko being the principal gateways. It's also possible to bus in from Tokyo straight to the Fuji Subaru Line Fifth Station (alternatively known as Kawaguchi-ko Fifth Station or Yoshidaguchi Fifth Station) on the mountain during the official climbing season. If you want to combine travel to Mt Fuji and Hakone, consider the Fuji Hakone Pass (p170) from Tokyo.

Coming from Western Japan (Kyoto, Osaka), you can take an overnight bus to Kawaguchi-ko.

BUS

Frequent **Keiō Dentetsu** (☑ 03-5376-2222; www.highwaybus.com) and **Fujikyū Express** (☑ 0555-72-6877; http://bus-en.fujikyu.co.jp) buses (¥1750, one hour and 45 minutes) run directly to Kawaguchi-ko Station, and to Fujisan Station in Fuji-Yoshida, from the **Shinjuku Highway Bus Terminal** (☑ 03-5376-2222; http://highway-buses.jp; ☒ JR Yamanote Line to Shinjuku, west exit).

Coming from Western Japan, the overnight bus departs from Osaka's Higashi-Umeda Subway Station (¥8700, 10.15pm) via Kyoto Station (¥8200, 11.18pm) to Kawaguchi-ko Station (arrives 8.32am).

TRAIN

JR Chūō line trains go from Shinjuku to Ōtsuki (*tokkyū* ¥2770, one hour; *futsū* ¥1320, 1½ hours), where you transfer to the Fuji Kyūkō line for Fujisan (the station for Fuji-Yoshida; ¥1020, one hour) and Kawaguchi-ko (¥1140, one hour and five minutes).

ℹ Getting Around

From Fujisan Station it's an eight-minute bus ride (¥240) or five-minute train ride (¥220) to Kawaguchi-ko Station.

The **Kawaguchiko-Saiko Sightseeing Bus** (two-day passes adult/child ¥1200/600) has hop-on-hop-off service from Kawaguchi-ko Station to all of the sightseeing spots around the western lakes. The red line follows Kawaguchi-ko's northern shore and western area, while the green line heads south and around Sai-ko and Aokigahara. There's also an **All Lines Sightseeing Bus** (two-day passes adult/child ¥1500/750), covering the above routes, in addition to the blue line, which travels around Shōji-ko to the eastern end of Motosu-ko.

There's a **Toyota Rent-a-Car** (Map p160; ☑ 0555-72-1100, in English 0800-7000-815; ☺ 8am-8pm) a few minutes' walk from Kawaguchi-ko Station; head right from the station, turning right at the next intersection. **Sazanami** (さざなみ; Map p160; ☑ 0555-72-0041; ☺ 7am-5pm summer, 9am-5pm winter), on Kawaguchi-ko's southeast shore, rents bicycles (¥400/1500 per hour/day), electric pedal-assisted bicycles (¥600/2600 per hour/day) and rowing boats (¥1000/2500 per hour/day).

Mt Fuji   富士山

Of all Japan's iconic images, Mt Fuji (3776m) is the real deal. Admiration for the mountain appears in Japan's earliest recorded literature, dating from the 8th century. Back then the now dormant volcano was prone to spewing smoke, making it all the more revered. In 2013, the year Fuji-san was granted World Heritage status, some 300,000 people climbed the country's highest peak.

The Japanese proverb 'He who climbs Mt Fuji once is a wise man, he who climbs it twice is a fool' remains as valid as ever. While reaching the top brings a great sense of achievement (particularly at sunrise), be aware that it's a gruelling climb not known for its beautiful scenery or for being at one with nature. During the climbing season routes are packed, and its barren apocalyptic-looking landscape is a world away from Fuji's beauty when viewed from afar. At the summit, the crater has a circumference of 4km, but be prepared for it to be clouded over.

🏃 Trails

The mountain is divided into 10 'stations' from base (First Station) to summit (Tenth). From the base station is the original pilgrim trail, but these days most climbers start from the halfway point at one of the four Fifth Stations, all of which can be accessed via bus or car. The intersection of trails is not well marked and it's easy to get lost, particularly on the way down, ending up at the wrong exit point; this is a good reason to climb with experienced guides.

To time your arrival for dawn you can either start up in the afternoon, stay overnight in a mountain hut and continue early in the morning, or climb the whole way at night. You do not want to arrive on the top too long before dawn, as it will be very cold and windy, even at the height of summer.

Fifth Station Routes

Around 90% of climbers opt for these more convenient, faster routes. The four routes are Kawaguchi-ko, also known as Yoshida (2305m); Subashiri (1980m); Fujinomiya (2380m); and Gotemba (1440m). Allow five to six hours to reach the top (though some climb it in half the time) and about three hours to descend, plus 1½ hours for circling the crater at the top.

The **Kawaguchi-ko Trail** is by far and away the most popular route. It's accessed from Fuji Subaru Line Fifth Station (aka Kawaguchi-ko Fifth Station), and has the most modern facilities and is easiest to reach from Kawaguchi-ko town.

The less trodden, but more scenic, forested **Subashiri Trail** is a good alternative. As it merges with the Kawaguchi-ko Trail at the Eighth Station, it's possible to combine the two by heading up via the Kawaguchi-ko path and descending via Subashiri by schussing down its loose volcanic sand. Though be aware you'll end up at Subashiri Fifth Station, so it might not be an option if you've parked your car at Kawaguchi-ko Fifth Station.

Other Fifth Stations are **Fujinomiya**, which is best for climbers coming from the west (Nagoya, Kyoto and beyond) and the seldom-used and neglected **Gotemba Trail**, a tough 7½-hour climb to the summit.

Traditional Route

Historically, Fuji pilgrims began at Sengen-jinja near present-day Fuji-Yoshida, paying their homage to the shrine gods before beginning their 19km ascent up the sacred mountain. Today the **Yoshidaguchi Trail** offers climbers a chance to participate in this centuries-old tradition. Purists will tell you this is the only way to climb, saying that the lower reaches are the most beautiful, through lush forests along an isolated path.

Mt Fuji Area

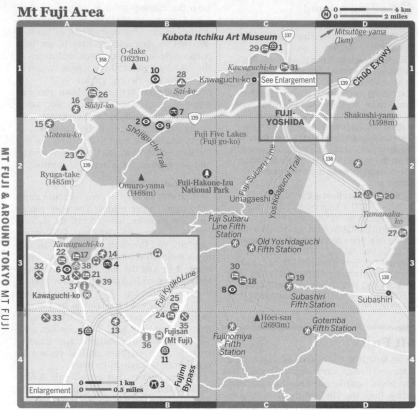

It takes about five hours to reach the old Yoshidaguchi Fifth Station – you can cut this by half by catching the climbing-season bus from Fujisan Station to Umagaeshi (¥500).

The trail meets up with the one leaving from the Fuji Subaru Line Fifth Station (also known as Kawaguchi-ko Fifth Station) at the Sixth Station. Count on around 12 hours to complete the climb from Fuji's base to summit.

Fuji Subaru Line Fifth Station

The road leading to the Fifth Station from Kawaguchi-ko, on the Fuji Subaru Line, stays open as long as the weather permits (from roughly mid-April to early December). Even when summiting is off-limits, it's still possible to take the bus here just to stand in awesome proximity to the snow-capped peak.

From roughly mid-May to late October, you can hike the flat Ochūdō (御中道) trail that

hugs the mountain at the tree line; it stretches 4km to Okuniwa (奥庭), where you'll have to double back. At either end of the climbing season, check conditions before setting out.

⛰ Tours

There are several reliable companies offering private tours with English-speaking guides.

Fuji Mountain Guides　　　　WALKING
(☑3-6883-4108; www.fujimountainguides.com/; 2-day Mt Fuji tours per person ¥44,000) Aimed at foreign visitors, these excellent tours are run both in and out of season by highly experienced and very professional American bilingual guides.

Discover Japan Tours　　　　TOURS
(www.discover-japan-tours.com/en; 2-day Mt Fuji tours per person ¥10,000) Reputable company offering guided tours from Tokyo for groups of two or more, and specialising in less-frequented routes.

Mt Fuji Area

MT FUJI & AROUND TOKYO MT FUJI

🛏 Sleeping & Eating

From the Fifth Stations up, dozens of mountain huts offer hikers simple hot meals in addition to a place to sleep. Most huts allow you to rest inside as long as you order something.

Conditions in mountain huts are spartan (a blanket on the floor sandwiched between other climbers), but reservations are recommended and are essential on weekends. It's also important to let huts know if you decide to cancel at the last minute; be prepared to pay to cover the cost of your no show.

Camping on the mountain is not permitted, other than at the designated campsite near the Fuji Subaru Line Fifth Station (aka Kawaguchi-ko Fifth Station).

Higashi Fuji Lodge　　　　　LODGE ¥
(東富士山荘; Map p160; ☑0555-75-2113; www4.tokai.or.jp/yamagoya; r ¥5000) This atmospheric rest hut at the Subashiri Fifth Station is convenient for off-season trekkers on Mt Fuji, and cooks up steaming soba (buckwheat noodles) with local mushrooms and Fuji herbs.

Fujisan Hotel　　　　　HUT ¥
(富士山ホテル; Map p160; ☑0555-22-0237; www.fujisanhotel.com; per person excl/incl 2 meals from ¥5950/8350) One of the largest and most popular rest huts open on Mt Fuji during the climbing season, the Fujisan Hotel is on the Kawaguchi-ko Trail. There are usually English-speaking staff here.

Taishikan　　　　　HUT ¥
(太子館; Map p160; ☑0555-22-1947; www.mfi.or.jp/w3/home0/taisikan; per person incl 2 meals from ¥8500) One of several rest huts open during the climbing season on Mt Fuji. There are usually English-speaking staff here, and vegetarian or halal meals are available if requested in advance.

ℹ Information

INTERNET

Free wi-fi is now available at Fifth Station access points and the summit, for 72 hours after you've acquired an access card at one of the Fifth Station information centres.

ℹ CLIMBING MT FUJI: KNOW BEFORE YOU GO

Make no mistake: Mt Fuji is a serious mountain, high enough for altitude sickness, and on the summit it can go from sunny and warm to wet, windy and cold remarkably quickly. Even if conditions are fine, you can count on it being close to freezing in the morning, even in summer. Also be aware that visibility can rapidly disappear with a blanket of mist rolling in suddenly.

At a minimum, bring clothing appropriate for cold and wet weather, including a hat and gloves. Also bring at least 2L of water (you can buy more on the mountain during the climbing season), as well as a map and snacks. If you're climbing at night, bring a torch (flashlight) or headlamp, and spare batteries. Also bring plenty of cash for buying snacks, other necessities and souvenirs from the mountain huts and to use their toilets (¥200).

Descending the mountain is much harder on the knees than ascending; hiking poles will help. To avoid altitude sickness, be sure to take it slowly and take regular breaks. If you're suffering severe symptoms, you'll need to make an immediate descent.

When to Climb

The official climbing season is from 1 July to 31 August. It's a busy mountain during these two months. To avoid the worst of the crush head up on a weekday, or start earlier during the day to avoid the afternoon rush and spend a night in a mountain hut.

Authorities strongly caution against climbing outside the regular season, when the weather is highly unpredictable and first-aid stations on the mountain are closed. Despite this, many people do climb out of season, as it's the best time to avoid the crowds. During this time, climbers generally head off at dawn, and return early afternoon – however, mountain huts on the Kawaguchi-ko Trail stay open through mid-September when weather conditions may still be good; a few open the last week of June, when snow still blankets the upper stations.

Outside of the climbing season, check weather conditions carefully before setting out (see www.snow-forecast.com/resorts/Mount-Fuji/6day/top), bring appropriate equipment, do not climb alone, and be prepared to retreat at any time. A guide will be invaluable.

Once snow or ice is on the mountain, Fuji becomes a very serious and dangerous undertaking and should only be attempted by those with winter mountaineering equipment and plenty of experience. It's highly advised that off-season climbers register with the local police department for safety reasons; fill out the form at the Kawaguchi-ko or Fuji-Yoshida Tourist Information Centers.

RESOURCES

Climbing Mt Fuji (www17.plala.or.jp/climb_fujiyama) and the Official Web Site for Mt Fuji Climbing (www.fujisan-climb.jp) are good online resources. The *Climbing Mt Fuji* brochure, available at the Fuji-Yoshida or Kawaguchi-ko Tourist Information Centers, is also worth picking up.

ℹ Getting There & Around

For those wanting to start trekking as soon as they arrive from Tokyo, **Keiō Dentetsu Bus** (p158) runs direct buses (¥2700, 2½ hours; reservations necessary) from the **Shinjuku Highway Bus Terminal** (p158) to Fuji Subaru Line Fifth Station (aka Kawaguchi-ko Fifth Station; it does not operate in winter).

Buses run from both Kawaguchi-ko Station and Fujisan Station to the starting point at Fuji Subaru Line Fifth Station (one way/return ¥1540/2100, one hour) roughly mid-April to early December. In the trekking season, buses depart hourly from around 6.30am until 7pm (ideal for climbers intending to make an overnight ascent). Returning from Fifth Station, buses head back to town from 8am to 8.30pm.

In the off-season, the first bus inconveniently leaves Kawaguchi-ko and Fujisan Stations at 8.40am, and the last bus returns at 6.15pm, meaning most trekkers will need to get a taxi in the morning to have enough time (around ¥12,000, plus ¥2100 in tolls), before getting the bus back. The bus schedule is highly seasonal; call **Fujikyū Yamanashi bus** (p158) or your hotel for details.

In the low season you should be able to find other trekkers to share a taxi at **K's House** (p165). Car hire is another option (particularly good if you're in a group), costing around ¥6800 per day plus fuel and tolls.

To get to the Subashiri Fifth Station trail, you can catch a bus from Kawaguchi-ko to Gotemba (¥1510), from where regular buses head to the Subashiri access point; Gotemba can also be accessed directly from Tokyo either by bus or train.

Fuji-Yoshida 富士吉田

☑ 0555 / POP 49,024

One of the main gateway towns for the Fuji Five Lakes area, Fuji-Yoshida is the location of the original inns that pilgrims stayed at before ascending Fuji. Its central district, Gekkō-ji, feels like the little town that time forgot, with original mid-20th-century facades. Fujisan Station is in the centre of Fuji-Yoshida. Pick up a map at the tourist information centre (p164) here to get oriented. But if you're heading straight to one of the hostels, the closer stop is Gekkō-ji (月江寺).

◉ Sights & Activities

Fuji Sengen-jinja SHINTO SHRINE
(富士浅間神社; Map p160; ☑ 0555-22-0221; http://sengenjinja.jp; 5558 Kami-Yoshida, Fuji-Yoshida; ⊘ grounds 24hr, staffed 9am-5pm) FREE A necessary preliminary to the Mt Fuji ascent is a visit to this deeply wooded, atmospheric temple, which has been located here since the 8th century. Notable points include a 1000-year-old cedar; its main gate, which is rebuilt every 60 years (slightly larger each time); and its two 1-tonne *mikoshi* (portable shrines) used in the annual festival Yoshida no Himatsuri (p163). From Fujisan Station it's a 20-minute uphill walk, or take a bus to Sengen-jinja-mae (¥150, five minutes).

Togawa-ke Oshi-no-ie
Restored Pilgrim's Inn HISTORIC BUILDING
(御師旧外川家住宅; Map p160; 3-14-8 Kami-Yoshida; adult/child ¥100/50; ⊘ 9.30am-4.30pm Wed-Mon) Fuji-Yoshida's *oshi-no-ie* (pilgrims' inns) have served visitors to the mountain since the days when climbing Mt Fuji was a pilgrimage rather than a tourist event. Very few still function as inns but Togawa-ke Oshi-no-ie offers some insight into the fascinating Edo-era practice of Mt Fuji worship.

Fuji-Q Highland AMUSEMENT PARK
(Map p160; www.fujiq.jp/en; 5-6-1 Shin-Nishihara; admission only adult/child ¥1500/900, day passes ¥5700/4300; ⊘ 9am-5pm Mon-Fri, to 8pm Sat & Sun) As well as a high-octane amusement park with spectacular roller coasters providing a memorable way to bag Fuji views, Fuji-Q's compound is home to Thomas Land (a theme park based on Thomas the Tank Engine), a resort hotel, onsen and shops. Fun for all the family, one stop west of Fujisan Station.

🎎 Festivals & Events

Yoshida no Himatsuri CULTURAL
(Yoshida Fire Festival; ⊘ 26-27 Aug) This annual festival is held to mark the end of the climbing season and to offer thanks for the safety of the year's climbers. The first day involves a *mikoshi* procession and the lighting of bonfires on Fuji-Yoshida's main street. On the second day, the focus is Sengen-jinja.

🛏 Sleeping & Eating

Fuji-Yoshida is known for its *te-uchi udon* (handmade wheat-flour noodles); some 60 shops sell them! The Fuji-Yoshida Tourist Information Center (p164) has a map and a list of restaurants.

Maisan-chi GUESTHOUSE ¥
(Map p160; ☑ 0555-24-5328; http://maisanchi.jimdo.com; 4-6-46 Shimo-Yoshida; dm/d with shared bathroom, incl breakfast ¥2900/6200; 🐾) On a backstreet and doubling up as a charming cafe specialising in desserts, this old Japanese-style building offers simple, friendly tatami-mat rooms and a dorm with bunk beds. At the time of research they had closed the guesthouse indefinitely for renovations – email ahead of your trip for an update.

Mt Fuji Hostel Michael's HOSTEL ¥
(Map p160; ☑ 0555-72-9139; www.mfi.or.jp/mtfujihostel; 2F 3-21-37 Shimo-Yoshida; dm/s/d ¥3000/3600/7200; ⊜❋🐾) Though this efficiently run, clean, modern Western-style hostel has no self catering facilities or common space, it's upstairs from the expat and local favourite **Michael's American Pub** (マイケルズアメリカンパブ; Map p160; ☑ 0555-24-3917; 3-21-37 Shimo-Yoshida; meals ¥600-1200; ⊘ 11.30am-4pm Sun-Fri, 7pm-2am Fri-Wed; 🅿), which serves reasonably priced Western and Japanese food. The English-speaking staff can also recommend some great local eateries.

Sakurada Udon JAPANESE ¥
(桜井うどん; Map p160; 5-1-33 Shimo-Yoshida; noodles ¥350; ⊘ 10am-2pm Mon-Sat) Just off the main drag, this tiny shop is a good spot to sample the local *te-uchi udon* while sitting cross-legged on tatami. Look for the blue *noren* (curtains) next to the Status Pub.

Izumiya JAPANESE ¥¥
(いづみや; Map p160; ☑ 0555-23-0270; 4-14-7 Shimo-Yoshida; meals ¥1200; ⊘ 11.30am-2.30pm & 5-9pm; 🅿) This friendly, family-run spot serves tasty, unfussy Japanese dishes including udon

and tempura, which you can enjoy seated either Japanese-style or at a Western-style table.

ℹ Information

Fuji-Yoshida Tourist Information Center
(Map p160; ☑ 0555-22-7000; ⊘ 9am-5pm)
Next to Fujisan (Mt Fuji) train station, the clued-up staff can provide info on climbing, and brochures and maps of the area.

Kawaguchi-ko　河口湖

☑ 0555 / POP 25,341

Even if you have no plans to climb Mt Fuji, the sprawling town of Kawaguchi-ko, set around the lake of the same name, is a great spot to hang out and enjoy what the Fuji Five Lakes region has to offer, including great mountain views. Also enquire with the tourist office about several public onsen in the area, for which they may have discount coupons.

◉ Sights & Activities

★ **Kubota Itchiku Art Museum**　MUSEUM
(久保田一竹美術館; Map p160; ☑ 0555-76-8811; www.itchiku-museum.com; 2255 Kawaguchi; adult/child ¥1300/400; ⊘ 9.30am-5.30pm Wed-Mon Apr-Nov, 10am-4.30pm Wed-Mon Dec-Mar) In an attractive Gaudí-influenced building, this excellent museum exhibits the kimono art of Kubota Itchiku (1917–2003). A small number of lavishly dyed kimonos from his life's work of continuous landscapes are displayed at any one time, in a grand hall of cypress.

You might see Mt Fuji in the wintertime, or the cherry blossoms of spring spread across oversized kimonos that have been painstakingly and intricately dyed, embroidered and hand-painted. Take the bus to the Kubota Itchiku Bijyutsukan-mae stop.

Fuji Viewing Platform　VIEWPOINT
(Map p160) If you're a Fuji admirer but not a hiker, consider this viewing platform, a popular way to go in Kawaguchi-ko. Weather permitting, your ride up the Kachi Kachi Yama Ropeway (p165) will reward you with dramatic views from the platform at the top (1104m).

Fujisan World Heritage Center　MUSEUM
(富士ビジターセンター; Map p160; ☑ 72-0259; www.fujisan-whc.jp; 6663-1 Funatsu; adult/child ¥420/free; ⊘ 8.30am-5pm, to 6pm or 7pm in peak season) Get up to speed on Mt Fuji at the new South Hall of this visitor centre. Its circular, beautifully designed exhibition hall features interpretive displays detailing the spiritual and geological history of the mountain (most accompanied by excellent English-language translations). Upstairs, you can view a gorgeously shot, eight-minute video (with sparse English subtitles), complete with mood lighting. An observation deck at the North Hall (free) affords great views of Mt Fuji.

Ide Sake Brewery　BREWERY
(Map p160; ☑ 0555-72-0006; www.kainokaiun.jp; 8 Funatsu; tours ¥500) Using the spring waters

---

BEST MT FUJI VIEWPOINTS

Mt Fuji has many different personalities depending on the season. Winter and spring months are your best bet for seeing it in all its clichéd glory; however, even during these times the snowcapped peak may be visible only in the morning before it retreats behind its cloud curtain. Its elusiveness, however, is part of the appeal, making sightings all the more special. Here are some of our top spots for viewing, both in the immediate and greater area:

Kawaguchi-ko On the north side of the lake, where Fuji looms large over its shimmering reflection.

Motosu-ko The famous view depicted on the ¥1000 bill can be seen from the northwest side of the lake.

Hakone The mountain soars in the background of Ashino-ko and the red *torii* (shrine gate) rising from the water.

Izu Peninsula Journey along the west coast to catch glimpses of Fuji and the ocean, bathed in glorious sunsets.

Panorama-dai (p167) The end of this hiking trail rewards you with a magnificent front-on view of the mountain.

Kōyō-dai (Map p160) Mt Fuji can be seen from this lookout, particularly stunning in the autumn colours.

from Mt Fuji, this small-scale sake brewery has been producing Japan's favourite tipple for 21 generations. Tours (9.30am and 3pm; around 40 minutes) provide a fascinating insight into the production process and include tastings of various sakes with a souvenir glass. Tours can be given in English, but reservations are essential.

Kachi Kachi Yama Ropeway   CABLE CAR

(カチカチ山ロープウェイ; Map p160; www. kachikachiyama-ropeway.com; 1163-1 Azagawa; one way/return adult ¥450/800, child ¥230/400; ⊙9am-5pm) On the lower eastern edge of the lake, this ropeway runs to the Fuji Viewing Platform (p164). If you have time, consider making the six-hour return hike from here to **Mitsutōge-yama** (三つ峠山; 1785m); it's an old trail with excellent Fuji views. Ask at Kawaguchi-ko Tourist Information Center (p166) for a map.

🛏 Sleeping

★K's House Mt Fuji   HOSTEL ¥

(Map p160; ☑0555-83-5556; http://kshouse.jp; 6713-108 Funatsu; dm from ¥2500, d with/without bathroom from ¥8800/7200; P ⊜@🛜) K's is expert at providing a welcoming atmosphere, spacious Japanese-style rooms and helpful English-speaking staff. There's a fully loaded kitchen, mountain bikes for hire, comfy common areas to meet fellow travellers/climbers and free pick-up from Kawaguchi-ko Station. Its bar, **Zero Station** (Map p160; ☑0555-72-9525; 6713-120 Funatsu; ⊙6pm-midnight), is stumbling distance away. Rooms fill up fast during the climbing season.

Kawaguchi-ko Station Inn   HOSTEL ¥

(河口湖ステーションイン; Map p160; ☑0555-72-0015; www.st-inn.com/english; 3639-2 Funatsu; dm/s/d ¥2800/4320/8700; P 🌢🛜) That pale-yellow building across from Kawaguchi-ko station is a spotless hostel offering mixed dorms (some with Fuji views), laundry facilities, English-speaking staff and a top-floor bath looking out to Mt Fuji in the distance. There's an 11.30pm curfew.

Tominoko Hotel   HOTEL ¥¥

(富ノ湖ホテル; Map p160; ☑72-5080; www. tominoko.net; 55 Asakawa; r per person incl 2 meals from ¥8925; P 🌢@🛜) Given its views of Fuji across the lake, this place is a steal. Rooms are modern, smart Western-style twins with plenty of space, and all guest rooms face the lake. Ask for one on an upper level to score a balcony. Also has a *rotemburo* (outdoor bath).

Sunnide Resort   HOTEL ¥¥

(サニーデリゾート; Map p160; ☑76-6004; www.sunnide.com; 2549-1 Ōishi; r per person incl 2 meals from ¥13,000, cottages excl meals from ¥13,000; P ⊜🌢@🛜) Offering views of Mt Fuji from the far side of Kawaguchi-ko, friendly Sunnide has hotel rooms and cottages with a delicious outdoor bath. You can splash out on the stylish suites or go for the discounted 'backpacker' rates (¥4400, no views), if same-day rooms are available. Note that in winter a heating surcharge of ¥3000 is tacked on to cottage rates.

★Kozantei Ubuya   RYOKAN ¥¥¥

(湖山亭うぶや; Map p160; ☑0555-72-1145; www.ubuya.co.jp; 10 Asakawa; r per person incl 2 meals from ¥20,100; P ⊜🌢@🛜) Elegant and ultra stylish, Ubuya offers unobstructed panoramic views of Mt Fuji reflected in Kawaguchi-ko that are simply unbeatable. Splash out on the more expensive suites to enjoy the scene while soaking in an outdoor tub on your balcony decking. One for the honeymooners.

Fuji Lake Hotel   HOTEL ¥¥¥

(富士レークホテル; Map p160; ☑0555-72-2209; www.fujilake.co.jp; 1 Funatsu; r per person incl 2 meals from ¥12,960; P 🌢@🛜) Located on Kawaguchi-ko's south shore, this stylish 1935 vintage hotel offers either Mt Fuji or lake views from its Japanese-Western combo rooms. Some rooms have a private *rotemburo* (outdoor bath); otherwise there's a common onsen.

🍴 Eating & Drinking

While in Kawaguchi-ko, be sure to try some *hōtō*, the local noodle speciality.

Akai   IZAKAYA ¥

(赤井; Map p160; ☑0555-72-5259; 1322-7 Funatsu; mains from ¥430; ⊙6-11pm Fri-Wed; 🍴) Great little *izakaya* (pub-eatery) serving sensational whole grilled fish and various *yaki-soba* (fried noodles). It's off Rte 137, behind the petrol station near the Ogino supermarket.

Idaten   TEMPURA ¥¥

(いだ天; Map p160; ☑0555-73-9218; 3486-4 Funatsu; meals from ¥800; ⊙11am-10pm; 🍴) Load up on some delicious, deep-fried goodness pre- or posthike at the Idaten counter, where you can watch the chefs prepare your tempura to order. Aside from Fujisan-themed lunch and dinner sets, you can also order a la carte (various vegetables are ¥90 to ¥180 apiece; a crab leg is ¥1000).

Hōtō Fudō
NOODLES ¥¥

(ほうとう不動; Map p160; ☎0555-72-8511; www.houtou-fudou.jp; 707 Kawaguchi; hōtō ¥1080; ☺11am-7pm; 🅿) Hōtō are Kawaguchi-ko's local noodles, hand-cut and served in a thick miso stew with pumpkin, sweet potato and other vegetables. It's a hearty meal best sampled at this chain with five branches around town. This is the most architecturally interesting one, an igloo-like building in which you can also sample basashi – horsemeat sashimi (¥1080).

Mt Fuji Base
BAR

(Map p160; ☎090-1699-0319; 3646-1 Funatsu; dishes ¥450-900; ☺11am-midnight Wed-Mon) While the army-base theme may not be your jam, all the camo decor here is balanced by petite potted plants on tables and the usual friendly Japanese hospitality you'll find in closet-sized cafes all over Japan. This is a great place for a bowl of ramen or a cocktail after a hike, with a fun crowd at any hour.

ℹ️ Information

Kawaguchi-ko Tourist Information Center (Map p160; ☎0555-72-6700; ☺8.30am-5.30pm Sun-Fri, to 7pm Sat), to the right as you exit Kawaguchi-ko Station, has English speakers as well as maps and brochures. It's always busy, so take a number and peruse brochures while you wait.

Sai-ko
紅葉台

Sai-ko is a quiet lake area good for hiking, fishing and boating. Mt Fuji is mostly obstructed but there are great views from the Kōyō-dai lookout, near the main road, and from the western end of the lake.

Sai-ko is served by the green line of the Kawaguchiko-Saiko Sightseeing Bus.

◉ Sights

Fugaku Fuketsu
CAVE

(富岳風穴; Map p160; ☎0555-85-2300; 2068-1 Aokigahara; adult/child ¥350/150; ☺9am-4.30pm) The Wind Cave (also known as the Lava Cave) was used to store silk-worm cocoons in the past. A combination ticket for this and Narusawa Hyōketsu is a good deal, as they're a 15-minute walk from one another.

Narusawa Hyōketsu
CAVE

(鳴沢氷穴; Map p160; ☎0555-85-2301; 8533 Narusawa-mura; adult/child ¥350/200; ☺9am-5pm) Not for the claustrophobic, the Narusawa Hyōketsu (ice cave) was formed by lava flows from an eruption of Mt Fuji in 864. It takes about 10 minutes to walk through to the end to see the ice pillars, which are at their peak in April (no ice from September to December). A 15-minute walk down the road is the similar Fugaku Fukestu.

Sai-ko
Iyashi-no-Sato Nenba
CULTURAL CENTRE

(西湖いやしの里根場; Map p160; ☎0555-20-4677; 2710 Nenba; adult/child ¥350/150; ☺9am-5pm) Built in 2006 on the site of historic thatched-roof houses washed away in a typhoon 40 years earlier, these reconstructed frames offer an insight into a forgotten time. There are demonstrations of silk and paper crafts as well as restaurants specialising in soba and hōtō. The green-line bus stops right out front.

🛏️ Sleeping & Eating

Saiko Camp Village Gnome
CAMPGROUND ¥

(西湖キャンプビレッジノーム; Map p160; ☎0555-82-2650; http://www.greatoutdoors.jp/Gnome/Welcome.html; 1030 Saiko; camping per person from ¥1000, 2-night tent rental ¥5000; 🖭) Ex-model and outdoors author Tokichi Kimura is the convivial English-speaking owner of this pleasant lakeside campsite opposite the Hamayou Resort; there are barbecue facilities, a simple cafe with wi-fi, and canoe rental (¥3000, three hours).

Shōji-ko
精進湖

☎0555 / POP 257

Further west from Sai-ko, low-key and tiny Shōji-ko is said to be the prettiest of the Fuji lakes and offers Mt Fuji views, fishing and boating.

Shōji-ko is served by blue-line buses from Kawaguchi-ko Station.

🛏️ Sleeping & Eating

There are a couple of restaurants at the tourist information area on the north side of the lake.

Murahamasō
MINSHUKU ¥¥

(村浜荘; Map p160; ☎0555-87-2436; www.murahamasou.com; 807 Shōji; r per person incl 2 meals ¥7500; 🖭) Traditional lodgings on quiet Shōji-ko where some rooms have lake and mountain (not Fuji) views and all have shared bathrooms. Some English is spoken. Find it near the Shōji-ko bus stop.

Motosu-ko 本栖湖

0555, 0556 / POP 134

For a preview of Motosu-ko, look at the ¥1000 bill to see an image of Mt Fuji rising majestically from the north shore. This is also naturally a popular setting for outdoor activities, including hiking to panoramic vista points, and recreation on and in the lake.

Blue-line buses from Kawaguchi-ko Station go as far as the east shore of Motosu-ko before heading back to the station.

🏃 Activities

Panorama-dai HIKING

(パノラマ台; Map p160) This trail ends in a spectacular, head-on view of Mt Fuji and, as advertised, panoramic views of the surrounding lakes and mountains. Midway through, stop at the signed viewpoint to spot Fuji-san between the trees. It's a one-hour hike through the woods from the trailhead, which starts at the Panorama-dai-shita bus stop. Take a blue-line bus (38 minutes from Kawaguchi-ko).

Kōan Motosu WATER SPORTS

(Map p160; 0556-38-0117; www6.nns.ne.jp/~k-ouan; 2926 Nakanokura; ⊙8am-4pm) Kōan Motosu offers paddleboarding (¥1500/4000 per hour/day), kayaking (¥2000 per person, one hour) and even scuba diving in the lake!

🛌 Sleeping & Eating

Kōan Motosu Inn CAMPGROUND ¥

(Map p160; 0556-38-0117; www6.nns.ne.jp/~k-ouan; 2926 Nakanokura; camping per person ¥600, tent rental ¥1000, 6-person cabin from ¥17,280) Kōan has two campgrounds on the lake, this one with Fuji views, a jacuzzi, a helpful English-speaking owner and an attached restaurant and shop, as well as cabins should you not wish to camp. It's a short walk downhill from the Tourist Information Center. Its second site occupies a more shaded forest area on the far west side of the lake.

Lake Motosu Campground CAMPGROUND ¥

(本栖湖キャンプ場; Map p160; 0555-87-2306; 18 Motosu; camping ¥3000, 4-/6-person bungalow ¥5250/6300) For those without a tent, this place also offers simple tatami-mat bungalows set in a wooded area on the lake, with campfires, shared bathroom blocks and a shop selling snacks, beer and camping items. Futon rental is ¥620 per set and no English is spoken. It's on the main road, about 300m on the left from the lake entrance.

Yamanaka-ko 山中湖村

The region's largest lake, Yamanaka-ko, is popular with locals. The southern shore is overdeveloped and has a tourist-trap feel but the northern side is more appealing with a sleepier vibe. One of the reasons to visit is for a soak at Benifuji-no-yu onsen.

The economical Sightseeing Bus pass (two-days ¥1340) for the Fuji-Yoshida and Yamanaka-ko areas can be bought at Fujisan Station or at the Asahigaoka Bus Terminal.

🏃 Activities

Benifuji-no-yu ONSEN

(山中湖温泉紅富士の湯; Map p160; 0555-20-2700; www.benifuji.co.jp; adult/child ¥800/300, face/bath towel rental ¥220/100; ⊙10am-9pm) Ignore the faded facade of this onsen near Yamanaka-ko. Inside, the views improve dramatically when Mt Fuji is clear in sight as you soak in the outdoor stone and *hinoki* (cypress) baths. If you'd like to dine here as well (meals from ¥3200), you'll have to reserve in advance.

🛌 Sleeping

Hotorinite GUESTHOUSE ¥

(ホトリニテ; Map p160; 0555-62-0548; 1464 Yamanaka-ko; r per person ¥3990; ☻❄@🛜) A beautiful refuge near Fuji-san, this warm, welcoming guesthouse is operated by an English-speaking owner who lends out bicycles and gives excellent local advice.

PICA Yamanaka-ko Village CABIN ¥¥

(PICA山中湖ヴィレッジ; Map p160; 0555-62-4155; yamanakako.pica-village.jp; 506-296 Hirano; 6-person cottage from ¥17,100; 🛜) On Yamanaka-ko's southern shore, this is a nicely designed complex of wooden cottages of varying sizes in a garden setting with attached restaurants, gift shop and a very popular hammock cafe. There are other PICA camps near Fuji-Yoshida and Sai-ko – see the website for details.

HAKONE 箱根

0460 / POP 11,717

Offering serene onsen, world-class art museums, traditional inns and spectacular mountain scenery crowned by Mt Fuji, Hakone can make for a blissful escape from Tokyo. Ashino-ko (芦ノ湖) is the lake at the centre of it all, the setting for the iconic image of

Hakone

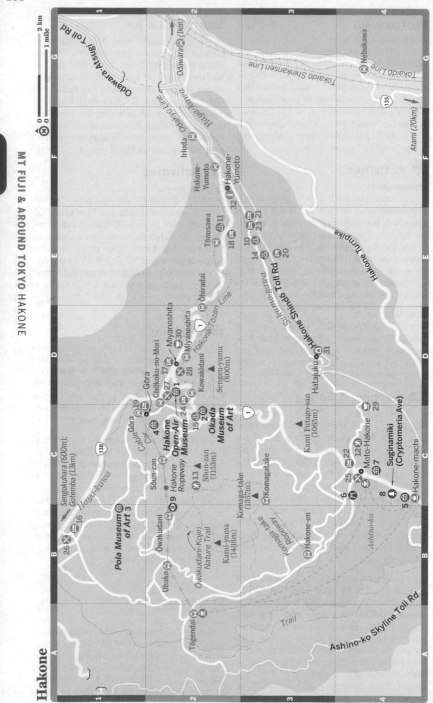

Hakone

Mt Fuji with the *torii* of Hakone-jinja rising from the water.

Naturally, this is all quite attractive, so it can feel crammed, particularly at weekends and holidays. If you follow the herd, it can also feel highly packaged. To beat the crowds, plan your trip during the week, go hiking and sample some of Hakone's offbeat gems.

◉ Information

LUGGAGE FORWARDING

At Hakone-Yumoto Station, deposit your luggage with **Hakone Baggage Delivery Service** (箱根キャリーサービス; Map p168; ☑ 0460-86-4140; 2nd fl, Hakone-Yumoto Station; per piece from ¥800; ⊙ 8.30am-7pm) by 12.30pm, and it will be delivered to your inn within Hakone from 3pm. Alternatively, you can check your bag at your inn by 10am and pick it up after 1pm at Hakone-Yumoto Station. Hakone Freepass holders get a discount of ¥100 per bag.

TOURIST INFORMATION

Try www.hakone.or.jp/en for online information. **Hakone-Yumoto Tourist Information Center** (Map p168; ☑ 0460-85-8911; www.hakone. or.jp; ⊙ 9am-5.45pm) Make your first stop at the most clued-up of several tourist information

centres scattered around Hakone. This is the best place for maps and information about hiking trails and all the attractions. Staffed by helpful English speakers, it's across the main road from the train station.

◉ Getting There & Away

The Odakyū line (www.odakyu.jp) from Shinjuku Station goes directly into Hakone-Yumoto, the region's transit hub. Use either the convenient Romance Car (¥2080, 90 minutes) or *kyūkō* (regular-express) service (¥1190, two hours); the latter may require a transfer at Odawara.

JR Pass holders can take the Kodama *shin-kansen* (¥3880, 50 minutes) or the JR Tōkaidō line (*futsū* ¥1790, one hour; *tokkyū* ¥2390, one hour) from Tokyo Station or the Shōnan-Shinjuku line from Shinjuku (¥1490, 80 minutes) to Odawara and change there for trains or buses for Hakone-Yumoto.

◉ Getting Around

Part of Hakone's popularity comes from the chance to ride assorted *norimono* (modes of transport): switchback train, cable car (funicular), ropeway (gondola), ship and bus.

The narrow-gauge, switchback Hakone-Tōzan line runs from Hakone-Yumoto to Miyanoshita

ⓘ HAKONE TRAVEL PASSES

Odakyū's Hakone Freepass, available at Odakyū stations and Odakyū Travel branches, is an excellent deal, covering the return fare to Hakone and unlimited use of most modes of transport within the region, plus other discounts at museums and facilities in the area. It's available as a two-day pass (adult/child from Shinjuku ¥5140/1500; from Odawara, if you're not planning on returning to Shinjuku, ¥4000/1000) or a three-day pass (adult/child from Shinjuku ¥5640/1750, from Odawara ¥4500/1250). Free-pass-holders need to pay an additional limited-express surcharge (¥890 each way) to ride the Romance Car.

If you plan to combine Hakone with Mt Fuji, also consider the Fuji Hakone Pass (adult/child ¥8000/4000), a three-day pass offering discount round-trip travel from Shinjuku as well as unlimited use of most transportation in the two areas.

(28 minutes, ¥270), Kowakidani (35 minutes, ¥360) and Chōkoku-no-Mori (38 minutes, ¥400) before continuing to its terminus at Gōra (40 minutes, ¥400).

From Gōra, a cable car (¥420, 10 minutes) heads up to near the 1153m-high summit of **Sōun-zan**, from where you can catch the **Hakone Ropeway** (p173) to Ōwakudani and Tōgendai. From Tōgendai, sightseeing boats criss-cross Ashino-ko to Hakone-machi and Moto-Hakone (one way/return ¥1000/1840, 30 minutes). Of course you can do the whole circuit in reverse. For more details, see www.odakyu.jp/english/course/hakone.

Two bus companies, Hakone-Tōzan and Izu Hakone, also service the Hakone area, linking most of the sights. Hakone-Tōzan buses, included in the Hakone Freepass, run between Hakone-machi and Odawara (¥1180, one hour) and between Moto-Hakone and Hakone-Yumoto (¥960, 35 minutes). Stops include Miyanoshita, Kowakidani and Senkyōrō-mae (for Sengokuhara).

Hakone-Yumoto
箱根湯元温泉

☑ 0460 / POP 3114

The onsen resort town of Hakone-Yumoto, spanning the Sukumo-gawa, is the starting point for most visits to Hakone. Though heavily visited, it offers a high concentration of good onsen, the main attraction here.

🏃 Activities

★ Hakone Yuryō   ONSEN
(箱根湯寮; Map p168; ☑ 0460-85-8411; www.hakoneyuryo.jp; 4 Tōnosawa; adult/child ¥1400/700, private bath from ¥3900; ◎ 10am-9pm Mon-Fri, to 10pm Sat & Sun) A free shuttle bus will whisk you in three minutes from Hakone-Yumoto station to this idyllic onsen complex ensconced in the forest. The *rotemburo* are spacious and leaf shaded, and you can book private ones up to a month in advance. No tattoos allowed (but if you book a private room, no one's the wiser).

It's about a five-minute walk from Tōnosawa Station on the Hakone-Tōzan line.

Furusato   ONSEN
(ふるさと; Map p168; ☑ 0460-85-5559; www.hakone-furusato.com; 191 Yumoto-chaya; ¥850; ◎ 9am-6pm Mon-Fri, to 8pm Sat & Sun) This classy ryokan has atmospheric *rotemburo* and indoor onsen that are open to day trippers. A minibus runs here from Hakone-Yumoto station (¥100, 9am to 6.30pm)

Yu-No-Sato   ONSEN
(湯の里; Map p168; ☑ 0460-85-3955; www.yunosato-y.jp; 191 Yumoto-chaya; adult/child ¥1450/600; ◎ 11am-11pm) A spa complex with several baths, including a *rotemburo* amid the fresh mountain air, jet bubble bath, plasma bath and private onsen for two, available by reservation.

Tenzan Tōji-kyō   ONSEN
(天山湯治郷; Map p168; ☑ 0460-86-4126; www.tenzan.jp; 208 Yumoto-chaya; adult/child ¥1300/650; ◎ 9am-10pm) Soak in *rotemburo* of varying temperatures and designs (one is constructed to resemble a natural cave) at this large, popular bath 2km southwest of town. To get here, take the 'B' course shuttle bus from the bridge outside Hakone-Yumoto Station (¥100). Tattoos are not a problem here.

🛏 Sleeping

K's House Hakone   GUESTHOUSE ¥
(Map p168; ☑ 0460-85-9111; http://kshouse.jp/hakone-e; 12-1 Yumoto-chaya; dm/s/d from ¥3300/6000/9000; P ✳ ⓐ) Above town on the south side of the river, K's House has spacious Japanese rooms, some overlooking the river, with a spotless shared kitchen, a lounge and private shower facilities. Staff are friendly, and knowledgeable about all the practicalities you're wondering about. The guesthouse is a 15-minute walk uphill from Hakone-Yumoto station, or a ¥200 bus ride

Omiya Ryokan RYOKAN ¥¥
(Map p168; ☑ 0460-85-7345; www.o-miya.com; 116 Yumoto-chaya; r incl breakfast from ¥9300, Sat or Sun incl 2 meals ¥13,400; ❄ ☎) Lower weekday prices make this simple ryokan an attractive proposition for its tatami rooms, some with mountain views. There's a small indoor onsen. To get here, take the 'B' course bus from Hakone-Yumoto Station.

★**KAI Hakone** RYOKAN ¥¥¥
(界箱根; Map p168; ☑ 050-3786-1144; www.hoshinoresorts.com; 230 Yumoto-chaya; s/d incl 2 meals from ¥31,000/62,000; ❄ @ ☎) Less than a 10-minute bus ride from Hakone-Yumoto, this sleek resort is nestled amid soaring stands of bamboo and overlooks the river. Spacious rooms mix traditional and contemporary styles. Highlights include infinity-style onsen pools, English-speaking staff and delicious *kaiseki* meals.

★**Fukuzumirō** RYOKAN ¥¥¥
(福住楼; Map p168; ☑ 0460-85-5301; www.fukuzumi-ro.com; 74 Tōnosawa; s/d per person incl 2 meals from ¥22,150/38,000; ❄ ☎) This exquisite 125-year-old inn sports detailed woodwork, public onsen baths and rooms with sun terraces with views of the Haya-kawa; the small, quiet room overlooking the garden was a favourite of author Kawabata Yasunori. It's about 10 minutes' walk down from Tōnosawa Station on the Hakone-Tōzan railway, or a short taxi ride from Hakone-Yumoto.

Miyanoshita & Kowakidani 宮ノ下・小涌谷

Miyanoshita is the first worthwhile stop on the Hakone-Tōzan railway heading towards Gōra, with antique shops, a small hiking trail and some good places to eat. Next stop along is Kowakidani, home to a giant onsen complex and the highly impressive collection of the Okada Museum of Art.

◉ Sights & Activities

★**Okada Museum of Art** MUSEUM
(岡田美術館; Map p168; ☑ 0460-87-3931; www.okada-museum.com; 483-1 Kowakidani; adult/student ¥2800/1800; ⏱9am-5pm) Showcasing the dazzling Japanese, Chinese and Korean art treasures of industrialist Okada Kazuo, this mammoth museum should not be missed. You could spend hours marvelling at the beauty of so many pieces, including detailed screen paintings and exquisite pottery. Interactive, multilingual interpretive displays enhance the experience. The museum is opposite the Kowakien bus stop.

An outdoor footbath cafe-restaurant in a traditional wooden villa and a lush hillside garden merging into the forest round out the experience.

Yunessun ONSEN
(箱根小涌園ユネッサン; Map p168; www.yunessun.com; 1297 Ninotaira; Yunessun adult/child ¥2900/1600, Mori-no-Yu ¥1900/1200, both ¥4100/2100; ⏱9am-7pm Mar-Oct, to 6pm Nov-Feb) Best described as an onsen amusement park with a whole variety of outdoor water slides and baths, including wine, coffee, green-tea and sake baths...yes, for putting your body in, not the other way round. Yunessun is mixed bathing so you'll need to bring a swimsuit. The connected Mori-no-Yu complex (11am to 8pm) is traditional single-sex bathing.

Take a bus from Hakone-machi, Gōra or Hakone-Yumoto to the Kowakien bus stop. There's also a variety of accommodation here.

🛏 Sleeping

Hakone Hostel 1914 HOSTEL ¥
(Map p168; hakonehostel1914@yahoo.co.jp; dm/d from ¥4000/9000; P ❄ ☎) This snug new hostel on Miyanoshita's main drag has a handful of rooms in a lovely old Western-style historical building. Dorms have spacious, curtained beds. All rooms share the modern bathroom facilities, and there's a streetside lounge with high, hammered-tin ceilings and a wall of windows allowing for good people-watching.

Fujiya Hotel HOTEL ¥¥¥
(富士屋ホテル; Map p168; ☑ 82-2211; www.fujiyahotel.jp; 359 Miyanoshita; d incl 2 meals from ¥22,150; ⏱❄ @ ☎) One of Japan's finest Western-heritage hotels, the beautifully detailed Fujiya opened in 1878 and played host to Charlie Chaplin back in the day (Room 45). Now sprawled across several wings, it remains dreamily elegant, although the dated rooms are underwhelming. Worth a visit for the retro atmosphere, a stroll through the gardens and greenhouse, and tea in the lounge.

✗ Eating & Drinking

Several options are clustered around the crossroads of Rtes 1 and 138 in Miyanoshita.

Yamagusuri JAPANESE ¥¥
(山藥; Map p168; ☑ 0460-82-1066; 224 Miyanoshita; meals ¥2300; ⏱7am-9pm; 🅿) Yamagusuri is a popular spot for substantial, healthy meal

sets featuring *tororo* (grated yam) that you pour over barley and rice. The dining room overlooks the forested gorge below.

Miyafuji
SUSHI ¥¥

(鮨みやふじ; Map p168; ☏ 0460-82-2139; www. miyanoshita.com/miyafuji; 310 Miyanoshita; meals from ¥1680; ◷ 11.30am-3pm & 5.30-8pm Fri-Wed; ▣) This friendly sushi shop is known for its *aji-don* (horse mackerel over rice). If you know how to fold an origami crane, ask to try their special challenge – using their impossibly small origami, fold a crane in under 10 minutes (they provide tweezers) and they'll add it to the shop's teeny-crane-festooned decor. Look for the English sign.

Naraya Cafe
CAFE

(ナラヤカフェ; Map p168; 404-13 Miyanoshita; coffee from ¥350; ◷ 10.30am-6pm, to 5pm Dec-Feb, closed Wed & 4th Thu of the month; ▣) Beside the station, this woodsy cafe and craft shop is a pleasant pit stop for drinks and light meals. You can also soak your toes in the footbath on the terrace looking out over the mountains.

Chōkoku-no-Mori & Gōra
彫刻の森・強羅

Chōkoku-no-Mori is the stop for the Hakone Open-Air Museum, one of the area's top attractions. The Hakone-Tōzan line terminates at the next station, Gōra, which is the starting point for the funicular and cable-car trip to Tōgendai on Ashino-ko.

◉ Sights

★ **Hakone Open-Air Museum** MUSEUM
(彫刻の森美術館; Map p168; ☏ 0460-82-1161; www.hakone-oam.or.jp; 1121 Ninotaira; adult/child ¥1600/800; ◷ 9am-5pm) In a rolling, leafy hillside setting, this safari for art lovers includes an impressive selection of 19th- and 20th-century Japanese and Western sculptures (including works by Henry Moore, Rodin and Miró) as well as an excellent Picasso Pavilion with more than 300 works ranging from paintings and glass art to tapestry.

Kids will love the giant crochet artwork/ playground with its Jengalike exterior walls, as well as the spiral staircase of the stained-glass Symphonic Structure. End the day by soaking your feet in the outdoor footbath. Hakone Freepass holders get ¥200 off the admission price.

Hakone Museum of Art
MUSEUM

(箱根美術館; Map p168; ☏ 0460-82-2623; 1300 Gōra; adult/child ¥900/free; ◷ 9.30am-4.30pm Fri-Wed, to 4pm in winter) Sharing grounds with a lovely velvety moss garden and teahouse (¥700 *matcha* green tea and sweet), this museum has a collection of Japanese pottery dating from as far back as the Jōmon period (some 5000 years ago). The gardens are spectacular in autumn.

🛏 Sleeping & Eating

★ **Hakone Tent** HOSTEL ¥
(Map p168; ☏ 0460-83-8021; http://hakonetent. com; 1320-257 Gora; dm/s/d/tr with shared bathroom ¥3500/4000/9000/13,500; ❄ ✳ @ 🛜) Best hostel by far in Hakone, with an ace contemporary design blending punk and trad elements in a stylish makeover of a rundown ryokan to include a sleek, wooden lobby bar and lounge and more traditional onsen. Run by a team of friendly young Japanese, the hostel has a relaxed and welcoming vibe. Great spot for an early-evening drink.

Yudokoro Chōraku
RYOKAN ¥

(湯処長楽; Map p168; ☏ 0460-82-2192; choraku. nakaji@gmail.com; 525 Kowakudani; r per person from ¥5150) Simple, homely ryokan with lovely owners (including the sprightly 93-year-old granny), enormous tatami rooms with kitchenettes and communal onsen with outdoor barrel tubs (available to nonguests, ¥550). If you're looking for a peaceful stay, this is a smashing deal. It's a 10-minute walk uphill from the Hakone Open-Air Museum (p172), on the left.

Kappeizushi
SUSHI ¥¥

(かっ平寿し; Map p168; ☏ 0460-82-3278; 1143-49 Ninotaira; meals from ¥1000; ◷ 10am-8pm Wed-Mon; ▣ ▣) A few doors downhill from the Hakone Open-Air Museum, this friendly sushi place also does tasty *chirashi-zushi* (rice topped with assorted sashimi). Look for the small sign in the window.

Itoh Dining by Nobu
JAPANESE ¥¥¥

(Map p168; ☏ 0460-83-8209; http://www. itoh-dining.co.jp/; 1300-64 Gōra; lunch/dinner from ¥3000/7000; ◷ 11.30am-3pm & 5-9.30pm; ▣ ▣) Savour some premium Japanese beef, cooked teppanyaki-style in front of you by the chef, at this elegant restaurant, a branch of the celeb chef Nobu's dining empire. It's just uphill from Koenshimo station on the funicular, one stop from Gōra.

Sōun-zan & Sengokuhara
早雲山・仙石原

Sengokuhara is a sizeable town with some good-value lodgings, places to eat and various niche interest museums, of which the standout is the brilliant Pola Museum of Art.

◉ Sights & Activities

★ Pola Museum of Art   MUSEUM
(Map p168; www.polamuseum.or.jp; 1285 Kozukayama; adult/child ¥1800/700; ⊕9am-5pm) Showcasing the top-drawer collection of the late Suzuki Tsuneshi, son of the founder of the Pola Group (a cosmetics company), this quality museum is located in an equally impressive architect-designed building. Artworks in the collection include those from such famous names as Van Gogh, Cézanne, Renoir, Matisse, Picasso and Rodin, in addition to Japanese artists painting in the Western style, including Kuroda Seiki and Okada Saburosuke.

Hakone Ropeway   CABLE CAR
(箱根ロープウェイ; Map p168; www.hakoneropeway.co.jp/foreign/en/; one way/return ¥1370/2410; ⊕9am-5pm Mon-Fri, to 4pm Sat & Sun, closed 2nd & 4th Thu of the month) The Hakone Ropeway is a 30-minute, 4km gondola ride, taking travellers to Tōgendai from Sōun-zan. It glides over the steaming crater of Ōwakudani, one of the stops along the way. At times, increased volcanic activity at Ōwakudani results in the ropeway not operating for the sake of public safety. In such cases, a bus runs from Tōgendai to Sōun-zan.

If you've bought a round-trip ticket and the ropeway is shut down before your return, there is a refund counter; those with the Hakone Freepass can pick up a bus ticket voucher here.

Hakone Geomuseum   MUSEUM
(Map p168; ☏0460-83-8140; www.hakonegeomuseum.jp; 1251 Sengokuhara; adult/child ¥300/200; ⊕9am-4.30pm) In the complex opposite the Ōwakudani ropeway station, this well-designed natural history exhibit is a fun way to learn about the volcanic forces that created Hakone. Good for kids and curious adults.

Ōwakudani   VOLCANO
(大桶谷; Map p168; www.kanagawa-park.or.jp/owakudani) FREE The 'Great Boiling Valley' was created 3000 years ago when Kami-yama erupted and collapsed, also forming Ashino-ko. Hydrogen sulphide steams from the ground here and the hot water is used to boil onsen *tamago*, eggs blackened in the sulphurous waters, which you can buy to eat (they're fine inside). At the time of writing, Ōwakudani was closing intermittently due to volcanic activity.

If conditions permit, you can hike the one-hour Ōwakudani-Tōgendai Nature Trail here, but don't linger, as the toxic gases are as dangerous as they are strong. Check conditions before your visit.

Sōun-zan   HIKING
(早雲山; Map p168) There are various hiking trails on this mountain including one to Kami-yama (1¾ hours) and another up to Ōwakudani (1¼ hours). The latter is sometimes closed due to the mountain's toxic gases. Check at the tourist information office.

🛏 Sleeping & Eating

Hakone Sengokuhara Youth Hostel   HOSTEL ¥
(箱根仙石原ユースホステル; Map p168; ☏0460-84-8966; www.theyh.com; 912 Sengokuhara; dm members/nonmembers from ¥3830/4470, r per person ¥5400; P⊛❋@⊕) This hostel, adjacent to and also run by the Fuji Hakone Guest House (p173), has Japanese-style shared and private rooms. Rates rise by ¥1000 to ¥2000 in high seasons. Take the T-course bus to Senkyoro-mae from the east exit of Odawara Station (lane 4; ¥1050, 50 minutes). It's a one-minute walk from the bus stop; look for the English sign.

★ Fuji Hakone Guest House   GUESTHOUSE ¥¥
(富士箱根ゲストハウス; Map p168; ☏0460-84-6577; www.fujihakone.com; 912 Sengokuhara; s/d from ¥5550/10,950; P⊛❋@⊕) Run by a welcoming English-speaking family, this long-running guesthouse is the best in the area, offering cosy tatami rooms, gorgeous indoor and outdoor onsen with divine volcanic waters, and a wealth of information on local sights and hiking. Take the T-course bus to Senkyōrō-mae from the east exit of Odawara Station (lane 4; ¥1050, 50 minutes); it's a one-minute walk from here.

There's an English sign nearby.

Hanasai   JAPANESE ¥
(花菜; Map p168; ☏0460-84-0666; 919 Sengokuhara; mains from ¥1000; ⊕11.30am-2.30pm & 5.30-9pm Wed-Mon; ⊚) Slurp noodles and tuck into hearty traditional stews as you soak up the old Japanese atmosphere of this friendly family-run restaurant.

Hakone-machi & Moto-Hakone
箱根町・元箱根

The sightseeing boats across Ashino-ko leave you at either Hakone-machi or Moto-Hakone, both well touristed and with sights of historical interest.

◉ Sights

Hakone Sekisho   MUSEUM
(箱根関所, Hakone Checkpoint Museum; Map p168; ☑0460-83-6635; www.hakonesekisyo.jp; 1 Hakone-machi; adult/child ¥500/250; ☺9am-4.30pm Mar-Nov, to 4pm Dec-Feb) You're free to walk through this 2007 reconstruction of the feudal-era checkpoint on the Old Tōkaidō Highway, but if you want to enter any of the buildings you'll need to buy a ticket. One displays Darth Vader–like armour and grisly implements used on lawbreakers. There are basic English explanations on only some displays.

Onshi Hakone Kōen   PARK
(恩賜箱根公園; Map p168; ☑0460-83-7484; 171 Moto-Hakone; ☺9am-5pm) **FREE** On a small peninsula near the Hakone Sekisho (p174) is this scenic park. Don't miss the elegant hilltop Western-style building, once used by the imperial family, and now a lovely cafe; weather permitting it has Fuji views across the lake.

Narukawa Art Museum   MUSEUM
(成川美術館; Map p168; ☑0460-83-6828; www.narukawamuseum.co.jp; 570 Moto-Hakone; adult/child ¥1300/600; ☺9am-5pm) Art comes in two forms here at Narukawa Art Museum – in the exquisite Japanese-style paintings, *nihonga,* on display, and in the stunning Mt Fuji views from the panorama lounge looking out across the lake. Be sure not to miss the cool kaleidoscope displays.

Hakone-jinja   SHINTO SHRINE
(箱根神社; Map p168; ☺9am-4pm) A pleasant stroll around Ashino-ko follows a cedar-lined path to this shrine set in a wooded grove, in Moto-Hakone. Its signature red *torii* (gate) rises from the lake; get your camera ready for that picture-postcard shot.

🛏 Sleeping & Eating

The path heading left from Moto-Hakone port is lined with little eateries.

Moto-Hakone Guesthouse   MINSHUKU ¥
(元箱根ゲストハウス; Map p168; ☑0460-83-7880; www.motohakone.com; 103 Moto-Hakone; s/tw/tr per person without bathroom ¥5000/10,000/15,000; ☺ @ 🛜) Offering simple, pleasant Japanese-style rooms and common areas, with laundry and breakfast available. Its location offers easy access to great hiking; note that there's a 10pm curfew. From Odawara Station, take the platform 3 bus to Hakone-machi or Moto-Hakone and get off at Ōshiba (¥1130, one hour); the guesthouse is a one-minute walk away.

Bakery & Table   INTERNATIONAL ¥¥
(Map p168; ☑0460-85-1530; www.bthjapan.com; 9-1 Moto-Hakone; mains ¥1000-2500; ☺bakery 10am-5pm, parlour 10am-3pm, cafe 8.30am-5pm, restaurant 11am-6pm) There are options that appeal to everyone at this lakeside venue with a footbath terrace outside. The takeaway bakery is on the ground floor, a cafe is one floor up, and the restaurant serving fancy open sandwiches and crêpes is above that.

WORTH A TRIP

OLD HAKONE HIGHWAY

Up the hill from the lakeside Moto-Hakone bus stop is the entrance to the stone-paved **Old Hakone Highway** (箱根旧街道; Map p168), part of the Edo-era Tōkaidō Highway that connected the shogun's capital with Kyoto. You can walk back to Hakone-Yumoto via the trail through the woods, which will take about 3½ hours.

About 30 minutes' walk from Moto-Hakone, you'll pass wonderful **Amazake-chaya** (甘酒茶屋; Map p168; ☑0460-83-6418; www.amasake-chaya.jp/; 395-1 Futoko-yama; amazake ¥400, snacks from ¥250; ☺7am-5.30pm), a thatched-roofed teahouse that has been serving naturally sweet *amazake* (a thick sweet drink made from the rice used to make sake) and seasoned *mochi* (sticky rice cakes, ¥250 to ¥750) for over 360 years.

Further along is the village of **Hatajuku** (畑宿), where you can visit the **Hatajuku Yosegi Kaikan** (畑宿寄木会館; Map p168; ☑0460-85-8170; 103 Hatajuku; ☺9am-4.30pm) to find out more about the craft of marquetry practised in the area.

LA POSADA

On the west coast of the Izu Peninsula, the seaside onsen town of Toi has thermal waters, the world's largest gold ingot and (allegedly) the world's largest clock made of flowers. But if these random attractions don't wow you, perhaps the Mexican-Japanese B&B, **La Posada** (ラポサーダ; Map p176; ☑ 0558-98-2227; www.laposada.jp; 46 Toi; per person incl half-board from ¥10,000; P ❋ ☎), will. Those who understand the allure of authentic Mexican cuisine will want to spend at least one night here to get their fill of delicious enchiladas, moles and tostadas, prepared with organic ingredients and served by a warmly hospitable Japanese family who lived for decades in Mexico. A day on the beach, an evening with a margarita and a soak in the onsen is like a mini Mexican getaway in this low-key Izu town. Buses to Toi run at least hourly from Shunzen-ji (¥1320, 45 minutes) and Dōgashima (¥910, 40 minutes).

IZU PENINSULA 伊豆半島

The Izu Peninsula (Izu-hantō), about 100km southwest of Tokyo in Shizuoka Prefecture, is where the famed *Kurofune* (Black Ships) of US Commodore Perry dropped anchor in 1854. Contemporary Izu has a cool surfer vibe, lush greenery, rugged coastlines and abundant onsen. Weekends and holidays see crowds descend on the east coast, particularly in summer. It's usually quieter on the rugged west coast, which has, weather permitting, Mt Fuji views over Suruga-wan (Suruga Bay).

Atami 熱海

☑ 0557 / POP 37,570

The onsen and seaside resort of Atami is both the gateway to Izu, and its largest town. Despite its dramatic hillside location, rampant development has robbed it of much of its charm. However, the seafront is pleasant enough for a stroll while you wait for a boat to the Izu Islands, and the newly renovated MOA Museum of Art is well worth a look.

◉ Sights

Sun Beach is an attractive sight in the evening, with its sands illuminated by coloured floodlights.

MOA Museum of Art MUSEUM
(MOA美術館; Map p176; ☑ 0557-84-2511; www.moaart.or.jp; 26-2 Momoyama-chō; adult/student ¥1600/800; ⊙ 9.30am-4.30pm Fri-Wed) Atami's hilltop MOA Museum of Art boasts an excellent collection of Japanese and Chinese pottery and paintings, spanning more than 1000 years and including national treasures. It also has a serene tea garden set among Japanese maples and bubbling brooks. The museum recently underwent an extensive renovation directed by artist Sugimoto Hiroshi and reopened on schedule in February 2017.

Buses run here from platform 8 outside Atami Station (¥170, eight minutes).

ⓘ Information

Atami Tourist Office (Map p176; ☑ 0557-85-2222; http://travel.ataminews.gr.jp/en/; ⊙ 9am-5.30pm Apr-Sep, to 5pm Oct-Mar), in the Atamix building across from Atami Station (immediately to the left as you enter the building), has discount tickets to **MOA Museum of Art** (p175) as well as town maps.

ⓘ Getting There & Away

JR trains run from Tokyo Station to Atami on the Tōkaidō line (Kodama *shinkansen* ¥4190, 50 minutes; Odoriko ¥3800, 1¼ hours; *kaisoku* ¥1940, 1½ hours).

Tokai Kisen (☑ 03-5472-9999; www.tokaikisen.co.jp) hydrofoils travel daily from Atami port to the island of Ō-shima (¥4280, 45 minutes). Prices are seasonal. To reach Atami port, take the bus from lane 7 outside Atami Station (¥230).

Itō

☑ 0557 / POP 68,325

A wonderfully laid-back seaside town, Itō houses some wonderful ryokan and onsen that provide a perfect antidote to the hectic city pace. Winding through town is the Matsukawa, alongside which runs an atmospheric riverside path.

◉ Sights & Activities

Itō's maritime history includes a relationship with the first Englishman to come to Japan – sailor William Adams, who was compelled by Tokugawa Ieyasu to teach the local shipbuilders to construct Western-style

Izu Peninsula

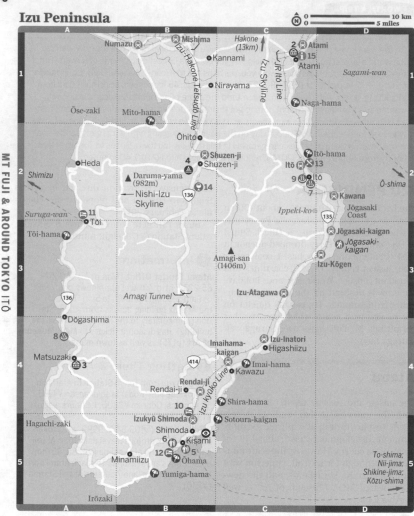

ships. There's a memorial to Adams near the bay, a short walk from the sculpture garden at the seaside **Nagisa Park** (なぎさ公園).

If you plan on hiking Jōgasaki-kaigan, pick up the one-day Itō Sightseeing Free Pass (¥1300) at the bus terminal.

Tōkaikan HISTORIC BUILDING
(東海館; ☎0557-36-2004; 12-10 Higashi Matsubara-chō; adult/child ¥200/100; ⊙9am-9pm, tearoom 10am-5pm, onsen 11am-7pm Sat & Sun) This inn, established in 1928, is now a national monument for its elegant woodwork. Each of its three storeys was designed

by a different architect. Architecture buffs will love comparing the subtle differences, and there's a convivial tearoom with river views on the ground floor. Pay ¥500 if you wish to take a dip in its onsen baths (big and small, alternating daily between male and female).

Ryokufuen ONSEN
(緑風園; Map p176; ☎0557-37-1885; www.ryokufuen.com; 3-1 Otonashi-chō; ¥1000; ⊙1.30-10pm) Soak away in this tranquil *rotemburo* with its rocky waterfall under a canopy of trees. K's House (p177) guests receive

Izu Peninsula

a 50% discount with voucher. Follow the river inland from K's House and you'll reach it in less than 10 minutes; it's next to Otonashi-jinja.

Yokikan
ONSEN
(陽気館; Map p176; ☑0557-37-3101; www.yokikan.co.jp; 2-24 Suehiro-chō; ¥1000; ⊙11am-3pm) Part of a hotel, this outdoor rooftop *rotemburo* has the novelty of only being accessible via a rickety in-house funicular. It's mixed bathing, with distant views over the town and the water.

Jōgasaki-kaigan
HIKING
(城ヶ崎海岸; Map p176) South of Itō is the striking Jōgasaki coast, with its windswept cliffs formed by lava. A moderately strenuous cliffside hike (about 6.5km), with volcanic rock and pine forests, winds south of the sci-fi-looking lighthouse to Izu-Kōgen Station. Add on another 1.5km for the walk from Jōgasaki-kaigan Station to the coast.

Along the way you'll cross the 48m-long Kadowaki-no-Umi suspension bridge with waves crashing 23m below. From Itō Station, take the bus heading to Jōgasaki-guchi (¥700, 40 minutes) and hop off at the lighthouse.

🛏 Sleeping

★ K's House Itō Onsen
HOSTEL ¥
(ケイズハウス伊東温泉; ☑0557-35-9444; http://kshouse.jp; 12-13 Higashi Matsubara-chō; dm/s/d ¥2950/4800/7600; ⊛🕸@🤶) A 100-year-old ryokan with a charming riverside setting full of carp and heron, K's House is the real reason to come to Itō. The Japanese-style dorms, private rooms and common areas are beautifully maintained and classically stylish. With a fully equipped kitchen, bicycle rental, helpful staff, and public and private onsen, this is an outstanding deal.

Yamaki Ryokan
RYOKAN ¥¥
(山喜旅館; ☑0557-37-4123; www.ito-yamaki.jp; 4-7 Higashi Matsubara-chō; r per person with/without meals from ¥16,200/8790; 🕸🤶) A block east of the Tōkaikan is this charming wooden inn from the 1940s with an onsen bath and pleasant rooms, some with ocean views. On weekends you can only book rooms with meals included. Limited English; ask for help making a reservation at the Tourist Information Center (p178).

🍴 Eating & Drinking

For a small seaside town, Itō is jam-packed with eateries and small bars. Fish, predictably, is a local speciality.

Hamazushi
SUSHI ¥
(はま寿司; Map p176; 546-40 Oyukawa; sushi Mon-Fri ¥90, Sat & Sun from ¥100; ⊙11am-10.30pm; ⊛🍴👶) In a town famous for fish, it says something about this *kaiten-sushi* (conveyor-belt sushi restaurant) place that people are prepared to queue for cheap and tasty morsels of seafood. Bonus: they even have touch screens for ordering in English. Opposite the beach near Marine Town.

Kunihachi
IZAKAYA ¥
(国八; ☑0557-37-9186; 10-2 Higashimatsubara-chō; dishes ¥370-800; ⊙5.30pm-midnight; 🕸🍴👶) A cute *izakaya* cluttered with eclectic decor. The menu caters to all with cheap and tasty dishes such as jumbo *okonomiyaki* (¥730) alongside more adventurous options such as fried crocodile and horse or deer sashimi. It has a great vegetarian selection, too.

Izu Kogen Brewery
PUB FOOD ¥¥
(伊豆高原ビール; ☑0557-38-9000; www.izu-beer.com; Marine Town, 571-19 Oyukawa; pizzas from ¥1000; ⊙10am-9pm) Enjoy delicious thin-crust pizzas while sipping microbrewed beer and looking out to the sea. Then soak

KANAYA RYOKAN

Built in 1929, the rambling wooden **Kanaya Ryokan** (金谷旅館; Map p176; ☎0558-22-0325; http://kanaya.la.coocan.jp; 114-2 Kouchi; r per person from ¥7690, with 2 meals from ¥16,350, onsen for nonguests ¥1000; 🅿 ❀ 🕾) is fabulously traditional, although the cheapest rooms are relatively simple. There are no restaurants nearby, so go for the inn's meals or pack your own. The star attraction is the biggest all-wood (*hinoki*) bath in the nation (mixed), called the *sennin-furo* (1000-person bath, a vast exaggeration).

Women can cover up with a towel (BYO or rent one for ¥300). The women-only bath is nothing to sneeze at, and both sides have private outdoor baths as well. Tattoos are totally acceptable here.

Kanaya Ryokan is in the town of Rendai-ji (蓮台寺). From Izukyū Shimoda Station take the Izukyūkō line to Rendai-ji Station (¥170, five minutes); note that the express doesn't stop here. Exiting the station, go straight across the river and main road to the T-junction and turn left; the onsen is 50m ahead on the right.

your toes in the foot onsen outside afterwards. Can life get any better?

Freaks BAR
(☎0557-37-4560; 2-3 Matsukawa-chō; ⊗8pm-2am) Intimate bar spinning soul and funk vinyl, on the main road towards the station from the Matsukawa.

ℹ Information

For online info, check out www.itospa.com.

Across from Itō Station, the **Tourist Information Center** (☎0557-37-6105; ⊗9am-5pm) has loads of info on the Izu Peninsula and a detailed Itō map.

ℹ Getting There & Away

The JR limited-express Odoriko service runs from Tokyo Station to Itō (¥3670, one hour and 40 minutes). Itō is connected to Atami by the JR Itō line (¥320, 22 minutes).

From Itō, the Izukyūkō (aka Izukyū) line goes to Shimoda (¥1620, one hour), stopping at Jōgasaki-kaigan (¥580, 25 minutes). There are six buses daily to Shuzen-ji (¥1130, one hour). **Tōkai Kisen** (東海汽船; ☎03-5472-9999; www.tokaikisen.co.jp; ⊗9.30am-8pm) jetfoils depart for Ō-shima (¥3560, 35 minutes), generally once daily, although during some periods they run only on weekends.

Shimoda 下田

☑0558 / POP 22,926

Shimoda holds a pivotal place in Japan's history as the spot where the nation officially opened to the outside world after centuries of near isolation. The small port's laid-back vibe is also perfectly suited to an exploration of its surrounding beaches, which are some of the best in Izu.

◉ Sights

★ **Perry Road** STREET
(ペリーロード; Map p180) It takes less than 10 minutes to walk end-to-end of this quaint cobbled street shadowing a narrow canal leading to Ryōsen-ji temple. However, the appealing ambience of old houses under willow trees now occupied by cafes, jazz bars, boutique shops and restaurants will encourage you to linger.

Ryōsen-ji & Chōraku-ji BUDDHIST TEMPLE
(了仙寺・長楽寺; Map p180) FREE A 15-minute walk south of Shimoda Station is **Ryōsen-ji**, site of the treaty that opened Shimoda, signed by Commodore Perry and representatives of the Tokugawa shogunate. The temple's **Museum of the Black Ship** (了仙寺宝物館, Hōmotsukan; Map p180; ☎0558-22-2805; www.mobskurofune.com; 3-12-12 Shimoda; adult/child ¥500/250; ⊗8.30am-5pm) stands streetside, with the temple beyond.

Behind and up the steps from Ryōsen-ji is **Chōraku-ji**, where a Russo-Japanese treaty was signed in 1854; look for the cemetery and *namako-kabe* (black-and-white lattice-patterned) walls.

Shimoda Kōen & Wakanoura Promenade Park PARK
(下田公園・和歌の浦遊歩道; Map p180) If you keep walking east from Perry Rd, you'll reach the pleasant hillside park of Shimoda Kōen, which overlooks the bay. It's loveliest in June, when the hydrangeas are in bloom.

Gyokusenji
TEMPLE

(玉泉寺; Map p176; 31-6 Kakisaki; museum adult/child ¥400/200; ⊗8am-5pm) Founded in 1590, this Zen temple is most famous as the first Western consulate in Japan, established in 1856. A small **museum** has artefacts of the life of American Townsend Harris, the first consul general. It's a 25-minute walk from Shimoda Station, or take bus 9 to Kakisaki-jinja-mae (¥170, five minutes).

👉 Tours

Nanz Village has a shopfront where you can book adventure tours (http://weekend-adventure.jp) on the Izu Peninsula, such as stand-up paddleboarding, sea kayaking and mountain biking. Take into consideration that English-language ability may be available but is generally limited.

Shimoda International Club
TOURS

(sicshimoda@yahoo.co.jp) Offers guided two-hour tours (¥200 per person) on weekends and holidays.

🛏 Sleeping

Yamane Ryokan
RYOKAN ¥

(やまね旅館; Map p180; ☎0558-22-0482; 1-19-15 Shimoda; r per person from ¥4500; ❄) You wouldn't guess that this place has been running for more than 60 years from its tidy, well-maintained Japanese-style rooms. The owners speak next to no English but are very friendly, and the central location is excellent. Facilities are shared among mostly repeat Japanese visitors, so it feels very safe and familial.

Kurofune Hotel
HOTEL ¥¥¥

(黒船ホテル; Map p180; ☎0120-715-841; www.kurofune-hotel.com; 3-8 Kakizaki; r per person from ¥13,800; P❄@📶☕) This retro-fabulous, old-line hotel has bay views, seafood dinners, palm trees by the *rotemburo* and a heated swimming pool. Rooms are Japanese-style, except for the suites, some of which have their own *rotemburo* (from ¥40,500 per person). You can't miss its peach-coloured presence across from the port complex.

🍴 Eating & Drinking

⭐ Gorosaya
JAPANESE ¥¥

(ごろさや; Map p180; ☎0558-23-5638; 1-5-25 Shimoda; set menus ¥1700-3300; ⊗11.30am-2pm & 5-9pm; 📷) Elegant, understated ambience and fantastic seafood. The *isōjiru* soup is made from more than a dozen varieties of shellfish and looks like a tide pool in a bowl. The *sashimi-don* (rice bowl), not on the English menu, is also excellent. Look for the wooden fish decorating the entrance.

Nanz Kitchen
INTERNATIONAL ¥¥

(Map p180; ☎0558-36-4318; 1-6-18 Shimoda; mains ¥900-1900; ⊗11.30am-2.30pm & 5.30-10pm; 🍴📷) The anchor of the new Nanz Village complex, this stylish restaurant serves seasonal French-esque, Japanese-ish cuisine, utilising as many fresh, locally sourced ingredients as possible, including venison and fish. There's a decent wine and cocktail list to complement your meal. The 'village' itself is one of the few places open in the evenings during low season.

SURFIN' SHIMODA

The beaches around Shimoda are some of Japan's best surf spots. While it's a year-round surfing destination, waves are best between June and September. **Shira-hama** (白浜海岸) is the most popular and its small but constant break gets packed in summer. There's also a **reef break** at the front of the Shimoda Prince Hotel, a short walk uphill from Papa's Restaurant. **Shirahama Mariner** (白浜マリーナ; ☎0558-22-6002; www.mariner.co.jp; 2752-16 Shirahama; ⊗9am-9pm) and **Irie Surf & Cafe** (☎0558-36-4333; 1737 Shirahama; ⊗10am-7pm Wed-Mon, hours vary off season) both rent boards (¥3000) and offer lessons (per two hours ¥5000).

The beaches in **Kisami** (きさみ), just south of Shimoda, are among some of the best. **Ōhama** (大浜) has the largest stretch of sand and consistent waves, **Irita** (入田) is especially good when a southerly rolls in, and **Tadato** (多々戸) has arguably the most consistent waves on the peninsula. **Baguse Surf School** (バグーススタダド&サーフィンスクール; Map p176; ☎0558-22-2558; http://baguse.jp; 58-8 Tadato; ⊗10am-4pm Apr-Nov), in Tadato, offers lessons and board rentals at Ōhama, as does **Real** (Map p176; ☎0558-27-0771; www.real-surf.jp; 1612-1 Kisami).

Shimoda

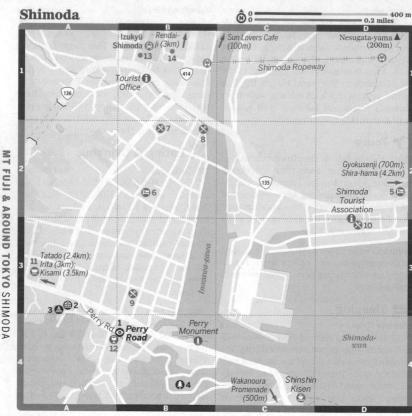

Ra-Maru CAFE ¥¥
(Map p180; ☎ 0558-27-2510; 1-1 Sotogaoka; burgers from ¥1000; ⊙ 10am-5pm; 🅿) Diner serving tasty Shimoda fish burgers with Camembert, and shrimp burgers with a big dollop of fresh avocado, plus a side of onion rings and cold beer. Just behind the harbour museum at the fishing port.

Porto Caro ITALIAN ¥¥
(ポルトカーロ; Map p180; ☎ 0558-22-5514; 2nd fl, 3-3-7 Shimoda; mains ¥840-1360; ⊙ 11.30am-2.30pm & 6-9pm Thu-Tue; 🖉🅿) This trattoria is run by Yokoyama Ikuyo, a friendly woman who wrote a book about Mishima Yukio (the famous writer, actor and film director), whom she met as a teenager – hence they have Mishima's favourite cake, the madeleine, on the menu. The Shimoda seafood pasta with a delicate wasabi sauce is excellent, as are the tasty simple pizzas.

Cubstar CAFE
(Map p180; ☎ 0558-27-3225; www.cubstar. com; 4-7-22 Shimoda; coffee/mains ¥500/1000; ⊙ 11am-10pm Wed-Mon, closed 2nd Mon of the month; 🐱) Run by a cool couple who abandoned Tokyo for the slower life of Shimoda, this quirkily decorated cafe offers excellent coffee, light meals and alcoholic beverages. Look for it opposite the green church.

Soul Bar Tosaya BAR
(土佐屋; Map p180; ☎ 0558-27-0587; 3-14-30 Shimoda; snacks from ¥600; ⊙ 7pm-2am) In the heart of Perry Rd, this unique place mashes up a traditional residence from the era of the Black Ships with a soul-music bar complete with disco ball. It also serves meals.

ℹ Information

Check the online guide at www.shimoda-city.info.
Pick up the useful *Shimoda Guidebook* (¥840),
a free walking map and book accommodation

Shimoda

at the **Shimoda Tourist Association** (Map p180; ☏ 0558-22-1531; 2nd fl, 1-1 Sotogaoka; ⊙ 9am-5pm) in the port area. You should find English-speaking staff here daily. At the **tourist office** (観光案内所; Map p180; ☏ 0558-22-1531; http://shimoda-city.info; 1-1 Sotogaoka; ⊙10am-5pm) opposite the station, staff speak very little English, but they will happily arm you with maps and can call the English-speaking staff at the port branch for you.

Sun Lovers Cafe (☏ 0558-27-2686; 1-21-9 Higashi-hongo; dishes ¥650-750; ⊙11am-5.30pm Tue-Sat; 🛜 🐾) offers free wi-fi, an English-language book swap, tourist info, kids' playroom and light meals.

ℹ Getting There & Away

Bus Tōkai buses run to Dōgashima (¥1360, one hour) via Matsuzaki.

Car Rental is available at **Nippon Rent-a-Car** (Map p180; ☏ 0558-22-5711; www.nipponrentacar.co.jp; Shimoda eki-mae; ⊙8am-8pm) and **Toyota Rent-a-Car** (トヨタレンタカー; Map p180; ☏ reservations in English 0800-7000-815; per day from ¥6500; ⊙8am-8pm) by the train station.

Ferry Serving the Izu Islands Kōzu-shima, Shikine-jima and Nii-jima (adult/child ¥5180/2590), **Shinshin Kisen** (神新汽船株式会社; Map p180; ☏ 03-3436-1146, 0558-22-2626; http://shin-shin-kisen.jp) ferries depart Shimoda on Mon-

day, Thursday and Saturday, and make return journeys on Tuesday, Friday and Sunday.

Train Shimoda is as far as you can go by train on the Izu Peninsula. Limited-express Odoriko *tokkyū* trains run to Shimoda from Tokyo Station (¥6090, 2¾ hours) or Atami (¥3400, 80 minutes); regular Izukyūko trains run from Atami (¥1890, 1½ hours) and Itō (¥1620, one hour). Try to catch Izukyū's *Resort 21* train, with sideways-facing seats for full-on sea views.

Shira-hama　　　白浜海岸

☏ 0558 / POP 21,534

Less than 10km north of Shimoda, Shirahama (meaning 'white-sand beach') is an attractive beach town that gets packed out with students in summer and on holiday weekends and is a popular spot with Kantō-area surfers.

Off the main road is the pleasant 2400-year-old **Shirahama-jinja** shrine, a nice spot to wander with a striking *torii* (gate) on the rocky edge of the beach.

🛏 Sleeping & Eating

There are some little guesthouses at the north end of the beach, as well as some nice ones up the hill from the south end. You're well advised to book ahead during the busy summer season.

Pension Sakuraya PENSION ¥
(ペンション桜家; ☏ 0558-23-4470; www.izu-sakuraya.jp; 2584-20 Shira-hama; r per person incl 1/2 meals from ¥5500/8000; ❋🛜) Around a 10-minute walk up a steep hill from the beach, this homely guesthouse has been welcoming visitors for almost 30 years. All rooms have fridges, as well as sea or mountain views. The English-speaking owner is a good source of info.

Pension Shirahama Mariner PENSION ¥¥
(☏ 0558-22-6002; www.mariner.co.jp; 2752-16 Shira-hama; dm/s/d from ¥3000/4800/7600; ❋🛜) Upstairs from Hana Cafe, rooms here are comfy with homely touches such as colourful bedspreads and rugs. There's a bit of traffic noise but with these spectacular ocean views, who cares?

Papa's Restaurant CAFE ¥¥
(☏ 0558-22-0225; pizzas from ¥1050; ⊙11am-3pm & 5-10pm, closed Tue) Cosy diner with vintage toy cars, gingham tablecloths and surfboards on the walls. Serves light fare such as shrimp tacos and pizza. It's about an eight-minute walk from Shirahama-jinja, away from the beach.

ⓘ Getting There & Away

Bus 9 runs from Shimoda to Shira-hama (¥330, 10 minutes).

Kisami きさみ

☑ 0558 / POP 2276

Our pick of Izu's seaside getaways is laid-back Kisami. It's most famous for its long surf beach **Ōhama** (大浜), but is also well placed for access to other nearby surf beaches **Irita** (入田) and **Tatado** (多々戸).

🛏 Sleeping & Eating

In season, Kisami has plenty of eating and drinking options. A great place to read up on further dining options in the area is Wabi Sabi guesthouse's blog: www.wabi sabishimoda.com/activities.

★ **Wabi Sabi** GUESTHOUSE ¥
(Map p176; ☑ 0558-22-4188; www.wabisabishimo da.com; 2735 Kisami; dm/s/d with shared bathroom from ¥3500/5000/8000; ❊🅟) An idyllic retreat enveloped by greenery but only five minutes' walk from Ōhama. The old Japanese house perfectly embodies the *wabi-sabi* (beauty in imperfection) aesthetic and is expertly managed by Angela and Yasu, who also run nearby **Tabi Tabi** (☑ 090-6513-5578; www.tabitabiizu. com; 1658 Kisami; s/d ¥6000/9000; ❊🅟), another appealing guesthouse. Wabi Sabi has a large shared kitchen, smart tatami rooms and shared bathrooms in a peaceful setting.

Ernest House B&B ¥¥
(アーネストハウス; ☑ 0558-22-5880; www. ernest-house.com; 1893-1 Kisami; r per person from ¥5400; 🅟😄❊@🅟) Two minutes' walk from Ōhama surf beach, this clean clapboard pension, named after Hemingway, has a quaint beach-house vibe.

The attached **Cafe Mellow** (☑ 0558-27-2327; 1893-1 Kisami; meals ¥1000-1500; ⊙11am-11pm, closed Tue, Fri & 2nd Wed of the month; 🅟) is a local hang-out offering outdoor decking with comfy chairs, and serving beach fare such as burgers, pizza and seafood barbecues (order a day ahead).

★ **South Cafe** INTERNATIONAL ¥¥
(☑ 0558-25-5015; www.southcafe.net; 918-2 Kisami; mains ¥1000-1200; ⊙noon-10pm Fri-Wed) The best combination of food, atmosphere and good-value prices in Kisami, this relaxed place is well worth dragging yourself away from the beach for. Excellent sandwiches, salads, pizzas and curries among other

things (including must-have brownies). It's a five-minute walk inland from the Kisami bus stop just past the convenience store Lawsons.

ⓘ Getting There & Away

From Izukyū Shimoda Station, hop onboard an Irōzaki-bound bus (lane 3 or 4; ¥270) to Kisami, from where Ōhama beach is a 15-minute walk.

Matsuzaki 松崎

☑ 0558 / POP 7021

Things are much quieter on the west coast of the Izu Peninsula. The sleepy port of Matsuzaki is known for its streetscapes and attractive setting on the Naka-gawa: some 200 traditional houses with *namako-kabe* plasterwork and tile lattice walls are concentrated in the south of town, on the far side of the river.

◎ Sights

Where the Naka-gawa curves towards the ocean, both sides of the river harbour quaint neighbourhoods full of buildings featuring *namako-kabe*. It's a nostalgic, stalled-in-time area to stroll around.

Nakaze-tei MUSEUM
(中瀬邸; Map p176; ☑ 0558-43-0587; 1-315 Matsuzaki; ¥100; ⊙9am-5pm) Explore the rooms and antique tools and curios in this old kimono shop and residence that is decorated with *namako-kabe*. Outside is a striking retro-design clock tower and a footbath.

🛏 Sleeping & Eating

Kaihin-sō MINSHUKU ¥¥
(海浜荘; ☑ 0558-42-0127; 207 Ena; per person incl 2 meals from ¥9000; ❊🅟) With a 200-year history, this *minshuku* (family-run guesthouse) continues to provide comfortable, traditional accommodation and onsen for visitors to Matsuzaki. It's also about a 30-second walk from the bus terminal. Not much English is spoken here, so have the Tourist Association (p183) help you make a reservation.

Mingei Sabo SHOKUDO ¥¥
(民芸茶房; ☑ 0558-42-0773; 495-7 Matsuzaki; sets ¥1050-3150; ⊙7.30am-3pm & 5-8.30pm) Here you'll find fishing paraphernalia on the walls and filling sets of fresh local seafood on the (picture) menu. It's near the port in Matsuzaki. From the art museum, walk straight across the river and keep going until the road comes around a curve; you'll see a painting of fish over the entrance.

Costa Forno BAKERY

(☎0558-36-4443; 495-37 Matsuzaki; ⊙9am-5pm, closed intermittently Mon & Tue) Run by a bright-eyed, bushy-tailed Nagano native, this heavenly bakery offers ¥100 cups of coffee to go with your Nagano blueberry jam (homemade, from harvest to bakery) and cream-cheese pull-apart bread, or Nagano apple Danish, or savoury Nagano-style *oyaki-pan* (small pie stuffed with hearty vegies). Great baked goods for picnics or enjoying right there at the little harbour.

ⓘ Information

Pick up an English map of the town at the **Tourist Association** (☎0558-42-0745; http://izumatsuzakinet.com; ⊙8.30am-5pm), which is about 10 minutes' walk south of the bus station, across the Naka-gawa. You can store your luggage in the bus station lockers for the day (¥300 to ¥500).

ⓘ Getting There & Away

From Shimoda Station buses run to Matsuzaki (¥1270, one hour).

Buses run to Shuzen-ji (¥2150, 1½ hours) via Dōgashima, complete with fantastic views over Suruga-wan to Mt Fuji.

Dōgashima 堂ヶ島

☑0558

Dōgashima has a dramatic coastline best enjoyed from the steamy perspective of an onsen, but a bay cruise or stroll along the waterfront path also offers excellent points of view.

🏃 Activities

Jagged rock formations line the seashore around Dōgashima, a short bus ride from Matsuzaki. View them up close and personal from Dōgashima Marine cruises, which depart from the jetty just below the Tourist Information Center in front of the village bus stop. The cliff-edge park here has excellent views too; don't miss the Tensōdō (天窓洞), a natural window in a cave's roof.

Dōgashima Marine CRUISE

(☎0558-52-0013; www.izudougasima-yuransen.com; 20/50 min cruises ¥1200/2300) Dramatic rock formations lining the seashore around Dōgashima are best seen from these cruises, which depart from the jetty just below the Tourist Information Center in front of the village bus stop.

BEST ONSEN

- ➡ Jinata Onsen (p186)
- ➡ Urami-ga-taki Onsen (p187)
- ➡ Kanaya Ryokan (p178)
- ➡ Hakone Yuryō (p170)

Sawada-kōen Rotemburo ONSEN

(沢田公園露天風呂; Map p176; 2817-1 Sawada Nishina; adult/child ¥600/200; ⊙9am-6pm Wed-Mon Oct-Feb, to 7pm Mar-May & Sep, to 8pm Jun-Aug) Set directly on a cliff overlooking an open view of the ocean is this small *rotemburo* (separate bathing). To get here, take a Matsuzaki-bound bus from Dōgashima and get off at Sawada-kōen. From here, walk towards the coast and skirt around the right side of the fisher's harbour. Keep heading for the buff-coloured bluffs, where the path leads directly to the onsen.

It can get very busy at sunset but at other times you may have the place to yourself.

🛏 Sleeping & Eating

As a popular holiday spot with limited accommodations, Dōgashima is a place where it's best if you don't simply turn up without a reservation.

During the day, you'll find several dining options near the jetty area.

Umibe-no-Kakureyu Seiryu RYOKAN ¥¥¥

(海辺のかくれ湯清流; ☎0558-52-1118; www.n-komatu.co.jp; 2941 Nishina; per person incl 2 meals from ¥17,800; 🅿❄@🛜) Traditional design meets contemporary standards at this seaside ryokan. A variety of baths are on offer; it has a sensational men's *rotemburo* right on the beach with crashing waves. The women's *rotemburo* is partially open-air and, while a step down from the men's, it overlooks the ocean from a geographically higher level. It's a five-minute walk from the Dōgashima bus stop.

ⓘ Information

Dōgashima Tourist Information Center (☎52-1268; www.nishiizu-kankou.com; ⊙8.30am-5pm Mon-Fri Sep-Jun, daily Jul & Aug)

ⓘ Getting There & Away

Buses run to Dōgashima from Shimoda (¥1400, one hour), via Matsuzaki (¥270, eight minutes).

Shuzen-ji Onsen
修善寺温泉

☑0558 / POP 16,328

Inland Shuzen-ji (修善寺温泉) is a quaint hot-spring village in a lush valley bisected by the rushing Katsura-gawa. The narrow lanes, bamboo forest path and criss-crossing red-lacquered pedestrian bridges are perfect for strolling. One of Japan's finest onsen ryokan is here as well.

◉ Sights & Activities

Shuzen-ji   BUDDHIST TEMPLE
(修善寺) FREE In the middle of the village is its namesake temple, said to have been founded over 1200 years ago by Kōbō Daishi, the priest credited with spreading Buddhism throughout much of Japan. You can wander the pleasant temple grounds for free but there's a fee if you wish to see inside the small **treasure museum** (修禅寺宝物殿; Map p176; ☑0558-72-0053; http://shuzenji-temple.com; 964 Shuzen-ji; adult/child ¥300/200; ⊗8.30am-4.30pm), which contains ancient carved buddhas and other religious works of art.

Shoko Kanazawa Museum   MUSEUM
(金澤翔子美術館; ☑0558-73-2900; www.shokokanazawa.net; 970 Shuzen-ji; adult/child ¥600/300; ⊗11am-3pm Fri-Wed) Kanazawa Shoko (www.k-shoko.org), who has Down's syndrome, has been doing calligraphy since she was five years old. Her vividly expressive pieces, as well as a video of her creating calligraphic work, are displayed in an annex of the Arai Ryokan.

Tokko-no-yu   ONSEN
(独鈷の湯, Iron-Club Waters; ⊗24hr) FREE Right on the river, complete with an open-air shelter, is this footbath. Legend says it was dug by hand by Kōbō Daishi himself.

Hako-yu   ONSEN
(筥湯; ☑0558-72-5282; 925 Shuzen-ji; ¥350; ⊗noon-9pm) Relax with a soak at this elegant, contemporary onsen facility identified by its 12m-high wooden tower.

🛌 Sleeping

Goyōkan   RYOKAN ¥¥
(五葉館; ☑0558-72-2066; www.goyokan.co.jp; 765-2 Shuzen-ji; r per person incl/excl 2 meals from ¥16,000/9500; P⊗❀❀) Stylish tatami rooms, some with river views, are offered at this sleek, small contemporary ryokan.

Shared (indoor) baths are made of stone and *hinoki* cypress. Some English is spoken here.

★**Arai Ryokan**   RYOKAN ¥¥¥
(新井旅館; ☑0558-72-2007; www.arairyokan.net; 970 Shuzen-ji; r per person incl 2 meals from ¥24,840; ❀❀❀) Long beloved by Japanese artists and writers, this gem of an inn was founded in 1872 and has kept its traditional, wood-crafted heritage. The main bath hall, designed by artist Yasuda Yukihiko, is grand, and the riverside rooms are magnificent in autumn, when the maples are ablaze. Take your pick between rooms looking on to the river or peaceful garden.

🍴 Eating & Drinking

You could meander the narrow streets, eating your way through Shuzen-ji, as there is no lack of dining options here.

Zenfutei Nana ban   NOODLES ¥¥
(禅風亭なゝ番; ☑0558-72-0007; 761-1-3 Shuzen-ji; meals ¥630-1890; ⊗10am-4pm Fri-Wed; 🅿) This institution serves the local speciality: *zendera soba* (¥1260), with a stalk of fresh wasabi root to grate yourself – they even give you a plastic bag in which to take home the precious leftover wasabi root. Look for the white and black shopfront with purple curtains on the road into town from Shuzen-ji Station.

Baird Brewery Beer Garden   BEER GARDEN
(Map p176; ☑0558-73-1225; www.bairdbeer.com; 1052-1 Ōdaira; ⊗noon-7pm Mon-Fri, 11am-8pm Sat & Sun) Sample some lovely craft beers in a peaceful setting, or take a brewery tour (check their website for tour times). From Shuzenji Station, take a Laforet Shuzenji Iriguchi-bound bus from lane 3 or 4.

ℹ Information

There's a **Tourist Information Office** (☑0558-72-0271; www.shuzenji.info; 838-1 Shuzen-ji; ⊗9am-5pm) at Shuzen-ji Station, where you can pick up a sightseeing map in English.

ℹ Getting There & Away

Bus Services connect Shuzen-ji Station to Shuzen-ji Onsen (¥220, 10 minutes), Itō (¥1130, one hour), Dōgashima (¥2030, 1½ hours) and Shimoda (¥3980, 1½ hours).

Train From Tokyo, take the Tōkaidō line to Mishima (Kodama *shinkansen* ¥4520, one hour) then transfer to the Izu-Hakone Tetsudō for Shuzen-ji (¥510, 35 minutes).

IZU ISLANDS 伊豆諸島

The peaks of a submerged volcanic chain extending 300km into the Pacific make up the Izu Islands (Izu-shotō). Soaking in an onsen while gazing at the ocean is the classic Izu Islands activity, as is hiking up the mostly dormant volcanoes and along the pristine beaches. Snorkelling, surfing and fishing are also popular. Island hopping is possible on daily ferries that run up and down the archipelago, but check schedules carefully, as they change frequently.

For more information on the whole chain, which includes To-shima (利島), Kōzu-shima (神津島), Miyake-jima (三宅島) and Mikura-jima (御蔵島), where it's possible to swim with dolphins, see www.tokyo-islands.com.

Booking ahead for the limited accommodation on the islands is a must during the summer, and a good idea the rest of the year.

ⓘ Getting There & Away

Though you can fly to the Izu Islands, the most economical and convenient way to get there is by hydrofoil. If you plan to spend any time on the Izu Peninsula, it's faster and cheaper to travel from Atami, Itō or Shimoda than from Tokyo.

Ō-shima 大島

POP 7762

The largest of the Izu Islands, the closest to Tokyo and generally the most interesting to visit is Ō-shima. It has a rustic charm and is particularly known for its profusion of scarlet camellia flowers (best viewed in February and March) as well as its active volcano Mihara-san, which last erupted in 1990.

◉ Sights & Activities

Hire a car or scooter in the main port of **Motomachi** (元町) to reach Ō-shima's rocky southernmost point, **Tōshiki-no-hana** (トウシキの鼻), with good swimming in sheltered pools below Tōshiki Camp-jō.

Discount tickets for **Gojinka Onsen** (御神火温泉; ☑04992-2-0909; 1-8 Nakanohara; adult/child ¥700/300; ☺6.30am-9pm on days of overnight ferry arrivals, 9am-9pm other days) and Motomachi Hama-no-yu (p185) are available from the souvenir shops near the port.

★ Mihara-san VOLCANO

(三原山) A road runs to the slope of the volcano, from where you can see Mt Fuji on a clear day. From here, you can hike 45 minutes to the 754m summit to peer into the still-steaming crater. It's another 45-minute hike around the rim of the crater, with stellar views 360 degrees around – it's fascinating to observe the path of previous lava flows. There's great interpretive signage in English at various points of interest (and concrete shelters, just in case).

Motomachi Hama-no-yu ONSEN

(元町浜の湯; adult/child ¥400/240; ☺1-7pm Sep-Jun, 11am-7pm Jul & Aug) Walkable from the port is this attractive outdoor onsen with great views of the ocean, and Mt Fuji, too, if the weather is clear; it's mixed, so bring your bathing suit.

⌂ Sleeping

The Ō-shima Tourist Association, near the pier in Motomachi, can assist in booking accommodation.

Tōshiki Camp-jō CAMPGROUND

(トウシキキャンプ場; ☑04992-2-1446) **FREE** Walkable from the Kaiyō kokusai kōkō-mae bus stop, this well-maintained stretch of grass has a nice location overlooking the sea, as well as showers and a communal cooking area. Advance booking is required; the Ōshima Town Office can help.

Island Izu Ō-shima CAPSULE HOTEL ¥

(アイランド伊豆大島; ☑04992-2-0665; www.izuoshimaisland.jp; 2-3-12 Motomachi; capsules from ¥5400; ☻✴☏) This is a top-quality capsule hotel with facilities for both men and women plus a friendly welcome. Just five minutes' walk uphill south of the port; look for the cheery green terrace out front.

ⓘ Information

The **Ō-shima Tourist Association** (大島観光協会; ☑04992-2-2177; www.izu-oshima.or.jp; ☺8.30am-5pm) is located near the pier in Motomachi. There are no English speakers but there is a free translation phone system, Gaikoku-go 110, by which they can call English-speaking volunteers from 8am to 8pm. Otherwise, they can usually call English-speaking staff at the town office.

Maps and sight descriptions can be found at www.town.oshima.tokyo.jp.

ⓘ Getting There & Away

Fly to Ō-shima from the Tokyo area with **New Central Airservice** (www.central-air.co.jp; ¥11,800, 30 minutes).

Tōkai Kisen (p178) hydrofoils service Ō-shima from Tokyo (¥6730, 1¾ hours), Atami (¥4280,

45 minutes) and Itō (¥3560, 35 minutes). In unfavourable weather, ferries will dock at **Okata** (岡田), on the northern end of the island, rather than at the Motomachi port on the west coast.

Nii-jima 新島

☑ 04992

Nii-jima attracts surfers from all over Kantō who converge on **Habushi-ura** (羽伏浦), a blazing 6.5km stretch of white sand that runs over half Nii-jima's length.

Aside from seductive beaches and surf spots, Nii-jima's main attraction is **Yuno-hama Onsen** (湯の浜温泉; ⊘24hr) **FREE**, a whimsical *rotemburo* with several tubs built into the rocks overlooking the Pacific.

Renting a bike is a great way of getting around this small island.

🛏 Sleeping & Eating

If you haven't booked ahead, stop at the Kurone port tourist information counter for help making a reservation.

Best to book meals with your accommodation, especially in slower seasons when shops close up early.

Habushi-ura Camp-jo　　　CAMPGROUND
(羽伏浦キャンプ場; ☑ 04992-5-1068) **FREE**
With a stunning mountain backdrop and spacious, grassy sites, this campground is a winner, and it's only about 10 minutes' walk to the beach. There are showers and plenty of barbecue pits to go around. Check in at the campground clubhouse.

B&B Seven　　　　　　　　INN ¥¥
(B&B セブン; ☑ 090-3304-5931, 04992-5-1106; per person ¥6000; ❋ 🛜) While the second 'B' is no more (it no longer offers breakfast), this simple inn is comfortable and friendly, with wood floors and a homely feel. The friendly owner here, Ōmura-san, speaks fluent English.

Sakae Sushi　　　　　　　SUSHI ¥¥
(栄寿司; ☑ 04992-5-0134; 5-2-9 Honson; meals ¥1850; ⊘11.30am-2pm & 6-10pm) This popular recommendation is a lovely spot to try *shima-zushi*, the local speciality in which fish marinated in island soy sauce is served atop rice.

ⓘ Information

The **Nii-jima Tourist Association** (新島観光協会; ☑ 04992-5-0001; ⊘7.30am-5pm, 8.30am-5pm in winter) has a helpful tourist information counter inside the ferry terminal at Kurone port.

ⓘ Getting There & Away

New Central Airservice (www.central-air.co.jp) operates flights to Nii-jima (¥14,100, 40 minutes).

Tōkai Kisen (p178) hydrofoils depart for Nii-jima (¥8560, 2½ hours) from Tokyo's Takeshiba pier. If ocean conditions aren't ideal, ferries will dock at Wakago port at the northern end of the island; from there, free buses shuttle passengers to the regular port of Kurone.

From Shimoda, **Shinshin Kisen** (p181) ferries serve Nii-jima (adult/child ¥5180/2590).

Shikine-jima 式根島

☑ 04992

About 6km south of Nii-jima, tiny Shikine-jima is not the island to visit if you're looking for some postcard-worthy, white-sand beaches, but its compact, rocky geography makes it the perfect place to unplug, camp out and explore via bicycle.

Several free, mixed-gender onsen on the island each feature unique chemical compositions and temperatures for enthusiasts of onsen and/or the best things in life. Don't miss **Jinata Onsen** (地鉈温泉; ⊘24hr) **FREE**, at the end of a narrow cleft in the rocky coastline. The waters, stained a rich orange from iron sulphide, are naturally 80°C; mixed with the cool ocean, they're just right. The tide affects the temperature, so bathing times change daily; check before making the steep descent.

Camping is free at Shikine-jima's well-maintained campgrounds, but visitors are required to register with the town office; stop by the **Tourist Association** (式根島観光協会; ☑ 04992-7-0170; ⊘8am-5pm) counter at the pier to do so.

Kamanoshita Camp-jo (釜の下キャンプ場; ☑ 04992-2-0004; ⊘Mar-Jun & Sep-Nov) **FREE** right near a fine beach and two free onsen is a good choice, though there are no showers. Campers should bring most of their provisions from Tokyo.

From Tokyo, jetfoils to Shikine-jima (¥8560, two hours 50 minutes) run at least four times a month; overnight ferries depart nightly at 10pm (¥5590, 11 hours).

Hachijō-jima 八丈島

☑ 04996

About 290km south of Tokyo, Hachijō-jima has a culture all its own. With two dormant volcanoes, 854m **Hachijō-Fuji** (八丈富士) and 700m **Mihara-yama** (三原山), and plenty of palms it attracts visitors for its hiking, diving and onsen.

Hike up Hachijō-Fuji for fantastic views from the rim of the crater. At the southern end of the island, a 30-minute drive from Sokodo Port, just below the road, **Urami-ga-taki Onsen** (裏見ケ滝温泉; ⊙10am-9pm) FREE overlooks a waterfall and is not to be missed; it's pure magic in the early evening. Soap and shampoo are prohibited here, and it's a mixed onsen, so bring your swimsuit.

The island is also famous in Japan for being riddled with bioluminescent mushrooms. If you go in June, the forests light up at night with more than seven different species.

Project WAVE (☑04996-2-5407; www. project-wave.jp/english.html; tours from ¥2500) offers a variety of ecotourism options, including hiking, birdwatching, sea kayaking and scuba diving.

In the centre of the island, **Hachijōjima Tourism Association** (八丈島観光協会; ☑04996-2-1377; ⊙8.15am-5.15pm) is next to the town hall on the main road.

While there are *minshuku* on the island, the **Sokodo Camp-jō** (底土キャンプ場; ☑04996-2-1121; 4188 Mitsune) FREE is an excellent free camping ground.

If you're self-catering, it's wise to bring any special food items from Tokyo, as you won't find so much variety on the island.

Ferries depart from Tokyo for Hachijō-jima (¥7820, 10½ hours) once daily at 8.50am, returning to Tokyo at 9.40am.

KAMAKURA 鎌倉

☑0467 / POP 172,902

The glory days of Japan's first feudal capital (from 1185 to 1333) coincided with the spread of populist Buddhism in Japan. This legacy is reflected in the area's proliferation of stunning temples. Kamakura also has a laid-back, earthy vibe complete with organic restaurants, summer beach shacks and surfers, which can be added to sunrise meditation and hillside hikes as reasons to visit. Only an hour from Tokyo, it tends to get packed on weekends and holidays, so plan accordingly.

History

In 1180 aspiring warlord Minamoto no Yoritomo set up his base at Kamakura, far away from the debilitating influences of Kyoto court life, close to other clans loyal to his family and, having the sea on one side and densely wooded hills on the other, easy to defend.

After victories over the old foes the Taira, Yoritomo was appointed shogun in 1192 and governed Japan from Kamakura. When he died without an heir, power passed to the Hōjō, the family of Yoritomo's wife. Ruling power remained in Kamakura until 1333, when, weakened by the cost of maintaining defences against threats of attack from Kublai Khan in China, the Hōjō clan was defeated by Emperor Go-Daigo. Kyoto once again became the capital.

By the Edo period, Kamakura was practically a village again. With the opening of a rail line at the turn of the last century, the seaside town was reborn as a summer resort. Summer homes of wealthy Tokyoites still line the Shōnan coast.

⊙ Sights

Engaku-ji BUDDHIST TEMPLE
(円覚寺; Map p188; ☑0467-22-0478; www.engaku-ji.or.jp; 409 Yamanouchi; adult/child ¥300/100; ⊙8am-4.30pm Mar-Nov, to 4pm Dec-Feb) One of Kamakura's five major Rinzai Zen temples, Engaku-ji was founded in 1282 as a place where Zen monks might pray for soldiers who lost their lives defending Japan against Kublai Khan. All of the temple structures have been rebuilt over the centuries; the Shariden, a Song-style reliquary, is the oldest, last rebuilt in the 16th century. At the top of the long flight of stairs is the Engaku-ji bell, the largest bell in Kamakura, cast in 1301.

Tōkei-ji BUDDHIST TEMPLE
(東慶寺; Map p188; www.tokeiji.com; 1367 Yamanouchi; adult/child ¥200/100; ⊙8.30am-5pm Mar-Oct, to 4pm Nov-Feb) Across the railway tracks from Engaku-ji, Tōkei-ji is famed as having served as a women's refuge. A woman could be officially recognised as divorced after three years as a nun in the temple precincts. Today, there are no nuns; the grave of the last abbess can be found in the cemetery, shrouded by cypress trees.

★**Kenchō-ji** BUDDHIST TEMPLE
(建長寺; Map p188; www.kenchoji.com; 8 Yamanouchi; adult/child ¥300/100; ⊙8.30am-4.30pm) Established in 1253, Japan's oldest Zen monastery is still active today. The central Butsuden (Buddha Hall) was brought piece by piece from Tokyo in 1647. Its Jizō Bosatsu statue, unusual for a Zen temple, reflects the valley's ancient function as an

Kamakura

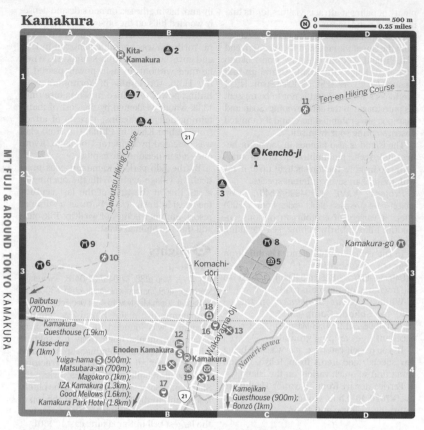

Kamakura

◎ Top Sights

◎ Sights

☺ Activities, Courses & Tours

▣ Sleeping

✕ Eating

♦ Drinking & Nightlife

▩ Shopping

ⓘ Transport

execution ground – Jizō consoles lost souls. Other highlights include a bell cast in 1253 and a juniper grove, believed to have sprouted from seeds brought from China by Kenchō-ji's founder some seven centuries ago.

Ennō-ji
BUDDHIST TEMPLE

(円応寺; Map p188; 1543 Yamanouchi; ¥200; ⏰9am-4pm Mar-Nov, to 3pm Dec-Feb) Ennō-ji is distinguished by its statues depicting the judges of hell. According to the Juo concept of Taoism, which was introduced to Japan from China during the Heian period (794–1185), these 10 judges decide the fate of souls, who, being neither truly good nor truly evil, must be assigned to spend eternity in either heaven or hell. Presiding over them is Emma (Yama), a Hindu deity known as the gruesome king of the infernal regions.

Tsurugaoka Hachiman-gū
SHINTO SHRINE

(鶴岡八幡宮; Map p188; http://hachimangu. or.jp; 2-1-31 Yukinoshita; ⏰5am-8.30pm Apr-Sep, 6am-8.30pm Oct-Mar) FREE Kamakura's most important shrine is, naturally, dedicated to Hachiman, the god of war. Minamoto no Yoritomo himself ordered its construction in 1191 and designed the pine-flanked central promenade that leads to the coast. The sprawling grounds are ripe with historical symbolism: the Gempei Pond, bisected by bridges, is said to depict the rift between the Minamoto (Genji) and Taira (Heike) clans.

Behind the pond is the **Kamakura National Treasure Museum** (鎌倉国宝館; Map p188; ☑0467-22 0753; 2-1-1 Yukinoshita, Kamakura Kokuhōkan; depending on exhibition ¥300-600; ⏰9am-4.30pm Tue-Sun), housing remarkable Buddhist sculptures from the 12th to 16th centuries.

★Daibutsu
MONUMENT

(大仏; ☑0467-22-0703; www.kotoku-in.jp; Kōtoku-in, 4-2-28 Hase; adult/child ¥200/150; ⏰8am-5.30pm Apr-Sep, to 5pm Oct-Nov) Kamakura's most iconic sight, an 11.4m bronze statue of Amida Buddha (*amitābha* in Sanskrit), is in Kōtoku-in, a Jōdo sect temple. Completed in 1252, it's said to have been inspired by Yoritomo's visit to Nara (where Japan's biggest Daibutsu holds court) after the Minamoto clan's victory over the Taira clan. Once housed in a huge hall, today the statue sits in the open, the hall having been washed away by a tsunami in 1498.

For an extra ¥20, you can duck inside to see how the sculptors pieced the 850-tonne statue together.

Buses from stops 1 and 6 at the east exit of Kamakura Station run to the Daibutsu-mae stop (¥190). Alternatively, take the Enoden Enoshima line to Hase Station and walk north for about eight minutes. Better yet, take the Daibutsu Hiking Course (p190).

Hase-dera
BUDDHIST TEMPLE

(長谷寺, Hase Kannon; ☑0467-22-6300; www. hasedera.jp; 3-11-2 Hase; adult/child ¥300/100; ⏰8am-5pm Mar-Sep, to 4.30pm Oct-Feb) The focal point of this Jōdo sect temple, one of the most popular in the Kantō region, is a 9m-high carved wooden *jūichimen* (11-faced) Kannon statue. Kannon (*avalokiteshvara* in Sanskrit) is the Bodhisattva of infinite compassion and, along with Jizō, is one of Japan's most popular Buddhist deities. The temple is about 10 minutes' walk from the Daibutsu and dates back to AD 736, when the statue is said to have washed up on the shore near Kamakura.

Sugimoto-dera
BUDDHIST TEMPLE

(杉本寺; http://sugimotodera.com; 903 Nikaidō; adult/child ¥200/100; ⏰8am-4.30pm) This small temple, founded in AD 734, is reputed to be the oldest in Kamakura. The fierce-looking guardian deities and statues of Kannon are its main draw. Take a bus from stop 5 at Kamakura Station to the Sugimoto Kannon bus stop (¥200, 10 minutes).

Hōkoku-ji
BUDDHIST TEMPLE

(報国寺; ☑0467-22-0762; www.houkokuji.or.jp; 2-7-4 Jōmyō-ji; bamboo garden ¥200; ⏰9am-4pm) Down the road from Sugimoto-dera, on the right-hand side, is this Rinzai Zen temple with quiet, landscaped gardens where you can relax under a red parasol with a cup of Japanese tea (¥500).

Jōmyō-ji
BUDDHIST TEMPLE

(浄妙寺; 3-8-31 Jōmyō-ji; adult/child ¥100/50; ⏰9.30am-4.30pm) This Tokasan temple of the Rinzaishu Kenchō-ji sect was originally a tantric Buddhist temple and converted to a Zen temple. The main reason to visit is for its atmospheric rock garden and teahouse where you can sip on *matcha* (green) tea in a traditional tea ceremony (¥600). To get here, take any bus from stop 5 at Kamakura Station's east exit and get off at the Jōmyō-ji stop from where it's a two-minute walk.

Behind the main temple is the Tomb of Ashikaga Sadauji, the father of Takauji, the founder of the Muromachi era.

Zuisen-ji
BUDDHIST TEMPLE

(瑞泉寺; www.kamakura-zuisenji.or.jp; 710 Nikaidō; adult/child ¥200/100; ⏰9am-5pm) The grounds of this secluded picturesque Zen temple make for a pleasant stroll and include gardens laid out by Musō Soseki, the temple's esteemed founder. To get here, take the bus from stop 4 at Kamakura Station and get off at Ōtōnomiya

MT FUJI & AROUND TOKYO KAMAKURA

(¥200, 10 minutes); turn right where the bus turns left in front of Kamakura-gū, take the next left and keep following the road for 10 or 15 minutes.

🏃 Activities

Daibutsu Hiking Course   HIKING
(Map p188) This 3km wooded trail connects Kita-Kamakura with the Daibutsu (p189) in Hase (allow about 1½ hours) and passes several small, quiet temples and shrines, including **Zeniarai-benten** (銭洗弁天; Map p188; 2-25-16 Sasuke; ☻8am-4.30pm) FREE, one of Kamakura's most alluring Shinto shrines.

The path begins at the steps just up the lane from pretty **Jōchi-ji** (浄智寺; Map p188; 1402 Yamanouchi; adult/child ¥200/100; ☻9am-4.30pm), a few minutes from Tōkei-ji. Near Zeniarai-benten a cavelike entrance leads to a clearing where visitors come to bathe their money in natural springs, with the hope of bringing financial success. From here, continue down the paved road, turning right at the first intersection, walking along a path lined with cryptomeria and ascending through a succession of *torii* to **Sasuke-inari-jinja** (佐助稲荷神社; Map p188; 2-22-10 Sasuke; ☻24hr) FREE before meeting up with the Daibutsu path once again. To hike in the opposite direction, follow the road beyond Daibutsu and the trail entrance is on the right, just before a tunnel.

Ten-en Hiking Course   HIKING
(天園ハイキングコース; Map p188) From Zuisen-ji (p189) you can access this trail, which winds through the hills for two hours before coming out at Kenchō-ji (p187). From Kenchō-ji, walk around the Hojo (Main Hall) and up the steps to the trail.

GET ZEN

Too many temples and before you know it you're feeling anything but 'Zen'. *Zazen* (seated meditation) can help you discover what you're missing – after all, temples were originally designed for this purpose (and not sightseeing). Both **Engaku-ji** (p187) and **Kenchō-ji** (p187) hold beginner-friendly, public *zazen* sessions. Instruction is in Japanese, but you can easily manage by watching everyone else; arrive at least 15 minutes early.

👉 Tours

Kamakura Welcome Guides   TOURS
(http://kamakura-info.secret.jp/kwga) FREE Offers free half-day tours on Fridays in English, French and Spanish, even Portuguese and Chinese on certain days, led by volunteer guides. You can also design your own adventure with five days' notice; see their website for details. Guests pay their own admission and transport fees.

🎊 Festivals & Events

Kamakura Matsuri   CULTURAL
(☻mid-Apr) A week of celebrations held from the second Sunday to the third Sunday in April. It includes a wide range of activities, most of which are centred on Tsurugaoka Hachiman-gū.

🛏 Sleeping

★**Kamakura Guesthouse**   GUESTHOUSE ¥
(鎌倉ゲストハウス; ☎0467-67-6078; www.kamakura-guesthouse.com; 273-3 Tokiwa; dm/q ¥3500/15,000; ☻❋☎) While it's away from the action, the cheap Japanese dorms and common area with *irori* set in a traditional cypress home make this a nice place to hang out. Take the Enoden bus from stop 1 at the east gate of Kamakura Station to Kajiwaraguchi (¥240); it's a one-minute walk from here.

There are bicycles for rent (per day ¥500) and a communal kitchen, and *zazen* meditation tours to Engaku-ji (p187) are offered during the week.

IZA Kamakura   HOSTEL ¥
(IZA 鎌倉; ☎0467-33-5118; http://izaiza.jp; 11-7 Sakanoshita; dm ¥3500, d or tw ¥8000; ☻❋☎) This surfie's hang-out hostel is steps from the beach and has a very studenty vibe, but is also handy for Hase's temples. There's a bar and bike rental (per day ¥1000).

★**Kamejikan Guesthouse**   GUESTHOUSE ¥¥
(亀時間; ☎0467-25-1166; www.kamejikan.com; 3-17-21 Zaimokuza; dm/d from ¥3500/9000; ☻@☎) A three-minute walk to the beach, this lovely guesthouse occupies a traditional house and has nice touches such as paper lampshades and a small cafe and bar (noon to 5pm Saturday and Sunday). Choose from six-bed dorms or private doubles, all with common tiled bathrooms. Catch bus 12, 40 or 41 to Kuhon-ji from Kamakura Station.

English-speaking owner Masa is a good source of info and rents bodyboards and bicycles (per day ¥500).

Hotel New Kamakura
HOTEL ¥¥

(ホテルニューカマクラ; Map p188; ☎0467-22-2230; www.newkamakura.com; 13-2 Onarimachi; s/d from ¥4200/6000; [P][❀][@]) Charming, slightly shabby, ultraconvenient and a steal, this hotel built in 1924 has both Western- and Japanese-style rooms, most of which share bathrooms. There's red carpet and a vintage vibe, though the economy rooms are rather plain – opt for Japanese-style. Exit west from Kamakura Station, then take a sharp right down the alley and up the left-hand stairs before the tunnel.

Kamakura Park Hotel
HOTEL ¥¥¥

(鎌倉パークホテル; ☎0467-25-5121; www.kamakuraparkhotel.co.jp; 33-6 Sakanoshita; s/tw from ¥16,000/19,000; [P][❀][@][☎]) A bit 1980s plush, the large Western-style rooms here come with ocean views and marble baths. It's a 12-minute walk along the coast from Hase Station.

✗ Eating

Vegetarians can eat well in Kamakura; pick up the free, bilingual *Vegetarian Culture Map* at the Tourist Information Center.

Cobakaba
JAPANESE ¥

(食堂コバカバ; Map p188; ☎0467-22-6131; 1-13-15 Komachi; meals ¥500-1000; ⊙8-10am & 11am-5pm Tue-Fri, to 9pm Sat & Sun, closed Mon; [☺][✆]) One of the few restaurants around town open for breakfast, Cobakaba offers clean Japanese-style breakfast sets – fried egg, rice, miso soup, salad and simmered vegies – from ¥500, and lunch options that change seasonally.

Wander Kitchen
INTERNATIONAL ¥

(Map p188; ☎0467-61-4751; http://wanderkitchen.net; 10-15 Onarimachi; sweets/lunch from ¥400/1000; ⊙noon-8pm; [☎]) It's worth searching out this charmingly decorated, retro-chic wooden house with a small garden out front for its cool vibe and tasty meals, cakes and drinks. It's tucked away just off the main street about five minutes' walk south of the west exit of Kamakura Station.

Bowls Donburi Café
JAPANESE ¥

(鎌倉どんぶりカフェbowls; Map p188; ☎0467-61-3501; http://bowls-cafe.jp; 2-14-7 Komachi; meals ¥880-1680; ⊙11am-3pm & 5-10pm; [☺][☎][✎][✆]) The humble *donburi* (rice bowl) gets a hip, healthy remake here at this modern bright cafe, with toppings such as roasted tuna, shredded cucumber or *daikon* (radish), avocado and *shirasu* (local tiny whitebait). You

---

WORTH A TRIP

ENOSHIMA

A short ride on the Enoden Line from Enoden Kamakura will take you to beachside Enoshima where rocky Enoshima Island is the main attraction. Cross the bridge that begins on the beach and head up the narrow cobblestone lane (or the escalator if you prefer) to **Enoshima-jinja** (江島神社; ☎0466-22-4020; http://enoshimajinja.or.jp; 2-3-8 Enoshima; ⊙8.30am-5pm) FREE, a shrine to the sea goddess Benzaiten. The island is a popular date spot, and cliffside restaurants offer sunset views along with local specialities including *sazae* (turban shell seafood). There's a park and some caves, too. During the summer, Enoshima's black-sand beach transforms into a sort of Shibuya-by-the-sea, as super-tanned teens crowd the sand.

---

get a discount if you discover the word *atari* (アタリ) at the bottom of the bowl. Also serves excellent coffee and has free wi-fi.

★ Bonzō
SOBA ¥¥

(梵蔵; ☎046/-/3-7315; http://bonzokamakura.com; 3-17-33 Zaimokuza; dishes ¥300-2000; set-course menu from ¥3500; ⊙11.30am-3pm & 6-9pm, closed Thu, [✆]) Intimate, rustic, Michelin-star restaurant that specialises in handmade *juwari* (100% soba), including *kamo seiro* (cold soba in hot broth) with wild duck imported from France. The homemade sesame tofu is incredibly creamy and not to be missed. Catch bus 12, 40 or 41 to Kuhon-ji and look for the brown shopfront next to the tiny post office.

★ Matsubara-an
NOODLES ¥¥

(松原庵; ☎0467-61-3838; http://matsubara-an.com/shops/kamakura.php; 4-10-3 Yuiga-hama; mains ¥860-1720; set meals from ¥2900; ⊙11am-10pm; [✆]) Dinner reservations are recommended for this upscale *soba* restaurant in a lovely old house. Try the tempura *goma seiro soba* (al dente noodles served cold with sesame dipping sauce). Dine alfresco or indoors where you can watch noodles being handmade. From Yuiga-hama Station (Enoden line) head towards the beach and then take the first right. Look for the blue sign.

Good Mellows
CAFE ¥¥

(☎0467-24-9655; 27-39 Sakanoshita; burgers from ¥850; ⊙10.30am-7pm Wed-Mon; [✆]) Americana meets Japanese kitsch opposite the beach, with neatly stacked, charcoal-grilled juicy burgers of bacon, mozzarella and avocado, plus perfect fries, washed down with a Dr Pepper or a cold California microbrew. Once a month or so they stay open till 11.30pm on Saturday with DJs playing.

Drinking & Nightlife

Kamakura has a thriving nightlife, featuring live music in tiny bars on either side of Kamakura's JR station.

Univibe   BAR

(Map p188; ☑ 0467-67-8458; www.univibe.jp; 2nd fl, 7-13 Onaricho; ⊙ 11am-3pm & 6pm-late; ⏰) Spacious upstairs bar kitted-out in retro vintage decor, with friendly bartenders, table football and a relaxed vibe. A five-minute walk from the Kamakura JR station.

Bar Ram   BAR

(バー・ラム; Map p188; ☑ 0467-60-5156; www. barram.net; 2-11-11 Komachi; drinks from ¥500; ⊙ 5pm-late) A hole in the wall in the lanes off Komachi-dōri, this *tachinomiya* (drink-while-standing bar) has plenty of old Rolling Stones vinyls and friendly banter. Look for the English sign.

Shopping

Kamakura Ichibanya   FOOD

(鎌倉壱番屋; Map p188; ☑ 0467-22-6156; 2-7-36 Komachi; packages from ¥80; ⊙ 10am-7pm) Specialises in *sembei* (rice crackers); watch staff grilling them in the window or buy some 50 packaged varieties, including curry, wasabi, garlic, *mentaiko* (spicy cod roe) or *uni* (sea urchin); look for the baskets on the corner.

Information

For information about Kamakura, see www.city. kamakura.kanagawa.jp (in Japanese).

Just outside the east exit of Kamakura Station, the English-speaking staff at the **Tourist Information Center** (鎌倉市観光総合案内所; Map p188; ☑ 0467-22-3350; ⊙ 9am-5pm) are helpful and can book accommodation. Pick up a guide to Kamakura's temples (¥1700), as well as free brochures and maps for the area.

Getting There & Away

JR Yokosuka–line trains run to Kamakura from Tokyo (¥920, 56 minutes) and Shinagawa (¥720, 46 minutes), via Yokohama (¥340, 27 minutes). Alternatively, the Shōnan Shinjuku line runs from the west side of Tokyo (Shibuya, Shinjuku and Ikebukuro, all ¥920) in about one

hour, though some trains require a transfer at Ōfuna, one stop before Kita-Kamakura. The last train from Kamakura back to Tokyo Station is at 11.20pm and Shinjuku at 9.16pm.

JR Kamakura-Enoshima Free Pass (adult/child ¥700/350) Valid for one day from Ōfuna or Fujisawa stations; unlimited use of JR trains around Kamakura, the Shōnan monorail between Ōfuna and Enoshima, and the Enoden Enoshima line.

Odakyū Enoshima/Kamakura Free Pass (from Shinjuku/Fujisawa ¥1470/610) Valid for one day; includes transport to Fujisawa Station (where it meets the Enoden Enoshima line), plus use of the Enoden.

Getting Around

You can walk to most temples and shrines from Kamakura or Kita-Kamakura Stations. Sites in the west, like the Daibutsu, can be reached via the Enoden line from Kamakura Station to Hase (¥200) or by bus from Kamakura Station stops 1 and 6.

Kamakura Rent-a-Cycle (レンタサイクル; Map p188; ☑ 0467-24-2319; per hr/day ¥800/1800; ⊙ 8.30am-5pm) is outside the east exit of Kamakura Station, and right up the incline.

YOKOHAMA　　　　　横浜

☑ 045 / POP 3.7 MILLION

Even though it's just a 20-minute train ride south of central Tokyo, Yokohama has an appealing flavour and history all its own. Locals are likely to cite the uncrowded, walkable streets or neighbourhood atmosphere as the main draw, but for visitors it's the breezy bay front, creative arts scene, multiple microbreweries, jazz clubs and great international dining.

History

Up until the mid-19th century, Yokohama was an unassuming fishing village. Things started to change rapidly, however, in 1853, when the American fleet under Commodore Matthew Perry arrived off the coast to persuade Japan to open to foreign trade.

From 1858, when it was designated an international port, through to the early 20th century, Yokohama served as a gateway for foreign influence and ideas. Among the city's firsts in Japan: a daily newspaper, gas lamps and a train terminus (connected to Shimbashi in Tokyo).

The Great Kantō Earthquake of 1923 destroyed much of the city, but the rubble was used to reclaim more land, including

Yamashita-kōen. The city was devastated yet again in WWII air raids; occupation forces were initially based here but later moved down the coast to Yokosuka. Despite all this, central Yokohama retains some rather fine early-20th-century buildings.

Sights & Activities

Minato Mirai 21

Over the last three decades Yokohama's former shipping docks have been transformed into this planned city of tomorrow ('Minato Mirai' means 'port future'), with plenty of pleasant recreation areas including the old **Akarenga Sōkō** (横浜赤レンガ倉庫; Map p194; www.yokohama-akarenga.jp; 1-1 Shinkō, Naka-ku; warehouse 1 10am-7pm, warehouse 2 11am-8pm; Bashamichi) red-brick warehouses, transformed into a shopping, dining and events space; the waterfront **Zō-no-hana Park** (象の鼻パーク; Map p194); and a series of breezy **promenades** connecting the area's main attractions.

Hara Model Railway Museum MUSEUM
(原鉄道模型博物館; Map p194; www.hara-mrm.com/english; 2nd fl, Yokohama Mitsui Bldg, 1-1-2 Takashima, Nishi-ku; adult/child ¥1000/500; 11am-5pm Wed-Mon; Yokohama) The result of Hara Nobutarō's lifelong obsession with trains, this superb collection of model trains and other railway-associated memorabilia is every kid's and trainspotter's dream come true. Even if you don't care much for trains, the sheer scale of the collection and beautiful detail of the exhibits is captivating. The highlight is the mammoth gauge-one diorama of moving locomotives where you can act as train driver.

Yokohama Museum of Art GALLERY
(横浜美術館; Map p194; 045-221-0300; www.yaf.or.jp/yma; 3-4-1 Minato Mirai, Nishi-ku; adult/child ¥500/free; 10am-6pm, closed Thu; Minato Mirai) The focus of the Yokohama Triennale (2017, 2020), this museum hosts exhibitions that swing between safe-bet shows with European headliners to more daring contemporary Japanese and up-and-coming Southeast Asian artists. There are also permanent works, including by Picasso, Miró and Dalí, in the catalogue.

Landmark Tower NOTABLE BUILDING
(ランドマークタワ; Map p194; www.yokohama-landmark.jp; 2-2-1 Minato Mirai, Nishi-ku; adult/child

ℹ MINATO BURARI PASS

The **Minato Burari** day pass covers municipal subway and bus rides (including the Akai-kutsu bus, but not the Minato Mirai line) around Minato Mirai and Yamashita-kōen (adult/child ¥500/250); purchase at any subway (blue line) station.

¥1000/500; 11am-8pm; Minato Mirai) Standing an impressive 296m high (70 storeys), the Landmark Tower has one of the world's fastest lifts (45km/h). On clear days the 69th-floor Sky Garden observatory affords views to Tokyo and Mt Fuji, and you can even get a glimpse into games taking place at Yokohama Stadium.

Yokohama Port Museum MUSEUM
(横浜みなと博物館; Map p194; 045-221-0280; www.nippon-maru.or.jp; 2-1-1 Minato Mirai, Nishi-ku; museum & ship adult/child ¥600/300; 10am-5pm Tue-Sun; Sakuragichō) Explore the docked **Nippon Maru** (日本丸; Map p194), a four-masted barque (built in 1930) that retains many original fittings. As you exit, the comprehensive, and somewhat dry, port museum takes you through the city's port history; kids will love the simulated ship ride.

★ Cup Noodles Museum MUSEUM
(Map p194; 045-345-0918; www.cupnoodles-museum.jp; 2-3-4 Shinkō, Naka-ku; adult/child ¥500/free; 10am-6pm Wed-Mon; Bashamichi) Dedicated to Momofuku Ando's instant ramen invention, this slickly designed, interactive museum includes a cutesy animated film on the history of the Cup Noodle. The highlight is the chance to design your own Cup Noodle (additional ¥300) by colouring your cup, selecting ingredients and having it air-sealed to take home to enjoy. Even though English signage is sparse, the underlying message of 'Never give up!' and going against the grain is worth the visit, especially for those with kids.

Yokohama Cosmoworld AMUSEMENT PARK
(横浜コスモワールド; Map p194; http://cosmoworld.jp; 2-8-1 Shinkō, Naka-ku; admission free, rides ¥100-800; 11am-9pm Mon-Wed & Fri, to 10pm Sat & Sun; Minato Mirai) Perfect for the kiddies, this busy amusement park is home to one of the world's tallest Ferris wheels, the 112.5m Cosmo Clock 21 (¥800).

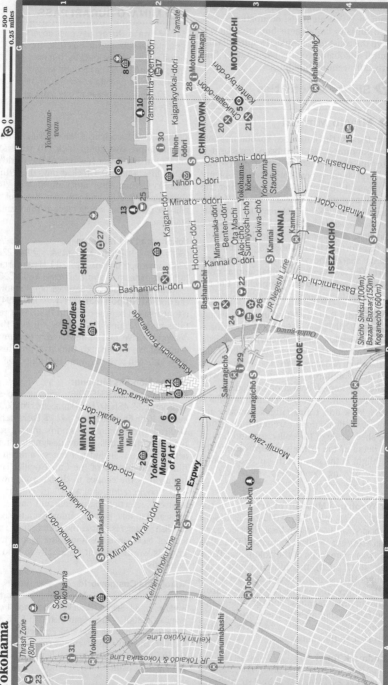

Yokohama

Yokohamatsu

Thrash Zone (80m)

Sogō Yokohama

Cup Noodles Museum

Kishamichi Promenade

SHINKŌ

MINATO MIRAI 21

Minato Mirai

Shin-takashima

Keihin-Tōhoku Line

Takashima-chō

Minato Mirai-ōdori

Yokohama Museum of Art

Expwy

Sakuragichō

Sakuragichō

NOGE

Keihin-Tōhoku Line

JR Tōkaidō & Yokosuka Line

Keihin Kyūkō Line

Hiranumabashi

Yokohama

Tobe

Kamonyama-kōen

Momiji-zaka

Hinodechō

Tōchinoki-dōri

Suzukake-dōri

Ichō-dōri

Keyaki-dōri

Sakura-dōri

Bashamichi-dōri

Bashamichi

Honchō-dōri

Kaigan-dōri

Minato-ōdori

Nihon-ōdori

Nihon Ō-dōri

Osanbashi-dōri

Osanbashi-dōri

Yamashita-kōen-dōri

Kaigankyōkai-dōri

Motomachi-dōri

Chūkagai-dōri

Kanteibyō-dōri

Motomachi-Chūkagai

Yamate

MOTOMACHI

CHINATOWN

Yokohama-kōen

Yokohama Stadium

KANNAI

Kannai

Kannai O-dōri

Tokiwa-chō

Sumiyoshi-chō

Ōta-chō

Aioi-chō

Benten-dōri

Minaminaka-dōri

Minato-ōdori

Bashamichi-dōri

ISEZAKICHŌ

Isezakichōjamachi

JR Negishi Line

Ōoka-gawa

Ishikawachō

Shicho Shitsu (100m);
Bazaar Bazaar (150m);
Koganechō (600m)

KANNAI

1
2
3
4
5
6
7 12
8
9
10
11
13
14
15
16 26
17
18
19
20
21
22
23
24
25
27
28
29
30
31

Yokohama

Yamashita-kōen

Seaside, landscaped park **Yamashita-kōen** (山下公園周辺; Map p194; [R] Motomachi-Chūkagai) is perfect for strolling and ship watching. Look for the sleek, award-winning **Ōsanbashi International Passenger Terminal** (大さん橋国際客船ターミナル; Map p194; ☎ 045-211-2304; https://osanbashi.jp; 1-1-4 Kaigan-dōri, Naka-ku; 🕑 24hr; [S] Nihon-ōdōri) [FREE] with its attractive roof deck.

BankART Studio NYK GALLERY
(Map p194; ☎ 045-663-2812; www.bankart1929.com; 3-9 Kaigan-dōri, Naka-ku; admission varies; 🕑 cafe 11.30am-5.30pm, gallery hours vary; [S] Bashamichi) In a former warehouse, this multifloor gallery is a fixture on the local arts scene. It hosts changing exhibitions from local and international artists, and you can sift through flyers for local events over drinks in the 1st-floor cafe before stocking up on art and design books in the excellent attached shop.

Yokohama Archives of History MUSEUM
(横浜開港資料館; Map p194; ☎ 045-201-2100; www.kaikou.city.yokohama.jp/en/; 3 Nihon-ōdōri, Naka-ku; adult/child ¥200/100; 🕑 9.30am-5pm, closed Mon; [S] Nihon-ōdōri) Inside the former British consulate, displays in English chronicle the city's history with paintings, sketches, model ships and photographs, from the opening of Japan at the Yokohama port through to the mid-20th century.

NYK Hikawa Maru MUSEUM
(氷川丸; Map p194; www.nyk.com; Yamashita-kōen, Naka-ku; adult/child ¥300/100; 🕑 10am-5pm Tue-Sun; [S] Motomachi-Chūkagai) Moored at the eastern end of Yamashita-kōen, this restored 1930s passenger ship has art-deco fixings and stories to tell. Inside, you can wander from the 1st-class cabins (one of the staterooms was used by Charlie Chaplin) to the engine room.

Chinatown, Motomachi and Yamate

Yokohama's frenetic Chinatown packs some 600 speciality shops and restaurants within a space of several blocks, marked by 10 elaborately painted gates. It's very touristy, but fun to visit for a meal or evening stroll. At its heart is the elaborately decorated temple **Kantei-byō** (関帝廟; Map p194; 140 Yamashita-chō; 🕑 9am-7pm; [S] Motomachi-Chūkagai) [FREE], dedicated to Kanwu, the god of business.

Across the nearby Nakamura River is **Motomachi**, a pleasant, upscale shopping and dining area overlooked by the bluff of **Yamate**, the old foreign quarter where you can find several preserved Western-style residences from the early 20th century. The most convenient subway for all these areas is Motomachi-Chūkagai.

👁 Koganechō

Prostitution was once rife in **Koganechō** (黄金町), an atmospheric Yokohama district squeezed between the train tracks connecting Hinodechō and Koganechō stations and the Ōka River, roughly 2km southwest of Minato Mirai. But since the local authorities cleaned up the red-light district in 2005, it has sprouted galleries, art studios, boutiques and fun cafes and bars such as **Shicho Shitsu** (試聴室; ☎045-251-3979; http://shicho.org; 7 Koganechō, Naka-ku; ⏰noon-8pm Wed-Mon, to late Sat; 🚆Koganechō), which has a packed schedule of live gigs. There are residencies for artists whose murals and installations decorate the area and whose work is then exhibited at the annual art festival **Koganechō Bazaar** (www.koganecho.net); check the website for other events throughout the year.

👁 Greater Yokohama

Shin-Yokohama Rāmen Museum MUSEUM

(新横浜ラーメン博物館; ☎045-471-0503; www.raumen.co.jp/ramen; 2-14-21 Shin-Yokohama, Kohoku-ku; adult/child ¥310/100, dishes around ¥900; ⏰11am-10pm Mon-Sat, 10.30am-10pm Sun; 🚆Shin-Yokohama) Nine ramen restaurants from around Japan were hand-picked to sell their wares in this inventive replica of a 1958 *shitamachi* (downtown district) that's lit to feel like perpetual, festive night-time. It's a short walk from the Shin-Yokohama station – ask for directions at the station's information centre. Most of the restaurants offer 'mini' sizes so you can sample a few.

Sankei-en GARDENS

(三渓園; ☎045-621-0634; www.sankeien.or.jp; 58-1 Honmoku-sannotani, Naka-ku; adult/child ¥500/200; ⏰9am-5pm) Opened to the public in 1906, this beautifully landscaped garden features walking paths among ponds, 17th-century buildings, several fine tea-ceremony houses and a 500-year-old, three-storey pagoda. The inner garden is a fine example of traditional Japanese garden landscaping. From Yokohama or Sakuragi-chō Station, take bus 8 to Honmoku Sankei-en-mae bus stop (10 minutes).

🛏 Sleeping

Yokohama has plenty of midrange business hotel chains. Those on a budget should head to Kotobukichō and Matsukage-chō near Ishikawachō Station where there's a high concentration of hostels. It's a neighbourhood known for the down and out, but it's perfectly safe, cheap and a five-minute walk to Chinatown.

Hostel Zen HOSTEL ¥

(Map p194; ☎342-9553; http://zen.ilee.jp/; 3-10-5 Matsukage-chō, Naka-ku; s/d incl breakfast from ¥3300/5000; ❄📶; 🚆Ishikawachō) The best of the area's many cheapo hostels is Zen, which offers bright, clean Japanese- and Western-style rooms. They vary in size, and a few have been given makeovers by artists, so ask the helpful staff to let you check a few out first. There's a good breakfast spread, shared kitchen and rooftop-decking area with funky furniture and umbrellas.

Hotel Edit HOTEL ¥¥

(Map p194; ☎045-680-0238; http://hotel-edit.com/en/; 6-78-1 Sumiyoshi-chō; s/d incl breakfast from ¥7000/8500; 🚭❄📶) This smart riverside hotel is an appealing choice, conveniently located about 10 minutes' walk from Sakuragichō Station. Priced like a business hotel but with an attractive, modern aesthetic and English-speaking staff, Hotel Edit is also surrounded by great places to eat and to taste local craft beer.

Hotel New Grand HOTEL ¥¥¥

(ホテルニューグランド; Map p194; ☎045-681-1841; www.hotel-newgrand.co.jp; 10 Yamashita-chō, Naka-ku; r from ¥13,000; 🚭❄@📶; [S]Motomachi-Chūkagai) Dating from 1927, the New Grand has a prime waterfront location and elegant old-world charm, particularly in its original lobby and lavishly decorated ballrooms. It was once a favourite of visiting foreign dignitaries such as General McArthur and Charlie Chaplin. Go for the bay-view rooms.

🍴 Eating

Charcoal Grill Green GRILL ¥¥

(Map p194; ☎045-263-8976; www.greenyokohama.com; 6-79 Benten-dōri, Naka-ku; mains ¥1100-1400; ⏰11.30am-2pm & 5pm-midnight; 📄; [S]Bashamichi) The most central branch of this convivial charcoal grill and bar with a number of craft beers on tap – and a well-rounded wine list –

to go with smoky steaks, barbecue pork and delicious prawn pizzas. Their lunch specials are a great deal.

Bills INTERNATIONAL ¥¥
(ビルズ; Map p194; ☎ 045-650-1266; www.bills-jp.net; Akarenga Sōkō Bldg 2, 1-1-2 Shinkō, Naka-ku; mains ¥1000-2000; ⏰ 9am-11pm Mon-Fri, 8am-11pm Sat & Sun; 🖉 📋; [S] Bashamichi) Australian celebrity chef Bill Granger's Yokohama outlet has been a huge hit with locals – expect to wait in line at weekends and holidays if you've not booked. Try his famous ricotta hotcakes or berry pancakes. Note that there are a couple of vegan options on the breakfast and dinner menus.

Masan-no-mise Ryūsen CHINESE ¥¥
(馬さんの店龍仙; Map p194; ☎ 045-651-0758; www.ma-fam.com; 218-5 Yamashita-chō, Naka-ku; mains from ¥1050; ⏰ 7am-3am; 📋; 🚉 Ishikawa-chō) You can't miss friendly old Mr Ma sitting outside his small Shanghai-style eatery, as he has done for years. The walls are literally wallpapered with photos of tasty-looking dishes. It has two other branches in Chinatown.

★**Araiya** JAPANESE ¥¥¥
(荒井屋; Map p194; ☎ 045-226-5003; www.arai-ya.co.jp; 4-23 Kaigan-dōri, Naka-ku; set lunch/dinner from ¥1300/3500; ⏰ 11am-2.30pm & 5-10pm; 📋; [S] Bashamichi) Yokohama has it's own version of the beef hotpot dish *sukiyaki*, called *gyū-nabe*. This elegantly designed restaurant with waitresses in kimonos is the place to sample it.

Manchinrō Honten CHINESE ¥¥¥
(萬珍樓本店; Map p194; ☎ 045-681-4004; www.manchinro.com; 153 Yamashita-chō, Naka-ku; lunch/dinner courses from ¥2800/6000; ⏰ 11am-10pm; 🚭 📋; 🚉 Motomachi-Chūkagai) This elegant Cantonese restaurant is one of Chinatown's oldest (1892) and most respected. It serves a great selection of dim sum from 11am to 4pm, all in opulent surrounds. Look for the English sign next to the traditional gate.

🍷 Drinking & Nightlife

Beer lovers rejoice! Yokohama is packed with microbreweries and quality craft-beer bars. **Yokohama Oktoberfest** is held over two weeks at Akarenga Sōkō (p193) in early October and features more than 100 beers and much carousing in the spirit of the German festival. Also popular is the **Great Japan Beer Festival Yokohama** (www.beertaster.org) in mid-April and mid-September, featuring around 200 craft beers from across Japan.

Bashamichi Taproom PUB
(馬車道 タップルーム; Map p194; ☎ 045-264-4961; www.bairdbeer.com; 5-63-1 Sumiyoshi-chō, Naka-ku; ⏰ 5pm-midnight Mon-Fri, noon-midnight Sat & Sun; [S] Bashamichi) Set over three floors with a rooftop beer garden, this Baird Brewing Company pub offers some 14 beers on tap, 10 of which are from the brewery itself, ranging from pale ales to chocolate flavours. Try a sampler set for ¥1000 if you're struggling to decide. It also dishes up authentic American-style barbecue dishes (meals from ¥700).

Zō-no-hana Terrace CAFE
(象の鼻テラス; Map p194; ☎ 045-661-0602; www.zounohana.com; 1 Kaigan-dōri, Naka-ku; dishes ¥750; ⏰ 10am-6pm; 👪; [S] Nihon-ōdōri) A life-size sculpture of an elephant (*zō* in Japanese) and baby elephants, plus food and drink with elephant-design themes, make this bay-side cafe a delightful place for a refreshing drink. There are often art shows and other events held here, too.

Yokohama Brewery BREWERY
(Map p194; www.yokohamabeer.com; 6-68-1 Sumiyoshi-chō, Naka-ku; ⏰ 11.30am-3pm & 6-11pm Mon-Fri, 11.30am-11pm Sat, 11.30am-9pm Sun; 🚉 Sakuragichō) Sample five on-tap beers from the oldest craft brewery in Japan at this spacious restaurant-bar. A tasting set of all five is ¥1500. The food, using organic ingredients from farms in Kanagawa prefecture, is also very tasty.

Grassroots BAR
(Map p194; ☎ 045-312-0180; http://grassroots.yokohama/; B1 fl, 2-13-3 Tsuruyachō, Kanagawa-ku; ⏰ 5pm-2am; 🚉 Yokohama) Gigs, live art shows and DJ events are held in this psychedelically decorated basement space a short walk north of Yokohama Station. They also serve a good selection of international beers and tasty pub meals (¥750 to ¥2500) such as fish burgers and grilled tuna steaks with avocado mash.

☆ Entertainment

Live music is prominent here, with Yokohama particularly noted for its love of jazz. The Kannai-Bashamichi area is considered the hub of jazz.

★**Kamome** LIVE MUSIC
(カモメ; Map p194; ☎ 045-662-5357; www.yokohama-kamome.com; 6-76 Sumiyoshi-chō, Naka-ku; cover ¥3000; ⏰ 7-10.30pm Mon-Fri, 6-10.30pm Sat & Sun; [S] Bashamichi) The best place for serious live music, with a line-up that includes veteran and up-and-coming talents playing

jazz, funk, fusion and bossa nova. The interior is stark and sophisticated, the crowd stylish and multigenerational.

Airegin
JAZZ

(エアジン; Map p194; ☑045-641-9191; http://airegin.yokohama/; 5-60 Sumiyoshi-chō, Naka-ku; cover incl 1 drink ¥2500; ☺7.30-11pm; ☒Bashamichi) Up a flight of stairs is where you'll find this intimate, smoky and genuine jazz bar that's been swinging since '72. It's run by a passionate jazz-loving couple and top-notch performances bring in an appreciative and knowledgeable audience.

ℹ️ Information

See www.yokohamajapan.com and www.yokohamaseasider.com as well as the following tourist offices, all of which have an English speaker.

Chinatown 80 Information Center (横浜中華街インフォメーションセンター; Map p194; ☑045-681-6022; ☺10am-8pm Sun-Thu, to 9pm Fri & Sat) A few blocks from Motomachi-Chūkagai Station.

Sakuragichō Station Tourist Information (Map p194; ☑045-211-0111; ☺9am-6pm) Has maps and brochures and can help with hotel bookings. It's outside the south exit of Sakuragichō Station.

Yokohama Convention & Visitors Bureau (Map p194; ☑045-221-2111; www.yokohamajapan.com; 1st fl, Sangyō-Bōeki Center, 2 Yamashita-chō, Naka-ku; ☺9am-5pm Mon-Fri) A 10-minute walk from Nihon-ōdori station, and is very helpful with recommendations, maps and brochures, all delivered in English. Check out their excellent website.

Yokohama Station Tourist Information Center (Map p194; ☑045-441-7300; ☺9am-7pm) Has helpful English-speaking staff who can book accommodation. It's the east-west corridor at Yokohama Station.

ℹ️ Getting There & Away

JR Tōkaidō, Yokosuka and Keihin Tōhoku lines run from Tokyo Station (¥470, 40 minutes) via Shinagawa (¥290, 18 minutes) to Yokohama Station. Some Keihin Tōhoku line trains continue along the Negishi line to Sakuragichō, Kannai and Ishikawachō. From Shinjuku, take the Shōnan-Shinjuku line (¥550, 32 minutes).

The Tōkyū Tōyoko line runs from Shibuya to Yokohama (¥270, 30 minutes), after which it becomes the Minato Mirai subway line to Minato Mirai (¥450, 33 minutes) and Motomachi-Chūkagai (¥480, 39 minutes).

The Tōkaidō *shinkansen* stops at Shin-Yokohama Station, northwest of town, connected to the city centre by the Yokohama line.

ℹ️ Getting Around

BOAT

Sea Bass ferries (www.yokohama-cruising.jp) connect Yokohama Station with Minato Mirai 21 (¥420, 10 minutes) and Yamashita-kōen (¥700, 15 minutes) from approximately 10am to 7pm. From Yokohama Station, take the east exit and pass through Sogō department store to reach the dock.

BUS

Although trains are more convenient, Yokohama has a good bus network. A special Akai-kutsu ('red shoe') bus loops every 20 minutes from 10am to around 7pm through the major tourist spots (adult/child ¥220/110 per ride).

SUBWAY & TRAIN

The Yokohama City blue line (*shiei chikatetsu*) connects Yokohama with Shin-Yokohama (¥240, 11 minutes), Sakuragichō (¥210, four minutes) and Kannai (¥210, six minutes).

JR trains link Yokohama with Shin-Yokohama (¥170, 14 minutes), Sakuragi-chō (¥140, four minutes) and Kannai (¥140, five minutes).

CHICHIBU & OKU-TAMA

Nature conquers concrete at the western edge of Tokyo, where there's great hiking in the mountains of Chichibu, which includes Takao-san, less than an hour from Tokyo, and Oku-Tama, once a popular destination for pilgrims (and today, Tokyoites).

Takao-san
高尾山

Gentle Takao-san (599m) is a highly popular day trip from Tokyo with year-round hiking. It's rather built up compared with other regional hikes, but can be a perfect family outing if you avoid busy weekends and holidays.

⊙ Sights & Activities

The most popular route up Takao-san is **Trail No 1**, which is paved all the way and passes by all the major points of interest. If you're after more of a walk-in-the-woods experience, we recommend hiking up the lovely Trail No 6, and descending via Trail No 1. If following this route, wear sturdy shoes as there are some stream crossings and places where the trail is narrow or slippery.

Takao 599 Museum
MUSEUM

(☑042-665-6688; www.takao599museum.jp; 2435-3 Takao-machi, Hachioji-shi; ☺8am-5pm Apr-Nov, to 4pm Dec-Mar) **FREE** This beautifully designed museum, opened in summer 2015, is flooded with natural light and arranged with visitors of all ages in mind – display cases of insects and fungi have step stools for curious kids, a nature wall shows taxidermic specimens of Takao-san's mammals and birds and there's even a small play area. Interpretive signage is in Japanese and English. Worth a look before or after your hike, and there's a small cafe, too.

Yakuō-in BUDDHIST TEMPLE
(薬王院; ☑042-661-1115; www.takaosan.or.jp; 2177 Takao-machi, Hachioji-shi; ⊙24hr) **FREE**
One of the chief attractions on Takao-san is this temple, best known for the **Hi-watari Matsuri** (Fire-crossing Ceremony), which takes place on the second Sunday in March, near Takaosanguchi Station. Priests walk across hot coals with bare feet amid the ceremonial blowing of conch shells. The public is also welcome to participate.

❶ Information

There's usually an English speaker on hand at the helpful **tourist information center** (☑042-643-3115; ⊙8am-5pm Apr-Nov, to 4pm Dec-Mar) just outside the station exit.

❶ Getting There & Away

From Shinjuku Station, take the Keiō line (*jun-tok-kyū*, ¥390, 50 minutes) to Takaosanguchi. The tourist village, trail entrances, cable car and chairlift are a few minutes away to the right. JR Pass holders can travel to Takao Station on the JR Chūō line (48 minutes) and transfer to the Keiō line to Takaosanguchi (¥130, two minutes).

Oku-Tama 奥多摩

☑0428
Oku-Tama is Tokyo's best spot for easy hiking getaways and for river activities along the Tama-gawa. From **Takimoto** (滝本), in the valley, you can either ride a **cable car** (www.mitaketozan.co.jp; one way/return ¥590/1110; ⊙7.30am-6.30pm) or hike up for around an hour via a beautiful ancient cedar-lined pilgrims' path to **Mitake-san** (御岳山; elevation 939m), a charming old-world mountain hamlet that seems light years from Tokyo's bustle.

If you're not spending the night on Mitake-san, note that the cable car operates 7.30am to 6.30pm.

❍ Sights & Activities

Near the Mitake Visitors Centre you'll find the pilgrims' lodge **Baba-ke Oshi-Jutaku**,

an amazing thatched roof building dating from 1866. From here, it's another 20-minute walk up the mountain and demon-riddled steps (look closely as you ascend) to Musashi Mitake-jinja.

Musashi Mitake-jinja SHINTO SHRINE
(武蔵御嶽神社; ☑0428-78 -8500; www.musashi mitakejinja.jp; 176 Mitake-san, Ome-shi; ⊙24hr) **FREE** Atop Mitake-san is this attractive Shintō shrine and pilgrimage site said to date back some 1200 years. The site commands stunning views of the surrounding mountains. The wolf imagery stems from folklore in which a lost pilgrim was led out of a blanket of fog on the mountain by a pair of wolves, who were then enshrined as gods of the mountain.

Ōtake-san HIKING
(大岳山) The five-hour round-trip hike from Musashi Mitake-jinja to the summit of Ōtake-san (1266m) is highly recommended. Although there's some climbing involved, it's a fairly easy hike and the views from the summit are excellent – Mt Fuji is visible on clear days.

Moegi-no-Yu ONSEN
(もえぎの湯; ☑0428-82-7770; www.okutamas.co.jp/moegi; 119-1 Hikawa, Okutama, Nishitama-gun; adult/child ¥780/410; ⊙9.30am-8pm Tue-Sun Apr-Jun, Oct & Nov, to 9.30pm Jul-Sep, to 7pm Dec-Mar; ⓡJR Ome line to Okutama) This is an excellent onsen to relax in after a day hiking in the Oku-Tama region and includes *rotemburo* and footbaths. It's a 10-minute walk from the JR Oku-Tama station.

Sleeping & Eating

If you're seeking respite from urban travel, spending a night or two on Mitake-san provides peace and luxurious quiet.

There are several small eateries at the end of the path leading to Mitake-san.

Komadori San-sō MINSHUKU ¥
(駒鳥山荘; ☑0428-78-8472; www.komadori.com; 155 Mitake-san, Ome-shi; r per person with shared bathroom from ¥4500, incl 2 meals from ¥10,000; @☎) Below Musashi Mitake-jinja, towards the back end of the village, this former pilgrims' inn brims with bric-a-brac and history – it's been in the same family for 17 generations. Rooms and the verandah have excellent views and the friendly English-speaking owners are a delight.

Meals are excellent and you can also arrange to take a dawn hike to a stand under a waterfall, an ascetic practice known as *takigyō*.

Mitake Youth Hostel
HOSTEL ¥

(御嶽ユースホステル; ☑0428-78-8774; www. jyh.or.jp; 57 Mitake-san, Ome-shi; dm member/ nonmember ¥2970/3570; ⊕❄☎) Part of the comfortable ryokan Reiun-sō, this hostel has fine tatami rooms inside a handsome old building that used to be a pilgrims' lodge. It's midway between the top of the cable car and Musashi Mitake-jinja, about a minute beyond the visitors centre.

Momiji-ya
NOODLES ¥

(紅葉屋; ☑0428-78-8475; 151 Mitake-san, Ome-shi; mains ¥750-1200; ⊙10am-5pm; 🅿) Near the gate of Musashi Mitake-jinja, this cosy shop has mountain views out the back windows and *kamo-nanban soba* (noodles in hearty duck broth).

❶ Information

Pick up trail maps at the **Mitake Visitors Centre** (御岳ビジターセンター; ☑0428-78-9363; 38-5 Mitake-san; ⊙9am-4.30pm Tue-Sun), 250m beyond the cable-car terminus, near the start of the village.

❶ Getting There & Away

Take the JR Chūō line from Shinjuku Station, changing to the JR Ōme line at Tachikawa Station or Ōme Station depending on the service, and get off at Mitake (¥920, 90 minutes). Buses run from Mitake Station to Takimoto (¥290, 10 minutes) for the cable car.

NIKKŌ & AROUND

North of Tokyo, the Kantō plain gives way to a mountainous, forested landscape providing a fine backdrop for the spectacular shrines of Nikkō and the beautiful nearby lake Chūzenji-ko. The whole area is within the 400-sq-km Nikkō National Park, sprawling over Fukushima, Tochigi, Gunma and Niigata Prefectures, offering some excellent hiking opportunities and remote onsen.

Nikkō
日光

☑0288 / POP 83,446

Ancient moss clinging to a stone wall; rows of perfectly aligned stone lanterns; vermilion gates; and towering cedars: this is only a pathway in Nikkō, a sanctuary that enshrines the glories of the Edo period (1600–1868). Scattered among hilly woodlands, Nikkō is one of Japan's major attractions, its key World Heritage Site temples and shrines an awesome display of wealth and power by the Tokugawa shogunate.

All this means that in high season (summer and autumn) and at weekends, Nikkō can be extremely crowded and the spirituality of the area can feel a little lost. Spending the night here allows for an early start before the crowds arrive. However, we highly recommend a couple of nights so you can explore the gorgeous natural scenery in the surrounding area, much of it national park, as well as Nikkō's other sights and activities, including an imperial palace and onsen.

History

In the middle of the 8th century the Buddhist priest Shōdō Shōnin (735–817) established a hermitage at Nikkō. For centuries the mountains served as a training ground for Buddhist monks, though the area fell gradually into obscurity. Nikkō's enduring fame was sealed, however, when it was chosen as the site for the mausoleum of Tokugawa Ieyasu, the warlord who established the shogunate that ruled Japan for more than 250 years.

Ieyasu was laid to rest among Nikkō's towering cedars at a much less grand Tōshō-gū in 1617. Seventeen years later his grandson, Tokugawa Iemitsu, commenced work on the colossal shrine that can be seen today, using an army of 15,000 artisans from across Japan, who took two years to complete the project.

◉ Sights

The Nikkō World Heritage Site is a top destination for domestic and foreign visitors alike – if you can visit during the week, the crowds may be a smidgen more manageable.

★ Tōshō-gū
SHINTO SHRINE

(東照宮; Map p202; www.toshogu.jp; 2301 Sannai; adult/child ¥1300/450; ⊙8am-4.30pm Apr-Oct, to 3.30pm Nov-Mar) A World Heritage Site, Tōshō-gū is a brilliantly decorative shrine in a beautiful natural setting. Among its notable features is the dazzling 'Sunset Gate' Yōmei-mon.

As the shrine gears up for its 400th anniversary, a major restoration program is underway. Until at least 2018, the Yōmei-mon and Shimojinko (one of the Three Sacred Storehouses) will be obscured by scaffolding. Don't be put off visiting, as Tōshō-gū remains an impressive sight. A new museum building also debuted in 2015.

The stone steps of **Omotesandō** lead past the towering stone *torii* (entrance gate), **Ishidorii** (Map p202), and the **Gōjūnotō** (五重塔; Five Storey Pagoda; Map p202), a 1819 reconstruction of the mid-17th-century original, to **Omote-mon** (表門; Map p202), Tōshō-gū's main gateway, protected on either side by Deva kings.

In Tōshō-gū's initial courtyard are the **Sanjinko** (三神庫; Three Sacred Storehouses; Map p202); on the upper storey of the Kamijinko (upper storehouse) are relief carvings of 'imaginary elephants' by an artist who had never seen the real thing. Nearby is the **Shinkyūsha** (神厩舎; Sacred Stable; Map p202), adorned with relief carvings of monkeys. The allegorical 'hear no evil, see no evil, speak no evil' simians demonstrate three principles of Tendai Buddhism.

Further into Tōshō-gū's precincts, to the left of the drum tower, is **Honji-dō** (本地堂; Map p202), a hall known for the painting on its ceiling of the Nakiryū (Crying Dragon). Monks demonstrate the hall's acoustical properties by clapping two sticks together. The dragon 'roars' (a bit of a stretch) when the sticks are clapped beneath its mouth, but not elsewhere.

Once the scaffolding comes off in 2018, the **Yōmei-mon** (陽明門; Sunset Gate; Map p202) will be grander than ever, its gold leaf and intricate, coloured carvings and paintings of flowers, dancing girls, mythical beasts and Chinese sages all shiny and renewed. Worrying that the gate's perfection might arouse envy in the gods, those responsible for its construction had the final supporting pillar placed upside down as a deliberate error.

Gōhonsha (御本社; Map p202), the main inner courtyard, includes the **Honden** (本殿; Main Hall) and **Haiden** (拝殿; Hall of Worship). Inside these halls are paintings of the 36 immortal poets of Kyoto, and a ceiling-painting pattern from the Momoyama period; note the 100 dragons, each different. *Fusuma* (sliding door) paintings depict a *kirin* (a mythical beast that's part giraffe and part dragon).

To the right of the Gōhonsha is **Sakashitamon** (坂下門; Map p202), into which is carved a tiny wooden sculpture of the **Nemuri-neko** (坂下門; Map p202) that's famous for its lifelike appearance (though admittedly the attraction is lost on some visitors). From here it's an uphill path through towering cedars to the appropriately solemn **Okumiya** (奥宮; Map p202), Ieyasu's tomb.

> ### ⓘ UNDER CONSTRUCTION
>
> A few of Nikkō's temples have been undergoing restoration work for the past few years and this is set to continue. At Rinnō-ji, Sanbutsu-dō, the temple's main hall, is undergoing major renovation works due for completion in 2019. At Tōshō-gū, the Yomei-mon (Sunset Gate) should be completed by 2018; until then, scaffolding will shroud the gate so visitors will be unable to fully view the shrine. Taiyūin-byō's Nitennmon Gate (second gate) was also being restored at time of research.
>
> While this does mean only partial exterior views of some temples may be possible, this shouldn't put people off visiting. The interiors are completely on display and the temples remain impressive sights. You can check in with the tourist information office for an update before you visit.

Bypassed by nearly everyone at Tōshō-gū is the marvellous **Nikkō Tōshō-gū Museum of Art** (日光東照宮美術館; Map p202; ☏0288-54-0560; www.toshogu.jp/shisetsu/bijutsu.html; 2301 Yamanouchi; adult/child ¥800/400; ⊗9am-5pm Apr-Oct, to 4pm Nov-Mar) in the old shrine offices, showcasing fine paintings on its doors, sliding screens, frames and decorative scrolls, some by masters including Yokoyama Taikan and Nakamura Gakuryo. Follow the path to the right of Omote-mon to find it.

Taiyūin-byō
SHINTO SHRINE

(大猷院廟; Map p202; adult/child ¥550/250; ⊗8am-4.30pm Apr-Oct, to 3.30pm Nov-Mar) Ieyasu's grandson Iemitsu (1604–51) is buried here, and although the shrine houses many of the same elements as Tōshō-gū (storehouses, drum tower, Chinese-style gates etc), the more intimate scale and setting in a cryptomeria forest make it very appealing.

Look for dozens of lanterns donated by *daimyō* (domain lords), and the gate Niōmon, whose guardian deities have a hand up (to welcome those with pure hearts) and a hand down (to suppress those with impure hearts).

Inside the main hall, 140 dragons painted on the ceiling are said to carry prayers to the heavens; those holding pearls are on their way up, and those without are returning to gather more prayers.

Nikkō

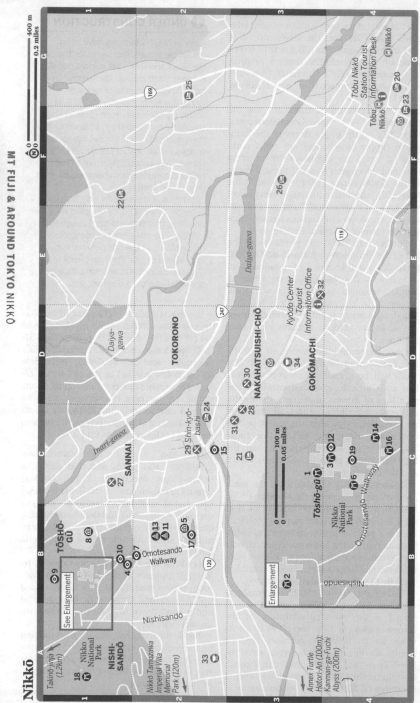

Nikkō

MT FUJI & AROUND TOKYO NIKKŌ

Rinnō-ji
BUDDHIST TEMPLE

(輪王寺; Map p202; ☏ 0288-54-0531; http://rinno ji.or.jp; 2300 Yamanouchi; adult/child ¥400/200; ⏰ 8am-5pm Apr-Oct, to 4pm Nov-Mar) This Tendai-sect temple was founded 1200 years ago by Shōdō Shōnin. Rinnō-ji's **Hōmotsu-den** (宝物殿, Treasure Hall; Map p202; ¥300; ⏰ 8am-5pm, to 4pm Nov-Mar) houses some 6000 treasures associated with the temple; the separate admission ticket includes entrance to the **Shōyō-en** (逍遥園; Map p202; ⏰ 8am-5pm Apr-Oct, to 4pm Nov-Mar) strolling garden.

Sanbutsu-dō
BUDDHIST TEMPLE

(三仏堂; Three-Buddha Hall; Map p202) The main hall of the temple Rinnō-ji houses a trio of 8m gilded wooden Buddha statues: Amida Nyorai (a primal deity in the Mahayana Buddhist canon) flanked by Senjū (deity of mercy and compassion) and Batō (a horse-headed Kannon). Its exterior is under wraps for restoration until 2019, with a life-size graphic adorning the building's scaffolding, *trompe l'œil* style.

Futarasan-jinja
SHINTO SHRINE

(二荒山神社; Map p202; www.futarasan.jp; adult/child ¥200/100) Set among cypress trees, this very atmospheric shrine was founded by Shōdō Shōnin; the current building dates from 1619, making it Nikkō's oldest. It's the protector shrine of Nikkō itself, dedicated to Nantai-san (2484m); the mountain's consort, Nyotai-san; and their mountainous progeny,

Tarō. There are other branches of the shrine on Nantai-san and by Chūzenji-ko.

Nikkō Tamozawa Imperial Villa Memorial Park
HISTORIC SITE

(日光田母沢御用邸記念公園; ☏ 53-6767; www.park-tochigi.com/tamozawa; 8-27 Hon-chō; adult/child ¥510/260; ⏰ 9am-5pm Wed-Mon, to 4.30pm Nov-Mar) About 1km west of Shin-kyō bridge, this splendidly restored imperial palace of more than 100 rooms showcases superb artisanship, with parts of the complex dating from the Edo, Meiji and Taishō eras. Apart from the construction skills involved there are brilliantly detailed screen paintings and garden views framed from nearly every window.

Visit in autumn to see the gardens at their most spectacular.

Takinō-jinja
SHINTO SHRINE

(滝尾神社) **FREE** Around one kilometre north of Futarasan-jinja, close by the Shiraito Falls, is this serene, delightfully less crowded shrine that has a history stretching back to 820. The stone gate, called **Undameshi-no-torii**, dates back to 1696. Before entering, it's customary to try your luck tossing three stones through the small hole near the top.

Maps available at the tourist offices show the route to the shrine, which also passes the tomb of Shōdō Shōnin.

Shin-kyō
HISTORIC SITE

(神橋; Map p202; crossing fee ¥300) This much-photographed red footbridge is located

WORTH A TRIP

OMIYA RAILWAY MUSEUM

The fascinating **Railway Museum** (鉄道博物館; ☎048-651-0088; www.railway-museum.jp/; 3-47 Onari-chō, Omiya-ku, Saitama-shi; adult/student/child ¥1000/500/200; ⏲10am-6pm Wed-Mon) in Omiya, 25km north of central Tokyo, charts the evolution from steam to modern-day technology of Japan's railways. It's packed with lovingly preserved rolling stock and is a must for rail enthusiasts, who can climb aboard classic carriages and even get behind the controls of a *shinkansen* (bullet train). The museum is linked to Omiya Station by the New Shuttle train (¥190, five minutes) and is easy to visit on the way to or from Nikkō.

at the sacred spot where Shōdō Shōnin is said to have been carried across the Daiya-gawa on the backs of two giant serpents. It's a reconstruction of the 17th-century original.

Kanman-ga-Fuchi Abyss PARK
(憾満ガ淵) Escape the crowds along this wooded path lined with a collection of Jizō statues (the small stone effigies of the Buddhist protector of travellers and children). After passing the Shin-kyō bridge (p203), follow the Daiya-gawa west for about 1km, crossing another bridge near Jyoko-ji temple en route. It's said that if you try to count the statues there and again on the way back, you'll end up with a different number, hence the nickname 'Bake-jizō' (ghost Jizō).

Tours

Tochigi Volunteer Interpreters & Guides Association TOURS
(nikkotviga@hotmail.co.jp) Offers free guided tours between November and March – 10 days' advance notice is preferred. Guests pay for their own admission and transport costs.

Festivals & Events

Tōshō-gū Grand Festival CULTURAL
(⏲17 & 18 May) Nikkō's most important annual festival features horseback archery on the first day and a 1000-strong costumed re-enactment of the delivery of Ieyasu's remains to Nikkō on the second.

There's a slightly scaled-down version of this **festival** in October.

Sleeping

★**Nikkorisou Backpackers** HOSTEL ¥
(にっこり荘バックパッカーズ; Map p202; ☎080-9449-1545; http://nikkorisou.com/eng.html; 1107 Kamihatsu-ishi-machi; dm/d with shared bathroom from ¥3000/6900; ❄📶) The closest hostel to the World Heritage Site offers a riverside location and relaxed, friendly vibe. As it's run single-handedly by the English-speaking Hiro, guests need to be elsewhere between 10am and 4pm, but at any other hour the kitchen, huge deck and cosy common area are havens for hanging out. Well-maintained hybrid mountain bikes are available for rent (¥500).

Nikkō Guesthouse Sumica GUESTHOUSE ¥
(日光ゲストハウス 巣み家; Map p202; ☎090-1838-7873; www.nikko-guesthouse.com; 5-12 Aioi-chō; dm/r per person without bathroom from ¥3500/7000; 📶) Run by a lovely, clued-up couple, this tiny guesthouse is set in an artfully renovated wooden house steps from both train stations. Dorms are a bit cramped, but they're tidy, as are the two private tatami-mat doubles; all with fan only and shared bathrooms. There's an 11pm curfew.

Rindō-no-Ie MINSHUKU ¥
(りんどうの家; Map p202; ☎53-0131; 1462 Tokorono; r per person without bathroom from ¥3500; 🚭❄@📶) Run by a lovely couple, this small but well-maintained *minshuku* offers tatami rooms, tasty meals and pick-up service. Breakfast/dinner is ¥700. It's across the river, a 15-minute walk northwest of the train station.

Nikkō Park Lodge GUESTHOUSE ¥
(日光パークロッジ; Map p202; ☎0288-53-1201; www.nikkoparklodge.com; 2828-5 Tokorono; dm/d from ¥2800/8980; 🚭❄@📶) In the wooded hills north of town, this well-kept guesthouse has Western-style rooms, a spacious dorm, a homely lounge with log fire and English-speaking staff who are a great source of info. There's an afternoon pick-up service, otherwise it's around ¥700 by taxi from the station. They also run an urban **lodge** (Map p202; ☎0288-25-3310; 11-6 Matsubara-chō; dm/r from ¥3000/7000) across from Tōbu Station.

Nikkō Inn INN ¥¥
(日光イン; ☎0288-27-0008; www.nikko-inn.jp; 333 Koshiro; s/d cottages from ¥8000/13,000; 📶) Located just 30 minutes' train ride from Nikkō in pastoral Shimo-goshiro, Nikkō Inn offers six Japanese-style cottages, sleeping between two and seven people and overlooking rice fields. Each wooden house has tatami

rooms with rice-paper screens and traditional verandahs, plus modern kitchen and bathroom facilities.

On the doorstep is a village of 1000 people and the mountains of Nikkō. Shimo-goshiro is on the Tōbu line from Asakusa (¥1160, 2¼ hours), four stops before Nikkō (¥350). The cottages are a five-minute walk from the station.

Annex Turtle Hotori-An INN ¥¥
(アネックスーほとり庵; ☑0288-53-3663; www. turtle-nikko.com; 8-28 Takumi-chō; s/tw from ¥6700/13,000; ◉❄@☎) Only steps away from the trailhead to Kanman-ga-Fuchi Abyss, this tidy, comfortable inn offers Japanese- and Western-style rooms, plus river views from the house onsen. It's a lovely spot in a quiet neighbourhood giving way to open space.

Stay Nikkō Guesthouse GUESTHOUSE ¥¥
(Map p202; ☑0288-25-5303; www.staynikko.com; 2-360-13 Inarimachi; s/d from ¥7500/7900; ❄☎) If your self-catering plans require nothing more than a microwave and fridge, this little yellow house might be your place. (If you require noise privacy, it might not be.) With only four private rooms, all sharing bathroom facilities, this spotless new riverside guesthouse is a only few blocks from downtown Nikkō, and yet a snug, peaceful space for escaping the bustle. Breakfast costs ¥800.

Nikkō Kanaya Hotel HOTEL ¥¥¥
(日光金谷ホテル; Map p202; ☑0288-54-0001; www.kanayahotel.co.jp; 1300 Kamihatsu-ishimachi; tw from ¥17,820; P❄@☎) This grand lady from 1893 wears her history like a well-loved, if not slightly worn, dress. The newer wing has Japanese-style rooms with excellent vistas, spacious quarters and private bathrooms; the cheaper rooms in the main building are Western style and have an appealing old-fashioned ambience.

Wi-fi in the lobby only, where you'll find the bar is deliciously dark and amenable to whisky drinkers. Rates rise steeply in high seasons.

✕ Eating

A local speciality is *yuba* (the skin that forms when making tofu) cut into strips; it's a staple of *shōjin-ryōri* (Buddhist vegetarian cuisine). You'll see it all over town, in everything from noodles (*yuba soba*) to fried bean buns (*age yuba manju*).

Hongū Cafe CAFE ¥
(本宮カフェ; Map p202; ☑0288-54-1669; www. hongucafe.com; 2384 Sannai; espresso ¥350,

dessert sets from ¥650; ◷10am-6pm Fri-Wed; ◨) Refresh with a cup of espresso, or a traditional Japanese dessert set of *matcha* and *yomogi-mochi* (mugwort dumplings topped with sweet *azuki*-bean paste) – it tastes better than it sounds. Set in a refurbished historic house near the entrance of the national park, this is a great place to take a breather après-shrine.

Hippari Dako YAKITORI ¥
(ひっぱり凧; Map p202; ☑0288-53-2933; 1011 Kamihatsu-ishimachi; meals ¥550-900; ◷11am-8pm; ☑◨) An institution for more than a quarter of a century among foreign travellers, as layers of business cards tacked to the walls testify, this no-frills restaurant serves comfort food, including curry *udon*, *yuba* sashimi and *yaki-udon* (fried noodles).

★ Meguri VEGAN ¥¥
(Map p202; ☑0288-25-3122; 909 Nakahatsuishimachi; lunch ¥1400; ◷11.30am-6pm Sat-Wed; ◨) A dedicated young couple dish up lovingly prepared tasty vegan Japanese meals in this former art shop with an amazing painting on its ceiling. Arrive at opening to secure lunch – it's a popular place and once they've run out of food it's sweets and drinks only.

Shiori JAPANESE ¥¥
(栞; Map p202; ☑0228-25-5745; 957-2 Shimohatsuishi-machi; dishes ¥400-1800; ◷6.30-10pm; ◨) As this is one of the few small restaurants open late, you'll find people queueing for it to open – consider making a reservation. This is a small-plates kind of place, with a tiny dish of *otōshi* (appetiser, ¥250) automatically served on arrival. Try some delicate *yuba* sashimi, served with spiral-cut *daikon* radish, wasabi and soy sauce.

Nagomi-chaya JAPANESE ¥¥
(和み茶屋; Map p202; ☑0288-54-3770; 1016 Kamihatsu-ishi; dishes/set meals from ¥450/1620; ◷11.30am-4pm Thu-Tue) A faithful picture menu makes ordering simple at this sophisticated arts-and-crafts-style cafe near the top of Nikkō's main drag. The beautifully prepared *kaiseki*-style lunches are a great deal.

★ Gyōshintei KAISEKI ¥¥¥
(尭心亭; Map p202; ☑0288-53-3751; www.meiji-yakata.com/gyoushin; 2339-1 Sannai; set lunch/dinner from ¥2100/4500; ◷11am-8pm Fri-Wed; ☑◨) Splash out on deluxe spreads of vegetarian *shōjin-ryōri*, featuring local bean curd and vegetables served half a dozen delectable ways, or the *kaiseki* courses which include

fish. The elegant tatami dining room overlooks a carefully tended garden which is part of the Meji-no-Yakata compound of chic restaurants close by the World Heritage Site.

♈ Drinking & Nightlife

★ Nikkō Coffee   CAFE
(日光珈琲; Map p202; http://nikko-coffee.com; 3-13 Honchō; coffee ¥550, meals from ¥1000; ☺10am-6pm Tue-Sun) A century-old rice shop has been sensitively reinvented as this retro-chic cafe with a garden, where expertly made hand-dripped coffee is served with cakes and snack meals such as bacon, cheese and egg galette (buckwheat pancake) or pork curry.

Yuzawaya   CAFE
(湯沢屋; Map p202; www.yuzawaya.jp; 946 Kamihatsu-ishimachi; tea sets from ¥450; ☺11am-4pm Mon-Fri, to 5pm Sat & Sun) In business since 1804, this teahouse specialises in *manju* (bean-jam buns) and other traditional sweets; look for the green-and-white banners.

❶ Information

At Tōbu Nikkō Station, there's a small **information desk** (Map p202; ☎ 0288-54-0864; ☺8.30am-

❶ NIKKŌ TRANSPORT PASSES

Tōbu Railway (www.tobu.co.jp/foreign) Offers two passes covering rail transport from Asakusa to Nikkō (though not the *tokkyū* surcharge, from ¥1040) and unlimited hop-on, hop-off bus services around Nikkō. Purchase at the **Tōbu Sightseeing Service Center** (p152).

Nikkō All Area Pass (adult/child ¥4520/2280) Valid for four days and includes buses to Chūzen-ji Onsen and Yumoto Onsen.

Nikkō City Area Pass (adult/child ¥2670/1340) Valid for two days and includes buses to the World Heritage Sites.

If you've already got your rail ticket, two-day bus-only passes allow unlimited rides between Nikkō and Chūzen-ji Onsen (adult/child ¥2000/1000) or Yumoto Onsen (adult/child ¥3000/1500), including the World Heritage Site area. The **Sekai-isan-meguri** (World Heritage Bus Pass; adult/child ¥500/250) covers the area between the stations and the shrine precincts. Buy at Tōbu Nikkō Station.

5pm) where you can grab a town map and get help in English to find buses, restaurants and hotels.

Kyōdo Center Tourist Information Office (Map p202; ☎ 0288-54-2496; www.nikko-jp.org; 591 Gokomachi; ☺9am-5pm; ☎) is Nikkō's main tourist information office, with English speakers (guaranteed between 10am and 2pm) and maps for sightseeing and hiking.

Tochigi Volunteer Interpreters & Guides Association (p204) offers free guided tours between November and March, but not of the World Heritage area. Contact in advance.

❶ Getting There & Away

Nikkō is best reached from Tokyo via the Tōbu Nikkō line from Asakusa Station. You can usually get last-minute seats on the hourly reserved *tokkyū* (limited-express) trains (¥2700, 1¾ hours). *Kaisoku* (rapid) trains (¥1360, 2½ hours, hourly from 6.20am to 5.30pm) require no reservation, but you may have to change at Shimo-imaichi. Be sure to ride in the last two cars to reach Nikkō (some cars may separate at an intermediate stop).

JR Pass holders can take the Tohoku *shinkansen* (bullet train) from Tokyo to Utsunomiya (¥4930, 54 minutes) and change there for an ordinary train to Nikkō (¥740, 45 minutes).

❶ Getting Around

Both JR Nikkō Station (designed by Frank Lloyd Wright) and the nearby Tōbu Nikkō Station lie southeast of the shrine area within a block of Nikkō's main road (Rte 119, the old Nikkō-kaidō). From the station, follow this road uphill for 20 minutes to reach the shrine area, past restaurants, souvenir shops and the main tourist information centre, or take a bus to the Shin-kyō bus stop (¥200). Bus stops are announced in English. Buses leave from both JR and Tōbu Nikkō Station; buses bound for both Chūzen-ji Onsen and Yumoto Onsen stop at Shin-kyō and other stops around the World Heritage Sites.

Chūzen-ji Onsen
中禅寺温泉
☎ 0288
This highland area 11.5km west of Nikkō offers some natural seclusion and striking views of Nantai-san from Chūzen-ji's lake, Chūzenji-ko. The lake itself is 161m deep and a fabulous shade of deep blue in good weather with the usual flotilla of sightseeing boats.

⊙ Sights

Kegon-no-taki   WATERFALL
(華厳ノ滝, Kegon Falls; 2479-2 Chūgūshi; adult/child ¥550/330; ☺7.30am-6pm May-Sep, 8am-5pm

KANIYU ONSEN

In the midst of the mountainous Okukino region of 'secret onsen', you'll find **Kaniyu Onsen** (加仁湯; ☑ 0288-96-0311; www.naf.co.jp/kaniyu; 871 Kawamata; r per person with 2 meals from ¥13,110, onsen day visitor ¥50; ☺ day visitors 9am-3pm), a rustic ryokan with milky sulphuric waters in its multiple outdoor baths, a few of which are mixed bathing. To get here from Nikkō, take the Tōbu line to Shimo-imaichi, change to a Kinugawa Onsen–bound train, then board the bus to Meoto-buchi (¥1540, 1½ hours, four daily). From here, it's a gentle 1½ hike up a beautiful river valley past several waterfalls.

You'll need to leave Nikkō before 9am to make it to Kaniyu and back in a day, and that will give you around only one hour at the onsen. If you'd prefer to take it at a more leisurely pace, plan an overnight stay. Either way, before setting off check the latest transport details with one of Nikkō's tourist offices.

Oct-Apr) The big-ticket attraction of Chūzen-ji is this billowing, 97m-high waterfall. Take the elevator down to a platform to observe the full force of the plunging water, or admire it from up high on the viewing platform.

Futarasan-jinja
SHRINE
(二荒山神社; 2484 Chūgūshi; ☺ 8am-4.30pm) **FREE** This shrine complements those at Tōshō-gū (p200), in Nikkō, and is the starting point for pilgrimages up Nantai-san. The shrine is about 1km west of Kegon Falls, along the lake's north shore.

Chūzen-ji Tachiki-kannon
BUDDHIST TEMPLE
(中禅寺立木観音; 2578 Chūgūshi; adult/child ¥500/200; ☺ 8am-3.30pm Dec-Feb, to 4pm Mar & Nov, to 5pm Apr-Oct) This eponymous temple, located on the lake's eastern shore, was founded in the 8th century and houses a 6m-tall Kannon statue from that time.

🛌 Sleeping & Eating

There are a couple of restaurants scattered around Lake Chūzenji, but most are clustered around the eastern corner.

Chūzenji Pension
INN ¥
(中禅寺ペンション; ☑ 0288-55-0888; www.chuzenji-pension.com; 2482 Chūgūshi; r per person incl dinner from ¥8500; ☺🅿️) A salmon-pink-painted hostelry set back from the lake's eastern shore with nine mostly Western-style rooms that feel like grandma's house. All rooms have lake views, it has onsen baths and, in the separate restaurant, a cosy fireplace. Bike rental (¥500 per hour) is also available.

KAI Nikko
RYOKAN ¥¥¥
(界日光; ☑ 050-3786-0099; http://kai-nikko.jp/; 1661 Chūgūshi; r per person incl 2 meals ¥30,000; ✳️📶) Hoshino Resorts took over this 20-year-old, 33-room mega-ryokan in

2014 and have given it some contemporary sparkle. Super-spacious tatami rooms feature Western-style beds and killer lake views. There are enormous onsen baths and a nightly Nikko Geta folk-dance show. English is spoken and the food is delicious.

ℹ️ Getting There & Away

Buses run from Tōbu Nikkō Station to Chūzen-ji Onsen (¥1150, 45 minutes) or use the economical Tōbu Nikkō Bus Free Pass (p206), available at Tōbu Nikkō Station.

Yumoto Onsen 湯元温泉
☑ 0288 / POP 298
Yumoto Onsen is a hot-springs village on the shore of Lake Yunoko. It's quieter than nearby Chūzen-ji Onsen and offers easy access to several hiking trails.

🏃 Activities

Senjōgahara Shizen-kenkyu-rō
HIKING
(戦場ヶ原自然研究路; Senjōgahara Plain Nature Trail) Take a Yumoto-bound bus and get off at **Ryūzu-no-taki** (竜頭ノ滝; ¥460, 20 minutes), a lovely waterfall overlooked by a teahouse that marks the trailhead. The hike follows the Yu-gawa across the picturesque marshland of **Senjōgahara** (mainly on wooden plank paths), alongside the 75m-high falls of **Yu-daki** (湯滝) to the lake **Yu-no-ko** (湯の湖), then around the lake to Yumoto Onsen.

Onsen-ji
ONSEN
(温泉時; adult/child ¥500/300; ☺ 9am-4pm) Towards the back of Yumoto Onsen, this temple has a humble bathhouse (with extremely hot water) and a tatami lounge for resting weary muscles. Look for a row of stone lanterns near the final village bus stop that leads to the temple.

STOPOVER IN NARITA

Long Layover?

The city of **Narita** (成田; population 131,230) is best known for **Narita International Airport** (p891), but it has a few charms of its own. If you have a five-hour layover (or more), you'll have time to take the train – either the private Keisei line (¥260, 10 minutes) or JR (¥200/240 from Terminal 2/1, 10 minutes) – into Narita, do some sightseeing and grab a bite to eat before heading back.

Pick up a map at the **Narita Tourist Information Center** (☑0476-24-3198; ◷8.30am-5.15pm), just outside the eastern exit of JR Narita Station. Then stroll down **Omote-sandō**, an atmospheric old road lined with souvenir, craft and medicinal shops, and restaurants to **Narita-san Shinshōji** (成田山新勝寺; www.naritasan.or.jp; 1 Narita; ◷24hr) FREE. The landscaped grounds of this venerable temple, founded in 940, are among the largest in Japan.

Narita is famous for its *unagi* (eel). At famous **Kawatoyo Honten** (川豊本店; ☑0476-22-2711; www.unagi-kawatoyo.com; 386 Naka-machi; meals from ¥2300; ◷10am-5pm Tue-Sun; 🖫), opposite the Tourist Pavilion, chefs expertly carve up live eels out the front (though you may prefer not to see this). Pay first, take a ticket and wait to be shown to your table.

Flight crews bunking in nearby hotels are a fixture of the local nightlife scene. **Jet Lag Club** (☑0476-22-0280; 508 Kamichō; ◷4pm-2am), run by a former flight attendant and usually packed with a mix of off-duty crew members, assorted locals and random tourists, is a comfortable spot to get your bearings (or lose them).

Early Flight?

Numerous chains operate hotels near the airport and in Narita town, and there are some great ryokan around Omote-sandō.

From Tokyo, the easiest way to get to Narita is via the Keisei line from Keisei Ueno Station, taking the Cityliner (¥1790, 41 minutes), or the express (*tokkyu*; ¥840, 71 minutes). Note that most JR Narita Express trains do not stop at Narita.

Ninehours Narita Airport (☑0476-33-5109; http://ninehours.co.jp; Narita International Airport Terminal 2; capsules excl/incl breakfast from ¥5900/7440; 🛜) You can hardly get closer to the airport than this brilliant white, futuristic-styled capsule hotel, which is in the basement car park of Terminal 2.

Kirinoya Ryokan (桐之屋旅館; ☑0476-22-0724; www.naritakanko.jp/kirinoya; 58 Tamachi; s/d with shared bathroom from ¥3500/9000, breakfast/dinner from ¥525/1050; P🌀🛜) The English-speaking owner of this workaday ryokan, a five-minute walk south of Narita-san temple, can trace his lineage back 50 generations, and his rambling old inn is filled with samurai armour and swords. Station pick-up/drop-off (until 7pm) is possible with advance notice or if staff is available.

🛏 Sleeping

If you opt to stay in Yumoto Onsen, you're most likely to take your meals at your accommodation, as there is very little else around.

Yu-no-Mori   RYOKAN ¥¥¥
(ゆの森; ☑0288-62-2800; www.okunikko-yunomori.com; Yumoto Onsen; r per person incl 2 meals from ¥20,000; 🛜) The 12 elegant rooms (Western-style on the 1st floor, Japanese-style on the 2nd) at this luxurious ryokan are decorated in natural tones, and each has a private wooden bath on a decked verandah.

❶ Getting There & Away

From Yumoto Onsen you can return to Nikkō by bus (¥1700, 1½ hours). You can also access Yumoto Onsen by bus from Chūzen-ji Onsen (¥890, 30 minutes), or by a rewarding three-hour hike on the **Senjōgahara Shizen-kenkyu-rō** (p207).

OGASAWARA ARCHIPELAGO
小笠原 諸島

About 1000km south of Ginza, but still within Tokyo Prefecture, the World Natural Heritage–listed Ogasawara Archipelago

(Ogasawara-shotō) is a nature-lover's paradise, with pristine beaches surrounded by tropical waters and coral reefs. Snorkelling, whale-watching, swimming with dolphins and hiking are all on the bill.

The only way to get here is by a 24-hour ferry ride (p210) from Tokyo. The ferry docks at Chichi-jima, the main island of the 30-strong group. A smaller ferry connects Chichi-jima to Haha-jima, the only other inhabited island.

History

Just as fascinating as the islands' natural attractions is their human history. Mapped by the Japanese in the 16th century, the islands' earliest inhabitants were a motley crew of Europeans and Pacific Islanders who set up provisioning stations for ships working the Japan whaling grounds in 1830. Around 100 descendants of these settlers, known as *obeikei*, still live on the islands, accounting for the occasional Western name and face. US Commodore Matthew Perry stopped here en route to Japan proper in 1853, when the archipelago was known as the Bonin Islands – it gained the name Ogasawara in 1875 when the Meiji government claimed the territory.

The gun emplacements at the ends of most of the islands' beaches were built by the Japanese during WWII, though the big battles were fought further south on Iwo-jima. After the war the islands were occupied by the US military until 1968 when they reverted back to Japan.

Chichi-jima 父島

☑ 04998 / POP 2061

Beautifully preserved, gorgeous Chichi-jima has plenty of accommodation, restaurants, even a bit of tame nightlife. But the real attractions are the excellent beaches, outdoor activities and access to the Ogasawara's amazing natural heritage.

🏃 Activities

The two best beaches for snorkelling are on the north side of the island, a short walk over the hill from the village. **Miya-no-hama** (宮之浜) has decent coral and is sheltered, making it suitable for beginners. About 500m along the coast (more easily accessed from town) is **Tsuri-hama** (釣浜), a rocky beach that has better coral but is more exposed.

Good swimming beaches line the west side of the island, getting better the further south you go. The neighbouring coves

of **Kopepe** (コペペ海岸) and **Kominato-kaigan** (小港海岸) are particularly attractive. From Kominato-kaigan, you can walk along a trail over the hill and along the coast to the beguiling white sand of **John Beach** (ジョンビーチ), but note that it's a two-hour walk in each direction and there is no drinking water – bring at least 3L per person.

👉 Tours

Pelan Sea Kayak Club   KAYAKING

(☑ 04998-2-3386; www.pelan.jp; full-day tours ¥9000, snorkelling gear rental ¥500) Run by Ryō-san from Pelan Village, here you can join tours to some of the island's more enchanting spots. Fees include rental of kayaking gear and meals cooked Pelan-style, on a wood-burning camp stove. Catching and grilling your own fish is optional.

Pink Dolphin   TOURS

(☑ 080-8849-7307; www.chichijimapinkdolphin.jp; half-/full-day tours ¥5000/10,000) Stanley Minami is the English-speaking skipper of the *Pink Dolphin*, a glass-bottom boat, offering dolphin- and whale-watching tours, and swimming with dolphins when sea conditions allow. Also runs trips to Minami-jima, an uninhabited island with a magical secret beach called Ōgi-ike (扇池). Tours must be booked in advance, by phone only.

Rao Adventure Tours   TOUR

(☑ 04998-2-2081) At Chichi-jima's Ōgiura Beach, Rao Adventure Tours organises jungle tours (¥5000 per half-day) and surf school (¥15,000 per day).

🛏 Sleeping

⭐ Pelan Village
CABIN ¥

(☑04998-2-3386; www.pelan.jp; r per person with shared bathroom from ¥5000; 🐾) 🖋 A Never-Never Land of cosy rough wooden cabins, walkways and ladders perched on a leafy mountainside, Pelan Village offers a sustainable ecoretreat ideal for self-caterers. It is not, however, for dilettantes – conventional soaps and detergents are banned because water run-off goes directly to the crops.

Banana Inn
GUESTHOUSE ¥

(バナナ荘; ☑04998-2-2050; www.chichijimapink-dolphin.jp/banana.html; s/d with shared bathroom ¥5000/9000; 🅿🕸❄@) Steps from the ferry pier, this humble inn has basic Japanese- and Western-style rooms but lots of hospitality. The owner, John Washington, an Ernest Hemingway–type who enjoys discussing local history, is usually in residence in March.

Tetsuya Healing Guest House
GUESTHOUSE ¥¥

(てつ家; ☑04998-2-7725; www.tetuyabonin.com; r per person incl breakfast from ¥9500; 😊❄@🐾) Offers thoughtfully designed rooms, open-air baths and multicourse meals that make innovative use of local ingredients. It's a five-minute walk from Kominato-kaigan Beach.

Rockwells
GUESTHOUSE ¥¥

(ロックウェルズ; ☑04998-2-3838; http://rockwells.co.jp/ogasawara; s/d with shared bathroom incl half-board from ¥8200/14,400; 😊❄🐾) A young and friendly English-speaking family run this simple guesthouse and bar right on Ōgiura Beach. The meals are delicious.

🍴 Eating & Drinking

There are a few options for dining on the island, although it's wise to book meals at your accommodation where possible, or self-cater.

Cafe Hale
JAPANESE ¥

(☑04998-2-2373; meals ¥1000; ⊙9am-8pm Fri-Tue; 🐾) Hale's deck, facing Chichi-jima's port, is a top spot to enjoy a delicious lunch of sashimi on a bowl of rice or a slice of lemon cheesecake.

Bonina
INTERNATIONAL ¥¥

(☑04998-2-3027; mains from ¥1000; ⊙11.30am-1.30pm & 6pm-midnight) Friendly restaurant and bar serving simple fare of rice dishes, pizza and tacos. Open for lunch on days when the Tokyo ferry is in town. It's in front of Futami Bay, steps from the port.

⭐ USK Coffee
CAFE

(☑04998-2-2338; https://uskcoffee.com/tag/chichijima; Kita-fukurozawa; ⊙1-5pm Thu & Fri, 10am-5pm Sat & Sun) Out of an Airstream caravan on the road to Kominato-kaigan beach, English-speaking Ku and Yusuke serve thirst-quenching caffeinated drinks, made from beans grown on their adjacent plot, along with homemade cookies and cakes. A top spot to relax and refresh.

Yankee Town
BAR

(ヤンキータウン; ☑080-2567-7168, 04998-2-3042; http://yankeetown.net; ⊙8pm-2am Thu-Tue) Follow the main coastal road towards Okumura for around 10 minutes east of the main pier to find this convivial driftwood bar run by island-born, English-speaking Rance Ohira. It's a great place to chill with a beer or cocktail. There's occasional live music, too, making it the town's liveliest bar.

ℹ Information

Find the **Chichi-jima Tourism Association** (父島観光協会; ☑04998-2-2587; ⊙8am-noon & 1.30-5pm) in the B-Ship building about 250m west of the pier, near the post office. Ask for the helpful *Guide Map of Chichi-jima;* English spoken. Right on the beach past the village office, the **Ogasawara Visitor Center** (小笠原ビジターセンター; ☑04998-2-3001; ⊙8.30am-5pm) has displays in English about the local ecosystem and history.

ℹ Getting There & Away

Ogasawara Kaiun (小笠原海運; ☑03-3451-5171; www.ogasawarakaiun.co.jp/english/) runs the *Ogasawara-maru*, which sails at least once a week between Tokyo's Takeshiba Pier (10 minutes' walk from Hamamatsu-chō Station) and Chichi-jima (2nd class from ¥22,260, 24 hours); check the website for exact details.

ℹ Getting Around

Rental scooters (available from ¥2400 per day) are the best way to get around as buses are infrequent and you'll be able to explore more of the island. You can rent them from **Ogasawara Kanko** (小笠原観光; ☑04998-2-3311; ⊙8am-6pm) if you have an international driving licence with the motorcycle permit included.

Haha-jima
母島

☑04998 / POP 465

Around 50km south of Chichi-jima is the much less developed Haha-jima. Outside the summer season, you may find yourself

NATURAL OGASAWARA

Known as the Galapagos of Japan, the Ogasawaras are oceanic islands that have never been connected with other land masses, meaning the nature here includes many rare endemic species. Of note are the Japanese wood pigeon, 90% of the snails on the island, and the Bonin flying fox. Between April and August, green turtles haul themselves ashore to lay their eggs on the islands' beaches. By day, botanists should look out for the white rhododendron boninense, while by night, bioluminescent 'green pepe' mushrooms glow in the dark.

For most visitors, it's the chance to watch whales and dolphins that is the Ogasawaras' big draw. From January to April, humpback whales come within 500m of shore. At other times you can see sperm whales around 10km to 30km offshore – if you're very lucky, one may rise with the fabled giant squid Architeuthis, photographed for the first time ever in 2004, in its mouth.

To protect the islands' unique ecosystems, camping and off-trail hiking are prohibited.

staring out over cerulean waters or spotting rare birds all by your lonesome.

◉ Sights & Activities

In town, a four-hour hike loops through rare indigenous flora to **Mt Chibusa** (乳房山; 463m), the highest peak on the island.

There are good snorkelling spots at the far north of the island at **Kita Minato** (北港湊).

Before leaving the only village on the island, scoot over to the **green turtle sanctuary** on the south side of the harbour – around 135 turtles are hatched here a year and released back into the sea.

Minami-zaki HIKING
(南崎) A road runs south from the village to the start of the **Minami-zaki Yūhodō** (南崎遊歩道), a hiking course that continues to Minami-zaki (literally 'southern point'). The route is jungly and at times slippery. Minami-zaki itself has a rocky, coral-strewn beach with ripping views of smaller islands to the south. Though tempting, the waters beyond the cove can whisk swimmers away.

Along the way you'll find **Hōraine-kaigan** (蓬莱根海岸), a narrow beach with a decent offshore coral garden, and **Wai Beach** (ワイビーチ), with a drop-off that sometimes attracts eagle rays. Above Minami-zaki you'll find **Kofuji** (小富士), an 86m-high peak with fantastic views in all directions.

☞ Tours

Club Noah DIVING
(クラブノア母島; ☎04998-3-2442; http://noah88.web.fc2.com; 1 dive ¥7980, gear rental ¥7500; ⓒcafe 9am-5pm) Dive shop Club Noah also runs jungle-hiking and marine-life eco-

tours (from ¥5200). It's in a white building next to the turtle sanctuary; inside there's a cafe serving light meals (from ¥500). Call ahead for reservations and current pricing.

🛏 Sleeping

Anna Beach Haha-jima Youth Hostel HOSTEL ¥
(アンナビーチ母島ユースホステル; ☎04998-3-2468; www.k4.dion.ne.jp/~annayh; dm members/nonmembers incl 2 meals ¥5780/6380; ⊝❋☎) A friendly family runs this tidy, cheery hostel in a bright-yellow Western-style house overlooking the fishing port.

Island Resort Nanpū HOTEL ¥¥
(民宿ナンプー; ☎0120-188-887; www.hahajima-nanpu.com/english; s/tw incl 2 meals from ¥12,000/20,000; ⊝❋@☎) Cosy, well-run lodge with glossy wood-panelled rooms, friendly owners and good food at its restaurant **Austro** (11.30am to 2pm and 6pm to 11pm), also open to nonguests.

ⓘ Information

Haha-jima Tourist Association (母島観光協会; ☎04998-3-2300; www.hahajima.com/en; ⓒ8am-noon & 1-5pm) is located in the passenger waiting room at the pier and only open on ferry days.

ⓘ Getting There & Around

The *Hahajima-maru* sails five times a week between Chichi-jima and Haha-jima (¥4220, two hours). Other operators run day cruises from Chichi-jima to Haha-jima.

Scooters (per day from ¥3000) are the best way to get around the island. They can be rented from most lodgings.

The Japan Alps & Central Honshū

Best Places to Eat

➜ Kaiseki Tsuruko (p256)

➜ Kyōya (p239)

➜ Sentō (p255)

➜ Gyōza Gishū (p228)

➜ Atsuta Hōraiken Honten (p221)

Best Places to Sleep

➜ Yarimikan (p245)

➜ Hōshi Onsen Chōjūkan (p294)

➜ Oyado koto no Yume (p239)

➜ Lamp no Yado (p262)

➜ Share Hotels Hachi (p254)

Why Go?

Japan's heartland in both geography and outlook, Central Honshū (本州中部; Honshū Chūbu) stretches out between the sprawling leviathans of Greater Tokyo and Kansai. The awesome Japan Alps rise sharply near the border of Gifu and Nagano Prefectures before rolling north to the dramatic Sea of Japan coast.

World-class skiing, hiking and onsen can be found in the region's photogenic alpine uplands. All but one of Japan's 30 highest peaks (Mt Fuji) are here. Kanazawa oozes culture: temples and tearooms that served lords and housed geisha are beautifully preserved. Takayama's riverside streetscapes satisfy admirers from Japan and abroad. Matsumoto's magnificent castle and alpine backdrop ensure its popularity.

Nagoya, Japan's fourth-largest city, is the gateway to Central Honshū, packing its share of urban delights with excellent transport connections to just about everywhere.

When to Go
Nagoya

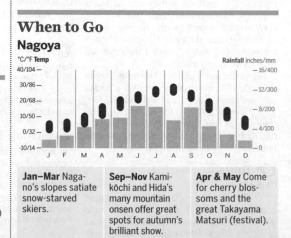

Jan–Mar Nagano's slopes satiate snow-starved skiers.

Sep–Nov Kamikōchi and Hida's many mountain onsen offer great spots for autumn's brilliant show.

Apr & May Come for cherry blossoms and the great Takayama Matsuri (festival).

Climate

Central Honshū's climate varies with its landscape. The best times to visit are generally April through May and late September to early November; temperatures are mild and clear skies prevail. Mid-April is the best time for *hanami* (cherry-blossom viewing) in the Alps. Expect heavy rains in the *tsuyu* (monsoon) season, typically a few weeks in June, then sticky summers capped with typhoons as late as October.

Road closures are commonplace in the Japan Alps when the snow sets in from November to March, although higher peaks might remain snowcapped as late as June. Hiking season runs from July to September, until autumn ushers in a brilliant display of *kōyō* (turning leaves), peaking in mid-October.

ⓘ Getting There & Away

AIR

Central Japan International Airport (NGO; ☑ 056-938-1195; www.centrair.jp/en), outside Nagoya, is an excellent gateway to the region with a variety of global connections. **Komatsu** (KMQ; www.komatsuairport.jp) and **Toyama** (TOY; www.toyama-airport.co.jp/english) airports to the north service domestic and a handful of intra-Asia routes, while **Shinshū Matsumoto Airport** (MMJ; Map p284; www. matsumoto-airport.co.jp) has daily flights to Fukuoka, Osaka and Sapporo.

TRAIN

Nagoya is a major rail hub on the Tōkaidō *shinkansen* (bullet train) line between Tokyo and Osaka. The new-in-2015 Hokuriku extension of the Nagano *shinkansen* connects Tokyo with Nagano and onward to Toyama and Kanazawa.

ⓘ Getting Around

BUS

Bus companies JR, Meitetsu, Nōhi and Alpico operate seasonal services from Nagoya, Takayama and Matsumoto to numerous destinations in Chūbu's mountainous middle.

CAR & MOTORCYCLE

While motorcycle rentals are not common, renting a car is well suited for trips to the Noto Peninsula, the Japan Alps and for those wanting to get up high and off the beaten track. Be prepared for slow, steep and winding roads that can be treacherous at times and are not for the faint-hearted; plan your explorations carefully.

The majority of rental cars include GPS navigation systems as standard equipment, an increasing number of which have English menus and guidance.

TRAIN

Rail access to this mountainous region is surprisingly good.

The north–south JR Takayama and Chūō lines have hubs in Takayama, Matsumoto and Nagano.

The JR Hokuriku line follows the Sea of Japan coast, linking Fukui, Kanazawa and Toyama, with connections to Kyoto and Osaka.

The Hokuriku and Jōetsu *shinkansen* lines open up the nation's alpine interior with quick and easy access to the peaks, from Tokyo, Kanazawa and Niigata.

NAGOYA & AROUND

Understated and under-appreciated Nagoya is the jumping off point for trips to the mountains and the sights of surrounding Aichi and Gifu Prefectures.

Inuyama and the nearby area has some excellent historical attractions, including a wonderful original hilltop castle (p225), while Tokoname is a must for pottery lovers. Almost a suburb of Nagoya, but a city in its own right, lovely Gifu is a good alternative base to Nagoya if you want to be close to the city but not right in the heart of the action.

Nagoya　名古屋

☑ 052 / POP 2.29 MILLION

Home-proud Nagoya, birthplace of Toyota and *pachinko* (a pinball-style game), is a manufacturing powerhouse. Although Nagoya's GDP tops that of many small countries, this middle child has grown accustomed to life in the shadow of its bigger brothers, Tokyo and Kansai.

In contrast to its industrial core, well-maintained parks and green spaces prevail in the inner wards. Nagoya has cosmopolitan aspects including some fantastic museums, significant temples and excellent shopping, and Nagoyans take pride in the unpretentious nature of their friendly, accessible city.

In spite of all this, the city still struggles to shake its reputation among Japanese (many who've never visited) as the nation's most boring metropolis. We're here to disagree.

In a prime spot between Tokyo and Kyoto/ Osaka on the Tōkaidō *shinkansen* line, Nagoya is the gateway to Chūbu's big mountain heart and a great base for day trips.

The Japan Alps & Central Honshū Highlights

1 **Nakasendō** (p230) Walking this ancient post road between Tsumago and Magome.

2 **Ainokura** (p248) Sleeping in a thatch-roofed house in this World Heritage–listed village.

3 **Miya-gawa Asa-ichi** (p241) Starting the day at this market in Takayama.

4 **Matsumoto-jō** (p267) Climbing to the top of the castle for magical vistas.

5 **Zenkō-ji** (p280) Seeking the key to enlightenment at this temple in Nagano.

6 **Kamikōchi** (p275) Hiking some of Japan's most breathtaking scenery.

7 **Tateyama-Kurobe Alpine Route** (p270) Getting around on high-altitude trolleys, cable cars and funiculars.

8 **Takaragawa Onsen** (p293) Soaking your troubles away by the river at this Minakami onsen.

9 **DT Suzuki Museum** (p252) Contemplating Zen and the art of contemplating in Kanazawa.

10 **JR SCMAGLEV & Railway Park** (p219) Entering trainspotter heaven, just outside Nagoya.

11 **Ichijōdani Asakura Clan Ruins** (p263) Re-imagining a shogun's reign in Fukui.

Central Nagoya

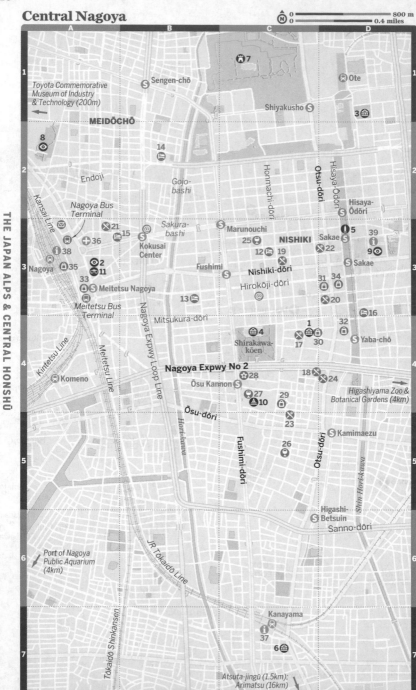

0 800 m
0 0.4 miles

Toyota Commemorative
Museum of Industry
& Technology (200m)

Sengen-chō

Shiyakusho

Ote

MEIDŌCHŌ

Shiyakusho

3

8

14

Endoji

Gojo-
bashi

Honmachi-dōri

Otsu-dōri

Hisaya-Ōdori

Hisaya-
Ōdōri

Nagoya Bus
Terminal

Sakura-
bashi

Marunouchi

NISHIKI

Sakae

5

39

21

15

Kokusai
Center

25

12   19

22

9

Nagoya

38

36

Fushimi

Nishiki-dōri

Sakae

35

2
11

Hirokōji-dōri

31 34

33

Meitetsu Nagoya

13

20

Meitetsu Bus
Terminal

Mitsukura-dōri

16

4

1

32

Shirakawa-
kōen

17 30

Yaba-chō

Komeno

Nagoya Expwy No 2

28

18

24

Ōsu Kannon

27

29

Higashiyama Zoo &
Botanical Gardens (4km)

10

Ōsu-dōri

23

Kamimaezu

Fushimi-dōri

26

Otsu-dōri

Shin Hori-kawa

Port of Nagoya
Public Aquarium
(4km)

JR Tōkaidō Line

Higashi-
Betsuin

Sanno-dōri

Tōkaidō Shinkansen

Kanayama

37

6

Atsuta-jingū (1.5km);
Arimatsu (16km)

Central Nagoya

History

As the ancestral home of Japan's 'three heroes' – Oda Nobunaga (unifier of Japan), Toyotomi Hideyoshi (second unifier of Japan) and Tokugawa Ieyasu (founder of Japan's last shogunate) – Nagoya's influence is long-standing, although it did not become a unified city until 1889.

In 1609, Tokugawa ordered the construction of Nagoya-jō, which became an important outpost for 16 generations of the Tokugawa family (also called the Owari clan), whose dictatorial yet prosperous reign in a time known as the Edo period held sway until 1868 when the restoration of Emperor Meiji saw the ultimate demise of feudal samurai culture in Japan.

Nagoya grew into a centre for commerce, industry and transport; during WWII some 10,000 Mitsubishi Zero fighter planes were produced here. Manufacturing prominence led to massive Allied bombing – almost 4000 citizens were killed, over 450,000 were forced to leave their homes and roughly one quarter of the city was destroyed. From these ashes rose the Nagoya of today with its wide avenues, subways, skyscrapers and parks.

⊙ Sights

⊙ Nagoya Station & Around

Sky Promenade   VIEWPOINT
(スカイプロメナード; Map p216; ☎052-527-8877; www.midland-square.com; 4-7-1 Meieki; adult/child ¥750/500; ⊗11am-9.30pm; ඹNagoya) On levels 44 to 46 of **Midland Square** (ミッドランドスクエア; Map p216; 4-7-1 Meieki; ⊗shops 11am-8pm, restaurants 11am-11pm), Sky Promenade features Japan's tallest open-air observation deck and a handful of high-altitude, high-priced eats. Reach them via adventurously lit passageways.

Toyota Commemorative Museum of Industry & Technology   MUSEUM
(トヨタテクノミュージアム産業技術記念館, Toyota Techno-museum Zangyō Gijutsu Kinenkan; ☎052-551-6115; www.tcmit.org; 4-1-35 Noritake-shinmachi; adult/child ¥500/300; ⊗9.30am-5pm Tue-Sat; ඹMeitetsu Nagoya line to

Sako) The world's largest car manufacturer had humble beginnings in the weaving industry. This interesting museum occupies the site of Toyota's original weaving plant. Revheads will find things textile heavy before warming to the 7900-sq-metre automotive and robotics pavilion. Science-minded folk will enjoy countless hands-on exhibits. Displays are bilingual and there's an English-language audio tour available.

Don't confuse this museum with the Toyota Exhibition Hall and factory tours.

Noritake Garden GARDENS
(ノリタケの森, Noritake no Mori; Map p216; ☎052-561-7290; www.noritake.co.jp; 3-1-36 Noritake-shinmachi; ⏰10am-6pm Tue-Sun; [S] Kamejima) Pottery fans will enjoy a stroll around Noritake Garden, the 1904 factory grounds of one of Japan's best-known porcelain makers, featuring remnants of early kilns and the pleasant **Noritake Gallery** (ノリタケの森ギャラリー; Map p216; ☎052-562-9811; ⏰10am-6pm Tue-Sun) [FREE]. You can also glaze your own dish in the **Craft Centre & Museum** (ノリタケクラフトセンター; Map p216; ☎052-561-7114; adult/senior/child ¥500/free/300; ⏰10am-5pm Tue-Sun), which demonstrates the production process. The 'Box Outlet Shop' has ironically unboxed wares at discounted prices. English signs throughout.

Nagoya-jō & Around

Nagoya-jō CASTLE
(名古屋城; Map p216; ☎052-231-1700; www.nagoyajo.city.nagoya.jp; 1-1 Honmaru; adult/child ¥500/free; ⏰9am-4.30pm; [S] Shiyakusho, exit 7) The original structure, built between 1610 and 1614 by Tokugawa Ieyasu for his ninth son, was levelled in WWII. Today's castle is a concrete replica (with elevator) completed in 1959. Renovations are ongoing. On the roof, look for the 3m-long gilded *shachi-hoko* – legendary creatures possessing a tiger's head and carp's body. Inside, find treasures, an armour collection and the histories of the Oda, Toyotomi and Tokugawa families. The beautiful year-round garden, **Ninomaru-en** (二の丸園) has a number of pretty teahouses.

Painstaking reconstruction of the **Honmaru Palace** (1624–44) using traditional materials and methods commenced in 2009. The project is scheduled for completion in 2018.

★**Tokugawa Art Museum** GALLERY
(徳川美術館, Tokugawa Bijutsukan; ☎052-935-6262; www.tokugawa-art-museum.jp/english; 1017 Tokugawa-chō; adult/child ¥1200/500; ⏰10am-5pm Tue-Sun; 🚌Me-guru stop 11) A must for anyone interested in Japanese culture and history, this museum has a collection of over 10,000 pieces that includes National Treasures and Important Cultural Properties once belonging to the shogun family. A priceless 12th-century scroll depicting *The Tale of Genji* is usually locked away, except during a short stint in late November; the rest of the year, visitors must remain content with a video.

Tokugawa-en GARDENS
(徳川園; ☎052-935-8988; www.tokugawaen.city.nagoya.jp; 1001 Tokugawa-chō; adult/senior ¥300/100; ⏰9.30am-5.30pm Tue-Sun; 🚌Me-guru stop 10) This delightful Japanese garden adjacent to the Tokugawa Art Museum was donated by the Tokugawa family to Nagoya city in 1931, but destroyed by bombing in 1945. From that time until a three-year restoration project was completed in 2004, the site was used as a park. Water is its key element – there's a lake, river, bridges and waterfall. Each spring 2000 peonies and irises burst into bloom, and maples ignite in the autumn.

Nagoya City Archives HISTORIC BUILDING
(名古屋市政資料館, Nagoya Shisei Shiryō-kan; Map p216; ☎052-953-0051; 1-3 Shirakabe, Higashi-ku; ⏰9am-5pm Tue-Sun; [S] Shiyakusho, exit 3) [FREE] Built in 1922 this grand Taisho-era Court of Appeal now houses the city archives. While the archives themselves are difficult to navigate for non-Japanese speakers, the attractive neo-baroque building, with its fine stained-glass ornamentation, is worth a look.

Fushimi & Sakae

The area between Fushimi and Sakae subway stations is ground zero for shopping and people-watching. **Hisaya-ōdōri-kōen** (Central Park) is usually bustling and Sakae's side streets fill with revellers well into the night.

Nagoya TV Tower TOWER
(名古屋テレビ塔; Map p216; ☎052-971-8546; www.nagoya-tv-tower.co.jp; 3-6-15 Nishiki; adult/child ¥1000/500; ⏰10am-9pm; [S] Sakae, exit 4b or 5a) Nagoya's much-loved TV tower, completed in 1954, was the first of its kind in Japan. The tower's central location makes its 100m-high **Sky Balcony** a great place to get the lay of the land. Better still, the sprawling beer garden and Korean barbecue at its base is unrivalled in town. Check the website for special events and occasional night-time illuminations.

Oasis 21 LANDMARK
(オアシス21; Map p216; ☑052-962-1011; www.
sakaepark.co.jp; 1-11-1 Higashi-sakura, Higashi-ku;
Ⓢ Sakae, exit 4a) Oasis 21 is a bus terminal and
transit hub with a difference. Its iconic 'galaxy
platform' – an elliptical glass-and-steel structure filled with water for visual effect and
cooling purposes – caused quite a stir when
it was first built. Feel free to climb the stairs
and walk around it while you're waiting for
your next ride; it's most fun at night when it's
adventurously lit.

Nagoya City Science Museum MUSEUM
(名古屋市科学館, Nagoya-shi Kagaku-kan; Map
p216; ☑052-201-4486; www.ncsm.city.nagoya.jp;
2-17-1 Sakae; adult/child ¥800/500; ⊙9.30am-5pm
Tue-Sun; ⓜ; Ⓢ Fushimi, exit 5) This hands-on museum claims the world's largest dome-screen
planetarium with some seriously out-of-this-
world projection technology. There's also a
tornado lab and a deep-freeze lab complete
with indoor aurora. Scheduled shows are
kid-centric and in Japanese, but the innovative technology of this impressive, centrally
located facility is worth experiencing.

**International Design
Centre Nagoya** GALLERY
(国際デザインセンター, Kokusai Dezain Sentaa;
Map p216; ☑052-265-2105; www.idcn.jp; 3-7F,
3-18-1 Sakae; ⊙11am-8pm Wed-Mon; Ⓢ Yaba-chō,
exit 5 or 6) FREE Housed in the swooping
Nadya Park complex is this secular shrine
to the deities of conceptualisation, form
and function. Everything from art deco to
postmodernism, Electrolux to Isamu Noguchi, Arne Jacobsen to the Mini Cooper and
everything in-between, is represented in these
significant galleries found on the 4th floor.

⊙ Ōsu Kannon & Kanayama

The area between Ōsu Kannon and Kamimaezu stations, crammed with retailers, eateries and street vendors, has a delightfully
young and alternative vibe. Patient shoppers
can be rewarded with funky vintage threads
and offbeat souvenirs.

From Kamimaezu Station, take exit 9 and
walk north two blocks. Turn left onto Ban-
shoji street (万松寺通), a covered shopping
arcade that becomes Ōsu Kannon street and
continues on to Ōsu Kannon temple. The
streets either side are alive with activity. Further south, the busy yet compact Kanayama
Station area is an alternative base to Meieki
and Sakae.

Ōsu Kannon BUDDHIST TEMPLE
(大須観音; Map p216; ☑052-231-6525; www.
osu-kannon.jp; 2-21-47 Osu, Naka-ku; ⊙24hr; Ⓢ Ōsu
Kannon, exit 2) FREE The much-visited Ōsu
Kannon temple traces its roots back to 1333.
The temple, devoted to the Buddha of Compassion, was moved to its present location
by Tokugawa Ieyasu in 1610, although the
current buildings date from 1970. The library
inside holds the oldest known handwritten
copy of the *kojiki* – the ancient mythological
history of Japan.

**Nagoya/Boston
Museum of Fine Arts** MUSEUM
(名古屋ボストン美術館, Nagoya Boston Bijutsukan; Map p216; ☑052-684-0101; www.nagoya-
boston.or.jp; 1-1-1 Kanayama-chō; adult/child/senior
¥1300/free/900; ⊙10am-7pm Tue-Fri, to 5pm Sat
& Sun; ℝ Kanayama, south exit) This collaborative effort between Japanese backers and the
Museum of Fine Arts Boston showcases an
impressive collection of Japanese and international masterpieces.

⊙ Greater Nagoya

★ **JR SCMAGLEV & Railway Park** MUSEUM
(JR リニア・鉄道館, JR Rinia Tetsudō-kan;
☑050-3772-3910; http://museum.jr-central.co.jp;
Kinjofuto 3-2-2; adult/child ¥1000/500, shinkansen
simulator ¥500; ⊙10am-5.30pm Wed-Mon; ℝ JR
Aonami line to Kinjofuto) Trainspotters will be
in heaven at this fantastic hands-on museum. Featuring actual maglev (the world's
fastest train – 581km/h), *shinkansen*, historical rolling stock and rail simulators, the
massive museum offers a fascinating insight
into Japanese postwar history through the
development of a railroad like no other. The
'hangar' is some 20 minutes from Nagoya
on the Aonami line, found on the Taiko-dōri
side of JR Nagoya Station.

Toyota Exhibition Hall MUSEUM
(トヨタ会館, Toyota Kaikan; ☑museum 0565-
29-3345, tours 0565-29-3355; www.toyota.co.jp/
en/about_toyota/facility/toyota_kaikan; 1 Toyota-
chō; ⊙9.30am-5pm Mon-Sat, tours 11am; ℝ Aichi
Kanjō line to Mikawa Toyota) FREE See up to 20
shiny examples of the latest automotive
technology hot off the production line and
witness first-hand how they're made here at
Toyota's global HQ. Fascinating two-hour
tours of Toyota Motor Corporation's main
factory begin at the Exhibition Hall, with
many exhibits fully revamped recently. Visit the museum any time it's open but daily

tours must be prebooked from two weeks to three months in advance. Check the website for full details.

Allow two hours to get to Toyota city from central Nagoya; refer to the website for directions and reservations.

Atsuta-jingū SHINTO SHRINE
(熱田神宮; ☎052-671-4151; www.atsutajingu.or.jp; 1-1-1 Jingū; [S] Jingū-mae or Jingū-nishi, exit 2) Although the current buildings were completed in 1966, Atsuta-jingū has been a shrine for over 1900 years and is one of the most sacred Shintō shrines in Japan. Nestled among ancient cypress, it houses the sacred *kusanagi-no-tsurugi* (grass-cutting sword), one of the three regalia that, according to legend, were presented to the Imperial Family by the sun goddess Amaterasu-Ōmikami. There's a changing collection of over 4000 Tokugawa-era swords, masks and paintings on display in the **Treasure Hall** (宝物館; adult/child ¥300/150; 🕘9am-4.30pm, closed last Wed & Thu of each month).

Festivals & Events

There are plenty of lively festivals and events to enjoy in a city of this size. A good, up-to-date resource is www.nagoya-info.jp/en/event.

Grand Sumō Tournament Nagoya SPORTS
(日本相撲協会名古屋場所, Nihon Sumō Kyōkai Nagoya Basho; ☎052-971-2516; www.sumo.or.jp; Aichi-ken Taiiku-kan, 1-1 Ninomaru; tickets from ¥3000; 🕘Jul) One of six annual sumo championship tournaments, Nagoya Basho is held over two weeks in July at Aichi Prefectural Gymnasium. Arrive early in the afternoon to watch the lower-ranked wrestlers up close.

World Cosplay Summit CULTURAL
(www.worldcosplaysummit.jp; 🕘Jul/Aug) If you're in Nagoya in July/August, be sure to see if your stay coincides with some of the events of this truly unique visual feast, when *cosplayers* (costume players) and anime (Japanese animation) fans from around the world come together to…well, play, in costume!

Nagoya Matsuri PARADE
(名古屋まつり; www.nagoya-festival.jp; 🕘mid-Oct) Nagoya's big sha-bang takes place mid-October in Hisaya-ōdōri-kōen. Celebrating Nagoya's 'three heroes', the lively procession includes costumes, *karakuri ningyō* (marionette) floats, folk dancing and decorated cars.

Sleeping

Guesthouse Mado GUESTHOUSE ¥
(ゲストハウスMADO; ☎050-7516-6632; www.guesthousemado.com; 924 Arimatsu; dm ¥3000; 🚉Meitetsu Arimatsu) This little guesthouse outside the hustle and bustle of downtown Nagoya in the pretty Arimatsu district really is an extension of the friendly owner's home, with two small shared rooms. If you're looking for a welcoming place to share stories and experience day-to-day life in Japan, you'll enjoy the vibe here.

Glocal Nagoya Hostel HOSTEL ¥
(グローカル名古屋ホステル; ☎052-446-6694; 1-21-3 Noritake; dm ¥3240; [S] Nagoya) This fabulously trendy hostel about seven-minutes' walk from Nagoya Station has its own cafe and bar that's popular with locals and guests alike. Friendly staff will make you feel welcome and are happy to dispense local advice and practise their already well-honed English skills.

the b Nagoya HOTEL ¥
(ザ・ビー 名古屋; Map p216; ☎052-241-1500; www.theb-hotels.com; 4-15-23 Sakae; s/d from ¥5200/6800; 🚭@; [S] Sakae, exit 13) A smart, well-managed hotel with a brilliant location opposite Hisaya-ōdōri-kōen, between Sakae and Yaba-cho subway stations. Well-designed rooms are tiny but tasteful. Online special rates including breakfast offer excellent value.

Kyoya Ryokan RYOKAN ¥¥
(京屋旅館; Map p216; ☎052-571-2588; www.kyoya.to; 2-11-4 Habashita, Nishi-ku; s/d incl 2 meals from ¥11,800/14,850; ❄📶; [S] Kokusai Center) This popular ryokan centred on an attractive Japanese garden can get a little noisy when busy, but it has a lovely common bath and an even lovelier self-contained private suite. It's a little bit of a hike from the station, but the friendly owners are eager to help and speak some English.

Royal Park Hotel The Nagoya HOTEL ¥¥
(ロイヤルパークホテル ザ 名古屋; Map p216; ☎052-300-1111; www.rph-the.co.jp; 3-2-13 Meieiki; s/d from ¥7000/14,000; [S] Kokusai Center) With lots of dark marble and cypress in the lobby and guestrooms furnished in fresh grey and cream tones, there's an element of sophistication about this newly built but otherwise standard business hotel. It's in an excellent location between Nagoya Station and the Kokusai Center subway.

Dormy Inn Premium Nagoya Sakae
HOTEL ¥¥

(ドーミーインPREMIUM名古屋栄; Map p216; ☑052-231-5489; www.hotespa.net/hotels/nagoya sakae; 2-20-1 Nishiki; s/d from ¥9240/11,990; 🚭❄🔊; Ⓢ Fushimi) Located in the heart of Nagoya's Sakae district, this busy tourist hotel is that little bit more luxe than the usual offering in the popular Dormy Inn chain, with stylish furnishings, an on-site restaurant, terrace and attractive communal baths.

★ Hilton Nagoya
HOTEL ¥¥¥

(ヒルトン名古屋; Map p216; ☑052-212-1111; www.hilton.com; 1-3-3 Sakae; s/d from ¥19,600/24,100; 🅿🚭❄@❄; Ⓢ Fushimi, exit 7) This characteristic Hilton benefits from an excellent location and features spacious, stylish rooms with Japanese accents, a selection of suites and an executive floor. There's also complimentary bicycle rental, a courtesy station shuttle service, two restaurants, three bars and a gym. Most rooms have good views.

✗ Eating

Nagoya may not be overburdened with tourist attractions, but it is a fantastic place to experience Japan's passion for food, with many local specialities. For cheap international eats, head to the storefronts of the Ōsu Shopping Arcade, where street vendors hawk everything from kebabs to *karaage* (deep-fried items), crêpes and pizza.

Sōhonke Ebisuya Honten
NOODLES ¥

(総本家えびすや本店; Map p216; ☑052-961-3412; 3-20-7 Nishiki; dishes/sets from ¥760/900; ⊙11am-1am; Ⓢ Sakae, exit 3) The massive noodle bowls at this, the head branch of one of Nagoya's best-known *kishimen* (flat, handmade wheat noodle) chains, are toasty, tasty and cheap. You can often see the noodles being made by the chef. There's a picture menu: try the *karē kishimen* (curry noodles).

Love Pacific Cafe
VEGAN ¥

(ラブ・パシフィックカフェ; Map p216; ☑052-252-8429; www.pacifit.jp/lovecafe.html; 3-23-38 Sakae; items from ¥600; ⊙11.30am-5pm Tue-Sun; ☑; Ⓢ Yaba-chō, exit 4) Lovers of wholesome, delicious, healthy foods are in for a treat at this trendy, friendly, vegan cafe preparing lunch sets and cafe items that are free of dairy, egg and white sugars. The changing menu usually features a choice of two soups, the organic salad bar and a main: the tofu teriyaki burgers are delicious.

NAGOYA CUISINE

The city is famous for bold local specialities that translate well to non-Japanese palates: *kishimen* are soft, flat, handmade wheat noodles; *miso-nikomi udon* are noodles in a hearty miso broth; and *miso-katsu* is a fried breaded pork cutlet topped with miso sauce. *Kōchin* (free-range chicken), *tebasaki* (chicken wings) and *hitsumabushi* (charcoal-grilled eel) are other local specialities.

★ Atsuta Hōraiken Honten
SEAFOOD ¥¥

(あつた蓬莱軒本店; ☑052-671-8686; www.houraiken.com; 503 Gōdo-chō; dishes ¥950, sets from ¥2500; ⊙11.30am-2pm & 4.30-8.30pm Thu-Tue; Ⓢ Temma-chō, exit 4) The head branch of this *hitsumabushi* chain, in business since 1873, is revered for good reason. Patrons queue during the summer peak season for *hitsumabushi*, eel basted in a secret *tare* (sauce) served atop rice in a covered lacquered bowl (¥3600); add green onion, wasabi and *dashi* (fish broth) to your taste. Other *teishoku* (set meals) include tempura and steak.

★ Trattoria Cesari
ITALIAN ¥¥

(トラットリア チェザリ; Map p216; ☑052-238-0372; www.cesari.jp; 3-36-44 Ōsu; pizza from ¥680, mains from ¥1200; ⊙11am-3pm & 6-10pm; ☑; Ⓢ Kamimaezu, exit 8) You may be surprised to find an Italian trattoria of this calibre and value smack bang in the heart of Nagoya. Prepare to queue on weekends as folks line up for chef Makishima's famous Napoletana pizzas. There's an extensive à la carte menu of Italian favourites, masterfully prepared and presented in an atmosphere reminiscent of the homeland.

Yabaton Honten
TONKATSU ¥¥

(矢場とん本店; Map p216; ☑052-252-8810; www.yabaton.com; 3-6-18 Ōsu; dishes ¥1080-2450; ⊙11am-9pm; ☑; Ⓢ Yaba-chō, exit 4) This has been the place to try Nagoya's famed *miso-katsu* (a type of *tonkatsu*) since 1947. Signature dishes are *waraji-tonkatsu* (schnitzel-style flattened, breaded pork) and *teppan-tonkatsu* (breaded pork cutlet with miso on a sizzling plate of cabbage). Walk under the expressway and look for the four-storey pig, across the street to your right. It's on the corner, next to McDonald's.

Check the website for other locations.

Misen

TAIWANESE ¥¥

(味仙; Map p216; ☑052-238-7357; www.misen.ne.
jp; 3-6-3 Ōsu; dishes ¥480-1500; ◷11.30am-2pm
& 5pm-1am Sun-Thu, to 2am Fri & Sat; ☑; ⑤Ya-
ba-chō, exit 4) Folks line up for opening at this
big Chinese joint where the *Taiwan rāmen* (
台湾ラーメン) induces rapture – it's a spicy
concoction of ground meat, chilli, garlic and
green onion, served over noodles in a hearty
clear broth. Other faves include *gomoku
yakisoba* (五目焼きそば; stir-fried noodles)
and *kinoko-itame* (stir-fried mushrooms).
There's a limited picture menu and some
dim-sum items.

Suzunami Honten

SEAFOOD ¥¥

(鈴波本店; Map p216; ☑052-261-1300; www.
suzunami.co.jp/shop/shop_honten.html; 3-7-23
Sakae; lunch sets ¥1300; ◷11am-2.30pm) Delightfully traditional but not overly formal,
this Nagoyan *kappo* institution specialises
in simple grilled fish lunches served with
miso soup, rice and pickles, and finished
off with *umeshu* (plum wine). You'll likely
have a short wait for a table.

Tarafuku

IZAKAYA ¥¥

(たら福; Map p216; ☑052-566-5600; 3-17-26
Meieki; small plates ¥470-1080; ◷5pm-1am Tue-
Sun; ⓓ; ⓡNagoya, Sakura-dōri exit) Atmosphere
seeps from this ambitious *izakaya,* which
transformed a decrepit building into an airy
urban oasis. French-influenced dishes made
with seasonal ingredients might include potato croquettes in a fried tofu crust, tomato and
eggplant au gratin, or house-cured beef in
wine sauce. There are wine and cocktail lists.

Torigin Honten

JAPANESE ¥¥¥

(鳥銀本店; Map p216; ☑052-973-3000; www.
torigin.co.jp; 3-14-22 Nishiki; kaiseki courses ¥3900-
10,000; ◷5pm-midnight; ⓓ; ⑤Sakae, exit 2)
Come here for a unique *kōchin kaiseki* experience with immaculately presented servers
and a wonderfully traditional atmosphere.
Courses consist of *kōchin* chicken served in
many forms, including *kushiyaki* (skewered),
karaage (deep-fried), *zōsui* (mild rice hotpot)
and sashimi (what you think it is).

🍸 Drinking & Nightlife

Grok

BAR

(グロック; Map p216; ☑052-332-2331; www.
grok-nagoya.com; 1-6-13 Tachibana; ◷5pm-midnight
Tue-Fri, noon-midnight Sat & Sun; ⑤Kamimaezu, exit
7) We love this friendly, colourful and a little
bit hippie two-storey cafe-bar. Whether you're
with friends or flying solo, you're bound to feel

comfortable. It's a little off the beaten track,
but that's part of its charm.

Coat of Arms

PUB

(コート・オブ・アームズ; Map p216; ☑052-
228-6155; www.coatofarms.jp; 2-6-12 Nishiki;
◷11.30am-midnight Tue-Sun; ⑤Marunouchi, exit 5)
This fresh and fun pub created by a bunch of
expats has an excellent outdoor patio (smoking permitted), two nonsmoking interior
floors, theme nights, weekly specials and a
range of unique craft beers and spirits to try.

Smash Head

PUB

(スマッシュヘッド; Map p216; ☑052-201-
2790; http://smashhead.main.jp; 2-21-90 Ōsu;
◷noon-midnight Wed-Mon; ⑤Ōsu Kannon, exit
2) Through the passageway to the left of the
main Ōsu Kannon temple building, you'll find
this teeny motorcycle and Vespa repair shop/
pub (that's right). Guinness and Corona are
the beers of choice, patrons are cool, and fish
and chips costs ¥850.

☆ Entertainment

Electric Lady Land

LIVE MUSIC

(エレクトリックレディランド; Map p216;
☑052-201-5004; www.ell.co.jp; 2-10-43 Ōsu; ⑤Ōsu
Kannon, exit 2) An intimate live venue showcasing the underground music scene in a cool,
post-industrial setting. Nationally known
bands play the 1st-floor hall, while up-and-
coming acts have the smaller 3rd.

🛍 Shopping

Nagoya's manufacturing roots make it a great
place to shop. Both Meieki and Sakae boast
gargantuan malls and department stores,
good for clothing, crafts and foods.

In Ōsu, along Akamon-dōri, Banshō-ji-dōri
and Niomon-dōri, are hundreds of funky vintage boutiques and discount clothing retailers. East of Ōsu, Otsu-dōri has a proliferation
of manga (Japanese comics) shops.

Regional crafts include *Arimatsu-narumi
shibori* (elegant tie-dyeing), cloisonné ceramics and *seki* blades (swords, knives etc).

Ōsu Kannon (p219) temple hosts a colourful antique market on the 18th and 28th of
each month, while **Higashi Betsuin** temple
has a flea market on the 12th of each month.

Komehyō

DEPARTMENT STORE

(コメ兵; Map p216; ☑052-242-0088; www.
en.komehyo.co.jp; 2-20-25 Ōsu; ◷10.30am-7.30pm
Thu-Tue; ⑤Ōsu Kannon, exit 2) Enjoy the genius
of Komehyō, Japan's largest discounter of
secondhand, well...everything. Housed over

WORTH A TRIP

TOKONOME POTTERY FOOTPATH

Clay beneath the ground has made the bayside community of Tokoname (常滑) a ceramic-making hub for centuries – at one time 400 chimneys rose above its centre. The area still produces some ¥60 trillion in ceramics annually and makes an interesting excursion from Nagoya or nearby Central Japan International Airport.

The **Pottery Footpath** (やきもの散歩道, Yakimono Sanpō-michi) is a hilly 1.8km trail around the town's historic centre. Start by collecting a walking map from the Tourist Information Center inside Tokoname Station. Lining the well-signposted path are kilns, cafes and galleries, with numbered plaques corresponding to the walking map indicating the stops along the way. A series of *maneki-neko* (ceramic 'lucky' cats) greets you as you head towards the beginning of the path. If you look up, you'll see **'Toko-nyan'**, the mother of all lucky cats, looming above: one for the Instagrammers.

At stop 8, the restored **Takita Residence** (瀧田家, Takita-ke; ☎0569-36-2031; 4-75 Sakae-machi; ¥300; ⏲9am-4.30pm Tue-Sun), c 1850, was the home of a shipping magnate. Inside are replicas of *bishu-kaisen* (local trading ships) and displays of ceramics, lacquerware and furniture. Continuing on, the pipe-and-jug-lined lane at **Dokan-zaka Hill** (stop 9) is particularly photogenic. Around the back of the Climbing Kiln Sq (**Noborigahama-hiroba**, stop 13) you'll find 10 of the square chimneys that served the gigantic 1887 kiln. It's a five-minute detour from here to the **Inax Live Museum** (イナックスライブミュージアム; ☎0569-34-8282; www1.lixil.co.jp/ilm/english; 1-130 Okueichō; adult/child ¥600/200; ⏲10am-5pm, closed 3rd Wed of month), showpiece of one of Japan's largest ceramics manufacturers, housing some 150 elaborately decorated Meiji- and Taisho-era toilets (you read correctly) and Japan's only tile museum.

When you need a rest, atmospheric **Koyō-an** (古窯庵; ☎0569-35-8350; 4-87 Sakae-machi; dishes ¥500-1800; ⏲11.30am-5pm Tue-Sun; 📖) serves homemade soba (buckwheat noodles) on beautiful local pottery. Alternatively, why not dine near the giant cat, at cosy **Nakamura-ya** (うなぎの中村屋; ☎0569-35-0120; 2-53 Sakae-machi; sets ¥1400-3600; ⏲11.30am-2.30pm Thu-Tue), whose specialities are *una-don* (eel on rice) and Nagoya's famous *hitsumabushi* (charcoal-grilled eel)?

The private Meitetsu line connects Tokoname with Nagoya (*tokkyū* ¥660, 33 minutes) and **Central Japan International Airport** (p213) (¥310, five minutes). The **Pottery Footpath** (p223) begins a few hundred metres from the train station.

seven floors in the main building, clothes, jewellery and accessories are of excellent quality and are sold at reasonable prices. With patience, you can find some real bargains, especially at 'yen=g' on the 7th floor, where clothing is sold by weight.

Loft Department Store DEPARTMENT STORE
(ロフト; Map p216; ☎052-219-3000; 3-18-1 Sakae, Nadya Park; ⏲10.30am-8pm; [S] Yaba-chō, exit 5 or 6) The Nagoya branch of one of Japan's coolest department stores has a definite design bent. You can't miss the yellow and black livery.

ℹ Orientation

Running east of the station, Sakura-dōri, Nishiki-dōri and Hirokōji-dōri are the three main drags, intersected first by Fushimi-dōri then Otsu-dōri. The majority of the mainstream action is found within this grid. Just east of Otsu-dōri is the long and narrow Hisaya-ōdōri-kōen (aka Central Park), Nagoya's much-loved Eiffel-esque **TV Tower** (p218) and the wacky **Oasis 21** (p219) complex. Following Otsu-dōri north will get you to **Nagoya-jō** (p218), while the vibrant Ōsu district, **Atsuta-jingū** (p220) shrine and bustling Kanayama Station area are to the south.

Nagoya's subway system has English signs and services all the hot spots – Fushimi and Sakae Stations are your mainstays for shopping, accommodation and nightlife.

ℹ Information

MEDICAL SERVICES

Aichi Prefectural Emergency Medical Guide (愛知県救急医療ガイド; ☎052-263-1133, automated service 050-5810-5884; www.qq.pref.aichi.jp) Phone or follow the English link on this prefectural homepage for a list of medical institutions with English-speaking staff, including specialities and hours of operation.

Tachino Clinic (たちのクリニック; Map p216; ☎052-541-9130; www.tachino-clinic.com; 3F

Dai-Nagoya Bldg, 3-26-8 Meieki; ⏰9.30am-1pm & 2.30-6pm Mon-Wed & Fri, 9.30am-1pm Thu & Sat; 🚉JR Nagoya, Sakura-dōri exit) This medical clinic a short walk from Nagoya Station has English-speaking staff.

TOURIST INFORMATION

English-language street and subway maps are widely available at Tourist Information Centers (TICs) and hotels. The *Nagoya Pocket Guide* (www.nagoyapocketguide.com) is particularly handy, as are the *Nagoya Navi Map* and *Nagoya Shopping & Dining Guide,* which you can also download at www.nagoya-info.jp/en/brochures.

Nagoya has three helpful TIC branches stacked with resources in English and Japanese and at least one English speaker on hand.

Tourist Information Center – Nagoya Station (名古屋駅観光案内所; Map p216; ☎052-541-4301; 1-1-14 Meieki; ⏰9am-7pm; 🚉JR Nagoya)

Tourist Information Center – Kanayama (金山観光案内所; Map p216; ☎052-323-0161; LOOP Kanayama 1F, 1-17-18 Kanayama; ⏰9am-7pm; 🚉Kanayama, north exit)

Tourist Information Center – Sakae (栄町観光案内所; Map p216; ☎052-963-5252; Oasis 21 B1F, 1-11-1 Higashisakura; ⏰10am-8pm; [S] Sakae)

Nagoya International Centre (名古屋国際センター; Map p216; ☎052-581-0100; www.nic-nagoya.or.jp; 1-47-1 Nagono; ⏰9am-7pm Tue-Sun; [S] Kokusai Center) This not-for-profit organisation provides information, consultation and referral services in English. There's also an internet corner on the 3rd floor (¥100 per 15 minutes) and a library with over 30,000 items in various languages.

USEFUL WEBSITES

There are a number of useful websites for up-to-date information on what's happening in Nagoya. The homepages of the Nagoya Convention and Visitors Bureau (www.nagoya-info.jp) and Nagoya International Center (www.nic-nagoya.or.jp) are brimming with information. Also try www.nagoya-info.com for English-language listings.

ℹ Getting There & Away

AIR

On an artificial island in Ise-wan, 35km south of the city, **Central Japan International Airport** (NGO; ☎056-938-1195; www.centrair.jp/en) has become a tourist attraction for locals who come for the dozens of well-priced shopping and dining options, to plane-spot from the enormous observation deck, or to soak in the **Fū-no-yu** (風の湯; ☎0569-38-7070; www.centrair.jp/interest/visit/relax/bath.html; SkyTown 4F; adult/child with towel ¥1030/620; ⏰8am-10pm) hot-spring baths. For travellers, the airport is far friendlier and less frantic than those in Tokyo and Osaka. With excellent transport connections, it's a great arrival port into Japan from around 30 international destinations in Europe, North America and Asia. Domestic routes serve around 20 Japanese cities, though some are reached faster by train.

BOAT

Taiheiyo Ferry (☎052-582-8611; www.taiheiyo-ferry.co.jp) sails snazzy ships between Nagoya and Tomakomai (Hokkaidō, from ¥9800, 40 hours) via Sendai (from ¥6700, 21¾ hours) every other evening at 7pm, with daily services to Sendai. Take the Meikō subway line to Nagoya-kō Station and go to Nagoya Port.

BUS

JR and Meitetsu Highway buses operate services between Nagoya and Kyoto (¥2560, 2½ hours, hourly), Osaka (¥3200, three hours, hourly), Kōbe (¥3350, 3½ hours), Kanazawa (¥4060, four hours, 10 daily), Nagano (¥4020, 4½ hours) and Tokyo (¥5060, six hours, 14 daily). Overnight buses run to Hiroshima (¥8600, nine hours).

New kid on the block, Willer Express (www.willerexpress.com) offers airline-style seating and online reservations in English at *heavily* discounted rates. Key routes from Nagoya include Tokyo (from ¥3400, six hours) and Fukuoka (from ¥6800, 11½ hours overnight).

Departure points vary by carrier and destination, although almost all highway buses depart from somewhere in Meieki (JR Nagoya Station). Some routes also depart from **Oasis 21** (p219). JR Highway buses depart from the **Nagoya Bus Terminal** (名古屋バスターミナル; Map p216) near the *shinkansen* entrance (north side) of JR Nagoya Station.

Meitetsu Highway buses depart from the **Meitetsu Bus Terminal** (名鉄バスターミナル; Map p216). Willer Express buses depart from a variety of locations, depending on the route. Be sure to confirm your departure location with your carrier at the time of booking.

TRAIN

All lines lead to Meieki (JR Nagoya Station), a hybrid terminus of the JR and private Meitetsu and Kintetsu train lines, as well as subway and bus stations. Here you'll find a labyrinthine world of passageways, restaurants and retailers, and above, the soaring JR Central Towers and **Midland Square** (p217) complexes. Be sure to leave plenty of time if making a rail transfer!

Nagoya is a major *shinkansen* hub, connecting with Tokyo (¥10,360, 1¾ hours), Shin-Osaka (¥5830, 50 minutes), Kyoto (¥5070, 35 minutes), Hiroshima (¥13,290, 2¼ hours) and Hakata/Fukuoka (¥17,500, 3¼ hours).

To get into the Japan Alps, take the JR Chūō line to Matsumoto (*Shinano tokkyū* ¥5510, two hours) or onwards to Nagano (¥7130, 2¾ hours). A separate line (JR Takayama line) serves Takayama (*Hida tokkyū* ¥5510, 2¼ hours).

The private Meitetsu line covers routes in and around Nagoya (Tokoname, Inuyama, Gifu).

ℹ️ Getting Around

BUS

The gold **Me-guru** (名古屋観光ルートバスメーグ ル; www.nagoya-info.jp/en/routebus; day pass adult/child ¥500/250) bus follows a one-way loop near attractions in the Meieki, Sakae and castle areas. Ticket holders receive discounted admissions to many attractions. It runs hourly from 9.30am to 5pm Tuesday to Friday and twice hourly on weekends. There's no bus on Mondays.

SUBWAY

Nagoya has an excellent subway system with six lines, clearly signposted in English and Japanese. Fares cost ¥200 to ¥320 depending on distance. One-day passes (¥740, including city buses ¥850), available at ticket machines, include subway transport and discounted admission to many attractions. On Saturday and Sunday the *donichi eco-kippu* (Saturday and Sunday eco-ticket) gives the same benefits for ¥600 per day.

Inuyama 犬山

📞 0568 / POP 74,319

In Inuyama, the Kiso-gawa, aka the 'Japanese Rhine', paints a pretty picture beneath its castle, a National Treasure. By day, the castle, quaint streets, manicured Uraku-en and 17th-century Jo-an teahouse make for pleasant strolling, while at night the scene turns cinematic as fishermen perform the ancient art of *ukai* (cormorant fishing) by firelight.

Just south of the castle are the picturesque Shintō shrines Haritsuna Jinja and Sankō-Inari Jinja, the latter with interesting statues of *komainu* (protective dogs).

Since 1635 townsfolk have celebrated the Inuyama Matsuri on the first weekend in April. A scaled-down version is held on the fourth Saturday in October. A government designated Intangible Cultural Asset, the festival features a parade of 13 three-tiered floats strewn with 365 lanterns. Atop each float, elaborate *karakuri ningyō* (marionettes) perform to music.

👁 Sights

👁 Central Inuyama

⭐ Inuyama-jō   CASTLE
(犬山城; Map p226; 📞0568-61-1711; www. inuyama-castle.jp; 65-2 Kitakoken; adult/child ¥550/110; ⏰9am-4.30pm; ℝMeitetsu Inuyama-yūen) A National Treasure, Japan's oldest standing castle is said to have originated as a fort in 1440. The current *donjon* (main keep) built atop a 40m rise beside the Kiso-gawa dates from 1537 and has resisted war, earthquake and restoration, remaining the penultimate example of Momoyama-era architecture. Inside are steep, narrow staircases and military displays – the view from the top is worth the climb. The castle is 15 minutes' walk from Meitetsu Inuyama-yūen Station.

Inuyama Artifacts
Museum/Castle & Town Museum   MUSEUM
(犬山市文化史料館・城とまちミュージ アム, Inuyama-shi Bunka Shiryō-kan/Shiro to Machi Myūjiamu; Map p226; 📞0568-62-4802; 8 Kitakoken; ¥100, free with admission to Inuyama-jō; ⏰9am-4.30pm; ℝMeitetsu Inuyama-yūen) This museum houses two of the Inuyama Matsuri floats and various artefacts related to cormorant fishing, Inuyama-jō and the town's history.

Karakuri Exhibition Room (Annex)   MUSEUM
(からくり展示館   (別館), Karakuri Tenji-kan (Bekkan); Map p226; 📞0568-61-3932; 69-2/69-3 Kitakoken; ¥100, free with admission to Inuyama-jō; ⏰9am-4.30pm; ℝMeitetsu Inuyama-yūen) This small annexe exhibits Edo- and Meiji-era *karakuri ningyō*. On Saturdays and Sundays at 10.30am and 2pm, you can see the wooden characters in action. On Fridays and Saturdays between 10am and 4pm, there are demonstrations of how the puppets are made by artisan Tamaya Shobei the 9th, who is the only living *karakuri ningyō* master from an unbroken lineage.

Uraku-en & Chashitsu Jo-an   GARDENS
(有楽苑・茶室如安; Map p226; 📞0568-61-4608; 1 Gomonsaki; adult/child ¥1000/600; ⏰9am-5pm Mar-Nov, 9am-4pm Dec-Feb; ℝMeitetsu Inuyama-yūen) Within the pretty garden of Uraku-en in the grounds of the Meitetsu Inuyama Hotel, you'll find 'Jo-an', one of the finest teahouses in Japan. One of Inuyama's National Treasures, Jo-an was built in 1618 in Kyoto by Oda Urakusai, younger brother of Oda Nobunaga, and relocated here in 1972. You can enjoy tea on the grounds for an additional ¥500.

Dondenkan   MUSEUM
(どんでん館; Map p226; 📞0568-65-1728; 62 Higashi-koken; adult/child ¥200/100; ⏰9am-4.30pm; ℝMeitetsu Inuyama) Four of the 13 impressive Inuyama Matsuri floats are on

Inuyama

Inuyama

◉ Top Sights

◉ Sights

◉ Activities, Courses & Tours

◉ Sleeping

◉ Eating

year-round display in this custom-made building.

◉ Greater Inuyama

★ Meiji-mura   MUSEUM

(明治村; ☎0568-67-0314; www.meijimura.com; 1 Uchiyama; adult/child/senior ¥1700/1000/1300; ⊙9.30am-5pm Mar-Oct, to 4pm Nov-Feb, closed Mon Dec-Feb) Few Meiji-era buildings have survived due to war, earthquakes and development. In 1965 this open-air museum was created to preserve this unique style, known for unifying Western and Japanese architectural elements. Over 60 buildings from around Japan were painstakingly dismantled, transported and reassembled in this leafy lakeside location. Favourites include the entry facade of Frank Lloyd Wright's Tokyo Imperial Hotel, Kyoto's St Francis Xavier's Cathedral, and Sapporo's telephone exchange.

Buses to Meiji-mura (¥410, 20 minutes) depart every 20 to 30 minutes from Inuyama Station's east exit. If you're driving, parking is ¥800.

★ Tagata-jinja   SHINTO SHRINE

(田県神社; 152 Tagata-chō; ⑧Meitetsu Komaki line to Tagata-jinja-mae) Izanagi, the male counterpart of female deity Izanami, is commemorated at this shrine, with countless wooden and stone phalluses to celebrate. You can buy souvenirs from ¥500. The **Tagata Hōnen-sai Matsuri** takes place on 15 March at Tagata-jinja, when the highly photogenic, 2m-long, 60kg 'sacred object' is paraded excitedly around the neighbourhood. Arrive well before the procession starts at 2pm. Tagata-jinja is five minutes' walk west of Tagata-jinja-mae Station on the Meitetsu Komaki line (¥290 from Inuyama, nine minutes).

Ōagata-jinja   SHINTO SHRINE

(大縣神社; ☎0568-67-1017; 3 Aza Miyayama; ⑧Meitetsu Komaki line to Gakuden) This ancient shrine set on a lovely hillside is dedicated to the female Shintō deity Izanami and attracts women seeking marriage or fertility. See if you can find the large *hime-ishi* (姫石; princess stone) and other items resembling giant female genitals. The popular **Hime-no-miya Matsuri** takes place here on the Sunday before 15 March (or on 15 March if it's a Sunday). Locals pray for good harvests and prosperity by parading through the streets bearing a *mikoshi* (portable shrine) with more replica vaginas.

Ōagata-jinja is a 25-minute walk from Gakuden Station (¥220 from Inuyama, seven minutes). To reach the shrine, turn right at the exit and follow Rte 177 east, all the way across the river and up the hill. Sadly, recent expansion of a nearby industrial landfill threatens the tranquillity of the shrine. Beware the many noisy, smelly dump trucks sharing the narrow road to your destination.

👉 Tours

Kiso-gawa Cormorant Fishing　　　BOATING
(木曽川鵜飼い, Kiso-gawa Ukai; Map p226; ☑0568-61-2727; www.kisogawa-ukai.jp; evening tours adult/child from ¥2600/1300) From June to the mid-October, the spectacle of *ukai* (cormorant fishing) takes place close to Inuyama-yūen Station, by the Twin Bridge Inuyama-bashi. Book your ticket on a Kisogawa Kankō spectator boat at the Inuyama Castle Tourist Information Center or near the cormorant-fishing pier. Up-close-and-personal tour boats depart nightly at 7pm from June to August and 30 minutes earlier in September and October.

Daylight tours depart at 11.30am and include a lunchbox (adult/child ¥3800/2900). You can always watch from a distance on the riverbank for free.

✨ Festivals & Events

In addition to **Inuyama Matsuri** (犬山まつり; ⊘Apr), the city hosts the summer **Nihon Rhine Matsuri**, culminating in fireworks, every 10 August on the banks of the river.

🛏 Sleeping & Eating

**Inuyama International
Youth Hostel**　　　HOSTEL¥
(犬山国際ユースホステル; ☑0568-61-1111; www.inuyama-hostel.com/en; 161 Himuro; s/d from ¥3600/4400; @; ☒Meitetsu Inuyama-yūen) This large hostel with a variety of room types and communal bathing is a little isolated, but reasonably priced. Meals must be reserved (breakfast/dinner ¥840/1580) and there are no facilities nearby. It's a 30-minute walk from Inuyama-yūen Station, or about ¥1350 in a taxi.

Rinkō-kan　　　RYOKAN¥¥
(臨江館; Map p226; ☑0568-61-0977; www.rinkokan.jp; 8-1 Nishidaimon; r per person incl 2 meals from ¥11,800; @; ☒Meitetsu Inuyama-yūen, west exit) Overlooking the river, this cheery 20-room ryokan has stone common baths, including *rotemburo* (outdoor baths). Some rooms have in-room bathrooms and a variety of packages are available, including good deals for single travellers.

Narita　　　FRENCH¥¥
(フレンチ創作料理なり多;Map p226; ☑0568-65-2447; www.f-narita.com; 395 Higashikoken;

5-course meal from ¥3400; ⊘11am-9pm; ☒Meitetsu Inuyama, west exit) Fancy five-course French cuisine in an Edo-period building with an attractive garden – lovely! From the station, turn right at the lights, walk two blocks to the next set of lights, then turn right. It's on your right.

ℹ Information

Inuyama has two TICs that dispense English-language materials and assist with accommodation and activities reservations. On the web, visit www.ml.inuyama.gr.jp.

Inuyama Station Tourist Information Center
(犬山市観光案内所・犬山駅); Map p226; ☑0568-61-6000; ⊘9am-5pm)

Inuyama Castle Tourist Information Center
(犬山市観光案内所・犬山城); Map p226; ☑0568-61-2825; 12 Kitakoken; ⊘9am-5pm)

ℹ Getting There & Away

Inuyama is connected with Nagoya (*tokkyū* ¥550, 25 minutes) and Gifu (¥450, 35 minutes) via the Meitetsu Inuyama line. The castle and *ukai* area are slightly closer to Inuyama-yūen Station than Inuyama Station.

Gifu 岐阜

☑058 / POP 406,866

Historically, Gifu has a strong association with Oda Nobunaga, *daimyō* (domain lord) of the castle and bestower of the city's name in 1567. It was later visited by famed haiku poet Matsuo Bashō, who witnessed *ukai* (cormorant fishing) here in 1688; Charlie Chaplin did the same in his day.

Although contemporary Gifu shows little evidence of those historic times (due to a colossal earthquake in 1891 and the decimation of WWII), redevelopment has created a vibrant and accessible downtown core. Noteworthy attractions include the lovely Gifu park and one of the three Great Buddhas of Japan. Add some pretty mountains, a wide river and excellent transport links, and a stopover here becomes a viable alternative to big city Nagoya.

⊙ Sights

Visitors generally arrive into JR Gifu or Meitetsu Gifu Stations, but sightseeing is centred about a 15-minutes bus ride north of this area around **Gifu-kōen** (岐阜公園; P; ☒N80, N32-N86 to Gifu-kōen), the Nagaragawa and the picturesque 'old-town' of Kawara-machi.

Shōhō-ji (Gifu Great Buddha)
BUDDHIST TEMPLE

(正法寺; ☎058-264-2760; 8 Daibutsu-chō; adult/child ¥200/100; ⊗9am-5pm; ⊠N80, N32-N86 to Gifu-kōen) The main attraction of this orange-and-white temple is the papier-mâché *daibutsu* (Great Buddha; c 1832), one of the three Great Buddha statues of Japan. It's 13.7m tall and is said to have been fashioned over 38 years using a tonne of paper sutras.

Nagara River Ukai Museum
MUSEUM

(長良川うかいミュージアム, Nagara-gawa Ukai Myūjiamu; ☎058-210-1555; www.ukaimuseum.jp; 51-2 Choryo; adult/child ¥500/250; ⊗9am-6.30pm Wed-Mon May–mid-Oct, 9am-4.30pm Wed-Mon mid-Oct–Apr; ☐city loop or N-line bus to Ukai-ya) Newly opened in 2012, this shiny museum is the only one of its kind and features exhibits on everything you could possibly want to know about cormorant fishing in Japan.

Gifu-jō
CASTLE

(岐阜城; ☎058-263-4853; 18 Tenshukaku; adult/child ¥200/100; ⊗9.30am-4.30pm; ⊠N80, N32-N86 to Gifu-kōen) Perched atop Mt Kinkazan with sweeping views over the cities of Gifu and Nagoya, this castle is a 1956 concrete replica of *daimyō* Oda Nobunaga's stronghold, destroyed in 1600, the ruins of which were finished off in WWII. There's an hourlong hiking trail from the park below.

➡ Kinka-zan Ropeway
CABLE CAR

(金華山ロープウエー; ☎058-262-6784; 257 Senjōjiki-shita; adult/child return ¥1080/540; ⊗9am-5pm year-round, extended hours during holiday periods) Gifu's castle is most easily reached by this cable car within Gifu-kōen, whisking you 329m to the summit in under five minutes.

Gifu City History Museum
MUSEUM

(岐阜市歴史博物館, Gifu-shi Rekishi Hakubutsukan; ☎058-265-0010; www.rekihaku.gifu.gifu.jp; 2-18-1 Ōmiya-chō; adult/child ¥300/150; ⊗9am-4.30pm Tue-Sun; ⊠N80, N32-N86 to Gifu-kōen) Located in the grounds of Gifu-kōen, this museum focuses on the Sengoku period, when Nobunaga was at the height of his power.

🖝 Tours

Nagara-gawa Cormorant Fishing
BOATING

(長良川鵜飼い, Nagara-gawa Ukai) The spectacle of *ukai* (cormorant fishing) and the glow of the lanterns drifting along the river east of the Nagara-bashi are a sight to see. For a closer view of the action, sightseeing boats depart nightly in season from the **Cormorant Fishing Viewing Boat Office** (鵜飼観覧船事務所; ☎058-262-0104; www.gifucvb.or.jp; 1-2 Minato-machi; adult/child ¥3400/1700; ⊗departures 6.15pm, 6.45pm & 7.15pm 11 May–15 Oct; ⊠N80, N32-N86, direction Takatomi, stop Nagara-bashi) below the bridge, which also takes reservations by phone (strongly advised). Food and drinks are not available on the boats.

🛌 Sleeping

There are plenty of modern, low-cost business/tourist hotels around the JR and Meitetsu station areas.

Dormy Inn Gifu Ekimae
HOTEL ¥¥

(ドーミーイン岐阜; ☎058-267-5489; www.hotespa.net/hotels/gifu; 6-31 Yoshino-machi; s/d from ¥7900/11,400; ❀🏠; ⓡJR Gifu, north exit) This new-ish hotel is five minutes' stroll along the elevated walkway from JR Gifu Station. Light-filled rooms are functionally compact with fresh, inviting decor. There's an on-site onsen and the guest laundry has gas-powered dryers (so you can actually get a decent amount of clothes dried). Breakfast is available.

Daiwa Roynet Hotel Gifu
HOTEL ¥¥

(ダイワロイネットホテル岐阜; ☎058-212-0055; www.daiwaroynet.jp/gifu; 8-5 Kanda-machi; s/d from ¥6000/8000; ⊜❀@; ⓡMeitetsu Gifu) Close to Meitetsu Gifu Station, there's a splash of colour in the rooms of this pleasant business hotel, where everything is at your doorstep.

🍴 Eating & Drinking

The narrow streets a couple of blocks north of JR Gifu Station and west of Meitetsu Gifu Station, between Kinkabashi-dōri and Nagarabashi-dōri, are dotted with open-air eateries and *izakaya*, and have a welcoming nocturnal vibe.

★ Gyōza Gishū
GYOZA ¥

(餃子専門店 岐州; ☎058-266-6227; 1-31 Sumidamachi; gyōza from ¥450; ⊗5.30pm until sold out Wed-Mon) This humming hole-in-the-wall does soupy, fried *gyōza* (dumplings) and *ebi chahan* (shrimp fried rice) and, of course, beer. Go straight from JR Gifu Station along the street between Kinkabashi-dōri and Nagarabashi-dōri. It's on the corner of the second block, to your right.

UKAI: THE ANCIENT ART OF CORMORANT FISHING

Inuyama and Gifu remain some of the few places in the world where the ancient (and some say barbaric) practice of cormorant fishing continues as it has done for centuries. Estimates date the practice, which falls under the auspices of the Imperial Household Agency (the first and finest fish of the year are sent to the emperor), at over 1300 years. The masters (called *ushō*) are so skilled that their craft is passed on from father to son.

During the *ukai* season (from May/June to 15 October), *ushō* set off after dusk in 13m traditional boats, with an iron basket containing a burning fire suspended by a pole at the front of the boat. Trained cormorants (large black, long-necked diving birds known for their voracious appetites) tethered by neck ropes to their masters, are released from the boats to dive for *ayu* (sweetfish). The ropes prevent the birds from swallowing the largest fish, which get lodged in their throats. Each bird will hold around six large fish until the master pulls it back into his boat and the fish are regurgitated. Although many shirk at this apparent cruelty, masters claim the birds are not harmed by their training.

While not for everyone, the spectacle of the fires reflected off the water and the opportunity to witness a unique and relatively unchanged traditional way of what was originally a means of feeding one's family, make watching *ukai* 'something different' if you're in the area.

Senryū JAPANESE ¥¥¥
(潜龍; ☑ 058-231-1151; www.senryu.co.jp; 14 Nagara; set menus from ¥10,000; ⊙11.30am-9.30pm) Since 1966 this delightful restaurant has been preparing succulent Hida beef in private tatami rooms in a traditional Japanese house. Set on the banks of the Nagara-gawa in view of Gifu-jō, and overlooking a manicured garden, the setting is delightful. If you're looking for an authentic teppanyaki experience (priced accordingly), you've found it. Some Japanese language ability is advantageous.

Utsuboya CAFE
(空穂屋; ☑ 058-215-7077; www.utsuboya.info; 38 Utsuboya-chō; ⊙10am-6pm Fri-Wed; 🚌N80, N32-N86, stop Hon-machi 3-chōme) In Kawaramachi, this charming cafe and antiques gallery makes homemade doughnuts (from ¥200). From the bus stop, walk east along Nagarabashi-dōri and then turn right on the second street; it's on the right in an old, tile-roofed shophouse.

🛍 Shopping

Gifu's craft tradition includes *wagasa* (oiled paper parasols/umbrellas) and elegantly painted *chōchin* (paper lanterns), though the number of real artisans is dwindling – souvenir shops sell mass-produced versions. The Tourist Information Center has a map of high-quality makers and retailers. Expect to pay ¥10,000 and over for the good stuff.

Sakaida Eikichi Honten ARTS & CRAFTS
(坂井田永吉本店; ☑ 058-271-6958; 27 Kanōnakahiroe-chō; ⊙9.30am-5.30pm Mon-Sat) This high-end maker of *wagasa* is a 10-minute walk from JR Gifu Station. Turn left from the south exit, then right at the second stoplight. It's on the next corner.

Ozeki Chōchin ARTS & CRAFTS
(オゼキ; ☑ 058-263-0111; www.ozeki-lantern. co.jp; 1-18 Oguma-chō; ⊙9am-5pm Mon-Fri; 🚌Ken-Sōgōchosha-mae) Find beautiful paper lanterns here, by Higashi Betsuin temple.

ⓘ Information

Tourist Information Center (観光案内所; ☑ 058-262-4415; JR Gifu Station; ⊙9am-7pm Mar-Dec, 9am-6pm Jan & Feb) Within Gifu Station; friendly staff can direct you to maps, accommodation and bicycle rentals (¥100 per day).

ⓘ Getting There & Away

Gifu is a blink from Nagoya on the JR Tōkaidō line (*tokkyū* ¥470, 20 minutes). Meitetsu trains take longer and are more expensive (¥550, 28 minutes) but also serve Inuyama (¥450, 35 minutes) and Central Japan International Airport (*tokkyū* ¥1340, 64 minutes).

JR Gifu and Meitetsu Gifu Stations are a few minutes' walk apart, joined by a covered elevated walkway.

ⓘ Getting Around

Buses to sights (¥200) depart from stops 11 and 12 of the bus terminal by JR Gifu Station's Nagara exit, stopping at Meitetsu Gifu en route. There's also a city-loop bus from stop 10. Check before boarding as not all buses make all stops.

Gujō-Hachiman 郡上八幡

☑ 0575 / POP 42,094

Nestled in the mountains at the confluence of several rivers, Gujō-Hachiman is a picturesque town famed for its Gujō Odori folk dance festival. It's also where plastic food models were invented.

Following a tradition dating to the 1590s, townsfolk engage in frenzied dancing on 32 nights between mid-July and early September. Visitor participation is encouraged, especially during *tetsuya odori,* the four main days of the festival (13 to 16 August), when the dancing goes all night.

Otherwise, the town's sparkling rivers, narrow lanes and stone bridges maintain appeal. A famous spring, Sōgi-sui, near the centre of town, is something of a pilgrimage site, named for a Momoyama-era poet. People who rank such things place Sōgi-sui at the top of the list for clarity.

🏃 Activities

Local resident Yuka Takada (Gujoinus) offers free English-language walking tours in the region. Email her at pupi@zd.wakwak.com.

Shokuhin Sample Kōbō   WORKSHOP
(食品サンプル工房創作館; ☑ 0575-67-1870; www.samplekobo.com; 956 Hachiman-chō; ⊗ 9am-5pm Fri-Wed) FREE Realistic food models have been one of life's great mysteries, until now. In an old merchant house, this hands-on workshop lets you see how it's done and try creating them yourself (reservations required). Tempura (three pieces, ¥1000) and lettuce (free) make memorable souvenirs. It's about five minutes' walk from Jōka-machi Plaza, across the river.

🛏 Sleeping

The town's few inexpensive ryokan and *minshuku* make spending a quiet night in this delightful hamlet a worthwhile consideration.

Nakashimaya Ryokan   RYOKAN ¥¥
(中嶋屋旅館; ☑ 0575-65-2191; www.nakashimaya.net; 940 Shinmachi; r per person from ¥6200; P) Nakashimaya Ryokan is a delightfully well-kept, compact and comfortable inn with shared facilities. It's between the train station and the Tourist Association. There's an organic cafe next door.

Bizenya Ryokan   RYOKAN ¥¥
(備前屋旅館; ☑ 0575-65-2068; www.gujyo-bizenya.jp; 264 Yanagi-machi; r per person from ¥5800; P)

This quietly upscale ryokan near Shin-bashi faces a lovely garden. Some rooms have private facilities; plans with or without meals are available.

ℹ Information

Tourist Association (観光協会; ☑ 0575-67-0002; www.gujohachiman.com/kanko; 520-1 Shimadani; ⊗ 8.30am-5pm) Pick up a walking map in English or rent a bicycle (¥300/1500 per hour/day) from this tourist office, located by Shin-bashi.

ℹ Getting There & Away

BUS

The most convenient access to Gujō-Hachiman is via bus from Gifu (¥1520, one hour). Be sure to get off at the Jōka-machi Plaza stop, which is not the end of the line. **Nōhi Bus** (濃飛バス; ☑ 0577-32-1688; www.nouhibus.co.jp) also operates services from Nagoya (¥1850, 1½ hours) and Takayama (¥1650, 1¼ hours), but these services only stop at the Gujō-Hachiman Highway Interchange on the outskirts of town.

TRAIN

The private Nagaragawa Tetsudō line serves Gujō-Hachiman from Mino-Ōta (¥1350, 80 minutes, hourly), with connections via the JR Takayama line to Nagoya (*tokkyū* ¥2320, 45 minutes; *futsū* via Gifu ¥1140, one hour) and Takayama (*tokkyū* ¥3770, 1¾ hours; *futsū* ¥1940, three hours), but the station is located a little inconveniently (about a 20-minute walk) away from the sights.

In late 2016, Nagaragawa Tetsudō (www.nagatetsu.co.jp) launched a new tourist train, Nagara, between Mino-Ōta and Gujō-Hachiman, with first-class seating, narration (in Japanese) and special French and Italian dining options. The train departs Mino-Ōta at 10.40am and arrives in Gujō-Hachiman at 12.16pm (Friday to Sunday). There is a ¥500 surcharge on top of the regular fare (¥1350).

KISO VALLEY NAKASENDŌ

The Nakasendō (中仙道) was one of the five highways of the Edo period connecting Edo (now Tokyo) with Kyoto. Much of the route is now followed by National Roads, however, in this thickly forested section of the Kiso Valley, there exist several sections of the twisty, craggy post road that have been carefully restored. The most impressive is the 7.8km stretch between Magome and Tsumago, two of the most attractive Nakasendō towns. Walking this route is one of Japan's most rewarding tourist experiences.

Along this historic highway, you'll find a handful of lovely, unpretentious *minshuku* and ryokan that won't break the budget. It's a nice idea to overnight in the area if walking a section of the Nakasendō.

Tsumago tends to be the more popular choice if only spending one night on the Nakasendō and has a bit more to choose from than the other towns in the valley. It's pretty hard to go wrong with this much atmosphere.

Dining is limited to a handful of options; most overnight visitors eat where they sleep, so to speak.

ⓘ Getting There & Away

The easiest way to reach the area is by *tokkyū* (limited express) Shinano trains on the JR Chūō line from Nagoya. Key stations include Nakatsugawa (for Magome), Nagiso (for Tsumago) and Kiso-Fukushima (for Kiso).

Magome 馬篭

☏ 0264

Located in the administrative district of Nakatsugawa, in Gifu Prefecture, pretty Magome-juku is the furthest south of the Kiso Valley post villages. Its buildings line a steep, cobblestone pedestrian road (unfriendly to wheelie suitcases); the rustic shopfronts and mountain views will keep your finger on the shutter.

🛏 Sleeping

Minshuku Tajimaya   MINSHUKU ¥¥
(民宿但馬屋; ☏ 0264-69-2048; www.kiso-tajimaya.com; 4266 Magome; r incl 2 meals from ¥9720; ⊕❄🅿) This pleasant historical inn has compact rooms and friendly staff, although the location of the bathrooms can be inconvenient. The array of local specialities served in the common dining area is impressive, as are the *hinoki* (cypress baths).

Magome-Chaya   MINSHUKU ¥¥
(馬籠茶屋; ☏ 0264-59-2038; www.magomechaya.com; 4296 Magome; r per person incl 2 meals from ¥8525; 🅿) This popular *minshuku* is almost halfway up the hill, near the waterwheel. Room-only plans are available.

ⓘ Information

Tourist Information Center (観光案内館;
☏ 0264-59-2336; 4300-1 Magome; ⊙9am-5pm)
Located somewhat inconveniently halfway up the

hill, to the right. A baggage forwarding service to Tsumago is available.

ⓘ Getting There & Away

Nakatsugawa Station on the JR Chūō line serves Magome, though it is some distance from the town. Nakatsugawa is connected with Nagoya (*tokkyū* ¥2500, 55 minutes) and Matsumoto (*tokkyū* ¥3770, 1¼ hours).

Buses leave hourly from Nakatsugawa Station for Magome (¥540, 30 minutes). There's also an infrequent bus service between Magome and Tsumago (¥600, 25 minutes), via Magome-tōge.

Meitetsu Bus (名鉄バス; ☏ 052-588-0876; www.meitetsu-bus.co.jp) operates highway buses that connect Tokyo's Shinjuku Station with Magome (¥4630, 4½ hours). Note that the stop is at the highway interchange; from there it's a 1.3km uphill walk, unless timed with the bus from Nakatsugawa.

Tsumago 妻籠

☏ 0264

Part of Nagiso town, Tsumago feels like an open-air museum, about 15 minutes' walk from end to end. It was designated by the government as a protected area for the preservation of traditional buildings, where modern developments such as telephone poles aren't allowed to mar the scene. The dark-wood glory of its lattice-fronted buildings is particularly beautiful at dawn and dusk. Film and TV crews are often spotted here.

On 23 November, the **Fuzoku Emaki** parade is held along the Nakasendō in Tsumago, featuring townsfolk in Edo-period costume.

⊙ Sights

**Waki-honjin (Okuya) &
Local History Museum**   MUSEUM
(脇本陣 (奥谷)・歴史資料館, Rekishi Shiryōkan; 2159-2 Azuma; adult/child ¥600/300; ⊙9am-5pm) The former rest stop for the *daimyōs'* (domain lords') retainers, this *waki-honjin* was reconstructed in 1877 by a former castle builder under special dispensation from Emperor Meiji. It contains a lovely moss garden and a special toilet built in case Meiji happened to show up; he never did. The adjacent Local History Museum houses elegant exhibitions about Kiso and the Nakasendō, with some English signage.

Tsumagojuku-honjin   HISTORIC BUILDING
(妻籠宿本陣; 2190 Azuma; adult/child ¥300/150; ⊙9am-5pm) It was in this building that the *daimyō* themselves would spend the night,

THE JAPAN ALPS & CENTRAL HONSHŪ KISO

DON'T MISS

MAGOME–TSUMAGO HIKE

From Magome (elevation 600m), the 7.8km hike to Tsumago (elevation 420m) follows a steep, largely paved road until it reaches its peak at the top of Magome-tōge (pass) – elevation 801m. After the pass, the trail meanders by waterfalls, forest and farmland. The route is easiest in this direction and is clearly signposted in English; allow three to six hours to enjoy it.

Both towns offer a handy baggage forwarding service from either Tourist Information Center to the other. Deposit your bags between 8.30am and 11.30am, for delivery by 1pm.

If fitness or ability prevent you from appreciating the amazing walk between Magome and Tsumago, there is an easier way. The Magome–Tsumago bus (¥600, 30 minutes, two to three daily in each direction) also stops at Magome-tōge. If you alight and begin the walk there, it's a picturesque 5.2km downhill run through to Tsumago.

although the building's architecture is more noteworthy than its exhibits. A combined ticket (adult/child ¥700/350) includes admission to Waki-honjin (Okuya) & Local History Museum, opposite.

🛏 Sleeping & Eating

★ Fujioto   RYOKAN ¥¥
(藤乙; ☑ 0264-57-3009; www.tsumago-fujioto.jp; r per person incl 2 meals from ¥10,800; ☺❋☏) The owner of this unpretentious, welcoming inn speaks some English, Italian and Spanish. It's a great place to have your first ryokan experience as most staff are able to communicate with travellers well, especially over the wonderful *kaiseki* dinner. Corner upstairs rooms have lovely views. You can also stop by for lunch – try the Kiso Valley trout (¥1350).

Oyado Daikichi   MINSHUKU ¥¥
(御宿大吉; ☑ 0264-57-2595; r per person incl 2 meals from ¥8600; ☺❋@) Popular with foreign visitors, this traditional-looking inn benefits from modern construction and has a prime location on the top of the hill – all rooms have a lovely outlook. It's at the very edge of town.

Hotel Kisoji   HOTEL ¥¥¥
(ホテル木曽路; ☑ 0264-58-2046; 2278 Azuma; r per person incl 2 meals from ¥16,500) A few kilometres above Tsumago, you'll find this resort hotel popular with inbound tour groups, whose main draw is its series of *rotemburo* with panoramic mountain vistas. There's a sprawling dining room, also with scenic views, and a souvenir shop.

Yoshimura-ya   NOODLES ¥
(吉村屋; ☑ 0264-57-3265; dishes ¥720-1540; ⏱ 10am-5pm; ☑❍) If you're hungry after a long walk, you can't go past a chilled bowl of handmade Kiso *zaru-soba*.

ℹ Information

Tourist Information Center (観光案内館; ☑ 0264-57-3123; www.tumago.jp/english; 2159-2 Azuma; ⏱ 8.30am-5pm) Tsumago's TIC is in the centre of town, by the antique phone booth. Some English is spoken and there's English-language literature. Ask here for any directions.

ℹ Getting There & Away

Nagiso Station on the JR Chūō line serves Tsumago, though it is some distance from the town. A few *tokkyū* daily stop in Nagiso (from Nagoya ¥2840, one hour); otherwise change at Magome's Nakatsugawa Station (*futsū* ¥320, 20 minutes).

There's an infrequent bus service between Magome and Tsumago (¥600, 25 minutes), via Magome-tōge.

Buses run between Tsumago and Nagiso Station (¥270, 10 minutes, eight daily).

Kiso   木曽町

☑ 0264 / POP 28,421

Kiso (*kiso-machi*) is larger and considerably more developed than its southern neighbours, and its historical significance as an important checkpoint on the Nakasendō, plus its pretty riverside position, make it a pleasant lunch stop en route to (or from) Matsumoto.

⊙ Sights

From Kiso-Fukushima train station, turn right and head downhill towards the town centre and the Kiso-gawa. Sights are well signposted. Look for **Ue-no-dan** (上の段), the historic district of atmospheric houses, many of which now house retailers.

Fukushima Checkpoint Site   MUSEUM
(福島関所跡, Fukushima Sekisho-ato; adult/child ¥300/150; ⏱ 8am-5pm Apr-Oct, 8.30am-

4pm Nov-Mar) This is a reconstruction of one of the most significant checkpoints on the Edo-period trunk roads. From its perch above the river valley, it's easy to see the barrier's strategic importance. Displays inside show the implements used to maintain order, including weaponry and *tegata* (wooden travel passes), as well as the special treatment women travellers received.

✖ Eating

There are a few good eateries in the village and by the train station.

★ Kurumaya Honten NOODLES ¥
(くるまや本店; ☑ 0264-22-2200; 5367-2 Kisomachi, Fukushima; mains ¥670-1775; ☺ 10am-5pm Thu-Tue; ☑ ◙) One of Japan's most renowned soba shops, where the classic presentation is cold *mori* (plain) or *zaru* (with strips of nori seaweed) with a sweetish dipping sauce. It's near the first bridge at the bottom of the hill; look for the gears above the doorway.

Bistro Matsushima-tei ITALIAN ¥¥
(ビストロ 松島亭; ☑ 0264-23-3625; 5250-1 Ue-no-dan; mains ¥1300-2200, lunch sets ¥1300-1900; ☺ lunch & dinner daily Jul-Oct, Thu-Tue Nov-Jun) In Ue-no-dan, Bistro Matsushima-tei serves a changing selection of handmade pizzas and pastas in an atmospheric setting befitting the building's history.

ⓘ Information

Kiso Tourist Information Center (木曽町観光協会, Kiso-machi Kankō Kyōkai; ☑ 0264-22-4000; 2012-10 Kiso-machi, Fukushima; ☺ 9am-4.45pm) Across from the train station, the friendly staff here have some English maps, but appreciate some Japanese-language ability.

Additional info can be found at www.nakasendoway.com, an excellent resource produced by Walk Japan.

ⓘ Getting There & Away

Kiso-Fukushima is on the JR Chūō line (*Shinano tokkyū*), easily reached from Matsumoto (¥2150, 38 minutes), Nakatsugawa (¥2150, 34 minutes) and Nagoya (¥4100, 1½ hours).

Narai 奈良井
☑ 0264
A lesser known but important example of a Nakasendō post town, little Narai is a gem tucked away in the folds of a narrow valley; it belongs to the city of Shiojiri, in Nagano.

Once called 'Narai of a thousand houses', it flourished during the Edo period when its proximity to the highest pass on the Nakasendō made it a popular resting place for travellers. Today, it's a conservation area with a preserved main street showcasing some wonderful examples of Edo-period architecture.

Narai is famed for *shikki* (lacquerware). Plenty of quality souvenir shops line the main street, many with reasonable prices.

◉ Sights

Nakamura House HISTORIC BUILDING
(中村邸; ☑ 0264-34-2655; adult/child ¥300/free; ☺ 9am-4pm) This wonderfully preserved former merchant's house and garden looks as if it has stood still while time passed by.

🛏 Sleeping & Eating

★ Echigo-ya RYOKAN ¥¥
(ゑちごや旅館; ☑ 0264-34-3011; www.naraijyuku-echigoya.jp; 493 Narai; r per person incl 2 meals from ¥15,660) In business for over 220 years, this charming family-run ryokan is one of a kind. With only two guestrooms, Echigo-ya provides a unique opportunity to experience the Japanese art of hospitality in its most undiluted form. Expect to feel like you've stepped back in time. Some Japanese-language ability will help make the most of the experience. Book well in advance. Cash only.

Oyado Iseya MINSHUKU ¥¥
(御宿伊勢屋; ☑ 0264-34-3051; www.oyado-iseya.jp; 388 Narai; r per person incl 2 meals from ¥9500) The street front of this former merchant house built in 1818 has been beautifully preserved. It's now a pleasant 10-room inn, with guestrooms in the main house and a newer building out back.

ⓘ HIKING RESOURCES

Central Honshū, a hiker's delight, is blessed with half of the nation's 100 famous mountains as well as many national parks. Enthusiastic hikers should pick up Lonely Planet's *Hiking in Japan*.

Numerous English-language maps and pamphlets are published by the Japan National Tourism Organization (JNTO) and local authorities. Most detailed hiking maps are in Japanese.

Matsunami SHOKUDO ¥
(松波; ☑0264-34-3750; 397-1 Narai; light meals
¥650-980; ⊙11.30am-8pm Wed-Mon) This delightful little eatery on a corner serves simple
favourites such as special-sauce *tonkatsu-don*
(deep-fried pork cutlet on rice).

ℹ Information

Narai Tourist Information Center (奈良井宿
観光協会; ☑0264-54-2001; www.naraijuku.
com; ⊙10am-5pm May-Oct) Inside Narai
Station, this tourist office has some English-
language leaflets and a map. Little English is
spoken.

ℹ Getting There & Away

Only *futsū* (local) trains stop at Narai, which is on
the JR Chūō line. It takes no more than an hour or
three to see the sights, making it a neat day trip
from Matsumoto (¥580, 50 minutes), but you
could easily pass a peaceful evening here. From
Nagoya, change trains at Nakatsugawa (¥1320,
1½ hours) or Kiso-Fukushima (¥410, 20 minutes).

HIDA REGION

Visitors flock to the utterly delightful, ancient, mountainous Hida Region (飛騨地域)
for its *onsen ryokan* (traditional hot-spring
inns); the World Heritage–listed villages of
Ogimachi and Ainokura, famed for their signature thatch-roofed *gasshō-zukuri* architecture; and its centrepiece, Takayama, one of
Japan's most likeable cities.

Whether you choose to bed down in a
gasshō-zukuri inn or opt for one of Takayama's many fantastic *minshuku* or ryokan,
the region's wide choice of accommodation
options makes it one of the best places to experience the Japanese art of hospitality.

ℹ Getting There & Around

The Hida Region is easily accessed by train or bus,
most directly by Nagoya to the south and Toyama
to the north.

BUS

There are two popular trunk routes in the area
with frequent services operated by a number of
carriers.

The first connects Takayama to Okuhida
Onsen-gō, Kamikōchi and sections of the
Northern Japan Alps, and Matsumoto. The
second links Takayama to Toyama/Kanazawa
via the *gasshō-zukuri* villages of Shirakawa-gō
and Gokayama.

A wide range of bus tours are also available.

If you're planning to explore the area in some
depth, the five-day Shōryūdō Highway Bus ticket
(¥14,000), which must be purchased online or
from a travel agent outside Japan, covers the Hida
Region extensively and includes travel to/from
Nagoya, Matsumoto and Kanazawa. You might
also benefit from purchasing a four-day Hida Open
bus ticket (adult/child ¥10,290/5150) offering
unlimited travel around the region, one of a variety
of discount passes available.

CAR & MOTORCYCLE

Getting to this mountainous region by car is neither cost nor time efficient and is not recommended for the inexperienced, especially in winter when
many roads become hazardous or impassable.

Once you're here, however, it's easy to rent a car
for shorter explorations in and around the region.

TRAIN

Sitting in the northernmost pocket of Gifu Prefecture, the Hida Region is accessed by *tokkyū* (limited express) rail services from Nagoya (¥5510,
2½ hours) to the south and Toyama (¥2840, 1½
hours) to the north. Both cities are now linked to
Tokyo by *shinkansen* (bullet train) lines.

Takayama 飛騨高山

☑0577 / POP 89,205
Takayama (officially known as Hida Takayama) boasts one of Japan's most atmospheric townscapes and best-loved festivals. A visit here should be considered a high priority
for anyone travelling in Central Honshū,
although its recent rise in popularity can
sometimes take the sparkle off what was a
little-known hamlet just a decade ago. Visiting during shoulder seasons affords a little
more tranquillity.

Its present layout dates from the late
17th century and incorporates a wealth of
museums, galleries and temples for a city
of its compact size. Meiji-era inns, hillside
shrines and temples, and a pretty riverside
setting beckon you. Excellent infrastructure
and friendly, welcoming locals seal the deal.
Give yourself two or three days to enjoy it all.
Takayama is easily explored on foot and is the
perfect start or end point for trips into the
Hida Region and the Northern Japan Alps.

◎ Sights

Most sights are clearly signposted in English
and are within walking distance of the train
station, which sits between the main streets
of Kokubunji-dōri and Hirokōji-dōri. Both
run east and cross the Miya-gawa where they
become Yasugawa-dōri and Sanmachi-dōri,

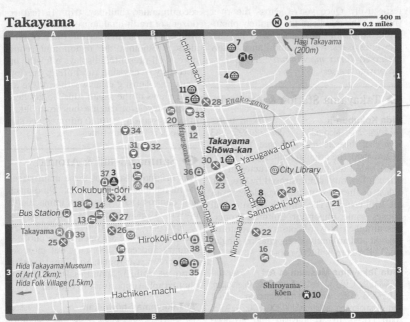

Takayama

respectively. Once you're across the river you're in the middle of the infinitely photogenic Sanmachi-suji district, with its sake breweries, cafes, retailers and immaculately preserved *furui machinami* (古い町並み; old private houses).

◉ Takayama Station & Around

Hida Kokubun-ji   BUDDHIST TEMPLE
(飛騨国分寺; Map p235; ☑ 0577-32-1395; 1-83 Sōwa-chō; treasure hall adult/child ¥300/250; ⊙ 9am-4pm) The original buildings of Takayama's oldest temple were constructed in the 8th century, but later destroyed by fire. The oldest of the present buildings dates from the 16th century. The temple's treasure hall houses some Important Cultural Properties, and the courtyard boasts a three-storey pagoda and an impressively gnarled gingko tree believed to be 1200 years old.

Hida Takayama Museum of Art   MUSEUM
(飛騨高山美術館, Hida Takayama Bijutsukan; ☑ 0577-35-3535; www.htm-museum.co.jp; 1-124-1 Kamiokamoto-chō; adult/child ¥1300/800; ⊙ 9am-5pm) Lovers of art-nouveau and art-deco glassware and furniture will appreciate this large private gallery set back from town with a ritzy cafe, its own London Bus shuttle (ask at the Tourist Information Center) and a spectacular glass fountain by René Lalique.

Hida Folk Village   MUSEUM
(飛騨の里, Hida-no-sato; ☑ 0577-34-4711; www.hidanosato-tpo.jp; 1-590 Kamiokamoto-chō; adult/child ¥700/200; ⊙ 8.30am-5pm) The sprawling, open-air Hida-no-sato is a highly recommended half-day trip. It features dozens of traditional houses and buildings, which were dismantled at their original sites throughout the region and rebuilt here. Well-presented displays offer the opportunity to envision rural life in previous centuries. During clear weather, there are good views of the Japan Alps. To get here, hire a bicycle or catch a bus from Takayama bus station (¥210, 10 minutes); be sure to check return bus times.

◉ Sanmachi-suji & Around

This original district of three main streets of merchants (Ichino-machi, Nino-machi and Sanno-machi) has been immaculately preserved. Sake breweries are designated by spheres of cedar fronds hanging above their doors; some are open to the public in January and early February, but most sell their brews year-round. You'll find artisans, antiques, clothiers and cafes. Day and night, photographic opportunities abound.

★ Takayama Shōwa-kan   MUSEUM
(高山昭和館; Map p235; ☑ 0577-33-7836; www.takayama-showakan.com; 6 Shimoichino-machi; adult/child ¥500/300; ⊙ 9am-5pm) This nostalgia bonanza from the Shōwa period (1926–89) concentrates on the years between 1955 and 1965, a time of great optimism between Japan's postwar malaise and pre-Titan boom. Lose yourself among the delightful mishmash of endless objects, from movie posters to cars and everything in-between, lovingly presented in a series of themed rooms.

THE JAPAN ALPS & CENTRAL HONSHŪ TAKAYAMA

GASSHŌ-ZUKURI ARCHITECTURE

Hida winters can be unforgiving. Its people braved the elements long before the advent of propane heaters and 4WD vehicles. The most visible symbol of their adaptability is *gasshō-zukuri* architecture, as seen in the steeply slanted, straw-roofed homes that dot the regional landscape.

Sharply angled roofs prevent snow accumulation, a serious concern in an area where most mountain roads close from December to April. The name *gasshō* comes from the Japanese word for prayer, because the shape of the roofs was thought to resemble hands clasped together. *Gasshō* buildings often feature pillars crafted from stout cedars to lend extra support. The attic areas are ideal for silk cultivation. Larger *gasshō-zukuri* buildings were inhabited by wealthy families, with up to 30 people under one roof. Peasant families lived in huts so small that today they'd only be considered fit for tool sheds.

The art of *gasshō-zukuri* construction is dying out. Most remaining examples have been relocated to folk villages, including Hida-no-sato (p236) and those at Ogimachi (p246), Suganuma (p248) and Ainokura (p248). Homes that are now neighbours may once have been separated by several days of travel on foot or sled. These cultural preservation efforts have made it possible to imagine a bygone life in the Hida hills.

Yoshijima Heritage House   HISTORIC BUILDING
(吉島家, Yoshijima-ke; Map p235; ☑0577-32-0038;
1-51 Ōjin-machi; adult/child ¥500/300; ◉9am-5pm
Mar-Nov, 9am-4.30pm Wed-Sun Dec-Feb) Design
buffs shouldn't miss Yoshijima-ke, which is
well covered in architectural publications.
Its lack of ornamentation allows you to focus
on the spare lines, soaring roof and skylight.
Admission includes a cup of delicious shiitake
tea, which you can also purchase for ¥600 per
can.

Kusakabe Folk Crafts Museum   MUSEUM
(日下部民藝館, Kusakabe Mingeikan; Map p235;
☑0577-32-0072; www.kusakabe-mingeikan.com;
1-52 Ōjin-machi; adult/child ¥500/300; ◉9am-
4.30pm Mar-Nov, 9am-4pm Wed-Mon Dec-Feb) This
building dating from the 1890s showcases
the striking craftsmanship of traditional
Takayama carpenters. Inside is a collection
of folk art.

**Takayama Museum
of History & Art**   MUSEUM
(飛驒高山まちの博物館, Hida-Takayama Machi
no Hakubutsukan; Map p235; ☑0577-32-1205; 75
Kamiichino-machi; ◉museum 9am-7pm, garden
7am-9pm) FREE Not to be confused with the
Hida Takayama Museum of Art, this free
museum is situated around pretty gardens
and features 14 themed exhibition rooms
relating to local history, culture, literature
and the arts.

Hida Folk Archaeological Museum   MUSEUM
(飛驒民族考古館, Hida Minzoku Kōkō-kan; Map
p235; ☑0577-32-1980; 82 Kamisanno-machi; adult/
child ¥500/200; ◉7am-5pm Mar-Nov, 9.30am-4pm
Dec-Feb) A former samurai house boasting interesting secret passageways and an old well
in the courtyard.

**Takayama Festival
Floats Exhibition Hall**   MUSEUM
(高山屋台会館, Takayama Yatai-kaikan; Map p235;
☑0577-32-5100; 178 Sakura-machi; adult/child
¥900/450; ◉8.30am-5pm Mar-Nov, 9am-4.30pm
Dec-Feb) A rotating selection of four of the 23
multi-tiered *yatai* (floats) used in the Takayama Matsuri (p237) can be appreciated here.
These spectacular creations, some dating
from the 17th century, are prized for their
flamboyant carvings, metalwork and lacquerwork. Some floats feature *karakuri ningyō*
(marionettes) that perform amazing feats
courtesy of eight accomplished puppeteers
manipulating 36 strings.

The museum is on the grounds of the stately **Sakurayama Hachiman-gū** (桜山八幡宮;

Map p235; ☑0577-32-0240; www.hidahachimangu.
jp) FREE, which presides over the festival.

Karakuri Museum   MUSEUM
(飛驒高山獅子会館・からくりミュージア
ム; Map p235; ☑0577-32-0881; www.takayama
karakuri.jp; 53-1 Sakura-machi; adult/child
¥600/400; ◉9am-4.30pm) On display here
are over 300 *shishi* (lion) masks, instruments and drums related to festival dances.
The main draw is the twice-hourly puppet
show where you can see the mechanical
karakuri ningyō in action.

◉ Teramachi, Shiroyama-kōen & Around

These lovely, hilly districts to the east are
linked by a well-signposted walking path. Teramachi has over a dozen temples and shrines
you can wander around before taking in the
greenery of Shiroyama-kōen. Various trails
lead through the park and up the mountainside to the ruins of the castle, **Takayama-jō**
(高山城跡; Map p235; Shiroyama-kōen).

Takayama-jinya   HISTORIC BUILDING
(高山陣屋; Map p235; ☑0577-32-0643;
1-5 Hachiken-machi; adult/child ¥430/380;
◉8.45am-4.30pm Sep-Jul, to 6pm Aug) These
sprawling grounds south of Sanmachi-suji
house the only remaining prefectural office building of the Tokugawa shogunate,
originally the administrative centre for the
Kanamori clan. The present main building
dates back to 1816 and was used as local
government offices until 1969. There's
also a rice granary, a garden and a torture
chamber with explanatory detail. Free
guided tours in English are available (reservations advised).

🍴 Courses

Green Cooking School   COOKING
(Map p235; ☑0577-32-9263; www.green-cooking.
com; 78 Shimo-sanno-machi; classes ¥4500-6500)
It's so nice to discover a Japanese cooking
school for foreign visitors in Takayama! Learn
about the basics of Japanese cooking, then
dine on your handiwork. Two days' notice and
a minimum of two participants are required
for classes to proceed.

🎊 Festivals & Events

Takayama Matsuri   PARADE
One of Japan's great festivals, the Takayama
Matsuri is in two parts. On 14 and 15 April is

the **Sannō Matsuri**, when a dozen decorated *yatai* (floats) are paraded through the town. **Hachiman Matsuri**, on 9 and 10 October, is a slightly smaller version.

In the evenings, the floats, with their carvings, dolls, colourful curtains and blinds, are decked out with lanterns and the procession is accompanied by sacred music.

🛏 Sleeping

One of Takayama's delights is its variety of excellent accommodation across all styles, for all budgets. If visiting during festival times, book accommodation months in advance and expect to pay a 20% premium. The Ryokan Hotel Association (www.takayamaryokan.jp) can assist with lodging enquiries.

Guesthouse Tomaru
GUESTHOUSE ¥

(飛騨高山ゲストハウスとまる; Map p235; ☑0577-62-9260; www.hidatakayama-guesthouse. com; 6-5 Hanasato-machi; dm ¥3000, s & d ¥7000, tr ¥10,000; ❄@🤶) Visitors love the friendly homestay vibe of this small, centrally located guesthouse. Pleasant rooms with homely touches are kept spotlessly clean. There's free wi-fi and a shared kitchen.

K's House Takayama
HOSTEL ¥

(Map p235; ☑0577-34-4410; www.kshouse.jp/takayama-e; 4-45-1 Tenman-machi; dm/s/d per person from ¥2900/4800/3600; ❄🤶) This sparkly hostel has caused a stir on the Takayama hostel scene. All rooms, including dorms, have private bathroom, TV and wi-fi. There's a kitchen and common area, and bicycle rentals are available. A second wing, K's House Oasis, offering similar but fresher facilities and closer to the train station, opened in 2016. Check the website for details of both properties.

★Rickshaw Inn
HOTEL ¥¥

(力車イン; Map p235; ☑0577-32-2890; www. rickshawinn.com; 54 Suehiro-chō; s without bathroom from ¥4200, tw with/without bathroom from ¥11,900/10,200; ⊕❄@🤶) Well positioned on the fringe of Takayama's entertainment district, this consistent travellers' favourite remains great value. There's a range of room types, a small kitchen, laundry facilities and a cosy lounge. Friendly English-speaking owners are founts of information about Takayama.

★Sumiyoshi Ryokan
RYOKAN ¥¥

(寿美吉旅館; Map p235; ☑0577-32-0228; www. sumiyoshi-ryokan.com; 4-21 Hon-machi; s/d from ¥8000/12,000; P@🤶) The kind owners of this delightfully antiquey inn, set in a Meiji-era merchant's house, have been wel-

coming guests from abroad for years. Some rooms have river views through panes of antique glass, and the common baths are made of wood and slate tiles. One room has a private bath. Add ¥4000 per person to include dinner and breakfast.

Hagi Takayama
RYOKAN ¥¥

(萩高山; ☑0577-32-4100; www.takayama-kh. com; 280 Hachiman-machi; r per person incl 2 meals from ¥12,600; P❄🤶) This elevated hotel on the immediate outskirts of downtown has wonderful views from all rooms and delightful communal bathing areas. Rooms in the main wing were refurbished most recently. Expect traditional service, fine local cuisine and a wonderful green location in the hills above Takayama, which makes it ideal for those with a car (parking in the town below can be tricky).

Honjin Hiranoya
RYOKAN ¥¥

(本陣平野屋; Map p235; ☑0577-34-1234; www. honjinhiranoya.co.jp; 1-5 Hon-machi; r per person incl 2 meals from ¥13,800; P❄🤶) For something a little different, choose the contemporary elegance of the executive rooms in the more expensive Kachoan wing. Otherwise opt for a classical river-view room in the Bekkan (Annexe) wing. There's a free shuttle bus from the train station, or it's a 10-minute walk. Expect the highest service levels, English-speaking staff and exquisite cuisine. Highly recommended.

Yamakyū
RYOKAN ¥¥

(山久; Map p235; ☑0577-32-3756; www.takayama-yamakyu.com; 58 Tenshōji-machi; r incl 2 meals from ¥7500; P@🤶) Occupying a lovely hillside spot opposite Hokke-ji temple, Yamakyū is a 20-minute walk from the train station. Inside, antique-filled curio cabinets, clocks and lamps line the red-carpeted corridors. All 20 tatami rooms have a sink and toilet, and the common baths are of a high standard. Some English is spoken. Yamakyū is an excellent choice for a ryokan experience without the expense.

Best Western Hotel
HOTEL ¥¥

(ベストウェスタンホテル高山; Map p235; ☑0577-37-2000; www.bestwestern.co.jp; 6-6 Hanasato-machi; s/d/tw from ¥7400/13,200/14,200; ⊕❄🤶) Popular with overseas guests, this tourist hotel's refurbished rooms have a splash of colour. Good-value rates can be found online and sometimes include a breakfast buffet. It's a hop, skip and a jump from the train station.

★ **Oyado koto no Yume** RYOKAN ¥¥¥
(おやど古都の夢; Map p235; ☑ 0577-32-0427; www.kotoyume-peace.com; 6-11 Hanasato-machi; d/ste from ¥22,000/40,000; ❉ ☎) You'll be impressed by the friendly, professional staff at this wonderful hybrid of a boutique hotel and a traditional ryokan, whose all-tatami rooms are furnished with a stylish fusion of old and new. Be sure to book the indoor rooftop *kazoku-buro* (family bath). Conveniently located near the train station. Great value.

Hōshōkaku RYOKAN ¥¥¥
(宝生閣; Map p235; ☑ 0577-34-0700; www.hoshokaku.co.jp; 1-88 Baba-machi; r per person incl 2 meals from ¥16,200; P ❉ ☎) Surrounded by the greenery of Shiroyama-kōen, this upscale hillside ryokan on the edge of town has wonderful outdoor rooftop hot springs with city views and sumptuous *kaiseki* (Japanese haute cuisine). If arriving by train, it's easiest to grab a taxi out here.

🍴 Eating

Takayama boasts a plethora of excellent dining options across many genres. Its specialities include soba (buckwheat noodles), *hoba-miso* (sweet miso paste grilled on a magnolia leaf), *sansai* (mountain vegetables) and *Hida-gyū* (Hida beef). Street foods include *mitarashi-dango* (soy-seasoned grilled rice-ball skewers) and *shio-sembei* (salty rice crackers). *Hida-gyū* turns up on *kushiyaki* (skewers), and in *korokke* (croquettes) and *niku-man* (steamed buns). Also look out for numerous bakeries.

Center4 Hamburgers BURGERS ¥
(Map p235; ☑ 0577-36-4527; www.tiger-center4.com; 94 Kamiichino-machi; burgers from ¥760; ◷ 11am-9.30pm; 🍴) Word has spread that this Japanese couple are living their dream, welcoming visitors from around the world – so you might have to wait for a table to enjoy their delicious comfort food. On the menu: juicy home-style burgers (including veggie), club sandwiches, and chilli and clam chowder, served in a funky dining room that feels like the extension of someone's home.

Jakuson JAPANESE ¥
(弱尊; Map p235; ☑ 0577-36-1810; 5-5 Tenman-machi; curry from ¥750; ◷ 11.30am-3pm & 5.30-9.30pm Fri-Wed) Pronounced 'Jackson' but having nothing to do with Michael or any of his gang, this unpretentious eatery dishes out some seriously delicious takes on Japanese curry, with a too-tempting

range of options that will likely see you coming back for a second visit.

Heianraku CHINESE ¥
(平安楽; Map p235; ☑ 0577-32-3078; 6-7-2 Tenman-machi; dishes from ¥740; ◷ 11.30am-1.30pm & 5-10pm Wed-Mon; 🍴) Atmospheric, inexpensive, welcoming and delicious are all words that spring to mind when describing this wonderful second-generation eatery serving up Chinese delights in a traditional Japanese shopfront on Kokubunji-dōri. It's a few steps before Hida Kokubun-ji (p236) on the opposite side of the street. The *gyōza* (dumplings) and meatballs are spot on. English is spoken.

Ebisu-Honten NOODLES ¥
(恵比寿本店; Map p235; ☑ 0577-32-0209; www.takayama-ebisu.jp; 46 Kamini-no-machi; noodle bowls from ¥880; ◷ 10am-5pm Thu-Tue; 🍴🍴) These folks have been making *teuchi* (handmade) soba since 1898. Try their cold *zaru soba* to strip it bare and taste the flavour of the noodles. The *tororo nameko soba* is also very good: noodles in a hot soup with boiled mushroom and grated mountain potato. The building has an interesting red-glass sign with white characters and a little roof on it.

iCafe Takayama CAFE ¥
(Map p235; www.icafe-takayama.com; 1-22-11 Showa-machi; light meals from ¥500; ◷ 7.30am-7pm; ☎) Run by the inspiring crew from Satoyama Experience (p242) in neighbouring Hida-Furukawa, this new-in-2016 cafe in the slick new-in-2016 Takayama Station is your one-stop shop for all things Hida. It's a great first port of call as you arrive into town, offering tasty snacks, good coffee and healthy servings of expert local knowledge. There's free wi-fi and oodles of baggage storage.

★ **Kyōya** SHOKUDO ¥¥
(京や; Map p235; ☑ 0577-34-7660; www.kyoya-hida.jp; 1-77 Ōjin-machi; mains ¥750-5200; ◷ 11am-10pm Wed-Mon; 🍴) This traditional eatery specialises in regional dishes such as *hoba-miso* and *Hida-gyū* soba. Seating is on tatami mats around long charcoal grills, under a cathedral ceiling supported by dark timbers. It's on a corner, by a bridge over the canal. Look for the sacks of rice over the door.

Kotarō TONKATSU ¥¥
(小太郎; Map p235; ☑ 0577-32-7353; 6-1 Tenman-machi; set meals ¥1050-2100; ◷ 11.30am-2pm & 5-9pm Thu-Tue; 🍴) Expect satisfaction from this compact workman-like eatery whose chef has spent over 25 years mastering the art of

tonkatsu (deep-fried pork cutlets) and other fried goodies. Generous *teishoku* (set meals) feature crispy, crunchy *katsu*, cooked to perfection, accompanied by perfectly balanced sides: fluffy rice, rich miso soup, fruit, salad and pickles. Try the cheese *katsu* for something different.

Takumi-ya BARBECUE ¥¥
(匠家; Map p235; ☑0577-36-2989; 2 Shimo-ni-no-machi; mains downstairs ¥680-980, upstairs from ¥1500; ☺11am-3pm & 5-9pm Thu-Tue; 🍴)
Hida-gyū on a burger budget. Adjacent to Takumi-ya's butcher shop is a casual restaurant specialising in ramen in Hida-beef broth and *Hida gyū-don* (beef and onion over rice). The pricier upstairs restaurant serves *yakiniku* (Korean-style barbecue).

★ Sakurajaya FUSION ¥¥
(さくら茶屋; ☑0577-57-7565; www.sakurajaya.jimdo.com; 3-8-14 Sowa-machi; dinner courses from ¥3000; ☺11.30am-2.30pm & 6-11pm Thu-Tue)
Sakurajaya is what you get when you take a Japanese man to Germany, introduce him to the European culinary arts, hone his craft over years then plonk him down in the quiet back lanes of Takayama. His wonderful artisanal creations draw from both German and Japanese lines. There's something here for all palates, including vegetarians. It's well worth the walk.

Shōjin Ryōri Kakushō VEGETARIAN ¥¥¥
(精進料理角正; Map p235; ☑0577-32-0174; www.kakusyo.com; 2-98 Baba-machi; kaiseki courses per person from ¥10,000; ☺11.30am-1.30pm & 5-8pm; 🍴) Experience the unique Japanese art of *shōjin-ryōri*, holistic vegetarian *kaiseki* dining in an atmospheric building and garden that's almost 200 years old, surrounded by ancient temples and mountains beyond. Sound dreamy? If you're a fan of the genre, it really, really is. If a burger and chips is your raison d'être, move on! Some English is spoken.

🍷 Drinking & Nightlife

★ Red Hill Pub PUB
(レッド・ヒル; Map p235; ☑0577-33-8139; 2-4 Sowa-chō; ☺7pm-midnight; 🔊) You'll feel like you're walking into a friend's living room in this cosy, dimly lit basement bar. The hip and happy owner, Hisayo, deftly adjusts the vibe to suit the patrons present. It's sometimes soulful and smooth, sometimes rocking and raucous. If it's quiet and you're alone, you'll still have someone fascinating to talk to – Hisayo speaks excellent English.

She also prepares tasty snacks and offers an excellent selection of brews and killer cocktails.

Bols SPORTS BAR
(Map p235; ☑0577-35-1762; 72-1 Suehiro-machi; ☺9pm-2am Tue-Sun) There's no cover charge at this friendly pub/sports bar with a great open patio out front. It's American-Euro styled but totally Japanese in all the best ways.

Fukutaro CAFE
(福太郎; Map p235; ☑0577-35-6777; www.fukutarou.com; 58 Shimosanno-machi; coffee ¥330, dango ¥70; ☺11am-5pm) Come to this authentic, century-old *machiya* (traditional Japanese townhouse) to enjoy good coffee, *dango* (sweet dumplings) and sesame *gohei-mochi* (sticky rice cakes).

Desolation Row BAR
(デゾレーション ロウ; Map p235; ☑090-8077-5966; 30 Asahi-machi; ☺8pm-late) If you're a Bob Dylan fan, you'll likely connect with Ken, the friendly owner of this mellow bar with a rustic charm. Ken speaks some English, but the language of music is universal. As is the language of whisky…and beer. Look for the galvanised iron front and the big blue door.

🔒 Shopping

Takayama is renowned for arts and crafts. Look for *ichi ittobori* (woodcarvings), *shunkei* lacquerware, and the rustic *yamada-yaki* and decorative *shibukusa-yaki* styles of pottery. Between Sanmachi-dōri and Yasugawa-dōri, near the Takayama Museum of History & Art (p237), are plenty of wonderful *kobutsu* (古物; antique) shops. With patience and smarts you can find some excellent deals – seeking them out is half the fun.

Takayama's most ubiquitous souvenirs are *saru-bobo* (monkey babies). These little red dolls with pointy limbs and featureless faces recall the days when grandmothers fashioned dolls for children out of whatever materials were available.

Washi no Yamazaki ARTS & CRAFTS
(和紙の山崎; Map p235; ☑0577-32-4132; 1-22 Hon-machi; ☺9am-5pm) This wonderful family-run store sells *washi* (handmade Japanese paper).

Suzuki Chōkoku ARTS & CRAFTS
(鈴木彫刻; Map p235; ☑0577-32-1367; 1-2 Hatsuda-machi; ☺9am-7pm Wed-Mon) Helmed by the one-time head of the local *ittobori*

(woodcarving) association, here you'll find figurines from ¥750 to *how much?*

ℹ️ Information

INTERNET ACCESS

Free wi-fi is available for visitors throughout the downtown area. Check in with the Tourist Information Center upon your arrival for the wi-fi password, which gets you access for one week.

City Library (高山市図書館; Map p235; 📞 0577-32-3096; 2-115 Baba-machi; 🕑 9.30am-9.30pm; 📶) Come for free internet access, or just to gawk at this wonderful historic building, east of Sanmachi-suji.

TOURIST INFORMATION

Tourist Information Center (飛騨高山観光案内所; Map p235; 📞 0577-32-5328; www.hida. jp; 🕑 8.30am-5pm Nov-Mar, 8.30am-6.30pm Apr-Oct) Directly in front of JR Takayama Station, knowledgeable English-speaking staff dispense English and other language maps and a wealth of pamphlets on sights, accommodation, special events and regional transport. Staff are unable to assist with accommodation reservations.

ℹ️ Getting There & Away

BUS

Nōhi Bus (濃飛バス; 📞 0577-32-1688; www.nouhibus.co.jp) operates highway bus services between Takayama and Tokyo's Shinjuku Station (¥6690, 5½ hours, several daily; reservations required), Matsumoto (¥3190, 2½ hours) and Kanazawa (¥3390, 2¼ hours). Schedules vary seasonally and some routes don't run at all during winter, when many roads are closed.

TRAIN

From Tokyo or cities to the south (Kyoto, Osaka, Hiroshima, Fukuoka), Takayama can be reached by catching a frequent *shinkansen* (bullet train) service to Nagoya, then connecting with the JR Takayama line (*tokkyū* ¥5510, 2½ hours).

Another option from Tokyo is to pick up the JR Takayama line from its northern terminus in Toyama (*tokkyū* ¥2840, 1½ hours). Get to Toyama on the shiny new-in-2015 Hokuriku Shinkansen: the trains are fabulous.

Either way, the mountainous train ride along the Hida-gawa is gorge-ous.

ℹ️ Getting Around

Most sights in Takayama can be covered easily on foot. You can amble from the train station to Teramachi in about 20 minutes. Takayama is bicycle-friendly but rentals can be expensive. Try **Hara Cycle** (ハラサイクル; Map p235; 📞 0577-32-1657; 61 Suehiro-chō; 1st hour ¥300, additional hour ¥200, per day ¥1300;

TAKAYAMA MORNING MARKETS

Daily *asa-ichi* (morning markets) are a wonderful way to wake up and meet people. The **Jinya-mae Asa-ichi** (陣屋前朝市; Map p235; www.jinya-asaichi.jp; 1-5 Hachiken-machi; 🕑 6am-noon) is in front of **Takayama-jinya** (p237); the larger **Miya-gawa Asa-ichi** (宮川朝市; Map p235; www.asaichi.net; 🕑 7am-noon) runs along the east bank of the Miya-gawa, between Kaji-bashi and Yayoi-bashi. Stalls range from farm-fresh produce to local arts and crafts. Autumnal apples are out of this world!

🕑 9am-8pm Wed-Mon). Some lodgings lend bikes for free.

Hida-Furukawa 飛騨古川

📞 0577 / POP 24,708

Just 15 minutes by train from Takayama, Hida-Furukawa is a relaxing riverside town with a friendly, ageing population, eager to preserve their local history and culture. Photogenic streetscapes, peaceful temples and interesting museums are framed by the Hida mountains. Each April the town comes to life for the Furukawa Matsuri.

👁️ Sights

Hida-Furukawa train and bus stations adjoin each other east of the town centre. Sights are within 10 minutes' walk of the train station.

Seto-kawa & Shirakabe-dōzō   HISTORIC SITE (瀬戸川と白壁土蔵街) You'll find this lovely historic canal district five minutes' walk from JR Hida-Furukawa Station, boasting white-walled shops, storehouses, private homes and carp-filled waterways. Across the canal, Ichino-machi is sprinkled with woodworking shops, sake breweries (marked by spheres of cedar fronds above the entrance) and traditional storehouses.

Honkō-ji   BUDDHIST TEMPLE (本光寺; 📞 0577-73-2938; 1-17 Furukawa-chō) Riverside Honkō-ji is Hida's largest wooden temple, showcasing the fine craftsmanship of Furukawa's carpenters. Originally established in 1532, the current buildings date from 1913 following a fire that destroyed 90% of the town.

Hida Carpentry Museum
MUSEUM

(飛騨の匠文化館, Hida no Takumi Bunkakan; ☑0577-73-3321; 10-1 Ichino-machi; adult/child ¥300/100; ☺9am-4.30pm Fri-Wed Dec-Feb, 9am-5pm daily Mar-Nov) This museum dedicated to the history of Japanese carpentry and its unique methods is a must for woodworkers and design fans. In a hands-on room, you can try assembling blocks of wood cut into different joint patterns – not as easy as it sounds.

👉 Tours

★ Satoyama Experience
CULTURAL

(☑0577-73-5715; www.satoyama-experience.com; 8-8 Nino-machi; half-day tours from ¥4700; ☺9am-6pm Fri-Wed) The fantastic crew at Satoyama Experience is eager to introduce you to its beloved region, culture and people. The small-group cycling tours include a friendly, English-speaking guide, mountain-bike rental and insurance. A variety of tours (including walking) cater to different levels of fitness, but all capture the spirit and scenery of Hida. Highly recommended.

The team can also connect you with some unique, traditional accommodation (for longer stays) in town and around – just ask.

🎎 Festivals & Events

Furukawa Matsuri
PARADE

(古川祭り; ☺Apr) Furukawa Matsuri – informally known as Hadaka Matsuri (Naked Festival) – takes place every 19 and 20 April with parades of *yatai* (festival floats). The highlight is an event known as Okoshi Daiko in which, on the night of the 19th, squads of boisterous young men dressed in *fundoshi* (loin cloths) and fuelled by sake, parade through town.

They compete to place small drums atop a stage bearing a giant drum. OK, it's not *naked* naked, but we didn't make up the name.

Kitsunebi Matsuri
PARADE

(きつね火祭り; ☺Sep) During the 'Fox Fire Festival' on the fourth Saturday in September, locals dress up as foxes, parade through the town by lantern light and enact a wedding at a local shrine, Okura Inari-jinja. The ceremony, deemed to bring good fortune, climaxes with a bonfire.

🛏 Sleeping & Eating

Hida Tomoe Hotel
HOTEL ¥¥

(飛騨ともえホテル; ☑0577-73-2056; www.tomoe-jp.com; 10-27 Kanamori-chō; r per person with/without meals from ¥11,290/6250; ❄@) This attractive business hotel by the train station has Western- and Japanese-style rooms, most with bath and toilet, as well as a pretty common bath. 'Including meals' means farm-fresh local *kaiseki* (Japanese haute cuisine) by the *irori* (fireplace).

Ichino-machi Cafe
CAFE ¥

(壱之町珈琲店; ☑0577-73-7099; 1-12 Ichino-machi; cakes from ¥400; ☺11am-5pm Wed-Mon; 🛜) Chiffon cake, melon bread and local Hida-beef curry are all items you might find on the menu at this handsome cafe within a restored traditional *machiya* (merchant house). Free wi-fi is a bonus.

ℹ Information

There's a Tourist Information Center at the bus station with some English maps and leaflets, though little English is spoken.

ℹ Getting There & Around

Hida-Furukawa is serviced by the *tokkyū* (limited express) Hida trains between Nagoya (¥5830, 2¾ hours) and Toyama (¥2670, 1¾ hours).

Local trains run frequently between Hida-Furukawa and Takayama, three stops south (¥240, 15 minutes).

From the train station, it's easy to stroll around central Furukawa, or you can hire bikes at nearby **Miyagawa Taxi** (☑0577-73-2321; 10-41 Furukawa-cho; bicycle rental per hour ¥200) or take a tour with **Satoyama Experience**.

Okuhida Onsen-gō

☑0577

Meaning 'deep Hida hot springs', Okuhida Onsen-gō – comprising the villages of Hirayu Onsen, Fukuji Onsen, Shin-Hirayu Onsen, Tochio Onsen and Shin-Hotaka Onsen – has a tough battle with Shirakawa-gō for being the jewel in Hida's crown. Certainly it's where you'll find some of the loveliest *onsen ryokan* (traditional hot-spring inns) and alpine scenery in all of Japan.

It's impossible to compare the two contenders and you'd be well advised to visit as much of the Hida Region as you can, but if time is limited, it's definitely well worth forking out the cash and taking the journey deep into the mountains to spend a tranquil evening here; if the weather is clear, take a ride on the Shin-Hotaka Ropeway (p244). Of the five villages, Hirayu, Fukuji and Shin-Hotaka Onsen have the most to offer visitors by way of their wonderful ryokan.

Some of Japan's most beautiful and peaceful *onsen ryokan* are found in the area's five villages: almost all are expensive, but worth every yen.

Hirayu has a higher concentration of accommodation than elsewhere in the Alps, save for Kamikōchi. It's a good place to base yourself if you're a single traveller, on a budget or you can't get a room in the region's more famous ryokan.

There's little by way of dining establishments in these mountain hamlets. Day trippers will benefit from stocking up at a convenience store before setting out. Those spending the night can look forward to savouring a true *kaiseki* dining experience at their ryokan.

ⓘ Getting There & Around

This remote alpine region can only be accessed by road, which can become treacherous or impassable in winter. Bus services from Matsumoto are operated by Alpico (p272) and from Takayama, by **Nōhi Bus** (p230).

If you don't get carsick and aren't scared of heights, consider renting a car from Takayama or Matsumoto for greater freedom to explore. However, self-driving is not recommended in winter.

Hirayu Onsen   平湯温泉

☑ 0578

Hirayu Onsen is a hub for bus transport and the best base for day trips to Kamikōchi, neighbouring Shirahone and Fukuji Onsen, and the Shin-Hotaka Ropeway. There is a pleasant, low-to-the-ground cluster of onsen lodgings, about half of which open for day bathers. Even the bus station has a rooftop *rotemburo* (outdoor bath; ¥600).

◉ Sights

Hirayu Folk Museum   MUSEUM
(平湯民俗館, Hirayu Minzoku-kan; ☑ 0578-89-3578; ¥500; ⊙ 8am-5pm) Admission to Hirayu Onsen's only attraction, a quaint museum of folk memorabilia, includes entrance to a rather lovely and lesser-known little *rotemburo*.

🛏 Sleeping

Hirayu Camping Ground   CAMPGROUND ¥
(平湯キャンプ場; ☑ 0578-89-2610; www.hirayu-camp.com; 768-36 Hirayu; campsites per adult/child ¥700/500, bungalows from ¥5800, parking from ¥1000; ⊙ late Apr-Oct; Ⓟ) To reach the small Hirayu Camping Ground, turn right from the bus station – it's about 700m ahead, on the left.

Hirayu-no-mori   RESORT ¥¥
(ひらゆの森; ☑ 0578-89-3338; www.hirayuno mori.co.jp; 763-1 Hirayu; s/d from ¥4000/8000; Ⓟ🛜) Practically in its own forest uphill from the bus station, this sprawling *onsen ryokan* boasts 16 different *rotemburo* pools, plus indoor and private baths. After 9pm they're exclusively for overnight guests. Rooms are Japanese-style, and meals are hearty and local.

Ryosō Tsuyukusa   MINSHUKU ¥¥
(旅荘つゆくさ; ☑ 0578-89-2620; www.tuyukusa-hirayu.com; 621 Hirayu; s/d incl 2 meals ¥9000/16,000; Ⓟ🛜) Ryosō Tsuyukusa is an eight-room mum-and-dad *minshuku* (Japanese guesthouse) with decent tatami rooms and a cosy mountain-view *rotemburo* of *hinoki* (cypress). Go downhill from the bus station and turn left at the first narrow street; it's on the left. Little English is spoken.

Okada Ryokan   RYOKAN ¥¥¥
(岡田旅館; ☑ 0578-89-2336; www.okadaryokan. com; 505 Hirayu; r per person incl 2 meals from ¥15,500; Ⓟ❄🛜) Although little English is spoken, the kind staff at this hulking ryokan downhill from the bus station provide a warm welcome. Large but dated rooms have private facilities and the common baths and *rotemburo* are excellent. Unlike many ryokan in the area, single travellers can sometimes get rates here without meals – but beware the slim pickings for nearby restaurants.

Miyama Ouan   RYOKAN ¥¥¥
(深山桜庵; ☑ 0578-89-2799; www.hotespa.net/ hotels/miyamaouan; 229 Hirayu; r per person incl 2 meals from ¥20,400; Ⓟ❄🛜) This recently built chain ryokan has traditional service, modern technology and intimate personal touches. Seventy-two rooms in a variety of sizes and styles are beautifully finished with cypress woods and chic design – all have private facilities. The private *kazoku-buro* (family use) *rotemburo* is a little piece of heaven. Staff will even collect you from the bus station.

ⓘ Information

Tourist Information Center (観光案内所; ☑ 0578-89-3030; 763-191 Hirayu; ⊙ 9.30am-5.30pm) Opposite the bus station; has leaflets and maps, and can book accommodation. Surprisingly, little English is spoken.

ⓘ Getting There & Away

Nōhi Bus operates regular express buses that stop at Hirayu Onsen, which is almost midway between Takayama (¥1570, one hour) and Matsumoto (¥2370, 1½ hours).

Buses between Takayama and Shin-Hotaka Onsen also stop at Hirayu Onsen.

Fukuji Onsen

☑ 0578

Tiny Fukuji Onsen, a short ride north of Hirayu Onsen, follows a steep hill with beautiful views and a handful of outstanding baths. Otherwise, there's not even a village here.

🏃 Activities

Mukashibanashi-no-sato (Isurugi-no-yu) ONSEN

(昔ばなしの里・石動の湯; ☑ 0578-89-2793; 110 Fukuji Onsen; bath ¥500; ⊙ 10am-4pm Thu-Tue) This restaurant-cum-onsen is set back from the street in a traditional farmhouse with fine indoor and outdoor baths, free on the 26th of each month. Out front is an unmissable vintage knick-knack shop adorned with Shōwa-era movie posters and advertisements. If travelling by bus, get off at Fukuji-Onsen-Kami bus stop.

🛏 Sleeping

★ **Yumoto Chōza** RYOKAN ¥¥¥

(湯元長座; ☑ 0578-89-0099; www.cyouza.com; 786 Fukuji; r per person incl 2 meals from ¥21,000; P ❄) Opposite Fukuji-Onsen-shimo bus stop, the entrance to Yumoto Chōza is reached by a rustic, covered walkway, as if to take you back in time. Think bold, dark woods and handsome traditional architecture. Half of the 32 rooms have en suites and *irori* (fireplaces), and there are five indoor baths and two stunning *rotemburo*. Advance reservations essential.

Day visitors can bathe between 2pm and 6pm for ¥750.

Yamazato-no-iori Soene RYOKAN ¥¥¥

(山里のいおり 草円; ☑ 0578-89-1116; www.soene.com; 831 Fukuji Onsen; r per person incl 2 meals from ¥17,800; P 🛜) This rustic ryokan is over 100 years old and atmosphere abounds. Its indoor and outdoor baths are absolutely delightful, as are the views. Rooms are spacious and have an air of romance about them. Delicious *kaiseki* is served in the dining room. A little English is spoken and

there's wi-fi in the lobby. Open year-round, this is one for all seasons.

ⓘ Getting There & Away

By bus from Hirayu Onsen, you can get off at the Fukuji-Onsen-Kami stop and walk downhill to check out the ryokan, then pick up the bus to return to Hirayu or travel onward to Shirahone Onsen.

Shin-Hotaka Onsen　新穂高温泉

☑ 0578

The delightful sleepy hollow of Shin-Hotaka Onsen is famed for the Shin-Hotaka Ropeway, Japan's longest, one of the largest *rotemburo* in the country, and its handful of magical lodgings, including an utterly lovable riverside *onsen ryokan* (traditional hot-spring inn).

🏃 Activities

★ **Shin-Hotaka Ropeway** CABLE CAR

(新穂高ロープウェイ; ☑ 0578-89-2252; www.shinhotaka-ropeway.jp; Shin-Hotaka; one way/return ¥1600/2900; ⊙ 8.30am-4.30pm) From a starting elevation of 1308m, two cable cars whisk you to 2156m towards the peak of Nishi Hotaka-dake (2909m). Views from the top are spectacular, both from observation decks and walking trails. In winter, snows can be shoulder deep. In season, properly equipped hikers with ample time can choose from a number of hikes beginning from the top cable-car station (Nishi Hotaka-guchi), including hiking over to Kamikōchi (three hours), which is much easier than going the other way.

Shin-Hotaka-no-yu ONSEN

(新穂高の湯; ☑ 0578-89-2458; Okuhida Onsengo Kansaka; ⊙ 8am-9pm May-Oct) FREE Exhibitionists will love this bare-bones *konyoku* (mixed bathing) *rotemburo* by the Kamata-gawa, visible from the bridge that passes over it. Entry is free (or by donation). Enter through segregated change rooms, and emerge into a single large pool. Be sure to mind your manners. When in Rome...

Nakazaki Sansou Okuhida-no-yu ONSEN

(中崎山荘奥飛騨の湯; ☑ 0578-89-2021; 710 Okuhida Onsengo Kansaka; adult/child ¥800/400; ⊙ 8am-8pm) Over 50 years old but completely rebuilt in 2010, this facility commands a spectacular vista of the mountains. The milky waters of its large indoor baths and *rotemburo* do wonders for dry skin.

🛏 Sleeping

Kazeya
RYOKAN ¥¥

(風屋; ☎ 0578-89-0112; www.kazeyatakayamajapan.com; 440-1 Kansaka; r per person incl breakfast from ¥8000; [P][❄][🛜]) Fresh from a 2014 renovation, this gorgeous little 10-room traditional inn has atmospheric rooms with private baths and two soak-worthy *rotemburo*. Deluxe rooms have their own onsen baths and offer some of the best value in this beautiful spot.

Karukaya Sansō
HOTEL ¥¥

(佳留萱山荘; ☎ 0578-89-2801; www.karukaya.co.jp; 555 Kansaka; r per person incl 2 meals from ¥14,000; [P][❄][🛜]) The tatami rooms at this friendly, riverside inn with lots of open space to explore are clean, tidy and unremarkable, but for the better ones with lovely views. What is remarkable are the enormous *konyoku rotemburo* (claimed to be the largest in Japan) with their sweeping mountain views.

Campsites are available (adult/child ¥3000/1500) or you can just come to use the *rotemburo* (¥600; 10am to 3pm).

Nonohana Sansō
INN ¥¥

(野の花山荘; ☎ 0578-89-0030; www.nono87.jp; r per person incl 2 meals from ¥14,000, day guests adult/child ¥800/500; ⊙day guests 10am-5pm; [P][❄][🛜]) Along a road that ascends from Rte 475, Nonohana Sansō opened its doors in 2010. All tatami guestrooms are traditionally styled and have private facilities, although the lobby and lounge are refreshingly contemporary. There's an open kitchen preparing local specialities and the large *rotemburo* have a fantastic outlook – they're open to day visitors.

★ Yarimikan
RYOKAN ¥¥¥

(槍見舘; ☎ 0578-89-2808; www.yarimikan.com; Okuhida Onsen-gun Kansaka; r per person incl meals from ¥18,510; [P][❄][🛜]) Yarimikan is a wonderfully traditional *onsen ryokan* on the Kamata-gawa, with two indoor baths, eight riverside *rotemburo* (some available for private use) and 15 rooms. Guests can bathe 24 hours a day (it's stunning by moonlight) and day visitors are accepted between 10am and 2pm for ¥500. Cuisine features local Hida beef and grilled freshwater fish.

It's just off Rte 475, a few kilometres before the Shin-Hotaka Ropeway.

ℹ Information

Oku-Hida Spa Tourist Information Center
(奥飛騨温泉郷観光案内所; ☎ 0578-89-2614; ⊙10am-5pm) On Hwy 471 before the bridge, as the road turns into Hwy 475 towards the ropeway.

ℹ Getting There & Away

Buses run from Takayama to Hirayu Onsen, then do a whistle-stop run to the **Shin-Hotaka Ropeway** (p244) terminus (¥2160, 1½ hours) at the far end of Shin-Hotaka Onsen.

From Matsumoto, an express bus to the Shin-Hotaka Ropeway terminus (¥2880, two hours) transits Hirayu Onsen.

Shirakawa-gō & Gokayama 白川郷・五箇山

The remote and mountainous districts of Shirakawa-gō and Gokayama, between Takayama and Kanazawa, are best known for farmhouses in the thatched *gasshō-zukuri* style. They're rustic and lovely whether set against the vibrant colours of spring, draped with the gentle mists of autumn, or peeking through a carpet of snow, and they hold a special place in the Japanese heart.

Most of Shirakawa-gō's sights are in Ogimachi, linked by expressway to Takayama and the most heavily visited village in the area. The less-crowded, more isolated villages of Suganuma and Ainokura, in the Gokayama district of Toyama Prefecture, have the most ambience; other sights are spread over many kilometres along Rte 156. All three villages are Unesco World Heritage Sites.

Passionate debate continues around the impact tour buses have upon these unique communities, and how best to mitigate disruption to daily life. To avoid the crowds, steer clear of weekends, holidays, and cherry-blossom and autumn-foliage seasons.

Be sure to bring enough cash – ATMs are sparse and credit cards rarely accepted.

To best appreciate life here, stay overnight in a *gasshō-zukuri* inn. Accommodation is basic and advance reservations are recommended. You can also come on a day trip from Takayama, Takaoka, Toyama or Kanazawa.

There's little in the way of dining options save for a few touristy cafes in the 'day-tripper' villages. Meals are generally provided by your accommodation if you're staying overnight.

ℹ Getting There & Around

The only way to get to these remote settlements is by bus or car.

A wide range of tours conducted by a variety of operators can be found departing Takayama, Takaoka, Toyama and Kanazawa.

THE JAPAN ALPS & CENTRAL HONSHŪ SHIRAKAWA-GŌ & GOKAYAMA

BUS

Nōhi Bus (濃飛バス; ☑ 0577-32-1688; www. nouhibus.co.jp) and its affiliates operate seven or more buses daily between Ogimachi (Shirakawa-gō) and Takayama (one way/return ¥2470/4420, 50 minutes), Kanazawa (¥1850/3290, 1½ hours) and Toyama (¥1700/3060, 1¾ hours). Some buses require a reservation. Weather delays and cancellations are possible between December and March.

Some buses on the Kanazawa–Takayama route stop in Suganuma. Nōhi Bus also offers day-return bus tours of Shirakawa-gō and Ainokura (adult/child ¥6690/4420) from Takayama.

Coming from the north, **Kaetsunou Bus** (加越能バス; ☑ 0766-22-4886; www.kaetsunou. co.jp) operates at least four buses a day between Shin-Takaoka Station on the JR Hokuriku Shinkansen line and Ainokura (¥1000, one hour), before continuing on to Ogimachi (¥1800, two hours) via all major sites. The fare between Ainokura and Ogimachi is ¥1300.

CAR & MOTORCYCLE

Self-driving is becoming an increasingly popular way to explore.

It's an easy drive on the Tokai-Hokuriku expressway from Takayama to Shirakawa-gō (Ogimachi).

From June through mid-November, the Hakusan White Rd (formerly the Hakusan Super-Rindō) is a 34km stretch of scenic toll road (one way ¥1600) between Hakusan and Ogimachi.

Ainokura (Gokayama) is directly accessible via the Tokai-Hokuriku expressway from Takayama.

For slower, more scenic explorations, get off the expressway at the Shirakawa-gō (Ogimachi) exit, then follow winding Rte 156 to the villages of Gokayama at your own pace.

In colder months, check conditions in advance with regional tourist offices before setting out on any National roads.

Ogimachi 荻町

☑ 05769 / POP 600

Ogimachi, the Shirakawa-gō region's central and most accessible settlement, has some 600 residents and the largest concentration of *gasshō-zukuri* buildings – over 110. Generally, the names Ogimachi and Shirakawa-gō are interchangeable for tourism purposes.

◉ Sights & Activities

Pick up free multilingual maps at the **Tourist Information Center** (白川郷観光案内所; ☑ 05769-6-1013; 2495-3 Ogimachi; ⊙ 9am-5pm) by the main bus stop outside the Folk Village.

Shiroyama Tenbōdai VIEWPOINT
(Observation Point) This lookout on the site of a former castle provides a lovely view of the valley. It's a 15-minute walk via the road behind the east side of town. You can climb the path (five minutes) from near the intersection of Rtes 156 and 360, or there's a shuttle bus (¥200 one way) from the Shirakawa-gō bus stop.

Gasshō-zukuri Folk Village MUSEUM
(合掌造り民家園, Gasshō-zukuri Minka-en; ☑ 05769-6-1231; www.shirakawago-minkaen.jp; 2499 Ogimachi; adult/child ¥600/400; ⊙ 8.40am-5pm Apr-Nov, 9am-6pm Fri-Wed Dec-Mar) Over two dozen *gasshō-zukuri* buildings have been relocated here, although the arrangement feels contrived. Several houses are used for demonstrating regional crafts such as woodwork, straw handicrafts and ceramics (in Japanese only, reservations required). Many items are for sale. You're free to wander the grounds for a picnic, but be sure to carry your rubbish out of town.

Wada-ke HISTORIC BUILDING
(和田家; ☑ 05769-6-1058; adult/child ¥300/150; ⊙ 9am-5pm) Shirakawa-gō's largest *gasshō* house is a designated National Treasure. It once belonged to a wealthy silk-trading family and dates back to the mid-Edo period. Upstairs you'll find silk harvesting equipment and a valuable lacquerware collection.

Myōzen-ji Folk Museum MUSEUM
(明善寺郷土館, Myōzen-ji Kyōdo-kan; ☑ 05769-6-1009; adult/child ¥300/150; ⊙ 8.30am-5pm Apr-Nov, 9am-4pm Dec-Mar) Adjacent to Myōzen-ji, Ogimachi's small temple, Myōzen-ji Folk Museum displays the traditional paraphernalia of daily rural life.

Ōshirakawa Rotemburo ONSEN
(大白川露天風呂; ☑ 05769-6-1311; ¥300; ⊙ 8.30am-5pm mid-Jun–Oct, to 6pm Jul & Aug) This tiny, middle-of-nowhere onsen is 40km from Ogimachi, along a mountainous winding road with blind curves, impassible much of the year. There's no public transport, which is part of the charm, as are the views of Lake Shiramizu. Getting here from Ogimachi takes at least 90 minutes and requires determination and a car, or a taxi and lots of cash.

✨ Festivals & Events

Shirakawa-gō's big festival is held on 14 and 15 October at **Shirakawa Hachiman-jinja** (other festivals continue until the 19th), and features groups of dancing locals taking part in the lion dance and *niwaka* (improvised buffoonery). The star is *doburoku,* a very potent unrefined sake.

🛏 Sleeping

For online reservations at one of Ogimachi's many *gasshō* inns, try www.japaneseguesthouses.com. Rates include two meals. Expect a nightly heating surcharge (¥400 and up) during cold weather. Otherwise, stay in Takayama or Kanazawa and visit as a day trip.

★ Magoemon INN ¥¥

(孫右ェ門; ☑ 05769-6-1167; 360 Ogimachi; r per person incl 2 meals from ¥10,260; 🅿 ❄ 🛜) This building is 300 years old and oozes history and charm – great for an authentic and atmospheric retreat. The friendly family owners speak no English and appreciate your efforts to communicate in Japanese. Meals are served around the handsome *irori* (hearth). Three of the six large rooms (shared facilities) face the river.

Shirakawa-gō-no-yu HUT ¥¥

(白川郷の湯; ☑ 05769-6-0026; www.shirakawagou-onsen.jp; 337 Ogimachi; r per person incl 2 meals from ¥10,800; ❄ 🛜) Day bathers (adult/child ¥700/300) in the town's only onsen can choose from a sauna, small *rotemburo* and large communal bath from 10am to 9.30pm. Overnight guests get to enjoy the facilities without the crowds. Pleasant, modern tatami rooms have shared facilities; the more expensive rooms (from ¥16,200) have private bathrooms. Western-style twin rooms are also available but lack appeal.

Toyota Shirakawa-gō Eco-Institute HOTEL ¥¥

(トヨタ白川郷自然学校; ☑ 05769-6-1187; www.toyota.eco-inst.jp; 223 Magari; d per person from ¥13,500; 🅿 ❄ 🛜) 🌱 Ten minutes' drive in the hills above Ogimachi brings you to this ecolodge, which caters heavily to groups, but also welcomes individual travellers. Countless activities are available and sumptuous French cuisine is served.

Kōemon INN ¥¥

(幸ェ門; ☑ 05769-6-1446; 546 Ogimachi; r per person incl 2 meals from ¥8860; 🅿 ❄ 🛜) In the centre of Ogimachi, Kōemon has five rooms with heated floors, dark-wood panelling and shared bathrooms. The fifth-generation owner speaks English well and his love of Shirakawa-gō is infectious.

DON'T MISS

BEST SCENIC VISTAS

➡ Kamikōchi (p275)

➡ Shin-Hotaka Ropeway (p244)

➡ Tateyama-Kurobe Alpine Route (p270)

➡ Utsukushi-ga-hara Open Air Museum (p268)

➡ Shiga Kōgen (p288)

Shimizu Inn INN ¥¥

(民宿志みづ, Minshuku Shimizu; ☑ 05769-6-1914; www.shimizuinn.com; 2613 Ogimachi; r per person incl 2 meals ¥8800; 🅿 ❄ 🛜) This home-style inn at the southern end of town enjoys a picturesque outlook. There are three small guestrooms and a common bath in a building that is over 200 years old.

🍴 Eating

Ochūdo CAFE ¥

(落人; ☑ 090-5458-0418; 792 Ogimachi; lunch ¥1000; ⊙ 10.30am-5pm; 🍴) Set around a large *irori* (hearth) in a 350-year-old *gasshō* house, this delightful cafe serves curry rice, tea and coffee.

Irori SHOKUDO ¥

(いろり; ☑ 05769-6-1737; 374-1 Ogimachi; dishes from ¥432, set menu from ¥1296; ⊙ 11am-3pm; 🚭 🍴) At the entrance to Ogimachi, this bustling eatery serves regional specialities such as *hoba-miso* (sweet miso paste grilled at the table on a magnolia leaf), *yaki-dofu* (fried tofu) and soba or udon *teishoku* (set meals). You can eat at tables or around the *irori*.

Gokayama District 五箇山

☑ 0763

North along the Shōkawa-gawa, in Toyama Prefecture, the Gokayama district is isolated and sparsely populated. Although there are a number of *gasshō-zukuri* buildings (a type of Japanese thatched-roof architecture) scattered along Rte 156, the villages of Suganuma and Ainokura have the best examples. To get here, drive north on Rte 156 from Shirakawa-gō. You'll reach Suganuma first, then Ainokura.

The **Gokayama Tourist Information Center** (五箇山観光総合案内所; ☑ 0763-66-2468; www.gokayama-info.jp; 754 Kaminashi; ⊙ 9am-5pm) is in the village of Kaminashi.

◉ Sights & Activities

Down a steep hill off Rte 156, 15km north of Ogimachi, **Suganuma** (菅沼) is a pretty riverside collection of nine *gasshō-zukuri* houses and a World Heritage Site. It feels more like a residential museum than a working village, and there's no accommodation here.

Enchanting **Ainokura** (相倉) is also a World Heritage Site. It is the most impressive of Gokayama's villages. The valley boasts over 20 *gasshō* buildings amid splendid mountain views. The village's remote location attracts fewer tour buses than Ogimachi, so it's much quieter. If you want to step back in time and hear the sound of your thoughts, spend a night here – it's quite magical after the buses leave.

From the Ainokura-guchi bus stop it's about a 400m uphill walk to Ainokura before the descent into the village.

Gokayama Minzoku-kan   MUSEUM
(五箇山民俗館; ☑ 0763-67-3652; 436 Suganuma; adult/child ¥300/150; ⊗ 9am-4.30pm) You can see items from traditional life and displays illustrating traditional gunpowder production, for which the area was once famed, at this folklore museum in Suganuma. If self-driving, parking is ¥500.

Kuroba Onsen   ONSEN
(くろば温泉; ☑ 0763-67-3741; 1098 Kamitaira-hosojima, Nanto; adult/child ¥600/300; ⊗ 10am-9pm Wed-Mon) About 1km north of Suganuma along Rte 156, Kuroba Onsen is a complex of indoor-outdoor baths with a lovely view. Its low-alkaline waters are good for fatigue and sore muscles.

Murakami-ke   HISTORIC BUILDING
(村上家; ☑ 0763-66-2711; www.murakamike.jp; 742 Kaminashi; adult/child ¥300/150; ⊗ 8.30am-5pm Apr-Nov, 9am-4pm Dec-Mar) Between Suganuma and Ainokura, in the hamlet of Kaminashi, you'll find Murakami-ke, one of the oldest *gasshō* houses in the region (dating from 1578). It's now a small museum; the proud owner delights in showing visitors around and might sing you some local folk songs. Close by, the main hall of **Hakusan-gū shrine** dates from 1502. It's an Important Cultural Property.

On 25 and 26 September, the **Kokiriko Matsuri** features costumed dancers performing with rattles that move like snakes. On day two, everyone joins in.

Ainokura Minzoku-kan   MUSEUM
(相倉民俗館; ☑ 0763-66-2732; 352 Ainokura; ¥210; ⊗ 8.30am-5pm) Stroll through the village to this interesting folklore museum, with displays of local crafts and paper. It's divided into two buildings, the former Ozaki and Nakaya residences (prominent local families).

Gokayama Washi-no-sato   GALLERY
(五箇山和紙の里; ☑ 0763-66-2223; www.gokayama-washinosato.com; 215 Higashinakae; ⊗ 8.30am-5pm) North of Ainokura on Rte 156 you'll find this roadside attraction, which explains the art of making *washi* (handmade paper) and gives you the chance to try making some yourself (from ¥500; reservations required, limited English is spoken). There's also a gift shop.

⌨ Sleeping

Remote Ainokura is a great place for a *gasshō-zukuri* stay. Some Japanese-language ability will help you with reservations and getting by. Rates may be higher in winter due to a heating charge.

Ainokura Campground   CAMPGROUND ¥
(相倉キャンプ場; ☑ 0763-66-2123; 611 Ainokura; per person ¥500; ⊗ mid-Apr–late Oct; Ⓟ) This lovely basic campground is about 1km from the village of Ainokura.

Minshuku Yomoshirō   MINSHUKU ¥¥
(民宿与茂四郎; ☑ 0763-66-2377; www.yomosiro.com; 395 Ainokura; per person incl 2 meals ¥8800) Try this welcoming four-room inn, whose owner will demonstrate the *sasara,* a kind of traditional percussion instrument, upon request.

Minshuku Chōyomon   MINSHUKU ¥¥
(民宿長ヨ門; ☑ 0763-66-2755; 418 Ainokura; per person incl 2 meals ¥8800; 🛜) You can't get much more rustic than this 350-year-old place in the centre of Ainokura village.

Minshuku Goyomon   MINSHUKU ¥¥
(民宿五ヨ門; ☑ 0763-66-2154; www.goyomon.burari.biz; 438 Ainokura; per person incl 2 meals ¥8800; 🛜) This is a small, family oriented homestay.

KANAZAWA & THE HOKURIKU COAST

The Hokuriku (北陸) region stretches along the Sea of Japan coast, encompassing Fukui, Ishikawa and Toyama Prefectures.

Long considered remote and off the beaten track, even among Japanese, the region got a big boost in 2015 with the opening of the Hokuriku Shinkansen line. With greatly improved access, tourism is booming.

The city of Kanazawa, in Ishikawa-ken (石川県), is the biggest draw. Once the power base of the feudal Maeda clan, Kanazawa was, at one time, at the forefront of wealth and culture in Japan – a legacy that can still be seen today, among the city's traditional architecture, artisan workshops and famous garden. To the north, the Noto Peninsula has sweeping seascapes and quiet fishing villages. For more information, see www.hot-ishikawa.jp.

To the west is little Fukui-ken (福井県), home to one of the world's most influential Zen centres, some pretty 'forgotten' towns and fascinating architectural ruins.

Toyama-ken (富山県), at the eastern end, is a manufacturing centre. Its bayfront capital city, Toyama, is the jumping-off point for explorations through the Tateyama mountain range.

❶ Getting There & Around

Useful regional airports include **Komatsu Airport** (p213), west of Kanazawa, and **Toyama Airport** (p213).

Frequent trains on the Hokuriku Shinkansen line travel between Tokyo and Kanazawa, via Toyama. The Hokuriku main line runs west from Kanazawa to Fukui and on to Kyoto and Osaka. A car is handy for exploring sights outside the larger cities.

Kanazawa 金沢

🎵 076 / POP 465,810

The array of cultural attractions in Kanazawa make the city the drawcard of the Hokuriku region and a rival to Kyoto as the historical jewel of mainland Japan. Best known for Kenroku-en, a castle garden dating from the 17th century, it also boasts beautifully preserved samurai and geisha districts, attractive temples, a wealth of museums and a wonderful market. A two- or three-day stay to take it all in is recommended.

History

During the 15th century Kanazawa was under the control of an autonomous Buddhist government, ousted in 1583 by Maeda Toshiie, head of the powerful Maeda clan. Kanazawa means 'golden marsh' – in its heyday the region was Japan's richest, producing about five million bushels of rice annually. This wealth allowed the Maeda to patronise culture and the arts. Kanazawa remains a national cultural hot spot.

An absence of military targets spared the city from destruction during WWII. Its myriad historical and cultural sites are wonderfully preserved and integrate neatly with the city's share of contemporary architecture.

⦿ Sights

Kanazawa is a sprawling city with two almost parallel rivers traversing its core. Most areas of interest are located a good distance from the impressive JR Kanazawa Station area, into which most visitors arrive. With the new-in-2015 Hokuriku Shinkansen speeding into town, this area is abuzz with activity. The terminus of the city's substantial bus network, which can at first seem a little confusing, is also here. Have patience: you'll orient yourself soon enough.

Heading south of the station along Hyakumangoku-dōri, you'll reach **Kōrinbō** (the shopping and business district) before arriving in **Katamachi**, by the banks of the Sai-gawa; this is the place to eat, drink and be merry. If you're staying near the station, note that buses stop early in the evening and taxis back from the action cost at least ¥1300. Tucked in-between Kōrinbō and the Sai-gawa, you'll find the former samurai district of **Nagamachi**.

Teramachi and **Nishi-chaya-gai** are over the bridge from Katamachi, but the mainstay of sights, including Kanazawa Castle Park and Kenroku-en, are to the east. To their north, on opposite sides of the Asano-gawa, lie the pretty **Kazuemachi-chaya-gai** and **Higashi-chaya-gai** teahouse districts in the shadow of hilly **Utatsuyama's** many temples. Heading west will loop you back to the station, passing Ōmi-chō Market, a must-see.

⦿ Kanazawa Station & Around

Ōmi-chō Market MARKET
(近江町市場; Map p250; 35 Ōmi-chō; ⊙9am-5pm) Between Kanazawa Station and Katamachi, you'll find this market, reminiscent of Tokyo's Tsukiji. A bustling warren of fishmongers, buyers and restaurants, it's a great place to watch everyday people in action or indulge in the freshest sashimi and local produce. The nearest bus stop is Musashi-ga-tsuji.

Kanazawa

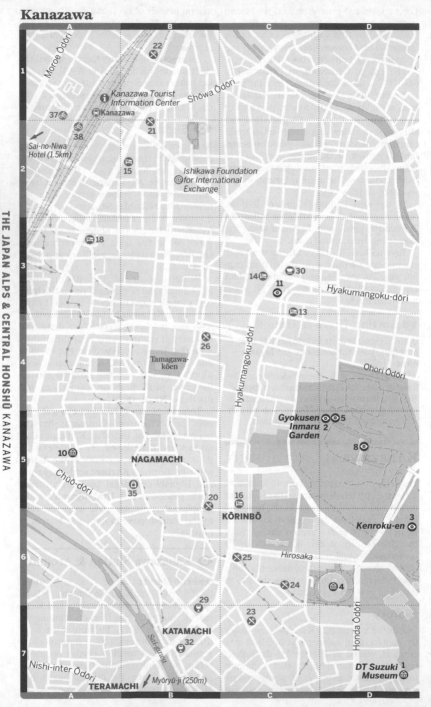

Moroe Ōdōri

22

Kanazawa Tourist
Information Center

Kanazawa

Shōwa Ōdōri

37

38

21

Sai-no-Niwa
Hotel (1.5km)

15

Ishikawa Foundation
for International
Exchange

18

14 30

11

Hyakumangoku-dōri

13

26

Tamagawa-
kōen

Hyakumangoku-dōri

Ohori Ōdōri

Gyokusen
Inmaru
Garden 5
2

8

10

NAGAMACHI

Chūō-dōri

35

20

16

KŌRINBŌ

Kenroku-en 3

25

Hirosaka

24

4

29

23

KATAMACHI

32

Honda Ōdōri

Nishi-inter Ōdōri

Myōryū-ji (250m)

TERAMACHI

DT Suzuki 1
Museum

Kanazawa

◎ Top Sights

◎ Sights

🛏 Sleeping

✕ Eating

🍷 Drinking & Nightlife

🎭 Entertainment

🛍 Shopping

ℹ Transport

THE JAPAN ALPS & CENTRAL HONSHŪ KANAZAWA

⊙ Nagamachi

Once inhabited by samurai, this attractive, well-preserved district (Nagamachi Buke-yashiki) framed by two canals features winding streets lined with tile-roofed mud walls.

Nagamachi Yūzen-kan   MUSEUM

(長町友禅館; Map p250; ☑076-264-2811; www.kagayuzen-club.co.jp; 2-6-16 Nagamachi; ¥350; ⊙9am-noon & 1-4.30pm Fri-Wed) Located in a non-traditional building at the edge of the Nagamachi district, the Nagamachi Yūzen-kan displays some splendid examples of *Kaga Yūzen* kimono dyeing and demonstrates the process. Enquire ahead about trying the silk-dyeing process yourself (¥4000).

⊙ Kenroku-en & Around

★Kenroku-en   GARDENS

(兼六園; Map p250; ☑076-234-3800; www.pref.ishikawa.jp/siro-niwa/kenrokuen/e/; 1-1 Marunouchi; adult/child ¥310/100; ⊙7am-6pm Mar–mid-Oct, 8am-4.30pm mid-Oct–Feb) Ranked as one of the top three gardens in Japan, this Edo-period garden draws its name (*kenroku* 'combined six') from a renowned Sung-dynasty garden in China that dictated six attributes for perfection: seclusion, spaciousness, artificiality, antiquity, abundant water and broad views. Kenroku-en has them all. Arrive before the crowds to increase your chances of silent contemplation.

It is believed that the garden, originally belonging to an outer villa of Kanazawa-jō, was developed from the 1620s to the 1840s and was so named in 1822. It was first opened to the public in 1871.

Kanazawa Castle Park   LANDMARK

(金沢城公園, Kanazawa-jō Kōen; Map p250; ☑076-234-3800; www.pref.ishikawa.jp/siro-niwa/kanazawajou/e/; 1-1 Marunouchi; buildings/grounds ¥310/free; ⊙grounds 5am-6pm Mar–mid-Oct, 6am-4.30pm mid-Oct–Feb, castle 9am-4.30pm) Originally built in 1580 this massive structure was called the 'castle of 1000 tatami' and housed the Maeda clan for 14 generations until it was ultimately destroyed by fire in 1881. The elegant surviving gate **Ishikawa-mon** (built in 1788) provides a dramatic entry from Kenroku-en; holes in its turret were designed for hurling rocks at invaders. Two additional buildings, the **Hishi-yagura** (diamond-shaped turret) and **Gojikken-nagaya** (armoury), were reconstructed by traditional means in 2001.

★Gyokusen Inmaru Garden   GARDENS

(玉泉院丸庭園, Gyokusen Inmaru Teien; Map p250; ☑076-234-3800; 1-1 Marunouchi; ⊙7am-6pm) FREE Adjacent to the Kanazawa Castle Park, this feudal pleasure garden was first constructed in 1634 but abandoned in the Meiji era. Its five-year reconstruction was completed in 2015. Features include a small waterfall, bridges and many traditional elements. While the garden's focal point is the Gyokusen-an Rest House, it's the overall picture of beauty and refinement that impresses most. The garden and teahouse are illuminated spectacularly on Friday and Saturday evenings between sunset and 9pm – have your camera at the ready.

➡ Gyokusen-an Rest House

(玉泉庵; Map p250; ☑076-234-3800; 1-1 Marunouchi; tea ceremony ¥720; ⊙9am-4.30pm) In the grounds of Gyokusen Inmaru Garden, this handsome teahouse is the perfect setting to experience *cha-dō* (a tea ceremony), one of Japan's oldest, most intricate and unique customs.

21st Century Museum of Contemporary Art   MUSEUM

(金沢21世紀美術館; Map p250; ☑076-220-2800; www.kanazawa21.jp; 1-2-1 Hirosaka; ⊙10am-6pm Tue-Thu & Sun, 10am-8pm Fri & Sat) FREE A low-slung glass cylinder, 113m in diameter, forms the perimeter of this contemporary gallery, which celebrated its 10th birthday in 2014. Entry to the museum is free, but admission fees are charged for exhibitions by contemporary artists from Japan and abroad. Inside, galleries are arranged like boxes on a tray. Check the English-language website for event info and exhibition fees.

★DT Suzuki Museum   MUSEUM

(鈴木大拙館; Map p250; ☑076-221-8011; www.kanazawa-museum.jp/daisetz; 3-4-20 Hondamachi; adult/child/senior ¥300/free/200; ⊙9.30am-4.30pm Tue-Sun) This spiritual museum is a tribute to Daisetsu Teitaro Suzuki, one of the foremost Buddhist philosophers of our time. Published in Japanese and English, Suzuki is largely credited with introducing Zen to the West. This stunning concrete complex embodies the heart of Zen. Come to learn about the man, and practise mindfulness by the water mirror garden.

Ishikawa Prefectural Museum of Traditional Products & Crafts   MUSEUM

(石川県立伝統産業工芸館; Map p250; ☑076-262-2020; www.ishikawa-densankan.jp; 2-1 Ken-

HAKUSAN NATIONAL PARK

Geared for serious hikers and naturalists, stunning Hakusen National Park (白山国立公園) straddles four prefectures: Ishikawa, Fukui, Toyama and Gifu. Within are several peaks above 2500m, the tallest being Hakusan (2702m), a sacred mountain that has been worshipped since ancient times. In summer, folks hike and scramble uphill for mountain sunrises. In winter, skiing and onsen bathing take over. The alpine section of the park is criss-crossed with trails, offering treks of up to 25km. For well-equipped hikers, there's a 26km trek to Ogimachi in the Shōkawa Valley.

For an overview of the hiking opportunities, check out www.kagahakusan.jp.

There is limited accommodation on the peaks, primarily offered in giant dorms at **Hakusan Murodō** (白山室堂; ☑ 076-273-1001; www.kagahakusan.jp/en/murodo; dm per person ¥5100; ⊘ May-Nov) and **Nanryū Sansō** (南竜山荘; ☑ 076-259-2022; www.city-hakusan.com/hakusan/naryusanso; dm incl 2 meals ¥7900, campsites ¥300, 5-person cabins ¥12,400; ⊘ 1 Jul–15 Oct). The latter has a campground and popular basic cabins – camping anywhere else is prohibited.

The villages of Ichirino, Chūgū Onsen, Shiramine and Ichinose have *minshuku* (guesthouses), ryokan and camping. Rates start at around ¥300 per person for campsites, or around ¥7900 for lodge dorms or rooms in inns, each including two meals.

Dining options are limited to a handful of choices in each of the villages near the park's borders. Simple meals are available in the lodges atop the peaks.

The closest access point is Bettōdeai. From here it's 6km to Hakusan Murodō (about 4½ hours' walk) and 5km to Nanryū Sansō (3½ hours).

Visiting Hakusen National Park requires commitment. The main mode of transport is the **Hokutetsu Kankō** (☑ 076-237-5115; www.hokutetsu.co.jp/en) bus from Kanazawa Station to Bettōdeai (¥2200, two hours). From late June to mid-October, up to three buses operate daily. If you're driving from the Shōkawa Valley, you might treat yourself and take the spectacular Hakusan White Rd toll route (one way/round-trip ¥1600/2600).

roku-machi; adult/child ¥260/100; ⊘ 9am-5pm, closed 3rd Thu of month Apr-Nov, closed Thu Dec-Mar) This small museum offers fine displays of over 20 regional crafts. Pick up the free English-language audio guide.

◉ Higashi-chaya-gai

Just north of Asano-gawa, Higashi-chaya-gai (Higashi Geisha District) is an enclave of narrow streets established early in the 19th century for geisha to entertain wealthy patrons. The slatted wooden facades of the geisha houses are romantically preserved.

Shima   MUSEUM
(志摩; Map p250; ☑ 076-252-5675; www.ochaya-shima.com; 1-13-21 Higashiyama; adult/child ¥500/300; ⊘ 9am-6pm) An Important Cultural Asset, this well-known, traditional-style former geisha house dates from 1820 and has an impressive collection of elaborate combs and *shamisen* (a three-stringed instrument resembling a lute or a banjo) picks.

Kaikarō   MUSEUM
(懐華樓; Map p250; ☑ 076-253-0591; www.ken-rokuen.jp; 1-14-8 Higashiyama; ¥700; ⊘ 9am-5pm) In Higashi-chaya-gai, Kaikarō is an early 19th-century geisha house refinished with contemporary fittings and art including a red lacquered staircase. Private banquets (approximately ¥28,000 per person) with two *geiko* (geisha) are available if you have the cash and a minimum of 10 diners.

Kanazawa Phonograph Museum   MUSEUM
(金沢蓄音器館; Map p250; ☑ 076-232-3066; 2-11-21 Owari-chō; ¥300; ⊘ 10am-5pm) Audio buffs will dig this museum of old-time phonographs and SP records, with daily demonstrations at 11am, 2pm and 4pm.

◉ Teramachi

This hilly neighbourhood on the south bank of the Sai-gawa, opposite Katamachi and adjacent to Higashi-chaya-gai, was established as a first line of defence and contains dozens of temples.

★ **Myōryū-ji**　　　　　　　　BUDDHIST TEMPLE
(妙立寺; ☑076-241-0888; www.myouryuji.or.jp;
1-2-12 Nomachi; adult/child ¥1000/700; ⊗9am-
4.30pm Mar-Nov, 9am-4pm Dec-Feb, reservations
required) In Teramachi, fascinating Myōryū-
ji (aka Ninja-dera), completed in 1643, was
designed to protect its lord in case of attack.
It contains hidden stairways, escape routes,
secret chambers, concealed tunnels and
trick doors. Contrary to popular belief, this
ancient temple has nothing to do with ninja.
Admission is by tour only (in Japanese with
an English guidebook). You must phone for
reservations (in English).

🎎 Festivals & Events

Kagatobi Dezomeshiki　　　　　　CULTURAL
(加賀鳶梯子出初式; ⊗Jan) In early January
scantily clad firemen brave the cold, imbibe
sake and demonstrate ancient firefighting
skills on ladders.

Hyakumangoku Matsuri　　　　　　PARADE
(百万石まつり; ⊗Jun) In early June Kanazawa's main annual festival commemorates
the first time the region's rice production
hit one million *koku* (around 150,000
tonnes). There's a parade of townsfolk in
16th-century costumes, *takigi nō* (torch-lit
performances of *nō* drama), *tōrō nagashi*
(lanterns floated down the river at dusk)
and a special *chanoyu* (tea ceremony). It's
held at Kenroku-en (p252).

Kanazawa Film Festival　　　　　　FILM
(かなざわ映画の会; www.eiganokai.com; ⊗Sep)
Having reached its 10th anniversary in 2016,
Kanazawa's increasingly popular film festival,
screening an wide-ranging mix of Japanese
and foreign-language films, has finally come
of age.

🛏 Sleeping

There are convenient options near Kanazawa Station, or you could go for a more
atmospheric choice in the Higashi-chaya
district

★ **Pongyi**　　　　　　　　　GUESTHOUSE ¥
(ポンギー; Map p250; ☑076-225-7369; www.
pongyi.com; 2-22 Rokumai-machi; dm/s/d
¥3000/5500/7000; @) Run by a friendly Japanese man who did a stint in Southeast Asia
as a monk, Pongyi is a charmingly renovated
old shop alongside a canal. Cosy dorms are
located in an annexed vintage *kura* (mud-
walled storehouse).

★ **Share Hotels Hachi**　　　　　GUESTHOUSE ¥
(Map p250; ☑03-5656-6916; www.thesharehotels.
com; 3-18 Hashiba-cho; dm/s from ¥3800/8800;
❉⧉) Ecofriendly, communal, arty, funky – it's
hard to tell what's hip and what's hype. Either
way, this brilliantly located guesthouse will
suit those who don't mind sharing facilities,
enjoy the company of others and like reading Taschen design books in their spare time.
Woody dorms and quirky private rooms are
available and there's a cafe on-site.

Minshuku Yōgetsu　　　　　　MINSHUKU ¥
(民宿陽月; Map p250; ☑076-252-0497; 1-13-22
Higashiyama; r per person with/without breakfast
from ¥5000/4500; ❉⧉) Located in the heart
of the picturesque Higashi-chaya-gai, this
200-year-old geisha teahouse has only three
rooms and features a *goemonburo* (caul-
dron-shaped bath). No English is spoken,
there's no wi-fi and it's tucked away, but it's
perfect if tranquillity, history and authentic-
ity are what you're after.

★ **Holiday Inn ANA
Kanazawa Sky**　　　　　　　　HOTEL ¥¥
(Map p250; ☑076-233-2233; www.holidayinn.com;
15-1 Musashi-machi; s/d from ¥7500/9200; ❉⧉)
Centrally located between JR Kanazawa Station and the sights, across the road from Ōmi-
chō Market, this recently renovated hotel is
an excellent midrange choice with comfortable bedding and great views. It's on top of the
M'Za department store, whose basement-level
food court is all too convenient.

**Hotel MyStays
Premier Kanazawa**　　　　　　　HOTEL ¥¥
(☑076-290-5255; www.mystays.com/en/hotel/
kanazawa/mystays-premier-kanazawa; 2-13-5 Hiroo-
ka; r from ¥7800) Spacious (guest rooms are 32
sq metres!), stylish, fresh and current are all
adjectives that could be used to describe this
smart tourist hotel in the station precinct. It
has real king-sized beds, a gym, a laundry
and an on-site cafe. Excellent value.

Kanazawa Sai-no-niwa Hotel　　　HOTEL ¥¥
(金沢彩の庭ホテル; ☑076-235-3128; www.
sainoniwa-hotel.jp; 2-4-8 Nagata; d from ¥10,000;
🅿❉⧉) New in 2015, this modern hotel does
an admirable job of combining traditional
Japanese and modern aesthetics in its comfortable, neutrally toned, oversized rooms,
some with separate living areas. A delightful
bonus are the traditional decorative gardens
and sizeable public baths. The downside? It's
out of the way in a non-touristy area 20 minutes' walk southwest of JR Kanazawa Station.

★ Hotel Nikkō Kanazawa
HOTEL ¥¥¥

(ホテル日航金沢; Map p250; ☑076-234-1111; www.hnkanazawa.jp; 2-15-1 Honmachi; r from ¥13,800; ✴ 🛜) Kanazawa's most luxurious hotel, near JR Kanazawa Station, has a wide range of room types from singles to lavish suites, and an impressive selection of on-site restaurants and bars. Most rooms have exceptional views. The hotel turned 20 in 2014, but all rooms have been refurbished. The 'Luxe Style' and 'Stylish' rooms are worth the extra coin.

Asadaya Ryokan
RYOKAN ¥¥¥

(浅田屋旅館; Map p250; ☑076-231-2228; www.asadaya.co.jp/ryokan; 23 Jikkenmachi; per person incl 2 meals ¥43,000; ✴🛜) Although more expensive than some of Japan's most lauded *onsen ryokan,* and without the views and outdoor baths, Asadaya's exceptional service, attention to detail and sublime *kaiseki* cuisine will be, for some, worth the expense. With only four rooms, the conveniently located inn (opened in 1867) has more staff than guests to ensure your stay epitomises the Japanese art of hospitality.

Hotel Trusty Kanazawa Kōrinbō
BOUTIQUE HOTEL ¥¥¥

(Map p250; ☑076-203-8112; http://ct.rion.mobi/trusty.kanazawa; 1-2-16 Kōrinbō; s/d from ¥14,000/21,000; ✴🛜) This classy, masculine hotel shares its enviable location in the heart of Kōrinbō's high-end shopping district with the likes of Gucci and Tiffany. Although it's by no means a luxury hotel, you're best not to turn up dishevelled: think yuppies, think business, think keeping up appearances. Rooms are deliciously dark, brooding and suitably stylish.

✖ Eating

The shiny, architecturally stunning JR Kanazawa Station building is brimming with eateries. Its neighbour, **Forus** (Map p250; ☑076-265-8111; www.forus.co.jp/kanazawa; 3-1 Horikawa Shin-machi; ⊙11am-10pm) department store, has excellent dining floors, as does the basement of Meitetsu M'Za department store, opposite the must-visit Ōmi-chō Market (p249) with its fresh-from-the-boat restaurants. Otherwise, the mainstay of nocturnal dining is found around the lanes of Kōrinbō and Katamachi.

★ Sentō
CHINESE ¥

(仙桃; Map p250; ☑076-234-0669; 88 Aokusa-machi, 2F Ōmichō Ichiba; dishes from ¥650, set

menus from ¥980; ⊙11am-3pm & 5-10.30pm Wed-Mon) Upstairs in Omi-chō Market, talented chefs from Hong Kong prepare authentic Szechuan- and Hong Kong–style dishes (including dim sum) from scratch. Healthy (yellow bean oil is used) and delicious lunch and dinner set menus are excellent value. The spicy, salted squid is exquisite, but we had to come back for a second bowl of *tantanmen* (sesame and chilli ramen). Sluuuurp!

Full of Beans
CAFE ¥

(フルオブビーンズ; Map p250; ☑076-222-3315; www.fullofbeans.jp; 41-1 Satomi-chō; meals from ¥800; ⊙11.30am-3.30pm & 5-10pm Thu-Tue) A variety of Japanese and *yōshoku* (Western-style meals) are served in this stylish cafe in the quieter backstreets of Katamachi – the website will give you a sense of the vibe. It's a good place to try the Kanazawa speciality, *hanton raisu,* a bowl of rice topped with an omelette, fried seafood, ketchup and tartare sauce. Yum.

Daiba Kanazawa Ekimae
IZAKAYA ¥

(台場金沢駅前店; Map p250; ☑076-263-9191; Kanazawa Miyako Hotel 1F, 6-10 Konohana-machi; items from ¥460; ⊙11am-3pm & 5pm-midnight; 🍴) This trendy spot in the Kanazawa Miyako Hotel building has a comprehensive Japanese menu and a limited English one with all the Western favourites and some local specialities. It's a great place for your first *izakaya* experience: lots of small plates and beer. Highly recommended.

Cottage
INTERNATIONAL ¥

(コテージ; Map p250; ☑076-262-3277; 2-8-16 Seseragi-dōri, rear of Kōrinbō 109; dishes from ¥800; ⊙noon-2.30pm & 6-9.30pm Thu-Tue) Thin-crust pizza, flavourful pastas and hearty Irish stews feature on the eclectic, rotating menu at this popular home-style restaurant run by a friendly Irish and Japanese husband-and-wife team.

Itaru Honten　　　　　　　IZAKAYA ¥¥
(いたる 本店; Map p250; ☑076-221-4194; www.
itaru.ne.jp/honten; 3-8 Kakinokibatake; sashimi for
2 from ¥2400; ☺5.30-11.30pm Mon-Sat; 🅿) One
of Kanazawa's favourite seafood *izakaya* is
as popular with locals as it is with international visitors, so you may have to queue for
a spot. Expect superlative sushi and sashimi
and daily specials based on the catch of the
day. There's an English menu and dinner sets
start at ¥3000.

Janome-sushi Honten　　　　SUSHI ¥¥
(蛇之目寿司本店; Map p250; ☑076-231-0093;
1-1-12 Kōrinbō; set menu ¥1200-3600, Kaga ryōri
sets from ¥4400; ☺11am-2pm & 5-11pm Thu-Tue;
🅿) One of our Japanese friends says that
when he eats at Janome-sushi Honten – regarded for sashimi and Kaga cuisine since
1931 – he knows he's really in Kanazawa.
You can't go wrong with the *saabisu ranchi*
(lunch specials; from ¥1000).

Restaurant Jiyūken　　　　SHOKUDO ¥
(レストラン自由軒; Map p250; ☑076-252-1996;
www.jiyuken.com; 1-6-6 Higashiyama; meals ¥700-
1890; ☺11.30am-3pm & 5-9pm) This *shokudō*
(all-round, inexpensive restaurant) in the
heart of Higashi-chaya-gai has been serving
yōshoku (Western food) – or at least Japanese takes on Western food, like omelettes,
hamburgers and curry rice – since 1909. Daily
set lunches (¥950) are good value.

Kanazawa Todoroki-tei　　　BISTRO ¥¥
(金沢とどろき亭; Map p250; ☑076-252-5755;
1-2-1 Higashiyama; plates from ¥1300; ☺11.30am-
2.30pm & 6-10pm) The art-deco, woody, can-
delit atmosphere of this Western-style bistro
near Higashi-chaya-gai is a big selling point.
The Taisho-era (1912–26) building with
vaulted ceilings is a little rough around the
edges, but that's part of its charm: it's not
too snooty. Eight-course dinners are good
value, starting at ¥3500 per person. Think
romance.

★ **Kaiseki Tsuruko**　　　JAPANESE ¥¥¥
(懐石 つる幸; Map p250; ☑076-264-2375; www.
turukou.com; 6-5 Takaoka-machi; lunch/dinner from
¥5000/15,000; ☺noon-3pm & 6-10pm) *Kaiseki*
dining is a holistic experience of hospitality,
art and originality: in no two presentations
are the colours, flavours and textures ever
quite the same. This outstanding restaurant is
a true gourmand's delight offering an authentic Japanese fine-dining experience beyond
what you might enjoy in a ryokan. Dress to
impress and budget accordingly.

🍷 **Drinking & Nightlife**

Most of Kanazawa's bars are jam-packed into
high-rises in Katamachi – many are barely disguised hostess bars. For a mellower evening,
soak in the ambience of Higashi-chaya-gai.

★ **Oriental Brewing**　　　　BREWERY
(Map p250; ☑076-255-6378; www.orientalbrewing.
com; 3-2-22 Higashiyama; ☺11am-10pm) You can't
miss this trendy brewhouse at the entrance to
Higashi-chaya-gai: it's always humming with
local and international guests who love the
mellow, friendly vibe and original yeasty ales.

Sturgis Rock Bar　　　　　BAR
(スタージス; Map p250; ☑076-262-9577; 4F Kin-
rin Bldg, 1-7-15 Katamachi; ☺8pm-3am) We almost
want to keep this fabulous, colourful, fun,
wild and original Kanazawan institution to
ourselves... With live rock and every manner
of everything hanging from the ceiling, you'll
feel like you're on an acid trip in San Francis-
co with a bunch of Japanese tourists paying
homage to the gods of rock and roll.

Curio Espresso & Vintage Design　　CAFE
(Map p250; ☑076-231-5543; 1-13 Yasue-cho;
☺9am-6pm Sat-Mon, from 8am Wed-Fri) Brewing
Seattle-style coffee that would satisfy even the
most hardened Melburnian coffee snob, this
sweet little cafe is a great spot to start your
day, with a variety of simple breakfast foods to
go with your latte.

Cambio APT　　　　　　　BAR
(Map p250; ☑076-207-7524; 2F Silk Bldg, 2-2-14
Katamachi; ☺7pm-midnight) Smack in the heart
of Katamachi you'll find this shiny, welcoming
bar. The friendly young owner spent time in
Canada and is happy to chat. There's a ¥400
seating charge.

☆ **Entertainment**

Ishikawa Prefectural Nō Theatre　　THEATRE
(石川県立能楽堂; Map p250; ☑076-264-2598;
www.nohgaku.or.jp; 3-1 Dewa-machi; performance
prices vary; ☺9am-4.30pm Tue-Sun) *Nō* theatre
is alive and well in Kanazawa. Weekly performances take place here during summer.

🔒 **Shopping**

The Hirosaka shopping street, between
Kōrinbō 109 department store and Kenroku-
en, has some upmarket craft shops on its
south side. Other major department stores
are towards JR Kanazawa Station (Forus,
Meitetsu M'za) and on Hyakumangoku-dōri
between Kōrinbō and Katamachi (Daiwa,

Atrio Shopping Plaza). The fresh and funky Tatemachi Shopping Promenade is also here.

Sakuda Gold Leaf Company ARTS & CRAFTS (金銀箔工芸さくだ; Map p250; ☑076-251-6777; www.goldleaf-sakuda.jp; 1-3-27 Higashiyama; ☺9am-6pm) Here you can observe the *kinpaku* (gold leaf) process and pick up all sorts of gilded souvenirs including pottery, lacquerware and, er...golf balls. It also serves tea containing flecks of gold leaf, reputedly good for rheumatism. Even the toilet walls are lined with gold and platinum.

Ishikawa Craft Store ARTS & CRAFTS (石川県観光物産館, Ishikawa-ken Kankō-bussankan; Map p250; ☑076-222-7788; www.kanazawa-kankou.jp; 2-20 Kenroku-machi; ☺10am-6pm) An overview of Kanazawa crafts, under one roof.

Murakami FOOD (村上; Map p250; ☑076-264-4223; 2-3-32 Nagamachi; ☺8.30am-5pm) If a flowering tree made of candy excites you, head to Murakami. At this handsome *wagashi* (Japanese sweets) shop you'll also find *fukusamochi* (red-bean paste and pounded rice in a crêpe) and *kakiho* (soybean flour rolled in black sesame seeds).

❶ Information

Online, check out www4.city.kanazawa.lg.jp for general city information.

Kanazawa Tourist Information Center (石川県金沢観光情報センター; Map p250; ☑076-232-6200, KGGN 076-232-3933; www.kggn.sakura.ne.jp; 1 Hirooka-machi; ☺9am-7pm) This brilliant office inside Kanazawa Station, one of Japan's best, has helpful staff and a plethora of maps and pamphlets in a variety of languages and the excellent free English-language magazine *Eye on Kanazawa*. The friendly folk from the Goodwill Guide Network (KGGN) are also here to assist with hotel recommendations and free guiding in English – two weeks' notice is requested.

Ishikawa Foundation for International Exchange (Map p250; ☑076-262-5931; www.ifie.or.jp; 1-5-3 Honmachi; ☺9am-8pm Mon-Fri, to

---

KANAZAWA'S TRADITIONAL CRAFTS

During the Edo period Kanazawa's ruling Maeda family fuelled the growth of important crafts. Many are still practised today.

Kanazawa & Wajima Lacquer

To create Kanazawa and Wajima lacquerware, decoration is applied to luminous black lacquerware through *maki-e* (painting) or gilding. Artists must take great care that dust does not settle on the final product.

Ōhi Pottery

The deliberately simple, almost primitive designs, rough surfaces, irregular shapes and monochromatic glazes of Ōhi pottery have been favoured by tea practitioners since the early Edo period. Since that time one family, with the professional name Chōzaemon, has been keeper of the Ōhi tradition.

Kutani Porcelain

Kutani porcelain is known for its elegant shapes, graceful designs and bright, bold colours. It dates back to the early Edo period and shares design characteristics with Chinese porcelain and Japanese Imari ware. Typical motifs include birds, flowers, trees and landscapes.

Kaga Yūzen Silk Dyeing

The laborious, specialised method of *Kaga Yūzen* silk dyeing is characterised by strong colours and realistic depictions of nature, such as flower petals that have begun to brown around the edges. White lines between elements where ink has washed away are a characteristic of *Kaga Yūzen*.

Gold Leaf

It starts with a lump of pure gold the size of a ¥10 coin, which is rolled to the size of a tatami mat, as little as 0.0001mm thick. The gold leaf is cut into squares of 10.9cm – the size used for mounting on walls, murals or paintings – or then cut again for gilding on lacquerware or pottery. Kanazawa makes over 98% of Japan's gold leaf.

5pm Sat & Sun) Offers information, a library, satellite-TV news and free internet access. It's on the 3rd floor of the Rifare building, a few minutes' walk southeast of JR Kanazawa Station.

❶ Getting There & Away

AIR

Nearby **Komatsu Airport** (p213) has air connections with major Japanese cities, as well as Seoul, Shanghai and Taipei.

BUS

JR Highway Bus operates express buses from in front of JR Kanazawa Station's east exit, to Tokyo's Shinjuku Station (¥8000, 7½ hours) and Kyoto (¥4100, 4¼ hours).

Meitetsu (p231) and **Hokutetsu Kankō** (☑ 076-237-5115; www.hokutetsu.co.jp) buses serve Nagoya (¥4180, four hours).

Nōhi Bus (濃飛バス; ☑ 0577-32-1688; www.nouhibus.co.jp) services Takayama, via Shirakawa-go (¥3390, 2¼ hours).

TRAIN

March 2015 marked the beginning of a new period of prosperity for Kanazawa with the arrival of the Hokuriku Shinkansen, slashing journey times from Tokyo by over an hour. The direct journey between Kanazawa and Tokyo (¥13,920) is now just 2½ hours.

The JR Hokuriku line links Kanazawa with Fukui (*tokkyū* ¥2500, 45 minutes; *futsū* ¥1320, 1½ hours), Kyoto (*tokkyū* ¥6380, 2¼ hours), Osaka (*tokkyū* ¥7130, 2¾ hours) and Toyama (*futsū* ¥980, one hour).

❶ Getting Around

BICYCLE

Full-size bikes can be rented from **JR Kanazawa Station Rent-a-Cycle** (駅レンタサイクル; Map p250; ☑ 076-261-1721; per hour/day ¥200/1200; ☺8am-8.30pm) and **Hokutetsu Rent-a-Cycle** (北鉄レンタサイクル; Map p250; ☑ 076-263-0919; per 4hr/day ¥630/1050; ☺8am-5.30pm), both by the train station's west exit.

There's also a pay-as-you-go bike rental system called 'Machi-nori'. The bikes are a little small for larger *gaijin* bodies, and not the most comfortable to ride, but, with a bit of planning, the system functions well. For the low-down in English, a downloadable map is available at www.machi-nori.jp.

BUS

Buses depart from the circular terminus in front of the station's east exit. Any bus from station stop 7, 8 or 9 will take you to the city centre (¥200).

The Kanazawa Loop Bus (single ride/day pass ¥200/500, every 15 minutes from 8.30am to 6pm) circles the major tourist attractions in 45 minutes. On Saturday, Sunday and holidays, the Machi-bus goes to Kōrinbō for ¥100.

Airport buses (¥1130, 45 minutes) depart from station stop 6. Some services are via Katamachi and Kōrinbō 109, but take one hour to reach the airport.

Day passes (¥500) offer excellent value, but since the influx of non-Japanese-speaking visitors to town began to inadvertently cause lost-in-translation style chaos across the network, they can no longer be purchased on board. Instead purchase them from the Hokutetsu Kankō service centre inside JR Kanazawa Station; there's another centre opposite the Omi-chō Market bus stop.

For more information, see www.hokutetsu.co.jp/en/en_round.

CAR & MOTORCYCLE

Numerous car-rental agencies are dotted around the train station's west exit.

Noto Peninsula　能登半島

Rugged seascapes, rural life, seafood and a light diet of cultural sights make Noto Peninsula (Noto-hantō) a pleasant escape from Kanazawa's urban sprawl. Lacquer-making town of Wajima is the hub of the rugged north, known as Oku-Noto, and the best place to stay overnight. Famous products include *Wajima-nuri* lacquerware, *Suzu*-style pottery, locally harvested sea salt and *iwanori* seaweed.

While the arrival of the Hokuriku Shinkansen has brought an increase in visitors to the peninsula, the area, slow to catch up, maintains its delightfully rural feel. Each of the peninsula's main towns has a handful of basic business hotels or *minshuku*, and there are a few unique and delightful ryokan to be found.

As you might imagine, seafood is king on the peninsula: you'll find plenty of sushi, sashimi and *kaisen* (seafood) restaurants. Outside of that, expect a limited range of dining options compared to nearby Kanazawa.

❶ Getting There & Around

AIR

In the centre of Oku-Noto, **Noto Satoyama (Wajima) Airport** (NTQ; Map p260; ☑ 0768-26-2000; www.noto-airport.jp) connects the peninsula with Tokyo (Haneda).

BUS

Hokutetsu Kankō (p258) runs buses between Kanazawa and Wajima (¥2200, two hours, 10 daily); some stop en route at Monzen (¥740, 35 minutes), halfway up the coast.

From Wajima, Ushitsu-bound buses for the **Senmaida Rice Terraces** (p261) stop in Sosogi (¥740, 40 minutes).

BICYCLE

Noto's mostly flat west coast appeals to cyclists, but cycling is not recommended on the Noto-kongō and east coasts because of steep, blind curves.

CAR & MOTORCYCLE

Self-driving from Kanazawa is easily the best way to see the peninsula. Most sights can be reached by road only: hiring a car from Kanazawa is recommended. The 83km Noto Yūryo (能登有料; Noto Toll Rd) speeds you as far as Anamizu (toll ¥1180).

Car rental companies can be found near Himi's and Hakui's train stations.

TRAIN

For the west Noto coast, take the JR Nanao line from Kanazawa to Hakui (*tokkyū* ¥1410, 45 minutes; *futsū* ¥760, one hour) and connect to infrequent local buses. For Oku-Noto, trains continue to Wakura Onsen, connecting to even less frequent local buses.

From Kanazawa, the JR Nanao line travels to Hakui (*tokkyū* ¥1410, 45 minutes; *futsū* ¥760, one hour) on the western coast of Noto and then cuts east to Wakura Onsen, from where you'll have to transfer to infrequent local buses. The JR Himi line connects Takaoka (in Toyama Prefecture) with Himi (*futsū* ¥320, 30 minutes).

Lower Noto Peninsula 能登半島下

☏ 0767

The small town of **Hakui** (羽咋) is Noto's western transit hub, with frequent train connections to Kanazawa and less frequent bus connections along Noto's west coast. With about twice the population, the town of **Himi** (氷見) in neighbouring Toyama Prefecture, about 40 minutes' drive east, is also a pleasant starting point from which to tackle the peninsula.

◉ Sights & Activities

★ **Myōjō-ji**   BUDDHIST TEMPLE
(妙成寺; Map p260; ☏ 0767-27-1226; Yo-1 Takidani-machi; ¥510; ⊗ 8am-5pm Apr-Oct, 8am-4.30pm Nov-Mar) Founded in 1294 by Nichizō, a disciple of Nichiren, the imposing Myōjō-ji remains an important temple for the sect. The grounds comprise 10 Important Cultural Properties, most notably the strikingly elegant five-storey pagoda. The Togi-bound bus from JR Hakui Station can drop you out at Myōjō-ji-guchi bus stop (¥430, 18 minutes); from there, it's less than 10 minutes' walk.

Cosmo Isle Hakui   MUSEUM
(コスモアイル羽咋; Map p260; ☏ 0767-22-9888; www.hakui.ne.jp/ufo; 25 Menda, Tsuruta-machi, Hakui-shi; ¥400; ⊗ 9am-5pm Wed-Mon) This quirky space and science museum is one for *The X-Files* fans, featuring '60s and '70s USSR space mission relics and a bunch of UFO and alien exhibits (including a replica of the alleged Roswell alien dissection).

Kita-ke   HISTORIC BUILDING
(喜多家; Map p260; ☏ 0767-28-2546; Ra 4-1 Kitaawashiri, Hodatsushimizu; adult/child ¥500/200; ⊗ 8.30am-5pm Apr-Oct, to 4pm Nov-Mar) During the Edo period, the Kita family administered over 200 villages from Kita-ke, the pivotal crossroads of the Kaga, Etchū and Noto fiefs. Inside this splendid, sprawling family home and museum are displays of weapons, ceramics, farming tools, fine and folk art, and documents. The garden has been called the Moss Temple of Noto.

It's about 1km from the Komedashi exit on the Noto Toll Rd. By train, take the JR Nanao line to Menden Station and walk for 20 minutes.

Chirihama Nagisa Driveway   SCENIC DRIVE
(千里浜なぎさドライブウエイ; Map p260) At times this 8km compacted strip of beach sand resembles Florida's Daytona Beach as buses, motorcycles and cars roar past the breakers, and revellers barbecue in the sun.

🛏 Sleeping

Route Inn Grantia Himi   HOTEL ¥¥
(ルートイングランティア氷見; Map p260; ☏ 0766-73-1771; www.hotel-grantia.co.jp; 443-5 Kanō; s/d from ¥6000/10,000; [P][※][⊚]) This smart, comfortable business hotel is a good resting point if you're driving to the Noto Peninsula from Toyama or Gokayama. It's in the car park of a shopping mall and there are plenty of shops and amenities nearby to keep you occupied.

Noto-kongō Coast 能登金剛

☏ 0767, 0768

This rocky, cliff-lined shoreline extends for about 16km between Fukūra and Sekinohana,

Noto Peninsula

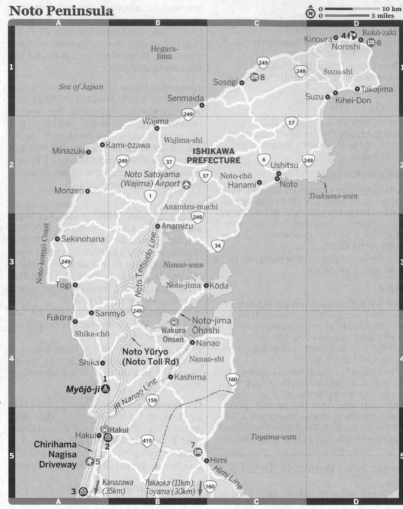

and is adorned with dramatic rock formations, best explored by road.

☉ Sights

Sōji-ji Soin BUDDHIST TEMPLE
(総持寺祖院; ☎0768-42-0005; 1-18-1 Monzen; adult/child ¥410/160; ☉8am-5pm) This beautiful temple in Monzen was established in 1321 as the head of the Sōtō school of Zen, but now functions as a branch temple. Temple buildings were damaged by the 2007 Noto earthquake and remain under fastidious reconstruction. Sōji-ji Soin welcomes visitors to experience one hour of *zazen*

(seated meditation; ¥300, 9am to 3pm), serves *shōjin-ryōri* (Buddhist vegetarian cuisine; ¥2500 to ¥3500) and can accommodate visitors (with two meals ¥6500; single women are prohibited). Reserve at least two days in advance.

Oku-Noto   奥能登

☎0768 / POP 27,205

About 20km northeast of Monzen, the fishing port of **Wajima** (輪島), historically famed for delicate *Wajima-nuri* (lacquerware), is the largest town in Oku-Noto, although it, too, is following a trend of rural

Noto Peninsula

depopulation. However, the arrival of the Hokuriku Shinkansen into Kanazawa in March 2015 seems to be helping things out with an injection of tourist spending.

◉ Sights

Travelling from Wajima towards the tip of the Noto Peninsula you'll pass the famous slivered *dandan-batake* (rice terraces) at **Senmaida** (千枚田) before arriving in the coastal village of **Sosogi** (曽々木) with its *mado-iwa* (窓岩; window rock) formation just offshore, and a number of hiking trails. In winter look for *nami-no-hana* (flowers of the waves), masses of foam that form when waves gnash Sosogi's rocky shore.

The road northeast from Sosogi village passes sea-salt farms as it winds its way onward to cape **Rokkō**, the peninsula's furthest point. Here, in the village of **Noroshi** (狼煙), you can amble up to the lighthouse for wonderful views, before circling around the tip of the peninsula southwards to the tiny outposts of **Suzu** and **Noto-chō**, from where the scenery becomes gradually less dramatic on the way back to civilisation.

Ishikawa Wajima
Urushi Art Museum   MUSEUM
(石川輪島漆芸美術館; ☑0768-22-9788; www.city.wajima.ishikawa.jp/art; 11 Shijukari Mitomori-machi; adult/student ¥620/150; ◷9am-4.30pm) This modern museum about a 15-minute walk west of the former train station, has a large, rotating collection of lacquerware in galleries on two floors. Phone ahead, as it closes between exhibitions.

Kiriko Kaikan   MUSEUM
(キリコ会館; ☑0768-22-7100; http://wajima-kiriko.com; 6-1 Marine Town; adult/child ¥620/360;

◷8am-5pm) Here you can view a selection of the impressive illuminated lacquered floats used in the Wajima Taisai festival, some up to 15m tall. Take the bus to Tsukada bus stop (¥150, six minutes).

Asa-ichi   MARKET
(朝市, Morning Market; ◷8am-noon, closed 10th & 25th of month) This entertaining morning market features a few hundred ageing fish-wives hawking fresh-off-the-trawler seafood, lacquerware, pottery and souvenirs, with sass and humour that transcends language. Haggle politely if you dare.

Senmaida Rice Terraces   LANDMARK
(白米千枚田段々畑) Once a common sight in Japan, the ancient method of rice farming is disappearing. These 'thousand' terraced rice paddies snaking up the hillside are both fascinating and beautiful in all seasons.

🎌 Festivals & Events

Ushitsu Abare Festival   CULTURAL
(宇出津あばれ祭り, Ushitsu Abare Matsuri; ◷Jul) Over the first Friday and Saturday in July, 40 *kiriko* lantern floats are paraded around the streets and showered in embers from giant torches. Who said fire and sake don't mix?

Gojinjō Daikō Nafune Matsuri   MUSIC
(御陣乗太鼓名舟大祭; ◷31 Jul) This festival features participants wearing demon masks and seaweed head gear and culminates in a frenzy of wild drumming.

Wajima Taisai   PARADE
(輪島大祭; ◷Aug) Wajima's famous, towering, illuminated *kiriko* festival floats parade through the streets to much excitement in late August.

🛏 Sleeping & Eating

Sodegahama
Camping Ground   CAMPGROUND ¥
(袖が浜キャンプ場; ☑0768-23-1146; 51 Sodegahama; campsites per person ¥1000; ℗) Take the local *noranke* bus (¥100) or Nishiho bus (direction Zōza, 雑座) to Sodegahama, or hike for 20 minutes to reach this beachfront campground.

★ Oyado Tanaka   RYOKAN ¥¥
(お宿たなか; ☑0768-22-5155; www.oyado-tanaka.jp; 22-38 Kawai-machi; r per person incl 2 meals from ¥10,950; ℗❀🌐) This immaculate 10-room inn has beds on tatami, hot-spring baths (including a private-use *rotemburo* for an extra

charge), dark woodwork, paper lanterns and ambience aplenty. The *kaiseki* meals here feature local seafood and laquerware.

Yokoiwaya
MINSHUKU ¥¥

(横岩屋; Map p260; ☑0768-32-0603; www.wajima.gr.jp/yokoiwaya; Ku-2 Machino-machi, Sosogi; r per person incl 2 meals from ¥8500; ℗) Waterfront *minshuku* Yokoiwaya in Sosogi has welcomed guests for over 150 years (and it shows). It's known for seafood dinners. Look for the paper lantern, or request pick-up from Sosogi-guchi bus stop (曽々木口バス停).

Route Inn Wajima
HOTEL ¥¥

(ホテルルートイン輪島; ☑0768-22-7700; www.route-inn.co.jp; 1-2 Marine Town; s/d from ¥7000/11,000; ℗❄⊙) With decent-sized rooms and great views from the upper floors, this modern, harbourside tourist hotel has all you need if you're passing through, including free breakfast.

★ Lamp no Yado
RYOKAN ¥¥¥

(ランプの宿; Map p260; ☑0768-86-8000; www.lampnoyado.co.jp; 10-11 Jike, Misaki-machi; r per person incl 2 meals from ¥21,000; ℗❄⊙⊠) Remote Lamp no Yado is a place of its own: a 13-room wooden waterside village beneath a cliff. The building goes back four centuries, to when people would escape to its curative waters for weeks at a time. It's been an inn since the 1970s. Decadent rooms have private bathrooms, and some have their own *rotemburo*. The pool is almost superfluous.

This is a romantic destination ryokan, but not for those on a budget.

Madara-yakata
SEAFOOD ¥

(まだら館; ☑0768-22-3453; www.madara-yakata.com; 4-103 Kawai-machi; dishes from ¥870; ⊙11am-7pm) This restaurant near the Asaichi (p261) serves local specialities including *zōsui* (rice hotpot), *yaki-zakana* (grilled fish) and seasonal seafood, surrounded by folk crafts.

Umi-tei Notokichi
SEAFOOD ¥¥

(海亭のと吉; ☑0768-22-6636; 4-153 Kawaimachi; dishes ¥620-2700; ⊙11am-2pm & 5-8pm Thu-Tue) Umi-tei Notokichi has been a popular local haunt for generations – you'll be hard pressed to better experience seafood elsewhere in Japan. Purists should keep it simple and go for the *sashimi moriawase* (sashimi of the day). It also does a mean version of *katsudon* (crumbed pork cutlet on rice).

❶ Information

Tourist Information Center (輪島観光協会; ☑0768-22-1503; ⊙8am-7pm) Limited English is spoken by the friendly staff at this office in the former Wajima train station, now the bus station. However, they do have English-language maps and can help with accommodation bookings.

Kaga Onsen 加賀温泉
☑0761

This broad area consisting of three hot-spring villages, Katayamazu Onsen, Yamashiro Onsen and Yamanaka Onsen, is centred on Kaga Onsen and Daishōji Stations along the JR Hokuriku line and is famed for its *onsen ryokan* (traditional hot-spring inns), lacquerware and porcelain.

Of the three villages, Yamanaka Onsen is the most scenic, straddling the Kakusenkei Gorge, through which the Daishoji-gawa flows. That said, the town's decaying buildings tell the regrettable and all-too-common tale of rural depopulation.

❂ Sights

Motorcar Museum of Japan
MUSEUM

(日本自動車博物館; ☑0761-43-4343; www.mmj-car.com; 40 Futatsunashi-machi, Komatsu; adult/child ¥1000/500; ⊙9am-5pm Thu-Tue; 🅿; 🚃JR Hokuriku line to Awazu) You're likely to be a little astounded by this significant collection of over 500 pristine Japanese (and foreign) vehicles housed over three floors, in a massive, elegant, though unmistakably modern, red-brick building, resembling an opulent mansion. Revheads and kids who loved the Pixar *Cars* films, will not want to miss this. The drawback: it's easiest to get to if you're self-driving.

The museum is located about 3km from JR Awazu Station on the Hokuriku Main line: don't mistake this for the Hokuriku Shinkansen line. Of course, there's plenty of parking.

Kutaniyaki Art Museum
MUSEUM

(石川県九谷焼美術館; ☑0761-72-7466; www.kutani-mus.jp/en; 1-10-13 Daishōji Jikata-machi; adult/child ¥500/free; ⊙9am-5pm Tue-Sun) Stunning examples of bright and colourful local porcelain are on display here, about an eight-minute walk from Daishōji Station.

Zenshō-ji
BUDDHIST TEMPLE

(全昌寺; ☑0761-72-1164; 1 Daishōji Shinmei-chō; ¥500; ⊙9am-5pm) The Daishōji Station area is crammed with temples including Zenshō-ji, which houses over 500 amusingly carved Buddhist arhat sculptures.

Activities

Kosōyu
ONSEN

(古総湯; Yamashiro Onsen; ¥500, Sōyu combined ticket ¥700; ⏱ 6am-10pm) Close to Kaga Onsen Station, Yamashiro Onsen is a sleepy town centred on a magnificent wooden bathhouse that was recently rebuilt. Kosōyu has beautiful stained-glass windows and a rest area on the top floor; neighbouring Sōyu is a larger, more modern bathhouse.

Yamanaka Onsen
ONSEN

The 17th-century haiku poet Bashō rhapsodised on the chrysanthemum fragrance of the local mineral springs in Yamanaka Onsen. It's still an ideal spot for chilling at the **Kiku no Yu** (菊の湯; ¥420; ⏱ 6.45am-10.30pm) bathhouse, and for river walks by the Kakusenkei Gorge, spanned by the elegant **Korogi-bashi** (Cricket Bridge) and the whimsical, modern-art **Ayatori-hashi** (Cat's Cradle Bridge).

Yamanaka Onsen is accessible by bus (¥420, 30 minutes) from Kaga Onsen Station.

Sleeping

The friendly folk at the **Yamanaka Onsen Tourism Association** (山中温泉観光協会; ☎ 0761-78-0330; www.yamanaka-spa.or.jp; 5-1 Yamanaka Onsen) and the **Yamashiro Onsen Tourist Association** (山代温泉観光協会; ☎ 0761-77-1144; www.yamashiro-spa.or.jp; 3-70 Hokubu; ⏱ 9am-5pm) can help with the difficult task of choosing from the many ryokan in this region: most are expensive, indulgent and delightful.

★ Beniya Mukayū
RYOKAN ¥¥¥

(べにや無何有; ☎ 0761-77-1340; www.mukayu.com; 55-1-3 Yamashiro Onsen; per person incl 2 meals from ¥36,000; Ⓟ❋@🛜) The friendly staff at this award-winning ryokan are committed to upholding the Japanese art of hospitality. Gorgeously minimalist, there's a sense of Zen pervading every aspect of the guest experience, from the welcoming private tea ceremony to the gentle morning yoga classes. Rooms are a beautiful fusion of old and new – most feature private outdoor cypress baths.

Mukayū's cuisine showcases only the best and freshest local seasonal ingredients, exquisitely prepared and presented. Spa treatments leave you gently breathless.

★ Kayōtei
RYOKAN ¥¥¥

(かよう亭; ☎ 0761-78-1410; www.kayotei.jp; 1-20 Higashi-machi, Yamanaka Onsen; per person incl 2 meals from ¥42,200; Ⓟ❋@🛜) This delightful, opulent ryokan along the scenic Kakusenkei Gorge has only 10 rooms, giving it an intimate feel. Some rooms have private outdoor baths, with views over the gorge and a beautiful hidden waterfall.

Kissho Yamanaka
RYOKAN ¥¥¥

(吉祥やまなか; ☎ 0761-78-5656; www.kissho-yamanaka.com; 1-14-3 Higashi-machi, Yamanaka Onsen; r per person incl 2 meals from ¥21,500; Ⓟ❋🛜) Most of the elegant Western- or Japanese-style rooms here have great views and are comfortably appointed, although this towering ryokan is showing its age. That said, dining and bathing here are both exceptional.

ⓘ Getting There & Away

The JR Hokuriku line links Kaga Onsen with Kanazawa (*tokkyū* ¥1510, 25 minutes; *futsū* ¥760, 44 minutes) and Fukui (*tokkyū* ¥1330, 21 minutes; *futsū* ¥580, 33 minutes).

Willer Express (http://willerexpress.com) operates bus services from Tokyo to Kaga Onsen, from ¥3500.

ⓘ Getting Around

Ride the 'O-sanpo' shuttle bus (two-day pass ¥500) around Yamanaka Onsen, and enquire at the **tourism association** or your accommodation about the irregular tour bus to **Daihonzan Eihei-ji**.

In Yamashiro Onsen, 'Can bus' (two-day pass ¥1200) operates a similar service around the various sights and onsen in the area.

Fukui
福井

☎ 0776 / POP 266,002

Unfortunate Fukui city was decimated in the 1940s, first by war, then by earthquake. Most of the sights of interest are scattered around the compact prefecture, a short drive from town. Consider car rental and an overnight stay: country roads make for easy driving and the scenery is lovely.

◉ Sights

★ Ichijōdani Asakura Clan Ruins
RUINS

(一乗谷朝倉氏遺跡, Ichijōdani Asakura-shi Iseki; ☎ 0776-41-2330; http://asakura-museum.pref.fukui.lg.jp; 4-10 Abaka; ¥210; ⏱ 9am-4.30pm) Designated a national historic site, this unexpected find boasts one of the largest town ruins in

Japan. Perched in a narrow valley between modest mountains, it's easy to see why the Asakura clan would have built their small fortified city here: it's very beautiful. You're free to wander along the restored street of merchants' houses and stroll through the lush grounds, following the remnants of the buildings up the hillside. It's a wonderful spot to sit, picnic and contemplate.

Daihonzan Eihei-ji   BUDDHIST TEMPLE
(大本山永平寺; ☑0776-63-3640; http://global.sotozen-net.or.jp/eng/temples/foreigner/Eihei-ji.html; 5-15 Shihi, Eiheiji; adult/child ¥500/200; ◎9am-5pm) In 1244 the great Zen master Dōgen (1200–53), founder of the Sōtō sect of Zen Buddhism, established Eihei-ji, the 'Temple of Eternal Peace', in a forest outside Fukui. Today it's one of Sōtō's two head temples, a palpably spiritual place amid mountains, mosses and ancient cedars. That said, day trippers visiting the complex of over 70 buildings might not find the constant throng of visitors and activities as peaceful as they might desire.

Aspirants affiliated with a Sōtō Zen organisation can attend Eihei-ji's four-day, three-night **sanzen experience program** (☑0776-63-3640), which follows the monks' training schedule – complete with 3.50am prayers, cleaning, zazen (seated meditation) and ritual meals in which not a grain of rice may be left behind. Knowledge of Japanese isn't necessary, but some self-discipline is helpful! Book well in advance.

The compound is often closed for periods varying from a week to 10 days for religious observance. Sanrō temple stays cost ¥8000 per night and must be booked a month in advance.

To get to Eihei-ji from Fukui, take the Keifuku bus (¥720, 30 minutes, hourly); buses depart from the east exit of JR Fukui Station.

ℹ TSURUGA FERRIES
From Tsuruga, a busy port and rail junction 60km south of Fukui city, Shin Nihonkai Ferry Company has daily sailings to Tomakomai, Hokkaidō (19½ hours nonstop, 30½ hours with stops). Several of these stop en route at Niigata (¥5350, 12½ hours) and Akita (¥6990, 20 hours). Buses timed to ferry departures serve Tsuruga-kō port from JR Tsuruga Station (¥350, 20 minutes).

Fukui Dinosaur Museum   MUSEUM
(福井県立恐竜博物館; ☑0779-88-0001; www.dinosaur.pref.fukui.jp; 51-11 Muroko-chō Terao, Katsuyama; adult/child ¥720/410; ◎9am-5pm) Kids love the larger-than-life replicas and fossilised relics of the Jurrasic Park–styled Fukui Dinosaur Museum, one of the three largest museums of its kind in the world. There are plenty of English explanations and over 40 main exhibits (including interactive ones) concerned with natural history, prehistoric flora, fauna and the dinosaurs that once roamed Japan and other parts of the world. The closest train station is Katsuyama on the privately owned Echizen line, but your best bet is self-driving.

🛏 Sleeping & Eating

Fukui Phoenix Hotel   HOTEL ¥¥
(福井フェニックスホテル; ☑0776-21-1800; www.phoenix-hotel.jp; 2-4-18 Ote; s/d/tw from ¥6500/10,000/12,000; ℗❉🛜) A hop, skip and a jump from JR Fukui Station, this refurbished hotel has tastefully decorated rooms, free wi-fi, a coin laundry and a variety of room types (including suites) for those wanting a little more room to spread out. Parking is available nearby for ¥1000.

Amida Soba Yūbuan   NOODLES ¥¥
(あみだそば遊歩庵; ☑0776-76-3519; www.amidasoba.jimdo.com; 1-9-1 Chūō; soba ¥600-1300; ◎11.30am-7pm) On the Rekishi-no-michi street outside the west exit of Fukui Station, you'll find this delightful variation on the usual soba theme. The speciality is *oroshi soba sanmai* (¥1300), a double serve of thick flattened soba noodles with three flavours to dip in: *oroshi* (grated daikon), *tororo* (puréed mountain potato) and wasabi.

ℹ Information

Fukui Tourist Information Center (福井市観光案内所; ☑0776-20- 5348; 1-2-1 Chūō; ◎8.30am-7pm) Enquire here, inside JR Fukui Station, for local maps and itineraries.

ℹ Getting There & Around

JR trains connect Fukui with Kanazawa (*tokkyū* ¥2500, 48 minutes; *futsū* ¥1320, 1½ hours), Tsuruga (*tokkyū* ¥2150, 35 minutes; *futsū* ¥970, 55 minutes), Kyoto (¥4420, 1½ hours) and Osaka (¥5510, two hours).

There is a bunch of car-rental options outside the east exit of JR Fukui Station, including Toyota Rent-a-Car.

WORTH A TRIP

ECHIZEN-ŌNO

Ringed by attractive mid-sized mountains and bathed in history, Echizen-Ōno (越前大野) was designed by Kanamori Nagachika in 1575 based on the layout of Kyoto at that time, earning it the nickname 'little Kyoto'. Today, the town is overlooked on most itineraries, but this little village has a special quality: even if the rest of the world seems to have forgotten it exists, its ageing population certainly hasn't. Even as its population grows increasingly older and the buildings start to decline, there's a palpable spirit of *ganbatte* (never give up) that shows in the immaculately clean, although sometimes almost empty, streets.

Ōno's **Teramachi** (temple row) features around 20 temples arranged side by side, some still operational, others closed down; most are still carefully cared for by their owners and patrons. It's a truly stirring spot for a contemplative walk, and an even better location for budding photographers.

Atop a hill overlooking the town, the little *yamashiro* (mountain castle) **Echizen Ōno-jō** (越前大野城; ☑ 0779-66-0234; 3-109 Shiromachi, Ōno; ¥200; ⊙ 9am-4pm Apr-Nov) is a true delight, even if it is a replica and you have to climb all those stairs. The original was built in 1576; today's version went up in 1968 to exacting specifications. The views of the surrounding valleys and mountains are something special. In the right conditions, the castle appears as if it were above a sea of clouds.

The friendly staff at the **tourist information center** (越前大野観光案内所; ☑ 0779-65-5521; www.ono-kankou.jp; 10-23 Motomachi; ⊙ 9am-4pm) speak little English but have some English-language publications to share.

If you have a rental car, it's a pleasant 45-minute drive along Rte 158 from Fukui, 30km to the west, to Echizen-Ōno.

By train, take the local JR Kuzuryu line from Fukui Station to Echizen-Ōno Station (¥670, one hour).

Toyama 富山

☑ 076 / POP 418,900

The most likely reason you'll find yourself in Toyama is to take a journey on the Tateyama-Kurobe Alpine Route (p270) or the Hokuriku Shinkansen.

In October 2014 Toyama's picturesque mountain-ringed bay was inducted into the Unesco-endorsed Most Beautiful Bays in the World Club, making it the second bay in Japan to be awarded this prestigious title, recognising both the natural beauty of the bay and its unique ecosystem. Toyama Bay's nutrient-dense waters are fed from nearby mountains and sustain a wide variety of marine life, including the uncommon *hotaruika* (firefly squid) and *shiroebi* (white shrimp).

⊙ Sights

Chōkei-ji   BUDDHIST TEMPLE
(長慶寺; ☑ 076-441-5451; 1882 Goso) This hilltop temple has a wonderful outlook, but you'll come to see the 500-plus stone statues of *rakan* (Buddha's disciples) lined up in the forest.

Kansui Park   PARK
(環水公園; ☑ 076-444-6041; Minatoirifune-chō) This immaculately maintained park built on reclaimed land around Toyama's canal and lock system is a wonderful place for a stroll or a picnic. It's a popular spot with locals in the warmer months and has plenty of attractions such as birdwatching enclaves and lovers' towers to keep you occupied.

Iwase   AREA
North of the city centre is the bayside Iwase neighbourhood, the well-preserved main street of the former shipping business district. Now it's filled with shops and private homes, and even the banks look interesting. Take the Portram light-rail line from Toyama Station's north exit to the terminus, Iwase-hama (¥200, 25 minutes), make a sharp left to cross the canal via Iwase-bashi (岩瀬橋) and you'll see signs in English. You can return via Higashi-Iwase Station on the Portram.

🛏 Sleeping & Eating

Thanks to the arrival of the Hokuriku Shinkansen, Toyama's station area has had a facelift and seen the construction of some new hotels; most are around the south exit.

WORTH A TRIP

KUROBE GORGE RAILWAY

For those wanting to do something a little different, consider the **Kurobe Gorge Railway** (黒部峡谷トロッコ電車; ☑ 0765-62-1011; www.kurotetu.co.jp; 11 Kurobe Kyokoku-guchi, Kurobe; one-way to Keyaki-daira ¥1710; ⊙ 9am-5pm). It is a unique (if not a little bumpy and chilly) exploration into the heart of the Kurobe Valley, running from Unazuki to Keyaki-daira, in tiny train carriages (originally used for the construction of the Kurobe Dam system). When you're not careering through seemingly endless tunnels, the views of the surrounding mountains are breathtaking, especially in autumn, and the opportunity to explore some truly remote and astounding mountain *rotemburo* (outdoor baths) and inns is definitely rewarding.

The new Kurobe Unazuki Onsen Station on the Hokuriku Shinkansen line has dramatically improved access and increased visitor numbers. From Shin-Kurobe Station (adjacent to the *shinkansen* station), catch a local train to Unazuki Onsen Station (¥630, 25 minutes), from where it's a short walk to Unazuki Station, terminus of the Kurobe Gorge Railway.

You must purchase tickets for each leg of the journey separately at each station; due to high passenger demand, this is not a hop-on, hop-off service. The entire journey from Unazuki to Keyaki-daira takes about 80 minutes. It's suggested you take the full journey, and, along the way, decide which stops you'd like to get off at on the way back. For full details on how to get there, what to see and how it works, refer to the website.

The remote **Kuronagi-onsen** is a must-see: look out for bears along the path. Also recommended is the **Iwa-buro** cave bath, a short walk from Kanetsuri Station. The restaurant at Keyaki-daira can get very busy at times – bring sandwiches and snacks with you for the journey, as well as some warm clothing: even in summer it can get very chilly in the tunnels.

Be sure to sit on the right side of the train for the outbound journey from Unazuki, and the left side of the train coming back, or you'll miss the best photo-ops and develop resentment towards your neighbouring passengers: carriages are allocated, but seats aren't reserved and it's first-come first-served.

Be sure to sample the plethora of seafood restaurants outside the station's south exit.

Toyama Excel Hotel Tōkyū HOTEL ¥¥¥
(富山エクセルホテル東急; ☑ 076-441-0109; www.toyama-e.tokyuhotels.co.jp; 1-2-3 Shintomi-chō; s/d from ¥11,900/19,400; ᴾ❄@) Toyama's fanciest digs has 210 rooms in a variety of configurations and two restaurants. Rooms on higher floors have fantastic views.

Shiroebi-tei SEAFOOD ¥¥
(白えび亭; ☑ 076-432-7575; www.shiroebiya.co.jp; 1-220 Meirin-cho; meal sets from ¥1200; ⊙ 10am-8pm; 📖) Locals swear by this workman-like institution on the 3rd floor of Toyama Station. The staple is *shiroebi ten-don* (white shrimp tempura over rice; ¥740). There's a picture menu.

❶ Information

Tourist Information Center (観光案内所; ☑ 076-432-9751; www.info-toyama.com; ⊙ 8.30am-8pm) Inside Toyama Station this office stocks maps and pamphlets on Toyama and the Tateyama-Kurobe Alpine Route. Some

English is spoken and bicycles can be rented for free.

❶ Getting There & Away

AIR

Daily flights operate between **Toyama Airport** (TOY; www.toyama-airport.co.jp/english) and major Japanese cities, with less frequent flights to Seoul and Shanghai.

BUS

Buses are available between Toyama, Takaoka and Gokayama; see www.info-toyama.com for details.

TRAIN

The Hokuriku Shinkansen connects Toyama with Kanazawa (¥2810, 20 minutes), Nagano (¥6900, one hour) and Tokyo (¥12,210, 2¾ hours).

The JR Takayama line runs south to Takayama (*tokkyū* ¥2770, 90 minutes) and Nagoya (*tokkyū* ¥6930, four hours). The JR Hokuriku line runs west to Kanazawa (*tokkyū* ¥2100, 39 minutes; *futsū* ¥950, one hour) and Osaka (*tokkyū* ¥7980, 3¼ hours), and northeast to Niigata (¥6620, three hours).

THE NORTHERN JAPAN ALPS
北日本アルプス

Boasting some of Japan's most dramatic scenery, the Northern Japan Alps of Gifu, Toyama and Nagano Prefectures contain stunning peaks above 3000m, accessible even to amateur hikers. Also called the Hida Ranges, the most spectacular scenery is protected within the 1743-sq-km Chūbu-Sangaku National Park (中部山岳国立公園). Highlights include hiking the valleys and peaks of Kamikōchi, doing it easy on the Shin-Hotaka Ropeway (p244) and soaking up the splendour of Hida's many mountain *rotemburo*.

Matsumoto, in the centre of north–south sprawling Nagano Prefecture, is the gateway city for the northern alps and also a worthwhile destination in its own right. It boasts a fantastic, original castle and some fine art museums.

❶ Information

Be sure you have enough cash before setting out for the mountains: to say that ATMs are scarce is an understatement.

❶ Getting There & Around

Matsumoto is the key transport hub of the region. **Shinshū Matsumoto Airport** (MMJ; Map p173; www.matsumoto-airport.co.jp) services a handful of domestic destinations.

The Matsumoto region is connected by highway buses to Tokyo (Shinjuku), Osaka, Nagoya and Kanazawa.

JR's *tokkyū* Super Azusa's trains link the region to Tokyo (Shinjuku) and Nagano, and *tokkyū* Shinano trains twist their way through the mountains, onward to Nagoya.

From Matsumoto travel is by bus, or a ride on the private Matsumoto Dentetsu train to Shin-Shimashima (don't you just love that name? It means 'new island island'!) and then a bus. Either way, the journey is breathtaking.

Within the Alps, schedules change seasonally. Alpico's 'Alps-wide Free Passport' (¥10,290) gives you four days unlimited travel on its network within Shinshu, the Chūbu-Sangaku National Park and Hida (including Shirakawa-gō).

Tourist Information Centers within the region will happily direct you to the latest schedules and fares, or check www.alpico.co.jp.

Hiring a car is a good option if winding roads don't bother you and you're not overnighting in

Kamikōchi – the road between Naka-no-yu and Kamikōchi is open only to buses and taxis.

Matsumoto 松本
☎ 0263 / POP 243,383

Embraced by seven great peaks to the west (including Yariga-take, Hotaka-dake and Norikura-dake, each above 3000m) and three smaller sentinels to the east (including beautiful Utsukushi-ga-hara-kōgen), Matsumoto occupies a protected position in a fertile valley no more than 20km across at its widest. Views of the regal Alps are never far away and sunsets are truly breathtaking.

Formerly known as Fukashi, Nagano Prefecture's second-largest city has been here since the 8th century. In the 14th and 15th centuries it was the castle town of the Ogasawara clan and it continued to prosper through the Edo period to the present.

Today, popular with young Japanese seeking a tree-change and perhaps signalling a new trend of rural repopulation, Matsumoto is one of Japan's finest cities – an attractive, cosmopolitan place loved by its residents. Admirers from around the world come to enjoy its superb castle, pretty streets, galleries, cafes and endearing vistas.

◉ Sights

◉ Matsumoto-jō & Around

★**Matsumoto-jō** CASTLE
(松本城; Map p268; ☎ 0263-32-9202; www.matsumoto-castle.jp; 4-1 Marunōchi; adult/child ¥610/420; ⊙ 8.30am-5pm early Sep–mid-Jul, to 6pm mid-Jul–early Sep) Must-see Matsumoto-jō is Japan's oldest wooden castle and one of four castles designated National Treasures – the others are Hikone, Himeji and Inuyama. The striking black-and-white three-turreted *donjon* (main keep) was completed around 1595, earning the nickname Karasu-jō (Crow Castle). You can climb steep steps all the way to the top, with impressive views and historical displays on each level. Don't miss the recently restored *tsukimi yagura* (moon-viewing pavilion). The **Goodwill Guide Group** (☎ 0263-32-7140) offers free one-hour tours by reservation.

Admission includes entry to Matsumoto City Museum of Art.

Matsumoto

Matsumoto City Museum of Art MUSEUM
(松本市美術館, Matsumoto-shi Bijutsukan; Map
p284; ☎0263-39-7400; www.matsumoto-art
muse.jp; 4-2-22 Chūō; adult/child ¥410/200;
⊙9am-5pm Tue-Sun) This sleek museum has
a good collection of Japanese artists, many
of whom hail from Matsumoto or whose
works depict scenes of the surrounding
countryside. Highlights include the striking
avant-garde works of local-born, internationally renowned Kusama Yayoi.

Former Kaichi School MUSEUM
(旧開智学校, Kyū Kaichi Gakkō; Map p284;
☎0263-32-5275; 2-4-12 Kaichi; adult/child
¥300/150; ⊙8.30am-4.30pm daily Mar-Nov,
Tue-Sun Dec-Feb) A few blocks north of the
castle, the former Kaichi School is both an
Important Cultural Property and the oldest
elementary school in Japan, founded in
1873. It opened its doors as an education
museum in 1965. The building itself is an
excellent example of Meiji-era architecture.

◉ Nakamachi 中町

The charming former merchant district of
Nakamachi by the Metoba-gawa, with its
namako-kabe kura (lattice-walled storehouses) and Edo-period streetscapes, makes
for a wonderful stroll. Many buildings have

been preserved and transformed into cafes, galleries and craft shops specialising in
wood, glass, fabric, ceramics and antiques.

Nawate-dōri AREA
(縄手道り; Map p268) Nawate-dōri, a few
blocks from the castle, is a popular place for
a stroll. Vendors along this riverside walk sell
antiques, souvenirs and delicious *tai-yaki*
(filled waffles in the shape of a carp) of varying flavours. Look for the big frog statue by
the bridge.

Matsumoto Timepiece Museum MUSEUM
(松本市時計博物館, Matsumoto-shi Tokei
Hakubutsukan; Map p268; ☎0263-36-0969; 4-21-
15 Chūō; adult/student ¥300/150; ⊙9am-5pm
Tue-Sun) Home to Japan's largest pendulum
clock (on the building's exterior) and over
300 other timepieces including fascinating
medieval Japanese creations, this museum

shows Japan's love of *monozukuri,* the art of creating things.

◉ Around Matsumoto

Northeast of downtown, **Utsukushi-ga-hara Onsen** (美ヶ原温泉; not to be confused with Utsukushi-ga-hara-kōgen) is a pretty spa village, with a quaint main street and views across the valley. **Asama Onsen** (浅間温泉) has a history that is said to date back to the 10th century and includes writers and poets, though it looks quite generic now. Both areas are easily reached by bus from Matsumoto's bus terminal.

To the east of Matsumoto, the stunning alpine plateau of **Utsukushi-ga-hara-kōgen** (美ヶ原高原; 2000m) boasts over 200 varieties of flora that come alive in the summer. It's a great day trip from Matsumoto, reached via an ooh-and-aah drive along twisty mountain roads called Azalea Line and Venus Line (open late April to early November). A car will give you the freedom to explore the beauty, but there's also a bus in season (¥1500 one way, 1½ hours).

Utsukushi-ga-hara
Open Air Museum   MUSEUM
(美ヶ原美術館, Utsukushi-ga-hara Bijutsukan; Map p284; ☏ 0263-86-2331; www.utsukushi-oam.jp; adult/child/student ¥1000/700/800; ◐9am-5pm late Apr-early Nov) Atop Utsukushi-ga-hara-kōgen plateau you'll find this seemingly random sculpture garden with some 350 pieces, mostly by Japanese sculptors. The surrounding countryside provides an inspiring backdrop. Nearby are pleasant walks and the opportunity to see cows in pasture (a constant source of fascination in Japan). Buses (¥1500, 1½ hours) run several times daily during the warmer months, although a rental car is a good option if winding roads don't faze you.

Japan Ukiyo-e Museum   MUSEUM
(日本浮世絵美術館; Map p284; ☏ 0263-47-4440; www.japan-ukiyoe-museum.com; 2206-1 Koshiba; adult/child ¥1200/600; ◐10am-5pm Tue-Sun) Housing more than 100,000 woodblock prints, paintings, screens and old books, this renowned museum exhibits but a fraction of its collection. The museum is approximately 3km from JR Matsumoto Station (about ¥1600 by taxi) or 15 minutes' walk from Ōniwa Station on the Matsumoto Dentetsu line (¥180, six minutes).

Matsumoto Open-Air
Architectural Museum   MUSEUM
(松本市歴史の里, Matsumoto-shi Rekishi-no-sato; Map p284; ☏ 0263-47-4515; 2196-1 Shimadachi; adult/child ¥400/300; ◐9am-4.30pm Tue-Sun) Adjacent to the better-known Japan Ukiyo-e Museum, amid fields and rice paddies beneath the gaze of the Alps, stand these five examples of striking late Edo- and early Shōwa-era architecture for you to explore. The museum is approximately 3km from JR Matsumoto Station (about ¥1600 by taxi) or 15 minutes' walk from Ōniwa Station on the Matsumoto Dentetsu line (¥180, six minutes).

✸ Festivals & Events

Locals love to celebrate – you're never far from a festival here.

Matsumoto-jō Sakura Matsuri   CULTURAL
(松本城桜祭り; ◐Apr) Three days after the cherry blossoms are declared in full bloom (early April), the castle and its *sakura* trees are illuminated spectacularly and entry to the inner compound is free.

Matsumoto-jō Taiko Matsuri   MUSIC
(松本城太鼓祭り; ◐Jul) The castle grounds and beyond ring out with the sound and energy of *taiko* drumming during this awesome festival, held the balmy last weekend of July.

Matsumoto Bonbon   PARADE
(松本ぼんぼん; ◐Aug) Matsumoto's biggest event takes place on the first Saturday in August, when over 25,000 people of all ages perform the 'bonbon' dance through the streets, well into the hot summer's night. Be prepared to be drawn into the action.

Takigi Nō Matsuri   THEATRE
(薪能まつり; ◐Aug) This atmospheric festival features outdoor *nō* performances (a stylised dance-drama performed on a bare stage) by torchlight in the park below the castle.

Saitō Kinen Festival   MUSIC
(サイトウ・キネン・フェスティバル松本; www.saito-kinen.com; ◐mid-Aug–mid-Sep) About a dozen classical music concerts are held in memory of revered Japanese conductor and music educator Saitō Hideo (1902–72) from mid-August to mid-September. Ozawa Seiji, conductor emeritus of the Boston Symphony Orchestra, is festival director.

Asama Onsen Taimatsu Matsuri   PARADE
(浅間温泉松明祭り; ◐Oct) Around the start of October, Asama Onsen celebrates the spectacular and slightly manic fire festival,

wherein groups of men, women and children, shouting 'wa-sshoi!', like a mantra, parade burning bales of hay through narrow streets to an enormous bonfire at Misha-jinja.

🛏 Sleeping

⭐ Nunoya   INN ¥

(ぬのや旅館; Map p268; ☎ 0263-32-0545; www. mcci.or.jp/www/nunoya; 3-5-7 Chūō; r per person from ¥4500; ❀✳🅟) Few inns have more heart than this simple, traditional charmer, meticulously kept by its friendly owner. The spotless lodgings have shiny dark-wood floors and atmospheric tatami rooms. No meals are served, but you're right in the heart of the best part of town. If you don't mind sharing a bathroom, the rate is a bargain for this much character.

Marumo   RYOKAN ¥

(まるも; Map p268; ☎ 0263-32-0115; www.avis.ne. jp/~marumo; 3-3-10 Chūō; r per person ¥5250; 🅟) Between Nakamachi and the river, this creaky wooden ryokan dates from 1868 and has lots of traditional charm, including a bamboo garden and coffee shop. Although the rooms aren't huge and don't have private facilities, it's quite popular, so book ahead.

Seifūsō   RYOKAN ¥

(静風荘; Map p284; ☎ 0263-46-0639; www. ryokanseifuso.jp; 634-5 Minami-asama; s/d from

---

TATEYAMA-KUROBE ALPINE ROUTE

From mid-April to mid-November, the popular seasonal 90km Tateyama-Kurobe Alpine Route (立山黒部アルペンルート) connects Tateyama (Toyama Prefecture) with Shinano-ōmachi (Nagano Prefecture) via a sacred mountain, a deep gorge, a boiling-hot spring and glory-hallelujah mountain scenery. It's divided into nine sections, with different modes of transport including your own two feet. Reservations are *strongly* advised.

Travel is possible in either direction; as the route is often only travelled one way, we'd suggest using the route to travel between Kanazawa/Toyama and Matsumoto. Full details can be found online at www.alpen-route.com. There are hundreds of steps en route and plenty of walking. Be sure to forward your baggage to your destination hotel before you set off (details on the website).

The fare for the entire route is ¥10,850 one way or ¥18,260 return; tickets for individual sections are available. It takes at least six hours, one way. If you're starting in Toyama and not heading to Matsumoto, you may find a return trip to Murodō (¥6710), the route's highest point (2450m), sufficient.

Start the journey before 9am at Dentetsu Toyama Station on the chug-a-lug regional Toyama Chiho line bound for Tateyama (¥1200, one hour). The first stage of the route is the cable car up to **Bijodaira** (美女平; seven minutes).

Next is a bus journey up to **Murodō** (室堂; 50 minutes) via the spectacular alpine plateau of **Midagahara Kōgen**, where you can break the trip and do the 15-minute walk to see **Tateyama caldera** (立山カルデラ), the largest nonactive crater in Japan. The upper part of the plateau is often covered with deep snow well into spring; snowploughs keep the road clear by pushing walls of snow to each side of the road, forming a virtual tunnel of ice.

Ten minutes' walk from Murodō is **Mikuri-ga-ike** (みくりが池) pond, where you'll find Japan's highest *onsen ryokan* (www.mikuri.com). Twenty minutes further on is **Jigokudani Onsen** (Hell Valley Hot Springs) – no bathing here, the waters are boiling! To the east, you can make the steep two-hour hike to the peak of **O-yama** (雄山; 3003m) for an astounding panorama. Experienced and equipped long-distance hikers can continue south to Kamikōchi.

When you're ready, board the trolley bus that tunnels through Mt Tateyama for 3.7km to **Daikanbō** (10 minutes). From here, the Tateyama Ropeway whisks you 488m down to **Kurobe-daira** (seven minutes) with breathtaking views of the valley. You're free to stop between sections at your own pace, or go with the flow of the crowds. The next step is the underground Kurobe cable car to **Kurobeko** (¥840, five minutes). You'll emerge to see the massive **Kurobe Dam**: it's a 15-minute walk across it to the impressive observation deck.

When you're ready to proceed, trolley buses (16 minutes) whisk you through a 5.8km tunnel to the end of your journey at **Ogizawa**. From here there's one last bus to **Shinano-ōmachi Station** (40 minutes; elevation 712m) – you made it!

Continue on to Azumino, Matsumoto or beyond at your leisure...

¥4390/8580; P @) Free pick-up (arrange in advance) and free bikes make up for the fact that this inn is closer to Asama Onsen than Matsumoto. It's run by a friendly family who love to welcome overseas guests. Japanese-style rooms are clean and bright, with a nice outlook and shared baths. Once you're there, take bus 2 to get back into town.

Matsumoto BackPackers
HOSTEL ¥
(Map p284; ☎ 0263-31-5848; www.matsumotobp.com; Shiraita 1-1-6; dm per person ¥3000; ✳ ☎) By the river, just a few minutes' walk from JR Matsumoto Station, you'll find this clean, friendly addition to the Matsumoto traveller's scene. These are the cheapest, most central dorm beds in town.

★ Marunouchi Hotel
HOTEL ¥¥
(丸の内ホテル; Map p268; ☎ 0263-35-4500; www.matsumoto-marunouchi.com; 3-5-15 Ōte; s/d from ¥6400/10,800; ✳ ☎) It's hard to fault this new hotel, occupying a prime spot near the castle. Right-priced rooms are refreshingly stylish and comfortable. Deluxe rooms approach Western standard sizes at 27 sq metres; standard rooms are more compact, but cheaper; while suites are a nice option for those wanting something special. Some rooms even have views of the castle.

★ Richmond Hotel
HOTEL ¥¥
(リッチモンドホテル松本; Map p268; ☎ 0263-37-5000; www.richmondhotel.jp; 1-10-7 Chūō; s/d from ¥7500/10,500; P ⊖ @) A few minutes' walk from JR Matsumoto Station, this 204-room business hotel is in great shape and in a great location. The deluxe double rooms are large by Japanese standards, and reasonably priced. There's a Gusto family restaurant (with picture menu) downstairs.

Dormy Inn Matsumoto
HOTEL ¥¥
(ドーミーイン松本; Map p268; ☎ 0263-33-5489; www.hotespa.net/hotels/matsumoto; 2-2-1 Fukashi; s/d from ¥5990/8590; P ✳ @) This newer property has compact, well-designed rooms with pleasant, neutral decor. There's an onsen featuring a sunny *rotemburo* and the breakfast buffet is decent. Otherwise, there's everything travellers need, including a good location and a functional laundry. Deals can be found online (in Japanese).

Sugimoto
RYOKAN ¥¥¥
(旅館すぎもと; Map p284; ☎ 0263-32-3379; www.ryokan-sugimoto.com; 451-7 Satoyamabe; r per person from ¥16,000; ✳ ☎; ⬚ Utsukushigahara Onsen line, Town Sneaker North Course) A lack of English-speaking staff at this upscale ryokan in Utsukushi-ga-hara Onsen may be its only downfall for non-Japanese speakers. With some fascinating elements, such as the art collection, underground passageway and bar full of single malts, this is a unique property. Rooms range in size and decor, but all are ineffably stylish and the cuisine is, appropriately, top-notch.

Hotel Buena Vista
HOTEL ¥¥¥
(ホテルブエナビスタ; Map p268; ☎ 0263-37-0111; www.buena-vista.co.jp; 1-2-1 Honjō; s/tw from ¥9760/19,740; P ✳ ✳ @ ☎) An oldie but a goodie – Matsumoto's sharpest Western hotel recently received a makeover in its public spaces and rooms, leaving it looking quite the part. The executive rooms and the suites are the way to go, if you're going to do it. Many rooms have exceptional views.

🍴 Eating

Menshō Sakura
RAMEN ¥
(麺匠佐蔵; Map p268; ☎ 0263-34-1050; 1-20-26 Chūō; ramen from ¥760; ⏱ 11.30am-3pm & 5.30-10pm) Miso and ramen fans should not go past this purveyor of fine noodles. *Miso-rāmen* and black *Kuro-miso rāmen* are the specialities of the house: both rank highly. The *gyōza* (dumplings) are crunchy and the beer is cold. Ask the friendly staff for help with the vending machine if you get stuck.

Delhi
JAPANESE CURRY ¥
(デリー; Map p268; ☎ 0263-35-2408; 2-4-13 Chūō; curry with rice ¥660-880; ⏱ 11.30am-6pm Thu-Tue; 🍴) One of our favourites, this little 'ma and pa' outfit has been serving delicious curry rice (Japanese style) in an adorable former storehouse by the river since 1970. If you like *tonkatsu* (deep-fried pork cutlets), you must try the *katsu karē* (pork cutlet, curry and rice). Cheap and cheerful.

Kane
TAIWANESE ¥
(香根; Map p268; ☎ 0263-36-1303; 2-8-5 Ōte; dishes ¥750-1100; ⏱ 5.30pm-2am; 🍴🍴) This simple Taiwanese eatery near the castle serves amazing spicy soups, noodles and veggies, as well as the standard array of Chinese fare at very reasonable prices. There's a picture menu.

Tōfu Ryōri Marui
TOFU ¥
(とうふ料理まるゐ; Map p268; ☎ 0263-46-0635; ESPA 7F, 1-2-30 Fukashi; set menus from ¥880; ⏱ 10am-9pm) On the 7th floor of the ESPA building opposite JR Matsumoto Station you'll find this outpost of an Asama Onsen

family business that has been making tofu for over 80 years. Lovers of the food's versatility will appreciate this delicious cuisine, but don't make the assumption that all dishes are vegetarian. Try the *agedashi teishoku* (fried silken tofu set menu).

Look for the orange and white *noren* (curtain).

Shizuka   IZAKAYA ¥

(しづか; Map p268; ☑0263-32-0547; 4-10-8 Ōte; plates from ¥480; ☺noon-11pm Mon-Sat; 📷) This wonderfully traditional *izakaya* serves favourites such as *oden* (a stew comprising fishcakes, tofu, vegetables and eggs simmered in a kelp-flavoured broth) and *yakitori* (grilled skewers of meat or vegetables), as well as some more challenging specialities…

Matsumoto Karaage Center   JAPANESE ¥¥

(松本からあげセンター; Map p268; ☑0263-87-2229; www.karacen.com; 1-1-1 Fukashi; lunch & dinner sets ¥780-1500; ☺10am-8.30pm) If you like *karaage* (deep-fried chicken), this standing-room-only shrine to the humble chook is a must, with tender, juicy boneless chicken pieces waiting to melt in your mouth. Enjoy it with a hearty serve of chicken-broth ramen or perhaps a crunchy chicken *katsu*.

Nomugi   NOODLES ¥¥

(野麦; Map p268; ☑0263-36-3753; 2-9-11 Chūō; soba from ¥1100; ☺11.30am-5pm Thu-Mon; 🖉) In Nakamachi, this is one of central Japan's finest soba shops. Its owner used to run a French restaurant in Tokyo before returning to his home town. Keeping things Zen, there are two dishes: *zaru-soba* (buckwheat noodles cold with dipping sauce) and *kake-soba* (buckwheat noodles in hot broth). Oh, and beer.

🍷 Drinking & Nightlife

Beer Garage Ganesha   CRAFT BEER

(Map p268; ☑0263-34-0665; www.beergarage ganesha.com; 2F Imai Bldg, 1-2-19 Chūō; ☺6.30pm-2am) A Belgian beer bar overlooked by Lord Ganesha, the Hindu 'God for every man', in the Japanese Alps. Quirky, but it works.

Old Rock   PUB

(オールドロック; Map p268; ☑0263-38-0069; 2-30-20 Chūō; mains from ¥750; ☺11.30am-2.30pm & 6pm-midnight) In the perfect spot a block south of the river, across from Nakamachi, you'll find this popular pub with good lunch specials and, appropriately, a wide range of beers.

Coat   BAR

(メインバーコート; Map p268; ☑0263-34-7133; 2-3-24 Chūō; ☺6pm-12.30am Mon-Sat) This sophisticated little whisky bar is run by a colourful character who'd love to pour you a single malt or one of his original cocktails.

🛍 Shopping

Matsumoto is synonymous with *temari* (embroidered balls) and doll-making. Takasago street, one block south of Nakamachi, has several doll shops. **Parco Department Store** is unmissable in the city centre.

Chikiri-ya   GLASS

(ちきりや; Map p268; ☑0263-33-2522; 3-4-18 Chūō; ☺9am-5pm) Glass and pottery aficionados will find this wonderful boutique a must.

Nakamachi Kura-chic-kan   ARTS & CRAFTS

(中町・蔵シック館; Map p268; ☑0263-36-3053; 2-9-15 Chūō; ☺9am-5pm) A pun on 'classic' in English, 'kura' in Japanese and 'chic' in French, Nakamachi Kura-chic-kan showcases locally produced arts and crafts.

Belle Amie   ARTS & CRAFTS

(ベラミ; Map p268; ☑0263-33-1314; 3-7-23 Chūō; ☺10am-6pm) *Temari* and dolls are found here. Doll styles include Tanabata and *oshie-bina* (dressed in fine cloth).

ℹ Information

TOURIST INFORMATION

Online, visit http://welcome.city.matsumoto.nagano.jp.

Matsumoto Tourist Information Center (松本市観光案内所; Map p268; ☑0263-32-2814; 1-1-1 Fukashi; ☺9.30am-5.45pm) This excellent TIC inside JR Matsumoto Station has friendly English-speaking staff and a wide range of well-produced English language materials on the area.

TRAVEL AGENCIES

JTB (Map p268; ☑0263-35-3311; 1-2-11 Fukashi; ☺10am-6pm Mon-Sat) For train and bus reservations.

ℹ Getting There & Away

AIR

Shinshū Matsumoto Airport (MMJ; Map p173; www.matsumoto-airport.co.jp) has daily flights to Fukuoka, Osaka and Sapporo.

BUS

Alpico (www.alpico.co.jp) runs buses between Matsumoto and Shinjuku in Tokyo (¥3400, 3¼ hours, 24 daily), Osaka (¥5850, 5¾ hours, two daily; one longer overnight service) and Nagoya (from ¥3600, 3½ hours, 10 daily). **Nōhi Bus** (p230) services Takayama (¥3900, 2½ hours, at least six daily). Reservations are advised. The **Matsumoto Bus Terminal** (Map p268) is in the basement of the ESPA building opposite JR Matsumoto Station.

CAR & MOTORCYCLE

Renting a car is a great way to explore the beauty outside town, but expect narrow, winding roads. There are several agencies around the train station. Rates start at around ¥6500 per day.

TRAIN

'Matsumotooo...Matsumotooo...' is connected with Tokyo's Shinjuku Station (*tokkyū* ¥6380, 2¾ hours, hourly), Nagoya (*tokkyū* ¥5510, two hours) and Nagano (Shinano *tokkyū* ¥2320, 50 minutes; Chūō *futsū* ¥1140, 1¼ hours). There are also infrequent direct services to Osaka (*tokkyū* ¥8850, 4½ hours).

ⓘ Getting Around

Matsumoto-jō and the city centre are easily covered on foot and free bicycles are available for loan – enquire at the Tourist Information Center. Three 'Town Sneaker' loop bus routes operate between 9am and 5.30pm for ¥200 per ride (¥500 per day); the blue and orange routes cover the castle and Nakamachi.

An airport shuttle bus connects Shinshū Matsumoto Airport with downtown (¥600, 25 minutes); a taxi costs around ¥5000.

Azumino 安曇野

📞 0263 / POP 95,297

The city of Azumino was formed in 2005, when the towns of Toyoshina, Hotaka, Akashina and three smaller villages amalgamated. It's also the traditional name of the picturesque valley in which they're located. An easy day trip from Matsumoto, the area is home to Japan's largest wasabi farm and is a popular starting point for mountain hikes.

⊙ Sights

Dai-ō Wasabi-Nōjo FARM
(大王わさび農場; 📞 0263-82-2118; www.daiowasabi.co.jp; 3640 Hotaka; ⊙9am-5pm) **FREE** Fancy some wasabi beer? This farm, a 15-minute bike ride from JR Hotaka Station, is de rigueur for wasabi lovers. An English map guides you among wasabi plants (130 tonnes of wasabi are grown in flooded fields here annually) amid rolling hills, restaurants, shops and work spaces. It's a fascinating and lovely place for a stroll and best of all, it's free!

Rokuzan Bijutsukan GALLERY
(碌山美術館; 📞 0263-82-2094; www.rokuzan.jp; 5095-1 Hotaka; adult/child ¥700/300; ⊙9am-4pm daily May-Oct, Tue-Sun Nov-Apr) Ten minutes' walk from JR Hotaka Station, Rokuzan Bijutsukan showcases the work of Meiji-era sculptor Rokuzan Ogiwara (aka 'Rodin of the Orient') and his Japanese contemporaries in a delightful garden setting.

NORTHERN JAPAN ALPS SAMPLE BUS FARES & DURATIONS

FROM	TO	FARE (¥, ONE WAY)	DURATION (MINUTES, ONE WAY)
Takayama	Hirayu Onsen	1570	55
	Kamikōchi	2720	80
	Shin-Hotaka	2160	90
Matsumoto	Shin-Shimashima	700 (train)	30
	Kamikōchi	2650	95
Shin-Shimashima	Naka-no-yu	1700	50
	Kamikōchi	1950	70
	Shirahone Onsen	1450	75
Kamikōchi	Naka-no-yu	770	15
	Hirayu Onsen	1160	25
	Shirahone Onsen	1350	35
Hirayu Onsen	Naka-no-yu	580	10
	Shin-Hotaka	920	30

WORTH A TRIP

A NIGHT ABOVE THE CLOUDS

If you're looking for something a little bit different, along the lines of isolation and indulgence, there are two very special places to rest your weary head in the mountains above Matsumoto. From April to November, consider a night at the singular **Ougatou Hotel** (王ヶ頭ホテル; Map p284; ☑0263-31-2751; www.ougatou.jp; d per person incl 2 meals from ¥16,500; 🅿✳🛜) atop the beautiful Utsukushi-ga-hara-kōgen. Rooms are plush, comfy and reasonably priced for their standard. Oversized suites have decadent baths overlooking the plateau and the cloud line: you'll think you're on Cloud Nine as you wake.

For something a little pricier, fancier and more traditional, the exclusive **Tobira Onsen Myōjin-kan** (扉温泉明神館; Map p284; ☑0263-31-2301; http://myojinkan.tobira-group.com; 8967 Iriyamabe; s/d per person incl 2 meals from ¥32,500/26,000; 🅿✳🛜) has been nestled quietly in the mountains above Matsumoto (on the way to Utsukushi-ga-hara-kōgen) since 1931. There's a variety of room types: many have private onsen baths, and each enjoys wonderful vistas of the natural surrounds. The communal indoor and outdoor baths will leave you feeling like you're floating on air. For your investment, expect nothing less than exquisite French cuisine and *kaiseki* (Japanese haute cuisine) and the epitome of customer service.

Both rare gems are best enjoyed with cash in your wallet and the freedom of a rental car.

🏃 Activities

Jōnen-dake   HIKING

(常念岳) From JR Hotaka Station it's 30 minutes by taxi (around ¥5000) to reach the Ichinosawa trailhead, from where experienced hikers can climb Jōnen-dake (2857m); the ascent takes about 5½ hours. There are many options for hikes extending over several days, but you must be properly prepared. Hiking maps are available at the Tourist Information Center, although the detailed ones are in Japanese.

🛏 Sleeping & Eating

★ Nakabusa Onsen   RYOKAN ¥¥

(中房温泉; ☑0263-77-1488; www.nakabusa.com; 7226 Nakabusa; r per person incl 2 meals from ¥9800; ☉Apr-Nov; 🅿) With over a dozen indoor, outdoor and sand baths, this rambling resort at the end of a twisty mountain road to nowhere will delight anyone seeking a peaceful retreat. The older *honkan* wing has basic rooms, while the newer *bekkan* wing is more comfortable. In late autumn gawk at stunningly colourful foliage against the backdrop of snowcapped peaks.

Day trippers can use one of the smaller *rotemburo* (¥700) between 9.30am and 4pm. Enquire at the Tourist Information Center for the limited bus schedule (¥1700, one hour) from Azumino to Nakabusa Onsen, or rent a car (and bring your nerves of steel).

★ Oyado Nagomino   RYOKAN ¥¥¥

(お宿なごみ野; ☑0263-81-5566; www.oyado-nagomino.com; 3618-44 Hotaka-ariake; r per person incl 2 meals from ¥19,440; 🅿✳🛜) In a lovely forested setting, this attractive modern ryokan is a little oasis on the way to Nakabusa Onsen. Although little English is spoken, the staff go to great lengths to ensure you have a pleasant stay. Guest rooms are typically styled, but the real draw here are the delightful communal baths and the exceptional locavore *kaiseki* cuisine, with seasonal menus.

Good Old Land   CAFE ¥

(☑0263-50-5085; www.goodoldland.com; 7542-85 Hotaka-ariake; items from ¥450; ☉10am-5pm Thu-Mon) The mostly locally sourced ingredients used to make such homely favourites as grandma's macaroni au gratin and hot-chilli brownies are preservative-free and often organic. The food seems to fit perfectly with the fabulous foresty vibe and the general glee of your good old hosts.

❶ Information

Tourist Information Center (観光案内所; ☑0263-82-9363; www.azumino-e-tabi.net; 5952-3 Hotaka; ☉9am-5pm Apr-Nov, 10am-4pm Dec-Mar) This friendly, home-proud tourist office opposite JR Hotaka Station has helpful English-speaking staff and rents out bicycles – a great way to explore the area. Be sure to check out the excellent English homepage.

ⓘ Getting There & Away

Hotaka is the gateway city to the Azumino valley. JR Hotaka Station is 28 minutes (*futsū* ¥320) from Matsumoto on the JR Ōito line.

Shirahone Onsen 白骨温泉

☏ 0263

Intimate, dramatic and straddling a deep gorge, Shirahone Onsen is one of Japan's most beautiful onsen hamlets – heavenly during autumn and a wonderland in winter. *Onsen ryokan* (traditional hot-spring inns) with open-air baths surround the gorge. It is said that bathing in the silky, milky-blue hydrogen-sulphide waters of Shirahone (meaning 'white bone') for three days ensures three years without a cold.

🏃 Activities

Kōkyō Notemburo ONSEN
(公共野天風呂; ☏ 0263-93-3251; ¥510; ⊗ 8.30am-5pm Apr-Nov) This riverside *rotemburo*, deep within the gorge at Shirahone Onsen, is separated by gender; the entrance is by the bus stop.

🛌 Sleeping

Tsuruya Ryokan RYOKAN ¥¥
(つるや旅館; ☏ 0263-93-2331; www.shirahone tsuruya.com; 4202-6 Shirahone Onsen; r per person incl 2 meals from ¥14,040; Ⓟ) Lovely Tsuruya Ryokan has both contemporary and traditional touches and great indoor and outdoor baths. Each of its 28 rooms has lovely views of the gorge; rooms with private toilet and sink are available for an extra charge. Book in advance.

★ Awanoyu Ryokan RYOKAN ¥¥¥
(泡の湯旅館; ☏ 0263-93-2101; www.awanoyu-ryokan.com; 4181 Shirahone Onsen; r per person incl 2 meals from ¥28,000; Ⓟ) Awanoyu Ryokan typifies mountain *onsen ryokan*. Uphill from Shirahone, it has been an inn since 1912 (the current building dates from 1940). Light-filled guest rooms have private facilities. There are also single-sex common baths and *konyoku* (mixed bathing): the waters are so milky that you can't see below the surface, so don't be shy. Reservations essential.

ⓘ Information

Tourist Information Center (白骨温泉観光案内所; ☏ 0263-93-3251; www.shirahone.org; 4197-4 Azumino; ⊗ 9am-5pm) The TIC maintains a list of inns that open their baths (admission from ¥600) to the public each day.

ⓘ Getting There & Away

From Matsumoto, take a train to Shin-Shimashima Station (¥700, 30 minutes) then catch a bus to Shirahone Onsen (¥1450, 70 minutes).

Kamikōchi 上高地

☏ 0260

In the late 19th century, foreigners 'discovered' this mountainous region and coined the term 'Japan Alps'. A British missionary, Reverend Walter Weston, toiled from peak to peak and sparked Japanese interest in mountaineering as a sport. He is now honoured with a festival on the first Sunday in June, the official opening of the hiking season. Kamikōchi has become a base for day trippers, hikers and climbers who come for snowcapped peaks, bubbling brooks, wild monkeys, wildflowers and ancient forests. That said, it wouldn't be Japan without the crowds: timing is everything.

Kamikōchi is closed from 15 November to 22 April; from late July to late August and during the foliage season in October, it can seem busier than Shinjuku Station.

It's perfectly feasible to visit as a day trip but you'll miss out on the pleasures of staying in the mountains and taking uncrowded early-morning or late-afternoon walks.

🏃 Activities

Bokuden-no-yu ONSEN
(卜伝の湯; ☏ 0260-95-2407; www.nakanoyu-onsen.jp/spa; ¥700; ⊗ noon-5pm) Not for the claustrophobic, the area's most unusual onsen – a tiny cave bath dripping with minerals – is found near the Naka-no-yu bus stop, to the left of the bus-only tunnel into Kamikōchi. Pay at the small shop for the key to the little mountain hut housing the onsen. It's yours privately for up to 30 minutes.

🛌 Sleeping & Eating

Accommodation in Kamikōchi is expensive and advance reservations are essential. Some lodgings shut down power in the middle of the night (emergency lighting stays on).

Dotted along the trails and around the mountains are dozens of spartan *yama-goya* (mountain huts), which provide two meals and a futon from around ¥8000 per person; some also serve simple lunches. Be sure to enquire before setting out to make sure there's one on your intended route.

The bus station has a small selection of eateries and beyond that there's little else. Bring essential munchies and take your rubbish with you. Unless you're camping, you'll be dining at your lodge of an evening.

Forest Resort Konashi CAMPGROUND ¥
(森のリゾート小梨, Mori no rizōto Konashi; ☑0260-95-2321; www.nihonalpskankou.com; 4468 Kamikōchi; campsites per person incl 2 meals from ¥800, cabins per person from ¥6000; ☺ office 7am-7pm) About 200m past the Kamikōchi Visitor Centre, this campground can get crowded. Rental tents are available from ¥7000 (July and August) and there's a small shop and restaurant.

Kamikōchi Gosenjaku Hotel & Lodge HOTEL ¥¥
(上高地五千尺ホテル・ロッヂ; ☑hotel 0260-95-2111, lodge 0260-95-2221; www.gosenjaku.co.jp; 4468 Kamikōchi; lodge skier's bed per person incl 2 meals from ¥12,000, hotel r from ¥17,500) By Kappa-bashi this compact lodge has 34 Japanese-style rooms and some 'skier's beds' (basically curtained-off bunks). Rooms all have sink and toilet, but baths are shared. The hotel is more upscale with a combination of comfortable Western and Japanese rooms, some with balconies.

★**Kamikochi Imperial Hotel** HOTEL ¥¥¥
(上高地帝国ホテル; ☑0260-95-2001; www.imperialhotel.co.jp; Azumino Kamikochi; r from ¥30,700; @) Expect exceptional service and rustic, European Alps–styled rooms in this historic red-gabled lodge completed in 1933. Prices are elevated, but a wide range of stay plans are available and the hotel occasionally offers excellent packages including French haute cuisine. You may have to book a year in advance!

Tokusawa-en INN ¥¥¥
(徳澤園; ☑0260-95-2508; www.tokusawaen.com; per person incl 2 meals dm ¥10,000, d from ¥14,900; ☺May-Oct) This is a marvellously secluded place in a wooded dell about 7km northeast of Kappa-bashi. It's both a camping ground (¥500) and a lodge, and has Japanese-style rooms (shared facilities) and hearty meals served in a busy dining hall. Access is by walking only, and takes about two hours.

HIKING & CLIMBING IN KAMIKŌCHI

The Kamikōchi river valley offers mostly level, short-distance, signposted walks.

A recommended four-hour hike begins east of Kappa-bashi, heading past Myōjin-bashi (one hour). By Myōjin-bashi, the idyllic Myōjin-ike (pond) marks the innermost shrine of Hotaka-jinja (admission ¥300). From Myōjin-bashi, continue on to Tokusawa (another hour) before returning the same way.

West of Kappa-bashi, you can amble alongside the river to Weston Relief (monument to Walter Weston; 15 minutes) or to Taishō-ike (40 minutes).

Popular hiking destinations include the mountain hut at Dakesawa (2½ hours up) and fiery Yake-dake (four hours up, starting about 20 minutes west of the Weston Relief, at Hotaka-bashi). From the peaks, it's possible to see all the way to Mt Fuji in clear weather.

Long-distance hikes vary in duration and have access to mountain huts; enquire at the **Tourist Information Center** (p277) for details. Japanese-language maps of the area show routes and average hiking times between huts, major peaks and landmarks. Favourite hikes and climbs (think human traffic jams during peak seasons) include Yariga-take (3180m) and Hotaka-dake (3190m). A stunning but steep hike connects Kamikōchi and Shin-Hotaka. From Kappa-bashi, the trail crosses the ridge below Nishi-Hotaka-dake (2909m) at Nishi-Hotaka Sansō (cottage; three hours) and continues to Nishi-Hotaka-guchi, the top station of the **Shin-Hotaka Ropeway** (p244). The hike takes nearly four hours in this direction but is far easier in reverse. Serious hikers should consider treks to pristine Nakabusa Onsen (three days) or Murodō (five days), the latter being the apex of the Tateyama-Kurobe Alpine Route (p270).

Hikers and climbers should be well prepared. Temperatures can plummet suddenly, sleeting rain or blinding fog set in rapidly and there's no refuge on the peaks during thunderstorms.

In winter, deserted Kamikōchi makes a beautiful cross-country skiing spot for the initiated: hike in from the entrance to the Kama Tunnel on Rte 158.

Kamikōchi Nishi-itoya Sansō INN ¥¥¥
(上高地西糸屋山荘; ☑0260-95-2206; www.
nishiitoya.com; 4469-1 Kamikōchi; per person incl
2 meals dm from ¥8800, d from ¥10,720; ⊕@☎)
This friendly lodge, west of Kappa-bashi, has
a cosy lounge and dates from the early 20th
century. Rooms are a mix of Japanese and
Western styles, all with toilet. The shared
bath is a large onsen facing the Hotaka
mountains.

Kamonji-goya SHOKUDO ¥
(嘉門次小屋; ☑0263-95-2418; www.kamonjigoya.
wordpress.com; dishes from ¥600; ⊙8.30am-4pm;
▥) Kamikōchi's signature dish is *iwana* (river trout) grilled whole over an *irori* (hearth).
This is *the* place to try it. The *iwana* set is
¥1500, or there's *oden* (fish-cake stew), soba
and *kotsu-sake* (dried *iwana* in sake) served
in a lovely ceramic bowl. It's just outside the
entrance to Myōjin-ike.

ⓘ Information

INSURANCE
Serious hikers should consider insurance (保
険, *hoken*; from ¥1000 per day), available at
Kamikōchi bus station.

TOURIST INFORMATION
Kamikōchi Tourist Information Center (上高地
インフォメーションセンター; ☑0260-95-2433;
⊙8am-5pm) This invaluable resource at the bus
station complex provides information on hiking
and weather conditions, and distributes the
English-language *Kamikōchi Pocket Guide* with a
map of the main walking tracks.
Kamikōchi Visitor Centre (上高地ビジター
センター; ☑0260-95-2606; ⊙8am-5pm) Ten
minutes' walk from Kamikōchi bus station along
the main trail, this is the place for information
on Kamikōchi's flora, fauna, geology and history.
You can also book guided walks to destinations
including Taishō-ike and Myōjin-ike (from ¥500
per person). English-speaking nature guides
(from ¥2000 per hour) and climbing guides
(around ¥30,000 a day) may be available.

ⓘ Getting There & Around
Visitors arrive at Kamikōchi's sprawling bus
station. A 10-minute walk along the Azusa-gawa
takes you to Kappa-bashi, a bridge named after a
legendary water sprite.

Private vehicles are prohibited between
Naka-no-yu and Kamikōchi; access is only by
bus or taxi as far as the Kamikōchi bus station.
Those with private cars can use car parks en
route to Naka-no-yu in the hamlet of Sawando
for ¥500 per day; shuttle buses (¥1800 return)
run a few times per hour.

Buses run via Naka-no-yu and Taishō-ike
to the bus station. Hiking trails commence at
Kappa-bashi, which is a short walk from the bus
station.

Hakuba 白馬
☑0261 / POP 8937
At the base of one of the highest sections
of the Northern Japan Alps, Hakuba is one
of Japan's main skiing and hiking centres.
In winter skiers from across Japan, and
increasingly overseas, flock to Hakuba's
seven ski resorts. In summer the region
draws hikers attracted by easy access to the
high peaks. There are many onsen in and
around Hakuba-mura, the main village,
and a long soak after a day of action is the
perfect way to ease your muscles.

The region was struck by a powerful 6.7
magnitude earthquake on 21 November 2014,
causing significant damage to Hakuba and
neighbouring villages, though tourism was
not greatly affected.

🏃 Activities
In summer you can take the gondola and the
two upper chairlifts, then hike along a trail for
an hour or so to Happō-ike on a ridge below
Karamatsu-dake (唐松岳; 2695m). From here,
follow a trail another hour up to Maru-yama,
continue for 1½ hours to the Karamatsu-dake
San-sō (mountain hut) and then climb to the
peak of Karamatsu-dake in about 30 minutes.

★**Tsugaike Nature Park** WALKING
(Map p284; www.tsugaike.gr.jp/english/trekking/
shizenen; Otari-mura; adult/child ¥300/250;
⊙Jun-Nov; ▥) Located in the Chūbu-Sangaku
National Park at an altitude of 1900m, Tsugaike Nature Park is an ideal place for families and novice hikers to experience the
alpine environment. Taking the 'Panorama
Way' gondola and cable car (round-trip
adult/child ¥3600/2050) required to get
there is half the fun.

It's a 5.5km round-trip walk across the
verdant moors from the park entrance to
the observation platform affording majestic
views of snowy Mt Shirouma.

★**Evergreen Outdoor** OUTDOORS
(☑0261-72-5150; www.evergreen-hakuba.com;
4377 Hokujō; half-day tours from ¥4000) This
gang of friendly, outdoorsy folk offers an
array of residential camps and half- to
multiday adventures with English-speaking
guides, year-round. On offer are canyoning,

mountain biking and hiking in the green season as well as snowshoeing and backcountry treks in winter. Visitors in July/August can even take an evening firefly canoe tour!

Happō-One Ski Resort SKIING
(八方尾根スキー所; ☎0261-72-3066; www. happo-one.jp; 1-day lift ticket ¥5200; ☺Dec-Apr) Host of the downhill races at the 1998 Winter Olympics, Happō-One is one of Japan's best ski areas, with superb mountain views and beginner, intermediate and advanced runs catering to skiers and snowboarders. For the low-down, read up on the excellent English-language homepage.

With a total of 23 lifts, half the terrain is rated intermediate, and there are more skiers than boarders. The resthouse at the top of the 'Adam' gondola, Usagidaira 109, is the ski area's centre point, with two chairlifts from there heading up to the highest elevation of 1830m.

From Hakuba Station, a five-minute bus ride (¥260) takes you into the middle of the lively little village of Hakuba-mura. In winter, shuttles make the rounds of the village, lodges and ski base.

Hakuba 47 Winter Sports
Park & Hakuba Goryū Ski Resort SKIING
(Hakuba47ウインタースポーツパーク・白馬五竜スキー場; www.hakuba47.co.jp; 1-day lift ticket ¥5000; ☺Dec-Apr) The interlinked areas of Hakuba 47 Winter Sports Park and Hakuba Goryū Ski Resort form the second major ski resort in the Hakuba area. There's a good variety of terrain at both areas, with about an equal number of skiers and boarders. Like Happō-One, this area boasts fantastic mountain views.

A free shuttle bus from Hakuba-mura and Hakuba-eki provides the easiest access.

Hakuba Cortina Kokusai SKIING
(白馬コルチナ国際; www.hakubacortina.jp/ski; 1-day lift ticket ¥4000; ☺Dec-Apr) At the northern end of the valley, Hakuba Cortina is popular with Japanese families who revel in the resort's facilities – a massive ski-in European-style structure with hotel, restaurants, ski rental and deluxe onsen – and those who want quieter slopes. Its seven lifts and 16 courses cater to all levels of skiers.

Mimizuku-no-yu ONSEN
(みみずくの湯; ☎0261-72-6542; www.hakuba-happo-onsen.jp/mimizukunoyu; 5480-1 Hokujō Happō-guchi; adult/child ¥600/300; ☺10am-

9.30pm, enter by 9pm) One of Hakuba's many onsen, many contend this has the best mountain views from the tub.

🛏 Sleeping

Hakuba has a huge selection of accommodation. The Hakuba Accomodation Information Centre can help arrange accommodation if you arrive without a reservation.

Snowbeds B&B HOSTEL ¥
(☎0261-72-5242; www.snowbedsjapan.com; 2937-304 Hokujo Eco-land; dm from ¥3900; ▣@🛜) This foreign-run backpackers has cheap but cramped bunk rooms and a nice communal area with a wood stove. It's close to the nightlife. Private rooms are also available.

★ Hotel Hifumi HOTEL, RYOKAN ¥¥
(ホテルひふみ; ☎0261-72-8411; www.hakubahifumi.jp; 4998 Happō; r per person incl breakfast from ¥11,880; ▣✳🛜) Closer to a ryokan than a hotel, this compact family-run establishment extends the feeling of family to its guests and welcomes visitors from around the world. Beautifully designed and recently renovated rooms are a fusion of modern and traditional styles; some rooms come with private outdoor baths to make this one of Hakuba's most rewarding places to stay.

Hakuba Echo Hotel BOUTIQUE HOTEL ¥¥
(☎0261-85-0931; www.hakubaechohotel.com; 3020-503 Hokujō; d & tw from ¥14,000; ▣✳🛜) Popular with families, this casual boutique hotel has spacious rooms with neutral decor and its own bar and restaurant. It occupies a good location within the main village.

Shiroumaso RYOKAN ¥¥
(白馬荘; ☎0261-72-2121; www.shiroumaso.com; 5004 Happō; s/d from ¥10,030/17,900) This lovely little ryokan in Happō has smart, though compact, traditionally styled rooms with lots of hinoki cypress detailing and lovely views.

Hakuba Panorama Hotel INN ¥¥
(白馬パノラマホテル; ☎0261-85-4031; www.hakuba-panorama.com; 3322-1 Hokujō; d per person incl breakfast from ¥7000; ▣🛜) About 300m from one of the lifts at Happō-One Ski Resort, this Australian-run outfit has bilingual Japanese staff, an on-site travel agency and a variety of room types with en-suite bathrooms. There's a guest laundry and a wonderful onsen.

★**Ridge Hotel & Apartments** HOTEL ¥¥¥
(📞0261-85-4301; www.theridgehakuba.com; 4608 Hakuba; d/apt from ¥12,800/38,000; 🅿🌐@🛜) Sophisticated, sexy and stylish, this stunning property has it all, year-round: location, amenities, views. A variety of room types range from the sublime (Western-style rooms with Japanese elements) to the ridiculous (a gorgeous loft balcony suite in the shadow of the slopes). Obliging, attentive staff speak English well. Splurge if you can.

Sierra Resort Hakuba RESORT ¥¥¥
(📞0261-72-3250; www.sierrahakuba.com; Kitaazumi; s/d from ¥17,500/22,500; 🚗) Open year-round, Hakuba's largest resort occupies over 10 hectares of forest at the northern border of the village and features elegant guest rooms with private jacuzzi, an outdoor pool in season and the beautiful Mizubasho Onsen facility on-site. There's plenty to keep the kids occupied while you enjoy the serenity.

Hakuba Tokyu Hotel HOTEL ¥¥¥
(白馬東急ホテル; 📞0261-72-3001; www.hakuba-h.tokyuhotels.co.jp; Happō-wadanomori; s/d incl breakfast from ¥20,200/28,200; 🅿🛜) This elegant year-round hotel has large rooms with great views and a wonderful garden, popular for weddings. The Grand Spa boasts the highest alkaline content in the area, and there's both French and Japanese restaurants.

Hakuba Highland Hotel HOTEL ¥¥¥
(白馬ハイランドホテル; 📞0261-72-3450; www.hakuba-highland.net; 21582 Hokujō; d per person incl 2 meals from ¥10,780; 🅿🛜) This older hotel has sensational views over the Hakuba range and a great indoor-outdoor onsen, but it's away from the action. In winter there's a free shuttle bus to the main resorts, each about 20 minutes' drive away. All rooms have wi-fi: not so common in the hills.

✕**Eating**

In winter there's plenty to choose from around the area's resorts. In summer you're limited to a handful of establishments around the station area.

Sounds Like Cafe CAFE ¥
(📞0261-72-2040; 3020-504 Hokujō; coffee from ¥350, breakfast items from ¥450; ⏱8am-6pm Sat-Wed) Breakfast, lunch and lattes done Aussie-style keep the hungry minions coming back for more. It's about as authentically Western a cafe can be in Japan and the food and coffee are both top-notch.

Ohyokkuri JAPANESE ¥
(おひょっくり; 📞0261-72-2661; www.shin-shuu-hakuba.com; 5081 Hokujō; meals from ¥650; ⏱11.30am-2pm & 5.30-9pm) Self-billed as 'Grandma's Hakuba home-style cooking', Ohyokkuri serves hearty soups and stews and traditional local dishes to an adoring crowd.

BC Hakuba CAFE ¥
(📞0261-85-4548; 6354 Hokujo; coffee from ¥350; ⏱9am-5pm; 🛜📱) Formerly the Bamboo Cafe, on the left as you exit JR Hakuba Station, this funky modern beanery serves delicious speciality coffees, sweet treats and savoury snacks. Free wi-fi makes it a great place to log on and get your bearings.

🍷**Drinking & Nightlife**

The rugged, sporty folk who hang around Hakuba have been known to down a beer or two at the end of a hard day skiing or hiking – join them at one of the few good year-round or plentiful seasonal bars.

When the powder's deep, there's usually live evening entertainment somewhere on the slopes and nightclub-style shenanigans on weekends.

Lucky Pete's Bar & Cafe SPORTS BAR
(📞0261-85-4458; www.luckypetes.com; Hakuba-eki; ⏱11am-9pm; 🚗) This chilled-out, family friendly, smoke free bar to your right as you exit JR Habuka Station serves juicy original burgers and your favourite comfort foods along with plenty of snow-cold beer.

Hakuba Bike Bar BAR
(白馬バイクバー; www.bikebar-hakuba.com; Hakuba Goryū) This fun, disco-lit basement bar in Hakuba Goryū Ski Resort has a refreshingly hippie vibe – these guys think they're pretty cool, and by many standards, they are. It's about 10 minutes' walk from the Sky 4 Gondola and has billiards, early-evening film nights for families (Ninja juice is served) and karaoke.

Tracks Bar BAR
(📞0261-75-4366; www.tracksbar.info; Hakuba Goryū) Located between Kamishiro Station and Goryū, this is a favourite night spot for the younger, foreign crowd, with live music, pool tables, wood-burner stoves and sports on a huge screen.

ℹ**Information**

Hakuba Accomodation Information Centre (白馬宿泊情報センター, Hakuba Shukuhaku Jōhō Sentā; 📞0261-72-6900; www.hakuba1.com;

⊙ 7am-6pm) For information, maps and lodging assistance. Located to the right of Hakuba Station.

Hakuba Tourist Information Center (白馬村観光案内所; ☑ 0261-72-3232; www.hakubavalley. jp; ⊙ 8.30am-5.30pm) Provides maps and leaflets relating to tourism in the area. In addition to all things winter, the website has detailed information on summer gondola operating schedules and fares. It's just outside Hakuba Station.

❶ Getting There & Away

BUS

Alpico group operates buses from Nagano Station (¥1600, approximately 70 minutes) and Shinjuku Nishi-guchi in Tokyo (¥4850, 4½ hours), as well as a direct service from Narita Airport (¥9500). See www.alpico.co.jp/traffic/express/narita_hakuba/en for details.

TRAIN

Hakuba is connected with Matsumoto by the JR Ōito line (*tokkyū* ¥2320, one hour; *futsū* ¥1140, 1½ hours). Continuing north, change trains at Minami Otari to meet the JR Hokuriku line at Itoigawa: it's a pretty journey on a little two-carriage train, taking an hour from Minami Otari to Itoigawa with connections to Niigata, Toyama and Kanazawa.

There is one direct service per day (Super Azusa #3) from Shinjuku to Hakuba, via Matsumoto (*tokkyū* ¥7780, four hours). It departs Shinjuku at 7.30am and returns from Hakuba at 2.38pm.

NAGANO & AROUND

Formerly known as Shinshū and often referred to as the 'Roof of Japan', Nagano Prefecture (長野県) is a wonderful place to visit for its regal mountains, rich cultural history, fine architecture and cuisine.

In addition to a hefty chunk of the Chūbu-Sangaku National Park, Nagano boasts several quasi-national parks that attract skiers, mountaineers and onsen aficionados.

Nagano, the prefectural capital and past host of the Olympic Games, is home to Zenkō-ji, a spectacular temple of national significance.

❶ Getting There & Away

Willer Express (www.willerexpress.com) operates services from Tokyo to a number of destinations in the prefecture.

Frequent *shinkansen* (bullet trains) depart Tokyo Station for Nagano.

The JR Shinonoi line connects Nagano with Matsumoto and Nagoya.

Nagano 長野

☑ 026 / POP 377,803

Mountain-ringed prefectural capital Nagano has been a place of pilgrimage since the Kamakura period, when it was a temple town centred on the magnificent Zenkō-ji, which still draws more than four million visitors per year.

Since hosting the Winter Olympics in 1998, the city has reverted to its friendly small-town self, while still retaining plenty of accommodation and some nice restaurants.

⊙ Sights

★**Zenkō-ji**   BUDDHIST TEMPLE
(善光寺; Map p282; ☑ 026-234-3591; www.zenkoji. jp; 491 Motoyoshi-chō; ⊙ 4.30am-4.30pm summer, 6am-4pm winter, varied hours rest of year) FREE
Founded in the 7th century, National Treasure Zenkō-ji is home to the revered statue Ikkō-Sanzon, said to be the first Buddhist image to arrive in Japan (AD 552). Not even 37 generations of emperors have seen the image, though millions of visitors flock here to view a copy every seven years during the Gokaichō Matsuri. Zenkō-ji's immense popularity stems partly from its liberal welcoming of pilgrims, regardless of gender, creed or religious belief.

Its chief officiants are both a priest and a priestess. The current building dates from 1707.

Any bus from bus stop 1 in front of JR Nagano Station's Zenkō-ji exit will get you to the temple (¥100, about 10 minutes); alight at the Daimon bus stop.

✿ Festivals & Events

Gokaichō Matsuri   RELIGIOUS
(⊙ Apr/May) Five million pilgrims come to Zenkō-ji every seven years from early April to mid-May to view a copy of Zenkō-ji's sacred Buddha image – the only time it can be seen. The festival will next be held in 2022.

🛏 Sleeping

Visitors have the unique opportunity to experience *shukubō* (temple lodging) at one of Zenkō-ji's subtemples. Contact Zenkō-ji (p280) to book at least one day in advance. Expect to pay ¥7000 to ¥10,000 per person with two meals.

★**Shimizuya Ryokan**   RYOKAN ¥
(清水屋旅館; Map p282; ☑ 026-232-2580; www.chuoukan-shimizuya.com; 49 Daimon-chō;

THE JAPAN ALPS & CENTRAL HONSHŪ NAGANO

r per person incl breakfast from ¥6800; @ 🛜) On Chūō-dōri, a few blocks south of Zenkō-ji, this ryokan has been in the family for 130 years. The rustic, dark-wood interior has plenty of interesting ups, downs, nooks and crannies. There are shared bathrooms and a laundry. Meal plans are available.

1166 Backpackers
HOSTEL ¥

(1166 バックパッカーズ; Map p282; ☎ 026-217-2816; www.1166bp.com; 1048 Nishi-machi; dm/r ¥2800/6000; @ 🛜) This intimate, woody hostel is set amid older buildings in the back streets near Zenkō-ji. Look for the beige building with a chalk signboard outside. No meals are served, but there's a kitchen and dining area for guests.

★ Hotel Metropolitan Nagano
HOTEL ¥¥

(ホテルメトロポリタン長野; Map p282; ☎ 026-291-7000; www.metro-n.co.jp; 1346 Minami-Ishido-chō; s/d from ¥9500/12,800; P @) Adjacent to JR Nagano Station, the Metropolitan has elegant and spacious rooms by Japanese standards. There's a cafe, restaurant and top-floor lounge with sweeping views.

Dormy Inn Nagano
HOTEL ¥¥

(ドーミーイン長野; Map p282; ☎ 026-291-5489; http://en.hotespa.net/dormyinn/hotel/17748; 1373-1 Kitaishido-chō; s/d from ¥8990/11,990; P ⊖ ❋ 🛜) Opened in July 2016, Nagano's newest member of the Dormy Inn family has all the plush comforts and electronic gadgetry you'd normally find squeezed into a business hotel of this brand. Plus there's the added bonus of a variety of delightful indoor and outdoor baths, a stone's throw from the station.

Matsuya Ryokan
RYOKAN ¥¥

(松屋旅館; Map p282; ☎ 026-232-2811; Zenkō-ji Kannai; r per person from ¥6300, incl 2 meals from ¥10,500; ❋) Six generations of the Suzuki family have maintained this traditional inn just inside Zenkō-ji's Niō-mon gate, next to the statue of Enmei Jizō. It's the closest lodging to the temple. Meals are seasonal *kaiseki*. Add ¥1000 per person for rooms with private facilities.

✖ Eating & Drinking

India the Spice
CAFE ¥

(インディア・ザ・すぱいす; Map p282; ☎ 026-226-6136; 1418 Minami-ishido-chō; curries from ¥860; ⏱ 11.30am-11pm Mon-Thu & Sun, to midnight Fri & Sat) This eccentric cafe is festooned with every kind of wall clock imaginable, and specialises in variations on the theme of curry; lunch set menus include *omu-karē* (rice wrapped in an omelette in keema curry sauce). Going up Chūō-dōri, turn right at

---

LEGENDS OF ZENKŌ-JI

Few Japanese temples inspire the fascination Zenkō-ji does, thanks in part to the legends related to it. The following are just a few:

The Key to Salvation Visitors may descend Okaidan (admission ¥500), a staircase to a twisting pitch-black tunnel beneath the altar. Not for the claustrophobic, the idea is that in the darkness, all are equal, seeking the same thing – a heavy metallic object said to be the key to salvation. Grope the right-hand wall while avoiding your fellow aspirants. Can you find it?

Ikkō-Sanzon Three statues of the Amida Buddha were brought to Japan from Korea in the 6th century and remain the temple's raison d'être, wrapped like a mummy and kept in an ark behind the main altar. It's said the image was not seen for 1000 years, but in 1702, to quell rumours that the ark was empty, the shogunate ordered a priest to confirm its existence and take measurements. That priest remains the last confirmed person to have viewed it.

The Doves of San-mon Legend claims there are five white doves hidden in the plaque of the San-mon gate; the five short strokes in the characters for Zenkō-ji do look remarkably dove-like. See if you can spot them too. In the upper character (善, Zen), they're the two uppermost strokes; in the middle character (光, kō), they're the strokes on either side of the top; and in the 'ji' (寺), it's the short stroke on the bottom left.

Binzuru It is said that Binzuru, one of Buddha's disciples, a healer, had attained enlightenment, but was instructed to remain on earth in service. You'll find his statue just inside, worn down where visitors have touched it to help heal ailments of the corresponding parts of their own bodies.

Nagano

N
0   400 m
0   0.2 miles

Nagano

◎ **Top Sights**
1 Zenkō-ji B1

🛏 **Sleeping**
2 1166 Backpackers A2
3 Dormy Inn Nagano B4
4 Hotel Metropolitan Nagano A4
5 Matsuya Ryokan B1
6 Shimizuya Ryokan B2

✖ **Eating**
7 Asian Night Market B2
8 Fujiki-an B2
9 Fujiya Gohonjin B2
10 India the Spice A4
11 Yayoi-za A2

🍷 **Drinking & Nightlife**
12 Shinshū Nagaya Sakaba A4

🎭 **Entertainment**
13 Jazz Square Groovy B3

ℹ **Information**
14 Nagano Tourist Information
    Center B4

There's a picture menu. *Seiro-mori soba* (cold soba on a bamboo mat) lets the flavour shine; other favourites are tempura, *kinoko* (mushroom) and *nishin* (herring).

the 'Joy Style' London bus, then take another right. There are vine leaves around the entrance.

Asian Night Market   THAI ¥
(アジアンナイトマーケット; Map p282; ☎026-214-5656; 2-1 Higashi-go-chō; dishes ¥620-1080; ☺noon-11pm; 🛜📱) This hippie joint is part boutique, selling clothes and knick-knacks from Southeast Asia, and part bar-restaurant, with English-speaking staff serving sumptuous Thai food. There's also free wi-fi. You can view the menu online. The Chinese broccoli and obligatory pad thai are wonderful.

Fujiki-an   NOODLES ¥¥
(藤木庵; Map p282; ☎026-232-2531; www.fujikian.co.jp; 67 Daimon-chō; mains ¥860-1800; ☺11am-3pm Wed-Mon; 🅿📱) Fujiki-an has been making fresh soba in the north of Nagano Prefecture since 1827, but you wouldn't know it by the clean contemporary lines of this outlet.

Yayoi-za   JAPANESE ¥¥
(弥生座; Map p282; ☎026-232-2311; www.yayoiza.jp; 503 Daimon-chō; dishes ¥600-4600; ☺lunch & dinner Wed-Mon, closed 2nd Wed each month; 📱) This establishment has been serving *seiro-mushi* (ingredients steamed in a wood and bamboo box) for over 150 years. The standard is *monzen seiro-mushi* (local beef and vegetables). For dessert, try *kurian cream* (chestnut-paste mousse).

★ **Fujiya Gohonjin**   FUSION ¥¥¥
(藤屋御本陣; Map p282; ☎026-232-1241; www.thefujiyagohonjin.com; 80 Daimon-chō; small plates from ¥750, courses ¥2600-7800; ☺lunch Mon-Fri, dinner nightly; 📱) Until recently this imposing 1923 building was Nagano's most venerable Hotel Fujiya, and had been since 1648. It has since been transformed into the city's most elegant Western restaurant and function centre. The spectacular dining room is called Wisteria and mixes Japanese and art-deco motifs.

Shinshū Nagaya Sakaba   PUB
(信州長屋酒場; Map p282; ☎026-269-8866; www.marutomisuisan.jpn.com/nagaya-shinsyu;

1418-12 Minami-ishidō-chō; dishes from ¥390; ⊙5pm-midnight) Some English is spoken at this lively *izakaya* with a great menu, a selection of sake and an ambience that is straight out of another era.

☆ Entertainment

Jazz Square Groovy LIVE MUSIC
(Map p282; ☑026-227-0480; www.facebook.com/jazz.square.groovy; 1398 Kitaishido-chō; cover ¥1000-3500; ⊙hours vary) A music spot popular with jazz lovers for its live shows; check the website for schedule info.

ℹ Information

The *Nagano Visitor's Guide* can be found online at www.nagano-cvb.or.jp.

Nagano Tourist Information Center (長野市観光情報センター; Map p282; ☑026-226-5626; ⊙9am-6pm) Inside JR Nagano Station, this friendly outfit has good English-language colour maps and guides to Nagano and the surrounding areas.

ℹ Getting There & Around

BUS

Local buses and buses to destinations further afield, like Togakushi (one way/return from ¥1250/2250) and Hakuba (¥1600, approximately 70 minutes) depart from the **bus terminal** (Map p282) outside the train station's Zenkō-ji exit.

TRAIN

Nagano's station buildings were revamped in preparation for the Hokuriku Shinkansen and the architects did a truly impressive job.

Frequent *shinkansen* depart Tokyo Station for Nagano (¥7680, 1¾ hours) and continue on to Kanazawa (¥8760, 70 minutes).

The JR Shinonoi line connects Nagano with Matsumoto (Shinano *tokkyū* ¥2320, 50 minutes; Chūō *futsū* ¥1140, 1¼ hours) and Nagoya (Shinano *tokkyū* ¥6810, three hours).

If you're travelling on *futsū* (local) trains on the JR Chūō line between Nagano, Matsumoto and beyond, don't schedule an onward connection too tightly as trains are occasionally delayed by weather and wild pigs!

Togakushi 戸隠

☑026
Popular with hikers in spring, summer and autumn, and with skiers in the winter, this pretty forested region in the mountains northwest of Nagano city makes a lovely day

SHINSHŪ SPECIALITIES

Nagano Prefecture is renowned for its food ranging from familiar to downright challenging. Local foods are usually preceded by the region's ancient name, '*Shinshū*' (信州).

ringo (りんご) Apples: we think these are the best in the world. Ubiquitous in autumn.

kuri (栗) Chestnuts, especially in Obuse.

teuchi soba (そば) Handmade buckwheat noodles, eaten either cold (*zaru-soba;* with wasabi and soy-based dipping sauce) or hot (*kake-soba;* in broth).

oyaki (おやき) Wheat buns filled with vegetables, baked or steamed.

wasabi (わさび) Japanese horseradish, grown in bogs particularly in Hotaka. Look out for wasabi cakes and ice cream.

basashi (馬刺し) Raw horse meat.

hachinoko (鉢の子) Bee larvae.

inago (稲子) Crickets.

trip or a peaceful overnight stay. Togakushi has been famed for soba (buckwheat noodles) for centuries.

Pick up English-language maps from the Nagano Tourist Information Center or download one at www.togakushi-21.jp.

◉ Sights

Comprising three sub-shrines – Togakushi-Hōkōsha, Togakushi-Chūsha and Togakushi-Okusha – each a couple of kilometres apart, **Togakushi-jinja** (戸隠神社; ☑026-254-2001) honours the 1911m-high Mt Togakushi. According to legend, the mountain is where sun goddess Amaterasu hid in a cave behind a stone door, plunging the world into darkness, before another deity flung the door away, luring her out and restoring light. Chūsha is the easiest shrine to get to, located in the middle of the village. From Okusha, avid alpinists can make the strenuous climb to the top of Mt Togakushi. In winter Okusha is inaccessible, except for hearty snowshoers, and businesses are closed.

Togakushi-Hōkōsha SHINTO SHRINE
(戸隠宝光社; Map p284) While apparently close to the village, access to the shrine

Nagano Prefecture

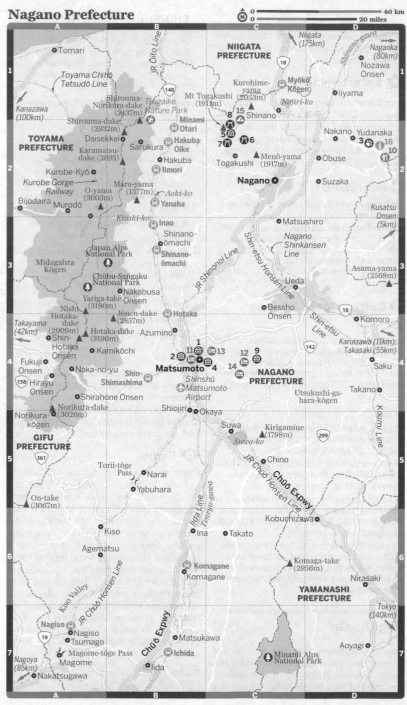

Nagano Prefecture

buildings of Togakushi-jinja's pretty, lower sub-shrine Hōkōsha, nestled among cedars, is via 274 (if we counted correctly) ancient and steep, stone steps, which those with mobility issues will find challenging.

Togakushi-Chūsha SHINTO SHRINE
(戸隠中社; Map p284) One of the three sub-shrines of Togakushi-jinja, intimate Chūsha, meaning 'middle shrine' is the most easily accessible, located prominently in the middle of the village. One tree here is said to be 700 years old.

Togakushi-Okusha SHINTO SHRINE
(戸隠奥社; Map p284) From Okusha bus stop it's 2km (40 minutes' walk) to Okusha (meaning Upper Shrine) – the innermost of Togakushi-jinja's three sub-shrines – via a magnificent 500m-long cedar-lined path (杉並木; suginamiki) planted in 1612, with plenty of twists, turns and many stone stairs. It's not an easy walk for the less mobile, but certainly a rewarding one, if you're able.

Togakushi Folk Museum & Ninja House MUSEUM
(戸隠民俗館・忍者からくり屋敷, Togakushi Minzoku-kan & Ninja Karakuri Yashiki; Map p284; ☎026-254-2395; 3688-12 Togakushi; adult/child ¥500/350; ◎9am-5pm mid-Apr–mid-Nov; ◻Okusha) Above the Okusha bus stop you'll find this museum housing artefacts from a time when local *yamabushi* (mountain monks) practised what became known as *ninpo* (the art of stealth). The Ninja House is the most fun, cleverly concocted with trick doors, hidden staircases and a room that slopes upwards.

🍽 Sleeping & Eating

Eating options are limited after dark; most visitors dine at their accommodation.

Togakushi Campground CAMPGROUND ¥
(戸隠キャンプ場; Map p284; ☎026-254-3581; www.togakusi.com/camp/; 3694 Togakushi; sites/bungalows/cabins/cottages from ¥3000/5000/9000/18,000; ◎late Apr–late Oct; ◻Togakushi Kyanpu-jo) This beautiful, sprawling campground a few kilometres from Okusha has its own babbling brook, 350 campsites, 30 bungalows, 33 cabins and six self-contained cottages. It's best in October when the leaves are turning and it's just about ready to close for the winter. Rental tents are available (¥4000). From Nagano, take the bus to Togakushi Kyanpu-jo stop.

Yokokura Ryokan RYOKAN ¥
(横倉旅館; Map p284; ☎026-254-2030; www.yokokura-inn.jp; 3347 Chūsha; dm with/without 2 meals from ¥5265/3245; r per person from ¥7800; ℗) Yokokura Ryokan is in a thatched-roof building from the early Meiji era, about 150m from the steps up to Chūsha shrine. It's both a hostel and a ryokan, with tatami-room dorms (gender separate) and private rooms. Room-only plans are available.

Uzuraya Soba NOODLES ¥
(うずら家そば; Map p284; ☎026-254-2219; 3229 Togakushi; soba from ¥780; ◎10.30am-4pm Thu-Tue; ◰) Revered in Japan by those who value soba (as many do), this wonderful noodle shop claims that Togakushi is the home of soba and it may just be right. It's directly across from the steps to Chūsha shrine. Tempura soba is king.

THE SNOW MONKEYS OF YUDANAKA

Pleasant in winter when shrouded in snow but far less appealing when seasonally bare, Yudanaka is a sprawling hot-spring town, best known for this wildly popular, though rundown, zoo, made famous by the 1992 film *Baraka*, where wild monkeys appear to bathe in natural onsen pools. In operation since 1964 and showing its age, **Jigokudani Monkey Park** (地獄谷野猿公苑, Jigokudani Yaen-kōen; Map p284; ☑ 0269-33-4379; www.jigokudani-yaenkoen.co.jp; 6845 Ōaza-heian; adult/child ¥500/250; ⊗ 8.30am-5pm Apr-Oct, 9am-4pm Nov-Mar) sees thousands flock here each year to view the over-photographed troupe of Japanese macaques who are lured into the pools with food.

They're at times a little savage as they run wildly around you on the paths to the artificial onsen. The monkeys are a few hundred steps' climb from the car park, which is itself at the end of a 1.6km winding uphill road.

The ruse is most convincing in winter when snow hides the industrial debris by the river; although the only way in is via a limited-operation shuttle bus on that slippery, winding road.

If you're determined to make the trip, take the Nagano Dentetsu line from Nagano to the Yudanaka terminus (*tokkyū* ¥1260, 45 minutes), then take the bus for Kanbayashi Onsen Guchi and get off at Kanbayashi Onsen (¥230, 15 minutes, eight daily). Walk uphill along the road about 400m until you see the sign reading 'Monkey Park', then begin your rather gruelling uphill climb.

Okusha no Chaya CAFE ¥

(奥社の茶屋; Map p284; ☑ 026-254-2222; 3506 Togakushi; mains from ¥840; ⊗ 10am-4.30pm late Apr–late Nov) By Okusha bus stop, Okusha no Chaya serves fresh soba and other staples behind a glass wall overlooking the forest. Delicious soft-serve ice cream comes in seasonal flavours such as tomato, chestnut and wasabi.

ⓘ Getting There & Away

Buses depart Nagano hourly (from 7am to 7pm) and arrive at Chūsha-Miyamae bus stop by Chūsha shrine in about an hour (one way/return ¥1250/2250). To Okusha the one-way/return fare is ¥1350/2400. The Togakushi Kōgen Free Kippu pass (¥2600) gives unlimited rides on buses to and around Togakushi for three days. Buy tickets inside the Alpico bus office in front of Nagano Station's Zenkō-ji exit.

Obuse 小布施

☑ 026 / POP 10,704

This lovely little town northeast of Nagano occupies a big place in Japanese art history and has a handful of interesting museums. The famed *ukiyo-e* (woodblock print) artist Hokusai (1760–1849) worked here during his final years. Obuse is also famed for *kuri* (chestnuts), which you can sample steamed with rice or in ice cream and sweets.

The town is increasingly popular with local day trippers – avoid weekends and holidays.

◉ Sights

Hokusai Museum GALLERY

(北斎館, Hokusai-kan; ☑ 026-247-5206; 485 Ōaza Obuse; adult/child ¥500/free; ⊗ 9am-5.30pm Apr-Sep, 9am-4.30pm Oct-Mar) Japan's most famous *ukiyo-e* (woodblock) artist, Hokusai, spent his final years in Obuse. Over 30 of his works are exhibited in this gallery, which recently reopened after extensive renovations. It's a 10-minute well-signposted walk from the Obuse train station.

Takai Kōzan Kinenkan MUSEUM

(高井鴻山記念館; ☑ 026-247-4049; 805-1 Ōaza Obuse; ¥300; ⊗ 9am-6pm Apr-Sep, 9am-5pm Oct-Mar) Takai Kōzan, woodblock artist Hokusai's friend and patron, was a businessman and an accomplished classical artist specialising in elegant Chinese-style landscapes. His life and work is commemorated in this small museum.

Taikan Bonsai Museum GALLERY

(盆栽美術館大観, Bonsai Bijutsukan Taikan; ☑ 026-247-3000; 28-7 Ōaza Obuse; adult/child ¥500/300; ⊗ 9am-5pm, closed winter) Come here to appreciate the delicate art of bonsai, including some rare species. Admission includes entry to a small gallery of landscapes.

Japanese Lamp & Lighting Museum MUSEUM

(日本のあかり博物館, Nihon no Akari Hakubutsukan; ☑ 026-247-5669; 973 Ōaza Obuse; adult/child ¥510/free; ⊗ 9am-4.30pm daily May, Aug, Oct

& Nov, Thu-Tue rest of year) Showcasing lighting through Japanese history, including oil lamps and lanterns, this neat museum will flip the switches of design aficionados.

🛏 Sleeping & Eating

You can count the town's lodging options on one hand. That said, they're all quite lovely.

Obuse has a handful of fanciful eateries in line with the town's artsy vibe. Expect to queue on weekends.

★ Masuichi Kyakuden   RYOKAN ¥¥¥
(桝一客殿; ☑ 026-247-1111; www.kyakuden.jp; 815 Oaza Obuse; d per person incl breakfast from ¥16,400; P✳🖥) Delightful, original, stylish and enchanting: all describe this reasonably priced gem in the heart of Obuse. Twelve rooms – huge by Japanese standards – beautifully synergise old and new, and are constructed from antique *kura* storehouses around a chestnut garden. Disappear into the peace, tranquillity and refinement.

Marrone   GELATO ¥
(マローネ; ☑ 026-214-3287; 973 Oaza Obuse; gelato from ¥400; ⏰ 10am-6pm) Even if it's cold out, be sure to stop by for some delicious, creamy, freshly churned gelato in a range of seasonal flavours. In summer, it's a must.

Chikufūdō   DESSERTS ¥
(竹風堂; ☑ 026-247-2569; 973 Oaza Obuse; desserts from ¥300; ⏰ 8am-6pm) Sample chestnut confections at Chikufūdō, established in 1893. *Dorayakisan* (chestnut paste in pancake dumplings) are the standard.

ℹ Information

A la Obuse Guide Centre (ア・ラ・小布施ガイドセンター; ☑ 026-247-5050; 789-1 Oaza Obuse; ⏰ 9am-5pm) You can get maps and hire bikes (¥400 for a half-day) here, en route to the museums from the Obuse train station. There's also a cafe, gift store and quaint guesthouse (single/twin from ¥8400/12,600).

ℹ Getting There & Away

Obuse is reached via the Nagano Dentetsu (Nagaden) line from Nagano (*tokkyū* ¥750, 26 minutes; *futsū* ¥650, 34 minutes).

Nozawa Onsen   野沢温泉

☑ 0269 / POP 3474

This wonderful working village tucked in a picturesque corner of the eastern Japan Alps is both a humming winter ski resort and a year-round onsen town – worth visiting any time of year.

Settled as early as the 8th century, Nozawa Onsen is compact and quaint, though the maze of narrow streets will challenge even the best of drivers. Dotted around the village are free public onsen and a range of excellent accommodation. Outside the busy ski season, it's possible to briefly escape modernity and get a sense of life in an ancient mountain village.

🏃 Activities

Onsen water is still wisely used by many villagers for laundry, cooking and heating. There are 13 free onsen (open 6am to 11pm) dotted about the town, each with a history. Our favourite is **Ō-yu**, with its fine wooden building, followed by the scalding-hot **Shin-yu**, and the atmospheric old **Kuma-no-te-arai** (Bear's Bathroom). The waters here are hot and full of minerals – if you have silver jewellery, leave it in your room unless you don't mind it temporarily turning black.

Some baths are cordoned off because they are so hot that only hardened locals are permitted to enter them!

**★ Nozawa Onsen
Snow Resort**   SNOW SPORTS
(野沢温泉スキー場; www.nozawaski.com; 1-day lift ticket ¥4800; ⏰ 8.30am-4.30pm Dec-Apr) Nozawa Onsen Snow Resort, one of Honshū's best, dominates the 'upper' village. The relatively compact resort with 21 lifts is easy to navigate and enjoy with a variety of terrain at all levels. The main base is around the Higake gondola station, where there are beginner and kid-friendly runs.

Snowboarders should try the **Karasawa** terrain park or the half-pipe at **Uenotaira**; advanced skiers will enjoy the steep and often mogulled **Schneider Course**. The lively village is great for after-ski action.

🎎 Festivals & Events

Dōsojin Matsuri   CULTURAL
(道祖神祭り; ⏰ Jan) Each year on 15 January crowds gather for the famous Dōsojin Matsuri, a kind of cleansing ritual for men aged 25 and 42, the so-called 'unlucky ages' in Japan. The 42-year-olds' task is to defend a purpose-built two-storey shrine, which they sit upon as it is besieged by fire at the hands of the 25 year olds and onlookers.

Copious amounts of sake are imbibed by all, the defenders come down after a while, and the shrine is set ablaze with great enthusiasm. Seriously!

🛏 Sleeping

Nozawa Onsen has a variety of accommodation, including some wonderful rustic ryokan, open year-round. In winter, it's buzzing: book ahead.

Lodge Nagano INN ¥
(ロッジながの; ☎050-5532-6026; www.lodge nagano.com; 6846-1 Toyosato; r per person incl breakfast from ¥4800, r in summer from ¥4200; ❀☎) This popular foreign-run guesthouse attracts lots of Aussie skiers – there's Vegemite in the dining room. It's a friendly, fun place with bunk dorms and tatami rooms, some with private bath.

Address Nozawa APARTMENT ¥¥
(アドレス野沢; ☎0269-67-0360; www. addressnozawa.com; 9535 Nozawa Onsen; studios from ¥9800; ❀@☎) This innovative, boutique property opened in 2011. In what was formerly a traditional inn, the new owners have created a space that combines Japanese and European design elements. Large Western-style rooms with tatami floors feature fresh colours, downy beds, bright bathrooms and a full kitchen stocked with breakfast provisions. There's an on-site onsen bath, kids' room, ski storage and plenty of technology.

Kiriya Ryokan RYOKAN ¥¥
(桐屋旅館; ☎0269-85-2020; www.kiriya.jp; 8714-2 Nozawa Onsen; r per person incl 2 meals from ¥14,500; ℗❀☎) This friendly ryokan has been in the family for generations. The owner's attentive service and excellent English ensure its abiding popularity with overseas guests. All rooms have private toilets; some have their own baths in addition to the large communal onsen baths. There's a guest laundry and a wonderful garden.

★ Mura-no-hoteru Sumiyoshi-ya RYOKAN ¥¥¥
(村のホテル住吉屋; ☎0269-85-2005; www. sumiyosiya.co.jp; 8713 Toyosato; r per person incl 2 meals from ¥18,820; ❀@) This wonderful ryokan, the oldest in town, has a wide range of inviting traditional room types, many with private bathrooms and great views. The communal onsen baths with stained-glass windows are dreamy. Limited English is spoken but the friendly staff are committed to excellence in service.

🍴 Eating & Drinking

Even in the low season, there's always a restaurant or two open in the village. In winter, you're spoiled for choice.

Kaze no Ie ITALIAN ¥
(風の家; ☎0269-85-3244; http://kazenoie.main.jp; 9494 Toyosato; pasta ¥590-990; ⏱5.30-11pm) You can't beat this little Italian trattoria for hearty pastas, tasty pizzas and delicious bruschetta. Excellent value.

Tōyō Rāmen RAMEN ¥
(東洋ラーメン; ☎0269-85-3363; 9347 Toyosato; bowls from ¥650; ⏱noon-10pm) Chunky ramen bowls and mouth-watering *tezukuri* (handmade) *gyōza* (dumplings) are dished out year-round in this 30-seat Chinese eatery.

Stay BAR
(ステイ; www.seisenso.com) Stay is a cosy basement bar that's open late and run by a music-loving Japanese man who has lived abroad.

ℹ Information

Nozawa Onsen Visitor Centre (野沢温泉ビジターセンター; ☎0269-85-3155; www. nozawakanko.jp; 9780-4 Toyosato; ⏱8.30am-6pm) In the centre of the village. There are English-speaking staff on hand here. They can assist with accommodation and tour bookings.

ℹ Getting There & Away

Since the arrival of the Hokuriku Shinkansen, access to Nozawa Onsen has changed: it's now quicker and easier than ever before.

To get here from Tokyo, take a *shinkansen* to Iiyama station (¥8110, 100 minutes) then connect to the Nozawa Onsen Liner bus to Nozawa Onsen (¥600, 25 minutes).

Direct buses operate between JR Nagano Station's east exit and Nozawa Onsen (¥1500, 90 minutes), but only in the winter season.

Shiga Kōgen 志賀高原
☎0269

The site of several events during the 1998 Nagano Olympics and the 2005 Special Olympics World Winter Games, Shiga Kōgen is Japan's biggest ski resort and one of the largest in the world: there are 21 linked areas covering 80 runs.

Outside winter the mountain's lakes, ponds and overlooks make it an excellent destination for hikers. In 1980, some 130 sq km of land was designated as a Unesco-protected Man and the Biosphere (MAB) Reserve.

If you don't ski or hike, the only compelling reason to visit is the glory-hallelujah green-season scenery of Rte 292 as it winds its way up from Yudanaka, then around twisty peaks, past active volcanic craters and lakes, down to the village of Kusatsu Onsen: it's one of mainland Japan's most rewarding drives.

🏃 Activities

Shiga Kōgen Ski Area   SKIING
(志賀高原スキー場; Map p284; ☑0269-34-2404; www.shigakogen.gr.jp; 1-day lift ticket ¥5200; ⊙8.30am-4.30pm Dec-Apr) This conglomeration of 21 ski areas is covered by one lift ticket, which gives access to all areas as well as the shuttle bus between various base lodges. Check out www.snow-japan.com for information on each of the individual areas.

There is a huge variety of terrain for all skill levels. In the Hasuike area, in front of the Shiga Kōgen ropeway station, the office has English speakers who can help you navigate the slopes and book accommodation. Hasuike ski area is central and good for learners and families; Nishitate-yama has long courses and great views; Yakebitai-yama is one of the biggest areas with a huge variety of terrain and panoramic views.

🛌 Sleeping & Eating

Ski resorts of all shapes and sizes dot the hills and valleys that make up Shiga Kōgen. There is no central village to speak of.

There is very little in the area by way of dining options outside ski season.

⭐ Villa Ichinose   INN ¥¥
(ヴィラ・一の瀬; Map p284; ☑0269-34-2704; www.villa101.biz; 7149 Hirao; s/d from ¥5500/10,000; P❸) With a great location in front of the Ichinose bus stop, English-speaking staff and a friendly atmosphere, this inn is popular with overseas guests. Japanese-style rooms have toilet only and Western-style rooms have their own bathroom. There's wi-fi in the lobby and a 24-hour public bath on the 2nd floor.

Chalet Shiga   INN ¥¥
(シャレー志賀; Map p284; ☑0269-34-2235; www.shigakogen.jp/chalet/en; r per person incl 2 meals from ¥10,200; P❸) Chalet Shiga is convenient to the slopes and has a popular sports

bar on-site. Both Western- and Japanese-style rooms are available.

ℹ Information

Shiga Kōgen Tourist Office (志賀高原観光協会; Map p284; ☑0269-34-2323; www.shigakogen.gr.jp; ⊙9am-5pm) In the Hasuike area, the Shiga Kōgen Tourist Office has English speakers who can help you navigate the slopes and book accommodation. It's in front of the Shiga Kōgen ropeway station.

ℹ Getting There & Away

Nagaden runs direct buses between JR Nagano Station and Shiga Kōgen (¥1700, 70 minutes), with frequent departures in ski season. You can also take a train from Nagano to Yudanaka and continue to Shiga Kōgen by bus – take a Haseike–bound bus and get off at the last stop (¥780, approximately 40 minutes).

Bessho Onsen   別所温泉
☑0268

With some interesting temples and reputedly excellent waters, mountain-ringed Bessho Onsen, part of Ueda city, is worth passing through if you're nearby, but overall lacks something cohesive as a destination.

Historically, it's been referred to as 'Little Kamakura' for the fact that it served as an administrative centre during the Kamakura period (1185–1333). It was also mentioned in *The Pillow Book* by the Heian-era poetess Sei Shōnagon – no doubt it was infinitely more appealing then. That said, it does have some lovely elements, a National Treasure temple and a stunning example of an *onsen ryokan* (traditional hot-spring inn).

◉ Sights & Activities

There are three central onsen (admission ¥150), each open from 6am to 10pm: Ō-yu (大湯) has a small *rotemburo*; Ishi-yu (石湯) is famed for its stone bath; and Daishi-yu (大師湯), most frequented by the locals, is relatively cool.

Kitamuki Kannon   BUDDHIST TEMPLE
(北向観音; ☑0268-38-2023; ⊙24hr) FREE The grounds of this Tendai temple have some impressive ancient trees and sweeping valley views. Once an awe-inspiring vista, there's no longer anything particularly contemplative about the valley development below. The temple's name comes from the fact that this Kannon image faces north, a counterpart to the south-facing image

at Zenkō-ji (p280) in Nagano. A 5km hike from here are the temples **Chūzen-ji** and **Zenzan-ji**, which do feel like a real escape.

Anraku-ji   BUDDHIST TEMPLE
(安楽時; ☑ 0268-38-2062; adult/child ¥300/100; ⊗ 8am-5pm Mar-Oct, 8am-4pm Nov-Feb) Of the Sōtō Zen sect, Anraku-ji is the oldest Zen temple in Nagano. Dating from AD 824–34, it's a National Treasure, renowned for its octagonal pagoda. The temple is a 10-minute walk from the Bessho Onsen train station.

🛏 Sleeping & Eating

There is a handful of reasonably priced eateries in the train station vicinity.

★ Ryokan Hanaya   RYOKAN ¥¥
(旅館花屋; ☑ 0268-38-3131; http://hanaya. naganoken.jp; 169 Bessho Onsen; r per person incl 2 meals from ¥13,880; ℗) Ryokan Hanaya is a step back in time to the Taishō era (1912–26) – a traditional gem set among wonderful manicured Japanese gardens. Fourteen beautiful, spacious (though ageing) tatami rooms open onto the scenery; each one has unique motifs and history. Little English is spoken, but the blissful *rotemburo* in the garden makes up for that.

Uematsu-ya   INN ¥¥
(上松屋; ☑ 0268-38-2300; www.uematsuya.com; 1628 Bessho Onsen; r per person incl 2 meals from ¥9800; ℗✳🛜) Uematsu-ya is a well-kept, good-value inn occupying a nine-storey building atop a hill. Its Japanese- and Western-style rooms all have their own bathrooms. Deluxe rooms are larger, on higher floors and have a private terrace. There are also indoor onsen and lovely *rotemburo*. Some English is spoken here.

❶ Information

Bessho Onsen Ryokan Association (別所温泉 旅館組合; ☑ 0268-38-2020; www.bessho-onsen.com; 1853-3 Bessho Onsen; ⊗ 9am-5pm) Located at the train station, this small office provides tourist information and can assist with lodging reservations, though some Japanese ability will be handy.

❶ Getting There & Away

Access is by train, via Ueda. From Nagano, take the JR *shinkansen* (¥1410, 12 minutes) or the private Shinano Tetsudō line (¥750, 42 minutes). From Tokyo, take the JR *shinkansen* (¥5980, 1½ hours). Once at Ueda, change to the private Ueda Dentetsu line to Bessho Onsen (¥570, 28 minutes).

Karuizawa   軽井沢

☑ 0267 / POP 19,005

Karuizawa is a picturesque resort town situated in a small, fertile valley beneath the shadow of Mt Asama, one of the most active volcanoes on Honshū. Its last significant eruption was in 2009, from which ashfall was reported as far as Tokyo. Despite the distant potential for volcanic cataclysm, Karuizawa has long been a popular retreat from Tokyo's summer heat. In 1957 a young Emperor Akihito met his future bride, Empress Michiko, on a tennis court here. Since then, the town has been a popular spot for weddings and an even more popular weekend destination for Tokyoites looking to escape the summer heat.

With easy access from Tokyo and Nagano by *shinkansen,* a range of accommodation, restaurants and a shopping outlet that even anti-shoppers will find hard to resist, Karuizawa makes a worthwhile day trip and a lovely, though expensive place to spend a night or two.

◉ Sights

Old Karuizawa (旧軽井沢; Kyū Karuizawa), also known as 'Old Karuizawa Ginza', is an attractive main street lined with classy boutiques, galleries and cafes. Follow Karuizawa-hondōri north from the train station for about 1km, then turn right onto Kyŭ-karuizawa Main Street – you can't miss it.

Usui Pass Lookout   VIEWPOINT
(碓氷峠見晴台, Usui Tōge Miharadai) FREE On the border of Gunma and Nagano Prefectures, about 4km northeast of Old Karuizawa, you'll find this observation platform with stunning views of Mt Asama and surrounding mountains. There's no public transport – for directions, ask at the Karuizawa Tourist Association office.

Mt Asama Magma Stone Park   PARK
(鬼押出し園, Onioshidashi-en; ☑ 0267-86-4141; www.princehotels.co.jp/amuse/onioshidashi; 1053 Kanbara, Tsumagoi-mura; adult/child ¥650/450; ⊗ 8am-4.30pm) Here's your chance to get up close and personal with Mt Asama – so close, you could almost touch it. Formed in 1783 by Asama's last violent eruption, this 'Hurled by Demons' park has a surreal landscape of jagged, hardened magma juxtaposed with verdant green fields; volcanic soil is extremely fertile. Enquire at the Karuizawa Tourist Association office for bus fares and times.

'Umi' Museum
of Contemporary Art
GALLERY

(軽井沢現代美術館, Karuizawa Gendai-bijutsukan; ☑0267-31-5141; www.moca-karuizawa.jp; 2052-2 Nagakura; adult/child/senior ¥1000/500/800; ☺10am-5pm Jul-Sep, 10am-5pm Fri-Mon Apr-Jun, Oct & Nov) This light-filled gallery showcases an impressive collection of contemporary works by Japanese artists who have found fame abroad. It's in a lovely forested spot.

Former Mikasa Hotel
MUSEUM

(旧三笠ホテル; ☑0267-42-7072; 1339-342 Karuizawa; ¥400; ☺9am-5pm) This property, one of the first Western hotels in Japan, welcomed guests from 1906 to 1970. An exceptional example of elaborate Meiji-era architecture, it's now a museum for you to explore, showcasing the building's unique architecture and memorabilia from the hotel's grand old days.

🛏 Sleeping

Karuizawa has a wide range of accommodation, from log cabins to business hotels, boutique resorts and hulking high-end hotels. Occupancy is generally high and room rates are among the dearest in Japan.

Cottage Inn Log Cabin
CABIN ¥¥

(☑0267 45-6007; www.log-cabin.co.jp; 3148-1 Naka-Karuizawa; per person s/tw from ¥13,000/6500; P✷) As the name suggests, these fully self-contained cabins have a rustic appeal in a forested setting, five minutes' walk from Naka-Karuizawa Station. It's a great option for travelling families.

★ Ancient Hotel
HOTEL ¥¥¥

(☑0267-42-3611; www.ancient-hotel.com; 2126 Nagakura; d per person incl 2 meals from ¥30,000; P✷🖥) Sleek lines, muted tones and gentle accents allow this beautifully designed hotel to blend gracefully into its natural surroundings, set away from town. It's a place of understated luxury, relaxation and tranquillity. This attention to detail and aesthetic sensibility flows through to the cuisine, which is presented so beautifully you'll have to eat very slowly indeed.

Hoshinoya
RYOKAN ¥¥¥

(星のや; ☑050-3786-0066; http://global.hoshinoresort.com/hoshinoya_karuizawa; Hoshino Karuizawa; d per person from ¥25,000; ✷🖥) ⏚ This stunning, though somewhat snobby, eco-resort in the onsen village of Hoshino, just outside Karuizawa, is anything but basic. Modern rooms and villas incorporate traditional design elements and are positioned around a pond in a beautiful forest setting. All have cypress tubs and are exquisitely furnished around the premise that less is more. Enjoy 24-hour room service from the resort's three restaurants.

You may have to share the decadent onsen pools with day visitors (¥1200).

APA Hotel Karuizawa Ekimae
HOTEL ¥¥¥

(APAホテル軽井沢駅前; ☑0267-42-0665; www.apahotel.com; 1178-1135 Karuizawa; s/d from ¥10,500/16,500; P✷@) Only two minutes' walk from the north exit of JR Karuizawa Station, this neat business hotel is a great choice if you're here to shop and looking for value and convenience.

🍴 Eating

Its reputation as a weekend playground for Tokyo's elite has seen Karuizawa become somewhat of a culinary destination in recent years. All manner of cuisine is represented here, with plenty of fancy restaurants in which to burn some yen.

Roast Chicken Kastanie
DINER ¥

(カスターニエ; ☑0267-42-3081; www.kastanie.co.jp; 23-2 Karuizawa-higashi; dishes from ¥600; ☺11am-2pm & 5-9pm Thu-Tue; 🖥) For something a little uncommon in Japan, pop into this original diner for succulent and tender roast chicken dinners, roast vegetables, sausage platters and all manner of Western treats, presented with Japanese attention to detail. Try the roast avocado with teriyaki sauce – yum!

Kawakami-an
FUSION ¥¥

(川上案; ☑0267-42-0009; www.kawakamian.com/shopkaruizawa; 6-10 Karuizawa; plates from ¥480; ☺11am-10pm) This is a wonderful place to sample a wide variety of Japanese and Western dishes, including an excellent large serve of *tempura soba* (¥1940) or, for something different, avocado and Camembert salad (¥790). Or just stop in for coffee and dessert.

🔒 Shopping

★ Karuizawa Prince
Shopping Plaza
MALL

(軽井沢・プリンスショッピングプラザ; ☑0267-42-5211; www.karuizawa-psp.jp; ☺10am-7pm) Outside the south exit of JR Karuizawa Station, this gargantuan outlet shopping mall has most of the big names. There's a high likelihood of finding bargains and hard-to-find or only-in-Japan merchandise. Shopaholics should allocate *plenty* of time.

Set among acres of grassland, with its own lake, plenty of dining options and great views to Mt Asama, it's easy to lose time here, even if you're not a big shopper.

ℹ️ Information

Karuizawa Tourist Association (軽井沢観光協会, Karuizawa Kankō Kyōkai; ☑ 0267-45-6050; www.karuizawa-kankokyokai.jp; ⊙ 9am-5pm) Grab your English-language publications and maps at this office inside the JR Karuizawa Station building. Some English is spoken.

ℹ️ Getting There & Around

Karuizawa is a stop on the Nagano *shinkansen* line, from Nagano (¥3160, 33 minutes) or Tokyo (¥5390, 70 minutes). There are twice-hourly services in both directions at most times.

Alternatively, the private Shinano Tetsudō line from Nagano operates local trains (¥1640, 1¼ hours) and there are five buses per day from Tokyo's Ikebukuro Station (¥2600, three hours).

Hiring a car will help you enjoy all the area has to offer.

GUNMA PREFECTURE

Mineral baths seem to bubble out of the ground at every turn in the mountainous landscape of Gunma Prefecture (群馬県; Gunma-ken). Its most famous onsen town is Kusatsu, but there are many others that are far less commercial. All that water and mountain adds up to great outdoor activities ranging from skiing in winter to rafting and canyoning in spring and summer.

ℹ️ Getting There & Around

Gateway to Gunma Prefecture, Takasaki is an important transport hub where the Jōetsu and Hokuriku *shinkansen* (bullet train) lines branch out in the directions of Niigata and Kanazawa (via Nagano) respectively.

The most popular onsen villages are reached by a combination of local trains and buses. If you don't mind driving on winding mountain roads, rent a car to make the journey more pleasurable.

Takasaki & Around

☑ 0273 / POP 370,751

Takasaki (高崎) is a pretty city, famed for *daruma* dolls, pasta and a handful of great day trips. It's an excellent *norikaeru-machi*:

place to change trains or stop over if you're travelling between Tōhoku and the Japan Alps. You'll find cheap eats and beds near the train station, which is the branching out point for the Jōetsu (to Niigata) and Hokuriku (to Nagano, Kanazawa and Toyama) *shinkansen* lines.

◎ Sights

★ **Tomioka Silk Mill** HISTORIC BUILDING
(富岡製糸場; ☑ 0274-64-0005; www.tomioka-silk.jp; 1-1 Tomioka, Tomioka; adult/child ¥1000/250; ⊙ 9am-5pm) Listed as a World Heritage Site in 2014, Tomioka Silk Mill provides a wonderful look into the history of silk production, with excellent English-language narration. Completed in 1872, the mill was once one of the largest producers of silk in the world. Today, its buildings are some of the only Meiji-era government factories preserved in excellent condition. To get here take the Joshin Dentetsu line from Takasaki to Joshu Tomioka Station, then walk 10 minutes.

It's a fascinating day trip from Takasaki.

Haruna Jinja SHINTO SHRINE
(榛名神社; ☑ 0273-74-9050; www.haruna.or.jp; 849 Harunasan-machi) Believed to be the home of the God of Water, Fire and Agriculture, there has been a shrine of some form here, amongst forested mountains, for almost 1400 years. It is said a visit brings good fortune for love and money. A 700m path to the shrine takes you to a tree that some date as old as 1000 years. Take a bus from JR Takasaki Station (70 minutes) or drive.

Usui Tōge Railway Village MUSEUM
(碓氷峠鉄道文化村, Usui Tōge Tetsudō Bunka Mura; ☑ 0273-80-4163; 407-16 Yokokawa; adult/child ¥500/free; ⊙ 9am-5pm) Kids, adults and trainspotters alike will love, love, love this rail graveyard-cum-beloved museum of the holy locomotive, with rolling stock, stations, carriages, simulators and years of Japanese rail history in a lovely rural setting. Take the train from Takasaki to Yokokawa Station (¥500, 30 minutes), the end of the Shinetsu main line.

The park is also within easy reach of Karuizawa (22km) for self-drivers.

Byakui Dai-kannon BUDDHIST STATUE
(白衣大観音; ☑ 0273-22-2269; www.takasakikannon.or.jp; 2710-1 Ishihara-machi; adult/child ¥300/100; ⊙ 9am-5pm) Built in 1936, this statue of Kannon (Goddess of Mercy) is one of the largest in Japan, standing at 41.8m tall and weighing over 6000 tonnes. You can walk

inside the statue up to her shoulder for excellent views. To get here, take the *gururin* bus (¥200, 20 minutes) from JR Takasaki Station to Jigen-in temple.

🛏 Sleeping

Takasaki has a wide variety of moderately priced business and tourist hotels clustered around the train station area.

Hotel Metropolitan Takasaki　　HOTEL ¥¥
(ホテルメトロポリタン高崎; ☑0273-25-3311; http://takasaki.metropolitan.jp; 222 Yashima-chō; s/d from ¥7700/13,900; ❄☎) Adjoining JR Takasaki Station, this hotel is Takasaki's most stylish and convenient, with excellent views from higher floors, and well-appointed rooms.

🍴 Eating & Drinking

There's no shortage of places to eat near Takasaki Station, with a variety of genres to choose from – a plethora of pasta restaurants, in particular, along with everything from Japanese to Indian and every popular franchise joint imaginable.

If you find yourself spending the night here, there are plenty of *izakaya* frequented by Japanese and a handful of more international watering holes to be found in the area radiating out from the train station's west exit.

ℹ Information

Takasaki Tourist Information Center (高崎観光案内所; ☑0273-27-2192; www.gtia.jp/kokusai/english; ⊗9am-8pm) Inside JR Takasaki Station, these friendly folks have a bunch of English-language publications and can advise how to get to sights further afield.

ℹ Getting There & Away

Frequent *shinkansen* (bullet train) services race into Takasaki from Tokyo (¥4410, one hour) onward to Karuizawa (¥2600, 15 minutes), Nagano (¥4530, 45 minutes), Toyama (¥9850, two hours) and Kanazawa (¥11,460, 2¼ hours).

You can also travel from here on the Jōetsu *shinkansen* to Niigata (¥7470, 1¼ hours) to begin your explorations of the Tōhoku region.

Minakami Onsen-kyo

☑0278 / POP 20,415
In the northern region of Gunma Prefecture you'll find Minakami Onsen-kyo, a sprawling onsen collective formed by the amalgamation

DON'T MISS

BEST ROTEMBURO
➡ Nakabusa Onsen (p274)
➡ Takaragawa Onsen (p293)
➡ Ōshirakawa Rotemburo (p246)
➡ Shin-Hotaka-no-yu (p244)
➡ Karukaya Sansō (p245)

of three smaller villages: Minakami-machi, Tsukiyo-no-machi and Niharu-mura.

Surrounded by beautiful natural forests and mountains, and cut through by the gushing Tone-gawa, the broader area is home to two of Japan's most adored *onsen ryokan* (traditional hot-spring inns), while the town of Minakami has become a year-round mecca for outdoor-adventure sports, hiking and skiing enthusiasts.

As most people arrive at Jōmō Kōgen Station, about half an hour from Minakami, it's hard to get a handle on the place at first. Looking a little worse for wear (like most mountain villages once the snow has melted), Minakami-machi is Minakami Onsen-kyo's main town, itself spread out and hard to pin down.

Gunma Prefecture's top-billing retreats Takaragawa Onsen (formerly of Minakami-machi) and Hōshi Onsen (of Niharu-mura) are remote, isolated and located in opposing directions. Although both are part of the Minakami Onsen group, neither are within striking distance of Minakami town at all.

It'd be a struggle to visit everything here in day; better to spend the night at one of the onsen ryokan here.

🏃 Activities

★**Takaragawa Onsen**　　ONSEN
(宝川温泉; ☑0278-75-2614; www.takaragawa.com; 1899 Fujiwara; ¥1500; ⊗9am-5pm) This stunning outdoor onsen offers four large rock pools cascading beside Tone-gawa and shaded by a lush forest riddled with meandering paths, wooden huts, and folk and religious statues. All the pools, bar one for women only, are mixed, but modesty towels are available (¥100). Buses run here hourly from Minakami Station (¥1150, 40 minutes).

You can also get off at Takaragawa Iriguchi (¥1050, 30 minutes), from where it's a 20-minute walk to the onsen. The curious junk and gems you'll pass on your way to the baths are decades' worth of gifts from local villagers.

ADVENTURE SPORTS IN MINAKAMI

Minakami is Japan's year-round adventure-sports destination, with the exception of November when many of the operators take a break before the start of the winter season.

In the spring melt (between April and June) the Tone-gawa (利根川) is the source of Japan's best white-water activities. Tour operators with English guides include **Canyons** (☑0278-72-2811; www.canyons.jp; rafting half/full day from ¥7500/16,000), **I Love Outdoors** (☑0278-72-1337; www.iloveoutdoors.jp; 169-1 Shikanosawa; half-day tours from ¥6500) and **H2O Guide Services** (☑0278-72 6117; www.h2o-guides.jp; rafting/canyoning tours from ¥8000). During summer, when water levels drop and it gets warmer, each outfitter offers canyoning trips. Both Canyons and I Love Outdoors can arrange packages in their own lodges.

A variety of mountain-biking tours are offered by **MTB Japan** (☑0278-72-1650; www.mtbjapan.com; tours from ¥6000), while the team at **Tenjin Lodge** (p294) offers hiking in the warmer months and off-piste skiing, snowboarding and snowshoeing in the winter. If none of that is heart-thumping enough for you, take a plunge with **Bungy Japan** (☑0278-72-8133; www.bungyjapan.com; 143 Obinata; 1st jump from ¥8000; ⊙10am-4pm Mon-Fri, 9am-5pm Sat & Sun Apr-Nov).

Serious climbers will want to tackle Tanigawa-dake (1977m), Tenjin-dake and Ichino-kura. Tanigawa-dake is suited to experienced climbers only: it has claimed quadruple the number of deaths of Mt Everest. When hiking, exercise caution for bears.

Several bears in cages are the only downside here.

Tanigawa-dake Ropeway
CABLE CAR
(谷川岳ロープウェイ; ☑0278-72-3575; www.tanigawadake-rw.com; return ¥2060; ⊙8am-5pm) Tanigawa-dake Ropeway takes you via gondola to the peak of Tenjin-daira, from where hiking trips, ranging from a couple of hours to all day, are available from May to November. There's skiing and snowboarding in winter. From Minakami Station, take a 20-minute bus ride to Ropeway-Eki-mae bus stop (¥670). Discounted combined ropeway and return bus tickets are available.

🛏 Sleeping

Most local adventure-sports operators have their own lodges, but if you're not the adventuring kind, the town feels like it has more ageing *minshuku* and ryokan than it does residents.

Tenjin Lodge
LODGE ¥
(天神ロッジ; ☑0278-25-3540; www.tenjinlodge.com; 220-4 Yubiso; r per person from ¥5000; ⊛) Ideally located at the foot of Tanigawa-dake, across from a lovely waterfall and nearby swimming holes, this lodge offers comfy, spacious Japanese- and Western-style rooms; ask for a riverside one. Welcoming hosts offer home-cooked meals (breakfast ¥800, dinner ¥1200) as well as plenty of local knowledge and adventure-sports options.

★ Takaragawa Onsen Ōsenkaku
RYOKAN ¥¥
(宝川温泉汪泉閣; ☑0278-75-2611; www.takaragawa.com; 1899 Fujiwara; s/d with 2 meals & shared bathroom from ¥13,400/20,600; ⊛⊛) 🍃 They hardly come more traditional than this riverside inn split over three buildings, the oldest of which is the riverside 1936 No 1 Annexe. Guests have 24-hour use of adjacent Takaragawa Onsen: early morning bathing gives you the opportunity to experience that sense of real tranquillity that can be hard to grasp during crowded peak times.

Note that the dinner banquet includes bear-meat soup; if you'd prefer not to eat this, ask for no *kuma-jiru* (熊汁) when reserving. A shuttle service is available.

★ Hōshi Onsen Chōjūkan
RYOKAN ¥¥
(法師温泉長寿館; ☑0278-66-0005; www.houshi-onsen.jp; 650 Nagai; r per person incl 2 meals from ¥15,500; ⊛⊛) Remote, rustic and supremely photogenic, this lodging is one of Japan's finest *onsen ryokan* (traditional hot-spring inns), with a stunning 1896 wooden bathhouse. From Gokan Station (two stops before Minakami), take a bus to Sarugakyō (¥730, 40 minutes), then change to an infrequent bus for Hōshi Onsen (¥590, 15 minutes). Otherwise take a taxi (¥3000).

Bathing for nonguests is also available (¥1000, 10.30am to 1.30pm Thursday to Tuesday).

✕ Eating & Drinking

La Biere PIZZA ¥
(ラ・ビエール; ☎0278-72 2959; www.3-sui.com/labiere.html; pizzas from ¥850; ⏰11am-2.30pm & 5-8.30pm Wed-Mon; 🖥) Simple and tasty wood-fired pizzas are served in this cute pizzeria with pot plants and umbrella-covered decking out the front. Takeaway is also available.

Kadoya SOBA ¥¥
(そば処角弥; ☎0278-72-2477; www.kadoya-soba.com; 189-1 Yubiso; soba ¥980-1480; ⏰11am-2.30pm) Expect to queue at this popular 'local' specialising in *hegi soba* (soba flavoured with seaweed and served on a special plate, a *hegi*). The noodles are hand-rolled fresh every day and the shop closes once they sell out.

Alpine Cafe BAR
(☎0278-72-2811; www.canyons.jp; 45 Yubiso; ⏰4pm-late Thu-Sun Dec-Oct; 🖥) Run by the Canyons (p294) crew, this popular cafe-bar offers riverside barbecues in the summer, a pool table, plenty of beer, hamburgers and occasional live music. It's also where you'll be put up if you're on one of Canyons' adventure-tour packages.

ⓘ Information

Minakami Onsen Tourist Information Center
(水上温泉旅館協同組合; ☎0278-72 2611; www.minakamionsen.com; ⏰8.30am-4.30pm Jun-Oct, 9am-4.30pm Nov-May) Adjacent to Jōmō Kōgen Station, this office has helpful English-speaking staff, brochures and bus schedules.

Also see www.enjoy-minakami.jp.

ⓘ Getting There & Away

From Ueno, take the Jōetsu *shinkansen* (¥4200, 50 minutes) or JR Takasaki line (¥1940, two hours) to Takasaki and transfer to the Jōetsu line (¥970, one hour).

Most JR Pass holders will catch the Jōetsu *shinkansen* direct to Jōmō Kōgen from Tokyo/Ueno (¥5390/5180, 1¼ hours), from where buses run to Minakami (¥620, 25 minutes).

ⓘ Getting Around

BUS
To get to Hōshi Onsen, take the bus from Jōmō Kōgen Station to Sarugakyō Onsen (¥880, 30 minutes) and change for the less frequent bus to Hōshi Onsen (¥640, 20 minutes).

If you're arriving by *tokkyū* train on the Jōetsu line, get off at Gokan Station (two stops before Minakami), then get the bus to Sarugakyō (¥730,

40 minutes), where you should change to the bus for Hōshi Onsen (¥590, 15 minutes).

Hourly buses depart Minakami Station for Takaragawa Onsen. All buses stop at Takaragawa Iriguchi bus stop (¥1050, 30 minutes), from where it's a further 20-minute walk to Takaragawa Onsen; some buses go all the way there (¥1150, 40 minutes).

Timetables can be found at http://global.kan-etsu.net/en/minakami/yunokoya.html.

CAR & MOTORCYCLE

If you don't mind driving winding mountain roads, renting a car from Jōmō Kōgen Station is by far the best way to experience the area, giving you freedom to explore the divine onsen, the town of Minakami and the ropeway.

See the friendly staff at **Toyota Rent-a-Lease** (トヨタレンタリース上毛高原駅前; ☎0278-62-0100; http://rent.toyota.co.jp; 766 Tsukiyono; ⏰8am-8pm), directly opposite Jōmō Kōgen Station.

Kusatsu Onsen

☎0279 / POP 6537
Consistently rated one of Japan's top onsen towns since the Edo period for its pungent, anti-bacterial, emerald-coloured waters, Kusatsu (草津温泉) is also a great base for winter skiing, suitable for all levels; see www.kusatsu-kokusai.com.

◉ Sights & Activities

Yubatake HOT SPRINGS
(湯畑) Yubatake is the main attraction in the town centre and the source of hot-spring water in the area. Its milky blue sulphuric water flows like a waterfall at 4000L per minute and is topped with wooden tanks from which Kusatsu's ryo-kan fill their baths. The area is atmospherically lit up at night.

Sai-no-kawara Rotemburo ONSEN
(西の河原露天風呂; ☎0279-88-6167; www.sainokawara.com; 521-2 Ōaza Kusatsu; adult/child ¥600/300; ⏰7am-8pm Apr-Nov, 9am-8pm Dec-Mar) In leafy Sai-no-kawara *kōen* (park) you'll find this atmospheric 500-sq-metre *rotemburo* separated by a bamboo wall into men's and women's baths. Each bath holds at least 100 people and frequently does: early morning visits afford greater privacy and tranquillity.

The baths are a 15-minute walk west from Yubatake or stop 15 on the Kusatsu Round Bus.

Ōtakinoyu
ONSEN

(大瀧乃湯; ☎0279-88-2600; www.ohtakinoyu. com; 596-13 Ōaza Kusatsu; adult/child ¥900/400; ⊙9am-9pm) Ōtakinoyu is known for its tubs at a variety of temperatures, some almost impossibly hot; try different ones for an experience known as *awase-yu* (mix-and-match waters). It's a five-minute walk downhill east of Yubatake.

🛏 Sleeping & Eating

Kusatsu gets extremely busy during holiday periods and on weekends, and there's little in the way of contemporary style that you may find at other resorts. Several of the town's many towering onsen hotels are more suited to the Japanese tour-group market than DIY international visitors, and many have seen better days.

Ijimakan
RYOKAN ¥

(飯島館; ☎0279-88-3457; www.iijimakan.com; 447-8 Kusatsu; r per person with shared bathroom & 2 meals/room only from ¥6690/4630; 🛜) Run by friendly owners, this is a good deal despite the mishmash of odd decor (stuffed animals, fake flowers and the like). Go for the upstairs rooms with balcony area and loads of natural light. It's a two-minute walk downhill from the bus terminal with no English sign.

Kusatsu Onsen Boun
RYOKAN ¥¥

(草津温泉望雲; ☎0279-88-3251; www.hotelboun. com; 433-1 Kusatsu-machi; r per person incl 2 meals from ¥14,040; ❄🛜) Beautiful Boun offers traditional decor with elegant touches, featuring tatami rooms and common areas brightened with ikebana artwork, mossy gardens, waterfalls and a bamboo decking atrium. There's a large onsen in a big wooden bathhouse and *rotemburo* with a garden outlook. A three-minute walk from Yubatake.

Hotel Sakurai
HOTEL ¥¥¥

(ホテル櫻井; ☎0279-88-3211; www.hotel-sakurai. co.jp; 465-4 Kusatsu-machi; r per person incl 2 meals from ¥28,000; 🅿❄🛜) Unmissable in town, in a central location, this towering, top-end onsen hotel has a wide range of luxurious room types, dining options and baths. Rooms on higher floors in the new wing feature lovely views over the town and countryside.

Mikuniya
NOODLES ¥

(三国家; ☎0279-88-2134; 386 Ōaza Kusatsu; dishes from ¥680; ⊙11am-2pm) Enjoy tasty bowls of *sansai soba* (buckwheat noodles with mountain vegetables; ¥800) at this popular place on the shopping street that runs behind Yubatake towards Sai-no-kawara. Look for the renovated wooden building with the black door curtains, or the line out the front.

☆ Entertainment

Netsu-no-yu Yumomi
LIVE PERFORMANCE

(☎0279-88-3613; www.kusatsu-onsen.ne.jp.e.uh. hp.transer.com/netsunoyu; 414 Kusatsu-machi; adult/child ¥600/300; ⊙performances 9am, 10am, 10.30am, 3.30pm, 4pm & 4.30pm) Although it's a touristy 30-minute show, this is a unique opportunity to see *yumomi*, in which local women stir the waters to cool them while singing folk songs. There's a chance to do it yourself at most shows (four or five daily) and the afternoon ones also include local dances.

ℹ Information

For more town info, see www.kusatsu-onsen.ne.jp.

City Hall Tourist Section (☎0279-88-0001; ⊙8.30am-5.30pm Mon-Fri) Stop in at this information spot next to the bus station. Occasionally there's an English speaker on hand and there is a touchscreen information terminal in English.

Kusatsu Onsen Ryokan Information Centre (草津温泉旅館案内センター; ☎0279-88-3722; ⊙9am-6pm) Located in the white building opposite the bus station, this place can help with accommodation bookings and has a recommended walking map.

ℹ Getting There & Away

JR buses connect Kusatsu Onsen to Naganohara-Kusatsuguchi Station (¥690, free for JR Pass holders, 25 minutes). *Tokkyū* Kusatsu trains run from Ueno to Naganohara-Kusatsuguchi Station (¥4750, 2½ hours) three times a day. Alternatively, take the Jōetsu *shinkansen* (bullet train) to Takasaki (¥5280, one hour) and transfer to the JR Agatsuma line (¥1140, 1½ hours).

JR Bus Kantō (☎03-3844-1950; www.jr buskanto.co.jp) offers direct service to Kusatsu Onsen (¥3600, four hours) from Shinjuku Station in Tokyo (departing from the New South exit); reservations required.

If you've rented a vehicle, you'll be stressed out trying to navigate the crowded, narrow streets of the village. However, the drive between Kusatsu Onsen and Karuizawa, 41km to the south, in Nagano region, affords excellent views of the active volcano Mt Asama.

Heading northwest on Rte 292 towards Shiga Kōgen, and onward to Yudanaka in Nagano, offers some of Japan's most spectacular spring and fall scenery, with no shortage of incredible vistas. The winding, high-altitude route is extremely popular (and slow) on weekends and is not recommended for those who get carsick easily.

Kyoto

POP 1.47 MILLION / ♪ 075

Best Places to Eat

➡ Kikunoi (p346)
➡ Omen (p346)
➡ Kyōgoku Kane-yo (p342)
➡ Yoshikawa (p344)
➡ Honke Owariya (p342)

Best Places to Sleep

➡ Hyatt Regency Kyoto (p336)
➡ Tawaraya (p334)
➡ Capsule Ryokan Kyoto (p332)
➡ Ritz-Carlton Kyoto (p334)
➡ Lower East 9 Hostel (p332)

Why Go?

Kyoto is old Japan writ large: quiet temples, sublime gardens, colourful shrines and geisha scurrying to secret liaisons. With 17 Unesco World Heritage Sites, more than 1000 Buddhist temples and over 400 Shintō shrines it is one of the world's most culturally rich cities. But Kyoto is not just about sightseeing: while the rest of Japan has adopted modernity with abandon, the old ways are still clinging on here. Visit an old *shōtengai* (market street) and admire the ancient speciality shops: tofu sellers, geisha sellers, *washi* (Japanese handmade paper) stores and tea merchants.

Traditional Japanese culture – and thus Kyoto itself – is intimately bound to the changing of the seasons. Everything shifts with the passage of time: the blooms in a temple garden, the garnishes on a plate served during a formal *kaiseki* (haute cuisine) meal, even the ornaments with which geisha adorn their hair. Whether this is your first visit or your 10th, the city is bound to surprise you with something new and extraordinary.

When to Go
Kyoto

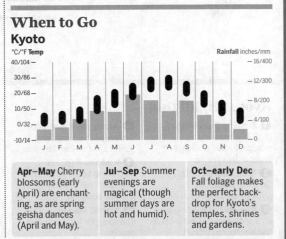

Apr–May Cherry blossoms (early April) are enchanting, as are spring geisha dances (April and May).

Jul–Sep Summer evenings are magical (though summer days are hot and humid).

Oct–early Dec Fall foliage makes the perfect backdrop for Kyoto's temples, shrines and gardens.

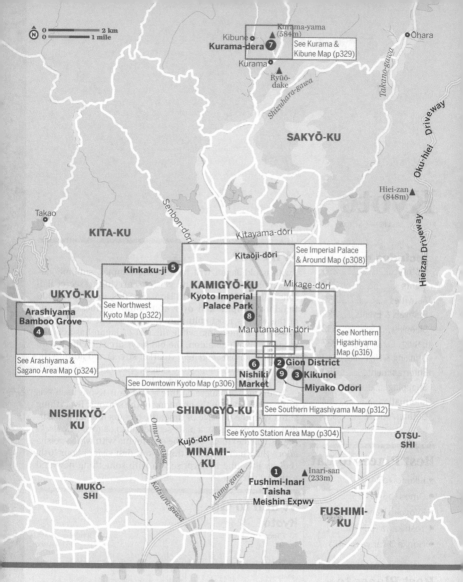

Kyoto Highlights

❶ Fushimi Inari-Taisha
(p303) Wandering through the magical tunnel of vermilion gates at this shrine.

❷ Gion district (p315) Strolling though the atmospheric district at night.

❸ Kikunoi (p346) Splurging on a once-in-a-lifetime meal of *kaiseki* (haute cuisine).

❹ Arashiyama Bamboo Grove (p323) Immersing yourself in this lush landscape.

❺ Kinkaku-ji (p321) Marvelling at the golden hall of this temple floating over its tranquil pond.

❻ Nishiki Market (p304) Shopping for local gourmet goods.

❼ Kurama-dera (p328) Climbing up to the mountain temple.

❽ Kyoto Imperial Palace Park (p308) Picnicking on the spacious grounds of the palace.

❾ Miyako Odori (p351) Being charmed by geisha at an annual performance of traditional dance.

History

Kyoto served as the capital of Japan for an almost unbroken stretch from the 8th century to the mid-19th century. (The city's nearly 1000-year reign was interrupted in the 12th and 13th centuries, when the first feudal government was established in Kamakura.) It was in Kyoto that the Heian-era (794–1185) court laid down the foundation for the Japanese aesthetic and here that the ascendant warrior class of the 15th and 16th centuries refined it, developing the tea ceremony, ikebana (art of flower arranging) and the elegant architectural style that can still be seen in the city's temples today.

When the emperor was reinstated as head of the country following the Meiji Restoration in 1868 and the imperial residence moved to Tokyo, the eastern city took on the mantle of nation's capital – though Kyoto remains in hearts and minds the cultural capital of the country.

◉ Sights

◉ Kyoto Station & South Kyoto

Kyoto Station   NOTABLE BUILDING
(京都駅; Map p304; www.kyoto-station-building.co.jp; Karasuma-dōri, Higashishiokōji-chō, Shiokōji-sagaru, Shimogyō-ku; 🚉 Kyoto Station) The Kyoto Station building is a striking steel-and-glass structure – a kind of futuristic cathedral for the transport age – with a tremendous space that arches above you as you enter the main concourse. Be sure to take the escalator from the 7th floor on the east side of the building up to the 11th-floor glass corridor, Skyway (open 10am to 10pm), that runs above the main concourse of the station, and catch some views from the 15th-floor Sky Garden terrace.

Kyoto Tower   NOTABLE BUILDING
(京都タワー; Map p304; Karasuma-dōri, Shichijō-sagaru, Shimogyō-ku; ¥770; ⊘9am-9pm, last entry 8.40pm; 🚉 Kyoto Station) Located right outside the Karasuma (north) gate of Kyoto Station, this retro tower looks like a rocket perched atop the Kyoto Tower Hotel. The tower provides excellent views in all directions and you can really get a sense for the Kyoto *bonchi* (flat basin). It's a great place to get orientated to the city upon arrival. There are free mounted binoculars to use and a cool touchscreen panel showing what the view looks like both day and night.

Higashi Hongan-ji   BUDDHIST TEMPLE
(東本願寺, Eastern Temple of the True Vow; Map p304; Karasuma-dōri, Shichijō-agaru, Shimogyō-ku; audio guide at information centre ¥500; ⊘5.50am-5.30pm Mar-Oct, 6.20am-4.30pm Nov-Feb; 🚉 Kyoto Station) FREE A short walk north of Kyoto Station, Higashi Hongan-ji is the last word in all things grand and gaudy. Considering its proximity to the station, the free admission, the awesome structures and the dazzling interiors, this temple is the obvious spot to visit when near the station. The temple is dominated by the vast **Goei-dō** (Main Hall), said to be the second-largest wooden structure in Japan, standing 38m high, 76m long and 58m wide.

The refurbished hall contains an image of Shinran, the founder of the sect, although the image is often hidden behind sumptuous gilded doors.

There's a tremendous **coil of rope** made from human hair on display in the passageway to the adjoining recently refurbished **Amida-dō** hall, where the Amida Buddha is enshrined on the central altar. Following the destruction of the temple in the 1880s, a group of female temple devotees donated their locks to make the ropes that hauled the massive timbers used for reconstruction.

Higashi Hongan-ji was established in 1602 by Shogun Tokugawa Ieyasu in a 'divide and conquer' attempt to weaken the power of the enormously popular Jōdo Shin-shū (True Pure Land) school of Buddhism. The temple is now the headquarters of the Ōtani branch of Jōdo Shin-shū.

Nishi Hongan-ji   BUDDHIST TEMPLE
(西本願寺; Map p304; Horikawa-dōri, Hanayachō-sagaru, Shimogyō-ku; ⊘5.30am-5pm Nov-Feb, to 5.30pm Mar, Apr, Sep & Oct, to 6pm May-Aug; 🚉 Kyoto Station) FREE A vast temple complex located about 15 minutes' walk northwest of Kyoto Station, Nishi Hongan-ji comprises five buildings that feature some of the finest examples of architecture and artistic achievement from the Azuchi-Momoyama period (1568–1603). The **Goei-dō** (Main Hall) is a marvellous sight. Another must-see building is the **Daisho-in** hall, which has sumptuous paintings, carvings and metal ornamentation. A small garden and two *nō* (stylised Japanese dance-drama) stages are connected with the hall. The dazzling **Kara-mon** has intricate ornamental carvings.

In 1591 Toyotomi Hideyoshi ordered the building of this temple to serve as the new headquarters for the Jōdo Shin-shū (True Pure Land) school of Buddhism. It was

Greater Kyoto

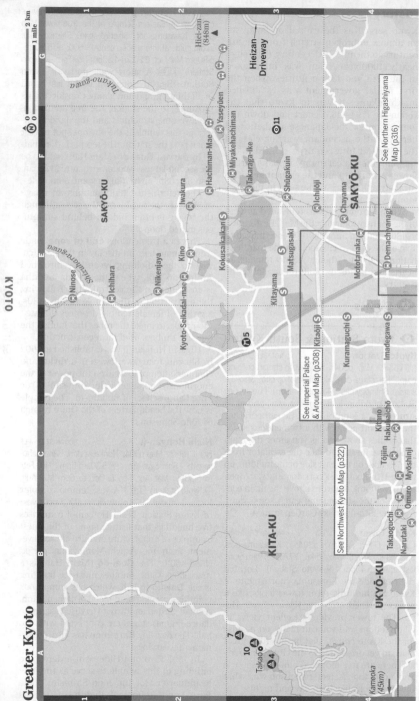

N 0 — 2 km
0 — 1 mile

Takano-gawa

Hiei-zan
(848m)

Hieizan
Driveway

SAKYŌ-KU

Yaseyūen
Hachiman-Mae
Miyakehachiman
Takaraga-ike
Shūgakuin
Ichijōji
Chayama
Iwakura
Kokusaikaikan Ⓢ
Matsugasaki
Kitayama Ⓢ
Mototanaka
Demachyanagi

See Northern Higashiyama Map (p316)

SAKYŌ-KU

Shizubara-gawa

Ninose
Ichihara
Nikenjaya
Kino
Kyoto-Seikadai-mae

Kitayama Ⓢ
Kitaōji Ⓢ
Kuramaguchi Ⓢ
Imadegawa Ⓢ

See Imperial Palace
& Around Map (p308)

KITA-KU

Kitano
Hakubaichō
Tōjiin
Myōshinji
Omuro
Takaoguchi
Narutaki

See Northwest Kyoto Map (p322)

UKYŌ-KU

Takao

Kameoka
(45km)

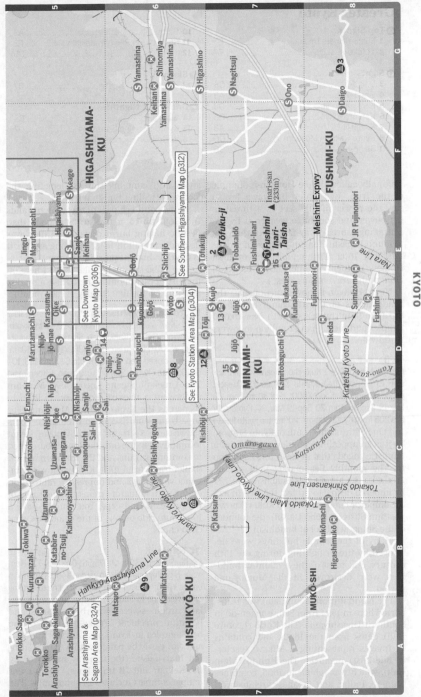

KYOTO

HIGASHIYAMA-KU

FUSHIMI-KU

MINAMI-KU

NISHIKYŌ-KU

MUKŌ-SHI

Ⓢ Yamashina
Keihan Ⓚ Ⓢ Shinomiya
Yamashina Ⓢ Yamashina
Ⓢ Higashino
Ⓢ Nagitsuji
Ⓢ Ono
⛰3 Ⓢ Daigo

Ⓢ Keage
Ⓚ Higashiyama
Ⓢ Higashiyama
Jingū- Ⓚ Sanjō
Marutamachi Keihan
Ⓢ Sanjō
Ⓢ Gojō

See Southern Higashiyama Map (p312)

▲ Inari-san (233m)
Ⓢ Shichijō
Ⓢ Tōfukuji ⛩ *Tōfuku-ji*
Ⓢ Tōbakaidō 2 Fushimi-Inari
Ⓢ Fushimi Inari-Taisha 16 1
Meishin Expwy

See Downtown Kyoto Map (p306)

Marutamachi Ⓢ
Nijō-
jō-mae Ⓢ
Ⓢ Karasuma-
Oike
Ⓢ Kyoto
Ⓢ Gojō
Ⓢ Kyōmizu-
Kiyomizu Ⓚ
Ⓢ Kujō 13 Ⓢ
Ⓢ Tōji
Ⓢ Jūjō
Ⓢ Jūjō
15 Ⓚ Kamitobaguchi
12 ⛩ Tōji
Ⓚ Fukakusa
Ⓚ Fujinomori
Ⓚ JR Fujinomori
Ⓢ Fujimori
Ⓢ Kuinabashi
Ⓢ Takeda
Ⓢ Sumizome
Ⓢ Fushimi
Nara Line

See Kyoto Station Area Map (p304)

Ⓢ Marutamachi
Nijō-
jō-mae Ⓢ
Ⓢ Ōmiya 14
Ⓢ Shijō-
Ⓢ Enmachi Ōmiya
Ⓚ Nijō Ⓢ
Nishijōji- Ⓚ
Oike Ⓢ Nishōji-
Ⓢ Sanjō
Ⓚ Sai Ⓢ Sai
Ⓚ Sai-in
Ⓚ Hanazono
Uzumasa- Ⓢ Tenjingawa
Yamanouchi Ⓚ
⛩8 Tanbaguchi Ⓚ
Ⓚ Nishikyōgoku
Ⓢ Nishōji

See Arashiyama & Sagano Area Map (p324)

Ⓚ Uzumasa
Katabira- Ⓚ
no-Tsuji
Ⓚ Kaikonoyashiro
Ⓚ Uzumasa Tokiwa
Ⓚ Kurumazaki
Torokko Saga Ⓚ
Torokko Ⓚ
Arashiyama Ⓚ Sagaekimae
Arashiyama Ⓚ
Arashiyama

Omuro-gawa
Katsura-gawa
Tōkaidō Shinkansen Line
Tōkaidō Main Line (Kyoto Line)
Hankyū Kyoto Line (Kyoto Line)
⛩6
Ⓚ Katsura
Ⓚ Mukōmachi
Ⓚ Higashimukō

Hankyū Arashiyama Line
Ⓚ Matsuo
Ⓚ Kamikatsura
⛰9

Kamo-gawa
Katsura-gawa
Kintetsu Kyoto Line

Greater Kyoto

originally called simple Hongan-ji (Temple of the True Vow). Later Tokugawa Ieyasu saw the power of this sect as a threat to his power and sought to weaken it by encouraging a breakaway faction of this sect to found Higashi Hongan-ji (*higashi* means 'east') in 1602. This temple, the original Hongan-ji, then became known as Nishi Hongan-ji (*nishi* means 'west').

Nishi Hongan-ji now functions as the headquarters of the Hongan-ji branch of the Jōdo Shin-shū school, with over 10,000 temples and more than 12 million followers worldwide.

Tō-ji
BUDDHIST TEMPLE

(東寺; Map p300; 1 Kujō-chō, Minami-ku; admission to grounds free, Kondō & Kōdō ¥500 each, pagoda, Kondō & Kōdō ¥800; ⊙8.30am-5pm 20 Mar-19 Sep, to 4pm 20 Sep-19 Mar; ⬛Kyoto City bus 205 from Kyoto Station, ⬛Kintetsu Kyoto line to Tōji) One of the sights south of Kyoto Station, Tō-ji is an appealing complex of halls and a fantastic pagoda that makes a fine backdrop for the monthly flea market held on the grounds. The temple was established in 794 by imperial decree to protect the city. In 823 the emperor handed it over to Kūkai (known posthumously as Kōbō Daishi), the founder of the Shingon school of Buddhism.

Many of the temple buildings were destroyed by fire or fighting during the 15th century, and most of the remaining buildings were destroyed in the Momoyama period.

The **Nandai-mon** (Main Gate) was transported here in 1894 from Sanjūsangen-dō in Southern Higashiyama. The **Kōdō** (Lecture Hall) dates from the 1600s and contains 21 images representing a Mikkyō (esoteric Buddhist) mandala. The **Kondō** (Main Hall), which was rebuilt in 1606, combines Chinese, Indian and Japanese architectural styles and contains statues depicting the Yakushi (Healing Buddha) trinity.

In the southern part of the garden stands the **Gojū-no-tō**, a five-storey pagoda that, despite having burnt down five times, was doggedly rebuilt in 1643. Standing at 57m, it is now the highest pagoda in Japan.

The Kōbō-san market fair is held here on the 21st of each month. There's also a market that runs on the first Sunday of each month.

Kyoto Railway Museum
MUSEUM

(梅小路蒸気機関車館; Map p300; www.kyoto-railwaymuseum.jp; Kankiji-chō, Shimogyō-ku; adult/child ¥1200/200, train ride ¥300/100; ⊙10am-5.30pm, closed Wed; ⬛; ⬛Kyoto City bus 103, 104 or 105 from Kyoto Station to Umekō-ji Kōen-mae) The Umekoji Steam Locomotive Museum underwent a massive expansion in 2016 to reopen as the Kyoto Railway Museum. This superb museum is spread over three floors showcasing 53 trains, from vintage steam locomotives in the outside Roundhouse Shed to commuter trains and the first *shinkansen* (bullet train) from 1964. Kids will love the interactive displays and impressive railroad diorama with miniature trains zipping through the intricate landscape. You can also take a 10-minute ride on one of the smoke-spewing choo-choos.

★ Tōfuku-ji
BUDDHIST TEMPLE

(東福寺; Map p300; ☑075-561-0087; 15-778 Honmahi, Higashiyama-ku; Hōjō garden ¥400, Tsūten-kyō bridge ¥400; ⊙9am-4pm; ⬛Keihan line to Tōfukuji or JR Nara line to Tōfukuji) Home to a spectacular garden, several superb structures and beautiful precincts, Tōfuku-ji is one of the best temples in Kyoto. It's well worth a visit and can easily be paired with a trip to Fushimi Inari-Taisha (the temples are linked by the Keihan and JR train lines). The present temple complex includes 24 subtemples. The

KYOTO SIGHTS

huge **San-mon** is the oldest Zen main gate in Japan, the **Hōjō** (Abbot's Hall) was reconstructed in 1890, and the gardens were laid out in 1938.

The northern garden has stones and moss neatly arranged in a chequerboard pattern. From a viewing platform at the back of the gardens you can observe the **Tsūten-kyō** (Bridge to Heaven), which spans a valley filled with maples.

Founded in 1236 by the priest Enni, Tōfuku-ji belongs to the Rinzai sect of Zen Buddhism. As this temple was intended to compare with Tōdai-ji and Kōfuku-ji in Nara, it was given a name combining characters from the names of each of these temples.

Tōfuku-ji offers regular Zen meditation sessions for beginners, but don't expect coddling or English-language explanations: this is the real deal. Get a Japanese speaker to enquire at the temple about the next session (it holds about four a month for beginners).

Note that Tōfuku-ji is one of Kyoto's most famous autumn-foliage spots, and it is invariably packed during the peak of colours in November. Otherwise, it's often very quiet.

★**Fushimi Inari-Taisha**　　　SHINTO SHRINE
(伏見稲荷大社; Map p300; 68 Yabunouchi-chō, Fukakusa, Fushimi-ku; ⊙dawn-dusk; ⓡJR Nara line to Inari or Keihan line to Fushimi-Inari) `FREE`
With seemingly endless arcades of vermilion *torii* (shrine gates) spread across a thickly wooded mountain, this vast shrine complex is a world unto its own. It is, quite simply, one of the most impressive and memorable sights in all of Kyoto.

The entire complex, consisting of five shrines, sprawls across the wooded slopes of Inari-san. A pathway wanders 4km up the mountain and is lined with dozens of atmospheric sub-shrines.

Fushimi Inari was dedicated to the gods of rice and sake by the Hata family in the 8th century. As the role of agriculture diminished, deities were enrolled to ensure prosperity in business. Nowadays, the shrine is one of Japan's most popular, and is the head shrine for some 40,000 Inari shrines scattered the length and breadth of the country.

As you explore the shrine, you will come across hundreds of stone foxes. The fox is considered the messenger of Inari, the god of cereals, and the stone foxes, too, are often referred to as Inari. The key often seen in the fox's mouth is for the rice granary. On an incidental note, the Japanese traditionally see the fox as a sacred, somewhat mysterious figure capable of 'possessing' humans – the favoured point of entry is under the fingernails.

The walk around the upper precincts of the shrine is a pleasant day hike. It also makes for a very eerie stroll in the late afternoon and early evening, when the various graveyards and miniature shrines along the path take on a mysterious air. It's best to go with a friend at this time.

KYOTO IN...

Two Days

Start your Kyoto experience by heading to the city's most important sightseeing district, Southern Higashiyama, to visit **Kiyomizu-dera** (p311), **Chion-in** (p314) and **Maruyama-kōen** (p313). If you've still got energy, walk off lunch with a stroll from **Nanzen-ji** (p315) up the Path of Philosophy to **Ginkaku-ji** (p319) in Northern Higashiyama. On the second day, head to the northwest corner of the city to see stunning **Kinkaku-ji** (p321) and the Zen garden at **Ryōan-ji** (p322). From here, hop in a taxi for Arashiyama, for the temple **Tenryū-ji** (p323) and its famous **bamboo grove** (p323). Finish up the evening with a stroll through the historic geisha districts, **Gion** (p315) and **Ponto-chō** (p305).

Four Days

With four days, we recommend doing the above in three days, rather than two, to give yourself more time to explore smaller sights en route and soak up the atmosphere. On the fourth day, take a break from temples to stroll around downtown, hitting the excellent **Nishiki Market** (p304) and nearby craft shops and department stores for souvenirs, maybe taking a walk along the **Kamo-gawa** or holding a picnic in **Kyoto Imperial Palace Park** (p308). Then head for a night out in the bars lining pretty Kiyomachi-dōri (p348). Alternatively, get out of the city and hike to **Kurama-dera** (p328).

Kyoto Station Area

Kyoto Station Area

On 8 April there's a Sangyō-sai festival with offerings and dances to ensure prosperity for national industry. During the first few days in January, thousands of believers visit this shrine as their *hatsu-mōde* (first shrine visit of the New Year) to pray for good fortune.

◉ Downtown Kyoto

★ Nishiki Market · · · · · · · · · · · · · · · MARKET
(錦市場; Map p306; Nishikikōji-dōri, btwn Teramachi & Takakura, Nakagyō-ku; ⏰ 9am-5pm; S Karasuma line to Shijō, 🚃 Hankyū line to Karasuma or Kawaramachi) Head to the covered Nishiki Market

to check out the weird and wonderful foods that go into Kyoto cuisine. It's in the centre of town, one block north of (and parallel to) Shijō-dōri, running west off Teramachi covered arcade. Wander past stalls selling everything from barrels of *tsukemono* (pickled vegetables) and cute Japanese sweets to wasabi salt and *yakitori* skewers. Drop into Aritsugu (p352) here for some of the best Japanese chef's knives money can buy.

Ponto-chō AREA

(先斗町; Map p306; Ponto-chō, Nakagyō-ku; [S] Tōzai line to Sanjo-Keihan or Kyoto-Shiyakusho-mae, [R] Keihan line to Sanjo, Hankyū line to Kawaramachi) There are few streets in Asia that rival this narrow pedestrian-only walkway for atmosphere. Not much to look at by day, the street comes alive at night, with wonderful lanterns, traditional wooden exteriors, and elegant Kyotoites disappearing into the doorways of elite old restaurants and bars.

Ponto-chō is also a great place to spot *geiko* (geisha) and *maiko* (apprentice geisha) making their way between appointments, especially on weekend evenings at the Shijō-dōri end of the street. Many of the restaurants and teahouses can be difficult to enter, but several reasonably priced, accessible places can be found. Even if you have no intention of patronising one of the businesses here, it makes a nice stroll in the evening, perhaps combined with a walk in nearby Gion.

Kyoto International Manga Museum MUSEUM

(京都国際マンガミュージアム; Map p306; www.kyotomm.jp; Karasuma-dōri, Oike-agaru, Nakagyō-ku; adult/child ¥800/100; ⏰10am-6pm, closed Wed; 👪; [S] Karasuma or Tōzai lines to Karasuma-Oike) Located in an old elementary school building, this museum is the perfect introduction to the art of manga (Japanese comics). It has 300,000 manga in its collection, 50,000 of which are on display in the Wall of Manga exhibit. While most of the manga and displays are in Japanese, the collection of translated works is growing. In addition to the galleries that show both the historical development of manga and original artwork done in manga style, there are beginners' workshops and portrait drawings on weekends.

Visitors with children will appreciate the children's library and the occasional performances of *kami-shibai* (humorous traditional Japanese sliding-picture shows), not to mention the artificial lawn where the kids can run free. The museum hosts six-month-long special exhibits yearly: check the website for details.

KYOTO'S BEST TEMPLES & SHRINES

➡ **Nanzen-ji** (p315) The one temple that has it all: expansive grounds, a fine *kare-sansui* (dry landscape) garden, intimate subtemples and soaring halls.

➡ **Ginkaku-ji** (p319) The famed 'Silver Pavilion' boasts one of Kyoto's finest gardens.

➡ **Kinkaku-ji** (p321) A golden apparition rises above a tranquil reflecting pond; it's arguably Kyoto's most impressive sight.

➡ **Heian-jingū** (p320) Colourful shrine with vast gardens.

➡ **Fushimi Inari-Taisha** (p303) A mountain covered with hypnotic arcades of *torii* (Shintō shrine gates).

➡ **Shōren-in** (p314) A rarely visited retreat on the main Southern Higashiyama tourist route with a superb garden.

➡ **Shimogamo-jinja** (p309) A historic and lovely shrine approached by a soothing tree-lined arcade.

★ **Nijō-jō** CASTLE

(二条城; Map p308; 541 Nijōjō-chō, Nijō-dōri, Horikawa nishi-iru, Nakagyō-ku; adult/child ¥600/200; ⏰8.45am-5pm, Ninomaru Palace 9am-4pm, closed Tue Dec, Jan, Jul & Aug; [S] Tōzai line to Nijō-jō-mae, [R] JR line to Nijō Station) The military might of Japan's great warlord generals, the Tokugawa shoguns, is amply demonstrated by the imposing stone walls and ramparts of their great castle, Nijō-jō, which dominates the surrounding area. Hidden behind these you will find a superb palace surrounded by beautiful gardens. As you might expect, a sight of this grandeur attracts a lot of crowds, so it's best to visit just after opening or shortly before closing.

This castle was built in 1603 as the official Kyoto residence of the first Tokugawa shogun, Ieyasu. The ostentatious style of its construction was intended as a demonstration of Ieyasu's prestige and also to signal

Downtown Kyoto

the demise of the emperor's power. As a safeguard against treachery, Ieyasu had the interior fitted with 'nightingale' floors, as well as concealed chambers where bodyguards could keep watch.

After passing through the grand **Karamon gate**, you enter **Ninomaru palace**, which is divided into five buildings with numerous chambers. The **Ōhiroma Yon-no-Ma** (Fourth Chamber) has spectacular screen paintings. Don't miss the excellent **Ninomaru Palace Garden**, which was designed by the tea master and landscape architect Kobori Enshū.

⊙ Imperial Palace & Around

Kyoto Imperial Palace HISTORIC BUILDING

(京都御所 , Kyoto Gosho; Map p308; ☎075-211-1215; www.kunaicho.go.jp; Kyoto Gosho, Nakagyō-ku; ⏲9am-5pm Apr-Aug, 9am-4.30pm Sep & Mar, 9am-4pm Oct-Feb, last entry 40min before closing, closed Mon; [S] Karasuma line to Marutamachi or Imadegawa) [FREE] The Kyoto Imperial Palace, known as the Gosho in Japanese, is a walled complex that sits in the middle of the Kyoto Imperial Palace Park (p308). While no longer the official residence of the Japanese emperor, it's still a grand edifice, though it

Downtown Kyoto

doesn't rate highly in comparison with other attractions in Kyoto. Visitors can wander around the marked route in the grounds where English signs explain the history of the buildings. Entrance is via the main Seishomon Gate where you'll be given a map.

The original imperial palace was built in 794 and was replaced numerous times after destruction by fire. The present building, on a different site and smaller than the original, was constructed in 1855. Enthronement of a new emperor and other state ceremonies are still held here, so at times the palace is closed to the public. Take note: the grounds are covered in gravel stones so wear shoes that are easy to walk in.

➡ **Sentō Gosho Palace**
(仙洞御所; Map p308; ☎075-211-1215; www.kunaicho.go.jp; Kyoto Gyōen, Nakagyō-ku; ⏰tours 9.30am, 11am, 1.30pm & 3pm; [S]Karasuma line to Marutamachi or Imadegawa) [FREE] The Sentō Gosho is the second imperial property located within the Kyoto Imperial Palace Park (the other one is the Imperial Palace itself). The structures are not particularly grand, but the gardens, laid out in 1630 by renowned landscape designer Kobori Enshū, are excellent. Admission is by one-hour tour only (in Japanese; English audio guides are free of charge). You must be over 18 years old and you will need to bring your passport for ID.

It was originally constructed in 1630 during the reign of Emperor Go-Mizunō as a residence for retired emperors. The palace was repeatedly destroyed by fire and reconstructed; it continued to serve its purpose until a final blaze in 1854, after which it was never rebuilt. Today only two structures, the **Seika-tei** and **Yūshin-tei** teahouses, remain.

You can book tickets in advance at the Imperial Household Agency (p310) office or online for morning tours; for afternoon tours tickets go on sale at the palace from 11am and are on a first-come, first-served basis until capacity is sold.

Imperial Palace & Around

→ Kyoto Imperial Palace Park

(京都御苑; Map p308; Kyoto Gyōen, Nakagyō-ku; ⏰dawn-dusk; Ⓢ Karasuma line to Marutamachi or Imadegawa) **FREE** The Kyoto Imperial Palace (p306) (Kyoto Gosho) and Sentō Gosho (p307) are surrounded by the spacious Kyoto Imperial Palace Park, which is planted with a huge variety of flowering trees and open fields. It's perfect for picnics, strolls and just about any sport you can think of. Take some time to visit the pond at the park's southern end, which contains gorgeous carp. The park is most beautiful in the plum- and cherry-blossom seasons (late February and late March, respectively).

The plum arbour is located about midway along the park on the west side. There are several large *shidareze-zakura* ('weeping' cherry trees) at the north end of the park, making it a great cherry-blossom destination. The park is between Teramachi-dōri and Karasuma-dōri (to the east and west)

and Imadegawa-dōri and Marutamachi-dōri (to the north and south).

Kyoto Botanical Gardens GARDENS

(京都府立植物園; Map p308; Shimogamohangi-chō, Sakyō-ku; adult/child gardens ¥200/free, greenhouse ¥200/free; ⏰9am-5pm, greenhouse 10am-4pm; Ⓢ Karasuma line to Kitayama) The Kyoto Botanical Gardens occupy 24 hectares and feature over 12,000 plants, flowers and trees. It is pleasant to stroll through the rose, cherry and herb gardens or see the rows of camphor trees and the large tropical **green-house**. This is a good spot for a picnic and also makes the perfect location for a *han-ami* (cherry-blossom viewing) party, and the blossoms here tend to hold on a little longer than those elsewhere in the city.

★Daitoku-ji BUDDHIST TEMPLE

(大徳寺; Map p308; 53 Daitokuji-chō, Murasakino, Kita-ku; admission to subtemples varies; ⏰hours for subtemples varies; Ⓢ Karasuma line to Kitaōji)

Imperial Palace & Around

Top Sights
1 Daitoku-ji B1
2 Kōtō-in A1
3 Nijō-jō B4

Sights
4 Kitano Tenman-gū A2
5 Kyoto Botanical Gardens C1
6 Kyoto Imperial Palace C3
7 Kyoto Imperial Palace Park C3
8 Sentō Gosho Palace C3
9 Shimogamo-jinja D1

Activities, Courses & Tours
10 Funaoka Onsen B2
11 Haru Cooking Class D2

Sleeping
12 Noku Kyoto C4
13 Palace Side Hotel C3
14 Ryokan Rakuchō C1

Eating
15 Café Bibliotec Hello! C4
16 Demachi Futaba C2
17 Falafel Garden D2
18 Papa Jon's C2
19 Sarasa Nishijin B2

Entertainment
20 Club Ōkitsu Kyoto C3
21 Kitano Odori A2

Transport
22 Demachiyanagi Bicycle Parking Lot D2
Rent a cycle EMUSICA ...... (see 22)

Daitoku-ji is a separate world within Kyoto – a world of Zen temples, perfectly raked gardens and wandering lanes. It's one of the most rewarding destinations in this part of the city, particularly for those interested in Japanese gardens. The eponymous Daitoku-ji temple (usually not open to the public) serves as the headquarters of the Rinzai Daitoku-ji school of Zen Buddhism. The highlights among the subtemples generally open to the public include **Daisen-in**, **Kōtō-in**, **Ōbai-in**, **Ryōgen-in** and **Zuihō-in**.

The main temple, Daitoku-ji, is on the eastern side of the grounds. It was founded in 1319, burnt down in the next century and rebuilt in the 16th century. The **San-mon** gate (1589) has a self-carved statue of its erector, the famous tea master Sen no Rikyū, on its 2nd storey.

The Karasuma subway line is the best way to get here. From Kitaōji Station, walk west along Kitaōji-dōri for about 15 minutes. You'll see the temple complex on your right. The main entrance is bit north of Kitaōji. If you enter from the main gate, which is on the east side of the complex, you'll soon find Daitoku-ji on your right.

★Kōtō-in

(高桐院; Map p308; 73-1 Daitokuji-chō, Murasakino, Kita-ku; ¥400; 9am-4.30pm; Karasuma line to Kitaōji) On the far western edge of the Daitoku-ji complex, the sublime garden of this subtemple is one of the best in all Kyoto and it's worth a special trip. It's located within a fine bamboo grove that you traverse via a moss-lined path. Once inside there is a small stroll garden that leads to the centrepiece: a rectangle of moss and maple trees, backed by bamboo. Take some time on the verandah here to soak it all up.

Shimogamo-jinja — SHINTO SHRINE

(下鴨神社; Map p308; 59 Izumigawa-chō, Shimogamo, Sakyō-ku; 6.30am-5pm; Kyoto City bus 205 to Shimogamo-jinja-mae, Keihan line to Demachiyanagi) FREE This shrine, dating from the 8th century, is a Unesco World Heritage Site. It is nestled in the fork of the Kamo-gawa and Takano-gawa, and is approached along a shady path through the lovely Tadasu-no-mori. This wooded area is said to be a place where lies cannot be concealed and is considered a prime location to sort out disputes. The trees here are mostly broadleaf (a rarity in Kyoto) and they are gorgeous in the springtime.

The shrine is dedicated to the god of harvest. Traditionally, pure water was drawn from the nearby rivers for purification and agricultural ceremonies. The **Hondō** (Main Hall) dates from 1863 and, like the **Haiden** hall at its sister shrine, Kamigamo-jinja, is an excellent example of *nagare*-style shrine architecture. The annual *yabusame* (horseback archery) event here is spectacular. It happens on 3 May in Tadasu-no-mori.

Kamigamo-jinja — SHINTO SHRINE

(上賀茂神社; Map p300; 075-781-0011; www.kamigamojinja.jp; 339 Motoyama, Kamigamo, Kita-ku; 6am-5pm; Kyoto City bus 9 to Kamigamo-misonobashi) FREE Around 2km north of the Botanical Gardens is Kamigamo-jinja,

ⓘ VISITING IMPERIAL HOUSEHOLD PROPERTIES

As of mid-2016, visitors no longer have to apply for permission to visit the **Kyoto Imperial Palace** (p306). The palace, situated inside the Imperial Palace Park, is open to the public from Tuesday to Sunday and you just need to go straight to the main gate for entry. Children are permitted with an accompanying adult.

Permission to visit the **Sentō Gosho** (p307), **Katsura Rikyū** (p326) and **Shūgaku-in Rikyū** (p321) is granted by the Kunaichō, the **Imperial Household Agency** (宮内庁京都事務所; Map p308; ☑075-211-1215; www.kunaicho.go.jp; ⊙8.45am-5pm, closed Mon; Ⓢ Karasuma line to Imadegawa), which is inside the **Imperial Palace Park** (p308). For morning tours, you have to fill out an application form and show your passport, or you can apply via its website, too. You must be over 18 years to enter each property. For afternoon tours, you can book tickets on the same day at the properties themselves from 11am. Only a certain number of tickets are issued each day, so it's first-come first-served. Sentō Gosho and Shūgaku-in tours run for 60 minutes, while the Katsura Rikyū runs for 80 minutes. All tours are free and are in Japanese with English audio guides available.

one of Japan's oldest shrines, which predates the founding of Kyoto. Established in 679, it is dedicated to Raijin, the god of thunder, and is one of Kyoto's 17 Unesco World Heritage Sites. The present buildings (more than 40 in all), including the impressive Haiden hall, are exact reproductions of the originals, dating from the 17th to 19th centuries.

◉ Southern Higashiyama

Southern Higashiyama, at the base of the Higashiyama (Eastern Mountains), is Kyoto's richest area for sightseeing. Thick with temples, shrines, museums and traditional shops, it's great to explore on foot, with some pedestrian-only walkways plus parks and expansive temple grounds. It's also home to the Gion entertainment district and some of the city's finest ryokan (traditional Japanese inns).

This is Kyoto's most popular sightseeing district, so it will be crowded during peak seasons. Walking or taking the train/subway is the way to go as traffic comes to a standstill.

Sanjūsangen-dō Temple BUDDHIST TEMPLE
(三十三間堂; Map p312; ☑075-561-0467; 657 Sanjūsangendōma wari-chō, Higashiyama-ku; adult/child ¥600/300; ⊙8am-5pm Apr–mid-Nov, 9am-4pm mid-Nov–Mar; 🚌Kyoto City bus 206 or 208 to Sanjūsangen-dō-mae, 🚆Keihan line to Shichijō) This superb temple's name refers to the 33 *sanjūsan* (bays) between the pillars of this long, narrow edifice. The building houses 1001 wooden statues of Kannon (the Buddhist goddess of mercy); the chief image, the 1000-armed Senju-Kannon, was carved by the celebrated sculptor Tankei in 1254. It is flanked by 500 smaller Kannon

images, neatly lined in rows. The visual effect is stunning, making this a must-see in Southern Higashiyama and a good starting point for exploration of the area.

The original temple, called Rengeō-in, was built in 1164 at the request of the retired emperor Go-shirakawa. After it burnt to the ground in 1249, a faithful copy was constructed in 1266.

If you look closely, you might notice that the supposedly 1000-armed statues don't have the required number. Just keep in mind that a nifty Buddhist mathematical formula holds that 40 arms are the equivalent of 1000 because each saves 25 worlds.

At the back of the hall are 28 guardian statues in a variety of expressive poses. The gallery at the western side of the hall is famous for the annual **Tōshiya festival**, held on 15 January, when archers shoot arrows along the length of the hall. The ceremony dates from the Edo period, when an annual contest was held to see how many arrows could be shot from the southern to northern end in 24 hours. The all-time record was set in 1686, when an archer successfully landed more than 8000 arrows at the northern end.

Kyoto National Museum MUSEUM
(京都国立博物館; Map p312; www.kyohaku. go.jp; 527 Chaya-machi, Higashiyama-ku; ¥520; ⊙9.30am-5pm, closed Mon; during special exhibitions, to 8pm Fri; 🚌Kyoto City bus 206 or 208 to Sanjūsangen-dō-mae, 🚆Keihan line to Shichijō) The Kyoto National Museum is the city's premier art museum and plays host to the highest-level exhibitions in the city. It was founded in 1895 as an imperial repository for art and treasures from local temples and shrines. In the original

main hall there are rooms with displays of over 1000 artworks, historical artefacts and handicrafts. The **Heisei Chishinkan**, designed by Taniguchi Yoshio and opened in 2014, is a brilliant modern counterpoint to the original building.

While the permanent collection is worth a visit, the special exhibitions are the real highlights. Check with the Kyoto Tourist Information Center (TIC) or the *Kyoto Visitor's Guide* to see what's on while you're in town.

Kawai Kanjirō Memorial Hall MUSEUM (河井寛治郎記念館; Map p312; 075-561-3585; 569 Kanei-chō, Gojō-zaka, Higashiyama-ku; ¥900; ⊙10am-5pm Tue-Sun; 📮Kyoto City bus 206 or 207 to Umamachi) This small memorial hall is one of Kyoto's most commonly overlooked little gems. The hall was the home and workshop of one of Japan's most famous potters, Kawai Kanjirō (1890–1966). The 1937 house is built in rural style and contains examples of Kanjirō's work, his collection of folk art and ceramics, his workshop and a fascinating *nobori-gama* (stepped kiln). The museum is near the intersection of Gojō-dōri and Higashiōji-dōri.

★ **Kiyomizu-dera** BUDDHIST TEMPLE (清水寺; Map p312; 🖉075-551-1234; www. kiyomizudera.or.jp; 1-294 Kiyomizu, Higashiyama-ku; ¥400; ⊙6am-6pm, closing times vary seasonally; 📮Kyoto City bus 206 to Kiyōmizu-michi or Gojō-zaka, 🚉Keihan line to Kiyomizu-Gojō) A buzzing hive of activity perched on a hill overlooking the basin of Kyoto, Kiyomizu-dera is one of Kyoto's most popular and most enjoyable temples. It may not be a tranquil refuge, but it represents the favoured expression of faith in Japan. The excellent website is a great first port of call for information on the temple, plus a how-to guide to praying here. Note that the Main

Hall is undergoing renovations and may be covered, though is still accessible.

This ancient temple was first built in 798, but the present buildings are reconstructions dating from 1633. As an affiliate of the Hossō school of Buddhism, which originated in Nara, it has successfully survived the many intrigues of local Kyoto schools of Buddhism through the centuries and is now one of the most famous landmarks of the city (for which reason it can get very crowded during spring and autumn).

The **Hondō** (Main Hall) has a huge verandah that is supported by pillars and juts out over the hillside. Just below this hall is the waterfall **Otowa-no-taki**, where visitors drink sacred waters believed to bestow health and longevity. Dotted around the precincts are other halls and shrines. At **Jishu-jinja**, the shrine up the steps above the main hall, visitors try to ensure success in love by closing their eyes and walking 18m between a pair of stones – if you miss the stone, your desire for love won't be fulfilled! You can ask someone to guide you, but if you do, you'll need someone's assistance to find your true love.

Before you enter the actual temple precincts, check out the **Tainai-meguri**, the entrance to which is just to the left (north) of the pagoda that is located in front of the main entrance to the temple (there is no English sign). We won't tell you too much about it as it will ruin the experience. Suffice to say that by entering the Tainai-meguri, you are symbolically entering the womb of a female bodhisattva. When you get to the rock in the darkness, spin it in either direction to make a wish.

The steep approach to the temple is known as **Chawan-zaka** (Teapot Lane) and is lined with shops selling Kyoto handicrafts, local snacks and souvenirs.

CHERRY BLOSSOMS

It can be a magical experience when the cherry trees blossom in Kyoto in early April. *Hanami* (cherry-blossom viewing parties) take place all over town. However, the city's main tourist sites will be mobbed. You'll need to book accommodation well in advance and anticipate that getting around will require more time and patience than usual (taxi ranks at Kyoto Station, for example, will have long queues).

Should you decide to join the party, **Maruyama-kōen** (p313) is one of the most popular *hanami* spots. The centrepiece is a massive *shidare-zakura* cherry tree; this is one of the most beautiful sights in Kyoto, particularly when lit up from below at night. Be sure to arrive early and claim a good spot high on the east side of the park, from where you can peer down on the mayhem below.

Other top spots include **Kyoto Imperial Palace Park** (p308) and the Kamo-gawa riverbanks. In the evening, join the crowds on Gion's Shimbashi.

Southern Higashiyama

KYOTO

Oike-dōri

Kyoto-Shiyakusho-mae
(Kyoto City Hall)

Oike-
Ōhashi

Sanjō
Keihan

Sanjō

Sanjō-dōri

Sanjō
Ōhashi

Hanami-kōji

Higashiyama

19

23
30

Higashiōji-dōri

37

4

Shōren-in

Ponto-chō

Kiyamachi-dōri

Furumonzen-dōri

39

1

Chion-in

Nawate-dōri

Shinmonzen-dōri

Shimbashi-dōri

25

SHINBASHI

Kiri-dōshi

14

33

Shijō-
Ōhashi

Kawaramachi

26

38

12

9

Shijō-dōri

Gion-
Shijō

36

31

GION

Hanami-kōji

HIGASHIYAMA-KU

Maruyama-kōen

35

Kawaramachi-dōri

Kawabata-dōri

Takasegawa

Kamo-gawa

Higashiōji-dōri

32

20

27

7

Gion

6

21

2

Yasui
Konpira-gū

15

P

22

34

Miyagawachō-dōri

Yasaka-dōri

28

17

13

10

Kiyomizu-michi

Sannen-zaka

Kawabata-dōri

Kiyomizu-
dera

Kiyomizu-
Gojō

Gojō-
Ōhashi

Gojō-dōri

16

Gojō-zaka
Bus Stop

29

Gojō-zaka

Chawan-zaka

3

24

Toiyamachi-dōri

Sayamachi-dōri

Yamatooji-dōri

5

Gojō-dōri

Syomen-dōri

Shibutani-dōri

8

Shichijō

Shichijō-dōri

18

11

Southern Higashiyama

Top Sights
- 1 Chion-in D2
- 2 Gion D4
- 3 Kiyomizu-dera D5
- 4 Shōren-in D2

Sights
- 5 Kawai Kanjirō Memorial Hall B6
- 6 Kennin-ji B4
- 7 Kōdai-ji D4
- 8 Kyoto National Museum B7
- 9 Maruyama-kōen D3
- 10 Ninen-zaka & Sannen-zaka Area C4
- 11 Sanjūsangen-dō Temple B7
- 12 Yasaka-jinja C3

Activities, Courses & Tours
- 13 Camellia Tea Experience C4
- 14 En C2
- 15 Maika A4

Sleeping
- Gion Hatanaka .... (see 35)
- 16 Gojō Guest House B5
- 17 Gojo Guesthouse Annexe B4
- 18 Hyatt Regency Kyoto B7
- 19 Koto Inn D1
- 20 Motonago C3
- 21 Old Kyoto B4
- 22 Ryokan Uemura C4
- 23 Sakara Kyoto C1
- 24 Seikōrō A5
- 25 Shiraume Ryokan B2

Eating
- 26 Kagizen Yoshifusa B3
- Kasagi-ya .... (see 10)
- 27 Kikunoi D3
- 28 Omen Kodai-ji D4
- 29 Sobadokoro Shibazaki C5

Drinking & Nightlife
- 30 Beer Komachi C1
- 31 Gion Finlandia Bar B3
- Tōzan Bar .... (see 18)

Entertainment
- 32 Gion Corner B3
- 33 Gion Odori C2
- 34 Kyō Odori A4
- 35 Kyoto Cuisine & Maiko Evening C3
- 36 Minami-za B3
- Miyako Odori .... (see 32)

Shopping
- 37 Ichizawa Shinzaburo Hanpu C2
- 38 Yojiya B3

Transport
- 39 Bicycle Parking Lot A2

Check the website for the scheduling of special night-time illuminations of the temple held in the spring and autumn.

Ninen-zaka & Sannen-zaka Area AREA
(二年坂・三年坂; Map p312; Higashiyama-ku; 🚌 Kyoto City bus 206 to Kiyomizu-michi or Gojō-zaka, 🚆 Keihan line to Kiyomizu-Gojō) Just downhill from and slightly to the north of Kiyomizu-dera, you will find one of Kyoto's loveliest restored neighbourhoods, the Ninen-zaka–Sannen-zaka area. The name refers to the two main streets of the area: Ninen-zaka and Sannen-zaka, literally 'Two-Year Hill' and 'Three-Year Hill' (the years referring to the ancient imperial years when they were first laid out). These two charming streets are lined with old wooden houses, traditional shops and restaurants.

Kōdai-ji BUDDHIST TEMPLE
(高台寺; Map p312; ☎075-561-9966; www.kodaiji.com; 526 Shimokawara-chō, Kōdai-ji, Higashiyama-ku; ¥600; ⏰9am-5.30pm; 🚌 Kyoto City bus 206 to Yasui, [S] Tōzai line to Higashiyama) This exquisite temple was founded in 1605 by Kita-no-Mandokoro in memory of her late husband, Toyotomi Hideyoshi. The extensive grounds include gardens designed by the famed landscape architect Kobori Enshū, and teahouses designed by the renowned master of the tea ceremony, Sen no Rikyū.

The temple holds three annual special night-time illuminations, when the gardens are lit by multicoloured spotlights. They are held from mid-March to early May, 1 to 18 August, and late October to early December.

Maruyama-kōen PARK
(円山公園; Map p312; Maruyama-chō, Higashiyama-ku; [S] Tōzai line to Higashiyama) Maruyama-kōen is a favourite of locals and visitors alike. This park is the place to come to escape the bustle of the city centre and amble around gardens, ponds, souvenir shops and restaurants. Peaceful paths meander through the trees, and carp glide through the waters of a small pond in the park's centre.

Yasaka-jinja SHINTO SHRINE
(八坂神社; Map p312; ☎075-561-6155; www.yasaka-jinja.or.jp; 625 Gion-machi, Kita-gawa, Higashiyama-ku; ⏰24hr; [S] Tōzai line to Higashiyama) [FREE] This colourful and spacious

OFF THE BEATEN TRACK

DAIGO-JI

Daigo-ji (醍醐寺; Map p300; 22 Higashiōji-chō, Daigo, Fushimi-ku; Kondō Hall, Sampō-in & pagoda ¥800, during spring ¥1500, Kami Daigo extra ¥500; ⏲9am-5pm Mar-Nov, to 4.30pm Dec-Feb; [S] Tōzai line to Daigo) is a World Heritage–listed sprawling temple complex located in the Daigo district of Kyoto, which lies on the east side of the Higashiyama Mountains, accessible by the Tōzai subway line. Outside of the cherry-blossom season (early April), it's not a high-priority destination, but it makes a good half-day trip for those who like hiking and want a break from the more famous temples in the city centre.

Daigo-ji was founded in 874 by Shobo, who named it Daigo ('the ultimate essence of milk'). This refers to the five periods of Buddha's teaching, which were compared to the five forms of milk prepared in India; the highest form is called *daigo* in Japanese.

The temple was expanded into a vast complex on two levels: **Shimo Daigo** (lower) and **Kami Daigo** (upper). Kami Daigo is atop **Daigo-yama**, behind the temple. During the 15th century those buildings on the lower level were destroyed, with the sole exception of the five-storey pagoda (**Garan**). Built in 951, this pagoda is treasured as the oldest of its kind in Japan and is the oldest existing building in Kyoto.

In the late 16th century, Hideyoshi took a fancy to Daigo-ji and ordered extensive rebuilding. It is now one of the Shingon school's main temples. To explore Daigo-ji thoroughly and at a leisurely pace, mixing some hiking with your temple-viewing, you will need at least half a day.

The subtemple **Sampō-in** is a fine example of the amazing opulence of that period. The Kanō paintings and the garden are special features.

From Sampō-in it's a steep and tiring 50-minute climb up to Kami Daigo. To get here, walk up the large avenue of cherry trees, through the Niō-mon gate, out the back gate of the lower temple, up a concrete incline and into the forest, past the pagoda.

To get to Daigo-ji, take the Tōzai line subway east from central Kyoto to the Daigo stop, and walk east (towards the mountains) for about 10 minutes. Make sure that the train you board is bound for Rokujizō, as some head to Hama-Ōtsu instead.

shrine is considered the guardian shrine of the Gion entertainment district. It's a bustling place that is well worth a visit while exploring Southern Higashiyama; it can be paired with Maruyama-kōen, the park just up the hill.

★Chion-in — BUDDHIST TEMPLE

(知恩院; Map p312; www.chion-in.or.jp; 400 Rinka-chō, Higashiyama-ku; inner buildings & garden adult/child ¥500/250, grounds free; ⏲9am-4.30pm; [S] Tōzai line to Higashiyama) A collection of soaring buildings and spacious courtyards, Chion-in serves as the headquarters of the Jōdo sect, the largest school of Buddhism in Japan. It's the most popular pilgrimage temple in Kyoto and it's always a hive of activity. For visitors with a taste for the grand, this temple is sure to satisfy.

Chion-in was established in 1234 on the site where Hōnen, one of the most famous figures in Japanese Buddhism, taught his brand of Buddhism (Jōdo, or Pure Land, Buddhism) and eventually fasted to death.

The oldest of the present buildings date to the 17th century. The two-storey **San-mon** temple gate is the largest in Japan. The immense main hall (Miei-dō Hall) contains an image of Hōnen. It's connected to another hall, the **Dai Hōjō**, by a 'nightingale' floor (that sings and squeaks at every move, making it difficult for intruders to move about quietly). Miei-dō Hall is currently under restoration and closed to the public. It's expected to be finished by 2019.

Up a flight of steps southeast of the main hall is the temple's **giant bell**, which was cast in 1633 and weighs 70 tonnes. It is the largest bell in Japan. The bell is rung by the temple's monks 108 times on New Year's Eve each year.

★Shōren-in — BUDDHIST TEMPLE

(青蓮院; Map p312; 69-1 Sanjōbō-chō, Awataguchi, Higashiyama-ku; ¥500; ⏲9am-5pm; [S] Tōzai line to Higashiyama) This temple is hard to miss, with its giant camphor trees growing just outside the walls. Fortunately, most tourists march right on past, heading to the area's more famous temples. That is their loss, because this intimate little sanctuary contains a superb landscape garden, which you can enjoy while drinking a cup of green tea (¥400, 9am to 4pm; ask at the reception office).

★**Gion** AREA

(祇園周辺; Map p312; Higashiyama-ku; S Tōzai line to Sanjō, R Keihan line to Gion-Shijō) Gion is the famous entertainment and geisha quarter on the eastern bank of the Kamo-gawa. While Gion's true origins were in teahouses catering to weary visitors to the nearby shrine Yasaka-jinja, by the mid-18th century the area was Kyoto's largest pleasure district. The best way to experience Gion today is with an evening stroll around the atmospheric streets lined with 17th-century traditional restaurants and teahouses lit up with lanterns. Start off on the main street **Hanami-kōji**, which runs north–south and bisects Shijō-dōri.

At the southern section of Hanami-kōji, many of the restaurants and teahouses are exclusive establishments for geisha entertainment. At the south end you reach Gion Corner (p351) and **Gion Kōbu Kaburen-jō Theatre** (祇園甲部歌舞練場).

If you walk from Shijō-dōri along the northern section of Hanami-kōji and take your third left, you'll find yourself on **Shimbashi** (often called Shirakawa Minami-dōri), which is truly one of Kyoto's most beautiful streets, especially in the evening and during cherry-blossom season. A bit further north lie **Shinmonzen-dōri** and **Furumonzen-dōri**, running east–west. Wander in either direction along these streets, which are packed with old houses, art galleries and shops specialising in antiques – but don't expect flea-market prices.

Kennin-ji BUDDHIST TEMPLE

(建仁寺; Map p312; www.kenninji.jp; 584 Komatsuchō, Yamatoōji-dōri, Shijo-sagaru, Higashiyama-ku; ¥500; ⏰10am-5pm Mar-Oct, to 4.30pm Nov-Feb; R Keihan line to Gion-Shijō) Founded in 1202 by the monk Eisai, Kennin-ji is the oldest Zen temple in Kyoto. It's an island of peace and calm on the border of the boisterous Gion nightlife district and it makes a fine counterpoint to the worldly pleasures of that area. The highlight at Kennin-ji is the fine and expansive *kare-sansui* (dry landscape). The painting of the twin dragons on the roof of the **Hōdō** hall is also fantastic.

Yasui Konpira-gū SHINTO SHRINE

(安井金比羅宮; Map p312; www.yasui-konpiragu. or.jp; 70 Simobenten-chō, Higashiyama-ku; ⏰24hr; R Kyoto City bus 204 to Higashiyama-Yasui) This interesting little Shintō shrine on the edge of Gion contains one of the most peculiar objects we've encountered anywhere in Japan: the **enkiri/enmusubi ishi**. Resembling some kind of shaggy igloo, this is a stone that is thought to bind good relationships tighter and sever bad relationships.

If you'd like to take advantage of the stone's powers, here's the drill: purchase a special piece of paper from the counter next to the stone and write your name and wish on it. If you want to bind your love tighter (figuratively, of course), grasp the paper and crawl through the tunnel in the stone from front to back. If you want out of your present relationship, crawl through from back to front. Then, use the glue provided and stick your wishing paper to the ever-huge collection of wishes decorating the stone.

⊙ Northern Higashiyama

At the northern end of the Higashiyama Mountains, this area is packed with first-rate attractions and soothing greenery, making it one of the best areas for relaxed sightseeing. The main area stretches from Nanzen-ji in the south to Ginkaku-ji in the north, two temples linked by the lovely Path of Philosophy (Tetsugaku-no-Michi). Other attractions include Hōnen-in, a quiet temple overlooked by the crowds, the superb Eikan-dō temple, and the museums around Okazaki-kōen.

Visit the big-name sights here (Ginkaku-ji, Eikan-dō and Nanzen-ji) early on a weekday morning to avoid the crowds. Alternatively, go right before closing.

★**Nanzen-ji** BUDDHIST TEMPLE

(南禅寺; Map p316; www.nanzenji.com; 86 Fukuchi-chō, Nanzen-ji, Sakyō-ku; Nanzen-in ¥300, Hōjō garden ¥500, San-mon gate ¥500, grounds free; ⏰8.40am-5pm Mar-Nov, to 4.30pm Dec-Feb; R Kyoto City bus 5 to Eikandō-michi, S Tōzai line to Keage) This is one of the most rewarding temples in Kyoto, with its expansive grounds and numerous subtemples. At its entrance stands the massive **San-mon**. Steps lead up to the 2nd storey, which has a great view over the city. Beyond the gate is the main hall of the temple, above which you will find the **Hōjō**, where the Leaping Tiger Garden is a classic Zen garden well worth a look.

➤ **Tenju-an**

(天授庵; Map p316; 86-8 Fukuchi-chō, Nanzen-ji, Sakyō-ku; ¥300; ⏰9am-5pm Mar–Nov, to 4.30pm mid-Nov–Feb; R Kyoto City bus 5 to Eikandō-michi, S Tōzai line to Keage) A subtemple of Nanzen-ji, Tenju-an is located on the south side of San-mon, the main gate of Nanzen-ji. Constructed in 1337, it has a splendid garden and a great collection of carp in its pond.

Northern Higashiyama

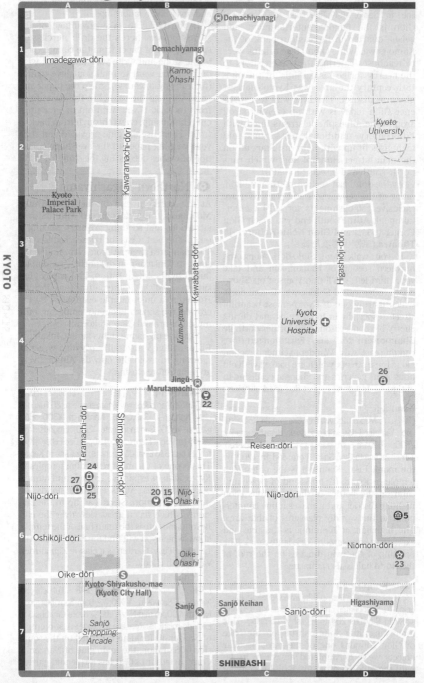

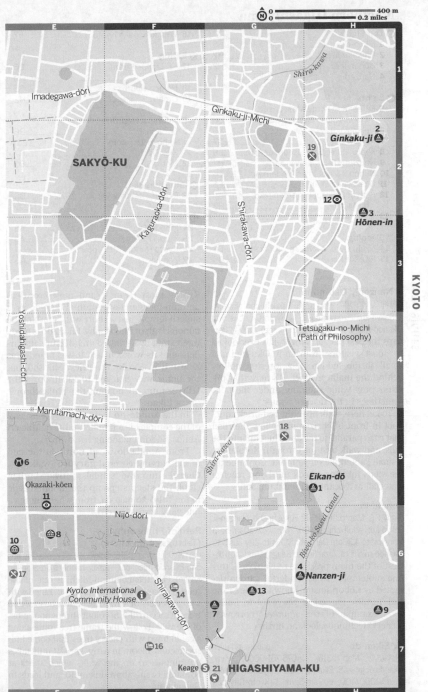

0
400 m
0
0.2 miles

Imadegawa-dōri

Shira-kawa

Ginkaku-ji-Michi

Ginkaku-ji 2

19

SAKYŌ-KU

12

Hōnen-in 3

Shirakawa-dōri

Kaguraoka-dōri

Tetsugaku-no-Michi
(Path of Philosophy)

Yoshidahigashi-cōri

Marutamachi-dōri

18

6

Eikan-dō 1

Okazaki-kōen

11

Shira-kawa

Biwa-ko Sosui Canal

8

Nijō-dōri

10

17

Nanzen-ji 4

9

Kyoto International
Community House

Shirakawa-dōri

14

13

7

16

Keage 21 **HIGASHIYAMA-KU**

Northern Higashiyama

KYOTO SIGHTS

➡ Nanzen-ji Oku-no-in

(南禅寺奥の院; Map p316; Fukuchi-chō, Nanzen-ji, Sakyō-ku; ⊙dawn-dusk; 🚍Kyoto City bus 5 to Eikandō-michi, 🚇Tōzai line to Keage) FREE Perhaps the best part of Nanzen-ji is overlooked by most visitors: Nanzen-ji Oku-no-in, a small shrine hidden in a forested hollow behind the main precinct. It's here that pilgrims pray while standing under the falls, sometimes in the dead of winter.

To get here, walk up to the red-brick aqueduct in front of Nanzen-in. Follow the road that runs parallel to the aqueduct up into the hills, and walk past (or through) Kōtoku-an, a small subtemple on your left. Continue up the steps into the woods until you reach a waterfall in a beautiful mountain glen.

Konchi-in   BUDDHIST TEMPLE
(金地院; Map p316; 86-12 Fukuchi-chō, Nanzen-ji, Sakyō-ku; adult/child ¥400/200; ⊙8.30am-5pm Mar-Nov, to 4.30pm Dec-Feb; 🚍Kyoto City bus 5 to Eikandō-michi, 🚇Tōzai line to Keage) Just southwest of the main precincts of Nanzen-ji, this fine subtemple has a wonderful garden designed by Kobori Enshū, known as the Crane and Tortoise garden. If you want to find a good example of the *shakkei* (borrowed scenery) technique, look no further.

★Eikan-dō   BUDDHIST TEMPLE
(永観堂; Map p316; 📞075-761-0007; www.eikando.or.jp; 48 Eikandō-chō, Sakyō-ku; adult/child ¥1000/400; ⊙9am-5pm; 🚍Kyoto City bus 5 to Eikandō-michi, 🚇Tōzai line to Keage) Perhaps

Kyoto's most famous (and most crowded) autumn-foliage destination, Eikan-dō is a superb temple just a short walk south of the famous Path of Philosophy. Eikan-dō is made interesting by its varied architecture, its gardens and its works of art. It was founded as Zenrin-ji in 855 by the priest Shinshō, but the name was changed to Eikan-dō in the 11th century to honour the philanthropic priest Eikan.

In the **Amida-dō** hall at the southern end of the complex is a famous statue of Mikaeri Amida Buddha glancing backwards.

From Amida-dō, head north to the end of the curving covered **garyūrō** (walkway). Change into the sandals provided, then climb the steep steps up the mountainside to the **Tahō-tō** pagoda, from where there's a fine view across the city.

**Path of Philosophy
(Tetsugaku-no-Michi)**   AREA
(哲学の道; Map p316; Sakyō-ku; 🚍Kyoto City bus 5 to Eikandō-michi or Ginkakuji-michi, 🚇Tōzai line to Keage) The Tetsugaku-no-Michi is one of the most pleasant walks in all of Kyoto. Lined with a great variety of flowering plants, bushes and trees, it's a corridor of colour throughout most of the year. Follow the traffic-free route along a canal lined with cherry trees that come into spectacular bloom in early April. It only takes 30 minutes to do the walk, which starts at Nyakuōji-bashi, above Eikan-dō, and leads to Ginkaku-ji.

The path takes its name from one of its most famous strollers: 20th-century philosopher Nishida Kitarō, who is said to have meandered lost in thought along the path.

During the day in the cherry-blossom season, you should be prepared for crowds; a night stroll will definitely be quieter.

★Hōnen-in BUDDHIST TEMPLE

(法然院; Map p316; 30 Goshonodan-chō, Shishigatani, Sakyō-ku; 🕓6am-4pm; 🚌Kyoto City bus 5 to Ginkakuji-michi) [FREE] One of Kyoto's hidden pleasures, this temple was founded in 1680 to honour the priest Hōnen. It's a lovely, secluded temple with carefully raked gardens set back in the woods. The temple buildings include a small gallery where frequent exhibitions featuring local and international artists are held. If you need to escape the crowds that positively plague nearby Ginkaku-ji, come to this serene refuge.

Hōnen-in is a 12-minute walk from Ginkaku-ji, on a side street above the Path of Philosophy (Tetsugaku-no-Michi); you may have to ask for directions.

★Ginkaku-ji BUDDHIST TEMPLE

(銀閣寺; Map p316; 2 Ginkaku-ji-chō, Sakyō-ku; adult/child ¥500/300; 🕓8.30am-5pm Mar-Nov, 9am-4.30pm Dec-Feb; 🚌Kyoto City bus 5 to Ginkakuji-michi stop) Home to a sumptuous garden and elegant structures, Ginkaku-ji is one of Kyoto's premier sites. The temple started its life in 1482 as a retirement villa for Shogun Ashikaga Yoshimasa, who desired a place to retreat from the turmoil of a civil war. While the name Ginkaku-ji literally translates as 'Silver Pavilion', the shogun's ambition to cover the building with silver was never realised. After Yoshimasa's death, the villa was converted into a temple.

Walkways lead through the gardens, which include meticulously raked cones of white sand (said to be symbolic of a mountain and a lake), tall pines and a pond in front of the temple. A path also leads up the mountainside through the trees.

Ginkaku-ji is one of the city's most popular sites, and it's almost always crowded, especially during spring and autumn. We strongly recommend visiting right after it opens or just before it closes.

Okazaki-kōen Area AREA

(岡崎公園; Map p316; Okazaki, Sakyo-ku; [S] Tōzai line to Higashiyama) Okazaki-kōen is an expanse of parks and canals that lies between Niōmon-dōri and Heian-jingū. Two of Kyoto's significant museums can be found here – the National Museum of Modern Art (p320) and Kyoto Municipal Museum of Art (p320) – as well as two smaller museums.

MACHIYA: KYOTO'S TRADITIONAL TOWNHOUSE

One of the city's most notable architectural features are its *machiya,* long and narrow wooden row houses that functioned as both homes and workplaces. The shop area was at the front of the house, while the rooms lined up behind it formed the family's private quarters. Nicknamed *'unagi no nedoko'* (eel bedrooms), the *machiya*'s elongated shape came about because homes were once taxed according to the amount of their street frontage.

A *machiya* is a self-contained world, complete with private well, store house, Buddhist altar, clay ovens outfitted with huge iron rice cauldrons, shrines for the hearth god and other deities, and interior mini-gardens.

Although well suited to Kyoto's humid, mildew-prone summers, a wooden *machiya* has a limited lifespan of about 50 years. Thus, as the cost of traditional materials and workmanship rose, and as people's desire for a more Western-style lifestyle increased, fewer and fewer people felt the urge to rebuild the old family home, as had been the custom in the past. Those considerations, plus the city's high inheritance tax, convinced many owners to tear down their *machiya,* build a seven-storey apartment building, occupy the ground floor, and live off the rent of their tenants.

The result is that Kyoto's urban landscape – once a harmonious sea of clay-tiled two-storey wooden townhouses – is now a jumble of ferro-concrete offices and apartment buildings.

Ironically, however, *machiya* are making a comeback. After their numbers drastically declined, the old townhouses began to acquire an almost exotic appeal. Astute developers began to convert them into restaurants, clothing boutiques and even hair salons. Today such shops are a major draw for the city's tourist trade, and not only foreign visitors – the Japanese themselves (especially Tokyoites) – love their old-fashioned charm.

WORTH A TRIP

BYŌDŌ-IN

Byōdō-in (平等院; ☎0774-21-2861; 116 Uji-renge, Uji-shi; ¥600, Hōō-dō guided tour extra ¥300; ⏰9am-5pm, gardens 8.30am-5.30pm, Hōō-dō 9.10am-4.10pm; 🚃JR Nara line or Keihan line to Uji) is the star attraction in the Kyoto suburb of Uji. It's home to one of the loveliest Buddhist structures in Japan: the Hōō-dō hall, which is depicted on the back of the Japanese ¥10 coin. Perched overlooking a serene reflecting pond, this refurbished hall is a stunning sight. Paired with a stroll along the banks of the nearby Uji-gawa, this temple makes a good half-day trip out of Kyoto City.

This temple was converted from a Fujiwara villa into a Buddhist temple in 1052. The **Hōō-dō** (Phoenix Hall), the main hall of the temple, was built in 1053 and is the only original building remaining. The phoenix used to be a popular mythical bird in China and was revered by the Japanese as a protector of Buddha. The architecture of the building resembles the shape of the bird and there are two bronze phoenixes perched opposite each other on the roof. Short guided tours inside the hall are in Japanese but there's an English leaflet.

The Hōō-dō was originally intended to represent Amida's heavenly palace in the Pure Land. This building is one of the few extant examples of Heian-period architecture, and its graceful lines make you wish that far more had survived the wars and fires that have plagued Kyoto's past. Inside the hall is the famous statue of Amida Buddha and 52 *bosatsu* (bodhisattvas) dating from the 11th century and attributed to the priest-sculptor Jōchō.

Nearby, the **Hōmotsukan Treasure House** contains the original temple bell and door paintings and the original phoenix roof adornments. Allow an hour to wander the grounds.

Uji can be reached by train in about 40 minutes from Kyoto on the Keihan Uji line or the JR Nara line.

If you find yourself in Kyoto on a rainy day, there's enough indoor sightseeing here to keep you dry.

Kyoto Municipal Museum of Art MUSEUM
(京都市美術館; Map p316; 124 Enshōji-chō, Okazaki, Sakyō-ku; admission varies; ⏰9am-5pm, closed Mon; 🚇Tōzai line to Higashiyama) This fine museum holds several major exhibitions a year, as well as a variety of free shows. It's always worth stopping by to see if something is on while you are in town. The pond behind the museum is a great place for a picnic.

National Museum of Modern Art MUSEUM
(京都国立近代美術館; Map p316; www.momak.go.jp; Enshōji-chō, Okazaki, Sakyō-ku; ¥430, extra for special exhibitions; ⏰9.30am-5pm, to 8pm Fri Apr-Sep, closed Mon; 🚇Tōzai line to Higashiyama) This museum is renowned for its Japanese ceramics and paintings. There is an outstanding permanent collection, which includes many pottery pieces by Kawai Kanjirō. The coffee shop here is a nice place for a break and overlooks a picturesque canal. The museum also hosts regular special exhibitions, so check the website for what's on.

Fureai-Kan Kyoto
Museum of Traditional Crafts MUSEUM
(みやこめっせ・京都伝統産業ふれあい館; Map p316; 9-1 Seishōji-chō, Okazaki, Sakyō-ku; ⏰9am-5pm; 🚇Tōzai line to Higashiyama) **FREE** Well worth a visit for anyone interested in traditional Kyoto arts and crafts, Fureai-Kan has excellent exhibits on display, including woodblock prints, lacquerware, bamboo goods and gold-leaf work, with information panels in English. It's in the basement of Miyako Messe (Kyoto International Exhibition Hall).

The attached museum shop sells a good range of gifts and souvenirs.

Heian-jingū SHINTO SHRINE
(平安神宮; Map p316; Nishitennō-chō, Okazaki, Sakyō-ku; garden adult/child ¥600/300; ⏰6am-5pm Nov-Feb, 6am-6pm Mar-Oct, garden 8.30am-4.30pm; 🚇Tōzai line to Higashiyama) One of Kyoto's more popular sights, this shrine was built in 1895 to commemorate the 1100th anniversary of the founding of the city. The shrine buildings are colourful replicas, reduced to a two-thirds scale, of the Imperial Court Palace of the Heian period (794–1185). About 500m in front of the shrine is a massive steel **torii** (shrine gate). Although it appears to be entirely separate, this is actually considered the main entrance to the shrine itself.

The vast **garden** here, behind the shrine, is a fine place for a wander and particularly lovely during the cherry-blossom season. With its large pond and Chinese-inspired bridge, the garden is a tribute to the style that was popular in the Heian period. It is well known for its wisteria, irises and weeping cherry trees.

One of Kyoto's biggest festivals, the **Jidai Matsuri**, is held here on 22 October. On 2 and 3 June, **Takigi nō** is also held here. Takigi nō is a picturesque form of *nō* (stylised dance-drama performed on a bare stage) performed in the light of blazing fires. Tickets cost ¥3000 if you pay in advance (ask at the Kyoto Tourist Information Center for the location of ticket agencies) or you can pay ¥4000 at the entrance gate.

Shūgaku-in Rikyū
Imperial Villa   NOTABLE BUILDING
(修学院離宮; Map p300; ☎075-211-1215; www.kunaicho.go.jp; Shūgaku-in, Yabusoe, Sakyō-ku; ⊗tours 9am, 10am, 11am, 1.30pm & 3pm Tue-Sun; ◪Kyoto City bus 5 from Kyoto Station to Shūgakuinrikyū-michi) FREE One of the highlights of northeast Kyoto, this superb imperial villa was designed as a lavish summer retreat for the imperial family. Its gardens, with their views down over the city, are worth the trouble it takes to visit. The eighty-minute tours are held in Japanese, with English audio guides free of charge; try to arrive early. You must be over 18 years to enter and you will need to bring your passport for ID.

Construction of the villa was begun in the 1650s by Emperor Go-Mizunō, following his abdication. Work was continued by his daughter Akeno-miya after his death in 1680.

The villa grounds are divided into three enormous garden areas on a hillside – lower, middle and upper. Each has superb tea-ceremony houses: the upper, **Kami-no-chaya**, and lower, **Shimo-no-chaya**, were completed in 1659, and the middle teahouse, **Naka-no-chaya**, was completed in 1682. The gardens' reputation rests on their ponds, pathways and impressive use of *shakkei* (borrowed scenery) in the form of the surrounding hills. The view from Kami-no-chaya is particularly impressive.

You can book tickets in advance at the Imperial Household Agency (p310) office or online for morning tours, but for afternoon tours tickets go on sale at the villa from 11am and are available on a first-come, first-served basis until capacity is sold.

⊙ Northwest Kyoto

Northwest Kyoto contains two of Kyoto's most important temples: Kinkaku-ji, also known as the Golden Pavilion, and Ryōan-ji, home of Japan's most famous Zen garden. Other noteworthy sights include the enclosed world of Myōshin-ji and the atmospheric Kitano Tenman-gū Shintō shrine.

Kitano Tenman-gū   SHINTO SHRINE
(北野天満宮; Map p308; www.kitanotenmangu.or.jp; Bakuro-chō, Kamigyō-ku; ⊗5am-6pm Apr-Sep, 5.30am-5.30pm Oct-Mar; ◪Kyoto City bus 50 from Kyoto Station to Kitano-Tenmangū-mae) FREE The most atmospheric Shintō shrine in Northwest Kyoto, Kitano Tenman-gū is also the site of Tenjin-San market, one of Kyoto's most popular flea markets. It's a pleasant spot for a lazy stroll and the shrine buildings themselves are beautiful. The present buildings were built in 1607 by Toyotomi Hideyori; the grounds contain an extensive grove of plum trees, which burst into bloom in early March.

Kitano Tenman-gū was established in 947 to honour Sugawara Michizane (845–903), a noted Heian-era statesman and scholar. It is said that, having been defied by his political adversary Fujiwara Tokihira, Sugawara was exiled to Kyūshū for the rest of his life. Following his death in 903, earthquakes and storms hit Kyoto, and the Imperial Palace was repeatedly struck by lightning. Fearing that Sugawara, reincarnated as Raijin (god of thunder), had returned from beyond to avenge his rivals, locals erected and dedicated this shrine to him.

Unless you're trying to avoid crowds, the best time to visit is during the **Tenjin-san** market fair, held on the 25th of each month. – December and January are particularly colourful.

★**Kinkaku-ji**   BUDDHIST TEMPLE
(金閣寺; Map p322; 1 Kinkakuji-chō, Kita-ku; ¥400; ⊗9am-5pm; ◪Kyoto City bus 205 from Kyoto Station to Kinkakuji-michi, Kyoto City bus 101 or 205 from Kyoto Station to Kinkakuji-mae) Kyoto's famed 'Golden Pavilion', Kinkaku-ji is one of Japan's best-known sights. The main hall, covered in brilliant gold leaf, shining above its reflecting pond is truly spectacular. Needless to say, due to its beauty, the temple can be packed any day of the year. It's best to go early in the day or just before closing, ideally on a weekday.

The original building was built in 1397 as a retirement villa for shogun Ashikaga Yoshimitsu. His son converted it into a temple. In 1950 a young monk consummated his obsession with the temple by burning it to the ground. The monk's story was fictionalised

KYOTO SIGHTS

Northwest Kyoto

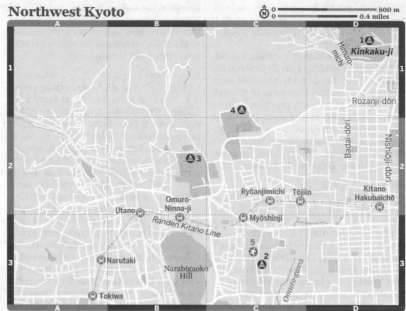

Northwest Kyoto

in Mishima Yukio's *The Golden Pavilion*. In 1955 a full reconstruction was completed that followed the original design, but the gold-foil covering was extended to the lower floors.

Ryōan-ji   BUDDHIST TEMPLE
(龍安寺; Map p322; 13 Goryōnoshitamachi, Ryōan-ji, Ukyō-ku; adult/child ¥500/300; ☙8am-5pm Mar-Nov, 8.30am-4.30pm Dec-Feb; 🚌Kyoto City bus 59 from Sanjō-Keihan to Ryoanji-mae) You've probably seen a picture of the rock garden here – it's one of the symbols of Kyoto and one of Japan's better-known sights. Ryōan-ji belongs to the Rinzai school and was founded in 1450. The garden, an oblong of sand with an austere collection of 15 carefully placed rocks, apparently adrift in a sea of sand, is enclosed by an earthen wall. The designer, who remains unknown to this day, provided no explanation.

Although many historians believe the garden was arranged by Sōami during the Muromachi period (1333–1568), some contend that it is a much later product of the Edo period. It is Japan's most famous **hira-niwa** (flat garden void of hills or ponds) and reveals the stunning simplicity and harmony of the principles of Zen meditation.

There is no doubt that it's a mesmerising and attractive sight, but it's hard to enjoy amid the mobs who come to check it off their 'must-see list'. An early-morning visit on a weekday is probably your best hope of seeing the garden under contemplative conditions. If you go when it's crowded, you'll find the less-famous garden around the corner of the stone garden a nice escape.

Ninna-ji   BUDDHIST TEMPLE
(仁和寺; Map p322; ☎075-461-1155; 33 Omuroōuchi, Ukyō-ku; temple & garden ¥500; ☙9am-5pm Mar-Nov, to 4.30pm Dec-Feb; 🚌Kyoto City bus 59 from Sanjō-Keihan to Omuro Ninna-ji, Kyoto City bus 26 from Kyoto Station to Omuro Ninna-ji) Few travellers make the journey all the

way out to this sprawling temple complex, but most who do find it a pleasant spot. It's certainly a good counterpoint to the crowded and more famous temples nearby.

Originally containing more than 60 structures, Ninna-ji was built in 888 and is the head temple of the Omuro branch of the Shingon school. The present temple buildings, including a **five-storey pagoda**, date from the 17th century.

On the extensive grounds you'll find a peculiar grove of short-trunked, multi-petalled cherry trees called Omuro-no-Sakura, which draw large crowds in April.

Separate admission fees (an additional ¥500 each) are charged for both the **Kondō** (Main Hall) and **Reihōkan** (Treasure House), which are only open April to May and October to November.

Myōshin-ji
BUDDHIST TEMPLE

(妙心寺; Map p322; www.myoshinji.or.jp; 1 Myoshin-ji-chō, Hanazono, Ukyō-ku; main temple free, other areas of complex adult/child ¥500/100; ⊙9.10-11.40am & 1-4.40pm; ⊒Kyoto City bus 10 from Sanjo-Keihan to Myōshin-ji Kita-mon-mae) Myōshin-ji is a separate world within Kyoto, a walled-off complex of temples and subtemples that invites lazy strolling. The subtemple of **Taizō-in** here contains one of the city's more interesting gardens. Myōshin-ji dates from 1342 and belongs to the Rinzai school. There are 47 subtemples, but only a few are open to the public.

From the north gate, follow the broad stone avenue flanked by rows of temples to the southern part of the complex. The eponymous Myōshin-ji temple is roughly in the middle of the complex. Your entry fee entitles you to a tour of several of the buildings of the temple. The ceiling of the **Hattō** (Lecture Hall) here features Tanyū Kanō's unnerving painting *Unryūzu* (meaning 'Dragon glaring in eight directions'). Your guide will invite you to stand directly beneath the dragon; doing so makes it appear that it's spiralling up or down.

Shunkō-in (p331), a subtemple of Myōshin-ji, offers regular *zazen* (seated Zen meditation) 60-minute sessions for foreigners with English explanations for ¥1500, or 90 minutes for ¥2500, including *matcha* (powdered green tea) and a sweet. This is highly recommended.

👁 Arashiyama & Sagano
嵐山・嵯峨野

Arashiyama and Sagano, two adjoining neighbourhoods at the base of Kyoto's western mountains, form the city's second-most-popular sightseeing district after Southern Higashiyama. Foreign and domestic tourists flock here to see Tenryū-ji, a temple with a stunning mountain backdrop, and the famous Arashiyama Bamboo Grove. There are also several small temples scattered around and a fine hilltop villa – Ōkōchi-Sansō – making it a great place to escape the city and simply wander.

Togetsu-kyo
BRIDGE

(渡月橋; Map p324; Saga Tenryū-ji, Susukinobaba-chō, Ukyō-ku; ⊒Kyoto City bus 28 from Kyoto Station to Arashiyama-Tenryuji-mae, ⊠JR Sagano/San-in line to Saga-Arashiyama or Hankyū line to Arashiyama, change at Katsura) The dominant landmark in Arashiyama, this bridge is just a few minutes on foot from either the Keifuku line or Hankyū line Arashiyama stations. The original crossing, constructed in 1606, was about 100m upriver from the present bridge.

★ Tenryū-ji
BUDDHIST TEMPLE

(天龍寺; Map p324; ☑075-881-1235; www.tenryuji.com; 68 Susukinobaba-chō, Saga-Tenryū-ji, Ukyō-ku; garden only ¥500, temple buildings & garden ¥800; ⊙8.30am-5.30pm, to 5pm mid-Oct–mid-Mar; ⊒Kyoto City bus 28 from Kyoto Station to Arashiyama-Tenryuji-mae, ⊠JR Sagano/San-in line to Saga-Arashiyama or Hankyū line to Arashiyama, change at Katsura) A major temple of the Rinzai school, Tenryū-ji has one of the most attractive gardens in Kyoto, particularly during the spring cherry-blossom and autumn-foliage seasons. The main 14th-century Zen garden, with its backdrop of the Arashiyama mountains, is a good example of *shakkei* (borrowed scenery). Unfortunately, it's no secret that the garden here is world class, so it pays to visit early in the morning or on a weekday.

It was built in 1339 on the old site of Go-Daigo's villa after a priest had a dream of a dragon rising from the nearby river. The dream was seen as a sign that the emperor's spirit was uneasy and so the temple was built as appeasement – hence the name *tenryū* (heavenly dragon). The present buildings date from 1900. You will find Arashiyama's famous bamboo grove situated just outside the north gate of the temple.

★ Arashiyama Bamboo Grove
PARK

(嵐山竹林; Map p324; Ogurayama, Saga, Ukyō-ku; ⊙dawn-dusk; ⊒Kyoto City bus 28 from Kyoto Station to Arashiyama-Tenruji-mae, ⊠JR Sagano/San-in line to Saga-Arashiyama or Hankyū line to Arashiyama, change at Katsura) **FREE** Walking into

Arashiyama & Sagano Area

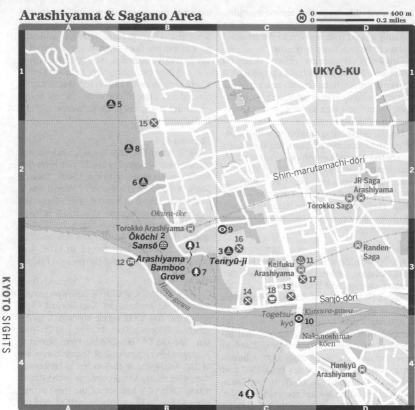

KYOTO SIGHTS

Arashiyama & Sagano Area

this extensive bamboo grove is like entering another world – the thick green bamboo stalks seem to continue endlessly in every direction and there's a strange quality to the light. You'll be unable to resist trying to take a few photos, but you might be disappointed with the results: photos just can't capture the magic of this place. The grove runs from outside the north gate of Tenryū-ji to just below Ōkōchi Sansō villa.

★ **Ōkōchi Sansō** HISTORIC BUILDING
(大河内山荘; Map p324; 8 Tabuchiyama-chō, Sagaogurayama, Ukyō-ku; ¥1000; ◷9am-5pm; 🚌Kyoto City bus 28 from Kyoto Station to Arashiyama-Tenryuji-mae, 🚇JR Sagano/San-in line to Saga-Arashiyama or Hankyū line to Arashiyama, change at Katsura) This is the lavish estate of Ōkōchi Denjirō, an actor famous for his samurai films. The sprawling gardens may well be the most lovely in all of Kyoto, particularly when you consider the brilliant views eastwards across the city. The house and teahouse are also sublime. Be sure to follow all the trails around the gardens. Hold onto the tea ticket you were given upon entry to claim the *matcha* (green powdered tea) and sweet that comes with admission.

Kameyama-kōen PARK
(亀山公園; Map p324; Sagaogurayama, Ukyō-ku; ◷24hr; 🚌Kyoto City bus 28 from Kyoto Station to Arashiyama-Tenryuji-mae, 🚇JR Sagano/San-in line to Saga-Arashiyama or Hankyū line to Arashiyama, change at Katsura) Just upstream from Tōgetsu-kyō and behind Tenryū-ji, this park is a nice place to escape the crowds of Arashiyama. It's laced with trails, one of which leads to a lookout over Katsura-gawa and up into the Arashiyama mountains. It's especially attractive during cherry-blossom and autumn-foliage seasons. Keep an eye out for monkeys, which occasionally descend from the nearby hills to pick fruit.

Jōjakkō-ji BUDDHIST TEMPLE
(常寂光寺; Map p324; 3 Ogura-chō, Sagaogurayama, Ukyō-ku; adult/child ¥400/200; ◷9am-5pm; 🚌Kyoto City bus 28 from Kyoto Station to Arashiyama-Tenryuji-mae, 🚇JR Sagano/San-in line to Saga-Arashiyama or Hankyū line to Arashiyama, change at Katsura) This temple is perched on top of a mossy knoll and is famed for its brilliant maple trees, which turn a lovely crimson red in November, and its thatched-roof Niō-mon gate. The *hondō* (main hall) was constructed in the 16th century out of wood sourced from Fushimi-jō.

Nison-in BUDDHIST TEMPLE
(二尊院; Map p324; 27 Monzenchōjin-chō, Saganison-in, Ukyō-ku; ¥500; ◷9am-4.30pm; 🚌Kyoto City bus 28 from Kyoto Station to Arashiyama-Tenryuji-mae, 🚇JR Sagano/San-in line to Saga-Arashiyama or Hankyū line to Arashiyama, change at Katsura) This is a popular spot with maple-leaf watchers. Nison-in was originally built in the 9th century by Emperor Saga. It houses two important Kamakura-era Buddha statues side by side (Shaka on the right and Amida on the left). The temple features lacquered nightingale floors.

Giō-ji BUDDHIST TEMPLE
(祇王寺; Map p324; www.giouji.or.jp; 32 Kozaka-chō, Sagatoriimoto, Ukyō-ku; adult/child ¥300/100; ◷9am-5pm; 🚌Kyoto City bus 28 from Kyoto Station to Arashiyama-Tenryuji-mae, 🚇JR Sagano/San-in line to Saga-Arashiyama or Hankyū line to Arashiyama, change at Katsura) This tiny temple near the north end of the main Arashiyama sightseeing route is one of Kyoto's hidden gems. Its main attraction is the lush moss garden outside the thatch-roofed hall of the temple.

Arashiyama Monkey Park Iwatayama PARK
(嵐山モンキーパークいわたやま; Map p324; ☎075-872-0950; http://monkeypark.jp/en; 8 Genrokuzan-chō, Arashiyama, Ukyō-ku; adult/child ¥550/250; ◷9am-5pm mid-Mar–Oct, to 4pm Nov–mid-Mar; 🚌Kyoto City bus 28 from Kyoto Station to Arashiyama-Tenryuji-mae, 🚇JR Sagano/San-in line to Saga-Arashiyama or Hankyū line to Arashiyama, change at Katsura) Though it is common to spot wild monkeys in the nearby mountains, here you can encounter them at a close distance and enjoy watching the playful creatures frolic about. It makes for an excellent photo opportunity, not only of the monkeys but also of the panoramic view over Kyoto. Refreshingly, it is the animals who are free to roam while the humans who feed them are caged in a box!

You enter the park near the south side of Tōgetsu-kyō, through the orange *torii* (shrine gate) of Ichitani-jinja. Buy your tickets from the machine to the left of the shrine at the top of the steps. Just be warned: it's a steep climb up the hill to get to the monkeys. If it's a hot day, you're going to be drenched by the time you get to the spot where they gather.

Saihō-ji BUDDHIST TEMPLE
(西芳寺; Map p300; 56 Jingatani-chō, Matsuo, Nishikyō-ku; ¥3000; 🚌Kyoto City bus 28 from Kyoto Station to Matsuo-taisha-mae, Kyoto bus 63 from Sanjō-Keihan to Koke-dera) Saihō-ji, one of Kyoto's best-known gardens, is famed for its superb moss garden, hence the temple's nickname: Koke-dera (Moss Temple). The heart-shaped garden, laid out in 1339 by Musō Kokushi, surrounds a tranquil pond. In order to limit the number of visitors, one must apply to visit and then copy a sutra with ink and brush before exploring the garden.

While copying a sutra might seem daunting, it's actually fairly self-explanatory and if you're lost, just glance at what the Japanese visitors are doing. It's not necessary to finish the entire sutra, just do the best you can. Once in the garden, you are free to explore on your own and at your own pace.

To visit Saihō-ji you must make a reservation. Send a postcard at least one week before the date you wish to visit and include your name, number of visitors, address in Japan, occupation, age (you must be over 18) and desired date (choice of alternative dates preferred). The address: Saihō-ji, 56 Kamigayachō, Matsuo, Nishikyō-ku, Kyoto-shi 615-8286, JAPAN.

Enclose a stamped self-addressed postcard for a reply to your Japanese address. You might find it convenient to buy an Ōfukuhagaki (send and return postcard set) at a Japanese post office.

Katsura Rikyū   HISTORIC BUILDING

(桂離宮; Map p300; ☎075-211-1215; www.kunaicho.go.jp; Katsura Detached Palace, Katsura Misono, Nishikyō-ku; ⊙tours 9am, 10am, 11am, 1.30pm, 2.30pm, 3.30pm; ᄆKyoto City bus 33 to Katsura Rikyū-mae, ᘓHankyū line to Katsura) **FREE** Katsura Rikyū, one of Kyoto's imperial properties, is widely considered to be the pinnacle of Japanese traditional architecture and garden design. Set amid an otherwise drab neighbourhood, it is (very literally) an island of incredible beauty. One-hour tours are in Japanese, with English audio guides free of charge. You must be over 18 years and you will need to bring your passport for ID.

The villa was built in 1624 for the emperor's brother, Prince Toshihito. Every last detail of the villa – the teahouses, the large pond with islets and the surrounding garden – has been given meticulous attention.

You can book tickets in advance at the Imperial Household Agency (p310) office or online for morning tours but for afternoon tours tickets go on sale at the palace from 11am and are on a first-come, first-served basis until capacity is sold.

It's a 15-minute walk from Katsura Station, on the Hankyū line. A taxi from the station to the villa costs around ¥700. Alternatively, Kyoto bus 33 stops at Katsura Rikyū-mae stop, which is a five-minute walk from the villa.

⊙ Kitayama Area & North Kyoto

The Kitayama (Northern Mountains) area contains several quaint villages that make great day trips out of the city: Kurama, Kibune, Ōhara and Takao. Kurama and Kibune are usually visited together via a hiking trail that connects them. Ōhara and Takao, usually visited separately, contain superb temples and pleasant rural scenery.

Ōhara   NEIGHBOURHOOD

Since ancient times Ōhara, a quiet farming town about 10km north of Kyoto, has been regarded as a holy site by followers of the Jōdo (Pure Land) school of Buddhism. The region provides a charming glimpse of rural Japan, along with the picturesque Sanzen-in, Jakkō-in and several other fine temples. It's most popular in autumn, when

---

HOZU-GAWA RIVER TRIP

The **Hozu-gawa river trip** (☎0771-22-5846; www.hozugawakudari.jp; Hozu-chō, Kameoka-shi; adult/child 4-12yr ¥4100/2700; ᘡ) is a great way to enjoy the beauty of Kyoto's western mountains without any strain on the legs. With long bamboo poles, boatmen steer flat-bottom boats down the Hozu-gawa from Kameoka, 30km west of Kyoto Station, through steep, forested mountain canyons, before arriving at Arashiyama.

Between 10 March and 30 November there are seven trips daily leaving on the hour from 9am to 3pm. During winter the number of trips is reduced to four per day (10am, 11.30am, 1pm and 2.30pm) and the boats are heated.

The ride lasts two hours and covers 16km through occasional sections of choppy water – a scenic jaunt with minimal danger. The scenery is especially breathtaking during cherry-blossom season in April and maple-foliage season in autumn.

The boats depart from a dock that is eight minutes' walk from Kameoka Station. Kameoka is accessible by rail from Kyoto Station or Nijō Station on the JR Sagano-San-in line. The Kyoto Tourist Information Center provides an English-language leaflet and timetable for rail connections. The fare from Kyoto to Kameoka is ¥400 one way by regular train (don't spend the extra for the express; it makes little difference in travel time).

HIEI-ZAN & ENRYAKU-JI

Located atop 848m-high Hiei-zan (the mountain that dominates the skyline in the northeast of the city), the **Enryaku-ji** (延暦寺; 4220 Honmachi, Sakamoto, Sakyō-ku; ¥700; ⊙ 8.30am-4.30pm, 9am-4pm winter; 🚌 Kyoto or Keihan bus to Enryakuji Bus Center) temple complex is an entire world of temples and dark forests that feels a long way from the hustle and bustle of the city below. A visit to this temple is a good way to spend half a day hiking, poking around temples and enjoying the atmosphere of a key site in Japanese history.

Enryaku-ji was founded in 788 by Saichō, also known as Dengyō-daishi, the priest who established the Tenzai school. This school did not receive imperial recognition until 823, after Saichō's death; however, from the 8th century the temple grew in power. At its height, Enryaku-ji possessed some 3000 buildings and an army of thousands of *sōhei* (warrior monks). In 1571 Oda Nobunaga saw the temple's power as a threat to his aims to unify the nation and he destroyed most of the buildings, along with the monks inside. Today only three pagodas and 120 minor temples remain.

The complex is divided into three sections: Tōtō, Saitō and Yokawa. The **Tōtō** (eastern pagoda section) contains the **Kompon Chū-dō** (Primary Central Hall), which is the most important building in the complex. The flames on the three dharma lamps in front of the altar have been kept lit for more than 1200 years. The **Daikō-dō** (Great Lecture Hall) displays life-sized wooden statues of the founders of various Buddhist schools. This part of the temple is heavily geared to group access, with large expanses of asphalt for parking.

The **Saitō** (western pagoda section) contains the Shaka-dō, which dates from 1595 and houses a rare Buddha sculpture of the Shaka Nyorai (Historical Buddha). The Saitō, with its stone paths winding through forests of tall trees, temples shrouded in mist and the sound of distant gongs, is the most atmospheric part of the temple. Hold on to your ticket from the Tōtō section, as you may need to show it here.

The Yokawa is of minimal interest and a 4km bus ride away from the Saitō area.

To get to Enryaku-ji, take the Keihan line north to the last stop, Demachiyanagi, and change to the Yase-Hiezan-guchi–bound Eizan Dentetsu Eizan-line train (be careful not to board the Kurama-bound train that sometimes leaves from the same platform). Travel to the last stop, Yase-Hiezan-guchi (¥260; about 15 minutes from Demachiyanagi Station), then board the cable car (¥540, nine minutes) followed by the funicular (¥310, three minutes) to the peak, from where you can walk down to the temples.

If you want to save money (by avoiding both the cable car and funicular), there are direct Kyoto buses from Kyoto and Keihan Sanjō stations to Hiei Sanchō bus stop, which take about 70 and 60 minutes respectively (both cost ¥820).

the maple leaves change colour and the mountain views are spectacular.

From Kyoto Station, Kyoto bus 17 or 18 runs to Ōhara bus stop. The ride takes about an hour and costs ¥550. From Keihan line's Sanjō Station, take Kyoto bus 16 or 17 (¥470, 45 minutes). Be careful to board a tan-coloured Kyoto bus, not a green Kyoto City bus of the same number.

Avoid Ōhara on busy autumn-foliage weekends in November. There's only one main road up there from Kyoto and you'll spend too much time sitting in traffic (and the temples will be crowded when you get there). Wait until Monday if you can.

➡ ★Sanzen-in

(三千院; 540 Raikōin-chō, Ōhara, Sakyō-ku; ¥700; ⊙ 9am-5pm Mar-Nov, to 4.30pm Dec-Feb; 🚌 Kyoto bus 17 or 18 from Kyoto Station to Ōhara) Famed

for its autumn foliage, hydrangea garden and stunning Buddha images, this temple is deservedly popular with foreign and domestic tourists alike. The temple's garden, **Yūsei-en**, is one of the most photographed sights in Japan, and rightly so. Sanzen-in is a 45-minute bus ride from central Kyoto and makes for an excellent day trip.

Take some time to sit on the steps of the **Shin-den** hall and admire the beauty of the Yūsei-en. Then head off to see **Ōjō-gokuraku-in** (Temple of Rebirth in Paradise), the hall in which stands the impressive Amitabha trinity, a large Amida image flanked by attendants Kannon (goddess of mercy) and Seishi (god of wisdom). After this, walk up to the garden at the back of the temple where, in late spring and summer, you can wander among hectares of blooming hydrangeas.

Sanzen-in was founded in 784 by the priest Saichō and belongs to the Tendai school. Saichō, considered one of the great patriarchs of Buddhism in Japan, also founded Enryaku-ji.

If you're keen for a short hike after leaving the temple, continue up the hill to see the rather oddly named **Soundless Waterfall** (Oto-nashi-no-taki; 音無の滝). Though, in fact, it sounds like any other waterfall, its resonance is believed to have inspired Shōmyō Buddhist chanting.

The approach to Sanzen-in is opposite the bus stop; there is no English sign but you can usually just follow the Japanese tourists. The temple is located about 600m up this walk on your left as you crest the hill.

➡ Jakkō-in

(寂光院; 676 Kusao-chō, Ōhara, Sakyō-ku; adult/child ¥600/100; ◷ 9am-5pm Mar-Nov, to 4.30pm Dec-Feb; 🚌 Kyoto bus 17 or 18 from Kyoto Station to Ōhara) Jakkō-in sits on the opposite side of Ōhara from the famous Sanzen-in. It's reached by a very pleasant walk through a quaint 'old Japan' village. It's a relatively small temple and makes an interesting end point to a fine walk in the country. Walk out of the bus stop up the road to the traffic lights, then follow the small road to the left. You might have to ask directions on the way.

The history of the temple is exceedingly tragic. The actual founding date of the temple is subject to some debate (it's thought to be somewhere between the 6th and 11th centuries), but it acquired fame as the temple that harboured Kenrei Mon-in, a lady of the Taira clan. In 1185 the Taira were soundly defeated in a sea battle against the Minamoto clan at Dan-no-ura. With the entire Taira clan slaughtered or drowned, Kenrei Mon-in threw herself into the waves with her son Antoku, the infant emperor; she was fished out – the only member of the clan to survive.

She was returned to Kyoto, where she became a nun and lived in a bare hut until it collapsed during an earthquake. Kenrei Mon-in was then accepted into Jakkō-in and stayed there, immersed in prayer and sorrowful memories, until her death 27 years later. Her tomb is located high on the hill behind the temple.

The main building of this temple burned down in May 2000 and the newly reconstructed main hall lacks some of the charm of the original. Nonetheless, it is a nice spot.

Kurama & Kibune   NEIGHBOURHOOD

Located roughly 30 minutes north of Kyoto, Kurama and Kibune are a pair of tranquil valleys that have been long favoured as places to escape the crowds and stresses of the city. Kurama's main attractions are its mountain temple and onsen (hot spring). Kibune, an impossibly charming little hamlet just over the ridge, is a cluster of ryokan overlooking a mountain river. Kibune is best in summer, when the ryokan serve dinner on platforms built over the rushing waters of Kibune-gawa, providing welcome relief from the heat.

The two valleys lend themselves to being explored together. In winter you can start from Kibune, walk 30 minutes over the ridge, visit Kurama-dera, then soak in the onsen before heading back to Kyoto. In summer the reverse route is better: start from Kurama, walk up to the temple, then down the other side to Kibune to enjoy a meal suspended above the cool river. Either way, a trip to Kurama and Kibune is probably the single best day or half-day trip possible from Kyoto city.

If you happen to be in Kyoto on the night of 22 October, don't miss the Kurama-no-hi Matsuri (p332) fire festival. It's one of the most exciting festivals in the Kyoto area.

To get to Kurama and Kibune, take the Eizan line from Kyoto's Demachiyanagi Station. For Kibune, get off at the second-last stop, Kibune-guchi, take a right out of the station and walk about 20 minutes up the hill or jump on the shuttle bus. For Kurama, go to the last stop, Kurama, and walk straight out of the station. Both destinations are ¥410 and take about 30 minutes to reach.

➡ ★Kurama-dera

(鞍馬寺; Map p329; 1074 Kurama Honmachi, Sakyō-ku; ¥300; ◷ 9am-4.30pm; 🚃 Eiden Eizan line from Demachiyanagi to Kurama) Located high on a thickly wooded mountain, Kurama-dera is one of the few temples in modern Japan that still manages to retain an air of real spirituality. This is a magical place that gains a lot of its power from its brilliant natural setting. The entrance to the temple is just up the hill from Kurama Station. A tram runs back and forth to the top for ¥100 each way, or you can hike up in about 30 minutes (follow the path past the tram station).

The temple also has a fascinating history: in 770 the monk Gantei left Nara's Toshōdai-ji in search of a wilderness sanctuary in which to meditate. Wandering in the hills north of Kyoto, he came across a white horse that led him to the valley known today as Kurama. After seeing a vision of the deity Bishamon-ten, guardian of the northern

Kurama & Kibune

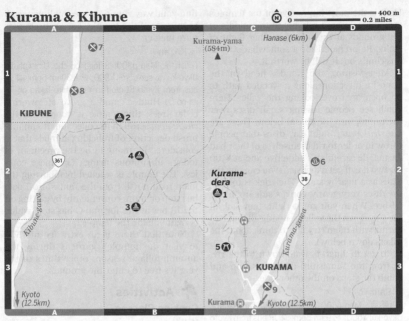

quarter of the Buddhist heaven, Gantei established Kurama-dera just below the peak of Kurama-yama. Originally belonging to the Tendai school of Buddhism, Kurama has been independent since 1949, describing its own brand of Buddhism as Kurama-kyō.

It's worth walking up the trail from the main entrance (if it's not too hot), since it winds through a forest of towering old-growth cryptomeria trees, passing by **Yuki-jinja** (Map p329), a small Shintō shrine, on the way. Near the peak, there is a court-yard dominated by the **Honden** (Main Hall); behind this a trail leads off to the mountain's peak.

At the top, you can take a brief detour across the ridge to **Ōsugi-gongen** (Map p329), a quiet shrine in a grove of trees. Those who want to continue to Kibune can take the trail down the other side. It's a 1.2km, 30-minute hike from the Honden to the valley floor of Kibune. On the way down are two mountain shrines, **Sōjō-ga-dani Fudō-dō** (Map p329) and **Okuno-in Maō-den** (Map p329), which make pleasant rest stops.

Takao   NEIGHBOURHOOD
The Takao area is tucked far away in the northwestern part of Kyoto. It is famed for autumn foliage and a trio of temples: Jingo-ji, Saimyō-ji and Kōzan-ji.

To reach Takao, take bus 8 from Nijō Station to the last stop, Takao (¥500, 40 minutes). From Kyoto Station, take the hourly JR bus to the Yamashiro Takao stop (¥500, 50 minutes).

➡ Jingo-ji
(神護寺; Map p300; 5 Takao-chō, Umegahata, Ukyō-ku; ¥600; ⊙9am-4pm; 🚌 JR Bus from Kyoto Station to Yamashiro-Takao) This mountaintop temple sits at the summit of a long flight of stairs that stretches from the Kiyotaki-gawa to the temple's main gate. The **Kondō** (Gold

Hall) is the most impressive of the temple's structures, located roughly in the middle of the grounds at the top of another flight of stairs. Be prepared for a somewhat strenuous climb, but it will be worth it.

After visiting the Kondō, head in the opposite direction along a wooded path to an open area overlooking the valley. Here you'll see people tossing small discs over the railing into the chasm below. These are *kawarakenage,* light clay discs that people throw in order to rid themselves of their bad karma. Be careful, it's addictive and at ¥100 for two it can get expensive (you can buy the discs at a nearby stall). The trick is to flick the discs very gently, convex side up, like a frisbee. When you get it right, they sail all the way down the valley – taking all that bad karma with them (try not to think about the hikers down below).

To get to Jingo-ji, walk down to the river from the Yamashiro-Takao bus stop and climb the steps on the other side.

➡ Saimyō-ji

(西明寺; Map p300; 2 Makino-chō, Umegahata, Ukyō-ku; ¥500; ☉9am-5pm; ☐ JR bus from Kyoto Station to Yamashiro-Takao) About five minutes' walk upstream from the base of the steps that lead to Jingo-ji, this is a fine little temple worth stopping at. See if you can find your way round to the small waterfall at the side of the temple. The grotto here is pure magic.

➡ Kōzan-ji

(高山寺; Map p300; 8 Toganoo-chō, Umegahata, Ukyō-ku; to see scroll ¥800; ☉8.30am-5pm; ☐ JR bus from Kyoto Station to Yamashiro-Takao or Toga-no-O) Hidden amid a grove of towering cedar trees, this temple is famous for the *chuju giga* scroll in its collection. It's an ink-brush depiction of frolicking animals that is considered by many to be the precursor of today's ubiquitous manga (Japanese comics). The temple is reached by following the main road north from the Yamashiro-Takao bus stop or, more conveniently, by getting off the JR bus at the Toga-no-O bus stop, which is right outside the temple.

Note that there is an extra fee of ¥500 to visit the temple's gardens during the autumn-foliage season; other times of the year it's free to enter the grounds.

🏃 Activities

Cooking Classes

Uzuki COOKING

(www.kyotouzuki.com; 2hr class per person ¥4500) If you'd like to learn how to cook some of the lovely foods you've tried in Kyoto, we highly recommend Uzuki, a small cooking

---

BUDDHIST IMAGES

There are dozens of images in the Japanese Buddhist pantheon, varying from temple to temple, depending on the religious school or period of construction. As you explore the temples of Kyoto, keep your eyes peeled for the following figures:

Nyorai (Buddhas) At the top of the Buddhist cosmic hierarchy, you will find *nyorai* (Buddhas). The four most common images are those of Shaka (Sanskrit: Sakyamuni), the Historical Buddha; Amida (Sanskrit: Amitabha), the Buddha of the Western Paradise; Miroku (Sanskrit: Maitreya), the Buddha of the Future; and Dainichi (Sanskrit: Vairocana), the Cosmic Buddha.

Bosatsu (bodhisattva) A *bosatsu* is a bodhisattva, a being who puts off entry into nirvana to help the beings stuck in the corrupt world of time. The most common *bosatsu* are Kannon (the god – or goddess – of mercy) and Jizō (the protector of travellers and children). Kannon is often depicted as standing in graceful flowing robes or with 1000 arms (to help all sentient beings). Jizō is often depicted as a monk with a staff in one hand and a jewel in the other. Other Jizō are barely distinguishable from stones with faintly carved faces or bodies. You might see these wearing red bibs, which reflects Jizō's role as protector of children.

Myōō (Kings of Light) These fierce-looking deities entered the Buddhist pantheon from Hinduism. You may see them arranged beside *nyorai* and *bosatsu* in Buddhist temples. The most common figure is Fudō Myōō, the Immovable God of Light. These figures act as protector figures and their wrathful forms are thought to snap people out of wrongful thinking.

Tenbu Usually directly translated as 'ten' or 'tenbu', these are a group of guardian figures inherited from Indian and Chinese cosmologies. A common example is the four heavenly kings, who guard the Buddha by surrounding him in the four directions.

class conducted in a Japanese home for groups of two to four people. You'll learn how to cook a variety of dishes and then sit down and enjoy the fruits of your labour.

You can consult beforehand if you have particular dishes you'd like to cook. The fee includes all ingredients. Reserve via website.

Haru Cooking Class COOKING
(料理教室はる; Map p308; www.kyoto-cooking-class.com; 166-32 Shimogamo Miyazaki-chō, Sakyō-ku; vegetarian/non-vegetarian per person from ¥5900/7900; ⊙classes from 2pm, reservation required) Haru Cooking Class is a friendly one-man cooking school located in a private home a little bit north of Demachiyanagi. The school's teacher, Taro, speaks English and can teach both vegetarian (though fish stock may be used) and non-vegetarian cooking in classes that run for three to four hours. Reserve by email.

Taro also offers tours of Nishiki Market once a week at noon (¥4000 per person).

Meditation

Shunkō-in MEDITATION
(春光院; Map p322; ☑075-462-5488; www.shunkoin.com; meditation class only ¥1500, class & guided tour ¥2500) A subtemple of Myōshin-ji (p323), Shunkō-in is run by a monk who has studied abroad and made it his mission to introduce foreigners to his temple and Zen Buddhism. Regular introductory meditation classes are held in English and there is the option of a guided tour of the temple; check website for class schedule. You can also stay overnight in the accommodation (p337) here.

Onsen

Kurama Onsen ONSEN
(鞍馬温泉; Map p329; ☑075-741-2131; 520 Kurama Honmachi, Sakyō-ku; outdoor bath only ¥1000, outdoor & indoor bath ¥2500; ⊙10am-9pm; ☒Eiden Eizan line from Demachiyanagi to Kurama) One of the few onsen within easy reach of Kyoto, Kurama Onsen is a great place to relax after a hike. The outdoor bath has fine views of Kurama-yama, while the indoor bath area includes some relaxation areas in addition to the tubs. For both baths, buy a ticket from the machine outside the door of the main building.

To get to Kurama Onsen, walk straight out of Kurama Station and continue up the main street, passing the entrance to Kurama-dera on your left. The onsen is about 10 minutes' walk on the right. There's also a free shuttle bus between the station and the onsen, which meets incoming trains.

MAIKO MAKEOVER

If you ever wondered how *you* might look as a *maiko* (apprentice geisha), Kyoto has many organisations in town that offer the chance. **Maika** (舞香; Map p312; ☑075-551-1661; www.maica.tv; 297 Miyagawa suji 4-chōme, Higashiyama-ku; maiko/geisha from ¥7500/9000; ⊙shop 9am-9pm; ☒Keihan line to Gion-Shijo or Kiyomizu-Gojo) is in the Gion district. Here you can be dressed up to live out your *maiko* fantasy. Prices begin at ¥7500 for the basic treatment, which includes full make-up and formal kimono. If you don't mind spending some extra yen, it's possible to head out in costume for a stroll through Gion (and be stared at like never before!). The process takes about an hour. Call to reserve at least one day in advance.

Funaoka Onsen ONSEN
(船岡温泉; Map p308; https://funaokaonsen.info; 82-1 Minami-Funaoka-chō-Murasakino, Kita-ku; ¥430; ⊙3pm-1am Mon-Sat, 8am-1am Sun & holidays; ☒Kyoto City Bus No 9 from Kyoto Station to Horikawa-Kuramaguchi) This old bath on Kuramaguchi-dōri is Kyoto's best. It boasts an outdoor bath, a sauna, a cypress-wood tub, an electric bath, a herbal bath and a few more for good measure. To get here, head west about 400m on Kuramaguchi-dōri from the Kuramaguchi and Horiikawa intersection. It's on the left, not far past Lawson convenience store. Look for the large rocks.

Be sure to check out the *ranma* (carved wooden panels) in the changing room. Carved during Japan's invasion of Manchuria, the panels offer insight into the prevailing mindset of that era. (Note the panels do contain some violent imagery, which may disturb some visitors.)

Arashiyama Station Foot Onsen ONSEN
(Map p324; Keifuku Arashiyama Randen Station; ¥200; ⊙9am-8pm, to 6pm in winter; ☒Keifuku Arashiyama, Randen, line to Keifuku Arashiyama) Give your feet a nice soak after all your temple-hopping at this foot onsen located at the end of the Keifuku Arashiyama Randen Station platform. Price includes a souvenir towel.

Tea Ceremony

★**Camellia Tea Experience** TEA CEREMONY
(茶道体験カメリア; Map p312; ☑075-525-3238; www.tea-kyoto.com; 349 Masuya-chō,

Higashiyama-ku; per person ¥2000; 🚌 Kyoto City bus 206 to Yasui) Camellia is a superb place to try a simple Japanese tea ceremony. It's located in a beautiful old Japanese house just off Ninen-zaka. The host speaks fluent English and explains the ceremony simply and clearly, while managing to perform an elegant ceremony. The price includes a bowl of *matcha* and a sweet. The website has an excellent map and explanation.

The 45-minute ceremonies are held on the hour from 10am to 5pm.

En　　　　　　　　　　　　TEA CEREMONY

(えん; Map p312; ☑ 080-3782-2706; www.teaceremonyen.com; 272 Matsubara-chō, Higashiyama-ku; per person ¥2000; ⊗ ceremonies 3pm, 4pm, 5pm & 6pm; 🚌 Kyoto City bus 206 to Gion or Chionin-mae) A small teahouse near Gion where you can experience the Japanese tea ceremony with a minimum of fuss or expense. Check the website for latest times, as these may change. English explanations are provided, and reservations are recommended in high season. It's a bit tricky to find: it's down a little alley off Higashiōji-dōri – look for the sign just south of Tenkaippin Rāmen.

✨ Festivals & Events

Daimon-ji Gozan Okuribi　　　　CULTURAL

(⊗ 16 Aug) This festival is celebrated as a means of bidding farewell to the souls of ancestors. Enormous fires, in the form of Chinese characters or other shapes, are lit on five mountains. The largest fire is burned on Daimon-ji-yama, just above Ginkaku-ji, in Northern Higashiyama. The fires start at 8pm and the best perspective is from the banks of the Kamo-gawa.

Kurama-no-hi Matsuri　　　　CULTURAL

(⊗ Oct) In perhaps Kyoto's most dramatic festival, the Kurama Fire Festival, huge flaming torches are carried through the streets of Kurama by men in loincloths on 22 October (the same day as the Jidai Matsuri). Trains to and from Kurama will be completely packed with passengers on the evening of the festival (we suggest going early and returning late).

Gion Matsuri　　　　　　　　　　PARADE

(⊗ Jul) Kyoto's most important festival, Gion Matsuri reaches a climax on 17 July with a parade of over 30 floats and a smaller parade on 24 July. On the three evenings preceding the 17th, people gather on Shijō-dōri dressed in beautiful *yukata* (light summer kimonos) to look at the floats and carouse from one street stall to the next.

Aoi Matsuri　　　　　　　　　　PARADE

(⊗ May) The Hollyhock Festival dates back to the 6th century and commemorates the successful prayers of the people for the gods to stop calamitous weather. These days the procession involves imperial messengers carried in ox carts and a retinue of 600 people dressed in traditional costume. On 15 May the procession leaves from the Kyoto Gosho and heads for Shimogamo-jinja.

🛏 Sleeping

When it comes to accommodation, you're spoiled for choice in Kyoto. You can choose from ryokan (traditional Japanese inns), luxury hotels, 'business hotels', chic boutique hotels, guesthouses, youth hostels and even capsule hotels. A huge range of hotels and budget guesthouses clutter around the Kyoto Station area, while the city's best ryokan can be found downtown, spread out in Higashiyama, and in the hills of Arashiyama.

🛏 Kyoto Station & South Kyoto

★ **Lower East 9 Hostel**　　　　HOSTEL ¥

(ザ ロウワー イースト ナインホステル; Map p300; ☑ 075-644-9990; www.lowereastnine.com; 32 Higashikujo, Minamikarasuma, Minami-ku; dm from ¥3800, private twin ¥18,000; ❋❋☎; Ⓢ Karasuma line to Kujō) LE9 is a design-savvy hostel in a quiet spot south of Kyoto Station. Dorms are spacious capsule-style with thoughtful details, while the twin private rooms come with private bathroom. It's kitted out with mid-century furniture and has a cool downstairs cafe-bar and inviting communal areas, so you might never want to leave. But if you do, you're right next to Kujō Station.

★ **Capsule Ryokan Kyoto**　　CAPSULE HOTEL ¥

(カプセル旅館京都; Map p304; ☑ 075-344-1510; www.capsule-ryokan-kyoto.com; 204 Tsuchihashi-chō, Shimogyō-ku; capsules from ¥4980, tw from ¥7980; ❋@☎; 🚊 Kyoto Station) The eight ryokan-style capsules here (meaning tatami mats inside the capsules) are unique as well as comfortable and cleverly designed. Each capsule has its own TV, while the private rooms have all the amenities you might need, including bathroom. Free wi-fi, earplugs, locker storage, laundry room and a guest-use kitchen round out the offering.

It's close to the southeast corner of the Horikawa and Shichijo intersection.

⭐**Tour Club**   GUESTHOUSE ¥
(ツアークラブ; Map p304; ☎075-353-6968; www.kyotojp.com; 362 Momiji-chō, Higashinakasuji, Shōmen-sagaru, Shimogyō-ku; d/tw/tr per person from ¥3490/3885/2960; ❄@🖥; 🚉Kyoto Station) This clean, well-maintained guesthouse remains a favourite of foreign visitors to Kyoto. Facilities include a small Zen garden, laundry, free tea and coffee, and free sake tasting every night. Most private rooms have a private bathroom and toilet, and there is a spacious quad room for families. This is probably the best choice in this price bracket.

Budget Inn   GUESTHOUSE ¥
(バジェットイン; Map p304; ☎075-344-1510; www.budgetinnjp.com; 295 Aburanokōji-chō, Aburanokōji, Shichijō-sagaru, Shimogyō-ku; tr/q/5-person r per person from ¥3660/3245/2996; ❄🌐@🖥; 🚉Kyoto Station) This well-run guesthouse is an excellent choice in this price bracket. Eight Japanese-style private rooms have TV and private bathroom, and can accommodate up to five people, making it good for families. The knowledgeable staff is very helpful and there is a guest-use kitchen, laundry room, wi-fi and thoughtful details, such as universal adaptors and a handy Kyoto information booklet in each room.

From Kyoto Station, walk west on Shiokōji-dōri and turn north one street before Horikawa and look for the English-language sign out the front.

Matsubaya Ryokan   RYOKAN ¥
(松葉家旅館; Map p304; ☎075-351-3727; www.matsubayainn.com; Kamijuzūyachō-dōri, Higashinotōin nishi-iru, Shimogyō-ku; r per person from ¥4600; 🌐@🖥; ⓈKarasuma line to Gojō, 🚉Kyoto Station) A short walk from Kyoto Station, this renovated ryokan has clean, well-kept rooms and friendly staff. Some rooms on the 1st floor look out on small gardens. Western (¥840 to ¥900) or Japanese breakfast (¥1080) is available. There are also several serviced apartments in its adjoining Bamboo House section – these would be great for anyone planning a longer stay in the city.

K's House Kyoto   GUESTHOUSE ¥
(ケイズハウス京都; Map p304; ☎075-342-2444; www.kshouse.jp; 418 Naya-chō, Dotemachi-dōri, Shichijō-agaru, Shimogyō-ku; dm from ¥2400, s/d/tw per person from ¥3800/3250/3250; ❄🌐@🖥; 🚉Kyoto Station) K's House is a large guesthouse with both

private and dorm rooms, which are simple but adequate. The rooftop terrace, patio and attached bar-restaurant make this a very sociable spot and a good place to meet other travellers and share information. There's bicycle hire, internet terminals, free wi-fi and a guest-use kitchen. It's a short walk from Kyoto Station.

Ryokan Shimizu   RYOKAN ¥
(京の宿しみず; Map p304; ☎075-371-5538; www.kyoto-shimizu.net; 644 Kagiya-chō, Shichijō-dōri, Wakamiya-agaru, Shimogyō-ku; r per person from ¥6000; ❄🌐@🖥; 🚉Kyoto Station) A short walk north of Kyoto Station's Karasuma central gate, this friendly ryokan has a loyal following of foreign guests, and for good reason: it's clean and well run. Rooms are standard ryokan-style and come with TV, private bathroom and toilet. Bicycle hire is available. Note there is a midnight curfew.

⭐**Ibis Styles Kyoto Station**   HOTEL ¥¥
(イビススタイルズ　京都ステーション; Map p304; ☎075-693-8444; www.ibis.com; 47 Higashikujō-Kamitonoda-chō, Minami-ku; s/d from ¥7800/10,000; ❄🌐@🖥; 🚉Kyoto Station) While the bright, clean rooms may be a tight squeeze, they are packed with features at this great business hotel just outside the south entrance to Kyoto Station. The staff and management is extremely efficient, there's free wi-fi and laundry rooms, and breakfast is included, making this a fantastic option for the price.

⭐**Hotel Granvia Kyoto**   HOTEL ¥¥¥
(ホテルグランヴィア京都; Map p304; ☎075-344-8888; www.granviakyoto.com; Karasuma-dōri, Shiokōji-sagaru, Shimogyō-ku; r from ¥28,000; ❄🌐@🖥; 🚉Kyoto Station) Imagine being able to step out of bed and straight into the *shinkansen* (bullet train). This is almost

KYOTO'S TOP RYOKAN

➡ **Tawaraya** A stay here is sure to be the memory of a lifetime.

➡ **Hiiragiya Ryokan** A true Kyoto classic.

➡ **Seikōrō** (p336) A lovely ryokan that combines great value and elegant rooms.

possible when you stay at the Hotel Granvia, which is located directly above Kyoto Station. The rooms are clean, spacious and elegant; some get a glimpse of the *shinkansen* on the tracks while others look out directly at the Kyoto Tower.

🛌 Downtown Kyoto

⭐ Royal Park Hotel The Kyoto   HOTEL ¥¥

(ロイヤルパークホテル　ザ　京都; Map p306; ☎ 075-241-1111; www.rph-the.co.jp; Sanjō-dōri, Kawaramachi higashi-iru, Nakagyō-ku; s/d from ¥11,000/13,000; ❄@🛜; Ⓢ Tōzai line to Kyoto-Shiyakusho-mae, Ⓡ Keihan line to Sanjō) Located on Sanjō-dōri, a stone's throw from the river, the Royal Park has a super-convenient location, with tons of shops and restaurants within easy walking distance. The hotel has a boutique-business feel, and rooms are slightly larger than most in the city. The French bakery downstairs is a perfect stop for breakfast pastries.

Tōyoko Inn Kyoto Gojō Karasuma   HOTEL ¥¥

(東横INN京都五条烏丸; Map p306; ☎ 075-344-1045; www.toyoko-inn.com; Gojō Karasuma-chō 393, Karasuma-dōri, Matsubara-sagaru, Shimogyō-ku; s/d/tw incl breakfast from ¥7130/8210/10,370; ❄@🛜; Ⓢ Karasuma line to Gojō) Those familiar with the Tōyoko Inn chain know that this hotel brand specialises in simple, clean, fully equipped but small rooms at the lowest price possible. Interesting extras include free breakfast, alcohol and snack vending machines, reduced rates on rental cars and laptops for rent. It's a little south of the city centre, but easily accessed by subway from Kyoto Station.

Hotel Sunroute Kyoto   HOTEL ¥¥

(ホテルサンルート京都; Map p306; ☎ 075-371-3711; www.sunroute.jp; 406 Nanba-chō, Kawaramachi-dōri, Matsubara-sagaru, Shimogyō-ku; s/d from ¥9000/11,000; ❄@🛜; Ⓡ Hankyū line to Kawaramachi) In a great location within easy walking distance of downtown, this

spic-and-span hotel is a superb choice in this price bracket. As you'd expect, rooms aren't large, but they have everything you need. It's well-run with friendly staff and rooms are clean and comfortable.

⭐ Tawaraya   RYOKAN ¥¥¥

(俵屋; Map p306; ☎ 075-211-5566; 278 Nakahakusan-chō, Fuyachō, Oike-sagaru, Nakagyō-ku; r per person incl 2 meals ¥55,900-74,500; ➡❄@🛜; Ⓢ Tōzai line to Kyoto-Shiyakusho-mae, exit 8) Tawaraya has been operating for more than three centuries and is one of the finest places to stay in the world. From the decorations to the service to the food, everything is simply the best available. It's a very intimate, warm and personal place that has many loyal guests.

It's centrally located within easy walk of two subway stations and plenty of good restaurants.

⭐ Hiiragiya Ryokan   RYOKAN ¥¥¥

(柊屋; Map p306; ☎ 075-221-1136; www.hiiragiya.co.jp; Nakahakusan-chō, Fuyachō, Aneyakōji-agaru, Nakagyō-ku; r per person incl 2 meals ¥30,000-90,000; ➡❄@🛜; Ⓢ Tōzai line to Kyoto-Shiyakusho-mae) This elegant ryokan has long been favoured by celebrities from around the world. Facilities and services are excellent and the location is hard to beat. Opt for the new wing if you prefer a polished sheen; alternatively, request an older room if you fancy some 'old Japan' *wabi-sabi* (imperfect beauty).

Room 14 played host to Japanese writer Yasunari Kawabata back in the day and is around 200 years old.

⭐ Ritz-Carlton Kyoto   HOTEL ¥¥¥

(ザ・リッツ・カールトン京都; Map p316; ☎ 075-746-5555; www.ritzcarlton.com; 543 Hokoden-chō, Nijō-Ōhashi-hotori, Nakagyō-ku; r ¥65,000-200,000; ❄@🛜🏊; Ⓢ Tōzai line to Kyoto-Shiyakusho-mae, Ⓡ Keihan line to Sanjō or Jingū-Marutamachi) The Ritz-Carlton is an oasis of luxury that commands perhaps the finest views of any hotel in the city – it's located on the banks of the Kamo-gawa and huge windows in the east-facing rooms take in the whole expanse of the Higashi-yama Mountains. The rooms are superbly designed and supremely comfortable, with plenty of Japanese touches.

Yoshikawa   RYOKAN ¥¥¥

(吉川; Map p306; ☎ 075-221-5544; www.kyoto-yoshikawa.co.jp; 135 Matsushita-chō, Tominokōji, Oike-sagaru, Nakagyō-ku; r per person incl 2 meals from ¥30,000; ✳@🛜; §Tōzai or Karasuma lines to Karasuma-Oike) Located in the heart of downtown, within easy walking distance of two subway stations and the entire dining and nightlife district, this superb ryokan has beautiful rooms and a stunning garden. The ryokan is famous for its attached tempura restaurant (p344) and its meals are of a high standard. All rooms have private bathrooms with wooden tubs and toilets.

Single occupancy is allowed at the higher rate of around ¥60,000.

Kyoto Hotel Ōkura   HOTEL ¥¥¥

(京都ホテルオークラ; Map p306; ☑075-211-5111; http://okura.kyotohotel.co.jp; 537-4 Ichinofunairi-chō, Kawaramachi-dōri, Oike, Nakagyō-ku; s/d/ste from ¥22,000/27,000/42,000; ☺✳@🛜✳; §Tōzai line to Kyoto-Shiyakusho-mae, exit 3) This towering hotel in the centre of town commands an impressive view of the Higashiyama Mountains. Rooms are clean and spacious and many have great views (7th floor and above), especially the excellent corner suites. You can access the Kyoto subway system directly from the hotel, which is convenient on rainy days or if you have luggage.

🛏 Imperial Palace & Around

Ryokan Rakuchō   RYOKAN ¥¥

(洛頂旅館; Map p308; ☑075-721-2174; www.rakucho-ryokan.com; 67 Higashi-hangi-chō, Shimogamo, Sakyō-ku; s/tw/tr ¥5300/9240/12,600; ☺✳@🛜; 🚌Kyoto City bus 205 to Furitsudaigaku-mae, §Karasuma line to Kitaōji) There's a lot to appreciate about this fine eight-room ryokan in the northern part of town: there's a nice little garden; it's entirely nonsmoking; and the rooms are clean and simple (no TV). Meals aren't served, but staff can provide a good map of local eateries. The downside is the somewhat out-of-the-way location.

Palace Side Hotel   HOTEL ¥¥

(ザ・パレスサイドホテル; Map p308; ☑075-415-8887; www.palacesidehotel.co.jp; Okakuen-chō, Karasuma-dōri, Shimotachiuri-agaru, Kamigyō-ku; s/tw/d from ¥6300/10,200/10,200; ☺✳@🛜; §Karasuma line to Marutamachi) Overlooking the Kyoto Imperial Palace Park, this great-value hotel looks a little dated but has a lot going for it, starting with friendly English-speaking staff, great service, washing machines, an on-site restaurant, well-maintained rooms and a communal guest-use kitchen. Free one-hour Japanese lessons are held in the evenings.

Noku Kyoto   BOUTIQUE HOTEL ¥¥¥

(ノク京都; Map p308; ☑075-211-0222; www.nokuroxy.com; 205-1 Okura-chō, Karasuma-dōri, Maratumachi-sagaru, Nakagyō-ku; r ¥18,000-33,000; ☺✳🛜; §Karasuma line to Marutamachi) Opened in late 2015, Noku (also known as Noku Roxy) is a stylish boutique hotel set over six floors within sight of the Imperial Palace Park and located next to Marutamachi Station. The minimalist elegant rooms all feature blonde wood with splashes of colour provided in the bedhead artwork. Some have park views and there's a basement bar and restaurant.

🛏 Southern Higashiyama

Gojo Guesthouse Annexe   GUESTHOUSE ¥

(五条ゲストハウス; Map p312; ☑075-525-2298; 11-26 Komatsu-chō, Higashiyam-ku; r from ¥3300; ✳🛜; 🚌Kyoto City bus 206 to Kiyomizu-michi) A short walk from the main Gojo Guest House, this homely quiet place offers private rooms with shared bathrooms and is decorated with vintage furniture in a tucked-away spot in the sightseeing area. The rooms are small but functional and there's a communal kitchen for guest use. There's a choice of Japanese- or Western-style rooms.

Gojō Guest House   GUESTHOUSE ¥

(五条ゲストハウス; Map p312; ☑075-525-2299; www.gojo-guest-house.com; 3-396-2 Gojōbashi higashi, Higashiyama-ku; dm/tw/tr ¥2600/3300/3500; ✳@🛜; 🚃Keihan line to Kiyomizu-Gojō) This is a fine budget guesthouse in an old wooden Japanese house, which makes the place feel more like a ryokan than your average guesthouse. There are male and female dorms, as well as private rooms, and the dining area and cafe is a good place to meet other travellers. The staff speak good English and can help with travel advice.

Shiraume Ryokan   RYOKAN ¥¥

(白梅; Map p312; ☑075-561-1459; www.shiraume-kyoto.jp; Gion Shimbashi, Shirakawa hotori, Shijōnawate-agaru, higashi-iru, Higashiyama-ku; r per person incl 2 meals ¥32,000-38,000; ✳@🛜; 🚃Keihan line to Gion-Shijō) Looking out over the Shirakawa Canal in Shimbashi, a lovely street in Gion, this ryokan offers excellent location, atmosphere and service. The decor is traditional with a small inner garden, and all rooms have their own private bathroom with nice wooden bathtubs. This is a great spot to sample the Japanese ryokan experience.

KYOTO SLEEPING

Ryokan Uemura RYOKAN ¥¥
(旅館うえむら; Map p312; uemura.ryokan3hsl@
gmail.com; Ishibe-kōji, Shimogawara, Higashiyama-ku;
r per person incl breakfast ¥9000; ❀✿☎; ◻Kyoto
City bus 206 to Higashiyama-Yasui) This beautiful
little ryokan is on a quaint, quiet cobblestone
alley, just down the hill from some of Kyoto's
most important sights. The owner prefers
bookings by fax or email. Book well in advance, as there are only four rooms. Take note:
there's a 10pm curfew.

★**Hyatt Regency Kyoto** HOTEL ¥¥¥
(ハイアットリージェンシー京都; Map p312;
☎075-541-1234; www.kyoto.regency.hyatt.com;
644-2 Sanjūsangendō-mawari, Higashiyama-ku; r
from ¥30,000; ❀✿@☎; ◻Keihan line to Shichijō)
The Hyatt Regency is arguably one of Kyoto's
best hotels and sits at the southern end of the
Southern Higashiyama sightseeing district.
The elegant and contemporary rooms feature
kimono tapestry walls and traditional paper
lanterns, and come packed with features including a tablet for ordering room service.
The staff are extremely efficient and helpful,
while the on-site restaurants and Tōzan Bar
(p349) are excellent.

Old Kyoto RENTAL HOUSE ¥¥¥
(Map p312; ☎075-533-7775; www.oldkyoto.com;
563-12 Komatsu-chō, Higashiyama-ku; per night
from ¥29,000; ✿☎; ◻Kyoto City bus 206 to
Higashiyama-Yasui, ◻Keihan line to Gion-Shijō)
The Old Kyoto group manage three beautiful traditional Japanese houses that stand
right on the edge of Gion and make for the
perfect getaway for those seeking a more
local experience. The Gion House, Amber
House and Indigo House are all kitted out
stylishly in Japanese meets mid-century decor and design, and can accommodate up to
four people. Minimum stay of five nights.

🛈 **KANSAI AIRPORT HOTEL**

The excellent **Hotel Nikkō Kansai
Airport** (ホテル日航関西空港; ☎072-
455-1111; www.nikkokix.com; Senshū Kūkō
Kita 1, Izumisano-shi, Osaka-fu; s/tw/d from
¥9500/11,000/14,500; @☎✿; ◻JR
Haruka Airport Express to Kansai Airport) is
connected to the main terminal building
by a pedestrian bridge (you can even
bring your luggage trolleys right to your
room). The rooms here are in good condition, spacious and comfortable enough
for brief stays.

Step outside the door of each property
and a few minutes' walk will bring you to
Gion's most atmospheric lanes. The houses
come with everything you need, including a
phone with a local SIM. Old Kyoto also manages the Gion Apartments, which are great
for long-term visitors (one-month minimum
stay from ¥12,000 per night).

Sakara Kyoto INN ¥¥¥
(桜香楽; Map p312; ☎075-708-5400; www.
sakarakyoto.com; 541-2 Furukawa-chō,
Higashiyama-ku; r ¥11,000-40,200; ✿@☎; ⓢTōzai
line to Higashiyama) This modern Japanese-style
inn is conveniently located in a covered pedestrian shopping arcade just south of Sanjō-
dōri, about 50m from Higashiyama Station.
It's great for couples and families. Each room
has bath/shower, kitchenette and laundry facilities. It also has rental houses in Gion.

Gion Hatanaka RYOKAN ¥¥¥
(祇園畑中; Map p312; ☎075-541-5315; www.
thehatanaka.co.jp; Yasaka-jinja Minami-mon mae,
Higashiyama-ku; d from ¥31,000; ❀☎; ◻Kyoto City
bus 206 to Higashiyama-Yasui) Gion Hatanaka is a
fine ryokan right in the heart of the Southern
Higashiyama sightseeing district (less than a
minute's walk from Yasaka-jinja). Despite being fairly large, this 21-room ryokan manages
to retain an intimate and private feeling. In
addition to bathtubs in each room, there is a
huge wooden communal bath. The rooms are
clean, well designed and relaxing.

This ryokan offers regularly scheduled
geisha entertainment (p350) that nonguests
are welcome to join.

Seikōrō RYOKAN ¥¥¥
(晴鴨楼; Map p312; ☎075-561-0771; www.seiko-
ro.com; 467 Nishi Tachibana-chō, 3 chō-me, Toiyamachi-dōri, Gojō-sagaru, Higashiyama-ku; r per
person incl 2 meals ¥25,000-55,000; ❀✿@☎;
◻Keihan line to Kiyomizu-Gojō) The Seikōrō is a
classic ryokan with a grandly decorated and
homely lobby. It's fairly spacious, with excellent, comfortable rooms, attentive service and
a fairly convenient midtown location. Several
rooms look over gardens and all have private
bathrooms featuring wooden bathtubs. Room
only without meals starts from ¥15,000.

Motonago RYOKAN ¥¥¥
(旅館元奈古; Map p312; ☎075-561-2087; www.
motonago.com; 511 Washio-chō, Kōdaiji-michi, Higashiyama-ku; r per person incl 2 meals ¥18,360-
29,160; ❀@✿☎; ◻Kyoto City bus 206 to Gion) This
ryokan may have the best location of any in
the city and it hits all the right notes for one

in this class: classic Japanese decor, friendly English-speaking staff, nice wooden communal bathtubs and a few small Japanese gardens. There are 11 rooms; some have private bathroom, and one room has twin Western beds for those not comfortable on a futon.

🛏 Northern Higashiyama

★ Westin Miyako Kyoto HOTEL ¥¥¥
(ウェスティン都ホテル京都; Map p316; ☎ 075-771-7111; www.miyakohotels.ne.jp/westinkyoto; Keage, Sanjō-dōri, Higashiyama-ku; d/tw from ¥26,460, Japanese-style r from ¥24,840; ☺✳@🛜🅿; Ⓢ Tōzai line to Keage, exit 2) Overlooking the Higashiyama sightseeing district (meaning it's one of the best locations for sightseeing in Kyoto), this *grande dame* of Kyoto hotels occupies a commanding position. Rooms on the north side have great views over the city to the Kitayama mountains. There is a fitness centre with a swimming pool (extra charge), as well as a private garden and walking trail.

Koto Inn RENTAL HOUSE ¥¥¥
(古都イン; Map p312; ☎ 075-751–2753; koto.inn@gmail.com; 373 Horiike-chō, Higashiyama-ku; per night for 2/3/4 people from ¥19,000/24,000/28,000; ☺✳🛜; Ⓢ Tōzai line to Higashiyama) Conveniently located near the Higashiyama sightseeing district, this vacation rental is good for families, couples and groups who want a bit of privacy. It's got everything you need and is decorated with lovely Japanese antiques. While the building is traditionally Japanese, all the facilities are fully modernised.

Kyoto Garden Ryokan Yachiyo RYOKAN ¥¥¥
(旅館八千代; Map p316; ☎ 075-771-4148; www.ryokan-yachiyo.com; 34 Fukuchi-chō, Nanzen-ji, Sakyō-ku; r per person incl 2 meals ¥16,500-82,500; ☺✳🛜; Ⓢ Tōzai line to Keage, exit 2) Located just down the street from Nanzen-ji, this large 20-room ryokan has a choice of traditional or modern rooms, all with private bathroom and TV. Some rooms look out over private gardens and four rooms come with an open-air bath. English-speaking staff are available.

🛏 Northwest Kyoto

Shunkō-in TEMPLE LODGE ¥
(春光院; Map p322; ☎ 075-462-5488; www.shunkoin.com; 42 Myōshinji-chō, Hanazono, Ukyō-ku; s ¥6500, d per person ¥5500; ☺@🛜; 🚆 JR Sagano/San-in line to Hanazono) This is a *shukubō* (temple lodging) at a subtemple in Myōshin-

ji (p323). It's very comfortable, with wi-fi and free bicycle hire, and the main priest here speaks fluent English. For an extra ¥500 you can try Zen meditation and go on a guided tour of the temple. Being in the temple at night is a very special experience.

🛏 Arashiyama & Sagano
嵐山・嵯峨野

★ Hoshinoya Kyoto RYOKAN ¥¥¥
(星のや京都; Map p324; ☎ 075-871-0001; www.hoshinoyakyoto.jp; Arashiyama Genrokuzan-chō 11-2, Nishikyō-ku; r per person incl meals from ¥81,000; 🚌 Kyoto City bus 28 from Kyoto Station to Arashiyama-Tenryuji-mae, 🚆 JR Sagano/San-in line to Saga-Arashiyama or Hankyū line to Arashiyama, change at Katsura) Sitting in a secluded area on the south bank of the Hozu-gawa in Arashiyama (upstream from the main sightseeing district), this modern take on the classic Japanese inn is quickly becoming a favourite of well-heeled visitors to Kyoto in search of privacy and a unique experience. Rooms feature incredible views of the river and the surrounding mountains.

The best part is the approach: you'll be chauffeured by a private boat from a dock near Togetsu-kyō bridge to the inn (note that on days following heavy rains, you'll have to go by car instead). This is easily one of the most unique places to stay in Kyoto. If you tire of just relaxing with the views, it also offers meditation classes as well as incense and tea ceremonies.

🍴 Eating

Kyoto is one of the world's great food cities. In fact, when you consider atmosphere, service and quality, it's hard to think of a city where you get more bang for your dining buck. You can pretty much find a great dining option in any neighbourhood but the majority of the best spots are clustered downtown.

BEST VALUE HOTELS

→ **Kyoto Hotel Ōkura** (p335) A first-class hotel with rates that are usually well below its nearest competitors.

→ **Palace Side Hotel** (p335) Great traveller's hotel with super-cheap rates.

→ **Tōyoko Inn Kyoto Gojō Karasuma** (p334) Business hotel at guesthouse rates.

KYOTO EATING

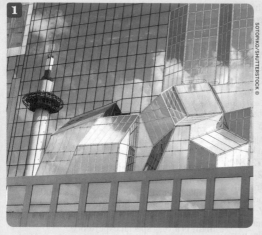

SOTOPIKO/SHUTTERSTOCK ©

1. Kyoto Station (p299)
Kyoto Tower is reflected in the facade of this futuristic building.

2. Daigo-ji (p314)
This Buddhist temple was founded in AD 874. Its five-storey pagoda (not pictured) is the oldest of its kind in Japan.

3. Nishiki Market (p304)
Offering a staggering range of weird and wonderful ingredients, this is a must-see for foodies.

4. Traditional dress (p872)
Women in kimono stroll past women dressed as geisha in Kyoto.

3

京都市北区北野上白梅町一六九

群馬県高崎市柳川町一七〇四

東京都荒飾区

大阪市鶴見区今津

東京都江戸川区東小岩四丁目

酒田市広栄町一七〇四

有酒田紙工

鈴木三恵

佐藤強也

山崎摯

木下物産

平成二十年十一月吉日建之

平成二十一月一日建之

平成二十二年十一月吉日建之

平成二十二年七月吉日建之

平成二十年六月吉日建之

CEZARY WOJTKOWSKI/SHUTTERSTOCK ©

1. Fushimi Inari-Taisha (p303)

Arcades of vermilion *torii* (shrine gates) spread across this vast Shintō shrine complex, one of Kyoto's most memorable sights.

2. Kyoto Station (p299)

Not just a transport hub, Kyoto Station is an architectural marvel of glass and steel.

3. Kiyomizu-dera (p311)

Set on a hill overlooking Kyoto, this popular, crowded Buddhist temple offers a look at how faith is expressed in Japan today.

🍴 Kyoto Station & South Kyoto

Kyoto Rāmen Kōji
RAMEN ¥

(京都拉麺小路; Map p304; ☎075-361-4401; www.kyoto-ramen-koji.com; 10F Kyoto Station Bldg, Karasuma-dōri, Shiokōji-sagaru, Shimogyō-ku; ramen ¥730-1150; ⏰11am-10pm; 🚻; 🚉Kyoto Station) If you love your noodles, do not miss this collection of nine ramen restaurants on the 10th floor of the Kyoto Station building (on the west end, take the escalators that start in the main concourse or access via the JR Isetan south elevator). Buy tickets from the machines (in English, with pictures) before queuing.

Eat Paradise
JAPANESE ¥

(イートパラダイス; Map p304; ☎075-352-1111; 11F Kyoto Station Bldg, Karasuma-dōri, Shiokōji-sagaru, Shimogyō-ku; ⏰11am-10pm; 🚻; 🚉Kyoto Station) On the 11th floor of the Kyoto Station building, you'll find this collection of decent restaurants. Among the choices here are **Tonkatsu Wako** for *tonkatsu* (deep-fried breaded pork cutlet), **Tenichi** for sublime tempura, and **Wakuden** for approachable *kaiseki*.

🍴 Downtown Kyoto

★ Honke Owariya
SOBA ¥

(本家尾張屋; Map p306; ☎075-231-3446; www.honke-owariya.co.jp; 322 Kurumaya-chō, Nijō, Nakagyō-ku; soba from ¥760; ⏰11am-7pm; 🚻; 🚇Karasuma or Tōzai lines to Karasuma-Oike) Set in an old sweets shop in a traditional Japanese building on a quiet downtown street, locals come here for excellent soba (buckwheat noodle) dishes. The highly recommended house speciality, *hourai soba* (¥2160), comes with a stack of five small plates of soba with a selection of toppings, including shiitake mushrooms, shrimp tempura, thin slices of omelette and sesame seeds.

★ Café Bibliotec Hello!
CAFE ¥

(カフェビブリオティックハロー！; Map p308; ☎075-231-8625; 650 Seimei-chō, Nijō-dōri, Yanaginobanba higashi-iru, Nakagyō-ku; meals from ¥1000, coffee ¥450; ⏰11.30am-midnight; ❄🛜🚻; 🚇Tōzai line to Kyoto-Shiyakusho-mae) As the name suggests, books line the walls of this cool cafe located in a converted *machiya* (traditional Japanese townhouse) attracting a mix of locals and tourists. It's a great place to relax with a book or to tap away at your laptop over a coffee or light lunch. Look for the huge banana plants out the front.

There's a great little bakery attached where you can grab tasty takeaway pastries and breads.

★ Kyōgoku Kane-yo
JAPANESE ¥

(京極かねよ; Map p306; ☎075-221-0669; 456 Matsugaechō, Rokkaku, Shinkyōgoku higashi-iru, Nakagyō-ku; unagi over rice from ¥1400; ⏰11.30am-9pm; 🚻; 🚇Tōzai line to Kyoto-Shiyakusho-mae) This is a good place to try *unagi* (eel). You can choose to either sit downstairs with a nice view of the waterfall, or upstairs on the tatami. The *kane-yo donburi* (eel over rice; ¥1400) set is excellent value. Look for the barrels of live eels outside and the wooden facade.

★ Ippudō
RAMEN ¥

(一風堂; Map p306; ☎075-213-8800; Higashinotōin, Nishikikōji higashi-iru, Nakagyō-ku; ramen ¥750-950; ⏰11am-2am; 🚻; 🚇Karasuma line to Shijō) There's a reason that there's usually a line outside this place at lunchtime: the ramen is fantastic and the bite-sized *gyōza* (dumplings) are to die for. The *gyōza* set meal (¥750 or ¥850 depending on your choice of ramen) is great value. It's on Nishikikōji-dōri, next to a post office and diagonally across from a Starbucks.

mumokuteki cafe
VEGETARIAN ¥

(ムモクテキカフェ; Map p306; ☎075-213-7733; www.mumokuteki.com; 2nd fl, Human Forum Bldg, 351 Iseya-chō, Gokomachi-dōri, Rokkaku-sagaru, Nakagyō-ku; meals from ¥1000; ⏰11.30am-10pm; 🌱🛜🚻; 🚉Hankyū line to Kawaramachi) This vegetarian cafe above a shop in the middle of the downtown area is a lifesaver for many Kyoto vegetarians. The food is tasty, varied and served in casual homely surroundings. Try the tofu and avocado burger paired with a fresh vegetable juice. Most of it is vegan, but non-vegan options are clearly marked on the picture menu.

Tsukimochiya Naomasa
SWEETS ¥

(月餅家 直正; Map p306; ☎075-231-0175; 530 Kamiōsaka-chō, Kiyamachi-dōri, Sanjō-agaru, Nakagyō-ku; tsukimochi ¥160; ⏰10am-6pm, closed Tue; 🚉Keihan line to Sanjō) This classic old sweet shop, located about 50m north of Sanjō-dōri on Kiyamachi-dōri, is a great place to get acquainted with traditional Kyoto sweets. Just point at what looks good and the friendly staff will wrap it up nicely for you. There's no English sign; look for the traditional Kyoto exterior and the sweets in the window.

Karafuneya Coffee Sanjō Honten
CAFE ¥

(からふねや珈琲三条本店; Map p306; ☑075-254-8774; 39 Daikoku-chō, Kawaramachi-dōri, Sanjō-sagaru, Nakagyō-ku; parfait from ¥690; ☺9am-11pm; ⓓ; ⓢTōzai line to Kyoto-Shiyakusho-mae, ⓡKeihan line to Sanjō) This coffee and dessert cafe is smack in the middle of Kyoto's main shopping district. In a country famous for its plastic food models, Karafuneya takes them to a whole new level – check out the centrepiece as you enter: the mother of all sundaes goes for ¥50,000! Lesser mortals can try the tasty *matcha* (powdered green tea) parfait (¥870).

Musashi Sushi
SUSHI ¥

(寿しのむさし; Map p306; ☑075-222-0634; www.sushinomusashi.com; Kawaramachi-dōri, Sanjō-agaru, Nakagyō-ku; plates ¥146; ☺11am-10pm; ⓓ; ⓢTōzai line to Kyoto-Shiyakusho-mae, ⓡKeihan line to Sanjō) If you've never tried a *kaiten-sushi* (conveyor-belt sushi restaurant), don't miss this place – most dishes are a mere ¥146. Not the best sushi in the world, but it's cheap, reliable and fun. It's also easy to eat here: you just grab what you want off the conveyor belt. If you don't see what you want, there's also an English menu to order from.

Musashi is just outside the entrance to the Sanjō covered arcade; look for the miniature sushi conveyor belt in the window.

Biotei
VEGETARIAN ¥

(びお亭; Map p306; ☑075-255-0086; 2nd fl, M&I Bldg, 28 Umetada-chō, Sanjō-dōri, Higashinotōin nishi-iru, Nakagyō-ku; lunch/dinner sets from ¥840/1300; ☺lunch 11.30am-2pm Sun-Fri, dinner 5-8.30pm Tue, Thu, Fri & Sat; ☑ⓓ; ⓢTōzai or Karasuma lines to Karasuma-Oike) Located diagonally across from Kyoto's main post office, this is a favourite of Kyoto vegetarians, serving daily sets of Japanese food with dishes such as deep-fried crumbed tofu and black seaweed salad with rice, miso and pickles. The seating is rather cramped but the food is excellent, beautifully presented and carefully made from quality ingredients.

It's on the corner. Go up the metal spiral staircase.

Nishiki Warai
OKONOMIYAKI ¥

(錦わらい; Map p306; ☑075-257-5966; www.nishikiwarai.com; 1st fl, Mizukōto Bldg, 597 Nishiuoya-chō, Nishikikōji-dōri, Takakura nishi-iru, Nakagyō-ku; okonomiyaki from ¥700; ☺11.30am-midnight; ⓓ; ⓢKarasuma line to Shijō, ⓡHankyū line to Karasuma) Nishiki Warai is a great place to try *okonomiyaki* (savoury pancakes) in casual surroundings. It can get a little smoky, but it's a fun spot to eat. Your *okonomiyaki* will

KYOTO CUISINE

Kyō-ryōri (Kyoto cuisine) is a style of cooking that evolved out of Kyoto's landlocked location and age-old customs of the imperial court. The preparation of dishes makes ingenious use of fresh seasonal vegetables and emphasises subtle flavours, revealing the natural taste of the ingredients. *Kyō-ryōri* is selected according to the mood and hues of the ever-changing seasons, and the presentation and atmosphere in which it's enjoyed are as important as the flavour.

Kaiseki (Japanese haute cuisine) is the pinnacle of refined dining, where ingredients, preparation, setting and presentation come together to create a dining experience quite unlike any other. Read more in Japanese Cuisine (p848); experience it at one of Kyoto's storied restaurants, like **Kitcho Arashiyama** (p347) or **Kikunoi** (p346), or at the more moderately priced (but still appealing), **Kiyamachi Sakuragawa** (p344).

be served ready-made to the hotplate at your table. It's about 20m west of the west end of Nishiki Market; look for the English sign in the window.

Shunsai Tempura Arima
TEMPURA ¥¥

(旬菜天ぷら 有馬; Map p306; ☑075-344-0111; 572 Sanno-chō, Muromachi-dōri, Takatsuji-agaru, Simogyō-ku; lunch/dinner sets from ¥1000/4750; ☺11.30am-2pm & 5.30-10.30pm, closed Thu; ⓓ; ⓢKarasuma line to Shijō) Tempura is one of Japan's most divine dishes and this friendly downtown restaurant is a great place to try it. It's a tiny family-run joint with a welcoming atmosphere. The English-language menus and set meals make ordering easy. It's on a corner with a small English sign.

Tōsuirō
TOFU ¥¥

(豆水楼; Map p306; ☑075-251-1600; www.tousuiro.com; Kiyamachi-dōri, Sanjō-agaru, Nakagyō-ku; lunch/dinner from ¥2494/3969; ☺11.30am-2pm & 5-9.30pm Mon-Sat, noon-3pm & 5-8.30pm Sun; ⓓ; ⓢTōzai line to Kyoto-Shiyakusho-mae) You will be amazed by the incredible variety of dishes that can be created with tofu at this specialist tofu restaurant. It's got great traditional Japanese decor and in summer you can sit on the *yuka* (dining platform) outside and take in a view of the river. You'll find it at the end of an alley on the north side off Kiyamachi-dōri.

At lunch the *machiya-zen* tofu set (¥2494) is highly recommended, while for dinner the Higashiyama tofu set (¥3969) is excellent.

Tsukiji Sushisei SUSHI ¥¥

(築地寿司清; Map p306; ☎075-252-1537; 581 Obiya-chō, Takakura-dōri, Nishikikōji-sagaru, Nakagyō-ku; sushi sets ¥1512-3456, per piece from ¥162; ⏲11.30am-3pm & 5-10pm Mon-Fri, 11.30am-10pm Sat, Sun & holidays; 📋; [S] Karasuma line to Shijō) On the basement floor, next to Daimaru department store, this simple sushi restaurant serves excellent sushi. You can order a set or just point at what looks good. You can see inside the restaurant from street level, so it should be easy to spot.

Tagoto Honten KAISEKI ¥¥

(田ごと本店; Map p306; ☎075-221-1811; www.kyoto-tagoto.co.jp; 34 Otabi-chō, Shijō-dōri, Kawaramachi nishi-iru, Nakagyō-ku; lunch/dinner from ¥1850/4000; ⏲11am-8.30pm; 📋; [R] Keihan line to Shijō or Hankyū line to Kawaramachi) Across from Takashimaya department store, this long-standing Kyoto restaurant serves approachable *kaiseki* fare in a variety of rooms, both private and common. Its *kiku* set (¥1850) includes some sashimi, tempura and a variety of other nibblies. *Kaiseki* dinner courses start at ¥6500 and you must make reservations in advance. Otherwise try the cheaper mini *kaiseki* dinner as a sampler (¥4000).

Kerala INDIAN ¥¥

(ケララ; Map p306; ☎075-251-0141; 2nd fl, KUS Bldg, Kawaramachi-dōri, Sanjō-agaru, Nakagyō-ku; lunch/dinner from ¥900/2600; ⏲11.30am-2pm & 5-9pm; ✏📋; [S] Tōzai line to Kyoto-Shiyakusho-mae) Kyoto's best Indian restaurant is a narrow upstairs spot on Kawaramachi-dōri. The ¥900 lunch set menu is an excellent deal, as is the vegetarian lunch (¥1200). Dinners run closer to ¥2600 per head and are of very high quality. Finish off the meal with the incredibly rich and creamy coconut ice cream.

Kerala is located on the 2nd floor; look for its sign out the front.

★Roan Kikunoi KAISEKI ¥¥¥

(露庵菊乃井; Map p306; ☎075-361-5580; www.kikunoi.jp; 118 Saito-chō, Kiyamachi-dōri, Shijō-sagaru, Shimogyō-ku; lunch/dinner from ¥4000/13,000; ⏲11.30am-1.30pm & 5-8.30pm; 🚭📋; [R] Hankyū line to Kawaramachi or Keihan line to Gion-Shijō) Roan Kikunoi is a fantastic place to experience the wonders of *kaiseki*. It's a clean, intimate space located right downtown. The chef takes an experimental and creative approach to *kaiseki* and the results are a wonder for the eyes and palate. Highly recommended. Reserve through your hotel or ryokan.

★Yoshikawa TEMPURA ¥¥¥

(吉川; Map p306; ☎075-221-5544; www.kyoto-yoshikawa.co.jp; 135 Matsushita-chō, Tominokōji, Oike-sagaru, Nakagyō-ku; lunch ¥3000-25,000, dinner ¥8000-25,000; ⏲11am-2pm & 5-8.30pm; 📋; [S] Tōzai line to Karasuma-Oike or Kyoto-Shiyakusho-mae) This is the place to go for delectable tempura. Attached to the Yoshikawa ryokan (p334), it offers table seating, but it's much more interesting to sit and eat around the small counter and observe the chefs at work. It's near Oike-dōri in a fine traditional Japanese-style building. Reservation required for tatami room; counter and table seating unavailable on Sunday.

Kiyamachi Sakuragawa KAISEKI ¥¥¥

(木屋町　櫻川; Map p306; ☎075-255-4477; Kiyamachi-dōri, Nijō-sagaru, Nakagyō-ku; lunch/dinner sets from ¥5000/10,000; ⏲11.30am-2pm & 5-9pm, closed Sun; [S] Tōzai line to Kyoto-Shiyakusho-mae) This elegant restaurant on a scenic stretch of Kiyamachi-dōri is an excellent place to try *kaiseki*. The modest but fully satisfying food is beautifully presented and it's a joy to watch the chef in action. The warmth of the reception adds to the quality of the food. Reservations are recommended and smart casual is the way to go here.

Mishima-tei JAPANESE ¥¥¥

(三嶋亭; Map p306; ☎075-221-0003; 405 Sakurano-chō, Teramachi-dōri, Sanjō-sagaru,

ℹ KYOTO TIPS FOR...

Luxury food on the cheap Many of Kyoto's elite *kaiseki* (Japanese haute cuisine) restaurants serve a delicious lunch set or *bentō* (boxed meal) for a fraction of their normal dinner offerings.

Hassle-free dining The upper floors of department stores (like Daimaru, Takashimaya etc) have good spreads of reliable Japanese and international restaurants, often with English menus; look to the basements for high-end takeaway options – perfect for a picnic.

Grabbing snacks for the train Porta, the shopping mall underneath the north side of Kyoto Station, is crammed with shops that sell takeaway food.

Nakagyō-ku; sukiyaki lunch/dinner from ¥7128/13,662; ⏱ 11.30am-9pm; 🅿 📱; Ⓢ Tōzai line to Kyoto-Shiyakusho-mae) Mishima-tei is a good place to sample sukiyaki (thin slices of beef cooked in sake, soy and vinegar broth, and dipped in raw egg) as the quality of the meat is very high, which is hardly surprising when there is a butcher right downstairs. It's in the intersection of the Sanjō and Teramachi covered arcades. You'll need your hotel to make a booking for you as it doesn't accept reservations without a Japanese telephone number.

🍴 Imperial Palace & Around

⭐ Papa Jon's
CAFE ¥

(パパジョンズカフェ　本店; Map p308; ☎ 075-415-2655; 642-4 Shokokuji-chō, Karasuma-dōri, Kamidachiuri higashi-iru, Kamigyō-ku; lunch from ¥850; ⏱ 10am-9pm; 🍴 📱; Ⓢ Karasuma line to Imadegawa) Just a three-minute walk from the north border of the Kyoto Imperial Palace Park, this clean, well-lit place serves brilliant New York cheesecake and hot drinks. Other menu items include pizza, homemade quiche, soup and tasty salads. Paintings by local artists are on display. There are a few branches around town, including a new convenient **downtown cafe** (Map p306; cnr Rokkaku-dōri & Sakaimachi-dōri, Higashi-iru, Nakagyō-ku; Ⓢ Karasuma or Tōzai lines to Karasuma-Oike).

Sarasa Nishijin
CAFE ¥

(さらさ西陣; Map p308; ☎ 075-432-5075; 11-1 Murasakino Higashifujinomori-chō, Kita-ku; lunch from ¥960; ⏱ noon-11pm, closed Wed; 🚌 Kyoto City bus 206 to Daitoku-ji-mae) This is one of Kyoto's most interesting cafes – it's built inside an old *sentō* (public bathhouse) and the original tiles have been preserved. Light meals and coffee are the staples here. Service can be slow but it's worth a stop for the ambience. Lines out the door are not uncommon. It's near Funaoka Onsen.

Demachi Futaba
SWEETS ¥

(出町ふたば; Map p308; ☎ 075-231-1658; 236 Seiryu-cho, Imadegawa-agaru, Kawaramachi-dōri, Kamigyō-ku; sweets from ¥175; ⏱ 8.30am-5.30pm, closed Tue; 🚃 Keihan line to Demachiyanagi) Join the queue of locals here for some of the city's tastiest sweets, with the *mame-mochi* (glutinous rice sweet with black beans) being the standout star. There's no English menu so just point to what takes your fancy. Look for the hanging paper signs and sweets on display.

🍴 Southern Higashiyama

Southern Higashiyama is filled with excellent restaurants and cafes, and one of the city's best *kaiseki* restaurants, the Michelin-starred Kikunoi.

⭐ Omen Kodai-ji
NOODLES ¥

(おめん　高台寺店; Map p312; ☎ 075-541-5007; 358 Masuya-chō, Kōdaiji-dōri, Shimokawara higashi-iru, Higashiyama-ku; noodles from ¥1150, set menu ¥1850; ⏱ 11am-9pm; 🚌 Kyoto City bus 206 to Higashiyama-Yasui) Housed in a remodelled Japanese building with a light, airy feeling, this branch of Kyoto's famed Omen noodle chain is the best place to stop while exploring the Southern Higashiyama district. The signature udon (thick, white wheat noodles) served in broth with a selection of fresh vegetables is delicious, and there are many other à la carte offerings.

⭐ Kagizen Yoshifusa
TEAHOUSE ¥

(鍵善良房; Map p312; ☎ 075-561-1818; www.kagizen.co.jp; 264 Gion machi, Kita-gawa, Higashiyama-ku; kuzukiri ¥900; ⏱ 9.30am-6pm, closed Mon; 📱; 🚃 Hankyū line to Kawaramachi, Keihan line to Gion-Shijō) This Gion institution is one of Kyoto's oldest and best-known *okashi-ya* (sweet shops). It sells a variety of traditional sweets and has a lovely tearoom out the back where you can sample cold *kuzukiri* (transparent arrowroot noodles) served with a *kuro-mitsu* (sweet black sugar) dipping sauce, or just a nice cup of *matcha* (powdered green tea) and a sweet.

Sobadokoro Shibazaki
NOODLES ¥

(そば処柴崎; Map p312; ☎ 075-525-3600; www.kyoto-shibazaki.com; 4-190-3 Kiyomizu, Higashiyama-ku; sushi per piece from ¥120, soba from ¥950; ⏱ 11am-9pm; 📱; 🚌 Kyoto City bus 206 to Kiyomizu-michi, 🚃 Keihan line to Kiyomizu-Gojō) This spacious, comfortable restaurant is a great spot to fuel up while sightseeing in the Kiyomizu-dera area, and has something to please everyone. Fill up on *kaiten-sushi* (conveyor-belt sushi) on the ground floor or head upstairs for excellent soba noodles and well-presented tempura sets and *unagi* (eel) dishes. While you're upstairs, check out the sublime collection of Japanese lacquerware.

Kasagi-ya
TEAHOUSE ¥

(かさぎ屋; Map p312; ☎ 075-561-9562; 349 Masuya chō, Kōdai-ji, Higashiyama-ku; tea & sweets from ¥600; ⏱ 11am-6pm, closed Tue; 📱; 🚌 Kyoto City bus 206 to Higashiyama-Yasui) At Kasagi-ya, on Sannen-zaka near Kiyomizu-dera, you can enjoy a nice cup of *matcha* and a variety of sweets. This funky old wooden shop has atmosphere to boot and friendly staff – which makes it worth the wait if there's a queue. It's hard to spot; you may have to ask one of the local shop owners.

★ **Kikunoi**   KAISEKI ¥¥¥

(菊乃井; Map p312; ☑ 075-561-0015; www.kikunoi.jp; 459 Shimokawara-chō, Yasakatoriimae-sagaru, Shimokawara-dōri, Higashiyama-ku; lunch/dinner from ¥8000/15,000; ⏱ noon-1pm & 5-8pm; ⊕ 🅿; 🚈 Keihan line to Gion-Shijō) This is one of Kyoto's true culinary temples, serving some of the finest *kaiseki* in the city by famous Michelin-starred chef Mutara. Located in a hidden nook near Maruyama-kōen, this restaurant has everything necessary for the full over-the-top *kaiseki* experience, from setting to service to exquisitely executed cuisine, often with a creative twist. Reserve through your hotel or ryokan concierge.

🍴 Northern Higashiyama

★ **Omen**   NOODLES ¥

(おめん; Map p316; ☑ 075-771-8994; www.omen.co.jp; 74 Jōdo-ji Ishibashi-chō, Sakyō-ku; noodles from ¥1150; ⏱ 11am-9pm; 🅿; 🚌 Kyoto City bus 5 to Ginkakuji-michi) This elegant noodle shop is named after the thick white noodles served in broth with a selection of seven fresh vegetables. Just say *omen* and you'll be given your choice of hot or cold noodles, a bowl of soup to dip them in and a plate of vegetables (put these into the soup along with sesame seeds).

★ **Goya**   OKINAWAN ¥

(ゴーヤ; Map p316; ☑ 075-752-1158; 114-6 Nishida-chō, Jōdo-ji, Sakyō-ku; meals from ¥680; ⏱ 11.30am-3.30pm & 5.30pm-midnight, closed Wed; 🅿🖥; 🚌 Kyoto City bus 5 to Ginkakuji-michi) This Okinawan-style restaurant has tasty food (with plenty of vegetarian options), a stylish interior and comfortable upstairs seating. It's perfect for lunch while exploring Northern Higashiyama and just a short walk from Ginkaku-ji. At lunch it serves simple dishes like taco rice (¥880) and *gōya champurū* (bitter melon stir-fry; ¥680), while dinners comprise a range of *izakaya* (Japanese pub) fare.

Falafel Garden   ISRAELI ¥

(ファラフェルガーデン; Map p308; ☑ 075-712-1856; www.falafelgarden.com; 15-2 Kamiyanagi-chō, Tanaka, Sakyō-ku; falafel from ¥410; ⏱ 11am-9.30pm; 🖥🅿; 🚈 Keihan line to Demachiyanagi) If you're in need of a break from Japanese food, head to this casual spot near Demachiyanagi Station for excellent and filling falafel pita sandwiches or plates with generous dollops of homemade hummus, or a side of green chilli sauce for more of a kick. Set menus (from ¥1100) are great value. There's a small garden courtyard for sunny days.

Hinode Udon   NOODLES ¥

(日の出うどん; Map p316; ☑ 075-751-9251; 36 Kitanobō-chō, Nanzenji, Sakyō-ku; noodles from ¥500; ⏱ 11am-3.30pm, closed Sun & occasionally Mon; 🅿; 🚌 Kyoto City bus 5 to Eikandō-michi) Filling noodle and rice dishes are served at this pleasant shop with an English menu. Plain udon are only ¥500, but we recommend you spring for the *nabeyaki udon* (pot-baked udon in broth) for ¥950. This is a good lunch spot when temple-hopping in the Northern Higashiyama area.

Au Temps Perdu   FRENCH ¥

(オ・タン・ペルデュ; Map p316; ☑ 075-762-1299; 64 Enshōji-chō, Okazaki, Sakyō-ku; tea & cake set from ¥1100; ⏱ 11am-7pm, closed Mon; 🅿; Ⓢ Tōzai line to Higashiyama) Overlooking the Shirakawa Canal, just across the street from the National Museum of Modern Art, this tiny indoor-outdoor French-style cafe is a lovely spot to take a break when sightseeing in the area. Check out the delicious cakes on display and pair them with a pot of tea, or spring for a light lunch along the lines of quiche and salad.

🍴 Arashiyama & Sagano
嵐山・嵯峨野

You won't be found hungry while exploring Arashiyama and Sagano as there are lots of great dining spots, including one of the city's finest *kaiseki* restaurants, Kitcho Arashiyama. The majority of the area's restaurants are clustered around the Keifuku Arashiyama Station, as well as some stand-out spots along the Hozu-gawa between the main street and the start of the Kameyama-kōen.

Arashiyama Yoshimura   NOODLES ¥

(嵐山よしむら; Map p324; ☑ 075-863-5700; Togetsu-kyō kita, Saga-Tenryū-ji, Ukyō-ku; soba from ¥1080, meals from ¥1600; ⏱ 11am-5pm; 🅿; 🚌 Kyoto City bus 28 from Kyoto Station to Arashiyama-Tenryuji-mae, 🚈 JR Sagano/San-in line to Saga-Arashiyama or Hankyū line to Arashiyama, change at Katsura) For a tasty bowl of soba noodles and an amazing view over the Arashiyama mountains and the Togetsu-kyō bridge, head to this extremely popular spot

DINING OVER THE RIVER IN KIBUNE

Visitors to Kibune from June to September should not miss the chance to dine at one of the picturesque restaurants beside the Kibune-gawa. Known as *kawa-doko*, meals are served on platforms suspended over the river as cool water flows underneath. Most of the restaurants offer a lunch special for around ¥4000. For a *kaiseki* (Japanese haute cuisine; ¥6000 to ¥12,000) spread, have a Japanese speaker call to reserve it in advance. Note that most restaurants don't accept solo diners, so either go with a friend or try your luck at lunchtime.

Hirobun (ひろ文; Map p329; ☑ 075-741-2147; 87 Kibune-chō, Kurama, Sakyō-ku; noodles from ¥1300, kaiseki courses from ¥8600; ⏱ 11am-9pm; 🅿; 🚃 Eiden Eizan line from Demachiyanagi to Kibune-guchi) is a good place to try. There's a friendly crew of ladies who run the show and the food is quite good. Note: it usually doesn't accept solo diners for *kaiseki* courses (but you can have noodles at lunch from 11am to 4pm). Look for the black-and-white sign and the lantern. Reserve for dinner.

just north of the famous bridge, overlooking the Katsura-gawa. There's an English menu but no English sign; look for the big glass windows and the stone wall.

Yoshida-ya SHOKUDO ¥
(よしだや; Map p324; ☑ 075-861-0213; 20-24 Tsukurimichi-chō, Saga Tenryū-ji, Ukyō-ku; soba & udon from ¥650; ⏱ 10am-4pm, closed Wed; 🅿; 🚃 Kyoto City bus 28 from Kyoto Station to Arashiyama-Tenryuji-mae, 🚃 JR Sagano/San-in line to Saga-Arashiyama or Hankyū line to Arashiyama, change at Katsura) This quaint and friendly little *teishoku-ya* (set-meal restaurant) is perfect for lunch while in Arashiyama. The standard *teishoku* favourites are on offer, including dishes like *oyakodon* (egg and chicken over a bowl of rice; ¥900) and filling bowls of udon and soba noodles. In summer, cool off with a refreshing *uji kintoki* (shaved ice with sweetened green tea; ¥600).

Komichi CAFE ¥
(こみち; Map p324; ☑ 075-872-5313; 23 Ōjōin-chō, Nison-in Monzen, Saga, Ukyō-ku; matcha ¥650; ⏱ 10am-5pm, closed Wed; 🚃 Kyoto City bus 28 from Kyoto Station to Arashiyama-Tenryuji-mae, 🚃 JR Sagano/San-in line to Saga-Arashiyama or Hankyū line to Arashiyama, change at Katsura) This friendly little teahouse is perfectly located along the Arashiyama tourist trail. In addition to hot and cold tea and coffee, it serves *uji kintoki* (shaved ice with sweetened green tea) in summer and a variety of light noodle dishes year-round. The picture menu helps with ordering.

★ **Shigetsu** VEGETARIAN, JAPANESE ¥¥
(篩月; Map p324; ☑ 075-882-9725; 68 Susukinobaba-chō, Saga-Tenryū-ji, Ukyō-ku; lunch sets ¥3500, ¥5500 & ¥7500, incl temple admission; ⏱ 11am-2pm; 🍴 🅿; 🚃 Kyoto City bus 28 from Kyoto Station to Arashiyama-Tenryuji-mae, 🚃 JR Sagano/

San-in line to Saga-Arashiyama or Hankyū line to Arashiyama, change at Katsura) To sample *shōjin-ryōri* (Buddhist vegetarian cuisine), try Shigetsu in the precincts of Tenryū-ji. This healthy fare has been sustaining monks for more than a thousand years in Japan, so it will probably get you through an afternoon of sightseeing, although carnivores may be left craving something. Shigetsu has beautiful garden views.

★ **Kitcho Arashiyama** KAISEKI ¥¥¥
(吉兆嵐山本店; Map p324; ☑ 075-881-1101; www.kitcho.com/kyoto/shoplist_en/arashiyama; 58 Susukinobaba-chō, Saga-Tenryūji, Ukyō-ku; lunch/dinner from ¥43,200/48,600; ⏱ 11.30am-3pm & 5-9pm, closed Wed; 🚃 JR Sagano/San-in line to Saga-Arashiyama) Considered one of the best *kaiseki* restaurants in Kyoto (and Japan, for that matter), Kitcho Arashiyama is the place to sample the full *kaiseki* experience. Meals are served in private rooms overlooking gardens. The food, service, explanations and atmosphere are all first rate. We suggest having a Japanese person call to reserve, or make a booking online via its website.

✖ Kitayama Area & North Kyoto

Most of the restaurants in Kurama and Kibune are clustered on the main strip in each town, and easy to spot.

★ **Yōshūji** VEGETARIAN ¥
(雍州路; Map p329; ☑ 075-741-2848; 1074 Honmachi, Kurama, Sakyō-ku; meals from ¥1080; ⏱ 10am-8pm, closed Tue; 🍴 🅿; 🚃 Eiden Eizan line from Demachiyanagi to Kurama) Yōshūji serves superb *shōjin-ryōri* in a delightful old Japanese farmhouse with an *irori* (open

DON'T MISS

LOCAL TOFU

Kyoto is famed for its tofu (soybean curd), a result of the city's excellent water and large population of (theoretically) vegetarian Buddhist monks. There are numerous *tofu-ya-san* (tofu makers) scattered throughout the city and a legion of exquisite *yudōfu* (tofu cooked in a pot) restaurants – many are located in Northern Higashiyama along the roads around Nanzen-ji and in the Arashiyama area. One typical Kyoto tofu by-product is *yuba*, sheets of the chewy, thin film that settles on the surface of vats of simmering soy milk. It turns up in many ryokan meals and *kaiseki* restaurants.

hearth). The house special, a sumptuous selection of vegetarian dishes served in red lacquered bowls, is called *kurama-yama shōjin zen* (¥2700). Or if you just feel like a quick bite, try the *uzu-soba* (soba topped with mountain vegetables; ¥1080).

You'll find it halfway up the steps leading to the main gate of Kurama-dera (p328); look for the orange lanterns out the front.

Kibune Club CAFE ¥

(貴船倶楽部; Map p329; ☎075-741-3039; 76 Kibune-chō, Kurama, Sakyō-ku; coffee from ¥500; 🕒11am-6pm; 📋; 🚆Eiden Eizan line from Demachiyanagi to Kibune-guchi) The exposed wooden beams and open, airy feel of this rustic cafe make it a great spot to stop for a cuppa and cake (sets from ¥800) while exploring Kibune. In winter it sometimes cranks up the wood stove, which makes the place rather cosy.

🍷 Drinking & Nightlife

Kyoto is a city with endless options for drinking, whether it's an expertly crafted single-origin coffee in a hipster cafe, a rich *matcha* (powdered green tea) at a traditional tearoom, carefully crafted cocktails and single malts in a sophisticated six-seater bar, or Japanese craft beer in a brewery.

🍷 Kyoto Station & South Kyoto

Vermillion Espresso Bar CAFE

(バーミリオン; Map p300; 85 Fukakusa-inari, Onmae-chō, Fushimi-ku; 🕒10am-5.30pm Mon-Wed & Fri, 9am-5.30pm Sat & Sun; 🚆JR Nara line to Inari) A Melbourne-inspired cafe, Vermillion takes its name from the colour of the *torii* gates of the nearby Fushimi Inari-Taisha shrine. It does standout coffee as well as a small selection of cakes. It's on the main street, just a short hop from Inari Station.

Kyoto Brewing Company BREWERY

(京都醸造株式会社; Map p300; ☎075-574-7820; www.kyotobrewing.com; 25-1 Nishikujō, Takahatacho, Minami-ku; 🕒most Sat & Sun 1-6pm; 🚆Kintetsu line to Jūjō) You'll find its beer in many of Kyoto's beer bars but it's worth a trip out to this small standing-room-only tasting room to sample it in a friendly local setting in South Kyoto. Check out the brewery vats as you sip on a selection of six beers on tap, including a few limited releases. Open most weekends in summer from 1pm to 6pm; check the website for details.

🍷 Downtown Kyoto

For a night out, your best bet is to head to Kiyamachi-dōri and the surrounding streets where you'll find bars and clubs around the Shijō-dōri end, and a great selection of restaurants and nightlife around the Sanjo-dōri end. But it pays to do some exploring as there are great bars hidden away in streets elsewhere.

★**Bungalow** CRAFT BEER

(バンガロー; Map p300; ☎075-256-8205; www.bungalow.jp; Shijō-dōri, Shimoji-ku, Nakagyō-ku; 🕒3pm-2am Tue-Sat, noon-11pm Sun; 🚆Ōmiya) Spread over two floors, Bungalow serves a great range of Japanese craft beer in a cool industrial space. The menu changes regularly but generally you'll find 10 beers on tap from all over Japan, from a Baird Brewery Scotch ale to a peach Weizen from Minoh. It also does excellent food, most of which is organic.

Weekenders Coffee Tominoko-ji COFFEE

(ウィークエンダーズ コーヒー; Map p306; ☎075-746-2206; www.weekenderscoffee.com; 560 Honeyana-chō, Nakagyo-ku; 🕒7.30am-6pm, closed Wed; 🚆Hankyū line to Kawaramachi) Weekenders is a standing-room-only coffee bar tucked away at the back of a parking lot in Downtown Kyoto. It's a strange spot but it's where you'll find some of Kyoto's best coffee being brewed by roaster-owner, Masahiro Kaneko.

Sama Sama BAR

(サマサマ; Map p306; ☎075-241-4100; 532-16 Kamiōsaka-chō, Kiyamachi, Sanjō-agaru, Nakagyō-ku; 🕒6pm-2am, closed Mon; [S]Tōzai line to Kyoto-Shiyakusho-mae) Sama Sama is an Indonesian-owned bar that feels like a very comfortable cave somewhere near the

Mediterranean. Scoot up to the counter or find a spot on the floor cushions and enjoy a wide variety of drinks paired with food, including Indonesian classics like *nasi goreng* (¥800). It's down an alley just north of Sanjō; look for the signboard.

Kaboku Tearoom
TEAHOUSE

(喫茶室嘉木; Map p316; Teramachi-dōri, Nijō-agaru, Nakagyō-ku; ⏰10am-6pm; Ⓢ Tōzai line to Kyoto-Shiyakusho-mae) A casual lovely tearoom attached to the Ippōdō Tea (p352) store, Kaboku serves a range of tea including *sencha*, *genmaicha* and *matcha*, and provides a great break while exploring the shops around the Teramachi covered arcade. Try the thicker *koicha*-style *matcha* and grab a counter seat to watch it being prepared.

Tadg's Gastro Pub
PUB

(ダイグ ガストロ パブ; Map p306; ☎075-213-0214; www.tadgs.com; 1st fl, 498 Kamikoriki-chō, Nakagyō-ku; ⏰11am-11pm; 🛜; Ⓢ Tōzai line to Kyoto-Shiyakusho-mae) Looking out on a scenic stretch of Kiyamachi-dōri, Tadg's is a great place for a drink in the evening and you can choose from an extensive selection of craft beers (including eight rotating Japanese beers on tap), along with a variety of wines, sake and spirits. Seating is available, including an enclosed garden out the back for smokers.

Bar K6
BAR

(バーK6; Map p316; ☎075-255-5009; 2nd fl, Le Valls Bldg, Nijō-dōri, Kiyamachi higashi-iru, Nakagyō-ku; ⏰6pm-3am, until 5am Fri & Sat; Ⓢ Tōzai line to Kyoto-Shiyakusho-mae, Ⓡ Keihan line to Jingu-Marutamachi) Overlooking one of the prettiest stretches of Kiyamachi-dōri, this upscale modern Japanese bar has a great selection of single malts and some of the best cocktails in town. There's even a local craft brew on offer. It's popular with well-heeled locals and travellers staying at some of the hotels nearby.

Atlantis
BAR

(アトランティス; Map p306; ☎075-241-1621; 161 Matsumoto-chō, Ponto-chō-Shijō-agaru, Nakagyō-ku; ⏰6pm-2am, to 1am Sun; Ⓡ Hankyū line to Kawaramachi) This is one of the few bars on Ponto-chō that foreigners can walk into without a Japanese friend. It's a slick, trendy place that draws a fair smattering of Kyoto's beautiful people, and wannabe beautiful people. In summer you can sit outside on a platform looking over the Kamo-gawa.

It's often crowded so you may have to wait a bit to get in, especially if you want to sit outside.

World
CLUB

(ワールド; Map p306; ☎075-213-4119; www.world-kyoto.com; Basement, Imagium Bldg, 97 Shin-chō, Nishikiyamachi, Shijō-agaru, Shimogyō-ku; cover ¥2000-3000; ⏰8pm-late; Ⓡ Hankyū line to Kawaramachi) World is Kyoto's largest club and it naturally hosts some of the biggest events. It has two floors, a dance floor and lockers where you can leave your stuff while you dance the night away. Events include everything from deep soul to reggae and techno to salsa.

Sake Bar Yoramu
BAR

(酒バー よらむ; Map p306; ☎075-213-1512; www.sakebar-yoramu.com; 35-1 Matsuya-chō, Nijō-dōri, Higashinotoin, higashi-iru, Nakagyō-ku; ⏰6pm-midnight Wed-Sat; Ⓢ Karasuma or Tōzai lines to Karasuma-Oike) Named for Yoramu, the Israeli sake expert who runs Sake Bar Yoramu, this bar is highly recommended for anyone after an education in sake. It's very small and can only accommodate a handful of people. Sake tasting sets start at around ¥1600 for a set of three. By day, it's a soba restaurant called Toru Soba.

Southern Higashiyama

There are a number of places to stop in for a drink in the many backstreets around Gion and the main strip, Shijō-dōri.

Beer Komachi
CRAFT BEER

(ビア小町; Map p312; ☎075-746-6152; www.beerkomachi.com; 444 Hachiken-chō, Higashiyama-ku; ⏰5-11pm Mon & Wed-Fri, 3-11pm Sat & Sun, closed Tue; 🛜; Ⓢ Tōzai line to Higashiyama) Located in the Furokawa-chō covered shopping arcade close to Higashiyama Station, this tiny casual bar is dedicated to promoting Japanese craft beer. There are usually seven Japanese beers on tap, which rotate on an almost daily basis. The excellent bar-food menu tempts with delights, such as fried chicken in beer batter and even a stout chocolate gateau for dessert.

Tōzan Bar
BAR

(Map p312; ☎075-541-3201; www.kyoto.regency.hyatt.com; Hyatt Regency Kyoto, 644-2 Sanjūsangendō-mawari, Higashiyama-ku; ⏰5pm-midnight; ⏰; Ⓡ Keihan line to Shichijō) Even if you're not spending the night at the Hyatt Regency (p336), drop by the cool and cosy underground bar for a tipple or two. Kitted out by renowned design firm Super Potato, the dimly lit atmospheric space features interesting touches, such as old locks, wooden beams, an antique-book library space and a wall feature made from traditional wooden sweet moulds.

Gion Finlandia Bar BAR
(ぎをん フィンランディアバー; Map p312; ☎075-541-3482; www.finlandiabar.com; 570-123 Gion-machi minamigawa, Higashiyama-ku; cover ¥500; ⏲6pm-3am; 🚆Keihan line to Gion-Shijō) This stylish, minimalist Gion bar in an old geisha house is a great place for a civilised drink. There's no menu, so just prop up at the bar and let the bow-tied bartender know what you like, whether it's an expertly crafted cocktail or a high-end Japanese single malt. Friday and Saturday nights can get busy, so you may have to queue.

🍷 Northern Higashiyama

Kick Up BAR
(キックアップ; Map p316; ☎075-761-5604; 331 Higashikomonoza-chō, Higashiyama-ku; ⏲7pm-midnight, closed Wed; [S] Tōzai line to Keage) Located just across the street from the Westin Miyako Kyoto (p337), this wonderful bar attracts a regular crowd of Kyoto expats, local Japanese and guests from the Westin. It's subdued, relaxing and friendly.

Metro CLUB
(メトロ; Map p316; ☎075-752-4765; www.metro.ne.jp; BF Ebisu Bldg, Kawabata-dōri, Marutamachi-sagaru, Sakyō-ku; ⏲about 8pm-3am; 🚆Keihan line to Jingū-Marutamachi) Metro is part disco, part live house and it even hosts the occasional art exhibition. It attracts a mix of creative types and has a different theme nightly, so check ahead in *Kansai Scene* to see what's going on. Metro is inside exit 2 of the Jingū-Marutamachi Station on the Keihan line.

🍷 Arashiyama & Sagano
嵐山・嵯峨野

% Arabica COFFEE
(Map p324; ☎075-748-0057; www.arabica.coffee; 3-47 Susukinobaba-chō, Saga-Tenryūji, Ukyō-ku; ⏲8am-6pm; 🚆JR Sagano/San-in line to Saga-Arashiyama) Peer through the floor-to-ceiling windows that look across the Hozu-gawa and mountain backdrop as you order coffee at this tiny cafe bringing excellent brew to Arashiyama. With just a few seats that can be 'rented', your best bet is to grab a takeaway and stroll along the river or nab a bench out front to take in the views.

☆ Entertainment

★Minami-za THEATRE
(南座; Map p312; ☎075-561-0160; www.kabuki-bito.jp; Shijō-Ōhashi, Higashiyama-ku; performances ¥5000-27,000; 🚆Keihan line to Gion-Shijō) The oldest kabuki theatre in Japan is the Minami-za in Gion. The major event of the year is the **Kaomise festival** (30 November to 25 December), which features Japan's finest kabuki actors. Other performances take place on an irregular basis – check the website for the schedule or enquire at the Kyoto Tourist Information Center (p354).

Kyoto Cuisine & Maiko Evening DANCE
(ぎおん畑中; Map p312; ☎075-541-5315; www.kyoto-maiko.jp; Hatanaka Ryokan, 505 Minami-gawa, Gion-machi, Yasaka-jinja Minamimon-mae, Higashiyama-ku; per person ¥19,000; ⏲6-8pm Mon, Wed, Fri & Sat; 🚆Kyoto City bus 206 to Gion

ROMANTIC WALKS IN KYOTO

Kyoto is one of the world's great walking cities, especially after dark. If you fancy an evening stroll with someone special, here are a few romantic routes:

Ponto-chō (p305) Take a short but sweet stroll through one of the most atmospheric lanes in all of Japan. Expect crowds in the evening.

Kiyamachi The section of Kiyamachi-dōri between Oike and Gojō is incredibly beautiful after dark, especially during cherry-blossom season. The section between Sanjō and Shijō is not as romantic as it's home to a lot of the city's clubs and nightlife.

Kiyomizu to Yasaka Clogged with tourists during the day, the main route from Kiyomizu-dera to Yasaka-jinja is usually almost deserted after dark. It's truly magical at this time.

Path of Philosophy (p318) The crowds are usually gone by 5pm here, leaving this scenic pathway to locals and savvy travellers.

Gion (p315) A brief stroll along Hanami-kōji, across Shijō, and over to Shimbashi is sure to seal the deal on any budding romance.

KYOTO'S GEISHA DANCES

Each year Kyoto's geisha (or, properly speaking, *geiko* and *maiko* – fully fledged and trainee geisha respectively) perform fantastic dances (known as *odori*), usually on seasonal themes. We highly recommend seeing one of these dances if you are in town when they are being held. Ask at the **Kyoto Tourist Information Center** (p354) or at your lodgings for help with ticket purchase. Tour companies can also help with tickets.

Kyō Odori (京おどり; Map p312; ☎ 075-561-1151; Miyagawachō Kaburenjo, 4-306 Miyagawasu-ji, Higashiyama-ku; nonreserved seat with/without tea ¥2800/2200, reserved seat with/without tea ¥4800/4200; ⊗ shows 1pm, 2.45pm & 4.30pm; ⊠ Keihan line to Gion-Shijō) Among the most picturesque of performances on the Kyoto calendar; held from the first to the third Sunday in April at the Miyagawa-chō Kaburen-jō Theatre (宮川町歌舞練場), east of the Kamo-gawa between Shijō-dōri and Gojō-dōri.

Miyako Odori (都をどり; Map p312; ☎ 075-541-3391; www.miyako-odori.jp; Gionkobu Kaburenjo, 570-2 Gion-machi minamigawa, Higashiyama-ku; nonreserved seat/reserved seat/reserved seat with tea ¥2500/4200/4800; ⊗ shows 12.30pm, 2pm, 3.30pm & 4.50pm; ⊠ Kyoto City bus 206 to Gion, ⊠ Keihan line to Gion-Shijō) Colourful, mesmerising dances held throughout April at Kyoto Art Theater Shunjuza (as of late 2016, while the regular venue, Gion Kōbu Kaburen-jō Theatre, undergoes renovations).

Kitano Odori (北野をどり; Map p308; ☎ 075-461-0148; Imadegawa-dōri, Nishihonmatsu nishi iru, Kamigyō-ku; admission/with tea ¥4300/4800; ⊗ shows 1.30pm & 4pm; ⊠ Kyoto City bus 50 to Kitano Tenmangu-mae) Performances by *maiko* and *geiko* of the Kamishichiken district; held in early April at Kamishichiken Kaburen-jō Theatre (上七軒歌舞練場), east of **Kitano Tenman-gū** (p321).

Kamogawa Odori (鴨川をどり; Map p306; ☎ 075-221-2025; Ponto-chō, Sanjō-sagaru, Nakagyō-ku; normal/special seat/special seat with tea ¥2300/4200/4800; ⊗ shows 12.30pm, 2.20pm & 4.10pm; ⊠ Tōzai line to Kyoto-Shiyakusho-mae) From 1 to 24 May at Ponto-chō Kaburen-jō Theatre (先斗町歌舞練場) in **Ponto-chō** (p305).

Gion Odori (祇園をどり; Map p312; ☎ 075-561-0224; Gion, Higashiyama-ku; admission/with tea ¥4000/4500; ⊗ shows 1.30pm & 4pm; ⊠ Kyoto City bus 206 to Gion) Charming dances put on by the geisha of the Gion Higashi district from 1 to 10 November at the Gion Kaikan Theatre (祇園会館), near **Yasaka-jinja** (p313).

For more on Kyoto's geisha culture, see Living Art of the Geisha (p872).

or Chionin-mae, ⊠ Keihan line to Gion-Shijō) If you want to witness geisha perform and then actually speak with them, one of the best opportunities is at Gion Hatanaka (p336), a Gion ryokan that offers a regularly scheduled evening of elegant Kyoto *kaiseki* food and personal entertainment by real Kyoto *geiko* (fully fledged geisha) as well as *maiko* (apprentice geisha). Children under seven years are not permitted.

ROHM Theatre Kyoto   THEATRE
(京都観世会館; Map p316; ☎ 075-771-6051; www.rohmtheatrekyoto.jp; 44 Okazaki Enshōji-chō, Sakyo-ku; tickets from ¥3000; ⊗ box office 10am-7pm; Ⓢ Tōzai line to Higashiyama) The Kyoto Kaikan Theatre was renovated in 2016 and became the ROHM Theatre Kyoto. Housed in a striking modernist building, it holds three multi-purpose halls with a 2000-seater main hall

hosting everything from international ballet and opera performances to comedy shows, music concerts and *nō* (stylised dance-drama performed on a bare stage).

Gion Corner   THEATRE
(ギオンコーナー; Map p312; ☎ 075-561-1119; www.kyoto-gioncorner.com; Yasaka Kaikan, 570-2 Gionmachi Minamigawa, Higashiyama-ku; adult/child ¥3150/1900; ⊗ performances 6pm & 7pm daily mid-Mar–Nov, Fri-Sun Dec–mid-Mar; ⊠ Kyoto City bus 206 to Gion, ⊠ Keihan line to Gion-Shijō) Gion Corner presents regularly scheduled one-hour shows that include a bit of tea ceremony, koto (Japanese zither) music, ikebana (art of flower arranging), *gagaku* (court music), *kyōgen* (ancient comic plays), *kyōmai* (Kyoto-style dance) and *bunraku* (classical puppet theatre). It's geared to tourists and is pricey for what you get. Arrive early for front-row seats.

Club Ōkitsu Kyoto JAPANESE CULTURE
(京都桜橘倶楽部「桜橘庵」; Map p308; ☎075-411-8585; www.okitsu-kyoto.com; 524-1 Mototsuchimikado-chō, Kamichōjamachi-dōri, Shinmachi higashi-iru, Kamigyō-ku; [S] Karasuma line to Imadegawa) Ōkitsu provides an upmarket introduction to various aspects of Japanese culture, including tea ceremony and the incense ceremony. The introduction is performed in an exquisite Japanese villa near the Kyoto Imperial Palace, and participants get a real sense of the elegance and refinement of traditional Japanese culture.

It also offers kimono dressing upon request (note that kimono dressing is not offered alone: it must be part of a package including tea ceremony and/or incense ceremony).

Shopping

Kyoto has a long history as Japan's artistic and cultural workshop: it's the place where the country's finest artisans used their skills to produce the goods used in tea ceremonies, calligraphy, flower arrangement and religious ceremonies, as well as in kimono fabrics and other textiles. Indeed, Kyoto is the best place to find traditional arts and crafts in Japan.

Of course, Kyoto has far more to offer than just traditional items. You will also find the latest fashions in the Shijō-Kawaramachi shopping district, the latest electronics on Teramachi-dōri and a wondrous assortment of food products in markets such as Nishiki.

Kyoto Station & South Kyoto

If you're looking to splash some cash in shopping malls, department stores and massive electronic shops, this is the area you'll want to head to. Branches of two of Japan's biggest electronics stores, **Yodobashi Camera** (ヨドバシカメラ; ☎075-351-1010; 590-2 Higashi Shiokōji-chō, Shimogyō-ku; 🕒9.30am-10pm; 🚆Kyoto Station) and **Bic Camera** (ビックカメラ; ☎075-353-1111; 927 Higashi Shiokōji-chō, Shimogyō-ku; 🕒10am-9pm; 🚆Kyoto Station), are here.

Downtown Kyoto

From multi-level department stores crammed with the latest fashion and gadgets to traditional shops selling exquisite arts and crafts, Downtown Kyoto is *the* place to part with your hard-earned cash.

★Zōhiko ARTS & CRAFTS
(象彦; Map p316; ☎075-229-6625; www.zohiko.co.jp; 719-1 Yohojimae-chō, Teramachi-dōri, Nijō-agaru, Nakagyō-ku; 🕒10am-6pm; [S] Tōzai line to Kyoto-Shiyakusho-mae) Zōhiko is the best place in Kyoto to buy one of Japan's most beguiling art and craft forms: lacquerware. If you're not familiar with just how beautiful these products can be, you owe it to yourself to make the pilgrimage to Zōhiko. There's a great selection of cups, bowls, trays and various kinds of boxes.

★Takashimaya DEPARTMENT STORE
(高島屋; Map p306; ☎075-221-8811; Shijō-Kawaramachi Kado, Shimogyō-ku; 🕒10am-8pm, restaurants to 9.30pm; 🚆Hankyū line to Kawaramachi) The *grande dame* of Kyoto department stores, Takashimaya is almost a tourist attraction in its own right, from the mind-boggling riches of the basement food floor to the wonderful selection of lacquerware and ceramics on the 6th floor. And don't miss the kimono display.

★Aritsugu HOMEWARES
(有次; Map p306; ☎075-221-1091; 219 Kajiya-chō, Nishikikōji-dōri, Gokomachi nishi-iru, Nakagyō-ku; 🕒9am-5.30pm; 🚆Hankyū line to Kawaramachi) While you're in Nishiki Market, pop into this store – it has some of the best kitchen knives in the world. Choose your knife – all-rounder, sushi, vegetable – and the staff will show you how to care for it before sharpening and boxing it up. You can also have your name engraved in English or Japanese. Knives start at around ¥10,000.

Founded in 1560, Aritsugu was originally involved in the production of swords and the blacksmith skills have been passed down over the years through generation after generation. It also carries a selection of excellent and unique Japanese kitchenware and whetstones for knife sharpening.

★Ippōdō Tea TEA
(一保堂茶舗; Map p316; ☎075-211-3421; www.ippodo-tea.co.jp; Teramachi-dōri, Nijō-agaru, Nakagyō-ku; 🕒9am-6pm; [S] Tōzai line to Kyoto-Shiyakusho-mae) This old-style tea shop sells some of the best Japanese tea in Kyoto, and you'll be given an English leaflet with prices and descriptions of each one. Its *matcha* makes an excellent and lightweight souvenir; 40g containers start at ¥500. Ippōdō is north of the city hall, on Teramachi-dōri. It has an adjoining teahouse, Kaboku Tearoom (p349); last order 5.30pm.

★Wagami no Mise ARTS & CRAFTS
(倭紙の店; Map p306; ☎075-341-1419; 1st fl, Kajinoha Bldg, 298 Ōgisakaya-chō, Higashinotōin-dōri, Bukkōji-agaru, Shimogyō-ku; 🕒9.30am-5.30pm

Mon-Fri, to 4.30pm Sat; ⓢKarasuma line to Shijō) This place sells a fabulous variety of *washi* (Japanese handmade paper) for reasonable prices and is a great spot to pick up a gift or souvenir. Look for the Morita Japanese Paper Company sign on the wall out the front.

Maruzen
BOOKS

(丸善; Map p306; basement, BAL, 251 Yamazaki-chō, Kawaramachi-sanjo sagaru, Nakagyō-ku; ⊙11am-9pm; ⓡHankyū line to Kawaramachi) Kyoto's most beloved bookshop closed in 2005 and finally reopened after 10 years in 2015. Occupying two basement floors of the BAL department store, this excellent bookshop has a massive range of English-language books across all subjects on basement level 2, plenty of titles on Kyoto and Japan, a great selection of Japanese literature, magazines from around the globe and travel guides.

Kyoto Design House
ARTS & CRAFTS

(Map p306; ☑075-221-0200; www.kyoto-dh.com; 1F Nikawa Bldg, Tominokōji-dōri, 105 Fukanaga-chō, Nakagyō-ku; ⊙11am-8pm; ⓢKarasuma or Tōzai lines to Karasuma-Oike) The Tadao Ando–designed Nikawa building is the perfect home for this design store, which stocks arts and crafts mainly designed by local Kyoto artists melding traditional with modern design. From handmade ceramics and *ohako* candy boxes to beautiful cushions using silk from the Nishijin textile district, this is the best place to pick up great gifts and souvenirs.

Tokyu Hands
DEPARTMENT STORE

(東急ハンズ京都店; Map p306; ☑075-254-3109; http://kyoto.tokyu-hands.co.jp; Shijō-dōri, Karasuma higashi-iru, Shimogyō-ku; ⊙10am-10.30pm; ⓢKarasuma line to Shijō) While the Kyoto branch of Tokyu Hands doesn't have the selection of bigger branches in Tokyo, it's still well worth a browse for fans of gadgets and unique homewares. It's a good place for an interesting gift or souvenir, from Hario coffee equipment and lacquerware bentō boxes to Lomography cameras, stationery and cosmetics.

Kamiji Kakimoto
ARTS & CRAFTS

(紙司柿本; Map p316; ☑075-211-3481; 54 Tokiwagi-chō, Teramachi-dōri, Nijō-agaru, Nakagyō-ku; ⊙9am-6pm; ⓡKeihan line to Jingū-Marutamachi) This is one of the best places to buy *washi* in Kyoto. It's got such unusual items as *washi* computer printer paper and *washi* wallpaper, along with great letter writing and wrapping paper. Look for the hanging white *noren* (curtain) out the front.

DON'T MISS

BEST SHOPPING FOR...

Tea Ippōdō Tea (p352)

Kitchenwares Aritsugu (p352)

Food Nishiki Market (p304)

Paper goods Wagami no Mise (p352)

Souvenirs Kyoto Handicraft Center (p354)

Kyūkyo-dō
ARTS & CRAFTS

(鳩居堂; Map p306; ☑075-231-0510; 520 Shimohonnōjimae-chō, Teramachi-dōri, Aneyakōji-agaru, Nakagyō-ku; ⊙10am-6pm Mon-Sat, closed Sun; ⓢTōzai line to Kyoto-Shiyakusho-mae) This old shop in the Teramachi covered arcade sells a selection of incense, *shodō* (calligraphy) goods, tea-ceremony supplies and *washi*. Prices are on the high side but the quality is good. This is your best one-stop shop for distinctively Japanese souvenirs.

Tsujikura
ARTS & CRAFTS

(辻倉; Map p306; ☑075-221-4396; www.kyototsujikura.com; 7th fl, Tsujikura Bldg, Kawaramachi-dōri, Shijō-agaru higashi-gawa, Nakagyō-ku; ⊙11am-7pm, closed Wed; ⓡHankyū line to Kawaramachi) Tsujikura is a small store stocking the beautiful *wagasa* (waxed-paper umbrellas) the company has been manufacturing since the 17th-century, which come in a mix of colours with traditional and modern design. It also has a small selection of Isamu Noguchi's famous Akari paper lamps. It's on the 7th floor of the same building as the tourist information office near the Shijō and Kawaramachi intersection.

BAL
DEPARTMENT STORE

(バル; Map p306; www.bal-bldg.com; 251 Yamazaki-chō, Kawaramachi-sanjo sagaru, Nakagyō-ku; ⊙11am-8pm; ⓡHankyū line to Kawaramachi) For all your high-end fashion needs, the chic and elegant BAL department store is the place to go. You'll find fashion by Helmut Lang and Diane von Furstenberg as well as botanical skincare from Neal's Yard, and the ever popular Muji. The two basement floors house the huge Maruzen (p353) bookstore.

Daimaru
DEPARTMENT STORE

(大丸; Map p306; ☑075-211-8111; Tachiuri Nishi-machi 79, Shijō-dōri, Takakura nishi-iru, Shimogyō-ku; ⊙10am-8pm, restaurants 11am-9pm; ⓢKarasuma line to Shijō, ⓡHankyū line to Karasuma) Daimaru has fantastic service, a great

DON'T MISS

KYOTO'S FLEA MARKETS

Kōbō-san Market kimonos, ceramics, antiques and more; on the 21st of the month at **Tō-ji** (p302).

Tenjin-san Market Everything from junk to treasures on the 25th of each month at **Kitano Tenman-gū** (p321).

selection of goods and a basement food floor that'll make you want to move to Kyoto.

Southern Higashiyama

The stretch of Shijō-dōri from Gion-Shijō Station to Yasaka-jinja is packed with souvenir stalls and shops selling everything from tea and sweets to *kokeshi* dolls and chopsticks.

★Ichizawa Shinzaburo Hanpu FASHION & ACCESSORIES
(一澤信三郎帆布; Map p312; ☎075-541-0436; www.ichizawa.co.jp; 602 Takabatake-chō, Higashiyama-ku; ⏲9am-6pm; [S] Tōzai line to Higashiyama) This company has been making its canvas bags for over 110 years and the store is often crammed with those in the know picking up a skillfully crafted Kyoto product. Originally designed as 'tool' bags for workers to carry sake bottles, milk and ice blocks, the current designs still reflect this idea. Choose from a range of styles and colours.

Pop upstairs to the workshop to get a look at how the bags are made. This is the one and only place where you can buy these bags – it's the sole store and they are not available online – making it the perfect souvenir.

Yojiya COSMETICS
(よーじや; Map p312; ☎075-541-0177; Shijō-dōri, Higashiyama-ku; ⏲10am-8pm; 🚆Keihan line to Gion-Shijō) Peruse the cosmetics and skincare here at one of Kyoto's most well-known brands. The famous oil-blotting facial papers make a great lightweight and cheap souvenir. There are a few branches around town – this one is on the corner of Shijō-dōri and Hanami-kōji; look for the logo of a face.

Northern Higashiyama

Kyoto Handicraft Center ARTS & CRAFTS
(京都ハンディクラフトセンター; Map p316; ☎075-761-7000; www.kyotohandicraftcenter.com; 17 Entomi-chō, Shōgoin, Sakyō-ku; ⏲10am-7pm; 🚌Kyoto City bus 206 to Kumano-jinja-mae) Split between two buildings, East and West, this store sells a good range of Japanese arts and crafts, such as Hokusai woodblock prints (from ¥5000), Japanese dolls, pearls, clothing and a great selection of books on Japanese culture and travel guides. There are English-speaking staff and currency exchange is available. It's within walking distance of the main Higashiyama sightseeing route.

ℹ Orientation

Central Kyoto is laid out in a grid and easy to navigate. The main hub of activity is the several blocks bracketed by Kawaramachi-dōri to the east and Karasuma-dōri to the west, and between Shijō-dōri to the south and Sanjō-dōri to the north. If you know your numbers in Japanese, navigating the city is even easier: Sanjō, for example, can be thought of as 'block three' (as 'san' means 'three'); Shijō as block four and so on. That said, most of the sights are on the fringes of the city, along the base of the eastern and western mountains (Higashiyama and Arashiyama, respectively).

ℹ Information

MEDICAL SERVICES

Kyoto University Hospital (京都大学医学部附属病院; Map p316; ☎075-751-3111; www.kuhp.kyoto-u.ac.jp; 54 Shōgoinkawahara-chō, Sakyō-ku; ⏲8.30am-11am Mon-Fri; 🚆Keihan line to Jingū-Marutamachi) Best hospital in Kyoto. There is an information counter near the entrance that can point you in the right direction.

TOURIST INFORMATION

Kansai International Airport Tourist Information Counter (関西国際空港関西観光情報センター; ☎0724-56-6160; ⏲7am-10pm) This counter is on the 1st floor of the international arrivals hall. Staff can provide information on Kyoto, Kansai and Japan.

Kyoto International Community House (京都国際交流開会, KICH; Map p316; ☎075-752-3010; 2-1 Torii-chō, Awataguchi, Sakyō-ku; ⏲9am-9pm, closed Mon; [S] Tōzai line to Keage, exit 2) An essential stop for those planning a long-term stay in Kyoto, KICH can also be useful for short-term visitors. It has a library with maps, books, newspapers and magazines from around the world, and a board with messages regarding work, accommodation, rummage sales etc.

You can use the wi-fi (register at the information counter) and pick up a copy of its excellent *Guide to Kyoto* map and its *Easy Living in Kyoto* book (note that both are intended for residents). You can also chill in the lobby and watch CNN news.

Kyoto Tourist Information Center (京都総合観光案内所, TIC; Map p304; ☎075-343-0548; 2F Kyoto Station Bldg, Shimogyō-ku; ⏲8.30am-7pm; [S] Karasuma line to Kyoto).

You'll find other small tourist offices dotted around the downtown area along Kawara-machi-dōri, such as the following office:

Kawaramachi Sanjo Tourist Information Center (Map p306; ☑ 075-213-1717; 1F Kyoto Asahi Kaikan Bldg, 427 Ebisu-cho, Kawara-machi-dōri, Sanjo-agaru; ⊙10am-6pm; S Tōzai line to Kyoto-Shiyakusho-mae) Convenient tourist information with plenty of brochures and maps, and helpful staff.

TRAVEL AGENCIES

Kansai Scene magazine advertises travel agencies that deal with foreigners.

KNT (近畿日本ツーリスト; Map p306; ☑ 075-255-0489; 437 Ebisu-chō, Kawaramachi-dōri, Sanjo-agaru, Nakagyō-ku; ⊙11am-7pm) A good place for domestic (within Japan) travel tickets.

USEFUL WEBSITES

Lonely Planet (www.lonelyplanet.com/kyoto) Destination information, hotel bookings, traveller forum and more.

Kyoto Visitor's Guide (www.kyotoguide.com) Great all-around Kyoto info.

HyperDia (www.hyperdia.com) Train schedules in English.

Inside Kyoto (www.insidekyoto.com) Monthly event information and much more.

Kyoto Travel Guide (www.kyoto.travel) Excellent resource on all things Kyoto.

❶ Getting There & Away

AIR

Most foreign visitors arrive in Kyoto via Kansai International Airport (KIX; Kyoto's main international entry point). Kyoto is also within reach of two other airports and it's sometimes cheaper to fly into Tokyo than into KIX.

Kansai International Airport

Built on an artificial island in Osaka Bay, Kansai International Airport (KIX) is about 75 minutes away from Kyoto by direct express trains.

KIX has a tourist information counter operated by the Osaka prefectural government. It's located roughly in the centre of the international arrivals hall, and can supply maps and answer questions.

If you'd prefer not to lug your bags into Kyoto, there are several luggage delivery services located in the arrivals hall.

When it comes time to depart, those travelling on Japanese airlines (JAL and ANA) can make use of an advance check-in counter inside the JR ticket office in Kyoto Station. This service allows you to check-in with your luggage at the station, which is a real bonus for those with heavy bags.

Osaka International Airport

Osaka International Airport, commonly known as Itami (ITM), is closer to Kyoto than KIX, but it handles only domestic traffic. Still, you might find that your international carrier will tack on a domestic leg from Tokyo to Itami.

You'll find an information counter with English-speaking staff in the main arrivals hall along with several luggage delivery services.

BUS

Overnight JR buses run between Tokyo Station (Nihonbashi-guchi/arrival, Yaesu-guchi/departure long-distance bus stop) and Kyoto Station Bus Terminal (京都駅前バスターミナル).

The trip takes about seven hours and the fare starts at around ¥5500 one way. There is a similar service to/from Shinjuku Station's Shin-minami-guchi in Tokyo.

Other JR bus transport possibilities include Kanazawa (one way from ¥3800) and Hiroshima (one way from ¥4450).

Willer Express (www.willerexpress.com) is a great budget option for long-distance and overnight buses. It operates between most major cities and Kyoto, and has comfortable reclining seats with personal monitors and a range of options from private seats to those with more legroom. From Tokyo's Shinjuku Station to Kyoto the fare starts at around ¥3600.

---

❶ KYOTO BUS & SUBWAY PASSES

To save time and money you can buy a *kaisū-ken* (book of five tickets) for ¥1000. There's also a *shi-basu Kyoto-bus ichinichi jōshaken kādo* (one-day card) valid for unlimited travel on Kyoto City buses and Kyoto buses (these are different companies) that costs ¥500. A similar pass *(Kyoto kankō ichinichi jōsha-ken)* that allows unlimited use of the bus and subway costs ¥1200. A *Kyoto kankō futsuka jōsha-ken* (two-day bus/subway pass) costs ¥2000. *Kaisū-ken* can be purchased directly from bus drivers. The other passes and cards can be purchased at major bus terminals, at the bus information centre at Kyoto Station or at the **Kyoto Tourist Information Center** (p354). The Kansai Thru Pass (p357) is useful if you're planning to do some exploring in the Kansai area.

The **Kyoto City Subway Pass** (adult/child ¥600/300) allows unlimited travel on the city's subway for one day, plus discounts on some sights. You can buy it from the Kyoto Tourist Information Center or any subway ticket office.

TRAIN

Kyoto Station is linked to nearby cities by several excellent train lines, including Japan Railways (JR). JR also has links to cities further afield, many of which are served by super-fast *shinkansen* (bullet trains). If you plan to do a lot of train travel around the rest of Japan, consider buying a Japan Rail Pass.

Private lines connect Kyoto Station with Nagoya, Nara, Osaka and Kōbe. Where they exist, private lines are always cheaper than JR. In particular, if you're travelling between Kyoto Station and Nara, you'll probably find a *tokkyū* (limited express) on the Kintetsu line to be faster and more comfortable than JR.

Kyoto Station is in the south of the city, just below Shichijō-dōri. The easiest way to get downtown from this station is to hop on the Karasuma subway line. There is a bus terminal on the north side of the station from where you can catch buses to all parts of town.

ⓘ Getting Around

TO/FROM THE AIRPORT
Kansai International Airport

Bus

Kansai International Airport Limousine Bus (☑ 075-682-4400; 1-way adult/child ¥2550/1280) runs frequent buses between Kyoto and KIX (about 90 minutes). In Kyoto, the buses depart from opposite the south side of Kyoto Station, in front of Avanti department store and Hotel Keihan.

Taxi

Perhaps the most convenient option is the **MK Taxi Sky Gate Shuttle limousine van service** (☑ 075-778-5489; www.mktaxi-japan.com), which will drop you off anywhere in Kyoto for ¥3600 – simply go to the staff counter at the south end of the KIX arrivals hall and they will do the rest. From Kyoto to the airport it is necessary to make reservations two days in advance staff will pick you up anywhere in Kyoto and take you to the airport.

ⓘ FOREIGNER-FRIENDLY TAXIS

In March 2016, Kyoto introduced a foreigner-friendly taxi service for a year-long trial. The service aims to make the taxi system more accessible to tourists, with drivers who can speak other languages, such as English and Chinese, and accepting payment by credit card. The taxis are clearly marked as 'foreigner friendly' and there is a separate taxi stand in front of the JR Kyoto Station

---

A similar service is offered by **Yasaka Taxi** (☑ 075-803-4800; www.yasaka.jp; one-way ¥3500). Keep in mind that these are shared taxis (actually vans), so you may be delayed by the driver picking up or dropping off other passengers.

Train

The fastest and most convenient way to move between KIX and Kyoto is the special JR Haruka airport express (reserved/unreserved ¥3370/2850, 75 minutes). First and last departures from KIX to Kyoto are at 6.30am and 10.16pm Monday to Friday (6.40am on weekends); first and last departures from Kyoto to KIX are at 5.45am and 8.30pm.

If you have time to spare, you can save money by taking the *kankū kaisoku* (Kansai airport express) between the airport and Osaka Station, and then taking a regular *shinkaisoku* (special rapid train) to Kyoto. The total journey takes about 95 minutes with good connections and costs around ¥1750.

Osaka International Airport

Bus

Osaka Airport Transport (☑ 06-6844-1124; www.okkbus.co.jp; 1-way ¥1310) runs frequent airport limousine buses between Itami and Kyoto Station (¥1310, 55 minutes). There are less frequent pick-ups and drop-offs at some of Kyoto's main hotels. The Itami stop is outside the arrivals hall – buy your ticket from the machine near the bus stop and ask one of the attendants which stand is for Kyoto. The Kyoto Station stop is in front of Avanti department store, which is opposite the south side of the station.

Taxi

MK Taxi Sky Gate Shuttle limousine van service (☑ 075-778-5489; www.mktaxi-japan. com) travels to/from the airport for ¥2400. Call at least two days in advance to reserve, or ask at the information counter in the arrivals hall.

BICYCLE

Kyoto is a great city to explore on a bicycle. With the exception of the outlying areas, it is mostly flat and there is a useful bike path running the length of the Kamo-gawa.

Many guesthouses hire or lend bicycles to their guests and there are also hire shops around Kyoto Station, in Arashiyama and in Downtown Kyoto. With a decent bicycle and a good map, you can easily make your way all around the city. Dedicated bicycle tours are available.

Unfortunately, Kyoto's bike parking facilities are pretty average – hence the number of bikes you see haphazardly locked up around the city. Many bikes end up stolen or impounded during regular sweeps of the city (particularly those near entrances to train/subway stations). If your bike does disappear, check for a poster (in both Japanese and English) in the vicinity indicating the time of seizure and the inconvenient place you'll have to go to pay the ¥2000 fine and retrieve your bike.

If you don't want to worry about your bike being stolen or impounded, we recommend using one of the city-operated bicycle and motorcycle parking lots. There is one downtown on Kiyamachi-dōri midway between Sanjō-dōri and Shijō-dōri, another near Kyoto Station, and another in the north of town near the Eizan Densha Station at Demachiyanagi. These places charge ¥150 per day (buy a ticket from the machine on your way in or out).

Hire

A great place to hire a bicycle is the **Kyoto Cycling Tour Project** (京都サイクリングツアープロジェクト, KCTP; Map p304; ☎ 075-354-3636; www.kctp.net; 552-13 Higashi-Aburanokoji-chō, Aburanokōji-dōri, Shiokōji-sagaru, Shimogyō-ku; ⏰ 9am-7pm; Ⓢ Karasuma line to Kyoto, Ⓡ JR line to Kyoto). These folk hire bikes (¥1000 per day) that are perfect for getting around the city. KCTP also conducts a variety of bicycle city tours with English-speaking guides, which are an excellent way to see Kyoto (check the website for details).

For exploring the Northern Higashiyama area, check out **Rent a cycle EMUSICA** (Map p308; 24 Tanaka Kamiyanagicho, Sakyo-ku; ⏰ 7.30am-11.30pm Mon-Fri, 9am-10.30pm Sat & Sun; Ⓡ Keihan line to Demachinayagi). Conveniently located right outside the Keihan Demachinaya Station and with access to the river and sightseeing areas, this place hires bikes for as little as ¥500 per day. A ¥2000 deposit is required.

Most hire outfits require you to leave a deposit and ID such as a passport.

BUS

Kyoto has an intricate network of bus routes providing an efficient way of getting around at moderate cost. Many routes used by visitors have announcements in English. Most buses run between 7am and 9pm, though a few run earlier or later.

In addition to the regular city buses, Kyoto now has a hop-on, hop-off sightseeing bus, **K'Loop** (www.kyoto-lab.jp/kloop; adult/child 1-day pass ¥2300/1000, 2-day pass ¥3500/1000), travelling around the city's World Heritage Sites.

The main bus information centre is in front of Kyoto Station. You can pick up bus maps, purchase bus tickets and passes (on all lines, including highway buses), and get additional information.

The Kyoto Tourist Information Center (TIC) stocks the *Bus Navi: Kyoto City Bus Sightseeing Map*, which shows the city's main bus lines. But this map is not exhaustive. If you can read a little Japanese, pick up a copy of the regular (and more detailed) Japanese bus map available at major bus terminals throughout the city, including the main bus information centre.

ⓘ KANSAI THRU PASS

The Kansai Thru Pass is a real bonus to travellers who plan to explore the Kansai area. It enables you to ride on city subways, private railways and city buses in Kyoto, Nara, Osaka, Kōbe, Kōya-san and Wakayama. It also entitles you to discounts at many attractions in the Kansai area. A two-day pass costs ¥4000 and a three-day pass costs ¥5200. It's available at the Kansai International Airport travel counter on the 1st floor of the arrivals hall and at the main bus information centre in front of Kyoto Station, among others. For more information, visit www.surutto.com.

Bus entry is usually through the back door and exit is via the front door. Inner-city buses charge a flat fare (¥230 for adults, ¥120 for children ages six to 12, free for those younger), which you drop into the clear plastic receptacle on top of the machine next to the driver on your way out. A separate machine gives change for ¥100 and ¥500 coins or ¥1000 notes.

On buses serving the outer areas, take a *seiri-ken* (numbered ticket) on boarding. When alighting, an electronic board above the driver displays the fare corresponding to your ticket number (drop the *seiri-ken* into the ticket box with your fare).

SUBWAY

Kyoto has two efficient subway lines, operating from 5.30am to 11.30pm. Minimum adult fare is ¥210 (children ¥110).

The quickest way to travel between the north and south of the city is the Karasuma subway line. It has 15 stops and runs from Takeda in the far south, via Kyoto Station, to the Kyoto International Conference Hall (Kokusaikaikan Station) in the north.

The east–west Tōzai subway line traverses Kyoto from Uzumasa-Tenjingawa Station in the west, meeting the Karasuma subway line at Karasuma-Oike Station, and continuing east to Sanjō-Keihan, Yamashina and Rokujizō in the east and southeast.

TRAIN

The main train station in Kyoto is Kyoto Station, which is actually two stations under one roof: JR Kyoto Station and Kintetsu Kyoto Station.

In addition to the private Kintetsu line that operates from Kyoto Station, there are two other private train lines in Kyoto: the Hankyū line that operates from Downtown Kyoto along Shijō-dōri and the Keihan line that operates from stops along the Kamo-gawa.

Kansai

Best Places to Eat

➡ Wanaka Honten (p376)

➡ Yoshino Sushi (p375)

➡ Shoubentango-tei (p376)

➡ Kōbe Plaisir (p387)

➡ Yokarō (p429)

Best Places to Sleep

➡ Hostel 64 Osaka (p373)

➡ Cross Hotel Osaka (p374)

➡ Oriental Hotel (p386)

➡ Nishimuraya Honkan (p432)

➡ Blue Sky Guesthouse (p418)

Why Go?

If you had to choose only one region of Japan to explore, Kansai (関西) would be an easy choice. It's the heart of Japan – there is nowhere else in the country you can find so much of historical and cultural interest in such a compact area.

Osaka, the region's hub and Japan's third largest city, shows off Japanese urban life in all its mind-boggling intensity, while Kōbe retains some of the international feeling that dates back to its days as a foreign treaty port. Nara, Japan's first permanent capital, is thick with traditional sights including Japan's largest Buddha at the awe-inspiring Tōdai-ji. Ise Grand Shrine in Mie Prefecture is one of the three most important sites in Shintō, In Wakayama-ken you'll find great onsen and hiking, a rugged coastline and the mountaintop Buddhist temple complex of Kōya-san, one of Japan's most intensely spiritual places.

Kyoto (p297) and Osaka are the main cities of Kansai and both make good bases for exploration.

When to Go
Osaka

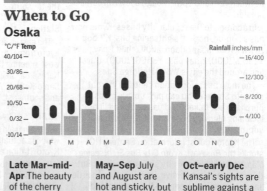

Late Mar–mid-Apr The beauty of the cherry blossoms is over the top.

May–Sep July and August are hot and sticky, but summer is a great time for festivals and street life.

Oct–early Dec Kansai's sights are sublime against a backdrop of bright red maple leaves.

ℹ Getting There & Around

By air, Osaka (p380) is the main hub for entry to the Kansai region, served by Kansai International Airport for international and domestic flights and Osaka Itami Airport for only domestic flights. By rail, Osaka (p382) and Kyoto (p356) are the main gateways, linked to major cities in the rest of the country via rail and *shinkansen* (bullet train).

There's an extensive network of Japan Rail and other ('private') train lines throughout Kansai. Within some of Kansai's outer reaches such as Kumano Kodō on the Kii Peninsula, bus may be the most efficient mode of public transportation. Renting a car is becoming increasingly popular, though take care if you'll be doing a lot of expressway driving as tolls can add up quickly.

OSAKA 大阪

📞 06 / POP 2,705,300

If Kyoto was the city of the courtly nobility and Tokyo the city of the samurai, then Osaka was the city of the merchant class. Japan's third-largest city is a place where things have always moved a faster, where people are a bit brasher and interactions are peppered with playful jabs – and locals take pride in this.

Osaka is not a pretty city in the conventional sense – though it does have a lovely river cutting through the centre – but it packs more colour than most. The acres of concrete are cloaked in dazzling neon, shopfronts are vivid, unabashed cries for attention. This is not a city that prefers to dress all in black.

Above all, Osaka is a city that loves to eat: it's unofficial slogan is *kuidaore* ('eat until you drop'). It really shines in the evening, when it seems that everyone is out for a good meal – and a good time.

History

Osaka (originally called 'Naniwa', a name still heard today) has been a key port and mercantile centre from the beginning of Japan's recorded history. From the 6th century onwards, it became Japan's base for trade with Korea and China – a gateway for goods but also ideas such as Buddhism and empire-building, and new technologies.

In the late 16th century, Osaka rose to prominence when the warlord Toyotomi Hideyoshi, having unified all of Japan after centuries of civil war, chose Osaka as the site for his castle. Merchants set up around the castle and the city grew into a busy economic centre. When Tokugawa Ieyasu moved the seat of power to Edo (now Tokyo) in the early 17th century, he adopted a hands-off approach to the city, allowing merchants to prosper unhindered by government interference. During the Edo period (1603–1868) Osaka served as Japan's largest distribution centre for rice (which was akin to currency at the time), earning it the nickname 'Japan's Kitchen'.

In the late 19th and 20th centuries, as economic influence became increasingly consolidated in Tokyo, Osaka reinvented itself as one of the most productive manufacturing centres in East Asia. Unfortunately this made it a bombing target during WWII. During the 1945 air raids, one-third of the city centre was levelled and over 10,000 people were killed.

Today commerce remains vital to Osaka – it is the business hub of western Japan – while the greater Keihanshin Industrial Zone, of which Osaka is part, is one of Japan's great manufacturing centres.

◉ Sights

Central Osaka is commonly divided into north (Kita), around Osaka and Umeda stations, and south (Minami), around Namba Station. Running east-west through the middle are two rivers, Dōjima-gawa and Tosabori-gawa; the island of Naka-no-shima divides the two. Sandwiched between the Tosabori-gawa and Minami is central Semba; landmark and top sight Osaka-jō is east of here.

Below Minami is Tennōji, a neighbourhood that has seen some recent redevelopment but is still rough around the edges. The bayside Tempōzan neighbourhood and Universal Studios are west of the city centre.

◉ Kita (Umeda) キタ

Kita ('north') is the city's centre of gravity by day in office buildings, department stores and shopping complexes – plus the transit hubs of JR Osaka and Hankyū Umeda Stations (and the multiple train and subway lines converging here). While there are few great attractions here, there is plenty of big-city bustle both on street level and in the extensive network of underground passages below.

Umeda Sky Building NOTABLE BUILDING
(梅田スカイビル; Map p362; www.kuchu-teien. com; 1-1-88 Ōyodonaka, Kita-ku; admission ¥700; ⊙ observation decks 10am-10.30pm, last entry 10pm; ® JR Osaka, north central exit) Osaka's landmark Sky Building (1993) resembles a 40-storey, space-age Arc de Triomphe. Twin towers are connected at the top by a 'floating garden' (really a garden-free observation deck), which

KANSAI OSAKA

Kansai Highlights

❶ Tōdai-ji (p394) Gazing in awe at Japan's largest Buddha at Nara's great temple.

❷ Dōtombori (p365) Feasting your eyes on the colourful human parade in this photogenic area of Osaka.

❸ Ise-jingū (p422) Feeling the power radiating from Japan's most sacred Shintō shrine.

❹ Oku-no-in (p410) Wandering the mystical forest of Kōya-san to visit this deeply spiritual Buddhist cemetery.

❺ Hongū (p417) Soaking in the restorative waters of the three nearby onsen.

❻ Kumano Kodō (p416) Walking the ancient pilgrimage trails in Wakayama.

❼ Kinosaki Onsen (p431) Donning a *yukata* (light cotton kimono) and strolling from onsen to onsen in this quaint town.

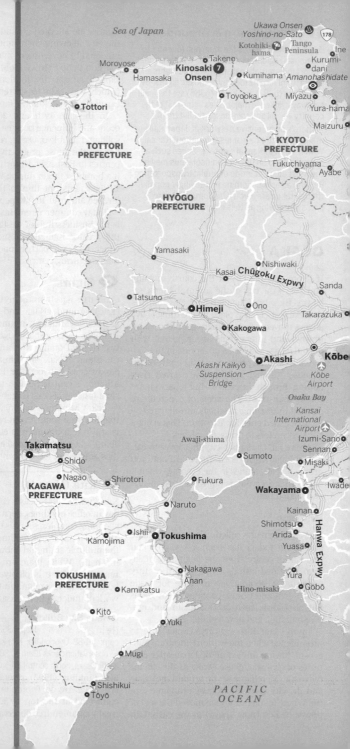

Osaka

was constructed on the ground and then hoisted up. The 360-degree city views from here are breathtaking day or night. Getting there is half the fun – an escalator in a see-through tube takes you up the last five storeys (not for vertigo sufferers). The architect, Hara

Hiroshi, also designed **Kyoto Station** (京都駅; www.kyoto-station-building.co.jp; Karasuma-dōri, Higashishiokōji-chō, Shiokōji-sagaru, Shimogyō-ku; ☒ Kyoto Station).

Access the building via an underground passage north of Osaka and Umeda stations.

Osaka

Top Sights

1	Osaka-jō	C4

Sights

2	Abeno Harukas	C6
	Abeno Harukas Art Museum	(see 2)
3	Billiken	B6
4	Liberty Osaka	B6
5	Museum of Oriental Ceramics	B3
6	Naka-no-shima-kōen	C4
7	Osaka Central Public Hall	B3
	Osaka City Hall	(see 7)
8	Osaka Museum of History	C4
9	Shin-Sekai	B6
10	Tsūten-kaku	B6
11	Umeda Sky Building	B3

Activities, Courses & Tours

12	Cycle Osaka	A3
13	Ofune Camome	C4
14	Spa World	B6

Sleeping

15	Arietta Hotel	B4
16	Hostel 64 Osaka	B4
17	Hotel Fūki	D3
18	Mitsui Garden Hotel Osaka Premier	B3
19	U-en	A3

Eating

20	Denki Soba	C3
	Ganso Kushikatsu Daruma Honten	(see 3)
21	Gout	C4
	Harannaka	(see 20)
22	Yoshino Sushi	B4

Drinking & Nightlife

23	Beer Belly	B4
24	Frenz Frenzy	B3
25	Leach Bar	A4
26	Moto Coffee	B4

Entertainment

27	Namba Bears	B5
28	National Bunraku Theatre	C5

Shopping

	Tower Knives	(see 10)

Information

29	Australian Consulate	D3
	German Consulate	(see 11)
30	Japan Red Cross Hospital	C5
31	Netherlands Consulate	C4
32	People's Republic of China Osaka Consulate	B4
33	UK Consulate	B4

O-hatsu Ten-jin SHINTO SHRINE

(お初天神, Tsuyu-no-Ten-jinsha; Map p364; ☎06-6311-0895; www.tuyutenjin.com; 2-5-4 Sonezaki, Kita-ku; 🕐6am-midnight; [S] Tanimachi line to Higashi-Umeda, exit 7, exit 15, [R] JR Osaka, Sakurabashi exit) [FREE] Hiding in plain sight amid the skyscrapers of Umeda, this 1300-year-old shrine owes its fame to one of Japan's best-known tragic plays (based on true events). Star-crossed lovers O-hatsu, a prostitute, and Tokubei, a merchant's apprentice, committed double suicide here in 1703, to remain together forever in the afterlife rather than live apart. The current shrine was constructed in 1957 (after WWII destroyed the previous one); it's popular with couples, who come to pray for strength in love – and happier endings.

The shrine is just southeast of Ohatsuten-jin-dōri arcade. There's a flea market here the first Friday of each month.

Naka-no-shima, Semba & Osaka-jō

South of Kita, sandwiched between the rivers Dōjima-gawa and Tosabori-gawa, the island of Naka-no-shima (中之島) is a pleasant oasis, with riverside walkways, art museums, early 20th-century architecture and the park, **Naka-no-shima-kōen** (中之島公園; Map p362; Naka-no-shima, Kita-ku; [S] Sakai-suji line to Kitahama, exit 26).

If coming from Kyoto, the Keihan line runs direct to Yodoyabashi Station; the island is a 15-minute walk south of JR Osaka Station.

Semba (船場), meaning 'ship's place', is the city's historic commercial district stretching along the southern bank of the Tosabori-gawa; there are some fashionable riverfront cafes here.

Museum of Oriental Ceramics MUSEUM

(大阪市立東洋陶磁美術館; Map p362; www.moco.or.jp; 1-1-26 Naka-no-shima; adult/student/child ¥500/300/free; 🕐9.30am-5pm, closed Mon; [S] Midō-suji line to Yodoyabashi, exit 1) This museum has one of the world's finest collections of Chinese and Korean ceramics, with smaller galleries of Japanese ceramics and Chinese snuff bottles. At any one time, approximately 400 of the gorgeous pieces from the permanent collection are on display, and there are often special exhibits (with an extra charge). The permanent collection has good English descriptions.

Kita (Umeda)

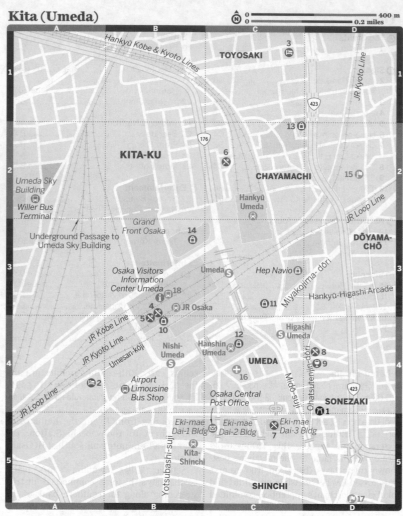

KANSAI OSAKA

From the station, cross the river and go right, passing the Central Public Hall.

★ Osaka-jō   CASTLE

(大阪城; Osaka Castle; Map p362; www.osaka castle.net; 1-1 Osaka-jō, Chūō-ku; grounds/castle keep free/¥600, combined with Osaka Museum of History ¥900; ⊙ 9am-5pm, to 7pm Aug; Ⓢ Chūo line to Tanimachi 4-chōme, exit 9, Ⓡ JR Loop line to Osaka-jō-kōen) After unifying Japan in the late 16th century, General Toyotomi Hideyoshi (p824) built this castle (1583) as a display of power, using, it's said, the labour of 100,000 workers. Although the present structure is

a 1931 concrete reconstruction (refurbished 1997), it's nonetheless quite a sight, looming dramatically over the surrounding park and moat. Inside is an excellent collection of art, armour, and day-to-day implements related to the castle, Hideyoshi and Osaka. An 8th-floor observation deck has 360-degree views.

Hideyoshi's original granite structure was said to be impregnable, yet it was destroyed in 1614 by the armies of Tokugawa Ieyasu (the founder of the Tokugawa shogunate). Ieyasu had the castle rebuilt – using the latest advancements to create imposing walls of enormous stones. The largest

Kita (Umeda)

stones are estimated to weigh over a 100 tonnes; some are engraved with the crests of feudal lords.

There are 13 structures, including several turrets, that remain from this 17th-century reconstruction. Osaka citizens raised money themselves to rebuild the main keep; in 1931 the new tower was revealed, with glittering gold-leaf tigers stalking the eaves.

At night the castle is lit with floodlights (and looks like a ghostly structure hovering above ground). Visit the lawns on a warm weekend and you might catch local musicians staging casual shows. The castle and park are at their best (and most crowded) in the cherry-blossom and autumn-foliage seasons.

Osaka Museum of History MUSEUM
(大阪歴史博物館, Osaka Rekishi Hakubutsukan; Map p362; www.mus-his.city.osaka.jp; 4-1-32 Ōtemae, Chūō-ku; adult/child ¥600/400, combined with Osaka Castle ¥900; ⊙9.30am-5pm, to 8pm Fri, closed Tue; Ⓢ Tanimachi or Chūō line to Tanimachi 4-chōme, exit 9) Built above the ruins of Naniwa Palace (c 650), visible through the ground floor, this museum tells Osaka's story from the era of this early palace to the early 20th century. English explanations are pretty sparse, though much of the displays are highly visible, including a walk-through recreation of old city life. You can also rent an English-language audio guide (¥200). There are great views of Osaka-jō from the 10th floor.

The museum is just southwest of the castle park, in a sail-shaped building adjoining the NHK Broadcast Center.

⊙ Minami ミナミ

Minami ('south'), which includes the neighbourhoods Namba, Shinsaibashi, Dōtombori and Amerika-Mura, is the funny man to Kita's straight man. It's here that you'll see the flashy neon signs and vibrant street life that you expect of Osaka. By day, Minami is primarily a shopping district; after dark, the restaurants, bars, clubs and theatres take over.

Namba and Shinsaibashi subway stations, both on the Midō-suji line, are convenient for this area.

⭐**Amerika-Mura** AREA
(アメリカ村, America Village, Ame-Mura; Map p366; Nishi-Shinsaibashi, Chūō-ku; Ⓢ Midō-suji line to Shinsaibashi, exit 7) West of Midō-suji, Amerika-Mura is a compact enclave of hip, youth-focused and offbeat shops, plus cafes, bars, tattoo and piercing parlours, nightclubs, hair salons and a few discreet love hotels. In the middle is **Triangle Park** (三角公園, Sanka-ku-kōen; Map p366), an all-concrete 'park' with benches to sit and watch the fashion parade. Come night, it's a popular gathering spot.

Around the neighbourhood, look for street lamps like stick-figure people, some painted by artists; the **Peace on Earth mural** (1983), painted by Osaka artist Seitaro Kuroda, and, of course, a mini **Statue of Liberty**.

Ame-Mura owes its name to shops that sprang up after WWII, selling American goods such as Zippo lighters and T-shirts.

⭐**Dōtombori** AREA
(道頓堀; Map p366; www.dotonbori.or.jp; Ⓢ Midō-suji line to Namba, exit 14) Highly photogenic Dōtombori has got to be the city's

KANSAI OSAKA

Minami (Shinsaibashi & Namba)

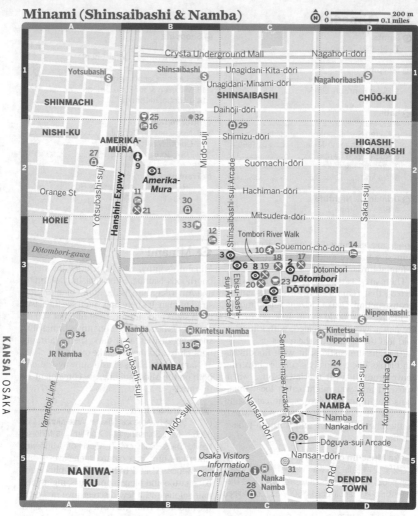

liveliest night spot and centre of the Minami (south) part of town. Its name comes from the 400-year-old canal, Dōtombori-gawa, now lined with pedestrian walkways and a riot of illuminated billboards glittering off its waters. Don't miss the famous **Glico running man** sign. South of the canal is a pedestrianised street that has dozens of restaurants vying for attention with the flashiest of signage.

For the best views, head to **Ebisu-bashi** (戎橋; Map p366), the bridge at the western end of the strip.

Hōzen-ji   BUDDHIST TEMPLE
(法善寺; Map p366; http://houzenji.jp; 1-2-16 Namba, Chūō-ku; S Midō-suji line to Namba, exit 14) This tiny temple hidden down a narrow alley houses a statue of Fudō Myō-ō (a deity of esoteric Buddhism), covered in thick moss. It's a favourite of people employed in *mizu shōbai* ('water trade' – a euphemism for the sexually charged nightworld), who pause before work to throw some water on the statue.

Hōzen-ji Yokochō (法善寺横丁, Hōzen-ji Alley; Map p366; S Midō-suji line to Namba, exit 14), the alley filled with traditional restaurants

Minami (Shinsaibashi & Namba)

Top Sights
1 Amerika-Mura B2
2 Dōtombori C3

Sights
3 Ebisu-bashi C3
4 Hōzen-ji C3
5 Hōzen-ji Yokochō C3
6 Kani Dōraku Honten C3
7 Kuromon Ichiba D4
8 Nakaza Cuidaore Building C3
9 Triangle Park B2

Activities, Courses & Tours
10 Tombori River Cruise C3

Sleeping
11 Capsule Hotel Asahi Plaza Shinsaibashi B2
12 Cross Hotel Osaka B3
13 First Cabin Midosuji Namba B4
14 Kaneyoshi Ryokan D3
15 Khaosan World Namba B4
16 Osaka Hana Hostel B2

Eating
17 Chibō C3
18 Daruma Dōtombori-ten C3
19 Imai Honten C3
20 Shoubentango-tei C3
21 Wanaka Amerika-mura-ten B2
22 Wanaka Honten C5
Za Ikaga .... (see 21)

Drinking & Nightlife
Circus .... (see 16)
23 Jun-kissa American C3
24 Misono Building D4
25 Rock Rock B1

Shopping
26 Dōguya-suji Arcade C5
27 Flake Records A2
28 Namba Parks C5
29 Shinsaibashi-suji Shōtengai C2
30 Standard Books B2

Information
31 Comic & Internet Cafe Aprecio C5
32 HIS Osaka Tourist Information Centre B1
33 South Korean Consulate B3

Transport
34 Osaka City Air Terminal A4

and bars, runs between the temple and the Sennichi-mae shopping arcade.

Kuromon Ichiba MARKET
(黒門市場, Kuromon Market; Map p366; www.kuromon.com; Nipponbashi, Chūō-ku; ⏲most shops 10am-5pm, closed Sun; [S] Sakai-suji line to Nipponbashi, exit 10) An Osaka landmark for over a century, this 600m-long market is equal parts functioning market and tourist attraction. Vendors selling fresh fish, meat, produce and pickles attract chefs and local home cooks; shops offering takeaway sushi or with grills set up (to cook the steaks, oysters etc that they sell) cater to visitors – making the market excellent for grazing *and* photo ops.

Tennōji & Around

Abeno Harukas NOTABLE BUILDING
(あべのハルカス; Map p362; www.abenoharukas300.jp; 1-1-43 Abeno-suji, Abeno-ku; observation deck ¥1500; ⏲observation deck 9am-10pm; [S] Midō-suji to Tennōji, 🚉 JR Loop line to Tennōji) This Cesar Pelli–designed tower, which opened in March 2014, is Japan's tallest building (300m, 60 storeys). It houses Japan's largest department store (Kintetsu, floors B2–14), the **Abeno Harukas Art Museum** (あべのハルカス美術館; Map p362; ☎06-4399-9050; www.aham.jp; 16th fl, Abeno Harukas, 1-1-43 Abeno-suji, Abeno-ku; admission varies by exhibition; ⏲10am-8pm Tue-Fri, to 6pm Sat & Sun), a hotel, offices and restaurants. The observatory on the 16th floor is free, but admission is required for the top-level **Harukas 300 observation deck**, which has 360-degree views of the whole Kansai region through windows that run several storeys high. There's also an open-top atrium up here.

Although Abeno Harukas is Japan's tallest building, the tallest *structure* is Tokyo Sky Tree (p105), at 634m.

Shin-Sekai AREA
(新世界; Map p362; Naniwa-ku; [S] Midō-suji line to Dōbutsuen-mae, exit 5) A century ago, Shin-Sekai ('new world') was home to an amusement park that defined cutting edge. Now this entertainment district mixes down-on-its-heels with retro cool. It's centred around the crusty, trusty, 103m-high steel-frame tower **Tsūten-kaku** (通天閣; Map p362; ☎06-6641-9555; www.tsutenkaku.co.jp; 1-18-6 Ebisu-higashi, Naniwa-ku; adult/student/child ¥700/500/300; ⏲9am-9pm; 🚉 JR Loop line

City Walk
Sights of Minami

START SHINSAIBASHI STATION
END SHINSAIBASHI STATION
LENGTH 2.5KM; 2½ HOURS

Head out before dusk to see the daylight fade and the neon lights of Dōtombori take over. Stroll down ❶ **Shinsaibashi-suji** (p369), Shinsaibashi's famous, and famously long, covered *shōtengai* (market street). Emerging from the arcade, you'll hit ❷ **Ebisu-bashi** (p366) bridge, the most popular place for photos down the canal, Dōtombori-gawa. Among the glowing signs that line the canal, look for the ever-joyful Glico running man.

Go left past ❸ **Kani Dōraku Honten**, the restaurant with the giant animated crab hanging over the entrance. This takes you to the main Dōtombori strip, past restaurants and food stands, marked with outlandish signage that takes the plastic food model concept to a new level – a giant octopus indicates, for example, a *tako-yaki* (octopus dumpling) stand. Look for the drumming mechanical clown Kuidaore Tarō at ❹ **Nakaza**

Cuidaore Building (p371), the mascot for the city's eating culture.

Before the big cow, take a right down Sennichi-mae arcade. Turn again at the cobblestoned alley with the wooden signboard for ❺ **Hōzen-ji Yokochō** (p366), and you're suddenly in an older, quieter Osaka, one charmingly lantern-lit in the evening. At the end, go left through the temple gateway to tiny ❻ **Hōzen-ji** (p366). Continue past the temple back around to the Dōtombori strip. Cross Tazaemon-bashi and head left on the ❼ **Tombori River Walk** – the promenade that runs alongside the canal.

Cross Shinsaibashi-suji and turn right, into Amerika-Mura, a fun place to spend the evenings. Grab some *ika-yaki* (grilled squid) at ❽ **Za Ikaga** (p376) or *tako-yaki* at the branch of famed ❾ **Wanaka** (p376) next door. Eat them here on the street or get 'em to go and head to ❿ **Triangle Park** (p365) – the district's popular local gathering spot. From here you can embark on an evening of bar-hopping Amerika-Mura, or make your way back to Shinsaibashi Station.

to Shin-Imamiya) – built 1912, rebuilt 1956 – and surrounded by ancient *pachinko* and mahjong parlours that draw some truly down-and-out characters. At the same time, Shin-Sekai draws plenty of visitors for nostalgia and cheap eateries behind over-the-top signage, especially for *kushikatsu* (p375) (deep-fried meat and vegetables on skewers).

Liberty Osaka MUSEUM
(大阪人権博物館, Osaka Human Rights Museum; Map p362; ☎06-6561-5891; www.liberty.or.jp; 3-6-36 Naniwa-nishi, Naniwa-ku; adult/student/child ¥500/300/200; ⏲10am 4pm Wed Fri, 1-5pm Sat, closed Sun, Mon & 4th Fri; [S] Midō-suji line to Daikoku-chō, exit 5, 🚆JR Loop line to Imamiya) Japan's first human rights museum began in 1985 as an archive of documents relating to the *burakumin* – the lowest caste under the old feudal system (against whom discrimination continued into the modern age). The museum has since grown to cover a variety of topics, from sexual politics to the struggles of Japanese of Korean ancestry. It's unflinching in its portrait of contemporary Japan. English is provided via an audio guide and a booklet with translations of some (though not all) exhibitions.

Sumiyoshi Taisha SHINTO SHRINE
(住吉大社; www.sumiyoshitaisha.net; 2-9-89 Sumiyoshi, Sumiyoshi-ku; ⏲dawn-dusk; 🚋Hankai line to Sumiyoshi-torii-mae, 🚆Nankai line to Sumiyoshi-taisha) [FREE] Dedicated to Shintō deities of the sea and sea travel, this graceful shrine was founded in the 3rd century and is considered the headquarters for all Sumiyoshi shrines in Japan. The buildings are faithful replicas of the ancient originals, with a couple that date back to 1810, and the grounds are criss-crossed by a tree- and lantern-lined waterway spanned by a bright orange drum bridge. It's a rare Shintō shrine that predates the influence of Chinese Buddhist architectural styles.

The Hankai line tram from Tennōji stops right in front of the *torii* (Shintō shrine gate).

👁 Tempōzan 天保山

Trudging through urban Kita or Minami, you could forget that Osaka is a port city. Remind yourself in Tempōzan, a bayside development with family-oriented attractions. Get the Chūō subway line to Osaka-kō Station, come down the stairs of exit 1 and head for the big wheel.

OSAKA IN ONE DAY

Start with a visit to Osaka-jō (p364); swing by Gout (p375) for pastries, to eat on the castle lawns. Next, take the Tanimachi subway line to Higashi-Umeda, to pay your respects to star-crossed lovers Ohatsu and Tokubei at O-hatsu Ten-jin (p363). Stop for an okonomiyaki lunch at nearby Yukari (p374).

Hop on the Midō-suji line at Umeda for Yodoyabashi and walk along the river to Moto Coffee (p377). Then take the subway down to Shinsaibashi, to stroll through **Shinsaibashi-suji Shōtengai** (心斎橋筋商店街; Map p366; www.shinsaibashi.or.jp) and over Ebisu-bashi (p366) before joining the nightly throngs in neon-lit Dōtombori (p365). There are plenty of places to eat here, like Imai Honten (p376) and Shoubentango-tei (p376). Then walk over to Amerika-Mura (p365), which is full of bars and clubs.

Osaka Aquarium Kaiyūkan AQUARIUM
(海遊館; ☎06-6576-5501; www.kaiyukan.com; 1-1-10 Kaigan-dōri, Minato-ku; adult/child ¥2300/1200; ⏲10am-8pm; [S] Chuō line to Osaka-kō, exit 1) Kaiyūkan is among Japan's best aquariums. An 800m-plus walkway winds past displays of sea life from around the Pacific 'ring of fire': Antarctic penguins, coral-reef butterflyfish, unreasonably cute Arctic otters, Monterey Bay seals and unearthly jellyfish. Most impressive is the ginormous central tank, housing a whale shark, manta and thousands of other fish. Note there are also captive dolphins here, which some visitors may not appreciate; there is growing evidence that keeping cetaceans in captivity is harmful for the animals.

There are good English descriptions, but the audio guide (¥500) gives more detail. Expect lots of families and school groups.

The **Osaka Kaiyu Ticket** (www.kaiyukan.com/language/eng/kaiyu.html; adult/child ¥2550/1300) combines entry to the aquarium, with one-day unlimited transport on city subways and discounted admission to other sites. Purchase at any subway station.

Giant Ferris Wheel FERRIS WHEEL
(大観覧車, Daikanransha; www.kaiyukan.com/thv/ferriswheel; 1-1-10 Kaigan-dōri, Minato-ku; admission ¥800; ⏲10am-10pm; [S] Chuō line to Osaka-kō, exit 1) Among the biggest in the world, this

MOMOFUKU ANDŌ INSTANT RAMEN MUSEUM

From its humble invention in 1958 by Andō Momofuku, (1910–2007; later chair of Nissin Foods), instant ramen has become a global business and one of Japan's most famous exports. Exhibits at this **museum** (インスタントラーメン発明記念館; ☑072-752-3484; www.instantramen-museum.jp; 8-25 Masumi-cho, Ikeda; ☺9.30am-4pm, closed Tue; ⓡHankyū line to Hankyū Ikeda, east exit) **FREE** illustrate the origin of Cup Noodles and how they're made; there's also a 'tunnel' of Nissin products that showcases a half-century of package design. The highlight, however, is getting to create your own custom blend Cup Noodles to take away (¥300), including decorating the cup.

Get the free English-language audio guide (¥2000 yen deposit). Expect long queues at weekends. It's a 10-minute walk from the station. Take the east exit, head down the stairs; go left and then right at the tourist information centre, and the museum will be on your right.

112m-high Ferris wheel offers unbeatable views of Osaka Bay and the seemingly endless Osaka/Kōbe conurbation. Give it a whirl at night to enjoy the vast carpet of lights.

⊙ Banpaku-kinen-kōen

Banpaku-kinen-kōen, also called Senri Expo Park, was the site of the 1970 World Fair – the first such event to be held in Japan and a big moment for Osaka. Little remains of the (for the time) future-forward installations; today it's a sprawling park with the city's best museum. Banpaku-kinen-kōen is a stop on the Osaka Monorail; the Midō-suji and Tanimachi subway lines intersect with the Osaka Monorail; so does the Hankyū Kyoto line.

★**National Museum of Ethnology** MUSEUM (国立民族学博物館; ☑06-6876-2151; www.minpaku.ac.jp; 10-1 Senri Expo Park, Suita; adult/child ¥420/110; ☺10am-5pm, closed Wed; ⌸Osaka Monorail to Banpaku-kinen-kōen) This ambitious museum showcases the world's cultures, showing them to be the continuous (and tangled) strings that they are. There are plenty of traditional masks, textiles and pottery but also Ghanaian barbershop signboards,

Bollywood movie posters and even a Filipino jeepney. Don't miss the music room, where you can summon street performances from around the globe via a touch panel. There are also exhibits on Okinawan history and Japan's indigenous Ainu culture. There's English signage but the audio guide gives more detail.

Tower of the Sun SCULPTURE (太陽の塔, Taiyō-no-tō; Senri Expo Park, Suita; ⌸Osaka Monorail to Banpaku-kinen-kōen) The 70m-tall Tower of the Sun was created by Japanese artist Okamoto Tarō for Osaka's Expo '70. While the curious three-faced creature (there's one face in the back) has been open to interpretation (and critique) for decades, there's no doubt that it has become the symbol of the expo and of the energy and optimism that surrounded it.

🏃 Activities

★**Spa World** ONSEN (スパワールド; Map p362; ☑06-6631-0001; www.spaworld.co.jp; 3-4-24 Ebisu-higashi, Naniwaku; 3hr/day pass Mon-Fri ¥2400/2700, Sat & Sun ¥2700/3000, additional ¥1300 midnight-5am; ☺10am-8.45am; ⓢMidō-suji line to Dōbutsu-enmae, exit 5, ⓡJR Loop line to Shin-Imamiya) 'Spa World' isn't a mere euphemism: this huge, seven-storey onsen (hot spring) complex contains many options from saunas to salt baths, styled after a mini-UN's worth of nations including Japan, Finland, Canada, ancient Rome and, er, Atlantis. 'Asian' and 'European' bathing zones are separated by gender (bathe in the buff, towels provided) and switch monthly. Swimsuits (rental ¥600, or bring your own) or special outfits (provided) are worn in swimming pools, eateries and *ganbanyoku* (stone baths; additional ¥800 to ¥1000).

Many visitors and splash for hours; there are casual restaurants here and even 'relaxation rooms' with armchairs where you can spend the night. Visitors with tattoos are not permitted.

Universal Studios Japan AMUSEMENT PARK (ユニバーサルスタジオジャパン, Universal City; ☑0570-200-606; www.usj.co.jp; 2-1-33 Sakura-jima, Konohana-ku; 1-day pass adult/child ¥7400/4980, 2-day pass ¥12,450/8420; ☺varies seasonally; ⓡJR Yumesaki line to Universal City) Modelled after sister parks in the US, 'USJ' bursts with Hollywood movie–related rides, shows, shops and restaurants. Top billing goes to the ¥45 billion (!) **Wizarding**

World of Harry Potter, opened in 2014, a painstakingly recreated Hogsmeade Village (shop for magic wands, Gryffindor capes and butterbeer) plus the 'Harry Potter and the Forbidden Journey' thrill ride through Hogwart's School. Wizarding World admission is by timed ticket. Maps and signage are in English, though narrations and entertainment are in Japanese.

Long queues are common at the park's major venues (1½ hours, or more, is not unusual for the Harry Potter ride). To shorten waits, USJ offers a variety of fast passes that allow you to bypass queues, at an extra charge.

Rumoured to be in the works for 2020: a Nintendo-themed attraction.

To get here, take the JR Loop line to Nishi-kujō Station, then switch to the JR Yumesaki line for Universal Studios (total trip ¥180, 15 minutes). There are also some direct trains from JR Osaka Station (same fare).

Tombori River Cruise CRUISE
(とんぼりリバークルーズ; Map p366; ☎06-6441-0532; www.ipponmatsu.co.jp/cruise/tombori.html; Don Quijote Bldg, 7-13 Sōemon-chō, Chūō-ku; adult/child ¥900/400; ⏰1-9pm Mon-Fri, 11am-9pm Sat & Sun; [S] Midō-suji line to Namba, exit 14) One way to beat the crowds in Dōtombori is to hop on a boat. Tombori's short, 20-minute trips past the neon signs run on the hour and the half-hour. Night time is best, though slots fill up quickly; tickets go on sale at the pier an hour before the first cruise of the day starts. Osaka Amazing Pass holders ride free.

Reception is on the 1st floor of the Don Quijote Bldg (identifiable by the oddly shaped Ferris wheel on top).

Tours

★ Cycle Osaka CYCLING
(Map p362; ☎080-5325-8975; www.cycleosaka.com; 2-12-1 Sagisu, Fukushima-ku; half-/full-day ¥5000/10,000; 🚉JR Loop line to Fukushima) English-speaking guides here lead well-organised tours to sights both well-known and less-well-known, along the river banks and through the markets. The food route (¥8000) is particularly recommended. Fees include bicycle and helmet rental, water and food.

Ofune Camome CRUISE
(御舟かもめ; Map p362; www.ofune-camome.net; cruises ¥2100-4200, child half-price; [S] Tanimachi line to Temmabashi, exit 18) This small wooden boat, with a few beanbags on the prow, cruises up and down the Yodo-gawa alongside Naka-no-shima; the small size means that, unless the tide is really high, it can go places that larger boats can't. The captain speaks some English and explains the significance of the buildings and bridges. It is advisable to book at least three days in advance.

Festivals & Events

★ Tenjin Matsuri CULTURAL
(天神祭; www.tenjinmatsuri.com; ⏰24 & 25 Jul) This is one of Japan's three biggest festivals. Try to make the second day, when processions of *mikoshi* (portable shrines) and people in traditional attire start at Osaka Tenman-gū and end up in hundreds of boats on the Ō-kawa. As night falls, there is a huge fireworks display.

OSAKA ICONS

New York has the Statue of Liberty and Brussels the Mannekin Pis; Osaka is doubly blessed with two icons. You'll see them pretty much all over town.

Kuidaore Tarō A clown (frankly a little creepy looking) banging a drum. Instantly recognisable by his red-and-white striped outfit and round glasses, he represents the city's culture of *kuidaore* ('eat until you drop'). Find the most famous Kuidaore Tarō in the vestibule of the **Nakaza Cuidaore Building** (中座くいだおれビル; Map p366; 1-7-21 Dōtombori, Chūō-ku; [S] Midō-suji line to Namba, exit 14) in Dōtombori.

Billiken (Map p362) Ever-smiling Billiken sits, toes out, like a golden Kewpie doll on a pedestal reading 'The God of Things as they Ought to Be' in English. He was created in the early 1900s as a good luck charm by an art teacher in Kansas City, Missouri, USA. Billiken debuted in Osaka for the opening of the Tsūten-kaku (p367) in 1912. A Billiken figurine is said to bring good fortune to its purchaser and even better fortune if received as a gift.

DON'T MISS

BUNRAKU

Bunraku is Japanese traditional puppet theatre. Almost-life-sized puppets are manipulated by black-clad, on-stage puppeteers, to evoke dramatic tales of love, duty and politics. The art form many not have originated in Osaka but it became popular here. Bunraku's most famous playwright, Chikamatsu Monzaemon (1653–1724), wrote plays about Osaka's merchants and the denizens of the pleasure quarters, social classes otherwise generally ignored in the Japanese arts at the time. Not surprisingly, the art form found a wide audience among them, and a theatre was established to stage Chikamatsu's plays in Dōtombori. Bunraku has been recognised on the Unesco World Intangible Cultural Heritage list, and the **National Bunraku Theatre** (p378) works to keep the tradition alive, with performances and an exhibition in the lobby about the history of bunraku and its puppeteers and main characters. Learn more at the Japan Arts Council's website, www2.ntj.jac.go.jp/unesco/bunraku/en.

Kishiwada Danjiri Matsuri CULTURAL
(岸和田だんじり祭; ☉Sep) Osaka's wildest festival, held over the 3rd weekend in September, is a kind of running of the bulls except with *danjiri* (festival floats), many weighing over 3000kg. The *danjiri* are hauled through the streets by hundreds of people using ropes – take care and stand back. Most of the action takes place on the second day.

The best place to see it is west of Kishiwada Station on the Nankai main line (from Nankai Station).

🛏 Sleeping

Osaka has plenty of accommodation in all budgets, including some stylish new hostels and guesthouses; at the midrange your best bet is a chain hotel. Higher end properties offer convenience and views. There are also ryokan and capsule hotels. Check websites for discounted rates; expect prices to rise by 10% to 20% on weekends. Base yourself in Minami for access to a larger selection of bars, restaurants and shops, or in Kita for fast access to long-distance transport.

🛏 Kita (Umeda)

U-en GUESTHOUSE ¥
(由苑; Map p362; ☑06-7503-4394; www.hostelosaka.com; 2-9-23 Fukushima, Fukushima-ku; dm/d from ¥2800/6600; ☉❄🛜; 🚃JR Loop line to Fukushima) Inside a restored, century-old townhouse down a quiet lane, U-en has seven upstairs rooms with a variety of bedding – futons and tatami mats in the private rooms and bunks or capsules (with curtains, lockers and shelves) in the dorms. It's beautifully done, though pretty touches like paper *shōji* doors mean sound does travel. Staff speak English; bicycle rental available (¥500 per day).

All of this sits atop an attractive cafe, where you can get coffee (from ¥400) and croissants in the morning (or beer in the evening).

Hearton Hotel Nishi-Umeda BUSINESS HOTEL ¥¥
(ハートンホテル西梅田; Map p364; ☑06-6342-1122; www.hearton.co.jp; 3-3-55 Umeda, Kita-ku; s/tw/tr from ¥8100/11,400/15,000; ☉❄🛜; 🚇Yotsubashi line to Nishi-Umeda, 🚃JR Osaka, Sakurabashi exit) At 18 storeys and 430 rooms, this large business hotel doesn't set any new style standards, but it has cheery staff, clean, comfy rooms, Japanese-Western breakfast buffet (¥1080 extra) and laundry machines, all a quick walk from JR Osaka Station and subway stops. Request a south-facing room unless you're OK with train noise.

Hotel Sunroute Umeda BUSINESS HOTEL ¥¥
(ホテルサンルート梅田; Map p364; ☑06-6373-1111; www.sunroute.jp; 3-9-1 Toyosaki, Kita-ku; s/d from ¥7020/12,960; ☉❄@🛜; 🚇Midō-suji line to Nakatsu, exit 4) Close enough to JR Osaka and Hankyū Umeda Stations to be convenient (about a 15-minute walk) but far enough away to be reasonably priced, Sunroute is a standard business hotel with small rooms and efficient service.

🛏 Naka-no-shima & Semba

Arietta Hotel HOTEL ¥¥
(アリエッタホテル大阪; Map p362; ☑06-6267-2787; www.thehotel.co.jp; 3-2-6 Azuchi-machi, Chūō-ku; s/d incl breakfast from ¥8800/13,500; ☉❄@🛜; 🚇Midō-suji line to Honmachi, exit 3) 10 minutes' walk north of the Minami District, the Arietta has good-sized rooms with wooden floors and tiled bathrooms, welcoming staff and a simple breakfast of breads, coffee and juice – all competitively priced. From the station, turn

right at the first corner, and it's two and a half blocks ahead on the right.

Mitsui Garden
Hotel Osaka Premier
HOTEL ¥¥¥

(三井ガーデンホテル大阪プレミア; Map p362; ☑06-6444-1131; www.gardenhotels.co.jp/osaka-premier; 3-4-15 Naka-no-shima, Kita-ku; s/d/tw from ¥18,000/28,000/32,000; ⊖✳🏠; Ⓢ Yotsu-bashi line to Higobashi, exit 3) On Naka-no-shima, this handsome hotel exudes contemporary cool. Rooms have wooden floors, clean, spare lines, lots of power outlets and large bathrooms with separate WC and bathing areas. There are also guest laundry machines and attractive common baths. Request an east-facing room for the best river views.

Check the website for significant discounts (some via the MGH Members club which has free registration). It's a five-minute walk from the subway station, along the river; the hotel has a shuttle service to JR Osaka Station.

🛏 Minami

★ Hostel 64 Osaka
HOSTEL ¥

(Map p362; ☑06-6556-6586; www.hostel64.com; 3-11-20 Shinmachi, Nishi-ku; dm/d from ¥3500/8100; ⊖✳@🏠; Ⓢ Chuō line to Awaza, exit 2) Osaka's most stylish hostel is inside a 1960s office building that's been kitted out with retro furniture. There are Japanese-and Western-style private rooms, a small dorm with beds separated by screens and a cosy lounge that doubles as a cafe-bar. It's in a quiet neighbourhood, a 20-minute walk northwest of Shinsaibashi. Staff are friendly and knowledgable.

Bathrooms are shared and there's no elevator. From the station, exit right, turn right at the third stoplight and make the first left. The hostel produces a bilingual Japanese-English map covering Osaka's hippest 'hoods.

Osaka Hana Hostel
HOSTEL ¥

(大阪花宿; Map p366; ☑06-6281-8786; http://osaka.hanahostel.com; 1-8-4 Nishi-Shinsaibashi, Chūō-ku; dm/tw/tr from ¥3000/7800/10,200; ⊖✳@🏠; Ⓢ Midō-suji line to Shinsaibashi, exit 7) This great budget option in the heart of Amerika-Mura has a variety of rooms. Besides six-bed dorms, there are private Japanese- and Western-style rooms, some with en suite bathrooms and kitchenettes. Shared facilities include two kitchen/lounge areas and coin-operated laundry machines. It's all managed by a helpful team of well-travelled, English-speaking staff. The only downside is some street noise.

Khaosan World Namba
HOSTEL ¥

(カオサンワールドなんば; Map p366; ☑06-6632-7373; http://khaosan-tokyo.com/en/namba; 1-2-13 Motomachi, Naniwa-ku; dm/d/q from ¥2800/7400/16,000; ⊖✳@🏠; Ⓢ Midō-suji line to Namba, exit 13) From the reliable Khaosan chain, this large hostel is run like an efficient hotel by a bevy of multilingual staff. The bunks are big and capsule-like; the more expensive six-bed rooms have showers. Cultural events are held regularly and there's a ground-floor bar that encourages a social vibe.

First Cabin Midosuji Namba
HOTEL ¥

(ファーストキャビン御堂筋難波; Map p366; ☑06-6631-8090; www.first-cabin.jp; 4th fl, Namba Midōsuji Bldg, 4-2-1 Namba, Chūō-ku; r per person from ¥5900; ⊖✳@🏠; Ⓢ Midō-suji line to Namba, exit 13) Imagine spending the night in a first-class suite of an Airbus A380 – inside an office building. Cabins, closed off by sliding screens, contain private TV, locker and power outlets. They're segregated by gender, as are large common baths and showers. It's a top location with direct subway access and friendly service, but noise can travel; pack earplugs (like on that plane).

Capsule Hotel Asahi
Plaza Shinsaibashi
CAPSULE HOTEL ¥

(カプセルホテル朝日プラザ心斎橋; Map p366; ☑06-6213-1991; www.asahiplaza.co.jp; 2-12-22 Nishi-Shinsaibashi, Chūō-ku; capsule from ¥3000; ⊖✳🏠; Ⓢ Midō-suji line to Shinsaibashi, exit 7) This is a classic capsule hotel, with over 400 pods on separate floors for men and women and communal baths, conveniently located in Ame-Mura. They're quite used to foreign guests, so this is a good choice for capsule hotel novices. Luggage that doesn't fit in the

---

ℹ OSAKA ACCOMMODATION TAX

On 1 January 2017, Osaka introduced an accommodation tax that is charged per person per night:

➡ ¥100 per person per night for lodgings that charge a rate of ¥10,000–14,999 per person per night

➡ ¥200 for lodgings that charge ¥15,000–19,999 per person per night

➡ ¥300 for lodgings that charge over ¥20,000 per person per night

It's likely that accommodations will charge fees as well as stated nightly rates.

LOCAL KNOWLEDGE

OSAKA'S BEST LOVE HOTEL

There are few love hotels – hotels intended for romantic encounters – like **Hotel Fūki** (ホテル富貴; Map p362; ☑ 06-6353-4135; www.hotelfuki.jp; 3-7-11 Higashi-Noda, Miyakojima-ku; r from ¥5600; ℝ JR Loop line to Kyobashi, north exit) left in Japan. The decor riffs on the courtesan boudoirs of the Heian era (794–1185), late 19th-century Europe and the swinging sixties. The more elaborate rooms (one has a bed in a wooden boat) cost ¥8950; there are pictures out front. Note that check-in is not until 7pm.

lockers provided can be held at the front desk (¥200 per day).

Kaneyoshi Ryokan
RYOKAN ¥¥

(かねよし旅館; Map p366; ☑ 06-6211-6337; www.kaneyosi.jp; 3-12 Sōemon-chō, Chūō-ku; per person from ¥6480; ✳ @ 🛜; Ⓢ Sennichimae line to Nipponbashi, exit 2) In business for nearly a century right by Dōtombori – try for a room at the back for river views – Kaneyoshi's current (1980s) building feels a bit dated, but there's eager-to-please staff, clean, comfy tatami (tightly woven floor matting) rooms with private bathrooms and a simple common bath on the top (6th) floor. Although it's in the nightlife district, doors close at 1am.

No nonsmoking rooms (though rooms are well aired).

Cross Hotel Osaka
HOTEL ¥¥¥

(クロスホテル大阪; Map p366; ☑ 06-6213-8281; www.crosshotel.com/osaka; 2-5-15 Shinsaibashi-suji, Chūō-ku; d/tw from ¥19,500; ⊜ ✳ @ 🛜; Ⓢ Midō-suji line to Namba, exit 14) The Cross Hotel rocks a trendy, urban look with a black, white and dark-red motif. Rooms are of average size, but spacious Japanese-style bathrooms are a rare treat. Service is excellent and you'd have to sleep under Ebisu-bashi bridge for a more central location. The breakfast buffet (¥2375) is cheaper if you book a package; rates rise about ¥3000 on weekends.

✗ Eating

✗ Kita (Umeda)

There are innumerable options just within Osaka and Umeda Stations, in the passages below ground and in the attached shopping centres. South of the station (close to Higashi Umeda Station), **Ohatsutenjin-dōri** (お初天神通り) has lots of cheap local options, as does **Hankyū Higashi-dōri** (阪急東通り), which runs east of Hankyū Umeda Station. Both get lively in the evenings, with commuters grabbing food on their way home.

Umeda Hagakure
NOODLES ¥

(梅田はがくれ; Map p364; ☑ 06-6341-1409; 2nd basement fl, Osaka Eki-mae Dai-3 Bldg, 1-1 Umeda, Kita-ku; noodles ¥600-1100; ⊘ 11am-2.45pm & 5-7.45pm Mon-Fri, 11am-2.30pm Sat & Sun; Ⓢ T-animachi line to Higashi-Umeda, exit 8, ℝ JR Osaka, south central exit) Two storeys underground and three decades old, this shop is cramped and workmanlike, but locals queue for udon noodles made before your eyes. Cold noodles are the speciality; try refreshing *nama-jōyu* (with soy sauce, ground *daikon* (radish) and sudachi lime) or *tenzaru* (with tempura). Order from the picture menu, and get hand-gestured eating instructions from the owner.

Avoid weekdays between noon and 1pm, when the office-worker lunch crowd descends.

Eki Marché
FOOD HALL ¥

(エキマルシェ大阪; Map p364; www.ekimaru.com; Osaka Station City, Kita-ku; ⊘ 10am-10pm; ℝ JR Osaka, Sakurabashi exit) This excellent collection of wallet-friendly eateries and takeaway counters is on the southwestern side of JR Osaka Station. Top picks include Kaiten Sushi Ganko, for conveyor-belt sushi, and **Kani Chahan-no-Mise** (かにチャーハンの店; Map p364; ☑ 06-6341-3103; Eki Maré, Osaka Station City, Kita-ku; mains from ¥680; ⊘ 10am-10.30pm; ⊜), for delectable crab fried rice.

Kaiten Sushi Ganko
SUSHI ¥

(回転寿司がんこ; Map p364; ☑ 06-4799-6811; Eki Maré, Osaka Station City, Kita-ku; plates ¥130-735; ⊘ 11am-11pm; ⊜ 🍴; ℝ JR Osaka, Sakurabashi exit) This *kaiten-sushi* (conveyor-belt sushi) shop is a popular choice for many hungry commuters, meaning the two whirring tracks of plates are continuously restocked with fresh options. It gets crowded at meal times. It's inside JR Osaka's Eki Marché food court.

There are also branches in Shin-Osaka Station and Abeno Harukas (p367).

Yukari
OKONOMIYAKI ¥¥

(ゆかり; Map p364; ☑ 06-6311-0214; www.yukarichan.co.jp; 2-14-13 Sōnezaki, Kita-ku; okonomiyaki ¥800-1460; ⊘ 11am-1am; Ⓢ Tanimachi line to Higashi-Umeda, exit 4, ℝ JR Osaka, south central exit) This popular restaurant in the Ohatsutenjin-dōri arcade serves up that great Osaka favourite, *okonomiyaki* (savoury pancakes), cooked on a griddle before you. There are lots to choose from on the picture menu, including veg options, but the *tokusen mikkusu yaki* (mixed *okonomiyaki* with fried pork, shrimp and squid; ¥1080) is a classic. Look for red and white signage out front.

Robatayaki Isaribi   IZAKAYA ¥¥
(炉ばた焼き漁火; Map p364; ☑ 06-6373-2969; www.rikimaru-group.com/shop/isaribi.html; 1-5-12 Shibata, Kita-ku; dishes ¥325; ☺ 5-11.15pm; ⓓ; Ⓢ Midō-suji line to Umeda, exit 2, Ⓡ Hankyū Umeda) Head downstairs to this spirited, friendly *izakaya* (pub eatery) for standards such as skewered meats, seafood, veggies fresh off the grill and giant pieces of *tori no karaage* (fried chicken). The best seats are at semi-circular counters, where your chef will serve you using a very, very longpaddle.

It's on the street along the western side of Hankyū Umeda Station, to the left of the signage featuring a guy wearing a headband, with white door curtains.

✖ Semba & Osaka-jō

Gout   BAKERY ¥
(グウ; Map p362; ☑ 06-6585-0833; 1-1-10 Honmachi, Chūō-ku; bread from ¥200; ☺ 7.30am-8pm Fri-Wed; ⊝; Ⓢ Tanimachi line to Tanimachi 4-chōme, exit 4) One of Osaka's best bakeries, Gout (think of it pronounced 'goo', as in French) sells baguettes, pastries, croissants, sandwiches and coffee to go or eat in the small seating area. It's perfect for picking up picnic supplies before heading to nearby Osaka-jō.

★ Yoshino Sushi   SUSHI ¥¥¥
(吉野鮨; Map p362; ☑ 06-6231-7181; www.yoshino-sushi.co.jp; 3-4-14 Awaji-machi, Chūō-ku; lunch/dinner from ¥3200/6500; ☺ 11am-1.30pm & 5.30-9.30pm Mon-Fri; Ⓢ Midō-suji line to Honmachi, exit 1) In business since 1841, Yoshino specialises in Osaka-style sushi, which is *hako-sushi* ('pressed sushi'). This older version (compared to the newer, hand-pressed Tokyo-style *nigiri-sushi*) is formed by a wooden mould, resulting in Mondrian-esque cubes of spongy

---

OSAKA SPECIALITIES

Okonomiyaki Thick, savoury pancakes filled with shredded cabbage and your choice of meat, seafood, vegetables and more (the name means 'cook as you like'). Often prepared on a *teppan* (steel plate) set into your table, the cooked pancake is brushed with a savoury Worcestershire-style sauce, decoratively striped with mayonnaise and topped with dried bonito flakes, which seem to dance in the rising steam. Slice off a wedge using tiny trowels called *kote*, and – warning – allow it to cool a bit before taking that first bite. Try it at Chibo (p376) in Dōtombori or Yukari (p374) in Umeda.

Tako-yaki These doughy dumplings stuffed with octopus (*tako* in Japanese) are grilled in special-made moulds. They're often sold as street food, served with pickled ginger, topped with savoury sauce, powdered *aonori* (seaweed), mayonnaise and bonito flakes and eaten with toothpicks. Nibble carefully first as the centre can be molten hot. Try it at Wanaka Honten (p376) in Namba.

Kushikatsu *Yakitori* refers to skewers of grilled meat, seafood and/or vegetables; *kushikatsu* is the same ingredients crumbed, deep fried and served with a savoury dipping sauce (double-dipping is a serious no-no). Goes well with beer. The Shin-Sekai neighbourhood is famed for *kushikatsu* restaurants. Try Ganso Kushikatsu Daruma Honten (p377).

Kaiten-sushi This Osaka invention (from the 1950s) goes by many names in English: conveyor-belt sushi, sushi-go-round or sushi train. It's all the same – plates of sushi that run past you along a belt built into the counter (you can also order off the menu). Though long considered downmarket, as Japan has gravitated toward cheap eats in the Great Recession, some *kaiten-sushi* have been raising the quality. Try it at at Kaiten Sushi Ganko (p374) in JR Osaka Station or at the branch in Abeno Harukas (p367).

Kappō-ryōri Osaka's take on Japanese haute cuisine is casual: the dishes are similar to what you might find at a Kyoto *ryōtei* (a formal restaurant with tatami seating) – incorporating intensely seasonal ingredients and elaborate presentation – but at *kappō* restaurants, diners sit at the counter, chatting with the chef who hands over the dishes as they're finished. Despite the laid-back vibe these restaurants can be frightfully expensive; try Shoubentango-tei (p376), which is reasonable.

omelette, soy-braised shiitake mushrooms, smokey eel and vinegar-marinated fish on rice. Reservations are required for dinner.

On the ground floor, the shop sells takeaway boxes priced under ¥2000. Look for the trees and brown curtains out front.

Harannaka
GYOZA ¥¥

(腹ん中; Map p362; ☑06-6809-5260; 2-4-13 Tenma, Kita-ku; gyōza 6 for ¥500; ⊘9pm-2am even-numbered days; Ⓢ Tanimachi line to Temmabashi, exit 2) This one-man show, set to a tribal soundtrack, revolves around a single hob, framed by a drum can, where a large pan of *gyōza* is set to sizzle. Service is slow, but reverential. The interior, hand-built by the owner, is punctuated with towers of stones. Standing only. Look for the green light bulb out front.

The same guy runs nearby **Denki Soba** (電気蕎麦; Map p362; ☑06-6809-5260; 3-5-1 Tenma, Kita-ku; soba from ¥800; ⊘9pm-2am odd-numbered days) on odd-numbered days.

✖ Minami

Lively Dōtombori has lots of street-food vendors and restaurants. As this area gets a lot of tourists, both English menus and English-speaking staff are common. Dōtombori can get extremely crowded in the evenings and you'll have to queue at the more popular spots. In Namba, the **Namba Parks** (なんばパークス; Map p366; www.nambaparks.com; 2-10-70 Namba-naka, Naniwa-ku; ⊘11am-9pm; Ⓢ Midō-suji line to Namba, exit 4) mall has a good spread of restaurants as well.

★ Wanaka Honten
STREET FOOD ¥

(わなか本店; Map p366; ☑06-6631-0127; http://takoyaki-wanaka.com; 11-19 Sennichi-mae, Chūō-ku; tako-yaki per 8 from ¥450; ⊘10am-10pm Mon-Fri, 8.30am-10pm Sat & Sun; Ⓢ Midō-suji line to Namba, exit 4) This famous *tako-yaki* (octopus dumplings) stand, just north of Dōguya-suji arcade, uses custom copper hotplates (instead of cast iron) to make dumplings that are crisper on the outside than usual (but still runny inside). There's a picture menu and tables and chairs in the back. One popular dish to try is *tako-sen* – two dumplings sandwiched between *sembei* (rice crackers).

There's also a convenient branch in **Ame-Mura** (わなかアメリカ村店; Map p366; ☑06-6211-3304; 2-12-8 Nishi-Shinsaibashi,

Chūō-ku; ⊘11am-10pm Mon-Fri, 10am-10.30pm Sat & Sun; Ⓢ Midō-suji line to Shinsaibashi, exit 7).

Za Ikaga
STREET FOOD ¥

(ザ・イカが; Map p366; ☑06-6212-0147; www.ikayaki.jp; 2-12-8 Nishi-Shinsaibashi, Chūō-ku; dishes from ¥300; ⊘6pm-4am Thu-Tue; Ⓢ Midō-suji line to Shinsaibashi, exit 7) The signature dish at this food stand is *ika-yaki* – grilled squid, served here in a thin crêpe splattered with egg, mayonaise and savoury, *okonomiyaki*-style sauce. There are a few seats inside at the counter and a few folding chairs on the street (perfect for watching the comings and goings in Amerika-Mura). There's a picture menu.

★ Chibo
OKONOMIYAKI ¥¥

(千房; Map p366; ☑06-6212-2211; www.chibo.com; 1-5-5 Dōtombori, Chūō-ku; mains ¥885-1675; ⊘11am-1am Mon-Sat, to midnight Sun; ⓒ; Ⓢ Midō-suji line to Namba, exit 14) Chibo is one of Osaka's most famous *okonomiyaki* restaurants. It almost always has a line, but it moves fast as there's seating on multiple floors (you might want to hold out for the coveted tables overlooking Dōtombori canal). Try the house special *Dōtombori yaki*, with pork, beef, squid, shrimp and cheese, and *tonpei-yaki* (omelette wrapped around fried pork).

★ Imai Honten
UDON ¥¥

(今井本店; Map p366; ☑06-6211-0319; www.d-imai.com; 1-7-22 Dōtombori, Chūō-ku; dishes from ¥765; ⊘11am-10pm Thu-Tue; ⊜ⓒ; Ⓢ Midō-suji line to Namba, exit 14) Step into an oasis of calm amid Dōtombori's chaos to be welcomed by kimono-clad staff at one of the area's oldest and most revered udon specialists. Try *kitsune udon* – noodles topped with soup-soaked slices of fried tofu. Look for the traditional exterior and the willow tree outside.

★ Shoubentango-tei
KAISEKI ¥¥¥

(正弁丹吾亭; Map p366; ☑06-6211-3208; 1-7-12 Dōtombori, Chūō-ku; dinner course ¥3780-10,800; ⊘5-10pm; ⓒ; Ⓢ Midō-suji line to Namba, exit 14) That this *kappō-ryōri* (Osaka-style haute cuisine) restaurant isn't more expensive is surprising considering its pedigree: established over 100 years ago, it was a literati hangout in the early 20th century. Even the cheapest course, which includes five dishes decided that day by the chef, tastes – and looks! – like a luxurious treat; reservations are necessary for all but the cheapest course. The restaurant is on Hōzen-ji Yokochō.

✕ Tennōji & Around

★Ganso Kushikatsu
Daruma Honten   KUSHIKATSU ¥¥

(元祖串かつ　だるま本店; Map p362; ☑06-6645-7056; www.kushikatu-daruma.com; 2-3-9 Ebisu-Higashi, Naniwa-ku; skewers ¥110-220; ⏰11am-10.30pm; 🅓; ⑤Midōsuji line to Dōbutsuen-mae, exit 5) Daruma has branches around town but, for many Japanese, a pilgrimage to the original shop in Shinsekai – opened in 1929 and said to be the birthplace of *kushikatsu* – is a necessary part of any visit to Osaka. There's room for maybe a dozen around the small counter. Start with the eight piece assortment (¥1140) of perfectly crisp skewers. There's a shop in **Dōtombori** (だるま　道頓堀店; Map p366; ☑06-6213-8101; 1-6-4 Dōtombori, Chūō-ku; skewers ¥120-230; ⏰11.30am-10.30pm; ⑤Midō-suji line to Namba, exit 14) but the line can be long.

🍷 Drinking & Nightlife

Osakans love to let loose: the city is teeming with *izakaya,* bars and nightclubs. Craft beer and coffee scenes are on the rise too; look for the *Osaka Craft Beer Map* (www.facebook.com/osakacraftbeermap). In the summer, rooftop beer gardens set up atop department stores. Check *Kansai Scene* (www.kansaiscene.com) for nightclub information; English-speaking bartenders at pubs popular with expats are another good information source.

🍷 Kita (Umeda)

Given that so many commuters either come or go through JR Osaka Station or Hankyū Umeda Station, the surrounding lanes, and especially to the south and the east of the train stations, have scores of bars and *izakaya.* Nearby Doyama-chō is western Japan's largest gay district with some 200 (tiny) bars.

Frenz Frenzy   GAY & LESBIAN

(Map p362; ☑06-6311-1386; http://frenz-frenzy. website; 18-14 Kamiyama-chō, Kita-ku; ⏰8pm-1am; ⑤Tanimachi line to Higashi-Umeda, exit 3) Frenz Frenzy calls itself a 'rainbow haven' and it means that literally: the whole place is awash in colour (including the front door, thankfully, because otherwise it would be impossible to find). Run by long-time expat Sari-chan, it's a welcoming first port of call for gay and lesbian travellers. There's no cover and drinks start at ¥500.

LOCAL KNOWLEDGE

URA-NAMBA

Ura-Namba (literally 'behind Namba') is an unofficial district made up of clusters of small restaurants and bars in the shadow of Namba Nankai Station. It's becoming an increasingly trendy place to hang out. A good place to start is the **Misono Building** (味園ビル; Map p366; 2nd fl, Misono Bldg, 2-3-9 Sennichi-mae, Chūō-ku; ⏰6pm-late; ⑤Sakai-suji line to Nipponbashi, exit 5), a once grand (and now wilting) structure, which has dozens of bars on the 2nd floor.

It's on the ground floor of a building with other bars, set back from the road.

Blarney Stone   PUB

(ザ・ブラーニーストーン; Map p364; www. the-blarney-stone.com; 6th fl, Sonezaki Center Bldg, 2-10-15 Sonezaki, Kita-ku; drinks from ¥500; ⏰5pm-1am Mon-Thu, to 5am Fri & Sat, 3.30pm-1am Sun; 🚈Tanimachi line to Higashi-Umeda, exit 4, 🚈JR Osaka, south central exit) Have a Guinness or two and relax in the friendly atmosphere of this Irish-style pub, well liked among local expats and Japanese for after-work drinks and the free live music on weekends. Bartenders speak English. It's in Umeda's Ohatsutenjin-dōri arcade; there's a sign at street level.

🍷 Naka-no-shima & Semba

★Beer Belly   CRAFT BEER

(Map p362; www.beerbelly.jp/tosabori; 1-1-31 Tosabori, Nishi-ku; ⏰5pm-2am Mon-Fri, 3-11pm Sat, 3-9pm Sun; ⑤Yotsubashi line to Higobashi, exit 3) Beer Belly is run by Osaka's best microbrewery, Minoh Beer. There are 10 taps and one hand pump featuring Minoh's award-winning classics and seasonal offerings (pints from ¥1000). Pick up a copy here of Osaka's *Craft Beer Map* to further your local beer adventures. From the subway exit, double back and take the road that curves behind the APA Hotel.

Moto Coffee   CAFE

(モトコーヒー; Map p362; ☑06-4706-3788; 2-1-1 Kitahama, Chūō-ku; ⏰noon-7pm; ☻; ⑤Sakai-suji line to Kitahama, exit 26) Sitting pretty in a small, whitewashed building next to the Kyū-Yodogawa, Moto serves quality coffee drinks (from ¥450) on its riverside terrace (or upstairs if the terrace is full).

Leach Bar   BAR

(リーチバー; Map p362; ☑06-6441-0983; www.rihga.co.jp/osaka; Ground fl, Rihga Hotel, 5-3-68 Naka-no-shima, Kita-ku; drinks from ¥1200; ⊙11am-midnight; ⒭Keihan Naka-no-shima line to Naka-no-shima, exit 3) Osaka's most attractive hotel bar doesn't have soaring views of the city; instead it has an interior designed by legendary potter Bernard Leach (who spent significant time in Japan). A few of his works and those of early 20th-century Japanese artists are on display here.

🍷 Minami

Visit Minami on a Friday night and you might think there's one bar for every resident – including *izakaya*, Irish pubs and cocktail lounges (as well as hostess and host bars, where the servers are flirtatious women and men, and the drinks are very pricey). Friday and Saturday nights are the big nights out (especially for clubs) but you'll usually have company on weeknights too. The English-speaking crowd tends to congregate in Amerika-Mura, which has lots of small, cheap bars that open on to the streets; the nightclubs are mostly here too.

★Circus   CLUB

(Map p366; ☑06-6241-3822; http://circus-osaka.com; 2nd fl, 1-8-16 Nishi-Shinsaibashi, Chūō-ku; ¥2000-2500; ⊙11pm-late; ⊛; ⓢMidō-suji line to Shinsaibashi, exit 7) This small club is the heart of Osaka's underground electronic scene, drawing a crowd more for the music than a pick-up scene. The dance floor is nonsmoking. It's open on Friday and Saturday nights and sometimes during the week. Look up for the small sign in English and bring a picture ID.

Jun-kissa American   CAFE

(純喫茶アメリカン; Map p366; ☑06-6211-2100; 1-7-4 Dōtombori, Chūō-ku; ⊙9am-11pm; ⓢMidō-suji line to Namba, exit 15) With its 1940s interior intact and waitresses in long skirts, American is a classic *jun-kissa* – a shop from the first wave of cafes to open in Japan, during the post-WWII American occupation. Come before 11am for a 'morning set' (¥620) of pillowy buttered toast, a hard-boiled egg and coffee. Look for the chrome sign out front.

Rock Rock   BAR

(ロックロック; Map p366; www.rockrock.co.jp; 3rd fl, Shinsaibashi Atrium Bldg, 1-8-1 Nishi-Shinsaibashi, Chūō-ku; ⊙6pm-5am Mon-Sat, to 1am Sun; ⓢMidō-suji line to Shinsaibashi, exit 7) Serving the music-loving community since 1995, Rock Rock has a history of hosting after parties for international acts and attracting celebs. Regular events with a modest cover charge (usually ¥1500, including one drink ticket) showcase some of Osaka's finest rock DJs (and famous guests).

☆ Entertainment

★Namba Bears   LIVE MUSIC

(難波ベアーズ; Map p362; ☑06-6649-5564; http://namba-bears.main.jp; 3-14-5 Namba-naka, Naniwa-ku; ⓢMidō-suji line to Namba, exit 4) For going on three decades this has been the place to hear underground music live in Osaka. It's a small, bare-concrete, smokey space – well suited to the punk, rock and indie bands that play here. In keeping with the alternative spirit, you can bring in your own beer. Most shows start at 7pm; tickets usually cost ¥2000 to ¥2500.

★National Bunraku Theatre   THEATRE

(国立文楽劇場; Map p362; ☑06-6212-2531, ticket centre 0570-07-9900; www.ntj.jac.go.jp; 1-12-10 Nipponbashi, Chūō-ku; full performance ¥2400-6000, single act ¥500-1500; ⊙opening months vary, check the website; ⓢSakai-suji line to Nipponbashi, exit 7) The classical performing art most associated with Osaka is bunraku, which makes dramatic use of highly sophisticated puppets. A visit to the theatre is a half-day event: shows, which include scenes from different plays, top four hours. Too long? Nonreserved, same-day single-act tickets are sold at the venue from 10am. Rent the English-language audio guide (full program/single act ¥700/300). Shows sell out quickly and single-act tickets are limited.

Sumo Spring Tournament   SPECTATOR SPORT

(Haru Bashō; www.sumo.or.jp; ⊙Mar) The big fellas rumble into Osaka in March for this major tournament, held in the Prefectural Gymnasium (府立体育館, Fu-ritsu Taiiku-kan) in Namba. Tickets (from ¥3800) go on sale in early February and can be purchased online.

Kyōcera Dome   BASEBALL

(京せらドーム; Map p362; ☑06-6586-0106; www.kyoceradome-osaka.jp; 3-2-1 Chiyozaki, Nishi-ku; ⓢNagahori Tsurumiryokuchi line to Dome-mae Chiyozaki) Also known as Osaka Dome, this futuristic stadium is home to the Orix Buffaloes baseball team. While the Buffaloes may not have the following of the mighty Hanshin Tigers, who play nearby in Kōbe (except for games in August, which they play here), they do have their own dedicated (and very vocal) fans. Same-day outfield tickets cost just ¥1800.

Shopping

Osaka is the biggest shopping destination in western Japan, with an overwhelming number of malls, department stores, shopping arcades, electronics dealers, boutiques and secondhand shops. More and more places are offering to waive the sales tax on purchases over ¥10,000. Look for signs in the window; passport is required. Flea markets take place every month at shrines and temples, including O-hatsu Ten-jin and Shitennō-ji.

Kita

Osaka Station is ringed by malls and department stores – they're all interconnected by underground passages, making the Umeda district one big shopping conurbation. You'll find outlets of all of Japan's most popular national chains here, like Uniqlo, Muji, Tokyū Hands and **Yodobashi Umeda** (ヨドバシ梅田; Map p364; www.yodobashi-umeda.com; 1-1 Ōfuka-chō, Kita-ku; ⏲ shops 9.30am 10pm, restaurants 11am-11pm; [S] Midō-suji line to Umeda, exit 4, 🚉 JR Osaka, Midō-suji north exit), along with literally hundreds of fashion boutiques.

★ Hankyū Umeda Department Store DEPARTMENT STORE
(阪急梅田本店; Map p364; www.hankyu-dept.co.jp/honten; 8-7 Kakuda-chō, Kita-ku; ⏲ 10am-8pm Sun-Thu, to 9pm Fri & Sat; [S] Midō-suji line to Umeda, exit 6, 🚉 Hankyū Umeda) Hankyū, which first opened in 1929, pioneered the now ubiquitous concept of the train-station department store. One of Japan's largest department stores, 'Ume-Han' is also among the most fashion-forward, with a good selection of edgy Japanese designers on the 3rd floor. Head to the 7th floor for artisan homewares and to the basement for a cornucopia of gourmet food items.

Maruzen & Junkudō Umeda BOOKS
(丸善&ジュンク堂書店梅田店; Map p364; www.junkudo.co.jp; Chaska Chayamachi Bldg, 7-20 Chayamachi, Kita-ku; ⏲ 10am-10pm; 🚉 Hankyū Umeda) This is the largest bookstore in Osaka, the result of two established chains joining forces. There's a big range of English-language books (on the 6th floor) and travel guides (3rd floor). It's in the Andō Tadao–designed Chaska Chayamachi building.

Kōbe-based Junkudō has a few other branches around town.

Minami

International high-end brands line Midō-suji, the main boulevard, between Shinsaibashi and Namba subway stations. A few blocks east, the jam-packed Shinsaibashi-suji (p369) arcade has popular local and international chain stores. Ame-Mura has youthful streetware and secondhand shops; on the other side of Midō-suji, the Minami-Horie district has trendy boutiques. Namba Station is anchored by the huge mall, Namba Parks (p376).

★ Dōguya-suji Arcade MARKET
(道具屋筋; Map p366; www.doguyasuji.or.jp/map_eng.html; Sennichi-mae, Chūō-ku; ⏲ 10am-6pm; [S] Midō-suji line to Namba, exit 4) This long arcade sells just about anything related to preparing, consuming and selling of Osaka's principal passion: food. There's everything from bamboo steamers and lacquer miso soup bowls to shopfront lanterns and, of course, moulded hotplates for making *tako-yaki* (octopus dumplings). Hours vary per store.

★ Standard Books BOOKS
(スタンダードブックストア; Map p366; ☎ 06-6484-2239; www.standardbookstore.com; 2-2-12 Nishi-Shinsaibashi, Chūō-ku; ⏲ 11am-10.30pm; [S] Midō-suji line to Shinsaibashi, exit 7) This cult-fave Osaka bookstore prides itself on not stocking any best sellers. Instead, it's stocked with small-press finds, art books, indie comics and the like, plus CDs and quirky fashion items and accessories.

Flake Records MUSIC
(Map p366; ☎ 06-6534-7411; www.flakerecords.com; No 201, 2nd fl, Sono Yotsubashi Bldg, 1-11-9 Minami-Horie, Nishi-ku; ⏲ noon-9pm; [S] Yotsubashi line to Yotsubashi, exit 6) Flake is Osaka's most in-the-know music shop, selling new and used, local and imported, CDs and records. The owner speaks some English; ask him for his recommendations on local bands. This is also a good place to pick up flyers for live music events.

Tennōji & Around

★ Tower Knives HOMEWARES
(タワーナイブズ; Map p362; ☎ 06-4395-5218; www.towerknives.com; 1-4-1 Ebisu-higashi, Naniwa-ku; ⏲ 10am-6pm; [S] Midō-suji line to Dōbutsuen-mae, exit 5) Tower Knives has a fantastic selection of kitchen knives – both carbon steel and stainless steel; some are

hand-forged by Osaka artisans. Best of all, the English-speaking staff will walk you through the different styles, let you try them out on some veggies (at your own risk: these knives are sharp!) and show you how to care for them. Duty-free shopping available.

ⓘ Information

DANGERS & ANNOYANCES

Osaka has a rough image in Japan, with the highest number of reported crimes per capita of any city in Japan – though it remains significantly safer than most cities of comparable size. Still, it's wise to employ the same common sense here that you would back home. Purse snatchings are not uncommon.

Nishinari-ku (also called Airin-chiku), south of Shinimamiya Station (just below Shin-Sekai), has a sizeable vagrant population and an organised-crime presence. There are a number of budget accommodations here targeting foreign travellers; while it's unlikely you'd encounter any real danger, female travellers, particularly solo female travellers, do risk drawing unwanted attention, especially at night.

INTERNET ACCESS

Most accommodations have wi-fi or internet access, as do an increasing number of cafes, and Osaka has been expanding free wi-fi in public areas (details at www.osaka-info.jp/en/wifi).

MEDICAL SERVICES

Every neighbourhood in Osaka will have at least one small clinic, though you're more likely to find English-speaking doctors at larger hospitals. Only Japanese health insurance is accepted at healthcare providers in Japan; however, if you are willing to pay the cost up front you should have little trouble finding treatment. Note that many smaller clinics only accept cash.

ⓘ NAVIGATING OSAKA

Fair warning: Osaka's larger stations can be disorienting, particularly Namba and the Umeda/JR Osaka Station area. Exits are often confusingly labelled, even for the Japanese, and English-language directional signage is lacking compared to similar stations in other Japanese cities.

Adding to the confusion, *shinkansen* (bullet trains) don't stop at any of these hubs, but at Shin-Osaka Station, three subway stops (about five minutes) north of Umeda and JR Osaka Station on the Midō-suji line.

Japan Red Cross Hospital (日本赤十字病院; Nihon Sekijyūji Byōin; Map p362; ☎06-6774-5111; www.osaka-med.jrc.or.jp; 5-30 Fude-gasaki-chō, Tennōji-ku; ⊙24hrs; 📵Kintetsu Ue-Honmachi) Emergency care; some doctors speak English.

Ohkita Medical Clinic (大北メディカルクリニック; Map p364; ☎06-6344-0380; www.ookita.com; 4th fl, Umeda Square Bldg, 1-12-17 Umeda, Kita-ku; ⊙10am-7pm Mon-Fri, to 1pm Sat; 📵JR Osaka, south central exit) English-speaking doctor for non-emergency care, near JR Osaka Station.

TOURIST INFORMATION

Osaka Visitors Information Center Umeda (大阪市ビジターズインフォメーションセンター・梅田; Map p364; ☎06-6345-2189; www.osaka-info.jp; JR Osaka Station; ⊙8am-8pm; 📵JR Osaka, north central exit) The main tourist office, with English information, pamphlets and maps, is on the 1st floor of the central north concourse of JR Osaka Station. There are also branches on the 1st floor of **Nankai Namba Station** (大阪市ビジターズインフォメーションセンター・なんば; Map p366; ☎06-6631-9100; Nankai Namba Station; ⊙9am-8pm; Ⓢ Midō-suji line to Namba, exit 4, 📵Nankai Namba) and at Kansai International Airport (KIX). Tourist offices can help book accommodation if you visit in person. The website is a good resource too.

TRAVEL AGENCIES

HIS Osaka Tourist Information Centre (HIS 大阪ツーリストインフォメーションセンター; Map p366; ☎06-6253-8866; http://his-osaka.com; 8th fl, Shinsaibashi OPA, 1-4-3 Nishi-Shinsaibashi, Chūō-ku; ⊙9am-9pm; Ⓢ Midō-suji line to Shinsaibashi, exit 7) English-speaking staff can book Osaka area tours and onward flights, exchange money and store luggage.

ⓘ Getting There & Away

AIR

Two airports serve Osaka: **Kansai International Airport** (KIX; 関西空港; Map p410; www.kansai-airport.or.jp) for all international and some domestic flights; and the domestic **Itami Airport** (ITM; 伊丹空港; ☎06-6856-6781; http://osaka-airport.co.jp; 3-555 Hotaru-ga-ike, Nishi-machi, Toyonaka), also confusingly called Osaka International Airport. KIX is about 50km southwest of the city, on an artificial island in the bay. Itami is located 12km northwest of Osaka.

To/From Osaka Itami Airport

Osaka Monorail Connects the airport to Hotarugaike (¥200, three minutes) and Senri-Chūō (¥330, 12 minutes), from where you can transfer, respectively, to the Hankyū Takarazaka line or Hankyū Senri line for Osaka Station.

Osaka Airport Limousine (www.okkbus.co.jp)
Frequent buses connect the airport with Osaka
Station (¥640, 25 minutes), Osaka City Air
Terminal (OCAT; ¥640, 35 minutes) in Namba
and Shin-Osaka Station (¥500, 25 minutes). At
Itami, buy your tickets from the machine outside
the arrivals hall.

To/From Kansai International Airport

KIX is well connected to the city with direct train
lines and buses.

Nankai Express Rapit (¥1430, 40 minutes)
All-reserved twice-hourly service (7am to 10pm)
between Nankai Kansai-Airport Station (in Terminal 1) and Nankai Namba Station; Nankai Airport
Express trains take about 10 minutes longer
and cost ¥920. To reach Nankai Kansai-Airport
Station from Terminal 2, you will need to take a
shuttle bus to Terminal 1.

JR Haruka Kansai-Airport Express Twice-
hourly service (6.30am to 10pm) between KIX
and Tennōji Station (unreserved seat ¥1710,
30 minutes) and Shin-Osaka Station (¥2330,
50 minutes). More frequent JR Kansai Airport
rapid trains also run between KIX, Tennōji
(¥1060, 50 minutes) and Osaka Station (¥1190,
68 minutes); the last train departs at 11.30pm.
All these stations connect to the Midō-suji
subway line. It departs from Terminal 1; you
need to take a free shuttle bus if you arrive at
Terminal 2.

KATE (www.kate.co.jp) Airport limousine
buses run to/from **Osaka City Air Terminal**
(OCAT; Map p366; ☑ 06-6635-3000; www.
ocat.co.jp) (¥1050, 50 minutes) in Namba, JR
Osaka Station (¥1550, one hour) and Tempōzan
(¥1550, one hour). Note that the trip, especially
to Umeda, can take longer depending on traffic.
After midnight, there is only an hourly service
to Osaka Station. Note that bus departures are
more frequent from Terminal 1.

Taxi There are standard taxi fares to Umeda
(¥14,500, 50 minutes), Namba (¥14,000, 50
minutes) and Shin-Osaka (¥18,000, one hour).
There is a late-night fare surcharge of ¥2500.

BOAT

Domestic

The following ferries depart from **Osaka Nankō
Port** (大阪南港; ☑ 06-6613-1571; 2-1-10 Nan-
kō-kita, Suminoe-ku; ☒ New Port Town line to
Ferry Terminal) for destinations in Shikoku,
Kyūshū and Okinawa:

Orange Ferry (www.orange-ferry.co.jp) Daily for
Ehime (from ¥5660, eight hours), on Shikoku.

Ferry Sunflower (www.ferry-sunflower.co.jp)
Daily for Beppu (from ¥11,200, 12 hours) and
Kagoshima (from ¥12,800, 16 hours), on Kyūshū.

City Line (www.cityline.co.jp) Twice-daily
for Kita-Kyūshū (¥6170, 12½ hours), north of
Fukuoka

---

① KANSAI TRAVEL PASSES

Three rail passes available only to travellers on temporary visitor visas (you'll
have to show your passport) offer inexpensive transit around Kansai.

JR West (www.westjr.co.jp) issues
two passes with different coverage
areas, durations and price points. The
Kansai Area Pass covers local and express trains (though not *shinkansen*)
on JR lines between Himeji and Kyoto,
including Kōbe, Osaka and Nara. The
Kansai Wide Area Pass covers all these
plus Wakayama Prefecture to the south,
Shiga Prefecture to the northeast and
Kinosaki to the northwest, and *shinkansen* as far west as Okayama.

Kansai also has an extensive network
of non-JR lines, for which the Kansai Thru
Pass (p903) offers unlimited travel, as
well as on municipal bus and subway
lines (though not on JR trains). It also
offers discounts at many attractions.

A Line Ferry (www.aline-ferry.com) Twice-weekly
for Naha (¥19,330, 40 hours) on Okinawa via
Amami-Oshima (¥15,120, 27 hours), off the coast
of Kyūshū. Purchase tickets online or from travel
agencies.

International

Ferries depart from the **Osaka Port International
Ferry Terminal** (大阪港国際フェリーターミナル;
Osaka-kō Kokusai Ferry Terminal; ☑ 06-6243-
6345; 1-20-52 Nan-kō-kita, Suminoe-ku; ☒ Chūō
line to Cosmo Square, ☒ Nankō Port Town Line
to Cosmo Square) journey to Shanghai, China,
and Busan, South Korea. The ferry terminal is a
15-minute walk from the subway.

Japan China International Ferry (日中国際フ
ェリー; ☑ 06-6536-6541; www.shinganjin.com)
departs every other Tuesday (alternating with
Kōbe) for Shanghai; **Shanghai Ferry Company** (
上海フェリー; www.shanghai-ferry.co.jp) departs
on Friday. One-way 2nd-class fares start from
¥20,000; the journey takes approximately 48
hours. Book tickets can be booked online in English or through a travel agent.

Panstar Ferry (パンスターフェリー; ☑ 06-
6614-2516; www.panstar.jp) leaves for Busan
(one-way 2nd-class fares from ¥13,000, 19 hours)
on Monday, Wednesday and Friday. Book through
a travel agency.

BUS

Highway buses depart from the **Willer Bus
Terminal** (Willerバスターミナル; Map p364;

🎫 reservation centre 0570-200-770; www.willerexpress.com; 1st fl, Umeda Sky Bldg Tower West, 1-1-88 Ōyodo-naka, Kita-ku; ⊗ 6am-12.30am; 🚇 JR Osaka, north central exit), next to the **Umeda Sky Building** (p359) for:

Hakata (Fukuoka, Kyūshū; ¥3920 to ¥10,800, eight to 10 hours)

Hiroshima (¥4200 to ¥6700, six to eight hours)

Matsuyama (Ehime, Shikoku; ¥3680 to ¥9980; seven to eight hours)

Takayama (¥3300 to ¥4700, five hours)

Tokyo (¥4400 to ¥11,100; eight to 10 hours)

Longer routes have overnight buses; check the website for more routes. Prices depend on the class of bus (nicer ones have roomy, reclining seats), season and day of departure (weekdays are cheaper). Purchase tickets online in English.

Slightly pricier, but convenient, **JR West Highway Bus** (www.nishinihonjrbus.co.jp) coaches run to similar destinations from the **JR Osaka Station Highway Bus Terminal** (大阪駅JR高速バスターミナル; Map p364; 🚇 JR Osaka), outside the station's north-central concourse. Book online five days prior to travel for better rates.

TRAIN

Shin-Osaka Station is on the Tōkaidō-Sanyō *shinkansen* line (between Tokyo and Hakata in Fukuoka) and the eastern terminus of the Kyūshū *shinkansen* to Kagoshima. Departures are frequent.

Destinations include Tokyo (¥14,140, three hours), Hiroshima (¥10,230, 1½ hours), Hakata (¥15,000, three hours) and Kagoshima (¥21,900, 4¾ hour).

To/From Kyoto

Tōkaidō-Sanyō shinkansen Run from Shin-Osaka Station one stop east to Kyoto Station (¥1420, 14 minutes), but from central Osaka it's easier to get the **JR Kyoto line** from Osaka Station to Kyoto (¥560, 28 minutes).

Hankyū Kyoto line *Tokkyū* (limited express) trains run from Hankyū Umeda Station to Karasuma (¥400, 40 minutes) and Kawaramachi (¥400, 44 minutes) in Kyoto.

Keihan Main line *Tokkyū* trains run from Osaka's Yodoyabashi Station, a stop on the Midō-suji subway line, to Gion-Shijō and Sanjō stations (¥410, 45 to 55 minutes) in Kyoto.

To/From Kōbe

Tōkaidō-Sanyō shinkansen Run from Shin-Osaka Station one stop west to Shin-Kōbe Station (from ¥1500, 13 minutes), but from central Osaka it's easier to get the **JR Kōbe line** from Osaka Station to Kōbe's central Sannomiya Station (¥410, 22 to 27 minutes).

Hankyū Kōbe line *Tokkyū* (limited express) trains run from Hankyū Umeda Station to Kōbe's

Sannomiya Station (¥320, 30 minutes) and are usually less crowded than the JR trains.

To/From Nara

JR Yamatoji line *Kaisoku* (express) trains run from Tennōji Station to JR Nara Station (¥470, 35 minutes) via Hōryū-ji (¥460, 25 minutes).

Kintetsu Nara line *Kaisoku* trains run from Namba (Kintetsu Namba Station) to Kintetsu Nara Station (¥560, 40 minutes).

ℹ Getting Around

BICYCLE

Hub Chari (📱 070-5436-2892; http://hubchari-english.jimdo.com; per hr/day ¥200/1000) rents city bikes at several stations around town. It's run by an NGO that supports Osaka's homeless community.

TRAIN & SUBWAY

Trains and subways should get you everywhere you need to go (unless you stay out past midnight, when they top running).

The JR Kanjō-sen – the Osaka loop line – makes a circuit south of JR Osaka Station, though most sights fall in the middle of it.

There are eight subway lines, but the one that short-term visitors will find most useful is the Midō-suji (red) line, running north–south and stopping at Shin-Osaka, Umeda (next to Osaka Station), Shinsaibashi, Namba and Tennōji stations. Single rides cost ¥180 to ¥370 (half-price for children).

KŌBE　神戸

📞 078 / POP 1,537,860

Perched on a hillside sloping down to the sea, Kōbe is one of Japan's most attractive and cosmopolitan cities. It was a maritime gateway from the earliest days of trade with China and home to one of the first foreign communities after Japan reopened to the world in the mid-19th century.

Kōbe's relatively small size makes it a pleasure for casual wandering and stopping in its high-quality restaurants and cafes. The most pleasant neighbourhoods to explore are Kitano-chō, Nankinmachi Chinatown and, after dark, the bustling nightlife districts around Sannomiya Station.

Kōbe's two main gateways are Sannomiya and Shin-Kōbe stations, with easy access to sights, lodging and dining on foot or a short train ride away. *Shinkansen* trains stop at Shin-Kōbe Station, uphill in the northeast corner of the city centre – a quick subway ride or 20-minute walk connects the two stations.

KANSAI KŌBE

⊙ Sights

At Sannomiya or Shin-Kōbe Stations, pick up a city map at one of the tourist information offices there. Shin-Kōbe is closest to Kitano-chō and the Nunobiki area, while most other sights are easier from Sannomiya. For the Nada-gogō neighbourhood of sake brewers, you'll want to take the Hanshin train line.

Kitano-chō   AREA

(北野町; Map p384; ijinkan ¥350-750, combination tickets ¥1300-3000; ◉most ijinkan open 9am-6pm, to 5pm Oct-Mar; 🅢 Shin-Kōbe, 🆁 Shin-Kōbe) For generations of Japanese tourists, this pleasant, hilly neighbourhood *is* Kōbe, thanks to the dozen or so well-preserved homes of (mostly) Western trading families and diplomats who settled here during the Meiji period. Its winding streets, nostalgic brick- and weatherboard-built *ijinkan* (literally 'foreigners' houses'), cafes, restaurants and, yes, souvenir shops are great for exploring. All lend a European-American atmosphere, though admittedly it's probably less intriguing for Western visitors than for Japanese.

Not sure you want to invest the time or effort? Stop for a coffee at the **Starbucks** (スターバックス異人館; Map p384; ☎078-230-6302; 3-1-31 Kitano-chō; ◉8am-10pm; 🆁Sannomiya) concept store in a former *ijinkan* c 1907. If you like it, continue uphill to the rest of the *ijinkan*.

Nunobiki Falls   WATERFALL

(布引の滝, Nunobikinotaki; 🅢 Shin-Kōbe, 🆁 Shin-Kōbe) 🆓 You'd never guess that such a beautiful natural sanctuary could sit so close to the city. This revered waterfall in four sections (the longest is 43m tall) has been the subject of art, poetry and worship for centuries – some of the poems are reproduced on stone tablets at the site. It's accessible by a steep 400m path, from Shin-Kōbe Station. Take the ground-floor exit, turn left and walk under the station building to the path.

Ikuta Shrine   SHINTO SHRINE

(生田神社, Ikuta Jinja; Map p384; ☎078-321-3851; 1-2-1 Shimo-Yamate-dōri; ◉7am-sunset; 🆁Sannomiya) 🆓 Said to date from AD 201, this peaceful, wooden shrine has played a key role in sake-brewing history; it has survived civil wars (notably as a hideout for the Heike clan) and WWII, and been a gathering place for residents after natural disasters such as the 1995 earthquake. Plaques in front of the main building commemorate generations of emperors' visits, and around the back a forest and landmark camphor tree provide a break from the city's bustle.

City Hall Observation Lobby   VIEWPOINT

(市役所展望ロビー; Map p384; ☎078-331-8181; 6-5-1 Kanō-chō, Chūō-ku; ◉8.15am-10pm Mon-Fri, 10am-10pm Sat & Sun; 🅢 Sannomiya Hanadoke-mae, 🆁Sannomiya) 🆓 Get a bird's eye orientation to the city (and appreciate its breadth) from the 24th floor of Kōbe City Hall. It's particularly romantic and impressive around sunset as the sky changes colours and the city lights up at your feet. During the day, weather permitting, you can see all the way to Kansai International Airport across Osaka Bay.

Kōbe City Museum   MUSEUM

(神戸市立博物館, Kōbe Shiritsu Hakubutsukan; Map p384; ☎078-391-0035; www.city.kobe.lg.jp/culture/culture/institution/museum; 24 Kyōmachi; admission ¥200, special exhibitions up to ¥1000; ◉10am-5pm Tue-Sun, longer hours during special exhibitions; 🆁Sannomiya) Ground yourself in Kōbe's history as a trading port and east–west meeting place, via art and artefacts with decent English signage. Items show foreign influence from clocks and oil lamps to hairstyles. It's pricey during special exhibitions but worth it, especially when they include the museum's collection of *namban* (literally 'southern barbarian') art, a school of painting that developed when early Jesuit missionaries taught Western painting techniques to Japanese students. The Greek revival-style building dates from 1935.

Nankinmachi   AREA

(南京町, Chinatown; Map p384; 🅢 Kaigan line to Kyūkyoryūchi-Daimaru-mae, 🆁JR or Hanshin lines to Motomachi) Four traditional gates mark the entrances to this gaudy, bustling, unabashedly touristy collection of Chinese restaurants and trinket and medicinal herb stores. The offerings should be familiar to anyone who's visited Chinatowns elsewhere, it's fun for a stroll, particularly at night when lights illuminate elaborately painted shop facades. Restaurants tend toward the overpriced and may disappoint sophisticated palates (set meals from about ¥850), although it's one of the few places in Japan where street snacking is condoned (snacks from about ¥200).

Kōbe Maritime Museum
& Kawasaki Good Times World   MUSEUM

(神戸海洋博物館 ＆カワサキワールド, Kōbe Kaiyō Hakubutsukan & Kawasaki Wārudo; ☎078-327-5401; www.khi.co.jp/kawasakiworld; 2-2 Hatoba-chō,

Kōbe

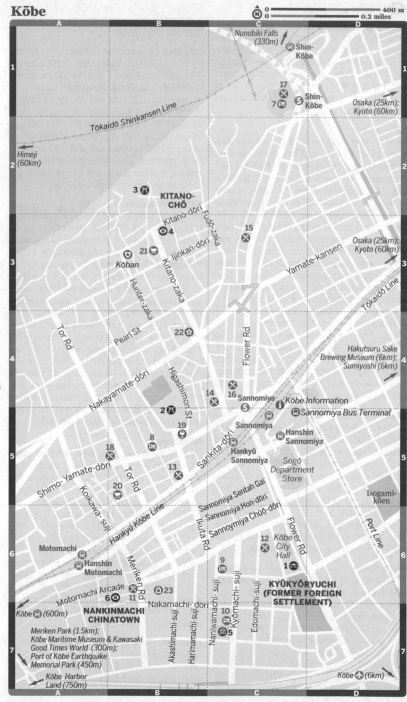

KANSAI KŌBE

0 400 m
0 0.2 miles

Nunobiki Falls (330m)

Shin-Kōbe

Osaka (25km);
Kyoto (60km)

Tōkaidō Shinkansen Line

Himeji (60km)

KITANO-CHŌ

Kitano-dōri

Ijinkan-dōri

Kōban

Hunter-zaka

Kitano-zaka

Fudō-zaka

Yamate-kansen

Osaka (25km);
Kyoto (60km)

Tōkaidō Line

Tor Rd

Pearl St

Nakayamate-dōri

Higashimon St

Flower Rd

Hakutsuru Sake
Brewing Museum (6km);
Sumiyoshi (6km)

Sannomiya

Kōbe Information

Sannomiya Bus Terminal

Sankita-dōri

Hankyū
Sannomiya

Hanshin
Sannomiya

Shimo-Yamate-dōri

Tor Rd

Koikawa-suji

Hankyū Kōbe Line

Sannomiya Sentah Gai

Sannomiya Hon-dōri

Sannoymiya Chūō-dōri

Sogō
Department
Store

Isogami-kōen

Port Line

Motomachi

Hanshin
Motomachi

Meriken Rd

Motomachi Arcade

Nakamachi-dōri

Akashimachi-suji

Harimamachi-suji

Naniwamachi-suji

Ikuta Rd

Kyomachi-suji

Edomachi-suji

Flower Rd

Kōbe
City
Hall

KYŪKYŌRYUCHI
(FORMER FOREIGN
SETTLEMENT)

NANKINMACHI
CHINATOWN

Kōbe (600m)

Meriken Park (1.5km);
Kōbe Maritime Museum & Kawasaki
Good Times World (300m);
Port of Kōbe Earthquake
Memorial Park (450m)

Kōbe Harbor
Land (750m)

Kōbe (6km)

Kōbe

Sights
1 City Hall Observation Lobby C6
2 Ikuta Shrine B5
3 Kitano Tenman-jinja B2
4 Kitano-chō B3
5 Kōbe City Museum C7
6 Nankinmachi B6

Sleeping
7 ANA Crowne Plaza Hotel Kōbe C1
8 B Kōbe B5
9 Hotel Trusty Kōbe Kyūkyoryuchi C6
10 Oriental Hotel C7

Eating
11 Daichi B6
12 Grill Jūjiya C6
13 Isuzu Bakery B5

14 Isuzu Bakery C4
   Kōbe Plaisir .... (see 8)
15 Mikami C3
16 R Valentino C4
17 Shin-Kōbe Oriental Avenue C1
18 Wanto Burger B5

Drinking & Nightlife
19 Izn't B5
20 Modernark B5
   Sake Yashiro .... (see 19)
21 Starbucks Ijinkan B3

Entertainment
22 Sone B4

Shopping
23 Daimaru Department Store B6

Chūō-ku; admission ¥600, Kōbe Port Tower combination ticket ¥1000; ⊙10am-5pm Tue-Sun; Ⓢ Kaigan line to Minato Motomachi, Ⓡ Kōbe or Motomachi) This building has two parts: an extensive collection of high-quality model ships and displays in the old-school **Maritime Museum**, and the fun, hands-on experience of modern technology in **Kawasaki Good Times World**. You've probably heard of Kawasaki's motorcycles, but this Kōbe-born company has also influenced tech from trains to robotics and aerospace. Clamber aboard a section of the original *shinkansen,* early aeroplanes and some very cool bikes. Yes, it's corporate promo, but it's also pretty impressive.

The museums are in Meriken Park, a seaside location crowned by the 108m-tall, metal lattice **Kōbe Port Tower** (1963), a city landmark, and the Earthquake Memorial Park.

Port of Kōbe
Earthquake Memorial Park MONUMENT
(神戸港震災メモリアルパーク; Meriken Park; Ⓢ Kaigan line to Minato Motomachi, Ⓡ Motomachi) **FREE** At 5.46am on 17 January 1995 the Great Hanshin Earthquake struck this region. It was Japan's strongest since the Great Kantō Quake of 1923 devastated Tokyo. Kōbe bore the brunt of the damage – 6000 killed, 40,000-plus casualties, toppled expressways and nearly 300,000 lost buildings. This simple, open-air, harbourside museum tells the story in artefacts and a video presentation in English. Most striking is a section of the dock that was left as it was after that devastating day.

Hakutsuru Sake Brewery Museum BREWERY
(白鶴造酒資料館; ☑078-822-8907; www.hakutsuru-sake.com; 4-5-5 Sumiyoshi Minami-machi, Higashinada-ku; ⊙9.30am-4.30pm; Ⓡ Hanshin main line to Sumiyoshi) **FREE** Hakutsuru is the dominant sake brewer in Kōbe's Nada-gogō district, one of Japan's major sake-brewing centres. The self-guided tour through its historic, wooden former brewery building (the current, giant brewery is behind it) is a fascinating look into traditional sake-making methods; life-sized models appear on old equipment, and a pamphlet and videos in English help explain. A free sake tasting is available after the tour.

Take the Hanshin line eight stops east from Sannomiya to Sumiyoshi Station (¥190, seven minutes if you switch trains at Mikage, 15 minutes if you take the *futsū* (local) train; express trains don't stop). Exit the station, walk south to the elevated highway and cross the overpass, make a U-turn at the bottom of the steps, take the first left, then a right; the entrance is on the right. Use the blue-and-white crane logo atop the factory as your guide.

Akashi Kaikyō Bridge BRIDGE
(明石海峡大橋; ☑Exhibition Centre 078-784-3339, Maikō Marine Promenade 078-785-5090; 2051 Higashi-Maikō-chō, Tarumi-ku; ¥310; ⊙promenade 9am-6pm, exhibition centre 9.15am-5pm Mar–mid-Jul & Sep-Nov, to 6pm mid-Jul–Aug, to 4.30pm Dec-Feb; Ⓡ JR Kōbe line to Maikō) West of central Kōbe is Japan's tallest bridge (283m), across the Akashi Strait. See it up close at the **Maikō Marine Promenade**, a 320m walkway 47m above sea level, over the bridge's northern end – try not to freak out over the glass floors!

KANSAI KŌBE

An indoor lounge features a 360-degree camera from atop a stanchion. Nearby, **Akashi Kaikyō Bridge Exhibition Centre** explains the science behind bridge building, through videos in English and exhibits including a cross-section of the 1.1m-diameter main cable.

🎊 Festivals & Events

Luminarie   LIGHT SHOW
(神戸ルミナリエ; ⊙ early Dec) Kōbe's biggest annual event is held every evening in early December in memory of the 6000 people who perished in the 1995 Great Hanshin Earthquake (p385), and to celebrate the city's miraculous recovery. The streets southwest of Kōbe City Hall are decorated with countless illuminated metal archways, which when viewed from within look like the interior of some otherworldly cathedral. Check with tourist offices for exact dates.

🛏 Sleeping

Although Kōbe is easily visited as a day trip from Osaka or Kyoto, an overnight stay will allow you to have those fantastic night time views and experience the city's nightlife. Hotels are concentrated around Sannomiya.

Hotel Trusty
Kōbe Kyūkyoryuchi   BOUTIQUE HOTEL ¥¥
(ホテルトラスティ神戸旧居留地; Map p384; ☑ 078-330-9111; http://ct.rion.mobi/trusty.kobe; 63 Naniwamachi, Chūō-ku; s/d/tw from ¥9800/ 15,400/18,900; ⊜ ❊ @; ℝ Sannomiya) The name screams 'standard-issue business hotel', but this intimate little hotel in Kyūkyoryuchi (the former foreigners' settlement) behind city hall is actually a super-stylish boutique property. Rooms are on the small side, but they are immaculate and have design touches. There's an indoor-outdoor terrace for breakfast or evening drinks.

★ Oriental Hotel   HOTEL ¥¥¥
(神戸旧居留地オリエンタルホテル;   Map p384; ☑ 078-326-1500; www.orientalhotel.jp; 25 Kyōmachi, Chūō-ku; r from ¥34,000; ❊ @; ℝ Sannomiya or Motomachi; Port Liner to Boeki Center) One of Japan's most historic hotels (1870), in Kyūkyoryuchi (the former foreigners' settlement), the Oriental was rebuilt after the 1995 earthquake and is now a sleek, elegant tower with a design sense deftly melding old Japan and new. Expect indulgent, English-speaking service and great views of the bay and mountains, from the 17th-storey lobby and restaurant. Significant discounts possible online.

Note: this hotel is not affiliated with Oriental hotels in other countries.

ANA Crowne Plaza Hotel Kōbe   HOTEL ¥¥¥
(ANAクラウンプラザ神戸; Map p384; ☑ 078-291-1121; www.anacrowneplaza-kobe.jp; 1-chome, Kitano-chō, Chūō-ku; s/d or tw from ¥9500/14,500; ⊜ ❊ @ 🛜; Ⓢ Shin-Kōbe, ℝ Shin-Kōbe) Survey the bright lights of Kōbe from this 37-storey tower perched atop the city. Adjacent to JR Shin-Kōbe Station, the Crowne Plaza offers clean, spacious rooms (even if the bathroom fixtures feel a bit dated), English-speaking staff, multiple bars and restaurants, and a pool and fitness centre (surcharge ¥1080). More restaurants are downstairs in the **Oriental Avenue shopping centre** (新神戸オリエンタ ルアベニュー; Map p384; http://shinkobe.net; 1 Kitano-chō; prices vary; ⊙ shop hours vary).

🍴 Eating

Kōbe is famous throughout Japan for beef, Japanese-Western fusion cuisine and tasty bakeries, a heritage of early Western residents. Best restaurant browsing is around Sannomiya Station (with plenty of *izakaya* surrounding Ikuta Shrine) and Nankinmachi Chinatown. Department-store food floors such as Sogo and Daimaru are happy grazing ground for take-out foods and some sit-down restaurants. Kōbe is also well-known for sake; the city's Nada-gogō district produces about one-third of Japan's total output.

Isuzu Bakery   BAKERY ¥
(イスズベーカリー; Map p384; ☑ 078-391-3963; www.isuzu-bakery.jp; 1-8-18 Nakayamate-dōri, Chūō-ku; bread & pastries ¥120-560; ⊙ 10am-11pm Mon-Thu, to midnight Fri & Sat, to 10pm Sun; ℝ Sannomiya) Kōbe is famous for baked goods, and this award-winning bakery (open since 1946) has been featured on national TV for creative treats like *toreron* (70cm-long sausage roll), *curry pan* (doughnut with curried beef tendon) and choco dome (exactly what it sounds like). Grab a tray and tongs to make your selections cafeteria-style, then pay at the cashier.

Other locations include **Ikuta Road** (イ スズベーカリー生田ロード店; Map p384; 078-333-4180; 2-1-14 Kitanagasa-dōri, Chūō-ku; ⊙ 9am-11pm).

Mikami   INTERNATIONAL ¥
(味加味; Map p384; ☑ 078-242-5200; www. kobe-mikami.com; 2-5-9 Kanō-chō; mains ¥480-1800, set meals from around ¥850; ⊙ 11.30am-3pm & 5-11pm Wed-Mon; 🚭; ℝ Sannomiya, ℝ Shin-Kōbe) This cheerfully eclectic and friendly

restaurant offers a giant menu of good-value lunches and dinners: noodles (Italian and Japanese), pizza, Chinese dishes and generous *teishoku* (set meals), plus plenty of beer and cocktails. It's on the block behind Green Hill Hotel; look for the many potted plants and the small English sign.

★ **Wanto Burger**   BURGERS ¥¥
(ワントバーガー; Map p384; ☑ 078-392-5177; www.wantoburger.com; 3-10-6 Shimo-Yamate-dōri; burgers ¥1080-3800; ⊙ noon-10pm Mon-Sat, to 5pm Sun; ⓡ Sannomiya) Run by a cool young crew, this spot looks like a vintage US diner, with long counter and a few tables, but that's where the resemblance ends. It's utterly different in both taste and price because the burgers are made with Kōbe beef (you can also order somewhat less expensive varieties of *wagyū*). Bonuses: cool tunes and cocktails!

Daichi   STEAK ¥¥
(大地; Map p384; ☑ 078-333-6688; www. koubegyuu.com/en/shop/daichi; 1-1-3 Motomachi-dori, Chūō-ku; steak meals from ¥2500; ⊙ 11am-9pm; Ⓢ Kaigan Line to Kyūkyorūchi-Daimaru-mae, ⓡ Motomachi) *Teppanyaki* steak (grilled on a steel plate) is notoriously expensive, but this friendly spot serves it at a fraction of the price charged at other places. Award-winning Kōbe and *wagyū* beef comes with simply grilled veggies, and lunches include soup, salad and rice. Prices vary by grade of meat and serving size: ¥2500 for 80g of basic *wagyū*, to ¥58,000 for 300g of Chateaubriand. Look for the giant bulls just inside Chinatown's east gate.

Grill Jūjiya   INTERNATIONAL ¥¥
(グリル十字屋; Map p384; ☑ 078-331-5455; 96 Edomachi, Chūō-ku; mains ¥850-2300; ⊙ 11am-8pm Mon-Sat; ⓡ Sannomiya) In this city thick with east-west heritage, this old-fashioned charmer specialises in *yōshoku,* early Japanese takes on Western cooking: beef stew, grilled chicken, fried seafood, *hayashi* rice (rice with hashed beef, onions and savoury sauce). Enjoy with Japanese craft beers. It's been in business since the 1930s, though the building is newer.

R Valentino   ITALIAN ¥¥
(アール ヴァレンティーノ; Map p384; ☑ 078-332-1268; www.r-valentino.com; 3rd fl, 4-5-13 Kanō-chō, Chūō-ku; mains ¥950-3200, lunch/dinner set menus from ¥1800/4000; ⊙ 11.30am-2pm & 5.30-9pm; ☑ⓘ; ⓡ Sannomiya) Run by Italians and popular with Japanese and foreign visitors, this easygoing eatery on a Sannomiya side street is casual, comfortable and cosy, with stone walls and rustic furniture. Choose from

KŌBE BEEF

For foodies worldwide, the name Kōbe is synonymous with great beef. The delicate marbling of Kōbe beef (Kōbe *gyū* in Japanese) lends a supple texture and, many say, sweetness that other varieties of beef lack. It accounts for a mere 0.06% of beef consumption nationwide, which helps explain its sky-high price. Kōbe beef is actually just one of many types of *wagyū* (Japanese beef); read more about Japan's premium beef in Japanese Cuisine (p846). There's no shortage of places in to try it yourself. We like **Kōbe Plaisir**, **Daichi** and **Wanto Burger**.

pasta and brick-oven pizza options, plus meat and fish mains. Eager staff help explain the specials and make recommendations.

★ **Kōbe Plaisir**   STEAK ¥¥¥
(神戸プレジール; Map p384; ☑ 078-571-0141; www.kobe-plaisir.jp; 2-11-5 Shimo-Yamate-dōri, Chūō-ku; lunch/dinner set menus from ¥3240/6480; ⊙ 11.30am-3pm & 5pm-10.30pm; Ⓢ Sannomiya, ⓡ Sannomiya) You can't get any more locavore than this – ingredients come directly from the local branch of the Japan Agricultural Cooperative. You choose your preparation of Kōbe or other steak – *seiro-mushi* (steamed), *teppanyaki* (grilled on a steel plate) or *shabu-shabu* (thinly sliced beef cooked with vegetables in boiling water and then dipped in sauce) – and sit back as a multicourse meat-and-veg feast unfolds before you. It's in the lobby beneath the **B Kōbe hotel** (ザ・ビー神戸; Map p384; ☑ 078-333-4880; www.theb-hotels.com/the-b-kobe; 2-11-5 Shimo-YamateB Kōbe, Chūō-ku; s/d from ¥13,000/22,000; ☺ ❋ @ 🛜).

🍷 Drinking & Nightlife

Kōbe has a large foreign community and a number of bars that see mixed Japanese and foreign crowds. Come evening, some cafes transform into bars.

Sake Yashiro   BAR
(さけやしろ; Map p384; ☑ 078-334-7339; 4-6-15 Ikuta-chō; ⊙ 4pm-11.30pm; ⓡ Sannomiya) Kōbe is one of Japan's great sake-producing cities, and this chill little standing bar and restaurant located just steps from Ikuta Shrine is a great spot to sample the varieties produced here. It stocks over 90 choices, including about 50

from local brewers. There's also a changing food menu of seasonal dishes.

Izn't
CLUB

(イズント; Map p384; ☎078-334-3040; http://iznt.net; 4th fl, 1-1-8 Shimo-Yamate-dōri; ◷5pm-midnight Sun, to 1am Mon-Thu, to 2am Fri & Sat; ☒Sannomiya) This large and lively bar brings Kōbe's Japanese and foreign community together with a rotation of salsa dancing, live bands, open mic, acoustic nights, sports broadcasts, cocktails, beer, wine and frozen mojitos. There's an international menu of bar snacks, from pizzas and burritos to tandoori wraps and sushi. And it's mostly nonsmoking. Enter off Higashimon Street.

Modernark
CAFE

(モダナーク; Map p384; ☎078-391-3060; 3-11-15 Kitanagasa-dōri, Chūō-ku; ◷11.30am-10pm; ☒Motomachi) Adorably funky, old-school cafe with a wood-accented room, glassed-in verandah and good-for-you gifts for sale. Modernark bills itself as a 'pharm cafe' and emphasises vegetarian and vegan options with its wraps, salads, cakes, coffees and teas (meals from ¥900). Look for the thicket of potted trees out front.

☆ Entertainment

Sone
JAZZ

(ソネ; Map p384; ☎078-221-2055; www.kobe-sone.com; 1-24-10 Nakayamate-dōri; cover charge from ¥1250; ◷5pm-midnight; ☒Sannomiya) Kōbe's go-to spot for jazz brings in Japanese and international performers, usually with four different acts nightly, and pub-style food and drink. Cover charges can vary, but the Sunday afternoon special snags you music and a beer for a mere ¥1000. The wooden, Bavarian-style interior might feel a bit dated, but it's been in business since 1969 – so why argue with success?

❶ Information

Kōbe Information (神戸市総合インフォメーションセンター; Map p384; ☎078-322-0220; www.feel-kobe.jp; Sannomiya Station; ◷9am-7pm; ☒Sannomiya) The city's main tourist information office is on the ground floor outside of JR Sannomiya Station's east gate. There's a smaller information counter on the 2nd floor of Shin-Kōbe Station, outside the main *shinkansen* gate. Both carry reasonably good free maps of the city, pamphlets and the *Kōbe Welcome Coupon* booklet, with discounts to sights and attractions.

❶ Getting There & Away

AIR

Itami Osaka Airport

There are direct limousine buses to/from Osaka's Itami Airport (p380) (¥1050, 40 minutes). In Kōbe, the buses stop on the southwestern side of Sannomiya Station.

Kōbe Airport

Kōbe Airport (www.kairport.co.jp) is served by ANA, Air Do, Skymark Airlines and Solaseed Air with most flights to Tokyo (Haneda; ¥12,890, one hour and 10 minutes), Sapporo (Chitose; ¥21,900, two hours) and Okinawa (Naha; ¥22,900, 2¼ hours).

Kansai International Airport

By train, the fastest way is the JR *shinkaisoku* to/from Osaka Station, and the JR *kanku kaisoku* between Osaka Station and the airport (total cost ¥1660, total time 1¾ hours with good connections). There is also a direct limousine bus to/from the airport (¥2000, 1¼ hours), which is more convenient if you have a lot of luggage. In Kōbe, the airport bus stop is on the southwestern side of Sannomiya Station

BOAT

The most fun connection between Kansai International Airport (KIX) and Kōbe is via the **Kōbe-Kansai Airport Bay Shuttle** (神戸関西空港ベイ・シャトル; www.kobe-access.jp; ◷5.30am-11.35pm) high-speed boat, which drops you off by Kōbe Airport (adult/concession ¥1850/1000, 31 minutes, approximately hourly), from where you can then take the **Port Liner** (ポートライナー; www.knt-liner.co.jp) monorail to the city.

There are regular ferries from Kōbe to Shinmoji (Kitakyūshū, Fukuoka Prefecture; from ¥6170) with **Hankyū Ferry** (阪九フェリー; ☎0120-56-3268; www.han9f.co.jp) and to Ōita (near Beppu on Kyūshū; from ¥12,000) with **Ferry Sunflower** (フェリーさんふらわあ; ☎toll free 0120-56-3268; www.ferry-sunflower.co.jp).

Orange Ferry (☎06-6612-1811; www.orange-ferry.co.jp) connects Kōbe Rokkō Port with Niihama Port (Ehime Prefecture, Shikoku; 2nd-class from ¥6690), Tuesday through to Saturday.

BUS

Willer Express (ウィラー・エクスプレス; http://willerexpress.com) overnight buses connect Kōbe's **Sannomiya Bus Terminal** (Map p384) and Tokyo (Shinjuku and Tokyo Stations). The journey costs from ¥5800 and takes 8½ hours.

TRAIN

Sannomiya Station is the hub for rail travel to/from Osaka on the private Hankyū and Hanshin lines and most JR trains. On the JR Tōkaidō line, *shinkaisoku* (special rapid trains) are the fastest between Sannomiya and Osaka Station (¥410, 20 minutes). Of the private lines, Hankyū is more convenient, connecting Kōbe Sannomiya Station and Hankyū Umeda Station (*tokkyū*, ¥320, 27 minutes), near Osaka Station.

Unless you're on the *shinkansen*, most trains to Kyoto require a transfer in Osaka or Umeda.

Shin-Kōbe Station is on the Tōkaidō/San-yō and Kyūshū *shinkansen* lines. Destinations include Fukuoka (Hakata Station; ¥14,160, 2¼ hours), Tokyo (¥14,160, 2¾ hours), and other major stops including Osaka, Kyoto, Nagoya, Hiroshima and Kagoshima.

ℹ Getting Around

JR, Hankyū and Hanshin railway lines run east to west through town. The Seishin-Yamate subway line connects Shin-Kōbe and Sannomiya Stations (¥210, two minutes), or you can walk it in about 20 minutes. Another subway line (the Kaigan line) runs from just south of Sannomiya Station to the Harbor Land area to the south.

A city-loop bus service (per ride/day pass ¥260/660) makes a grand-circle tour of most of the city's sightseeing spots and main stations; look for the retro-style green buses.

Kobelin (⌨ toll free 0120-040-587; www.kobelin.jp; per hr ¥100, each additional 30min ¥100, per day ¥500), the new municipal bike system, has stations all over town; look for red bikes with the Hanshin Tigers baseball team logo. To use, first register your credit card using your smart phone.

HIMEJI　　姫路

⌨ 079 / POP 535,807

A visit to Himeji in the Hyōgo Prefecture is a must for any lover of Japanese history and in particular of Japanese castles. The recently renovated Himeji Castle, the finest in all of Japan, towers over this quiet city. Nearby, Kōkō-en is a rambling collection of nine meticulously reconstructed samurai houses and their gardens.

You can visit Himeji, on the *shinkansen* route, as a day trip from Kyoto, Nara, Osaka or Kōbe, or as a stopover en route to Okayama or Hiroshima. The city is flat and easily walkable, or free rental cycles are available from the tourist information office at the train station.

◉ Sights

★ **Himeji-jō**　　CASTLE

(姫路城, Himeji Castle; Map p389; 68 Honmachi; adult/child ¥1000/300, combination ticket with Kōkō-en ¥1040/360; ⊘ 9am-5pm Sep-May, to 6pm

Himeji

KANSAI HIMEJI

Himeji

Jun-Aug) Japan's most magnificent castle, Himeji-jō, is a Unesco World Heritage Site, national treasure and one of only a handful of original castles remaining (most are modern concrete reconstructions). It's nicknamed Shirasagi-jō ('White Egret Castle') for its lustrous white plaster exterior and stately form on a hill rising from the plain. There's a five-storey main *tenshū* (keep) and three smaller keeps, all surrounded by moats and defensive walls punctuated with rectangular, circular and triangular openings for firing guns and shooting arrows.

The main keep's walls also feature *ishiotoshi* – narrow openings that allowed defenders to pour boiling water or oil onto anyone trying to scale the walls after making it past the other defences. We recommend visitors to pay the admission charge and enter the castle by legitimate means!

Although there have been fortifications in Himeji since 1333, today's castle was built in 1580 by Toyotomi Hideyoshi and enlarged some 30 years later by Ikeda Terumasa. Ikeda was awarded the castle by Tokugawa Ieyasu when the latter's forces defeated the Toyotomi armies. In the following centuries it was home to 48 successive lords. More recently, the castle reopened in 2014 after a five-year renovation.

It takes approximately 1½ hours to follow the arrow-marked route around the castle. Last entry is an hour before closing.

★ **Kōkō-en** GARDENS
(好古園; Map p389; 68 Honmachi; adult/child ¥300/150, combination ticket with Himeji Castle ¥1040/360; ⊙9am-6pm May-Aug, to 5pm Sep-Apr) Across Himeji Castle's western moat is this stunning reconstruction of the former samurai quarters. Nine Edo period–style homes boast gardens with various combinations of waterfalls, koi ponds, intricately pruned trees, bamboo, flowering shrubs and a wisteria-covered arbor. If it feels like you're on a movie set amid the stone and plaster walls lining the paths, you would be right; many Japanese historical dramas have been shot here. It is particularly lovely in spring and during the autumn foliage season.

In the teahouse, ¥500 gets you *matcha* (powdered green tea) and a Japanese sweet, presented by a kimono-clad server, and the restaurant **Kassui-ken** (活水軒) serves a *bentō* (boxed meal) of *anago* (conger eel, a local speciality; ¥2080).

★☆ Festivals & Events

Nada-no-Kenka Matsuri FESTIVAL
(灘のけんか祭り; ⊙14-15 Oct) Nada-no-Kenka involves a battle between three *mikoshi* (palanquins), which are battered against each other until one smashes. Try to go on the second day, when the festival reaches its peak (around noon). It is held five minutes' walk from Shirahamanomiya Station (10 minutes from Himeji Station on the Sanyō-Dentetsu line); follow the crowds.

🛏 Sleeping

Himeji is easily visited on a day trip from elsewhere in Kansai, but an overnight stay at one of the hotels just south of the station can give you a head start on the morning crowds.

Dormy Inn Himeji BUSINESS HOTEL ¥¥
(ドーミーイン姫路; Map p389; www.hotespa. net/hotels/himeji; 160-2 Toyozawa-chō; s/d/tw from ¥7800/11,000/15,600; ⊛❄@🅿🛜) Despite compact rooms, this 12-storey hotel has lots going for it: top-floor indoor-outdoor onsen baths (though only showers in most rooms), sauna, laundry machines, crisp, modern-meets-rustic style, Chinese-style PJs instead of the usual *yukata* (bathrobe), all nonsmoking rooms and free ramen service nightly. The breakfast buffet (¥1200 surcharge) includes local specialties like *anago* (eel) over rice and almond toast.

It's one block south of the station, behind the Hotel Nikko.

★ **Hotel Nikkō Himeji** HOTEL ¥¥¥
(ホテル日航姫路; Map p389; ☎079-222-2231; www.hotelnikkohimeji.co.jp; 100 Minami-ekimae-chō; s/d from ¥13,000/20,000; ⊛❄@🛜🏊) Across from the station's south exit, Himeji's top hotel offers stylish (if somewhat dated) and fairly spacious rooms with Western-style bathtubs, several restaurants (Japanese, Chinese, Western) and a bar with beautifully framed castle views. Our favourite part is the fitness center (¥1500 surcharge) with well-equipped gym, 20m pool, jacuzzi, sauna and Japanese-style common baths. Significant discounts may be available online.

✕ Eating & Drinking

Menme NOODLES ¥
(めんめ; Map p389; ☎079-225-0118; 68 Honmachi; noodles ¥550-950; ⊙noon-6pm Thu-Tue; 🅿) They make their own noodles at this homey, cheerful little joint on the main

street a few minutes' walk from the castle. It's not fancy, but it serves an honest, tasty bowl of udon with your choice of toppings to power you through the day. Look for the white *noren* (doorway curtain) showing noodles being rolled out.

★Fukutei
JAPANESE ¥¥

(福亭; Map p389; ☑ 079-222-8150; 75 Kamei-chō; dishes ¥480-980, set menus lunch ¥1350-2700, dinner ¥3200-4000; ☺ 11.30am-2pm & 5-10pm Mon-Fri, 11.30am-2.30pm & 5-9pm Sat & Sun; ⓞ) This approachable contemporary restaurant of Japanese stucco walls and marble floors is a great choice for a civilised experience. The speciality are the set menus: a little sashimi, some tempura and the usual nibbles on the side. At lunch try the daily special *omakase-zen* (tasting set), *kaisen-don* (seafood donburi) or *oden* set (fish cake and veggie hotpot).

It's just east of the Miyuki-dōri shopping arcade.

★Kokoromi
BAR

(こころみ; Map p389; ☑ 079-280-6172; www. kokoromi.in; 125 Minami-ekimae, Vierra Arcade; sake ¥110-1250; ☺ 1-9pm Tue-Fri, noon-8pm Sat & Sun; ☺) It's all about local sake at this modern and sophisticated standing bar, which stocks some 270 varieties from Hyōgo, Himeji's prefecture. Touch screens let you search and order in English by taste, price and grade (search West Harima for Himeji) and your 65ml pour also comes with an English explanation card and a picture of the bottle for future reference. Background music: cool jazz.

It's in the Vierra arcade just east of the train station; walk past Daily Yamazaki convenience store, and you'll see sake casks on your left.

❶ Information

Pick up the *Places of Interest Downtown Himeji* map or *Himeji Tourist Guide & Map* from the **Himeji Tourist Information Office** (姫路市観光案内所 [姫路観光なびポート]; Map p389; ☑ 079-287-0003; Ground Fl, Himeji Station; ☺ 9am-7pm). You can also book volunteer guides here or borrow bicycles for free – first come, first served.

❶ Getting There & Away

If you've got a Japan Rail Pass or are in a hurry, take the *shinkansen* from Kyoto (from ¥4770, 55 minutes), Hiroshima (¥7790, one hour), Shin-Osaka (¥3240, 35 minutes) and Shin-Kōbe (¥2600, 16 minutes). Otherwise, slower *shinkaisoku* trains on the JR Tōkaidō line run from Kyoto (¥2270, one hour and 34 minutes),

Osaka (¥1490, one hour) and Kōbe's Sannomiya Station (¥970, 40 minutes).

NARA & AROUND

From the emperors to sake, much of Japanese history started in Nara Prefecture. The city of Nara was Japan's first permanent capital and retains an important place in the nation's cultural legacy.

Southern Nara-ken is the birthplace of imperial rule and is rich in historical sites easily accessible on day trips from Osaka, Kyoto or Nara; make sure to set out early. Of particular interest are the *kofun* (burial mounds) that mark the graves of Japan's first emperors, concentrated around Asuka. Elsewhere, several isolated temples provide an escape from the crowds. Further afield, the historic refuge and mountaintop town of Yoshino is one of Japan's cherry blossom meccas.

Nara
奈良

☑ 0742 / POP 360,439

Japan's first permanent capital, Nara is one of the country's most rewarding destinations. With eight Unesco World Heritage Sites, it's second only to Kyoto as a repository of Japan's cultural legacy.

The centrepiece is the Daibutsu (Great Buddha), which rivals Mt Fuji and Kyoto's Golden Pavilion (Kinkaku-ji) as Japan's single most impressive sight. The Great Buddha is housed in Tōdai-ji, a soaring temple that presides over Nara-kōen, a park filled with other fascinating sights that lends itself to relaxed strolling amid greenery and tame deer.

Nara is also compact: it's quite possible to pack the highlights into one full day. Many people visit as a side trip from Kyoto, but with an overnight stay (there's high-quality accommodation for all budgets) you might spend one day around the city centre, another exploring west and southwest of here (areas called Nishinokyō and Ikaruga, respectively) and/or another exploring more far-flung historical destinations.

History

Nara is at the northern end of the Yamato Plain, where members of the Yamato clan rose to power as the original emperors of Japan. Until the 7th century, however, Japan had no permanent capital, as Shintō taboos concerning death stipulated that the capital

Nara

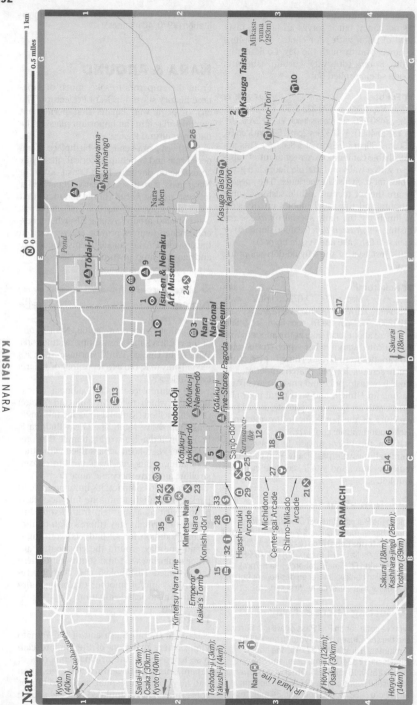

Nara

KANSAI NARA

be moved with the passing of each emperor. This practice died out under the influence of Buddhism and with the Taika reforms of 646, when the entire country came under imperial control.

At this time it was decreed that a permanent capital be built. Two locations were tried before a permanent capital was finally established at Nara (then known as Heijōkyō) in 710. 'Permanent' status, however, lasted a mere 75 years. When a priest named Dōkyō seduced an empress and nearly usurped the throne, it was decided to move the court out of reach of Nara's increasingly powerful clergy. The new capital was eventually established at Kyoto, about 35km north.

Although brief, the Nara period was extraordinarily vigorous in its absorption of influences from China, laying the foundations of Japanese culture and civilisation. Except for an assault on the area by the Taira clan in the 12th century, Nara was subsequently spared the periodic bouts of destruction wreaked upon Kyoto, and a number of magnificent buildings have survived.

⊙ Sights

Nara retains its 8th-century Chinese-style grid pattern of streets. There are two main train stations: JR Nara and Kintetsu Nara. JR Nara Station is a little west of the city centre (but still within walking distance of the sights), while Kintetsu Nara is right in the centre of town. Nara-kōen, which contains most of the important sights, is on the eastern side, against the bare flank of Wakakusa-yama mountain. It's easy to cover the city centre and the major attractions in nearby Nara-kōen on foot, although buses and taxis do ply the city.

Nara Visitor Center & Inn (p402) runs interesting experiential programs like tea ceremony and origami for free or a nominal charge.

⊙ Nara-kōen & Around

Many of Nara's most important sites are located around Nara-kōen (奈良公園), a fine park that occupies much of the eastern side of the city. The park is home to about 1200 deer, which in pre-Buddhist times were considered messengers of the gods and today enjoy the status of National Treasures. They roam the park and surrounding areas in search of handouts from tourists, often descending on petrified children who have the misfortune to be carrying food. You can buy *shika-sembei* (deer biscuits; ¥150) from vendors to feed to the deer, and *shika-no-fun* (deer poo) chocolates for yourself.

★ **Nara National Museum** MUSEUM

(奈良国立博物館, Nara Kokuritsu Hakubutsukan; Map p392; ☎ 050-5542-8600; www.narahaku.go. jp; 50 Noboriōji-chō; admission ¥520, special exhibitions ¥1120-1420; ☺ 9.30am-5pm, closed Mon) This world-class museum of Buddhist art is divided into two sections. Built in 1894 and strikingly renovated in 2016, the Nara Buddhist Sculpture Hall & Ritual Bronzes Gallery displays a rotating selection of about 100 *butsu-zō* (statues of Buddhas and bodhisattvas) at any one time, about half of which are national treasures or important cultural properties. Each image has detailed English explanations and the excellent booklet *Viewing Buddhist Sculptures* provides even more detail and is well worth the additional ¥500 donation.

Chinese bronzes in the ritual bronzes gallery are as old as the 15th century BC.

The newer east and west wings, a short walk away, contain the permanent collections (sculptures, paintings and calligraphy).

A special exhibition featuring the treasures of the Shōsō-in Hall, which holds the treasures of Tōdai-ji (p394), is held from late October to early November (dates vary slightly each year). The exhibits include priceless items from the cultures along the Silk Road. This exhibit (admission ¥1100) is well worth it, but be prepared for crowds.

Kōfuku-ji BUDDHIST TEMPLE

(興福寺; Map p392; www.kohfukuji.com; grounds free, Tōkondō ¥300, National Treasure Museum ¥600, combined ticket ¥800; ☺ grounds 24h, Tōkondō 9am-5pm) Another of Nara's sights on the Unesco World Heritage List, this temple was founded in Kyoto in AD 669 and relocated here in 710. The original Nara temple complex had 175 buildings, and although only a dozen remain after fires and destruction due to power struggles, many of those are national treasures. Two pagodas – one of three and the other of **five storeys** (五重塔; Map p392) – date from 1143 and 1426 respectively. The taller one is Japan's second tallest, outclassed by the one at Kyoto's **Tō-ji** (p302) by a few centimetres.

The temple grounds are free to visit, but some of the buildings require admission.

Among them, the Tōkondō (Eastern Golden Hall) is a national treasure dating from AD 726AD, rebuilt in 1415, and enshrining a variety of national treasure and Buddhist statuary. The Kōfuku-ji National Treasure Museum contains a variety of statues and art objects salvaged from previous structures. It is scheduled to close for renovation for all of 2017.

★ **Isui-en & Neiraku Art Museum** GARDENS

(依水園・寧楽美術館; Map p392; 74 Suimon-chō; admission museum & garden ¥900; ☺ 9.30am-4.30pm Wed-Mon, daily Apr, May, Oct & Nov) This exquisite, contemplative Meiji-era garden features abundant greenery, ponds and walkways with stepping stones designed for each to be observed as you walk, to appreciate their individual beauty. For ¥850 you can enjoy a cup of tea on tatami mats overlooking the garden. Admission covers the adjoining **Neiraku Art Museum**, displaying Chinese and Korean ceramics and bronzes in a quiet setting.

Yoshiki-en GARDENS

(吉城園; Map p392; 68 Noboriōji-chō; Japanese/foreign visitors ¥250/free; ☺ 9am-5pm Mar-Dec) FREE This garden, located next door to Isui-en (to the right as you enter), is a stunner. Originally a residence of the high priest of Tōdai-ji, the present garden was laid out in 1918 and contains a lovely thatched-roof cottage, a pond and several walking paths. It's particularly lovely in November and early December, when the maples turn a blazing crimson. Look for the small English sign.

★ **Tōdai-ji** BUDDHIST TEMPLE

(東大寺; Map p392; 406-1 Zōshi-chō; Daibutsu-den admission ¥500, combination ticket with Tōdai-ji Museum ¥800; ☺ Daibutsu-den 8am-4.30pm Nov-Feb, to 5pm Mar & Oct, 7.30am-5.30pm Apr-Sep) Nara's star attraction is the famous **Daibutsu (Great Buddha)**, centrepiece of this grand temple on the Unesco World Heritage List, with origins going back to AD 728. The Daibutsu statue itself is one of the largest bronze figures in the world and was originally cast in 746. The present statue, recast in the Edo period, stands just over 16m high and consists of 437 tonnes of bronze and 130kg of gold.

The Daibutsu is located in Tōdai-ji's Daibutsu-den (大仏殿, Great Buddha Hall), which itself is the largest wooden building in the world. Incredibly, the present structure, rebuilt in 1709, is a mere two-thirds of the size of the original. Except for the Daibutsu-den, most of Tōdai-ji's grounds can be visited free of charge.

The Daibutsu is an image of Dainichi Nyorai (also known as Vairocana Buddha), the cosmic Buddha believed to give rise to all worlds and their respective Buddhas. Historians believe that Emperor Shōmu ordered the building of the Buddha as a charm against smallpox, which ravaged Japan in preceding years. Over the centuries the statue took quite a beating from earthquakes and fires, losing its head a few times (note the slight difference in colour between the head and the body).

As you circle the statue towards the back, you'll see a wooden column with a hole through its base. Popular belief maintains that those who can squeeze through the hole, which is exactly the same size as one of the Great Buddha's nostrils, are ensured of enlightenment. There's usually a line of children waiting to give it a try and parents waiting to snap their pictures. A hint for bigger 'kids': try going through with one or both arms above your head – someone on either end to push and pull helps too.

Though Tōdai-ji is often packed with tour groups and schoolchildren from across the country, it's big enough to absorb huge crowds and it belongs at the top of any Nara itinerary. Also be sure to check out the Nandai-mon.

Tōdai-ji Nandai-mon
BUDDHIST TEMPLE

(東大寺南大門; Map p392) The great south gate of Tōdai-ji (p394) contains two fierce-looking Niō guardians. These recently restored wooden images, carved in the 13th century by the famed sculptor Unkei, are some of the finest wooden statues in all of Japan, if not the world. They are truly dramatic works of art and seem ready to spring to life at any moment. The gate is about 200m south of the Tōdai-ji temple enclosure.

Nigatsu-dō & Sangatsu-dō
BUDDHIST TEMPLE

(二月堂・三月堂; Map p392; Nigatsu-dō free, Sangatsu-dō ¥500; ⊙ Nigatsu-dō 24hr, Sangatsu-dō 8am-4.30pm Nov-Feb, to 5pm Mar & Oct, 7.30am-5.30pm Apr-Sep) These sub-temples of Tōdai-ji are uphill from the Daibutsu-den and far less clamorous. Climb a lantern-lined staircase to Nigatsu-dō, a national treasure from 1669 (originally built c 750). Though the interior is private, the verandah's sweeping views across the town (especially at dusk) may remind you of Kyoto's Kiyomizu-dera (p311). Nara's Omizutori (p399) Matsuri is held here. A short walk south of Nigatsu-dō is Sangatsu-dō, the oldest building in the Tōdai-ji complex and home to a small collection of fine Nara-period statues.

The halls are an easy walk east (uphill) from the Daibutsu-den. Instead of walking straight up the hill, we recommend taking a hard left out of the Daibutsu-den exit, following the enclosure past the pond and turning up the hill. This pathway is one the most scenic walks in all of Nara.

Tōdai-ji Museum
MUSEUM

(東大寺ミュージアム; Map p392; ☑ 0742-20-5511; Nara-shi, Suimon-chō 100; admission ¥500, joint ticket with Daibutsu-den ¥800; ⊙ 9.30am-5.30pm Apr-Sep, to 5pm Mar & Oct, to 4.30pm Nov-Feb) Not far from the Daibutsu-den and Nandai-mon, the stately Tōdai-ji Museum displays several priceless bodhisattva and other temple treasures, especially appealing to scholars and serious fans of early Nara Buddhism. The air-conditioning is welcome on hot summer days.

★ Kasuga Taisha
SHINTO SHRINE

(春日大社; Map p392; 160 Kasugano-chō; ⊙ dawn-dusk) FREE Founded in the 8th century, this sprawling shrine on the Unesco World Heritage List lies at the foot of a deeply forested hill, where herds of sacred deer await handouts. Until the end of the 19th century, Kasuga Taisha was completely rebuilt every 20 years, according to Shintō tradition. Pathways are lined with hundreds of lanterns, with many hundreds more in the shrine itself. They're illuminated during the twice-yearly Mantōrō (p399) lantern festivals, held in early February and mid-August.

Mornings at 8.50am, the public is welcome to observe the daily *chōhai* chanting ceremony in the *Naoraiden* (Ceremony Hall), in which a half-dozen priests lead worshipers in the *Norito* prayer for the safety and peace of nature and the Japanese people. This practice was begun after the Great Tohoku Earthquake of 2011.

There are several subshrines around the main hall, among an impressive 61 subshrines throughout the city. It's worth walking a few minutes south to the nearby subshrine of **Wakamiya-jinja** (若宮神社; Map p392).

Tōdai-ji

VISIT THE GREAT BUDDHA

The Daibutsu (Great Buddha) at Nara's Tōdai-ji is one of the most arresting sights in Japan. The awe-inspiring physical presence of the vast image is striking. It's one of the largest bronze Buddha images in the world and it's contained in an equally huge building, the Daibutsu-den Hall, which is among the largest wooden buildings on earth.

Tōdai-ji was built by order of Emperor Shōmu during the Nara period (710–784) and the complex was finally completed in 798, after the capital had been moved from Nara to Kyoto. Most historians agree the temple was built to consolidate the country and serve as its spiritual focus. Legend has it that over two million labourers worked on the temple, but this is probably apocryphal. What's certain is that its construction brought the country to the brink of bankruptcy.

The original Daibutsu was cast in bronze in eight castings over a period of three years. It has been recast several times over the centuries. The original Daibutsu was covered in gold leaf and one can only imagine its impact on Japanese visitors during the eighth century AD.

The temple belongs to the Kegon school of Buddhism, one of the six schools of Buddhism popular in Japan during the Nara period. Kegon Buddhism, which comes from the Chinese Huayan Buddhist sect, is based on the Flower Garland Sutra. This sutra expresses the idea of worlds within worlds, all manifested by the Cosmic Buddha (Vairocana or Dainichi Nyorai). The Great Buddha and the figures that surround him in the Daibutsu-den Hall are the perfect physical symbol of this cosmological map.

Kokuzo Bosatsu
Seated to the left of the Daibutsu is Kokuzo Bosatsu, the bodhisattva of memory and wisdom, to whom students pray for help in their studies and the faithful pray for help on the path to enlightenment.

The Daibutsu (Great Buddha)
Known in Sanskrit as 'Vairocana' and in Japanese as the 'Daibutsu', this is the Cosmic Buddha that gives rise to all other Buddhas, according to Kegon doctrine. The Buddha's hands send the messages 'fear not' and 'welcome'.

FACT FILE

THE DAIBUTSU

Height 14.98m

Weight 500 tonnes

Nostril width 50cm

THE DAIBUTSU-DEN HALL

Height 48.74m

Length 57m

Number of roof tiles 112,589

Komokuten

Standing to the left of the Daibutsu is Komokuten (Lord of Limitless Vision), who serves as a guardian of the Buddha. He stands upon a demon *(jaki)*, which symbolises ignorance, and wields a brush and scroll, which symbolises wisdom.

Buddhas Around Dainichi

Sixteen smaller Buddhas are arranged in a halo around the Daibutsu's head, each of which symbolises one of the Daibutsu's different manifestations. They are graduated in size to appear the same size when viewed from the ground.

Tamonten

To the right of the Daibutsu stands Tamonten (Lord Who Hears All), another of the Buddha's guardians. He holds a pagoda, which is said to represent a divine storehouse of wisdom.

Hole in Pillar

Behind the Daibutsu you will find a pillar with a 50cm hole through its base (the size of one of the Daibutsu's nostrils). It's said that if you can crawl through this, you are assured of enlightenment.

oirin Kannon

ted to the right of the Daibutsu is Nyoirin non, one of the esoteric forms of Kannon hisattva. This is one of the bodhisattva that side over the six different realms of karmic rth.

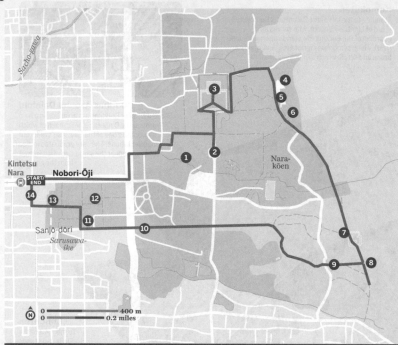

🏃 City Walk
Nara-kōen

START KINTETSU NARA STATION
END KINTETSU NARA STATION
LENGTH 5KM; HALF A DAY

Start at Kintetsu Nara Station and walk up Nobori-Ōji, passing Kōfuku-ji on your right. Go left for ❶ **Isui-en** (p394), one of Nara's finest gardens. Walk north from the garden entrance, take the next major right after 100m and walk east to come out in front of Tōdai-ji. Go right to see the ❷ **Nandai-mon** (p395), the main gate. Admire the Niō guardians and continue to ❸ **Tōdai-ji** (p394).

Take the southeast exit, then a left and walk along the temple enclosure. Past the pond, go right up the hill following the stone-paved path. An atmospheric stretch takes you to an open plaza in front of ❹ **Nigatsu-dō** (p395) and ❺ **Sangatsu-dō** (p395) halls. Climb the steps to Nigatsu-dō to enjoy the view from the verandah, taking in the curves of Daibutsu-den and the Nara plain.

Return to the plaza and exit heading south, passing between a log-cabin-like structure

and gaudy ❻ **Tamukeyama-hachimang**, a small shrine overlooking the plaza. Follow the path through the woods, descend two staircases and follow the 'Kasuga Shrine' signs. Follow the road leading uphill to the left, passing under the slopes of Wakakusa-yama. At Musashino Ryokan, walk down the steps, cross a bridge, head left, and at the T-intersection take a left to ❼ **Kasuga Taisha** (p395) – walk around the side for the main entrance.

Exit via the main entrance and bear left up to ❽ **Wakamiya-jinja** (p395), passing several small shrines. Go back towards Kasuga Taisha and turn left down the steps leading back to town. You pass through ❾ **Ni-no-Torii**, a large Shintō shrine gate, and then continue down the wooded arcade to ❿ **Ichi-no-Torii**, another shrine gate. Cross the street and you'll see ⓫ **Kōfuku-ji's five-storey pagoda** (p394). Walk through the grounds, passing between the ⓬ **Nanen-dō** and ⓭ **Hokuen-dō** halls, and take the lane that leads to ⓮ **Higashi-muki Arcade**. A quick right brings you back to where you started: Kintetsu Nara Station.

⊙ Naramachi

South of Sanjō-dōri and Sarusawa-ike pond, Naramachi (奈良町) is a traditional neighbourhood with many well-preserved *machiya* (shophouses) and *kura* (storehouses). It's a mellow place for a stroll away from the busier sights around Nara-kōen. There are several good restaurants, shops, cafes, inns and a creative energy that residents are eager to share with travellers.

Naramachi Kōshi-no-le　HISTORIC BUILDING
(ならまち格子の家; Map p392; ☑ 0742-23-4820; 44 Gangōji-chō; ⊙ 9am-5pm Tue-Sun) **FREE** This well-preserved merchant's house is an excellent place to explore details of traditional Japanese architecture: lattice front, beamed ceilings, old kitchen, *tansu* (chest of drawers) stairs and inner garden; an English-language leaflet is available.

⌖ Tours

Nara Walk　TOURS
(奈良ウォーク; Map p392; ☑ 090-9708-0036; www.narawalk.com; Nara Park ¥3000, Old Town ¥2000; ⊙ Mar-Nov or by appointment) Nara Walk offers well-regarded walking tours in English, including a morning tour around Nara Park (Tōdai-ji, Kasuga Taisha etc) and an afternoon Old Town stroll (through Naramachi). Other tours to Tōshōdai-ji, Yakushi-ji, Hōryū-ji and Tōdai-ji are available by appointment.

Nara Student Guides　TOURS
(☑ 0742-26-4753; www.narastudentguide.org) Volunteer guides have been showing international visitors around Nara since 1964.

⚑ Festivals & Events

The dates for some festivals vary, so it's best to check with the Nara or Kyoto tourist information offices.

Mantōrō　CULTURAL
(Lantern Festival; ⊙ early Mar & mid-Aug) The Lantern Festival involves the lighting of 3000 stone and bronze lanterns around Kasuga Taisha at 6pm one night in early February – it's impossibly atmospheric. A *bugaku* (dance piece played by court orchestras in ancient Japan) takes place in the Apple Garden on the last day. This festival is also held around 14 August in the O-Bon (Festival of the Dead) holiday period.

Omizutori　CULTURAL
(⊙ 1-14 Mar) During this two-week festival in early March, the monks of Tōdai-ji parade huge flaming torches around the balcony of Nigatsu-dō and rain down embers on the spectators to purify them, in a nightly ceremony called Otaimatsu. On the evening of 12 March, the monks hold a water-drawing ceremony from which the festival takes its name (*mizutori* means 'to take water'), performed after midnight.

Yamayaki　CULTURAL
(Grass Burning Festival; ⊙ 4th Sat of Jan) In January (the day before Seijin-no-hi, or Coming-of-Age Day), the Grass Burning Festival commemorates a feud that was had many centuries ago between the monks of Tōdai-ji and Kōfuku-ji: Wakakusa-yama is set alight at 6pm, with an accompanying display of fireworks.

⌂ Sleeping

Although Nara can be visited as a day trip from Kyoto or Osaka, spending the night will allow a more relaxing pace. There's fine accommodation for all budgets, with some especially good choices for budget travellers.

★**Naramachi
Hostel & Restaurant**　HOSTEL ¥
(ナラマチホステルアンドレストラン; Map p392; ☑ 0742-93-3390; www.naramachihostel.com; 939-1 Takabatake-chō; dm ¥3300, 4-person r ¥13,200; ⊙ restaurant 11am-11pm; ⊜ ❋ ◉ ﹫) This place rocks. A Nara important cultural property, this former landowner's estate reopened in 2016 after extensive renovation. Now Japan's largest hostel (62 beds, multiple rooms), its Edo period shell contrasts beautifully with 21st-century facilities (untreated wood walls, Washlets, showers), terraces, a 100-year-old pine tree, BBQ grill, coin laundry, and even a Jacuzzi (swimsuit required).

The atmospheric restaurant-bar in the former *kura* (storehouse) prepares lovely Japanese-Western fusion cuisine (lunch mains ¥1000–1600, dinner ¥1200–2900), made from local ingredients.

★**Guesthouse
Nara Backpackers**　GUESTHOUSE ¥
(ゲストハウス 奈良バックパッカーズ; Map p392; ☑ 0742-22-4557; www.nara-backpackers.com; 31 Yurugichō; dm ¥2400, r per person without bathroom ¥3800; ⊜ ❋ ﹫) An utterly charming stay in a traditional 1920s building, which was once a tea master's home. Choose from bunk-bed dorm rooms or five different-sized private

tatami-mat rooms, some with garden views. Bathing facilities are shared (bring your own toiletries and towel, or buy or rent them here) and there's a shared kitchen for self-caterers. Per night rates fall the longer you stay.

Children under 10 are not permitted, to preserve the home's *shōji* (sliding paper doors) and antique glass windows. It's about eight minutes on foot from Kintetsu Nara Station.

Ryokan Matsumae
RYOKAN ¥

(旅館松前; Map p392; ☑ 0742-22-3686; www.matsumae.co.jp; 28-1 Higashi-terabayashi-chō; r per person from ¥5400, s/d with bathroom ¥8640/12,960; ⊛❋@⊜) This very friendly little ryokan, conveniently located in Naramachi, has Japanese-style rooms with TVs and toilet, some with private bath. The overall feeling is warm and relaxing. Bonus: occasional lessons in yoga, calligraphy and *kyōgen* (traditional theatrical farce). Japanese or Western breakfast is available for an additional ¥756.

Guesthouse Sakuraya
GUESTHOUSE ¥¥

(桜舎; Map p392; www.guesthouse-sakuraya.com; 1 Narukawa-chō; s/d incl breakfast ¥6200/10,400; ⊜❋⊜) This atmospheric stunner in Naramachi has just three quiet guest rooms in a one-time Edo-period ink-maker's workshop. It integrates both traditional and contemporary touches around a lovely courtyard garden and common room and baths. One room has an en suite toilet. The owner offers cultural experiences (tea ceremony, calligraphy, kimono) for ¥3000. If you're looking for a party, head elsewhere.

Hotel Fujita Nara
HOTEL ¥¥

(ホテルフジタ奈良; Map p392; ☑ 0742-23-8111; www.fujita-nara.com; 47-1 Shimosanjō-chō; s/d/tw from ¥8500/12,000/14,000; ❋@⊜) In the heart of downtown Nara, about five minutes' walk from either main train station, this efficient, immaculate (if a bit plain) hotel offers reasonable prices, some English-speaking staff, lovely garden views from the lobby lounge and a Japanese-Western breakfast buffet (¥1800).

★ Nara Hotel
HOTEL ¥¥¥

(奈良ホテル; Map p392; ☑ 0742-26-3300; www.narahotel.co.jp; 1096 Takabatake-chō; s/tw from ¥19,010/34,450; ⊜❋@⊜) Founded in 1909, this grande dame has hosted dignitaries from Edward VIII and Albert Einstein to Audrey Hepburn and the Dalai Lama. It retains a Meiji-era style in its traditional exterior, high ceilings, gorgeous

woodwork, refined Japanese and Western restaurants, tea lounge and beautifully landscaped grounds. Rooms are spacious and comfortable with big beds, though some have cramped unit bathrooms.

For historic atmosphere and all nonsmoking rooms, we recommend the Honkan (main building) over the Shinkan (new building).

Wakasa Bettei
RYOKAN ¥¥¥

(和鹿彩別邸; Map p392; ☑ 0742-23-5858; www.n-wakasa.com; 1 Kita-handahigashi-machi; r per person incl 2 meals ¥34,546, without meals ¥22,727; ❋⊜) This friendly, contemporary ryokan aims to please. The 11 stylish, large Japanese- and Western-style rooms have private facilities including stone or wooden bathtub, and the top-floor common bath has views of Tōdai-ji and Wakakusa-yama. We recommend the newer Bettei over the original (though still friendly) Hotel New Wakasa next door.

✗ Eating

Nara is chock-a-block with good restaurants, mostly near the train stations and in Naramachi. For restaurant browsing, the covered arcade **Higashi-muki Shōtengai**, between Kintetsu Nara Station and Sanjō-dōri, has about a dozen restaurants: udon, sushi, Italian, fast food and coffee-and-sandwich chains.

Nara considers itself the birthplace of sake, so Nara-style cuisine often uses sake lees (the leftover bits after brewing), which give a heady umami to pickles, marinated dishes, soups and hotpots. Another local speciality is *kaki-no-ha sushi* (individual pieces of sushi wrapped in persimmon leaves – don't eat the leaf!).

Kameya
OKONOMIYAKI ¥

(かめや; Map p392; ☑ 0742-22-2434; 9 Taruichō; mains ¥650-1400, okonomiyaki around ¥700; ⊙ 11am-10pm; ◈) A giant red lantern marks the entrance to this casual, spirited *okonomiyaki* joint, going strong since the 1960s. There's a seemingly infinite number of combinations for the savoury pancakes cooked on steel griddles at your table. The 'mix *okonomiyaki*' contains squid, shrimp, pork and scallops, while the *yaki-soba* roll has fried noodles inside.

★ Washokuya Happoh
IZAKAYA ¥¥

(和食屋八寳; Map p392; ☑ 0742-26-4834; 22 Higashimuki-nakamachi; dishes ¥360-1380, lunch menus ¥750-1050; ⊙ 11.30am-10.30pm Mon-Sat, to 10pm Sun; ◈) This large, cheery, modern farmhouse-style spot salutes Nara as sake's birthplace, in both drink and food. Alongside *izakaya* standards like sashimi and *karaage* (fried chicken pieces), we loved the dishes marinated in sake lees (especially pork) and seared *wagyū* sushi. The wide-ranging, fastidiously detailed menu gets props for cute pictures of ingredients, for diners with allergies or dietary restrictions.

Look for the wooden beams on your right, inside the Higashimuki Arcade, a short walk south of Kintetsu Nara Station.

★ **Kura** IZAKAYA ¥¥
(蔵; Map p392; ☎0742-22-8771; 16 Kōmyōin-chō; dishes ¥100-1000; ⊙5-10pm; ▣) This friendly spot in Naramachi is styled like an old storehouse and has just 16 seats around a counter amid dark-wood panels and an old beer sign. Indulge in *mini-katsu* (mini pork cutlets), *yakitori* (grilled chicken skewers) and *oden* (fish cake and veggie hotpot). Order Nara's own Kazenomori sake (from ¥600), and everyone will think you're a sake sage.

★ **Sakura Burger** BURGERS ¥¥
(さくらバーガー; Map p392; ☎0742-31-3813; http://sakuraburger.com; 6 Higashimuki-kitamachi; burgers & sandwiches ¥490-1230; ⊙11am-4pm & 5-9pm Thu-Tue; ▣) This unassumingly gourmet burger joint is steps north of Kintetsu Nara Station. Expect a lunchtime queue for burgers, sandwiches and hot dogs with your choice of toppings. The namesake Sakura burger comes piled with veggies and a thick slice of house-smoked bacon. They even make their own ketchup. Dessert (while it lasts) is homemade apple pie or caramel walnut tart.

Yumekaze Plaza FOOD HALL ¥¥
(夢風ひろば; Map p392; ☎0742-25-0870; www.yume-kaze.com; 16 Kasuganochō; ⊙hours vary by shop, mostly lunch & dinner; ▣) Adjacent to Nara-kōen and across from the Nara National Museum, this convenient collection of a dozen restaurants offers everything from handmade *soba* to Italian pasta and panini sets, and *kamameshi* (rice hotpot), noodles and *wagashi* (Japanese sweets) in attractively updated old-style buildings.

🍸 Drinking & Nightlife

Nara Izumi Yūsai BAR
(なら泉勇斎; Map p392; ☎0742-26-6078; 22 Nishi-Terabayashi-chō; ⊙11am-8pm Fri-Wed) Drop in on this small standing bar in Naramachi for tastings (¥200 to ¥600) of sakes produced in Nara Prefecture (120 varieties from 29 makers, also available to buy). There is a useful English explanation sheet.

Drink Drank CAFE
(ドリンクドランク; Map p392; ☎0742-27-6206; 8 Hashimoto-chō; smoothies ¥700-900; ⊙11am-8pm Thu-Tue) Fruit smoothies are a relatively new thing in Japan; find them at this charming, contemporary cafe near the eastern end of Sanjō-dōri. Besides traditional fruits, look for only-in-Japan and local seasonal flavours like pumpkin-banana and melon-persimmon. Food offerings include daily lunch specials (¥880) and light meals (¥580 to ¥650) of crêpes and panini (grilled sandwiches).

Mizuya-chaya TEAHOUSE
(水谷茶屋; Map p392; ☎07542-22-0627; 30 Kasugano-chō; ⊙10am-4pm Thu-Tue) In a small wooded, brookside clearing between Nigatsu-dō and Kasuga Taisha, this quaint thatched-roof teahouse is one of Nara's most atmospheric spots. Stop for a cup of *matcha* (powdered green tea; ¥700 including a sweet), *onigiri* (rice balls; ¥350 to ¥400) or a bowl of udon (¥580 to ¥850) for a pick-me up.

In warm seasons, sit outside among the greenery and enjoy *kakigōri* (shaved ice with toppings of condensed milk, sweet red beans or fruit-flavoured syrups).

🛍 Shopping

Nipponichi ARTS & CRAFTS
(日本市; Map p392; ☎0742-23-5650; 1-1 Tsuno-furi-shinyamachi; ⊙10am-7pm) From humble beginnings as a linen merchant in 1716, this retailer has evolved to repurpose traditional craft-making (clothing, towels, housewares and accessories) for the 21st century in Japan's sweet spot of cool, adorable, fun and quietly chic. Because this is Nara, make sure to look for deer motifs: paper clips, handkerchiefs and *shika-sembei* (crackers for deer), though these are for human consumption.

Ikeda Gankōdō ARTS & CRAFTS
(池田含香堂; Map p392; 16 Tsunofuri-chō; ⊙9am-7pm, closed Mon Sep-Mar) For six generations, this little shop on Sanjō-dōri has been making traditional-style fans. Lovely *sensu* (folding fans) may pack more easily, but the local speciality is Nara *uchiwa*, paddle-style fans whose *washi* paper covering has been intricately carved with local and nature scenes. Silk backing makes them surprisingly durable. Prices span from ¥2000 to ¥25,000.

ℹ️ Information

All the information offices in Nara stock useful maps and can assist with same-day hotel reservations. They even keep a supply of loaner umbrellas in case you get caught in the rain!

JR Nara Station Information Centre (Map p392; 📞 0742-22-9821; www.narashikanko. or.jp; ⊙9am-9pm; 📶) Located in the old Nara Station building just outside the east exit of JR Nara Station. This is the city's main tourist information centre and English speakers are usually on hand. You can store luggage here (¥500 per piece per day).

Kintetsu Nara Station Information Office (Map p392; 📞 0742-24-4858; ⊙9am-9pm; 📶) If arriving at Kintetsu Nara Station, try this helpful information office, which is near the top of the stairs above exit 3 from the station.

Nara City Tourist Information Centre (奈良市観光センター; Map p392; 📞 0742-22-3900; 23-4 Kami-Sanjō-chō; ⊙9am-9pm) Located only a short walk from JR Nara or Kintetsu Nara Stations.

Nara Visitor Center & Inn (奈良県猿沢イン; Nara-ken Sarusawa Inn; Map p392; 📞 0742-81-7461; www.sarusawa.nara.jp; 3 Ikeno-chō; ⊙8am-9pm) This visitor centre is on the southern side of Sarusawa Pond. It has a daily roster of cultural happenings, including popular tea-ceremony and kimono experiences.

ℹ️ Getting There & Away

BUS

There's an overnight bus service between Tokyo's Shinjuku neighborhood and Nara (one way ¥5980 to ¥9500; rates vary by day). In Nara, call **Nara Kōtsū Bus** (📞 0742-22-5110; www.narakotsu.co.jp/kousoku) or check with the **Nara City Tourist Information Centre** (p402) for more details. In Nara, overnight buses leave from stop 4 in front of JR Nara Station's east exit and from stop 20 outside Kintetsu Nara Station. In Tokyo, call **Kantō Bus** (📞 03-3371-1225; www.kanto-bus.co.jp) or visit the Shinjuku highway bus terminal.

TRAIN
Kyoto

The Kintetsu Nara line is the fastest and most convenient connection between Kyoto (Kintetsu Kyoto Station, in Kyoto Station) and central Nara (Kintetsu Nara Station). Comfortable, all-reserved *tokkyū* trains (¥1130, 35 minutes) run directly; *kyūkō* trains (express; ¥620, 45 minutes) usually require a change at Yamato-Saidaiji.

For Japan Rail Pass holders, the JR Nara line connects JR Kyoto Station with JR Nara Station (*kaisoku*, rapid; ¥710, 45 minutes) with several departures per hour.

Osaka

The Kintetsu Nara line connects Osaka (Namba Station) with Nara (Kintetsu Nara Station). *Kaisoku* and *futsū* services take about 40 minutes and cost ¥560. All-reserved *tokkyū* trains take five minutes less but will cost you almost double.

For Japan Rail Pass holders, the JR Kansai line links JR Nara Station with Osaka (Namba and Tennō-ji stations), via *kaisoku* trains (¥540, 45 minutes and ¥450, 30 minutes respectively).

ℹ️ Getting Around

BUS
To/From the Airport

Nara Kōtsū operates a **limousine bus service** (奈良交通; Nara Kōtsū; www.narakotsu.co.jp/kousoku/limousine/nara_kanku.html) between Nara and Kansai International (¥2050, 1½ hours) and Osaka Itami (¥1480, one hour) airports, with departures roughly every hour during the day. Buses depart from stop 4 in front of JR Nara Station's east exit and stop 20 (for Kansai International Airport) and 12 (for Itami Airport) outside Kintetsu Nara Station. Tickets can be purchased at the ticket offices at the respective stations or the airports.

To skip the 15-minute walk between JR Nara Station and the temple and shrine districts (about five minutes from Kintetsu Nara), take the bus (¥210 per ride). Two circular bus routes cover the Nara-kōen area: bus 1 (anticlockwise) and bus 2 (clockwise). For more than two trips, a one-day Free Pass costs ¥500. On Saturday, Sunday and holidays, a tourist-friendly Gurutto Bus covers major sights (¥100 per ride) several times per hour from about 9am to 5pm.

Temples Southwest of Nara

While Nara city has some impressive ancient temples and Buddhist statues, three temples southwest of Nara take you to the roots of Japanese Buddhism: Hōryū-ji, Yakushi-ji and Tōshōdai-ji.

Hōryū-ji is one of Japan's most historically important temples. However, its appeal is more academic than aesthetic and it's a slog through drab suburbs to get there. For most people we recommend a half-day trip to Yakushi-ji and Tōshōdai-ji, which are easy to reach from Nara and pleasant for strolling.

If you want to visit all three temples, head to Hōryū-ji first (it's the most distant from the centre of Nara) and then continue by bus 97 or 98 (¥560, 39 minutes) up to Yakushi-ji and Tōshōdai-ji, which are a 10-minute walk apart.

Several buses ply the southwest temple route, but bus 97 is most convenient, with English announcements and route maps.

★ **Hōryū-ji** BUDDHIST TEMPLE

(法隆寺; Map p404; www.horyuji.or.jp; admission ¥1000; ◎8am-5pm Feb-Oct, to 4.30pm Nov-Mar) Hōryū-ji was founded in 607 by Prince Shōtoku, considered by many to be the patron saint of Japanese Buddhism. It's a veritable shrine to Shōtoku, renowned not only as the oldest temple in Japan, but also as a repository for some of the country's rarest treasures. Several of the temple's wooden buildings have survived earthquakes and fires to become the oldest of their kind in the world. There's an entire gallery of Hōryū-ji treasures at the Tokyo National Museum (p97).

The temple is divided into two parts: **Sai-in** (West Temple) and **Tō-in** (East Temple); pick up a detailed map and guidebook in English.

The main approach proceeds from the south along a tree-lined avenue and through the Nandai-mon and Chū-mon gates before entering the Sai-in precinct. As you enter, you'll see the **Kondō** (Main Hall) on your right and a pagoda on your left.

The Kondō houses several treasures, including the triad of the Buddha Sakyamuni with two attendant bodhisattvas. One of Japan's great Buddhist treasures, it's dimly lit and barely visible – you will need a torch (flashlight) to see it. Likewise, the pagoda contains clay images depicting scenes from the life of Buddha, which are barely visible without a torch.

East of Sai-in are the two concrete buildings of the **Daihōzō-in** (Great Treasure Hall), containing numerous treasures from Hōryū-ji's long history. Continue east through the Tōdai-mon to Tō-in, where Prince Shōtoku is believed to have meditated and received help with problem sutras from a kindly, golden apparition in the **Yumedono** (Hall of Dreams).

Given the admission costs and the time it takes to get here from central Nara, we recommend you give careful thought to committing at least half a day to visiting this temple. Take the JR Kansai line from JR Nara Station to Hōryū-ji Station (¥220, 11 minutes). From here, bus 72 travels the short stretch between the station and the bus stop Hōryū-ji Monmae (¥180, eight minutes). Alternatively, take bus 52 or 97 from either JR Nara Station (stop 10) or Kintetsu Nara Station (stop 8) and get off at the Hōryū-ji-mae stop (¥760, one hour). Walk west about 50m, cross the road and you'll see the tree-lined approach to the temple.

Yakushi-ji BUDDHIST TEMPLE

(薬師寺; Map p404; 457 Nishinokyō; admission ¥500; ◎8.30am-5pm) Another Nara site on the Unesco World Heritage List, this temple houses some of the most beautiful Buddhist statues in all Japan. It was established by Emperor Temmu in 680 as a prayer for the healing of his wife. With the exception of the East Pagoda, which dates to 730 (and is due to be under renovation until 2018), the present buildings either date from the 13th century or are very recent reconstructions.

Entering from the south, turn right before going through the gate with guardian figures and walk to the **Tōin-dō** (East Hall), where a famous, 7th-century Shō-Kannon image shows obvious influences of Indian sculptural styles, making it the progenitor of other Kannon statues throughout Japan.

Then walk west to the **Kondō** (Main Hall). Rebuilt in 1976, it houses several images, including the famous **Yakushi Triad** (the Yakushi Nyorai – healing Buddha – flanked by the bodhisattvas of the sun and moon), dating from the 8th century. They were originally gold, but a fire in the 16th century turned the images an appealingly mellow black.

Behind (north of) the Kondō is the **Kōdō** (Lecture Hall), which houses yet another fine Buddhist trinity, this time Miroku Buddha with two bodhisattva attendants. Exit to the north behind this hall and head to Tōshōdai-ji.

To get to Yakushi-ji, take bus 70 or 72 from JR Nara Station (stop 10) or Kintetsu Nara Station (stop 8) and get off at the Yakushi-ji Parking Lot stop (Yakushi-ji Chūshajō in Japanese; ¥250, 15 minutes). Bus 97 from the same stations runs to the Yakushi-ji Higashiguchi stop (¥250, 15 minutes). From here, walk 100m south (in the direction the bus was travelling) to a petrol station, cross the road and walk west across a canal. From the main road it's 250m to the temple's southern entrance.

Alternatively, trains on the Kintetsu Kashihara line (connecting Kyoto and Kashiharajingū-mae) stop at Nishinokyō Station, about a 200m walk northwest of Yakushi-ji (and 600m walk south of Tōshōdai-ji). From Kintetsu Nara station (¥260, 11 to 15 minutes), change trains at Yamato-Saidaiji (about four minutes) for the short train ride to Nishinokyō Station. From Kyoto, some trains run direct to Nishinokyō (*kyūkō* ¥620, 46 minutes; *tokkyū* ¥1130, 32 minutes); others require a transfer at Yamato-Saidaiji.

KANSAI TEMPLES SOUTHWEST OF NARA

Around Nara

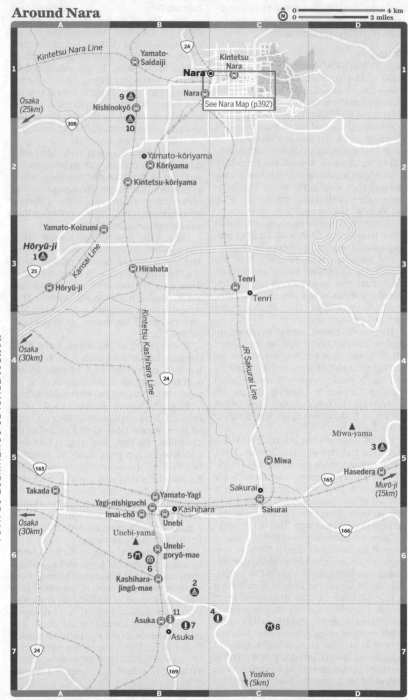

0 — 4 km
0 — 2 miles

Kintetsu Nara Line

Yamato-Saidaiji

Nara

Kintetsu Nara

Nara

See Nara Map (p392)

Osaka (25km)

308

Nishinokyō

9

10

Yamato-kōriyama

Kōriyama

Kintetsu-kōriyama

Yamato-Koizumi

Hōryū-ji

1

25

Kansai Line

Hōryū-ji

Hirahata

Tenri

Tenri

Osaka (30km)

Kintetsu Kashihara Line

24

JR Sakurai Line

Miwa-yama

3

5

165

Hasedera

Murō-ji (15km)

Takada

Miwa

Yagi-nishiguchi

Yamato-Yagi

Sakurai

Osaka (30km)

Imai-chō

Kashihara

Sakurai

Unebi

166

Unebi-yama

5

6

Unebi-goryō-mae

Kashihara-jingū-mae

2

Asuka

11

4

7

8

Asuka

24

169

Yoshino (5km)

Around Nara

Tōshōdai-ji   BUDDHIST TEMPLE
(唐招提寺; Map p404; www.toshodaiji.jp; 13-46 Gojo-chō; admission ¥600; ☺8.30am-5pm, last entry by 4.30pm) This temple was established in 759 by the Chinese priest Ganjin (Jian Zhen), who had been recruited by Emperor Shōmu to reform Buddhism in Japan. The temple grounds are pleasantly wooded and mossy, making a good contrast to nearby Yakushi-ji (Tōshōdai-ji is about a 500m walk north of Yakushi-ji's northern gate), which is largely devoid of greenery. The Kondō (Golden Hall), roughly in the middle, contains a stunning Senjū (thousand-armed) Kannon image. Behind it, the Kōdō (Lecture Hall), contains a beautiful image of Miroku Buddha.

Its buildings, also in contrast to the bright colors of Yakushi-ji, have been allowed to age, but you can still see remnants of the colors on the back of the hall.

To reach Tōshōdai-ji from Nara, take the Kintetsu Nara line to Yamato-Saidaiji Station and transfer to the Kintetsu Kashihara line to Nishinokyō Station. The temple is 500m north. Alternatively, buses 70 and 72 stop at Tōshōdai-ji bus stop. Bus 97 stops nearby at Tōshōdai-ji-*higashiguchi*; all buses stop here on the way to Nara. From JR Nara Station the ride takes 15 minutes and costs ¥260; it's another five minutes to Kintetsu Nara.

Yamato Plain   大和平野

The Yamato Plain in central Nara Prefecture is where the forerunners of Japan's ruling Yamato dynasty cemented their grip on power. In these pre-Buddhist days, deceased em-

perors were entombed in huge *kofun* (also know as *tumuli*, or earthen burial mounds) around Asuka. A comprehensive archaeological museum in Kashihara covers it.

ⓘ Getting There & Around

The most convenient transport hub for sights here is Yamato-Yagi, reached on the Kintetsu line from Osaka, Kyoto or Nara. We suggest renting a car here as some of the sights are far flung and hard to reach by public transportation.

From Kyoto take the Kintetsu Nara/Kashihara line direct (kyūkō, ¥880, 65 minutes).

From Nara take the Kintetsu Nara line to Yamato-Saidaiji and change to the Kintetsu Kashihara line (kyūkō, ¥440, 40 minutes with transfer).

From Osaka's Tsuruhashi Station, take the Kintetsu Osaka line direct (kyūkō, ¥560, 35 minutes). Japan Rail Pass holders can reach the Kashihara area from Nara by taking the JR Mahoroba line and getting off at Unebi (¥500, 39 minutes).

Kashihara   橿原

The town of Kashihara, three stops south of Yamato-Yagi, is best known for its archaeological museum and sprawling shrine. Reach them via Kashihara-jingū-mae Station (¥210 from Yamato-Yagi, five minutes, all trains stop). You can also take the JR Nara/Sakurai line from Nara.

Kashihara-jingū   SHINTO SHRINE
(橿原神宮; Map p404; ☎0744-22-3271; www.naranet.co.jp/kashiharajingu; FREE) This vast, graceful shrine, at the foot of Unebi-yama and alongside a pond, offers park-like grounds and classical Shintō architecture. Many of the buildings were moved here from the Kyoto Imperial Palace (p306) and are in the same style as those at Ise-jingū (p422). The shrine is dedicated to Japan's mythical first emperor, Jimmu, and a festival is held here each 11 February, the anniversary of his enthronement.

The shrine is five minutes' walk from Kashihara-jingū-mae Station; take the central exit and follow the main street toward the mountain.

Nara Prefecture Kashihara Archaeological Museum   MUSEUM
(奈良県橿原考古学研究所付属博物館, Nara Ken-ritsu Kashihara Kōkogaku Kenkyūjo Fuzoku Hakubutsukan; Map p404; ☎0744-24-1185; Japanese/foreign visitors ¥400/free; ☺9am-5pm Tue-Sun) FREE This museum and research

centre is an important visit for students of ancient Japanese history. Artefacts come from various archaeological sites in the area, including several *kofun* (earthen burial mounds), and date as far back as the Jōmon period (10,000 years ago). The permanent collection is well labeled in English. Foreigners can enter for free (bring your passport) and receive a glossy pamphlet guide book, but expect an extra charge during special exhibitions.

The museum is a five-minute walk west of Unebi Goryō-mae Station. Alternatively, from Kashihara-jingū (p405) shrine, exit the northern gate (to your left with your back to the main hall), follow the wooded avenue for five minutes, cross the main road, continue for 100m and turn left at the first intersection. It's on the left.

Sakurai 桜井

Sakurai is a hub of historic temples and shrines and can be reached directly from Nara on the JR Nara/Sakurai line (*futsū*, ¥320, 33 minutes). Connections from Kyoto require a change of trains at Yamato-Yagi to the Kintetsu Osaka line (*tokkyū* and *junkyū*, ¥1840, one hour). Sights within the region are quite spread out, so renting a car is suggested to see them all in one day.

Hase-dera BUDDHIST TEMPLE
(長谷寺; Map p404; admission ¥500; ⊙8.30am-5pm Apr-Sep, 9am-4.30pm Oct-Mar) Climb 399 covered steps to the Hondō (main hall) to view a 10m-tall image of Kannon (deity of mercy), Japan's largest wooden sculpture crafted in 1538. There are splendid views from a balcony built on stilts over the mountainside. Expect lots of visitors in spring – for the explosion of blooming peonies and cherry blossoms which seem to swirl upward in the wind – and autumn, when maples turn vivid red. No wonder it's nicknamed *hana no mitera* (flower-viewing temple).

Hase-dera Station is two stops east of Sakurai on the Kintetsu Osaka line (¥210, six minutes). It's a 20-minute walk to the temple; go through the archway, down several flights of steps, turn left, cross the river, then go right onto the main street toward the temple.

Murō-ji BUDDHIST TEMPLE
(室生寺; Sakurai; admission ¥600; ⊙8.30am-5pm Mar-Nov, to 4pm Dec-Feb) Secluded in a thick forest, this temple (founded in the 9th century) is associated with the Shingon

sect of Esoteric Buddhism. It's nicknamed 'Women's Kōya-san' because, unusually, it welcomed female students. Top sights include two national treasures: a 9th century, eleven-headed Kannon (deity of mercy) with female forms and, uphill, a five-storey pagoda built in the late 8th century and restored after damage from a 1998 typhoon. Next continue to Oku-no-in, the innermost sanctum, atop another very steep flight of steps.

Tanzan-jinja SHINTO SHRINE
(談山神社; Map p404; Sakurai; admission ¥500; ⊙8.30am-4.30pm) Centred around an attractive 13-storey pagoda, this shrine is best viewed against a backdrop of maples ablaze with autumn colours (November to early December). It enshrines Nakatomi no Kamatari, patriarch of the Fujiwara clan, which effectively ruled Japan for nearly 500 years. According to legend, Nakatomi met here secretly with Prince Naka no Ōe over games of kickball to discuss the overthrow of the ruling Soga clan. This is commemorated in scroll paintings and by priests playing kickball on 29 April and 3 November.

The shrine can be reached by Sakurai City Community Bus from stand 1 outside the southern exit of Sakurai Station (¥490, 25 minutes).

Asuka 飛鳥

Some of Japan's best-preserved *kofun* (burial mounds) are around Asuka (say Ahs-ka), about an hour south of Nara. Nowadays, the picturesque rolling hills are covered with rice terraces and farmland for crops such as strawberries. Also worth visiting is the very old temple, Asuka-dera.

There's a **tourist information office** (Map p404; ☑54-3624; Asuka Station; ⊙8.30am-5pm) outside Asuka Station; it didn't stock any useful maps on our last visit. The best way to explore the area is by bicycle. **Manyō Rent-a-Cycle** (レンタサイクル万葉; Asuka; bike rental per hour/day ¥300/900), across the street from the station, rents bikes and also stocks a useful English map of the area.

Asuka can be reached in just 12 minutes from Yamato-Yagi (¥230); change at Kashihara-jingū-mae on the Kintetsu Yoshino line.

Takamatsuzuka-kofun MONUMENT
(高松塚古墳; Map p404; museum admission ¥250; ⊙9am-5pm) Located in a pleasant wooded park, about 1.2km from Asuka Station, this ancient tomb looks like a grassy

mound. The interior of the *kofun* is closed to the public, but a hall next door shows painstaking reproductions of the murals inside. Curiously, these murals depict Korean motifs and nobles in Korean court dress, suggesting that the early Yamato nobility may have come from, well, somewhere else. As there is no written documentation as to who was entombed here, one can only wonder.

Asuka-dera
BUDDHIST TEMPLE

(飛鳥寺; Map p404; admission ¥350; ⊙9am-5.30pm Apr-Sep, to 5pm Oct-Mar) Considered the first true Buddhist temple in Japan (founded 596), Asuka-dera houses the Asuka Daibutsu, Japan's oldest remaining Buddha image (609). Weighing 15 tonnes and originally covered in gold, it's said that the statue has never been moved from this spot, meaning that many of the greats of Japanese history have likely stood before it. It's flanked by the Amida Buddha and Prince Shōtoku, the saint credited with bringing Buddhism to Japan.

Ishibutai-kofun
MONUMENT

(石舞台古墳; Map p404; Asuka; admission ¥250; ⊙8.30am-5pm) Composed of vast rocks in an open area, this tomb in Asuka is said to have housed the remains of Soga no Umako but is now completely empty.

Yoshino
吉野

📞 0746 / POP 7398

At the northern end of the Kii Mountain Range, the Yoshino (Omine) District is on the Unesco World Heritage List as the birthplace of Japan's unique Shugendō religion and has a unique history as a place of refuge. In spring it's also Japan's top cherry-blossom destination, renowned for the *hito-me-sen-bon* (1000 trees in a glance) viewpoint. For a few weeks from early to mid-April, the blossoms form a floral carpet that gradually ascends the mountainsides, and thousands of visitors jam the hilltop village's narrow streets. For the rest of the year Yoshino reverts to a sleepy hamlet where some important shrines and temples – and distinctive local foods – entertain day trippers and overnight guests.

◉ Sights

Yoshimizu-jinja
SHINTO SHRINE

(吉水神社; admission ¥400; ⊙9am-4.30pm) This shrine on the Unesco World Heritage List was for centuries a refuge for important historical figures. It now displays scrolls, armour, *nō* (stylised dance-drama) masks and painted *fusuma* (sliding doors) from those times. Among the refugees, swordsman/general Minamoto Yoshitsune fled here after incurring the wrath of his brother, the first Kamakura shogun. After a dispute for succession in Kyoto, emperor Go-Daigo set up a rival court in Yoshino. Toyotomi Hideyoshi hosted a 5000-person *hanami* (blossom-viewing) party here in 1594.

From Kimpusen-ji, continue 300m to a side road to the left (the first turn past the post office) leading to this shrine. There are good views back to Kimpusen-ji and the *hito-me-sen-bon* (1000 trees in a glance) viewpoint.

Kimpusen-ji
TEMPLE

(金峯山寺; admission ¥500; ⊙8.30am-4.30pm, enter by 4pm) A national treasure and Unesco World Heritage Site, this is the head temple of Shugendō, a sect based in Buddhism but borrowing liberally from other traditions. Check out the fearsome Kongō Rikishi (guardian figure statues) in the gate and continue to the Zaō-dō Hall, said to be Japan's second-largest wooden building. Early risers can observe morning *otsutome* (worship service), incorporating *taikō* drumming and the sounding of the *horagai* (giant conch shell), reminiscent of storied *yamabushi* (mountain monks).

The temple's trio of central deity statues are a symbol of the city with their fearsome blue faces. They're opened to the public for a short period each year (check at tourist offices for dates); they will close to the public in 2022.

The stone steps to the temple's Niō-mon gate are about 400m uphill from the cable-car station.

Nyoirin-ji
BUDDHIST TEMPLE

(如意輪寺; Map p410; admission ¥400; ⊙9am-4pm May-Mar, 7am-5pm Apr) This marvelously atmospheric temple, about 30 minutes on foot from central Yoshino, preserves both the relics of Emperor Go-Daigo's unlucky court and his tomb. In the Hōmotsu-den (treasure hall) is a trio of scroll paintings each with 1000 Buddhas. Legend says that if you look hard enough, you'll find one that looks like yourself. To get here, take the left fork on the road just above Yoshimizu-jinja and the dilapidated Katte-jinja (勝手神社), through the Naka-sen-bon forest of 1000 cherry trees.

🛏 Sleeping & Eating

There are a number of small inns around town. During cherry blossom season, book well ahead or expect to slog it from elsewhere with the throngs of day trippers.

★ Ryokan Katō   RYOKAN ¥¥

(旅館歌藤; ☏0746-32-3177; www.kato-yoshino. jp; 3056 Yoshinoyama; r per person incl breakfast ¥9720, without meals ¥7560; P❉🐾🛜) In business for two centuries but marvelously up to date, thanks to warm, young owners, design flair, rough-hewn wooden furniture and a *rotemburo* (outdoor bath) of local stone. We especially like the modern, log-house-style back building, with a glassed-in rotunda for cherry-tree viewing and communing around a wood stove. All 14 Japanese-style rooms have shared bathroom; half of them have private toilet. It's about a five-minute walk from the cable car.

Accommodating staff will cook your choice of Japanese- or Western-style meals (advance reservation requested).

Chikurin-in Gumpōen   RYOKAN ¥¥¥

(竹林院群芳園; ☏0746-32-8081; www.chikurin. co.jp; 2142 Yoshinoyama; r per person incl 2 meals from ¥14,040, without bathroom ¥12,960-18,360, single surcharge ¥5250; ❉@🛜) Generations of emperors have stayed at this temple that also operates as a ryokan, and it's easy to see why. The main building dates from the 1790s with frequent additions and updates. Its 43 rooms span humble *shukubō* (temple lodging) to Japan-posh, and baths and the temple garden have sweeping valley views. Some staff speak English. Reservations are essential for cherry-blossom season and recommended at all other times.

Even if you don't stay overnight, at least visit the temple's splendid garden (admission ¥300).

Kakinohasushi Tatsumi   SUSHI ¥

(柿の葉すしたつみ; ☏0746-32-1056; 559-3 Yoshinoyama; per piece ¥130-140, bento from about ¥1000; ⊙9am-5pm, longer hours in cherry blossom season) This tiny, family-run takeaway shop serves about the simplest menu in town: *kakinoha-sushi,* a local speciality of pressed sushi wrapped in persimmon leaves. Choose your fish – salmon (*sake*), mackerel (*saba*) or both (*combi*) – and quantity (single piece to large *bentō*) and you're set. Look for samples and a wooden sushi press in the window.

It may close early if supplies run out.

Nakai Shunpūdō   SWEETS ¥

(中井春風堂; ☏0746-32-3043; 545 Yoshinoyama; kuzumanju ¥125; ⊙10am-5pm Thu-Tue, Sat & Sun only in winter; 🍴) You can watch the chef make *kuzu* (arrowroot gelatin) sweets in the shop window here – it's kind of like magic as it transforms from starch to edibles (simple English translation explains the process). Then try it as *kuzumanju* (filled with bean paste) or in noodle form dipped in black honey in the spiffy cafe.

ℹ Information

There is no tourist information centre in central Yoshino, but you can phone the **Yoshino Visitors Bureau** (吉野ビジターズビューロー; ☏0746-34-2522; yoshino-kankou.jp; 2060-1 Kami-ichi, Yoshino-chō; ⊙8.30am-5.15pm Mon-Fri) for help with ryokan and *minshuku* reservations. Some staff speak English. It's located across from Yamato Kami-ichi Station on the Kintetsu Yamato line.

ℹ Getting There & Around

Visitors to Yoshino first arrive at Yoshino Station, and then make their way up to the village proper by the **Yoshino Ropeway** (吉野大峯ケーブル; one-way/return ¥360/610; ⊙9.20am-5.40pm, 7.40am-7.40pm apr) (cable car) or on foot. The ropeway is Japan's oldest aerial tram (1929) and takes about five minutes to climb the 350m.

To reach Yoshino Station from Kyoto, take the Kintetsu line to Kashihara-jingū-mae and change trains (*kyūkō* ¥1230, 2¼ hours; *tokkyū* ¥2550, one hour and 36 minutes). From Nara, change trains twice at Yamato-Saidaiji and Kashihara-jingū-mae (*kyūkō*, ¥850, about one hour 40 minutes; *tokkyū* ¥1780, about 1¼ hours).

From Osaka, direct trains run on the Kintetsu Minami Osaka–Yoshino line from Abeno-bashi Station (by Tennō-ji Station) to Yoshino (*kyūkō* ¥970, one hour and 33 minutes; *tokkyū* ¥1480, 1¼ hours).

The closest JR station to Yoshino is Yoshino-guchi, which has connections with Nara, Osaka and Wakayama. From here, you'll have to take the Kintetsu line (*kyūkō* ¥380, 35 minutes; *tokkyū* ¥890, 26 minutes).

KII PENINSULA   紀伊半島

The remote and mountainous Kii Peninsula (Kii-hantō) is a far cry from central Kansai's bustling urban sprawl. Most attractions are in Wakayama Prefecture (Wakayama-ken), including the mountaintop temple complex of Kōya-san, one of Japan's most important

YUASA, BIRTHPLACE OF SOY SAUCE

Like many great inventions, soy sauce was essentially an accident, and it happened here in Yuasa, on the Kii Peninsula's west coast. Some 750 years ago a clever monk tasted the deep, mahogany-coloured liquid by-product of miso making and realised it had potential. By the mid-Edo period, there were over 90 makers of *shōyu* (soy sauce) here, and today it's hard to imagine Japanese cooking without it.

Yuasa Station is on the JR Kinokuni line between Wakayama and Kii-Tanabe. About 10 minutes' walk northeast of the station, the **Yuasa Soy Sauce Factory** (湯浅醤油工場; Map p410; ☎0737-62-2100; www.yuasasyouyu.co.jp; 1466-1 Yuasa; ⊙9am-4pm) FREE gives tours and tastings (and – surprise! – has a well-stocked shop); their traditional soy-sauce production method takes about two years! About 10 minutes northwest of the station is a special-preservation zone of buildings from the Edo period, when soy sauce production was at its height. Their fine architectural details (lattice fronts, tile roofs, distinctive windows etc) front exhibition spaces about soy-sauce making, as well as galleries and souvenir shops.

Buddhist centres, and the ancient pilgrimage trails and onsen of the Kumano Kodō.

Along the coast are the beachside onsen resort of Shirahama on the west coast, and the rugged coastline of Shiono-misaki and Kii-Ōshima at the southern tip.

ℹ Getting There & Around

The JR Kinokuni line runs around the peninsula's coast, linking Shin-Osaka and Nagoya Stations (some to Kyoto Station). Special Kuroshio and Nankii *tokkyū* trains can get you around the peninsula fairly quickly.

Once you step off the express train to the peninsula, you're at the mercy of slow local trains and buses. For most freedom of movement, renting a car is the best way to get around the area. All of Japan's major car rental companies have branches at airports, in big cities and some small towns.

Kōya-san 高野山

☎0736 / POP 3343

Kōya-san is a raised tableland in northern Wakayama-ken, covered with thick forests and surrounded by eight peaks. The major attraction is the Kōya-san monastic complex, which is the headquarters of the Shingon school of Esoteric Buddhism. Though not quite the Shangri-la it's occasionally described as, Kōya-san is one of Japan's most rewarding destinations, for the natural setting of the area and the opportunity to stay in temples and get a glimpse of long-held traditions of Japanese religious life.

Keep in mind that Kōya-san tends to be around 5°C colder than down on the plains, so bring warm clothes if you're visiting in winter, spring or autumn.

Whenever you go, you'll find that getting there is half the fun – near the end of its journey, the train winds through a series of tight valleys with soaring mountains on all sides, and the final vertiginous cable-car leg is not for the faint of heart.

History

The founder of the Shingon sect of Esoteric Buddhism, Kūkai (known after his death as Kōbō Daishi), established a religious community here in 816. Kōbō Daishi travelled as a young priest to China and returned after two years to found the school. He is one of Japan's most famous religious figures and is revered as a bodhisattva, calligrapher, scholar and inventor of the Japanese *kana* syllabary.

Followers of Shingon believe that Kōbō Daishi is not dead, but rather that he is meditating in his tomb in Kōya-san's Oku-no-in Cemetery, awaiting the arrival of Miroku (Maitreya, the future Buddha). Food is ritually offered in front of the tomb daily to sustain him during this meditation. When Miroku returns, it is thought that only Kōbō Daishi will be able to interpret his heavenly message for humanity. Thus, the vast cemetery here is like an amphitheatre crowded with souls gathered in expectation of this heavenly sermon.

Over the centuries, the temple complex grew in size and attracted many followers of the Jōdo (Pure Land) school of Buddhism. During the 11th century, it became popular with both nobles and commoners to leave hair or ashes from deceased relatives close to Kōbō Daishi's tomb.

Kōya-san is now a thriving centre for Japanese Buddhism, with more than 110 temples. It is the headquarters of the Shingon sect,

410

Kii Peninsula

KANSAI KŌYA-SAN

which has 10 million members and presides over nearly 4000 temples all over Japan.

◉ Sights

The precincts of Kōya-san are divided into two main areas: **Garan (Sacred Precinct)** in the west, where you will find interesting temples and pagodas, and **Oku-no-in**, with its vast cemetery, in the east.

A joint ticket (*shodōkyōtsu-naihaiken*; ¥2000) that covers entry to Kongōbu-ji, the Kondō, Dai-tō, Reihōkan, the Tokugawa Mausoleum and more can be purchased at the Kōya-san Shukubō Association (p414) office and the venues themselves.

★ Oku-no-in
BUDDHIST TEMPLE

(奥の院; Map p412; ⊙24hr) **FREE** One of Japan's most intensely spiritual places, Oku-no-in is a memorial hall to Kōbō Daishi surrounded by a vast, forested Buddhist cemetery. The tall cedars and thousands of peaked stone stupas along the stone path can be utterly gripping, especially in swirling mist. Important Japanese Buddhists have had their remains, or at least a lock of hair, interred here to ensure pole position when the Buddha of the Future (Miroku Buddha) comes to earth.

Oku-no-in is easily reached on foot from the town centre, or you can take the bus east to the Ichi-no-hashi-mae bus stop. From here cross the bridge, **Ichi-no-hashi** (一の橋; Map p412), and head into the cemetery. Buses return to the town centre from Oku-no-in-mae bus stop (or walk it in about 30 minutes).

➡ **Miroku-ishi**

(みろく石; Map p412) Inside Oku-no-in (p410) is a wooden building the size of a large phone booth, which contains the Miroku-ishi. Pilgrims reach through the holes in the wall to try to lift a large, smooth boulder onto a shelf. The weight of the stone is supposed to change according to your weight of

Kii Peninsula

sin. We can only report that the thing was damn heavy!

➤ Mimyo-no-hashi

(御廟橋; Map p412) This bridge is inside Oku-no-in, on the way to Tōrō-dō. To the right of the bridge, worshippers ladle river water from a trough and pour it over the nearby Jizō statues as an offering to the dead. To the left, the inscribed wooden plaques in the river are in memory of aborted babies and those who died by drowning.

➤ Tōrō-dō

(燈籠堂, Lantern Hall; Map p412; ⊘6am-5.30pm) **FREE** At the northern end of the Oku-no-in cemetery is the complex's main building, Tōrō-dō. It houses hundreds of lanterns donated by dignitaries including emperors; two lanterns are believed to have been burning for more than 900 years. Here guests are invited to write letters to Kōbō Daishi.

➤ Kūkai Mausoleum

(空海の墓; Map p412) At the very end of the path through Oku-no-in, this is perhaps the holiest place in Japan. In front of the fence enclosing the mausoleum, you may well find pilgrims offering bouquets of flowers and chanting sutras.

Kongōbu-ji   BUDDHIST TEMPLE

(金剛峯寺; Map p412; ☎0736-56-2011; www.koyasan.or.jp; 132 Kōya-san; admission ¥500; ⊘8.30am-5pm) This sprawling temple is the headquarters of the Shingon sect and the residence of Kōya-san's abbot. The main gate is the temple's oldest structure (1593); the present main hall dates from the 19th century; and the newest annexe was constructed as late as 1984, the 1150th anniversary of Kōbō Daishi's passing. The Great Main Hall has ornate *fusuma* (sliding screen door) masterpieces of landscapes and seasonal scenes by famed 17th-century painters, including those of the Kanō school.

The Banyutei rock garden (1984) is Japan's largest (2349 sq metres). It contains 140 large granite stones brought from Shikoku (Kōbō Daishi's birthplace) and white gravel from Kyoto, which are collectively meant to represent two protector dragons rising from a sea of clouds.

The annexes (Betsuden and Shin-Betsuden) are filled with more contemporary paintings of seasons and images inspired by Kōbō Daishi's sojourn in China.

Admission includes tea and rice cakes served beside the stone garden.

Garan   BUDDHIST TEMPLE

(伽藍; Map p412; admission to each bldg ¥200; ⊘8.30am-5pm) At the western end of central Kōya-san, this complex of eight principal buildings (temples, pagodas) and several other structures is one of Kōya-san's most important sites, along with Oku-no-in and Kongōbu-ji. Sometimes also called Danjo Garan or Dai Garan, the name comes from Sanskrit for monastery. Among the most important buildings are the Kondō, Konpon Daitō (p412) and Chūmo. Even if many of the buildings are 20th- and 21st-century reconstructions, the Garan is well worth a visit.

➤ Kondō

(金堂, Main Hall, Golden Hall; Map p412; admission ¥200; ⊘8.30am-5pm) The Garan's *kondō* is the main hall and enshrines Yakushi Nyorai, the Buddha of medicine and healing. First constructed in the early 9th century, it was destroyed by fire six times; the current structure dates from 1934. The Yakushi Nyorai is hidden, but there are plenty of other mandalas and wall paintings of Bodhisattvas and Buddhist teachings.

KANSAI KŌYA-SAN

Kōya-san

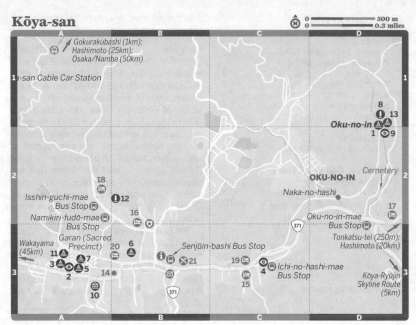

Gokurakubashi (1km);
Hashimoto (25km);
Osaka/Namba (50km)

-san Cable Car Station

Oku-no-in

8
13
1
9

18
Isshin-guchi-mae
Bus Stop
12

Namikiri-fudō-mae
Bus Stop
16

OKU-NO-IN

Cemetery

Naka-no-hashi

Oku-no-in-mae
Bus Stop

17

Wakayama
(45km)
Garan (Sacred
Precinct)
20
6

11
3
7
5
2
14

10

371

Senjūin-bashi Bus Stop

21

Tonkatsu-tei (250m);
Hashimoto (20km)

19

4

15

Ichi-no-hashi-mae
Bus Stop

Kōya-Ryūjin
Skyline Route
(5km)

Kōya-san

→ **Konpon Daitō**

(根本大塔, Great Pagoda; Map p412; admission ¥200) Most recently rebuilt in 1934 after a fire, this 50m tall, bright-orange pagoda in the Garan (p411) is said to be the centre of the lotus-flower mandala formed by Kōya-san's eight mountains. The main object of worship is Dainichi-nyōrai (Cosmic Buddha) and his four attendant Buddhas, painted on pillars, said to combine to form a single mandala. Originally, it's said, the pillars were painted by Kōbō Daishi himself. Even though it's since been repainted, it's an awesome sight.

Reihōkan   MUSEUM

(霊宝館, Treasure Museum; Map p412; admission ¥600; ⊙8.30am-5.30pm May-Oct, to 5pm Nov-Apr) The Treasure Museum has a compact display of Buddhist works of art, all collected in Kōyasan. There are some very fine statues, painted scrolls and mandalas.

Tokugawa Mausoleum   MONUMENT

(徳川家霊台, Tokugawa-ke Reidai; Map p412; admission ¥200; ⊙8.30am-5pm) Built in 1643, the Tokugawa Mausoleum is actually two adjoining mausoleums in a clearing: Tokugawa Ieyasu is on the right and Tokugawa Hidetada on the left, the first and second Tokugawa shoguns, respectively. They are ornately decorated, as are most structures associated with the Tokugawa regime. The mausoleum is near the Namikiri-fudō-mae bus stop (波切不動前バス亭).

👉 Tours

Kōyasan Cross-Cultural Communication Network
TOURS

(Map p412; ☏090-3263-5184, 0736-56-2270; www.koyasan-ccn.com; 347 Kōya-san, Daishi Kyōkai Bldg; 1½hr group tours per person ¥1500; ☉tours Oku-no-in Wed 9am, Garan & Kongōbu-ji Wed 1pm & 3pm Mar-Nov) On Wednesdays, this outfit offers tours of Kōya-san in English with guides from the Koyasan Interpreter Guide Club. Wednesday morning Oku-no-in tours meet at Ichi-no-hashi, and afternoon tours of Garan and Kongōbu-ji meet at the visitor information center in the network's office. They also offer customised private tours (eg two-/four-hour tours ¥10,000/15,000) for up to 10 people.

🎊 Festivals & Events

Rōsoku Matsuri
CULTURAL

(ろうそく祭り; ☉13 Aug) This captivating festival is held in remembrance of departed souls. Thousands of people come to light some 100,000 candles along the approaches to Oku-no-in.

Aoba Matsuri
CULTURAL

(☉15 Jun) Held to celebrate the birth of Kōbō Daishi. Various traditional ceremonies are performed at the temples around town.

🛏 Sleeping

Although it is technically possible to visit Kōya-san as a day trip from Nara, Kyoto or Osaka, we don't recommend it. Instead, take it slow and stay overnight in one of the town's excellent *shukubō* (temple lodgings).

More than 50 temples in Kōya-san offer *shukubō*, which serve *shōjin-ryōri* (Buddhist vegetarian cuisine; no meat, fish, onions or garlic) and typically hold morning prayer sessions that guests are welcome to join or observe.

Lodgings start at about ¥9720 per person including two meals, with a surcharge for solo guests. Prices can vary widely, both between temples and within them, depending upon room (most without en suite bath and toilet), meals and season; generally, the more you pay, the better the room and the meals. Most *shukubō* ask that you check in by 5pm.

Reserve at least a week in advance through the Kōya-san Shukubō Association (p414); you can fill out a request form online, in English.

Many lodgings do not have air-con but do provide fans during warmer months and space heaters during colder months.

⭐ Koyasan Guest House Kokuu
GUESTHOUSE ¥

(高野山ゲストハウスKokuu; Map p412; ☏26-7216; http://koyasanguesthouse.com; 49-43 Kōyasan; capsules from ¥3500, s/d/tr from ¥6000/9000/12,000; @🛜) This convivial place puts the Kōya-san experience within range of even the most budget-conscious backpackers. It's intimate, clean, woodsy, light and airy with capsule-style and private rooms and shower cabinets down the hall. Knowledgable English-speaking staff can help arrange morning prayers and night-time tours, and prepare inexpensive breakfasts and light meals, like Indian curry, for dinner.

Reserve directly, not through the Shukubō Association.

Ekō-in
SHUKUBO ¥¥

(惠光院; Map p412; ☏0736-56-2514; www.ekoin.jp; 497 Kōya-san; r per person with meals from ¥10,800; P😊@🛜) This lovely hillside temple is run by a friendly bunch of young monks, and rooms look onto beautiful gardens. Ekō-in is known for its nighttime tours of Oku-no-in (in English) and as one of the two temples in town (the other is Kongōbu-ji) where you can study seated meditation; call ahead. There's no solo-traveller surcharge.

Fukuchi-in
SHUKUBO ¥¥

(福智院; Map p412; ☏0736-56-2021; www.fukuchiin.com; 657 Kōya-san; r per person with meals from ¥12,960, single travellers ¥16,200; P❄@🛜) This fine temple has outdoor baths with onsen water and a lovely garden designed by the famous designer Shigemori Mirei. Wi-fi is available for limited durations near the temple office. It's occasionally busy with Japanese bus tours. Some staff speak English.

Rengejō-in
SHUKUBO ¥¥

(蓮華定院; Map p412; ☏0736-56-2233; r per person with meals from ¥9720, single travellers ¥11,880; P😊❄🛜) This stately temple has superb rooms, a wealth of gardens, fine painted *fusu-ma* (sliding screen doors) and interesting art on display. English is spoken and sometimes an explanation of Buddhist practices and meditation is available in the early evening.

Shōjōshin-in
SHUKUBO ¥¥

(清浄心院; Map p412; ☏0736-56-2006; www.shojoshinin.jp; 566 Kōya-san; r per person with meals from ¥9,720, with bathroom from ¥16,200; P😊🛜)

A friendly spot with in-room wi-fi and no extra charge for solo travellers. There's an atmospheric old kitchen under a tall wooden ceiling and gold-leaf *fusuma* (sliding screen doors). It's the closest *shukubō* to the Oku-no-in entry.

Sōji-in
SHUKUBO ¥¥¥

(総持院; Map p412; ☑0736-56-2111; www.soujiin.or.jp; r per person with meals from ¥18,360, single travellers ¥29,380; ❋🐾) At home with foreign guests and across the street from the Garan, this pleasantly modern temple has a lovely garden, some rooms with en suite baths and a wheelchair-accessible room with Western-style beds. The top rooms here are among the best in Kōya-san, and the high-quality meals also account for the price differential.

✕ Eating

The culinary speciality of Kōya-san are *shōjin-ryōri,* elaborate and very tasty Buddhist vegetarian meals served at temple lodgings. If you're not staying the night, reserve a *shōjin-ryōri* lunch at a temple; contact the Kōya-san Shukubō Association ahead of time. Prices are fixed at ¥2700, ¥3800 and ¥5400, depending on the number of courses. Otherwise, most eateries around town close by late afternoon. For snacks and simple meals there are a couple of convenience stores.

★ Bononsha
CAFE ¥

(梵恩舎; Map p412; ☑0736-56-5535; 730 Kōyasan; lunch set menu ¥1200; ☉9am-5pm Wed-Sun; 🚗) Japanese, English and French are spoken by the delightful couple who own

this charming cafe with great old wooden beams. It's a relaxing spot for coffees, organic mains and cakes like chocolate cake and tofu cheesecake. Daily lunch set menus are served until they run out (arrive early). It's also a gallery of local pottery.

Tonkatsu-tei
SHOKUDO ¥

(とんかつ亭; ☑0736-56-1039; 49-48 Kōyasan; mains ¥650-950, set meals from ¥1300; ☉11am-2pm & 5-10pm Wed-Sun; 📖) If after all that Buddhist vegetarian cooking you just need some meat, this mom-and-pop shop on the edge of town serves up an assortment of deep-fried goodness: the namesake *tonkatsu* (pork cutlet), chicken, grilled fish and curry rice. No English is spoken, but the sweet older couple who own it make a good go. Look for the yellow roof.

❶ Information

In the centre of town in front of the Senjūin-bashi bus stop (千手院橋バス停), Kōya-san's well-equipped tourist information centre **Kōya-san Shukubō Association** (高野山宿坊協会; Map p412; ☑0736-56-2616; http://shukubo.net; ☉8.30am-4.30pm Dec-Feb, to 5pm Mar-Jun & Sep-Nov, to 5.45pm Jul & Aug; 🐾) stocks maps and brochures, and English speakers are usually on hand. The association also makes *shukubō* and dining reservations (in advance) and rents bikes and English-language audio guides (¥500) to important sights around town.

❶ Getting There & Away

Without a rental car, access to Kōya-san is via the Nankai Railway from Osaka. Trains from Namba Station (*kyūkō* ¥1260, one hour and 40

WORTH A TRIP

RYŪJIN ONSEN

Deep in central Wakayama Prefecture, this village of peaks and gorges along the Hidakagawa has onsen waters that are said to rank among Japan's most beautifying. Try them at ryokan like **Kirari** (季楽里; Map p410; ☑0739-79-0331; www.kirari-ryujin.com; 189 Ryūjin; s/d incl 2 meals from ¥10,000/18,000; 🅿❄❋🐾) or the public bath **Ryūjin Onsen Motoyu** (龍神温泉元湯; Map p410; ☑0739-79-0726; 37 Ryūjin; admission ¥700; ☉7am-9pm). One of Kansai's most prestigious ryokan is also here; **Kamigoten** (上御殿; Map p410; ☑0739-79-0005; www.kamigoten.jp; 42 Ryūjin; r per person incl 2 meals from ¥19,050; 🅿❋🐾) is now in its 29th generation, originally built for the *daimyō* of the Kii fief, a relative of the Tokugawas. For a quick meal, try **Yuzuyume Cafe** (ゆず夢カフェ; Map p410; ☑0739-79-8025; 165-1 Ryūjin; mains ¥860-1240; ☉9am-6pm Mon-Fri, to 7pm Sat & Sun, closing hours vary; 🅿📖) for curry rice, pizza and handmade desserts; it's by the gorge.

If you're travelling between Kōya-san and Kumano Kodō, an overnight in Ryūjin will allow you a meaningful morning or afternoon of sightseeing in those places; otherwise, you'll spend the best part of the day in transit.

minutes; *tokkyū* ¥2040, 43 minutes) terminate at Gokurakubashi, at the base of the mountain, where you can board a cable car (gondola; five minutes, price included in train tickets) up to Kōya-san itself. From the cable car station (Map p412), take a bus into central Kōya-san; walking is prohibited on the connecting road.

Nankai's **Kōya-san World Heritage Ticket** (¥3400, www.nankaikoya.jp/en/stations/ticket. html) covers return train fare (including one-way *tokkyū* fare from Osaka), buses on Kōya-san and discounted admission to some sites.

From Kyoto, if you've got a Japan Rail Pass, take the JR line to Hashimoto, changing at Nara, Sakurai and Takada en route. At Hashimoto, connect to the Nankai line to Kōya-san (¥830, 50 minutes). Without a Japan Rail Pass, it's easier and quicker to connect to the Nankai line at Namba.

To continue on from Kōya-san to Hongū on the Kumano Kodō, return to Hashimoto on the Nankai line and transfer to the JR line to Gōjō (¥210, 15 minutes), then continue by bus to Hongū (¥3200, four hours).

ⓘ Getting Around

Buses run on three routes from the top cable-car station via the town centre to Ichi-no-hashi and Oku-no-in (¥410) via the tourist office at Senjūin-bashi (¥290). The bus office by the top cable-car station sells an all-day bus pass (*ichi-nichi furee kippu*; ¥830), but once up the hill, the sights are easily walkable in about 30 minutes. Take note of bus schedules before setting out, as buses run infrequently.

Bicycles can be rented (per hour/day ¥400/1200) at the Kōya-san Shukubō Association office.

Along the Kumano Kodō

Tanabe, on the west coast of the peninsula, is the biggest transport hub for the pilgrimage routes along the Kumano Kodō; Shingū is its smaller counterpart on the east coast. South of Shingū are the sacred sights in Nachi and Kii-Katsuura. In the centre of the peninsula is Hongū, a major pilgrimage town.

Tanabe   田辺

♪ 0739 / POP 74,777

Tanabe, a small city on the west coast of Wakayama, is the main gateway to the Kumano Kodō. The government of this friendly town has made huge efforts to welcome foreign tourists with lots of info in English and English-speaking staff members at the tourist office.

JAPAN'S UME CAPITAL

The Tanabe region is known for its high production of *ume* (oo-may), the slightly sour, slightly umami fruit with its distinctively Japanese taste. It's usually translated as 'Japanese plum', but don't say that here – locals insist that it's really in the apricot family. Sample it at **Umeshu de Kanpai** (梅酒で乾杯; ♪ 0739-26-5225; 993-3 Minato; ⊙ 10am-7pm), which has tastings of *umeshu* (*ume* wine) and also sells *umeboshi* (pickled *ume*), ever popular among Japanese.

⊙ Sights

Takijiri-ōji   SHINTO SHRINE
(滝尻王子; Map p410; 859 Kurisugawa, Tanabe-shi) One of five important Ōji shrines, Takijiri-ōji marks the beginning of the passage into the mountains, where pilgrims in the 12th and 13th centuries performed ablutions before setting out (the river waters to the right were said to have healing powers). That said, it's been scaled back greatly since those times.

🛏 Sleeping & Eating

Spending the night in Tanabe will enable you to get an early start on the Kumano Kodō and experience small-town life. The tourism bureau (p416) can provide info on lodging.

The epicentre of eats in Tanabe is Ajik-ōji (Flavour Alley), an atmospheric maze of narrow streets that connects dozens of *izakaya* (Japanese pub-eateries), a short walk from Kii-Tanabe Station. Even if English is not spoken, many are well equipped to deal with non-Japanese speakers thanks to English-language menus. Pick up a 'gourmet map' of local restaurants with English menus at the tourism bureau (p416).

Miyoshiya Ryokan   RYOKAN ¥
(美吉屋旅館; ♪ 0739-22-3448; www.miyoshiya-ryokan.com; 739-7 Minato; r per person from ¥3200; 🅿 ❄ ✷ 🤚) Miyoshiya is a simple travellers' ryokan from the 1940s and the knowledgeable English-speaking owner makes a stay here worth it. Most of the Japanese-style rooms have shared facilities and there's a stone common bath. It is a three-minute walk from Kii-Tanabe Station (turn left at the first traffic signal, walk about 300m and it will be on your right).

There are coin laundry facilities, and breakfast costs an extra ¥800.

Konyamachiya
RENTAL HOUSE ¥¥

(紺屋町家; www.kumano-travel.com/index/en/action_ContentsDetail_Detail/id209; 74 Konya-machi; one/two/three guests ¥8640/10,800/14,580; P) This beautifully renovated guesthouse is an exercise in Japanese modernist minimalism, all dark wood posts and beams, white plaster, a mini-kitchen, beautiful bath and even laundry machines and a little deck. There are two Japanese-style bedrooms. The only downside: it's a bit far, a 15-minute walk or 5-minute taxi ride from Kii-Tanabe Station.

PIck up the key and get directions at the Tanabe City Kumano Tourism Bureau (p416).

Shinbe
IZAKAYA ¥¥

(しんべ; 0739-24-8845; www.jpcenter.co.jp/shinbe; Ajikoji; dishes ¥300-1300; 5pm-10.30pm Mon-Sat;) In Ajikoji, this boisterous, family-run *izakaya* is famous for *ebi-dango* (shrimp paste balls) with house-made mayo, croquettes and ridiculously fresh fish that the chef himself might have just pulled in from local waters. Sit at the counter for lots of local colour and tons of fun.

ℹ Information

By the train station, the excellent **Tanabe City Kumano Tourism Bureau** (田辺市熊野ツーリズムビューロー; 0739-34-5599; www.tb-kumano.jp; 9am-6pm) offers detailed info on the region and lodging options, as well as useful maps including a 'gourmet map' of local restaurants with English menus.

ℹ Getting There & Away

The JR Kinokuni line connects Kii-Tanabe with JR Shin-Osaka Station (*tokkyū*, ¥4750, 2¼ hours).

Buses running between Tanabe and Hongū (¥2060, two hours, from stop 2) make a loop of the three surrounding onsen towns (Watarase, Yunomine and Kawa-yu). These buses also stop at several places, which serve as trail heads for the Kumano Kodō.

KUMANO KODŌ: JAPAN'S ANCIENT PILGRIMAGE ROUTE

From earliest times, the Japanese believed the wilds of the Kii Peninsula to be inhabited by *kami*, Shintō deities. When Buddhism swept Japan in the 6th century, these *kami* became *gongen* – manifestations of the Buddha or a bodhisattva – in a syncretic faith known as *ryōbu*, or 'dual Shintō'.

Japan's early emperors made pilgrimages to the area. The route they followed from Kyoto – via Osaka, Tanabe and over the inner mountains of Wakayama – is known today as the Kumano Kodō: the Kumano Old Road. Over time, the popularity of this pilgrimage spread from nobles to *yamabushi* priests (wandering mountain ascetics) and common folk.

The Kumano faith is based on prehistoric forms of nature worship; over the centuries it has mixed with other religions, such as Buddhism. The focal points of worship are the Hongū Taisha (p417), Hayatama Taisha (p418) and Nachi Taisha (p419) 'grand shrines', which are connected via the Kumano Kodō pilgrimage routes. Interestingly, the Kumano faith is not defined or standardised, and is open to reinterpretation by those who visit; it's a universal sacred site.

In 2004 Unesco declared the Sacred Sites and Pilgrimage Routes in the Kii Mountain Range to be World Heritage sites. Many sections of the route have been restored and there is good accommodation en route, making it possible to perform your own 'pilgrimage' through the mountains of Wakayama.

The best way to visit Kumano would probably be to follow the general flow of pilgrims from the 9th century – how could over 1000 years of pilgrimage tradition be wrong? Come down the west coast of the Kii Peninsula from Kyoto or Osaka to Tanabe where there are some great *izakaya* (pub-eateries) and you can get an early start the next morning. Typical routes involve taking a bus from Tanabe, and walking for two days to Hongū, but many variations and longer or shorter trips are possible.

Along the way, most routes converge in Hongū, home of the Hongū Taisha (grand shrine) and some excellent onsen, including Yunomine (p417) and Kawa-yu; many visitors spend a few nights here.

The Tanabe City Kumano Tourism Bureau (p416), one of the most progressive tourism outfits in all Japan, has detailed information and maps of the routes and an English-language accommodation booking site on its homepage, making trip-planning a snap.

Hongū 本宮

Home to a Unesco World Heritage Site shrine, Hongū is also a good starting point for visiting the onsen nearby – Watarase, Yunomine and Kawa-yu. Other highlights include Kumano Hongū Taisha and Kumano Hongū Heritage Centre, and some important Shintō sites. Throw in a lovely guesthouse and cafe and you have the makings of a nice stay.

◎ Sights & Activities

Kumano Hongū Taisha   SHINTO SHRINE
(熊野本宮大社; Map p410; FREE) Kumano Hongū Taisha is one of the three famous shrines of the Kumano Sanzan, collectively a Unesco World Heritage Site; the others are Kumano Nachi Taisha (p419) and Kumano Hayatama Taisha (p418). It's dramatically perched on a tree-covered ridge and reached via a long stone staircase. It's near Hongū Taisha-mae bus stop.

Kumano Hongū Heritage Centre   MUSEUM
(世界遺産熊野本宮館; Map p410; ☑0/35-42-0751; 100-1 Hongū; ☺9am-5pm) FREE This spiffy, modern multimedia museum has detailed information in English about the Unesco World Heritage Sites around the sacred Kumano region. Amid rice paddies behind the heritage centre is Japan's largest *torii* (Shintō shrine gate; 39.9m tall), made out of steel and painted dramatic black.

It also serves as the town's tourist office and post office. Public buses stop right in front.

Onsen

Yunomine, Watarase and Kawa-yu onsen are among Kansai's best, each with its own distinct character and conveniently located to each other. The picture-perfect village of Yunomine (湯峰温泉), said to be one of Japan's first onsen towns, is nestled around a rapidly flowing, narrow river in a wooded valley, with onsen in small ryokan and public baths. Watarase Onsen (わたらせ温泉), between Yunomine and Kawa-yu, is basically one large onsen operation, with a bathing complex surrounded by large inns, while Kawa-yu (川湯温泉) lives up to its name: river-hot water. Onsen water flows from beneath the river into the stones that make the riverbed, and visitors carve out their own baths!

It's possible to walk between the three onsen. The tunnel at the western end of the village at Kawa-yu connects to the Watarase Onsen (the total journey is a bit less than 1km). From Watarase Onsen, it's about 3km west along Rte 311 to reach Yunomine.

Yunomine Sentō   SENTO
(Map p410; Yunomine; admission sentō ¥260, kusuri-yu ¥390; ☺6am-10pm) There are two baths that make up this *sentō* (public bath) in the middle of Yunomine. We suggest the *kusuri-yu* (medicine water), which is 100% pure hot-spring water. Soap and shampoo are not provided, but they are for sale.

Admission to Tsubo-yu Onsen also includes both baths at this *sentō*.

Tsubo-yu Onsen   ONSEN
(つぼ湯温泉; Map p410; Yunomine; admission ¥770; ☺6am-10pm, enter by 9.30pm) Right in the middle of Yunomine, this hot spring is inside a tiny wooden shack built on an island in the river. Buy a ticket at the *sentō* (public bath) next to Tōkō-ji, the temple in the middle of town, and it's yours for up to 30 minutes. Tsubo-yu Onsen admission includes the *sentō*.

Watarase Onsen   ONSEN
(わたらせ温泉; Map p410; Watarase; admission ¥700; ☺6am-10pm, entry by 9.30pm) Built around a bend in the river, Watarase is a large onsen complex, with not as much character as its onsen neighbours Yunomine and Kawa-yu, though it does boast a nice collection of multiple *rotemburo* (outdoor baths) in a rustic, wooded vale. Baths get progressively cooler as you work your way out from the inside bath.

There's also a simple *shokudō* with soba and udon (mains ¥500 to ¥700).

Sennin Buro   ONSEN
(仙人風呂; Map p410; Kawa-yu; ☺6.30am-10pm) FREE This onsen at Kawa-yu is a natural wonder: geothermally heated water percolates up through the gravel banks of the river. In the winter, from December to the end of February, bulldozers are used to turn the river into a giant *rotemburo* (outdoor bath). It's name means 'thousand-person bath', though whether it holds 1000 people is anyone's guess.

The rest of the year, you can make your own bath by digging out some of the stones and letting the hole fill with hot water; then spend the day jumping back and forth between the bath and the cool river water. The best spots are in front of Fujiya ryokan (p418). Bring a bathing suit year-round.

Sleeping & Eating

Yunomine has about a dozen *minshuku* and ryokan, and there are some larger inns in Watarase. If you are on a tight budget it's possible to camp on the riverbanks around Kawa-yu and Watarase Onsen.

If you're not eating at your inn, there's a public hot spring in Yunomine where people boil eggs, corn and more (a nearby shop sells them; closing days vary).

★ **Blue Sky Guesthouse** GUESTHOUSE ¥¥
(蒼空げすとはうす; ☑ 0735-42-0800; www.kumano-guesthouse.com; 1526 Hongū, Hongū-chō; r per person incl breakfast from ¥6000, single travellers ¥7000; P❋❄️) An excellent modern B&B in a glen near central Hongū, with immaculate, comfortably minimalist design, lots of English-language sightseeing info and laundry machines. Its four Japanese rooms have private facilities.

It's approximately a minute on foot from the Kumano-Hongū bus stop. Or from the Hongū Information Centre (p417), walk along the main highway towards the southern end of town for about 10 minutes and look for signs in English.

★ **Fujiya** RYOKAN ¥¥
(冨士屋; Map p410; ☑ 0735-42-0007; www.fuziya.co.jp; 1452 Kawa-yu, Hongū-cho; r per person with meals from ¥16,350, single surcharge ¥5000-10,000; ❋❄️) This upmarket ryokan features tasteful and spacious rooms, all with river views and private facilities in addition to onsen baths. It's closest to the Sennin Buro (p417). There are some Western rooms too, usually an afterthought in most ryokan, but here they're actually beautiful with nature-theme design and private *rotemburo* (outdoor bath).

Ryokan Yoshino-ya RYOKAN ¥¥
(旅館よしのや; Map p410; ☑ 0735-42-0101; 359 Yunomine; r per person without/with 2 meals from ¥6090/9500, single surcharge ¥1080/2160; P❋❄️) In Yunomine Onsen, just steps from Tsubo-yu, is this atmospheric place with a lovely private *rotemburo* (outdoor bath). It's fairly new, the owners are very friendly, and the location has gorgeous riverside views. Rooms have no private facilities. Wi-fi in the lobby.

Minshuku Yunotanisō MINSHUKU ¥¥
(民宿湯の谷荘; Map p410; ☑ 0735-42-1620; www.kumano-travel.com; 168-1 Yunomine; r per person incl 2 meals ¥8640; P❋❄️) At the upper end of the village of Yunomine Onsen, this six-room *minshuku* is exactly what a *minshuku* should be: simple, clean and welcoming. The food is good, and there are rustic wood-built indoor baths, but make sure to visit the tiny *rotemburo: sweeeeet!* Most rooms do not have a private toilet.

The inn doesn't have its own website. Reservations can be made online through the municipal Kumano Travel Bureau.

★ **Cafe Bonheur** VEGAN ¥¥
(カフェボヌール; Map p410; ☑ 0735-42-1833; 436-1 Hongū; lunch mains ¥850-1000, dinner set meal ¥3000; ⊙ 11am-3pm, dinner by reservation; ❄️🌿) An unexpected treasure at Hongū's southern end is this vegan cafe in a former post office (with the wood floors and clapboard walls to prove it). It does lovely lunches like green curries and delectable sandwiches on housemade bagels. For dinner, ask your innkeeper to make a reservation. The charming owner used to be a designer in Tokyo and Osaka.

ℹ️ Getting There & Around

Hongū is served by infrequent buses from JR Gojō Station (¥3200, four hours) and Kintetsu Yamato-Yagi Station (¥3950, five hours and 10 minutes), both in the north; Kii-Tanabe (¥2000, two hours) in the west; and more frequent departures from Shingū (¥1500, 60 to 80 minutes) in the southeast. Most Hongū buses also stop at Kawa-yu, Watarase and Yunomine Onsen (in that order), but be sure to ask before boarding.

Since bus departures are limited, exploring the area by rental car is a good idea. Tanabe, Shirahama and Wakayama City have good rental options.

Shingū 新宮

☑ 0735 / POP 29,334

The small city of Shingū on the east coast of Wakayama is a useful transport hub for access to the Kumano Kodō pilgrimage route and the onsen village of Hongū. The end of the pilgrimage route is here, at Kumano Hayatama Taisha.

◎ Sights

Kumano Hayatama Taisha SHINTO SHRINE
(熊野速玉大社; Map p410; 0735-22-2533; 1 Shingū) **FREE** At the end of the Kumano Kodō pilgrimage route, this shrine dates from prehistory and celebrates Hayatama-no-Okami, the god said to rule the workings of nature and, by extension, all life. Meticulously maintained orange pavilions (some tied with impressively thick *shimenawa*, sacred rope) stand in sharp

contrast to the greenery all around, including what's said to be Japan's oldest conifer.

In town there's a stone staircase, after which a 15-minute climb takes you to a large stone where it is said that the gods originally descended, at Kamikura Shrine.

🛏 Sleeping & Eating

There are a few restaurants in the station area.

Kishū   RYOKAN ¥
(紀州; ☑0735-22-6599; 1-2-15 Isada-chō; r without/with bathroom from ¥3500/4000; ❄@🛜) Cheap and cheerful Kishū calls itself a 'business hotel', but it's really a small, family-run inn with futon bedding and minifridges on tatami or carpeted floors. Laundry machines available.

Hotel New Palace   BUSINESS HOTEL ¥¥
(ホテルニューパレス; ☑0735-28-1500; www.hotel-newpalace.com; 7683-18 Shingū; s/d/tw ¥7000/11,500/13,000; 🅿❄@🛜) For a break from roughing it on the Kumano Kodō pilgrimage route, this new business hotel is a welcome relief, about a five-minute walk from the station. Largish, Western-style rooms offer contemporary design; there are coin-op laundry machines and there's a large common bath in addition to en suites. Breakfast costs extra (buffet/Japanese breakfast set ¥800/1,500).

Tensui   JAPANESE ¥¥
(天酔; ☑0735-21-3175; 1-3-12 Isada-chō; mains ¥630-1800; ⊘11am-2pm & 5pm-10.30pm Wed-Mon) This easygoing, comfortably contemporary cluster of rooms serves a large selection of Japanese specialities – including sashimi, tempura and 100% buckwheat soba and even some Western dishes like pasta.

Look for the black lattice facade across from Kishū.

ℹ Information

There's a helpful **information office** (新宮市観光協会, Shingū-shi Kankō Kyōkai; ☑0735-22-2840; 2-1-1 Jofuku, Shingū Station; ⊘9am-5.30pm; 🛜) at the station.

ℹ Getting There & Around

The JR Kinokuni line connects Shingū with Nagoya Station (*tokkyū*, ¥6870, three to 3½ hours) and Shin-Osaka Station (*tokkyū*, ¥6690, four hours). Shingū can also be reached from Ise with a change of trains (multiple options, from ¥4420, 2½ hours).

There are buses between Shingū and Hongū, about half of which make a loop of the three surrounding onsen (Watarase, Yunomine and Kawa-yu).

The **information office** (p419) rents out bikes (per two hours/day ¥500/1000); get there at least half an hour before closing.

Nachi & Kii-Katsuura
那智・紀伊勝浦

The Nachi and Kii-Katsuura area has several sights grouped around sacred Nachi-no-taki, Japan's highest waterfall (133m). One highlight of the year is the fire festival Nachi-no-Ōgi Matsuri, held in mid-July.

⊙ Sights

Nachi Taisha   SHINTO SHRINE
(那智大社; Map p410) FREE The Shintō shrine Nachi Taisha, near the waterfal **Nachi-no-taki** (那智の滝; Map p410), was built in homage to the waterfall's *kami* (spirit god). It's one of the three great shrines of Kii-hantō, and worth the climb up the steep steps for the inspirational views that cross the gorges to the waterfall and down to the Pacific. After visiting the shrine, walk down to the falls.

The most atmospheric approach to the falls and the shrine is the fantastic tree-lined arcade of Daimon-zaka (大門坂). To get to here, take a bus from Nachi or Kii-Katsuura Station and get off at the Daimon-zaka stop (ask the bus driver to drop you at Daimon-zaka and he'll point you in the right direction from the stop). It's roughly straight uphill just in from the road. From the bus stop to the shrine is roughly 800m, most of it uphill. It's fine in winter, but in summer you'll be a sweaty mess, so consider doing it in reverse (check bus schedules carefully before setting out).

Sanseiganto-ji   BUDDHIST TEMPLE
(山青岸渡寺; Map p410; pagoda admission ¥300) FREE Next to the Shintō shrine Nachi Taisha is this fine old Buddhist temple; the gong above the offering box in the main hall is the largest in Japan, a gift from Toyotomi Hideyoshi.

Nachiyama-oku-no-in   BUDDHIST TEMPLE
(那智山奥の院; Map p410; admission ¥300) At the base of Nachi-no-taki (p419) waterfalls is this Buddhist temple, where you can pay to hike up to a lookout with a better view of the falls.

OFF THE BEATEN TRACK

KII PENINSULA SOUTH COAST

For some stunning coastal scenery, continue down the coast from Shirahama to the southern tip of the peninsula at Kushimoto (串本). Here you'll find **Hashigui-iwa** (Map p410), an amazing natural rock formation is a line of about a dozen spire-like boulders extending 900m into the water like the supports of a bridge. It's popular for a ramble at low tide and for photos at sunrise, and the adjacent visitor centre sells soft ice cream flavoured from local *ponkan* tangerines.

Kushimoto can be reached from Shirahama by JR *tokkyū* (¥1940, 50 minutes) and also from Shin-Osaka (¥5940, 3½ hours). Without your own transport, the best way to explore the area is by renting a bike (per three hours/day ¥1500/2000) at the **Kushimoto Town Tourism Association** (串本町観光協会; ☑ 0735-62-3171; www.kankou-kushimoto.jp; 33 Kushimoto, Kushimoto Station). Buses from the station are few and far between.

🎇 Festivals & Events

Nachi-no-Ōgi Matsuri   CULTURAL
(Fire Festival; ⊙14 Jul) This lively festival takes place at the Nachi-no-taki waterfalls (p419). *Mikoshi* (portable shrines) are brought down from the mountain and met by groups bearing flaming torches.

🛏 Sleeping & Eating

There are a few *minshuku* and guesthouses in Kii-Katsuura.

There are a few informal shops and restaurants near the station.

Minshuku Kosakaya   MINSHUKU ¥¥
(民宿小坂屋; Map p410; ☑ 0735-52-0335; http://kosakaya.jp; 1-18 Kitahama, Nachi-Katsuura-chō; r per person without/with meals from ¥5150/7950; ▣❄🛜) The fourth-generation Kosaka family of innkeepers opened this modern and polished *minshuku* in 2015. The current generation Kosaka-san doesn't speak much English, but he does just fine with his energetic manner and seemingly permanent smile. Hearty meals usually include the local catch of the day. There are onsen common baths, and some rooms have private bath (extra charge). Laundry machines available.

From Kii-Katsuura Station, walk through the arch, and it's about 300m ahead on the right.

ℹ Getting There & Around

Nachi and Kii-Katsuura (two stops apart) can be reached by JR Kinokuni line trains from Shin-Osaka Station (*tokkyū*, ¥6160, three hours and 45 minutes) and from Nagoya Station (*tokkyū*, ¥7200, three hours and 40 minutes).

Buses to the waterfall and shrine leave from Nachi Station (¥470, 17 minutes) and Kii-Katsuura Station (one-way/return ¥620/1000, 25 minutes). Buses to the Daimon-zaka stop leave from Nachi Station (¥330, 11 minutes) and Kii-Katsuura Station (¥420, 19 minutes).

Shirahama   白浜

☑ 0739 / POP 21,534

Shirahama, on the southwest coast of the Kii Peninsula, is Kansai's leading beach resort and has all the trappings of a major Japanese tourist attraction – huge resort hotels, aquariums, amusement parks etc. It also has several good onsen, a great white-sand beach and rugged coastal scenery.

Because the Japanese like to do things according to the rules – and the rules say the only time you can swim in the ocean is from late July to the end of August – the place is almost deserted outside the peak season. It's a great place to visit in June or September, and we've swum here as late as mid-October.

⊙ Sights

The main sights in the town of Shirahama can be divided into two categories: a variety of public onsen (mostly in the town centre), from indoors to seaside, and inspirational coastal attractions south of the town centre.

The natural wonders of Sandan-beki and Senjō-jiki can be reached on foot, or you can bicycle from the main beach in around 30 minutes; you can also take a bus from the station (¥430, 20 minutes to bus stop 'Senjō-guchi').

Sandan-beki   NATURAL FEATURE
(三段壁, Three-Step Cliff; http://sandanbeki.com; lift ¥1300; ⊙lift 8am-5pm) Sandan-beki is a 50m cliff face which drops away vertiginously into the sea. You can pay to take a lift down to a cave at the base of the cliff, or simply clamber along the rocks to the north of the cliff – it's stunning, particularly when the big rollers are pounding in from the Pacific.

Senjō-jiki BEACH

(千畳敷) Senjō-jiki is a wildly eroded point with layer after horizontal layer of stratified rock; this explains its name in Japanese, translating to Thousand Tatami Mat Point.

Shirara-hama BEACH

(白良浜) The town's main beach is famous for its white sand. If it reminds you of Australia, you're not wrong – the town had to import sand from Down Under after the original stuff washed away. This place is packed during July and August, but in the low season it can be quite pleasant. The beach parallels the western side of town.

🏃 Activities

Sakino-yu Onsen ONSEN

(崎の湯温泉; 1668 Shirahama-chō Yusaki, Nishimuro-gun; admission ¥420; ⏰8am-6pm Apr-Jun & Sep, 7am-7pm Jul-Aug, 8am-5pm Oct-Mar, closed Wed year-round) Mentioned in Japan's earliest history book, *Nihon Shōki*, this fantastic bath sits in rocks next to the ocean (taller waves might spill into the lower bath). It's 1km south of the main beach along the seafront road, below Hotel Seamore. No soap or shampoo provided, and gents, note that your side of the bath isn't entirely private.

Come early in the day to beat the crowds.

Shirara-yu ONSEN

(白良湯; 3313-1 Shirahama-chō; admission ¥420; ⏰7am-10pm Fri-Wed) At the northern end of Shirara-hama sits this lovely wooden building with a verandah. Baths are on the 2nd floor and have great ocean views. Enter next to Family Mart.

Shirasuna-yu ONSEN

(しらすな湯; 864 Shirahama-chō; admission May-Sep ¥100, Oct-Apr free; ⏰10am-3pm Tue-Sun, to 7pm daily Jul–mid-Sep) This open-air onsen in the middle of Shirara-hama's boardwalk is a foot bath most of the year. Between June and mid-September you can wear a swimsuit to soak then dash into the ocean to cool off.

🛏 Sleeping & Eating

Shirahama has a mix of towering resort hotels geared toward Japanese package tourists, as well as smaller guesthouses, waterside hotels and *minshuku*.

There's a huge variety of restaurants close to the beach: fish and sushi, burgers, pizza, ramen and more. On the southern edge of town is a collection of restaurants in **Fisherman's**

Wharf Shirahama (フィッシャーマンズワーフ白浜; ☎0739-43-1700; 1667-22 Shirahama-chō; prices vary; ⏰hours vary; ✤), or there's a 24-hour supermarket for self-caterers.

Uminoyado GUESTHOUSE ¥

(海の宿; ☎0739-34-3205; 1393-6 Shirahama-chō; s/d incl breakfast from ¥4000/6000; 🅿❄🐾🤶) This modernised classical Japanese building, a former *okiya* (geisha house), has just reopened as a guesthouse with Western-style rooms (including some bunk beds) and bread and coffee for breakfast. Facilities (down the hall) include design-y baths with natural onsen waters. The really unique point is the kabuki dance show held in a small theatre room (¥1000, 40 minutes), 9pm nightly except Wednesday.

★ Hotel Luandon Shirahama HOTEL ¥¥

(ホテルルアンドン白浜; ☎0739-43-3477; www.luandon-sh.com; 3354-9 Shirahama-chō; r per person from ¥6200; 🅿❄🐾🤶) It's an inconvenient 10-minute walk from the beach area, but you're rewarded with en suite bathrooms and crisp, modern room design. You'll also enjoy bang-on views of Shirahama's inner harbour from the balconies and en suite bathrooms of the fairly spacious and up-to-date Western-style rooms. Add ¥500 for a breakfast set (egg, toast, salad and a drink).

Kiraku SHOKUDO ¥

(喜楽; ☎0739-42-3916; 890-48 Shirahama-chō; mains ¥650-800, set menus from ¥1200; ⏰11am-2pm & 4.30-9pm Wed-Mon; 🍴) This well-kept, cheerful little *shokudō* serves *teishoku* (set meals) like *tonkatsu* (deep-fried pork cutlet) tempura, *katsuo tataki* (lightly roasted bonito) and a popular local fish called *kue* (long-tooth grouper). On Miyuki-dōri, head away from the beach and make the second right, about 150m. It's the traditional building next to the arch over the street.

❶ Information

Shirahama Tourist Association (白浜観光協会; 1384 Shirahama-chō; ☺8.30am-6pm) For tourist information in town, visit this info centre just across from the beach. Enter via the little street by Shirahama Beach bus stop.

Tourist Information Office (☏0739-42-2900; JR Shirahama Station; ☺9.30am-6pm) At Shirahama Station, pick up a map of sights and accommodation.

❶ Getting There & Around

Shirahama is on the JR Kinokuni main line. There are *tokkyū* trains from Shin-Osaka Station (¥5080, two hours and 35 minutes). The same line also connects to Kushimoto, Nachi, Shingū and Wakayama City. A cheaper alternative is offered by **Meikō Bus** (☏0739-42-2112; www.meikobus.jp; ☺9am-6pm), which runs buses between JR Osaka Station and Shirahama via Tanabe (one way/return ¥2700/5000, about 3½ to four hours).

From Shirahama Station, you'll need to take a bus to the main sights (one-way/day pass ¥340/1100, 15 minutes to the beach).

ISE-SHIMA

☏0596 / POP 127,868

The Ise (伊勢, 'ee-say') region, on Mie ('me-ay') Prefecture's Shima Peninsula, is home to Ise-jingū, Japan's most sacred Shintō shrine and one of its most impressive. Its only rival is Nikkō's Tōshō-gū, which is as gaudy as Ise-jingū is austere. To preserve their purity (and, no doubt, the ancient building techniques), the shrine buildings are rebuilt every 20 years! Some interesting historic districts and a variety of inns and restaurants round out the scene in central Ise.

Down the coast is the Shima region, where coastal scenery feels like something out of an Edo-period woodblock print.

Ise is easily reached from Nagoya, Kyoto or Osaka and makes a good two-day trip from any of these cities (you can even do it as a day trip if you take Kintetsu express trains).

❶ Sights

Ise-jingū SHINTO SHRINE
(伊勢神宮, Ise Grand Shrine) FREE Dating back to the 3rd century, Ise-jingū is Japan's most venerated Shintō shrine. It's in two parts – Gekū (p424), the outer shrine,

and the more impressive Naikū (p422), the inner shrine, which are several kilometres apart – both set on sprawling, deeply forested precincts. According to tradition, shrine buildings are rebuilt every 20 years, with exact imitations on adjacent sites according to ancient techniques – no nails, only wooden dowels and interlocking joints. The present buildings were rebuilt in 2013.

Upon completion of the new buildings, the god of the shrine is ritually transferred to its new home in the Sengū No Gi ceremony, first witnessed by Western eyes in 1953. The wood from the old shrine is then used to reconstruct the *torii* (Shintō shrine gate) at the shrine's entrance, or it is sent to shrines around Japan for use in rebuilding their structures.

The buildings are stunning examples of pre-Buddhist Japanese architecture, so you may be surprised to discover that the main shrine buildings are almost completely hidden from view behind wooden fences. Only members of the imperial family and certain shrine priests are allowed to enter the inner sanctum. Don't despair, though, as determined neck craning over fences allows glimpses of the upper parts of buildings (if you're tall enough). You can get a good idea of the shrine's architecture at the Sengūkan museum or at lesser shrines nearby, which are smaller scale replicas.

Smoking is prohibited throughout the grounds of both shrines and photography is forbidden around their main halls. Many Japanese dress fairly neatly to visit the shrines. You might feel distinctly out of place in anything too casual, but you don't have to dress formally – you can even wear shorts, but opt on the side of neatness.

Gekū is an easy 10-minute walk from Iseshi Station; Naikū is accessible by bus from the station or from the stop outside Gekū.

★**Naikū** SHINTO SHRINE
(内宮, Inner Shrine) FREE The Inner Shrine of Ise-jingū (p422) is thought to date from the 3rd century and enshrines the sun goddess, Amaterasu-Ōmikami, considered the ancestral goddess of the imperial family and guardian deity of the Japanese nation. Naikū is held in even higher reverence than its counterpart Gekū (p424) because it houses the sacred mirror of the emperor, one of the three imperial regalia (the other two are sacred beads, at the **Imperial Palace** (皇居; Kōkyo; ☏03-5223-8071; http://sankan.kunaicho.go.jp/english/guide/koukyo.html; 1 Chiyoda, Chiyoda-ku; tours usually 10am & 1.30pm Tue-Sat; Ⓢ Chiyoda line to Ōtemachi, exits

Ise-Shima

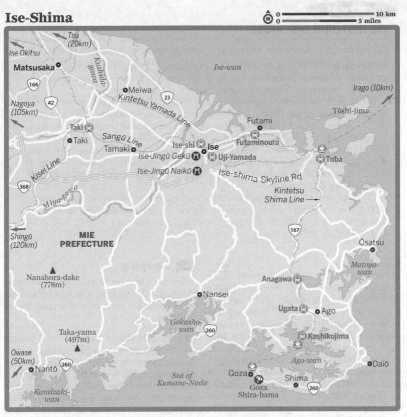

C13b & C10) **FREE** in Tokyo, and the sacred sword, at **Atsuta-jingū** (熱田神宮; ☑052-671-4151; www.atsutajingu.or.jp; 1-1-1 Jingū; Ⓢ Jingū-mae or Jingū-nishi, exit 2) in Nagoya).

Pick up an English-language leaflet (same one given out at Gekū) at the stall just before the shrine entrance. Next to the stall, the bridge **Uji-bashi** crosses the crystal-clear river Isuzu-gawa into the sprawling shrine precincts. Just off the main gravel path is a *mitarashi*, the place for pilgrims to purify themselves in the river before entering the shrine.

The path continues along an avenue lined with towering cryptomeria trees to the **Goshōden**, the main shrine building. As at Gekū, you can only catch a glimpse of the top of the structure from here, past four rows of wooden fences. Closed-circuit TV cameras not so cleverly disguised as trees keep an eye out for potential fence-jumpers!

To get to Naikū, take bus 51 or 55 from bus stop 11 outside Ise-shi Station's south exit (walk south on the main street) or the stop on the main road in front of Gekū (¥410, 15 to 20 minutes). Get off at the Naikū-mae stop. From Naikū, return buses depart from bus stop 2. Alternatively, taxi fare between Ise-shi Station and Naikū costs about ¥2000.

Sengūkan MUSEUM
(せんぐう館; ☑0596-22-6263; 126-1 Toyokawa-chō; admission ¥300; ⊘9am-4.30pm, closed 4th Tue of the month) On the Gekū (p424) premises, this stunning museum illustrates Shikinen-Sengū, the ceremonial reconstruction of the buildings of the Ise shrines and transfer of the deities. There are pristine displays of techniques and tools and a 1:20 scale model of Gekū's buildings. The highlight is a full-size replica of Goshōden (the main shrine building); the real one is off limits to all but the emperor and highest priests. Pick up the English-language leaflet or an audio guide.

ISE HISTORIC DISTRICTS

Outside the shrines are some well-preserved and restored historic districts worth visiting.

Gekū-sandō (外宮参道) is easiest to find; head straight through the *torii* (Shintō shrine gate) from JR Ise-shi Station toward Ise-jingū's Gekū, and soon you'll be in a retro, Shōwa-period street of restaurants and souvenir shops.

Naikū has its own historic district, **Oharai-machi** (おはらい町), a pedestrian street along the Edo-period pilgrimage route to the shrine, packed with several dozen beautifully restored storefronts with shops, restaurants, cafes, sake and beer breweries. There are a few locations of Akafuku (赤福), a landmark teahouse established in 1707, which continues to do a gangbuster business in *mochi* (pounded rice cakes) covered in sweet bean paste. About halfway down the street, turn left onto **Okage-yokochō** (おかげ横町) for more modern recreations of shops and a pavilion with occasional performances. Oharai-machi begins just left of Uji-bashi.

On the other side of central Ise, behind the stations, atmospheric **Kawasaki Kaiwai** (河崎界隈) is lined with traditional houses and shops. From the Ise Pearl Pier Hotel, take the side street by Eddy's Supermarket, and turn left about 50m before the canal. The old buildings begin about 200m north.

Gekū

SHINTO SHRINE

(外宮, Outer Shrine; ☉sunrise-sunset) FREE
Gekū, the Outer Shrine of Ise-jingū (p422), dates from the 5th century and enshrines the god of food, clothing and housing, Toyouke-no-Ōkami. Daily offerings of rice are made by shrine priests to the deity, who is charged with providing food to Amaterasu-Ōmikami, the goddess enshrined in Ise's other main shrine, Naikū (p422). A stall at Gekū's entrance provides a leaflet in English with a map. The main shrine building here is Goshōden, about 10 minutes' walk from the entrance.

Across the river from Goshōden are three smaller shrines worth a look (and usually less crowded).

From Ise-shi Station or Uji-Yamada Station it's a 10-minute walk southwest down the main street, Gekū-sandō, to the shrine entrance. It's slightly easier to find if you start from Ise-shi Station (exit the JR station side, across from Gekū-sandō).

✦ Festivals & Events

As Japan's most sacred shrine, it's not surprising that Ise-jingū is a favourite destination for *hatsu-mōde* (the first shrine visit of the new year). Most of the action takes place in the first three days of the year, when millions of worshippers pack the area and accommodation is booked out for months in advance.

Kagura-sai

PERFORMING ARTS

(☉late Apr & mid-Sep) The Kagura-sai is a good chance to see performances of *kagura* (sacred dance), *bugaku* dance, *nō* and Shintō music.

🛏 Sleeping

There are a number of lodgings for all budgets around the area, from ryokan to business hotels. Most are concentrated around Ise-shi Station.

★ Ise Guest House Kazami

HOSTEL ¥

(風見荘, Kazami-sō; ☎0596-64-8565; www.ise-guesthouse.com; 1-6-36 Fukiage; dm/s/d ¥2600/4000/6000; ☉❄@�📶) This hostel may be budget, but it's got a chill, comfy handmade vibe thanks to wood panelling, driftwood 'trees' and whimsical murals. There are rental bikes (¥500 per day) available, and after sightseeing, you can relax over a beer in the lobby at night. Check-in is 4pm to 10pm, and doors are locked at 11.30pm. It's a two-minute walk from JR Ise-shi Station.

Asakichi Ryokan

RYOKAN ¥¥

(麻吉旅館; ☎0596-22-4101; fax 0596-22-4102; 109 Nakano-chō; r per person with/without 2 meals ¥12,920/7560; P❄❄📶) This atmospheric six-room ryokan, partially dating from the late Edo period, sits a short ride outside Ise's city centre. There's a nice common bath and four rooms have en suite baths. Take bus 1 or 2 from stop 7 outside Ise-shi Station or stop 2 outside Uji-Yamada Station (towards Urata-chō) and get off at Nakano-chō. Taxis from the stations cost about ¥1000.

Staff recommend reserving through a travel agent.

Hoshide-kan

RYOKAN ¥¥

(星出館; ☎0596-28-2377; www.hoshidekan.jp; 2-15-2 Kawasaki; s/d/tr from ¥5350/10,500/15,575, incl breakfast ¥6300/12,500/18,750; @☎) A foreign travellers' favourite, this quaint, 10-room ryokan has heaps of traditional atmosphere, old woodwork and a central garden crisscrossed by a red bridge. But there are no private facilities. From the Ise-shi station area, go straight past Ise City Hotel, and it's on the right at the second light (400m); look for the traditional building with cedars poking in tiny gardens.

Ise Pearl Pier Hotel BUSINESS HOTEL ¥¥
(パールピアホテル; ☎0596-26-1111; www.pearlpier.com; 2-26-22 Miyajiri; s/d/tw ¥8100/16,200/17,280, deluxe s/tw ¥8640/19,400; P⊗❄@☎) This pleasant, updated business hotel has decent restaurants, a small sauna and common bath (¥540 extra) and coin-op laundry machines. It's worth upgrading to a 'deluxe' twin room for more space. It's a two-minute walk from Ise-shi Station's north exit; request a room facing away from the tracks if you're sensitive to noise.

Ise Shinsen RYOKAN ¥¥¥
(伊勢神泉; ☎0596-26-0100; www.iseshinsen.jp; r per person without/with meals ¥15,000/24,000; P⊗❄☎) A modern Japanese cool permeates this new ryokan across from Ise-shi Station, from the views of Gekū's greenery from the 5th-floor lobby to the public bath (day use for nonguests ¥1230). There's a mix of Japanese- and Western-style rooms, all with indoor showers and onsen *rotemburo* (outdoor bath) with ceramic tubs on the balconies, discreetly hidden from outside view.

🍴 Eating

The areas around the two main shrines are filled with restaurants and snack shops. Local specialities are fish and seafood from nearby waters, including *tekone-sushi* (bonito dipped in soy sauce and served atop a rice bowl), and *gyū-don* (a bowl of thinly sliced marinated beef with smothered onion served over a bowl of rice). The local sweet of record is Akafuku *mochi* (pounded rice cakes covered in sweet bean paste), which you can find for sale in souvenir shops around the region.

★Butasute JAPANESE ¥¥
(豚捨; ☎0596-23-8802; Okage-yokochō; gyū-don ¥1000; ⊗9am-6pm Apr-Sep, to 5pm Oct-Mar) This atmospheric local institution specialises in *gyū-don* (beef bowls), with the meat thinly sliced, simmered in hearty sauce and served with onions over rice. It's in the far left corner of Okage-yokochō. There's another by Gekū.

Magatama-tei BUFFET ¥¥
(勾玉亭, ☎0596-22-7788; 2nd fl, 1-1-31 Iwabuchi, Hōon-kan, 豊恩間; lunch/dinner buffet ¥1620/2375; ⊗11am-2.30pm & 6-9pm Thu-Tue, closed 2nd & 4th Tue of the month) This spiffy buffet restaurant serves some 25 dishes made from local ingredients. The market menu selection changes daily, but look for dishes like Ise *udon* and *tekone-sushi*. Expect queues at peak times. Turn left near the Gekū end of Gekū-sandō, and look for the white building with 2nd-floor balcony; it's above a local food-products shop.

Sushi-kyu SUSHI ¥¥
(すし久; ☎0596-27-0229; Oharai-machi; set meal ¥1250-2900; ⊗10.30am-7.30pm; ▣) This former ryokan in Oharai-machi oozes Edo-period charm, from the wooden floors to the large tatami room. It serves the local speciality *tekone-sushi* (bonito dipped in soy sauce and served atop a rice bowl). The 'ume' set is usually enough for most people. It's on the right, just before the Okage-yokochō entrance.

Daiki SHOKUDO ¥¥
(大喜; ☎0596-28-0281; http://ise.ne.jp/daiki; 2-1-48 Iwabuchi; meals from ¥1080, set meals incl lobster from ¥5400; ⊗11am-9pm; ▣) Signage reading 'Japan's most famous restaurant' and 'Royal Family Endorsed' may be an exaggeration, but this is a polished place to sample seafood, including *ise-ebi* (Japanese lobster). Simpler meals include sushi and a tempura *teishoku* (set meal). Look for the wooden building outside and to the right of Uji-Yamada Station.

ℹ Information

Across the street from Gekū (about 10 minutes' walk from Ise-shi Station), **Ise Tourist Information Centre** (伊勢市観光協会; ☎0596-28-3705; 16-2 Honmachi; ⊗8.30am-5pm) has the useful *Map of Ise* and can answer your questions and help you find accommodation. There are smaller information offices in both Ise-shi Station and Uji-Yamada Station.

ℹ Getting There & Away

There are two stations in Ise: Ise-shi Station and Uji-Yamada Station, only a few hundred metres apart (most trains stop at both). Ise-shi Station is the most useful for sights and accommodation.

Ise-shi is connected with Nagoya, Osaka and Kyoto on both the JR and the Kintetsu lines. With a Japan Rail Pass, best connections are via JR Nagoya Station (even if coming from Kyoto/Osaka; take a *shinkansen*) via JR *kaisoku* Mie train to Ise-shi Station (¥2000, 1½ hours).

KANSAI ISE-SHIMA

Without a Japan Rail Pass, the Kintetsu line is most convenient, via comfortable, fast *tokkyū* trains. Kintetsu fares and travel times to/from Ise-shi include Nagoya (*tokkyū*, ¥2770, one hour and 20 minutes), Osaka (Uehonmachi or Namba stations, *tokkyū*, ¥3120, one hour and 46 minutes) and Kyoto (*tokkyū*, ¥3620, two hours).

SHIGA PREFECTURE　　滋賀県

Just across the Higashiyama mountains from Kyoto, Shiga Prefecture (Shiga-ken) is dominated by Biwa-ko, Japan's largest lake. At the southern reach of the lake is Ōtsu, a jumping-off point for two excellent temples. Hikone, with its rare, original castle, and Nagahama, with its well-preserved old downtown, are on the eastern shore. With easy rail connections, these destinations can easily be visited as excursions from Kyoto.

Ōtsu　　大津

📞 077 / POP 340,972

Ōtsu, Shiga-ken's capital, has developed from a 7th-century imperial residence (for five years it was Japan's capital) into a lake port and major post station on the Tōkaidō highway between eastern and western Japan. The big attractions here are two impressive temples, Mii-dera and Ishiyama-dera.

◉ Sights

Mii-dera Temple　　BUDDHIST TEMPLE
(三井寺; 246 Onjōji-chō; admission ¥600; ⊗8am-5pm) Just past its 1200th anniversary (in 2014), these rambling, deeply wooded precincts at the edge of central Ōtsu are the head temple of the Jimon branch of Tendai Buddhism. Four of its buildings are national treasures, while others are important cultural properties. The Niō-mon gate here is unusual for its roof, made of layers of tree bark rather than tiles. Mii-dera is a short walk northwest of Mii-dera Station on the Keihan Ishiyama-Sakamoto line (from Kyoto, change trains at Hama-Ōtsu Station).

Ishiyama-dera　　BUDDHIST TEMPLE
(石山寺; 1-1-1 Ishiyama-dera; admission ¥500; ⊗8am-4.30pm) This Shingon-sect temple was founded in the 8th century. Climb the many steps past a garden of massive boulders to the *hondō* (main hall), famed as the place where Lady Murasaki wrote *The Tale of Genji*. Continue exploring on trails winding further uphill through a lovely forest, including the one that leads up to Tsukimitei hall, for great views over Biwa-ko. The temple is a 10-minute walk from Keihan Ishiyama-dera Station (continue along the road in the direction that the train was travelling).

From Kyoto Station, take the JR Tōkaidō line to Ishiyama Station (*kaisoku* or *futsū* trains only, ¥240, 13 minutes) and switch to the Keihan line for the short journey to Ishiyama-dera Station (¥160). Alternatively, from central Kyoto take the Kyoto subway Tōzai line to Keihan Hama-Ōtsu and transfer to an Ishiyama-dera–bound train (from Sanjo Station: ¥560, 42 minutes including transit time).

⭐ Festivals & Events

Biwa-ko Dai-Hanabi Taikai　　FIREWORKS
(Great Fireworks Festival; ⊗early Aug) For the best views of Ōtsu's Great Fireworks Festival head to the waterfront near Keihan Hama-Ōtsu Station. Trains to/from Kyoto are packed for hours before and afterward.

Hikone　　彦根

📞 0749 / POP 113,819

On the eastern shore of Biwa-ko, Hikone is of special interest for its lovely, historic castle, which dominates the town; it's one of five national-treasure castles for being well preserved since feudal times. The adjoining garden is also a classic and there are remnants of the town's days as a stop along the old Nakasen-dō Road. Visitors also enjoy browsing and snacking in and around the preservation district Yumekyō-bashi Castle Rd.

◉ Sights

★ Hikone Castle　　CASTLE
(彦根城, Hikone-jō; 1-1 Konki-chō; combined admission with Genkyū-en ¥600; ⊗8.30am-5pm) Completed in 1622, this diminutive castle of the Ii family of *daimyō* (domain lords) is considered a national treasure; much of it remains in its original state. One unusual feature is the *teppōzama* and *yazama*, outlets for shooting guns and arrows, designed to be invisible from the outside until being popped out for use. Upper storeys have great views across Biwa-ko. Surrounded by over 1200 cherry trees, the castle's also very popular for springtime *hanami* (cherry blossom viewing).

Shiga Prefecture

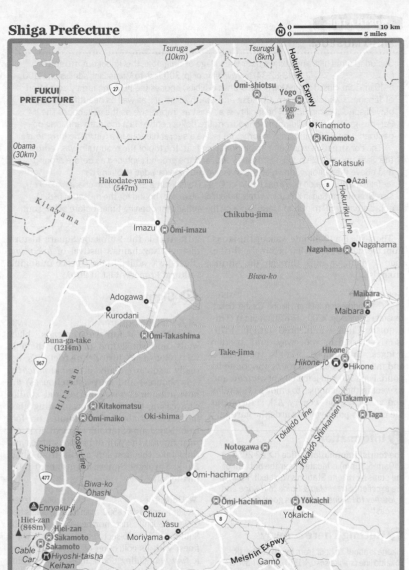

MIHO MUSEUM

Secluded amid hills and valleys near the village of Shigaraki, this knockout **museum** (ミホミュージアム; ☑ 0748-82-3411; www.miho.or.jp; 300 Tashiro Momodani; admission ¥1100; ⊙10am-5pm, closed some Mon & Tue & btwn exhibits) houses the Koyama family collection of Japanese, Middle Eastern, Chinese and South Asian art, as well as beautifully displayed special exhibitions. The facility is at least as impressive as the collection. The IM Pei–designed main building, reached from the ticket centre via a footpath and long pedestrian tunnel opening onto a gorge, feels like a secret hideout in a futuristic farmhouse.

The construction was quite an engineering feat: the top of the mountain was removed, the glass and marble building constructed, and the ground replaced as before around and above the building, down to the massive red pine (a video explains it).

Take the JR Tōkaidō line from Kyoto or Osaka to Ishiyama Station, then change to a **Teisan Bus** (Teisan Konan Kōtsu; www.teisan-konan-kotsu.co.jp) bound for the museum (¥820, approximately 50 minutes). Double-check the website for opening times before setting out.

The castle is a 10-minute walk up the street from the station (take a left before the shrine, then a right, or walk through the shrine grounds).

Genkyū-en
GARDENS

(玄宮園; admission incl in Hikone Castle ticket, separate admission ¥200; ⊙8.30am-5pm) This exquisite Chinese-influenced garden (1679) is criss-crossed by waterways and wooden bridges. Tree-topped islands, peninsulas and interestingly shaped rocks punctuate its pond. For ¥500 you get a cup of *matcha* and a sweet in the teahouse, to enjoy as you relax and gaze over the scenery. Ask someone at the castle to point you towards the garden.

❶ Information

The **tourist information office** (☑ 22-2954; ⊙9am-5.30pm) is located near the bottom of the steps by Hikone Station's west exit. Pick up the excellent *Street Map & Guide to Hikone* and *A Journey to Hikone*, which has good detail on the castle.

❶ Getting There & Away

Hikone is about an hour from Kyoto on the JR Tōkaidō line (*shinkaisoku*, ¥1110). If you have a Japan Rail Pass or are in a hurry, you can take the *shinkansen* to Maibara (¥3300, 20 minutes from Kyoto) and then backtrack on the JR Tōkaidō line to Hikone (¥190, five minutes).

Nagahama   長浜

☑ 0749 / POP 118,230

Easily paired with a trip to Hikone, Nagahama is a well-preserved little town and historic glass-making centre on the northeastern shore of Biwa-ko. The main attraction is the Kurokabe Square historic district. Nagahama's festival of *hikiyama* (floats) was added to the Unesco Intangible Cultural Property List in 2016.

◉ Sights

★ Kurokabe Square
AREA

(黒壁スクエア) *Kurokabe* means 'black walls', and you'll find plenty of them in this photogenic historic district (it's not really a square). Many of the old *machiya* (townhouses) and *kura* (storehouses) are now antique shops, galleries and studios showcasing the town's longstanding glass industry. It's about five minutes on foot from Nagahama Station's east exit. Exit left, turn right at the pair of bronze statues and then take the first left across from Shiga Bank; Kurokabe Square begins about 100m further on.

★ Daitsū-ji
BUDDHIST TEMPLE

(大通寺; admission ¥500, main hall & grounds free; ⊙9am-4.30pm) Just northeast of Kurokabe Square, this Jōdo-sect temple rivals Kyoto's finest with its collection of dozens of historic *fusuma* (sliding door) and *byōbu* (folding screen) paintings of landscapes and wildlife on gold leaf, including important cultural properties by members of the Kanō school. There's also a stunning inner garden. Even if that's not of interest, take a peek at the stately main hall and grounds.

Nagahama Hikiyama Museum
MUSEUM

(長浜曳山博物館; ☑ 0749-65-3300; 14-8 Motohama-chō; admission ¥600; ⊙9am-5pm) A selection of the elaborately ornamented *hikiyama* (festival floats) used during

Nagahama's famous festival Nagahama Hi-kiyama Matsuri are on display here for the rest of the year.

✨ Festivals & Events

Nagahama Hikiyama Matsuri   PARADE
(長浜曳山祭り; ⏱14-16 Apr) The town's famous festival, Nagahama Hikiyama Matsuri, takes place from 14 to 16 April. The highlight is costumed five- to 13-year-old children performing kabuki (stylised Japanese theatre) plays aboard elaborately ornamented *hikiyama* (festival floats). Floats are about 6m high and weigh about 4.6 tonnes. The event was added to the Unesco World Heritage List of Intangible Cultural Properties in 2016.

✕ Eating

The signature dish in town is *yakisaba sōmen* (grilled mackerel over thin noodles). The local beef variety, *Ōmi-gyū*, can be found in restaurants and at stalls around town including as street food such as *niku-man* (steamed wheat buns).

★ **Yokarō**   NOODLES ¥
(翼果楼; ☎63-3663; 7-8 Motohama-chō; mains ¥650-900, set meals ¥1340-2040; ⏱11am-5pm) With its tatami room and garden, this intimate, 200-plus-year-old restaurant positively oozes 'old Japan' charm. The signature dish is *yakisaba-sōmen* (grilled mackerel over thin noodles), which is also available in a set with *yakisaba* (grilled mackerel) sushi. Order from the picture menu. It's on the western side of Kurokabe Square.

ⓘ Information

There's a **Tourist Information Office** (JR Nagahama Station; ⏱10am-4.45pm Mon-Fri, 9.15am-5pm Sat & Sun) located inside JR Nagahama Station, to the right as you exit the ticket gate. Not much English is spoken, but you can ask for maps and restaurant guides. The office also serves as the station's waiting room.

ⓘ Getting There & Away

From Kyoto, *shinkaisoku* (special rapid trains; ¥1320, one hour and 10 minutes) run direct to Nagahama. Alternatively, you can take a *Kodama shinkansen* and transfer in Maibara, a nine-minute ride south of Nagahama (¥2300, 40 minutes including transfer time).

NORTHERN KANSAI

The spectacular coastline of northern Hyō-go and Kyoto Prefectures bursts with sandy beaches, rugged headlands, rocky islets and a laid-back atmosphere. JR trains serve some destinations, but to really explore the coastline you'll want wheels: rental car, motorbike, bicycle or thumb.

Without a doubt, the best place to base yourself for exploration is the onsen town of Kinosaki Onsen, about 1½ hours from Himeji or two hours from Kyoto by comfortable JR express trains.

Miyama-chō   美山

♪ 0771 / POP 33,161 (NANTAN CITY)

The antidote to the urban centres of Kyoto, Osaka and Nara is a visit to Miyama-chō, a sprawling collection of tiny rural hamlets in the Kitayama (Northern Mountains) north of Kurama in Kyoto Prefecture. Miyama-chō has two great sights: Ashū, a hiker's paradise; and Kayabuki-no-Sato, a collection of thatched-roof houses. En route, you can stop at the temple of Bujō-ji.

While you can reach all three by public transport, with a car you can hit them all and even do a quick hike in Ashū in one long day. The northern section of the district continues up the Saba Kaido (Mackerel Route), which historically supplied food from the Sea of Japan to Kyoto.

◉ Sights & Activities

Kayabuki-no-Sato   VILLAGE
(かやぶきの里; ☎0771-77-0660; Kita, Miyama-chō) FREE Along Rte 38 in the village of Kitamura, you'll find Miyama-chō's star attraction, a hamlet boasting a cluster of some 50 thatched-roof farmhouses, said to be the thickest concentration of these buildings in Japan. Many are now repurposed as museums – such as the Folk Museum (美山民俗資料館, Minzoku Shiryōkan) and Little Indigo Museum (ちいさな藍美術館, Chīsa na Aibijutukan) – shops, cafes and inns, amid private homes and temples. Allow an hour or more for a good ramble.

In 1994 the village was designated a national preservation site; since then the local government has been generously subsidising the exorbitant cost of re-thatching the roofs (at an average cost of ¥6 million – around US$60,000).

KANSAI MIYAMA-CHŌ

Bujō-ji
TEMPLE

(峰定寺; Hanase-Harachi-chō; admission ¥500, children under 12yr not permitted; ☺9am-3.30pm, closed on rainy/snowy days & Dec-Mar) Remote Bujō-ji is a *Shugendo* (mountain asceticism) temple that is also called 'the Northern Omine', a reference to Omine-san in Nara Prefecture, which is a centre for Japan's *yamabushi* (mountain mystics). It's a 430-step climb to the main hall.

First, you surrender your bags and cameras, and get a special pilgrim's bag and staff plus a printout of a mantra to chant as you climb. Only then can you pass through the gate and climb to the hall. Just before the hall, ring the bell, focus your thoughts and then climb to the verandah to soak up the views.

It's located off Rte 38, 2km east of the Daihizan-guchi bus stop.

Ashū
HIKING

(芦生) Reached by narrow, twisty mountain road (take the turn off Rte 38 after descending from Sasari-tōge pass), this remote, *tiny* village on the eastern edge of Miyama-chō is known for its 4200-hectare virgin forest. Administered by Kyoto University's Department of Agriculture, it's about the only remaining virgin forest in Kansai. Hiking trails enter from above the stone hut at Sarari-tōge pass and from Ashū at the bottom of the pass; register at the office in Ashū before entering the forest.

The most basic walk follows old train tracks along the undammed river Yura-gawa. More involved hikes continue beyond the tracks up the river or up side valleys. If you intend to do serious hiking here, grab a copy of Shobunsha's Yama-to-Kogen *Kitayama* map at a Kyoto bookshop.

🛏 Sleeping

Miyama Heimat Youth Hostel
HOSTEL ¥

(美山ハイマートユースホステル; ☎0771-75-0997; www.jyh.or.jp; 57 Obuchinakasai, Miyama-chō, Nantan; dm members/nonmembers ¥3460/4100; P⊜❀🛜) A real rarity, even in Japan: a youth hostel in a *kayabukiya* (thatched-roof house) – you can see some exposed beams built into the ceiling – with both Japanese- and Western-style bedding. Breakfast (¥700) and dinner (¥1240 to ¥4300) cost extra. It's located in far western Miyama-chō, so you'll probably want your own transport as it's quite a distance to sights and activities and buses are not frequent.

Asiu Yama-no-Ie
GUESTHOUSE ¥¥

(芦生山の家; ☎0771-77-0290; www.cans.zaq.ne. jp/asiuyamanoie; Ashū, Miyama-chō, Nantan-shi; r per person incl 2 meals ¥7560; P❀) Built in the early Aughts, this well-kept, spacious, eight-room wooden guesthouse is super convenient for hikers visiting the virgin forest of Ashū, which is practically next door. Rooms sleep up to four on Japanese-style futons or Western-style bunk beds. Have a Japanese speaker call to reserve.

Matabe
MINSHUKU ¥

(またべ; ☎0771-77-0258; Kita, Miyama-chō, Nantan-shi; r per person incl 2 meals from ¥8700, solo travellers ¥9200; P⊜❀🛜) In the Kayabuki-no-Sato village of thatched-roof homes, this three-room *minshuku* (family-run inn) is traditional on the outside yet clean and modern on the inside, with Japanese-style rooms with shared facilities. Have a Japanese speaker call to reserve.

Kigusuriya
RYOKAN ¥¥¥

(きぐすりや; ☎0771-76-0015; www.kigusuriya. com; 8-1 Imayasu Tsurugaoka; r per person with two meals from ¥17,280; P❀🛜) In northern Miyama-chō and surrounded by farmland, this four-room family-run inn started as a drugstore on the old road connecting Kyoto with the sea. The kindly owners place great importance on the delicious meals. They've just opened additional guest rooms in a renovated farmhouse a few doors down. Get the English-language walking map for a rustic neighbourhood stroll.

If you don't have your own car, you can avail of a shuttle service to Sonobe Station and Kayabuki-no-Sato.

🍴 Eating & Drinking

Morishige
NOODLES ¥

(もりしげ; ☎0771-75-1086; Taninoshimo 15, Uchi-kubo, Miyama-chō; noodle dishes from ¥750; ☺11am-3pm Wed-Sun) This thatched-roof place on the road to Kayabuki-no-Sato serves simple but tasty noodle dishes as well as *nabe* (hotpot) dishes. Look for it behind the cluster of shrubs and pines.

Yururi
JAPANESE ¥¥¥

(厨房　ゆるり; ☎0771-76-0741; http://youluly. umesao.com; 15 Sano-mae, Morisato; lunch/dinner sets ¥3240/5400) A wonderfully elegant restaurant serving *kappō-ryōri* (gourmet set menus) in a fine thatched-roof house. It's about 30 minutes north of the Miyama-chō centre by car. Reservations are required.

Saika CAFE
(采花; ☎ 0771-77-0660; Kayabuki-no-Sato; ⊙ 11am-5pm) This delightful little cafe and gallery specialises in sweets handmade from local ingredients.

❶ Getting There & Away

To get here by train and bus, take the JR Sagano/San-in line from Kyoto Station to Hiyoshi Station (¥760, 50 minutes), then a bus from Hiyoshi to Kita (Kayabuki-no-Sato; ¥610, 50 minutes). Note that this bus runs only on Sunday and holidays; on other days, it's necessary to change midway at Miyawaki.

The fastest road to Miyama-chō is Rte 162 (Shūzankaidō), but there is a lovely but longer (two-hour) option (routes 38/477) via Kurama and over Hanase-tōge and Sasari-tōge passes. This route is also a good option for getting to Bujō-ji.

You can also get to Bujō-ji and Ashū (but not Kita) via Kyoto bus 32 from Demachiyanagi Station in Kyoto. If you're only going to Bujō-ji, get off at Daihizan-guchi bus stop (¥930, 95 minutes) and walk 2km east on the narrow road. If you're going to Ashū, continue to Hirogawara (¥1100, 110 minutes) and hike over Sasari-tōge. From Hirogawara follow the road to the pass and then take the trail down to Ashū (use Shobunsha's Yama-to-Kogen series *Kitayama* map).

Kinosaki Onsen 城崎温泉

☑ 0796 / POP 3778

In northern Hyōgo Prefecture, Kinosaki Onsen is one of Japan's best places to sample the classic onsen experience. A willow-lined canal runs through the town centre, and many of the houses, shops and restaurants retain their traditional charm. Add to this the delights of crab fresh from the Sea of Japan in winter, and you'll understand why this is one of our favourite overnight trips from the cities of Kansai.

Kinosaki Onsen is flat and easily walkable. It's about 20 leisurely minutes from one end to the other. Trains arrive at Kinosaki Onsen Station, in the southwest corner of town. From here, Eki-dōri heads north and intersects with the willow-lined river Ōtani-gawa. Turn left on the streets paralleling the river, Kitayanagi-dōri and Minamiyanagi-dōri (north and south willow streets) to reach most onsen, inns and restaurants. Should your feet grow weary, there are a number of *ashi-yu* (foot baths) along the way.

◉ Sights

Genbudō CAVE
About 5km south of Kinosaki Onsen proper, Genbudō is a collection of five mysterious caves with otherworldly surfaces of pillar-like ripples formed by basalt lava 1.6 million years ago. The route there along the Maruyama-gawa, amid rolling hills and rice fields, is lovely by bike or car and explodes with maples in autumn. Look for the signboards for San-in Kaigan National Park.

✗ Activities

Kinosaki Onsen's biggest attraction is its seven onsen, in various styles from simple to over the top. Overnight guests clip-clop around the canal from bath to bath wearing *yukata* (light cotton kimono) and *geta* (wooden sandals). You can get a map of local onsen from the information office (p433) or your lodging. Paying individually at each onsen can add up quickly, so the *yumeguri* pass (¥1200) is a great deal.

★ **Gosho-no-yu** ONSEN
(御所の湯; Yunosato-dōri; admission ¥800; ⊙ 7am-11pm, enter by 10.30pm, closed 1st & 3rd Thu of the month) If you have time for only one of Kinosaki's onsen, make it this one. The entry area is decorated like the Kyoto Imperial Palace it is known for lovely log construction, a nice two-level *rotemburo* and fine maple colours in autumn. It has pride of place among the onsen on the main street, Yunosato-dōri.

Sato-no-yu ONSEN
(さとの湯; admission ¥800; ⊙ 1-9pm Tue-Sun, enter by 8.40pm) This onsen has a fantastic variety of baths, including Arab-themed saunas, rooftop *rotemburo* and a 'Penguin Sauna' (basically a walk-in freezer – good after a hot bath). Women's and men's baths shift floors daily, so you'll have to go two days in a row to sample all of the offerings. It's the closest onsen to JR Kinosaki Onsen Station.

Ichi-no-yu ONSEN
(一の湯; admission ¥600; ⊙ 7am-11pm Thu-Tue, enter by 10.30pm) This onsen has two sections, a main bath that shows its age and a wonderful 'cave' bath. It's near where Kitayanagi-dōri meets Yunosato-dōri.

🛏 Sleeping

A big part of the fun of a visit here is a ryokan stay, and there's a variety of inns for budgets from midrange to sky high. Most lodgings have their own *uchi-yu* (private baths), but also provide their guests with free tickets to the *soto-yu* (public baths).

Ryokan Yamamotoya
RYOKAN ¥¥

(旅館山本屋; ☑ 0796-32-2114; www.kinosaki.com; 643 Yushima, Kinosakichō; r per person incl meals from ¥16,200; ❄️ 🛜) This fine, 15-room ryokan with a 350-year history offers lovely rooms, cosy indoor-outdoor baths and excellent food. It's in the middle of town, near Ichi-no-yu onsen. Rooms have river or mountain views but no private bath (sink and toilet only). Solo travellers are accepted in the spring and autumn only and must pay a single supplement.

Suishōen
RYOKAN ¥¥

(水翔苑; ☑ 0796-32-4571; www.suisyou.com; 1256 Momoshima; r per person without meals ¥6,480-15,876, with meals from ¥18,360; ❄️ 🛜) This excellent modern 34-room ryokan boasts great indoor and outdoor onsen baths, sauna and Japanese rooms with en suite baths, around a fabulous garden where *nō* plays are projected on a stage. It's a short drive northeast from the town centre, but they'll whisk you to and from the onsen of your choice in their own London taxi. It's a strangely pleasant feeling to ride in the back wearing only a *yukata*!

Western-style rooms are also available, with sink and toilet but no bath.

Mikuniya
RYOKAN ¥¥

(三国屋; ☑ 0796-32-2414; www.kinosaki3928.com; 221 Yushima; r per person without/with meals from ¥9,720/16,200; ❄️ @ 🛜) This charming, well-kept ryokan offers comfy Japanese rooms (12 in a main building and an annexe) with a toilet and sink, onsen baths for private use, and friendly, English-speaking owners. Heading into town from the station, it's about 150m on the right; look for the rickshaw.

Dinner is served in rooms; if you want Western breakfast, head to the inn's nearby cafe.

★ Nishimuraya Honkan
RYOKAN ¥¥¥

(西村屋本館; ☑ 0796-32-2211; www.nishimuraya.ne.jp/honkan; 469 Yushima; r per person incl 2 meals from ¥32,550, single travellers from ¥43,350; ❄️ @ 🛜) In its seventh generation and tops in town, this luxurious ryokan is the real deal. Its maze-like layout lends a sense of privacy, the two onsen baths are exquisite, most rooms look out over private gardens, and there's a private gallery of art and historical artefacts. Seasonal *kaiseki* (Japanese haute cuisine) meals are the final touch.

🍴 Eating

Fresh *kani* (crab) is a speciality in Kinosaki Onsen during the winter months (and frozen during other times). It is often enjoyed in *kani-suki* (crab *sukiyaki* – in sake, soy and vinegar broth), cooked at your table with vegetables. Note that many visitors opt for a two-meal option at their ryokan, so some restaurants in town shut down early.

Masuya
NOODLES ¥¥

(ますや; ☑ 0796-32-2642; 654 Yushima; meals ¥900-1550; ⏱️ 11am-9.30pm; 🅿️) This soba and udon specialist has been in business for half a century and shows it, with atmospheric woodwork and walls festooned with old farm and home implements. Go for dishes like *kamozaru* (chilled soba with duck), *tendon* (prawn tempura rice bowl) or curry udon. Even their *dashi* (fish stock) is made in house.

It's by the old-fashioned post box on Kitayanagi-dōri, east of Yanagi-yu onsen.

Okeshō
SEAFOOD ¥¥

(おけしょう海中苑; ☑ 0796-29-4832; 132 Yushima; kaisendon ¥1400-1950; ⏱️ 11am-6pm; 🛜🅿️) This restaurant above a fish market serves a varied menu: sushi, fried dishes, tempura, salads etc. In addition to its signature *kaisendon* (seafood rice bowl), deep-pocketed crab lovers can order a full-on *kani* menu (per person ¥9500, minimum two orders). Budget crab lovers should try the *kani zosui* (rice porridge with crab), the ultimate comfort food.

Staff will prepare fish purchased downstairs at roughly twice the retail price (four times for crab). There are many windows to look out on Eki-dōri below. Look for the sea-blue awning with a ship's stern sticking out from above the entrance.

Gubigabu
PUB FOOD ¥¥

(グビガブ; www.gubigabu.com; 646 Yushima; mains ¥650-2700; ⏱️ 11.30am-10pm Fri-Wed, closed 3rd Wed of the month; 🅿️) This craft-beer pub near the town centre has four house beers on tap and serves a diverse menu of pasta, *jidori* (local chicken), curry rice and beer snacks. Look for pancakes made with beer batter, or go nuts with the Tajima beef steak.

Koyume
IZAKAYA ¥¥

(こ夢; ☑ 0796-32-2695; 691 Yushima; dishes ¥150-1500; ⏱️ 11.30am-2.30pm Nov-Mar, 5.30-11pm year-round) Rub shoulders with locals at this kindly, tiny *izakaya*, over a varied menu including *kani-kamameshi* (crab over steamed rice), *kushikatsu* (fried skewers), *agedashi-tofu* (creamy, deep-fried tofu), *moro-kyu* (cucumber with sweet miso) and plenty of sake. There's a half-dozen counter seats plus *hori-kotatsu* (well-in-the-floor) seating. It's on the small street behind Jizo-yu and Yanagi-yu onsen.

★ **Irori Dining Mikuni** STEAK ¥¥¥
(いろりダイニング三國; ☑ 0796-32-4870; 2nd fl, 219 Yushima; lunch mains ¥1500-3800, dinner sets ¥2000-3600; ⏱ 11am-2.30pm & 6-10pm Thu-Tue) If you want a break from Kinosaki seafood, this new, cosy, whitewashed spot on Eki-dori serves Tajima beef (both a cousin and a neighbour of Kōbe beef). Get yours atop *donburi* (rice bowl; our favourite), in croquettes, or as steak dinners (¥5300). To preserve the grownup atmosphere, kids of primary school age and younger are not permitted at dinner time.

It's just south of Mikuniya Ryokan.

ⓘ Information

There are two information centres opposite the station.

Kinosaki Onsen Ryokan Service Centre (お宿案内所; ☑ 0796-32-4141; 78 Yushima; ⏱ 9am-6pm) At this office operated by the local ryokan association, staff will gladly help you find a place to stay and make bookings, as well as provide town maps. It also rents bicycles and operates a luggage delivery service (¥100 per piece) for guests at member ryokan. No English spoken, but they do work with a translation service.

Sozoro (そぞろ; ☑ 0796-32-0013; www.kinosaki-info.com; 96 Yushima; ⏱ 9am-6pm; 🛜) This new tourist information centre is focused on sightseeing and activities and can help arrange tours around the region. Reservations can be made online.

ⓘ Getting There & Around

Kinosaki is on the JR San-in line; there are a few daily *tokkyū* from Kyoto (¥4320, two hours and 25 minutes), Osaka (¥5080, two hours and 40 minutes) and Himeji (¥3340, one hour and 45 minutes).

There's a free shuttle bus operated by the ryokan association, timed to train arrivals to take you to member inns for check-in. Ask at your inn for information. If travelling on foot, you can drop your luggage at the tourist information office for delivery to your inn (¥100 per piece).
Kinosaki Onsen Ryokan Service Centre (p433) rents bicycles (per two hours/day ¥400/800; return by 5pm).

Tango Peninsula 丹後半島

The peninsula Tango-hantō juts up into the Sea of Japan on the north coast of Kyoto Prefecture. The peninsula's interior is covered with thick forest, terraced farms, idyllic mountain villages and babbling streams, while the serrated coast alternates between good sandy beaches, gumdrop-shaped islands, bays, inlets and rocky points. Follow the coastal Route 178 around the peninsula for truly spectacular scenery.

At the base of the peninsula, on the east side, **Amanohashidate** (天橋立, Bridge to Heaven) **FREE** has been rated for centuries as one of Japan's 'three great views'. The 'bridge' is really a 3.5km long, narrow sand spit covered with some 8000 pine trees. You can cross Amanohashidate on foot, by bicycle or on a motorcycle of less than 125cc capacity. Bicycles can be hired at a number of places for ¥400 for two hours or ¥1600 per day. (Be warned though that it's a bit of a tourist circus.)

Up the coast is **Ine** (伊根), a village sitting on a perfect little bay where boats moor as if in car ports under special houses called *funaya*, built right over the water. Just around the tip of the peninsula is the hillside onsen complex, **Ukawa Onsen Yoshino-no-Sato** (宇川温泉 よし野の里; ☑ 0772-76-1000; www.ukawaonsen.jp; 1562 Kyusō; bathing ¥600; ⏱ 11am-9pm, longer hours in summer), with views down to the sea. There's a simple cafe and a shop selling local farm products here.

On the west coast, make a stop at **Kotohiki-hama** (琴引浜; Amino; parking per day ¥1000; ⏱ campground Apr-Oct), a beautiful beach hemmed in by pine-topped hills, with a tiny seaside onsen pool (bring your swimsuit). There are also bare-bones but pretty camping facilities (campsites ¥3000; first come, first served) with simple toilets and showers.

The nicest place to stay is **Totoya** (と卜屋; www.kyoto-sea.com; 566 Taiza, Tango-chō; r per person without meals/with 2 meals from ¥4900/11,900; Ⓟ 😊 ❄ 🛜), a 10-room inn with shared hot spring baths seemingly in the middle of nowhere, and that's kind of the point. The gregarious owner can arrange activities for guests, including kimono-wearing, fabric dyeing, fruit-picking and sea-cave exploring. With advance notice, pickup is available from Amino Station on the Kyoto Tango Railway (Tantetsu) line.

Hiroshima & Western Honshū

Best Places to Eat

➡ Okonomi-mura (p442)

➡ Takadaya (p471)

➡ Mamakari-tei (p472)

➡ Yabure-Kabure (p500)

➡ Sabō Kō (p489)

Best Places to Sleep

➡ Hattōji International Villa (p459)

➡ Benesse House (p463)

➡ Hiroshima Inn Aioi (p442)

➡ Hinoyama Youth Hostel (p499)

➡ Iwasō Ryokan (p448)

Why Go?

Travellers to Western Honshū (本州西部) will find a tale of two coastlines. San-yō (literally 'sunny side of the mountains'), looking out over the Inland Sea, boasts the bigger cities, the narrow-laned portside and hillside towns, ceramic history and the fast train. This is the coast that holds the region's big name – indelibly scarred, thriving, warm-hearted Hiroshima.

On the other side of the dividing Chūgoku mountain range, San-in (literally 'in the shade of the mountains') gazes out across the expanse of the Sea of Japan. Up here, it's all about an unhurried pace, onsen villages that see few foreigners, historic sites, wind-battered coastlines and great hospitality.

Head inland for hikes along gorges and through caves, or escape the mainland altogether – you could take a trip to the Inland Sea and its galaxy of islands, or lose yourself in the remote and rugged Oki Islands (Oki-shotō) in the Sea of Japan.

When to Go
Hiroshima

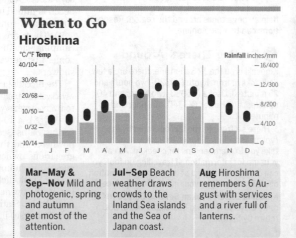

| Mar–May & Sep–Nov Mild and photogenic, spring and autumn get most of the attention. | Jul–Sep Beach weather draws crowds to the Inland Sea islands and the Sea of Japan coast. | Aug Hiroshima remembers 6 August with services and a river full of lanterns. |

ⓘ Getting There & Around

The *shinkansen* (bullet train), linking Osaka and Kyoto with Okayama, Hiroshima and other cities on the way to Shimonoseki, is the fastest way to get around along the Inland Sea coast of Western Honshū. Along the Sea of Japan the *shinkansen* is not an option. Trains operate all the way from Tottori to Hagi, hugging some beautiful rugged coastline on the way, but services are generally infrequent and it's hard to avoid the slow 'local' services. If you're really in a hurry up here (and to get way off the beaten track), it's worth hiring a car. There are few train and bus lines servicing inland destinations – the major rail link between the two coasts runs between Okayama and Yonago.

Setouchi Seaplanes (www.setouchi-seaplanes. com) offer sightseeing flights around the Seto Inland Sea from ¥32,000 for a 50-minute trip.

HIROSHIMA & AROUND

It's easy to beeline it to Miyajima to glance at the floating *torii*, or to Hiroshima's Peace Memorial Park to witness how locals have transformed a tragedy into a firm call for peace.

Yet there are other quiet wonders worth exploring in the region around Hiroshima. Stroll narrow cobbled streets in the seaside town of Tomo-no-ura, go temple hunting in Onomichi, sip sake at one of many breweries in Saijō, and save some time for reflection in an ancient Shintō shrine in Ōmi-shima.

Hiroshima 広島

♪ 082 / POP 1,196,800

To most people, Hiroshima means just one thing. The city's name will forever evoke thoughts of 6 August 1945, when Hiroshima became the target of the world's first atomic-bomb attack. Hiroshima's Peace Memorial Park is a constant reminder of that day, and it attracts visitors from all over the world with its moving message of peace. And leafy Hiroshima, with its wide boulevards and laid-back friendliness, is far from a depressing place. Present-day Hiroshima is home to an ever-thriving cosmopolitan community, and it's worth spending a couple of nights here to experience the city at its vibrant best.

⊙ Sights

⊙ Peace Memorial Park

Hugged by rivers on both sides, Peace Memorial Park (平和記念公園; Map p438; Heiwa-kinen-

kōen; 🚋 Genbaku-dōmu-mae) is a large, leafy space criss-crossed by walkways and dotted with memorials. Its central feature is the long tree-lined Pond of Peace leading to the **cenotaph** (原爆死没者慰霊碑; Map p438). This curved concrete monument holds the names of all the known victims of the bomb. Also at the pond is the **Flame of Peace** (平和の灯; Map p438), set to burn on until all the world's nuclear weapons are destroyed.

Look through the cenotaph down the pond and you'll see it frames the Flame of Peace and the Atomic Bomb Dome across the river – the park was planned so that these features form a straight line, with the Peace Memorial Museum at its southern end.

Just north of the road through the park is the **Children's Peace Monument** (Map p438) FREE, inspired by Sadako Sasaki, who was two years old at the time of the atomic bomb. When Sadako developed leukaemia at 11 years of age, she decided to fold 1000 paper cranes. In Japan, the crane is the symbol of longevity and happiness, and she believed if she achieved that target she would recover. She died before reaching her goal, but her classmates folded the rest. A monument was built in 1958. Sadako's story inspired a nationwide spate of paper-crane folding that continues to this day. Surrounding the monument are strings of thousands of colourful paper cranes sent here by school children from around the country and all over the world.

Nearby is the **Korean Atomic Bomb Victims Memorial** (韓国人原爆犠牲者慰霊碑; Map p438). Many Koreans were shipped over to work as slave labour during WWII, and Koreans accounted for more than one in 10 of those killed by the atomic bomb. Just north of this memorial is the **Atomic Bomb Memorial Mound** (Map p438) – the ashes of thousands of unclaimed or unidentified victims are interred in a vault below.

There are other monuments and statues throughout the park, and plenty of benches, including those along the riverside looking across to the Atomic Bomb Dome; they make this a pleasant area to take a break and reflect.

★ Atomic Bomb Dome HISTORIC SITE

(原爆ドーム, Genbaku Dome; Map p438; 🚋 Genbaku-dōmu-mae) FREE Perhaps the starkest reminder of the destruction visited upon Hiroshima in WWII is the Atomic Bomb Dome. Built by a Czech architect in 1915, it was the Industrial Promotion Hall until the bomb exploded almost directly above it. Everyone inside was killed, but the building

Hiroshima & Western Honshū Highlights

1 Hiroshima (p435) Reflecting on a tragic past in this cosmopolitan city.

2 Naoshima (p460) Marvelling at nature meeting contemporary art on this island.

3 Miyajima (p445) Photographing the floating shrine and staying at a ryokan.

4 Shimanami Kaidō (p451) Island-hopping by bicycle via this chain of bridges to Shikoku.

5 Taikodani-Inari-jinja (p490) Walking through the shrine gates in the mountain town of Tsuwano.

6 Onomichi (p449) Following in the footsteps of cats on a temple hunt.

7 Izumo Taisha (p484) Seeing where the gods go on holiday.

8 Oki Islands (p478) Getting way off the beaten track in these nature- and culture-rich islands.

9 Matsue (p474) Strolling around the moated castle and soaking up a gorgeous sunset.

10 Iwami Ginzan (p485) Exploring the World Heritage silver mine district.

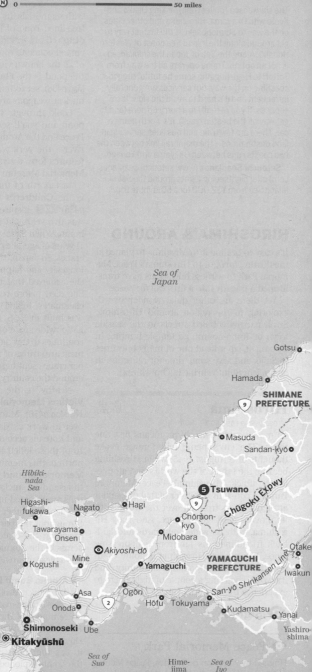

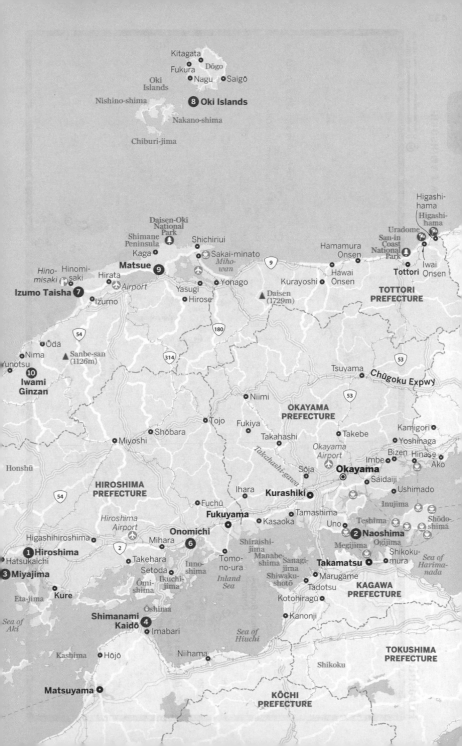

Hiroshima

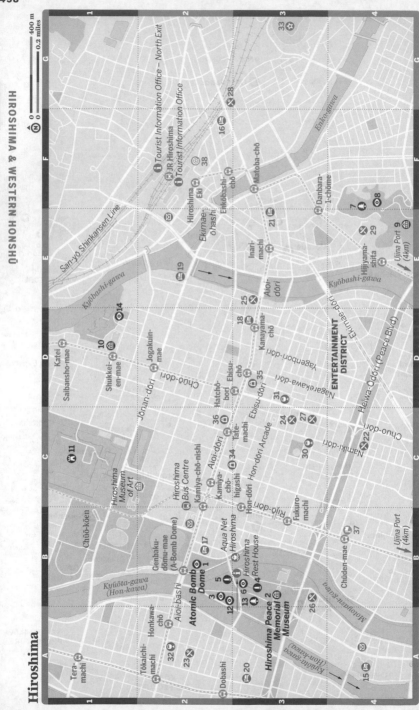

Hiroshima

was one of very few left standing near the epicentre. A decision was taken after the war to preserve the shell as a memorial.

★ Hiroshima Peace Memorial Museum

MUSEUM

(広島平和記念資料館; Map p438; www.pcf.city. hiroshima.jp; 1-2 Nakajima-chō, Naka-ku; adult/child ¥200/free; ⊗8.30am-7pm Aug, to 6pm Mar-Jul & Sep-Nov, to 5pm Dec-Feb; ⓖGenbaku-dōmu-mae or Chūden-mae) The main building of Hiroshima's premier museum houses a collection of items salvaged from the aftermath of the atomic bomb. Displays are confronting and personal – ragged clothes, a child's melted lunch box, a watch stopped at 8.15am – and there are grim photographs. While upsetting, it's a must-see in Hiroshima. The east building presents a history of Hiroshima and of the development and destructive power of nuclear weapons.

At the exit, don't miss the first-person video accounts and guest book of world-leader visitors – including the first visit by a sitting US President, Barack Obama in 2016, who gifted origami cranes.

The museum is undergoing major renovations. The main building will close in February 2017 until a 2018 grand reopening. During its closure, some items from the main building will be on display in the east building. Check the website for the latest developments as there have been delays.

⊙ Hiroshima-jō & Around

Hiroshima-jō

CASTLE

(広島城, Hiroshima Castle; Map p438; 21-1 Motomachi; ⊗9am-6pm Mar-Nov, to 5pm Dec-Feb; ⓖKamiya-chō) Also known as Carp Castle (Rijō; 鯉城), Hiroshima-jō was originally constructed in 1589, but much of it was dismantled following the Meiji Restoration. What remained was totally destroyed by the bomb and rebuilt in 1958. There's a small museum with historical items, but most impressive is the moat, and the surrounding park is a pleasant place for a stroll.

Shukkei-en

GARDENS

(縮景園; Map p438; 2-11 Kami-nobori-chō, Naka-ku; ¥260; ⊗9am-6pm Apr-Sep, to 5pm Oct-Mar; ⓖShukkei-en-mae) Modelled after West Lake in Hangzhou, China, Shukkei-en was built in 1620 for *daimyō* (domain lord) Asano Nagaakira. The garden's name means 'contracted view', and it attempts to recreate grand vistas in miniature. Pathways lead through a series of 'landscapes' and views around an island-dotted pond.

Shukkei-en was destroyed by the bomb, though many of the trees and plants survived to blossom again the following year, and the park and its buildings have long since been restored to their original splendour.

Hiroshima
Prefectural Art Museum   GALLERY
(広島県立美術館; Map p438; www.hpam.jp; 2-22 Kami-nobori-chō, Naka-ku; ¥510; ⊙9am-5pm Tue-Sun; 🚋Shukkei-en-mae) Next to the Shukkei-en garden you'll find this prefectural art museum, with a small collection featuring Salvador Dalí's *Dream of Venus* and the artwork of Hirayama Ikuo, who was in the city during the atomic bombing. The ground floor has a large light lounge area with floor-to-ceiling windows and garden views.

⊙ Hijiyama-kōen & Around

Hiroshima City Manga Library   LIBRARY
(広島市まんが図書館; Map p438; 🖀082-261-0330; www.library.city.hiroshima.jp/manga; 1-4 Hijiyama-kōen; ⊙10am-5pm Tue-Sun; 🚋Hijiyama-shita) An obvious pit stop for manga (Japanese comics) enthusiasts, this library has a small section of foreign-language manga and a collection of vintage and rare manga. Grab the English-language pamphlet and head up to the 2nd floor.

Hiroshima City Museum
of Contemporary Art   GALLERY
(広島市現代美術館, MOCA; Map p438; www.hiroshima-moca.jp; 1-1 Hijiyama-kōen; ¥370; ⊙10am-5pm Tue-Sun; 🚋Hijiyama-shita) Fans of contemporary art should visit this modern museum in Hijiyama-kōen, where the exhibits change regularly and may include anything from large-scale installations to video. Outside is a sculpture garden. Check ahead before your visit as there are sometimes special exhibitions (additional fees may apply).

⊙ Greater Hiroshima

Mazda Museum   MUSEUM
(マツダミュージアム; 🖀082-252-5050; www.mazda.com/about/museum; ⊙by reservation Mon-Fri) **FREE** Mazda is popular for the chance to see the impressive 7km assembly line. There are English-language tours (90 minutes) available at 10am weekdays, but it's best to check the website or with the tourist office for the current times. Reservations are required and can be made online or by phone.

The museum is a short walk from JR Mukainada (向洋) Station, two stops from Hiroshima on the San-yō line.

Naka Incineration Plant   ARCHITECTURE
(環境局中工場, Kankyō-kyoku Naka Kōjō; 1-5-1 Minami-Yoshijima, Naka-ku; ⊙9am-4pm) **FREE** Exploring a garbage-processing plant might not sound appealing, but if you're an architecture fan this building is worth a visit. The waterfront building is an imposing sleek-lined glass-and-metal construction designed by Taniguchi Yoshio, architect of the MoMA redesign in New York. Don't miss the tree-lined central atrium, the Ecorium, where you can see the surprisingly clean and quiet internal workings of the plant. Head up to

---

THE FIRST ATOMIC BOMB

On 6 August 1945, the US B-29 bomber *Enola Gay* released the 'Little Boy' atomic bomb over Hiroshima. The 2000°C (3630°F) blast obliterated 90% of the city and instantly killed 80,000 people. The bomb exploded over the centre of Hiroshima, which was filled with wooden homes and shops. This created intense firestorms that raced through the city for three days and destroyed 92% of the structures, fuelled by broken gas pipes and electrical lines. Toxic black rain fell 30 minutes after the blast, carrying 200 different types of radioactive isotopes, contaminating the thirsty wounded who drank it.

Around 350,000 people were present that day. In the following months, 130,000 more died of radiation exposure and other secondary effects, including intensive burns. Most casualties were civilians, including firefighters and 90% of the city's doctors who came to help; 20,000 forced Korean labourers; and 6,000 junior-high-school students who had been working in the city clearing fire breaks in anticipation of a regular attack.

The Japanese government says there were around 187,000 atomic bomb survivors still alive in 2015, many living through the mental trauma, cancers, and other effects of radiation. (No residual radiation remains today.)

the level 6 viewing gallery for views across the water.

Visitors can walk through the Ecorium and the viewing gallery independently. There are information panels dotted around, and the office on level 6 can give you a pamphlet (note no English is spoken and this isn't a tourism office). To get to the plant, take bus 24 for Yoshijima Eigyō-sho and get off at Minami-Yoshijima (¥220, 20 minutes). Walk back to the intersection and turn right. You won't smell garbage in the area, but you may get a waft of *furikake* (seasoning) from a nearby factory.

Tours

Hiroshima Sightseeing Loop Bus   BUS
(www.chugoku-jrbus.co.jp; single/day pass ¥200/400) The loop bus *(meipurū-pu)* has two overlapping routes – orange and green – taking in the city's main sights and museums, including the Peace Memorial Park and Atomic Bomb Dome. Both routes begin and end on the *shinkansen* entrance (north) side of Hiroshima Station, running from about 9am to 6pm (the green route runs later during summer).

Passengers can get on and off at any stop. There is a bus about every 15 minutes – both orange and green route buses run every half-hour. Purchase tickets and day passes from the driver. Those with a JR Pass (not JR West passes) ride for free. On the bus there are announcements in English, though the background info on the sights is all in Japanese.

Festivals & Events

Peace Memorial Ceremony   MEMORIAL SERVICE
On 6 August, the anniversary of the atomic bombing, a memorial service is held in Peace Memorial Park and thousands of paper lanterns for the souls of the dead are floated down the Kyūōta-gawa from in front of the Atomic Bomb Dome.

Sleeping

Hiroshima's accommodation is clustered around the station, near Peace Memorial Park, and along the main thoroughfares of Aioi-dōri and Heiwa-Ōdōri, but the city is compact enough that wherever you base yourself you're never more than a short walk or tram ride away from the main sights.

★ **Hana Hostel**   HOSTEL ¥
(広島花宿; Map p438; 082-263-2980; www.hiroshima.hanahostel.com; 1-15 Kojin-machi; dm/tw from

HIROSHIMA READING

➡ *Hiroshima* (1946) by John Hersey – book of the article (available on newyorker.com) by Pulitzer Prize–winning writer.

➡ *Hiroshima: Three Witnesses* (1990); ed Richard H Minear – translation of first-hand accounts of three authors.

➡ *Black Rain* (1965) by Masuji Ibuse – a novel depicting the lives of survivors.

➡ *Sadako and the Thousand Paper Cranes* (1977) by Eleanor Coerr – aimed at younger readers, based on the true story of Sadako Sasaki.

¥2500/6800; ❄❀@📶) Hana has a choice of Japanese- or Western-style private rooms, some with a private toilet or full (very small) en suite. Cosy lamp lighting and traditional decoration make the tatami rooms the best pick. The only downside is occasional street and train noise. Solo travellers can book a private room at the cost of a twin.

From the station's south exit go immediately left along the train tracks, continue past the railway crossing (not over it) and turn right. It's opposite the temple.

★ **K's House Hiroshima**   HOSTEL ¥
(ケイズハウス広島; Map p438; 082-568-7244; www.kshouse.jp/hiroshima e; 1-8-9 Matoba-chō; dm/s/tw from ¥2600/4800/7400; ❄❀@📶; Matoba-chō) K's House has a great location not far from the station. There are small dorms and comfortable tatami rooms with shared shower rooms, or pay a little more for a Western room with en suite. The kitchen-lounge is modern and a good size, there's a rooftop terrace, and staff are helpful.

The entrance is at the back of the block – turn left off Aioi-dōri to find it.

J-Hoppers Hiroshima   HOSTEL ¥
(ジェイホッパーズ広島ゲストハウス; Map p438; 082-233-1360; http://hiroshima.j-hoppers.com; 5-16 Dobashi-chō; dm/tw from ¥2500/6000; ❄❀@📶; Dobashi) This clean old favourite near the Peace Park feels more like someone's house than a standard hostel. Not only private rooms get tatami treatment; dorms too have private-feeling capsules. It's a small but cosy place with a friendly English-speaking crew and cheap laundry and bike use. Singles come at the price of a twin.

★ **Hotel Active Hiroshima**   HOTEL ¥¥
(ホテルアクティブ広島; Map p438; ☑082-212-0001; www.hotel-active.com/hiroshima; 15-3 Nobori-chō; s/d incl breakfast from ¥5380/7300; ☞✳@ぐ; 🚊Kanayama-chō) With its satiny coverlets and backlit headboards, Hotel Active tries for a little more style than the average business hotel. It's right in the heart of things, and extras such as free drink machines, a spa and an included buffet breakfast make this a good-value option.

Some English is spoken; it may be easier to book by phone than via the Japanese website.

**Aster Plaza
International Youth House**   HOTEL ¥¥
(広島市国際青年会館; Map p438; ☑082-247-8700; http://hiyh.pr.arena.ne.jp; 4-17 Kako-machi; s/tw from ¥4200/6420; ☞✳@ぐ; 🚊Funairi-machi or Shiyakusho-mae) With good views from the top floors of a huge cultural complex, this city-run hotel (not a hostel despite the name) is excellent value for foreign travellers, who get roomy well-equipped modern accommodation at budget prices. Rooms have LAN internet access and there's wi-fi in the lobby. Note that the building is locked at 1am.

Hotel Flex   HOTEL ¥¥
(ホテルフレックス; Map p438; ☑082-223-1000; www.hotel-flex.co.jp; 7-1 Kaminobori-chō; s/d incl breakfast from ¥7150/12,100; ☞✳@ぐ) Curves and concrete are the features at this riverside hotel. Standard rooms are small, but there is a more spacious maisonette and high-ceiling room option. All rooms are light with large windows; naturally, the ones facing the river have the views. There's a bright, breezy cafe downstairs where the included breakfast of a sandwich and drink is served.

★ **Hiroshima Inn Aioi**   RYOKAN ¥¥¥
(広島の宿相生; Map p438; ☑082-247-9331; www.galilei.ne.jp/aioi; 1-3-14 Ōtemachi; r per person with meals from ¥19,900; ☞✳@; 🚊Genbaku-dōmu-mae) At this fine traditional inn, kick back in *a yukata* and enjoy city and park views from your tatami room, or while lazing in the large bath on the 7th floor. The meals are an elaborate traditional spread of dishes, and you can opt for breakfast or dinner only.

Welcoming staff speak just a little English, but do their best to accommodate.

✕ Eating

Hiroshima is famous for oysters and *okonomiyaki* (savoury pancakes; batter and cabbage, with vegetables and seafood or meat cooked on a griddle). The local version, *Hiroshima-yaki,* features individual layers and noodles as the key ingredient.

The sweet (and edible) souvenir of choice from the Hiroshima area is the *momiji-manjū,* a maple-leaf-shaped waffle-like cake filled with a sweet-bean paste.

★ **Okonomi-mura**   OKONOMIYAKI ¥
(お好み村; Map p438; www.okonomimura.jp; 2nd-4th fl, 5-13 Shintenchi; dishes ¥800-1300; ⊙11am-2am; 📶; 🚊Ebisu-chō) This Hiroshima institution is a touristy but fun place to get acquainted with *okonomiyaki* and chat with the cooks over a hot griddle. There are 25 stalls spread over three floors, each serving up hearty variations of the local speciality. Pick a floor and find an empty stool at whichever counter takes your fancy.

Look for the entrance stairs off Chūō-dōri, on the opposite side of the square to the white Parco shopping centre.

★ **Hassei**   OKONOMIYAKI ¥
(八誠; Map p438; ☑082-242-8123; 4-17 Fujimi-chō; dishes ¥600-1300; ⊙11.30am-2pm & 5.30-11pm Tue-Sat, 5.30-11pm Sun; 📶; 🚊Chūden-mae) The walls of this popular *okonomiyaki* specialist are covered with the signatures and messages of famous and not-so-famous satisfied customers. The tasty, generous servings are indeed satisfying – a half-order is probably more than enough at lunchtime.

Hassei is on a side street one block south of Heiwa-Ōdōri.

Mequl   CAFE ¥
(喫茶めくる; Map p438; ☑082-296-9023; www.mequl.jp; 1-6-29 Tōkaichimachi; meals ¥880-1080; ⊙8am-6pm Thu-Tue; ☞✳🖋📶; 🚊Honkawa-cho) The lovely owners' personalities show in this cafe, decorated like a hip, high-ceilinged refurb with upcycled wooden furniture, plants, and homemade treats on display. Coffee and breakfasts are good, and set lunch *teishoku* include raw salmon with avocado. Cash only. From the Atomic Bomb Dome, cross the bridge, take the third left and second right.

Shanti Vegan Cafe   VEGAN ¥
(Map p438; ☑082-247-8529; 2nd fl, 2-20 Mikawatyo; menu ¥1500, Sat & Sun ¥2000; ⊙noon-3pm Tue-Fri, to 5pm Sat & Sun; 🅿☞✳ぐ🖋📶; 🚊Totemachi) 🍃 Enter this clean, tranquil space and sit on the tatami for tasty *shōjin-ryōri* dishes, a Buddhist style that includes a balance of five colours and flavours in each meal. Here this means beautiful set lunches featuring wild rice, salads, breadless burgers, dessert and tea.

HIROSHIMA IN ONE DAY

Hop on the Sightseeing Loop Bus (p441) or a tram at Hiroshima Station to breakfast at cute Mequl (p442), then walk nearby to the Hiroshima Peace Memorial Museum (p439) for quiet contemplation and education before the crowds. Outside in the Peace Memorial Park (p435), continue the reflection at the Flame of Peace (p435) and be brightened up by origami cranes sent by kids from across the world at the Children's Peace Monument (p435). Witness the Atomic Bomb Dome (p435), a surviving building from the epicentre of the explosion.

Head to the Museum of Contemporary Art (p440) and nearby Manga Library (p440), then recharge on Hiroshima-style okonomiyaki at Tanpopo (p443) near Hiroshima Station. Next, stroll around either the castle moat of Hiroshima-jō (p439), or Chinese-styled Shuk-kei-en (p439) and adjacent Prefectural Art Museum (p440) to check out the artwork of Hirayama Ikuo, who was in the city during the atomic bombing.

At night, try Hiroshima's famous oysters at Oyster Conclave Kaki-tei (p443) and finish at Organza (p443), a smoky lounge-bar with live events..

Everything is meat and dairy free, and organic. Soy smoothies are also good.

Tanpopo
OKONOMIYAKI ¥

(たんぽぽ; Map p438; ☑ 082-263-2077; 3-4 Higashi-kōjin-machi; okonomiyaki ¥770-1070; ◷11am-9pm; ✳ⓘ) Far from the crowds, the husband and wife team here have been making spicy *Hiroshima-yaki* for years. There are only a few tables, but the long bar is where the action is; dig into satisfying layers of cabbage, soba and crispy squid with a metal spatula, straight off the hotplate.

It's next to the train line; look for the green awning and yellow lanterns.

★ Tōshō
TOFU ¥¥

(豆匠; Map p438; ☑ 082-506-1028; www.toufu-tosho.jp; 6-24 Hijiyama-chō; sets ¥1620-3240; ◷11am-3pm & 5-10pm Mon-Sat, to 9pm Sun; ☑ⓘ; ◉Danbara-1-chōme) In a traditional wooden building overlooking a large garden with a pond and waterfall, Tōshō specialises in homemade tofu, served in a variety of tasty and beautifully presented forms by kimono-clad staff. Even the sweets are tofu based. There's a range of set courses, with some pictures and basic English on the menu. Vegetarians can be accommodated.

From the tram stop, continue walking in the direction of the tram and turn left uphill after Hijiyama shrine.

Oyster Conclave Kaki-tei
SEAFOOD ¥¥

(牡蠣亭; Map p438; ☑ 082-221-8990; www.kakitei.jp; 11 Hashimoto-chō; mains ¥800-1800; ◷11.30am-2.30pm & 5-10pm, closed Tue & 1st & 3rd Wed of the month; ⓘ; ◉Kanayama-chō) Come to this intimate riverside bistro for local oysters prepared in a range of mouth-watering ways.

Lunch is a set menu of oysters in various guises, served with salad and soup; an à la carte menu is available in the evenings.

Ristorante Mario
ITALIAN ¥¥

(リストランテマリオ; Map p438; ☑ 082-248-4956; www.sanmario.com; 4-11 Nakajima-chō; mains ¥1200-1800; ◷11.30am-2.30pm & 5-10pm; ⓘ; ◉Chūden-mae) This cosy ivy-covered place across from the Peace Park serves honest Italian food with good service and boasts a romantic atmosphere in the evenings. Reservations are recommended for weekends.

🍷 Drinking & Nightlife

Hiroshima is a great city for a night out, with bars and pubs to suit every mood. The main entertainment district is made up of hundreds of bars, restaurants and karaoke joints crowding the lanes between Aioi-dōri and Heiwa-Ōdōri. Most places also serve light meals or snacks, and some have live music.

★ Organza
BAR

(ヲルガン座; Map p438; ☑ 082-295-1553; www.organ-za.com; 2nd fl, Morimoto Bldg, Tōkaichi-machi; ◷5.30pm-2am Tue-Fri, 11.30am-2am Sat, 11.30am-midnight Sun; ◉Honkawa-chō) Bookshelves, old-fashioned furniture, a piano and a stuffed deer head all add to the busy surrounds at this smoky lounge-bar. Organza hosts an eclectic schedule of live events (from acoustic guitar to cabaret), some with a cover charge, and food is also served. Lunch on weekends only.

★ Koba
BAR

(コバ; Map p438; ☑ 082-249-6556; 3rd fl Rego Bldg, 1-4 Naka-machi; ◷6pm-2am Thu-Tue; ◉Ebisu-chō) It'll be a good night if you drop into this laid-back bar, where the friendly metal-loving

SAKE TOWN SAIJŌ

Saijō (西条), just east of Hiroshima, has been producing sake for around 300 years. There are seven breweries clustered within easy walking distance of the town's train station – and most open up their doors to curious and thirsty visitors for free sake tastings. A beginner's guide to sake and what makes each local brewery special is available at www.saijosake.com.

Among the most well known of Saijō's sake breweries, **Kamotsuru** (賀茂鶴; ☎ 082-422-2121; www.kamotsuru.jp; 4-31 Saijō-honmachi; ⊗ 9am-4.30pm) is worth a look as it has a large tasting room, and screens a video about the district. One of Saijō's oldest sake breweries, **Hakubotan** (白牡丹; ☎ 082-422-2142; www.hakubotan.co.jp; 15-5 Saijō-hon-machi) has a lovely broad-beamed display and tasting room with Munakata woodblock prints on the wall. When you're done sake tasting, you can pay your respects to the god of sake at **Matsuo-jinja**, a short walk to the north of Saijō Station.

If you're in the Hiroshima area on the second weekend of October, don't miss the **Saijō Sake Matsuri** (西条酒祭り; www.sakematsuri.com), when crowds descend on Saijō for hours of sampling and events.

Saijō is 35 minutes by train from Hiroshima (¥580) on the Sanyō line. The **tourist office** (2nd fl, Saijō station; ⊗ 10am-4pm Tue-Sun) on the 2nd floor of the station has a good walking map in English, showing the location of each sake brewery.

---

musician owner 'Bom-san' can be found serving drinks and cooking up small tasty meals. There is occasional live music.

It's up the stairs in a concrete building, just behind Stussy.

Molly Malone's PUB
(Map p438; ☎ 082-244-2554; www.mollymalones.jp; 4th fl, Teigeki Bldg, 1-20 Shintenchi; ⊗ 5pm-1am Mon-Thu, to 2am Fri, 11.30am-2.30am Sat, 11.30am-midnight Sun; ⓔ Ebisu-chō) A reliable Irish-style pub with a welcoming Irish expat manager, good beer, good food and occasional live music. It draws a mixed crowd of local expats and Japanese.

☆ Entertainment

Mazda Zoom Zoom Stadium STADIUM
(Hiroshima Municipal Stadium; Map p438; 2-3-1 Minami-Kaniya) This stadium is a good place to catch a baseball game and see the beloved local team, the Carp. It's a short walk southeast of the Hiroshima Station – follow the signs and the red-marked pathways.

A love of baseball is not a prerequisite for having a great time – it's fun just watching the rowdy yet organised enthusiasm of the crowd, especially when the despised Yomiuri (Tokyo) Giants come to town. For schedule information in English, see www.japanball.com, or ask at the tourist office.

🛍 Shopping

Browse the busy shop-filled Hon-dōri covered arcade for clothes, shoes, accessories and more. There are also conveniently placed cafes for when you need a break. Namiki-dōri is another shopping street, with a range of fashionable boutiques. Hiroshima also has branches of the big-name department stores, such as **Tokyu Hands** (東急ハンズ広島店; Map p438; http://hiroshima.tokyu-hands.co.jp; 16-10 Hatchō-bori; ⊗ 10am-8pm Sun-Thu, to 8.30pm Fri & Sat; ⓔ Tate-machi), packed with homewares, must-have gadgets, and gifts; and classy **Mitsukoshi** (広島三越; Map p438; http://mitsukoshi.mistore.jp/store/hiroshima; 5-1 Ebisu-chō; ⊗ 10.30am-7.30pm; ⓔ Ebisu-chō), with its designer labels and great basement-floor food hall.

ℹ Information

INTERNET ACCESS

Hiroshima has a free (sometimes patchy) wi-fi service accessible in a number of spots around the city, including at the Peace Park, along Hon-dōri and Ebisu-dōri, and in some museums. Look for 'Hiroshima Free Wi-fi' to connect. Users need to register when they first connect and usage is limited to 30-minute periods, though you can reconnect as often as you like. There are also computers with internet access at **Global Lounge** (グローバル・ラウンジ; Map p438; www.hiroshima-no1.com/lounge.html; 2nd fl, Kensei Bldg, 1-5-17 Kamiya-chō; ⊗ 11.30am-9pm Mon-Thu, to 11pm Fri & Sat; ⓔ Kamiya-chō-higachi).

MONEY

Higashi Post Office has currency-exchange services and ATMs that accept international cards.

ATMs in 7-Elevens also take international cards. The tourist offices have lists of banks and post-offices that change money and travellers cheques.

TOURIST INFORMATION

In addition to the tourist offices, check out the Hiroshima Navigator website (www.hcvb.city. hiroshima.jp) for tourism and practical information and downloadable audio guides to the sights. *Get Hiroshima* (www.gethiroshima.com), an expat-run website and magazine, has an events calendar, restaurant and bar reviews, and regular feature articles.

Hiroshima Rest House (広島市平和記念公園レストハウス; Map p438; ☏ 082-247-6738; www.mk-kousan.co.jp/rest-house; 1-1 Nakajima-machi; ⊙ 8.30am-7pm Aug, to 6pm Mar-Jul & Sep-Nov, to 5pm Dec-Feb; ☐ Genbaku-dōmu-mae) In Peace Memorial Park next to Motoyasu-bashi bridge, this air-conditioned tourist office has comprehensive information, English-speaking staff, and a small shop selling souvenirs.

Tourist Information Office (観光案内所; Map p438; ☏ 082-261-1877; ⊙ 9am-5.30pm) Inside the station near the south exit, with English-speaking staff. There is another branch at the **north (shinkansen) exit** (Map p438; ☏ 082-263-6822; ⊙ 9am-5.30pm).

🛈 Getting There & Away

AIR

Hiroshima Airport (☏ 082-231-5171; www.hij.airport.jp) is 40km east of the city, with bus connections to/from Hiroshima Station (¥1340, 45 minutes, every 15 to 30 minutes). Buses operate from the airport from 8.20am to 9.40pm; buses run from Hiroshima Station (*shinkansen* exit) from 6am to 7.20pm.

BOAT

There are connections from Hiroshima port to Matsuyama in Shikoku with **Setonaikai Kisen Ferry** (瀬戸内海汽船フェリー; ☏ 082-253-1212; www.setonaikaikisen.co.jp), via standard car ferry (adult/child ¥3600/1800, two hours and 40 minutes, 10 daily) or high-speed 'Super Jet' (adult/child ¥7100/3550, 1¼ hours, 12 daily). The port (広島港) is the last stop on trams 1, 3 and 5 bound for Ujina (宇品).

Setonaikai also offers high-speed ferry services to Miyajima (p449) (one-way ¥1850, 30 minutes) every one to two hours.

BUS

Long-distance buses connect Hiroshima with all the major cities. Buses depart from the **Hiroshima Bus Centre** (広島バスセンター; Map p438; www.h-buscenter.com; 6-27 Motomachi; ☐ Kamiya-chō-nishi), located on the 3rd floor between the Sogo and AQ'A shopping centres in the city centre.

HIROSHIMA ON FILM

The Japanese crowd-funded animated film *In This Corner of the World* (2016; この世界の片隅に, *Kono Sekai no Katasumi ni*) paints a picture of life in Hiroshima in the 1930s.

TRAIN

Hiroshima Station is on the JR San-yō line, which passes westwards to Shimonoseki. It's also a stop on the Tokyo–Osaka–Hakata *shinkansen* line. If you're travelling from Tokyo or Kyoto, you may need to change trains at Osaka or Okayama en route. Example *shinkansen* fares from Hiroshima:

Hakata ¥9150, 65 minutes
Osaka ¥10,440, 1½ hours
Tokyo ¥19,080, four hours

🛈 Getting Around

Most sights in Hiroshima are accessible either on foot or with a short tram (street-car) ride. There is also a convenient hop-on, hop-off **sightseeing bus** (p441) that links the main attractions.

BICYCLE

Hiroshima is fairly compact and easy for cycling. Many hostels and hotels have bikes for hire from around ¥500 per day.

TRAM

Hiroshima's trams (www.hiroden.co.jp) will get you almost anywhere you want to go for a flat fare of ¥160. You pay by dropping the fare into the machine by the driver as you get off the tram. If you have to change trams to get to your destination, you should ask for a *norikae-ken* (transfer ticket).

If you'll be taking at least four tram trips in a day, get a one-day trip card, which gets you unlimited travel for ¥600. A one-day card that covers trams plus return ferry to Miyajima is ¥840. The three-day Visit Hiroshima Tourist Pass (Small Area) is a good deal at ¥1000, covering tram rides, the sightseeing loop bus, loop buses, and Miyajima ferry. Buy passes from the tram terminal at the station, from the conductors on board (one-day cards only), or at various hotels and hostels.

Miyajima   宮島

☏ 0829 / POP 2015

The small island of Miyajima is a Unesco World Heritage Site and one of Japan's most visited tourist spots. Its star attraction is the oft-photographed vermilion *torii* (shrine gate) of Itsukushima-jinja, which seems to float on the waves at high tide – a scene that

Miyajima

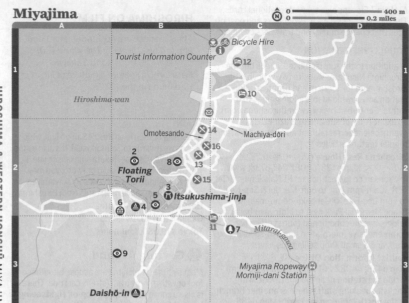

Miyajima

⊙ Top Sights

⊙ Sights

⊚ Sleeping

⊗ Eating

has traditionally been ranked as one of the three best views in Japan. It is also at its evocative best at sunset, or when lit up after dark.

Besides this feted view, Miyajima has some good hikes on sacred Misen, temples, and cheeky deer that do what they want, when they want, and will eat your map (or JR Pass) right out of your pocket if you're not careful.

⊙ Sights

To head straight to the *torii* (shrine gate) of Itsukushima-jinja, turn right as you emerge from the ferry terminal and follow the waterfront for 10 minutes.

The main shopping street, Omotesandō, is a block back from the waterfront and packed with souvenir outlets and restaurants. This is also where you'll find the world's largest *shakushi* (rice scoop).

★ **Itsukushima-jinja** SHINTO SHRINE
(厳島神社; Map p446; 1-1 Miyajima-chō; ¥300; ⊙6.30am-6pm Jan-Nov, to 5pm Dec) With origins from as far back as the late 6th century, Itsukushima-jinja gives Miyajima its real name.

The shrine's pier-like construction is a result of the island's sacred status: commoners were not allowed to set foot on the island and had to approach by boat through the **torii** (shrine gate; 大鳥居; Map p446) in the bay. Much of the time, though, the shrine and *torii* are surrounded by mud: to get the classic view of the 'floating' *torii,* come at high tide.

The shrine's present form dates from 1168, when it was rebuilt under the patronage of Taira no Kiyomori, head of the doomed Heike clan. One side has a **floating nō stage** (能舞台; Map p446), built by local lord Asano Tsunanaga in 1680 and used for *nō* (stylised dance-drama) performances every year from 16 to 18 April as part of Toka-sai Festival.

Senjō-kaku   NOTABLE BUILDING

(Map p446; 1-1 Miyajima-chō; ¥100; ⊙8.30am-4.30pm) Dominating the hill to the north of Itsukushima-jinja is this huge pavilion built in 1587 by Toyotomi Hideyoshi. The atmospheric hall is constructed with massive pillars and beams, and the ceiling is hung with paintings. It looks out onto a colourful five-storey **pagoda** (五重塔) dating from 1407.

Daigan-ji   BUDDHIST TEMPLE

(大願寺; Map p446; 3 Miyajima-chō; ⊙9am-5pm) FREE Miyajima has several important Buddhist temples, including the 1201 Daigan-ji, just south of Itsukushima-jinja, which dates back to the Heian period and is dedicated to Benzaiten, the Japanese name for Saraswati (the Hindu goddess of good fortune). The seated image of Yakushi Nyorai here is said to have been carved by Kōbō Daishi.

★ Daishō-in   BUDDHIST TEMPLE

(大聖院; Map p446; 210 Miyajima-chō; ⊙8am-5pm) FREE Just south of town at the foot of Misen, Daishō-in is a worthwhile stopping point on the way up or down the mountain. This Shingon temple is crowded with interesting things to look at: from Buddhist images and prayer wheels to sharp-beaked *tengu* (bird-like demons) and a cave containing images from each of the 88 Shikoku pilgrimage temples. Daishō-in is a 15-minute walk from the ferry terminal; it's another 90 minutes if you intend to hike to Misen's summit.

Momiji-dani-kōen   PARK

(紅葉谷公園; Momiji-dani Park; Map p446) Momiji means 'maple', and their leaves come alive in autumn here in this pretty park along the river. It's at the foot of Misen, close to the ropeway station.

Tahō-tō   PAGODA

(多宝塔; Map p446) South of Itsukushima-jinja, stone steps (before the History & Folklore Museum) lead up from the road to this picturesque pagoda. There's a pleasant, short path looping around from here and back down to the road.

Miyajima History & Folklore Museum   MUSEUM

(歴史民俗資料館; Map p446; 57 Miyajima-chō; ¥300; ⊙8.30am-5pm Tue-Sun) This museum combines a 19th-century merchant house with exhibitions on trade in the Edo period, as well as displays connected with the island.

🏃 Activities

★ Misen & Ropeway   HIKING

(弥山; www.miyajima-ropeway.info; ropeway one-way/return adult ¥1000/1800, child ¥500/900; ⊙ropeway 9am-5pm) Covered with primeval forest, the sacred, peaceful Misen is Miyajima's highest mountain (530m), and its ascent is the island's finest walk. Avoid most of the up-hill climb by taking the two-stage **ropeway** with its giddying sea views, which leaves you with a 30-minute walk to the top, where there is an excellent observatory.

At the summit observatory, you can laze on wooden platforms while enjoying 360-degree views – on clear days you can see across to the mountain ranges of Shikoku.

Close to the summit is a temple where Kōbō Daishi meditated for 100 days following his return from China in the 9th century. Next to the main temple hall is a flame that's been burning continually since Kōbō Daishi lit it 1200 years ago. From the temple, a path leads down the hill to Daishō-in and Itsukushima-jinja. The descent takes a little over an hour, or you can take the ropeway back down. While on the mountain you might see monkeys and deer around the ropeway station.

The ropeway station (Momiji-dani Station) to ascend Misen is about a 10-minute walk on from Momiji-dani-kōen, or a few minutes on the free shuttle bus, which runs every 20 minutes from a stop near Iwasō Ryokan.

👉 Tours

Paddle Park   KAYAKING

(☑0829-50-4340; www.paddlepark.com; half-/full-day course ¥6480/10,800) For a different perspective on the floating *torii,* try a kayaking tour. Paddle Park offer half- and full-day courses, or a night-time tour, heading out from the mainland near Maezora Station, which is one stop from Miyajima-guchi. Depending on the conditions on the day, you may even get to kayak through the *torii* itself.

✨ Festivals & Events

★ Kangen-sai   RELIGIOUS

This Shintō ritual sees decorated wooden boats float by to the sound of traditional drums and flutes. It's held in summer, starting early evening on the 17th of the sixth lunar-calendar month (late July/early August) – check with the tourist office for exact dates for the year you're in town.

🛏 Sleeping

It's worth overnighting on the island to enjoy the evening quiet once the crowds have left and the floating *torii* is lit up. For many, staying in Hiroshima (or near the mainland ferry) and making a day trip to the island is enough.

Backpackers Miyajima   HOSTEL ¥

(バックパッカーズ宮島; ☑ 0829-56-3650; www.backpackers-miyajima.com; 1-8-11 Miyajima-guchi; dm ¥2900; ❷@🛜) This hostel with attached cafe is not actually on Miyajima, but is a good budget base a short walk from the mainland ferry terminal in Miyajima-guchi. Cash only.

★ Guest House Kikugawa   RYOKAN ¥¥

(ゲストハウス菊がわ; Map p446; ☑ 0829-44-0039; www.kikugawa.ne.jp; 796 Miyajima-chō; s/tw from ¥6800/11,880; ❷🌼@🛜) This charming good-value inn is built in traditional style with wooden interiors. There are tatami rooms with futons and rooms with beds, all with attached bathrooms. The tatami rooms are slightly larger – the most spacious with a cosy mezzanine sleeping area. Dinners are available, as is a no-frills Western-style breakfast.

Heading inland from the ferry terminal, walk through the tunnel; turn right after this and look for Kikugawa on the left opposite Zonkō-ji (存光寺) temple.

Yamaichi Bekkan   RYOKAN ¥¥

(山一別館; Map p446; ☑ 0829-44-0700; www.yamaichibekkan.com; r per person from ¥8500; 🅿🌼❀) Just across from the ferry terminal, Yamaichi Bekkan offers simple, clean lodgings in one Western-style and three tatami rooms. Bathrooms are all private. The lady of the house couldn't be more welcoming and speaks some English.

Breakfast and dinner can be arranged at the on-site restaurant and vegetarians can be looked after.

★ Iwasō Ryokan   RYOKAN ¥¥¥

(岩惣; Map p446; ☑ 0829-44-2233; www.iwaso.com; Momiji-dani Miyajima-chō; r per person with 2 meals from ¥21,000; ❷🌼@) The Iwasō, open since 1854, offers a grand ryokan experience amid exquisite gardens. There are three wings; a stay in a lovely 'Hanare' cottage will set you back the most. Not all rooms have private bathrooms, but you can soak in the onsen in the main building. It's especially stunning in autumn when Momiji-dani (Maple Valley) explodes with colour.

It's about a 15-minute walk from the ferry port, or a pick-up can be arranged.

🍴 Eating

There are plenty of places to eat along and around the main shopping strip of Omotesandō and near the waterfront. Just one street back from the main strip is the much quieter Machiya-dōri, with a few cafes and eateries. Most restaurants shut down after the crowds go home – the tourist office has a list of those that stay open for dinner.

★ Cafe Lente   CAFE ¥

(☑ 0829-44-1204; 1167-3 Miyajimachō; mains ¥800; ⏰ 11am-9pm Wed-Mon; 🌼❀📶📶) This comfortable cafe boasts excellent views of the *torii* and sea. Open and airy, it serves handsome-looking lunches – think Japanese chicken curry or vegan risotto – to go with the quietly stylish decor. Organic coffee or wine are other excuses to drop by.

Baccano   GELATO ¥

(バッカーノ; Map p446; 435 Miyajima-chō; ice cream from ¥450; ⏰ 10am-6pm; 📶) Baccano gelateria dishes up refreshing swirls of handmade ice cream, from fruity standards to interesting local flavours like roasted green tea and black sesame.

Sarasvati   CAFE ¥

(Map p446; ☑ 0829-44-2266; www.sarasvati.jp; 407 Miyajima-chō; meals ¥990-1500; ⏰ 8.30am-8pm; 📶) The aroma of roasting coffee beans lures people into this cafe inside a former storehouse building from the early 1900s. Bare wooden floors and tables match a simple menu of traditional coffees (from ¥500: espresso, latte, cappuccino), plus cakes, sandwiches and pasta sets.

★ Mame-tanuki   IZAKAYA ¥¥

(まめたぬき; Map p446; ☑ 0829-44-2131; www.miyajima-mametanuki.com; 1113 Miyajima-chō; dishes ¥500-1500, lunch sets ¥1400-2500; ⏰ 11am-3.30pm & 5-11pm; 🛜📶) By day at Mame-tanuki there are lunch sets, such as the tasty *anago meshi* (steamed conger eel with rice) and fried oysters; at night it's one of the few places open late, serving drinks and *izakaya*-style small dishes. Look for the blue curtain; there's a menu signboard outside.

No smoking in the evening.

⭐**Yakigaki-no-hayashi** SEAFOOD ¥¥
(焼がきのはやし; Map p446; ☑0829-44-0335; www.yakigaki-no-hayashi.co.jp; 505-1 Miyajima-chō; dishes ¥900-1700; ⊙10.30am-5pm Thu-Tue; 🗊) The oysters in the tank and on the barbecue outside are what everyone is eating here. Try a plate of *nama-gaki* (raw oysters) or *kaki-furai* (crumbed, fried oysters), or go for oysters on udon noodles. It's not all about the bivalves – there are other meals on the menu, such as curry and eel sets.

ℹ Information

Tourist Information Counter (宮島観光案内所; Map p446; ☑0829-44-2011; http://visit-miyajima-japan.com; ⊙9am-5pm) Tourist info inside the ferry terminal on Miyajima. There is also a counter between the two ferry wharves on the mainland side.

ℹ Getting There & Away

Miyajima is accessed by ferry and is an easy day trip from Hiroshima.

The mainland ferry terminal is a short walk from Miyajima-guchi Station on the JR San-yō line, halfway between Hiroshima (¥410, 30 minutes) and Iwakuni. The **ferry terminal** (Map p446) can also be reached by tram 2 from Hiroshima (¥260, 70 minutes; not JR), which runs from Hiroshima Station, passing the Atomic Bomb Dome on the way. Ferries operated by two companies shuttle regularly across to the island from Miyajima-guchi (¥180, 10 minutes). JR Pass holders can travel on the JR ferry for free.

Setonaikai Kisen (p445) operates high-speed ferries (¥1850, 30 minutes, six to eight daily) direct to Miyajima from Hiroshima's Ujina port. Another option is to take the **Aqua Net ferry** (Map p438; ☑082-240-5955; www.aqua-net-h.co.jp/en) directly from Peace Memorial Park in central Hiroshima (one way/return ¥2000/3600, 45 minutes, 10 to 15 daily). These boats cruise under the bridges of Kyūōta-gawa before coming out into the bay towards Miyajima. No reservation is required.

ℹ Getting Around

Everywhere on Miyajima is within easy walking distance. For **bicycle hire** (Map p446; per hour ¥100; ⊙9am-5pm), go to the JR office in the ferry terminal. There are also taxis on the island – ask at the tourist office for details.

Iwakuni 岩国

☑0827 / POP 137,120

About an hour away from Hiroshima by train or bus, Iwakuni makes for a worthwhile half-day trip, or a stop-off en route between Yamaguchi and Hiroshima. The main reason to come here is to see the graceful, five-arched bridge **Kintai-kyō** (錦帯橋; ¥300, combination incl cable car & castle ¥940; ⊙24hr).

Originally built in 1673 during the rule of feudal lord Kikkawa Hiroyoshi, it has since been restored several times, but its high arches remain an impressive sight over the wide river, with Iwakuni-jō atop the green hills behind. Across the bridge, what remains of Iwakuni's old samurai quarter now forms pleasant **Kikkō-kōen** (吉香公園).

It's also possible to watch traditional cormorant fishing (birds trained by fishermen) here during the summer.

There are small eateries in the park and stalls down along the riverside. Local specialities include *iwakuni-zushi*, a sushi made in large square moulds, and *renkon* (lotus root) cooked in *korokke* (croquette) form.

ℹ Information

Tourist Information (☑0827-21-6050; ⊙10am-5pm Tue-Sun) Inside JR Iwakuni Station. There is another office at **Shin-Iwakuni Station** (⊙10.30am-3.30pm Thu-Tue).

ℹ Getting There & Away

The bridge and park are a 20-minute bus ride (¥300) from JR Iwakuni Station. There are also regular buses to the bridge (¥350, 15 minutes) from Shin-Iwakuni. JR Iwakuni Station is on the San-yō line, west of Hiroshima (¥760, 55 minutes). Shin-Iwakuni is on the San-yō *shinkansen* line, connecting to Hiroshima (¥1620, 15 minutes) and Shin-Yamaguchi (¥3910, 30 minutes).

If coming from Hiroshima without a JR Pass, you may find it more convenient to get the Iwakuni bus from Hiroshima bus centre, as it handily drops you at Kintai-kyō (one-way/return ¥930/1700, 50 minutes, nine daily).

Onomichi 尾道

☑0848 / POP 141,810

Onomichi is a gritty, old-timey seaport town with hills full of temples and literary sites. Film director Ōbayashi Nobuhiko was born in Onomichi, and the town has featured in a number of Japanese movies, notably Ozu's *Tokyo Story*. For many travellers,

Onomichi is the base from which to cycle the Shimanami Kaidō, the system of road bridges that allows people to island-hop their way across the Inland Sea to Shikoku.

Sights & Activities

The modern town stretches east from the station along a thin corridor between the railway tracks and the sea. Most places of interest are in the series of steep flagstoned lanes that ladder the hillside behind the tracks. There are some interesting sights on the islands accessible by ferry or bike from Onomichi; nearby Ikuchi-jima (p452) is a popular half-day trip.

★ Temple Walk
WALKING

(古寺めぐり) FREE This picturesque trail takes in 25 old temples in the hills behind the town, following narrow lanes and steep stone stairways, where cats laze about in the sunshine. Along the route is a **ropeway** (千 光寺山ロープウェイ; one way/return ¥320/500; every 15min 9am-5.15pm) to an observation tower and a park area (Senkō-ji-kōen), home to Onomichi's best-known temple, **Senkō-ji** (千光寺). There are cute cafes, gift shops and galleries dotted between the temples.

The temple walk starts just east of the station: take the inland road from the station and cross the railway tracks by the statue of local author Hayashi Fumiko. To walk the whole trail takes a couple of hours. You can cut back down into town at various points along the way, or take the ropeway.

Sleeping

★ Onomichi Guesthouse Anago no Nedoko
HOSTEL ¥

(あなごのねどこ; ☑ 0848-38-1005; http://anago. onomichisaisei.com; 2-4-9 Tsuchidō; dm from ¥2800; ❸❈@☎) Within a traditional old wooden house restored as part of an NPO project to give life to vacant dwellings, Anago is a budget option with character. As well as the dorms (accessed via narrow stairs), there are private tatami rooms (from ¥3300), a kitchen and a school-room-themed cafe. The entrance is in the *shōtengai* (shopping arcade).

★ Hotel Cycle
HOTEL ¥¥¥

(☑ 0848-21-0550; www.onomichi-u2.com; U2 complex, 5-11 Nishi-gosho-cho; tw from ¥17,000; ❸❈@☎) Hotel Cycle is within the large U2 complex on the waterfront boardwalk, clearly aimed at both the cycling crowd and those with an eye for design. The softly lit rooms (all twins) feature bike storage and spacious baths perfect for a soak after a long cycle.

U2 also houses a cafe (where you can 'ride through'), bar, restaurant, bakery and Giant bicycle shop.

Uonobu Ryokan
RYOKAN ¥¥¥

(魚信旅館; ☑ 0848-37-4175; www.uonobu.jp; 2-27-6 Kubo; r per person with 2 meals from ¥16,800) Elegantly old-fashioned Uonobu is a good pick for a ryokan experience, but it's probably best if you can speak a little Japanese. It's renowned for its seafood; non-guests can eat here if they reserve by 5pm the previous day. Find it about a 20-minute walk east from the station, just after the city hall (市役所).

Eating

Onomichi is known for its ramen, and you'll find lots of places serving this speciality, which uses a soup base of chicken and *dashi* (dried fish stock), and sometimes also pork fat.

Go east from the station to find eateries along the waterfront and in the arcade one block inland. There are also cafes dotted on the hill to refresh temple hunters.

Onomichi Rāmen Ichibankan
RAMEN ¥

(尾道ラーメン壱番館; ☑ 0848-21-1119; www. f-ichibankan.com; 2-9-26 Tsuchidō; noodles ¥580-950; 11am-7pm Sat-Thu; ⬤) Opposite the Sumiyoshi shrine, a 15-minute walk from the station, this popular noodle shop is a good place to try Onomichi ramen, characterised by thick slabs of juicy pork. Its best seller is the *kaku-ni rāmen* (noodles with eggs and tender cuts of fatty pork).

Neko-no-Te Pan
BAKERY ¥

(ネコノテパン; http://pan.catnote.co.jp; 7-7 Higashi-tsuchidō-chō; items ¥120-450; 10am-dusk Thu-Mon) Could this be Japan's smallest bread shop? Pop into 'cat's-paw bakery' for a sweet or savoury baked treat and judge for yourself. It's on the steep path that leads to Senkō-ji.

Hana Akari
SUSHI ¥¥

(花あかり; ☑ 0848-24-2287; 1-12-13 Tsuchidō; meals ¥1300-1630; 11am-10pm; ❸❈⬤) Every table has a sea view at this homely little seafood restaurant. The lively owner brightens up any lunch, and here it features good-quality (and excellent-value) sashimi, sushi and tempura. Beware, the included *chawanmushi* (savoury seafood egg-custard) is an acquired taste and not a dessert. It's a five-minute walk east along the port road from Onomichi Station. Look for the orange perspex sign.

CYCLING THE SHIMANAMI KAIDŌ

The **Setouchi Shimanami Kaidō** (瀬戸内しまなみ海道; Shimanami Sea Route) is a chain of bridges linking Onomichi in Hiroshima Prefecture with Imabari in Ehime Prefecture on Shikoku, via six Inland Sea islands. Besides being remarkable feats of engineering (the monster Kurushima-kaikyō trio at the Imabari end are among the longest suspension bridges in the world), the bridges make it possible to cycle the whole way across. Breezing along 50m or more above the island-dotted sea is an amazing experience, and a highlight of any trip to this part of Japan. Needless to say, it's best enjoyed when the weather is fine.

The Route

The route begins on Mukai-shima (a quick boat ride from Onomichi) and crosses Inno-shima (p452), Ikuchi-jima (p452), Ōmi-shima (p453), Hakata-jima and Ōshima, before the final bridge to reach Imabari. The 'recommended' route is well marked with information boards and maps, but there's nothing stopping you from taking detours along the minor routes around the islands and plotting your own course from bridge to bridge. Much of the recommended route is fairly flat, with the odd minor hill, but there are long, thigh-burning inclines leading up to each bridge entrance. The ride takes you through towns and villages, rural areas, past citrus groves and along the coastline, but does also hit some less-pretty built-up industrial patches.

Distance & Time

The total recommended route from Onomichi to Imabari is roughly 70km and could be done in eight or so hours, depending on your fitness and propensity to stop and take pictures. You could take the ferry part of the way, such as to Ikuchi-jima, and bike the rest (where the ferry does not go). Or, a good day trip from Onomichi is to cycle to Ikuchi-jima (about 30km) and return to Onomichi on the ferry in the afternoon. Some cyclists opt to spend a night on one of the islands on the way across – Ikuchi-jima is a popular stopover point. Alternatively, take it easy and just spend a few hours cycling a section of the route on one of the islands.

Information

The tourist office (p452) in Onomichi, and those on each of the islands, can help with all the information you need, including an excellent map in English showing the routes, distances, sights and locations of bike terminals along the way. There's some information in English at www.go-shimanami.jp, from where you can download the English map. You'll also find basic maps, plus bus and ferry schedules, at www.city.onomichi. hiroshima.jp.

If you need to get heavy luggage across, try Kuroneko Yamato (www.kuronekoyamato. co.jp), whose *takkyūbin* service will deliver it for you by the next business day (from around ¥1000 depending on size). It picks up from many convenience stores.

Bikes & Costs

Bike hire is ¥1000 per day, plus ¥1000 deposit. You don't get the deposit back if you return the bike to a different rental place along the route. There are large bike-hire terminals in Onomichi and in Imabari, and on each island in between. Electric-assist bicycles are also available for ¥1500 per day; these have to be returned to the same rental terminal. It's not necessary to reserve a bike, though it's possible to do so and you may want to consider it if you're planning to cycle on a major holiday. Note that reservations can't be made less than a week in advance.

Cyclists do not need to pay bridge tolls and can cross for free as fees have been waived until March 2018. This promotion is likely to be extended, but check tourist offices for the latest. Otherwise fees are between ¥50 and ¥200 per bridge. No one actually collects this money; you're trusted to drop the coins into the box at the bridge entrances.

To take a bike on a ferry costs up to ¥300.

ℹ️ Information

Tourist Information Office (☏ 0848-20-0005; www.ononavi.jp; ⊙ 9am–6pm) Supplies local maps, information on the Shimanami Kaidō, and can help with accommodation. It's inside JR Onomichi Station.

ℹ️ Getting There & Away

BICYCLE

Onomichi Port Rent-a-Cycle (☏ 0848-22-5332; per day ¥1000, deposit ¥1000; ⊙ 7am–6pm) Located in the car park next to the ferry terminal, with multiple bikes. Bikes with gears and electric-assist bikes available.

BOAT

Setouchi Cruising (☏ 0865-62-2856; www.s-cruise.jp) ferries travel from Onomichi to Setoda port on Ikuchi-jima (¥1050, 40 minutes, eight daily). There are frequent ferries to Mukai-shima (¥110, five minutes). It costs up to an additional ¥300 to take a bicycle on the ferries.

BUS

Regular buses run to Imabari (¥2250) in Shikoku from Onomichi Station (some originating in Shin-Onomichi Station), most with a 15- to 40-minute transfer at Inno-shima, but three daily run direct. It takes up to two hours, depending on the connection, or 90 minutes direct. Buses also run between Onomichi and Setoda port on Ikuchi-jima (¥1030, one hour, four to seven daily).

TRAIN

Onomichi is on the main JR San-yō line, east of Hiroshima (¥1490, 1½ hours). The Shin-Onomichi *shinkansen* station is 3km north. Regular buses (¥190, 15 minutes) connect the two.

Shimanami Kaidō Islands

Inno-Shima   因島

Famed for its flowers and fruit, Inno-shima is connected by bridge to Mukai-shima, facing Onomichi, and Ikuchi-jima to the west. The Inland Sea was once a haven for pirates, and Inno-shima was the base of one of the three Murakami pirate clans. Today you can get a taste for that time at the modern-replica **pirate castle** (因島水軍城, Suigun-jō; ¥310; ⊙ 9.30am–5pm Fri-Wed), which has some displays of weaponry. Worth cycling (or driving) up to is **Shirataki-yama** (白滝山), a collection of sculptures of the 500 Rakan disciples of the Buddha.

The local bittersweet *hassaku* orange is featured in the Inno-shima speciality *daifuku*, a rice-flour dessert filled with sweet bean paste and the orange segments.

Setouchi Cruising (www.s-cruise.jp) ferries from Onomichi to Setoda port on Ikuchi-jima stop in at Inno-shima at Shigei-Higashi port (¥550, 20 minutes, eight daily). Bikes are an additional ¥300.

Inno-shima is 22km away from Onomichi along the cyclist-friendly Shimanami Kaidō.

Ikuchi-jima   生口島

Ikuchi-jima is known for its citrus groves and beaches, including Sunset Beach on the west coast.

There's not much doing in the main port town of **Setoda**, but it does have a glaringly ostentatious temple complex and an interesting art gallery.

◉ Sights

⭐ **Ikuo Hirayama Museum of Art**   GALLERY
(平山郁夫美術館; www.hirayama-museum.or.jp; ¥900; ⊙ 9am–5pm) The Ikuo Hirayama Museum of Art is dedicated to the life and work of the famous and well-travelled Setoda-born artist. The collection here includes several striking works inspired by Ikuo's journeys in India and along the Silk Road.

Kōsan-ji   BUDDHIST TEMPLE
(耕三寺; www.kousanji.or.jp; adult/child ¥1400/free; ⊙ 9am–5pm) Buddhist theme park, anyone? A short time after the death of his beloved mother in 1934, local steel-tube magnate and arms manufacturer Kanemoto Kōzō became a Buddhist priest and sank his fortune into a series of garishly coloured temple buildings. The result is the remarkabe Kōsan-ji, a sprawl of over-the-top Buddhist kitsch, consisting of some 2000 exhibits. Be sure not to miss the 1000 Buddhas Cave and its series of graphically illustrated hells.

Kōsan-ji is a 15-minute walk from Setoda port.

🛏️ Sleeping & Eating

Ikuchi-jima is a good place to overnight if you're cycling the Shimanami Kaidō.

The arty, white-marble cafe inside Kōsan-ji has impressive sea views. Seafood is, unsurprisingly, popular.

Setoda Private Hostel RYOKAN ¥
(瀬戸田垂水温泉; Setoda Tarumi Onsen; ☎0845-27-3137; http://setodashimanami.web.fc2.com; 58-1 Tarumi Setoda-chō; r per person with/without meals ¥4800/3000) The cheap-and-cheerful Setoda Private Hostel on Sunset Beach has its own onsen, with accommodation in basic, individual tatami rooms; payment is by cash only. If you're not arriving on two wheels, a pick-up can be arranged from Setoda ferry port. The tourist office in Onomichi can help with reservations. Breakfast (¥600) and dinner (¥1200) sets are also available separately.

ⓘ Getting There & Away

Setouchi Cruising (www.s-cruise.jp) ferries travel from Onomichi Ekimae port (in front of Onomichi Station) to Setoda port (¥1050, 40 minutes, eight daily) on Ikuchi-jima. It is an additional ¥300 to take a bicycle.

For cyclists, it's 31km from Onomichi along the picturesque Shimanami Kaidō road to Setoda port. If you rented a bicycle from Onomichi port and have had enough of riding, there are bicycle return points here.

Ōmi-shima 大三島

The mountainous island of Ōmi-shima is connected by bridge to Ikuchi-jima to the east and Ō-shima to the southeast. It is home to one of the oldest Shintō shrines in western Japan, **Ōyamazumi-jinja** (大山祇神社; Treasure Hall & Kaiji Museum ¥1000; ⊙8.30am-5pm), near Miyaura port. The deity enshrined here is the brother of Amaterasu, the sun goddess. The present structure dates from 1378, but in the courtyard is a 2600-year-old camphor tree, and the treasure hall contains the most important collection of ancient weapons found anywhere in Japan.

It's worth getting off the 'recommended' cycling route to explore Ōmi-shima. With more time on the island, don't miss the **Tokoro Museum** (ところミュージアム大三島; http://museum.city.imabari.ehime.jp/tokoro; ¥300; ⊙9am-5pm Tue-Sun), a small but interesting collection of modern sculpture. It's a hilly ride up to the museum, but you're rewarded with fabulous sea views.

There are a few guesthouses here, including a converted school. The tourist office (p452) in Onomichi can book accommodation.

Ōmi-shima is 42km along the Shimanami Kaidō from Onomichi, or 36km from Imbari Station on the other end of the cycling road. Ōmi-shima is one of the hillier islands on the bike route so may take more time to explore.

The nearest ferry port is on Ikuchi-jima at Setoda port, which connects with Onomichi and allows bringing bicycles.

Tomo-no-ura 鞆の浦

☎084 / POP 5000

Perfectly situated in the middle of the Inland Sea coast, Tomo-no-ura flourished for centuries as a stopping-off point for boats travelling between western Japan and the capital, until the arrival of steam put an end to the town's glory days. It's now a sleepy port town – at the old harbour, fishing boats quietly bob on the water, and the narrow cobbled streets that surround it retain much of the flavour of the Edo-period heyday. Inland from the harbour there are a dozen or so temples, some tucked within residential streets, and stone steps lead up the hillside to views of the Inland Sea. It all makes for a good few hours of strolling.

For film buffs: Tomo-no-ura was the setting for some scenes in *The Wolverine* (2013). It also provided inspiration for renowned Studio Ghibli director Miyazaki Hayao, who spent two months in the town while developing *Ponyo* (*Gake no ue no Ponyo*; 2008).

⊙ Sights

★**Sensui-jima** ISLAND
(仙酔島) The island of Sensui-jima is just five minutes across the water from Tomo-no-ura town. There's a walking path that hugs the coast, passes by interesting rock formations and offers lovely sunset views across the water. After a stroll or swim at the beach, drop into Kokuminshukusha Sensui-jima (p454), where non-guests can take a soak in a range of baths for ¥525 (from 10am to 9pm).

The ferry that shuttles passengers across to the island is modelled on the Edo-era steamboat *Iroha Maru*.

There are no English signs on the island, so check with the tourist office in Tomo-no-ura town if you have specific questions on where to go. The ferry (one-way ¥240) runs to the island every 20 minutes (7.10am to 9.35pm).

★**Ōta Residence** HISTORIC BUILDING
(太田家住宅; ¥400; ⊙10am-4.30pm Wed-Mon) On the corner of a lane leading back from the harbour area, this former Ōta residence is a fine collection of restored buildings from the mid-18th century. Guided tours (included in the admission) take you through the impressive family home and workplace, where

hōmēshu (sweet medicinal liquor) was once brewed. Some English information available.

Iō-ji

BUDDHIST TEMPLE

(医王寺) FREE Up a steep hill on the western side of Tomo-no-ura, Iō-ji was reputedly founded by Kōbō Daishi in the 900s. A path leads from the temple to the top of a bluff, from where there are fabulous views.

Fukuzenji

BUDDHIST TEMPLE

(福禅寺; ¥200; ⊗ 8am-5pm) Close to the waterfront, this temple dates back to the 10th century. Adjoining the temple is **Taichōrō** (対潮楼), a reception hall built in the 1690s. This is where you go for the classic view across the narrow channel to the uninhabited island of Benten-jima and its shrine.

Jōyatō

LIGHTHOUSE

(常夜燈) Looking over the harbour area of Tomo-no-ura is this large stone lantern, which used to serve as a lighthouse and has become a symbol of the town.

🛏 Sleeping & Eating

If you're interested in spending the night, it's worth staying on Sensui-jima. There are a few guesthouses in Tomo-no-ura town, and nearby Fukuyama has a bunch of decent hotels in the station area. The Fukuyama Station tourist office and the Tomo-no-ura tourist office can help with local accommodation bookings.

The greatest number of eating options are around or near the port. During the week, restaurants dotted around town may be closed.

Kokuminshukusha Sensui-jima

RYOKAN ¥¥

(国民宿舎仙酔島; ☑ 084-970-5050; www.tomonoura.co.jp/sen; 3373-2 Ushiroji Tomo-chō; r per person with 2 meals from ¥8800; ☯) This is a reasonably priced ryokan option on Sensui-jima, right on the beach, with Japanese- and Western-style rooms and a range of baths. Meals, unsurprisingly, feature local seafood.

★ Tabuchiya

CAFE ¥¥

(田渕屋; www.tomonoura-tabuchiya.com; 838 Tomo-chō-tomo; set lunch ¥1300; ⊗ noon-5pm Mon-Sat) At this former merchant building only one meal is served – *hayashi raisu* (beef in a rich tomato-based sauce on rice) – but it's served very well. The set lunch comes with a tea or coffee. Walk past the Ōta Residence away from the harbour and look for the white *noren* (door curtains).

Tomo-no-ura @Cafe

CAFE ¥¥

(www.facebook.com/tomonouraacafe; Jōyatō-mae, Tomo-chō; meals ¥600-1600; ⊗ 10am-6pm Thu-Tue; 🛜🍴📶) This friendly, modern cafe is in a 150-year-old building beside the stone lighthouse on the harbour. There's a small menu of sandwiches and set menus that can include seafood pasta and vegetarian options.

ℹ Information

Tomo-no-ura Tourist Information Centre
(鞆の浦観光情報センター; ☑ 084-982-3200; 416-1 Tomo-chō-tomo; ⊗ 6.30am-10pm) Opposite the Tomo-no-ura bus stop; doubles as a souvenir shop. It has English maps, information on the locations used in films, and it rents out audio guides (¥500).

ℹ Getting There & Around

Bus 5 runs to Tomo-no-ura every 20 minutes from outside JR Fukuyama Station (¥520, 30 minutes). The tourist office is located at the Tomo-no-ura stop; the bus continues on another 450m or so to the Tomo-kō stop (Tomo port), which is closest to the central harbour area. JR Fukuyama Station is a main hub and *shinkansen* stop on the San-yō line.

It's easy and most convenient to get around the town on foot. Bikes can be hired (¥300 for two hours) from a booth (10am to 4.30pm) next to the terminal where the ferries leave for Sensui-jima.

OKAYAMA & AROUND

Okayama Prefecture (岡山県; Okayama-ken) is known for its rural character. The area is home to Kurashiki with its well-preserved merchant quarter and picturesque canal, and the historic ceramic-making centre of Bizen – both within easy reach of prefectural capital Okayama. The coastline in this area also provides jumping-off points for some of the most popular islands in the Inland Sea, including arty Naoshima.

ℹ Getting There & Away

Okayama is the main transport hub for the region. Okayama is on the JR San-yō line and *shinkansen* line, connecting to Osaka in the east and Hiroshima to the west. Yonago in Tottori Prefecture is on the limited express Yakumo.

Naoshima and the other 'art islands' can be accessed from Uno port south of Okayama, and also Takamatsu in Kagawa, which can make a more convenient base for Naoshima than Okayama. There are rail links to Takamatsu, from where there are ferries to Naoshima and Shōdo-shima.

Okayama　岡山

♫ 086 / POP 721,170

The most many travellers see of Okayama is the blur of colour as they fly through on the *shinkansen* to Hiroshima. But it's worth stepping off the train, if only to spend a few hours strolling around Kōraku-en, one of Japan's top three gardens, which is overlooked by the city's crow-black castle. If you have a few days up your sleeve, make Okayama your base for day trips to other attractions in the region and side trips to islands in the Inland Sea.

The city is proud of its connection to Momotarō, the demon-quelling 'Peach Boy' hero of one of Japan's best-known folk tales. You'll spot his face beaming out at you all over town.

◎ Sights

★ Kōraku-en　GARDENS

(後楽園; Map p456; www.okayama-korakuen. jp; 1-5 Kōraku-en; ¥400; ⊙ 7.30am-6pm Apr-Sep, 8am-5pm Oct-Mar, also to 9.30pm late Jul to mid Aug) Kōraku-en draws the crowds with its reputation as one of the three most beautiful gardens in Japan. It has expansive lawns broken up by ponds, teahouses and other Edo-period buildings, including a *nō* theatre stage; it even has a small tea plantation and rice field. In spring the groves of plum and cherry-blossom trees are stunning, white lotuses unfurl in summer, and in autumn the maple trees are a delight for photographers. There are also seasonal events (fancy some harvest-moon viewing?).

Built on the orders of *daimyō* Ikeda Tsunemasa, the garden was completed in 1700 and, despite suffering major damage during floods in the 1930s and air raids in the 1940s, it remains much as it was in feudal times. It was opened to the public in 1884.

In summer, from late July to mid-August, the garden and castle are dreamily lit up and stay open to 9.30pm.

From Okayama Station, take the Higashi-yama tram to the Shiroshita stop, from where it's about 10 minutes on foot. Bus 18 from the station will drop you right outside the garden (Kōraku-en-mae stop). Walking the entire way will take about 25 minutes.

Okayama-jō　CASTLE

(岡山城; Map p456; 2-3-1 Marunouchi; ¥300, additional charge for special exhibitions; ⊙ 9am-5pm, to 9.30pm late Jul to mid Aug) Nicknamed U-jō (烏城; Crow Castle) because of its colour, the striking black Okayama Castle has an imposing exterior with gilded-fish gargoyles flipping their tails in the air. You can appreciate it for nix from the grounds or from across the river. In summer the castle and nearby Kōraku-en are lit up and stay open late. Inside the *donjon* (main keep), some modern finishes detract from the 16th-century feel, but there are a few interesting museum displays and views from the top floor.

Hayashibara Museum of Art　MUSEUM

(林原美術館; Map p456; ♫ 086-223-1733; www. hayashibara-museumofart.jp; 2-7-15 Marunouchi; ¥300; ⊙ 10am-5pm Tue-Sun) This is a small museum with exhibits of scrolls, armour and paintings that were once the property of the Ikeda clan (who ruled Okayama for much of the Edo period). It's near the rear entrance of Okayama-jō. Look for the traditional black-and-white building.

✦ Festivals & Events

Saidai-ji Eyō　CULTURAL

(Saidai-ji; ⊙ 3rd Sat in Feb) Also known as the Hadaka Matsuri ('Naked Festival'), this event takes place at the Kannon-in temple

---

MOMOTARŌ, THE PEACH BOY

Okayama Prefecture and Kagawa Prefecture, on the island of Shikoku, are linked by the legend of Momotarō, the Peach Boy, who emerged from the stone of a peach and, backed up by a monkey, a pheasant and a dog, defeated a three-eyed, three-toed people-eating demon. The island of Megi-jima, off Takamatsu in Shikoku, is said to be the site of the clash with the demon. Momotarō may actually have been a Yamato prince who was deified as Kibitsuhiko. His shrine, Kibitsu-jinja, lies along the route of the Kibiji cycling route.

There are statues of Momotarō at JR Okayama Station, he and his sidekicks feature on manhole covers, and the city's biggest street is named after him. One of the most popular souvenir treats from Okayama is also Momotarō's favoured sweet, *kibi-dango*, a soft *mochi*-like dumpling made with millet flour. And if you can sing the first couple of lines of the well-known old children's tune, *Momotarō's Song*, you'll impress the locals no end. All together now: *Momotarō-san, Momotarō-san, o-koshi ni tsuketa kibi-dango...*

Okayama

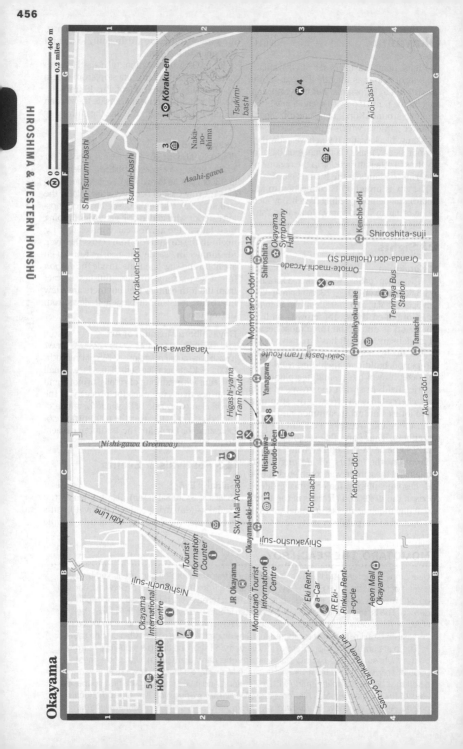

0 400 m
0 0.2 miles

HŌKAN-CHŌ

Nishiguchi-suji

Okayama International Centre

Tourist Information Counter

JR Okayama

Kibi Line

Momotarō Tourist Information Centre

Eki Rent-a-Car

JR Eki-Rinkun-Rent-a-cycle

Sanyō Shinkansen Line

Aeon Mall Okayama

Kenchō-dōri

Honmachi

Shiyakusho-suji

Okayama-eki-mae

Sky Mall Arcade

Nishi-gawa Greenway

Nishigawa-ryokudo-kōen

Higashi-yama Tram Route

Yanagawa

Seki-bashi Tram Route

Yanagawa-suji

Kōrakuen-dōri

Momotarō-Ōdori

Shin-Tsurumi-bashi

Tsurumi-bashi

Asahi-gawa

Naka-no-shima

Kōraku-en 1

3

4

Tsukimi-bashi

2

Aioi-bashi

Kenchō-dōri

Shiroshita

Okayama Symphony Hall

Omote-machi Arcade

Oranda-dōri (Holland St)

Shiroshita-suji

Yūbinkyoku-mae

Tenmaya Bus Station

Tamachi

Akura-dōri

12

9

8

6

10

11

13

5

7

Okayama

in Saidai-ji, where a chaotic crowd of around 10,000 men in loincloths fight over two sacred *shingi* (wooden batons) while freezing water is poured over them. It begins at 10pm, though there's also a version for elementary-school boys earlier in the evening.

Only men are allowed to participate, but anyone can watch.

🛏 Sleeping

Kamp Hōkan-chō Backpacker's Inn & Lounge   HOSTEL ¥
(キャンプ; Map p456; ☑086-254-1611; http://kamp.jp; 3-1-35 Hōkan-chō; dm/tw with shared bathroom ¥3000/7000; ⊖❄🛜) Dorm rooms are basic (with rather thin walls) but clean at this fresh hostel option on the west side of Okayama Station – rare for this hotel-filled area. There is plenty of space to relax in the large lounge and bar downstairs, where events and live performances are sometimes held. Find it on a side street just off an old-style sleepy shopping arcade.

★ Kōraku Hotel   HOTEL ¥¥
(後楽ホテル; Map p456; ☑086-221-7111; www.hotel.koraku.co.jp; 5-1 Heiwa-chō; s/tw from ¥6000/8600, cnr room from ¥13,200; ⊖❄@🛜) Kōraku has classy touches such as local museum pieces displayed on each floor, and pampering extras such as complimentary aroma pots for your room. The corner rooms, with large curved windows, are especially spacious. Staff members speak English (and other languages), as does the enthusiastic manager, who you may bump into mingling with guests in the lobby.

There are good discounts for longer stays, and a buffet breakfast or lunch for ¥980.

Saiwai-sō   HOTEL ¥¥
(ビジネスホテル幸荘; Map p456; ☑086-254-0020; http://w150.j.fiw-web.net; 24-8 Ekimoto-chō; s/tw ¥4300/7600; ⊖❄🛜) This 'happy house' declares itself Okayama's first business hotel, but it's not typical of that genre, having mostly tatami rooms (go for one of these) in a warren-like building. Some rooms have shared bathrooms. Groups and families are welcomed (up to six people from ¥3800 per person), and what other business hotel has an old-school video-game table in the lounge?

Breakfast is available for ¥600. The owners are very welcoming, but note that they don't speak English.

🍴 Eating & Drinking

★ Okabe   TOFU ¥
(おかべ; Map p456; ☑086-222-1404; 1-10-1 Omote-chō; set meals ¥820-870; ⊙11.30am-2.30pm Mon-Wed, Fri & Sat) Squeeze in at the counter at this small, simple lunch joint and watch the team of women preparing delicious tofu meals. There are only three things on the (picture) menu; try the *okabe teishoku* for a set of several types of tofu. The restaurant is on a corner – look for the big illustration of a heavily laden tofu seller in a straw hat.

The menu is meat free but contains fish stock.

Ajitsukasa Nomura   TONKATSU ¥
(味司野村; Map p456; ☑086-222-2234; 1-10 Heiwa-chō; meals ¥900-1400; ⊙11am-9pm; ⊖📷) Step into this quiet bamboo-themed restaurant to try local speciality *demi-katsudon* – deep-fried pork cutlets with a thick, rich demi-glace sauce, served on rice. Place your order by purchasing a ticket from the machine inside the entrance.

OFF THE BEATEN TRACK

CYCLING THE KIBI PLAIN

The largely rural Kibiji district around Okayama is best explored on two wheels, following a mostly flat cycling route across the Kibi plain between Bizen-Ichinomiya (備前一宮) and Sōja (総社). The roughly 15km route takes in several interesting temples and shrines, and an ancient burial mound, passing through rice fields along the way. It can take as little as a couple of hours if you're just pedalling through, but allow at least three or four if you want to wander around the sights or take a few detours (or get lost) here and there.

Among the highlights is the **Kibitsu-jinja** (吉備津神社; www.kibitujinja.com; 931 Kibitsu, Kita Ward; ⊙ 8.30am-4pm) FREE, a major shrine dedicated to an ancient warrior who subdued a local bandit/demon called Ura and brought the area under central control. Many believe that these exploits were the ultimate source of the Momotarō legend. The route also passes nearby the 5th-century **Tsukuriyama-kofun** (造山古墳; ☑ 086-270-5066; ⊙ 24hr) FREE, the fourth-biggest *kofun* tomb (keyhole-shaped burial mound) in Japan, thought to mark the final resting place of a local king who ruled the Kibi region when this area was a rival power to the Yamato court (which eventually came to rule the country). Another major stop is **Bitchū Kokobun-ji** (備中国分寺; ☑ 0866-92-0037; 1046 Kanbayashi, Soja; ⊙ 7.30am-5pm) FREE, a temple with a picturesque five-storey pagoda. The oldest buildings here date from the Edo period, but the first temple on this site was built in the 8th century.

To start cycling from Bizen-Ichinomiya Station, take a local JR Kibi line train from Okayama (¥210, 11 minutes) and hire a bike from **Uedo Rent-a-Cycle** (レンタサイクルウエド; ☑ 086-284-2311; Bizen-Ichinomiya Station; ⊙ 9am-6pm), on the right at the front of the station. It sometimes closes in bad weather. If no one is around, ask the guard at the nearby bike parking lot, who may be able to call and get it opened. At the Sōja end, hire bikes from **Araki Rent-a-Cycle** (荒木レンタサイクル; ☑ 0866-92-0233; 2 Chome-1-5 Ekimae, Soja; ⊙ 9am-6pm), at the side of the bus area in front of the station. Trains run between Okayama and Sōja on the JR Momotarō line (¥410, 40 minutes) and JR Hakubi line (¥500, 30 minutes).

Bike rental is ¥1000 for the day if you hire from one office and drop it at the other. Follow the route map you receive with the bike, and the blue 'Kibiji District' road signs along the course. If you wander off track, locals will be able to set you straight – just ask them for the *Kibiji jitensha dōro* (Kibiji bike path).

The machine doesn't have English, but the separate menu does and staff can assist.

Teppan-Ku-Ya   JAPANESE ¥¥
(テッパン クウヤ; Map p456; ☑ 086-224-8880; http://teppan-ku-ya.com; 1-1-17 Nodayachō; meals ¥2500-5000; ⊙ 6pm-midnight; ✱ 🖶) An extremely popular fusion restaurant for Japanese classics such as *tako-yaki* (grilled octopus dumplings). The best bet is the set six-course meal, which includes French-leaning flavours in pumpkin soup, grilled prawn, Wagyu beef or salmon steak, and sweet green-tea ice cream. The warm fuss-free atmosphere, English-speaking staff, wine options and Western-style service make this a foreigner-friendly, good-value choice.

Saudade na Yoru   BAR
(サウダーヂな夜; Map p456; www.saudade-ent.com/saudade; 2nd fl, Shiroshita Bldg, 10-16 Tenjin-chō; ⊙ 6pm-3am Mon-Fri, 3pm-3am Sat & Sun) This 2nd-floor lounge bar overlooking the Symphony Hall building makes all the right retro-chic moves, with mismatched furniture,

ornate-glass lighting and eclectic background (and sometimes live jazz) music. It has a good drinks list (most priced around ¥700), coffees and a limited food and snacks menu. A ¥300 cover charge applies after 8pm.

Izayoi no Tsuki   IZAKAYA
(いざ酔いの月; Map p456; ☑ 086-222-2422; 1-10-2 Ekimae-chō; ⊙ 5pm-midnight) A convivial atmosphere (though it's fine to sit at the counter solo), walls decorated with sake labels, and an enormous drinks menu – just what you want from a local *izakaya*. There are numerous sakes from Okayama Prefecture and beers from local microbreweries. Try the Doppo pilsner or a Kibi Doteshita Bakushu ale.

Izayoi is just off the Sky Mall arcade. Look for the sign written across a yellow moon.

☆ Entertainment

Okayama Symphony Hall   THEATRE
(岡山シンフォニーホール; Map p456; ☑ 086-234-2001; www.okayama-symphonyhall.or.jp; 1-5-1 Omotechō) Okayama's concert hall, in an

impressive circular building, hosts a wide range of international and local music and dance performances.

ℹ Information

Momotarō Tourist Information Centre (もも たろう観光センター; Map p456; ☑086-222-2912; www.okayama-kanko.net/sightseeing; ◷9am-8pm; ☏) Large office with maps and information on Okayama and the region, as well as coupons for small discounts on the major sights. The helpful staff speak some English and there's free wi-fi. It's in the basement complex below the station – follow the underground signs.

Okayama International Centre (岡山国際交流センター; Map p456; ☑ 086-256-2914; www.opief.or.jp/oicenter; 2-2-1 Hōkan-chō; ◷9am-5pm Mon-Sat) Information and resources mostly aimed at foreign residents, with some maps and pamphlets. Free internet access (30 minutes).

Tourist Information Counter (観光案内所; Map p456; ◷9am-6pm) In the station, by the entrance to the *shinkansen* tracks.

ℹ Getting There & Away

BOAT

Ferries run to Shōdo-shima and Naoshima from Shin-Okayama port (40 minutes away) and Uno port (one hour away).

BUS

Highway buses connect Okayama with big cities across the region. Buses also run between Okayama Station and Kansai International Airport (3¼ hours, one-way/return ¥4650/7700, seven daily).

Buses to Shin-Okayama port (¥490, 40 minutes, one or two per hour) leave from Okayama Station, stopping at **Tenmaya bus station** (Map p456) in the city centre on the way.

TRAIN

Okayama is on the JR San-yō line and *shinkansen* line, connecting to Osaka (¥6020, 50 minutes) in the east and Hiroshima (¥6020, 40 minutes) to the west. There are rail links to Takamatsu in Kagawa (¥2030, 55 minutes) south of Naoshima on the JR Marine Liner, and Yonago in Tottori Prefecture on the limited express Yakumo (¥5270, 135 minutes).

WORTH A TRIP

FARMHOUSE GETAWAY IN HATTŌJI

As you head up through the hills past the farms and thatched-roof houses to Hattōji (八塔寺), a little over an hour northeast of Okayama, the crowds and vending-machine-packed streets of big-city Japan begin to feel delightfully out of reach.

The chief reason to journey out here is to stay at the **Hattōji International Villa** (八塔寺国際交流ヴィラ; ☑086-256-2535; www.international-villa.or.jp; Kagami Yoshinaga-chō, Bizen-shi; s/d ¥4100/7200, whole house up to 8 people/9-13 people ¥25,700/41,000; ◷❄), a restored farmhouse that is one of two remaining places established by the prefectural government in the late 1980s as accommodation for foreigners. Spending a night or two here is an excellent way to get a sense of Japan outside the well-touristed urban centres.

In the farmhouse are four large tatami rooms separated by sliding doors, a shared bathroom and kitchen, and bicycles that are free to use. In the common area you can burn charcoal in the open hearth, and near the villa you'll find hiking tracks, shrines and temples (where it's possible to join morning meditation). Check availability and make reservations online. Payment is cash only. There are a couple of eateries in the area, but hours are irregular – stock up on groceries in Okayama or Yoshinaga before you come to Hattōji.

Buses (¥200, 30 minutes, five to six daily Monday to Saturday) run to Hattōji from Yoshinaga (吉永) on the JR San-yō line, accessible by train (¥580, 40 minutes, roughly every hour) from Okayama. The bus drops you near the villa entrance. See the International Villa Group website for the latest schedule.

While you're near Yoshinaga Station, it's worth visiting the historic Edo-period **Shizutani Gakko** (閑谷学校; Shizutani School; ☑0869-67-1427; www.shizutani.jp; 784 Shizutani, Bizen; ¥300; ◷9am-5pm), the first public school in Japan. The building boasts wood interiors and beautifully preserved Bizen-yaki roof tiles. The school is about 3km from the station. There are infrequent buses, but it's walkable; ask at the station for directions.

WORTH A TRIP

POTTERY TOWN BIZEN

The Bizen (備前) region has been renowned for its ceramics since the Kamakura period (1185–1333). The pottery produced here tends to be earthy and subdued, and has been prized by dedicated tea-ceremony aficionados for centuries. Travellers with an interest in pottery will find the sleepy Bizen town of **Imbe** (伊部) and its kilns a worthwhile trip from Okayama.

Most places of ceramic interest are within easy walking distance of Imbe Station. The **Imbe information counter** (☑0869-64-1001; www.touyuukai.jp; ☉9am-6pm Wed-Mon), inside the souvenir shop on the left as you exit the platform, has a very good *Inbe Walk* map in English, showing the locations of kilns, shops and other sites.

Kibido (黄薇堂; ☑0869-64-4467; www.bizenyakikibido.com; 714 Inbe; ☉9am-5pm Mon-Sat, noon-5pm Sun) FREE is a kiln and gallery-shop run by the Kimura family, one of the six original families granted official permission in the early 1600s to produce pottery in the Bizen region. Here it's possible to take a free tour in English (email them in advance) of the traditional step-style *nobori-gama* kiln and see the current generation of Kimura artists at work. The free information pamphlet has an excellent short explanation in English of the traditional process of producing Bizen ware – a good place to start a visit to the town. From opposite the station, walk up and to the left.

Tempogama (天保窯) is a large kiln ruin (c 1832) a short walk up a lane leading off the main street. The kiln is fenced off for protection. Look for the red iron roofing.

To learn more about Bizen-yaki (Bizen pottery), stop by Imbe's **Okayama Prefectural Bizen Ceramics Art Museum** (岡山県備前陶芸美術館; ☑0869-64-1400; 1659-6 Inbe; ¥700; ☉9.30am-5pm Tue-Sun), which exhibits pieces from the Muromachi (1333–1568) and Momoyama (1568–1600) periods, plus work by several modern artists who have been designated 'Living National Treasures'.

Try your hand at making your own Bizen-yaki (Bizen pottery) at **Bishūgama** (備州窯; ☑0869-64-1160; www.gift.or.jp/bisyu; 302-2 Imbe; ☉9am-3pm). Creating a piece costs ¥2700 or ¥3780, depending on the type of firing you choose, though firing happens later and international delivery can cost as much as the product. No bookings are required and information (but not instruction) in English is available.

There is one direct train an hour to Imbe from Okayama (¥580, 40 minutes) on the Akō line (赤穂線), bound for Banshū-Akō (播州赤穂) and Aioi (相生).

ℹ Getting Around

Okayama can be seen on foot or by taking a couple of short tram rides. The Higashi-yama line takes you to the main attractions, going from the station's east exit all the way up Momotarō-Ōdōri (get out at the last stop on this street to visit nearly all of the sights), then turning right. The Seiki-bashi line turns right earlier at the large roundabout, passing Okayama Central Post Office. Travel within the central city area costs ¥100. Okayama is also a good city for cycling.

JR Eki-Rinkun Rent-a-cycle (レンタサイクル駅リンくん; Map p456; ☑086-223-7081; 1-2 Motomachi; rental per day ¥350; ☉7am-9.50pm) Bike rental on the east side of Okayama Station.

Eki Rent-a-Car (駅レンタカー; Map p456; ☑086-224-1363; www.ekiren.co.jp; rental per day from ¥5940; ☉8am-8pm) Car rental office located on the east side of Okayama Station.

Naoshima 直島

☑087 / POP 3135

As the location of the Benesse Art Site, the island of Naoshima has become one of the region's biggest tourist attractions, offering a unique chance to see some of Japan's best contemporary art in lovely natural settings.

The Benesse project started in the early '90s, when the Benesse Corporation chose Naoshima as the setting for its growing collection of modern art. Since then, Naoshima has continued to transform – once home to a dwindling population subsisting on the proceeds of a small fishing industry, it now has a number of world-class art galleries and installations, and has attracted creative types from all over the country to set up businesses here. The art movement has not stopped at Naoshima's shores, either, with museums and art sites popping up on other islands in the Inland Sea.

In addition to the museums, numerous outdoor sculptures are situated around the coast, including **Yellow Pumpkin** (⏱24hr) `FREE` by Kusama Yayoi, which has become a symbol of Naoshima.

◉ Sights & Activities

Most sights and activities are clustered around the Honmura (本村), Miyanoura (宮ノ浦) and Benesse Art Site areas.

During holiday seasons the museums can become quite crowded and you may find you have to queue.

★ Art House Project   ART INSTALLATION
(家プロジェクト; www.benesse-artsite.jp/ en/art/arthouse.html; single/combined ticket ¥410/1030; ⏱10am-4.30pm Tue-Sun) In Honmura, half a dozen traditional buildings have been turned over to contemporary artists to use as the setting for creative installations, often incorporating local history. Highlights include Ōtake Shinrō's shack-like **Haisha** (はいしゃ; ¥410), its Statue of Liberty sculpture rising up through the levels of the house; James Turrell's experiment with light in **Minami-dera** (南寺; ¥410), where you enter in total darkness...and wait; and Sugimoto Hiroshi's play on the traditional **Go'o Shrine** (護王神社; ¥410), with a glass staircase and narrow underground 'Stone Chamber'.

The sites are within walking distance of each other. Take the Naoshima bus to the Nōkyō-mae stop to start exploring. Buy a ticket at the tourist counter in the Miyanoura ferry terminal, at Honmura Lounge, or at the tobacco shop near the bus stop.

Benesse House Museum   GALLERY
(ベネッセハウス; Map p462; www.benesse-art-site.jp/en/art/benessehouse-museum.html; adult/child/hotel guests ¥1030/free/free; ⏱8am-9pm) Award-winning architect Andō Tadao designed this stunning museum and hotel on the south coast of the island. Among the works here are pieces by Andy Warhol, David Hockney, Jasper Johns, and Japanese artists such as Ōtake Shinrō. Art installations are dotted across the adjacent shoreline and forest, blending architecture into nature.

Chichū Art Museum   GALLERY
(地中美術館; Map p462; www.benesse-artsite. jp/en/art/chichu.html; adult/child ¥2060/free; ⏱10am-6pm Tue-Sun Mar-Sep, to 5pm Oct-Feb) A short walk from Benesse House is this Andō Tadao creation. A work of art itself, the museum consists of a series of cool concrete-walled spaces sitting snugly underground. Lit by natural light, it provides a remarkable setting for several Monet water-lily paintings, some monumental sculptures by Walter De Maria and installations by James Turrell. Outside is the Chichū garden, created in the spirit of Monet's garden in Giverny.

At peak times a 'timed ticket' system may be in place, designating the time you are able to purchase a ticket and enter.

Lee Ufan Museum   GALLERY
(李禹煥美術館; Map p462; www.benesse-artsite. jp/en/art/lee-ufan.html; adult/child ¥1030/free; ⏱10am-6pm Tue-Sun Mar-Sep, to 5pm Oct-Feb) Adding to Benesse's suite of museums is yet another design from the irrepressible Andō Tadao. It houses works by renowned Korean-born artist (and philosopher) Lee Ufan, who was a leading figure in the Mono-ha movement of the 1960s and '70s.

★ Naoshima Bath – I Heart Yū   SENTO
(直島銭湯; Map p462; www.benesse-artsite.jp/en/ art/naoshimasento.html; adult/child ¥510/210; ⏱2-9pm Tue-Fri, 10am-9pm Sat & Sun) For a unique bathing experience, take a soak at this colourful fusion of Japanese bathing tradition and contemporary art, designed by Ōtake Shinrō, where there really is an elephant in the room. It's a couple of minutes' walk inland from Miyanoura port. Look for the building with the palm trees out front.

The name is a play on words – 'yū' refers to hot water in Japanese.

🎊 Festivals & Events

★ Setouchi Triennale   ART
(瀬戸内国際芸術祭; Setouchi International Art Festival; www.setouchi-artfest.jp) This festival of art, music, drama and dance comes around every three years and has a packed calendar of events occurring on multiple Inland Sea islands, many on Naoshima. Previous schedules have been spread across the three seasons spring, summer and autumn.

Check the excellent website for the low-down on events and ferry passes. The three-season festival 'passport' ticket (¥4000 if bought in advance, or ¥5000 on site), which covers entry to almost all sites, offers significant savings for those visiting a number of sites and museums and is highly recommended. Book your accommodation well ahead if you plan on staying on Naoshima or even in Takamatsu during the festival.

Naoshima

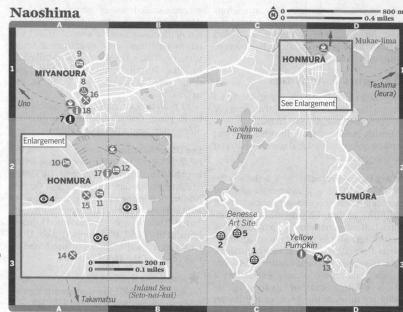

Naoshima

◎ Sights

1 Benesse House Museum	C3
2 Chichū Art Museum	C3
3 Go'o Shrine	B2
4 Haisha	A2
5 Lee Ufan Museum	C3
6 Minami-dera	A3
7 Red Pumpkin	A2

◎ Activities, Courses & Tours

8 Naoshima Bath – I Heart Yū	A1

◎ Sleeping

Benesse House	(see 1)
9 Cin.na.mon	A1
10 Gallery Inn Kuraya	A2
11 Minshuku Oyaji-no-Umi	A2

12 Naoshima Backpackers Guesthouse	B2
13 Tsutsuji-sō	D3

◎ Eating

14 Cafe Salon Naka-Oku	A3
15 Genmai-Shinshoku Aisunao	A2
Museum Restaurant Issen	(see 1)
16 Shioya Diner	A1

◎ Information

17 Honmura Lounge & Archive	A2
18 Marine Station Tourist Information Centre	A1

◎ Transport

Cafe Ougiya Rent-a-Cycle	(see 18)

🛏 Sleeping

The accommodation scene is dominated by privately run *minshuku* (guesthouses). Not a lot of English is spoken, but locals are becoming increasingly used to foreign guests. If you prefer hotel-style facilities, Benesse House hotel is your only real option. Alternatively, stay in Okayama or Uno port on the mainland, or Takamatsu in Shikoku, and visit as a day trip. Rates increase at most places during high season.

★**Tsutsuji-sō**   CAMPGROUND ¥
(つつじ荘; Map p462; ☎087-892-2838; www.tsutsujiso.com; tents/cottages per person from ¥3780/4760; ❄) Located on the beachfront not far from the Benesse Art Site area is this camp of Mongolian-style *pao* tents. The cosy tents sleep up to four, have a small fridge and heater (but no air-con), and shared bathroom facilities. The tent-averse can opt instead for one of the caravans or cottages. Meals are available if reserved in advance. Cash only.

Naoshima Backpackers Guesthouse
HOSTEL ¥

(Map p462; ☑080-9130-2976; www.naoshima backpackers.wixsite.com/backpackers; 845-9 Nao-shimachō; dm ¥2500; ➌✴✿) The dorms here may just be wooden capsules, but hey it's cheap, has free bike use and an excellent location near Honmura port and the sights. Prior reservations only, as they might not hear the doorbell! From the Honmura local bus stop, head straight towards the water and look for a white sign.

Gallery Inn Kuraya
GUESTHOUSE ¥

(ギャラリーインくらや; Map p462; ☑087-892-2253; www.kuraya-naoshima.net; r per person from ¥4000; ➌✿) Kuraya Gallery offers accommodation when it's not occupied by visiting artists. There's a tatami room in the house, or you can sleep in the small wood-floored gallery room opposite. Both share the bathroom. The lovely owner speaks very good English and there is a small cafe attached (irregular hours).

Kuraya is near Honmura port, on the left if you're walking towards the Art House Project's *Ishibashi*.

Minshuku Oyaji-no-Umi
MINSHUKU ¥

(民宿おやじの海; Map p462; ☑090-5261-7670; www.ameblo.jp/naosima-oyajinoumi; r per person from ¥4200; @✿) This is a good option for friendly, family-style lodgings, with tatami rooms (separated by sliding doors) and shared bathroom, in an old house close to the Art House Project in Honmura. The owners don't speak English; it's best to book via email or the website if you don't speak Japanese. The entrance is next to the Cat Cafe.

Cin.na.mon
GUESTHOUSE ¥

(シナモン; Map p462; ☑087-840-8133; www.cin-na-mon.jp; r per person incl breakfast ¥4000; ➌✴✿) Above this cafe-bar near the port in Miyanoura are three comfortable tatami rooms with shared bathroom.

Uno Port Inn
RYOKAN ¥¥

(☑0863-21-2729; www.unoportinn.com; 1-4-4 Chikko, Tamano; s/d from ¥6900/9900; ✴✿) You'll find this cosy ryokan with 12 rooms mixing futons or regular beds between Uno Station and Uno port on the mainland. Spaces are small, so some private bathrooms are across the hall. The sleepy port area has few restaurants, but the ryokan's own cafe is good. Staff speak English, and it makes a convenient base to explore both Naoshima and Teshima.

★ Benesse House
BOUTIQUE HOTEL ¥¥¥

(☑087-892-3223; www.benesse-artsite.jp/en/stay; tw/ste from ¥32,000/59,000; ℗➌✴@✿) A unique Andō-designed hotel-museum, this is a treat for art and architecture enthusiasts. Accommodation is in four different wings – Museum, Oval, Park and Beach – each with a clean, modern, clutter- and TV-free design, and decor featuring artworks from the Benesse collection. Reserve well in advance.

A monorail takes guests up to the hilltop Oval wing (the most expensive of the options), where rooms are arranged around a pool of water open to the sky, and there are stunning views from the grassed rooftop. Rooms in Oval are spacious (though the bathrooms are standard-issue) and large windows make the most of the views; you may not want to come back down once you're up here. The Beach wing is a newer building by the sea, from where you can see the *Yellow Pumpkin* sculpture. Or stick close to the art with a stay in the Museum lodgings.

Children under seven years old aren't permitted in the Oval and Museum wings.

✗ Eating

There are a few cafes, and the only convenience store, near the port at Miyanoura, and some restaurants and cafes plus a small supermarket in the Art House Project area in Honmura. Not many places open in the evenings and hours can be irregular.

★ Shioya Diner
CAFE ¥

(シオヤダイナー; Map p462; ☑087-892-3290; dishes ¥400-1000; ◷11am-9pm Tue-Sun; ✿⛯) With rock 'n' roll music, retro furniture and kitsch knick-knacks, Shioya is an odd mix of American diner and grandma's kitchen. The menu features tacos and chilli dogs and they sometimes charcoal-grill Cajun chicken on the barbecue out front. It's a great place to relax over a meal near Miyanoura port and chat to the English-speaking Japanese owners.

★ Cafe Salon Naka-Oku
CAFE ¥

(カフェサロン中奥; Map p462; ☑087-892-3887; www.naka-oku.com; lunch ¥600-790, dinner ¥400-750; ◷11.30am-9pm Wed-Mon; ✿⛯) Up on a small hill at the rear of a farming plot, Na-ka-Oku is a good option in the Honmura area, and one of only a few of places open in the evenings here. It's all wood-beamed warmth and cosiness, with homey specialities like *omuraisu* (omelette filled with fried rice) at lunchtime and small dishes with drinks in the evening.

WORTH A TRIP

BEYOND NAOSHIMA: MORE ARTY ISLANDS OF THE INLAND SEA

Naoshima and Teshima draw the largest art-loving crowds, leaving Inujima, Megijima and Ogijima for quieter exploration.

The drawcard on **Inujima** (犬島) is the excellent **Inujima Seirensho Art Museum** (犬島精錬所美術館; Inujima; incl Inujima Art House Project ¥2060; ⊙10am-4.30pm Wed-Mon, closed Wed & Thu Dec-Feb), a copper refinery converted into an eco-building displaying Yanagi Yukinori's surreal take on environmental issues. This is more an interactive experience than a traditional gallery – you enter through a dark maze of mirrors with the burning sun at its end and continue past floating furniture. Inujima also boasts smaller art sites converted from Japanese houses, and cute little cafes. A future project, 'Inujima Stay', will allow you to spend extended periods of time with local islanders.

Is **Megijima** (女木島) the mythical Onigi-shima, the 'Ogre's Island' where legendary Momotarō went to fight? Head up to the caves to see the comically colourful ogre statues and you might become a believer – or at least the kids will, while you appreciate the panoramic views. You can also explore the beach and Oni Cafe & Gallery, or *Mecon*, a work by Ōtake Shinrō (of *Naoshima Bath – I Heart Yū* fame) that places neon-coloured frameworks around actual school grounds to express the hope that locals remain on the island.

Tiny **Ogijima** (男木島) is only 2km long and has even less flat ground among the green mountain tops, but this makes it an interesting 'museum without walls'. The narrow roads wind up in a maze through the sleepy village, but can suddenly open onto outdoor art installations. Look for a 'wallalley' – one of a few colourful paintings made from discarded lumber and scrapped vessels.

Ferries run between Inujima and Ieura port (¥1030, 25 minutes, three daily) on Teshima, or Hoden port (¥300, 10 minutes, eight daily) on the mainland. A bus from Okayama Station (¥750, 50 minutes, three daily, outside of Triennale Saturday and Sunday only) terminates a two-minute walk from Hoden port.

A ferry runs six times a day from Takamatsu calling first at Megijima (¥240, 20 minutes) then Ogijima (¥510, 40 minutes). Warning: the last two ferries to Ogijima give you little or no time to catch the last return ferry!

Genmai-Shinshoku Aisunao   CAFE ¥
(玄米心食あいすなお; Map p462; www.aisunao. jp; meals ¥600-900; ⊙11am-5.30pm; ⊝⊛🖉📵)
🖉 A tranquil rest stop within the Art House Project area, Aisunao has seating on raised tatami flooring and a decidedly health-conscious menu – try the tasty Aisunao lunch set, with local brown rice, soup and veggies. Desserts (such as soy-milk ice cream), juices and fairtrade coffees are also on offer.

Look for the blue *noren* (door curtains) or sign with a picture of a bowl of rice. It's opposite the guesthouse of the same name.

Museum Restaurant Issen   KAISEKI ¥¥¥
(日本料理一扇; Map p462; ☑087-892-3223; www. benesse-artsite.jp/en/stay/benessehouse/restaurant_cafe.html; breakfast ¥2495, lunch sets ¥2000-2900, dinner sets ¥7720-9540; ⊙7.30-9.30am, 11.30am-2.30pm & 6-9.45pm; ⊝📵) The artfully displayed *kaiseki* (multi-course) dinners at this contrastingly austere Benesse House restaurant are almost too pretty to eat. Courses feature seafood, but there is a veg-dominated option (request a couple of days ahead) and

the menu changes with the seasons. Breakfast and lunch are also served. Reservations are recommended.

ⓘ Information

LEFT LUGGAGE

For day trippers: there are some luggage lockers at Miyanoura port, and luggage can also be left at the Honmura Lounge & Archive.

MONEY

The ATMs at the post offices in Miyanoura and Honmura take international cards, as does the 7-Eleven near Miyanoura port. Ask at the tourist office for directions.

TOURIST INFORMATION

Honmura Lounge & Archive (Map p462; ☑087-840-8273; ⊙10am-4.30pm Tue-Sun) Tourist information next to Honmura port, with a rest area and left luggage service. Tickets for Art House Project can be purchased.

Marine Station Tourist Information Centre (Map p462; ☑087-892-2299; www.naoshima. net; ⊙8.30am-6pm) At the Miyanoura ferry port. Has a comprehensive bilingual map of the island (also downloadable from the website), a walking map and a full list of accommodation options. Note that staff don't make accommodation reservations. Tickets for Art House Project can also be purchased here.

❶ Getting There & Away

Naoshima can be visited on a day trip from Okayama or Takamatsu and it makes a good stopover if you're travelling between Honshū and Shikoku. Extra-large lockers or left-luggage services are available at the ports.

From Okayama, take the JR Uno line to Uno (¥580, about an hour); this usually involves a quick change of trains at Chayamachi, crossing the same platform. Ferries go to Naoshima's main port of **Miyanoura** from the port near Uno Station (¥290, 15 to 20 minutes, hourly). There are also ferries from Uno to the **Honmura port** (¥290, 20 minutes, five daily). Heading back to Okayama at night, you may find trains from Uno have finished or are two hours away, in which case it can be better to take a bus to Okayama Station (¥650, one hour, one to two hourly) from outside Uno Station at bus stop 1.

Takamatsu is connected to the port of Miyanoura by standard ferry (¥520, 50 minutes, nine daily) and high-speed boat (¥1220, 25 minutes, four daily on Fridays, weekends and holidays between March and November, one daily at other times).

Ferry route maps and the latest timetables can be found on the Benesse Art Site website (www. benesse-artsite.jp/en/access) or at the tourist offices in Okayama and Takamatsu.

❶ Getting Around

Bicycle or the town bus are the best options for getting around Naoshima, though it's possible on foot if you have time – for example, it's just over 2km from Miyanoura port to Honmura and the Art House Project area. There is one **taxi** (☏ 087-892-3036) on Naoshima, taking up to nine passengers – this has to be reserved in advance of coming to the island.

BICYCLE

Naoshima is great for cycling and there are a few rental places around Miyanoura ferry port. **Cafe Ougiya Rent-a-Cycle** (☏ 090-3189-0471; rental per day ¥300-500; ☺9am-7pm Mar-Nov, to 6pm Dec-Feb) is inside the Marine Station at the port. A few electric bikes (¥1000 per day) and scooters (¥1500 per day) are also available. Prices are similar at the other rental shops nearby.

BUS

Naoshima 'town bus' minibuses run between Miyanoura, Honmura, and the Benesse House area (Tsutsuji-sō campground stop) in the south once or twice an hour – expect queues during the Triennale. It costs ¥100 per ride (no change given).

From Tsutsuji-sō, there's a free Benesse shuttle, stopping at all the Benesse Art Site museums. In busy seasons buses can fill up quickly, especially towards the end of the day when people are returning to the port to catch ferries. Be sure to check timetables and allow enough buffer time.

Teshima 豊島

If there's not enough to inspire you on Naoshima, get yourself across to Teshima, a small island sitting between Naoshima and Shōdo-shima with a number of art sites. You can spot these larger sibling islands across the sea from lofty vantage points as you make your way over the hills, winding up by lemon trees and old Japanese houses.

◉ Sights

★ **Teshima Yokoo House**   GALLERY
(豊島横尾館; www.benesse-artsite.jp/en/art/teshima-yokoohouse.html; ¥510; ☺10am-5pm Wed-Mon Mar-Sep, to 4pm Oct-Feb, closed Wed & Thu Dec-Feb) Close to Ieura port, an old house has been converted into exhibition spaces, with a colourful take on a traditional Japanese rock garden outside (which locals helped create). Don't miss stepping inside the tower 'waterfall' installation, which is lined with thousands of postcards of waterfalls and seems to go on forever below your feet. Even the giddying, all-chrome bathrooms are worth checking out.

Les Archives du Cœur   MUSEUM
(心臓音のアーカイブ; www.benesse-artsite.jp/en/art/boltanski.html; adult/child ¥510/free; ☺10am-5pm Wed-Mon Mar-Sep, to 4pm Oct-Feb, closed Wed & Thu Dec-Feb) For an fascinating and unique experience, visit this 'heartbeat archive' on a small bay near the Karato port area. There are tens of thousands of registered heartbeats from around the world, and you can listen to them on a loop in surround sound in the dark 'heart room'. While you're here, why not register and record your own heartbeat and get a keepsake CD (¥1540)?

Teshima Art Museum   MUSEUM
(豊島美術館; www.benesse-artsite.jp/en/art/teshima-artmuseum.html; ¥1540; ☺10am-5pm Wed-Mon Mar-Sep, to 4pm Oct-Feb, closed Wed & Thu Dec-Feb) Teshima's art 'museum' is a large concrete shell, forming a low tear-drop-shaped dome on the hillside. Visitors wander through the peaceful, contemplative space, where cutouts in the shell frame snapshots of blue sky, clouds, or the green of the surrounding hills.

Look down to see small globules of water being rolled about the floor on the breeze.

The attached shop (also in concrete) has a small cafe.

Sleeping & Eating

The majority of the *minshuku* and ryokan on Teshima are small homes with little English spoken. Staff at the tourist information office near the Ieura ferry terminal can help book accommodation.

There are cafes dotted around the island that offer *teishoku* (set-menu) lunches.

Takamatsu-ya   RYOKAN ¥
(古宿　たかまつ屋; ☑080-5275-8550; www.takamatsu-ya.jp; r per person with shared bathroom from ¥3000; ⓟ☀🖨) This guesthouse has witnessed ample history as a sanatorium and ryokan for infants or the down and out. Not that you would know it now looking at the seven immaculate tatami rooms. The English-speaking staff, breakfast (¥500) among the lemon trees, and location just a short walk from the Ieura ferry terminal make it as welcoming as ever.

ℹ Information

Pick up maps and information (some English spoken) at the tourist office near the Ieura ferry terminal.

ℹ Getting There & Away

Eight ferries a day travel from Uno port on the mainland to Ieura port (¥770, 25 to 40 minutes), with six continuing around to Karato port (¥1030); these ferries also continue to the island of Shōdo-shima. From Takamatsu, three to five ferries go to Ieura daily (¥1330, 35 minutes), some also stopping at Honmura on Naoshima. Two ferries a day go from Naoshima's Miyanoura port to Ieura (¥620, 35 minutes; not every day in low season), continuing on to the island of Inujima.

Current timetables are available on the Benesse website at www.benesse-artsite.jp/en/access.

ℹ Getting Around

Cycling on the island is highly recommended for getting around; travelling by bus and walking is easier, just more time consuming. Hire bikes at the Ieura port area for ¥500 per day; electric-assist bikes (¥1000 per four hours, ¥100 per additional hour) are also available (but go quickly during the Triennale) and are a good if you're cycling across the hilly island to Karato. There's an infrequent shuttle bus connecting Ieura and Karato (¥200), with additional buses during the Triennale.

Shōdo-shima 小豆島

☑0879 / POP 31,200

Famed for its olive groves and as the setting of the classic film *Nijūshi-no-hitomi* (*Twenty-Four Eyes;* it tells the story of a village school teacher and her young charges), Shōdo-shima makes an enjoyable day trip or overnight escape from big-city Japan. It has a smattering of sights, but is mainly appealing for its mountainous landscape, scenic coastal roads and Inland Sea vistas.

Tonoshō is the main town and port, and also where you can see the 'world's narrowest navigable strait' (Dobuchi Strait), which runs through the centre of town. The island is popular during summer and when the autumn leaves are at their peak in October and November. Come out of season and you'll find a sleepy isle with very few fellow travellers.

◎ Sights

★ Marukin Soy Sauce Historical Museum   MUSEUM
(マルキン醤油記念館; Map p467; www.moritakk.com; ¥210; ⊙9am-4pm) Shōdo-shima was famous for its soy beans long before olives arrived, and several old soy-sauce companies are still in business here. Marukin has a small museum with displays of the sauce-making process, old implements, photos and interesting facts you never knew about the ubiquitous brown stuff. There are good English explanations, and you can try the surprisingly tasty soy-sauce-flavoured ice cream.

It's on the main road between Kusakabe and Sakate.

Nakayama Rice Fields   LANDMARK
(中山千枚田; Nakayama Senmaida; Map p467) About 4km inland from the Ikeda ferry terminal are Nakayama's 'thousand rice fields'. The terraces are pretty in any season but are especially picturesque after rice planting in late April or early May, when the water-filled fields become a hillside of mirrors.

Twenty-Four Eyes Movie Village   MUSEUM
(二十四の瞳映画村; Map p467; www.24hitomi.or.jp; ¥700, combined ticket with Misaki Branch School ¥790; ⊙9am-5pm) Just north of Sakate is the turn-off to the picturesque fishing village of Tanoura (田ノ浦), site of the village school that featured in the film *Twenty-Four Eyes*. The film was based on a

Shōdo-shima

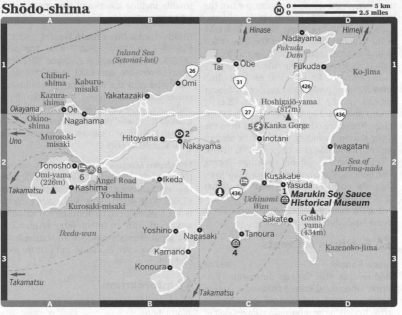

Shōdo-shima

◎ Top Sights

◎ Sights

✪ Activities, Courses & Tours

🛌 Sleeping

ℹ Information

ℹ Transport

novel by local writer Tsuboi Sakae and was
a huge hit in postwar Japan. At this movie
village you can see the set used in the 1980s
remake of the original 1954 B&W film.

Misaki Branch School   HISTORIC BUILDING
(岬の分教場; Map p467; www.24hitomi.or.jp;
¥200, combined ticket with Twenty-Four Eyes Movie Village ¥790; ⊙9am-5pm) Worth visiting
in Tanoura is this perfectly preserved 1902
school, setting for the *Twenty-Four Eyes* story and the 1954 film. It's a short walk from
the movie village on the road back to Sakate.

Shōdo-shima Olive Park   PARK
(小豆島オリーブ公園; Map p467; www.ol-
ive-pk.jp; Nishimura-misaki 1941-1; ⊙8.30am-
5pm) FREE This park is where the island's
olive-growing activities are celebrated with
several whitewashed buildings, some fake
Grecian ruins, a museum, and opportunities to buy olive-themed souvenirs. It's
worth tolerating the kitsch for the **Sun Olive Onsen** (サン・オリーブ温泉; Map p467;
¥700; ⊙noon-9pm), where you can enjoy fabulous views of the Japanese Aegean from a
variety of herbal baths.

🏃 Activities

★ **Kanka Gorge & Ropeway**   OUTDOORS
(寒霞渓; Map p467; www.kankakei.co.jp; ropeway
one-way/return ¥750/1350; ⊙ropeway 8.30am-
5pm) The cable car (寒霞渓ロープウエイ)
is the main attraction at Kanka-kei in the
central mountains, making a spectacular

trip through the gorge, particularly when the foliage is ablaze with autumn colours (drawing scores of leaf-peepers). You can also take in the breathtaking views of the Inland Sea from the area around the upper cable-car station without taking the ride.

An alternative for keen walkers is to climb between the lower and upper cable-car stations via the Omote 12 Views (表12景; 2.3km) and Ura Eight Views (裏8景; 1.8km) tracks. There are other scenic walks from the upper station, including a hike to the eastern peak of Hoshigajō-yama (星ヶ城東峰; 817m).

On weekends, and on weekdays during peak periods, there are four buses a day from Kusakabe port to the lower cable-car station (紅雲亭; Kōuntei), with additional services during the autumn leaf-viewing season. There are no buses during winter.

✹ Festivals & Events

Nōson Kabuki   THEATRE
Shōdo-shima was famous during the Edo period for its rural kabuki (stylised Japanese theatre), and two 17th-century thatched theatres survive in the mountain villages east of Tonoshō. Performances are held on 3 May at the Rikyū Hachiman Shrine in Hitoyama (肥土山) and on the second Sunday in October at the Kasuga Shrine in Nakayama (中山).

🛏 Sleeping & Eating

Shōdo-shima has a variety of hotels, particularly along the road running straight back from the waterfront in Tonoshō.

For its size, eating out on this island does not present the number of options you might expect. Head to the road running straight back from the waterfront in Tonoshō for simple cafes and some *izakaya* and ramen joints. Resorts and large hotels usually include meals and have restaurants for nonguests.

Shōdo-shima Olive Youth Hostel   HOSTEL ¥
(小豆島オリーブユースホステル; Map p467; ☑ 0879-82-6161; www.jyh.gr.jp/shoudo; 1072 Nishimura, Uchinomi-chō; dm ¥3400; ◉ 🛜) This pleasant hostel near the waterfront has bunk-bed dorms and tatami rooms. Meals, bike rental and laundry are available. Buses stop right in front of the hostel (at the Shōdoshimi Orību-Yūsu-mae stop) or it's about a 20-minute walk from Kusakabe port.

Minshuku Maruse   MINSHUKU ¥
(民宿マルセ; Map p467; ☑ 0879-62-2385; www. new-port.biz/maruse/1.htm; r per person from ¥3700; ◉ 🌀 @ 🛜) This welcoming, neatly kept place next to Tonoshō's post office is a short walk from the ferry terminal. It has Japanese-style rooms with shared bathrooms. Meals are available and feature local seafood.

❶ Information

Check www.town.shodoshima.lg.jp for local information.

Tourist Information Booth (Map p467; ☑ 0802-853-5857; ◷ 8.30am-6pm) Inside the Tonoshō ferry terminal with English-speaking staff.

❶ Getting There & Away

There are several ferry routes to and from Shōdo-shima's ports.

If you're going to Shōdo-shima from Okayama, pick up a *Kamome bus kippu* (one-way ¥1300), a discounted combination ticket covering the bus from Okayama Station to Shin-Okayama port plus the ferry to Shōdo-shima. They're sold at the booth in the bus terminal of Okayama Station, and in the Tonoshō ferry terminal.

FERRIES TO SHŌDO-SHIMA

ORIGIN	DESTINATION	FARE (¥)	DURATION	FREQUENCY (PER DAY)
Himeji	Fukuda	1520	1hr 40min	7
Shin-Okayama	Tonoshō	1050	70min	13
Takamatsu	Tonoshō (regular)	690	1hr	15
Takamatsu	Tonoshō (high speed)	1170	30min	16
Takamatsu	Ikeda	690	1hr	8
Takamatsu	Kusakabe (regular)	690	1hr	5
Takamatsu	Kusakabe (high speed)	1170	45min	5
Uno	Tonoshō (via Teshima)	1230	1½hr	6

ⓘ Getting Around

The most convenient way to see the island is by car and it's definitely worth hiring one for the day to take in all the scenic routes. Buses do not go everywhere and services are infrequent.

BICYCLE

Cycling can be enjoyable around the coast if you have plenty of time, but you'd want to be very keen to venture inland as there are some serious climbs. Bikes can also be rented at the youth hostel near Kusakabe.

Asahiya Rent-a-Cycle (旭屋レンタサイクル; Map p467; ☑ 0879-62-0162; gearless bikes per 3hr/5hr/1day ¥300/600/1000; ⊘7am-7pm) Inside the Asahiya hotel, opposite the post office in Tonoshō, a short walk from the ferry terminal.

Ishii Rent-a-Cycle (石井レンタサイクル; Map p467; ☑ 0879-62-1866; www.ishii-cycle.com; Olive-dōri; gearless bikes per day ¥1000, mountain & electric bikes ¥2000; ⊘8.30am-5pm) It's worth the walk here to get a bicycle with gears. It's about 2km from Tonoshō port. Ask at the ferry terminal for a town map with directions.

BUS

Shōdo-shima Olive Bus (小豆島オリーブバス; www.shodoshima-olive-bus.com) operates services around the island. The most frequent bus, at one or two per hour, runs between Tonoshō and Kusakabe ports, passing Ikeda and Olive Park. Some continue on to Sakate port, passing the Marukin Soy Sauce Historical Museum; some head north to Fukuda port. There are infrequent services along the north coast, inland to Nakayama, and to Tanoura. A one-/two-day pass is ¥2000/2500, though if you're only taking the bus a couple of times it's cheaper to pay the individual fares (¥150 to ¥300) as you go.

CAR & MOTORCYCLE

There are a handful of car-rental places. Note you can bring a car on some ferries, but it can cost more than hiring one on the island.

Orix Rent-a-Car (オリックスレンタカー小豆島; Map p467; ☑ 0879-62-4669; http://car.orix.co.jp; 6hr from ¥4725; ⊘8.30am-6pm) Has a basic touring map in English. Walk about two minutes along the road heading right out of the Tonoshō ferry terminal.

Kurashiki 倉敷

☑ 086 / POP 477,980

The main attraction in Kurashiki is its atmospheric Bikan quarter (美観地区), an area of historic buildings along an old willow-edged canal, where a picturesque group of black-and-white warehouses has been converted into museums, and laneways are lined with old wooden houses and shops. By night, lamp-light reflecting off the canal creates a cinematic mood in the small area.

In the feudal era the warehouses here were used to store rice brought by boat from the surrounding countryside. Later, the town became an important textile centre, under the Kurabō Textile Company. Owner Ōhara Magosaburō built up a collection of European art and opened the Ōhara Museum of Art in 1930, which today draws many Japanese tourists.

◉ Sights

★ Ōhara Museum of Art GALLERY

(大原美術館; Map p470; www.ohara.or.jp; 1-1-15 Chūō; adult/child ¥1300/500; ⊘9am-5pm, closed Mon except late Jul-Aug & Oct) This is Kurashiki's premier museum, housing the predominantly Western art collection amassed by local textile magnate Ōhara Magosaburō (1880–1943), with the help of artist Kojima Torajirō (1881–1929). The varied assemblage of paintings, prints and sculpture features works by Picasso, Cézanne, El Greco and Matisse, and one of Monet's water-lilies paintings (said to have been bought from the man himself by Torajirō while visiting Monet's home in 1920).

While no rival to the major galleries of Europe, it's an interesting collection and one of the town's biggest attractions for Japanese tourists.

The valid-all-day ticket gets you into the museum's **Craft & Asiatic Art Gallery**, the **contemporary Japanese collection** housed in an annexe behind the main building, plus the **Kojima Torajirō Memorial Hall** (児島虎次郎記念館; Map p470; ☑ 086-422-0005; www.ivysquare.co.jp/cultural/torajiro.html; 7-2 Honmachi; ¥500; ⊘9am-5pm Tue-Sun).

★ Ōhashi House HISTORIC BUILDING

(大橋家住宅; Map p470; www.ohashi-ke.com; 3-21-31 Achi; adult/child ¥550/350; ⊘9am-5pm Tue-Sun) Between the station and the canal area is the beautifully restored Ōhashi House, built in 1793. The wooden house belonged to one of Kurashiki's richest families and was built at a time when prosperous merchants were beginning to claim privileges that had previously been the preserve of the samurai.

Japan Rural Toy Museum MUSEUM

(日本郷土玩具館; Map p470; 1-4-16 Chūō; adult/child ¥400/200; ⊘9am-5pm) Four rooms are crammed with displays of wooden toys, masks, dolls and spinning tops (including a world-record breaker), and a colourful array

Kurashiki

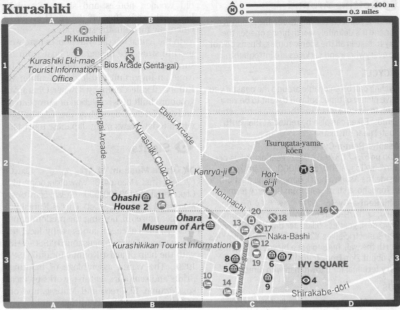

Kurashiki

of kites just beckoning to be put on a breeze. You can purchase a new toy of your own in the shop, which also sells crafts and regional artwork.

Kurashiki Museum of Folk-craft MUSEUM (倉敷民芸館; Map p470; www.kurashiki-mingeikan. com; 1-4-11 Chūō; ¥700; ⊙9am-5pm Tue-Sun Mar-Nov, to 4.15pm Dec-Feb) This museum is housed in an attractive complex of rice warehouses dating from the late 18th century, with interesting exhibits of exquisite household items

from across Japan, including ceramics, glassware, textiles and furniture.

Momotarō Karakuri Hakubutsukan MUSEUM (桃太郎のからくり博物館; Map p470; ☑086-423-2008; http://momotarounokarakuri hakubutsukan.sitemix.jp; 5-11 Honmachi; adult/ child ¥600/400; ⊙10am-5pm; 🚼) Part gallery and part fun-house, this small museum is devoted to local legend Momotarō (p455), with memorabilia, toys and depictions of the peach boy from over the years. On the ground floor is a collection of amusing displays designed to trick the eye – here you can get a photo of yourself emerging from a peach like Momotarō himself. The 'interactive' displays are dated (think high-school projects before computers), but this is part of the charm. Silly fun for a rainy day.

Ivy Square
SQUARE

(アイビースクエア; Map p470) Present-day Ivy Sq was once the site of Ōhara's Kurabō textile factories. The company moved into more modern premises a long time ago, and the ivy-covered red-brick factory buildings (dating from 1889) now house a hotel, restaurants, tourist-driven shops, and museums (most 9am to 5pm), including the **Kurabō Memorial Hall** (倉紡記念館; Map p470; www.kurabo.co.jp/kurabo_kinenkan; 7-1 Honmachi; ¥350; ◎9am-5pm), where you can learn all about the history of the Japanese textile industry. Enter from the west.

Achi-jinja
SHINTO SHRINE

(阿智神社; Map p470; 12-1 Honmachi) `FREE` A short walk from Kurashiki's Bikan canal area are the steep stone steps that lead up to this shrine in **Tsurugata-yama-kōen**, a park that overlooks the old area of town. The shrine is home to a wisteria tree thought to be 300 to 500 years old.

🛏 Sleeping

★ Cuore Kurashiki
HOSTEL ¥

(クオーレ倉敷; Map p470; ☎086-486-3443; www.bs-cuore.com; 1-9-4 Chūō; dm/s/tw ¥3500/4500/7500; ◎🛜) Artistic and quirky touches in the rooms and common areas, which were decorated by staff, and a large lounge-cafe-bar area on the ground floor make this a great budget option. The cubby-hole-style dorm beds are a cosy change from a standard bunk, and the 'VIP' private room has a good-sized shower. The cafe opens to midnight, later than most in the area.

Yuji Inn
HOSTEL ¥

(ゆうじいん; Map p470; ☎086-441-1620; www.yuji-inn.com; 1-10-13 Chūō; dm ¥4000; ◎🛜) Comfortable and extremely clean shared tatami rooms tucked back from the canal make this family-run house an excellent budget choice for visitors who don't need a hostel vibe. There is a large lounge and eating area if you do feel like a chat with the English-speaking owner.

Dormy Inn Kurashiki
HOTEL ¥¥

(ドーミーイン倉敷; Map p470; ☎086-426-5489; www.hotespa.net/hotels/kurashiki; 3-21-11 Achi; s/tw from ¥6000/8500; ◎🛜@🛜) The pick of the Western-style chains, Dormy Inn is not far from the historic district and has something extra to tip the scales in its favour – an onsen on the top floor. There are also complimentary soba noodles in the evening.

★ Ryokan Kurashiki
RYOKAN ¥¥¥

(旅館くらしき; Map p470; ☎086-422-0730; www.ryokan-kurashiki.jp; 4-1 Honmachi; s/d with 2 meals from ¥48,300/73,600; P◎🛜) By the canal in the heart of the historic district and incorporating several beautifully restored Edo-period buildings, this is probably the best ryokan in town. The spacious suites all have tatami lounge areas with attached twin-bed rooms and bathrooms. Dinner is a multi-course *kaiseki* affair featuring delicacies from the Inland Sea. Some English is spoken.

Ryokan Tsurugata
RYOKAN ¥¥¥

(鶴形; Map p470; ☎086-424-1635; www.turugata.jp; 1-3-15 Chūō; r per person with 2 meals from ¥17,820; ◎🛜) This welcoming ryokan in a converted building right in the historic area has tatami rooms overlooking a garden, and meals featuring local seafood. Prices vary according to room size and most have shared bathrooms. A little English is spoken.

🍴 Eating & Drinking

Within the historic area there are numerous eateries and you'll pay a little more for the atmosphere that goes with your food. You'll find cheaper, quick-eats options along Chūō-dōri and in the arcades running from the station.

★ Takadaya
BARBECUE ¥

(高田屋; Map p470; ☎0120-810-190; 11–36 Honmachi; skewers ¥120-420; ◎5-10pm Tue-Sun; 🛜) This bar is in perfect balance. It manages to have loads of old-Japan charm, while maintaining a cocktail list that features plum wine and *shōchū*. Plus its small space isn't intimidating for solo diners, thanks to the English-speaking staff and English menu. Delicious grilled skewers include *shiso-maki* (Japanese basil rolled around chicken) and *gyū-kushi* (beef sirloin).

Takadaya is on a corner with a red lantern.

Bukkake Udon
NOODLES ¥

(ぶっかけうどん; Map p470; 2-3-23 Achi; dishes ¥470-870; ◎7am-9pm; 🛜) In the Bios Arcade across from the station, this local chain serves up the tasty Kurashiki udon speciality – called *bukkake udon* (from *bukkakeru,* meaning to pour or splash) because you tip the sauce over the noodles – hot or cold - yourself. Look for the sign with a ぶ *(bu)* in a yellow oval. Picture and English menu.

KuKu
INDIAN ¥

(クウクウ; Map p470; ☎086-424-3075; 11-19 Honmachi; meals ¥750-1200; ⊙11.30am-5.30pm Thu-Tue; ⊛🍴📶) White adobe-style walls and South Asian knick-knacks set the scene at this diminutive cafe-restaurant. There's a menu of simple Indian curries (and a Thai green curry), and there are good-value set courses at lunch (11.30am to 2pm) including salad, dessert and a tasty cup of chai.

★Mamakari-tei
SEAFOOD ¥¥

(ままかり亭; Map p470; ☎086-427-7112; www. hamayoshi-kurashiki.jp; 3-12 Honmachi; dishes ¥800-1500; ⊙11am-2pm & 5-10pm Tue-Sun; 📶) This traditional eatery, in a 200-year-old warehouse with chunky beams and long wooden tables, is famed for *mamakari,* the sardine-like local speciality. The tasty fish is supposed to induce bouts of uncontrollable feasting, so that people are obliged to *kari* (borrow) more *mama* (rice) from their neighbours in order to carry on with their binge.

There are sets at lunch and *kaiseki*-style course options (from ¥4200; reservations recommended) available at dinner, as well as an à la carte menu.

Kurashiki Coffee-Kan
CAFE

(倉敷珈琲館; Map p470; ☎086-424-5516; www. kurashiki-coffeekan.com; 4-1 Honmachi; ⊙10am-5pm) The low-ceilinged, wood-and-brick interior of this caffeine lovers' paradise is thick with the aroma of freshly roasted beans. The menu features coffee and coffee only (¥500 to ¥850), though you can choose hot or cold. It's on the canal next to Ryokan Kurashiki.

🛍 Shopping

★Tsuneki Tea Shop
DRINKS

(つねき茶舗; Map p470; www.tsuneki.net; 3-9 Honmachi; ⊙10am-6pm Mon-Sat) Follow the earthy aroma of roasting leaves to this specialist tea shop, where a machine in front churns out fresh *hōjicha* (roasted green tea) to be sold by the bag. You can also buy *mugicha* (barley tea), and tea-brewing instructions in English are available.

ℹ Information

MONEY
The Bikan historical area lacks 24-hour ATMs. The nearest machines accepting foreign cards are at the train station and in the 7-Eleven on Chūō-dōri.

TOURIST INFORMATION

Kurashiki Eki-mae Tourist Information Office (倉敷駅前観光案内所; Map p470; ☎086-424-1220; 2nd fl, Kurashiki City Plaza, 1-7-2 Achi; ⊙9am-7pm Apr-Sep, to 6pm Oct-Mar) Out of the station on the second level and to the right.

Kurashikikan Tourist Information (倉敷館観光案内所; Map p470; ☎086-422-0542; www. kurashiki-tabi.jp; 1-4-8 Chuō; ⊙9am-6pm; 🛜) The main tourist centre, in the Bikan quarter, with multilingual staff.

ℹ Getting There & Around
Kurashiki is on the JR San-yō main line just west of Okayama (¥320, 15 minutes). Shin-Kurashiki, on the *shinkansen* line, is two stops from Kurashiki Station (¥200, nine minutes).

Kurashiki is easily explored on foot. It's possible to get around by bike, though this may end up being more of a nuisance than convenience, as the lanes are narrow and often crowded.

Kasaoka Islands 笠岡諸島

Located between Kurashiki and Fukuyama, the port of Kasaoka is the jumping-off point for six small islands connected to the mainland only by boat. In particular, the islands of Shiraishi-jima and Manabe-shima are worth visiting to enjoy the slower pace of life as it used to be lived all over the Inland Sea.

The only sleeping option on Manabe-shima is a ryokan, while Shiraishi-jima boasts a villa and has family run *minshuku,* but it is worth organising your visit before you arrive, especially if you don't speak Japanese. Tourism offices can help book accommodation, and the owners of the Moooo! Bar are very knowledgable.

ℹ Getting There & Away
Kasaoka is 45 minutes west of Okayama (¥760) and 30 minutes west of Kurashiki (¥500) on the JR San-yō line. From the station, it's a seven-minute stroll down to the port for boats to Shiraishi-jima and on to Manabe-shima.

Manabe-shima 真鍋島
☑0865 / POP 325

Manabe-shima is home to more cats than people, and its one small town is an atmospheric maze of old wooden houses, a solitary village shop that has been in business since the Meiji period, and an old-fashioned school. As with everywhere in this part of Japan, Kōbō Daishi got here first – the great man spent time at the **Enpukuji** (円福寺) temple. More recently, the island and all its characters have been wonderfully captured in Florent Chavouet's illustrated book *Manabé Shima*. The locals are sure to show you a copy (and point themselves out in it).

Sleeping & Eating

There are few places to eat out on the island (most with irregular hours) – the helpful staff at the ferry terminal office can give you some tips.

★**Santora** RYOKAN ¥¥
(島宿三虎; ☑0865-68-3515; www.santora.biz; r per person with 2 meals from ¥10,800; ☺🐾) ⚓ At this waterfront ryokan you can laze about in the outdoor saltwater bath while watching boats sail by. The rooms are spacious, the shared indoor bathroom has sea views, and the meals feature local seafood and veggies grown by the friendly owners (no English spoken). There is a range of rooms and plans. It's a 10- to 15-minute walk from Honura port.

ⓘ Getting There & Away

Eight **Sanyo Kisen** (三洋汽船; ☑0865-62-2866; www.sanyo-kisen.com) ferries run a day to Manabe-shima from the port in Kasaoka. There are four regular services (¥1020, 70 minutes) and four high-speed services (¥1760, 45 minutes), all going via Shiraishi-jima. Checked luggage is ¥230. A water taxi is a convenient alternative option if heading to Santora ryokan, especially for groups, as these can take you from Kasaoka direct to the pier at the ryokan (saving you the 10- to 15-minute walk from Honura port). Water taxis are ¥10,000 for up to 10 people – Santora can help with details. Clear timetable and fare information in English is on the official Kasaoka Islands website, www. kasaoka-kankou.jp.

Shiraishi-jima 白石島

☑0865 / POP 525

Sleepy Shiraishi-jima is popular in the summer for its beaches and there are some good walking paths. Go-everywhere Buddhist saint Kōbō Daishi stopped off here on his way back from China in 806; the temple associated with him, **Kairyū-ji** (開龍寺; ☑0865-68-3014; 855 Shiraishi-jima), incorporates a trail of small shrines leading to a huge boulder on top of the hill.

Sleeping & Eating

Visitors can stay at the great-value **Shiraishi Island International Villa** (☑086-256-2535; www.international-villa.or.jp; r per person ¥3500). The villa is a large house atop a hill, with spacious living areas and kitchen, and an outdoor deck with views of the sea. It's particularly good for groups or families.

There are a handful of eateries on the island, though hours are irregular outside of summer. If you're staying at the Villa, make sure you bring groceries along with you. During summer, resident expat Amy Chavez runs the **Moooo! Bar** (www.moooobar.com; ☺daily Jul & Aug, Sun Jun & Sep) on the beach.

ⓘ Getting There & Away

Eight **Sanyō Kisen** (p473) ferries run a day to Shiraishi-jima from the port in Kasaoka, about seven minutes from Kasaoka Station. There are four regular services (¥660, 35 minutes) and four high-speed services (¥1100, 22 minutes).

There's also the larger Shiraishi Ferry (which also takes cars), running four times a day to Shiraishi-jima from Kasaoka (¥530, 45 minutes). It departs from a different dock in Kasaoka, about 20 minutes' walk from the station.

Clear timetable and fare information in English is on the official Kasaoka Islands website, www. kasaoka-kankou.jp.

MATSUE & THE SAN-IN COAST

The San-in coast stretches along the Japan Sea side of western Honshū. This whole regions is off-the-beaten-track territory – yet there are plenty of reasons to visit. Matsue, the capital of Shimane Prefecture (島根県; Shimane-ken), has a fantastic castle; to the west, the shrine at Izumo is among Japan's most sacred spots. The Oki Islands are as dramatic and remote as they come. To the east, Japan's least populated prefecture, Tottori-ken (鳥取県), has has plenty of coastal scenery, sand dunes, onsen and volcanoes.

Out this way, cities are few and far between, the pace of life is decidedly slower than on the San-yō coast and the people are particularly friendly towards visitors.

Although Tottori Prefecture (鳥取県; Tottori-ken) is the least populous of Japan's 47 prefectures and probably gets less tourist love than most prefectures, it has plenty of coastal scenery, sand dunes, onsen and volcanoes. The snag is it takes time and a bit of planning to get to some areas – this is a good place to hire a car. Summer is the best time to visit to get the most out of the beaches.

🛈 Getting There & Around

The area is serviced domestically by **Izumo Airport** (IZO; ☑ 0853-72-7500; www.izumo-airport.co.jp), west of Matsue, and **Yonago Airport** (YGJ; ☑ 0859-45-6121; www.yonago-air.com), east of Matsue.

The San-in main line runs from Kyoto to Shimonoseki, stopping at Tottori and Matsue. Limited express Yakumo trains run from Okayama (¥5510, 2½ hours).

Highway buses ply a popular route between Matsue and Hiroshima city (¥4060, 3½ hours). At the time of writing a year-long promotion to increase visitor numbers had been extended, offering tickets on the route for just ¥500! Inquire at **Matsue International Tourist Information Office** (p477) to check if it is still available at this price.

If you want to explore beyond the main sights, a car is recommended.

Matsue 松江

☑ 0852 / POP 206,400

With its fine castle and crowd-pleasing sunsets over Shinji-ko (Lake Shinji), Matsue is an appealing city with some interesting historical attractions. The city straddles the Ōhashi-gawa, which connects Shinji-ko with Nakanoumi, a saline lake. Most of the main attractions are in a compact area in the north, where you'll find the castle – a rare original. Matsue is also a good base for trips to other places of interest in Shimane Prefecture and you could easily spend a few lazy days here.

👁 Sights

★ Matsue-jō
CASTLE

(松江城, Matsue Castle; Map p475; ☑ 0852-21-4030; www.matsue-tourism.or.jp/m_castle; 1-5 Tono-machi; ¥560, foreigners with ID ¥280; ⊗ 8.30am-6.30pm Apr-Sep, to 5pm Oct-Mar) Dating from 1611, picturesque Matsue-jō has a wooden interior showcasing treasures belonging to the Matsudaira clan. Known as Plover Castle for the graceful shape of its gable ornaments, Matsue-jō is one of only 12 original keeps left in Japan, making it well worth having a look inside. There are dioramas of the city, as well as displays of armoury, including a collection of helmets – the design of each helmet is said to have reflected the personality of its wearer.

From the top of the castle there are great unobstructed views. It's also pleasant to walk around the castle grounds (free entry) and along the surrounding moat, with its charming bridges and pines reaching out across the water. A good way to see the castle area is via a trip on a Horikawa Sightseeing Boat (p476).

Matsue History Museum
MUSEUM

(松江歴史館; Map p475; ☑ 0852-32-1607; www.matsu-reki.jp; 279 Tono-machi; ¥510, foreigners with ID ¥250; ⊗ 8.30am-6.30pm Apr-Sep, to 5pm Oct-Mar, closed 3rd Thu of the month) Matsue's excellent modern museum gives a broad-ranging introduction to the history of the regional clans and development of local industry and crafts. Among the displays are old town maps, ceramics, letters and the local speciality Matsue *wagashi* (sweets) – you can taste modern versions in the attached shop. The free English audio guide is very good.

Koizumi Yakumo (Lafcadio Hearn) Memorial Museum
MUSEUM

(小泉八雲記念館; Map p475; ☑ 0852-21-2147; www.matsue-tourism.or.jp/yakumo; 322 Okudani-chō; ¥300, foreigners with ID ¥150; ⊗ 8.30am-6.30pm Apr-Sep, to 5pm Oct-Mar) This memorial museum has displays on the life and work of former Matsue resident Lafcadio Hearn, as well as some of the writer's personal effects, including his dumb-bells, spectacles and a stack of Japanese newspapers on which he wrote words and phrases to teach English to his son. Hearn enthusiasts should pop round next door to have a look at his **old residence** (小泉八雲旧居; Map p475; ☑ 0852-23-0714; 315 Kitahori-chō; ¥300, foreigners with ID ¥150; ⊗ 8.30am-6.30pm Apr-Sep, to 5pm Oct-Mar).

Buke Yashiki Samurai Residence
HISTORIC BUILDING

(武家屋敷; Map p475; ☑ 0852-22-2243; www.matsue-tourism.or.jp/buke; 305 Kitahori-chō; ¥300, foreigners with ID ¥150; ⊗ 8.30am-6.30pm Apr-Sep, to 5pm Oct-Mar) You'll take lots of pictures as you stroll around this immaculately preserved house and garden built for a middle-ranking samurai family during the early 18th century.

Shimane Prefectural Art Museum
GALLERY

(島根県立博物館; Map p475; www.shimane-art-museum.jp; 1-5 Sodeshi-chō; ¥300, foreigners with ID ¥150; ⊗ 10am-6.30pm Wed-Mon Oct-Feb, to 30min after sunset Mar-Sep) With its white undulating roof and huge glass windows facing the lake, the museum building itself is an impressive sight. Inside, it displays rotating exhibits from its collection of woodblock prints (there are some Hokusai among them), as well as European paintings and

Matsue

Matsue

◉ Top Sights
1 Matsue-jō	B2

◉ Sights
2 Buke Yashiki Samurai Residence	B1
3 Koizumi Yakumo (Lafcadio Hearn) Memorial Museum	B1
4 Lafcadio Hearn Old Residence	B1
5 Matsue History Museum	B1
6 Shimane Prefectural Art Museum	B4

◉ Activities, Courses & Tours
7 Horikawa Sightseeing Boat	B2

◉ Sleeping
8 Green Rich Hotel Matsue	C4
9 Hotel Knut	C3
10 Minamikan	B3
11 Ryokan Terazuya	C4

◉ Eating
12 Kawa-kyō	B3
13 Naniwa	B3
14 Tsurumaru	C3
15 Yakumo-an	B1

◉ Drinking & Nightlife
Cafe Bar EAD	(see 13)

contemporary art. The sunset views from the museum's 2nd-floor platform or outside by the water also draw crowds here. The museum is a 15-minute walk west of the station.

Yūshien Garden　　　GARDENS
(由志園; ☎0852-76-2255; www.yuushien.com; 1206-2 Hanyū, Yatsuka-chō; adult/child ¥600/300; ☺8.30am-5.30pm) This pretty garden occupying an area of around 40,000 sq metres

WORTH A TRIP

ADACHI MUSEUM OF ART

East of Matsue in Yasugi is this excellent museum (足立美術館; ☎0854-28-7111; www.adachi-museum.or.jp; 320 Furuka-wa-chō, Yasugi-shi; ¥1150; ⊙9am-5pm; P). founded by local businessman and art collector Adachi Zenkō. The collection includes over 100 paintings by Yokoyama Taikan (1868–1958) and a good selection of works by other major 20th-century Japanese painters. There's also a delightful 'pictures for children' gallery.

For many, however, the real attraction are the stunning gardens, regularly voted among the best in Japan. Sit and contemplate the perfectly clipped mounds of the Dry Landscape Garden – in the distance, mountains rise up as though part of the garden itself.

From Matsue, take the JR line to Yasugi (安来; ¥410, 22 minutes), where there's a free shuttle bus to the museum (11 daily from 9.05am). The bus also leaves from Yonago Station (12.25pm and 1.15pm, 45 minutes).

was established privately in 1975 on Lake Nakaumi's Daikonshima Island, between Matsue and Sakai Minato. Best known for its peonies, there's also rock gardens, water features and plenty of traditional Japanese elements to enjoy. Catch an Ichibata bus from JR Matsue Station (¥470, 25 minutes).

👉 Tours

Horikawa Sightseeing Boat　　　BOATING
(Map p475; ☎0852-27-0417; www.matsue-horikawa meguri.jp; 507-1 Kuroda-chō; ¥1230, foreigners with ID ¥820; ⊙every 15-20min 9am-5pm) The characterful boatmen circumnavigate the castle moat and then zip around the city's canals and beneath a series of bridges. There are a few boarding points; the main one is near the castle entrance.

🎊 Festivals & Events

Matsue Suitōro　　　CULTURAL
(松江水燈路; www.suitouro.com; Matsue-jō) In Matsue's night festival of water and light, hand-painted lanterns create atmospheric paths of light around the moat and up to the castle grounds of Matsue-jō, where there are group drumming battles and outdoor food

stalls. Held every Saturday, Sunday and holiday in October.

🛏 Sleeping

⭐**Hotel Knut**　　　BOUTIQUE HOTEL¥
(ホテルクヌート; Map p475; ☎0852-61-1400; www.hotel-knut.jp; 481-7 Asahi-machi; s/d ¥3100/5300; ❀🅿) If you don't mind the fact that the single hotel-style rooms all have shared toilets and bathrooms, you might just love this fresh, young conversion of what was once an old business hotel. Try for an airy corner double room at the front of the hotel. The foyer of the hotel hosts a popular cafe-bar with cheap eats and good drinks.

Ryokan Terazuya　　　RYOKAN¥
(旅館寺津屋; Map p475; ☎0852-21-3480; www. mable.ne.jp/~terazuya; 60-3 Tenjin-machi; r per person with/without breakfast ¥5300/4600; @🅿) You'll find a warm welcome and simple tatami rooms at this family-run inn, opposite a shrine. The owners speak a little English and can collect you from the station. The bathroom is shared, there's a 10pm curfew, and coffee and toast is included if you haven't paid for the full breakfast. Cash only.

A canal runs behind the ryokan, as does the JR line – fortunately there's little traffic at night.

Green Rich Hotel Matsue　　　HOTEL¥¥
(グリーンリッチホテル松江駅前; Map p475; ☎0852-27-3000; www.gr-matsue.com; 493 1 Asahi machi; s/tw from ¥5900/10,300; ❀❉@🅿) A modern chain hotel going for a designer look with dark-toned furnishings and backlit headboards. Most inviting is the large, sunken public bath and sauna. A buffet breakfast is an additional ¥500.

⭐**Minamikan**　　　RYOKAN¥¥¥
(皆美館; Map p475; ☎0852-21-5131; www. minami-g.co.jp/minamikan; 14 Suetsugu Hon-machi; r per person with 2 meals from ¥23,000; P❀🅿) A refined inn on the edge of the lake, Minamikan has a choice of 'modern', 'retro' and 'classic' rooms, all with broad views across the water. The top-end 'modern' has a tatami room with twin beds and private cypress-wood onsen. The cheaper 'classic' has seen the likes of literary great Kawabata Yasunari pass through.

There is also an excellent restaurant. The ryokan entrance is set back from the road.

KAI Izumo　　　RYOKAN¥¥¥
(会出雲; ☎0570-073-011; www.hoshinoresorts. com; 1237 Tamayu-chō, Tamatsukuri Onsen; r per

person with 2 meals from ¥25,000; P ❄ 🛜) Whilst not in Izumo at all, this modern ryokan in Tamatsukuri Onsen, about 9km from downtown Matsue, has a minimalist but traditional aesthetic along the (clean) lines of less is more. Each room has a private, onsen-fed indoor/outdoor bath and the service and dining will leave you feeling elevated. One for those who like the finer things in life.

🍴 Eating & Drinking

Matsue has plenty of good restaurants to tempt you during your stay. The food court at JR Matsue Station has some excellent, convenient options to dine in or take out.

Turn left from the station's north exit and walk one block to the Asahi-chō intersection, then turn right to find a healthy selection of *izakaya* and the town's nightlife district radiating off from the main drag.

★ Yakumo-an   NOODLES ¥
(八雲庵; Map p475; www.yakumoan.jp; 308 Kita-Horiuchi; dishes ¥700-1150; ⏰10am-3pm; 🅿) This busy soba restaurant and its beautiful grounds are an excellent place to sample the local *warigo soba*. Try the tasty *soba kamo nanban* (noodles with slices of duck in broth). Look for a sign on a piece of wood outside.

★ Kawa-kyō   IZAKAYA ¥¥
(川京; Map p475; 🕿0852-22-1312; 65 Suetsugu Hon-machi; dishes ¥800-1575; ⏰6-10.30pm Mon-Sat; 🍴🅿) You can count on a friendly welcome at this small *izakaya*, which specialises in the 'seven delicacies' from Shinji-ko and is a good place to try some local sake. The daughter of the owners speaks English. Look for the bamboo-roofed menu display outside. Weekends get busy so book ahead.

Tsurumaru   SEAFOOD ¥¥
(鶴丸; Map p475; www.tsurumaru2.net; 1-79 Higashi Hon-machi; dishes ¥620-1400; ⏰noon-2pm & 5.30-10.30pm Mon-Sat; 🅿) The smell of fish grilling over coals permeates this restaurant, which specialises in the cuisine of the Oki Islands. The menu features meals such as *eri-yaki konabe* (hot spicy soup cooked over a flame at your table) and sashimi. You'll know it by the *noren* with the crane on it and the rustic folk singing that drifts into the street. There's a limited English menu.

Naniwa   JAPANESE ¥¥¥
(なにわ; Map p475; 🕿0852-21-2835; http://honten.naniwa-i.com; 21 Suetsugu Hon-machi; meals ¥2260-11,000; ⏰11am-9pm) Next to Matsue-ōhashi, this bright, wood-themed

---

MATSUE SPECIALITIES

Matsue's *kyodo ryōri* (regional cuisine) includes the 'seven delicacies' from Shinji-ko –

➡ *suzuki* – bass, paper-wrapped and steam-baked

➡ *shirauo* – whitebait, as tempura or sashimi

➡ *amasagi* – smelt, as sweet tempura or teriyaki

➡ *shijimi* – freshwater clams, usually in miso soup

➡ *moroge ebi* – shrimp, steamed

➡ *koi* – carp, baked in sauce

➡ *unagi* – freshwater eel, grilled.

---

restaurant is a tranquil spot for *unameshi* (eel and rice; ¥2700). Otherwise, opt for one of the delicately prepared *kaiseki* spreads, such as the Shinji-ko course (¥4320).

Cafe Bar EAD   BAR
(カフェバーEAD; Map p475; 🕿852-28-3130; www.ameblo.jp/bar-ead; 36 Suetsugu Hon-machi; ⏰9pm-1am Thu-Mon) Low lighting, sofas and a broad terrace with a river view make this relaxed cafe-bar a nice place to end your evening. Snacks include homemade pizzas. It's on the 3rd floor of a building just near the bridge.

ℹ Information

INTERNET ACCESS

There's free wi-fi in the lobby area (also accessible from outside at all hours) of the large **Matsue Terrsa building** (松江テルサ; Map p475; ⏰9am-9pm Mon-Fri, to 8pm Sat & Sun; 🛜) near the station.

TOURIST INFORMATION

Matsue International Tourist Information Office (松江国際観光案内所; Map p475; 🕿0852-21-4034; www.kankou-matsue.jp; 665 Asahi-machi; ⏰9am-7pm Jun-Oct, to 6pm Nov-May; 🛜) Excellent, friendly assistance in English, French and other languages directly in front of JR Matsue Station. Free wi-fi.

ℹ Getting There & Away

Matsue is on the JR San-in line, which runs along the San-in coast. You can get to Okayama via Yonago on the JR Hakubi line. It's ¥500 to Yonago (30 minutes), then ¥5270 to Okayama by *tokkyū*

LAFCADIO HEARN: JAPAN'S ADOPTED SON

Born to a Greek mother and an Anglo-Irish army surgeon on the island of Lefkada in the Ionian Sea, Patrick Lafcadio Hearn (1850–1904) grew up in Dublin and studied in England before being packed off at 19 with a one-way ticket to America. He worked as a journalist in Cincinnati, and in New Orleans wrote about voodoo and developed taste for the exotic that would characterise his writing on Japan. After two years in the French West Indies, Hearn accepted an assignment from *Harper's* magazine to travel to the Land of the Rising Sun.

Hearn soon became famous for his articles and books about his new home. Eager to stay on after his contract with *Harper's* ran out, he took a job teaching English. For 15 idyllic months he lived in Matsue, where he married Koizumi Setsu, the daughter of a local samurai family. After stints elsewhere, he settled in Tokyo – 'the most horrible place in Japan' – where he was appointed professor of English Literature at Tokyo Imperial University.

Although Japan has changed almost beyond recognition since Hearn lived here, his best pieces are still well worth reading today. His first Japan-themed collection, *Glimpses of Unfamiliar Japan* (1894), contains his famous essay on Matsue – 'Chief City of the Province of the Gods', as well as an account of his trip to Izumo, where he was the first European allowed inside the gates of the ancient shrine. Children still read Hearn's Japanese folk tales, ghost stories and legends, which may have been lost had Hearn not documented them.

(2¼ hours). Highway buses go to Japan's major cities from the terminal in front of the station.

ⓘ Getting Around

It's possible to walk around the sights. Matsue is also a good place to explore by bicycle; these can be rented close to Matsue Station at **Times Car Rental** (タイムズカーレンタル; Map p475; ☑0852-26-8787; 590-4 Asahi-machi; bike rental per day ¥300; ⊙8am-6.30pm) (where you could also rent a car) and returned to your choice of six different locations.

The easiest way to get to all the sights is via the handy city-loop bus. The red streetcar-like Lake Line buses follow a set route around the attractions every 20 minutes. One ride costs ¥200; a day pass is available for ¥500.

Sakai Minato

☑0859 / POP 34,200

Although not the most visually appealing little town, Sakai Minato is a boarding point for boats to the Oki Islands and home to the Mizuki Shigeru Museum, showcasing the life and work of one of Japan's best-loved anime artists, who was born and raised here. Fans of Mizuki's work flock to this little port from across Japan, Asia and around the world.

🛏 Sleeping & Eating

Oyado Nono SPA HOTEL ¥¥
(御宿野乃; ☑0859-44-5489; www.hotespa. net/hotels/sakaiminato; s/d from ¥6990/10,990; Ⓟ❄🌐) New in 2016, this towering 195-room, all-tatami (take off your shoes in the lobby!) hotel looks like it has been plopped in the middle of nowhere. Popular with tour groups for its comfortable, compact rooms and convenient location, the best bit is the rooftop *rotemburo* with sweeping views: you can even see Daisen on a clear day.

Genki-tei SEAFOOD ¥¥
(元気亭; ☑0859-42-3551; 38 Taisho-machi; dishes ¥1200-2600; ⊙11am-3pm & 5.30-10pm Fri-Wed) This restaurant is proud that its *kaisen-don* (seafood over rice) has featured on Japanese TV. The friendly owner will help you navigate the menu and advise on the daily specials: fish fresh off the boat. There are a few *izakaya*-style items on the menu, or you can just stop in for some delicious *gyōza* and beer.

ⓘ Getting There & Away

From Matsue, change at Yonago to the colourfully decked-out local trains of the JR Sakai line for Sakai Minato. Many anime pilgrims come just to ride these very trains. The journey takes an hour or so depending on how long you have to transfer between trains and costs ¥840.

The port is also the jump-on/off point for boats to the Oki Islands.

Oki Islands　　隠岐諸島

North of Matsue in the Sea of Japan are the remote and spectacular Oki Islands (Oki-shotō), within the Oki Islands Geopark, and with coastal areas that are part of the Daisen-Oki National Park (大山隠岐国立公園). These islands were once used to exile officials (including two emperors) who came out on the losing side of political squabbles. Four of the islands are inhabited: the three Dōzen Islands – Nishino-shima, Chiburi-jima and Nakano-shima – and the larger Dōgo island. Being cut off from the mainland, there are cultural and religious practices preserved here that aren't observed elsewhere in Japan, the pace of life is decidedly slower, and there's a refreshing lack of development at the tourist spots. Allow at least a couple of days to visit and keep in mind that ferry services are subject to change and halt in bad weather.

🛏 Sleeping & Eating

All the islands have ryokan, *minshuku* and campgrounds (although you'll need to bring your own tent).

Before you set out it's advisable to contact the tourism associations of the islands you wish to visit; staff will be able to book your accommodation and tell you how to get there – essential, as lodgings can be spread out and resemble a regular house.

These are remote islands and much of the produce here is brought in by ferry: expect higher prices for regular commodities. You'll find an abundance of seafood on local menus. Each island's handful of eateries open irregular hours outside the busier summer season. Best to chill like the locals and play it by ear.

ℹ Information

MONEY
All of the four main islands have a post office with an ATM that accepts international cards.

TOURIST INFORMATION
Each island has a tourism association with a tourist information office that has free wi-fi and at least one native English speaker who can book activities and accommodation.

For more on the natural and cultural features of the islands, the **Oki Islands Geopark Promotion Committee** (📞 08512-2-9636; www.oki-geopark.jp) produces a very good English guide and map.

ℹ Getting There & Away

AIR
The islands' Oki Airport (📞 08512-2-0703; www.oki-airport.jp) on Dōgo is serviced by regular direct flights from Izumo and Osaka (Itami) airports.

BOAT
The most common way to reach the islands is by ferry or hydrofoil (the 'Rainbow Jet'). Services, operated by **Oki Kisen** (📞 08512-2-1122; www.oki-kisen.co.jp) depart from Shichirui port in Shimane Prefecture and Sakai Minato port in Tottori Prefecture.

Depending on your port of embarkation and ultimate destination, boats do an island-hop en route. Sample routes and fares include Sakai Minato to Dōgo (ferry ¥3240, 2½ hours; hydrofoil ¥6170, 70 minutes) and Nishino-shima (ferry ¥3240, 1½ hours; hydrofoil ¥6170, one hour).

While there are some seated areas on the ferry, most locals sprawl out on the grubby carpet and sleep. Blanket rentals are available! Once on board, you can 'upgrade' to a private cabin from ¥4000 if you feel like a splurge. The Rainbow Jet is fully seated.

Buying tickets seems more complicated than it should be, even if you speak Japanese. You can reserve the Rainbow Jet in advance, but only pay for your ticket on the day. You'll need to fill in an embarkation card before proceeding to the ticket counter at all of the Oki Kisen offices. Make sure

---

MIZUKI SHIGERU'S HORROR MANGA

Eyeballs on taxis and ghostly murals on ferries and ports in the Oki Islands – this is the horror manga of artist Mizuki Shigeru (水木 しげる), Sakai-minato's most famous resident.

His adorably evil *yōkai* (spirit demons) from manga series GeGeGe No Kitarō are a take on Japanese folklore. They plaster four train exteriors and interiors from Yonago to Sakai-minato – even announcements are made by one of his characters.

Legions of fans make the trip especially to Mizuki Shigeru Rd – outside Sakai-minato Station – to pose with the 134 bronze *yōkai* statues and visit the **Mizuki Shigeru Museum** (水木しげる記念館; 📞 0859-42-2171; http://mizuki.sakaiminato.net; 5 Hon-machi; ¥300; ⏰ 9.30am-5pm; 🅿), plus the inevitable souvenir stores. The multimedia museum explains all things ghoulish, with free English audio guides, and has rooms that recreate ancient Japan.

Mizuki's undead cast includes Kitarō, the boy born in a cemetery; his father Medama-oyaji, a reborn eyeball; Neko Musume, the 'Cat Girl' with fangs and a Jekyll and Hyde personality; and Nezumi Otoko, the unwashed 'Rat Man' who uses flatulence as a weapon. Kids love it.

you allow yourself enough time before departure. When in doubt, phone a tourism office.

Buses go to Shichirui from Matsue Station (¥1000, 40 minutes) and Yonago Station (¥870, 40 minutes). Sakai-minato is at the end of the JR Sakai train line, which connects with the JR San-in line at Yonago (¥320, 45 minutes).

❶ Getting Around

You can get to some of the main attractions by bike, but to see all of the islands it's best to hire a car or make use of a taxi or ecotour guide service.

The **inter-island ferry** (☑ 089514-6-0016; 1 trip ¥300) service operates the Isokaze and Dōzen ferries between islands.

Dōgo 島後

☑ 08512 / POP 14,850

While Dōgo, the Oki group's largest island, has notably more signs of civilisation than the Dōzen trio, the pace here is as delightfully slow and there's still barely a franchised or recognisable brand to be found. The island is notable for its giant, wizened old cedar trees: the 800-year-old **Chichi-sugi tree** is believed to be the home of a deity; and the **Yao-sugi** tree at **Tamakawasu-no-mikoto-jinja** is thought to be 2000 years old, its gnarled sprawling branches propped up with posts.

The island boasts nature and coastal walks, and boat tours in the Saigō port area and along the northern Shirashima Coast. Bull sumo is an attraction throughout the year – not big guy versus bull, but bull versus bull.

🏃 Activities

Oki Onsen GOKA SENTO
(隠岐温泉GOKA; ☑ 08512-5-3200; 296-1 Nanpō; admission ¥500; ⊘2-8pm Tue-Sun) Dōgo's only *sentō* is delightfully dated and refreshingly quiet. It's on the northwest corner of the island, about 25 minutes' drive from Saigō port.

🛌 Sleeping & Eating

Kichiura Campground CAMPGROUND ¥
(吉浦野営場, Kichiura yaeijō; ☑ 08512-5-2211; Hisami, Okinoshima-chō; campsite per person ¥200; ⊘Jun-Sep) Tucked away in the island's northwest, this attractive, isolated campground with modern facilities runs down a steep hill towards a little beach. Rental tents are available (¥1500).

Hotel Uneri HOTEL ¥¥
(ホテル海音里; ☑ 08512-5-3211; www.oki-island. jp/search/uneri.php; cabins from ¥14,200; ▣)

Deliciously isolated about 16km from Saigō port on the island's northwestern flank, Hotel Uneri has log cabins in a peaceful location near the water; you can either self-cater or have a prearranged dinner and breakfast.

Cafe Spuntino CAFE ¥
(☑ 08512-2-7417; meals ¥600-950; ⊘11am-5pm Tue-Sun) This modern cafe run by hip young islanders makes a delicious melty cheese curry and decent coffee. It's opposite the ferry terminal.

❶ Information

Okinoshima Tourist Information Center (隠岐の島観光案内所; ☑ 8512-2-0787; www.oki-dougo.info; ⊘9am-5pm; 🖥) Opposite the ferry port – follow the signs.

❶ Getting Around

Renting a car at the ferry port is really the best way to see and explore the island. Contact the Okinoshima Tourist Information Center for advance reservations.

Dōzen Islands

West of Dōgo, **Nishino-shima** (西ノ島) boasts the stunningly rugged Kuniga coastline, with the sheer 257m Matengai cliff. The coastal hike here is a must-do. The island is also home to interesting shrines, including Yurahime-jinja, near a small inlet. Legend has it that squid come en masse to this inlet every year in autumn/winter as a way to ask forgiveness from the deity (there are pictures at the shrine to prove it). Nishino-shima is also known for horses, which you'll see roaming the hillsides.

The small **Chiburi-jima** (知夫里島), or 'Chibu', where the local slogan is *nonbiri Chiburi* (carefree Chiburi), is home to more impressive coastline, featuring the striking Sekiheki, an expanse of rust-coloured cliffs. You can also see stone-wall remains on the island – what is left of a crop-rotation practice that began here in the middle ages.

The Akiya coast and Oki-jinja are draws on **Nakano-shima** (中ノ島), also known locally as Ama.

🏃 Activities

Club Noah Oki KAYAKING, DIVING
(クラブノア隠岐; ☑ 08514-6-0825; www.oki. club-noah.net; night dive ¥8400, sunset cave kayaking ¥5500) Diving and kayaking with sunset cave

tours, and night diving. Instructors know the essentials in English.

🛏 Sleeping & Eating

Kuniga-so
RYOKAN ¥¥

(☎08514-6-0301; www.kunigasou.com; 192 Urago; s/d from ¥7020/12,040; P❀) Nishino-shima's best lodging is operated by a friendly family and features rooms with floor-to-ceiling windows overlooking the bay and a communal bath sharing the same vista. In the 1990s, the decor would have been at the height of style. Today, it's delightfully outdated and island-y. Meal plans are available.

Oki Seaside Hotel Tsurumaru
HOTEL ¥¥

(隠岐シーサイドホテル鶴丸; ☎08514-6-1111; www.oki-tsurumaru.jp; d with 2 meals from ¥21,600; P) On Nishino-shima, Oki Seaside Hotel Tsurumaru has a pleasant waterfront location and a large restaurant, and it runs regular cruises. The owners also have an affiliated restaurant in Matsue on the Japan mainland.

Hotel Chibu-no-Sato
HOTEL ¥¥

(ホテル知夫の里; ☎08514-8-2500; www.tibuno sato.com; Chibu 1242-1; d with 2 meals from ¥21,600; P) Hotel Chibu-no-Sato is a great choice for accommodation on Chiburi-jima. The balconied rooms have fabulous sea views and there's an open-air bath (April to October) and free bicycle use for guests.

Sawano
CHINESE ¥

(☎08514-6-0181; 367 Urago; dishes ¥700-1280) If you can speak some Japanese you might indulge in a heart-warming conversation with the friendly owner of this cosy Chinese joint, who spent a year travelling the length and breadth of Japan in the '70s before starting a family on the island. He makes fat, juicy dumplings and delicious vegetable-laden *miso-rāmen*, among other dishes.

ℹ Information

Nishino-shima Tourist Information Office
(☎08514-7-8888; www.nkk-oki.com; ⏰8.30am-7pm Jun-Oct, to 5.30pm Nov-May; 📶)

ℹ Getting Around

There's a local bus on Nishino-shima that goes to the Kuniga coast, though it's infrequent.

Bike hire on the smaller islands can suffice, but it's best to rent a car if you're planning to explore larger Nishino-shima. The tourism offices of each island can help with reservations.

It costs ¥300 to ride on the regular inter-island ferry service between the Dōzen Islands.

Daisen 大山
☎0859

Although it's not one of Japan's highest mountains, at 1729m Daisen looks impressive because it rises straight from sea level – its summit is only about 10km from the coast. Daisen is part of the Daisen-Oki National Park (大山 隠岐国立公園).

The popular climb up the volcano is a five-to six-hour return trip from **Daisen-ji temple** (大山寺; ☎0859-52-2158; 9 Daisen; treasure hall ¥300; ⏰9am-4pm Apr-Nov). From the summit, there are fine views over the coast and, in perfect conditions, all the way to the Oki Islands.

The mountain catches the northwest monsoon winds in the winter, bringing lots of snow to what is western Japan's top skiing area. Among the slopes are **Daisen White Resort** (大山ホワイトリゾート; ☎0859-52-2315; www.daisen-resort.jp; day lift ticket adult/child from ¥4300/3500) and **Daisen Masumizu-kōgen Ski Resort** (大山ますみず高原スキー場; ☎0859-52-2420; www.masumizu.net/ski; day lift ticket adult/child ¥4000/3000).

⊙ Sights

★ Shōji Ueda Museum of Photography
MUSEUM

(植田正治写真美術館; ☎0859-39-8000; www.japro.com/ueda; 353-3 Sumura, Hōki-chō; adult/child ¥900/500; ⏰9am-5pm Wed-Mon Mar-Nov) Showcases the works of prominent Tottori Prefecture photographer Shōji Ueda (1913–2000), in a large minimalist concrete building with fabulous views across to the mountain.

Ōgamiyama-jinja
SHINTO SHRINE

(大神山神社) Surrounding Daisen-ji are temples, ruins and forest walking tracks, and you can walk up the stone path to this shrine, the oldest building in western Tottori Prefecture.

🛏 Sleeping

Limited accommodation options are scattered around the towns and villages at the base of the mountain, but you won't be spoiled for choice.

★ Bayside Square Kaike Hotel
HOTEL ¥¥

(ベイサイドスクエア皆生ホテル; ☎0859-35-0001; www.kaikehotel.com; 4-21-1 Kaike-onsen, Yonago; s/d from ¥6500/12,000) In Yonago, about 17km from Daisen, you'll find this smart, modern beachfront hotel with simple, stylish rooms, a fabulous onsen, and lovely views over the Sea of Japan.

ℹ Information

Daisen-ji Information Centre (大山寺観光案内所; ☏0859-52-2502; ☺8.30am-6pm) Located at the temple; stocked with brochures, maps and hiking information. Staff can arrange bookings at the local ryokan.

For info online in English, check out http://en.go-to-japan.jp/daisenguide.

ℹ Getting There & Away

The closest station to Daisen is Yonago, about 30 minutes from Matsue (in Shimane) and one to 1½ hours from Tottori on the San-in line.

The Daisen Loop bus (one-/two-day pass ¥1000/2000) runs to Daisen-ji from Yonago Station on weekends and holidays in May and from August to November. It stops at all the main sights around the mountain.

Regular buses run to the temple from Yonago (¥830, 50 minutes, five daily) with **Nihon Kōtsū** (☏0857-23-1121; www.nihonkotsu.co.jp).

Tottori　鳥取

☏0857 / POP 193,770

If you're into camels, geological science, crumbling country railroads, fading post-WWII architecture and sand...little Tottori might be worth your while. Its big-in-Japan sand dunes and sand sculpture museum are the main draw here.

⦿ Sights

There are beaches (though wash-up pollution levels can be grim) and scenic stretches of coastline within the San-in Coast National Park; this is a good side trip from Tottori city.

★ Tottori-sakyū (The Dunes)　DUNES

(鳥取砂丘) Used as the location for Teshigahara Hiroshi's classic 1964 film *Woman in the Dunes*, the Tottori sand dunes are on the coast about 5km from the city. There's a viewing point on a hillside overlooking the dunes, along with parking and the usual array of tourist schlock. You can even get a 'Lawrence of Arabia' photo of yourself accompanied by a camel. Pick up maps at the Sand Pal Tottori Information Centre (p483).

The dunes stretch for over 10km along the coast and, at some points, can be about 2km wide. Buses to the dunes also stop at the Sakyū-Sentā (砂丘センター; Dunes Centre),

on the hillside, from where you can take a cable car (one-way/return ¥200/300) down to the sand.

★ Sand Museum　MUSEUM

(砂の美術館; ☏0857-20-2231; www.sand-museum.jp; 2083-17 Fukubecho Yuyama; ¥600; ☺9am-8pm Apr-Jan) You came to see sand? There's truckloads at this impressive museum of sand sculptures, where sand aficionados from all over the world are invited to create huge, amazingly detailed works based on a particular theme. The exhibition changes each year: check at the tourist office for this year's theme and opening months. The museum is near the sand dunes.

🛏 Sleeping & Eating

Drop Inn Tottori　HOSTEL ¥

(ホステル　ドロップイン鳥取; ☏0857-30-0311; www.dropinn-tottori.com; 2-276 Imamachi; dm from¥3900; ☀❀☞) New in 2016, Tottori's only hostel has smart mixed and single-sex dorm rooms with flat-screen TVs and great coffee in the cafe downstairs.

Matsuya-sō　MINSHUKU ¥¥

(松屋荘; ☏0857-22-4891; 3-814 Yoshikata Onsen; s/tw from ¥3880/6580) This *minshuku*-style lodging has no wi-fi or mod cons, but offers large, clean tatami rooms with washbasins and shared bathrooms. From the station, go straight up the main street and turn right onto Eiraku-dōri (永楽通り). Look for Matsuya-sō on the left after a few blocks; it's about a 15-minute walk from the station. The owners speak some English.

Tottori-ya　YAKITORI ¥

(とっ鳥屋; ☏0857-26-3038; 771 Suehiro Onsen-chō; skewers from ¥85; ☺5pm-1am; 🅐) This bustling *yakitori* (skewers of grilled chicken) place has a large menu of individual sticks and rice dishes. Get an assortment of six skewers for ¥626 or 12 for ¥1242. As well as chicken there are grilled veg options. It's on Suehiro-dōri, east of the intersection with Eki-mae-dōri. Look for the rope curtain hanging over the door and ask for the English menu.

Sumibi Jujuan　GRILL, SEAFOOD ¥¥

(炭火焼ジュジュアン; ☏0857-21-1919; http://sumibi-jujuan.info; 751 Suehiro Onsen-chō; mains ¥980-3000; ☺11am-3pm & 5-11pm) Fresh seafood and local beef *sumibiyaki* (charcoal grilled) are the specialities in this airy restaurant. It does *shabu-shabu*, and set courses, such as the *kaisen gozen* (grilled seafood and vegetables with sides), with a seasonal menu that may include crab and other locally sourced goodies. It's on Suehiro-dōri, east of the intersection with Eki-mae-dōri.

❶ Information

Sand Pal Tottori Information Centre (サンドパルとっとり; 083-17 Yūyama, Fukube-chō; ⊘9am-6pm) Specialises in all things sand-sculpture and sand-dune related, but can also offer advice on excursions around the nearby coastline.

Tourist Information Office (鳥取市観光案内所; ☑0857-22-3318; www.torican.jp; ⊘9.30am-6.30pm) To the right as you exit the station, with English-language pamphlets, maps and English-speaking staff who can book the 1000 Yen Taxi for tourists. Accommodation is only booked at the other tourism office just inside the station entrance.

❶ Getting There & Away

Tottori is on the coastal JR San-in train line. JR Pass holders going south and west (eg towards Himeji, Okayama, Osaka) must pay a cash fee on board or when booking of around ¥1800 for using non-JR tracks; JR-only alternatives add hours. Major destinations:

Matsue ¥2270, two to three hours; express service ¥4620, 1½ hours

Okayama express via Kamigōri ¥5010, two hours

Toyooka local service ¥1490, 2½ hours

There are also long-distance buses to major cities in the region.

❶ Getting Around

BUS

The Kirinjishi loop bus (¥300/600 per ride/day pass) operates on weekends, holidays and between 20 July and 31 August. It passes the main sights and goes to the dunes. Red- and blue-roofed Kururi minibuses (¥100 per ride) ply inner-city loops from the station every 20 minutes, passing by the main city attractions. Regular city buses depart from the station and travel to the dunes area (¥360, 20 minutes). There are maps and timetables available at the information office.

BICYCLE

Rent-a-Cycle (per day ¥500; ⊘8am-6.30pm) Outside the station. You can also rent bikes at the Sand Pal Tottori Information Centre near the dunes.

CAR & MOTORCYCLE

Cal Rent-a-Car (☑0857-24-0452; www.cal-rent.net; 1-88 Tomiyasu; 24hr from ¥3800; ⊘8am-8pm) Take the main road leading straight out from the south side of the station, then take a left turn at the first major intersection; this rental outlet is in a petrol station on the right.

TAXI

1000 Yen Taxi (www.torican.jp; per car for foreigners with ID ¥1000; ⊘8.30am-5.30pm) A great deal for visiting a few sites in a short time. Up to four passengers can hire a taxi for up to three hours, including waiting time at any sites. Passengers are also given a coupon card that can be used with some sites for discounts and free souvenirs (mostly trinkets). Book at the tourist info office.

San-in Coast National Park 山陰海岸国立公園

The coastline east from the Tottori dunes stretching all the way to the Tango Peninsula in Kyoto Prefecture is known as the San-in Coast National Park (San-in Kaigan Kokuritsu-kōen), which boasts sandy though polluted beaches, rugged headlands and pines jutting into the blue sky.

Near the edge of Hyōgo Prefecture, the **Uradome Kaigan** (浦富海岸; Uradome Coastline) features a scenic stretch of islets and craggy cliffs with pines clinging precariously to their sides. Two popular beaches, **Uradome** (浦富) and **Makidani** (牧谷) lie a few kilometres further east.

Along this stretch of coast are walking tracks that are part of the **Chūgoku Shizen Hodō** (中国自然歩道; Chūgoku Nature Walking Path), linking to tracks in neighbouring prefectures.

❶ Information

Uradome Tourism Association (浦富観光協会; ☑0857-72-3481; ⊘9am-6pm Tue-Sun) This info centre is located a stone's throw from JR Iwami Station. From here you can rent bicycles and staff can help arrange accommodation in the area or show you how to you take a bus to the beach.

❶ Getting There & Away

While it is possible to reach some of the area's sights by combination of bus and train, services can be infrequent and stations aren't always conveniently located to what you want to see.

An exception is **Higashi-hama** (東浜), one of the best of the swimming beaches along the coast, easily accessed by train from Tottori – it's just near Higashi-hama Station (¥410, 30 minutes).

Iwami, on the JR San-in line, is the closest station to the Uradome Kaigan from Tottori (¥320, 23 minutes).

If you're really keen to explore the area, your best bet is to rent a car: there is a number of car-rental companies around Tottori Station.

Izumo 出雲

☎ 0853 / POP 171,580

Just southwest of Matsue, breezy Izumo is a lovely little city with one heavyweight attraction – the great Izumo Taisha shrine, which ranks with Ise-jingū (in Kansai) as one of the most important shrines in Japan. The shrine and surrounding area can be visited on a day trip from Matsue.

⊙ Sights

Izumo Taisha is 8km northwest of central Izumo. The shrine area is basically one street, lined with eateries and shops, that leads up to the shrine gates. The Ichibata-line Izumo Taisha-mae Station is at the foot of the street.

★ **Izumo Taisha**   SHINTO SHRINE
(出雲大社; ☎ 0853-53-3100; 195 Kizuki-higashi, Taisha-chō; ⊗ 6.30am-8pm) FREE Izumo Taisha is also known as Izumo Ōyashiro and is perhaps the oldest Shintō shrine of all. It is second in importance only to Ise-jingū, the home of the sun goddess Amaterasu. This shrine, dedicated to Ōkuninushi, God of marriage and bringer of good fortune, is as old as Japanese recorded history – there are references to Izumo in the *Kojiki*, Japan's oldest book – and its origins stretch back into the age of the gods.

Visitors to the shrine summon Ōkuninushi by clapping four times rather than the usual two. According to tradition, the deity ceded control over Izumo to the sun goddess's line – he did this on the condition that a huge temple would be built in his honour, one that would reach as high as the heavens.

Impressive as the structure is today, it was once even bigger. Records dating from AD 970 describe the shrine as the tallest building in the country; there is evidence that the shrine towered as high as 48m above the ground during the Heian period. It may well have been too high for its own good – the structure collapsed five times between 1061 and 1225, and the roofs today are a more modest 24m.

The current appearance of the main shrine dates from 1744. The main hall underwent one of its periodic rebuildings in 2013, to be done again in another 60 years.

Huge *shimenawa* (twisted-straw ropes) hang over the entry to the main buildings. Those who can toss and lodge a coin in them are said to be blessed with good fortune. Visitors are not allowed inside the main shrine precinct, most of which is hidden behind huge wooden fences. Ranged along the sides of the compound are the *jūku-sha*, which are long shelters where Japan's myriad deities stay when they come for their annual conference.

When former-Princess Noriko married the eldest son of the head priest of Izumo Taisha – a 'commoner' – she relinquished her royal status and now lives in a house near the shrine.

**Shimane Museum of
Ancient Izumo**   MUSEUM
(島根県立古代出雲歴史博物館; 99-4 Kizuki-higashi, Taisha-chō; ¥300; ⊗ 9am-6pm Mar-Oct, to 5pm Nov-Feb, closed 3rd Tue of the month) Just to the right of the Izumo Taisha shrine's front gate, this museum contains exhibits on local history. These include reconstructions of the shrine in its pomp, and recordings of the annual ceremonies held to welcome the gods to Izumo. There is also a superb collection of bronze from the ancient Yayoi period.

Izumo Cultural Heritage Museum   MUSEUM
(出雲文化伝承館, Izumo Bunka Denshokan; ☎ 0853-21-2460; http://izumo-zaidan.jp/tag/izumobunkadensyoukan/; 520 Hama-chō; ⊗ 9am-5pm) FREE This free cultural museum in the beautifully restored former home of the lords of Izumo, the Ezumi clan, is worth a visit if only to stroll around the pretty Japanese garden. Although there's not much by way of English exhibits, the artefacts and architecture alone give some insight into the history of the area, inhabited since ancient times.

⚗ Festivals & Events

Kamiari-sai   RELIGIOUS
The 10th month of the lunar calendar is known throughout Japan as Kan-na-zuki (Month without Gods). In Izumo, however, it is known as Kami-ari-zuki (Month with Gods), for this is the month when all the Shintō gods congregate at Izumo Taisha.

The Kamiari-sai is a series of events to mark the arrival of the gods in Izumo. It runs from the 11th to the 17th of the 10th month according to the old calendar; exact dates vary from year to year.

⭙ Sleeping & Eating

For a city with such a well-known tourist attraction, accommodation options are limited. Your best bet is to grab a room at one of the low-cost but comfortable business hotels near the station.

There are plenty of well-priced restaurants on both sides of Izumo Station, with seafood a common culinary theme. A higher concentration is found on the northern side.

Green Hotel Morris　　　BUSINESS HOTEL ¥¥
(☑0853-24-7700; www.hotel-morris.co.jp/izumo; 2-3-4 Ekiminami-machi; s/d from ¥4900/7800; P@⊛) With rooms bigger than typical business hotels in Japan, self-serve pillow bars, friendly professional staff, a good communal bath with outdoor area, and an excellent breakfast buffet, all at a seriously reasonable price, it's hard to go past Green Morris. The hotel is just outside the station's south exit.

Uosensuisan Izumo-eki Minamiguchi-ten　　　IZAKAYA ¥¥
(魚鮮水産出雲市駅南口店; ☑0853-24-7091; chimney.co.jp; 1-2-6 Ekiminami-machi; dishes ¥575 2380) This hulking seafood *izakaya* around the corner from the station is always loud and packed – you may have to wait. It'll be worth it if you're a fan of all-you-can-drink plans and seafood done every which way. The substantial picture menu has lots of other popular Japanese treats, from tofu to teriyaki, on offer.

Gyōza-ya　　　GYŌZA ¥
(餃子屋; ☑0853-22-5053; 1268-6 Imaichi chō; gyōza ¥400-800; ⊙6.30-11pm) At that moment when you think you'll go crazy if you see another Izumo soba restaurant, proceed immediately to this cheap and cheery station-area eatery specialising in humble *gyōza:* they're fat and juicy, and crispy fried on the outside, just the way they should be. Order a beer and...'*kanpai!*'.

ℹ Information

Taisha Tourist Information Office (退社観光案内所; ☑0853-30-6015; 1346-9 Kizuki-minami, Taisha-chō; ⊙9am-5.30pm) Not far from Izumo Taisha-mae Station on the main street.

ℹ Getting There & Away

The private, old-fashioned Ichibata line starts from Matsue Shinjiko-onsen Station in Matsue and trundles along the northern side of Shinji-ko to Izumo Taisha-mae Station (¥810, one hour), with a transfer at Kawato (川跡).

The JR line runs from JR Matsue Station to JR Izumo-shi Station (¥580, 40 minutes), where you can transfer to an Ichibata train to Izumo Taisha-mae (¥490, 20 minutes), or to a bus to the shrine (¥510, 25 minutes).

Long-distance buses run from a few major cities in the region, including Hiroshima, Okayama and Kyoto.

Iwami Ginzan　　　石見銀山

Southwest of Izumo, about 6km inland from Nima Station on the San-in coast is the former Iwami Ginzan silver mine, a Unesco World Heritage Site. In the early 17th century, the mine produced as much as 38 tonnes of silver annually, making it the most important mine in the country at a time when Japan was producing around a third of the world's silver every year. The Tokugawa shogunate had direct control over 500 or so mines in the area.

⊙ Sights

The site is spread along a valley, with the small town of Ōmori at its centre. The main streets and the walking path along the river roughly form a long narrow loop, with mine shafts, temples, historic residences and ruins dotted along it and in the wooded hillsides. It's about 2km from one end to the other; allow at least four or more hours to do the loop on foot and to see the various sites at leisure.

Kumagai Residence　　　HISTORIC BUILDING
(熊谷家住宅; ☑0854-89-9003; http://kumagai.city.ohda.lg.jp; 63 Omori-chō Hachi; ¥300; ⊙9.30am-5pm Tue-Sun) The lovingly restored Kumagai Residence was rebuilt in 1801 after an earthquake destroyed most of the town the previous year. The house belonged to a merchant family who made their fortune as officials in the silver trade.

Gohyakurakan　　　BUDDHIST SITE
(五百羅漢) Crowded into two small caves at Gohyakurakan, there are 500 diminutive stone statues of the Buddha's disciples, each showing a different expression – some smiling, some turning their head to chat to their neighbour. The collection was completed in 1766, after 25 years of work.

Iwami Ginzan World Heritage Centre　　　MUSEUM
(石見銀山世界遺産センター; ☑0854-89-0183; http://ginzan.city.ohda.lg.jp; 1597-3 Omori-chō; ¥200; ⊙8.30am-6pm, closed last Tue of the month) The Iwami Ginzan World Heritage Centre has exhibits with explanations in English on the history of the mines and the surrounding area.

Shimizudani Refinery Ruins
HISTORIC BUILDING

(清水谷製錬所跡; ☑0854-89-9090) FREE The stone remains of a silver-mine refinery, now delightfully overgrown with apricot trees.

Ryūgenji Mabu Shaft
MINE

(龍源寺間歩; ☑0854-82-1600; ¥200; ◉9am-5pm Apr-Nov, to 4pm Dec-Mar) The Ryūgenji Mabu Shaft is a tunnel into the silver mine. It has been widened substantially from its original size and one glance at the old tunnel that stretches beyond the fence at the end of the accessible area should be enough to make most people glad they weren't born as 17th-century miners.

🛏 Sleeping & Eating

Jōfuku-ji Youth House
HOSTEL ¥

(城福寺ユースハウス; ☑0854-88-2233; www14. plala.or.jp/joufukuji; 1114 Nima-machi, Nima-chō; dm with/without meals ¥4500/3000; @) This is a great option for accommodation in comfortable tatami rooms in a Buddhist temple near Nima Station. Meals are available, and the owners can collect you from the station.

Chaya Yamabuki
CAFE

(茶屋やまぶき; ☑0854-89-0676; 28 Omori-chō; donuts ¥120; ◉10am-5pm Thu-Tue Apr-Oct, to 4pm Nov-Mar) For a drink and a sweet treat, stop in at Yamabuki, where the speciality is sweet-potato doughnuts. Look for the wooden sign.

ℹ Information

There is a booth near the Ōmori Daikansho Ato stop where you can pick up a map and audio guide (¥500), also available at the **Tourist Information Office** (☑0854-89-0333; ◉9am-5pm, to 4pm Oct-Apr) by the car park close to Rakan-ji.

Additional information can be found at www. ginzan-wm.jp.

ℹ Getting There & Around

Iwami Ginzan can be visited as a day trip from Matsue, but it would be a long day. You could also combine a trip here with a stay in nearby Yunotsu.

Buses run to the Ōmori Daikansho Ato stop about every half-hour from Ōda-shi Station (¥620, 25 minutes), and from Nima Station (¥400, 15 minutes, four or five per day). There is also a long-distance bus to Hiroshima.

Within the mine area, shuttle buses connect Ōmori Daikansho-ato and the World Heritage Centre every 15 minutes (¥200).

Bike rental is available (¥500 for three hours, ¥700 for an electric-assist bike for two hours).

YAMAGUCHI & AROUND

Yamaguchi-ken (山口県), Honshu's southernmost prefecture, doesn't get a lot of the attention is rightfully deserves: most visitors' experience of Yamaguchi is but a blur as they whiz through it on the *shinkansen* bound for Kyūshū.

If you should choose to disembark, you'll find that temperate Yamaguchi is full of surprises, with white sandy beaches that somehow avoid the float-up pollution that has spoiled Japan's coastline, active volcanoes, a gargantuan limestone cave, rolling hills and farmlands, historic villages and Unesco World Heritage Sites.

ℹ Getting There & Around

The main *shinkansen* lines linking eastern and western Japan run through Yamaguchi making access a breeze, especially if you have a JR Pass.

The slower, more scenic San-in line hugs the coast from Shimonoseki and heads north through Shimane and Tottori before dropping back down towards Kyoto.

If you're coming from Tokyo, you can often get good deals on flights from Haneda to **Yamaguchi Ube Airport** (UBJ; www.yamaguchiube-airport.jp) in Ube city, although access is a bit inconvenient.

Be sure to pick up a copy of the excellent *Enjoy Driving in Yamaguchi* brochure, produced by the Yamaguchi Prefectural Tourism Federation (www.oidemase.or.jp), from any of the region's tourist information centres. It's a must for anyone considering driving around the prefecture and contains a wealth of hidden gems.

Yamaguchi
山口

☑083 / POP 197,500

During the 100 years of civil war that bedevilled Japan until the country was reunited under the Tokugawa in the early 17th century, Yamaguchi prospered as an alternative capital to chaotic Kyoto. In 1550 Jesuit missionary Francis Xavier paused for two months here on his way to the imperial capital, and quickly returned when he was unable even to find the emperor in Kyoto. Yamaguchi today is a surprisingly small prefectural capital with a handful of sights.

👁 Sights

★ Kōzan-kōen
PARK

(香山公園; Map p487) North of the town centre is Kōzan Park, where the five-storey pagoda of **Rurikō-ji** (瑠璃光寺), a National

Yamaguchi

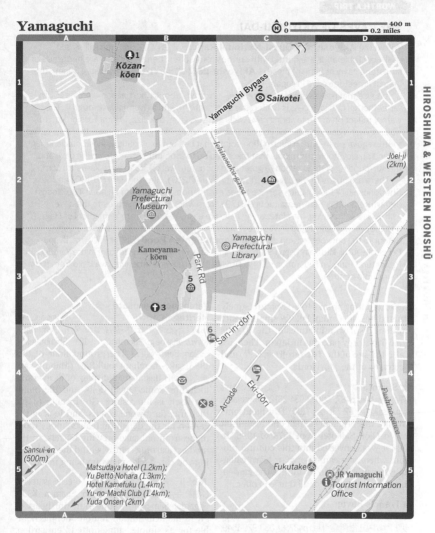

Yamaguchi

◎ Top Sights
1 Kōzan-kōen...B1
2 Saikotei C1

◎ Sights
　Christian Museum ....(see 3)
3 St Francis Xavier Memorial Church B3
4 Yamaguchi Furusato Heritage
　Centre..C2

5 Yamaguchi Prefectural Art Museum....B3

🛏 Sleeping
6 Sunroute Kokusai Hotel B4
7 Taiyō-dō Ryokan....................................C4

🍴 Eating
8 Sabō Kō B4

WORTH A TRIP

THE CAVES OF AKIYOSHI-DAI

Within the **Akiyoshi-dai Quasi-National Park** (秋吉台国定公園), the rolling Aki-yoshi-dai tablelands are dotted with curious rock spires, beneath which are hundreds of limestone caverns. One of these is **Akiyoshi-dō** (秋芳洞; ¥1200; ⊙8.30am-4.30pm), the largest limestone cave in Japan.

It is size that makes the cave impressive. It extends about 10km, at some points 100m wide (though public access is limited to a 1km section), and a river flows through it. The watery reflection of the towering cave walls at times gives the dizzying impression you're walking over a deep ravine. But you can leave the spelunking gear at home – there's a paved route, regular push-button information points that belt out explanations in various languages, and an elevator in the middle that takes you up to a lookout. For more on the cave and the surrounding plateau region (a great area for nature walks), go to www.karusuto.com.

There are buses to the cave from Yamaguchi (¥1210), Higashi-Hagi (¥1800) and Shimonoseki (¥1800). Each service takes a little more or less than an hour. The closest departure point is Shin-Yamaguchi (¥1170), from where it's 45 minutes to the cave.

If you're self-driving, the plateau and cave are easily reached from Yamaguchi or Hagi, and they make a good stop en route between the two. You could also consider a slight detour to the unexpected and delightful **Beppu Benten Pond** (別府弁天池湧水, Beppu Benten Ike Yūsui; Mizukami Beppu Shuho-cho, Mine-shi). Both locations feature in the Yamaguchi Prefectural Tourism Federation's *Enjoy Driving in Yamaguchi* brochure, available from most tourist info centres.

Treasure dating from 1404, is picturesquely situated beside a small lake. A small on-site museum displays miniatures of the 50-plus other five-storey pagodas in Japan. The park is also the site of the **Tōshun-ji** (洞春寺) and the graves of the Mōri lords.

★ Saikotei
CULTURAL CENTRE

(菜香亭; Map p487; ☎ 083-934-3312; www.c-able.ne.jp/~saikou/; 1-2-7 Tenge; ¥100) This handsome building was originally a high-end restaurant named Gion Saikotei from 1878 to 1996. In 2004 it was converted into this cultural museum where you can observe or learn calligraphy, wear a kimono or admire the garden. Check the homepage for all that's on offer.

St Francis Xavier Memorial Church
CHURCH

(ザビエル記念聖堂; Map p487; ☎ 083-920-1549; www.xavier.jp; 4-1 Kameyama-chō; donation ¥100; ⊙visiting hours 9am-5pm Thu-Tue) Yamaguchi was a major centre of Christian missionary activity before the religion was outlawed in 1589. This church resembles a large tent and sits above the town in Kameyama-kōen. Built in 1952 in honour of St Francis Xavier, it burned down in 1991 and was rebuilt in 1998. The ground-floor **Christian museum** (Map p487; ¥300; ⊙9am-5pm) covers the life of Xavier and the early history of Christianity in Japan, mostly in Japanese only. Steps opposite the church lead uphill to views of Yamaguchi.

Yamaguchi Furusato Heritage Centre
HISTORIC BUILDING

(山口ふるさと伝承総合センター; Map p487; www.c-able.ne.jp/~denshou; 12 Shimotatekōji; ⊙9am-5pm) FREE The ground floor of this 1886 sake-merchant building (Manabi-kan; まなび館) has a small display of local crafts, including some Ōuchi dolls, and the building itself is interesting. Go upstairs to see the large dark-wood beams, and look in the garden for the delightful tea-ceremony room made from old sake-brewing barrels. In the modern learning centre behind the old building you can see lacquerware being made.

Jōei-ji
BUDDHIST TEMPLE

(常栄寺; 2001 Miyano-shimo; garden ¥300; ⊙garden 8am-5pm) About 4km northeast of JR Yamaguchi Station, temple Jōei-ji is notable for its simple, stone-dotted Zen garden, **Sesshutei**, designed by painter Sesshū. From the garden, a trail leads uphill through the woods to several more temples. You can reach the temple by bike or taxi (about ¥1300) from central Yamaguchi. Or take the train two stops to Miyano and from there it's about 1km to walk.

🏃 Activities

Just west of Yamaguchi city is the 800-year-old Yuda Onsen (湯田温泉). The area is full of hotels and bathing facilities, mostly along a busy main road, which isn't really a place for tottering between baths in your *yukata*. Still, a soak here is a nice way to spend a few hours.

You can take a dip in the indoor and outdoor baths of **Yu-no-Machi Club** (湯の町 倶楽部; ☑ 083-922-0091; 4-6-4 Yudaonsen; not incl towel ¥800; ⊙ 11am-10pm). Use the baths at **Hotel Kamefuku** (ホテルかめ福; ☑ 083-922-7000; www.kamefuku.com; 4-5-2 Yudaonsen; ¥800; ⊙ 11.30am-10pm) or, for luxury and a peaceful garden setting, head to **Sansui-en** (山水園; ☑ 083-922-0560; www.yuda-sansuien.com; 4-60 Midori-chō; ¥1600; ⊙ 10am-9pm).

For a full list and map of the baths and hotels, drop in first at the **tourist information office** (☑ 083-901-0150; 2-1-23 Yuda Onsen; ⊙ 9am-7pm, foot bath 10am-10pm) on the main road, which also has a free foot bath and towels for sale.

JR and Bōchō Buses run regularly to Yuda Onsen bus stop from Yamaguchi Station (¥220, 15 minutes). They drop you on the main strip, Yuda Onsen-dōri, a short walk from the tourist office (just keep walking in the direction of the bus). Yuda Onsen also has a station, one stop on the local train line from Yamaguchi (¥140) or 20 minutes from Shin-Yamaguchi (¥240). From the station, follow the quiet red road for about 1km to get to the busy main T-intersection and turn right for the tourist office.

🛏 Sleeping & Eating

Taiyō-dō Ryokan RYOKAN ¥
(太陽堂旅館; Map p487; ☑ 083-922-0897; 2-3 Komeya-chō; r per person from ¥3200; 🛜) The Taiyō-dō is a friendly old ryokan in the shopping arcade just off Eki-dōri. The tatami rooms are quite a good size and there are large communal bathrooms (which you may have private use of, depending on how busy it is). No English spoken.

Yu Bettō Nohara RYOKAN ¥¥
(湯別当野原; ☑ 083-922-0018; www.yubettou-nohara.com; 7-8 Yuda Onsen; r per person with 2 meals from ¥9800; ⊜ ❀) You'll be welcomed by keen staff at this centrally located ryokan in Yuda Onsen. Most rooms are of the traditional tatami variety; some have both tatami and an area with two single beds. Not all have private bathrooms. Meals are *kaiseki*-style with a seafood focus, and you can stay without meals or with breakfast only.

Sunroute Kokusai Hotel HOTEL ¥¥
(サンルート国際ホテル山口; Map p487; ☑ 083-923-3610; www.hsy.co.jp; 1-1 Nakagawara-chō; s/tw from ¥5500/11,775; 🅿 ⊜ ❀ @ 🛜) This

modern hotel has stylish, neutral-toned rooms, and is in a good location in the centre of town at the base of tree-lined Park Rd.

★ Matsudaya Hotel RYOKAN ¥¥¥
(ホテル松田屋; ☑ 083-922-0125; www.matsudayahotel.co.jp; 3-6-7 Yuda Onsen; r per person with 2 meals from ¥22,800; ❀ @ 🛜) This centuries-old, now modernised, ryokan, allows you to bathe in history – right in the tub where once dipped the plotters of the Meiji Restoration. The ryokan's garden setting and excellent service will likely ease any present-day rebellious thoughts. Matsudaya is on the main drag in Yuda Onsen.

★ Sabō Kō CAFE ¥
(茶房幸; Map p487; 1-2-39 Dōjōmonzen; dishes ¥620-980; ⊙ 11.30am-6pm Wed-Mon; ⊜) A cosy atmosphere prevails in this low-ceilinged little eatery, where customers perch on wooden stools sipping coffee. The speciality on the Japanese-only menu is the generous, rustic *omuraisu* (omelette filled with fried rice), but there are also curries and soba. Look for the small wood-covered place with ceramic pots sticking out of the exterior plasterwork.

★ Mottimo Pasta Yuda Onsen ITALIAN ¥¥
(モッチモパスタ 山口湯田店; ☑ 083-941-6447; 2-5-41 Yoshikishimo-higashi; pastas ¥850-1200; ⊙ 11am-3pm & 5-10pm Thu-Tue) A variety of Japanese twists on Italian faves including eight kinds of delicious hot, buttery, flavoured bread sticks (think honey, basil and custard cream!), a small selection of pizzas and a range of delicious pastas. Lunch specials are available and there's a picture menu.

ⓘ Information

Tourist Information Office (山口観光案内所; Map p487; ☑ 083-933-0090; www.yamaguchi-city.jp; ⊙ 9am-6pm) Inside Yamaguchi Station. There's also an office at **Shin-Yamaguchi** (☑ 083-972-6373; 2nd fl, Shin-Yamaguchi Station; ⊙ 9am-6pm), *shinkansen* exit side.

ⓘ Getting There & Away

BUS
Chūgoku JR Bus (☑ 083-922-2519; www.chugoku-jrbus.co.jp) runs nine to 11 buses daily to Hagi (Higashi-Hagi Station; ¥1780, 70 minutes) from Yamaguchi Station, some originating at Shin-Yamaguchi. **Bōchō Bus** (☑ 0834-32-7733; www.bochobus.co.jp) runs buses to Higashi-Hagi Station (¥2080, 1½ hours, at least hourly) from Shin-Yamaguchi.

TRAIN

Yamaguchi Station is on the JR Yamaguchi line. Shin-Yamaguchi Station is 10km southwest in Ogōri on the San-yō *shinkansen* line, which connects to Shimonoseki and Hiroshima, and to Osaka in the east. The Yamaguchi local service connects the Shin-Yamaguchi and Yamaguchi Stations (¥240, 25 minutes).

The **SL Yamaguchi** (www.c571.jp; adult/child ¥1660/830) steam train trundles through the scenic valleys from Shin-Yamaguchi to Tsuwano between mid-March and late November on weekends and holidays. It's a fun way to travel and is very popular; check the latest schedules and book well ahead at JR and tourist information offices.

❶ Getting Around

You can walk to the central sights from Yamaguchi Station, but it's handy to hire a bicycle for the outlying temple areas. Jōei-ji, for example, is about 4km away (closer to Miyano Station). A taxi might be an easier option if you don't want to walk or cycle. For bikes, try **Fukutake** (福武; Map p487; ☑ 083-922-0915; 1-4-6 Eki-dōri; rental per day ¥700; ⊙ 8am-7pm) just across from the station.

Yuda Onsen is served by bus or train from Yamaguchi and Shin-Yamaguchi.

Tsuwano 津和野

☑ 0856 / POP 7660

A highlight of this region, utterly delightful Tsuwano is a quiet, 700-year-old mountain town straddling a pretty river and boasting an important shrine, a ruined castle and an evocative samurai quarter. It also has a wonderful collection of carp swimming in the roadside water channels – in fact, there are far more carp here than people.

◉ Sights

Only the walls and some fine old gates from the former samurai quarter of Tonomachi (殿町) remain, but it's an attractive area for strolling. The water channels that run alongside the picturesque Tonomachi Road are home to numerous carp, bred to provide food in case of emergency. As you're walking, look out for *sugidama* (cedar balls) hanging outside a few old sake breweries.

★ Taikodani-Inari-jinja   SHINTO SHRINE

(太鼓谷稲成神社; Map p491; ⊙ 8am-4.30pm) Just above the castle chairlift station, this thriving shrine, built in 1773 by the seventh lord Kamei Norisada, is one of the five major Inari shrines in Japan. Walk up the hillside to it through a tunnel created by hundreds of *torii*, which are lit up at night, creating a beautiful sight from the town. There are fabulous views of the valley and mountains from the top.

Tsuwano-jō   CASTLE

(津和野城; Map p491; chairlift one-way ¥450; ⊙ chairlift 9am-5pm, irregular hours winter) The broken walls of Tsuwano-jō brood over the valley. A slightly rickety chairlift takes you slowly up the hillside, and there's a further 15-minute walk through the woods to the castle ruins. There's nothing here but the walls, but there are of course great views.

Morijuku Museum   MUSEUM

(杜塾美術館; Map p491; 542 Morimura; ¥500; ⊙ 9am-5pm) This museum is housed in a 150-year-old building that once served as the home of a *shōya* (village headman). Downstairs is a collection of soft-edged scenes painted by local-born artist Nakao Shō, a roomful of bullfight sketches by Goya, and a framed set of beautifully embroidered Taishō-era kimono collars. The caretaker will gladly point out the features of the building, including the pinhole camera hidden away upstairs.

Chapel of St Maria   CHAPEL

(乙女峠マリア聖堂, Otometoge Maria Kinenseido; Map p491; ☑ 856-72-0251) The tiny Maria-dō dates from 1951. More than 150 'hidden Christians' were imprisoned in a Buddhist temple on this site in the early years of the Meiji Restoration; some 36 of them died before a law allowing freedom of religion was passed in 1873. A procession is held here on 3 May.

Anno Art Museum   GALLERY

(安野光雅美術館; Map p491; ☑ 0856-72-4155; 60-1 Ushiroda; ¥800; ⊙ 9am-5pm, closed 2nd Thu in Mar, Jun, Sep & Dec) Tsuwano-born Anno Mitsumasa is famous for his wonderfully detailed illustrated books, including *Anno's Alphabet* and *Anno's Journey*. You can see his work at this traditional-looking white building near the station, where the large collection is rotated throughout the year.

Tsuwano Catholic Church   CHURCH

(津和野カトリック教会; Map p491; Tonomachi; ⊙ 8am-5.30pm Apr-Nov, to 5pm Dec-Mar) The church here is a reminder of the town's Christian history. Hidden Christians from Nagasaki were exiled here in the early Meiji period. It's interesting to peep inside to see tatami mats instead of pews.

Tsuwano

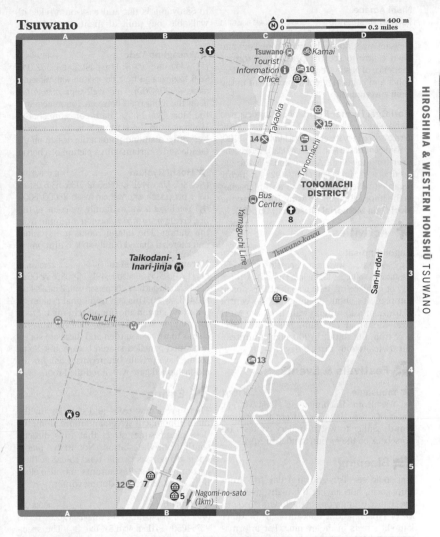

Tsuwano

**Nishi Amane
Former Residence** HISTORIC BUILDING
(西周旧居; Map p491; ◎9am-5pm) FREE It's a pleasant walk down the river from Tsuwano town centre to see the peaked-roof former residence of Nishi Amane (1829–97), a philosopher and political scientist prominent in the Meiji government.

Mori Ōgai Former Residence HISTORIC BUILDING
(森鴎外旧宅; Map p491; ☑856-72-3210; www.town.tsuwano.lg.jp/shisetsu/ougai.html; ¥100; ◎9am-5pm, closed Mon Dec-early Mar) Across the river from the Nishi Amane house is the old residence of Mori Ōgai (1862–1922), a highly regarded novelist who served as a physician in the Imperial Japanese Army. It's next to the **Mori Ōgai Memorial Museum** (Map p491).

🏃 Activities

Nagomi-no-sato ONSEN
(なごみの里; www.nagomi-nosato.com; 256 Washibara; ¥600; ◎10am-9pm Fri-Wed) After a day of sightseeing, take a soak at this onsen complex. It's about 2.5km from the centre of town, or a 15-minute walk from the Mori Ōgai Memorial Museum. Buses do travel here from the station (¥200, eight minutes), but there are only three a day.

🎉 Festivals & Events

★ Yabusame CULTURAL
At Washibara Hachiman-gū (鷲原八幡宮), south of town about 4km from the station, crowds gather to watch archery contests on horseback on the second Sunday in April.

🛏 Sleeping

You could see Tsuwano in a day trip from Yamaguchi, but staying the night gives you the chance to enjoy one of the town's *minshuku* or ryokan, and a walk through the quiet lamp-lit streets in the evening. For information in English online, go to www.gambo-ad.com/english and click on 'Tsuwano' – a few of the local ryokan are listed.

Shokudō Minshuku Satoyama MINSHUKU ¥
(食堂民宿　さと山; Map p491; ☑080-1913-9396; www.genki-ya.com/sato; 345 Washibara; s/tw from ¥2700/4700; P✳@🛜🐕) Satoyama has a spectacular countryside setting. The Japanese-style rooms have mountain views and strong wi-fi, though neglected shared bathrooms. The English-speaking owner cooks decent meals and there is a free-use clothes washer. The mountain-hugging road

to Satoyama is flat and easy on a bike; it's walkable, but unlit at night. Look for the white house, blue *noren* and red banners.

Wakasagi-no-Yado MINSHUKU ¥
(民宿わかさぎの宿; Map p491; ☑0856-72-1146; 98-6 Morimura-guchi; r per person with/without 2 meals ¥7700/4700) This well-kept *minshuku* is on the main road between Tonomachi and the Mori Ōgai house. Bathrooms are shared. Walking from the station, look for the building with a diamond-pattern tile design on the facade and a curtain with a picture of a heron.

★ Hoshi Ryokan MINSHUKU ¥¥
(星旅館; Map p491; ☑0856-72-0136; 53-6 Ushiroda; r per person with/without meals ¥8000/6000; 🛜) You'll get a warm, family welcome at this big, creaky *minshuku* located a minute from the station. The tatami rooms are spacious and there's a shared family-style bathroom.

Noren Yado Meigetsu RYOKAN ¥¥
(のれん宿明月; Map p491; ☑0856-72-0685; 665 Ushiroda-guchi; r per person with 2 meals from ¥10,400; ✳🛜) This is a traditional ryokan on a narrow lane in the Tonomachi area. *Fusuma* (sliding screen doors) glide open in the rooms to reveal a garden and there are soothing, wood-panelled shared bathrooms. Some rooms have private bathrooms. Look for the old-fashioned gate with a red-tiled roof.

🍴 Eating

There are a few cafes and eateries on the main Tonomachi street, and more along the (less picturesque) street that runs directly south from the station. Not many places open at night as people tend to eat at their accommodation. Restaurants may also close if it's quiet, especially during winter.

★ Tsurube NOODLES ¥
(つるべ; Map p491; 384-1 Ushoroda-guchi; dishes ¥575-1050; ◎11am-4pm Sat-Thu; 🏮) The speciality here is fresh wheat noodles handmade onsite, going into filling dishes such as *sansai udon* (noodles with wild vegetables) and *umeboshi udon* (noodles with dried plum). For a little extra, have a side of *omusubi* (rice ball). Tsurube is next to a small graveyard.

Yūki SEAFOOD ¥¥
(遊亀; Map p491; ☑0856-72-0162; 271-4 Ushiroda; meals ¥1400-2800; ◎11am-3pm) The *Tsuwano teishoku* (a carp-themed sampler of local dishes) is recommended at this elegantly rustic restaurant, which has wooden tables and the sound of running water. There are koi

(carp) in a pool in the floor here, and more on the menu. Look for the old-fashioned building with a small pine tree outside. Dinner by reservation only.

ℹ️ Information

Tourist Information Office (津和野町観光協会; Map p491; 📞0856-72-1771; www.tsuwano-kanko. net; ⏱9am-5pm; 📶) Immediately to the right as you exit the station. Audio sightseeing guides are available for rent (¥300 per day) and there's free wi-fi, accessible even when closed.

ℹ️ Getting There & Away

Tsuwano is on the JR Yamaguchi line, which runs from Shin-Yamaguchi and Yamaguchi in the south, to Masuda on the Sea of Japan coast (which connects to the San-in line). The *Super Oki* service from Yamaguchi or Shin-Yamaguchi shaves 25 to 35 minutes off the trip, but costs more than double the standard fare (or free for JR Pass holders).

Masuda ¥580, 40 minutes

Shin-Yamaguchi ¥1140, 100 minutes

Yamaguchi ¥970, 80 minutes

Long-distance buses go from the **Tsuwano Bus Centre** (Map p491) to Higashi-Hagi (¥2190, 1¾ hours, five daily 8.10am to 5.10pm; JR passes not valid). There are also overnight buses to Kōbe/Osaka and Tokyo.

ℹ️ Getting Around

Most attractions are within walking or cycling distance of the station. There is a local bus service, but it's not of much use to travellers and runs only a few times a day. The easiest way to explore is to rent a bike from **Kamai** (貸自転車かまい; Map p491; bike hire per 2/24hr ¥500/800; ⏱8am-sunset), across from the station.

Hagi 萩

📞0838 / POP 49,580

The jewel in Yamaguchi's crown, Hagi is known for producing some of the finest ceramics in Japan and has a well-preserved old samurai quarter. During the feudal period, Hagi was the castle town of the Chōshū domain, which, together with Satsuma (corresponding to modern Kagoshima in southern Kyūshū), was instrumental in defeating the Tokugawa government and ushering in a new age after the Meiji Restoration. The importance of Hagi's role in the modernisation of Japan was recognised in 2015 by Unesco, who decreed World Heritage status on five historical industrial sites.

Western and central Hagi are effectively an island created by the two rivers Hashimoto-gawa and Matsumoto-gawa; eastern Hagi (with the major JR station Higashi-Hagi; get off there for the main sights) lies on the eastern bank of the Matsumoto-gawa.

Hagi's proximity to the Sea of Japan, quiet pace and bucolic vistas make it the prefecture's most worthwhile destination.

Because historically Hagi wasn't on the radar for international visitors, many service providers weren't used to the vagaries of *gaijin* and not a lot of English was spoken. While that's largely still the case, the town's new and cherished World Heritage status has meant an increase in visitors from abroad, so things are changing. Have patience with the kind and often elderly townsfolk as they do their bit to catch up.

👁️ Sights

Hagi is a sprawling city which hugs every inch of land between the shoreline and its enfolding mountain range. The city's main areas of interest are its picturesque samurai district, **Jōkamachi** (also called 'Hagi Castle town' since its inclusion in the Unesco World Heritage camp) – the streets of which are lined with whitewashed walls enclosing beautiful villas – and its World Heritage Sites. Most attractions are spread apart and renting a car or bicycle can be a good idea.

⭐**Kikuya Residence** HISTORIC BUILDING (菊屋家住宅; Map p494; 1-1 Gofuku-machi; ¥520; ⏱9.30am-5.30pm) The Kikuya family were merchants rather than samurai. As official merchants to the *daimyō*, their wealth and connections allowed them to build a house well above their station. This house dates from 1604 and has a fine gate and attractive gardens, and numerous interesting displays of items used in daily life, including an old public phone box. Don't miss the large old maps of Hagi, which show just how little has changed in the town layout.

Shizuki-kōen PARK (指月公園; Map p494) Within this park, there's not much of the old **Hagi-jō** (萩城; Map p494; 📞0838-25-1826; 500 Horiuchi; incl Asa Mōri House ¥210; ⏱8am-6.30pm Mar-Oct, to 4.30pm Nov-Feb) to see, apart from the castle's typically imposing outer walls and the surrounding carp-filled moat. The castle was built in 1604 and dismantled in 1874 following the Meiji Restoration. The inner grounds hold a pleasant park, with spring cherry blossoms; the

Hagi

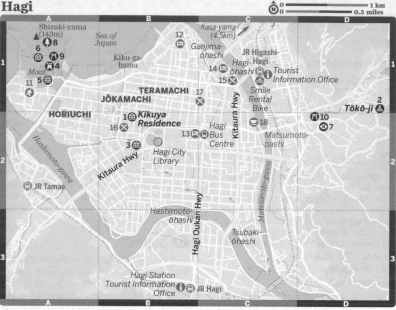

Hagi

Shizuki-yama-jinja (志都岐山神社; Map p494); the mid-19th century **Hanano-e Tea House** (花江茶亭; Map p494); and other buildings, including a *nagaya* (Japanese long house) known as **Asa Mōri House**.

From the castle ruins you can climb the hillside to the 143m peak of Shizuki-yama.

Hagi Uragami Museum   MUSEUM
(山口県立萩美術館・浦上記念館; Map p494; ☎0838-24-2400; www.hum.pref.yamaguchi.lg.jp; 586-1 Hiyako; ¥300; ⏰9am-5pm Tue-Sun) In this appealing modern building you'll find a superb collection of ceramics and woodblock prints, with fine works by Katsushika Hokusai and Utamaro Kitagawa. There are also regular special exhibitions.

★ Tōkō-ji   BUDDHIST TEMPLE
(東光寺; Map p494; www.toukouji.net; 1647 Chintō; ¥300; ⏰8.30am-5pm) East of the river, near Shōin-jinja, stands pretty Zen Tōkō-ji, built in 1691 and home to the tombs of five Mōri lords. The stone walkways on the

hillside behind the temple are flanked by almost 500 stone lanterns, which were erected by the lords' servants.

Shōin-jinja
SHINTO SHRINE

(松陰神社; Map p494) This shrine, with a garden and small complex, was founded in 1890 and is dedicated to Meiji Restoration movement leader Yoshida Shōin. His **former house** (吉田松陰幽囚の旧宅, Yoshida Shōin Yūshū-no-kyūtaku; Map p494; ⊗8am-5pm) **FREE** and the school where he agitated against the shogunate in the years leading up to the revolution are also here, as well as a **treasure house** (宝物館; Map p494; ¥500; ⊗9am-5pm). The shrine is located southeast of Higashi-Hagi Station. The circle bus drops you out the front.

Shoka Sonjuku Academy
HISTORIC BUILDING

(松下村塾; Map p494; ☑0838-22-4643; 1537-1 Chinto) **FREE** Although the word 'academy' conjures images of Ivy League schools, this humble schoolhouse is anything but that. Here in the 1850s Yoshida Shōin lectured students who would go on to play instrumental roles in the Meiji Revolution.

Itō Hirobumi House
NOTABLE BUILDING

(伊藤博文旧宅; Map p494; 1515 Chinto; ¥100; ⊗9am-5pm) About 200m from Shōin-jinja is the thatched early home of the four-term prime minister, who was a follower of Yoshida Shōin, and who later drafted the Meiji Constitution. It's interesting to see the contrast between this humble place and the impressive mansion he lived in during his years in Tokyo, which is next door, having been moved to Hagi after his death.

Kasa-yama
MOUNTAIN

(笠山) About 5km northeast of the town is this 112m dormant volcano. The top has gorgeous views of the Sea of Japan and a tiny 30m-deep crater. There is also a walking track around the coast. From late February to late March a beautiful grove of camellias blooms here.

The pond at the mountain's base, **Myōjin-ike** (明神池), is connected to the sea and shelters a variety of saltwater fish. Look and listen for birdlife in the surrounding trees.

About a five-minute walk up the mountain from the pond is **Hagi Glass** (萩ガラス工房; ☑0838-26-2555; www.hagi-glass.jp; ⊗9am-6pm, demonstrations 9am-noon & 1-4.30pm) **FREE**, where quartz basalt from the volcano is used to make extremely tough Hagi glassware. The showroom and shop display beautiful coloured vases and you can

watch the glass-blowing process. Next door is Hagi's own beer and citrus-juice factory, **Yuzuya Honten** (柚子屋本店; www.e-yuzuya.com; 1189 Chintō; ⊗9am-5pm) **FREE**. Stop in here to see the very small team at work, taste juice in the attached shop, or have a refreshing *mikan*-flavoured (*satsuma*) soft cream.

Buses go to Kasa-yama from Higashi-Hagi Station once every one to 1½ hours (¥280, 15 minutes); get off at the Koshi-ga-hama stop, about eight minutes' walk from the base of the mountain and Myōjin-ike.

Unrinji Temple
TEMPLE

(雲林寺; 2489 Kibekami) **FREE** About 22km east of Hagi, this unique temple is dedicated to the humble moggy and features cats, cats, everywhere! Well, carved ones, anyway. Serious cat people won't mind renting a car to get out here.

🛏 Sleeping

★ Guesthouse Ruco
HOSTEL ¥¥

(ゲストハウスRuco; Map p494; ☑0838-21-7435; www.guesthouse-ruco.com; 92 Karahimachi; dm/d with shared bathroom ¥2800/7500; ⊛❄🖏) Ruco is a modern wonderland of handmade furniture and vintage decor. Effortlessly stylish and minimalist, from the the cafe-bar through to the bathrooms, the design theme makes you feel like you're spending the night in a Muji store. Cramped but clean dorms use clever personal curtains, while Japanese-style doubles are spacious. Helpful staff speak some English. Exit left from Hagi Bus Centre and then left again.

Guesthouse Hagi Akatsukiya
HOSTEL ¥

(古民家ゲストハウス萩・暁屋; Map p494; ☑050-3624-4625; www.guesthouse-hagi-akatsukiya.jimdo.com; 237-1 Hamasakimachi; dm ¥2600-2800; ⊛❄🖏) This polished-up Japanese house just two minutes from the beach has a cute garden and soft bunk beds for a tranquil rest. The well-travelled owner provides good local knowledge, speaks English and rents bikes (¥500 per 24 hours). Akatsukiya is beside a shrine – from the northernmost beach, go down the road opposite the blue-tiled toilets and cross the saw mill.

★ Hagi Kankō Hotel
HOTEL ¥¥

(萩観光ホテル; ☑0838-25-0211; www.hagikan.com; 1189 Chintō; r from ¥10,560; 🅿❄) At the base of Kasa-yama, this solid tourist hotel has wonderfully friendly yet formal staff who'll do anything to assist, even if English

HAGI POTTERY

During his Korean peninsula campaigns in 1592 and 1598, Toyotomi Hideyoshi abducted whole families of potters as growing interest in the tea ceremony generated desire for the finest Korean ceramics. The firing techniques brought over all those centuries ago live on in Japanese ceramics today.

Hagi-yaki (Hagi ceramicware) is noted for its fine glazes and delicate pastel colours, and connoisseurs of Japanese ceramics rank it as some of the best. At a number of shops and kilns, such as **Hagi-jō Kiln** (萩城窯; Map p494; ☎0838-22-5226; 2-5 Horiuchi; ⏱8am-5pm) **FREE**, you can watch artisans at work and browse the finished products. The **tourist office** (p496) has a complete list of kilns in the area. At workshop **Jōzan** (城山; Map p494; ☎0838-25-1666; 31-15 Horiuchi Nishi-no-hama; lessons ¥1730; ⏱8am-4pm) you can try your hand at making pottery in this large workshop; once fired, items can be shipped anywhere in Japan. Look for the building next to the large kiln.

is a challenge for them. Smart, ryokan-style rooms have beautiful views over the bay to the mountains in the distance, as does the gorgeous *rotemburo*.

★Hagi no Yado Tomoe
RYOKAN ¥¥¥

(萩の宿常茂恵; Map p494; ☎0838-22-0150; www.tomoehagi.jp; 608-53 Kōbō-ji Hijiwara; r per person from ¥18,850; ⊕✳@) The finest inn in Hagi, the historic Tomoe has gorgeous Japanese rooms with garden views, beautifully prepared cuisine and luxurious baths. Prices vary according to season, and there are discounted plans on the website (if you don't read Japanese, it may be easier to reserve via email). Cross the bridge from the station and take the road along the river.

✗ Eating & Drinking

Hagi Seaside Market
SEAFOOD ¥

(道の駅 萩しーまーと; ☎0838-24-4937; www. seamart.axis.or.jp; 4160-61 Chinto; ⏱9.30am-6pm) There's all manner of fresh and wild delights to sample here at this busy market, with plenty of eateries as well as straight-from-the-source sellers if you're planning your own barbecue somehow.

★Hotoritei
CAFE ¥¥

(畔亭; Map p494; ☎0838-22-1755; www. hotoritei.com; 62 Minami-Katakawa; meals ¥1100-1850; ⏱11am-5pm Fri-Wed Feb-Dec) A tranquil rest stop near the Jōkamachi area, Hotoritei is within a large house surrounded by gardens. It mainly serves coffees, teas and cakes – try the fluffy, cream-filled *matcha* (green-tea) roll. There are a few lunch sets; the menu has some pictures. Look for the entrance set back from the road, next to Sam's Irish pub.

Maru
IZAKAYA ¥¥

(まる; Map p494; ☎0838-26-5060; 78 Yoshida-chō; dishes ¥750-1850; ⏱5-11pm Mon-Sat) This lively *izakaya* specialises in dishes prepared using fresh local produce. There's a predictable seafood theme going on, with lots of sushi and sashimi to enjoy, but a range of other hot items are available.

Hagi Shinkai
SEAFOOD ¥¥¥

(萩心海; Map p494; ☎0838-26-1221; www.hagi shinkai.com; 370-71 Hijiwara; set meals ¥2500-7000; ⏱11am-2.30pm & 5-9pm) Seating here is around a large open tank, so you can watch as the doomed fish are plucked out by the staff while you eat. There are various set-meal options, or ask for the manager-recommended *Shinkai teishoku* (¥1080/1990 at lunch/dinner), which isn't on the menu and includes sashimi, tempura and *chawanmushi* (steamed savoury egg custard). Look for the white building with the lighthouse.

Cafe Tikal
CAFE

(長屋門珈琲・カフェティカル; Map p494; ☎838-26-2933; www.hagi-nagayamoncoffee.jimdo. com; 298-1 Hijiwara; ⏱9.30am-8pm Tue-Sat, to 6pm Sun) Through the old gate of the Kogawa family residence is this small cafe with large windows looking on to a pleasingly unkempt garden. Sit among the games and books at one of the wooden tables and choose from a range of coffees (from ¥380), including a hilly cappuccino. Cakes are also served.

ℹ Information

Tourist Information Office (萩市観光案内所; Map p494; ☎0838-25-3145; ⏱9am-5.45pm Mar-Nov, to 5pm Dec-Feb) Located inside Higashi-Hagi Station. Staff speak English and provide a good English cycling and walking map. There's another tourist office near **Hagi**

Station (萩駅観光案内所; Map p494; ☎ 0838-25-3145; 2997 Chintō; ⏱ 9am-5pm).

ⓘ Getting There & Away

BUS

Bus connections from Higashi-Hagi Station, via the **Hagi Bus Centre** (Map p494) include:
Shin-Yamaguchi ¥2100, 1½ hours, at least hourly
Tsuwano ¥2290, 1¾ hours, five daily
Yamaguchi ¥1860, 70 minutes, nine to 11 daily; JR Passes can be used on this service

TRAIN

Hagi is on the JR San-in line, which runs along the coast from Tottori and Matsue. Local services between Shimonoseki and Higashi-Hagi (¥1940) take up to three hours, depending on transfers. If you're going to Tsuwano from Higashi-Hagi, go by train up the coast to Masuda (¥970, 70 minutes), then change to the JR Yamaguchi line (¥580, 40 minutes) or *Super Oki* (¥580, 30 minutes) for Tsuwano. All these journeys are free with a JR Pass. If you have to wait long transferring at sleepy Masuda, try the hidden restaurant street one block north of the station.

ⓘ Getting Around

It's easy to walk around central Hagi and the Jōkamachi area, but many sights, including the World Heritage locations, are on the edges of town. It helps to have wheels of some kind.

BUS

The *māru basu* (まぁ〜るバス; circle bus) takes in all of central Hagi's attractions. There are east- (東回り) and west-bound (西回り) loops, with two services per hour at each stop. A trip costs ¥100, and one-/two-day passes cost ¥500/700. Both routes stop at Higashi-Hagi Station.

BICYCLE

Smile Rental Bike (Map p494; ☎ 0838-22-2914; bike hire per 1/24hr ¥200/1000; ⏱ 8am-5pm) The first of two rental sheds directly left as you exit Higashi-Hagi Station. Smile allows taking bikes overnight whereas the other doesn't.

Shimonoseki 下関

☎ 083 / POP 268,620

At the southwestern tip of Honshū, Shimonoseki is separated from Kyūshū by a narrow strait, famous for a decisive 12th-century clash between rival samurai clans. The expressway crosses the Kanmon Straits (関門海峡; Kanmon-kaikyō) on the Kanmon-bashi, while another road, the *shinkansen* railway line and the JR railway line all tunnel underneath. You can even walk to Kyūshū through a tunnel under the water. Shimonoseki is also a key connecting point to South Korea. The town is famous for seafood, particularly *fugu*, the potentially lethal pufferfish.

⊙ Sights

★Karato Ichiba   MARKET

(唐戸市場; Map p498; www.karatoichiba.com; 5-50 Karato; ⏱ 5am-1pm Mon-Sat, 9am-3pm Sun) A highlight of a trip to Shimonoseki is an early-morning visit to the Karato fish market. It's a great opportunity to try sashimi for breakfast or lunch and the fish doesn't get any fresher – a fair bit of it will still be moving. The best days to come are Friday to Sunday, when stallholders set up tables selling *bentō* of sashimi and cooked dishes made from the day's catch. Note that the market is closed on some Wednesdays.

You can take away meals or eat at the counters on the mezzanine level. Buses to Karato (¥220) leave from outside the station and take about seven minutes.

Akama-jingū   SHINTO SHRINE

(赤間神宮; Map p498; 4-1 Amidaiji-chō; ⏱ 24hr) Akama-jinjū is a shrine dedicated to the seven-year-old emperor Antoku, who died in 1185 in the battle of Dan-no-ura. On the left is a statue of Mimi-nashi Hōichi (Earless Hōichi), the blind bard whose musical talents get him into trouble with ghosts in a story made famous by Lafcadio Hearn.

The bright vermilion shrine is between Karato and Hino-yama, about a five-minute walk from the Karato market area. From the station, get off the bus at the Akama-jingū-mae bus stop (¥260, 10 minutes).

Former British Consulate   HISTORIC BUILDING

(旧下関英国領事館, Kyu Shimonoseki Eikoku Ryōjikan; Map p498; ☎ 083-235-1906; www.kyu-eikoku-ryoujikan.com; 4-11 Karato-cho; ⏱ 9am-5pm Wed-Mon) FREE Built in 1906, this handsome example of Meiji architecture, one of the few such remaining original buildings in Japan (most were destroyed or relocated), is now a quaint little museum with a small (and very British!) cafe-pub-restaurant.

Hino-yama-kōen   PARK

(火の山公園; Map p498) About 5km northeast of Shimonoseki Station, this park has superb views over the Kanmon Straits from the top of 268m-high Hino-yama. To get to the lookout's **ropeway** (火の山ロープウエイ; Map p498; one-way/return ¥300/500; ⏱ 10am-

Shimonoseki

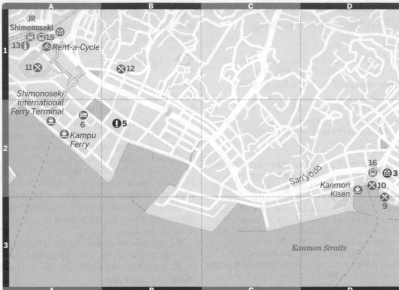

Shimonoseki

5pm Thu-Mon Mar-Nov), get off the bus at Mimosusōgawa (¥260, 12 minutes). From here it's a steep 10-minute walk to the ropeway entrance. There are also buses from Shimonoseki Station that drop you at the ropeway entrance at the Hino-yama ropeway stop (¥290, 15 minutes, hourly).

Kōzan-ji   BUDDHIST TEMPLE
(功山寺; ☎083-245-0258; 1-2-3 Chōfukawabata; ⊙9am-5pm) This National Treasure is the family burial temple of the local Mōri lords, and has a Zen-style hall dating from 1327, making it the oldest example of Zen Buddhist architecture in Japan. The narrow streets in the area nearby feature old walls and gates.

🎆 Festivals & Events

**Kanmon Straits
Fireworks Festival**   FIREWORKS
(Hanabi Taikai) A spectacular fireworks display occurring on both sides of the straits at the same time. Held on 13 August.

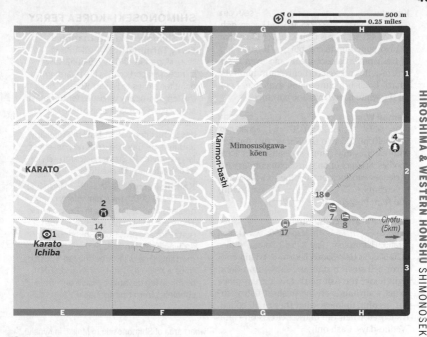

Sentei Festival CULTURAL

Held at Akama-jingū from 2 to 4 May to remember the Heike women who worked as prostitutes to pay for rites for their fallen relatives. On 3 May women dressed as Heian-era courtesans form a colourful procession at the shrine.

🛏 Sleeping

⭐Hinoyama Youth Hostel HOSTEL ¥

(火の山ユースホステル; Map p498; ☎083-222-3753; www.e-yh.net/shimonoseki; 3-47 Mimosusōgawa-chō; dm¥3300; ⊜@🛜) Amazing views of the straits and welcoming service make this one of the best youth hostels in western Honshū. You can take a bus from the station to Hino-yama Observatory (¥290, 15 minutes, hourly), from where it's a short walk. Note that the caretakers sometimes need to pop out – let them know if you're coming to drop off your bags.

Dormy Inn Shimonoseki HOTEL ¥¥

(ドーミーイン下関; Map p498; ☎083-223-5489; www.hotespa.net/hotels/shimonoseki; 3-40 Shinmachi; s/d from ¥6800/10,890; ⊜※@🛜) This modern hotel gets a vote for having a top-floor onsen, where you can look out over the straits and bathe under a *fugu*-shaped lantern. Rooms are stylish, though small, and

it's in a good central location. There's a courtesy shuttle to the station in the morning and from the station in the evening (though it's not far to walk).

Kaikyō View Shimonoseki HOTEL ¥¥¥

(海峡ビューしものせき; Map p498; ☎083-229-0117; www.kv-shimonoseki.com; 3-58 Mimosusogawa-chō; r per person with 2 meals from ¥11,800; P※🛜) Perched up on Hino-yama, Kaikyō View has professional service and the choice of Japanese- or Western-style rooms. Some of the Japanese-style rooms don't have private bathrooms. The hotel has a fabulous onsen with sea views – nonguests can also use it from 11am to 4pm Thursday to Tuesday (¥720, last entry 3pm).

🍴 Eating

For easy eating near the station, head to the upper floors of the **Sea Mall Shimonoseki** (Map p498; ☎083-232-4705; 4-8 Takezaki-chō; ⊙8am-9pm) shopping complex. There are restaurants serving local and international food, all with menus and displays in the windows.

There are a few cafes dotted around Chōfu.

Note that whale meat *(kujira)* is on the menu at many seafood places in Shimonoseki. Check for くじら or クジラ if you'd rather avoid it.

Kawaku SEAFOOD ¥
(河久; Map p498; ☑083-235-4129; 5-1 Karato; dishes ¥220-780, set menus from ¥500; ☺10am-6pm; 🅿) No puffed-up decor, but you'll catch lots of fresh pufferfish set meals and even a sea breeze at this relaxed corner restaurant on the wharf. English picture menu available. Look for the white *noren* over the entrances.

Kamon Wharf SEAFOOD ¥
(Map p498; ☑083-228-0330; 6-1 Karato-cho; ☺9am-10pm) Close to the Karato fish market, with eateries and shops specialising in local goodies. Seekers of only-in-Japan culinary experiences can look out for the *uni*-flavoured ice cream (うにソフトクリーム; sea urchin) and *fugu* burgers (ふぐバーガー).

Kaiten Karato Ichiba Sushi SUSHI ¥
(海転からと市場寿司; Map p498; www.kaiten karatoichibazusi.com; 2nd fl, 5-50 Karato; dishes ¥120-600; ☺11am-3pm & 5-9pm; 🅿) This conveyor-belt sushi restaurant on the 2nd floor, right above the fish market, is a great place to get your hands on the freshest fish without needing to know what they're all called. It's closed when the market closes on some Wednesdays. Cash only.

★ **Yabure-Kabure** SEAFOOD ¥¥¥
(やぶれかぶれ; Map p498; ☑083-234-3711; www.yaburekabure.jp; 2-2-5 Buzenda-chō; lunch sets ¥3240, dinner sets ¥5000-12,000; ☺11am-9pm) There's only one thing on the menu in this boisterous spot: pick from a range of *fugu* sets, such as the dinner Ebisu course, which features the cute little puffer in raw, seared, fried and drowned-in-sake incarnations, or a lunchtime *tetsuyaki setto* (set meal with grilled *fugu*). You can also order individual dishes. Look for the blue-and-white pufferfish outside.

ℹ Information

Shimonoseki Station Tourist Information Office (下関駅観光案内所; Map p498; ☑083-232-8383; www.city.shimonoseki.lg.jp; ☺9am-6pm) Just downstairs upon exiting the ticket barriers, opposite a supermarket.

Shin-Shimonoseki Station Tourist Information Office (☑083-256-3422; ☺9am-6pm) A small booth as you exit the ticket gates.

ℹ Getting There & Away

BOAT
Kanmon Kisen (Map p498; ☑083-222-1488; www.kanmon-kisen.co.jp) ferries run about every 20 minutes (6am to 9.29pm) from the Karato

SHIMONOSEKI–KOREA FERRY

The **Shimonoseki International Ferry Terminal** (下関港国際ターミナル; Map p498; ☑083-235-6052; www.shimonoseki-port.com) is the boarding point for ferries to Busan, Korea. Check the ferry company websites for the latest schedules. Companies also have offices inside the terminal. The port website also has some information, but isn't regularly updated. Shimonoseki has no passenger ferry services to Shanghai (cargo services only), though Osaka does.

Kampu Ferry (関金フェリー; Map p498; ☑083-224-3000; www.kampuferry.co.jp) operates the Shimonoseki–Busan ferry. There are daily departures at 7.45pm (gate closes 7pm) from Shimonoseki, arriving in Busan at 8am the following morning. One-way fares start at ¥9000 (plus a ¥300 fuel surcharge and ¥610 terminal fee payable by cash only at check-in) from Shimonoseki.

wharf area of Shimonoseki to Mojikō in Kyūshū (adult/child ¥400/200, five minutes).

TRAIN
JR Shimonoseki is the end of the San-yō line and connects to the San-in line, which runs north to Nagato and beyond along the Sea of Japan coast.

JR Shin-Shimonoseki *shinkansen* station is two stops from JR Shimonoseki (¥200, 10 minutes).

There's very little around the Shin-Shimonoseki Station area, and there's a long tunnel connecting the local lines to the *shinkansen* lines. Trains don't always connect well so be prepared for a long and boring wait between trains.

ℹ Getting Around

The main sights outside of the city centre are accessible by regular buses from the **train station** (Map p498). To reach the Karato wharf and fish market area, you can also take a pleasant 2km walk east following the water's edge. Shimonoseki is also great for cycling. Bikes can be hired from outside the station from a **booth** (Map p498; rental per day ¥500; ☺8am-7pm) in the car park beside the bus terminal area.

If you're taking more than a couple of bus rides in Shimonoseki, pick up a **one-day bus pass** (*ichinichi furī jōsha-ken*; ¥700) from the booth at the bus terminal outside the station or at the Karato bus terminal. It's good value – a trip to Chōfu and back alone normally costs more than ¥700 – and it saves you the hassle of paying coins each time you get off the bus.

Northern Honshū (Tōhoku)

Best Places to Eat

➜ Kosendō (p542)
➜ Kadare Yokochō (p531)
➜ Azumaya Honten (p515)
➜ Aji Tasuke (p508)
➜ Mitsutaya (p567)

Best Places to Sleep

➜ Komatsukan Kofu-tei (p511)
➜ Zao Shiki no Hotel (p549)
➜ Tsuru-no-yu Onsen (p544)
➜ Urashima (p560)
➜ Westin (p508)

Why Go?

Stretching out above Tokyo is the fabled Tōhoku (東北; 'northeast') – starring Miyagi, Yamagata, Iwate, Fukushima, Akita and Aomori prefectures – where ice monsters and river imps inhabit the imagination. Hugging the west coast is Niigata-ken, a skiing and hiking wonderland that also includes rugged and remote Sado Island (Sado-ga-shima).

Three national parks – alternating between thick mountain forests, stark volcanoes and coastal marshes – offer year-round outdoor pursuits, while the spectacular lakes Tazawa ko and Towada-ko welcome summertime swimmers. Sendai is the pick of the prefectural capitals for those seeking an urban fix.

Feudal-era remnants are well represented in numerous places – Hiraizumi and Kakunodate being the most historically notable – and traditional cultures are still alive and well.

This region suffered greatly in the 2011 earthquake and tsunami, and some coastal areas along the glorious Sanriku Kaigan, in particular, will welcome your visit as they continue to rebuild.

When to Go
Aomori

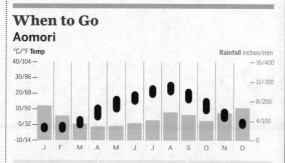

Dec–Feb Skiing galore, magnificent winter festivals and loads of mountain retreats.

Jun–Aug Dry summers, with a feast of food and cultural festivals, and lush green landscapes.

Sep & Oct Photographers and nature lovers flock here for spectacular displays of autumn foliage.

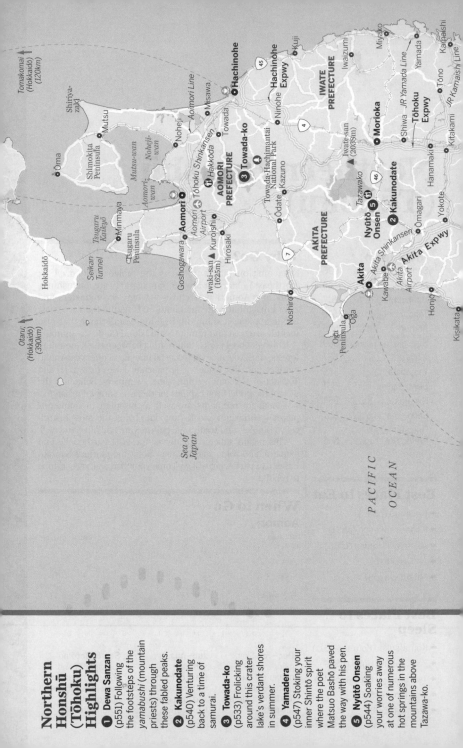

Northern Honshū (Tōhoku) Highlights

1 Dewa Sanzan
(p551) Following the footsteps of the *yamabushi* (mountain priests) through these fabled peaks.

2 Kakunodate
(p540) Venturing back to a time of samurai.

3 Towada-ko
(p533) Frolicking around this crater lake's verdant shores in summer.

4 Yamadera
(p547) Stoking your inner Shintō spirit where the poet Matsuo Bashō paved the way with his pen.

5 Nyūtō Onsen
(p544) Soaking your worries away at one of numerous hot springs in the mountains above Tazawa-ko.

6 Zaō Onsen

(p548) Dodging the 'ice monsters' at this pretty little onsen and ski town.

7 Matsushima

(p510) Whiling away a weekend by the beautiful bayside town of Matsushima.

8 Naeba (p564)

Honouring the site of the Fuji Rock Festival, and shredding the slopes come winter.

9 Hiraizumi

(p517) Feeling the feudal glory of this untouched Unesco site.

10 Sanriku Kaigan

(p522) Discovering one of Japan's much-loved coastal stretches in post-tsunami rebuild mode.

ℹ️ JR EAST PASS

The **JR East Pass** (www.jreast.co.jp/e/eastpass) now has two options: 'Niigata & Nagano' (¥17,000) or 'Tōhoku' (¥19,000). Both offer unlimited rail travel around Tokyo and their respective regions. It's cheaper than the full JR Pass and good for five flexible days in a two-week period. Exchange orders for passes must be purchased from selected agencies outside Japan and surrendered for the actual pass at the JR ticket windows of Narita Airport station or JR Travel Service Centres at major train stations. Passes are only valid for foreign passport holders on a temporary visitor visa and do not cover travel on JR buses.

History

Tōhoku has been populated since at least the Jōmon period (13,000–400 BC), but first entered historical records when, in the 8th century, the newly formed central government in Nara enlisted generals to subjugate the indigenous Emishi people. By the mid-9th century the land, then known as Michinoku (literally 'the land beyond roads'), was, if only tenuously, under imperial control.

In the 11th century the Ōshu Fujiwara clan established a short-lived settlement at Hiraizumi that was said to rival Kyoto in its opulence. However, it was the warrior and leader Date Masamune, in the 17th century, who would bring lasting notoriety to the region. Masamune transformed the fishing village of Sendai into the capital of a powerful domain. His descendants ruled until the Meiji Restoration brought an end to the feudal system, and an end to Tōhoku's influence, by restoring imperial control.

Blessed with rich alluvial plains, the coast along the Sea of Japan became an agricultural centre supplying rice to the imperial capital and, as a result, picked up more influence from Kyoto. Farming was less productive on the Pacific side, and the coastline rocky, wind-battered and difficult to navigate, resulting in a strong culture of perseverance born of hardship and isolation.

National Parks

Sprawling over Fukushima, Niigata and Yamagata Prefectures, **Bandai-Asahi National Park** (磐梯朝日国立公園), at 1870 sq km, is the third-largest protected area in Japan. The region is defined to the south by the Bandai-Azuma mountain range and to the north by the holy peaks of Dewa Sanzan.

The **Rikuchū-kaigan National Park** (陸中海岸国立公園) runs 180km along the Pacific coast, from Kuji in Iwate Prefecture to Kesennuma in Miyagi Prefecture. It is characterised by sheer cliffs, crashing waves and, to the south, deep inlets and rocky beaches.

Further north, the 855-sq-km **Towada-Hachimantai National Park** (十和田八幡平国立公園) is a vast wilderness area of beech forests, volcanic peaks, crater lakes and alpine plateaus that straddles Akita and Aomori Prefectures.

The Unesco-protected **Shirakami-sanchi** (白神山地) is a primeval beech forest, also on the Akita–Aomori border. One of the last of its kind in east Asia, it harbours a number of protected species, such as the Asiatic black bear and the golden eagle.

ℹ️ Getting There & Away

The JR Tōhoku *shinkansen* (bullet train) line travels as far as Aomori. From there, limited express and local trains run further north to Hokkaidō. The Akita and Yamagata *shinkansen* branches run through central Tōhoku to the Sea of Japan coast.

The JR Tōhoku main line follows roughly the same route as the Tōhoku *shinkansen*, but with regular local and express trains and only as far as Morioka, after which private lines take over. A combination of JR and private lines runs along the east and west coasts. This is the perfect place to upgrade to the Green Car if you're travelling on a JR Rail Pass as you'll almost always get a seat.

Buses are a much cheaper option for moving between the major cities, although smaller networks can be quite costly, particularly in remote areas. Renting a car is the most affordable and efficient way to get off the beaten track.

Decent domestic airports are found in Niigata, Sendai, Akita and Aomori.

ℹ️ Getting Around

Exploring the more remote parts of Tōhoku is possible on local trains and buses, but renting a car is a great way to cover destinations such as the Shimokita Peninsula, Towada-ko, Tazawa-ko and Sado-ga-shima, where stunning vistas beckon and driving those winding rural roads is just plain fun. Be sure to confirm your rental has GPS with English capabilities (most now do).

Have patience and *'go-yukkuri'* – take your time: speed limits are generally between 40km/h to 80km/h and there are many cautious, elderly drivers on roads in the region.

Tōhoku has a solid network of tolled expressways and well-maintained roads, signposted in romaji (romanised Japanese). Traffic is lighter than in central Honshū, although facilities can be more spread out. Driving between November and April can be subject to frequent road closures caused by heavy snow and ice, and is not recommended for those without appropriate driving experience.

The new **Treasureland Tōhoku Highway Bus Ticket** allows unlimited bus travel in and between Aomori, Akita, Iwate, Yamagata, Miyagi and Fukushima Prefectures on most major routes. Four-/seven-day tickets cost ¥10,000/13,000.

A number of novelty trains (p512) in this region can add the perfect mix of style and kitsch to your trip.

MIYAGI PREFECTURE 宮城県

Sendai, the capital of Miyagi-ken, is Tōhoku's largest, most happening city and a principle transit hub for the region – though it is nonetheless pretty laid-back and hassle-free. Venture outside the center city and things get rural pretty fast. Coastal Matsushima has some superb ocean-facing ryokan, which make a great base for exploring the rejuvenated post-tsunami coastline, while Naruko Onsen is a justifiably popular mountain escape.

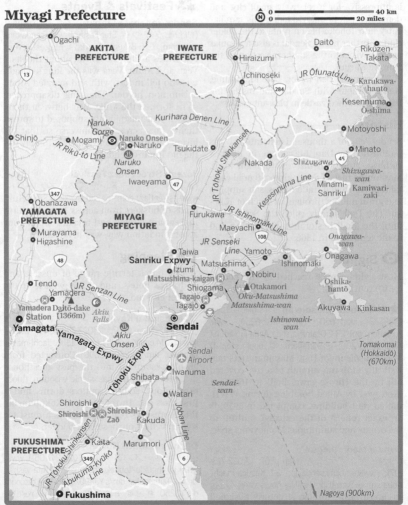

Miyagi Prefecture

🛏 Sleeping

Sendai has the best range of hotel accommodation in northern Honshū. Elsewhere, Naruko Onsen has many options for rural escapes, while Matsushima has a long tradition of high-quality, sea-facing ryokan.

Sendai 仙台

☎ 022 / POP 1,063,100

Sendai is a lively regional city and the pick of Tōhoku's urban centres. The city's wide, tree-lined streets fill up in summer for spectacular Tanabata Matsuri, one of Japan's most famous festivals. At other times, the nightlife district is impressive for a relatively small city, and domestic visitors enjoy making this familiar entry into Tōhoku life en route to the wilder climes further north. Sendai is also a popular base for visits to the southern section of the Sanriku Kaigan.

The samurai benefactor, Date Masamune, is synonymous with Sendai, and his lasting legacy is a ruined castle in pleasant gardens.

History

Sendai, 'city of a thousand generations', was established by Date Masamune in 1600. A ruthless, ambitious *daimyō* (domain lord), Masamune turned Sendai into a feudal capital that controlled trade routes, salt supplies and grain milling throughout much of Tōhoku. The Date family ruled the Sendai-han until the Meiji Restoration brought an end to the feudal era in 1868.

⊙ Sights

Most sights can be reached by the Loople (p510) tourist bus.

★ Zuihō-den Mausoleum HISTORIC BUILDING

(瑞鳳殿; Map p507; ☎ 022-262-6250; www.zuihoden.com; 23-2 Otamaya-shita, Aoba-ku; adult/child ¥550/200; ⊙9am-4pm; 🚌 Loople stop 4) The mausoleum of Date Masamune sits majestically atop the summit of a tree-covered hill by the Hirose-gawa. Built in 1637 but destroyed by Allied bombing during WWII, the current building, completed in 1979, is an exact replica of the original, faithful to the ornate and sumptuous Momoyama style.

Sendai Mediatheque LIBRARY

(仙台メディアテーク; Map p507; ☎ 022-713-3171; www.smt.city.sendai.jp; 2-1 Kasuga-machi, Aoba-ku; ⊙9am-10pm, gallery hours vary) FREE In an award-winning structure designed by Japanese architect Itō Toyō, this cultural hub includes a library, art galleries and event space. Check the website to see if anything is going on when you're in town.

Sendai Castle Ruins CASTLE

(仙台城跡; Map p507; ☎ 022-261-1111; www.sendaijyo.com; 1 Kawauchi, Aoba-ku; 🚌 Loople stop 6, regular bus stop 'Sendai Jō Ato Minami') Built on Aoba-yama in 1602 by Date Masamune and destroyed during Allied bombing, Sendai-jō still looms large over the city. Giant moss-covered walls, as imposing as they are impressive, are still intact and the grounds offer sweeping views over the city.

✸ Festivals & Events

Sendai Tanabata Matsuri CULTURAL

(仙台七夕まつり, Star Festival; www.sendaitanabata.com; ⊙6-8 Aug) Sendai's biggest event celebrates a Chinese legend about the stars Vega and Altair. Vega was the king's daughter who fell in love with and married Altair, a common herder. The king disapproved, so he formed the Milky Way between them. Once a year magpies are supposed to spread their wings across the universe so that the lovers can meet – traditionally on 7 July (on the old lunar calendar).

Jōzenji Street Jazz Festival MUSIC

(定禅寺ストリートジャズフェスティバル; www.j-streetjazz.com; ⊙2nd weekend Sep) Hundreds of buskers from across Japan perform in Sendai's streets and arcades. Book your accommodation way, way in advance.

🛏 Sleeping

Sendai has a terrific range of upscale and midrange hotels, and a fair whack at the budget end too.

★ Minshuku Keyaki MINSHUKU ¥

(民宿欅; Map p507; ☎ 022-796-4946; http://keyaki2014.com/english.html; 13-4 Tachi-machi, Aoba-ku; dm/d ¥2800/5600) Converted from an old restaurant into the best guesthouse in Sendai, Keyaki has sleek wooden floors throughout, stylish, spotless dorms and a first-class bar. In the heart of Kokubunchō, this represents real value and is a must for solo travellers or those on a budget.

Dōchū-an Youth Hostel HOSTEL ¥

(道中庵ユースホステル; ☎ 022-247-0511; www.jyh.or.jp/yhguide/touhoku/dochuan; 31 Kita-yashiki, Ōnoda, Taihaku-ku; dm/s ¥3890/4645, YHA discount dm ¥3250; 🅿 ☻ @ �{?}) You'll need some resolve

Central Sendai

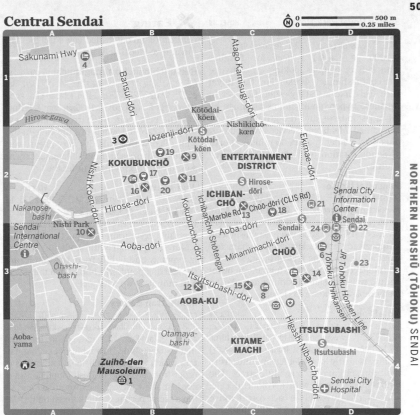

Central Sendai

to find this former farmhouse, but it's worth it. Go to Taishidō station (¥180, eight minutes from Sendai Station) on the JR Tōhoku line, from where it's a six-minute walk (get a map at the station). Trees surround the humble property, which has been cleverly designed to accommodate independent travellers on a budget. There's a fantastic cedar bath.

Sendai Royal Park Hotel
HOTEL ¥¥

(仙台ロイヤルパークホテル; ☏022-377-1111; www.srph.co.jp; 6-2-1 Teraoka, Izumi; d ¥14,000; P🅿️❄️🛜) Perfect for families with kids or couples looking for a luxurious, old-fashioned weekender, the Royal Park feels like a Gatsby-esque film set in Japanese hypercolour. Rooms are huge by Miyagi standards and the grounds beg to be roamed. Meals and service are fabulous, plus there's a day spa. It's 30 minutes north of Sendai Station (call ahead for the free shuttle).

Bansuitei Ikoiso
RYOKAN ¥¥

(晩翠亭いこい荘; Map p507; ☏022-222-7885; www.ikoisouryokan.co.jp; 1-8-31 Kimachi-dori, Aoba; per person ¥8500) The best traditional ryokan in town is a humble, good-value establishment. It appeals to those seeking a more character-filled abode than the typical business hotel. The old creaky floorboards, fragrant oil burners and well-kept shared bathrooms make it a memorable Japanese experience.

Hotel Foliage
HOTEL ¥¥

(ホテルフォーリッジ仙台; Map p507; ☏022-221-3939; www.libraryhotel.jp/hotelfoliage.html; 4-7-1 Chūō; s incl breakfast from ¥8000; ❄️🛜) Foliage is neatly located a few minutes from the train station on a busy little street. The lobby shares space with a colourful cafe, and silver feature walls in each corridor give the place an edge. Rooms feel like upmarket university dorms. Staff have a good handle on the local nightlife.

★ Westin
HOTEL ¥¥¥

(ウェスティンホテル仙台; Map p507; ☏022-722-1234; www.westin.com; 1-9-1 Ichiban-chō, Aoba-ku; r from ¥14,500; P🅿️❄️🛜) Set atop a chic shopping complex (with excellent restaurants and masseurs) on the main thoroughfare running through Sendai, the Westin is the best five-star chain hotel in the whole far north. The cocktail bar affords magnificent views, while the rooms themselves are decadently comfortable and as large as most posh suites.

Hotel Metropolitan Sendai
HOTEL ¥¥¥

(ホテルメトロポリタン仙台; Map p507; ☏022-268-2525; www.sendaimetropolitan.jp; 1-1-1 Chūō, Aoba-ku; s/d from ¥10,500/21,000; 😊@🛜) Impressive renovations lift the Metropolitan to clear-winner status among the train-station business hotels. The 'Japanese Suite Room' is the plushest, while the 'Character Room' is a child's cartoon wonderland.

✖ Eating

Gyūtan (charcoal-grilled cow's tongue) is a much-loved local delicacy.

Rikyu Ichibancho Yanagimachi
JAPANESE ¥

(牛たん炭焼 利久 一番町やなぎ町店; Map p507; ☏022-722-3550; 1-10-1 Ichiban-chō, Aoba-ku; dishes from ¥650; ⏱11.30am-3pm & 5-11pm; 🍴) The best *gyūtan* (charcoal-grilled cow's tongue) place in town is this tiny hole-in-the-wall filled with locals. It's very cheap, very fresh and there is an English-language menu so you don't accidentally order the tail.

Jogi Tofuten
VEGETARIAN ¥

(定義とうふ店; Map p507; ☏022-393-2035; 1-2 Okura, Aoba-ku; snacks from ¥400; ⏱11am-11pm) It's soybeans at every turn at this large tofu speciality restaurant in a quiet street in Aoba-ku and popular with students. Triangular, spongy and lightly fried, the tofu is only the starting point. Mix and match the sauces and mop it all up with glee.

Manhattan Bakery
BAKERY ¥

(マンハッタンベーカリー; Map p507; ☏022-208-5566; 1-7-18 Chūō, Aoba-ku; sandwiches from ¥380; ⏱7am-8pm) Japanese bakeries often make sugary, limp bread, but not so Manhattan, which whips up delicious sandwiches to order from a variety of fresh toppings. There are just a few tables, so expect to get and go (on a picnic perhaps). You'll find it off the Clis Rd shopping street (before Marble Rd).

Gengo Chaya
CAFE ¥

(源吾茶屋; Map p507; ☏022-222-2830; 1-1 Sakuragaoka-kōen, Aoba-ku; snacks from ¥350; ⏱11am-6pm; 🍴🍴) In business for 130 years, this teahouse is known for its *zunda-mochi*, pounded rice cakes topped with a jam made from fresh soybeans – a Sendai speciality. It's on the eastern edge of Nishi Park, with white *noren* (sunshade) curtains out front.

★ Ohisamaya
VEGETARIAN ¥¥

(おひさまや; Map p507; ☏022-224-8540; 4-8-17 Chūō, Aoba-ku; meals from ¥1200; ⏱11.30am-2.30pm Mon-Sat; 🍴) The vegetable curries, macrobiotic tofu and fresh, colourful salads are the highlights of this stalwart of healthy dining, which rotates its menu regularly from a library of cookbooks on display. The occasional fish product may sneak into view.

Aji Tasuke
JAPANESE ¥¥

(味太助; Map p507; ☏022-225-4641; www.aji-tasuke.co.jp; 4-4-13 Ichiban-chō, Aoba-ku; mains from ¥1470; ⏱11.30am-10pm Wed-Mon; 🍴) In a city of fans of charcoal-grilled cow tongue, this little *gyūtan* has been steadily among the top few for some time now. Perch at the counter to watch – and smell – the grilling in action. It's next to a small *torii* (shrine gate), and usually has a queue.

Jiraiya   IZAKAYA ¥¥
(地雷也; Map p507; ☎022-261-2164; www.jiraiya. com/pc; basement fl, 2-1-15 Kokubunchō, Aoba-ku; dishes from ¥1100; ⓧ5.30pm-late; 🖻) Named after a Song-era fantasy epic, this classic *izakaya* (Japanese pub-eatery) specialises in charcoal-grilled *kinki* (also called *kichiji*, or rockfish), which is nibbled by sake-sipping customers propped at the bar. Jiraiya's entrance is on a side street, marked by a giant red lantern.

Santarō   JAPANESE ¥¥¥
(三太郎; Map p507; ☎022-224-1671; www.san tarou.jp; 1-20 Tachi-machi, Aoba-ku; dishes from ¥1200, sets from ¥1700, kaiseki courses per person ¥8000-16,000; ⓧ11.30am-2pm & 5-10pm) Spectacular evening *kaiseki* (Japanese haute cuisine) courses and crunch-for-lunch tempura are served in this evocative traditional building in the heart of Kokubunchō. Best for dining with two or more.

🍷 Drinking & Nightlife

The Kokubunchō area is Tōhoku's largest entertainment district. It's noisy, slightly chaotic and bright, with everything from hole-in-the-wall bars and British-styled pubs to raging dancing clubs and seedy strip shows. Note that there are a fair number of hostess and host clubs here, as well as seemingly ordinary bars, that levy steep cover charges.

★ Peter Pan   BAR
(ロックカフェ　ピーターパン; Map p507; ☎022-264-1742; 2-6-1 Chōme, Kokubunchō) A music-loving father-and-son team runs this lounge-room-vibe 'rock' bar. Dad provides the soundtrack with his extensive, alternative-rock vinyl collection, while Son busies himself with the clientele. Coffee, booze, cake and conversation.

Craftsman Sendai   CRAFT BEER
(クラフトマン; Map p507; ☎050-7576-4480; http://craftsman-sendai.com; 1F, 2-2-38 Chūō, Aoba-ku; mains from ¥1300; ⓧ11.30am-1am) When there's a global trend, like craft beer, the Japanese are never far behind. This small Craftsman outlet (there are a few popping up around the country) combines casual Italian dining with Japan's independent beer scene.

Patrons prop at the bar or on leather seats around tiled tables and talk loudly over indie tunes and the regular chinking of glasses.

Gallo   BAR
(ガッロ; Map p507; ☎022-765-7493; 2-12-23 Kokubunchō, Aoba-ku; cover charge ¥500; ⓧ7pm-2am, closed irregularly) Bar Gallo is a tiny basement bar that keeps the tempo low and slow and mixes fruit-infused cocktails with a Japanese twist. Our pick is the lemon-and-ginger-spiked *umeshū* (plum wine, ¥650). The city's more eclectic DJs play smooth beats on rotation. Look out for special party nights and you're likely to make more friends than at a regular Kokubunchō superclub.

Club Luxs   CLUB
(ラックスセンダイ; Map p507; ☎0222-16-3921; www.luxs-sendai.com; 14-3 Tachi-machi; ⓧ9pm-late Thu-Sun) This is a great place to see Japanese club music in all its bouncy, uptempo brilliance. Lots of MCs, drum machines and glow sticks, and frenetic clubbers hidden under hoodies.

ℹ Information

Sendai City Hospital (仙台市立病院; Map p507; ☎022-266-7111, 24hr emergency hotline 022-216-9960; http://hospital.city.sendai. jp; 3-1 Shimizu-kōji, Wakabayashi-ku; ⓧoutpatient service 8.30-11.30am Mon-Fri)

Sendai City Information Center (仙台市観光案内所; Map p507; ☎022-222-4069; www. sentabi.jp; 2nd fl, JR Sendai Station; ⓧ8.30am-7pm) Pick up English maps and brochures here.

Sendai International Centre (仙台国際センター; Map p507; ☎022-265-2471; www.sira. or.jp/icenter/english/index.html; Aoba-yama, Aoba-ku; ⓧ9am-8pm) English-speaking staff, plus an international newspaper library and bulletin board.

ℹ Getting There & Away

AIR

From Sendai airport, 18km south of the city centre, flights head for Tokyo, Osaka, Nagoya, Hiroshima, Sapporo and many other destinations.

The Sendai Kūkō Access line leaves for the airport from Sendai Station roughly every 20 minutes (¥630, 25 minutes).

BOAT

From the port of Sendai-kō, **Taiheyo Ferry** (☎022-263-9877; www.taiheiyo-ferry.co.jp/ english/index.html) has one daily ferry to Tomakomai on Hokkaidō (from ¥7200, 15 hours), and three to four ferries per week to Nagoya (from ¥6700, 22 hours).

NORTHERN HONSHŪ (TŌHOKU) MATSUSHIMA

ⓘ SENDAI MARUGOTO PASS

The **Sendai Marugoto Pass** (仙台まるごとパス; adult/child ¥2670/1330) covers unlimited travel for two days on the **Loople** tourist bus, Sendai subway, and area trains and buses going as far as Matsushima-kaigan, Akiu Onsen and Yamadera (in Yamagata Prefecture). Pick one up at JR Sendai Station.

Buses leave from stop 34 at Sendai Station for Sendai-kō (¥530, 40 minutes), but only until 6pm.

BUS

Highway buses depart from the West Bus Terminal outside the east exit of the train station, and connect Sendai to major cities throughout Honshū. Purchase tickets at the **JR Tōhoku Bus Center** (Map p507; ☎022-256-6646; www.jrbustohoku.co.jp; ⊙6.50am-7.30pm), next to bus stop 42.

CAR & MOTORCYCLE

The Tōhoku Expressway (東北自動車道) runs between Tokyo and the greater Sendai area. **Toyota Rent a Car** (Map p507; ☎022-293-0100; https://rent.toyota.co.jp; 1-5-3 Tsutsujigaoka, Miyagino-ku; ⊙8am-8pm) has an office a few blocks east of the train station.

TRAIN

The JR Tōhoku *shinkansen* runs hourly between Tokyo and Sendai (¥11,200, two hours), and between Sendai and Morioka (¥6460, 45 minutes).

There are several daily *kaisoku* (rapid trains) on the JR Senzan line between Sendai and Yamagata (¥1140, 1¼ hours), via Yamadera (¥840, one hour). Local trains on the JR Senseki line connect Sendai and Matsushima-kaigan (¥410, 35 minutes); make sure to get one going all the way to Takagi-machi, or you'll have to transfer at Higashi-Shiogama.

ⓘ Getting Around

The **Loople** (Map p507; single ride/day pass ¥250/600) tourist trolley leaves from the west bus pool's stop 15-3 every 30 minutes from 9am to 4pm, making a useful loop around the city in a clockwise direction.

Sendai's single subway line runs from Izumichūō in the north to Tomizawa in the south, but doesn't cover any tourist attractions; single tickets cost ¥200 to ¥350.

Matsushima 松島

☎022 / POP 14,733

Matsushima is heavily romanticised by Japanese travellers due to its status as one of Japan's Three Great Sights (Nihon Sankei).

It was also immortalised by the poet Matsuo Bashō who revered its glorious bay's 260-odd pine-covered islands, battered by wind and sea to form a kind of Zen rock garden in the ocean. When the sun sets and a storm rolls in, the effect on the islands is mesmerising. The main village itself has some fine ancient temples, impressive ryokan, seafood shacks and a quaint by-the-sea feel. Try to avoid the high-summer weekend crowds.

◉ Sights & Activities

Matsushima-kaigan, where the sights are, is really a small village, easily navigated on foot.

Zuigan-ji　　BUDDHIST TEMPLE
(瑞巌寺; ¥700; ⊙8am-5pm Apr-Sep, closes earlier Oct-Mar) Tōhoku's finest Zen temple, Zuigan-ji was established in AD 828. The present buildings were constructed in 1606 by Date Masamune to serve as a family temple. Zuigan-ji is undergoing a major restoration that will take until 2019 to complete. As a result, some buildings are closed and others are sheathed in tarps, though it's possible to enter them. Still open is the excellent **Seiryūden** (temple museum), which has a number of well-preserved relics from the Date family, including national treasures.

The temple is 500m north of Matsushima-kaigan Station. Follow the signs.

Godai-dō　　BUDDHIST TEMPLE
(五大堂) Date Masamune constructed this small wooden temple in 1604. Although it stands on an island in the bay, connected to the mainland by a short bridge, it was miraculously untouched by the 2011 tsunami. The temple doors open to the public only once every 33 years (next in 2039). Come instead for the sea views and to see the 12 animals of the Chinese zodiac carved on the eaves.

Godai-dō is located in the park across from Matsushima-kaigan Station, about a 600m walk, past the boat wharves.

Fuku-ura-jima　　ISLAND
(福浦島; ¥200; ⊙8am-5pm Mar-Oct, to 4.30pm Nov-Feb) You can't miss the 252m-long red wooden bridge connecting Fuku-ura-jima to the mainland. The shady trails here, which wind along the coast through native pines and a botanic garden, make for a pleasant hour-long stroll.

Matsushima-wan　　CRUISE
(松島湾; www.matsushima.or.jp; adult/child ¥1500/750; ⊙9am-3pm) To get a sense of the scale of the bay and its dense cluster of

pine-topped islands, which sit like so many bonsai floating in a giant's backyard pond, cruise boats depart hourly from the central ferry pier, completing a 50-minute loop. Between April and October, you can opt for a longer course (¥2700, 1¾ hours) that goes all the way to Oku-Matsushima.

🛏 Sleeping & Eating

There are numerous charming Japanese-style hotels and coastal ryokan here, but mostly at the top end of the price scale.

Matsushima has a few fine casual restaurants near the ferry terminal; otherwise, eat at your accommodation.

Minshuku Kami-no-Ie　　　　　MINSHUKU ¥
(☑ 0225-88-4141; 16-1 Mura, Miyato, Higashi-Matsushima; per person incl 2 meals ¥8000; P ❄ @) This simple inn has become a symbol of post-tsunami sustainable tourism in the small community of Higashi-Matsushima, which bore the full force of the 2011 disaster. The six tatami-mat rooms are bright and airy, while the seafood dinners are salty fresh. If it's full, ask about possible farmstays in the region.

★ Komatsukan Kofu-tei　　　　RYOKAN ¥¥¥
(松島小松館 好風亭; ☑ 0223-54-5065; 35-2 Matsushima; per person incl 2 meals ¥29,000; P ❄ 🛜) This classy seaside ryokan/hotel has inimitable, understated Japanese style. Rooms are exercises in balance and modernism, with artworks and homewares to fill a designer catalogue. The outdoor onsen is comfortable, though relatively small, but the foot bath overlooking the bay provides a special travel moment. The *kaiseki* (Japanese haute cuisine) meals are as good as anything you'll find on your travels.

Santori Chaya　　　　　　　JAPANESE ¥
(さんとり茶屋; ☑ 050-5796-4571; 24-4 1 Senzui; meals from ¥980; ⏱ 11.30am-3pm & 5-10pm Thu-Tue) Perennial local favourites from land and sea such as *kaisen-don* (mixed sashimi on rice) and *gyūtan* (chargrilled cow's tongue) feature here, along with seasonal specialities such as Matsushima's famous oysters. Seating is on floor cushions on the 2nd level; get a table by the window. It's in a beige building with an indigo banner and has a picture menu.

🛍 Shopping

Matsushima Yukitakeya　　GIFTS & SOUVENIRS
(松島雪竹屋; ☑ 0223-54-2612; 109-Senzui; ⏱ 10am-5.30pm) Opposite the ferry terminal

---

OFF THE BEATEN TRACK

OKU-MATSUSHIMA

Oku-Matsushima (奥松島) is a geographically stunning peninsula 20km southwest of Matsushima proper, which was devastated by the 2011 tsunami. It's still possible to visit Ōtakamori (大高森), a hill in the middle of the peninsula's main island (Miyato Island) that offers stunning views of the bay. The 20-minute trek up and down is highly recommended, but only if you have a rental car to get there (you can drive across an access bridge) – public transport has all but ceased.

---

is this chic bakery and gift shop selling handmade jewellery and homewares, and delicious baked goodies, including hand-sized rice crackers.

ℹ Information

Tourist Information Center (松島観光協会; ☑ 022-354-2263; www.matsushima-kanko. com; Matsushima-kaigan Station; ⏱ 9.30am-4.30pm Mon-Fri, 8.30am-5pm Sat & Sun) At the train station, come here for English brochures, accommodation bookings and the latest info on Oku-Matsushima.

ℹ Getting There & Away

Frequent trains on the JR Senseki line connect Sendai and Matsushima-kaigan (¥410, 35 minutes).

Sights are at Matsushima-kaigan Station, not Matsushima Station – an easy mistake. To confuse further, Matsushima is on the Jōban line (Sendai, platform 3), while Matsushima-kaigan is on the Senseki line (Sendai, platform 10 – *jūban*, in Japanese).

The service between Takagi-machi and Rikuzen-Ono reopened in 2015 after significant rebuilding.

By road, Matsushima can be reached from Sendai via the Sanriku Expressway (三陸自動車道).

Ishinomaki　　　　石巻
☑ 0225 / POP 145,805

Ishinomaki is the largest city on the Sanriku Coast, a beautiful stretch that was decimated by the 2011 tsunami. Many travellers move on quickly, but this easily accessible place is a shining example of creative urban renewal in post-disaster Japan – loads of hip new businesses have opened up – and it certainly rewards a longer visit.

◉ Sights

Ishinomori Mangattan Museum MUSEUM
(石ノ森萬画館; ☑ 0225-96-5055; 2-7 Nakase; adult/child ¥800/200; ⊙ 9am-5pm) This popular manga (Japanese comics) museum's other-worldly spaceship structure survived the tsunami largely intact, while the collection has since been restored and rejuvenated. The work of influential *manga-ka* (cartoonist) and local hero Shōtarō Ishinomori, most famous for creating the *Cyborg 009* and *Kamen Rider* series, is the star attraction here. It's a 20-minute walk from the train station.

Hiyori-yama Kōen PARK
(日和山公園) In the hills above Ishinomaki, 56m above sea level, this beautiful park stands on the site of the former Ishinomaki castle. Offering sweeping views over the city, it's a wonderful spot to relax. On a more sombre note, it's also the best vantage point to comprehend the scale of the 2011 tsunami's destruction.

⌸ Sleeping & Eating

There's only a handful of decent places to stay, mostly business hotels near the station, but a few guesthouses are starting to emerge. Ask at the Tourist Information Center for the latest

---

TŌHOKU'S NOVELTY TRAINS

Tetsudō otaku (train geeks) will love a ride on one of a number of colourful themed trains that have been launched in Tōhoku. These sleek 'joyful' trains offer travellers a novel and stylish way of flitting about the countryside. Best of all, they can be boarded with a standard JR Pass or JR East Pass (subject to seat availability) for no extra cost. If you don't have one of those, then just pay the usual fare between the two destinations. Either way, you can book your seat at any JR office. Visit www.jreast.co.jp/e/joyful/index.html for a full listing of novelty trains, including times and routes. Following are our personal favourites:

Resort Shirakami If you plan to travel from Akita to Aomori, consider making the ocean-facing, three-hour journey on the wondrous *Resort Shirakami* (¥3350). The beechwood interior is light and spacious, allowing maximum viewing of the Sea of Japan. Trains leave Akita at 8.20am, 10.40am and 2.17pm. From Aomori, go at 8.10am or 1.51pm.

Toreiyu Tsubasa Cut through the stunning Yamagata mountains with your feet in a hotspring bath (advanced reservation needed), or seated on a tatami floor sipping local sake. Trains (¥4940) depart Fukushima at 10.02am and return from Shinjo at 3pm.

FruiTea Fukushima This fruit-themed train-cafe on wheels travels six times a day from Kōriyama to Aizu-Wakamatsu (¥1140). Sip citrus teas, eat fruit-laden cake or just crunch an apple and enjoy the colourful ride. Trains leave Kōriyama at 9.41am and 12.44pm for the 90-minute trip. You can also catch a train from Aizu-Wakamatsu at 11.08am and 3.06pm.

SL Ginga A very special SL Ginga series steam locomotive has recommenced service along the route from Hanamaki to Kamaishi (¥1680) via Tōno, inspired by the novel *Night on the Galactic Railroad*. The design is reminiscent of the Meiji era with soft leather lounges, period photographs and decorative brass awnings. Trains depart Hanamaki at 10.37am (4½ hours) or leave the other way from Kamaishi at 10.55am.

Genbi Shinkansen Art and/or train lovers should check out the *Genbi Shinkansen* 'art train', which operates between Niigata and Echigo-Yuzawa (¥5380) six times daily. It's a short and fast ride featuring a contemporary art gallery, a children's art area and a stylish stand-up cafe-bar. Trains depart Echigo-Yuzawa at 8.24am, 12.44pm and 3.20pm, or from Niigata at 11.26am, 2.02pm and 6.18pm.

Pokemon Train From the cartoon exterior to the extensive on-board playground facilities, this one is squarely for the kids. It runs once daily from Ichinoseki to Kesennuma (¥2960) and back again. Leaves Ichinoseki at 11.05am and Kesennuma at 3.08pm.

Tōhoku Emotion There's train travel and then there's *train* travel: this stunning service running daily between Hachinohe and Kuji (¥4430) definitely falls into the latter category. Gourmet cuisine is served and the decor and service are worthy of far higher fares. The service was initiated as a way to attract travellers back to the tsunami-affected region and your patronage is graciously welcomed. Leaves from Hachinohe at 11.05am or Kuji at 2.20pm.

listings. While you're there, pick up a copy of *Ishinomaki Navi*, which has up-to-date listings of the many pop-up cafes around town.

Long Beach House GUESTHOUSE ¥
(ロングビーチハウス; ☎ 0225-98-4714; http://longbeachhouse.wixsite.com/lbh314/; 47-1 Watanoha Hamasone-no-ichi; dm/s/d from ¥2200/3800/5500; P �) Part of the new generation of socially conscious creatives setting up shop in Ishinomaki, the folk at Long Beach House have built a minimalist guesthouse with a terrific boho vibe. On-site is a Japanese and modern Spanish restaurant serving stiff cocktails, which may seduce you to stay over.spcnd the night.

Cho-de-Burger BURGERS ¥
(☎ 080-6006-9054; 8-9 Chūō 2-chōme; burgers from ¥800; ⊙ 10am-9pm) Beautiful young things play soulful tunes and flip juicy burgers at this shiny silver van-cafe on the river, part of a pop-up food/entertainment area called Common. It's quite the recipe and their upbeat approach typifies the mood at street level.

ⓘ Information

Tourist Information Center (石巻観光案内所; ☎ 0225-93-6448; www.i-kanko.com; ⊙ 9am-5.30pm) Inside the JR train station.

ⓘ Getting There & Away

A rapid service on the JR Senseki line connects Sendai and Ishinomaki (¥840, one hour). Direct highway buses also leave for Ishinomaki roughly twice an hour from stop 33 in front of Sendai Station (¥800, 1½ hours).

Naruko Onsen 鳴子温泉

☎ 0229 / POP 8000
A lovely day trip or overnighter from Sendai, Naruko Onsen is a rural town known for the magnificent Naruko Gorge and nine distinct hot springs, whose waters have different compositions of minerals and thus different healing qualities.

🏃 Activities

★ Taki-no-yu ONSEN
(滝の湯; ¥150; ⊙ 7.30am-10pm) This fabulously atmospheric wooden bathhouse has hardly changed in 150 years and is a sheer delight. Water gushes in from *hinoki* (cypress) channels, carrying with it various elements and minerals including sulphur, sodium bicarbonate and sodium chloride. This onsen is

particularly famous for its therapeutic relief of high blood pressure and hardened arteries.

Naruko Gorge HIKING
(鳴子峡, Naruko-kyō) Northwest of Naruko town, this 100m-deep gorge is particularly spectacular in the fall when the leaves change colour. The trail leading to the gorge from town has been closed for repairs for some time, but should reopen in 2017. There's an alternative course though, which takes about an hour to loop around two bridges.

The latter trail can be reached from Nakayama-daira Onsen Station, which is a short bus trip from Naruko Onsen Station (¥180, five minutes), or an easy, well-signed walk. This path also intersects with a 10km stretch of the old foot highway, walked by the haiku poet Matsuo Bashō, which is now a hiking trail. Pick up maps and the latest trail info at the Tourist Information Center.

🛏 Sleeping & Eating

You can eat a decent meal at one of the restaurants near the train station, or at the cafe at the Tourist Information Center. If you're sleeping over, fine meals will be included.

Ryokan Onuma RYOKAN ¥¥
(旅館大沼; ☎ 0229-83 3052; www.ohnuma.co.jp/en; 34 Narukonsen Akayu, Osaki; per person incl 2 meals from ¥14,000; ✴ email) Alight the train at Naruko Goten-yu and walk 500m west until you reach this peaceful ryokan with an indefatigable staff who will soak, feed and replenish you in style. Each room has access to its own private onsen bath, plus there is an outdoor onsen on the forest floor. Rooms are large and spotless.

Yusaya Ryokan RYOKAN ¥¥
(ゆさや旅館; ☎ 0229-83-2565; www.yusaya.co.jp; 84 Yumoto; r per person incl 2 meals from ¥14,800; P email) Among the many charms of this country inn is its impressive *rotemburo* (outdoor bath) in an isolated building surrounded by a dense thicket of trees. The main building, dating to 1936, has tatami-lined sleeping quarters separated from Western-style sitting areas by sliding *shoji* (rice-paper screens). Meals are elegant banquets of river fish and mountain vegetables.

ⓘ Information

Tourist Information Center (鳴子観光・旅館案内センター; ☎ 0229-83-3441; www.naruko.gr.jp; ⊙ 8.30am-6pm) Located just outside the train station.

❶ NORTHERN TŌHOKU WELCOME CARD

The **Northern Tōhoku Welcome Card** offers discounts on admission, lodging and even transport from participating vendors – identified by a red-and-white Welcome Card sticker – in Iwate, Aomori and Akita Prefectures. Pick one up at most JR stations in these regions. Its use is technically restricted to foreign travellers staying in Japan for less than a year.

❶ Getting There & Away

There is an hourly service on the JR Tōhoku *shinkansen* (bullet train) between Sendai and Furukawa (¥3220, 15 minutes). The JR Tōhoku line also runs regular services from Sendai to Furukawa via Kogota (¥920, one hour). Hourly trains run on the JR Rikū-tō line between Furukawa and Naruko Onsen (¥670, 45 minutes).

IWATE PREFECTURE 岩手県

There are few physical reminders of the pre-eminent, turbulent position of Iwate-ken in Japanese feudal history – aside from the glorious temples of Hiraizumi – but its stature as the country's second-largest prefecture suggests a hefty natural environment to explore. Sleepy valleys, a rugged coastline and some pretty serious mountains attract discerning hikers and those looking for a village-change, but it's perhaps the Tōno valley, where countless folk tales are still born and told, where travellers glimpse that all-too-rare Lost Japan.

The coastal communities here have re-grouped admirably since the Great East Earthquake and those with their own wheels, or travelling on slow trains, will be rewarded with glorious sunrises and welcoming hosts.

🛏 Sleeping

Morioka has the usual cluster of similar business hotels, but most travellers opt for the traditional ryokan and guesthouses in the gorgeous Tōno valley.

Morioka 盛岡

🎵 019 / POP 299.169

Three rivers flow through Morioka, an attractive park commands attention near the centre, and Iwate-san stands proudly in the background, but the prefectural capital is fairly unremarkable for visitors, aside from its convenience as a transport hub and range of smart noodle restaurants. Morioka is also known for its cast-iron artisan work.

◉ Sights

Rock-Splitting Cherry Tree   LANDMARK
(石割桜; Ishiwari-zakura; Map p516) A few blocks north of Iwate-kōen, in front of the Morioka District Court, is this much-loved local attraction: a 300-year-old cherry tree, which sprouted from the crack in a huge granite boulder. There is still some conjecture over whether or not the tree actually grew through the wall; we suspect otherwise.

🛏 Sleeping

A few business hotels near the train station are convenient and welcoming.

Hotel Ace Morioka   BUSINESS HOTEL ¥¥
(ホテルエース盛岡; Map p516; ☑034-510-8651; www.hotel-ace.co.jp; 2-11-35 Chūō-dōri; s/d from ¥6000/8000; ❂❄🛜) This hotel is newly renovated and pretty stylish, despite having some of the pokiest rooms known to travel writers! The lobby and bathrooms are very spiffy, while management bows to your every need (well, even more so than usual in Japan). It's a 10-minute walk east of the train station.

Kumagai Ryokan   RYOKAN ¥¥
(熊ヶ井旅館; Map p516; ☑019-651-3020; www.kumagairyokan.com; 3-2-5 Ōsawakawara; s/d ¥5000/9000; ❂@🛜) Morioka is no tourist destination, but travellers will find reason to linger in this spacious ryokan surrounded by a pleasant garden filled with various folk crafts. The communal areas are kitschy cool and there's a neat *iwa-buro* (rock bath) for evening soaks. The inn is located about 800m east of the train station (behind the church).

Hotel Shion   HOTEL ¥¥¥
(ホテル紫苑; ☑019-689-2288; www.aishinkan.co.jp/shion_e; 74-2 Yunotate, Tsunagi; per person incl 2 meals ¥29,000; P❄🛜) In a very attractive setting overlooking Gosho Lake 14km west of Morioka, Hotel Shion is a decadent onsen hotel catering largely to groups. The rest of us won't be denied its real charms though; enjoy the multiple bathing options and the well-organised Western- and Japanese-style rooms. Meals are phenomenal. Pick-ups can be arranged from JR Morioka Station.

Iwate Prefecture

🍴 Eating

Noodle fans note: Morioka has some delicious and unusual varieties, including *wanko-soba* (わんこそば), buckwheat noodles served in tiny wooden bowls. Eating them is like a competition between you and the waiter, who'll top up your bowl faster than you can say you're full.

Prefer to savour at your own pace? Try *jaja-men* (じゃじゃめん), udon-like noodles heaped with cucumber, miso paste and ground meat (add vinegar, spicy oil and garlic to taste).

Karē Kōbō Chalten JAPANESE CURRY ¥
(カレー工房チャルテン; Map p516; ☎019-651-1223; 1-8-1 Nakanohashi-dōri; curries from ¥850; ⏱11.30am-3pm & 6-8pm Mon-Sat) Serving the best curry we tried in the whole of northern Japan, this small, charming curry house makes nothing else but creamy plates of curry, and rice and salad. The wonderful vegetarian option uses eight different vegetables diced to a near pulp. Choose your heat from one to five (three was pretty intense!). The *masala chai* (¥400) goes well.

Pairon Honten UDON ¥
(白龍本店; Map p516; ☎019-624-2247; 5-15 Uchi-maru; noodles from ¥350; ⏱9am-9pm Mon-Sat, 11.30am-6pm Sun) *Jaja-men* (flat noodle with miso and minced meat) joints are all over town, but this hole-in-the wall icon is still the leader. Ordering is a breeze: just ask for *shō* (small), *chū* (medium) or *dai* (large). When you're finished, crack a raw egg (¥50) into the bowl and the staff will add hot soup and more of that amazing miso paste.

On a side street, you'll know you've found it when you find the queue.

Azumaya Honten SOBA ¥¥
(東屋本店; Map p516; ☎019-622-2252; www.wankosoba-azumaya.co.jp; 1-8-3 Nakanohashi-dōri; wanko-soba from ¥2700; ⏱11am-8pm; 🅿)

Morioka

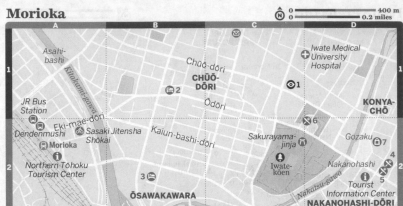

Morioka

◉ Sights
1 Rock-Splitting Cherry Tree.................C1

⬤ Sleeping
2 Hotel Ace Morioka............................B1
3 Kumagai Ryokan...............................B2

✖ Eating
4 Azumaya Honten...............................D2
5 Karē Kōbō Chalten............................D2
6 Pairon Honten..................................D2

◉ Shopping
7 Kamasada Honten.............................D2

Customers line up and tour buses roll in for this hugely popular *wanko-soba* restaurant. A Morioka tradition, the waiter refills your tiny bowl with *soba* (buckwheat noodles) as soon as you've put the last one down. Fifteen bowls equal one ordinary bowl – but the average customer puts away 50 (and 100, or 200, is not unheard of).

🛍 Shopping

Gozaku, the area just east of the Nakatsu-gawa, is the old merchants' district, now home to craft studios and cafes.

Kamasada Honten   HOMEWARES
(釜定本店; Map p516; ☑019-622-3911; 2-5 Kon-ya-chō; ⊙9am-5.30pm Mon-Sat) Morioka is known for its *nanbu tekki* (cast ironware), notably tea kettles. There are some beautiful examples at this venerable old shop, along with more affordable items, such as wind chimes and incense holders.

ℹ Information

Iwate Medical University Hospital (岩手医科大学附属病院; Map p516; ☑24hr emergency hotline 019-651-5111; www.iwate-med.ac.jp/hospital; 19-1 Uchi-maru; ⊙outpatient services 8.30-11am & 1-4pm Mon-Fri)

Northern Tōhoku Tourism Center (北東北観光センター; Map p516; ☑019-625-2090; ⊙9am-5pm) Located on the 2nd floor of JR Morioka Station, with English speakers and help available to book accommodation.

Tourist Information Center (盛岡観光コンベンション協会; Map p516; ☑019-604-3305; www.hellomorioka.jp; 2nd fl, Odette Plaza, 1-1-10 Nakanohashi-dōri; ⊙9am-6pm, closed 2nd Tue of month; ☎) The friendly staff near the Nakanohashi district speak some English and are happy to welcome you to Morioka.

ℹ Getting There & Away

BUS

Regional buses depart from the JR Bus Station (Map p516), which is outside the east exit of the train station, and connect Morioka with Sendai (¥2890, 2½ hours) and Hirosaki (¥2980, 2¼ hours). Night buses depart for Tokyo (¥7870, 7½ hours) also from the east exit.

CAR & MOTORCYCLE

If you're driving, the Tōhoku Expressway (東北自動車道) runs between Tokyo and the greater Morioka area.

TRAIN

There are hourly *shinkansen* on the JR Tōhoku line between Tokyo and Morioka (¥14,740, 2½ hours), and Morioka and Shin-Aomori (¥6130, 1¼ hours).

Frequent trains run on the JR Akita *shinkansen* line between Morioka and Akita (¥4620, 1½ hours) via Tazawa-ko (¥2030, 30 minutes) and Kakunodate (¥2840, 50 minutes). The local Tazawa-ko line covers the same route in about twice the time for around half the price; you may need to transfer at Ōmagari.

❶ Getting Around

The charmingly named Dendenmushi ('electric transmission bug') tourist trolley makes a convenient loop around town (single ride/day pass ¥250/600), departing in a clockwise direction from stop 15 in front of JR Morioka Station (anticlockwise from stop 16) between 9am and 7pm.

Bicycles can be rented from **Sasaki Jitensha Shōkai** (佐々木自転車商会; Map p516; ☑ 019-624-2692; 10-2 Morioka Eki-mae-dōri; per hr/day ¥200/1000; ⊗ 8.30am-6pm), near JR Morioka Station.

Hiraizumi 平泉

☑ 0191 / POP 8000

Tōhoku's first Unesco World Heritage listing, Hiraizumi is a handsome feudal town with architectural remnants courtesy of the gold-mining Ōshu Fujiwara clan who ruled here throughout the 12th century. Dedicated to the principles of Buddhism, the town has been thoughtfully integrated into the natural surrounds. While feudal strife eventually brought the town's demise, visitors will appreciate its understated charm.

History

Hiraizumi's fate is indelibly linked to that of Japan's favourite tragic hero, Minamoto-no-Yoshitsune. A great warrior, he earned the jealous contempt of his elder half-brother – Japan's first shogun, Minamoto-no-Yoritomo – and fled east, eventually taking refuge at Hiraizumi in 1187. This gave Yoritomo the perfect excuse to attack, resulting in both the defeat of the Ōshu Fujiwara and the death of Yoshitsune. Yoritomo was said to be so impressed with the temples of Hiraizumi that he allowed them to remain, and it was the Kamakura shogunate (military government) that later sponsored the construction of the first wooden hall to protect the Konjiki-dō mausoleum.

◎ Sights

★ **Chūson-ji** BUDDHIST TEMPLE
(中尊寺; Map p518; ☑ 0191-46-2211; www.chusonji.or.jp/en; adult/child ¥800/300; ⊗ 9am-5pm) Established in AD 850 by the priest Ennin, this complex was expanded by the Ōshu Fujiwara

family in the 12th century. A total of 300 buildings with 40 temples were constructed. Ironically, the family's grand scheme to build a Buddhist utopia was destroyed when a massive fire ravaged nearly everything in 1337. Only two of the original constructions, the Konjiki-dō and Kyōzō, remain alongside more recent reconstructions. The sprawling site is reached via a steep cedar-lined avenue.

Konjiki-dō BUDDHIST TEMPLE
(金色堂, Golden Hall; Map p518; ⊗ 8am-4.30pm Apr-Oct, 8.30am-4pm Nov-Mar) With gilding up to its eaves, elaborate lacquerwork and mother-of-pearl inlay, the Konjiki-dō was at the cutting edge of Heian-era artistry when it was created in 1124 – and it still impresses today. Beneath the three altars are the mummified remains of three generations of the Ōshu Fujiwara family. Given Hiraizumi's unlucky history, it seems a miracle that the Konjiki-dō has survived. To avoid tempting fate, the pavilion is now behind glass inside a fireproof enclosure.

The adjacent treasury (讃衡蔵; Sankōzō) contains the coffins and funeral finery of the Fujiwara clan – scrolls, swords and images transferred here from long-vanished halls and temples.

Kyōzō BUDDHIST TEMPLE
(経蔵; Sutra Repository; Map p518) This understated Sutra Repository guarded by Kishi Monju Bosatsu and Four Attendants formerly stored sacred sutras and artefacts.

Mōtsū-ji GARDENS
(毛越寺; Map p518; ☑ 0191-46-2331; ¥500; ⊗ 9am-5pm) Established by the priest Ennin in AD 850 at the same time as Chūson-ji, Mōtsū-ji was once Tōhoku's largest and grandest temple complex. The buildings are all long gone, but the enigmatic 12th-century 'Pure Land' gardens, designed with the Buddhist notion of creating an earthly paradise, remain.

Hiraizumi Cultural Heritage Center MUSEUM
(平泉文化遺産センター; Map p518; 44 Hanadate; ⊗ 9am-5pm) FREE Modest, friendly museum charting Hiraizumi's rise and fall, with English explanations throughout.

🏃 Activities

Geibi Gorge BOATING
(厳美渓; 90min cruise ¥1600; ⊗ 8.30am-4pm) Singing boatmen on flat-bottomed wooden boats steer passengers down the Satetsu River, which cuts through a ravine flanked

Hiraizumi

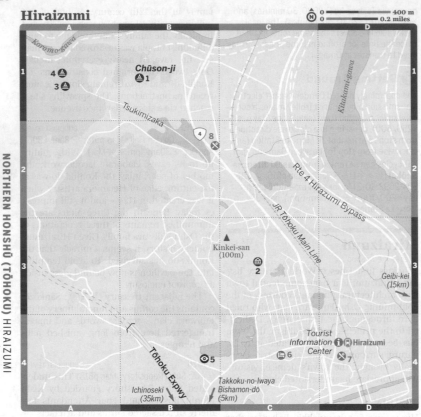

N

0 ———————— 400 m
0 ———————— 0.2 miles

Hiraizumi

by towering limestone walls. Geibi-kei is 15km east of Hiraizumi; take the hourly bus from stop 7 outside Ichinoseki Station (¥660, 40 minutes) or the *kaisoku* (rapid train) from Ichinoseki to Geibi-kei Station on the JR Ōfunato line (¥500, 30 minutes).

🛏 Sleeping & Eating

Minpaku Hiraizumi   MINSHUKU ¥
(民泊平泉町; Map p518; ☑ 090-267-7889; 117-17 Hiraizumi Shirayama; per person incl breakfast ¥6000; P✴☎) The two rooms in this charming house are regularly booked out for good reason. The friendly older couple in charge present their home in exquisite fashion, from the bright and stylish sleeping areas to the hearty breakfasts and peaceful sitting room. A very welcome addition to the town.

O-shokuji-dokoro Sakura   JAPANESE ¥
(お食事処さくら; Map p518; ☑ 0191-46-5651; 73-4 Hiraizumi-ya; snacks/meals from ¥100/700; ☉8.30am-7pm; 🅿) Station-side Sakura looks more like a local lunch counter than a tourist restaurant and, fittingly, the menu is packed with tasty home-style dishes. The speciality

here is the handmade *hatto gozen* (wheat dumplings) – try with the sweet sesame sauce.

Sobadokoro Yoshiie SOBA¥
(そば処義家; Map p518; ☑0191-46-4369; 43 Koromonoseki; meals from ¥800) Next to the Konjiki-dō (p517) exit, this small tourist-friendly restaurant dishes up *wanko-soba* (わんこそば; buckwheat noodles) by the mini-bowlful. Rural Japanese fast food at its finest.

ⓘ Information

Tourist Information Center (平泉町観光協会; Map p518; ☑0191-46-2110; ⊗8.30am-5pm) Located next to the train station, with English pamphlets available. Ask about bicycle rental.

ⓘ Getting There & Away

Hourly *shinkansen* run along the JR Tōhoku line between Sendai and Ichinoseki (¥4020, 30 minutes). Local trains (¥1660, two hours), running every hour or two, ply the same route on the JR Tōhoku main line and also connect Ichinoseki and Hiraizumi (¥230, 10 minutes).

Ichinoseki is connected to Morioka by the JR Tōhoku *shinkansen* (¥4020, 40 minutes) and the JR Tōhoku main line *futsū* (¥1660, 1½ hours).

Tōno 遠野

☑0198 / POP 27,262
Tōno has enjoyed a renaissance among domestic travellers in search of an antidote to a harried urban existence. It provides an accessible dip into agricultural life, watched over by a dramatic mountain range, and its infamous folklore, the basis for so many spooky stories about *yōkai* (ghosts, demons, monsters and spirits), adds an intriguing spiritual dimension. The sights are spread out, so a car, or better yet a bicycle, is recommended to make the most of your stay.

Tōno is also the gateway for journeys south through the coastal region known as Sanriku Kaigan (p522).

⊙ Sights

Tōno Folk Village MUSEUM
(とおの昔話村, Tōno Mukashibanashi-mura; Map p520; ☑0198-62-7887; 2-11 Chūō-dōri; ¥300; ⊗9am-5pm) Housed in the restored ryokan where Yanagita Kunio penned his famous work *Legends of Tōno*, this evocative museum has audiovisuals of some of the tales

CAUTION: MISCHIEVOUS RIVER IMPS AHEAD

At the beginning of the 20th century, writer and scholar Yanagita Kunio (1875–1962) published *Tōno Monogatari* (遠野物語; *Legends of Tōno*), a collection of local folk tales based on interviews with Sasaki Kyōseki, an educated man from a peasant family who had committed to memory more than 100 *densetsu* (local legends). The book captured the nation's imagination, bringing into focus the oral traditions of a region that had previously been ignored. Read the English translation before you visit, if you can.

A weird and wonderful cast of characters and situations draws heavily on the concept of animism, whereby an individual spirit is attributed to everything that exists, including animals and objects. Of particular importance to Tōno is the story of Oshira-sama. It begins with a farm girl who develops a deep affection for her horse; eventually the two marry, against her father's will. One night, the father finds her sleeping in the stables and, outraged, slaughters the animal. Distraught, the daughter clings to the horse's head and together they are spirited up to the heavens, becoming the deity, Oshira-sama.

There are also shape-shifting foxes and *oni* (ogres) who live in the hills and eat lost humans; but best known are the *kappa* (yes, from Super Mario Bros fame): impish water sprites with thick shells, scaly skin and pointed beaks, responsible for all sorts of mischief and grief. Tōno's many *kappa* reputedly have a nasty habit of pulling people's intestines out through their bum to feed on their *shirikodama*, a mythical ball that humans would call a soul and *kappa* would call delicious.

Points to note: *kappa* love cucumbers, so keep some handy – your generosity might earn you a temporary reprieve. (Astute connoisseurs of sushi will note that a *kappa-maki* is none other than a cucumber hand roll.) If you meet a *kappa* in the woods, remember to bow, as it will return the gesture, spilling out the water stored in its head and becoming temporarily powerless. *Kappa* will always repay a favour and are highly knowledgeable in medicine, agriculture and games of skill.

Throughout all of the *Tōno Monogatari* stories is a common theme: the struggle to overcome the everyday problems of rural life.

Tōno Valley

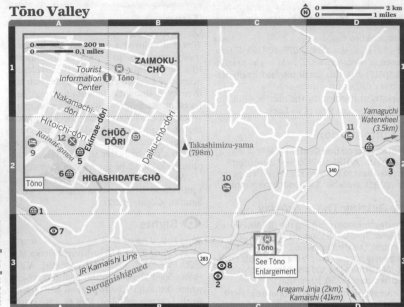

Tōno Valley

and memorabilia pertaining to Yanagita. Several times a day, local storytellers regale visitors with *mukashi-banashi* (old-time stories); however, given the heavy country dialect, even Japanese visitors may have trouble understanding them.

Tōno Municipal Museum　　　MUSEUM
(遠野市立博物館; Map p520; ☎0198-62-2340; 3-9 Higashidate-chō; ¥310; ⊙9am-5pm) With exhibits depicting some of Tōno's famous legends, this museum provides a good measure of background information and context for what's to come in the valley beyond.

✿✿ Festivals & Events

Tōno Matsuri　　　CULTURAL
(遠野祭り; ⊙3rd weekend Sep) This flamboyant spectacle, involving prayers for a bountiful harvest, is deeply connected with the legends of Tōno. There are *yabusame* events (horseback archery, in this case a 700-year-old event), traditional dances and costume parades through the city.

🛏 Sleeping & Eating

There are loads of excellent guesthouses in the town and surrounding countryside; just ask at the Tourist Information Center (p522) if you don't have a booking.

A handful of *izakaya* (Japanese pub-eateries) serve dinner, but otherwise you'll need to depend on your hosts for an evening meal.

Tōno Youth Hostel　　　HOSTEL ¥
(遠野ユースホステル; Map p520; ☎0198-62-8736; 13-39-5 Tsuchibuchi-chō; dm from ¥3800; breakfast/dinner ¥700/1400; P ⊕ @ 🛜) ⚐ If

you're after a gentle rural experience, then this hostel, set inside a converted farmhouse, is a worthy choice. The communal library and dining hall invite lingering, and the open-air baths suggest a simpler time when mythical creatures stirred the locals' imaginations. The dorms are fairly plain, but the silence, soft pillows and Iwate wine will induce a restful sleep.

From Tōno Station, take a bus bound for Saka-no-shita to the Nitagai stop (¥290, 12 minutes). From there, it's a 10-minute walk, with the hostel signposted along the way (look for the small wooden signs at knee-level).

Aeria Tohno
HOTEL ¥¥

(あえりあ遠野; Map p520; ☑ 0198-60-1700; 1-10 Shin-machi; s/d incl breakfast from ¥8230/14,300; ℗ 🟦 🟦) This is a very hospitable, upscale hotel near the town museum. Staff are high-ly knowledgeable about the local area and encourage guests to venture out from their spacious, elegant rooms often booked out by conference delegates and tour groups. It's by far the pick of the town at the higher end. Dinner can be added for ¥4300.

Kuranoya
MINSHUKU ¥¥

(くら乃屋; Map p520; ☑ 0198-60-1360; www. kuranoya-tono.com; 45-136 Sanchiwari, Kōkōji, Matsuzaki-chō; s/d from ¥6500/12,000) Guests rave about Kuranoya, a classic Japanese homestay with urbane owners who sought refuge from the city in Tōno's hills. They speak magnificent English, are passionate about the history and future of their town, and are keen to share it with you. Accommodation is modern Japanese of the highest standard. A wholesome dinner costs ¥1000. Call ahead for pick-ups.

CYCLING AROUND TŌNO

A fantastic riverside trail draws leisure cyclists (no need for lycra), as the Tōno Valley opens up into some beautiful terrain, particularly to the east. Most of the sights following are dotted throughout the valley. Finding them is half the fun. Rent a bicycle, grab a walking map from the Tourist Information Center (p522) and don't be (too) afraid to explore. The mythical world is well signposted in English, but don't let that stop you setting off down unmarked roads – you never know what you might find.

About 2.5km southwest of Tōno Station is **Unedori-sama** (卯子酉様; ☑ 0198-62-2111; Shimokumi-chō), the matchmaking shrine. According to legend, if you tie a strip of red cloth around one of the pines, using only your left hand, you'll meet your soul mate. In the hills above, the **Gohyaku Rakan** (五百羅漢) are eerie, moss-covered rock carvings of 500 disciples of Buddha fashioned by a priest to console the spirits of those who died in a 1754 famine. It's a truly unique site – approach respectfully.

If you continue west along Rte 283 towards Morioka for about 8km, you'll eventually come to **Tsuzuki-ishi** (続石), a curious rock that rests amid aromatic cedars; it's either a natural formation or a dolmen (primitive tomb). A short, steep hike rewards you with views across the valley, but take heed as hungry ogres (p519) and bears are reported to lurk in these parts. One kilometre past Tsuzuki-ishi is the **Chiba Family Magariya** (南部曲り家千葉家; ☑ 0198-62-9529; adult/child ¥310/100; ⊙ 9am-4pm), a grand 200-year-old farmhouse in the traditional L-shaped Tōno style.

About 5km east of the town centre is **Tōno Denshōen** (遠野伝承園; ☑ 0198-62-8655; www.densyoen.jp; 6-5-1 Tsuchibuchi, Tsuchibuchi-chō; ¥300; ⊙ 9am-4pm), another traditional farmhouse containing a small cultural museum. The highlights here are the 1000 Oshira-sama deities fashioned from mulberry wood. A few hundred metres southeast is **Jōken-ji** (常堅寺; ☑ 0198-62-1333; 7-50 Tsuchibuchi, Tsuchibuchi-chō), a peaceful temple dedicated to the deity image of Obinzuru-sama. Behind the temple is the *kappa-buchi pool*, where Tōno's famous water sprites lurk. It is said that if pregnant women worship at the shrine on the riverbank, they'll produce plenty of milk, but only if they first produce a breast-shaped offering. The tiny altar is filled with small red or white cloth bags, most replete with nipple.

Otherwise, see if you can find **Aragami Jinja** (荒神社; 21 Nakazawa, Aozasa-chō), an insanely photogenic little shrine in the middle of a luminous yellow field of canola – you'll need a guide – or head on to the **Yamaguchi Waterwheel** (山口の水車), a delightful thatch-roofed waterwheel once used for milling crops, now preserved as a symbol of Tōno's past. From here it's a 12km ride back to town.

Itō-ke SOBA ¥
(伊藤家; Map p520; ☎0198-60-1110; 2-11 Chūō-dōri; mains from ¥650; ⊙11am-5pm) Among the soba varieties served here, try *hitsuko soba* (ひつこそば), eaten with chicken, mushrooms, onion and raw egg. Otherwise go for *hittsumi* (ひっつみ), hand-cut noodles served with chicken-and-vegetable dumplings in a hot broth. The restaurant is in a traditional dark-wood building adjacent to the Tōno Folk Village (p519); look for the wooden sign over the sliding doors.

❶ Information

Tourist Information Center (遠野市観光協会; Map p520; ☎0198-62-1333; www.tonojikan.jp; ⊙9am-5pm; ☎) Across from the train station, friendly, helpful staff await your arrival with bicycle rentals (¥1000 per day), English maps and free internet.

❶ Getting There & Away

Trains run hourly on the JR Tōhoku line between Hiraizumi and Hanamaki (¥840, 45 minutes). The JR Kamaishi line connects Hanamaki to Tōno (¥840, one hour), while the JR Tōhoku line connects Hanamaki to Morioka (¥670, 45 minutes).

If you're coming from Sendai, take the Tōhoku *shinkansen* to Shin-Hanamaki (¥5700, one hour) and transfer to the JR Kamaishi line for Tōno (¥760, 45 minutes). The *shinkansen* also connects Shin-Hanamaki to Morioka (¥3030, 15 minutes).

The Sennin-Tōge expressway links up with Rte 283 between Tōno and Kamaishi, for journeys around the Sanriku Kaigan.

SANRIKU KAIGAN 三陸海岸

Extending from Aomori Prefecture in the north, through Iwate and Miyagi Prefectures to the south, the vast Sanriku Kaigan (Sanriku Coast) is a rugged and beautiful stretch of coastline marked by steep rocky cliffs and a 'ria' topography. A ria is characterised by having a broad estuary that funnels into a long narrow inlet. It's on the low-lying land around the rias of the Sanriku Kaigan that communities developed. Ironically, these peculiarities that sustain life here also amplify tsunami – sadly the Sanriku Coast bore the brunt of destruction and the greatest loss of life when the Great East Japan Earthquake and subsequent tsunami struck in March 2011.

Almost all the low-lying areas of towns and villages here were levelled. It's a humbling experience to see what remains firsthand and to try to imagine what was here before. Businesses are emerging and re-establishing themselves, while new restaurants and hotels are popping up everywhere.

If you're interested in seeing where things are at, we recommend self-driving. The towns of Tōno to the north and Ichinoseki to the south are the two major inland towns you're likely to pass through, but if you come this far then you really should take your time and stay at least a night or two to get a better understanding of how travel can nurture healing.

✦ Festivals & Events

Tour de Sanriku CYCLING
(www.tour-de-sanriku.com; ⊙late Sep) The annual Tour de Sanriku was started in 2012 as a means to assist the recovery efforts since the tsunami. It's now an annual event that runs 65km through the region. Leisurely competitors are very welcome.

🛏 Sleeping & Eating

Tōno or Ichinoseki are good bases for trips along the coast, however, a number of coastal villages, such as Rikuzen-takata, Kesennuma and Kamaishi, are now able to host travellers in a range of smart new hotels and ryokan.

The food scene here is incredibly dynamic, as many young creatives and community groups have come together to open both hip and wholesome establishments to jump-start local economies.

A few savvy chefs in Rikuzen-takata have come together to create Hota-waka Go-zen, a 12-dish degustation laid out on tiered wooden trays and featuring scallops and seaweed. Check out www.rikuzentakata-hotatewakame.com for more information.

❶ Information

Kamaishi Tourist Information Society (釜石観光物産協会; ☎0193-22-5835; 22-1 Suzuko-chō, Kamaishi; ⊙9am-5pm) By Kamaishi Station, friendly staff are able to assist with information and maps on the surrounding areas.

❶ Getting There & Around

Depending on how much you wish to explore, car rental (from Morioka, Sendai or Ichinoseki) is highly recommended. Roads in, out and around the area are in excellent shape, with many new roads and highways now in action.

Rail services on the JR Kamaishi line are fully operational, but buses have replaced trains on a small section of the JR Ōfunato Kesennuma and Yamada lines.

The private Sanriku Tetsudō's coastal Kita-Riasu (between Miyako and Kuji) and Minami-Riasu (between Sakari and Kamaishi), which were heavily damaged by the tsunami, are running full services again. The Kita-Riasu line connects with the JR Hachinohe line in Kuji, for journeys north as far as Hachinohe, in Aomori Prefecture, from where it's possible (though time-consuming) to continue to Aomori city, or north to the Shimokita Peninsula, on the private Aoimori line. As schedules are subject to change, visit www.hyperdia.com for information on connections, travel times and prices.

Minami-Sanriku & Kesennuma 南三陸・気仙沼

Minami-Sanriku is a coastal town in Miyagi prefecture at the southern end of the Sanriku Kaigan. In 2011, 95% of the town was destroyed, yet thousands of people reached higher ground and survived. Roughly 40km to the north, Kesennuma is one of the coast's bigger cities. Life in the hilly suburbs above this port has returned to something like normal since 2000 people died here in 2011. Two excellent 'Recovery Markets' here are fascinating examples of Japanese community-mindedness. Kesennuma was also the site for the iconic photo of a ship – the *Kyotoku Maru 18* – beached atop an ocean of rubble. The eerie wreck was finally removed in 2013.

◉ Sights

Minami-Sanriku

Crisis Management Centre MEMORIAL
(南三陸防災対策庁舎; Minami-Sanriku) The steel shell is all that remains of this three-storey building, standing alone in what once was Minami-Sanriku. It's been preserved by the locals as a touching memorial to the lives that were lost here.

Ue-no-yama Ryokuchi PARK
(上の山緑地; Minami-Sanriku) This little park in Minami-Sanriku was one of the elevated evacuation zones during the 2011 tsunami. From here you can see the sheer scale of the devastation and reconstruction. Say a prayer or ring the bell at the nearby shrine.

★ RIAS Ark Art Gallery MUSEUM
(リアスアーク美術館; ☎0226-24-1611; www.riasark.com; 138-5 Akaiwamakisawa, Kesennuma; ¥300; ⊙9.30am-4.30pm Wed-Sun) High in the hills above Kesennuma, this local art museum houses the largest collection of photographs

and artefacts in existence relating to the 2011 Great East Japan Earthquake and tsunami. A comprehensive booklet containing an English translation of each exhibit is available. The sheer volume and nature of the collection is a little overwhelming.

⌶ Sleeping

Accommo Inn Kesennuma BUSINESS HOTEL ¥¥
(アコモイン気仙沼; ☎0226-21-2565; www.accommo-inn.com; 2-1 Shinden, Kesennuma; s/d ¥6200/12,400; P⊖❀❀) Built in 2013, the low-rise Accommo Inn has very modern rooms with soft colours, quality linen, small desks and lots of natural light. The complimentary breakfast is a Japanese take on the full English.

Rikuzen-takata & Ōfunato 陸前高田・大船渡

Located just over the prefectural border from Kesennuma, in southern Iwate, the small town of Rikuzen-takata was largely swept away in 2011. A vast network of conveyor belts ferried soil from neighbouring mountains into the town to raise the ground level. It's now an attractive seaside village with a decent travel infrastructure (namely hotels and restaurants) and makes a great base for trips in the region.

The port town of Ōfunato, 15km north of Rikuzen-takata, saw 24m-high waves travel 3km inland during the 2011 tsunami. Residents heeded warnings and loss of life was comparatively small.

◉ Sights & Activities

Rikuzen-takata Ippon-matsu MEMORIAL
(陸前高田一本松; www.city.rikuzentakata.iwate.jp/kategorie/fukkou/ipponmatu/ipponmatu.html; Rikuzen-takata) Thousands of pine trees lined the coastline around Rikuzen-takata. Remarkably, all but one were destroyed in the 2011 tsunami. That tree survived for over a year, until salination from the inundation caused its demise. A replica was constructed in its place and serves as a touching memorial, symbolising hope. A park is due to open here in 2017.

Goishi Kaigan BEACH
(碁石海岸; Ōfunato) This 6km scenic stretch of rocky coastline and picturesque beaches around Ōfunato is part of the **Sanriku Recovery National Park**. Around 4km of walking trails hug the clifftops.

THE GREAT EAST JAPAN EARTHQUAKE

At 2.46pm (JST) on 11 March 2011, a magnitude 9.0 earthquake struck off the eastern coast of Tōhoku.

During the Great East Japan Earthquake (東日本大震災; Higashi-nihon Dai-shinsai), the most powerful to hit Japan since record-keeping began in the early 20th century, and among the five strongest recorded worldwide, the ground shook for a mind-boggling six minutes. It is a testament to Japan's earthquake preparedness that many people received a warning on their mobile phones one minute prior to the event, the same warning stopping high-speed train services automatically: both measures saved countless lives. Due to stringent building codes, few structures collapsed from the shaking.

It was, however, the series of tsunami that followed just 15 minutes later, with wave heights of a staggering 38m in some areas, that caused the devastation. Coastal communities along a continuous 500km stretch of the Sanriku Kaigan (p522) were levelled completely and more than 15,000 lives were lost.

Travelling in the Region

More than five years on, the reconstruction efforts in this beautiful coastal region have been a testament to the resilience and community spirit of the Japanese. Domestic tourists continue to support the rebuilding by spending time and money here; tourism is seen as one of the best ways to revitalise the local economies.

Ever-popular Matsushima, partly protected by one of Japan's most beautiful bays, escaped relatively unscathed, but other villages were far less fortunate. Oku-Matsushima, Ishinomaki, Kamaishi, Ofunato and Rikuzen-takata were almost annihilated, but new guesthouses, onsen hotels, restaurants and community tourism initiatives have emerged and are helping survivors to move on with purpose.

It's a powerful experience to rent a car and drive along the coast here, visiting the towns most affected by the disaster – many travellers count it as a highlight of their visit to Japan.

Rail travel is up and running except for a handful of stations on the Ōfunato line, which have been replaced by bus services. See www.jreast.co.jp/e/eastpass for details.

Kurosaki Senkyo Onsen ONSEN

(黒崎仙境温泉; ☑0192-57-1126; www.kurosaki-onsen.com; 9-41 Hirotacho Kurosaki, Rikuzen-takata; up to 4hr ¥500, towel ¥240; ⊙9am-9pm) A spiffy new complex down by the sea, this onsen has lovely views and an on-site noodle restaurant to fill tummies between plunges.

🛏 Sleeping & Eating

Hakoneyama Terrace BOUTIQUE HOTEL ¥¥

(はこねやまテラス; ☑0192-22-7088; www.hakoneyama-terrace.jp; 1-Myoga, Otomocho; per person incl 1/2 meals ¥7000/8000) This beautiful wooden building is in an elevated location among tall trees. The ocean and mountains provide a wonderful backdrop for sharing travel stories on the huge shared terrace. Cedar and pine rooms are pristine, and come with quality towels and linen, and loads of natural light. A healthy breakfast is included. There's a ¥1000 surcharge on Saturday night.

Reisen Tamanoyu Onsen HOTEL ¥¥

(霊泉玉乃湯; ☑0192-55-6866; 104-8 Takekoma-chō, Rikuzen-takata; per person incl 2 meals ¥12,000;

🅿🌢🛜) This is a lovely rural escape, with a number of piping-hot baths and a separate building for Japanese-style accommodation. Day trippers can make use of the bathing facilities for ¥500.

Capital Hotel 1000 HOTEL ¥¥¥

(キャピタルホテル1000; ☑0192-55-3111; www.capitalhotel1000.jp; 0-1 Nagasuna Takata-chō, Rikuzen-takata; s/d ¥9000/17,000; 🅿🌢🛜) A symbol of the reconstruction effort, the Capital Hotel 1000 was reborn in 2013 and is now a grey rectangular building in an industrial style with excellent rooms, most with a small couch. The surrounding area is a hive of reconstruction. Breakfasts are delicious.

Riku Café JAPANESE ¥

(りくカフェ; ☑0192-22-7311; www.rikucafe.jp; 22-9 Naruishi Takata-chō, Rikuzen-takata; dishes from ¥900; ⊙9am-9pm) The main community centre in Rikuzen-takata is also a lively cafe with home-cooked food, decent coffee and the odd performance. It's an unofficial information centre, too, so drop in if you're travelling independently.

Frypan Farmers Cafe
JAPANESE ¥

(農家フライパンカフェ; ☎0192-55-3358; 2-63 Aza Tonokuchi, Rikuzen-takata; mains from ¥990; ⏱10am-4pm; ♿) This family oriented cafe serves popular *teishoku* (set meals) using local produce. There's a lovely kids' area so mums and dads can sit back and savour the yummy fruit salads and cakes.

Waiwai
JAPANESE ¥

(わいわい; ☎0192-47-3102; 93-1 Osumi Takata-chō, Rikuzen-takata; dishes from ¥750; ⏱11am-2.30pm & 5.30-8.30pm) This friendly local eatery has novel food items including *nattō*-filled fish cake and the refreshing alcoholic orange *nacchiku* drink. The owner is a mini celebrity around these parts.

Kamaishi & Ōtsuchi 釜石・大槌町

Due east of Tōno, Kamaishi is an industrial and fishing town where low-lying areas were flattened and 1250 lives were lost. A famed Buddhist statue towers over the town. Flanked by Chojamori-san and Komagamori-san, the small fishing village of Ōtsuchi, 10km north of Kamaishi, blooms with azaleas in spring. Roughly 10% of the town's 16,000 people were lost in 2011.

◉ Sights

Kamaishi Dai-kannon
BUDDHIST MONUMENT

(釜石大観音; ☎0193-24-2125; www.kamaishi-daikannon.com; 3-9-1 Ōdaira, Kamaishi; adult/child ¥500/300) In the hills above Kamaishi, this enormous (48.5m) statue of the Goddess of Mercy has witnessed much tragedy below, but remains a source of hope for thousands of pilgrims each year. You can climb the inside of the structure for eye-opening views.

☞ Tours

★ Yume-no-hiroba
WALKING

(夢の広場; ☎0193-55-5120; www.oragaotsuchi.jp; 23-37-3 Ōtsuchi; tours per person from ¥1000; ⏱by appointment) The resilient, forward-thinking and compassionate folk at this local organisation run individual and group tours around Ōtsuchi, sharing personal, firsthand accounts of the 2011 Tōhoku earthquake and tsunami, and educating visitors on disaster management and humanitarian concerns. Prepare to have your heart melt a little (OK, a lot). Very highly recommended.

⛏ Sleeping & Eating

Hotel Route Inn Kamaishi
HOTEL ¥¥

(ホテルルートイン釜石; ☎0193-22-0301; www.route-inn.co.jp; 2-5-17 Ōhara, Kamaishi; s/d from ¥7300/12,000; ℗❋🛜) This business hotel has compact, state-of-the-art rooms and on-site onsen baths.

Hamabeno Ryouriyado Houraikan
RYOKAN ¥¥¥

(浜べの料理宿宝来館; ☎0193-28-2526; www.houraikan.jp; 2-1 Shinden, Kamaishi; r incl 2 meals ¥28,000) A little luxury has returned to the region at last. The dining experience at this ryokan is exceptional for such a remote placc and the onsen facility includes a Zen garden surrounding a large wooden bath, and stunning views from the indoor hot and cold pools. Rooms are light and stylish, with a largely Western decor, save the tatami flooring.

It's not cheap, but you won't need to touch your wallet once you arrive and it's supremely comfortable.

Sunfish Kamaishi
MARKET ¥

(サン・フィッシュ釜石; www.sunfish-kamaishi.sakura.ne.jp; opposite Kamaishi Station; sushi box of 10 from ¥1100; ⏱7am-4pm) A great spot to pick up fresh sushi on the way through Kamaishi, Sunfish market also has a few small restaurants on the 1st floor.

Ririshiya
JAPANESE ¥¥

(凛々家; ☎0193-44-2366; 1-3-53 Kiri Kiri, Ōtsuchi; mains from ¥850; ⏱11am-2.30pm & 5.30-9.30pm) When in Ōtsuchi, stop for a special seafood *donburi* (rice bowl) at this popular restaurant run by a former fisherman. Lots of local vegetables from the surrounding mountains also feature on the eclectic menu.

🔒 Shopping

Fukko Kirari Shōtengai
MARKET

(23-9 Daichiwari, Ōtsuchi; ⏱9am-6pm) Ōtsuchi's 'Recovery Market' has developed into a full commercial zone and rewards a little time and money being spent. Most towns in the region have similar set-ups.

AOMORI PREFECTURE 青森県

Travellers to the northern tip of Honshū often speed through the peculiar-shaped Aomori prefecture en route to the island of Hokkaidō. However, for geographical extremity – and remarkably few tourists – you needn't go so far. Disembark the bullet train before it reaches the sea, rent a car and explore the axe-shaped Shimokita Peninsula, the sacred volcanoes around Osore-zan, and the snowy Hakkōda highlands. It's seriously wild stuff. In summer, the beaches around Towada-ko are a lovely surprise too. Meanwhile, Hirosaki, the former capital, is a stylish town with cool clothing stores and a rather fine park.

Aomori 青森

☑ 017 / POP 288.029

In the upper reaches of Japan's main island is the quiet prefectural capital of Aomori, with a very pleasant harbourfront area near the train station. The wilds of Hokkaidō draw many travellers here for a brief stopover, but the savvy wanderer will use it as a base for exploring this vastly under-visited prefecture. The most famous draw is its Nebuta festival, in August, but the rest of the time the city maintains a sleepy seaside feel. It's sunny and delightfully cooler than most of Japan in summer, but winter here is an icy, frigid state of affairs.

◉ Sights

★ Sannai Maruyama Site
ARCHAEOLOGICAL SITE

(三内丸山遺跡; ☑ 017-766-8282; www.sannai maruyama.pref.aomori.jp; Sannai Maruyama 305; ⊙ 9am-5.30pm Jun-Sep, 9am-4.30pm Oct-May) FREE Excavation of this site turned up an astonishing number of intact artefacts from Japan's Jōmon era (10,000 to 2000 years ago), which are on display at the museum here. Clay figures, jade beads and large chestnut pillars head the collection, and there are also some reconstructed dwellings. Sannai Maruyama is approximately 5km west of JR Aomori Station. City buses leaving from stop 6 for Menkyō Center stop at Sannai Maruyama Iseki-mae (¥300, 20 minutes).

Aomori Museum of Art
MUSEUM

(青森県立美術館; ☑ 017-783-3000; www.aomori-museum.jp/en/index.html; 185 Chikano, Yasuta; adult/child ¥510/300; ⊙ 9am-5pm; ☼) There are terrific offerings for kids in the fun and quirky pieces by contemporary artists from Aomori Prefecture featured heavily in the permanent collection here. These include pop icon Yoshitomo Nara – and his 9ft dog – master printmaker Munakata Shikō, and Tohl Narita, who designed many of the monsters from the iconic *Ultraman* television

show. The museum is about 5km west of JR Aomori Station, adjacent to the Sannai Maruyama Site.

City buses leaving from stop 6 at the JR station for Menkyō Center stop at Kenritsu-bijyutskan-mae (¥270, 20 minutes), where you should get off.

Nebuta no Ie Wa Rasse
MUSEUM

(ねぶたの家ワ・ラッセ; Map p528; ☑ 017-752-1311; www.nebuta.or.jp/warasse; 1-1-1 Yasukata; adult/child ¥600/250; ⊙ 9am-5pm) Even if you missed the Nebuta festival, you can still gawk at the awesome craftsmanship of the floats displayed at this new museum on the waterfront. On weekends there are dancing and drumming performances.

✨ Festivals & Events

Aomori Nebuta Matsuri
PARADE

(青森ねぶた祭り; www.nebuta.or.jp/english/index_e; ⊙ 2-7 Aug) The Nebuta Matsuri has parades of spectacular illuminated floats, accompanied by thousands of rowdy, chanting dancers. The parades start at sunset and last for hours; on the final day, the action starts at about noon. As this is one of Japan's most famous festivals, you'll need to book accommodation way in advance.

🛏 Sleeping

Aomori has the usual gamut of business hotels, mostly on the walk north from the train station along the Shinmachi covered arcade.

Art Hotel Color
HOTEL ¥

(アートホテル カラー; ☑ 017-775-4311; www.arthotelcolor.com; 2-5-6 Shin-machi; s/d from ¥3200/5300; ☏☺☎) Friendly management who aim to please welcome solo travellers and couples to their minuscule, but ever-so-slightly hip rooms. The 'color' is found on the top floor – insist on a room up there – and in the communal dining area, which has a very enticing set-up come morning.

Hyper Hotels Passage
HOTEL ¥¥

(ハイパーホテルズパサージュ; Map p528; ☑ 017-721-5656; 1-8-6 Shin-machi; s/d from ¥5080/7180; ☏☺☎) Sometimes the thought of exiting the train station can be too daunting. Luckily, Japanese urban planners have perfected the covered arcade, which includes fabulous little hotels like this business number with a chandelier in the lobby, spotless rooms, bubbly management and larger-than-average rooms.

Aomori Prefecture

🍴 Eating & Drinking

Seafood is the star in this port city; there are loads of purveyors of the famed local scallop.

★ Shinsen Ichiba
MARKET ¥

(新鮮市場; Map p528; ☏ 017-721-8000; basement fl, Auga Bldg, 1-3-7 Shin-chō; meals from ¥580; ⊙ 5am-6.30pm) Cut out the middle man and head straight for the famed Aomori seafood market where piles of produce including scallops, codfish, apples, pickled vegetables and many other foods are laid out for restaurateurs to hand-pick. There are also a few counter restaurants selling ramen and *sanshoku-don* (rice topped with scallops, fish roe and sea-urchin roe). Cheap and ridiculously cheerful.

Osanai
SEAFOOD ¥

(おさない; Map p528; 1-1-17 Shin-machi; items from ¥450; ⊙ 7am-9.30pm Tue-Sun) In a town that knows how to handle a bivalve, Osanai has the stellar reputation among locals for its simple and cheap *hotate* (scallop) recipes. Located at the beginning of busy Shinmachi-dōri, the menu here includes *marucchi tsumire soba* (dumplings made from apple and scallops on hot soba noodles). We preferred ours simply hot and buttery.

Ringobako
JAPANESE ¥¥

(りんご箱; Map p528; ☏ 017-763-5155; 1-3-7 Shin-machi; mains from ¥900; ⊙ 6-11pm) This brightly lit basement restaurant stars musicians wielding *shamisen* (three-stringed instruments resembling a lute or a banjo) entertaining seafood lovers with their high-pitched twang. It's a lovely place to enjoy fresh sashimi, curried scallops and multiple ales among a very festive audience.

A-Factory
BREWERY

(エーファクトリー; Map p528; ☏ 017-752-1890; 1-4-2 Yanagigawa; meals from ¥600; ⊙ 11am-8pm) The A-Factory food hall has a fairly broad

Aomori

N 0   0.2 km
0   0.1 miles

Aomori

⊙ Sights
1 Nebuta no Ie Wa Rasse A2

🛏 Sleeping
2 Hyper Hotels Passage.........................B2

✕ Eating
3 Osanai...A2
4 Ringobako..A2
Shinsen Ichiba...............................(see 4)

🍷 Drinking & Nightlife
5 A-Factory A2

ⓘ Information
6 Aomori Station Tourist
Information Center...........................A2
7 Shin-Aomori Station Tourist
Information Center...........................A2

selection of Japanese and Western holes-in-
the-wall, but its on-site apple cider brewery
is what makes it special – the sweet drink is
available by the glass or bottle. This is a delightful place to while away an afternoon un-
impeded.

ⓘ Information

Aomori City Hospital (青森市民病院; ☑24hr
emergency hotline 017-734-2171; 1-14-20

Katsuda; ⊙ outpatient services 9am-5pm Mon-
Fri) The hospital is 3km southeast of the train
station, off Rte 103.

Aomori Station Tourist Information Center (
青森市観光交流情報センター; ☑ 017-723-4670;
www.city.aomori.aomori.jp/contents/english;
⊙8.30am-7pm) Everything you need to know
about Aomori, in English.

**Shin-Aomori Station Tourist Information
Center** (あおもり観光情報センター; ☑017-
752-6311; ⊙ 8.30am-7pm) On the 2nd floor
of the *shinkansen* terminus; ask here for info
on all things Aomori and for journeys north to
Hokkaidō.

ⓘ Getting There & Away

AIR

From Aomori Airport, 11km south of the city
centre, there are flights to and from Tokyo, Osaka,
Sapporo and Seoul. Airport buses (¥700, 40
minutes) are timed for flights and depart from
stop 11 in front of JR Aomori Station.

BOAT

Sii Line (シイライン; Map p528; ☑ 017-722-
4545; www.sii-line.co.jp) ferries depart twice
daily for Wakinosawa (¥2610, one hour) from
Aomori-kō Ryokyaku Fune Terminal (青森港旅
客船ターミナル).

Tsugaru Kaikyō (津軽海峡; ☑ 017-766-4733;
www.tsugarukaikyo.co.jp) operates eight
ferries daily between Aomori and Hakodate
(from ¥2220, three hours) year-round. Ferries
depart from Aomori Ferry Terminal (青森フェリ
ーターミナル) on the western side of the city,
a 10-minute taxi ride from JR Aomori Station
(about ¥1600).

BUS

JR highway buses connect Aomori to Sendai
(¥6000, five hours) and Tokyo (from ¥9000, 9½
hours). Alight at the JR Highway Bus Stop.

Aomori city buses depart from stop 11 for Hakkōda (¥1180, 50 minutes) and Towada-ko (¥3200,
three hours); schedules vary seasonally and run
infrequently during winter. Some English schedules can be found at www.jrbustohoku.co.jp.

CAR & MOTORCYCLE

The Tōhoku Expressway (東北自動車道) runs
between Tokyo and greater Aomori.

Toyota Rent a Car (トヨタレンタカー; ☑017-
782-0100; http://rent.toyota.co.jp/en/index.
html; 104-79 Takama, Ishie; ⊙8am-10pm) can
be found outside the west exit of the Shin-
Aomori *shinkansen* station and has branches
a few blocks from JR Aomori Station.

TRAIN

The Tōhoku *shinkansen* (bullet train) runs
roughly every hour from Tokyo Station, by

way of Sendai and Morioka, to the terminus at Shin-Aomori Station (¥17,350, 3½ hours).

Futsū (local) trains on the JR Ōu main line connect Aomori with Shin-Aomori (¥190, five minutes) and Hirosaki (¥670, 45 minutes). A few JR Tsugaru *tokkyū* (limited express) trains run daily between Aomori and Akita (¥5400, three hours) on the same line.

Hourly *tokkyū* trains run on the JR Tsugaru-Kaikyō line between Aomori and Hakodate on Hokkaidō (¥3240, two hours), via the Seikan Tunnel.

One daily *kaisoku* (rapid train) on the JR Ōmino-to line connects Aomori and Shimokita (¥2700, 1½ hours). Otherwise, take a *futsū* train on the private Aoimori Tetsudō line and transfer at Noheji for the JR Ōminato line (¥2180, 1¾ hours).

❶ Getting Around

Shuttle buses (single ride/day pass ¥200/500) circle the city, connecting Shin-Aomori Station, JR Aomori Station, Aomori Ferry Terminal and most city sights. They may be less direct than regular municipal buses, but are the most economical way to get around the city. Buses depart from the **Aomori City Buses** (Map p528) terminal, plus numerous smaller stops in between.

Hirosaki 弘前

📞 0172 / POP 176,590

Hirosaki is an enigmatic historic town with rightful claims as the cultural capital of the prefecture, a step up from the blander capital just a few stops down the train line. Set in the shadow of the impressive Iwaki-san (p531), the town has a youthful vitality that belies its feudal past under the Tsugaru clan. Its semi-rural setting is complemented by beautiful parks, a wonderful temple district and some living history to be discovered in the spread-out backstreets, while its variety of hip boutique fashion stores and stylish urban landscapes create a lasting impression.

◉ Sights

Apple Park   PARK
(リンゴ公園; 📞 0172-36-7439; www.city.hirosaki. aomori.jp/ringopark/; Shimizu Tomita Aza Terasawa 125; ⊘apple season Aug-Nov; 🚗) In season, an excursion to this working orchard in full view of regal Iwaki-san (p531) is an ideal family activity. Pick as many apples as you can carry (2kg for ¥200) – they're so good! It's possible to ride bikes here, but driving or catching the bus from the train station can be a better option: check the website for details.

Hirosaki-kōen   PARK
(弘前公園; Map p530) Perfect for picnicking, this enormous public park has been shaped over the centuries by three castle moats, and landscaped with overhanging cherry trees (more than 5000 in total!) that bloom in late April or early May. The remains of Hirosaki-jō lie at the heart of the park.

Fujita Memorial Garden   GARDENS
(藤田記念庭園; Map p530; 📞 0172-37-5525; 8-1 Kamishiro-gane; adult/child ¥310/100; ⊘9am-5pm Tue-Sun Apr-Nov) The former home and garden of the wealthy Fujita family, this beautiful example of a manicured Japanese garden is the second largest in Tōhoku. It features a wonderful teahouse and Western-styled Meiji-era mansion, which now serves as a cafe, replete with grand piano.

Neputa Mura   NOTABLE BUILDING
(ねぷた村; Map p530; 📞 0172-39-1511; 61 Kamenoko-machi; adult/child ¥550/350; ⊘9am-5pm) Come here to see some of Hirosaki's Neputa festival floats and try your hand at the giant *taiko* (drums). There are also exhibitions of local crafts. It's a short walk from the Bunka Center stop on the Dote-machi Loop Bus.

Chōshō-ji   BUDDHIST TEMPLE
(長勝寺; 📞 0172-32-0813; 1-23-8 Nishi-Shigemori; ¥300; ⊘9am-4pm) A 10-minute walk southwest of the Hirosaki-jō ruins brings you to an atmospheric temple district redolent of feudal times. At the top of the hill, Chōshō-ji comprises the oldest wooden building in Aomori-ken and rows of mausoleums built for the rulers of the Tsugaru clan. Views of Iwaki-san (p531) from the imposing stupa to the right of the main temple building are inspiring.

Hirosaki-jō   CASTLE
(弘前城; Map p530; ¥300; ⊘9am-5pm Apr-Nov) At the heart of Hirosaki-kōen lie the ancient remains of this castle, originally constructed in 1611. Rather tragically, only 16 years after it was built, the castle was struck by lightning and burnt to the ground. Two centuries on, one of the corner towers was rebuilt and today it has a small museum housing samurai weaponry.

🎊 Festivals & Events

Hirosaki Neputa Matsuri   PARADE
(弘前ねぷたまつり; ⊘1-7 Aug) Hirosaki's Neputa Matsuri is famous for the illuminated floats parading each evening to the accompaniment of flutes and drums. The festival is considered to signify ceremonial

Hirosaki

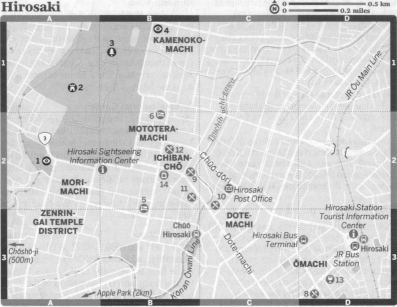

Hirosaki

◎ Sights
1 Fujita Memorial Garden A2
2 Hirosaki-jō A1
3 Hirosaki-kōen B1
4 Neputa Mura B1

🛌 Sleeping
5 Dormy Inn Hirosaki B2
6 Ishiba Ryokan B2
7 Super Hotel Hirosaki C3

✖ Eating
8 Curry House Hōryū D3
9 Kadare Yokochō B2
10 Kikufuji C2
11 Manchan B2
12 Yamakazi B2

🍷 Drinking & Nightlife
13 Robbin's Nest D3

🛍 Shopping
14 Tanaka-ya B2

preparation for battle, expressing sentiments of bravery for what lies ahead and heartache for what lies behind.

Hirosaki Castle
Snow Lantern Festival   LIGHT SHOW
(ひろさきじょ ゆきどうろう まつり; ⊙Feb)
In Hirosaki-kōen (p529), more than 200 snow lanterns and 300 miniature igloos light up the winter night.

🛌 Sleeping

★**Ishiba Ryokan**   RYOKAN ¥
(石場旅館; Map p530; ☑0172-32-9118; www.
ishibaryokan.com; 55 Mototera-machi; r per person
from ¥4860; ℗🛜) Ishiba is the only decent

ryokan in Hirosaki, but luckily it's also excellent value. Set inside a late-19th-century property a block from the castle, the bright, large tatami rooms have attractive floor mats and drapes and face onto a tree-filled garden. Meals and rental bicycles are available.

Super Hotel Hirosaki   BUSINESS HOTEL ¥¥
(スーパー ホテル弘前; Map p530; ☑0172-35-
9000; 148 Dote-machi; s/d ¥6200/9500; ℗❄🛜)
In the hip part of Dote-machi is this discreet business hotel, whose dull, grey-brick facade belies the personal touches awaiting inside. Pillow menus, a small onsen, bicycle hire and an effortless check-in lift this hotel above its many competitors.

Dormy Inn Hirosaki

HOTEL ¥¥

(ドーミーイン弘前; Map p530; ☑ 0172-37-5489; www.hotespa.net/hotels/hirosaki; 71-1 Hon-machi; s/d from ¥8700/10,200) This colourful inn is perfectly placed on a hill near Hirosaki-kōen (p529), affording glorious views from the rooftop onsen and *rotemburo* (outdoor bath). It's also on the edge of a lively nightlife area. Rooms are spotless and functional and there's complimentary ramen from 9pm to 11pm. It's a short taxi ride from the station.

🍴 Eating & Drinking

The best restaurants are along Dote-machi.

Hirosaki has some interesting bars and clubs and an upbeat, youthful vibe on weekends. Keep an eye on the posters around the shops and streetlamps on Dote-machi for the latest club nights.

★ Kadare Yokochō

FOOD HALL ¥

(かだれ横丁; Map p530; ☑ 0172-38-2256; www.kadare.info; 2-1 Hyakkoku-machi; ☻ 11am-2am; ☑) In the evening, university students flock to this nondescript office building housing eight tiny restaurants, most doubling as bars. It's a lively local hang-out. Hinata-bokko (日向ぼっこ), with the orange *noren* curtains, is particularly recommended, turning out excellent *hotate misoyaki* (grilled scallops in miso; ¥600) and *ikamenchi* (fried minced squid; ¥400). The Nepalese Curry House does a fine vegetable thali (¥800).

Curry House Hōryū

JAPANESE CURRY ¥

(カレーハウス芳柳; Map p530; ☑ 0172-33-2189; 2-1-2 Ōmachi; meals ¥600-800; ☻ 11am-3pm & 5-8.30pm) Nearly 50 years of churning out sweet, creamy curries has led to mastery of spice and consistency at Curry House Hōryū. It's remarkably cheap and draws a steady crowd despite the quiet area. The menu is easy to understand: there are only six choices and a daily special – all curry. The 'vegetarian' curry is cooked in pork stock.

Manchan

CAFE ¥

(万茶ン; Map p530; ☑ 0172-35-4663; 36-6 Dote-machi; dessert from ¥600; ☻ 11am-6.30pm) In business since 1929, this old-fashioned cake and tea shop is said to be the oldest in Tōhoku. Expect to see arty types with pen in hand (or finger on screen), nibbling on a slice of famed apple pie coddled in cream. Look for the bifurcated cello out front.

Kikufuji

JAPANESE ¥¥

(菊富士; Map p530; ☑ 0172-36-3300; www.kikufuji.co.jp; 1 Sakamoto-chō; meals from ¥900; ☻ 11am-3.30pm & 5-9pm) A true local restaurant offering a variety of set meals of hearty stews and delicate seafood concoctions. There's also an extensive list of Aomori sake, which you can try in an *otameshi* (sampler) set of three. Paper lanterns and folk music add atmosphere without being kitschy. Look for the vertical white sign out front.

Yamakazi

MODERN FRENCH ¥¥¥

(やまかじ; Map p530; ☑ 0172-38-5515; 41 Oyakata-machi; 5-course set meal from ¥5000; ☻ 10am-10pm) This impressive eatery morphs from patisserie by day to casual French dining at night. Solo patrons sip coffee at the bar, while others enjoy the highly recommended

NORTHERN HONSHŪ (TŌHOKU) HIROSAKI

IWAKI-SAN & SHIRAKAMI-SANCHI

Looming over Hirosaki, sacred Iwaki-san (岩木山; Mt Iwaki; 1625m) looks remarkably like Fuji-san from certain angles and at times seems so close you could almost touch it. Should you wish to, daily buses depart the Hirosaki Station bus terminal for **Iwaki-san-jinja** (岩木山神社; ¥720, 40 minutes, April to October), where tradition dictates summit-bound travellers should first make an offering before attempting the ascent. The views from the top are remarkable. A different trail takes you down, past the smaller peak of **Tori-no-umi-san** (鳥ノ海山) to the village of **Dake-onsen** (岳温泉), from where infrequent buses chug back to Hirosaki (¥1050, one hour). The entire 9km hike should take you about seven hours.

If you *were* wondering, Iwaki-san's last recorded eruption was in 1863.

Southwest of Iwaki-san is the isolated Shirakami-sanchi (白神山地), a Unesco-protected virgin forest of Japanese beech trees. From the bus stop at Anmon Aqua Village, an hour-long trail leads into the woods to the three **Anmon Falls** (暗門の滝; Anmon-no-taki), the longest of which is 42m. This is part of the park's 'buffer zone' – open to the public without permit. Two buses depart Hirosaki Station bus terminal each morning for Anmon Aqua Village (one way/return ¥1650/2470, 1½ hours, May to October) and return in the afternoon.

Enquire at the helpful Hirosaki Sightseeing Information Center (p532) for maps and timetables if you intend on making either of these trips.

WORTH A TRIP

AONI ONSEN

You can't get much more rustic, romantic and isolated than **Rampu-no-yado** (ランプの宿; ☑0172-54-8588; www.yo.rim.or.jp/~aoni; 1-7 Aoni-sawa, Taki-no-ue, Okiura, Kuroishi; r per person incl 2 meals from ¥9870, day bathing ¥520; ⊙day bathing 10am-3pm; ℗) ⬆ in little Aoni Onsen (青荷温泉). Plopped in a deep valley surrounded by heavily forested mountains, it's the ultimate escape from civilisation and the modern day: oil lamps (rampu) are used to light the corridors, though electricity has now reached the basic tatami rooms. As the sun goes down and the stars come out, the effect is magical. Have your camera and tripod ready.

Numerous indoor baths and rotemburo (outdoor baths) are spread over several small wooden buildings along both sides of a stream, crossed by a footbridge. With the lack of distractions, you'll have lots of time to soak and think about what's important. Dining is a delicious and communal affair, featuring hearty, healthy, mostly vegetarian, locavore cuisine.

Aoni Onsen is alongside Rte 102 between Hirosaki and Towada-ko. Getting here requires effort or a rental car. Without a car, take the private Kōnan Tetsudō line from Hirosaki to Kuroishi (¥460, 30 minutes), then connect with a Kōnan bus for Niji-no-ko (¥830, 30 minutes) from where shuttle buses run to Aoni (free, 30 minutes, four daily). From December through March, the narrow lane that winds down to Aoni Onsen is closed to private vehicles; if you're coming by car, park at the Niji-no-ko bus station and catch the free shuttle bus.

Advance reservations essential.

---

five-course set meals on red tablecloths. Staff speak limited English, but the produce is invariably local, featuring mostly pork, chicken and fresh vegetables. Desserts are exquisite.

Robbin's Nest PUB
(ロビンズネスト; Map p530; ☑090-6450-1730; www.robbins-nest.jp; 1-3-16 Ōmachi; ⊙5pm-late) This is an excellent Japanese rendition of a British pub. It's intimate, and there's no cover charge (except sometimes when bands are playing), frequent live music, Guinness on tap and a few tables out front (in warmer months) for alfresco drinking.

🛍 Shopping

Tanaka-ya ARTS & CRAFTS
(田中屋; Map p530; ☑0172-33-6666; www.tugarunuri.jp; Ichiban-chō-kado; ⊙10am-7pm) Tanaka-ya deals in high-grade works by local artisans. The prices aren't cheap, but even if you're not looking to buy it's worth stopping in for a peek at the boldly coloured tsugaru-nuri (lacquerware of the Tsugaru region), produced in-house. A second store has opened up across the road.

ℹ Information

Hirosaki Sightseeing Information Center
(弘前市立観光館; Map p530; ☑0172-37-5501; www.en-hirosaki.com; 2-1 Shimoshirogane-chō; ⊙9am-6pm) Situated inside the Kankōkan (tourism building), you can rent bikes and grab all manner of English-language

materials here. Be sure to check out the plaza and surrounds.

Hirosaki Station Tourist Information Center
(弘前市観光案内所; Map p530; ☑0172-26-3600; ⊙8.45am-6pm; ☎) On the ground floor of JR Hirosaki Station. The best way to see the city is by bicycle – rent one here for an hour (¥200) or all day (¥500; return by 5pm). Very helpful staff.

ℹ Getting There & Away

Tokkyū (limited express) trains on the JR Ōu main line run hourly between Aomori and Hirosaki (¥670, 50 minutes), and Hirosaki and Akita (¥4450, two hours).

For bus services to other cities, the JR Bus Station (Map p530) is directly in front of the JR Hirosaki Station.

The Tsugaru free pass (adult/child ¥2060/1030) covers area buses and trains, including those out to Iwaki-san and Shirakami-sanchi, for two consecutive days, plus a few good nearby onsen. Enquire at the **Hirosaki Station Tourist Information Center**.

ℹ Getting Around

The Dote-machi Loop Bus (¥100 per ride), which travels the downtown area, leaves from in front of JR Hirosaki Station.

Catch buses around the town from the Hirosaki Bus Terminal (Map p530), 200m further west from the west exit of the JR station.

Bicycle rental (¥500 daily, 9am to 5pm) is available at either tourist information centre from May through November.

Towada-ko 十和田湖

☎ 0176 / POP 6000

Hemmed in by rocky coastlines and dense forests, Towada-ko is the largest crater lake in Honshū (52km in circumference) and a fabulous natural attraction for those seeking solitude and, in summer, an unrivalled open-water swim. Towada-Hachimantai National Park once bore witness to a series of violent volcanic eruptions; today, the only action is the quiet trickle of the Oirase Keiryū (mountain stream), winding its way to the Pacific Ocean. The main tourist hub of Yasumiya will lower your pulse to that of a prehistoric amoeba lining the lake bed.

🏃 Activities

★ Oirase Keiryū   HIKING
(奥入瀬渓流; Map p533) This meandering river is marked by cascading waterfalls, carved-out gorges and gurgling rapids. Casual hikers can follow its path for a 14km stretch connecting Nenokuchi, a small tourist outpost on the eastern shore of the lake, to Yakeyama, from where relatively frequent buses return to either Nenokuchi (¥680, 30 minutes) or of Yasumiya (¥1210, one hour).

The hike should only take about three hours. Set out in the early morning or late afternoon to avoid slow-moving coach parties.

☞ Tours

Towada-ko   BOATING
(十和田; Map p533; ⊙8am-4pm) To get a sense of the lake's enormous scale, consider a 40-minute scenic cruise from Yasumiya (¥1400, April to November). A ferry also operates between Yasumiya and Nenokuchi (¥1400). You can rent rowboats and paddleboats next to the dock.

🛌 Sleeping & Eating

Hotel rates peak during August (summer holidays) and October, when autumn leaves blaze red.

A few simple restaurants and a grocery store are at Towado-ko bus station in Yasumiya. Best to eat meals at your accommodation.

Towadako Backpackers   HOSTEL ¥
(十和田湖バックパッカーズ; Map p533; ☎0176-75-2606; www.laketowada.wordpress.com; 116-201 Yasumiya, Towada-ko; dm/s incl 2 meals ¥4000/6000; P@) This unassuming hostel has a terrific communal atmosphere. Shared facilities are clean and spacious, while the

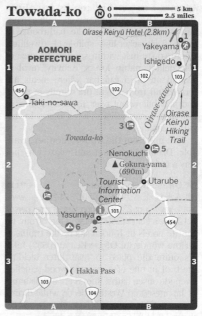

Towada-ko

dormitories are Western-style and comfortable, if a little congested; the twin cottages are preferable. The location is wonderful, just a 10-minute steep walk to the lake. Free bike rental available.

Towadako Oide
Camping Ground   CAMPGROUND ¥
(十和田湖生出キャンプ場; Map p533; ☎0176-75-2368; www.bes.or.jp/towada/camp.html; 486 Yasumiya, Towada-kohan; per person ¥300, campsite ¥200, powered sites ¥3000; ⊙25 Apr–5 Nov; P) This pretty riverside campground has well-maintained facilities, and rental supplies (tents etc) available.

★ That Sounds Good   PENSION ¥¥
(ペンションサウンズグッド; Map p533; ☎0187-43-0127; www.hana.or.jp/~takko; 160-58

Kata-mae; r per person incl breakfast from ¥6200; Ｐ❋🛜) This pension's rooms range from quaint cottages with private bathrooms to more flashpacker-like split-level dwellings where you're just within snoring distance of your fellow nature-lovers. Activity revolves around an open cafe-bar where meals are served and from where the sounds of weekend jazz billow out over Towada-ko. One of the more cosmopolitan places to stay in this part of Japan.

Pick-ups from the train station are available. Drop in, tune out and relax...why not stay a few days?

★Oirase Keiryū Hotel HOTEL ¥¥
(奥入瀬渓流ホテル; ☏0176-74-2121; www. oirase-keiryuu.jp; 231 Tochikubo, Oirase; r per person incl 2 meals from ¥12,500; Ｐ🛜) One of our favourite hotels in Tōhoku sits by the trailhead for the wonderful Oirase Keiryū (p533) hike. It's quite the place to relax after tackling the trail in one of numerous wood-panelled riverside onsen baths. Rooms are a stylish mix of Japanese and Western decor, while dining occurs in a kind of forest-facing hardwood cathedral that fills with natural light.

Free transfers from Shin-Aomori Station are available. All-round exceptional value.

Towada Hotel HOTEL ¥¥
(十和田ホテル; Map p533; ☏0176-75-1122; www. towada-hotel.com; Namariyama, Kosaka-machi; r per person incl 2 meals from ¥15,500; Ｐ) The pre-WWII Towada Hotel has a dramatic lobby of hulking timbers, rising to a chandelier-lit cathedral ceiling. The historic main building has elegant Japanese-style rooms (with and without baths); avoid the drab Western-style annexe. All have lake views, as do the communal baths. Dining is a treat.

A path leads from the hotel to the lake's secluded southwestern shore.

❶ Information

Tourist Information Center (十和田湖総合案内所; Map p533; ☏0176-75-2425; ⊗8am-5pm) Next to the bus station in Yasumiya, with English-language pamphlets available.

❶ Getting There & Around

Renting a car from Aomori or Hirosaki allows you to make the most of this picturesque, remote area. Route 103 runs south of Aomori to Towada-ko.

JR buses run from Aomori, through Yakeyama (¥2300, two hours) to Towada-ko-eki in Yasumiya (¥1000, three hours); departures are highly seasonal and infrequent in winter.

A limited network of local buses runs around the lakeside. Infrequent connections are reason enough to bring your own wheels.

Hakkōda-san 八甲田山

🎵 017
Honshū's northernmost volcanic range is a paradise for hikers between May and October, while in winter months, serious powder fiends descend, off-piste, for some of the most untapped skiing and snowboarding in Japan. For those needing to thaw, Hakkōda-san is home to one of Tōhoku's best onsen, Sukayu.

The Hakkōda-san area is synonymous with a sad history: in 1902 a regiment of 210 Japanese soldiers on a winter training exercise were caught here in a severe snow storm. All but 11 men perished, carving out a place for Hakkōda-san in the collective Japanese psyche.

◉ Sights & Activities

Hakkōda Ropeway CABLE CAR
(八甲田山ロープウェー; ☏017-738-0343; www.hakkoda-ropeway.jp; 1-12 Kansuizawa, Arakawa; one way/return ¥1180/1850; ⊗9am-4.20pm; Ｐ) For anyone wanting a taste of the alpine without having to brave the steep ascent, this scenic ropeway whisks you quickly up to the summit of Tamoyachi-dake (田茂萢岳; 1324m). From there, you can follow an elaborate network of hiking trails, although purists prefer the magnificent one-day loop that starts and finishes just outside the Sukayu Onsen Ryokan.

★Hakkōda-san HIKING
(八甲田山) Hakkōda-san's gruelling but rewarding 12km day-return hike begins near Sukayu Onsen Ryokan, in the shadow of Ōdake (大岳; 1584m). The ridge trail continues to Ido-dake (井戸岳; 1550m) and Akakura-dake (赤倉岳; 1548m) before connecting via Tamoyachi-dake (田茂萢岳; 1324m) and looping via the ropeway back to Sukayu ryokan.

Things start out relatively flat as you wind through marshlands, but eventually the pitch starts to increase: a good level of fitness and some hiking experience is recommended. If you time your hike for mid- to late October, expect to whip your camera out for the early autumn foliage.

Hakkōda Ski Park SNOW SPORTS
(八甲田スキー場; ☏017-738-0343; www.hakkoda-ropeway.jp; 5-ride pass ¥5050; ⊗9am-4.20pm) For all its fluffy white goodness,

Tamoyachi-dake (田茂萢岳; 1324m) is a fairly modest set-up, with only two official runs (intermediate) beginning at the top of the Hakkōda Ropeway. However, the 5km **Forest Course** cuts through the treeline and has some very challenging sections; it's for serious players only. Weather conditions can suddenly become severe and getting lost is easy.

Come spring, it's possible to explore a network of unofficial trails that extend to some of the nearby peaks. Even experienced alpinists should only go backcountry with a local guide. Equipment rental (¥3500 per day) and a handful of dining options are available in the ropeway terminals.

🛏️ Sleeping & Eating

Come prepared with snacks for hiking around this area; most accommodation options can provide proper meals.

Sukayu Camping Ground   CAMPGROUND ¥
(酸ヶ湯キャンプ場; ☎017-738-6566; www.sukayu.jp/camp; per person ¥500, campsite from ¥500; ⊙late Jun–late Oct; P) A good spot to pitch a tent, with clean facilities and rental supplies. It's at the end of a small access road immediately south of Sukayu Onsen Ryokan.

★ Sukayu Onsen Ryokan   RYOKAN ¥¥
(酸ヶ湯温泉; ☎017-738-6400; www.sukayu.jp; r per person incl 2 meals from ¥12,000, day bathing ¥610; ⊙day bathing 7am-5.30pm; P) Straight from an *ukiyo-e* (woodblock print), Sukayu's cavernous, dark-wooded bathhouse is a delight for the senses. The

water is hot, acidic and sulphurous (don't get it in your eyes) – nothing beats the feel of its penetrating heat. Note that the main bath is *konyoku* (mixed bathing). Rooms in the sprawling old-fashioned inn are simple but comfortable, with shared facilities.

Hakkōda Hotel   HOTEL ¥¥¥
(八甲田ホテル; ☎017-728-2000; www.hakkodahotel.co.jp; 1 Minami-arakawayama, Arakawa; s/d incl breakfast from ¥17,000/26,000) The huge rooms at this mountain lodge appeal to muscle-sore skiers who like to dump their gear and pass out, then wake up at dinnertime to eat like royalty. It's open and spacious, and close to Hakkōda's best trails. Great for hungry powder-hounds in the winter and hikers in summer. It's not cheap, but you can save by self-catering at dinner.

ℹ️ Getting There & Away

JR buses leave from stop 11 outside JR Aomori Station, stopping at Hakkōda Ropeway train station (¥1100, 50 minutes) and the next stop, Sukayu Onsen (¥1350, one hour). The bus continues to Towada-ko train station (¥2070, 1½ hours). Bus schedules vary seasonally.

Shimokita Peninsula   下北半島

☎0175

Wild, short-legged horses, craggy rock formations and a frontier history give the remote, axe-shaped Shimokita-hantō the air of

---

DELICACIES OF THE DEEP NORTH

Eating in Tōhoku is all about simple seasonal pleasures – the bounty of the land and sea:

gyū-tan (牛タン) Cow's tongue, grilled over charcoal (Sendai).

Yonezawa-gyū (米沢牛) Yonezawa's premium-grade beef.

kiritanpo-nabe (きりたんぽ鍋) Kneaded rice wrapped around bamboo spits, barbecued over a charcoal fire then served in a chicken and soy-sauce hotpot with vegetables (Akita).

inaniwa udon (稲庭うどん) Thinner-than-usual wheat noodles (Akita).

wanko-soba (わんこそば) All-you-can-eat noodles (Morioka).

jaja-men (じゃじゃ麺) Flat wheat noodles topped with sliced cucumber, miso paste and ground meat (Morioka).

kamaboko (かまぼこ) Steamed fish paste (Sendai).

Aomori Prefecture's seafood is king:

uni (うに) Sea urchin.

hotate (ホタテ) Scallops.

maguro (まぐろ) Tuna; the village of Ōma, at the tip of Honshū, is said to have the finest in the country.

travel legend. Jet-black ravens swarm about its sulphur-infused tributaries where locals believe Buddhist souls come if they cannot rest; Japanese come to pay tribute at a powerful Buddhist shrine.

There are three main towns on the peninsula: Mutsu (first if arriving by car or train), Wakinosawa (if arriving by ferry) and Ōma, the furthest point north on the Japanese mainland – get here by car or bus. However you arrive, it's a long, slow ride. The region is centred on Osore-zan (恐山; 874m), a barren volcano that is regarded as one of the most sacred places in all of Japan.

◉ Sights & Activities

★ Osorezan-bodaiji BUDDHIST TEMPLE
(恐山菩提寺; ☏0175-22-3825; ¥500; ◷6am-6pm May-Oct; ℗) This holy shrine at Osorezan's summit is a moving, mesmerisingly atmospheric and beautiful place honouring Jizō Bosatsu, protector of children and a much-loved deity in Japanese mythology. It's also said to be located at the entrance to hell: a small brook that flows into the beautiful crater lake, Usori, is said to represent the legendary Sanzu river, which souls must cross on their way to the afterlife. Fittingly, people visit mourning lost children or seeking to commune with the dead.

Several stone statues of Jizō overlook hills of craggy, sulphur-strewn rocks and hissing vapour. Visitors are encouraged to help lost souls with their underworld penance by adding stones to the cairns. You can even bathe on hell's doorstep at the free onsen off to the side as you approach the main hall. Allow an hour or two to wander the landscape in deep contemplation.

Hotoke-ga-ura BOATING
(仏ヶ浦) The western edge of the peninsula is a spectacular stretch of coastline dotted with 100m-high wind-carved cliffs, which are said to resemble images of Buddha. Boats depart for sightseeing round trips from Wakinosawa to Hotoke-ga-ura between April and October at 10.45am and 2.55pm (¥3900, two hours). Services are often suspended in poor weather.

Popular 30-minute boat trips (¥2400) are also available from the gorgeous village of Sai (佐井村). Check out www.saiteikikanko.jp.

✦✦ Festivals & Events

Osore-zan Taisai CULTURAL
(恐山大祭; ◷20-24 Jul & 9-11 Oct) These two annual festivals attract huge crowds of people, who come to consult *itako* (mediums) in order to contact deceased family members.

⌁ Sleeping & Eating

A few basic business hotels are found in Ōma and Mutsu, close to the Shimokita train station.

★ Wakinosawa Youth Hostel HOSTEL ¥
(脇野沢ユースホステル; ☏0175-44-2341; www.wakinosawa.com; 41 Senokaname, Wakinosawa; dm ¥3900, breakfast/dinner ¥630/1050; ℗⊜⬆) ⌁ Run by a wildlife photographer who takes pride in the region's natural attractions (including snow monkeys!), this remote hostel is perched on a hillside at Wakinosawa, about 15 minutes west of the ferry pier – call ahead for a pick-up if you don't have a car. There's a homely feel about the wooden rooms, which are a touch above typical hostel standard.

ŌMA TUNA

Ōma, at the tip of the Shimokita Peninsula, may look like the end of the Earth, but it's the centre of the universe when it comes to tuna. The frigid waters of the Tsugaru Strait directly off the coast are said to yield the tastiest *maguro* (bluefin tuna) in Japan. At the height of the season, a prize catch can sell for ¥25,000 per kilogram.

Ōma's fishing co-ops catch fish the old-fashioned way, with hand lines and live bait (and a lot of muscle). It's a way of life that sets them squarely against large-scale commercial interests and in favour of greater regulation to protect the bluefin population.

Kaikyōsō (海峡荘; ☏0175-37-3691; 17-734 Ōma-taira, Ōma; meals from ¥1100; ◷11am-3pm late Apr–early Nov), in a bright-green building that looks more like a hardware store than a purveyor of fine raw fish, is a popular place to sample locally caught tuna. Try the *maguro-don* (tuna sashimi over rice) with thick, melt-in-your-mouth cuts of *akami* (lean red meat), *chū-toro* (medium-grade fatty tuna) and *ō-toro* (top-grade fatty tuna).

Tuna is caught fresh between late August and January, although most shops close up by mid-November when the cold winds turn fierce.

While it helps to speak a bit of Japanese, the genial owners are very accommodating.

❶ Getting There & Away

BOAT

Sii Line (p528) runs two daily ferries between Wakinosawa and Aomori (¥2610, one hour).

Tsugaru Kaikyō (p528) runs two to three ferries daily from Ōma to Hakodate on Hokkaidō (from ¥1810, 1¾ hours).

TRAIN

One daily *kaisoku* (rapid train) on the JR Ōminato line connects Aomori, Shimokita and Ōminato (¥2700, 1½ hours).

Otherwise, take a *futsū* (local train) on the private Aoimori Tetsudō line from Aomori. Transfer at Noheji for the JR Ōminato line (¥2180, 1¾ hours).

❶ Getting Around

It's best to have a car to explore these parts.

From May to October, there are up to five buses departing from JR Shimokita Station for Osore-zan (¥750, 45 minutes). Year-round, buses connect Shimokita and Ōma (¥1990, two hours). There are a few buses each day to Wakinosawa from JR Ōminato Station (¥1800, 70 minutes).

AKITA PREFECTURE   秋田県

Akita-ken nestles between the Sea of Japan and the spectacular Oū-sanmyaku and Dewa ranges, where hikers and pilgrims navigate their way to shrines and summits. In a prefecture overflowing with high-altitude hot springs, Nyūtō Onsen stands out for its variety of accommodation and its proximity to Tazawa-ko, an under-visited volcanic lake perfect for swimming in summer. The charming feudal city of Kakunodate is the cultural highlight of the region – its old samurai houses and pine-tree-lined streets make it one of the most photogenic historic towns in Japan.

🛏 Sleeping

Akita has many smart business hotels, while Kakunodate has some decent cheap guesthouses. In the mountainous areas, look for ryokan and onsen hotels, especially around Nyūtō Onsen. Tazawa-ko has the best traditional youth hostel.

Akita's countryside has dozens of *nōka minshuku* (farmhouse inns). For a complete list (in Japanese), see www.akita-gt.org/stay.

Akita   秋田
🎧 018 / POP 315,374

Akita is a busy and compact industrial city in the northeast of the prefecture, which serves as a transport hub for travel along the west coast or as a base for trips to Kakunodate. Like many Japanese cities, there's a fine public museum and park complex, and a better-than-average entertainment district.

Central Akita, where all the sights are, is easily walkable.

◉ Sights

Senshū-kōen   PARK

(千秋公園; Map p540; 🎧018-832-5893) Originally constructed in 1604, Akita's castle was destroyed with other feudal relics during the Meiji Restoration. The moat still guards the entrance to this leafy park; though hardly sinister, it becomes choked with giant waterlilies in summer. There are also a few pieces of the castle foundation remaining, along with plenty of grassy patches and strolling paths. A reconstruction of a guard tower in the north corner offers views over the city.

Akita Museum of Art   MUSEUM

(秋田県立美術館; Map p540; 🎧018-853-8686; http://common3.pref.akita.lg.jp/art-museum; 1-4-2 Naka-dōri; adult/child ¥300/200; ⊙10am-6pm) Akita's most famous painting, Tsuguharu Fūjita's *Events of Akita*, is also reputed to be the world's largest canvas painting, measuring 3.65m by 20.5m and depicting traditional Akita life through the seasons. It's the clear highlight of an otherwise fairly underwhelming collection in the Andō Tadao–designed museum, but the public square is worth the visit alone. Visitors can rest in the 2nd-floor cafe, from where the reflecting pool seems to run directly into Senshū-kōen's moat.

Akarenga-kan Museum   MUSEUM

(赤れんが郷土館, Akarenga Kyōdokan; Map p540; 🎧018-864-6851; www.city.akita.akita.jp/city/ed/ak; 3-3-21 Ō-machi; ¥200; ⊙9.30am-4.30pm) Once the opulent headquarters of Akita Bank, this brick structure built in 1912 is now a folk museum. Inside, you'll find fascinating woodblock prints of traditional Akita life by self-taught artist Katsuhira Tokushi.

🎎 Festivals & Events

Akita Kantō Matsuri   CULTURAL

(秋田竿燈まつり; www.kantou.gr.jp/english/index.htm; ⊙3-6 Aug) At summer's height, Akita celebrates its visually stunning Pole Lantern

Akita Prefecture

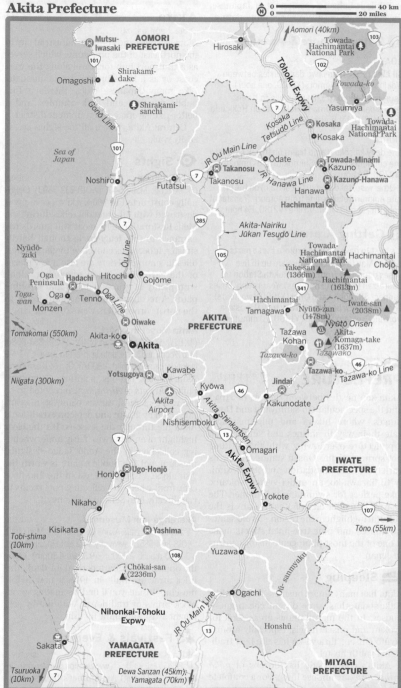

0   40 km
0   20 miles

Aomori (40km)

AOMORI PREFECTURE

Mutsu-Iwasaki

101

Omagoshi

Shirakami-dake

Shirakami-sanchi

Hirosaki

Towada-Hachimantai National Park

103

102

Tōhoku Expwy

Towada-ko

Yasumiya

Kosaka Tetsudō Line

Kosaka

Kosaka

Ōdate

Towada-Hachimantai National Park

JR Ōu Main Line

Noshiro

Futatsui

7

Takanosu

Takanosu

JR Hanawa Line

Towada-Minami
Kazuno

Kazuno-Hanawa

Hanawa

Gonō Line

Sea of Japan

101

Ōu Line

285

105

Akita-Nairiku Jūkan Tesudō Line

Hachimantai

Hachimantai

Nyūdō-zaki

Oga Peninsula

Hadachi

Hitochi

Gojōme

Towada-Hachimantai National Park

Yake-san (1366m)

Hachimantai Chōjō

Hachimantai (1613m)

Iwate-san (2038m)

Toga-wan

Oga

Tennō

Monzen

Oga Line

Oiwake

341

Hachimantai

Tamagawa

Nyūtō-zan (1478m)

Nyūtō Onsen

Akita-Komaga-take (1637m)

Tomakomai (550km)

Akita-ko

Akita

AKITA PREFECTURE

Tazawa Kohan

Tazawa-ko

Tazawako

Niigata (300km)

Yotsugoya

Kawabe

Kyōwa

46

Jindai

Tazawa-ko

Tazawa-ko Line

46

Akita Airport

Akita Shinkansen

Kakunodate

Nishisemboku

13

Ōmagari

Akita Expwy

IWATE PREFECTURE

Honjō

Ugo-Honjō

7

Yokote

107

Tōno (55km)

Nikaho

Kisikata

Tobi-shima (10km)

Yashima

108

Yuzawa

Ou-sanmyaku

Chōkai-san (2236m)

Ogachi

Honshū

Nihonkai-Tōhoku Expwy

JR Ōu Main Line

13

Sakata

YAMAGATA PREFECTURE

MIYAGI PREFECTURE

Tsuruoka (10km)

7

Dewa Sanzan (45km); Yamagata (70km)

Festival. As evening falls on the city centre, more than 160 men skilfully balance giant poles, weighing 60kg and hung with illuminated lanterns, on their heads, chins, hips and shoulders, to the beat of *taiko* drumming groups.

🛏 Sleeping

Naniwa Hotel
MINSHUKU ¥¥

(ホテルなにわ; Map p540; ☏018-832-4570; www.hotel-naniwa.jp; 6-18-27 Naka-dōri; r per person incl 2 meals ¥6500; 🅿 🕙 @) A lovely *mama-san* oversees this quaint budget guesthouse. The rooms are on the small side, but the beautiful 24-hour *hinoki* (cypress) bath, massage chairs and homemade meals more than compensate for the cramped quarters. Pick-ups from the station are possible if you speak some Japanese, though it's not far to walk. It's in a red building with a wooden entrance.

Akita Castle Hotel
HOTEL ¥¥

(秋田キャッスルホテル; Map p540; ☏018-834-1141; www.castle-hotel.co.jp; 1-3-5 Naka-dōri; s/d from ¥9200/15,000; 🅿 🕙 @ 🛜) In a prime position near the park, Akita Castle Hotel is the most distinguished in the city. Service is measured and thorough; ask for one of the rooms overlooking the former castle's moat.

🍴 Eating & Drinking

Kawabata-dōri, lined with restaurants and bars both classic and seedy, is the city's main nightlife strip. For a picnic lunch, stop by the supermarket in the Naka-Ichi centre.

Kanbun Gonendō
UDON ¥

(寛文五年堂; Map p540; ☏0120-17-2886; www.kanbun5.jp; 1-4-3 Naka-dōri; noodles from ¥800; 🕙11am-10.30pm; 🖍) This well-regarded *inaniwa udon* (thin wheat noodle) speciality shop is very popular among locals who seek out the chewy delicacy, often served cold with various sauces, while on shopping forays around the Naka-Ichi centre. Vegetarian dishes are available; ask before ordering.

Cafe Pamplemousse
CAFE ¥

(パンプルムゥス 秋田; Map p540; ☏018-801-6677; 3-1-6 Ō-machi; items from ¥400; 🕙11am-9pm) This peculiar concept cafe enjoys a lovely riverside locale and is run by a busy young team of foodies who specialise in desserts, fancy teas and organic produce. The cafe's signature is enormous fluffy pancakes (too big for one). The 'super-cute' decor includes piles of kids' books, lo-fi Japanese CDs for sale and an unnerving number of yellow rubber duckies.

Nagaya Sakaba
IZAKAYA ¥¥

(秋田長屋酒場; Map p540; ☏018-837-0505; 4-16-17 Naka-dōri; small dishes from ¥600; 🕙5pm-late) Highly regarded by locals, Nagaya Sakaba is easy to spot due to the massive red-faced Namahage demon overlooking the entrance. Sake flows freely once you've negotiated the Japanese-only menu. If in doubt, just shout *o-susume* and staff will happily bring various fish dishes accompanied by the signature pounded rice cake.

Hinai Jidoriya
JAPANESE ¥¥

(秋田比内地鶏や; Map p540; ☏018-874-7282; 7-2-1 Naka-dōri; set meals from ¥1200; 🕙10am-9pm) Yummy *oyako-don* (chicken and egg on rice) set meals are the pick of this busy train station restaurant, plus a decent crack at the local hotpot speciality (*kani*; crab) often sold for far more yen elsewhere in town.

ℹ Information

Akita Red Cross Hospital (秋田赤十字病院; ☏24hr emergency hotline 018-829-5000; www.akita-med.jrc.or.jp; 222-1 Nawashiro-sawa; 🕙outpatient services 8-11.30am Mon-Fri) Located 5km southeast of the train station, off Rte 41.

Tourist Information Center (秋田市観光案内所; Map p540; ☏018-832-7941; www.akitacity.info; 🕙9am-7pm) Opposite the *shinkansen* tracks on the 2nd floor of JR Akita Station.

ℹ Getting There & Away

AIR

From Akita Airport, 21km south of the city centre, flights go to/from Tokyo, Osaka, Nagoya, Sapporo and Seoul. Frequent buses (¥930, 40 minutes) leave for the airport from platform 1 in front of JR Akita Station.

BOAT

From the port of Akita-kō, 8km northwest of the city, **Shin Nihonkai** (新日本海; ☏018-880-2600; www.snf.jp) has ferries to Tomakomai on Hokkaidō (from ¥4530, 10 hours), departing at 7am on Tuesday, Wednesday, Friday, Saturday and Sunday. A connecting bus leaves at 6.05am from platform 11 outside JR Akita Station for Akita-kō (¥440, 30 minutes).

BUS

Highway buses (Map p540) depart from the west exit of the train station, and connect Akita to major cities throughout Honshū.

CAR & MOTORCYCLE

The Akita Expressway (秋田自動車道) runs east from Akita until it joins with the Tōhoku

Akita

0 —— 400 m
0 —— 0.2 miles

Akita

⦿ Sights
1 Akarenga-kan Museum.........................A2
2 Akita Museum of Art A2
3 Senshū-kōen B1

🛏 Sleeping
4 Akita Castle Hotel A2
5 Naniwa Hotel B3

🍴 Eating
6 Cafe Pamplemousse A2
7 Hinai Jidoriya...B2
8 Kanbun Gonendō A2
9 Nagaya Sakaba B2

ℹ Information
Tourist Information Center ....(see 7)

ℹ Transport
10 Bus Station..B2
11 Toyota Rent a Car..................................B2

Expressway. The Nihonkai-Tōhoku Expressway (日本海東北自動車道) runs south along the coast.

Rental-car outlets are scattered around the train station, including the reliable **Toyota Rent a Car** (トヨタレンタカー; Map p540; ☏ 018-833-0100; 4-6-5 Naka-dōri; ⊙8am-10pm), a few minutes' walk west.

TRAIN

The JR Akita *shinkansen* (bullet train) runs hourly between the northern terminus of Akita and the southern terminus of Tokyo (¥17,460, four hours) via Kakunodate (¥3020, 45 minutes) and Tazawa-ko (¥3360, one hour).

Infrequent local trains also run on the JR Ōu main line between Akita and Kakunodate (¥1320, 1½ hours), with a change at Ōmagari to the JR Tazawako line. There are a few *tokkyū* (limited express) trains each day on the JR Inaho line, connecting Akita with Niigata (¥7210, 3¾ hours).

Kakunodate   角館

☏ 0187 / POP 28,300

Descendants of the Satake clan in Kakunodate can look back proudly at the architectural and aesthetic vision of their forebears. The *buke yashiki* (samurai district) is arguably the finest in the country; most of its buildings are still in perfect working order and are open to visitors. Horticulturalists, too, will delight in the manicured gardens and cherry trees that welcome trainloads of domestic tourists as they approach this living relic of feudal Japan.

The town was established in 1620 by Ashina Yoshikatsu, the lord of the Satake clan, and is well protected by mountains on three sides.

⦿ Sights

Half-a-dozen villas are open to the public, lining a street shaded by cherry trees a 20-minute walk northwest of the train station. The more elaborate ones are set up like miniature museums; others are simply left as they were and are free for visitors to peek inside.

Andō Brewery   BREWERY
(安藤醸造; ☏ 0187-53-2008; 27 Shimo-Shinmachi; ⊙11am-5pm) FREE Rows of Hinamatsuri dolls welcome visitors to this centuries-old brewery overseen by one of the oldest families in Akita-ken. Andō makes soy sauce and miso (sorry, tipplers, not that kind of brewery!) in a beautiful, brick storehouse from the late 19th century. You can tour a few rooms and sample some pickles and miso soup (for free!) in the cosy cafe.

Bukeyashiki Ishiguro-ke   HISTORIC BUILDING
(武家屋敷石黒家; ☏ 0187-55-1496; 1 Omotemachi; adult/child ¥300/200; ⊙9am-5pm) Built in 1809 as the residence of the Ishiguro family, advisers to the Satake clan, this is one of the oldest buildings in the district. Descendants of the family still live here, and offer tours

TŌHOKU FAMOUS FESTIVALS

Tōhoku festivals are the stuff of Japanese legend, and many Japanese legends live on in Tōhoku's wild public celebrations. Particularly through the warmer months, you've a decent chance of passing a city, town or village in full flight. The following festivals are non-negotiable (just be sure to book accommodation months in advance):

Sendai Tanabata Matsuri (p506) Thousands of coloured streamers around Sendai's downtown area honour a tale of star-crossed lovers.

Aomori Nebuta Matsuri (p526) Local artists outdo each other creating elaborate floats, and a multitude of merrymakers take to Aomori's streets.

Akita Kantō Matsuri (p537) Stunning acrobatics are performed in Akita with towering bamboo poles hung with lanterns.

around parts of the house. In addition to samurai gear, don't miss the weathered maps and the precision scales for doling out rice.

Aoyagi Samurai Manor Museum MUSEUM
(角館歴史村青柳家; Kakunodate Rekishi-mura Aoyagi-ke; ☑ 0187-54-3257; www.samuraiworld. com; 3 Omote-machi; adult/child ¥500/300; ⏰ 9am-4pm) The Aoyagi family compound is impressive in its own right, but inside each well-maintained structure is a fascinating exhibition of family heirlooms. The collection spans generations and includes centuries-old samurai weaponry, folk art and valuable antiques, along with gramophones and classic jazz records. Luckily for the kids, it's OK to handle some of the items.

Kakunodate Cherry-Bark Craft Center ARTS CENTRE
(角館樺細工伝承館, Kakunodate Kabazaiku Denshōkan; ☑ 0187-54-1700; 10-1 Omote-machi; adult/child ¥300/150; ⏰ 9am-4.30pm) Inside are exhibits and demonstrations of *kabazaiku*, the craft of covering household or decorative items in fine strips of cherry bark. This pursuit was first taken up by lower-ranking and masterless samurai in times of hardship.

Festivals & Events

Kakunodate Sakura CULTURAL
(角館の桜; ⏰ mid-Apr–early May) On the river embankment, a 2km stretch of cherry trees becomes a tunnel of pure pink during the *hanami* (blossom viewing) season. Some of the *shidare-zakura* (drooping cherry) trees in the *buke yashiki* (samurai district) are up to 300 years old.

Kakunodate O-matsuri CULTURAL
(角館祭り; ⏰ 7-9 Sep) As they have done for 350 years, festival participants haul around enormous 7-tonne *yama* (wooden carts) to

pray for peaceful times, accompanied by folk music and dancing.

Sleeping & Eating

Room rates rise sharply during cherry-blossom and festival seasons.

Near the train station are a number of pleasant eateries, but the best options are in the old town.

Iori MINSHUKU ¥
(☐; ☑ 0187-55-2262; www.akita-gt.org/stay/minshuku/iori.html; 65 Maeda, Ogata; r per person/incl 2 meals ¥4500/6000) Kakunodate is still a largely agricultural community, and this working farm 3km north of the train station provides an authentic opportunity to get your hands dirty, or just unplug in a peaceful rural setting. Accommodation is in stylish, minimalist cabins with whitewashed walls, dark-wood beams, fresh tatami and indigo cushions; it's a great deal, especially with meals included.

Pick-up from Kakunodate Station can be arranged.

Tamachi Bukeyashiki Hotel BOUTIQUE HOTEL ¥¥
(田町武家屋敷ホテル; ☑ 0187-52-1700; www. bukeyashiki.jp; 23 Ta-machi; r per person/incl 2 meals from ¥8500/13,800; ☐❋☎) With an idyllic location in the historic Bukeyashiki area, Tamachi is a surprisingly modern hotel, blending Japanese and Western aesthetics. All rooms have the requisite dark wooden beams and paper lanterns, but the communal areas are largely typical of European boutique hotels.

Wabizakura RYOKAN ¥¥¥
(わびざくら; ☑ 0187-47-3511; www.wabizakura. com/en/; 2-8 Sasayama, Nishikichokadoya; per person incl 2 meals ¥35,000; ☐❋☎) Located 15km north of Kakunodate, the 200-year-old house

that constitutes this stunning ryokan was deconstructed then relocated from Iwate Prefecture. With distinct Western interior-design influences, Wabizakura (a type of cherry blossom) is popular with well-off Tokyoites seeking refined solitude in a historical setting. The 10 suites include their own outdoor onsen and stylish lounge area. Very hard to leave.

Kosendō   SOBA ¥¥
(古泉洞; ☎ 0187-53-2902; 9 Higashi-katsurakuchō; noodles from ¥1050; ⊙10am-4pm; 🖂) The best noodles in town are found in this 250-year-old Edo-era wooden schoolhouse. The house speciality is *buke-soba* served with *takenoko* (bamboo) and tempura-fried *ōba* (large perilla leaf). Little has changed here in years, including the regular clientele and the travellers who seek it out.

It's in the middle of the *buke yashiki* (samurai district); look for the wooden sign above the entrance. There's a pleasant gift shop out the back.

Nishi-no-miyake   JAPANESE ¥¥
(西宮家レストラン北蔵; ☎ 0187-52-2438; 11-1 Kami-chō, Tamachi; meals from ¥1100; ⊙11am-5pm; 🅿🖂) Halfway between the train station and the sightseeing district, this samurai house has been partly converted into a delightful cafe-restaurant. The menu spans the ages, but mostly serves classic *yōshoku* (Japanese-style Western food). The tea and cake selection is equally tempting.

❶ Information

Tourist Information Center (角館町観光協会; ☎ 0187-54-2700; ⊙9am-5pm) Pick up English maps outside the train station in a small building shaped like a *kura* (traditional Japanese storehouse).

❶ Getting There & Around

Several of the *shinkansen* on the Akita line run hourly between Kakunodate and Tazawa-ko (¥1590, 15 minutes), and between Kakunodate and Akita (¥3020, 45 minutes).

Local trains also run infrequently on the JR Tazawako line between Kakunodate and Tazawa-ko (¥320, 20 minutes), and between Kakunodate and Akita (¥1320, 1½ hours), with a change at Ōmagari to the JR Ōu main line.

Bicycle rentals are available across from the train station for ¥300 per hour.

Tazawa-ko   田沢湖
☑ 0187 / POP 12,500

Popular with domestic travellers in the warmer months, Tazawa-ko feels isolated despite being accessible by the *shinkansen*. There are some well-serviced beaches, plus a few where you'll have the natural world to yourself. Some strange creatures from the blue lagoon may have yet to surface – at 423m, Tazawa-ko is Japan's deepest lake.

The nearby mountains offer excellent views of the lake, and four seasons of activity, including skiing. It's highly recommended to pick up a rental car at Tazawa-ko Station for a night or two to make the most of the lake and nearby Nyūtō Onsen.

◉ Sights & Activities

Tazawa-ko   LAKE
(田沢湖) The under-visited beach at **Shirahama** (白浜) is a real find for open-water swimmers and beach bums due to its clear-blue water, shallow entry and breathtaking mountain backdrop, but is only recommended during summer months when the crispness is out of the air. Rent pleasure-craft at the nearby boathouse from spring to autumn. Romantic sunset strolls are highly recommended any time of year: on the lake's eastern shore, you'll find Tazawa-ko's famed bronze statue of the legendary beauty Tatsuko, sculpted by Funakoshi Yasutake.

A 20km road wraps around the lake, perfect for a slow drive or vigorous cycle – bike rentals are available in the small village of Tazawa Kohan (¥400 per hour). Sightseeing buses depart Tazawa-ko Station and loop around the lake, stopping for 15 minutes to admire the statue of Tatsuko.

★ Akita Komaga-take   HIKING
(秋田駒ヶ岳) These mountains straddling the border with Iwate Prefecture are admired for summer wildflowers, autumn foliage and a rare prevalence of both dry and wet plant species. Over two days you can pursue a 17km course that takes in three peaks, overnights in a picturesque mountain hut and ends with a rewarding soak in the reportedly healing waters of Nyūtō Onsen.

Access the trailhead at Komaga-take Hachigōme (eighth station) by taking one of seven daily buses (all departing before 1.30pm) from Tazawa-ko Station (¥1120, one hour). From the eighth station, it's a two-hour hike to the summit of Oname-dake (男女岳;

1637m) before pressing on to the eastern edge of the oval-shaped pond below and claiming your space at the Amida-ike Hinan Goya (阿弥陀池避難小屋) unstaffed mountain hut; it's recommended that you leave a small tip (¥1000). You can also double-back for 20 minutes or so and scale O-dake (男岳; 1623m).

On the second day, it's a seven-hour descent to Nyūtō Onsen, including first reaching the summit of Yoko-dake (横岳; 1583m). The trail down follows the ridge line most of the way before winding through expansive marshlands rich with bird life. Emerge at the Nyūtō Onsen bus stop, from where it's a short stroll to a heavenly bath.

Tazawako Ski Park SNOW SPORTS
(田沢湖スキー場; ☑ 0187-46-2011; www.tazawako-ski.com; 73-2 Shimo-Takano; 1-day lift ticket adult/child ¥4000/1000, gear rental per day ¥3600; ☉ Dec-Apr) Skiers in northern Japan are spoiled for choice, so it's no surprise that setups like Tazawako Ski Park, the venue for the 2016 World Cup Freestyle Moguls, are rarely visited by foreigners. Of the 13 or so trails, all but the 1.6km Kokutai and Shirakaba runs are on the shorter side, but with an even mix of beginner, intermediate and advanced.

The views down the hill to the nearby shores of Tazawa-ko are breathtaking.

There's English signage on the mountains and eateries. In the winter months, buses leaving Tazawa-ko Station for Nyūtō Onsen stop at Tazawako Sukī-jō (¥550, 30 minutes).

🛏 Sleeping & Eating

Many elect to bed down in one of neighbouring Nyūtō Onsen's excellent ryokan (p544).

A number of restaurants near the lake serve lunch and dinner, but ideally you'll need a car to explore.

Tazawa-ko Youth Hostel HOSTEL ¥
(田沢湖ユースホステル; ☑ 0187-43-1281; www.jyh.or.jp/yhguide/touhoku/tazawako/index.html; 33-8 Kami-Ishigami; dm ¥3890, with YHA discount ¥3240, breakfast/dinner ¥650/1050; ℗) Although it looks very dodgy from the outside, this older hostel is actually pretty decent, especially for backpackers who struggle to find value in the area. Shared tatami rooms are clean and overlook the lake. Bathing is a communal affair. Meals are hearty and home-style. It's a few minutes' walk from the lake.

Tamagawa Onsen Ryokan RYOKAN ¥¥
(玉川温泉旅館; ☑ 0187-58-3000; www.tamagawa-onsen.jp; Shibukurosawa, Tamagawa; r per

THE LEGEND OF TATSUKO

Legend has it that long ago, a local maiden, Tatsuko, believing that the spring water would make her youthful beauty last forever, drank so much water that she was turned into a dragon and remains in the lake to this day. One version of the mythology adds another dragon, formerly a prince, as her lover. Their passionate nocturnal antics are said to be the reason why Tazawa-ko doesn't freeze in winter!

person incl 2 meals from ¥8300, baths ¥600; ☉ day bathing 7am-5pm; ℗ 🛜) This new, very local onsen resort is affordable and fun, especially for those well versed in Japanese custom (or those happy enough to bumble along!). The long rows of baths are known for their high acidity, which is supposed to detox internal organs. The dining area is cafeteria-style, and the rooms are remarkably spacious, many with Western beds.

Hutte Birke RYOKAN ¥¥
(ヒュッテ ビルケ; ☑ 0187-46-2833; 72 Shimotakano, Obonai; per person incl 2 meals ¥8000; ℗ ✳ 🛜) This modest, very welcoming ryokan servicing the Tazawa-ko ski fields is very well priced and perfect for families. Some of the spacious rooms (only eight available) interconnect and the friendly owners are flexible with meal times.

Orae FUSION ¥
(☑ 0187-58-0608; www.orae.net; 37-5 Haru-yama; meals from ¥700; ☉ 11.30am-5pm) Delicious, organic lakeside cafe known for its starring role in a Korean film. Salads, soups and local beer make for a very satisfying lunch.

Tazawako Beer Brewery Restaurant FUSION ¥¥
(☑ 0187-44-3988; www.warabi.or.jp; 430 Waseda; 300/500ml beer ¥380/600, set meals from ¥1050; ☉ 11am-8pm) A great discovery for beer lovers is this lakeside brewery tapping into fine hops and water from the region. The casual dining is impressive too, especially the *donburi* set meals and the desserts. Non-drivers can attempt to find value in the all-you-can-drink-in-an-hour deal for ¥1300.

ℹ Information

Tourist Information Center (田沢湖観光情報センター, Folake; ☑ 0187-43-2111; ☉ 8.30am-5.30pm) Inside the train station; free internet.

❶ Getting There & Around

JR Tazawa-ko Station is located a few kilometres southeast of the lake and serves as the area's main access point.

The Akita *shinkansen* runs several times an hour between Tazawa-ko and Tokyo (¥15,830, three hours) and between Tazawa-ko and Akita (¥3360, one hour) via Kakunodate (¥1590, 15 minutes).

Frequent local buses run between JR Tazawa-ko Station and Tazawa Kohan (¥370, 10 minutes), the tourist hub on the eastern shore of the lake.

If you're driving, Rte 46 connects the Akita Expressway (秋田自動車道) with Tazawa-ko. Buses run to Nyūtō Onsen (¥690, 45 minutes). Services terminate after sunset.

Nyūtō Onsen 乳頭温泉

☎ 0187

Named for the bosom-shaped hills from where the milky-white waters recede, Nyūtō Onsen (*nyūtō* means 'nipple') is a well-known onsen village at the end of a mountain road. Offering the practice of *konyoku* (mixed-gender bathing), there's hardly a better place to enjoy nature in all its glory. Better yet, eight onsen can be visited on a single pass. When it all gets too hot, head downhill for a refreshing dip in, or a wander around, splendid Tazawa-ko.

🏃 Activities

Kuroyu Onsen ONSEN
(黒湯温泉; ☎ 0187-46-2214; www.kuroyu.com; 2-1 Kuroyu-zawa; day bathing ¥510; ⊗ day bathing 9am-4pm May-Nov) Perhaps best visited as a 'day bather' (the accommodation is fairly

❶ NYŪTŌ ONSEN PASS

It's possible to enjoy Nyūtō Onsen's waters without the expense of staying overnight, as a day bather. The excellent-value *hi-gaeri* (day-return) pass is available from most inns (¥1800), which open their baths between check-out and check-in (usually between 10am and 3pm). The pass gets you admission to eight onsen. Otherwise, you'll need to pay admission (between ¥500 and ¥1000) at each onsen you visit. You'll also need to bring your own towel, or buy one. The caveat is that much of the ambience is lost when you're sharing your stunning mountain *rotemburo* (outdoor bath) with coachloads of tourists with the same idea.

underwhelming for the price), 300-year-old Kuroyu ryokan has a lovely old-fashioned feel. The sulphur smell may be a little strong for some, but the forest setting is the lushest in the area and little touches including waterfall jets, complimentary towels and rustic wooden change rooms suggest a keen awareness of bathers' wants.

🛏 Sleeping & Eating

For the complete list of Nyūtō's inns and some onsen eye-candy, see www.nyuto-onsenkyo.com. If you have the time, you'll appreciate spending a night in these divine surrounds; meals are uniformly special, and there's no better way to enjoy these fine outdoor baths beneath moonlight or in private.

All ryokan provide half-board; otherwise, you will need to head down the mountain to Tazawa-ko for a restaurant or supermarket.

⭐ **Tsuru-no-yu Onsen** RYOKAN ¥¥
(鶴の湯温泉; ☎ 0187-46-2139; www.tsurunoyu.com; 50 Kokuyurin, Sendatsui-zawa; r per person incl 2 meals ¥8790-16,350, day bathing ¥500; ⊗ day bathing 10am-3pm Tue-Sun; 🅿) Tsuru-no-yu is the epitome of the Japanese ryokan: discreet, atmospheric and totally sumptuous. At every turn there's another photographic moment, from the slick suites opening up to the forest floor to the Edo-era artworks lining the halls. Evenings are a nostalgic affair, distinguished by memorable meals and guests in *yukata* (light cotton kimonos) socialising by lantern light. Reservations are essential.

The newer Yamanoyado buliding is 1km inland and very comfortable.

According to lore, the onsen became the official bathhouse of Akita's ruling elite after a hunter once saw a crane (*tsuru*) healing its wounds in the spring. Its milky-white waters are rich in sulphur, sodium, calcium chloride and carbonic acid. The mixed *rotemburo* (outdoor bath) is positively jubilant, although shyer folk can take refuge in the indoor sex-segregated baths.

Ganiba Onsen RYOKAN ¥¥
(蟹場温泉; ☎ 0187-46-2021; 4-1 Komagatake; per person incl 2 meals from ¥9870; 🅿❄📶) 'Crab' Onsen is a delightfully unpretentious affair with a gorgeous mixed-gender onsen and superb Japanese cuisine. The rooms are large and comfortable, though a little worn (ask to see a few). It's the last stop on the bus so the day trippers tend to stay away.

Tae-no-yu
RYOKAN ¥¥

(妙乃湯; ☑0187-46-2740; www.taenoyu.com; 2-1 Komagatake; r per person incl 2 meals from ¥13,100, day bathing ¥720; ☺day bathing 10am-3pm Wed-Mon; P🖦) 🖋 This small ryokan is the most modern in Nyūtō Onsen. The stylish lodging is the right mix of urbane sensibility in a forest setting; think a Parisian apartment with tatami floors. Exquisite locavore meals incorporate wild plants foraged from the grounds. Bathing options are comprehensive, including private family onsen, reclining cypress tubs and heavenly *rotemburo* (outdoor bath). Single travellers are welcomed.

ⓘ Getting There & Around

Buses run to Nyūtō Onsen (¥690, 45 minutes) from Tazawa-ko every hour from sunrise until sunset. Tazawa-ko can be reached by train from Akita (¥3360, one hour) via Kakunodate (¥1590, 15 minutes).

Renting a car from Tazawa-ko gives you the freedom to truly get the most out of a visit to this area.

YAMAGATA PREFECTURE
山形県

The three sacred peaks of Dewa Sanzan – and much of mountainous Yamagata-ken – have climbed into the consciousness of Japanese travellers thanks largely to the poet Matsuo Bashō. His cherished accounts of the region's aesthetic beauty and his championing of the *yamabushi's* (local priests') ascetic practice have elevated the prefecture to its current status as somewhere to seek tranquillity and reflection.

Further inland, the remarkable clifftop temple of Risshaku-ji (p547), near the village of Yamadera, makes a mesmerising day trip from the big cities, while Zaō Onsen, with its dramatic caldera lake, fine hiking trails and challenging ski slopes, attracts a more active wanderer. The coastal train from Tsuruoka to Sakata is utterly charming, as are many train lines weaving through the interior, but renting a car is the best way to explore the mountains.

🛏 Sleeping

Yamagata and Tsuruoka have a decent business hotel selection. Most travellers will head for Zaō Onsen, Ginzan Onsen or Dewa Sanzan though, where both luxurious and rustic mountain retreats await.

Yamagata
山形

☑023 / POP 252,600

Yamagata is a bustling *inaka* (rural) capital that makes a comfortable base for exploring the mountain trails around Yamadera and as a stopover en route to Zaō Onsen and Ginzan Onsen, tucked away in the surrounding countryside. When night falls, there is plenty of action to be found in the entertainment district near the train station. Hirashimizu is a respectable pottery district nearby.

⊙ Sights & Activities

Hirashimizu Pottery District   HISTORIC SITE
(平清水焼陶芸地域) In the 19th century there were dozens of fiery kilns lining the Hazukashi-gawa turning out beautiful bluish-grey mottled pieces known as *nashi-seiji* (pear skin), but now only a few remain. You can purchase ceramics from a number of onsite gift shops, which cater to a steady trade of tour buses. Buses bound for Nishi-Zaō or Geikō-dai run hourly or half-hourly from stop 5 outside Yamagata Station to the Hirashimizu stop (¥290, 15 minutes).

Shichiemon-gama   POTTERY MAKING
(·七右エ門窯; ☑023-642-7777; 153 Hirashimizu; ☺8.30am-5.30pm, pottery making 9am-3pm) Try your hand at making your own pottery at this renowned studio in the Hirashimizu Pottery District. Lessons (in Japanese) are 90 minutes and priced according to the amount of clay you use (¥2000 per kilogram; shipping fee extra). Finished pieces ship to an address in Japan one month later.

✰ Festivals & Events

Yamagata International Documentary Film Festival   FILM
(www.yidff.jp; ☺Oct) This biennial event takes place over one week in October and screens films and retrospectives from all over the world, and also hosts symposiums.

🛏 Sleeping & Eating

Guesthouse Mintaro Hut   GUESTHOUSE ¥
(ゲストハウスミンタロハット; ☑090-2797-1687; www.mintarohut.com; 5-13 Ōte-machi; s/d ¥3500/6000; P@🖦) Guesthouses where hosts and guests interact freely with each other are a rare thing in Japan, which makes the childhood home of English-speaking Sato-san all the more fabulous. The common area is built around a radiant stove, ensuring a warm and familial atmosphere

Yamagata Prefecture

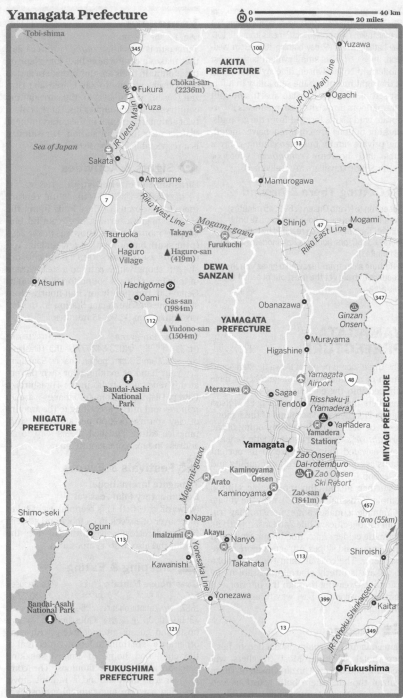

0 — 40 km
0 — 20 miles

Tobi-shima

345

AKITA PREFECTURE

108

Yuzawa

Fukura
Chōkai-san
(2236m)

Yuza

7

JR Ōu Main Line

Ogachi

13

Sea of Japan

Sakata

JR Uetsu Main Line

7

Amarume

Mamurogawa

Riko West Line

Mogami-gawa

Shinjō

47

Mogami

Takaya

Furukuchi

Riko East Line

Tsuruoka

Haguro Village

Haguro-san
(419m)

DEWA SANZAN

Atsumi

Hachigōme

Ōami

Gas-san
(1984m)

112

YAMAGATA PREFECTURE

Obanazawa

347

Ginzan Onsen

Yudono-san
(1504m)

Murayama

Higashine

Yamagata Airport

48

NIIGATA PREFECTURE

Bandai-Asahi National Park

Aterazawa

Sagae

Tendō

Risshaku-ji
(Yamadera)

Yamadera

Yamadera Station

Yamagata

Zaō Onsen
Dai-rotemburo

Zaō Onsen
Ski Resort

Kaminoyama Onsen

Arato

Kaminoyama

Zaō-san
(1841m)

457

Tōno (55km)

Shimo-seki

Oguni

113

Nagai

Mogami-gawa

Imaizumi

Akayu

Nanyō

Shiroishi

Kawanishi

Yonesaka Line

Takahata

113

399

Kaita

Bandhi-Asahi National Park

Yonezawa

349

JR Tōhoku Shinkansen

121

13

FUKUSHIMA PREFECTURE

Fukushima

MIYAGI PREFECTURE

conducive to chatting with fellow travellers, and the kitchen is stocked with supplies for self-caterers. Terrific value.

It's located on the northeast corner of the central park.

Yamagata Kokusai Hotel HOTEL ¥¥
(山形国際ホテル; ☑ 023-633-1313; www.kokusai hotel.com; 3-4-5 Kasumi-chō; s/d ¥6000/9000; ❄ ☎) This very comfortable independent hotel is in a fun part of the city next to popular *izakaya* and a high school. English-language TV, locally sourced breakfasts and warm, knowledgeable staff are all big ticks.

Sobadokoro Shōjiya SOBA ¥
(そば処庄司屋; ☑ 023-622-1380; 14-28 Saiwai-chō; bowls from ¥600; ⏰ 11-2.30pm & 5-8.30pm) Delicious chewy udon and signature soba bowls (hot or cold) are served with simple elegance here. The accompanying tempura and miso are respectively light and tangy.

Kitanosuisan IZAKAYA ¥¥
(北野水産; ☑ 023-624-0880; 2nd fl, 1-8-8 Kasumi-chō; table charge ¥500, dishes ¥300-1500; ⏰ 5pm-12am) Come here to sample sake and local Yamagata specialities, such as *imo nabe* (potato stew) and *dongara* (cod), cooked in practically every possible way. The menu is on a wooden board and includes pictures. Take the first left outside the train station's east exit and look for the blue sign across the 2nd floor.

🛈 Information

Tourist Information Center (山形市観光案内センター; ☑ 023-647-2266; ⏰ 9am-5.30pm) On the 2nd floor of Yamagata Station, in a small glass booth.

🛈 Getting There & Away

The *shinkansen* between Tokyo and Yamagata (¥10,450, 2¾ hours) runs hourly, as do *kaisoku* (rapid trains) on the JR Senzan line between Yamagata and Yamadera (¥240, 15 minutes).

Alternatively, JR highway buses make an overnight trip between Yamagata and Tokyo (¥6400, 6½ hours).

Yamadera　山寺
☑ 023

Immortalised by the itinerant haiku master, Matsuo Bashō in *The Narrow Road to the Deep North* (1689), Yamadera is home to some very special mountain temple buildings. The town was founded in AD 860 by

WORTH A TRIP

YONEZAWA

Yonezawa (米沢) is an attractive, secluded medieval town with some fine feudal-era streetscapes – though it's best known for its local beef, tender *Yonezawa-gyū*, said to rival Kōbe's own. There are dozens of places in town to try it, but 100-year-old **Tokiwa** (登起波; ☑ 0238-24-5400; www.yonezawabeef. co.jp/info/eng.html; 7-2-3 Chūō; meals from ¥4200; ⏰ 11am-9pm, closed Tue) is the best known. Ask the tourist information centre staff in Yonezawa Station for directions – it's a bit out of the way.

The town is also home to the ruined 17th-century castle of the Uesugi clan. The foundations of the castle now form the boundaries of **Matsugasaki-kōen** (松ヶ崎公園), a pretty park framed by a placid moat filled with lotus flowers.

Yonezawa is a stop on the Yamagata *shinkansen* (bullet train) and regular *futsū* (local) trains plough the JR Ōu main line between Yonezawa and Yamagata (¥840, 45 minutes).

priests who carried with them the sacred flame from Enryaku-ji near Kyoto, believing that Yamadera's rock faces were the boundaries between this world and the next. Supposedly that flame remains lit to this day. Although it's possible (though precarious) to visit Yamadera during winter, a visit in the warmer months will be more enjoyable.

⊙ Sights

★ **Risshaku-ji** BUDDHIST TEMPLE
(立石寺; ☑ 023-695-2843; www.rissyakuji.jp; ¥300; ⏰ 8am-5pm) The 'Temple of Standing Stones', more commonly known as Yamadera, rests atop a rock-hewn staircase weathered over the centuries by unrelenting elements. At the foot of the mountain, guarded by a small lantern, is the sacred flame **Konpon-chūdō** (根本中堂; admission ¥200), said to have been transported from Kyoto many centuries ago.

The **San-mon** (山門) gate marks the start of the climb, some 1000 steps that take you past carvings so mossy and worn they appear to be part of the landscape. It's a steep ascent – a sort of walking meditation – but one that makes the views from the top, of the surrounding mountains and bucolic countryside below, that much more spectacular.

MATSUO BASHŌ

Born into a samurai family, Matsuo Bashō (1644–94), regarded as Japan's master of haiku, is credited with elevating this poetic form's status from comic relief to Zen-infused enlightenment. Comparisons have been made between his haiku and Zen *kōan* (short riddles), intended to bring about a sudden flash of insight in the listener. Influenced by the natural philosophy of the Chinese Taoist sage Chuangzi, his work contemplated the rhythms and laws of nature. Later he developed his own poetic principle by drawing on the concept of *wabi-sabi*, a kind of spare, lonely beauty.

When he reached his 40s, Bashō abandoned his career in favour of travelling throughout Japan, seeking to build friendships and commune with nature as he went. He published evocative accounts of his travels, including *The Records of a Weather-Beaten Skeleton* and *The Records of a Travel-Worn Satchel,* but his collection *The Narrow Road to the Deep North,* detailing his journey throughout Tōhoku in 1689, is the most famous.

During the summer months, the electric whir of the cicadas is almost overpowering.

Past the **Nio-mon** (仁王門), through which only those with pure souls may enter (be honest now!), the path splits, heading in one direction to the **Oku-no-in** (奥の院; Inner Sanctuary) and in the other to the **Go-daidō** (五大堂). The latter, an 18th-century pavilion perched on the cliffside, has the most arresting views.

For a better shot at a measure of the meditative bliss that so inspired Bashō, visit early in the morning or late in the afternoon. It's possible to visit Yamadera during the winter, although if you arrive just after a snowfall, the paths may not yet be shovelled.

Sleeping & Eating

A few simple ryokan can be found near the train station.

Lots of street stalls sell yummy *tamakon*, gooey balls of pounded root vegetable on a stick. These, and a few pleasant noodle shops, are about the extent of Yamadera's culinary offerings.

Getting There & Away

Hourly *kaisoku* (rapid trains) travel the JR Senzan line between Yamagata and Yamadera (¥240, 15 minutes), continuing to Sendai (¥840, one hour).

Zaō Onsen 蔵王温泉

023 / POP 13,800

Hidden at the end of a winding, misty mountain road, Zaō Onsen is a cute resort village equally suited to adventure and convalescence. In warmer months, Zaō promises scenic hiking and the chance to soak in some special sulphur-infused *rotemburo*

(outdoor baths). In ski season, experts and beginners speed and stumble down huge slopes and dodge the creepy *juhyō* (ice monsters) – conifers that have been frozen solid by harsh Siberian winds – a phenomenon unique to the area.

Activities

★ **Zaō Onsen Ski Resort**   SNOW SPORTS
(蔵王温泉スキー場; ☑ 023-647-2266; www.zao-spa.or.jp; 1-day lift ticket ¥3500-5000; ☉ Dec-Apr) Distinguished by its broad and winding runs (some up to 10km long!) and famous **Juhyō Kōgen** (樹氷高原; Ice Monster Plateau), which reaches peak ferocity in frigid February, Zaō has more than 40 ropeways and 14 spidery courses with multiple offshoots, including a huge breadth of beginner and intermediate runs. English signage is excellent and full equipment rental is available.

Nightly 'ice-monster' illuminations (January to February) are fun for all (adult/child, ¥2500/1300). Newbies will love that it's possible to ski from the mountain's highest point to the base without accidentally turning down a black diamond or getting stuck in a field of moguls, while experienced skiers will appreciate the sheer scope and variety of terrain.

Zaō Sanroku Ropeway   CABLE CAR
(蔵王山麓ロプウェー; ☑ 023-694-9518; one way/return ¥1500/2600; ☉ 8.30am-5pm Apr-Nov) This succession of cable cars whisks you over the conifers and up **Zaō-san** (蔵王山) to within spitting distance of **Okama** (御釜), a crater lake of piercing cobalt blue. The walk to the lake passes Buddhist statues and monuments hidden among the greenery, before the terrain breaks up into a sunset-coloured crumble of volcanic rock.

You can extend the hike (and save money) by taking one of the other two shorter ropeways, the **Zaō Chūō Ropeway** or the **Zaō Sky Cable**, up or down.

Zaō Onsen Dai-rotemburo ONSEN
(蔵王温泉大露天風呂; ☏023-694-9417; ¥450, locker ¥100; ◎6am-7pm May-Oct) Above the village, at the base of the mountain, you'll find this huge open-air hot-spring pool. The sulphur-stained rocks set the stage for the spectacle of dozens of complete strangers bathing naked together in joyful unison. If you arrive for first light in the warmer months, you'll have the place to yourself.

Shinzaemon-no-Yu ONSEN
(新左衛門の湯; ☏023-693-1212; www.zaospa. co.jp; 905 Kawa-mae; adult/child ¥700/400; ◎10am-6.30pm Mon-Fri, to 9.30pm Sat & Sun) An upmarket bathing option, this modern hotspring complex has several spacious pools. The nicest are outside, set in stone and with wooden canopies.

🛏 Sleeping

Accommodation abounds, but reservations are essential if you're visiting during the ski season or on weekends in summer.

Yoshida-ya RYOKAN ¥
(吉田屋; 13 Zaō Onsen; r per person from ¥5000, breakfast/dinner ¥800/2000; P🛜) Right in the heart of the modest action, Yoshida-ya has a more international feel than most due to the presence of young, foreign adventurers and helpful English-speaking staff. It's a modern building, about a 500m uphill walk from both the bus station and the Zaō Sky Cable.

Pension Boku-no-Uchi PENSION ¥
(ペンションぼくのうち; ☏023-694-9542; www.bokunouchi.com; 904 Zaō Onsen; r per person/incl 2 meals from ¥3700/6800; P🛜) This is a skiers' lodge through and through, from the posters on the wall of the sociable dining room to the prime location right in front of Family Mart and the Zaō Chūō Ropeway. Rooms are Japanese-style with communal facilities, including a 24-hour sulphur bath. Don't be put off by the weathered exterior.

Zao Shiki no Hotel HOTEL ¥¥
(蔵王四季のホテル; ☏023-693-1211; www. zao-shikinohotel.jp/en; per person incl 2 meals from ¥10,800; P◉❈🛜) Massive Japanese- or Western-style rooms, many with broad mountain views, are the selling point of this fastidious ski hotel, with a wonderful outdoor

onsen and lively communal dining area. It's very popular with Japanese weekenders who come for the value, trail access and comfort.

Tsuruya Hotel HOTEL ¥¥
(つるやホテル; ☏023-694-9112; www.tsuruya hotel.co.jp; 710 Zaō Onsen; r per person incl 2 meals from ¥10,950) Conveniently located opposite the bus terminal, the friendly staff of this small hotel do their best to ensure you have a wonderful stay. Handsome tatami rooms have beautiful views and a variety of indoor and outdoor baths beckon to soak your troubles away. Great value for budget ski-travellers; a shuttle to the ski lifts is available.

★ Takamiya RYOKAN ¥¥¥
(高見屋; ☏023-694-9333; www.zao.co.jp/takam iya; 54 Zaō Onsen; r per person incl 2 meals from ¥32,000; P🛜) Takamiya is an atmospheric, upmarket ryokan that has been in business for nearly three centuries. There are several beautiful baths here, both indoor and outdoor, made of stone or aromatic cedar. Meals are traditional *kaiseki ryōri* (formal, multiple-course banquets), with top-grade local beef as the headliner. The spacious rooms have tatami sitting areas and fluffy *wa-beddo* (thick futons on platforms).

It's not cheap, but it's a true destination and worth the splurge, especially with a loved one.

Oomiya Ryokan RYOKAN ¥¥¥
(おおみや旅館; ☏023-694-2112; www.oomiya ryokan.jp/en; per person incl 2 meals from ¥16,200; P❈🛜) Constructed in the style of the Taishō era, retro Oomiya is our favourite ryokan in pretty little Zaō. It's highly functional for skiers and hikers, especially with children, yet charming enough to lend a sense of significance to your stay. Very good value for these parts, too.

🍴 Eating & Drinking

Mongolian barbecues are popular in Zaō, where the style of cooking is known as *jingisukan*, with the hotplate oddly resembling Genghis Khan's hat.

Marumo CAFE ¥
(まるも; ☏0948-60-2438; 55-10 Zaō Onsen; ◎8am-7pm) The pizza at this informal, friendly place not only fills a void for hungry skiers seeking Western food, it's actually pretty good.

Robata BARBECUE ¥¥
(ろばた; ☏023-694-9565; 42-7 Kawara; courses from ¥1200; ◎11am-11pm Fri-Wed; 🖨) The best

DON'T MISS

BEST ONSEN
....
➡ Nyūtō Onsen (p544)

➡ Sukayu Onsen (p535)

➡ Zaō Onsen (p548)

➡ Akiu Onsen (p512)

Mongolian barbecue or *jingisukan* restaurant in Zaō is a sharp operation where diners do the grunt work on plates of raw lamb and veggies. It's good smoky fun, well supported by a drinks menu including fruit sake and, everyone's favourite, yoghurt liqueur.

Oto-chaya BAR
(音茶屋; ☑023-694-9081; 935-24 Zaō Onsen; meals from ¥850; ⊙11am-9pm Thu-Tue; 🐾) Oto-chaya is a hub for convivial pre- and post-ski rendezvous. Come for coffee, casseroles, Chinese tea sets, stews, sake and beer, and occasional live tunes, too. Look for the wooden sign with the teapot, on the main road beyond the Zaō Chūō Ropeway.

ℹ️ Information

Tourist Information Center (蔵王温泉観光協会; ☑023-694-9328; www.zao-spa.or.jp; 708-1 Zaō Onsen; ⊙9am-6pm) English-language info available, just inside the bus terminal.

ℹ️ Getting There & Away

Buses run hourly between the bus terminal in Zaō Onsen and JR Yamagata Station (¥1060, 40 minutes).

At the height of the ski season, private companies run overnight shuttles between Tokyo and Zaō. Prices can be as low as ¥7000 return – enquire at travel agencies in Tokyo for more information.

Ginzan Onsen 銀山温泉

☑ 0237 / POP 17,500

With its century-old inns forming mirror images on either side of the peaceful Obana-zawa, Ginzan Onsen, an out-of-the-way collection of ryokan in the classic Taishō-era style (which adds romantic Western flourishes to traditional architecture), was once the setting for *Oshin,* an enormously popular historical drama from the 1980s. Most romantic in the evening or when draped in snow, Ginzan is a pleasant day trip from Yamagata. Several ryokan open their baths for *hi-gaeri* (day) bathing.

🛏️ Sleeping & Eating

Ginzan Onsen's single heritage-listed street is filled with traditional Japanese ryokan.

All ryokan offer at least half-board, though there are a few restaurants serving local dishes.

Ginzan-so RYOKAN ¥¥¥
(☑0237-28-2322; www.ginzanso.jp; 1-/2-spa suite per person incl 2 meals from ¥16,500/19,500) A picture of the artist Kenji Uchino greets guests to Ginzan-so, an enchanting mountain hotel with spacious, traditional accommodation where soft interiors are accentuated by beautiful paper lamps. Go for the in-room spas overlooking the trees. The included meals are delicious.

Notoya Ryokan RYOKAN ¥¥¥
(能登屋旅館; ☑0237-28-2327; www.notoya ryokan.com; 446 Ginzan Shin-hata, Obanazawa; r per person incl 2 meals from ¥18,900; 🅿️) Three storeys high, complete with balconies, elaborate woodwork and a curious garret tower, Notoya is a classical ryokan originally constructed in 1922. Make sure you get a room in the main building overlooking the river.

ℹ️ Getting There & Away

Take the Yamagata *shinkansen* to its terminus in Ōishida (¥1940, 30 minutes), or the JR Ou train (¥670, 50 minutes), then transfer to one of up to five daily buses leaving for Ginzan Onsen (¥710, 40 minutes) from the west exit bus pool.

Tsuruoka 鶴岡

☑ 0235 / POP 129,700

This laid-back, compact city on the Shōnai Plain is the ideal transit point for visits to the mountains of Dewa Sanzan. Established by the Sakai clan, one of feudal Yamagata's most important families, today Tsuruoka is the second-largest city in the prefecture with a handful of modest sights to lure travellers.

⊙ Sights

Kamo Aquarium AQUARIUM
(加茂水族館; ☑0235-33-3036; 657-1 Ōkubo, Imaizumi; adult/child ¥1000/500; ⊙9am-5pm) The world's largest jellyfish tank – containing 30 to 40 species at any one time – was given a spark by a Nobel Prize–winning scientist who discovered a fluorescent protein in belt jellyfish and taught the aquarium how to make the jellyfish glow. Ever since, the *Aequorea coerulescens* have put on a surreal

show. Elsewhere, seals frolic to the signal of instructors. From Tsuruoka Station, take the bus bound for Yunohama Onsen and get off at the Kamo Suizokukan stop (30 minutes).

The building looks like a streamlined boat pointed towards the ocean.

Zenpō-ji
TEMPLE

(善寶寺) Seven kilometres west of Tsuruoka is this Zen Buddhist temple, complete with five-tier pagoda and large gateway. It dates from the 10th century, when it was dedicated to the Dragon King, guardian of the seas. Near the temple is a more contemporary attraction, the famous *jinmen-gyo* (human-faced carp). When viewed from above, these curious fish actually do appear to have human faces. From the station, take a bus bound for Yunohama Onsen to the Zenpō-ji stop (¥580, 30 minutes).

🛏 Sleeping

Tsuruoka has some comfortable business hotels from where you can travel to nearby Dewa Sanzan. Two reliable, if impersonal, options include **Hotel Route Inn Tsuruoka Ekimae** (ホテルルートイン鶴岡駅前; ☑0235-28-2055; www.route-inn.co.jp; 1-17 Suehiro-machi; s/d ¥6900/10,350), in front of Tsuruoka train station, and **Tokyo Daiichi Hotel Tsuruoka** (東京第一ホテル鶴岡; ☑0235-24-7611; www.tdh-tsuruoka.co.jp; 2-10 Nishiki-machi; s/d from ¥8800/12,700; 🅿@), connected to the S-Mall shopping centre a few minutes' walk away.

🍴 Eating & Drinking

Downtown is pretty sleepy; if you need a bite to eat or snacks for the road, try the S-Mall shopping centre, a few minutes on foot from the train station.

Sapporo Rāmen
RAMEN ¥

(サッポロラーメン; ☑0235-23-4300; 15-16 Suehiro-machi; bowls from ¥600; ⊙11.30am-2pm & 5.30-10pm) A little ramen joint that lasts for decades must be good given Japan's high culinary standards. The husband-and-wife team here prepare buttery noodles with thin, sweet pork and/or heaped leafy green vegetables. It's cheap and cheery. Exiting the train station, turn left: it's within two blocks, on your left.

High Noon Diner
BAR

(ハイヌーン; ☑0235-25-0081; 15-18 Suehiro-machi; ⊙7pm-1am Wed-Mon) Turning left from the train station, walk not even two blocks until you see the neon pink flamingo in the window of this cosy retro bar with Guinness on tap, popular with visitors and locals alike.

ℹ Information

Tourist Information Center (鶴岡市観光案内所; ☑0235-25-7678; ⊙10am-5pm) To the right as you exit the train station, come here for information, bus timetables and English maps for Dewa Sanzan and other attractions.

ℹ Getting There & Away

A few daily *tokkyū* (limited-express trains) run on the JR Uetsu main line between Tsuruoka and Akita (¥4130, 1¾ hours) and between Tsuruoka and Niigata (¥4450, 1¾ hours).

Buses leave from in front of Tsuruoka Station and from the bus depot at S-Mall for Haguro village (¥1000, 35 minutes). There are a few buses each day between Tsuruoka and Yamagata (¥2470, 1¾ hours), though services are often cut back during winter.

Dewa Sanzan
出羽三山

☑ 0235 / POP 30,000

Haguro-san (Birth), Gas-san (Death) and Yudono-san (Rebirth) represent both the cycle of life and the stages you may go through when tackling the three famous peaks of Dewa Sanzen. The folk religion Shugendō's white-clad devotees worship a hybrid of Buddhism and Shintō and can be seen trekking the well-worn trail with wooden staff, sandals and straw hat, alongside fleece-clad hikers equipped with poles and waterproof boots.

Mountain priests go that extra step in their unmistakable conch shells, chequered jackets and voluminous white pantaloons. Come winter, you can join them beneath an icy waterfall to discipline both body and spirit, or just watch them pass from the comfort of your temple lodging at either end of the journey.

👁 Sights & Activities

If you want to tackle all three mountains – possible from June through September – you need two full days, though three are advised and accommodation should be booked in advance. Tradition dictates that you start hiking at Haguro-san and finish at Yudono-san. You can do the pilgrimage in the opposite direction, though the ascent from Yudono-san to Gas-san is painfully steep. For many, a visit to Haguro-san is rewarding enough.

★ Haguro-san
MOUNTAIN

(羽黒山) The 2446 stone steps through ancient cedars to Haguro-san's summit (419m) have been smoothed by centuries of pilgrims. The climb, taking up to two hours, passes **Gojū-no-tō** (五重塔), a beautiful wooden five-storey pagoda dating from the 14th century. At the top, marvel at the **San-shin Gōsaiden** (三神合祭殿), a vivid red hall that enshrines the deities of Dewa San-zan's three mountains.

If you're completing the circuit, you must catch the bus from the parking lot beyond the shrine, bound for **Hachigōme** (八合目; eighth station), where the trail to the top of Gas-san picks up again. The last bus leaves just after 2pm. Most of the old 20km pilgrim trail along the ridge line to Gas-san became overgrown after a road was built in the 1960s.

★ Gas-san   MOUNTAIN

(月山) Accessible from July to September, Gas-san (1984m) is the highest of Dewa San-zan's sacred mountains. From **Hachigōme** (八合目; eighth station), the route passes through an alpine plateau to **Kyūgōme** (九合目; ninth station) in 1¾ hours, then grinds uphill for another 1¼ hours to the top.

From here, the pilgrimage route presses on towards the steep descent to Yudono-san (p552). This takes another three hours or so, and you'll have to carefully descend rusty ladders chained to the cliff sides and pick your way down through a slippery stream bed at the end of the trail.

Gassan-jinja   SHINTO SHRINE

(月山神社; ¥500; ⏱5am-5pm Jul–mid-Sep) At the peak of Gas-san (p552) is the deeply spiritual Shintō shrine of Gassan-jinja. Before entering, you must be 'purifed': bow to receive the priest's benediction, then brush yourself head-to-toe with the slip of paper, placing it afterwards in the fountain. Beyond the gate, photography is prohibited.

★ Yudono-san   MOUNTAIN

(湯殿山) Accessible from May to October, Yudono-san (1504m) is the spiritual culmination of the Dewa Sanzan trek. Coming from Gas-san, it's a short walk from the stream bed at the end of the descent to Yudono-san-jinja.

To finish the pilgrimage, it's a mere 10-minute hike down the mountain to the trailhead at **Yudono-san Sanrōsho** (湯殿山参籠所), marked by a *torii* (gate) and adjacent to the Sennin-zawa (仙人沢) bus stop.

Yudono-san-jinja   SHINTO SHRINE

(湯殿山神社; ¥500; ⏱9am-5pm, closed Nov-Apr) Beyond the giant red *torii* (gate) of this shrine, ancient tradition – and stern-faced priests – forbid disclosure of what you witness. It's forbidden to photograph and taboo

to discuss this sacred natural shrine, so you'll just have to find out for yourself. It's quite remarkable. Strict rituals prevail: remove your shoes, bow your head before the priest for purification rites then follow the other pilgrims.

A bus stop is a mere 200m from the shrine should modern life, or a busy itinerary, have pilfered enough of your time already to make the pilgrimage hike a bit of an inconvenience.

Daishōbō   MEDITATION

(大聖坊; 99 Haguro-machi; 2-night training program ¥30,000) The new generation of *yamabushi* (mountain priests) have opened up their *shukubō* (temple lodging) to us everyday folk in need of reconnecting with nature. The masters dressed in white deliver three-day training programs twice monthly for those wanting to take their trip to the next level.

It's a tremendous opportunity to become versed in the austere spiritual practices of Shugendō devotees, revered across Japan for their mythical powers.

The sleeping quarters are more than pleasant, and the vegetarian meals come highly recommended. Guests can expect morning worship, educational nature walks, Shugendō incantations and even exorcism.

🎏 Festivals & Events

The peak of Haguro-san is the site of some lively festivals.

Hassaku Matsuri   CULTURAL

(八朔祭; ⏱31 Aug) *Yamabushi* (mountain priests) perform ancient fire rites throughout the night to pray for a bountiful harvest.

Shōrei-sai   CULTURAL

(松例祭; ⏱31 Dec) On New Year's Eve, *yamabushi* perform similar rituals to those of the mountain priests at the Hassaku Matsuri, competing with each other after completing 100-day-long austerities.

🛏 Sleeping

Reservations are essential if you plan to stay up here. You can choose to stay at either end of the pilgrimage path, in Haguro-san or Yudono-san, and a few places in-between.

★ Saikan   TEMPLE LODGE ¥¥

(斎館; ☎0235-62-2357; 7 Tōge, Haguro-machi; r per person incl 2 meals ¥7700; 🅿) ✿ Elegantly perched atop Haguro-san (p551), templeside, and accessed by an imposing gate, Saikan is a destination for reflective, quiet travel. The main building is sparingly furnished, but rooms are spotless and comfortable, and each is a few steps from valley views. Meals (lunch also available) are *shōjin ryōri* (Buddhist cuisine) with foraged mushrooms and mountain vegetables. A very special place.

Gas-san Shizu Onsen
Ochimizu no Yu Tsutaya
HOTEL ¥¥

(月山志津温泉変若水の湯つたや; ☑0237-74-4119; www.gassan-shizuonsen.net; per person incl 2 meals ¥15,000) Perform some *toji* (restorative bathing) at this mellow onsen hotel in Shizu village, then walk the attractive streets in between feasting on mountain plants and river fish. The tatami rooms include a tea-drinking area.

Midahara Sanrōsho
HUT ¥¥

(御田原参籠所; ☑090-2367-9037; r per person incl 2 meals ¥7650; ☺closed Oct-Jun) At the eighth station on Gas-san, this mountain hut is a convenient place to break up the long three-mountain hike. Futons are laid out in one big communal room (sans shower), but the meals are filling and the close quarters conducive for swapping stories. Catch the sunrise and you'll be on your way to the peak before the tour buses arrive.

Yudono-san Sanrōsho
LODGE ¥¥

(湯殿山参籠所; ☑0235-54-6131; 7 Rokujuri-yama, Tamugimata; r per person incl 2 meals from ¥7560; ☺closed Dec-Mar; Ⓟ) This airy mountain lodge at the bottom of Yudono-san has a hot bath and is full of jovial pilgrims celebrating the completion of their multiday circuit. Hearty meals, beer and sake are available and generally gratefully received. Tasty lunch sets (from ¥1575) are served here as well, even for non-lodgers.

✖ Eating & Drinking

There are some delightful, welcoming noodle stands at the entrance to Haguro-san, many serving fresh mountain-vegetable dishes.

Ni-no-saka-chaya
TEAHOUSE

(二の坂茶屋; tea sets ¥700; ☺8.30am-5pm Apr-Nov) Ni-no-saka-chaya is a charming teahouse marking the halfway resting place for hikers on Dewa Sanzan's three-mountain trek. Here you'll be greeted by marvellous views and smiling women selling refreshments.

ℹ Information

Stock up on maps at the **tourist information center** (p551) in Tsuruoka.

DON'T MISS

BEST HIKES
....
➡ Dewa Sanzan (p551)

➡ Hakkōda-san (p534)

➡ Iwaki-san (p531)

➡ Akita Komaga-take (p542)

➡ Oirase Keiryū (p533)

ℹ Getting There & Away

During the summer climbing months, there are up to 10 buses daily (the earliest leaving at 6am) from Tsuruoka to Haguro village (¥820, 35 minutes), most of which then continue to Haguro-sanchō (Haguro summit; ¥1180, 50 minutes). Outside the high season, the schedule is greatly reduced.

From early July to late August, and then on weekends and holidays until late September, there are up to four daily buses from Haguro-sanchō to **Gas-san** as far as Hachigōme (¥1560, one hour).

Between June and early November, there are up to four daily buses from the Yudono-san Sanrōsho trailhead to Tsuruoka (¥1880, 1¼ hours), which also pass by Ōami (¥1200, 35 minutes). Transport can grind to a halt once snows begin.

Sakata
酒田

☑0234 / POP 105,000

Sakata flourished in the Edo period when it was a wealthy port cultivated by nobles and merchants. Today, first glances allude to a sad story of a fading rural town with an ageing population. Closer inspection reveals a wealth of cultural and historical attractions waiting to be uncovered. There's a surprising amount of English signage here and plenty to see and do if you have a few hours and sunny weather.

◎ Sights

Historical
Abumiya Residence
HISTORIC BUILDING

(旧鐙屋; ☑0234-22-5001; 14-20 1-chōme; adult/child ¥320/210; ☺9am-4.30pm) Opposite the city hall, this private home once belonged to a wealthy shipping agent. With a beautiful garden and a fascinating variety of room divisions using *shōji* screens, it's a wonderful place to contemplate the Japanese aesthetic of bringing the outside in.

Historical Obata
('NK Agent') Building
HISTORIC BUILDING

(旧割烹小幡　　(NKエージェント)事務所; ☑0234-26-5759; 2-9-37 Hiyoshi-machi; ¥100; ☺9am-5pm) This wonderful, unique museum, or rather, the building that houses it, featured in the 2009 Academy Award–winning Best Foreign Language film, *Okuribito* (おくりびと; *Departures*). A bunch of other locations around town were used in the film too – ask about them here.

🛏 Sleeping

A few basic business hotels are found near the train station, but there are also some worthy ryokan for a small town.

Despite being on the sea, Sakata is close enough to the mountains to make a worthy alternative to Tsuruoka as a base.

Wakaba Ryokan　　　　　　RYOKAN ¥¥
(若葉　旅館; ☑0967-44-0500; 2-3-9 Honcho; per person incl 2 meals ¥11,500) Wakaba is the pick of the town's ryokan due to its friendly, English-speaking owners and a fine location within walking distance of shops and restaurants. Rooms are bright and clean.

🍴 Eating & Drinking

Sakata Kaisen Ichiba　　　　SEAFOOD ¥
(酒田海鮮市場; ☑0234-23-5522; 5-10 2-chōme; sushi box from ¥1000; ⊙8am-6pm) You can eat at a variety of places at this indoor seafood market or grab some mouth-watering sushi and picnic goodies.

Kumura no Sakaba　　　　　IZAKAYA ¥
(久村の酒場; ☑0234-24-1935; 1-41 Kotobukicho; dishes from ¥700; ⊙5-10pm) While many believe Sakata is an underrated town, Kumura no Sakaba is definitely an underrated *izakaya* (Japanese pub-eatery). The atmosphere is propelled by buoyant, local Japanese sharing simple seafood, chicken and vegetable dishes, and the beer flows freely on most tables.

Kerun　　　　　　　　COCKTAIL BAR
(ケルン; ☑0234-23-0128; 2-4-20 Naka-machi; ⊙noon-9pm) In business for decades, Kerun is run by an octogenarian Japanese man who whisks up frothy whisky sours from a well-stocked bar surrounded by lots of mirrors and booth seating. You can also get lovely filter coffee and iced chocolates during the day.

ℹ Information

Tourist Information Office (酒田駅観光案内所; ☑0234-24-2454; www.sakata-kankou.com; ⊙9am-5pm) The staff at the tourist information office within Sakata Station don't speak much English, but they rent bikes for free and have an excellent English-language walking map.

ℹ Getting There & Away

Sakata is an easy day trip from Tsuruoka on the local *futsū* train (¥500, 35 minutes) or a pleasant stop en route to Akita (limited express ¥1940, two hours) on the scenic, coast-hugging Uetsu main line.

NIIGATA PREFECTURE　　　新潟県

Skirting the western coast of Tōhoku, Niigata-ken is known for its supreme ski runs, rocky coastal stretches and established onsen villages. In summer, thousands descend on the small village of Naeba for the famed Fuji Rock Festival (p564), while in winter city-slickers carve up the slopes around Myōkō Kōgen and Echigo-Yuzawa Onsen. Its sprawling capital city is an industry and transport hub and easily accessible from Tokyo. The attractive port area is a gateway to quiet Sado-ga-shima, a working island with an interesting history and a rugged natural beauty.

Niigata　　　新潟

☑025 / POP 810,514

Niigata is the prefectural capital, the largest city on the Sea of Japan coast and a decent place to spend a night or so en route to the ski fields or Sado-ga-shima. Highlights include a lively restaurant district serving the region's famed rice and sake, an attractive city **park** (白山公園; ☑025-228-1000; 1-2 Ichiban Hori-dori-chō; ⊙dawn-dusk) and the handsome Shina-no-gawa running through the centre. Head up to the impressive **Nippō** (新潟日報メディアシップそらの広場; ☑025-385-7500; 1-1-3 Chome, Bandai; ⊙8am-11pm) FREE observation deck to get a sense of where you are in the world.

🛏 Sleeping

Niigata has the usual range of business hotels near the train station and a couple of smart options near the Sado-ga-shima ferry terminal. North of the river you'll find a few more decent hotels (and love hotels) in the entertainment district.

Hotel Nikkō Niigata　　　　HOTEL ¥¥
(ホテル日光新潟; ☑025-240-1888; www.jalhotels.com/domestic/chubu_hokuriku/niigata; 5-1 Bandai-jima; s/d from ¥7200/12,000; P✿) Starting on the 23rd floor of the tallest building in the prefecture, the Nikkō looms

over the mouth of Shinano-gawa and the Sado-ga-shima ferry terminal. Rooms are pushing five-star, with ample space, pleasing colour schemes and fantastic views. The breakfast buffet spans Japanese and Western tastes with exquisite skill; the coffee is nice and strong.

ANA Crowne Plaza Niigata　　　HOTEL ¥¥
(ANAクラウンプラザホテル新潟;　　☎025-245-3333; www.ihg.com; 5-11-20 Bandai; s/d from ¥7275/10,250; ⓟ⚡) A 10-minute walk from the station and easy access to the river makes the Crowne Plaza a convenient choice for affordable luxury. The Japanese suites

are the best value if you have a friend or two, though guest rooms come in a variety of shapes and sizes.

✖ Eating & Drinking

Pulp Fiction　　　　　　FUSION ¥¥
(パルプフィクション;　　　☎025-378-0677; 7-1545-2 Nishibori-dōri; meals from ¥1200; ⊙6pm-late) This beer-and-bourbon bar's chef sizzles amazing *yakitori*, curates cured meat and cheese plates, and whips up various fried delicacies to complement the fiery cocktails. The decor is polished wood, lava lamps and movie posters. No English is spoken.

Niigata Prefecture

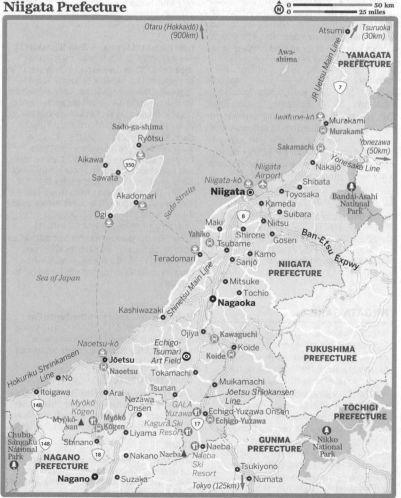

Pia Bandai
MARKET ¥¥

(ピアBandai; ☑025-249-2560; 2-10 Bandai-shima, Chūō-ku; meals from ¥1000; ⊙9am-9pm; P) Conveniently located on the way to the Sado Kisen (p556) ferry terminal, this sprawling complex includes markets and eateries – so you can gawk at the bounty of Niigata's coast and sample it, too. If you're in Niigata with time to eat, a visit here is a must. You'll be spoiled for choice: if you're overwhelmed, **Benkei's** (弁慶) *kaiten-sushi* (conveyor-belt sushi) ranks highly.

Craft Beer Kan
CRAFT BEER

(クラフトビールかん; ☑025-278-7622; 500ml glass from ¥400; ⊙noon-11pm) Near the south exit of Niigata Station is this fun little stand-up beer bar at the forefront of the city's craft-beer renaissance. Forty-odd beers are on tap; buy tickets from a machine. The owners can point you to their second branch in the entertainment district.

Ponshukan
DISTILLERY

(ぽんしゅ館; ☑025-240-7090; http://ponshukan-niigata.com; 1-96-47 Hanazono; ⊙11am-10pm) This charming sake shop just outside the train station sells hundreds of different types in the *kikizake* style, where you can purchase five small samples for ¥500. Gourmet nibbles are also served to line the stomach. Don't miss your train!

❶ Information

Niigata University Medical & Dental Hospital (新潟大学医歯学総合病院; ☑025-227-2460, after hours 025-227-2479; www.nuh.niigata-u. ac.jp/index_e.html; 1-757 Asahimachi-dōri, Ichiban-chō; ⊙outpatient service 8.30-11.30am Mon-Fri)

NIIGATA SAKE

Niigata Prefecture is one of Japan's top sake-producing regions, known in particular for a crisp, dry style called *tanrei karakuchi*. The long, cold winters produce plenty of fresh mountain snow melt for the valleys below, which translates into delicious rice and then delicious sake. Tipplers should be sure to treat themselves while passing through. In March, a mammoth bacchanal in Niigata city, called **Sake-no-jin** (酒の陣; www.niigata-sake.or.jp/en; ⊙Mar), highlights more than 90 varieties of sake from around the prefecture.

Tourist Information Center (新潟駅万代口観光案内センター; ☑025-241-7914; www.nvcb. or.jp/en; ⊙9am-6pm) Lovely, helpful staff dispense English maps and information to the left of Niigata Station's Bandai exit. The website is good too!

❶ Getting There & Around

AIR

Niigata Airport (KIJ), 13km north of the city centre, has domestic flights to Sapporo, Nagoya, Osaka, Fukuoka and Okinawa and international flights to Khabarovsk, Vladivostok, Seoul, Shanghai, Harbin and Guam.

Buses to the airport run from stop 5 outside Niigata Station's south exit roughly every half-hour from 6.30am to 6.40pm (¥410, 25 minutes); a taxi should cost about ¥2500.

BOAT

From the port of Niigata-kō, **Shin-Nihonkai** (新日本海; ☑025-273-2171; www.snf.jp) ferries depart at 10.30am daily, except Monday, for Otaru on Hokkaidō (from ¥6480, 18 hours). To get to Niigata-kō, take any bus bound for Rinko-nichōme from stop 6 at the Bandai exit bus pool in front of Niigata Station and get off at Suehiro-bashi (¥200, 25 minutes). A taxi should cost about ¥1500.

Sado Kisen (佐渡汽船; ☑025-245-1234; www.sadokisen.co.jp; ⊙8am-6pm) runs frequent car ferries (from ¥1930, three hours) and hydrofoils (¥6130, one hour) to Ryōtsu on Sado-ga-shima. Buses to the ferry terminal (¥200, 15 minutes) leave from stop 5 at the Bandai exit bus pool 45 minutes before sailing. A taxi should cost about ¥1000; alternatively, you can walk there in about 40 minutes.

The 2½-hour journey from the port of Naoetsu-kō to Ogi on Sado-ga-shima costs ¥2720 per person and ¥19,500 including a car. At least one service runs each day outside December to February.

BUS

Highway buses depart from the **Bandai Bus Center** (万代シティバスセンター), a big yellow building 1km northwest of the train station, and connect Niigata to major cities throughout Honshū.

CAR & MOTORCYCLE

If you're driving, the Kan-Etsu Expressway (関越自動車道) runs between Tokyo and the greater Niigata area. The Nihonkai-Tōhoku Expressway (日本海東北自動車道) connects Niigata with Akita.

TRAIN

Shinkansen on the Jōetsu line run approximately twice an hour between Niigata and Tokyo (¥10,570, 2¼ hours), via Echigo-Yuzawa (¥5380, 45 minutes).

There are a few *tokkyū* (limited express trains) each day on the JR Uetsu line between Niigata and Tsuruoka (¥4450, 1¾ hours) and between Niigata and Akita (¥7000, 3¾ hours).

To access the port of Naoetsu-kō, where you can grab a ferry or hydrofoil to the town of Ogi on Sado-ga-shima, there are a few *tokkyū* each day on the JR Shinetsu line between Niigata and Naoetsu (¥4940, 1½ hours). From Naoetsu Station, it's a 10-minute bus ride (¥200) or about ¥1000 for a taxi to the port.

Sado-ga-shima 佐渡島

🎵 0259 / POP 62,313

The S-shaped Sado-ga-shima is a remote, sparsely populated island with a unique cultural heritage and dramatic natural landscape. Its history as a penal colony, gold mine, religious retreat, and a bastion of cultural preservation gives Sado a special place in the Japanese psyche, even if foreign travellers are still rather thin on the ground.

Crowds peak during the third week in August for the Earth Celebration, headlined by the world-famous Kodō Drummers. Outside of the summer holiday season, it's blissfully quiet.

History

Sado has always been something of a far-flung destination, just not always a voluntary one. During the feudal era, the island was a notorious penal colony where out-of-favour intellectuals were forever banished. The illustrious list of former prisoners includes Emperor Juntoku, *nō* (stylised dance-drama) master Ze-Ami and Nichiren, the founder of one of Japan's most influential Buddhist sects. When gold was discovered near the village of Aikawa in 1601, there was a sudden influx of miners, who were often vagrants press-ganged from the mainland and made to work like slaves.

🎎 Festivals & Events

Sado is bursting at the seams with culture and known throughout Japan for its many festivals – a testament to the islanders' commitment to a more traditional way of life. *Nō* (stylised dance-drama) theatre has a strong following here, with several different groups performing at shrines around the island, often for free. For a full list of all the weird and wonderful events on Sado, including the well-known Earth Celebration (p561), see www. visitsado.com and http://sado-biyori.com/en.

🛏 Sleeping

Sado has a number of excellent ryokan and some smaller *minshuku* (guesthouses), but few typical business hotels. The best places to stay are in or around Ogi, Sawata and Mano.

ℹ Getting There & Away

Sado Kisen (佐渡汽船; Map p558; www.sado kisen.co.jp) runs car ferries and passenger-only hydrofoils between Niigata and Ryōtsu. There are up to six ferries per day (one way per person/car from ¥2510/17,900, 2½ hours) and 11 jetfoils (one way ¥6520, one hour) in peak season. Service is greatly reduced outside the summer months. It's generally cheaper to rent a car on the island than take one on the ferry.

From Naoetsu-kō, about 90km southwest of Niigata, there are also up to three daily car-ferry services to **Ogi** (Map p558) (one way per person/car from ¥2720/19,500, 2½ hours); these are particularly useful during **Earth Celebration**.

From March to November, there are one to three daily high-speed ferries (one way ¥2960, one hour) between Akadomari and Teradomari, 45km south of Niigata.

ℹ Getting Around

BICYCLE

Cycling is an enjoyable way to move around the towns, but steep elevations make long-distance rides a challenge. Tourist information centres in each town rent electric bikes for a hefty ¥2000 per day (or ¥500 for two hours). Local shops in Ryōtsu and Ogi rent regular bikes for slightly less.

BUS

The island is well served by buses, but services are slow, infrequent and can be confusing.

The Minami line connects Ryōtsu with Mano (¥670, 45 minutes). The Hon line runs from Ryōtsu to Aikawa (¥820, one hour), by way of the large hub of Sawata (¥620, 40 minutes). The Ogi line connects Ogi with Mano (¥820, 55 minutes) and Sawata (¥820, 1¼ hours). Along the northern coast, a few buses run on the Kaifu line each day between Aikawa and Iwayaguchi (¥820, one hour). The Uchikaifu line connects Iwayaguchi and Ryōtsu (¥820, 1½ hours).

The unlimited-ride bus pass (two weekdays/weekend ¥2500/2000) is good value if you plan to cover a lot of ground.

CAR & MOTORCYCLE

Renting a car on the island is the best way to explore: it's much cheaper than bringing a car over on the ferry. Sights and accommodation options are spread out. Expect to pay ¥6000 to ¥10,000 per day, depending on size and availability. **Sado Kisen Car Rental** (Map p558; 🎵 0259-27-5195)

Sado-ga-shima

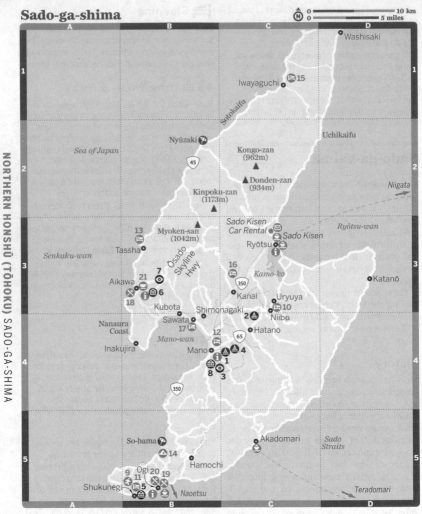

NORTHERN HONSHŪ (TŌHOKU) SADO-GA-SHIMA

in the ferry terminal is a friendly, helpful operator. Gas stations are few and far between outside the main towns, but you'll often pay a per-kilometre fee for gas and not be required to return the car with a full tank. Unless you plan to circumnavigate the island or stay a long time, you're unlikely to use a full tank.

Aikawa   相川

The former Edo-era gold-mining town of Aikawa was once 50,000-strong, but today the main draws are the remnants of Kamidera-machi, an area above town once home to scores of temples, and the remains

of the mines themselves. The town's stunning location ain't half bad either.

Buses run almost hourly between Aikawa and Sawata.

◉ Sights

Sado Hanga-mura Museum   MUSEUM
(佐渡版画村美術館; Map p558; ☑0259-74-3931; 38-2 Aikawa Komeyamachi; adult/child ¥400/200; ⊙9am-5pm Mar-Nov; P) Lovers of Japanese art will appreciate this rambling gallery where local artists display *hanga* woodblock prints depicting country life in Sado. Workshops (in Japanese) are available.

Sado-ga-shima

Sado Kinzan HISTORIC SITE

(佐渡金山; Map p558; ☎0259-74 2389; www.sado-kinzan.com/en; 1305 Shimo-Aikawa; 1/2 tunnels ¥900/1400; ⊙8.30am-4.30pm; 🅿) You'll have to venture up a steep mountain to access this gold mine, which produced large quantities of gold and silver until its demise in 1989. Descend into the chilly depths, where you'll encounter robots that dramatise the tough existence of former miners. Three hundred metres up the mountain is **Dōyū-no-Wareto**, the original opencast mine where you can still see the remains of the workings. There is no public transport here.

Ask for directions to the **Kami-Aikawa** walk, starting from car park 3: it's a fascinating downhill ramble past hidden temples along a historic street with wonderful vistas.

🍴 Eating & Drinking

A handful of restaurants and cafes flank the bus-stop area and Aikawa Yaoya-machi.

Isonoya SOBA ¥

(磯の家; Map p558; ☎0259-74-2213; 16 Aizawa Edozawa-machi; noodles from ¥600; ⊙11am-8pm; 🅿) From the bus stop, walk north for 200m, turn right in front of the police station and, where the road bends, look for the blue *noren* curtain to discover this popular soba shop that does a delicious tempura set.

Kyōmachi Chaya CAFE

(京町茶屋; Map p558; ☎080-1093-6341; 5 Aikawa Yaoya-machi; refreshments from ¥300; ⊙9am-5pm Wed-Mon) Grab a slice of fluffy chiffon cake and an iced coffee at this cafe and gallery in a restored merchant's house.

The views and sea breezes from inside or the small plaza outside are magnificent.

ℹ Information

Tourist Information Center (相川観光案内所; Map p558; ☎0259-74-2220; 15 Aikawa Ilaneda machi; ⊙9am-5pm Apr-Oct) A five-minute walk from the bus stop, behind the police station.

Mano & Sawata 真野・佐和田

Sawata is the main 'hub' of the island, but it's still a fairly sleepy place with a couple of blocks of street life catering to local administration and a few tourists happy to have made it this far.

About 20 minutes southeast is Mano, the capital and cultural centre of the island from early times until the 14th century. It's now a deathly quiet seaside village with a few attractive wooden buildings and some more recently planted willows.

◉ Sights

A peaceful 7km nature trail east of town winds through paddy fields and past Mano's attractions. The entrance is near the Danpū-jō bus stop, along the Minami bus route between Ryōtsu and Sawata. From the trailhead, it's a short walk to **Myōsen-ji** (妙宣寺; Map p558; ☎0259-55-2061; ⊙dawn-dusk) `FREE`, which was founded by one of the Buddhist monk Nichiren's disciples and features a distinctive five-storey pagoda.

From Myōsen-ji, it's a 10-minute walk through farmland and up old wooden steps set into the hillside to **Kokubun-ji** (国分寺;

Map p558; ☑0259-55-2059; 113 Kokubun-ji; ◉dawn-dusk) FREE, Sado-ga-shima's oldest temple, dating from AD 741. Another 3km takes you past marvellous lookout points to **Mano Go-ryō** (真野御陵; Map p558; ◉10am-5pm), the tomb of Emperor Juntoku. From there, it's a short walk down to the **Sado Museum of History & Tradition** (佐渡歴史伝説館; Sado Rekishi Densetsukan; Map p558; ☑0259-55-2525; www.sado-rekishi.jp; 655 Mano; adult/child ¥800/400; ◉8am-5.30pm; ℗), where tireless animatrons act out scenes from Sado's dramatic past.

🛏 Sleeping & Eating

Mano has a couple of nice ryokan and a handful of restaurants lining the attractive main thoroughfare. Sawata has a few ryokan too, along with bakeries and small delis and pleasant waterfront cafes.

★**Urashima** RYOKAN ¥¥
(浦島; Map p558; ☑0259-57-3751; www.urashima.com; 978-3 Kubota; r per person incl 1/2 meals ¥9000/13,000; ℗❋⊛) Industrial design by the sea, Urashima is a former fishmongers redesigned by two prominent Japanese architects. The result is a total destination hotel, combining traditional Japanese elements with a distinct European sensibility. This is the best place on the island to stay for a few days, especially with children. The lawn running alongside the sea offers a sense of space.

It's about 400m west of Sawata on the bus route to Mano.

Itōya Ryokan RYOKAN ¥¥
(伊藤屋; Map p558; ☑0259-55-2019; www.itouyaryokan.com; 278 Mano Shin-machi, Mano; r per person/incl 2 meals ¥5300/7300; ℗⊛) This welcoming ryokan in the quiet village of Mano suits solo travellers. Rooms and common areas are full of handicrafts from across the island, and evening dishes feature seafood prominently. The inviting *hinoki* (wooden bath) is filled with ocean water to permeate your bones. It's just 50m southwest of the Shin-machi traffic signal.

ℹ Information

Tourist Information Center (真野観光案内所; Map p558; ☑0259-55-3589; 488 Mano Shin-machi; ◉9am-5pm, closed irregularly) Pick up information about hikes and temples in the vicinity here, in front of the Mano Shin-machi bus stop. Also rents bikes (¥300/800 per hour/day).

ℹ Getting There & Away

Sawata can be reached by bus from the ferry terminal in Ryōtsu (¥880, 50 minutes). Mano is 10 minutes down the road and can also be accessed easily from the ferry terminal (¥820, 45 minutes).

Ogi & Shukunegi 小木・宿根木

Ogi is a tiny village on the southwestern tip of the island and one of the most popular places to visit. The drive along the beautiful rocky shoreline is cathartic if you crave remote destinations, and its splendid isolation is evident in the cultural practices that have changed little in 400 years. Ogi is also the heart of the famed Earth Celebration festival.

Shukunegi, about 3km west of Ogi, is a rarer jewel – a tiny, gated, traditional fishing village that feels like a museum, with its weathered wooden merchant houses, narrow alleyways and stone staircases snaking up the hillside.

◉ Sights & Activities

Ogi is famous for its *taraibune,* round boats made from huge barrels designed for collecting shellfish in the many coastal inlets. Today, they're mainly used by women in traditional fisher-folk costumes to give **rides** (¥500, 10 minutes) to tourists. Buy tickets at the marine terminal, to the west of the ferry pier.

For travellers with their own wheels (two or four will do), the coast west of Ogi is riddled with caves and coves ripe for exploring: follow the road. Further around the point, the rocky coast gives way to sandy beaches, such as **So-bama** (素浜), along Mano-wan.

Ogi Folk Museum MUSEUM
(小木民俗博物館; Ogi Minzoku Hakubutsukan; Map p558; ☑0259-86-2604; 270-2 Shukunegi; adult/child ¥500/200; ◉9am-5pm) Come to this former 1920s schoolhouse, saved from demolition to take up a new life as a folk museum, to gawk at all manner of Sado's cultural artefacts (more than 30,000 items) and a life-size replica of a 19th-century *sengokubune* freight ship.

Sado Island Taiko Centre MUSIC
(佐渡太鼓体験交流館; Sado Taiko Taiken Tatakō-kan; Map p558; ☑0259-86-2320; www.sadotaiken.jp; 150-3 Ogi-kanetashinden; ◉9am-5pm Tue-Sun) Come to this beautiful hall perched on a hill overlooking the ocean to have a drumming lesson with members from the elite Kodō Drummers. Pop in to have a look any time, but lessons must be

DON'T MISS

SADO'S EARTH CELEBRATION

A highlight of any trip to Japan (that coincides with the third week in August), **Earth Celebration** (アース・セレブレーション; www.kodo.or.jp/ec/en; ⊘ mid-Aug) is a one-of-a-kind, three-day, music, arts and environmental love-in, celebrating the diversity of Japanese traditions, the importance of community and the magical power of music. Since 1988, dedicated followers have been returning to Sado to take part in the many activities designed to inform, entertain and bring people together.

The event features a smorgasbord of performances and hands-on workshops, but the main draws are the nightly outdoor performances by the world-renowned Kodō Drummers. If you've never experienced *taiko* drumming, you're in for a real treat. Considered one of the most elite drumming groups on the planet, Kodō members are required to adhere to strict physical, mental and spiritual training regimens and spend much of the year on tour.

Rain, hail or shine, themed evening performances proceed to the sheer thrill of adoring fans: it's a pleasure to watch the excitement build up with the heat of the day as crowds gather patiently in groups at **Kisaki Shrine** for the best viewing spots, before ascending the steep path to the beautiful amphitheatre in **Shiroyama Park**. By the time the frenetic drumming commences as the sun starts to set and the temperature cools, the atmosphere is electric. Earth Celebration remains one of those rare and unique opportunities to witness and be part of a historical and cultural lineage, on its home soil.

Earth Celebration's main concerts and workshops take place in and around the village of Ogi, but optional activities and tours are scheduled all over the island. The festival is already well known worldwide, so accommodation is limited and books up well in advance. Commit to the journey and you will be rewarded.

booked in advance – generally ¥2000 per person, minimum five people.

🛏 Sleeping & Eating

There are a few ryokan here and a decent place to camp, but call ahead as places fill up in the high season. Visit the tourist information center if needed.

So-bama Campground　CAMPGROUND ¥
(素浜キャンプ場; Map p558; ☑0259-86-3200; site per person/rental tent from ¥300/1700; ⊘May-Oct; P) Right across the road from a tempting stretch of sand and only 6km from Ogi, this attractive campground reaches peak popularity during Earth Celebration, when shuttle buses between it and the festival run several times a day. You'll need a car to access it easily.

★**Hana-no-ki**　RYOKAN ¥¥
(花の木; Map p558; ☑0259-86-2331; www.sado-hananoki.com; 78-1 Shukunegi; r per person/incl 2 meals from ¥6500/9000; P😊🛜) If you make it this far, you'll need to find somewhere worthwhile to rest your weary head. Luckily this 150-year-old former farmhouse has been relocated to the rice paddies of Shukunegi to serve exactly that purpose. Accommodation is in Japanese-style rooms in the main building or detached cottages in the garden. Call ahead for pick-up from Ogi.

Uohara　SEAFOOD ¥¥
(魚晴; Map p558; ☑0259-86-2085; 415-1 Ogi-machi; meals from ¥1100; ⊘11am-5pm, closed irregularly) The speciality here is *awabi* (abalone), grilled as a steak (at market rate) or, more affordably, barbecued with a sweet soy-sauce marinade and served over rice. Follow the shop-lined road snaking up the hill behind the tourist information center for 250m until you see a white building with red and blue writing on the side. There's a picture menu.

Shichiemon　SOBA ¥
(七右衛門; Map p558; ☑0259-86-2046; 643-1 Ogi-machi; noodles from ¥700; ⊘11am-2pm) This long-established eatery serves slightly flatter-than-usual *teuchi* (handmade) soba (buckwheat noodles) in all your favourite ways.

ℹ Information

Tourist Information Center (小木観光案内所; Map p558; ☑0259-86-3200; 1935-26 Ogi-machi; ⊘8.30am-5.30pm) English maps and bicycle rentals, a few minutes' walk west of the bus and ferry terminals.

ℹ Getting There & Away

Buses to Ogi from Ryōtsu (¥1430, 90 minutes) via Mano leave at least once an hour until dark from outside the ferry terminal. In between

Mano and Ogi (¥880, 40 minutes) you can flag down the bus from anywhere.

Ryōtsu 両津

Ryōtsu serves as the main ferry access point to Sado-ga-shima, but there is no reason to stick around. A short drive inland, however, will soon give way to rice fields, rustic farmhouses and ancient temples.

⊙ Sights

Konpon-ji BUDDHIST TEMPLE
(根本寺; Map p558; ☑0259-22-3751; 1837 Niibo Ōno; ¥300; ⊗9am-4.30pm; P) This rustic wooden temple, with its thatched roof and pleasant gardens, is where the Buddhist monk Nichiren was first brought when exiled to Sado in 1271. Any bus on the Minami line from Ryōtsu can drop you off at the Konpon-ji-mae bus stop.

🛏 Sleeping & Eating

A few cafes line the exit from the ferry terminal, and there are a couple of satisfactory restaurants within a 10-minute walk south.

Green Village Patio House HOSTEL ¥
(グリーンヴィレッジパティオハウス; Map p558; ☑0259-22-2719; www.e-sadonet. tv/~gvyh/eng; 750-4 Niibo Uryuya; dm/s per person ¥3500/3800, breakfast/dinner ¥700/1500; P⊗@🛜) Staying at a Western-style B&B in Sado's heart is a strange feeling, but the English-speaking hosts here do a fine job of creating a congenial environment. Accommodation is in six-person dormitories or private rooms with shared facilities. From Ryōtsu, regular buses on the Minami line can drop you off at Niibo Yubinkyoku-mae, about 100m past the hostel's turn-off.

Tōkaen MINSHUKU ¥¥
(桃華園; Map p558; ☑0259-63-2221; www.on.rim. or.jp/~toukaen; 1636-1 Kanai-Shinbo; r per person/ incl 2 meals from ¥4500/8800; P🛜) 🍃 On the central plains outside Ryōtsu is this isolated *minshuku* (guesthouse) where you can ride horses and receive salt therapy in a roasting sauna. The tatami-lined rooms are open and bright and you certainly won't go hungry at mealtime. If you don't have a car, take a Honline bus from Ryōtsu to Undōkōen-mae and tell the driver you're going to Tōkaen. Otherwise it's a 3km walk.

The owners are experts on Sado's many hidden hiking trails.

ℹ Information

Tourist Information Center (佐渡観光協会; Map p558; ☑0259-27-5000; www.visitsado. com/en; 2nd fl, Sado Kisen Ferry Terminal; ⊗8.30am-6pm) There's an excellent selection of English maps and pamphlets here, including walking and cycling guides for all of the island's main areas. English-speaking staff can help arrange car rental.

Ryōtsu Post Office (両津郵便局; Map p558; ☑0259-27-3634; 2-1 Ryōtsu-ebisu; ⊗9am-5pm Mon-Fri) This main post office has an international ATM. Another branch inside the ferry terminal has shorter opening hours.

ℹ Getting There & Away

Ryōtsu is the first port of call, literally, for travellers coming from Niigata-shi. Buses leave for destinations across the island from a well-marked bus terminal to the right as you exit from the ferry.

Sotokaifu 外海府

Sado's rugged northern coast is a dramatic landscape of sheer sea cliffs dropping off into deep blue waters. Roads along Sotokaifu are narrow and windy; think harrowing/ exhilarating coastal drives. Buses from Aikawa pass hourly.

🛏 Sleeping & Eating

A few simple hostels are spread out around here, but you'll need a car to find them.

Small noodle shops and seafood-inspired restaurants exist, but don't go looking for food after dark because you won't find any.

Sado Belle Mer Youth Hostel HOSTEL ¥
(佐渡ベルメールユースホステル; Map p558; ☑0259-75-2011; http://sado.bellemer.jp; 369-4 Himezu; dm incl breakfast ¥4320; P⊗) Fishing, hiking and hanging out by the windswept sea are the activities of choice at this established hostel, which immerses guests in Japanese village life (whether they want immersion or not!). The owners know at least one fabulous secret beach. Rooms are basic dorms, and almost all have sea views. Meals are available. It's near the Minami-Himezu bus stop.

Sotokaifu Youth Hostel HOSTEL ¥
(外海府ユースホステル; Map p558; ☑0259-78-2911; www.sotokaifu.jp; 131 Iwaiguchi; dm incl 2 meals ¥6000; P⊗) Tucked away in a tiny fishing hamlet, this cosy hostel will appeal. It's in a traditional Sado house, complete with central hearth, refitted with shared and private rooms. Filling meals include fresh seafood.

The hostel is right in front of the Iwayaguchi (岩谷口) bus stop. Think remote.

Echigo-Yuzawa Onsen 越後 湯沢温泉

♪ 025 / POP 7972

If Kawabata Yasunari's famous novel *Yuki-guni (Snow Country)*, set here, is to be believed, Echigo-Yuzawa Onsen was once a hot-spring retreat where geisha competed for guests' affection. Then came skiing and the *shinkansen*. Winter visitors generally head straight to the slopes of Gala Yuzawa and then back home, but there are still plenty of great onsen here, year-round.

◉ Sights & Activities

Echigo-Tsumari Art Field ARTS CENTRE

(越後妻有大地の芸術祭の里; www.echigo-tsumari.jp/eng) In 2000 this open-air gallery was conceived as a way to bring people back to this rapidly depopulating, though enchantingly beautiful rural area of green fields and historical wooden farmhouses. Spread out over 770 sq km are scores of installations by Japanese and international artists, set as naturally as possible in the surrounding landscape. Catch a train from Echigo-Yuzawa Onsen to Tōkamachi (¥610, 30 minutes) and download maps online. You'll need a car to make the most of it all.

The area really comes to life during the summer-long Echigo-Tsumari Triennial (next up in 2018).

Yuzawa Town History Museum MUSEUM

(雪国館; Yukiguni-kan; ☑025-784-3965; 354-1 Yuzawa; ¥500; ⊙9am-4.30pm Thu-Tue) This wonderful little museum displays memorabilia from the life of Kawabata Yasunari, the first Japanese recipient of the Nobel Prize for Literature, in addition to interesting displays about life in snow country that bring his classic book to life. From the west exit of Echigo-Yuzawa Station, turn right and walk about 500m.

Gala Yuzawa SNOW SPORTS

(ガーラ湯沢; www.galaresort.jp/winter/english; day lift tickets ¥4600; ⊙Dec-Apr) With its own *shinkansen* (bullet train) stop at the base of the mountain, it's possible to wake up in Tokyo, hit the slopes here after breakfast and be back in the big smoke for dinner: the slopes can get predictably packed. Three quad lifts alongside six triple and double lifts help to thin the crowds. Expect queues at peak times.

Runs range the gamut from beginner to intermediate and advanced, with the longest stretching 2.5km. English is spoken everywhere, and you'll see plenty of other foreigners. Full equipment rental is available for a somewhat pricey ¥5200 per day. Tokyo travel agents can often arrange cheap packages that include lift and train fare, especially if you're planning to head up on a weekday.

🛏 Sleeping & Eating

Most visitors are day trippers from the capital, but you can spend the night to take advantage of the hot springs and aim to be the first one on the slopes the following day.

The train station area has some excellent restaurants that do a brisk trade during winter. Otherwise, eat meals at your lodging up the mountain.

Hotel Futaba HOTEL ¥

(☑0257-84-3357; www.hotel-futaba.com; 419 Yuzawa; per person/incl 2 meals from ¥8500/14,000; P❄🛜) The full onsen hotel experience is accessible at Futaba, which also provides a free shuttle service to Gala Yuzawa. The common areas are a little impersonal, but the Japanese-style rooms are large and cosy, and the food is sublime.

★Hatago Isen INN ¥¥

(HATAGO井仙; ☑025-784-3361; www.hatago isen. jp; 2455 Yuzawa; r per person incl 1/2 meals from ¥8800/13,075; P❄🛜) 🍃 This sumptuous ryokan perfects the aesthetic of an old-time travellers' inn with dim lighting and dark wood, while maintaining modern conveniences. Rooms vary from humble singles to deluxe suites with private *rotemburo* (outdoor baths). Meals feature local ingredients and are unusually flexible: you can choose from three different dinner courses and even elect to swap breakfast for lunch and a later checkout.

NASPA New Ōtani HOTEL ¥¥¥

(NASPAニューオータニ; ☑025-780-6111; www. naspanewotani.com; 2117-9 Yuzawa; r per person incl 2 meals & lift pass from ¥18,500; P⊖@ 🛜🍴) This family- and foreigner-friendly resort has its own backyard ski park that is particularly suited to beginners and small children. Rooms are Western-style and reasonably spacious, and there's a whole range of resort facilities, including an onsen. Free shuttles take just five minutes to run between Echigo-Yuzawa Station and the resort.

BEST SKIING

→ Zaō Onsen (p548)

→ Naeba (p564)

→ Tazawa-ko (p543)

→ Myōkō Kōgen (p565)

→ Gala Yuzawa (p563)

Kikushin
SOBA ¥

(菊新; ☑ 025-784-2881; 1-1-2 Yuzawa; bowls from ¥900; ⊙ 11am-2pm & 5.30-9pm Wed-Mon) Just outside the train station's east exit, on the corner, Kikushin serves delicious soba (buckwheat noodles; hot or cold) and crunchy tempura (including mountain mushrooms) – perfect on a cold day.

Moritaki
UDON ¥¥

(森瀧; ☑ 0257-84-3600; 357-5 Yuzawa; mains from ¥1100; ⊙ 5pm-late) The family at this fabulous little *nabe* (hotpot) restaurant prepares handmade udon noodles and various small beer-drinking sides. It's intimate and always busy.

ⓘ Getting There & Away

BUS

Echigo-Yuzawa Onsen is connected to Naeba by regular local buses (¥650, 40 minutes). A free shuttle runs between Echigo-Yuzawa Station and Gala Yuzawa (p563).

TRAIN

There are several hourly *shinkansen* on the Jōetsu line from Tokyo to Echigo-Yuzawa (¥6670, 1¼ hours). Trains continue from Echigo-Yuzawa to Niigata (¥5380, 50 minutes).

Naeba
苗場

☑ 025

Not much more than a bus stop and a ski resort, Naeba nonetheless enjoys a gorgeous mountain location. Expect some serious talent on the slopes (and at the welcoming àpres-ski scene). Indie music lovers across the world know Naeba for the wondrous summertime Fuji Rock Festival, Japan's biggest outdoor music festival.

🏃 Activities

Naeba Ski Resort
SNOW SPORTS

(苗場スキー場; ☑ 025-789-4117; www.prince hotels.co.jp/ski/naeba; 202 Mikuni, Yuzawa; day lift ticket/combined Naeba & Kagura ¥5000/5700; ⊙ Dec-Apr; ⛷) The longest of Naeba's 20-plus runs (4km) winds through birch forests and mogul fields prior to dropping a full kilometre. The snow tends to be dry and light, and there are plenty of ungroomed areas where you can carve up some serious powder. English is widespread. Equipment hire starts at ¥5000 per day.

There's also a **snow park** for kids and a freestyle snowboarding course complete with rails, half pipes and kickers. At the bottom of the hill, you'll find the **N-Plateau**, a massive complex with food court, onsen, convenience store and ski shop.

The awesomely named **Dragondola** (ド ラゴンドラ), covering a distance of 5.5km, is reportedly the longest gondola in the world and whisks you away to neighbouring Kagura resort in just 15 minutes.

Kagura Ski Resort
SNOW SPORTS

(かぐらスキー場; ☑ 025-788-9221; www. princehotels.co.jp/ski/kagura; 742 Mitsumata, Yuzawa; day lift ticket/combined Naeba & Kagura ¥5000/5700; ⊙ Nov-May) Contiguous with Naeba, Kagura is an impressive mountain in its own right with an additional 20-plus runs from beginner to advanced and a lax policy on backcountry skiing: experienced alpinists can really have an extreme adventure up here. For those who feel more comfortable sticking to the trails, one of the courses here reaches an impressive 6km.

With the combined pass, you can travel freely between Naeba and Kagura on the Dragondola at any time. Free shuttle buses depart from the bottom of the Mitsumata area.

🎉 Festivals & Events

Fuji Rock Festival
MUSIC

(www.fujirockfestival.com; ⊙ late Jul) The Fuji Rock Festival now ranks among the most prominent music festivals in the world. Big-name acts across a variety of genres – with ample indie, pop and electronica – take the stage over three days. It's a peaceful scene and a gorgeous mountain setting. Certainly a must-do for contemporary music lovers.

🛏 Sleeping

A lot of folk choose to sleep down the mountain in Yuzawa Onsen where there's more action, but if you like to beat the morning rush there are some decent options in the village itself.

There is nowhere of note to eat here outside the resorts.

Wadagoya Mountain Hut
HUT ¥

(和田小屋; ☎025-789-2211; www.princehotels.com/en/ski/mtnaeba/accommodation; Mt Kagura; dm per person incl 2 meals ¥7800; ☺Dec-May) The Prince Hotel runs this mountain hut on Mt Kagura. Sleeping elbow-to-elbow on futons in a communal room, you'll make friends and cut first tracks in the morning. Arrive in Naeba by 3pm in order to catch the sequence of lifts up to the hut.

Prince Hotel Naeba
HOTEL ¥¥

(プリンスホテル苗場; ☎025-789-2211; www.princehotels.co.jp/naeba; 202 Mikuni, Yuzawa; r from ¥8000; P☺@☎) All of the ski action in Naeba centres on this monolithic resort at the base of the mountain. On offer is a range of Western-style rooms and suites that vary considerably in size, amenities and price – check online for specials – in addition to bars, cafes, restaurants and health and fitness facilities.

🛈 Getting There & Away

Naeba is connected to Echigo-Yuzawa Onsen by regular local buses (¥650, 40 minutes). Free shuttle buses to the **Prince Hotel** run this route for registered guests.

At the height of ski season, **Seibu Travel** (☎03-5910-2525; http://bus.seibutravel.co.jp/en) runs a shuttle bus between the Shinagawa Prince Hotel in Tokyo and Naeba (¥3600, four hours).

Myōkō Kōgen
妙高高原

☎0255 / POP 32,829

The Myōkō mountain range is a well-known destination among powder-hounds and ski-bunnies – its proximity to the Sea of Japan means Myōkō gets snow before anywhere else – but there are plenty of other attractions in the many stylish, accessible resorts here for other connoisseurs of alpine living.

🏃 Activities

Akakura Onsen Ski Park
SNOW SPORTS

(赤倉温泉スキー場; ☎0255-87-2169; www.akakura-ski.com; day lift ticket ¥4200; ☺Dec-Apr; ⛷) Akakura Onsen Sukī-Jō is one of the more popular resorts, especially among travellers with small children. All but two of the 20 runs were laid out with the needs of novice skiers in mind, and even the black diamonds are little more than short chutes. But the high-quality powder and picturesque setting ensure a good time for everyone.

Family restaurants, many drawing inspiration from European chalets, are scattered around the slopes. English signage is generally available.

👉 Tours

Dancing Snow
SNOW SPORTS

(ダンシングスノー; ☎090-1433-1247; www.dancingsnow.com) For off-piste excitement, check out these local experts for guided tours through the backwoods terrain and snowshoe treks, as well as personalised one-on-one instruction – all in English. Prices depend on the length and type of tour. Check the website for details.

🛏 Sleeping & Eating

Akakura Onsen, a cosy mountain village nearby, is the perfect base for a long stay. There are plenty of restaurants there and around the train station.

Hotel Alp
INN ¥¥

(ホテルアルプ; ☎0255-87-3388; www.alp.myoko.com/english/index.html; 585-90 Akakura Onsen; r per person incl 1/2 meals from ¥11,000/14,000; P☺@☎) The tranquil Hotel Alp lies at the base of the slopes and is extremely conducive to a ski-in, ski-out holiday. There are fewer than 20 rooms on the premises, allowing for a sense of intimacy not found at the resort hotels. Be sure to spend some quality time in the therapeutic sauna and hot-spring bath, perfect for thawing out your joints.

Red Warehouse
LODGE ¥¥¥

(インターナショナルロッジ; 赤の蔵; ☎0255-78-7828; 25-549 Akakura Onsen; dm/s from ¥4900/17,900) Knowledgeable, English-speaking hosts oversee this terrific homestyle retreat where guests stay in clean, simple rooms ideal for families. It's good value too, given the easy access to the ski fields, spotless communal areas and uncomplicated travel vibe.

🛈 Information

Tourist Information Center (妙高市観光協会; ☎0255-86-3911; www.myoko.tv/english; 291-1 Taguchi; ☺9am-5pm) Enquire here about multiple-mountain and monthly passes especially for overseas travellers, as well as accommodation, rentals and ski schools with English instructors. The office is located to the right of Myōkō Kōgen Station, past the bus stop.

🛈 Getting There & Around

The Nagano *shinkansen* runs once or twice every hour between Tokyo and Nagano (¥8200, 1¾ hours). Nagano is connected to Myōkō Kōgen by the JR Shinano line; hourly *kaisoku* (rapid trains; ¥830, 45 minutes) ply this route. From Myōkō Kōgen Station, shuttle buses and taxis run to **Akakura Onsen Sukī-Jō** (p565) and other ski resorts.

FUKUSHIMA PREFECTURE 福島県

Fukushima-ken, Japan's third-largest prefecture, runs from the Pacific Ocean in the east through to vast mountainous terrain in the west. In the centre awaits the lush, peaceful Bandai Plateau where the medieval capital of Aizu-Wakamatsu makes an ideal base for hikers and campers to explore the many traditional villages hidden along rickety train lines. In winter, skiers seek out remote runs, and onsen fill up on weekends.

The Fukushima Dai-ichi Exclusion Zone only applies to about 10% of the prefecture, and it is clearly signposted and safeguarded.

Aizu-Wakamatsu 会津若松

☎ 0242 / POP 122,715

Aizu-Wakamatsu is a former feudal capital with a number of interesting historical attractions and a bucolic location on the Bandai Plateau. A leisurely cycle around its wide, quiet streets – Nanoka-machi-dōri has

a number of old-fashioned shops selling local crafts – is a pleasant way to spend time between forays along rickety train lines to traditional villages in the surrounding foothills. If your spirits run low, there are a number of famous sake breweries around town that do tours and tastings.

History

Aizu-Wakamatsu was once the capital of the Aizu clan, whose reign came to an end in the Bōshin civil war of 1868, when the clan sided with the Tokugawa shogunate against the imperial faction. The fall of Aizu is famous throughout Japan on account of the Byakkotai (White Tigers). This group of teenage samurai committed *seppuku* (ritual suicide by disembowelment) when they saw Tsuruga Castle shrouded in smoke. In reality, it was the surrounding area that was ablaze and it took weeks before defeat was final, but the White Tigers emerged as a powerful symbol of loyalty and fraternity.

◉ Sights

The main sights in Aizu are arrayed around the fringes of downtown. English signage makes it easy to get around on foot: expect a decent amount of walking. Be sure to visit the area around Iimori-yama.

FIGHTING THE FALLOUT: FUKUSHIMA

Like Chernobyl, Fukushima (in English) has become a dirty word, far removed from its ancient origin. The characters *fuku* (福) and *shima* (島) mean 'luck, good fortune' and 'island'. It's a cruel irony for the disenfranchised people of this large region that their name has become synonymous with one of the great man-made misfortunes of our time.

Following the Great East Japan earthquake and tsunami, nuclear power plant Fukushima Dai-ichi experienced a meltdown in three of its reactors and an explosion in its fourth, severely damaging the building in which highly radioactive spent nuclear fuel is stored. It's an unprecedented and ongoing nuclear disaster. More than 55,000 people were permanently evacuated from their homes. Many still live in crowded, temporary housing and are not allowed to return to their home towns.

For many travellers to this region, the big question is whether there are any risks. However, risks faced by long-term residents far outweigh those encountered by short-term travellers and, according to the *Journal of Radiological Protection* (2015), there is essentially no health risk outside the 20km exclusion zone, which is on the coast 58km from the capital city of Fukushima and 80km from Sendai.

Research the event, the nuclear industry and how radiation affects humans, animals and plants: there's excellent free content on the Fairewinds Energy Education site at www.fairewinds.org. For up-to-the-minute scientific data and radiation readings, visit www.ieaa.org.

Fukushima is Japan's third-largest prefecture and the 20km exclusion zone is a mere fraction of the overall region. Your presence in this part of the country, particularly in the coastal regions hit by the tsunami, will help show locals they've not been forgotten.

Aizu Bukeyashiki   HISTORIC BUILDING

(会津武家屋敷; Map p569; ☎0242-28-2525; Innai Higashiyama-machi; adult/child ¥850/450; ◎9am-4.30pm; P) This is a superb reconstruction of the *yashiki* (villa) of Saigō Tanomo, the Aizu clan's chief retainer. Wander through the 38 rooms, which include a guest room for the Aizu lord, a tea-ceremony house, quarters for the clan's judge and a rice-cleaning mill, presented here in full, noisy working order.

Tsuruga-jō   CASTLE

(鶴ヶ城; Map p569; ☎0242-27-4005; www. tsurugajo.com; 1-1 Ōte-machi; adult/child ¥410/150; ◎8.30am-4.30pm) The towering 1965 reconstruction of Tsuruga-jō sits in sprawling grounds framed by the original moat and some ruins of the old castle walls. Inside is a museum with historical artefacts from battles and daily life, but the real drawcard is the view from the 5th-floor lookout. Experience a tea ceremony (¥1000) in **Oyakuen**, the 400-year-old teahouse (rescued by a local family when the original castle was destroyed), returned here in 1990.

Iimori-yama   HISTORIC SITE

(飯盛山; Map p569) On the eastern edge of Aizu is Iimori-yama, the mountain where the White Tigers samurai killed themselves during the Bōshin civil war (1868). You can take an escalator (¥250) or walk to the top to visit their graves. There are also some creepy old monuments here, gifted by the former fascist regimes of Germany and Italy, in honour of the samurai's loyalty and bravery.

Sazae-dō   HISTORIC BUILDING

(さざえ堂; Map p569; ☎0242-22-3163; 1404 Bentenshita; ¥400; ◎9am-5pm) Halfway up Iimori-yama, Sazae-dō is a weird and wonderful hidden gem in a Buddhist temple complex. Built in 1796, the 16.5m-high hexagonal wooden structure houses 33 statues of Kannon, the Buddhist goddess of mercy. Once inside you follow a fabulous, spiral, Escher-esque staircase that allows you to journey up and back down again without retracing your steps.

White Tigers Memorial Hall   MUSEUM

(白虎隊記念館, Byakkotai Kinenkan; Map p569; ☎0242-24-9170; 33 Bentenshita; adult/child ¥410/200; ◎8am-5pm Apr-Nov, 9am-4pm Dec-Mar) At the foot of Iimori-yama, the White Tigers Memorial Hall tells the story of the dramatic suicides of the teenage samurai who died during the Bōshin civil war of 1868. The hall also houses their personal possessions.

🛏 Sleeping

Aizuno Youth Hostel   HOSTEL ¥

(会津野ユースホステル; Map p569; ☎0242-55-1020; www.aizuno.com; 88 Kaki-yashiki, Terasaki, Aizu-Takada-chō; dm/s ¥3600/4600; P ➔ @) Blissfully (or painfully) quiet, this renovated rural property is a good budget option, though it's a little like a school camp in layout. There is an on-site bar if birdsong is not your thing, or you need to celebrate a day's hiking. It's about 20 minutes by foot from Aizu-Takada Station along the Tadami line from Aizu-Wakamatsu (¥240, 20 minutes).

Pick-up from the station is possible if you call ahead.

Minshuku Takaku   MINSHUKU ¥

(民宿多賀来; Map p569; ☎0242-26-6299; www. naf.co.jp/takaku; 104 Innai Higashiyama-machi; r per person/incl 2 meals ¥4200/6300; P ➔ @) Aesthetically Japanese in nature, fitting for this feudal-era town, Minshuku Takaku is fairly modest, but the tatami rooms are adequate, there's a pleasant *o-furo* (bath) and an elegant communal dining area. It's located just east of the Aizu Bukeyashiki bus stop; from there, continue along the road, turn left at the post office and it's just behind, on the left.

🍴 Eating

Aizu is famous for *wappa-meshi,* steamed fish or vegetables over rice, prepared in a round container made from tree bark, which adds a woody fragrance.

Mitsutaya   JAPANESE ¥

(満田屋; Map p569; ☎0242-27-1345, 0242-27-1345; 1-1-25 Ō-machi; skewers from ¥120; ◎10am-5pm Thu-Tue; P) The versatile soybean is pounded and skewered to perfection at this former bean-paste mill dating from 1834. The speciality here is *dengaku,* bamboo skewers of tofu, *mochi* (pounded rice cake) or vegetables basted in sweet miso paste and baked over charcoal. Just point at what you want, or go for the *dengaku cōsu* (tasting course; ¥1150 for seven skewers).

Sakuranabe Tsuruga   JAPANESE ¥¥

(さくら鍋 鶴我; Map p569; ☎0242-29-4829; www.turuga829.com; 4-21 Higashisakae-machi; mains from ¥1100; ◎11.30am-2pm & 5-10pm) Horse meat is a delicacy in Japan (and growing in acceptance elsewhere in the world). Try every part of the animal here, and various other Japanese culinary delights, washed down with wooden cupfuls of sake from an extensive list.

Takino   JAPANESE ¥¥

(田季野; Map p569; ☑ 0242-25-0808; www.takino.jp; 5-31 Sakae-machi; wappa meshi from ¥1480; ⊙ 11am-9pm; P ☑ ⊕) One of the most popular places to try the sublime *wappa meshi*. Takino offers several versions including salmon, crab and wild mushroom. It's not particularly cheap for the size of the portions, but it's easy to order and quick to reach your table.

ℹ Information

Tourist Information Center (会津若松観光案内所; Map p569; ☑ 0242-33-0688; www.e.samurai-city.jp; ⊙ 9am-5.30pm) Inside the JR station; staff speak limited English but have plenty of literature to dispense.

ℹ Getting There & Away

BUS

Highway buses connect Aizu-Wakamatsu and Tokyo (¥4970, 4½ hours).

CAR & MOTORCYCLE

The Tōhoku Expressway (東北自動車道) runs between Tokyo and Kōriyama, while the Ban-etsu Expressway (磐越自動車道) connects Kōriyama and Aizu-Wakamatsu.

TRAIN

The JR Tōhoku *shinkansen* (bullet train) runs hourly between Tokyo and Kōriyama (¥8200, 1¼ hours). Kōriyama is connected to Aizu-Wakamatsu by the JR Ban-etsu-saisen line; hourly *kaisoku* (rapid trains; ¥1140, 1¼ hours) ply this scenic route. There are a couple of daily *kaisoku* on the JR Ban-etsu West line between Aizu-Wakamatsu and Niigata (¥2270, three hours).

ℹ Getting Around

The retro **Classic Town Bus** (まちなか周遊バス; Map p569; single/day pass ¥210/500) departs from outside the train station and does a slow loop of the main sights.

Bicycle rental is available at several points around town for ¥500 per day; enquire at the **tourist information centre**.

Bandai Plateau   磐梯高原

☑ 0241 / POP 4000

The Bandai Plateau is part of the Bandai-Asahi National Park (磐梯朝日国立公園). Its spectacular scenery and vast potential for independent exploration attract hikers,

climbers, fishing enthusiasts, skiers and snowboarders. In the centre is Bandai-san (1819m), a once-dormant volcano that erupted suddenly in 1888, spewing forth a tremendous amount of debris that's said to have lowered the mountain's height by 600m. The eruption destroyed dozens of villages and completely rearranged the landscape, resulting in the vast, lake-dotted plateau now known as Bandai-kōgen.

🏃 Activities

Goshiki-numa   HIKING

(五色沼; Map p569) The popular, 3.7km Goshiki-numa nature trail weaves around a dozen or so pools known as the Five Colours Lakes. Mineral deposits from the 1888 eruption imparted various hues to the waters – cobalt-blue, emerald-green, reddish-brown, which change with the weather. Trailheads begin at Goshiki-numa Iriguchi and Bandai-kōgen bus stops, the main transport hubs beside Hibara-ko, the largest of the Ura-Bandai lakes.

Buses depart from the town of Inawashiro. In April, the Goshiki-numa trail may still be covered in packed snow, and November marks the start of the long Tōhoku winter.

Bandai-san   HIKING

(磐梯山; Map p569; ⊙ summit accessible May-Oct) Six trails lead to Bandai-san summit and its panorama of mountain ranges and Inawashiro Lake. From JR Inawashiro Station, catch the bus to Bandai-kōgen to reach the **Ura-Bandai Tozan-guchi** (裏磐梯登山口) trail: this is the easiest to reach by public transport and the most challenging hike, at seven hours return.

After climbing through ski grounds, the path meets the **Happō-dai** (八方台) trail, the shortest, most popular route.

Snow Paradise Inawashiro   SNOW SPORTS

(猪苗代スキー場; Map p569; ☑ 0242-62-5100; 7105 Hayama, Inawashiro-machi; 1-day lift ticket adult/child ¥4600/3800, equipment rental per day ¥4000; ⊙ Dec-Mar; ⊕) Bandai-san's original ski area, Inawashiro has 16 runs – most are beginner and intermediate, which, in conjunction with scant weekday crowds makes this resort a great choice for novices and families. Veterans may grow bored with the limited options. The slopes are located in the hills above Inawashiro town. Frequent shuttles run between JR Inawashiro Station and the resort, in season.

Bandai Plateau & Around

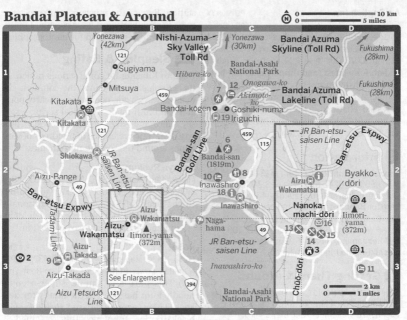

Bandai Plateau & Around

◎ Sights
1 Aizu Bukeyashiki	D3
2 Iimori-yama	A3
Sazae-dō	(see 4)
3 Tsuruga-jō	D3
4 White Tigers Memorial Hall	D2
5 Yamatogawa Sake Brewing Museum	A1

✪ Activities, Courses & Tours
6 Bandai-san	C2
7 Goshiki-numa	C1
8 Snow Paradise Inawashiro	C2

🛏 Sleeping
9 Aizuno Youth Hostel	A3
10 An English Inn	C2
11 Minshuku Takaku	D3
Sasaya Ryokan	(see 5)
12 Urabandai Youth Hostel	C1

✖ Eating
Genraiken	(see 5)
Kōhei	(see 5)
13 Mitsutaya	C3
14 Sakuranabe Tsuruga	D3
15 Takino	D3

ℹ Information
16 Aizu-Wakamatsu Post Office	D3
17 Tourist Information Center	D2
18 Tourist Information Center	C2
Tourist Information Center	(see 5)
Ura-Bandai Visitors Center	(see 7)

ℹ Transport
19 Bandai-kōgen Bus Stop	C1
Classic Town Bus	(see 17)
Goshiki-numa Iriguchi Bus Stop	(see 7)

🛏 Sleeping & Eating

Inawashiro has the widest selection of accommodation and is the best place to find a meal.

Urabandai Youth Hostel   HOSTEL ¥
(裏磐梯ユースホステル; Map p569; ☏ 0241-32-2811; http://homepage3.nifty.com/urabandai/indexe.html; 1093 Kengamine, Hibara, Kita-Shiobara; camping per person ¥1080, dm/incl 2 meals from ¥3780/5630, cabin from ¥5900; ⊙ May-Oct; P @ �🔊) Soothe your hiker's soul at this lovable hostel beside the Goshiki-numa trailhead, a seven-minute walk from the Goshiki-numa Iriguchi bus stop (p570) (there are signs). Choose a dorm room for a social atmosphere, camp at the annexed Goshiki Paradise Campground to rough it, or share a romantic cabin in the woods with your better half.

An English Inn PENSION ¥¥
(アン・イングリッシュ・イン; Map p569;
☑ 0242-63-0101; http://aei.inawasiro.com; 3449-84
Higashi-Nakamaru, Osada; r per person incl 1/2 meals
from ¥6500/9200; P☺☏) A rather English
bed-and-breakfast (and dinner) is found here
at An English Inn run by an English-Japanese
couple. A quaint dining room lends itself to
après-ski chats, and the cosy Western-style
rooms with shared bathrooms invite long lie-
ins. There's a fine onsen, too.

❶ Information

Tourist Information Center (裏磐梯観光協会;
Map p569; ☑ 0242-62-2048; ☺8.30am-5pm)
Outside JR Inawashiro Station; get trail maps
here for **Bandai-san** hikes and beyond.
Ura-Bandai Visitors Center (裏磐梯ビジター
センター; Map p569; ☑ 0241-32-2850; 1093-
697 Kengamine, Hibara; ☺9am-4pm) Near the
Goshiki-numa Iriguchi trailhead.

❶ Getting There & Around

Several *kaisoku* (rapid trains) run daily along the
JR Ban-etsu West line (¥500, 30 minutes) between Aizu-Wakamatsu and Inawashiro.

From outside JR Inawashiro Station, frequent
buses depart from stop 3 for the **Goshiki-numa
Iriguchi** (Map p569) trailhead (¥770, 25 minutes), before heading on to the Bandai-kōgen
bus stop (Map p569; ¥890, 30 minutes).

Kitakata 喜多方

☑ 0241 / POP 49,900

An old Kitakata saying goes: 'A man is not
a man unless he has built at least one *kura*
(mud-walled storehouse)'. Scattered around
this area near Aizu-Wakamatsu, thousands
of unique *kura,* constructed between the late
18th and early 20th centuries, remain. Kitakata, however, is likely more famous for ramen than its *kura* obsession. There are a few
historical attractions here, but not much to
hold the traveller beyond a day or so, unless
you're using it as a base for hiking excursions.

◉ Sights

**Yamatogawa Sake
Brewing Museum** MUSEUM
(大和川酒蔵北方風土館; Map p569; ☑ 0241-
22-2233; 4716 Teramachi; ☺9am-4.30pm) FREE
Step into the Yamatogawa Sake Brewing
Museum to peek inside a *kura* (mud-walled
storehouse) that dates from 1790 and, until
20 years ago, functioned as a sake brewery.
It's a 15-minute walk north of Kitakata train

station. East of the museum and across the
river, Otazukikura-dōri has a cluster of pretty
kura that are a drawcard for photographers.

🛏 Sleeping & Eating

Head to Kitakata for some serious ramen. In
the 120-plus ramen joints, the common element is wavy, wide noodles in a hearty pork-
and-fish broth made with local spring water,
soy sauce and sake. There's no 'best': pick
based on your preference of hundreds of variations around the soy and miso themes.

Sasaya Ryokan RYOKAN ¥
(笹屋旅館; Map p569; ☑ 0241-22-0008; 4844
3-Chōme; r from ¥5500; 🚍Burain-go stop B9)
In the heart of Kitakata, this traditionally
styled ryokan has lots of dark wood, a Meiji-
era ambience and its own art collection.

Kōhei RAMEN ¥
(こうへい; Map p569; ☑ 0241-22-4328; 6981
Numata; bowls from ¥600; ☺11am-8pm Thu-
Tue) This pure and simple, super-friendly
noodle joint has been in the family for decades. Their secret soy-based *shikkoku* (jet
black) ramen, for which they're famed, is
rich and soupy. Look for the red awning on
a side street near the NTT tower.

Genraiken RAMEN ¥
(源来軒; Map p569; ☑ 0241-22-0091; 7745
Ippongi-ue; bowls from ¥650; ☺10am-7.30pm Wed-
Mon) There are only so many bowls of ramen
one can eat in a day (roughly eight by last
count), so best to eat them at the oldest and
most well-known ramen joint. Find it one
block north and one block east of the train
station, with a red facade.

❶ Information

Tourist Information Center (喜多方観光案
内所; Map p569; ☑ 0241-24-5200; ☺8.30am-
5pm) Inside the train station; there are excellent
English maps, but no English-speaking staff.

❶ Getting There & Around

Kitakata can be reached from Aizu-Wakamatsu
by frequent trains along the JR Ban-etsu West
line (¥320, 25 minutes). For drivers, Rte 121 runs
between Aizu and Kitakata.

Bicycle rentals are available across the street
from the train station for ¥500 per day.

The town is spread out but easy to navigate with
the English-language map from the **tourist information centre**. From April to November, catch the
hop-on, hop-off 'Burain-go' tourist bus (¥500 per
day), which loops around the city's sights.

Sapporo & Hokkaidō

Best Places to Eat

➡ Menya Saimi (p584)

➡ Kikuyo Shokudo (p639)

➡ Niseko Loft Club (p592)

➡ Robata Chidori (p618)

➡ Poronno (p630)

Best Places to Sleep

➡ Marukibune (p632)

➡ Momoiwa-sō Youth Hostel (p618)

➡ SappoLodge (p582)

➡ Lodge Nutapukaushipe (p610)

Why Go?

Hokkaidō (北海道) is the Japan of wide-open spaces, with 20% of the country's land area but only 5% of its population. There are large swathes of wilderness here, with primeval forests, tropical-blue caldera lakes, fields of alpine wildflowers and bubbling, in-the-rough hot springs. In the summer, all this (plus the cooler, drier weather) draws hikers, cyclists and strollers.

Winter is a different beast entirely: cold fronts from Siberia bring huge dumps of light, powdery snow, which has earned Hokkaidō a reputation as a paradise for skiers and snowboarders; there are international-level resorts here, but also remote back-country opportunities.

The island's stunning natural scenery and the promise of outdoor adventure tend to overshadow everything else Japan's northernmost island has to offer, which is a lot: there is excellent food, especially seafood; a vibrant capital city; and a compelling history, starting with the legacy of Hokkaidō's indigenous people, the Ainu.

When to Go
Sapporo

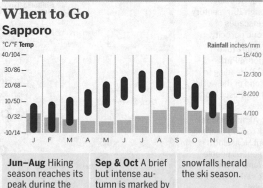

Jun–Aug Hiking season reaches its peak during the holidays of July and August.

Sep & Oct A brief but intense autumn is marked by changing leaves.
Dec–Mar Subzero chill and Siberian snowfalls herald the ski season.

Sapporo & Hokkaidō Highlights

1 Daisetsuzan National Park (p609) Charting a path through the wilderness in Japan's largest national park, nicknamed the 'rooftop of Hokkaidō'.

2 Niseko (p589) Carving fresh tracks in the famous powder of Asia's top ski destination.

3 Sapporo (p577) Getting your urban fix in the restaurants and bars of Susukino and drinking Sapporo beer straight from the source.

4 Noboribetsu Onsen (p598) Saying goodbye to stiff muscles in steaming baths of natural hot spring water.

5 Rishiri-Rebun-Sarobetsu National Park (p617) Taking the ferry to the remote islands of Rishiri-tō and Rebun-tō for hiking and *uni* (sea urchin).

6 Hakodate (p636) Strolling through 19th-century streetscapes of a historic port city.

7 Shiretoko National Park (p623) Heading to the 'end of the world' at this Unesco World Heritage Site.

8 Akan National Park (p627) Learning about Hokkaidō's indigenous people, the Ainu, in the park's lakeside *kotan* (village).

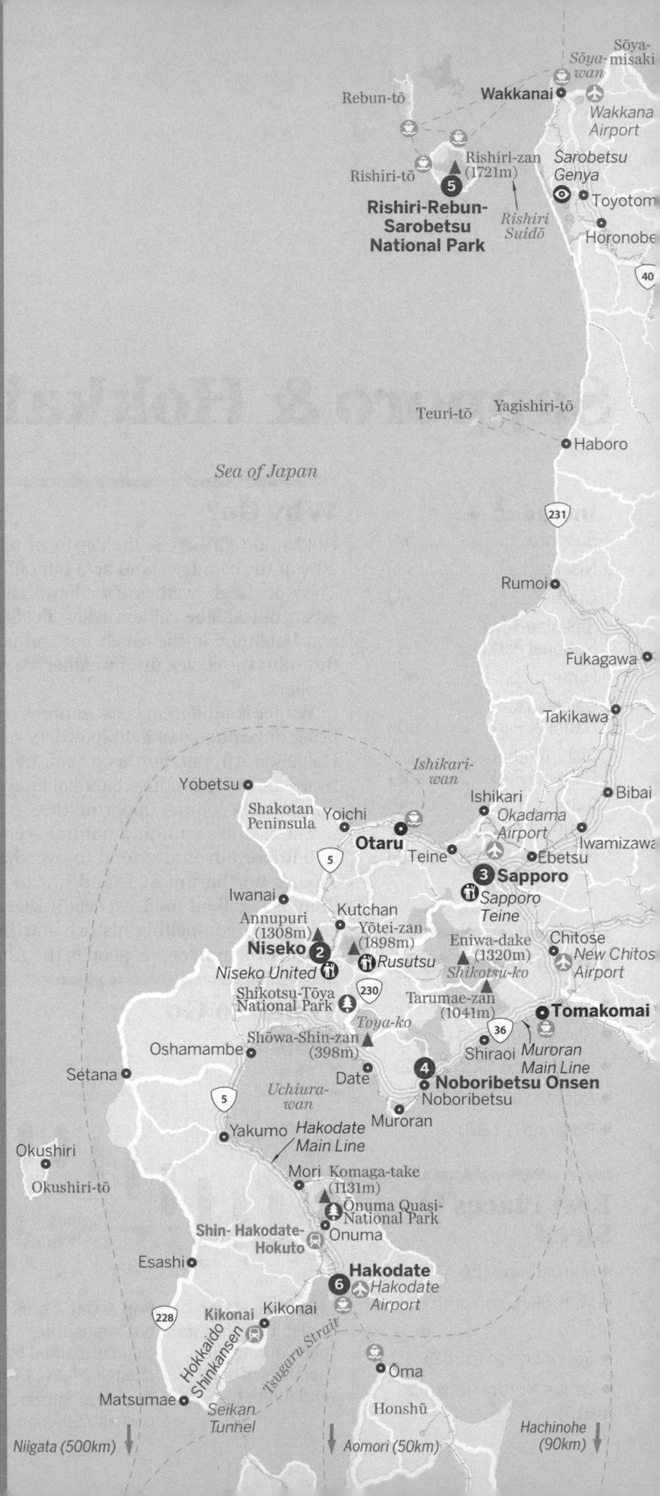

Sea of Okhotsk

PACIFIC OCEAN

History

Hokkaidō was connected to northern Asia via Sakhalin, the large island to the north, and the Kuril Islands, a long archipelago reaching from the Kamchatka peninsula towards eastern Hokkaidō, during the glacial age. It is believed that humans moved into the region around 30,000 years ago, following the mammoths and bison that once roamed these parts. In the 12th or 13th century, influenced by both the burgeoning Japanese civilisation to the south and the hunting and fishing tribes to the north (in Sakhalin and beyond), a distinct culture formed. The people called themselves Ainu, which meant 'human' and their land Mosir, which meant 'world'.

Prior to 1869, the Japanese called the island Ezo (or Yezo) and its people *emishi* (basically, barbarians). Hokkaidō was a foreign land. As the Japanese empire solidified and expanded in the 14th and 15th centuries, many Japanese people moved north, lured by the promise of profit in trade. Conflicts erupted occasionally between the Ainu and the Japanese settlers, but they remained important trading partners: the Japanese coveted the dried fish, seaweed pelts and furs of the Ainu; the Ainu had come to depend on the iron goods imported from the south.

Then, in 1590, the Matsumae clan of northern Honshū was given permission by shogun Toyotomi Hideyoshi to extend their domain over the southern reach of Ezo – in order to better protect Japan from 'barbarian' attack. In 1604 the newly established Tokugawa shogunate granted the Matsumae clan exclusive trading rights in Ezo. With consolidated authority (and occasional force), the Matsumae were able to push forward with trade and production regulations that resulted in the Ainu working for the Japanese (in fisheries, for example) in order to receive the same goods they had previously acquired through trade.

Japanese authority crept ever northward throughout the 18th and 19th centuries, with colonialisation beginning in earnest following the Meiji Restoration. In 1869, the new government formally annexed Ezo, renamed it Hokkaidō ('northern sea territory'), and established the Kaitakushi (Development Commission) to promote settlement and introduce agriculture and manufacturing to the region. Among those who were encouraged to move north were the newly unemployed (and potentially troublesome) samurai class and luckless second sons (as first-born sons traditionally inherited everything).

The primary purpose of this push northward was to halt Russian expansion southward, but it was devastating for the Ainu. While the Ainu had previously been prohibited from dressing like Japanese – in order to distinguish them – new regulations demanded assimilation, banning the Ainu language and traditional ways of life.

Following the Japanese victory in the 1904–05 Russo-Japanese War, Japan took control of the whole of the island of Karafu-tō (now Sakhalin). By 1940, 400,000 Japanese were living there as part of a continuing colonial effort. In the final days of WWII, Russia recaptured Sakhalin, as well as the Southern Kuril Islands, which were then part of Japan (and now referred to in Japan as the Northern Territories).

Still today Japan continues to dispute the ownership of the latter, which were captured after Japan's surrender to the western European powers (Russia was not party to that treaty). The islands remain a point of contention between Japan and Russia, to the point that the two countries have yet to sign a peace treaty ending the war.

Climate

Surprisingly, Sapporo, at around 43°N, is about the same latitude as Marseille in the south of France and southern Oregon in the USA. The freezing winters for which Hokkaidō are known are a result of the island's proximity to Siberia and cold northwesterly winds, which bring significant snowfall, especially on the Sea of Japan side of the island.

Summers in Hokkaidō are relatively cool and dry compared to hot and humid Honshū to the south (making the island a popular escape). The typhoons that can wreck travel plans in the southern half of Japan don't usually reach this far – though one did, in 2016, causing enough damage to suspend some rail lines for months. Winter comes early: Daisetsuzan gets its first snowfall in October (and sometimes late September). This range of mountains in the dead centre of Hokkaidō is the coldest region in Japan, where temperatures can drop to -20°C.

National Parks

Hokkaidō has six national parks, including Japan's largest, Daisetsuzan National Park. As much of this protected landscape was formed by volcanic activity, all parks (except for Kushiro-shitsugen) have natural hot springs.

Akan (p627) Caldera lakes set in pristine forests of fir and spruce.

Daisetsuzan (p609) A true wilderness of primeval forests, covering 2267 sq km, with 15 peaks higher than 2000m.

Kushiro-shitsugen (p635) Japan's largest wetland and an important habitat for the endangered red-crowned crane.

Rishiri-Rebun-Sarobetsu (p617) Isolated islands and marshlands with endemic flora.

Shikotsu-Tōya (p595) Clear caldera lakes and active volcanoes.

Shiretoko (p623) A remote, wild peninsula with little human intervention (and lots of wildlife).

Dangers & Annoyances

Wildlife and weather pose the biggest threats in Hokkaidō. Hikers need to be wary of bears (p626) and foxes. It's estimated that 40% of Hokkaidō's foxes carry the parasitic worm *echinococcus* so keep away from them and boil your water if camping. If you're driving, keep an eye out for deer, especially at night, and inquire about road conditions if you're heading up into the mountains outside of the summer season.

ℹ Getting There & Away

AIR

Flying to Hokkaidō is often the cheapest way to get there. Sapporo's **New Chitose Airport** (新千歳空港; CTS; ☑ 0123-23-0111; www.new-chitose-airport.jp/en) is the main port of entry, seeing an increasing number of direct international flights wing in from around Asia and the Pacific, including Taiwan, Hong Kong, China, Korea, Thailand, Guam and Hawaii.

Hokkaidō-based budget carrier **Air Do** (www.airdo.jp) flies direct from Tokyo's Haneda Airport to New Chitose and also to regional airports such as Asahikawa, Hakodate, Kushiro, Memanbetsu and Obihiro; it also flies to New Chitose from Hiroshima, Kobe, Nagoya and Sendai.

ANA (www.ana.co.jp) has flights to New Chitose Airport from cities around Japan and also direct flights from Tokyo to some of Hokkaido's regional airports, such as Asahikawa, Hakodate, Kushiro, Memanbetsu, Obihiro and Wakkanai.

The following budget airlines offer cheap flights, from as low as ¥4000 one way, to New Chitose Airport from Tokyo. If you buy a ticket from Narita, be sure to factor in the cost and time required for the trip to the airport.

Jetstar (www.jetstar.com) Also flies to/from Nagoya and Osaka.

ℹ RAIL PASSES

In addition to the country-wide Japan Rail Pass, the following options are available for Hokkaidō-bound travellers. Passes can be purchased from travel agents abroad or from JR information centres in Hokkaidō and Tokyo, including those at Narita, Haneda and New Chitose Airports. For details, see: www2. jrhokkaido.co.jp/global.

Hokkaidō Rail Pass Unlimited fixed-day (three/five/seven ¥16,500/22,000/24,000, children half-price) and four-day flexible (¥22,000, children half-price) travel on Hokkaidō's network of limited express and local trains (*shinkansen* excluded).

JR East-South Hokkaidō Rail Pass (adult/child ¥27,000/13,500) Six-day unlimited, flexible travel (within 14 days) on *shinkansen* trains between Tokyo and Hakodate and limited express trains between Hakodate and Sapporo (via Niseko).

Peach (www.flypeach.com) Also flies to/from Osaka.

Skymark (www.skymark.jp)

Vanilla Air (www.vanilla-air.com)

BOAT

Ferries make the journey from Honshū to Hokkaidō. This is pretty much never the cheapest way to get anywhere, and is always the least time-efficient, but the ferries themselves can be a lot of fun: long-haul ones have communal bathhouses, dining halls and even karaoke rooms.

Tomakomai is the main port of entry for long-haul ferries. Shorter runs from Aomori, the northernmost prefecture on Honshū, go to Hakodate. Ferries up the Japan Sea coast travel to Otaru.

The following companies operate ferries to/from Hokkaidō:

MOL Ferry (www.sunflower.co.jp) Between Tomakomai and Ōarai (Ibaraki-ken) – the closest port to Tokyo.

Shin-Nihonkai Ferry (www.snf.jp) Down the Japan Sea side of Honshū, between Tomakomai, Akita, Niigata and Tsuruga (Fukui-ken); and between Otaru, Niigata and Maizuru (Kyoto-fu).

Silver Ferry (www.silverferry.jp) Between Tomakomai and Hachinohe (Aomori-ken).

Taiheiyō Ferry (www.taiheiyo-ferry.co.jp) Down the Pacific coast of Honshū, between Tomakomai, Sendai and Nagoya.

ROAD TRIPPING HOKKAIDŌ

Japan may not scream 'road trip!' in most people's minds but that's because Hokkaidō is not most people's image of Japan. Here the roads are long and straight, with little traffic. Instead of densely populated cities, Hokkaidō is punctuated by caldera lakes and soaring volcanoes. In between, it's vast stretches of fields and undeveloped land; on the fringes, long stretches of forlorn sea. You can follow your nose to hot sulphur springs or be lured by the colourful siren banners of fishing town diners. And you get all this without having to compromise on infrastructure.

Best Drives

➥ Rte 334 between Utoro and Rausu, via the soaring **Shiretoko Pass** (p625) in Shiretoko National Park.

➥ Rte 237 from Furano to Biei with detours along the **Patchwork Road** and **Panorama Road**, past fields of flowers.

➥ Rte 243 from Abashiri to Kawayu Onsen, via the **Bihoro Pass** (p631), which has fantastic views over Kussharo-ko in Akan National Park.

➥ The **Ororon Line** (オロロンライン; Rte 231), from Otaru to Wakkanai, with the Japan Sea on one side and the marshes of **Sarobetsu** (p614) on the other.

➥ Rte 273 on the eastern edge of Daisetsuzan National Park, via the Mikuni Pass and alongside the gorges of Sōunkyō.

➥ The **Oiwake Soran Line** (追分ソーランライン; Rte 228) along the winding coast of Southern Hokkaidō, from Hakodate to Esashi.

➥ The long, empty coastline from Wakkanai to Abashiri on the **Okhotsk Line** (オホーツクライン; Rte 238).

Tips for Drivers

➥ The best time of year to drive around Hokkaidō is mid-May through mid-October. Any later and snow threatens to cover mountain passes and ice can be a problem; coastal routes will be windy then, too. Note that Daisetsuzan is the first place in Japan to see snow, usually in September. Driving in the mountains in winter, outside of established resort areas such as Niseko, is not advised. July and August will have the most crowds.

➥ Hokkaidō's roads are well paved and well signposted in English. What you won't see noted in English, however, is road closures; if you're travelling around the shoulder periods (April, May, October and November), it's a good idea to run your route by someone before heading out.

➥ You'll also need to keep an eye on the speedometer (as the limits can be irrationally low and police are out to enforce them) and look out for wildlife, such as deer.

➥ Most towns will have a petrol station and a convenience store, though it is wise to not let yourself get under half a tank. Many petrol stations close around 7pm or 8pm.

➥ Outside of Sapporo, most places have free parking.

➥ As Japanese addresses can be complicated (and hard to read, even for Japanese), it's often easiest to enter the phone number of your destination in the car's navigation system.

➥ For more information on driving in Hokkaidō, see the tourism bureau's downloadable handbook (www.hkd.mlit.go.jp/topics/toukei/chousa/h20keikaku/e/e_all.pdf), in English.

Tsugaru Kaikyō Ferry (www.tsugarukaikyo.co.jp) Between Hakodate and Aomori, and Hakodate and Ōma (at the northernmost tip of Honshū).

TRAIN

With the opening of the Hokkaidō Shinkansen in 2016, it's now possible to take a *shinkansen* (bullet train) all the way from Tokyo to Hakodate, the terminus in southern Hokkaidō. Travel on the Hokkaidō Shinkansen is included in the country-wide Japan Rail Pass.

ℹ️ Getting Around

AIR

Flying is a good option if you are short on time and want to hit remote, and distant, points.

ANA (www.ana.co.jp) Flies from **New Chitose Airport** (p575) to most Hokkaidō regional airports, including Rishiri-tō (1 June to 30 September).

Hokkaidō Air System (HAC; www.hac-air.co.jp) Flies mainly from Sapporo's secondary airport, **Okadama** (p587), including flights to Rishiri-tō.

BICYCLE

Hokkaidō is a great place to tour by bike and cyclists are a common sight all over the island, especially during summer. The Cycle Tourism Hokkaido Promotion Network has a helpful booklet, called *Hokkaido Cycle Tourism*, that covers routes, climate, guidelines for taking bikes on public transport and more. Download it at www.hkd.mlit.go.jp/kanribu/chosei/hct_e.pdf.

BUS

Buses tend to be the cheapest way to get around Hokkaidō, based on individual fares, and there is an extensive network of routes. Most city-to-city coaches require reservations; purchasing a return ticket usually results in a slight discount. Bus terminals tend to be conveniently located: either next to the train station or, when the station is outside of town, in a central location. **Chūō Bus** (p592), based in Sapporo, is the biggest operator, connecting the capital with pretty much everywhere.

CAR & MOTORCYCLE

With the advent of multilingual car navigation systems, more and more travellers are choosing to tour Hokkaidō by car. There is an expanding pay-your-way expressway system (高速道路; *kōsoku-dōro*), which is relatively expensive and you won't need to use unless you're in a hurry. A reduced-price **Hokkaidō Expressway Pass** (www.driveplaza.com/trip/drawari/hokkaido_expass) is available for foreign visitors and can be purchased through rental-car companies.

The easiest place to pick up a car is at **New Chitose Airport** (p575). Shuttles take you to the airport car depots, where friendly English-speaking staff will get you on your way.

Prices are comparable among major agencies, between ¥7000 and ¥10,000 per day (depending on the season), plus the cost of fuel. The following are reliable and can be booked online in English:

JR Hokkaido Rent a Car (www.jrh-rentacar.com) With outlets at major train stations, good for short-term rentals combined with rail travel.

Nippon Rent-a-Car Hokkaido (www.nrh.co.jp) Outlets in Sapporo, Hakodate and most regional airports.

Nissan Rent a Car (http://nissan-rentacar.com) Outlets in Sapporo, Hakodate and most regional airports.

Toyota Rent-a-Car (www.toyotarentacar.net) Outlets in Sapporo and Niseko.

TRAIN

While the *shinkansen* only runs as far as Hakodate, a number of 'limited express' (*tokkyū*) trains make quick runs between major cities, as far north as Wakkanai and as far east as Kushiro. Sapporo is the main transit hub for these trains. Local trains ply the same routes and others, for less, but take much longer and often require multiple transfers.

SAPPORO 札幌

🎵 011 / POP 1.96 MILLION

Japan's fifth-largest city, and the prefectural capital of Hokkaidō, Sapporo is a dynamic urban centre that offers everything you'd want from a Japanese city: a thriving food scene, stylish cafes, neon-lit nightlife, shopping galore – and then some. While many travellers see the city as a transit hub from which to access Hokkaidō's mountains and hot springs, there are enough worthwhile attractions to keep you here for days. Summer is the season for beer and food festivals. In February, despite the bitter cold, Sapporo's population literally doubles during the famous Snow Festival (p582).

History

Looking out over the city from one of its many observatories, it's hard to imagine that, until the mid-1800s, Sapporo was just a small trading post. The Ainu gave it the name Sari-poro-betsu or 'a river which runs along a plain filled with reeds'. The site was chosen for the capital of the new province of Hokkaidō in 1868 because it would be easier to defend than the already established port cities of Hakodate and Otaro. Also, the wide-open plain would allow for growth.

Sapporo's development was carefully planned: here was a chance for Meiji-era bureaucrats to create the modern, orderly city of their dreams, incorporating fashionable European and American urban planning concepts (which were responsible for the city's central oasis, Ōdōri-kōen.

Growth remained slow until the postwar period: Sapporo wasn't as heavily bombed

Sapporo

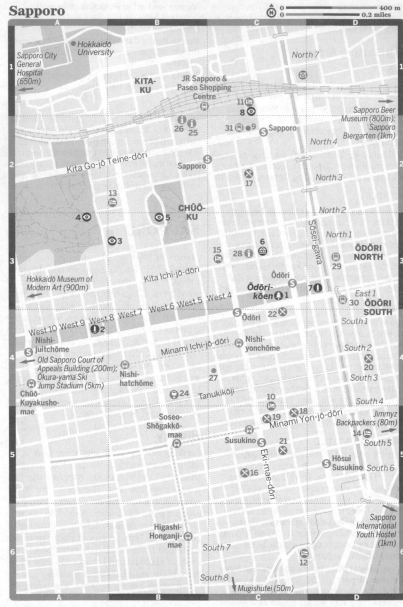

0 | 400 m
0 | 0.2 miles

Sapporo City General Hospital (650m)

Hokkaidō University

KITA-KU

JR Sapporo & Paseo Shopping Centre

North 7

Sapporo Beer Museum (800m); Sapporo Biergarten (1km)

North 4

North 3

North 2

North 1

ŌDŌRI NORTH

Kita Go-jō Teine-dōri

Sapporo

CHŪŌ-KU

Hokkaidō Museum of Modern Art (900m)

Kita Ichi-jō-dōri

Ōdōri

Ōdōri-kōen

West 10 West 9 West 8 West 7 West 6 West 5 West 4

East 1

Ōdōri

South 1

ŌDŌRI SOUTH

Nishi-juitchōme

Old Sapporo Court of Appeals Building (200m); Ōkura-yama Ski Jump Stadium (5km)

Nishi-hatchōme

Minami Ichi-jō-dōri

Nishi-yonchōme

South 2

South 3

Chūō-Kuyakusho-mae

Tanukikōji

South 4

Soseo-Shōgakkō-mae

Minami Yon-jō-dōri

Jimmyz Backpackers (80m)

Susukino

South 5

Hōsui Susukino

South 6

Higashi-Honganji-mae

South 7

Sapporo International Youth Hostel (1km)

South 8

Mugishutei (50m)

during WWII as cities further south and populations swelled in the war's aftermath as many sought a fresh start up north. In 1972 the city made its debut on the world stage as the host of the first Olympic Winter Games in Japan.

While population is declining around Japan, Sapporo continues to hold steady: as a relatively new city, it lacks the same degree of entrenched hierarchies found elsewhere in Japan and draws young (and not-so-young) dreamers looking for fresh opportunities.

Sapporo

◎ Sights

High season runs from April to October; most attractions have reduced hours the rest of the year.

◎ Sapporo Station, Ōdōri-kōen & Around

★ **Sapporo Beer Museum**   MUSEUM
(サッポロビール博物館; ☎011-748-1876; www.sapporoholdings.jp/english/guide/sapporo/; N7E9 Higashi-ku; ⊙11.30am-8pm; Ⓟ; ☒88 to Sapporo Biiru-en, Ⓢ Tōhō line to Higashi-Kuyakusho-mae, exit 4) FREE This legendary Sapporo attraction is in the original Sapporo Beer brewery, a pretty, ivy-covered brick building. There's no need to sign up for the tour; there are plenty of English explanations throughout about Japan's oldest beer (the brewery was founded in 1876). At the end there's a tasting salon (beers ¥200 to ¥300) where you can compare Sapporo's signature Black Label with Sapporo Classic (found only in Hokkaidō) and Kaitakushi Pilsner, a recreation of the original recipe (found only here).

Afterwards, head next door to the Sapporo Biergarten (p586) for more beer and *jingisukan* (all-you-can-eat lamb dish).

From the subway it's a 10-minute walk; the bus stops right out front.

★ **Ōdōri-kōen**   PARK
(大通公園; Map p578; www.sapporo-park.or.jp/odori/; Ⓢ Tōzai, Tōhō & Namboku lines to Ōdōri) This haven in the heart of the city is fully 13 blocks (1.5km) long, with the TV Tower at its eastern end. Among the green lawns and flower gardens are benches, fountains and sculptures; don't miss Noguchi Isamu's elegant Black Slide Mantra (ブラックスライドマントラ). This is also where many of the city's major events and festivals take place.

The park is a 10-minute walk south from JR Sapporo Station along Eki-mae-dōri.

Sapporo TV Tower   TOWER
(さっぽろテレビ塔, Sapporo Terebi-tō; Map p578; www.tv-tower.co.jp; Ōdōri-nishi 1-chōme; adult/child ¥720/200; ⊙9am-10pm; Ⓢ Tōzai, Tōhō & Namboku lines to Ōdōri, exits 2 & 7) Beating Tokyo Tower by two years, Sapporo TV Tower (147m) arrived in 1956, bringing with it the modern television age. It was designed by 'Dr Tower' Naitō Tachū, who also designed Nagoya TV Tower (1954), Osaka's Tsūtenkaku (1956) and Tokyo Tower (1958). The observation deck at 90m is rather cramped, but you do get a view straight down Ōdōri-kōen.

Sapporo Clock Tower   HISTORIC BUILDING
(札幌市時計台; Sapporo Tokei-dai; Map p578; http://sapporoshi-tokeidai.jp; N1W2 Chūō-ku; adult/child ¥200/free; ⊙8.45am-5pm; Ⓢ Tōzai, Tōhō

& Namboku lines to Ōdōri, exit 31) No Japanese tourist can leave Sapporo without snapping a photo of the city's signature landmark and oldest building, the clock tower. Built in 1878, the clock has not missed tolling the hour for more than 130 years. Inside is a **museum** on the tower.

Old Sapporo Court of Appeals Building MUSEUM
(札幌市資料館; Shiryokan; ☎011-251-0731; www.s-shiryokan.jp/; W13 Ōdōri; ⏲9am-7pm Tue-Sun; [S] Tōzai line to Nishi-juitchōme, exit 4) [FREE] This impressive building at the western end of Ōdōri-kōen (p579) was built in 1926, of tuff stone, to serve as Sapporo's High Court. Inside are a few galleries with exhibitions on local history.

Hokkaidō Museum of Modern Art MUSEUM
(北海道立近代美術館, Hokkaidō Ritsukindai-bijutsukan; http://www.dokyoi.pref.hokkaido.lg.jp/hk/knb/index.htm; N1W17, Chūō-ku; ¥500; ⏲9.30am-5pm Tue-Sun; [S] Tōzai line to Nishi-juhatchōme, exit 4) Hokkaidō's top collection of modern art includes many works from artists who were born here, lived here or were inspired by the northern island. Exhibitions vary, so check the schedule ahead of time.

Hokkaidō University Botanical Garden GARDENS
(北大植物園, Hokudai Shokubutsuen; Map p578; ☎011-221-0066; www.hokudai.ac.jp/fsc/bg; N3W8 Chūō-ku; adult/child ¥420/300; ⏲9am-4pm Tue-Sun; 🚉JR Sapporo, south exit) Among the highlights of this meandering, 14-hectare outdoor garden maintained by Hokkaidō University, is a collection of 200 plants and herbs historically used by the Ainu as medicine, food and raw materials for clothing. There's also a landscaped section that evokes the alpine scenery of a mountain in Daisetsuzan, in northern Hokkaidō.

Hokkaidō Ainu Center CULTURAL CENTRE
(北海道アイヌ協会, Hokkaidō Ainu Kyōkai; Map p578; ☎011-221-0462; www.ainu-assn.or.jp/english/eabout01.html; 7th fl, Kaderu 2.7 Bldg, N2W7 Chūō-ku; ⏲9am-5pm Mon-Sat; 🚉JR Sapporo, south exit) [FREE] In an office building across the street from Hokkaidō University Botanical Garden, this cultural centre is run by the Hokkaidō Ainu Association and has a small display of artefacts and historical information.

If you really want to learn more, the reading room here has pretty much every book published in English on the Ainu (past and present).

Old Hokkaidō Government Office Building NOTABLE BUILDING
(北海道庁旧本庁舎; Map p578; ☎011-204-5019; N3W6 Chūō-ku; ⏲8.45am-6pm; [S] Namboku & Tōhō lines to Sapporo-eki, exit 10) [FREE] Known by all as Akarenga (red bricks), this magnificent neo-baroque building was constructed of bricks in 1888 and is surrounded by lovely lawns and gardens. There are various historical exhibits and shows from local artists inside. While Akarenga closes at 6pm, the gardens are open until 9pm and are a popular place for a stroll.

Tower Three-Eight OBSERVATORY
(タワースリーエイト; T38; Map p578; ☎011-209-5500; www.jr-tower.com/t38; JR Tower, JR Sapporo Station; adult/child ¥720/300; ⏲10am-11pm; 🚉JR Sapporo, east exit) Defeating Sapporo TV Tower (p579) when it comes to views and class (but not cultural significance!), the 38-floor JR Tower (173m) has a spacious observatory with seats and sofas. Best at night. Enter from the 6th floor of JR Tower East.

👁 Maru-yama & Moiwa-yama

Moiwa-yama Ropeway CABLE CAR
(もいわ山ロープウェイ; ☎011-561-8177; www.sapporo-dc.co.jp/eng; adult/child return ¥1700/850; ⏲10.30am-10pm; 🚋Rōpuwei-iriguchi) At 531m, Moiwa-yama has fantastic, panoramic views over the city. Part of the fun is getting there. First you take a gondola for five minutes, then switch to a cute little cable car for two more minutes. Free shuttle buses run to the ropeway from the Rōpuwei-iriguchi tram stop; otherwise it's a 10-minute walk.

Hokkaidō-jingū SHINTO SHRINE
(北海道神宮; www.hokkaidojingu.or.jp/eng/index.html; 474 Miyagaoka Chūō-ku; [S] Tōzai line to Maruyama-kōen, exit 1) [FREE] Dating back to 1869, this is one of the oldest shrines in Hokkaidō. It's known for its spectacular cherry and plum blossoms in spring. It's inside sprawling, woodsy Maruyama-kōen (円山公園).

👁 Greater Sapporo

★Ōkura-yama Ski Jump Stadium MUSEUM
(大倉山ジャンプ競技場; ☎011-641-8585; www.sapporowintersportsmuseum.com; 1274 Miyanomori, Chūō-ku; combined lift & museum ticket ¥1000; ⏲8.30am-6pm May-Oct, 9am-5pm Nov-Apr; [P]) This ski-jump slope was built on the side of Ōkura-yama for the 1972 Sapporo

Winter Games. At 133.6m it's just slightly shorter than Sapporo TV Tower (p579), with a 33-degree incline. What would it feel like to whiz down that? You can hazard a guess after taking the rickety old lift up to the top and staring down the slope. Keep that image in mind when you try the highly amusing computerised simulator in the museum below.

There are a few other simulators in the museum, as well as photos and equipment from the 1972 Games – which show just how far winter sports technology (and fashion!) has come in the last 45 years.

The stadium is still in use and if you're lucky, you might catch a practice session.

To reach Ōkura-yama, take the Tōzai subway line to Maruyama Kōen (円山公園), and then take exit 2 for the Maruyama bus terminal. Next, take bus 14 to Ōkurayama-kyōgijō-iriguchi (大倉山競技場入り口; ¥210, 15 minutes); from here, it's a 10-minute walk uphill to the stadium.

Moerenuma-kōen SCULPTURE, PARK
(モエレ沼公園; ☎011-790-1231; www.sapporo-park.or.jp/moere/english; 1-1 Moerenuma-kōen; ⏱7am-10pm; P; 🚌69 or 79 to Moerunuma-kōen Higashi-guchi, S Tōhō line to Kanjo-dōri Higashi) FREE Completed in 2005, this former waste-treatment plant to the northeast of the central city is now an impressive reclaimed green belt. It was originally designed by the acclaimed Japanese-American artist Noguchi Isamu before his death in 1988. In addition to works by Noguchi in stone (on which children are free to climb), there are sculptures of land and water.

To reach the park, take bus 69 or 79 (¥210, 25 minutes, every 10 to 30 minutes) from the Kanjo-dōri Higashi subway stop.

Hokkaidō Museum MUSEUM
(北海道博物館; Hokkaidō hakubutsukan; ☎011-898-0466; www.hm.pref.hokkaido.lg.jp; 53-2 Konopporo, Atsubetsu-chō, Atsubetsu-ku; adult/child/student ¥600/free/300; ⏱9.30am-5pm May-Sep, to 4.30pm Oct-Apr; P) This recently renovated museum does an admirable job of explaining Hokkaidō's multilayered history, from the age of the woolly mammoths to the age of the steam locomotives, with English throughout. The museum is east of central Sapporo, in Nopporo Shinrin-kōen.

From Shin-Sapporo Station, take bus 新22 (¥210, 15 minutes, every 30 minutes) from bus stop 10 for Kaitaku-mura (開拓の村) and get off at the Hokkaidō hakubutsukan stop.

SAPPORO BEER

Sapporo Brewery, founded in 1876, was Japan's first brewery. Its first brewmaster, Nakagawa Seibei, trained in Germany, bringing home knowledge of the beverage, considered exotic in Japan. Today, Sapporo is the most popular Japanese beer outside of Japan – though much of what is sold overseas is produced overseas. For die-hard beer fans, a trip to Hokkaidō means not only getting to sample Sapporo from the source, but also tasting Sapporo Classic, a beer in the Sapporo line-up sold only in Hokkaidō. You can try both at the original factory, now the **Sapporo Beer Museum** (p579), or the newer factory, **Hokkaidō Brewery**.

Centennial Memorial Tower MONUMENT
(百年記念塔; Hyaku-nen Kinen-tō; 53-2 Konopporo, Atsubetsu-chō, Atsubetsu-ku; P) Construction of this modernist tower, designed by architect Iguchi Ken, started in 1968 to mark Sapporo's centennial (it was completed in 1970). The footprint is a hexagon, to evoke a six-sided snowflake; a cross-section reveals the kanji for 'north' (北; *kita*). It's in Nopporo Shinrin-kōen, a short walk behind the Hokkaidō Museum.

Kaitaku-mura HISTORIC BUILDING
(開拓の村; ☎011-898-2692; www.kaitaku.or.jp; 50-1 Konopporo, Atsubetsu-chō, Atsubetsu-ku; adult/child/student ¥800/free/600; ⏱9am-5pm May-Sep, 9am-4.30pm Tue-Sun Oct-Apr; P) This expansive collection of historical buildings (and some recreations), in Nopporo Shinrin-kōen east of central Sapporo, shows the diversity of experience in 19th-century Hokkaidō. There are ornate, Victorian town halls; equally grand villas built by herring barons in the traditional Japanese style; and thatched-roof pioneer cabins. Most of the buildings you can enter.

From Shin-Sapporo Station, take bus 新22 (¥210, 15 minutes, every 30 minutes) from bus stop 10 for Kaitaku-mura (開拓の村), the last stop.

Hokkaidō Brewery BREWERY
(サッポロビール北海道工場; ☎011-748-1876; www.sapporoholdings.jp/english/guide/hokkaido/; 542-1 Toiso, Eniwa; ⏱tours 10am-4pm Tue-Sun) FREE This is one of the current brewing and bottling facilities for Sapporo beer. Guided tours are led (in Japanese only) by very enthusiastic brand ambassadors past windows that

allow visitors to peer into the high-tech factory. You need to make reservations by 5pm the day before (best get a Japanese-speaker to do this). Note that the facility is not in operation every day; when you reserve be sure to ask. Either way, you get two free beers at the end!

Hokkaidō Brewery is a 40-minute train ride from Sapporo; take the JR Chitose line towards the airport and get off at JR Sapporo Beer Teien Station. There are a few luggage-sized lockers here if you're coming from/going to the airport.

🏃 Activities

Sapporo Teine SNOW SPORTS
(サッポロテイネ; ☑ 011-223-5830, bus pack reservations 011-223-5901; www.sapporo-teine.com/snow; day pass adult/child ¥4900/2400; ⏰ 9am-4pm; 🚌) You can't beat Teine for convenience, as the slopes, which hosted skiing events for the 1972 Winter Olympics, lie quite literally on the edge of Sapporo. Teine has two zones: the lower, more beginner- and family-oriented **Olympia Zone**; and the higher, more challenging **Highland Zone**. There are 15 runs and nine lifts. A variety of packages bring the price down.

If you're travelling as a family, take advantage of the 'family pack' plan, which also comes with savings on equipment rentals. The 'bus pack' (adult/child ¥6700/4300) gives you round-trip bus service from JR Sapporo Station plus a seven-hour lift ticket; this deal requires pre-booking by 3pm the day before. Full equipment rental for skiers/snowboarders is available for ¥5100 per day.

Just 10 minutes from Sapporo by local train, Teine can get very crowded, particularly on weekends and school holidays. Frequent trains on the JR Hakodate line run between Sapporo and Teine (¥260). From JR Teine Station, shuttle buses conveniently run to both zones.

👉 Tours

Hokkaidō Chūō Bus Tours BUS
(北海道中央バス; Map p578; ☑ 011-231-0500, English 090-2878-8237; http://teikan.chuo-bus.co.jp/en; 2nd fl, Sapporo Eki-mae Bus Terminal; ⏰ 7.30am-6pm) Half-day city tours (adult/child ¥2600/1300) take in awkward-to-reach-by-public-transport sights including the Winter Sports Museum (p580) and the Central Wholesale Market. There are also longer tours to Otaru, Furano, Shikotsu-ko and Tōya-ko (to name a few). All have multilingual

audio options. Visit the information counter inside the bus terminal.

🎊 Festivals & Events

For a list of festivals and events, see www.welcome.city.sapporo.jp/cal/?lang=en.

★ **Sapporo Yuki Matsuri** CULTURAL
(さっぽろ雪まつり, Sapporo Snow Festival; www.snowfes.com/english; ⏰ Feb; 🚌) Held in early February, this is one of Japan's top festivals. From humble beginnings in 1950, when local high-school students built six snow statues in Ōdōri-kōen (p579), the festival now hosts an international snow sculpture contest and draws over two million visitors annually.

It's not just ice statues in Ōdōri-kōen and around town: there are frozen stages for musical acts and ice slides and mazes for kids. There are plenty of food and drink vendors and you can expect all kinds of drunken revelry, particularly once the sun sets (at these latitudes, it's quite early!). Finding reasonably priced accommodation can be extremely difficult, so book as far in advance as possible.

Sapporo Summer Matsuri BEER
(札幌夏まつり; http://sapporo-natsu.com; ⏰ mid-Jul–mid-Aug) The big names plus microbrewers set up outdoor beer gardens in Ōdōri-kōen (p579) from mid-July to mid-August. A whole month of beer drinking in the sun! During the mid-August, weeklong **Obon Festival**, part of the summer *matsuri*, traditional dances are performed.

🛏 Sleeping

Budget options have gotten a whole lot better in Sapporo, with a slew of hip new hostels opening recently. There are a lot of midrange choices, too; prices often correlate with decor (if you're not picky you can find very reasonable rooms). Book well in advance during festivals (especially the Snow Festival, holiday weekends and summer. Rates usually increase (by ¥1000 to ¥3000) on Friday and Saturday nights.

★ **SappoLodge** GUESTHOUSE ¥
(サッポロッジ; Map p578; ☑ 011-211-4314; http://sappolodge.com; S5E1-1-4 Chūō-ku; dm/tw from ¥3000/8000; ➿ @ 🛜; Ⓢ Namboku line to Susukino, exit 5) A little slice of mountain life a stone's throw from Susukino – you can use the climbing wall to get to the 2nd-floor dorms instead of the stairs – SappoLodge is a magnet for outdoorsy types who find themselves in the city. The only downside is the noise from the (fun,

popular) ground-floor bar until 'quiet time' is enforced at midnight.

Owner (and Sapporo native) Nara-san is a real adventurer. He worked as a guide for 14 years and this is his form of 'retirement' – though he still takes guests on hiking and backcountry excursions to his favourite spots (shoot him an email if you're keen).

⭐ Ino's Place   HOSTEL ¥

(イノーズプレイス; ☎ 011-832-1828; http://inos-place.com/e/; 3-4-6-5 Higashi-Sapporo, Shiroishi-ku; dm/s/d from ¥2900/4300/7600; ☺ ✳ @ 🛜; Ⓢ Tōzai line to Shiroishi, exit 1) This is a popular backpackers' spot with all the fixings: friendly, bilingual staff, clean rooms with modern bunks, private lockers, free coffee and tea, no curfew, a Japanese bath, laundry facilities, a kitchen and a communal lounge space. Bonus: the owner is a juggler and the hostel doubles as a shop for juggling goods.

From the subway exit (don't go to JR Shiroishi Station!), walk straight for a few minutes along the main street towards the Eneos petrol station. Turn right at the fourth traffic light and you'll see a detached two-storey white building – you've arrived! The English website tells you all you need to know.

Untapped Hostel   HOSTEL ¥

(☎ 011-788-4579; http://untappedhostel.com; N18 W4 Kita-ku; dm/d from ¥3200/8000; ☺ ✳ 🛜; Ⓢ Namboku line to Kita-juhachi-jō, exit 2) This is one of Sapporo's new hipster hostels – think raw wood and concrete – inside an old *unagi* (eel) shop a minute's walk from the subway. The rooms, with Western-style beds and bunks, are spotless, though it's a hike up to the 3rd-floor dorms. Common space includes a lounge, kitchen and laundry room.

The folks who run it are currently working on renovating the house behind the hostel for more space.

Jimmyz Backpackers   HOSTEL ¥

(☎ 011-206-8632; www.jimmyzbp.com/english; S5 E3 Chūō-ku; per person ¥2950; ☺ @ 🛜; Ⓢ Tōhō line to Hōsui Susukino, exit 5) With only 10 beds in total – six in a mixed dorm and four in a female dorm – Jimmyz is small, filling two upstairs rooms of a typical Japanese home. Downstairs there's a cosy lounge with free tea and coffee and a shared kitchen. The owner speaks good English.

Capsule Inn Sapporo   CAPSULE HOTEL ¥

(カプセル・イン札幌; Map p578; ☎ 011-251-5571; www.capsuleinn-s.com/english; S3W3 Chūō-ku; per person ¥3100; ☺ ✳ @ 🛜; Ⓢ Namboku line to Susukino, exit 1) If you're a man of simple needs who doesn't get scared easily by small spaces, this XY-chromosome-only capsule hotel offers your standard berth plus a sauna, large bathroom, coin-laundry machines and free morning coffee – just a stone's throw from the main Susukino crossing. Check-in from 1pm; check-out by 10am.

Its website has a full English explanation on how to make the most of a capsule hotel.

Sapporo International Youth Hostel   HOSTEL ¥

(札幌国際ユースホステル; ☎ 011-825-3120; www.youthhostel.or.jp/kokusai; 6-5-35 Toyohira 6-jō, Toyohira-ku; dm/r per person from ¥3200/3800; Ⓟ ☺ ✳ @ 🛜; Ⓢ Tōhō line to Gakuen-mae, exit 2) This oddly upmarket youth hostel – which looks like a modern apartment building – is great value, though it's a little out of the way. Both Western- and Japanese-style private rooms are available, as well as 'dorm rooms' featuring four full-sized beds that double as family rooms. It fills up quickly.

The hostel is just two minutes from the subway station, behind the Sapporo International Student Centre.

Nakamuraya Ryokan   RYOKAN ¥¥

(中村屋旅館; Map p578; ☎ 011-241-2111; www.nakamura-ya.com/english.html; N3W7-1 Chūō-ku; s/d from ¥7560/14,800; ☺ ✳ @ 🛜; Ⓢ JR Sapporo, south exit) Located on a side street near the entrance to the Hokkaidō University Botanical Garden (p580), a 10 minute walk from JR Sapporo Station, this charming Japanese-style inn is a wonderful introduction to traditional hospitality. Sleeping is on futons on tatami floors and you can soak in the big communal *o-furo* (bath). The owner-managers are friendly and used to foreign travellers.

Meals are available, too; enquire when booking. Be sure to read up on the inn's colourful beginnings on the website.

Marks Inn Sapporo   HOTEL ¥¥

(マークスイン札幌; Map p578; ☎ 011-512-5001; www.marks-inn.com; S8W3 Chūō-ku; s/d from ¥4800/7000; ☺ ✳ @ 🛜; Ⓢ Namboku line to Nakajima-kōen, exit 1) For private accommodation, you really can't get cheaper or more convenient than this business hotel on the edge of the Susukino entertainment district, right across from the canal. Rooms are a bit cramped, but the beds are soft and breakfast is free.

Sapporo Grand Hotel   HOTEL ¥¥¥

(札幌グランドホテル; Map p578; ☎ 011-261-3311; www.grand1934.com/english/index.html; N1W4

Chūo-ku; s/d from ¥19,000/29,000; ⊛❋@☞; Ⓡ JR Sapporo, south exit) Established in 1934 as the first European-style hotel in Sapporo, this grand old dame now occupies three adjacent buildings that lie at the southeast corner of the former Hokkaidō government building. Rooms vary considerably; those in the Honkan (main wing) offer the best balance of style and price.

JR Tower Hotel Nikko Sapporo HOTEL ¥¥¥

(JRタワーホテル日航札幌; Map p578; ☑ 011-251-2222; www.jrhotels.co.jp/tower; N5W2-5 Chūo-ku; s/d/tw from ¥26,000/34,000/46,500; ⊛❋@☞; Ⓡ JR Sapporo, east exit) You can't beat the location of this lofty hotel, virtually on top of JR Sapporo Station. Rooms are plush, service is genteel and the views are fantastic. Downer: there's a spa with a natural hot spring but even staying guests pay an extra ¥1600 to use it.

✗ Eating

Sapporo is a fantastic place to eat. It has its own food culture and, as Hokkaidō's capital city and regional transit hub, it also gets all the seafood (like crab), produce (like potatoes and corn) and dairy products (like butter and cream) for which Hokkaidō is famous. You can eat well without leaving the JR Sapporo Station-Ōdōri-Susukino corridor, though there are some detour-worthy destination restaurants.

★ Menya Saimi RAMEN ¥

(麺屋彩未; ☑ 011-820-6511; Misono 10-jō Toyohiraku; ramen from ¥750; ☉ 11am-3.15pm & 5-7.30pm Tue-Sun; Ⓟ ☺; Ⓢ Tōhō line to Misono, exit 1) Sapporo takes its ramen very seriously and Saimi is oft-voted the best ramen shop in the city (and sometimes the country) – and it's not overrated. You'll have to queue, which is annoying, but you'll be rewarded with a mind-blowing meal for the same price as a convenience store *bentō*. Get the miso ramen.

Kōhīhausu JAPANESE CURRY ¥

(こうひいはうす; ☑ 011-561-9115; S20W15-3; meals from ¥800; ☉ 11.30am-9pm Mon, Tue & Thu-Sat, to 3pm Wed, to 8pm Sun; Ⓟ ☺; Ⓡ Rōpuwei-iriguchi) This soup curry shop close to the Moiwa-yama Ropeway (p580) comes highly recommended by Sapporo locals. Most popular: the chicken curry (チキンカレー; *chikin karē*) with a 'medium' (中; *chū*) spice level. Get it with coffee for ¥1000. Kōhīhausu is an unhurried, dimly lit place strewn with antiques.

Saera SANDWICHES ¥

(さえら; Map p578; ☑ 011-221-4220; 3rd basement fl, W2 Ōdōri; sandwiches ¥600-850; ☉ 10am-6pm Thu-Tue; ⊛ 🅹; Ⓢ Tōzai, Tōhō & Namboku lines to Ōdōri, exit 19) This Sapporo institution serves sandwiches of the genteel sort (crusts-off, lightly stuffed), with dozens of fillings. Two to try: the king-crab sandwich and the curious fruit sandwich, filled with mandarins and whipped cream. It's in Ōdōri subway station; at exit 19 go downstairs instead of up. An extra ¥200 gets you coffee.

Milk Mura ICE CREAM ¥

(ミルク村; Map p578; ☑ 011-219-6455; S4W3-7-1; per serving ¥1300; ☉ noon-11pm Tue-Sun; ☺; Ⓢ Namboku line to Susukino, exit 1) A grown-up twist on the classic ice-cream parlour, Milk Mura serve mugs of soft-serve ice cream accompanied by three tiny chalices of your choice of liquors – and there are literally hundreds to choose from. Bottles, some ancient-looking, cover the counters, fairy lights twinkle and chansons play in the background. Bonus: one free refill of ice cream.

Ramen Yokochō RAMEN ¥

(元祖さっぽろラーメン横丁; Map p578; www.ganso-yokocho.com; S5W3 Chūo-ku; ramen from ¥800; ☉ 11am-3am; Ⓢ Namboku line to Susukino, exit 3) This famous alleyway in the Susukino entertainment district is crammed with ramen shops, including branches of several venerable Hokkaidō shops. It's been around since 1952, and is keen to distinguish itself from all the new 'imposter' ramen alleys.

It can be a little tricky to find (old as it is, it doesn't glow as bright as everything else in Susukino), but all locals know where it is. Hours for individual shops vary.

Daruma BARBECUE ¥¥

(だるま; Map p578; ☑ 011-552-6013; http://best.miru-kuru.com/daruma/index.html; S5W4; plates from ¥750; ☉ 5pm-3am; Ⓢ Namboku line to Susukino, exit 5) This is where Sapporoites take friends visiting from out of town for the local speciality, *jingisukan* (all-you-can-eat lamb dish). There's nothing fancy here, just quality meat and a warm homey vibe. Daruma, in business for more than 60 years, is popular and has a few branches around town, which is good because the main shop draws long lines.

Come early or late to beat the crowds, or check the website for other locations.

Sushi-no-uo-masa SUSHI ¥¥

(鮨の魚政; ☑ 011-644-9914; www.asaichi-maruka.jp; Chūo Oroshi-uri-ichiba Maruka Centre

1F, N12W21, Chūō-ku; set ¥2800; ⊙6-11am Mon, Tue & Thu-Sat; P 🅿 🔲; S Tōzai line to Nijū-yonken, exit 5, R JR Hakodate line to Sōen) This is something special: sushi for breakfast out at the fish market. It takes an effort to get here, but the sushi is excellent and you can wander around the market before and after eating. Sushi-no-uo-masa is smack in the middle of the stalls on the ground floor of the Maruka Centre (マルカセンター).

Not to be confused with Ni-jō Ichiba (p586), the Central Wholesale Market (Chūō Oroshi-uri-ichiba; 中央卸売市場) is a 10-minute walk from either the subway or the train station.

EATING IN HOKKAIDŌ: WHAT, WHERE & WHEN

Want to make the most of your meals in Hokkaidō? Look for the following regional delicacies. To this list we'd add anything from Seico Mart, the only-in-Hokkaidō convenience store chain; if you're driving, good local food can be found at Michi-no-eki (p604) road stops.

Seafood

For many Japanese travellers, Hokkaidō is synonymous with crab. Winter is the season for *tarabagani* (タラバガニ; king crab), *zuwaigani* (ズワイガニ; snow crab) and *kegani* (毛蟹; horse hair crab) from the frigid waters of the Sea of Okhotsk. Restaurants in Sapporo and resort areas like Niseko do lavish crab feasts. But you don't have to spend heaps: *kani-jiru* (かに汁) – miso soup made with crab – is a decadent treat that many *shokudō* will serve.

Summer, meanwhile, is *uni* (うに; sea urchin) season. The islands of Rebun-tō and Rishiri-tō are particularly famous for it. So is Shakotan, which means you can get good *uni* in season in southern and central Hokkaidō, too. Fish markets, sushi restaurants and *shokudō* serve *uni-don* (うに丼), a bowl of rice topped with a mountain of fresh roe; you can also get it with other toppings on a *kaisen-don* (海鮮丼; mixed seafood on rice). Summer is also the season for the blooming red *hanasakigani* (花咲ガニ; spiny king crab), found only around Nemuro. In autumn you can get fresh *ikura* (salmon roe).

Spring is the start of squid season, which moves slowly north through autumn. Hakodate, which peaks in June, is particularly known for squid (it even has a squid festival!). Try *ika-sōmen* (イカそうめん), raw squid sliced thin like noodles.

Ramen

Hokkaidō has no fewer than three ramen cities, each specialising in a different style. In Sapporo the signature style is hearty miso-ramen (味噌ラーメン); in Asahikawa it's *shōyu* ramen (醤油ラーメン; soy-sauce-seasoned ramen); and in Hakodate, *shio* ramen (塩ラーメン), a light, salt-seasoned broth. In a nod to two of the prefecture's staple products, butter and corn, you'll often have the option to top off your ramen with either (or both!).

Jingisukan

This dish of charcoal-grilled mutton is the unofficial symbol of Hokkaidō, a legacy of the island's short-lived 19th-century sheep-rearing program. Its name – a Japanese rendering of Genghis Khan – comes from the unique shape of the cast-iron hotplate used to grill the meat, thought to resemble the warlord's helmet. The meat is grilled on the peak of the hotplate, allowing the juices to run down the sides to the onions and leeks sizzling on the brim. Jingisukan (ジンギスカン) is served all over the island, though especially in the heartland, and is best accompanied by copious amounts of beer.

Ainu Cuisine

From a gourmand's perspective, it is something of a tragedy that little remains of Hokkaidō's indigenous cuisine. From 19th-century anthropological reports and travellers' diaries, we know that it made use of ingredients such as wild-caught salmon and deer, shoots and roots foraged from forests, seaweed, millet, bear fat and fish oil.

There are a handful of restaurants in Akan National Park that serve the few Ainu dishes that have survived, including *ruibe* (ルイベ), salmon that has been left out in the Hokkaidō midwinter freeze, sliced up sashimi style, and then served with soy sauce and water peppers; *pocche* (ポッチェ), traditional dumplings made from fermented potato mash; and *ohaw* (オハウ), a soup of salmon or venison and wild vegetables.

Ni-jō Ichiba MARKET ¥¥
(二条市場; Map p578; S3E1&2 Chūō-ku; meals ¥800-3500; ⌚7am-6pm; Ⓢ Tōzai, Tōhō & Namboku lines to Ōdōri, exit 34) Sapporo's original fish market is now mostly a tourist spot (since the wholesale market moved to a big modern facility outside the city centre). There are several shops selling *kaisen-don* (raw seafood on rice) for upwards of ¥3000, but you can also get a tasty breakfast of *yaki-zakana* (grilled fish) for one-third of the price.

Kani-honke SEAFOOD ¥¥¥
(札幌かに本家; Map p578; ☎011-222-0018; www.kani-honke.jp/e; N3W2 Chūō-ku; lunch/dinner from ¥2600/4400; ⌚11.30am-10pm; 📄; 🚂 JR Sapporo, south exit) These are *the* crab guys! The frigid seas surrounding Hokkaidō are bountiful and yield some of the tastiest crustaceans around. Try the 'kani-suki' (¥4400 per person), a crab version of sukiyaki; after the crab and vegetables are cooked in the pot, rice and egg are added to the remaining soup.

You can't miss it: there's a huge crab sign on the building. There's also a **branch** (かに本家すすきの店; Map p578; ☎011-551-0018; S3W6 Chūō-ku; ⌚11.30am-11pm; Ⓢ Namboku line to Susukino, exit 5) near Susukino crossing.

Drinking & Nightlife

Sapporo offers far and away the best nightlife in Hokkaidō. While bigger cities such as Tokyo have multiple nightlife districts catering to different demographics, in Sapporo it all comes together in Susukino, home to craft-beer bars, hostess bars, flashy nightclubs and jazz cafes.

★Sapporo Biergarten BREWERY
(サッポロビール園; ☎reservation hotline 0120-150-555; www.sapporo-bier-garten.jp; N7E9 Higashi-ku; ⌚11.30am-10pm; 🚌88 to Sapporo Biiru-en, Ⓢ Tōhō line to Higashi-Kuyakusho-mae, exit 4) This complex next to the Sapporo Beer Museum (p579) has no fewer than five beer halls, the best of which is Kessel Hall, where you can tuck into all-you-can-eat *jingisukan* (a lamb dish) washed down with all-you-can-drink draught beer direct from the factory (per person ¥3900). Reservations highly recommended.

From the subway it's a 10-minute walk; the bus stops right out front.

Mugishutei BAR
(麦酒亭; Map p578; ☎011-512-4774; www.mugishutei.com; S9W5 Chūō-ku; ⌚7pm-3am; Ⓢ Nakajima-kōen, exit 2) At Sapporo's original hub for craft-heads you can choose from a selection of 300 beers, including many from owner Phred Kauffman's line of Ezo beers, produced and bottled by Portland's Rogue Brewery. Beer aside, we love the off-beat vibe, from the bottle cap mosaics to the '80s MTV clips played on the TV. Warning: cover charge ¥900.

Cafe Morihiko CAFE
(森彦; ☎011-622-8880; www.morihiko-coffee.com; S2N26-2-18 Chūō-ku; ⌚11am-9.30pm Mon-Fri, 10am-9.30pm Sat & Sun; 🚭; Ⓢ Tōzai line to Maruyama-kōen, exit 4) Set in a teeny-tiny old wooden house, with red eaves and clinging ivy, this cafe delivers big on ambience. The hand-poured coffee (¥550 to ¥680) and homemade cakes are good, too!

TK6 BAR
(Map p578; ☎011-272-6665; http://tk6.jp; S2W6 Chūō-ku; ⌚4pm-late; 📶; Ⓢ Namboku line to Susukino, exit 2) Sapporo's top sports bar, TK6 keeps everybody bubbling with happy hour from 4pm to 7pm daily (when beers are just ¥400), and international sports events on the big screen. Get some tips on what to do in town from the locals, both Japanese and foreign. The bar food is as good as the beer.

Entertainment

Sapporo Dome BASEBALL
(札幌ドーム; ☎011-850-1000, dome tour reservations 011-850-1020; www.sapporo-dome.co.jp; 1 Hitsujigaoka, Toyohira-ku; Ⓢ Tōhō line to Fukuzumi, exit 3) Built for the 2002 FIFA World Cup, Sapporo Dome is home to both baseball's Hokkaidō Nippon Ham Fighters (www.fighters.co.jp) and J-League soccer's Consadole Sapporo (www.consadole-sapporo.jp). The stadium switches surfaces depending on the sport being played: the Fighters play on an artificial surface; when Consadole has a match, a natural grass pitch is slid into the stadium.

The Fighters in particular have extremely boisterous crowds and a trip to the Dome is a great way to see parochial Japan in action. Check out the website for schedules. When nothing is on, tours of the dome are held on the hour from 10am to 4pm for ¥1000; reservations necessary. It's a 10-minute walk from the subway.

Orientation

Unlike most Japanese cities, Sapporo is laid out in an easy-to-navigate Western-style grid pattern. Centre city blocks are labelled East

(東; *higashi*) or West (西; *nishi*) and North (北; *kita*) or South (南; *minami*). Addresses are generated accordingly; so, for example, the famous landmark Clock Tower (p579) is in the block of North 1, West 2 (Kita Ichi-jo, Nishi Ni-chōme) – or N1W2.

Ōdōri-kōen (p579) is the border between north and south; the canal-like Sōsei-gawa (創成川) divides east and west. Sapporo TV Tower (p579) is roughly the centre point, which makes it easy to get your bearings. South of Ōdōri is the downtown shopping district. Susukino, the entertainment district, is located mainly between the South 2 and South 6 blocks.

Sapporo is a very walkable city for much of the year – it gets bitterly cold in winter. This is the time to take advantage of the *chika-ho* (チカホ), the underground passageway that runs from JR Sapporo Station to the Susukino subway station.

ⓘ Information

MEDICAL SERVICES
Sapporo City General Hospital (市立札幌病院; ☏ 011-726-2211; www.city.sapporo.jp/hospital; N11W13 1-1 Chuo-ku; ⊗ outpatient reception 8.45-11am, emergency room 24hr; ⓡ Hakodate main line to Sōen) Twenty-four-hour emergency care.

TOURIST INFORMATION
There is a tourist help desk in the basement of the arrivals hall at New Chitose Airport (p575).
Hokkaidō-Sapporo Food & Tourist Information Centre (北海道さっぽろ「食と観光」情報館; Map p578; ☏ 011-213-5088; www.welcome.city.sapporo.jp/english; JR Sapporo Station; ⊗ 8.30am-8pm; ⓡ JR Sapporo, west exit) This huge info centre has maps, timetables, brochures and pamphlets in English for Sapporo and all of Hokkaidō. Staff speak English and are helpful. It's located on the ground floor of Sapporo Stellar Pl, inside the north concourse of JR Sapporo Station.
JR Information Desk (Map p578; JR Sapporo Station; ⊗ 8.30am-7pm; ⓡ JR Sapporo, west exit) English-language assistance regarding JR trains and rail passes, in the north concourse of JR Sapporo Station.
Sapporo International Communication Plaza (札幌国際プラザ; Map p578; ☏ 011-211-3678; www.plaza-sapporo.or.jp/en; 3rd fl, MN Bldg, N1W3 Chūō-ku; ⊗ 9am-5.30pm Mon-Sat; ☏; ⓢ Tōzai, Tōhō & Namboku lines to Ōdōri, exit 31) Opposite the Sapporo Clock Tower (p579), this place is set up to cater for the needs of foreign residents and visitors, with an extensive list of English resources and helpful, friendly staff.

ⓘ Getting There & Away

AIR
New Chitose Airport (p575) is located 45km southeast of Sapporo, in Chitose. With flights to more than 25 cities in Japan and many cities in Asia, this is where most travellers will arrive.

In Sapporo, **Okadama Airport** (丘珠空港; Okadama Kūkō; ☏ 011-785-7871; www.okadama-airport.co.jp; Okadama-chō, Higashi-ku) runs short-haul flights to Hakodate, Kushiri, Rishiri and Misawa (in Aomori).

BUS
Highway buses tend to be cheaper than trains. Sapporo has three central bus stations:
Sapporo Eki-mae Bus Terminal (札幌駅前バスターミナル; Map p578; ⓡ JR Sapporo) Sapporo's main bus depot, beneath the Esta building on the south side of JR Sapporo Station.
Chūō Bus Terminal (中央バスターミナル; Map p578; Ōdōri E1; ⓢ Namboku line to Bus Center-mae, exit 2) Most buses departing from Sapporo Eki-mae Bus Terminal also stop here, convenient for travellers staying around Ōdōri or Susukino.
Ōdōri Bus Terminal (大通バスターミナル; Map p578; S1E1; ⓢ Namboku line to Bus Center-mae, exit 1) Mostly for destinations in greater Sapporo.

ⓘ SAPPORO AREA TRANSPORT PASSES

Common Use One-Day Card Includes the use of subways, trams and city buses for ¥1000 per day.

Kitaca (http://www2.jrhokkaido.co.jp/global/english/kitaca/) JR Hokkaidō's rechargeable pay-in-advance microchipped (IC) card that can be used on trains, subways, trams and buses in any zone that accepts IC cards (greater Sapporo and also cities like Tokyo). Enquire at JR info desks in New Chitose Airport (p575) or JR Sapporo Station.

Sapica Rechargeable pay-in-advance IC card that covers Sapporo's subways, city buses and trams. Bonus: you accrue points for using the card, so you get 11 rides for the price of 10.

Sapporo-Otaru Welcome Pass (¥1700) Gives you return travel between Sapporo and Otaru plus 24-hour unlimited use of Sapporo subway lines – a saving of ¥410 if you use your time well. Available at JR info desks in JR Sapporo Station.

Buses run from Sapporo Eki-mae Bus Terminal, via Chūō Bus Terminal to the following destinations:

Abashiri ¥6390, six hours, eight daily

Asahikawa ¥2060, two hours, every 30 minutes

Furano ¥2260, three hours, hourly

Hakodate ¥4810, 5½ hours, eight daily (including one night bus)

Niseko ¥2240, three hours, departures vary by season

Noboribetsu Onsen ¥1850, two hours, hourly

Shin-Hakodate-Hokuto (Hokkaidō Shinkansen station) ¥4810, five hours, eight daily (including one night bus)

Tōya-ko Onsen ¥2700, 2¾ hours, four daily

From Ōdōri Bus Terminal, buses run to Wakkanai (¥6000, six hours, six daily including one night bus).

CAR & MOTORCYCLE

The best place in Hokkaidō to pick up a rental car is New Chitose Airport (p575). There are a dozen companies located in the arrivals area on the 1st floor. Most companies have outlets in Sapporo.

TRAIN

From Sapporo Station, JR Limited Express trains run to the following destinations:

Abashiri (Okhotsk Liner) ¥9910, 5½ hours, four daily

Asahikawa (Super Kamui Liner) ¥4810, 90 minutes, every 30 minutes

Hakodate (Hokuto Liner) ¥8830, 3½ hours, hourly

Kushiro (Super Ōzora Liner) ¥9370, four hours, six daily

Noboribetsu Onsen (Hokuto Liner & Suzuran Liner) ¥4480, 70 minutes, hourly

Shin-Hakodate-Hakuto (Hokuto Liner) ¥8830, 3¼ hours, hourly

Wakkanai (Super Sōya Liner and Sarubetsu Liner) ¥10,450, six hours, three daily

JR Hakodate line trains run to Kutchan (for Niseko; ¥2360, two hours) via Otaru (¥640, 45 minutes).

🛈 Getting Around

TO/FROM THE AIRPORT
New Chitose Airport

Rapid Airport trains (¥1070, 36 minutes) depart every 15 minutes for JR Sapporo Station. Frequent buses (¥1030, 70 minutes) also make the trip, stopping not just at JR Sapporo Station but also at major hotels. For a taxi to central Sapporo, budget about ¥10,000.

Okadama Airport

Hokuto Airport Shuttle buses depart from the south side of JR Sapporo Station (¥400, 30 minutes) and are timed to match departures. A taxi from JR Sapporo Station should take 20 minutes (¥2500).

BICYCLE

Porocle (ポロクル; 📞 011-242-4696; https://porocle.jp/; 24hr ¥1080, after 3pm ¥540; ⏰ 7.30am-9pm) Sapporo's flat grid is made for cycling. With a smartphone and a passport you can access the city's easy-to-use bike-share program, which has 30-plus kiosks around downtown. Sign up at the Hokkaidō-Sapporo Food & Tourist Information Centre (p587), inside the train station, or at the Grand Hotel (p583).

BUS

The 'Sapporo Stroller's Bus' (single rides ¥300, day pass ¥750) runs a useful loop around the city's major attractions, including the **Museum of Modern Art** (p580), **Hokkaidō-jingū** (p580) and the **Winter Sports Museum** (p580). It starts and finishes at JR Sapporo Station.

Bus 88 loops around from JR Sapporo Station to the **Sapporo Beer Museum** (p579), **Ōdōri Park** (p579) and the **Clock Tower** (p579); a one-day pass costs ¥750, single trips are ¥210. Catch the bus from the south exit of the train station, in front of the Tokyū department store.

CAR & MOTORCYCLE

A car is a drag in central Sapporo as traffic and parking are constant hassles; however, some of the city's more far-flung (but worthwhile) sights are awkward to reach by public transport. It's worth renting a car for a day to hit those.

SUBWAY

Sapporo has three useful subway lines that run from 6am to midnight: the east–west Tōzai line; the north–south Nambou line; and the curving Tōhō line. Fares start at ¥200.

One-day passes cost ¥830 and only ¥520 on weekends (half-price for children).

TAXI

Taxis are easy to hail. Flagfall is ¥670, which gives you 1.6km; then ¥80 per 300m (or two minutes in traffic).

TRAM

Sapporo has a cute streetcar that loops from Ōdōri down to the base of **Moiwa-yama** (p580) and back (7am to 10pm). The fare is a flat ¥170.

CENTRAL HOKKAIDŌ 道央

Given that the capital and transport hub Sapporo is here, Central Hokkaidō (Dō-ō) represents the island at its most accessible –

perfect for a shorter trip. It's got everything you'd want and expect from Hokkaidō covered: for world-class ski slopes there is Niseko, with its legendary powder snow; for caldera lakes and steaming onsen towns there is Shikotsu-Tōya National Park; and for a bit of history, there's the 19th-century port town Otaru.

Niseko ニセコ

♪ 0136 / POP 4920

Hokkaidō is dotted with world-class ski resorts, but the reigning prince of powder is unquestionably Niseko. There are four interconnected resorts with more than 800 skiable hectares along the eastern side of the mountain, Niseko Annupuri. Soft and light powdery snow and an annual average snowfall of more than 15m make Niseko popular with international skiers. Many own second homes here – resulting in a diverse dining and nightlife scene that is atypical of far-flung rural Japan. English is spoken virtually everywhere. While it's possible to do Niseko on a tight budget, be warned that it is getting increasingly difficult.

Spread around the eastern base of the mountain are several towns and villages that compose Niseko 'resort'. Most of the restaurants and bars are clustered together in Hirafu (ひらふ), while Annupuri (アンヌプリ), Niseko Village (ニセコビレッジ, also called Higashi-yama Onsen) and Hanazono (花園) are much quieter and less developed. Further east are Kutchan (倶知安) and Niseko (ニセコ) proper, towns with more permanent population centres and less of a resort feel.

🏃 Activities

Niseko is making a big push to become a year-round destination. The buzz isn't quite there yet, but the infrastructure is building, with operators offering rafting, kayaking and mountain-biking tours. The combination of mountains and farmlands means Niseko is excellent for hiking and cycling, too. There are also 25 onsen in the area, from luxurious hotel baths to mountain hideaways.

⭐ Niseko United   SNOW SPORTS

(ニセコユナイテッド; Map p596; www.niseko. ne.jp/en; adult/child ¥7400/4500; ⊙8.30am-8.30pm Nov-Apr) Niseko United covers the four resorts on Niseko Annupuri (1308m): Annupuri, Niseko Village, Grand Hirafu and Hanazono. While you can buy individual passes for each, part of what makes Niseko

so great (in addition to that famous powder) is that you can buy a single all-mountain pass, an electronic tag that gives you access to 18 lifts and gondolas and 60 runs.

All the resorts have terrain for all levels, though quieter Hanazono is considered best for families. The all-mountain pass also gets you free rides on the hourly shuttle that runs between the resorts. Eight-hour and multiday passes are available, too.

As so many skiers and snowboarders here are from abroad, there are plenty of English-speaking instructors and backcountry guides; the many rental shops also typically have a few foreign staff on hand.

Niseko takes a pretty hard stance against rope ducking. Avalanches do happen; when conditions are deemed safe, gates to select off-piste areas are opened.

Moiwa   SKIING

(モイワ; ♪0136-59-2511; http://niseko-moiwa.jp; 448 Niseko, Niseko-chō; lift ticket ¥4300; ⊙8am-4pm) Moiwa (not to be confused with Sapporo's Moiwa) is Niseko's 'fifth Beatle', right next to Annupuri but not part of Niseko United. It's a small resort that's quietly built up a loyal following for its deep powder and backcountry opportunities. Moiwa follows Niseko's policy of no rope-ducking – it just doesn't have any ropes.

Experienced skiers can ski from Moiwa over to Annupuri (if the gate is open). As always, check the daily avalanche report (http://niseko.nadare.info).

Goshiki Onsen   ONSEN

(五色温泉; ♪0136-58-2707; 510 Niseko, Niseko-chō; ¥700; ⊙8am-8pm May-Oct, 10am-7pm Nov-Apr) At the base (750m) of active volcano

WORTH A TRIP

SKIING IN RUSUTSU

Rusutsu Resort (ルスツリゾート; Map p596; ☑0136-46-3111; http://en.rusutsu.co.jp; 13 Izumi-kawa, Rusutsu; lift tickets adult/child ¥5800/2900, after 4pm ¥2500/1200; ⏱9am-9pm Nov-Apr) gets snow that almost rivals Niseko's and has both well-groomed trails and fantastic tree runs. The resort caters equally to skiers and snowboarders of all levels, has 18 lifts, more than three-dozen runs, a half-pipe and numerous off-piste options. It's less developed and thus usually less crowded than Niseko, and makes for a good day trip.

Besides a handful of pensions, the only place to stay here is the resort's official hotel, **Rusutsu Resort Hotel** (ルスツリゾートホテル; Map p596; ☑0136-46-3111; http://en.rusutsu.co.jp/accommodations; 13 Izumi-kawa, Rusutsu; d incl breakfast from ¥31,000; P❄❅❆), which sits atop an indoor amusement park so kitschy as to be almost endearing. As a self-contained facility, with plenty of restaurants, it's great for families (and also a beacon for tour groups). Discounted packages including room, lift ticket and meal plan are often available. Note that there are few amenities outside the resort.

Rusutsu is only a 20- to 30-minute drive away from Niseko, off Rte 230, on the way to Tōya-ko. Various operators offer Rusutsu day trips if you don't have your own wheels.

Iwaonupuri, Goshiki Onsen has soaring views from the outdoor baths and sulphur-rich, highly acidic (pH 2.6!) waters. It's attached to a deeply rustic ryokan, but most visitors just come for the baths. You need a car to get here; some lodgings do excursions to the baths.

Niseko Circuit HIKING

Just above Goshiki Onsen (p589), a trail heads off into the wilderness. At the first fork, you can opt for the 70-minute roundtrip up Iwaonupuri (イワオヌプリ; 1116m) or go deeper towards the pond Ō-numa (大沼). From Ō-numa you can carry on, completing the epic nine-hour, 16km loop that goes up and over Nitonupuri (ニトヌプリ; 1080m) and Chisenupuri (チセヌプリ; 1134m) before returning to Goshiki Onsen.

Pick up a map and info on trail conditions at the Goshiki Onsen Information Centre (p592), at the start of the trail.

Niseko Adventure Centre (NAC) OUTDOORS

(ニセコアドベンチャーセンター; ☑0136-23-2093; www.nacadventures.jp; Yamada, Kutchan-chō; ⏱8am-9pm) These guys are the innovators in Japan, following examples set in other mountain resorts throughout the world. In winter they offer everything from ski and snowboard lessons to snowshoe and backcountry tours with experienced English-speaking guides. In summer they offer rafting, cycling, sea kayaking and canyoning tours...plus more!

They're based in a massive purpose-built building in Hirafu with an 11m indoor climbing wall and **Jojo's Café & Restaurant** (ジョジョズカフェ; www.nacadventures.jp/jojos-restaurant; Yamada, Kutchan-chō; mains from ¥1000; ⏱11am-9pm; P❄❅⊙❆).

🛏 Sleeping

Hirafu, followed by Annupuri have the most accommodation options, while Niseko Village is centred on the upmarket Hilton. Most places will provide pick-up and drop-off for the slopes in winter, or you can take buses and shuttles to move about. It's strongly recommended that you book well in advance in winter. Prices are increasing by the year, though low season remains a steal.

Eki-no-yado Hirafu MINSHUKU ¥

(駅の宿ひらふ; ☑0136-22-1956; http://hirafu-eki.com; 594-4 Hirafu, Kutchan-chō; d ¥3500-4000; P❄⊙@❆) This is Japan's only train station *minshuku* (family-run guesthouse) and it is wonderfully eccentric. It's literally part of tiny JR Hirafu Station: to reach the bathhouse you need to walk out onto the platform. While it's convenient to arrive by train, the station is not convenient for Hirafu proper; however, the guesthouse offers ski field transfers for ¥200.

In summer the station 'master' hosts barbecues on the train platform; there's a small kitchen, too, well set up for self-catering.

Youth Hostel Karimpani Niseko HOSTEL ¥

(ユースホステルカリンパニ・ニセコ藤山; Map p596; ☑0136-44-1171; www.karimpani-niseko.com/english; 336 Niseko, Niseko-chō; dm/d from ¥4900/9800, breakfast/dinner ¥600/1200; P@❆) In an 80-year-old converted schoolhouse, former classrooms now house dorms and concerts are held regularly in the gymnasium. Friendly owners Max and Yūko speak excellent English and do free pickups and transfers to the Annupuri slopes (a five-minute drive away). Private rooms are Japanese-style; rates are lower in the low season. Meals are first-class.

Niseko Annupuri Youth Hostel HOSTEL ¥
(ニセコアンヌプリユースホステル; ☎ 0136-58-2084; www.annupuri-yh.com; 479-4 Niseko, Niseko-chō; dm from ¥4000; ⊗ closed mid-Oct–early Dec; P ⊕ ⊚) This friendly mountain lodge, which sees many repeat customers, is constructed entirely from hardwood and sits conveniently within a five-minute walk of the Annupuri ski grounds. In the evenings, guests congregate in front of the fire, swapping ski tips. Breakfast is available for ¥800.

Moiwa Lodge 834 CAPSULE HOTEL ¥¥
(☎ 050-3171-5688; www.thelodgebythnf.com; 447-5 Niseko, Niseko-chō; dm incl 2 meals ¥14,000; P ⊕ ⊛ ⊚) The world's only ski-in, ski-out capsule hotel, Moiwa Lodge 834, in front of the Moiwa lifts, is popular with powder hounds who have no patience for the morning queues in Hirafu. The lodge has done a pretty good job tweaking the capsule format: there's plenty of secure space for your gear. Capsule rooms are sex-segregated.

Buffet meals (of mostly Western food) are served in the cosy lounge, which looks out towards the mountain. The hotel does free pick-ups from the nearest highway bus stop at Kanronomori.

Outside the snow season, rates drop to ¥4300 per night with no meals.

Hotel Niseko Alpen HOTEL ¥¥¥
(ホテルニセコアルペン; ☎ 0136-22-1105; www.grand-hirafu.jp/hotel_niseko-alpen/en; 204 Yamada, Kutchan-chō; d incl breakfast from ¥23,300; P ⊕ ⊛ @ ⊚) This utilitarian block is in need of an overhaul and we hope it never happens – because this is currently the most economical ski-in, ski-out option left in Niseko. It's right in front of the Grand Hirafu gondola, rooms are plain but comfortable and the breakfast buffet has a good spread. Look for package deals that include lift tickets.

Hilton Niseko RESORT ¥¥¥
(ニセコヒルトンヴィレジ; Map p596; ☎ 0136-44-1111; www.placeshilton.com/niseko-village; Higashi-yama Onsen; d from ¥29,000; P ⊕ ⊛ @ ⊚) The Hilton enjoys the best location of all – it is quite literally attached to the **Niseko Gondola** (ニセコアンヌプリゴンドラ; Map p596; ☎ 0136-58-2080; http://annupuri.info; one way/return ¥750/1240; ⊗ 9am-4.30pm). Spacious Western-style rooms are complemented by a whole slew of amenities, including an onsen bath that faces Yōtei-zan, spread out across a self-contained village.

Check the website before arriving as special deals are usually available, which combine discounted room rates with breakfast and dinner buffets.

Annupuri Village CHALET ¥¥¥
(アンヌプリ・ヴィレジ; Map p596; ☎ 0136-59-2111; www.annupurivillage.com; Niseko Annupuri; chalets for 4-12 people ¥83,900-196,900; P ⊕ ⊚) If you're travelling with a large group of friends, consider giving the resort hotels a pass and renting an immaculate ski chalet in Annupuri Village, located at the base of the Annupuri ski slopes. The natural hardwoods, picture windows and stone fireplace are complemented by spa-quality bathroom fixtures and a kitchen full of appliances. Concierge and catering services available, too.

✕ Eating & Drinking

The slopes have plenty of pizza, ramen and other snacks. After hours, Hirafu has an international spread of restaurants and buzzes during ski season (many places shut in the low season). Year-round, Kutchan town has lots of *izakaya* (Japanese-style pubs), especially on Miyako-dōri; there's a supermarket next to JR Kutchan Station.

★ **Graubunden** CAFE ¥
(グラウビュンデン; ☎ 0136-23-3371; www.graubunden.jp; 132-26 Yamada, Kutchan-chō; ⊗ 8am-7pm Fri-Wed; P ⊕ ⊚ @ ☎) This is Niseko's original hang-out spot, in Hirafu East Village, a favourite with season regulars and long-time expats for its yummy sandwiches, omelettes and cakes. You won't find a better breakfast in Niseko than the classic bacon, egg and cheese sandwich here. Friendly service, too.

Sobadokoro Rakuichi SOBA ¥
(そば処 楽一; ☎ 0136-58-3170; 431 Niseko, Niseko-chō; lunch from ¥900; dinner course ¥8000; ⊗ lunch from 11.30am, dinner from 5pm Fri-Wed; P ⊕) Niseko's most famous noodle shop is also famously hard to find, though its secluded location (accessed via a wooden boardwalk) is a big part of the appeal. The other part is watching chef Tatsuri Rai behind the counter hand-make the soba (buckwheat noodles) you just ordered. Simple is best: go for the *namako uchi seiro* (生粉打ちせいろ; fresh-made cold noodles) – just ¥900.

Rakuichi is known to draw huge lines for the first lunch seating at 11.30am (it stops serving lunch when it runs out). So unless you're willing to commit a lot of time, this is one for the low season. Dinner is reservations only, but lunch is better. It's off the access road to Annupuri; look for the banner. No children under 12.

Green Farm Café
CAFE ¥

(☏ 0136-23-3354; http://nisekogreenfarm.com; 67-6 Yamada, Kutchan-chō; meals ¥900-1500; ☺8am-4pm summer, 8am-10pm winter; ☺☜ ☂🖥) 🍃 Veggie wraps, banana pancakes and granola – not to mention a location in the heart of Hirafu – make this a popular pit stop. The same folks run Niseko Green Farm, an organic farm outside town, and their produce shows up in the dishes.

★ Niseko Loft Club
BARBECUE ¥¥

(ニセコロフト倶楽部; Map p596; ☏ 0136-44-2883; 397-5 Sōga, Niseko-chō; per 300g ¥1900; ☺5.30-9.30pm; P☜🖥) Down the road from the Annupuri slopes, Loft Club glitters with fairy lights and the warm, glowing promise of a filling meal washed down with beer and lively conversation. The speciality here is *yak-iniku* (grill-it-yourself meat), but rather than just the usual beef and pork, there's lamb and venison on the menu, too. Dishes are to share.

Niseko Pizza
ITALIAN ¥¥

(ニセコピザ; ☏ 0136-55-5553; 167-3 Yamada, Kutchan-chō; pizzas from ¥1700; ☺11am-11pm; ☺🖥) This authentic family-run pizzeria headed by the affable Cezar does thin-crust, wood-fired pizzas with a mouth-watering variety of toppings (plus pastas and steaks). Bonus: it delivers. In central Hirafu, downhill from the gondola; reduced hours low season.

Milk Kōbō
SWEETS

(ミルク工房, Milk Factory; Map p596; ☏ 0136-44-3734; www.milk-kobo.com; 888-1 Sōga, Niseko-chō; ☺9.30am-6pm; 🖥) On the road up to Niseko Village, this popular complex brings together a number of Hokkaidō's signature dairy products under one roof: ice cream, yoghurt, cheese tarts and cream puffs, plus espresso drinks made with local milk.

Sprout
CAFE

(スプラウト; ☏ 0136-55-5161; http://sprout-project.com; N1W3-10, Kutchan-chō; coffee from ¥400; ☺8am-8pm Wed-Mon; ☺🖥) This popular hang-out run by a former outdoor guide serves Niseko's best coffee. It's 100m up the road from Kutchan Station, decked out like a very cool campsite. There's a huge library of outdoor books and magazines (in Japanese) here, too.

ℹ Information

Goshiki Onsen Information Centre (五色温泉インフォメーションセンター; ☏ 0136-59-2200; 510 Niseko, Niseko-chō; ☺8am-5pm Jun-Oct) English hiking maps and information on the latest weather and trail conditions. Just above Goshiki Onsen (p589), at the start of the hiking trail.

Hirafu Welcome Centre (ひらふウエルカムセンター; ☏ 0136-22-0109; www.grand-hirafu.jp/winter/en/index.html; 204 Yamada, Kutchan-chō; ☺8.30am-9pm) Near the Hirafu gondola (and where direct buses to/from New Chitose Airport originate and terminate), with English-language information. Open only during the snow season.

Information Centre Plat (☏ 0136-22-3344; www.niseko.co.jp; Kita 1 Nishi 2, Kutchan-chō; ☺10am-7pm Tue-Sun; ☎) Lots of English brochures and maps (for Niseko and beyond), 200m down the street outside JR Kutchan Station. There's a smaller information centre (open 9am to 6pm) in the train station.

Niseko Tourist Information (ニセコ観光案内所; ☏ 0136-44-2468; www.nisekotourism. com; Chūō-dōri, Niseko-chō; ☺8am-5pm; ☎) At JR Niseko Station, with pamphlets, maps, bus timetables; can help with bookings. It also has a centre at the View Plaza Michi-no-Eki on Rte 66 heading into town.

ℹ Getting There & Away

BUS

During the ski season, **Chūō Bus** (中央バス; ☏ Hakodate terminal 0128-22-3265, Sapporo terminal 011-231-0600; www.chuo-bus.co.jp) coaches run from Sapporo Eki-mae Bus Terminal (one way/return ¥2240/4000, three hours) and New Chitose Airport (one way/return ¥2600/4500, 3¾ hours) to Niseko; travel times are dependent on weather conditions. Drop-off points include the Welcome Centre in Hirafu, the Hilton (p591) and Annupuri. Reservations are necessary, and it's recommended that you book well ahead of your departure date.

CAR & MOTORCYCLE

Scenic Rte 5 winds from Sapporo to Otaru around the coast, and then cuts inland through the mountains down to Niseko. Having a car will make it easier to move between the various ski slopes, though you'll need to drive with extreme caution. In summer (low season), public transport services drop off, which provides more incentive to pick up a car in Sapporo or at New Chitose Airport (p575). There are also outlets of major car rental companies in Hirafu.

TRAIN

The JR Hakodate line runs from Sapporo to Kutchan (¥2360, two hours), Hirafu (¥2360, 2½ hours) and Niseko (¥2680, three hours) stations. You will need to transfer in Otaru, where you can also get trains directly to New Chitose Airport (p575).

Note that JR Hirafu Station is actually inconvenient for central Hirafu, unless you've arranged for pick-up.

ℹ Getting Around

Buses (¥300, 15 minutes) run irregularly (and infrequently in summer) between Kutchan Station and the ski villages; it's better to arrange pick-up.

During snow season, Niseko United Shuttle (www.niseko.ne.jp) runs a service (roughly hourly 8am to 11pm) between Hirafu, Niseko Village and Annupuri (free for all-mountain pass holders). From 5pm to 11pm, the shuttle route extends to Kutchan Station, giving you more dining options. Pick up a schedule from any of the tourist information centres.

Niseko suffers from a chronic taxi shortage during the ski season, as most are booked up in advance. Most likely your lodging will offer to shuttle you around (for a fee), which is usually cheaper than taxis and more reliable. If you need to use a taxi, have your accommodation call ahead for you.

Otaru 小樽

☎ 0134 / POP 121,000

Otaru was the financial centre of Hokkaidō – a bustling center of trade with Russia and China – in the early 20th century. The city's elite invested those riches in the construction of grand, Western-style buildings of stone and brick – the style of the time – many of which line the town's central canal. This exotic (for Japan) atmosphere makes Otaru very popular with domestic visitors. While the town is definitely touristy, it's evocative of an interesting slice of Hokkaidō history and makes for an easy day trip or one-night excursion from Sapporo.

◎ Sights & Activities

Otaru's sights are clustered around its canal, a 10-minute walk straight down Chūō-dōri from Otaru Station. The area is easily walkable.

★ Otaru Canal   CANAL

(小樽運河; Map p594) Historic Otaru canal is lined with warehouses from the late 19th and early 20th centuries. This was a time when traditional Japanese architecture was infused with Western-style building techniques, so some of the buildings are quite interesting. Most have been restored and now house museums and cafes. Unfortunately the canal itself is half-buried by a major thoroughfare, despite the best lobbying efforts of local preservationists.

Otaru Museum   MUSEUM

(小樽市総合博物館; Map p594; ☎ 0134-22-1258; 2-1-20 Ironai; adult/child ¥300/free; ⊙ 9.30am-5pm) This annexe of the Otaru Museum, known as the Ungakan (運河館), is housed in a restored warehouse dating from 1893 near the canal. It does a good job of illustrating (with an English-language supplement) Otaru's rise, thanks to the herring industry, its peak in the early 20th century and the city's subsequent decline.

Former Nihon
Yūsen Building   HISTORIC BUILDING

(旧日本郵船株式会社小樽支店; ☎ 0134-22-3316; 3-7-8 Ironai; adult/child ¥300/150; ⊙ 9.30am-5pm Wed-Mon) This is where trade orders were processed during Otaru's golden age. When the stone building was completed in 1906, it represented the latest construction technology and the height of fashion – don't miss the gilded, embossed wallpaper made of rice paper. It's at the northern end of the canal.

Bank of Japan
Otaru Museum   HISTORIC BUILDING

(日本銀行旧小樽支店金融資料館; Map p594; ☎ 0134-21-1111; 1-11-16 Ironai; ⊙ 9.30am-5pm Thu-Tue) FREE The former Otaru branch of the venerable Bank of Japan (日本銀行), completed in 1912 and designed by the same architect who did Tokyo Station, has been so thoroughly restored as to look rather contemporary. Don't miss the owl keystones on the exterior, which pay homage to the Ainu guardian deity.

Nichigin-dōri   AREA

(日銀道り; Map p594) Once known as the 'Wall Street of the North', Nichigin-dōri is lined with elegant buildings that speak to Otaru's past life as a prominent financial centre.

Otaru Canal Cruise   CRUISE

(Map p594; ☎ 0134-31-1733; http://otaru.cc/en/; 5-4 Minato-machi; day cruise adult/child ¥1500/500, night cruise ¥1800/500) The view of the canal is prettiest from this vantage point on the water. Cruises depart from Chūō-bashi and last 40 minutes; though recommended, no advance booking is necessary.

🛏 Sleeping

Otaru is an easy day trip from Sapporo, though it also works as a convenient stopover on the way to Niseko. There are plenty of

Otaru

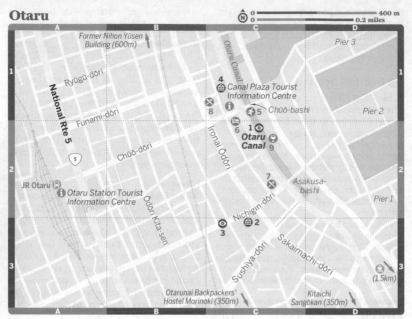

Otaru

places to stay here, the best (and priciest) of which have rooms overlooking the bay.

★Otarunai Backpackers' Hostel Morinoki

HOSTEL ¥

(おたるないバックパッカーズホステル 杜の樹; ☑0134-23-2175; www.infotaru.net; 4-15 Aioi; dm ¥3000; ᴾ⊝@🛜) While the sights of Otaru can be done in a day, if you're looking for somewhere to hole up for a few, this is a fantastic choice. Morinoki is an old, sprawling house perched on a stone embankment. Accommodation is in fairly simple male and female dormitories, but there are kitchen and laundry facilities, bilingual staff and super-comfy lounging areas.

Meals are good and exceedingly reasonable (breakfast/dinner ¥390/500). The hostel is about a 15-minute walk from JR Otaru Station, and can be a little tricky to find.

Hotel Nord Otaru

HOTEL ¥¥¥

(ホテルノルド小樽; Map p594; ☑0134-24-0500; www.hotelnord.co.jp/en/index.php; 1-4-16 Ironai; s/d/q from ¥9200/16,200/23,760; ⊝❄@🛜) This is a reliable higher-end option, in a restored warehouse along the canal. Rooms are priced according to size and view – the larger, canal-facing rooms naturally being the prize.

🍴 Eating & Drinking

★Kita-no Aisukurīmu-ya-san

ICE CREAM ¥

(北のアイスクリーム屋さん; Map p594; ☑0134-23-8983; 1-2-18 Ironai; ice cream from ¥300; ⊙9.30am-6pm; 🚶) Housed in a converted warehouse that was built in 1892, just back from the canal, this legendary Otaru ice-cream parlour scoops up some seriously 'special' ice cream flavours. The *ika-sumi* (squid ink) is actually just mildly sweet. We were afraid to try the *uni* (sea urchin). Melon, a more ice-cream friendly local speciality, is divine.

Otaru Sushi-kō   SUSHI ¥¥
(小樽すし耕; Map p594; ☑ 0134-21-5678; 2-2-6 Ironai; sushi sets ¥1900-4000; ☺ noon-8.30pm Thu-Tue; ◙) Come here for excellent sushi sets and *kaisen-don* (bowls of rice topped with sashimi) featuring Hokkaidō specialities such as *sake* (salmon), *ikura* (salmon roe), *uni* (sea urchin) and *kani* (crab). Note that it often closes for a few hours in the afternoon and fills up fast at dinner, so reservations are recommended.

Otaru Sōko No 1   PUB
(小樽倉庫　No 1; Map p594; ☑ 0134-21-2323; http://otarubeer.com/jp; 5-4 Minato-machi; beer ¥500-1300; ☺ 11am-11pm) Come to this convert-ed warehouse on the canal to taste the local microbrew, Otaru Beer, on tap. Its pilsner and dunkel beers are the best.

🛍 Shopping

Local glassmaker **Kitaichi** (北一硝子三号館; ☑ 0134-33-1993; www.kitaichiglass.co.jp; 7-26 Sakai machi; ☺ 8.45am-6pm) has numerous shops in town. There are also a few antique stores.

ℹ Information

Canal Plaza Tourist Information Centre (運河プラザ観光案内所; Map p594; ☑ 0134-33-1661; ☺ 9am-6pm) Housed in Otaru's oldest warehouse, with lots of pam-phlets and brochures in English for Otaru and surrounding areas.

Otaru Station Tourist Information Centre (小樽駅観光案内所; Map p594; ☑ 0134-29-1333; ☺ 9am-6pm) If you're arriving by train, pick up an English map at this kiosk in the station.

ℹ Getting There & Away

BOAT

Shin-Nihonkai Ferry (新日本海フェリー; ☑ 0134-22-6191; www.snf.jp; 7-2 Chikkō) runs ferries down the Japan Sea coast, connecting Otaru to Niigata (18 hours) and Maizuru (Kyoto-fu; 20 hours). Prices and departures are seasonal, but the latest information is posted in English on the website.

When ferries are running, buses (¥220, 30 minutes) depart from stop 4 in front of JR Otaru Station for the ferry terminal at 8.59am, 5.29pm (Sundays only) and 9pm, to coincide with ferry departures. From the ferry terminal, buses depart at 9.30pm for Otaru.

TRAIN

Twice-hourly *kaisoku* trains on the JR Hakodate line connect Otaru and Sapporo (¥1160, 30 minutes); hourly local trains take 45 minutes (¥640). Less frequent trains on the same line continue to Kutchan (¥1070, 1¼ hours).

Shikotsu-Tōya National Park　支笏洞爺国立公園

Shikotsu-Tōya National Park (993 sq km) is an oddly non-contiguous park, with pockets of wilderness carved out of a large area. Highlights include two caldera lakes, Shikotsu-ko and Tōya-ko, two popular hot spring towns, Jōzankei and Noboribetsu, and numerous mountains, the most im-pressive of which is Yōtei-zan (p598), also known as Ezo-Fuji, because it resembles famous Mt Fuji. Within easy striking dis-tance of Sapporo, to the south and south-west, the park is an attractive getaway with much to offer.

As Shikotsu-Tōya National Park is spread out, public transport between the different sections of the park is difficult; only Nobor-ibetsu and Tōya-ko have a direct bus link. A car is best if you want to explore the whole area.

Jōzankei   定山渓
☑ 011 / POP 2250

Jōzankei sits along the Toyohira-gawa, deep in a gorge. It's the closest major onsen town to Sapporo and an easy escape for those after some R&R. The resort is especially pretty (and popular) in autumn, when the leaves change colour – a sight that can be viewed from many an outdoor bath. Only an hour's bus or car ride from Sapporo, Jōzankei works well as a day trip. Most hotels and ryokan allow nonguests to use their onsen baths for a fee (¥500 to ¥1500). There's also Hōheikyō (p597) further up the road, often voted one of Hok-kaidō's best onsen.

⊙ Sights & Activities

Ainu Culture Promotion Centre   CULTURAL CENTRE
(札幌ピリカコタン, Sapporo Pirka Kotan; ☑ 011-596-5961; www.city.sapporo.jp/shimin/pirka-kotan/en; 27 Kogane-yu, Minami-ku; adult/child ¥200/free; ☺ 9am-5pm Tue-Sun; 🅿) Unlike museums where artefacts are kept behind glass, exhibitions here consist of replicas, handmade by members of Sapporo's Ainu

Niseko & Shikotsu-Tōya National Park

- Jōzankei
- Jōzan-ko
- Kutchan
- 4
- 8
- Hirafu
- 7
- 10
- 14
- 15
- Niseko
- Kyōgoku
- 276
- 230
- Nakayama Pass
- Yōtei-zan (1898m)
- Kimobetsu
- Makkari
- 13
- 5
- Otaki
- 230
- Tōya
- Tōya-ko
- Naka-jima
- Tōya-ko Onsen
- Shōwa-Shin-zan (398m)
- Sōbetsu
- Abuta
- Usu-zan (729m)
- 2
- Tōya
- Dō-ō Expwy
- 1
- Noboribetsu Onsen
- 37
- Date
- Noboribetsu
- Mareppu
- Horobetsu
- Uchiura-wan
- Orofure Pass
- Muroran Main Line
- Sakimori
- Higashi-Muroran
- Muroran
- Wanishi
- Muroran
- Chikyū-misaki

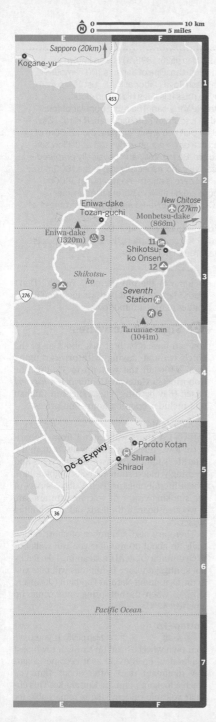

Niseko & Shikotsu-Tōya National Park

community using their own family heirlooms as models. As a result, you can touch everything on display, feeling, for example, the linen-like softness of textiles made from tree bark. The centre is in Kogane-yu, 3km east of Jōzankei.

The Sapporo–Jōzankei bus stops at Kogane-yu (¥650, 50 minutes); the museum is a short walk up from the bus stop.

Iwato Kannon-dō BUDDHIST TEMPLE
(岩戸観音堂; ☏ 011-598-2012; 3 Jōzankei Onsen-higashi; ☺ 7am-8pm) This small temple fronts a 120m-long cave that has 33 statues of Kannon, the Buddhist deity of compassion, and is dedicated to road workers who lost their lives constructing roads in the area. There are also lovely old photographs of Jōzankei on display and, next door, a free *ashi-yu* (foot bath).

★**Hōheikyō** ONSEN
(豊平峡; ☏ 011-598-2410; www.hoheikyo.co.jp; 608 Jōzankei; adult/child ¥1000/500; ☺ 10am-10.30pm) Home to Hokkaidō's largest outdoor bath, Hōheikyō is a stunner, set above town on the gorge's forested slope. The whole rambling structure is shack-like, which just adds to the appeal of having stumbled upon something great. The door curtains indicating which

WORTH A TRIP

HIKING YŌTEI-ZAN

The perfect conical volcano **Yōtei-zan** (羊蹄山; Map p596; 1898m) is also known as Ezo-Fuji because of its striking resemblance to Fuji-san. One of Japan's 100 Famous Mountains, it sits in its own little pocket of Shikotsu-Tōya National Park, just 10km from Niseko. It's a stunning backdrop: the only way to miss it is if it's hidden in cloud.

Be prepared for a big climb if you want to tackle Yōtei-zan. The most popular of four trailheads is Yōtei-zan tozan-guchi (羊蹄山登山口), south of Kutchan near JR Hirafu Station at 350m. Do your maths and you'll calculate that you are in for more than 1500m of vertical climb. Most people climb and descend in a day – get an early start and allow six to nine hours return, depending on how fit you are. Be mentally and physically prepared – the weather can change quickly on this exposed volcano, especially above the 1600m tree line. Make sure you have enough food and drink. There is an emergency hut at 1800m.

The upper reaches of Yōtei-zan are covered in alpine flowers during the summer. From the peak, the Sea of Japan, the Pacific Ocean and Tōya-ko are all visible – unless, of course, you are inside a cloud!

If you want to attempt this by public transport, you have to catch the 6.40am bus (¥300, 11 minutes, Monday to Saturday) from JR Kutchan Station; the last return bus is at 8.07pm. Hiking season is roughly mid-June through mid-October.

baths are for men and which are for women are swapped daily.

Oddly enough, there's an Indian restaurant on the ground floor. The Sapporo-Jōzankei bus continues on to Hōheikyō (¥840, 1¼ hours), its final stop.

ℹ Information

Tourist Information Centre (☏ 011-598-2012; http://jozankei.jp; 3-222 Jōzankei Onsen-higashi; ⊙ 9am-5pm) Right on Rte 230, the main road through the valley, with English brochures and maps, an English-speaker, and a small museum with photos of Jōzankei in the booming years of days gone by.

ℹ Getting There & Away

Five buses run between **Sapporo Eki-mae Bus Terminal** (p588) and Jōzankei daily (¥770, one hour).

Noboribetsu Onsen 登別温泉

☏ 0143 / POP 49,525

Noboribetsu Onsen is a serious onsen: you can smell the sulphur from miles away. While the town is small, there are countless springs here, sending up mineral-rich waters. The baths received great fame when the town was designated as a health resort for injured soldiers following the 1904–05 Russo-Japanese War and remain Hokkaido's most famous onsen today.

The source of the waters is Jigoku-dani, a hissing, steaming volcanic pit above town. According to legend, this hellish landscape is home to the *oni* (demon) Yukujin. Don't worry: he's kind and bestows luck. You'll find statues of him around town.

◉ Sights & Activities

You can have a bath at just about all of the hotels without staying, with prices ranging from ¥400 all the way up to ¥2000. The Noboribetsu Gateway Center has a *higaeri onsen* (day bathing) cheat sheet in English that includes opening hours and prices.

Jigoku-dani   HOT SPRINGS

(地獄谷) A short walk uphill from Noboribetsu town reveals what may await us in the afterlife: sulphurous gases, hissing vents and seemingly blood-stained rocks. Jigoku-dani, which literally means 'Hell Valley', is part of the smoking crater of volcanic Kuttara-san. A wooden boardwalk leads out to a boiling geyser.

There are also a number of short hiking trails. In about 30 minutes you can walk out to Ōyu-numa (大湯沼), a steaming lake fed by hot springs; another 15 minutes will take you to the Ōyu-numa Natural Footbath (大湯沼天然足湯), where the hot spring water comes up a perfect 42°C.

Kuttara-ko   LAKE

(倶多楽湖; クッタラコ; Map p596) If you have your own wheels, head up through town past Jigoku-dani on Rte 350 as it becomes a narrow mountain road. After about 4km you reach a lookout point for Kuttara-ko. This circular volcanic caldera lake is remarkable for two things: there's not a single river flowing into or out of it and it has been left almost completely untouched by human hands. You can't drive any further, as traffic has been cut off to protect the lake.

⭐**Onsen Tengoku**   ONSEN

(温泉天国; www.takimotokan.co.jp/english/onsen; Dai-ichi Takimoto-kan, 55 Noboribetsu Onsen-chō; ¥2000, after 4pm ¥1500; ◷9am-6pm) The bathhouse attached to the Dai-ichi Takimoto-kan hotel deserves singling out because it is truly spectacular, an 'onsen heaven' (*tengoku* means 'heaven'). The sprawling complex, awash in pastel tiles, fountains and mirrors, has more variety than any others here, with seven different springs (all purportedly good for something) and several outdoor baths.

🛏 Sleeping & Eating

With its compact layout and decent bus links, Noboribetsu is the best place to base yourself in Shikotsu-Tōya National Park if you're getting around by public transport. There are about 10 hotels here, all with onsen baths.

There is a little more life here after dark than in most rural onsen towns, with a handful of ramen shops and convenience stores lining Gokuraku-dōri, the (small, walkable) main drag.

Shōkōin   MINSHUKU ¥

(聖光院; ☑0143-84-2359; http://jodo.jp/01-063; 119-1 Noboribetsu Onsen-chō; per person ¥3400; P ⎙) Not many temples look like an office building, but this one does! The entrance is on the ground floor, the temple rooms are on floor two, and the priest's wife runs a *minshuku* on floor three, with small but well-kept tatami rooms. The shared bath, which can be used privately and is open 24 hours, has onsen water.

The temple is known locally as Kannon-ji (観音寺). Morning prayers (if you like) are at 8am.

Dai-ichi Takimoto-kan   HOTEL ¥¥¥

(第一滝本館; ☑0143-84-3322; www.takimotokan.co.jp/english; 55 Noboribetsu Onsen-chō; s/d incl 2 meals from ¥18,900/24,840; P ❉ ⎙) This sprawling onsen hotel, with its escalators and kiosks and constant buzz, feels a bit like a gaily decorated airport terminal. That's not meant to be critical: with 24-hour complimentary use of the excellent bathhouse, Onsen Tengoku, this is a fine place to stay. Go for the Japanese-style rooms (the Western rooms are rather dowdy). Meals are served buffet-style.

Note that wi-fi is only available in the Honkan (main wing) and Minami-kan (south wing).

Aji no Daiō   RAMEN ¥

(味の大王; ☑0143-84-2415; 29-9 Noboribetsu Onsen-chō; ramen ¥800-1150; ◷11.30am-3pm & 9pm-midnight, closed 1st, 3rd & 5th Tue of the month; 📷) Noboribetsu's landmark ramen shop serves up fiery red 'jigokudani' noodles that would make the local *oni* (devils) proud. Entry level is a totally manageable kick; you can add ¥50 to step it up a notch, all the way to 10. (Warning: there are far more celebrity signings on the walls here than photos of customers who have successfully finished level 10 bowls.)

ℹ Information

Noboribetsu Gateway Center (登別ゲートウェイセンター; ☑0143-83-3111; 26 Noboribetsu Onsen-chō; ◷8.30am-6pm) Part of the Noboribetsu Onsen bus terminal, with bus schedules, English maps and luggage storage (¥500 per day).

Noboribetsu Park Service Centre (登別パークサービスセンター; ☑0143-84-3141; www.noboribetsu-spa.jp; Noboribetsu Onsen-chō; ◷8am-6pm) English brochures and hiking maps, at the entrance to **Jigoku-dani**.

ℹ Getting There & Away

Limited express trains run to JR Noboribetsu Station on the JR Muroran line from Hakodate (¥6890, 2½ hours), Sapporo (¥4480, 1¼ hours) and JR Tōya Station (¥2720, 40 minutes).

Frequent buses (¥340, 15 minutes) connect the train station with Noboribetsu Onsen bus terminal, at the southern end of town; a taxi ride between the train station and town should cost ¥2000.

Direct highway buses run between Noboribetsu Onsen bus terminal and Sapporo (¥1950, 100 minutes), as well as New Chitose Airport (¥1370, one hour).

Shikotsu-ko   支笏湖

Directly south of Sapporo and surrounded by soaring volcanoes, Shikotsu-ko is Japan's second-deepest lake and renowned for its clear water. While it is 250m above sea level, its deepest spot is 363m, 113m below sea level. You'll need your own wheels to get here, but it's a superb spot for independent exploration and excellent for campers.

Shikotsu-ko Onsen (支笏湖温泉), on the eastern side of the lake, is the only town. This compact little resort village has some nice short walks, including a nature trail for bird-watchers. Sightseeing boats head out onto the lake and there are rental bicycles, boats and canoes.

🏃 Activities

Tarumae-zan
HIKING

(樽前山; Map p596) On the southern side of the lake is Tarumae-zan (1041m), an active volcano that is the area's most popular hike. The crater itself is usually closed – it has a still-smoking lava dome – but you can reach and go around the rim from the seventh station (650m; only accessible by private car, off Rte 141). Allow 1½ hours for the return hike to the rim.

From the same trailhead you can also climb Fuppushi-dake (風不死岳; 1102m) in five to six hours return, which offers excellent views of the lake and park. Locals suggest a bear bell is essential for this hike.

Marukoma Onsen
ONSEN

(丸駒温泉; Map p596; ☑0123-25-2341; 7 Horobinai, Chitose; ¥1000; ◷10am-3pm) On the surface, Marukoma Onsen is a typical ageing resort hotel, but the concrete facade hides a fantastic collection of baths, which are open to day trippers. The large *rotemburo* (outdoor bath) looks right over Shikotsu-ko.

🛏 Sleeping & Eating

There are a handful of small pensions in town, plus two attractive campgrounds: **Morappu** (モラップキャンプ場; Map p596; ☑0123-25-2201; Shikotsu-ko Onsen, Chitose; adult/child ¥800/500; ◷late Apr–mid-Oct; P), near town, and **Bifue** (美笛キャンプ場; Map p596; ☑090-5987-1284; Bifue, Chitose; adult/child ¥1000/500; ◷early May–mid-Oct), on the quiet, sandy western shore (both accessed by Rte 276).

There are very few places to eat here and they all close by 5pm or 6pm. Either secure meals at your lodging or pack food.

Log Bear
MINSHUKU ¥¥

(ログベアー; Map p596; ☑0123-25-2738; http://logbear.moto-nari.com/shikotsu/Welcome.html; Shikotsu-ko Onsen, Chitose; per person ¥5500; 🛜) Log Bear is right in the middle of Shikotsu-ko Onsen, and is run by a real character called Robin. There are only two simple rooms: one twin and one quad. On the ground floor is a coffee shop (open 9am to 10pm), where complimentary breakfast is served along with the town's best coffee.

ⓘ Information

Shikotsu-ko Visitor Centre (支笏湖ビジターセンター; Map p596; ☑0123-25-2404; http://shikotsukovc.sakura.ne.jp; Shikotsu-ko Onsen; ◷9am-5.30pm Apr-Nov, 9.30am-4.30pm Dec-Mar) Before heading up any trails, check for closures and bear sightings on the map here. Staff are helpful and they also rent out bicycles for ¥500 per day.

ⓘ Getting There & Away

There is no public transport to Shikotsu-ko, unfortunately; however, the lake is only 25km from New Chitose Airport (p575) – a short drive if you pick up a car at the airport.

Tōya-ko
洞爺湖

At the southwestern side of Shikotsu-Tōya National Park, Tōya-ko is an almost classically round caldera lake with a large island (Naka-jima) sitting in the middle. What sets it apart is its truly active volcano, Usu-zan (有珠山; 729m), which has erupted four times since 1910, most recently in 2000.

Usu-zan is a mixed blessing: residents know that it will erupt again, covering their town in ash, and possibly rock; however, it was the 1910 eruption that led to the discovery of hot springs here and the development of Tōya-ko Onsen (洞爺湖温泉), the small resort on the lake's southern shore.

⊙ Sights & Activities

Tōya-ko Onsen has free hand baths and foot baths throughout town (think of it as an onsen treasure hunt!) and many hotels' baths can be used during the day (¥500 to ¥1500). There's a fireworks display on the lake every night from April until October at 8.45pm, and paddle steamers running lake cruises. The 50km circumference of the lake can be rounded by car or bicycle.

Volcano Science Museum
MUSEUM

(火山科学館; ☑0142-75-2555; www.toyako-vc.jp; 142-5 Tōya-ko Onsen; ¥600; ◷9am-5pm; P) The eruptions at Uzu-san were among the first to be recorded by modern means (and work here significantly advanced science in early detection). Here you can see video footage of eruptions in action, and before and after photos that clearly show new land masses forming.

The museum, a short walk west from the Tōya-ko Onsen bus terminal, is part of the Tōya-ko Visitor Centre, which also has excellent (and free!) information on the local topography and indigenous flora and fauna.

Usu-zan
MOUNTAIN

(有珠山; Map p596; ☎0142-74-2401; www.
wakasaresort.com; 184-5 Shōwa Shin-zan, Sōbetsu-
chō; ropeway adult/child return ¥1500/750;
⏰8.30am-5pm) Here is a rare chance to bear
witness to modern mountain-making: Shōwa
Shin-zan (昭和新山; 398m) – whose name
means 'the new mountain of the Shōwa period' – arose from a wheat field following
the 1943 eruption of Usu-zan. The **Usu-zan
Ropeway** runs up to a viewing platform for
Shōwa Shin-zan, with Tōya-ko behind it.

From the observation deck a trail heads out
on a 90-minute circuit (open May to October)
around the outer rim of Usu-zan, with views
of Tōya-ko and Yōtei-zan (p598). Buses (one
way/round trip ¥340/620, 10.10am, 12.45pm,
1.40pm and 3.50pm) run four times a day
from the Tōya-ko Onsen bus terminal to the
ropeway. A taxi should cost ¥1800; all the way
from JR Tōya-ko Station, ¥3000.

🛏 Sleeping

In addition to some pricier resorts, Tōya-ko
Onsen has quite a few budget ryokan.

Daiwa Ryokan
RYOKAN ¥¥

(大和旅館; ☎0142-75-2415; http://daiwa-ryokan.
jp; 105 Tōya-ko Onsen; s/d from ¥5200/9200; P🅿🛜)
This is a simple, homey budget ryokan with
character; adopting an early Shōwa (1926–89)
theme, it's strewn with old knick-knacks. The
owners are friendly, the bath is 100% natural
onsen and there's a small garden. Nonguests
can use the onsen here for ¥500.

ℹ Information

Tōya-ko Tourist Information Centre (洞爺
湖観光情報センター; ☎0142-75-2446; www.
laketoya.com; 142 Tōya-ko Onsen; ⏰9am-
6pm; 🛜) Inside the Tōya-ko Onsen bus terminal, with maps, pamphlets and bus schedules
in English.

Tōya-ko Visitor Centre (洞爺湖ビジター
センター; ☎0142-75-2555; www.toyako-vc.jp;
142-5 Tōya-ko Onsen; ⏰9am-5pm) Excellent
(and free!) information on the local topography as well as indigenous flora and fauna, a
short walk west from the Tōya-ko Onsen bus
terminal.

ℹ Getting There & Away

Limited express trains on the JR Muroran line
link JR Tōya Station with Hakodate (¥5490,
two hours), Sapporo (¥5920, two hours) and
Noboribetsu (¥2720, 40 minutes). From the
train station, it's a 15-minute bus (¥330, twice
hourly) or taxi ride (¥1800) to the bus terminal
in Tōya-ko Onsen.

There are four buses daily between the Tōya-ko
Onsen bus terminal and Sapporo (¥2780, 2¾
hours).

Tomakomai
苫小牧

☎0144 / POP 173,285

Tomakomai is actually a sizeable industrial
city on Hokkaidō's south-central coast, though
most travellers know it only as the main port
of entry for long-distance ferries.

TOMAKOMAI FERRY ROUTES

Four operators, Shin-Nihonkai Ferry (www.snf.jp), Silver Ferry (www.silverferry.jp), MOL Ferry (www.sunflower.co.jp) and Taiheiyō Ferry (www.taiheiyo-ferry.co.jp), run ferries between
Tomakomai and the following destinations on Honshū. Note that schedules and prices are
subject to seasonal fluctuations.

DESTINATION	COST (¥; 2ND CLASS)	DURATION (HR)	FREQUENCY	OPERATOR
Akita	4530	10	Mon-Sat	Shin-Nihonkai Ferry
Hachinohe (Aomori-ken)	5000	7½	4 daily	Silver Ferry
Nagoya	9800	40	alternate days	Taiheiyō Ferry
Niigata	6480	18	Mon-Sat	Shin-Nihonkai Ferry
Oarai (Ibaraki-ken)	8740	17	1-2 daily	MOL Ferry
Sendai	7200	15	daily	Taiheiyō Ferry
Tsuruga (Fukui-ken)	9570	19	daily	Shin-Nihonkai Ferry

🛏 Sleeping & Eating

There really is no reason to stay in Tomakomai unless you are arriving or departing by ferry and won't be able to make your travel connections otherwise. There are plenty of business hotels here, including the major chains, for this very purpose.

The **Toyoko Inn Tomakomai Eki-mae** (東横イン苫小牧駅前; ☑0144-32-1045; www.toyoko-inn.com/e_hotel/00108/index.html; 3-2-21 Ōji-machi; s/d from ¥6265/7885; ❄❊@❋), in front of JR Tomakomai Station, is a reliable choice.

There are restaurants near the hotels. If you're catching a ferry it's advisable to eat beforehand and stock up on snacks as the food on-board is terrible (if you just arrived by ferry, you already know that).

ℹ Getting There & Away

JR Tomakomai Station is on the JR Muroran line, one hour from Sapporo (¥1450). Dōnan Bus (www.donanbus.co.jp) runs between the ferry terminal and JR Tomakomai Station (¥250, 15 minutes); a taxi should cost about ¥1500.

Chūō Bus (www.chuo-bus.co.jp) runs highway buses between Tomakomai Ferry Terminal and Sapporo Eki-mae Bus Terminal (¥1310, 1¾ hours).

NORTHERN HOKKAIDŌ 道北

Northern Hokkaidō (Dō-hoku) is where the majestic grandeur of the natural world takes over. Southeast of Asahikawa, Hokkaidō's second-largest city, is Daisetsuzan National Park, Japan's largest national park. It's a raw virgin landscape of enormous proportions. Way up north, west of Wakkanai and in the shadow of Siberia, Rishiri-Rebun-Sarobetsu National Park is a dramatic island-scape famous for its wildflowers. For hikers and extreme skiers the possibilities are tantalising. South of Asahikawa, Furano offers a somewhat mellower alternative: a family-friendly ski resort in winter and, in summer, picturesque fields through which you can drive, cycle or just stroll.

Asahikawa 旭川

☑0166 / POP 343,400

Asahikawa, Hokkaidō's second-largest city, carries the dual honour of having the most days with snowfall in all of Japan, as well as the record for the coldest temperature (−40°C). It is mainly used by travellers as a transit point for Wakkanai to the north, Daisetsuzan National Park to the southeast, and Biei and Furano to the south; however, if you find your travel plans waylaid by bad weather, this a pleasant city in which to spend a day or two, with a handful of sights and plenty of eating and drinking options.

Heiwa-dōri, a large pedestrian strip, extends north of JR Asahikawa Station for eight blocks. Most hotels and many restaurants are here, within walking distance of the station.

◉ Sights

Kawamura Kaneto
Ainu Memorial Hall   MUSEUM
(川村カ子トアイヌ記念館; Map p606; ☑0166-51-2461; http://ainu-museum.sakura.ne.jp; 11 Hokumon-chō; adult/child ¥500/300; ⊙9am-5pm) Recently celebrating its 100th anniversary, this museum is less a collection of artefacts (though it has those too) and more the story of a local Ainu family desperate to keep the old ways alive; there are many fascinating, unstaged photographs from the early 20th century. Its founder was Kaneto Kawamura, an Ainu chief and master surveyor, who helped lay the tracks for many challenging rail projects in Japan; he used his savings to start the museum.

Take bus 24 from stop 14 in front of JR Asahikawa Station to the Ainu Kinenkan-mae stop (¥190, 15 minutes, hourly).

Asahiyama Zoo   ZOO
(旭山動物園; Map p606; ☑0166-36-1104; www.city.asahikawa.hokkaido.jp/asahiyamazoo/; Kuranuma, Higashi-Asahigawa; adult/child ¥820/free; ⊙9.30am-5.15pm May-Oct, 10.30am-3.30pm Nov-Apr) Known Japan-wide, the country's northernmost zoo attracts visitors with its stars from cold climates: polar bears and penguins. More interesting to travellers might be the enclosures featuring Hokkaidō native species, including Blakiston's Fish Owl, *higuma* (brown bear) and *ezo-jika* (Hokkaidō deer).

Shuttle buses (¥440, 40 minutes) run every 30 minutes from bus stop 6 in front of JR Asahikawa Station for the zoo.

🎆 Festivals & Events

For local events, visit www.asahikawa-daisetsu.jp/event.

Asahikawa Winter Matsuri   CULTURAL
(旭川冬祭り; http://www1.city.asahikawa.hokkaido.jp/files/kankou/awf/) Held every February

and into its sixth decade, Asahikawa's winter festival is second only to Sapporo's. The **International Ice Sculpture Competition** is a highlight, along with local food and fun events.

Kotan Matsuri CULTURAL
(コタン祭り; ⊙ Sep) Held on the autumn equinox in September on the banks of the Chubestu-gawa, south of the city. There are traditional Ainu dances, music and prayer ceremonies offered to the deities of fire, the river, *kotan* (the village) and the mountains.

🛏 Sleeping

There's a good spread of national hotel chains around the train station.

Guest House Asahikawa HOSTEL ¥
(ゲストハウス旭川; ☎ 0166-73-8269; www.
guesthouseasahikawa.jp; 7-31-10 6-jō-dōri; dm ¥3000; ➔@🛜) On the 2nd floor of what used to be an office building, this hostel has been crafted with loving care. It's a bit squashy, but the owners are enthusiastic, and there's free coffee, a kitchen, games and a book exchange. It's about a 10-minute walk from JR Asahikawa Station, straight up the pedestrian strip.

Art Hotel Asahikawa HOTEL ¥¥
(アートホテル旭川; ☎ 0166-25-8811; www.
arthotelsasahikawa.com; 6 7-jō-dōri; s/d from ¥8000/10,000; ➔✳🛜) An easy-to-spot white tower block, the Art Hotel is Asahikawa's top hotel. It's not fancy, but it is clean and comfortable with very professional staff. Book early online for good deals. It's a 10-minute walk from JR Asahikawa Station, one block west of the pedestrian strip.

There's a spa in the basement, though admission is extra (ask for a discount ticket at the front desk).

🍴 Eating & Drinking

Asahikawa is famous for its *shōyu* (soy sauce) ramen; there are countless shops, the best of which are highly debated. The shopping centre attached to JR Asahikawa Station has a food court and a supermarket. There are also options along Heiwa-dōri.

Ramen Aoba RAMEN ¥
(らーめん青葉; ☎ 0166-23-2820; 8 2-jō-dōri; ramen from ¥750; ⊙ 9.30am-2pm & 3-7.45pm Thu-Tue; 🍴) The city's oldest ramen shop (70 years and counting!) serves delicious al dente noodles in a *shōyu*-seasoned, *assari* (light) broth – classic Asahikawa-style. The elderly proprietor

truly loves foreign customers and will likely ask you to sign her notebook.

It's a five-minute walk from JR Asahikawa Station, one block east of the pedestrian strip, on Midori-bashi-dōri; look for the orange door curtains.

Furarīto Alley JAPANESE ¥¥
(ふらりーと小路; www.furari-to.com; ⊙ 5-11pm) This rambling collection of 18 tiny restaurants runs the length of an alley between 4-jō-dōri and 5-jō-dōri about a 10-minute walk north of the train station. Wander along (loosely translated, *furarīto* means wander) and see what looks good – options include *yakitori* (grilled chicken skewers), *izakaya* (Japanese-style pubs) and even a tapas restaurant. Prices vary, but none of these restaurants is expensive.

★ Tirol CAFE
(チロル; ☎ 0166-26-7788; http://cafe-tirol.com/; 8-7 3-jō-dōri; ⊙ 8.30am-6pm) Tirol may have only opened a few years ago, but the owner has kept the 70-year-old building lovingly intact, with a suitably vintage interior and jazzy soundtrack. The coffee (¥550), roasted in-house, is fantastic. Come before 11am to get the 'morning set' (モーニングセット; ¥650), which includes coffee, toast and a hard-boiled egg.

It's a five-minute walk from JR Asahikawa Station; walk up the pedestrian strip and turn right one block before the Lawson convenience store and the shop will be on your right.

ℹ Information

Asahikawa International Centre (旭川国際交流センター; ☎ 0166-25-7491; http://asahikawaic.jp/en; 7th fl, Feeeal Asahikawa Bldg, 8 1-jō-dōri; ⊙ 10am-7.30pm; 🛜) This centre for foreign residents has a useful help desk and info-exchange bulletin board.

Tourist Information Counter (旭川観光案内所; ☎ 0166-26-6665; www.asahikawa-daisetsu.jp; ⊙ 8.30am-7pm Jun-Sep, 9am-7pm Oct-May) Inside JR Asahikawa Station on the ground floor, with English maps, brochures and bus timetables, and helpful English-speaking staff.

MICHI-NO-EKI

Country roads are dotted with Michi-no-eki (道の駅; road stations), like highway service areas, but for smaller, toll-free byways. In addition to toilets, tourist information and coffee, Michi-no-eki sell fresh produce, food products and crafts – all locally sourced. There is usually a cafeteria, too. In most cases, the staff and cooks are farmers' wives – which means these can be great places to sample local cooking. They're well signposted and when you've gone miles without seeing anything, they appear like beacons of promise.

ⓘ Getting There & Away

AIR

Asahikawa Airport (旭川空港; Map p606; ☑ 0166-83-3939; www.aapb.co.jp/en; E2-16-98, Higashi-Kagura) is 10km southeast of the city, in between Asahikawa and Biei. There are domestic flights to Tokyo, Nagoya and Osaka, as well as international flights to Beijing, Shanghai and Taipei. Airport shuttle buses (¥620, 30 minutes) depart from bus stop 9 in front of JR Asahikawa Station and are timed to meet arrivals and departures. A taxi should run around ¥4000.

BUS

Buses depart every 30 minutes from the **Chūō Bus Asahikawa Terminal** (中央バス旭川ターミナル; ☑ 0166-25-3000; ⊙ 5.45am-9.30pm) for Sapporo (¥2060, two hours; reservations necessary).

There are four daily buses to/from Asahidake Onsen (¥1430, 1½ hours), departing from bus stop 9 in front of JR Asahikawa Station.

Furano Bus (www.furanobus.jp) has eight daily runs to/from Furano (¥880, 1¾ hours) via Biei (¥620, 50 minutes), departing from bus stop 22 or 23 in front of the Aeon Mall next to JR Asahikawa Station.

Dōhoku Bus (www.dohokubus.com) has seven daily runs to/from Sōunkyō Onsen (¥2160, two hours), departing from bus stop 7 in front of JR Asahikawa Station.

CAR & MOTORCYCLE

Rental cars are available at Asahikawa Airport or from agencies near JR Asahikawa Station.

TRAIN

JR Limited Express Super Kamui, Okhotsk, Super Sōya and Sarubetsu Liner trains run between Asahikawa and Sapporo (¥4290, one hour, hourly).

Okhotsk Liner trains continue to Abashiri (¥8170, 3¾ hours, four daily). There are slightly more frequent trains on the JR Sekihoku line, but you'll need to transfer at Kamikawa.

Super Sōya and Sarubetsu Liner trains continue to Wakkanai (¥8500, four hours, three daily). Local trains require multiple transfers.

Hourly JR Furano trains run to Biei (¥540, 40 minutes); most go on to Furano (¥1070, 1¼ hours).

Biei 美瑛

☑ 0166 / POP 10,950

More or less halfway between Asahikawa and Furano, with the dramatic mountains of Daisetsuzan National Park in the background, Biei boasts some of the prettiest countryside in Hokkaidō. There is little in the way of sights here, but plenty of meandering country lanes passing through fields of sunflowers, lavender and white birch. Biei is primarily a summer destination, with visitors coming to explore the countryside and maybe pick up local produce from farm stands and/or spend an afternoon in a cute, little cottage cafe.

Biei has two scenic routes, **Patchwork Road** (パッチワークの路) and **Panorama Road** (パノラマロード). The former stitches together a collection of small farms. The latter is a network of lanes with vistas over the countryside. Both are well signposted, and possible to traverse by car, bicycle or, if you get an early start, on foot. The tourist information office has a map in English.

🛏 Sleeping & Eating

Biei has a handful of pensions, the best of which are out in the countryside. The tourist information office has a list, but it's better to book ahead in summer. Note that only a few places stay open year-round.

There are some places to eat around the train station, but the better options, which include restaurants, bakeries and cafes, are among the fields outside of town.

★ **Biei Potato-no-Oka**   INN ¥¥
(美瑛ポテトの丘; Map p606; ☑ 0166-92-3255; www.potatovillage.com/eng/top.html; Ōmura Murayama; dm/r per person from ¥4960/6600, breakfast/dinner ¥800/1500; ⊙ closed mid-Nov–mid-Dec & mid-Mar–mid-Apr; ℗ ⊖ ☎ 🛜) 🍴 Among the fields of Biei's pretty 'Patchwork Road', charming Potato-no-Oka, though small, has a big variety of accommodation, including dorm rooms, private Western- and Japanese-style rooms, and some cottages. Dinners are a treat, using fresh produce from neighbours. The owner is

friendly and speaks English. Free shuttle service is possible from Biei station if you book ahead.

ℹ Information

Biei Tourist Information Office (美瑛観光案内所; Map p606; ☑ 0166-92-4378; www.biei-hokkaido.jp; ⊗ 8.30am-7pm Jun-Sep, 8.30am-5pm Oct-May) Pick up the excellent English-language Biei map, which even includes GPS map codes for key viewpoints. To the left as you exit the train station.

ℹ Getting There & Away

JR Furano line trains run hourly between Biei and Asahikawa (¥540, 32 minutes) and every two hours between Biei and Furano (¥640, 36 minutes).

Furano buses make eight runs daily between JR Asahikawa Station and JR Furano Station via **Asahikawa Airport** and Biei. The ride from Asahikawa Airport to Biei takes 15 minutes (¥370).

Rte 237 runs between Asahikawa, Biei and Furano.

ℹ Getting Around

Pick up a car in Asahikawa if you plan on driving around Biei. Rental bicycles are available from a few shops around the station for ¥200/1000 per hour/day. Most bicycle rental shops will mind your bags for you.

Furano   富良野
☑ 0167 / POP 22,800

Furano is one of Japan's most inland towns and considered the centre of Hokkaidō – a distinction that has earned it the cute nickname Heso-no-machi (Belly-Button Town). It is equally attractive in summer and winter: summers are almost hot (but not quite) and there are fields of flowers, farm-fresh produce and ice-cream stands to be enjoyed, plus plenty of opportunities for walking, hiking and cycling. Winters, on the other hand, are very cold – resulting in extreme amounts of powdery snow. Furano is one of the country's top skiing and snowboarding destinations, though it lacks the international recognition of rival Niseko.

◉ Sights & Activities

In summer (and peaking in July) fields of lavender bloom in and around Furano. This is a big draw for domestic travellers, which means things can get crowded.

Farm Tomita   FARM
(ファーム富田; Map p606; ☑ 0167-39-3939; www.farm-tomita.co.jp/en; 15-gō, Kisen-kita, Naka-Furano; ⊗ 9am-4.30pm Oct–late Apr, 8.30am-6pm late Apr–Sep; Ⓟ) **FREE** Until snow falls in October, Tomita's fields are covered in a rainbow array of flowers. With the mountains of Daisetsuzan National Park as a backdrop, this is one of the most photographed spots in Hokkaidō. It's particularly known for its lavender (which peaks in early July), packaged in an array of goods – from pot-pourri to tea – that are sold here.

This place is so popular that from June to September, JR actually opens up a temporary train station known as Lavender Batake (ラベンダー畑; Lavender Farm) to accommodate the large influx of visitors. Otherwise, the closest station is JR Naka-Furano.

Furano Ski Area   SNOW SPORTS
(富良野スキー場; Map p606; www.princehotels.com/en/ski/furano/index.html; lift ticket full day/night ¥5200/1600, children 12yr & under free; ⊗ day 8.30am-7.30pm, night 4.30-7.30pm; ♿) Furano, open from December until the start of May, gets excellent, light and dry snow yet remains relatively undiscovered by foreign visitors, compared to Niseko. The slopes are predominantly beginner and intermediate, though there are some steep advanced runs. If you're travelling as a family, a major bonus here is that children aged 12 and under get a free lift pass.

Eleven lifts, including the fastest gondola in Japan, help to keep the crowds in check. The resort is anchored by two large Prince hotels with ski-in, ski-out access, restaurants and bars. Full equipment rental is available for ¥5600 per day (¥3700 for children). English signage is adequate.

Kitanomine Gondola   CABLE CAR
(北の峰ゴンドラ; Map p606; ☑ 0167-22-1111; return ¥1900; ⊗ 6.30-9am Jul & Aug, 5.45-8.15am Sep) From July to September, this gondola makes early morning runs up to 940m for day-break views over the sea of clouds below. It doesn't run every day or in bad weather, so call ahead. (During snow season, it's one of the two main Furano lifts.)

🎊 Festivals & Events

Hokkai Heso Matsuri   CULTURAL
(北海へそ祭り; ⊗ Jul) Taking its humorous nickname, Heso-no-machi (Belly-Button Town), to heart, Furano celebrates the

Furano, Biei & Daisetsuzan National Park

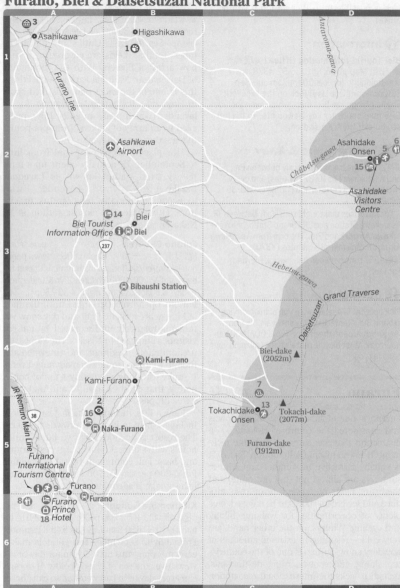

Hokkai Heso Matsuri 'navel festival' on 28 and 29 July. If you're in town at this time, take the opportunity to strip off, have a silly face painted on your midriff and join the Belly-Button Dance.

🛏 Sleeping

Furano is full of pensions and *minshuku* and staying in one out in the countryside is one of the main reasons to visit (you'll need your own transport, though).

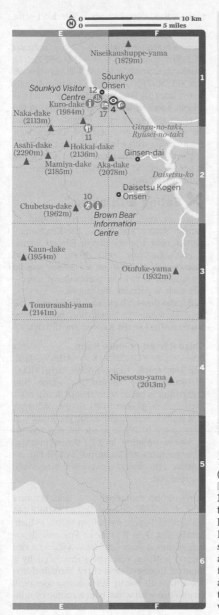

Furano, Biei & Daisetsuzan NP

◎ Sights

◑ Activities, Courses & Tours

⌂ Sleeping

ⓐ Shopping

★ **Alpine Backpackers** HOSTEL ¥
(アルパインバックパッカーズ; Map p606;
☑ 0167-22-1311; www.alpn.co.jp/english/index.html;
14-6 Kitanomine-chō, Furano; dm per person ¥2800,
tw/q ¥5600/11,200; P ⊛ @ 🕏) Conveniently
located just a few minutes' walk from the
Kitanomine Gondola (p605), this is a great
spot for skiers and active types. Backpackers
are well catered for with cooking and laundry
facilities, and a boiling onsen. There are also
all sorts of activities from rafting to fishing
to hot-air ballooning on offer. Check out the
website.

Furano Hostel HOSTEL ¥
(富良野ホステル; Map p606; ☑ 0167-44-4441;
http://furanohostel.sakura.ne.jp/english.htm; 3-20
Oka-machi, Naka-Furano; dm incl breakfast & dinner
¥3450; P @) Five minutes' walk west of JR
Naka-Furano Station (not JR Furano Station!), this hostel occupies a big farmhouse

If you're here to ski, zero in on lodging in
the Kitanomine area, which is nearest the
slopes. Note that many places close in the
in-between season, from mid-November to
mid-December and April. It's best to call
ahead to confirm.

WORTH A TRIP

BEAR MOUNTAIN

A 15-hectare forested enclosure in northern Tokachi, **Bear Mountain** (ベアマウンテン; ☑ 0156-64-7007; www.sahoro.co.jp/language/english/green/bear/bear.html; Karikachi-kogen, Shintoku; adult/child ¥1840/1080, with bus option ¥2920/2160; ⊙9am-4pm late Apr-Oct; 🅿) is home to 12 male *higuma* (who range in size from 300kg to 400kg!). The clever viewing facilities include a boardwalk 5m above ground and, for a little more yen, a heavily fortified bus – that looks like it was built for *Jurassic Park* – that cruises the park. The bears seem little fazed by both, and you're almost guaranteed to see at least one hanging around.

You'll need your own wheels to get to Bear Mountain. It's part of the Sahoro Resort (サホロリゾート) complex on Rte 38, 54km northeast of Obihiro and 66km southeast of Furano. Bear Mountain is, naturally, closed during the winter as all the bears are hibernating.

overlooking the countryside. It's exceptional value: breakfast and dinner are on the house (except Sunday night – the chef takes a break). Meals are simple, tasty and feature local produce. Private rooms may be available for an extra ¥2100 per room.

The owners are very kind and will give you a lift to the Furano ski slopes.

New Furano Prince Hotel   HOTEL ¥¥¥
(新富良野プリンスホテル; Map p606; ☑ 0167-22-1111; www.princehotels.com/en/newfurano; s/d incl lift ticket & breakfast from ¥22,300/33,600; 🅿❀❄@❀) The nicer of the two Prince hotels offers comfortable, classy, though not terribly stylish, rooms, decent restaurants and efficient service – all at the base of the Furano Ropeway. It's also got a few neat quirks, like the **Ningle Terrace** (ニングルテラス; Map p606; ☑ 0167-22-1111; ⊙10am-8.45pm Jul & Aug, noon-8.45pm Sep-Jun) outdoor craft centre and a coffee house and lounge bar down a path in the woods.

Note that while children 12 and under get free lift tickets to the ski resort, those aged seven and above are charged the adult rate at this hotel. Book through the Japanese site for better rates.

The bus from Asahikawa Airport (p604) to Furano terminates here (¥930, 80 minutes),

making this a good choice if you don't want to drive.

Furano Natulux Hotel   HOTEL ¥¥¥
(富良野ナチュラクスホテル; ☑ 0167-22-1777; www.natulux.com/en/index.html; 1-35 Asahi-chō; s/d from ¥15,850/21,000; 🅿❀❀) Located directly across from JR Furano Station, this hotel has a fresh, modern feel. Rooms here are on the smallish side but they're stylishly done, and the nicer ones have views of Tokachi-dake. There's a spa with a bath and sauna, too.

It's a bit inconvenient to get to the ski slopes though, if that's what you're here for, without your own car.

✖ Eating & Drinking

There are restaurants clustered around JR Furano Station and also in the Kitanomine district near the ski slopes. Furano actually produces some pretty decent wines and cheeses, which you'll see on menus around town, along with more humble local specialities such as potatoes and onions.

Furano doesn't have anything close to the après-ski scene that Niseko has, though there are some bars in the Kitanomine district.

Chīzu Rāmen-no-mise Karin   RAMEN ¥
(チーズラーメンの店かりん; ☑ 0167-22-1692; 9-12 Moto-machi, Furano; dishes from ¥1000; ⊙11am-8pm; 🖪) Testing the adage that everything is better with cheese, Karin adds local Furano cheese to its ramen. Whether that sounds amazing or awful, you know you have to try it! It's in a nondescript brown-and-white building (look for the red curtain) a few minutes' walk southwest of JR Furano Station. The elderly owners will be ecstatic to greet you.

Kunen-kōbō Yamadori   JAPANESE CURRY ¥
(くんえん工房 Yamadori; ☑ 0167-39-1810; 4-14 Asahi-machi, Furano; meals from ¥1080; ⊙11am-3pm Fri-Wed; 🅿❀🖪) One of Furano's signature dishes is *omu-karē* (オムかれー) – rice topped with an omelette surrounded by a moat of Japanese-style curry. Yamadori ups the ante with bacon. It's a cutesy-cool pink farmhouse with white trim a couple of minutes' walk from JR Furano Station.

🔒 Shopping

Furano Marche   FOOD & DRINKS
(フラノマルシェ; ☑ 0167-22-1001; www.furano.ne.jp/marche; 13-1 Saiwai-chō, Furano; ⊙10am-7pm) This one-stop shop for made-in-Furano food and drink is stocked with local wines, cheeses,

cured meats, yoghurts and puddings. There's also a produce market and food court here.

🛈 Information

Furano International Tourism Centre (富良野国際観光センター; Map p606; ☎0167-22-5777; 1st fl, Kitanomine Terminal, 18-Kitanomine-chō; ☺9am-6pm) Tourist information counter inside the **Kitanomine Gondola** (p605) terminal.

Tourist Information Office (富良野観光案内所; ☎0167-23-3388; www.furanotourism.com; ☺9am-6pm) Stock up on English maps and pamphlets here, next to JR Furano Station. Staff can also help with bookings.

🛈 Getting There & Away

BUS

Ten buses daily run between Sapporo and Furano (¥2260, 2½ hours), stopping at Kitanomine Iriguchi, for the Kitanomine district, before the terminus at JR Furano Station.

Furano Bus (www.furanobus.jp) makes eight runs daily between Furano and Asahikawa (¥880, 1½ hours), stopping at Biei and **Asahikawa Airport** (p604). It takes one hour from Asahikawa Airport (¥770).

There are three buses daily between Furano and Obihiro (¥2160, 2½ hours).

CAR & MOTORCYCLE

Rte 237 runs between Asahikawa, Biei and Furano. It is 59km to Asahikawa by road, 125km from **New Chitose Airport** (p575) and 142km to Sapporo. Be extremely careful in the winter months as roads in this area can be icy and treacherous.

TRAIN

JR Furano line trains run roughly hourly from Asahikawa to Furano (¥1070, 1¼ hours), via Kami-Furano and Naka-Furano.

For Sapporo (¥4140, 2½ hours), take a *futsū* (local train) on the JR Nemuro line to Takikawa, then change to the hourly JR Limited Express Super Kamui Liner.

🛈 Getting Around

Buses running from Asahikawa to JR Furano Station continue to the Furano Prince Hotel and the New Furano Prince Hotel, which are, respectively, at the bases for the **Kitanomine Gondola** (p605) and the Furano Ropeway. Buses do not run in the morning, so if you're staying in town and want to ski, you'll need to have your own car or arrange transport with your accommodation.

Bicycle rentals can be found around JR Furano and JR Naka-Furano stations for ¥200 per hour.

Daisetsuzan National Park 大雪山国立公園

Daisetsuzan National Park is Japan's largest national park, designated in 1934 and covering more than 2300 sq km. It's a vast wilderness area of soaring mountains – Daisetsuzan literally means 'Big Snow Mountain' – active volcanoes, remote onsen, clear lakes and dense forests. Virtually untouched by human hands, the park has minimal tourism, with most visitors basing themselves in the hot-spring villages on the periphery. The three main access points into the park are Asahidake Onsen in the northwest, Sōunkyō Onsen in the northeast and Tokachidake Onsen in the southwest. Another special spot on the eastern side of the park is Daisetsu Kōgen Onsen.

🏃 Activities

Some ski and snowboard operators in Furano run backcountry tours to Asahi-dake (p610) and Kuro-dake (p611). If you come

---

THE BLAKISTON LINE

It was an Englishman, Thomas Blakiston, who first noticed that the native animals of Hokkaidō are different species from those on the southern side of the Tsugaru straits on Honshū. Blakiston lived in Japan from 1861 to 1884, spending most of his time in Hokkaidō in Hakodate, and his name is now used to describe the border in the distribution of animal species between Hokkaidō and the rest of Japan – 'the Blakiston Line'.

While Hokkaidō had land bridges to north Asia via Sakhalin and the Kuril Islands, southern Japan's land bridges primarily connected it to the Korean peninsula. Bears found on Honshū are Asiatic black bears while Hokkaidō's bears are Ussuri brown bears, found in northern Asia. On the southern side of the straits, Japanese macaque monkeys are found on Honshū as far north as Aomori, but not in Hokkaidō. Among other species north of the Blakiston Line are Siberian chipmunks, Hokkaidō red squirrels, the *ezo-jika* (Hokkaidō deer), *kita-kitsune* (northern fox), northern pika and Blakiston's Fish Owl.

on your own, it's advisable to hire a local guide; your accommodation should be able to help with that (just remember to ask well in advance).

ℹ️ Getting Around

While public transport can get you to the various access points around the park, it's not good at getting you from one point to another. If you want to visit multiple places, you will have to do some serious back-tracking; it's better to have a car. If you're driving though, be aware that snow can fall on base roads as early as October.

Asahidake Onsen   旭岳温泉

☎ 0166

Asahidake Onsen sits at 1100m, at the base of Asahi-dake, Hokkaidō's tallest peak. It's the easiest access point into the park, with regular buses from Asahikawa. There are plenty of hiking options in summer plus downhill and cross-country skiing in winter. All of this can be followed by a soak in the healing onsen found in the town's inns; most are open for day use to the general public for a fee (¥500 up to ¥1500).

Be prepared: there are no ATMs, shops or restaurants at Asahidake Onsen. The nearest amenities are a 30-minute drive away in Higashikawa.

ℹ️ HIKING IN DAISETSUZAN NATIONAL PARK

Winter comes early to Daisetsuzan. While elevation may seem 'low' (at 2000m) compared to mountains in Honshū that top 3000m, conditions are similar. Snow is still common on trails through early July (and snowy gorges are visible year-round). High season is late July to early August, when the alpine flowers bloom. Coloured leaves appear in mid-September and the first snow falls later that month. By October, even the trailheads are snowed under and you'll need winter mountaineering experience and gear.

Staff at the visitor centres in both Asahidake Onsen and Sōunkyō Onsen can give you the latest information on trail and weather conditions, necessary gear, bear sightings etc. This is bear country, so you'll need to take precautions; a bear bell is advised.

🏃 Activities

★ Asahi-dake   HIKING

(旭岳; Map p606) Asahi-dake, Hokkaidō's tallest peak (2290m) and one of Japan's 100 Famous Mountains, offers amazing views and can be done in a day (June to September). Take the **ropeway** (旭岳 ロープウェイ; Map p606; ☎ 0166-68-9111; http://asahidake.hokkaido.jp/en/; one way/return 1 Jun–20 Oct ¥1800/2900, 21 Oct–31 May ¥1200/1800; ⏰ 6am-5.30pm Jul–mid-Oct, 9am-4pm mid-Oct–Jun) to Sugatami, from where it's a 2½-hour steep hike to the top (allow four to five hours total for the return). Alternatively, you could do an easier, hour-long circuit around Sugatami-daira (姿見平), also from Sugatami.

From the summit of Asahi-dake it is possible to carry on over to Kuro-dake and take the ropeway down to Sōunkyō Onsen. Start early, check conditions at the visitors centre and allow seven to nine hours for this mission.

Asahi-dake Skiing   SKIING

(Map p606; http://asahidake.hokkaido.jp/en; day pass ¥4200; ⏰ 1 Dec–6 May) This is an extreme skiing experience on a smoking volcano – not for beginners. The only lift is the Asahi-dake Ropeway (p610), but it is possible to hike up higher. There is plenty in the way of dry powder and scenic views, but it is recommended you ski with an experienced mountain guide, as visibility can be bad.

For up-to-date information, check out www.snowjapan.com.

🛏️ Sleeping

★ Lodge Nutapukaushipe   LODGE ¥¥

(ロッジ・ヌタプカウシペ; Map p606; ☎ 0166-97-2150; r per person incl 2 meals from ¥8000; 🅿️😊🛜) 🍴 This log-cabin-style place is an absolute joy, run by a real character who has handcrafted most of the furniture and fittings from local timber. The onsen is superb, as are the meals. You'll have to make a bit of an effort though as there isn't a website. Pick up the phone and speak slowly. You won't be disappointed.

Daisetsuzan Shirakaba-sō   INN ¥¥

(大雪山白樺荘; Map p606; ☎ 0166-97-2246; http://shirakabasou.com/; incl 2 meals, dm from ¥7890, r per person ¥8940; 🅿️🛜) A cross between a youth hostel and a ryokan, this mountain lodge near the lower terminal of the ropeway (p610) offers comfortable Japanese- and Western-style rooms and hot-spring baths. There is a large kitchen available if you're self-catering,

DAISETSUZAN GRAND TRAVERSE

The Ainu called the area now known as Daisetsuzan National Park *kamui mintara*, meaning 'the playground of the gods'. Those gods being the animals, most notably the brown bear – the god of the mountains – that had the run of the land. For experienced hikers, the park offers an amazing opportunity to really get out into the wilderness.

The 55km Daisetsuzan Grand Traverse covers the length of the park in anywhere from five to seven days. You could start at either Asahidake Onsen or Sōunkyō Onsen and you'll finish at Tokachidake Onsen. There are some extremely bare-bones huts along the way, but it's better to have a tent and camping gear. You'll need to carry in your own food and cooking supplies.

The best time of year to attempt this is from mid-July through August. Any earlier and there will likely still be snow and ice; any later and you might have trouble finding water. Check in with the staff at the visitor centre at either the Asahidake Onsen or Sōunkyō Onsen, and carry a copy of Shōbunsha's *Yama-to-Kōgen Chizu Map 3: Daisetsuzan* (昭文社山と高原地図３大雪山).

It's also possible, with a very early start, to do a one-day traverse, from **Asahi-dake** (p610), in Asahidake Onsen, to **Kuro-dake** (p611), in Sōunkyō Onsen, going up one ropeway and down the other.

SAPPORO & HOKKAIDŌ DAISETSUZAN NATIONAL PARK

but it's worth going for the meal plan. Lots of options, so check out the website. Nonguests can use the onsen for ¥500.

ℹ Information

Asahidake Visitors Centre (旭岳ビジターセンター; Map p606; ☏ 0166-97-2153; www.town.higashikawa.hokkaido.jp/vc; ◷ 9am-5pm Jun-Oct, 9am-4pm Nov-May) There are excellent maps here that the staff will mark with daily track conditions. If you're heading out on a long hike, inform them of your intentions.

ℹ Getting There & Away

There are four buses daily between bus stop 9 in front of JR Asahikawa Station and Asahidake Onsen (¥1430, 1½ hours). The first bus leaves Asahikawa at 7.40am, returning from Asahidake Onsen at 6pm. Buses run via the Asahikawa Airport (¥1000, either direction).

Sōunkyō Onsen　　層雲峡温泉

☏ 01658

Sōunkyō Onsen (670m), at the foot of Kuro-dake on the northeast side of the park, is a good base for forays into Daisetsuzan's interior. In addition to alpine treks, there is also the natural spectacle of the surrounding gorges.

There are more amenities here (including ATM facilities, restaurants and a few convenience stores) than in the other gateway villages. Still, if you are heading out into the backcountry, you'd be better off organising supplies before coming. There's no petrol station.

◉ Sights & Activities

Sōunkyō　　　　　　　　GORGE
(層雲峡; Layer Cloud Gorge; Map p606) Sōunkyō is a string of gorges 15km long formed by the Ishikari River, the very same Ishikari River that empties out into the Sea of Japan just north of Sapporo. A few kilometres southeast of town on Rte 39, there's a popular viewing station where you can see the waterfalls **Ryūsei-no-taki** (流星の滝; Shooting Stars Falls) and **Ginga-no-taki** (銀河の滝; Milky Way Falls). Well worth a detour if you're driving.

Kuro-dake　　　　　　　　HIKING
(黒岳; Map p606) Take the **Sōunkyō Kuro-dake Ropeway** (大雪山層雲峡・黒岳ロープウェイ; Map p606; www.rinyu.co.jp/kurodake; one way/return ¥900/1700; ◷ 8am-7pm Jun-Aug, 7am-5pm Sep-May, closed intermittently winter) and chairlift to the mountain's 7th station (1520m), from where it's a 90-minute trek to the summit at 1984m. This hike, doable between June and early October (check at the visitor centre about early snow), is a favourite with alpine plant and flower enthusiasts.

Kuro-dake Skiing　　　　　SKIING
(Map p606; www.rinyu.co.jp/kurodake; pass ¥3800) Kuro-dake gets heaps of fantastic snow and is becoming a word-of-mouth destination for hard-core enthusiasts who like vertical and challenging terrain. The season is December to early May, though the ropeway and chairlift close for maintenance for parts of January and February – time your

visit well. This is not a place for beginners; avalanche gear is required for backcountry skiing.

A guide is recommended. For up-to-date info, check out www.snowjapan.com.

Kurodake-no-yu   ONSEN

(黒岳の湯; Map p606; ☑01658-5-3333; www.sounkyo.com/kurodakenoyu.html; ¥600; ☺10am-9pm) After a hard day of play, Kurodake-no-yu offers handsome hot-spring baths, including a 3rd-floor *rotemburo* – it's on the town's main pedestrian street. You can also soothe your aching feet in the free foot bath next to the Ginsenkaku Hotel.

🛏 Sleeping

Sōunkyō Youth Hostel   HOSTEL ¥

(層雲峡ユースホステル; Map p606; ☑01658-5-3418; www.youthhostel.or.jp/sounkyo/en/index.html; dm per person incl/excl 2 meals ¥5550/3800; ☺Jun-Oct; P☺@☎) Expect a warm welcome at this humble wooden hostel, a 10-minute walk up-hill from the bus station. There are bunk-bed dorms and a few private family rooms (book well ahead for the latter). This is a great place to meet other hikers before tackling the trails in the park. Summer season only.

Note that kitchen facilities are minimal, so it's best to sign up for the basic, but filling, meal plan.

Pension Yama-no-ue   PENSION ¥¥

(ペンション山の上; Map p606; ☑01658-5-3206; www.p-yamanoue.com; tw incl/excl 2 meals ¥18,900/11,600; P☎) This friendly, family-run place is in the middle of the village, straight down from the ropeway terminal. There are nature photos everywhere and the meals are prepared with great care. Rooms are tatami-style with shared facilities; the bath gets the same hot-spring water as Kurodake-no-yu next door.

ℹ Information

Sōunkyō Visitor Centre (層雲峡ビジターセンター; Map p606; ☑01658-9-4400; http://sounkyovc.net; ☺8am-5.30pm Jun-Oct, 9am-5pm Nov-May) Near the bottom of the Sōunkyō ropeway, this is an excellent visitor centre with displays, photos and maps (some in English). Run your hiking plans by the helpful staff.

ℹ Getting There & Away

There are seven daily buses in both directions between Sōunkyō Onsen and Asahikawa (¥2160, two hours) via Kamikawa.

JR Rail Pass holders can take the JR Sekihoku line from Asahikawa to Kamikawa, and then catch the bus from Kamikawa to Sōunkyō Onsen (¥870, 35 minutes).

There are two buses daily to Kushiro (¥4930, five hours) via Akanko Onsen (¥3350, four hours) in Akan National Park and one bus daily to Obihiro (¥2260, 2¼ hours).

If you're driving, Rte 39 connects Sōunkyō Onsen to Asahikawa in the west and Abashiri in the east.

Daisetsu Kōgen Onsen   大雪高原温泉

☑01658

On the eastern side of the park about 20km south of Sōunkyō Onsen, Daisetsu Kōgen Onsen is about as remote as it gets! Ten kilometres up an unsealed road in the middle of nowhere you'll find a couple of buildings in the heart of the national park. Make the effort – this is a highly recommended mountain adventure.

There are no shops, ATMs or petrol stations here.

🏃 Activities

Kōgen-numa Meguri Hike   HIKING

(高原沼めぐり登山コース; Map p606; ☺22 Jun–10 Oct) This four-hour hiking course around the Kōgen-numa (small lakes) is your best chance to see a brown bear in the wild. It's strictly regulated. Hikers must listen to a lecture at the Brown Bear Information Centre and are only allowed to head out on the hike between 7am and 1pm. Hikers must be off the track by 3pm.

Staff are out on the track each day, radioing in bear whereabouts and keeping an eye on both the hikers and the bears. This is a wonderful day hike beneath the high peaks. Soak in the onsen at Daisetsu Kōgen Sansō after your walk.

🛏 Sleeping & Eating

★ Daisetsu Kōgen Sansō   LODGE ¥¥

(大雪高原山荘; Map p606; ☑01658-5-3818; www.daisetsu-kogen.com; per person incl meals from ¥12,570; ☺10 Jun–10 Oct; P☺☎) Make the most of your foray into the mountains: this inn, only open 123 days each year, is like staying at a mountain hut without having to walk five hours to get there. Rooms are simple with shared facilities, but the food is good, the onsen is hot and the air is fresh.

The lodge also operates a *shokudō* (casual eatery) between 11.30am and 1pm, with simple meals such as ramen and curry rice.

There are two shuttle buses per day from Sōunkyō Onsen for overnight guests (reservations necessary), but having your own wheels is the best option. If you're not staying, you can use the onsen for ¥700. Note that prices increase to ¥17,430 for the second half of September, when the autumn leaves are the major attraction.

ⓘ Information

Brown Bear Information Centre (ヒグマ情報センター; Map p606; ⏰ 22 Jun–10 Oct) A must-visit before heading out on the **Kōgen-numa Meguri Hike**, with info on bears and recent sightings, latest trail conditions and closures, advice and hiking maps in English.

ⓘ Getting There & Away

Daisetsu Kōgen Onsen is at the end of a 10km unsealed road off Rte 273 to the east of the park. The turn-off is signposted about 15km southeast from Sōunkyō Onsen.

Alternatively, make a booking for the night at Daisetsu Kōgen Sansō and use its twice-daily shuttle service for guests from Sōunkyō Onsen.

Tokachidake Onsen

☏ 0167

At 1270m, remote Tokachidake Onsen is the highest of the gateway villages for Daisetsu-zan. It is also the least developed, with no ropeway and just two inns, and is thus the least crowded – though it's relatively easy to access from Furano. In addition to being the end point for the epic Grand Traverse hike, Tokachidake Onsen is also a great spot for starting day hikes into the park. There are no shops, ATMs or petrol stations – not even a visitor centre – so you need to come prepared.

🏃 Activities

★ **Fukiage Roten-no-yu** ONSEN
(吹上露天の湯; Map p606) FREE If the idea of sitting naked in pools of hot steaming water surrounded by pristine forest appeals to you, then head to Fukiage Roten-no-yu. The turn-off, 2km before Tokachidake Onsen on Rte 291, is signposted. There's a parking lot, from where it's a 200m walk through the woods to the springs.

There's nothing there except two hot pools; the one higher up is hotter than the other. It's not for the shy: strip off and hop in! There's no

614

> **DON'T MISS**

BEST ONSEN

- ➡ Hōheikyō (p597)
- ➡ Onsen Tengoku (p599)
- ➡ Goshiki Onsen (p589)
- ➡ Mizunashi Kaihin Onsen (p639)
- ➡ Fukiage Roten-no-yu (p613)

charge...and this place is *konyoku*, meaning men and women bathe together. You can take a small 'modesty towel' if you prefer.

Tokachi-dake HIKING
(十勝岳; Map p606) A return trip up Tokachi-dake (2077m), an active volcano and one of Japan's Hyakumeizan (100 Famous Mountains), will take six to eight hours return and reveal some marvellous volcanic landscapes – if you're lucky enough to get clear weather.

About 40 minutes in, the trail splits, with one branch heading up to the Tokachi-dake summit and another veering south to Furano-dake (富良野岳; 1912m); the return trip up the latter will take four to six hours.

🛏 Sleeping

Kamihoro-sō LODGE ¥¥
(カミホロ荘; Map p606; ☏ 0167-45-2970; http://tokachidake.com/kamihoro; d incl 2 meals from ¥19,500; 🅿🖨🐕) A good place to unwind after hiking, with pleasant Japanese-style rooms, filling meals and hot-spring baths fronting the mountains. Nonguests can use the baths for ¥600.

When it's not crowded it may be able to accommodate solo travellers – call ahead.

ⓘ Getting There & Away

Buses (¥500, 45 minutes) run three times daily to Tokachidake Onsen from JR Kami-Furano Station, 15 minutes north of Furano on the JR Furano line.

Wakkanai 稚内

☏ 0162 / POP 35,700

Wakkanai, Japan's northernmost city at 45°N, changes wildly with the seasons. From November to March, it's something akin to a remote Siberian outpost, home to hearty fishers, kelp farmers and a harp-seal colony. Outside the winter months, it's a pleasantly mild port city that serves as a departure point for ferries to the islands of Rishiri-tō and Rebun-tō.

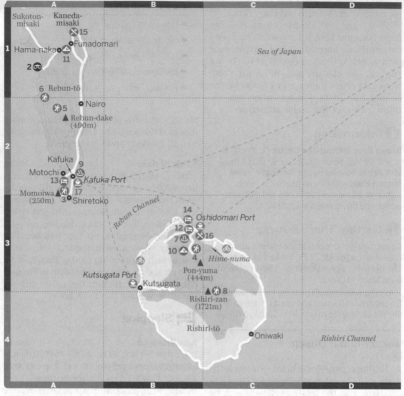

◉ Sights

Sarobetsu Wetlands   NATURE RESERVE
(サロベツ原野; Sarobetsu Genya; Map p614)
Part of Rishiri-Rebun-Sarobetsu National
Park, these marshlands are 40km southwest of Wakkanai. Fields of wild flowers
bloom here in summer, which can be appreciated from boardwalks built over the
marsh. Infrequent trains on the JR Sōya
line run between Wakkanai and Toyotomi
(*futsū* ¥930, 50 minutes; *tokkyū* ¥1550, 40
minutes). Buses (¥400, 10 minutes) run
from JR Toyotomi Station to the **Sarobetsu
Wetlands Centre** (サロベツ原野セン
ター; ☎0162-82-3232; http://sarobetsu.or.jp;
8662 Sarobetsu, Toyotomi-chō; ☺9am-5pm May-
Oct, 10am-4pm Nov-Apr, closed Mon Nov-Apr) at
8.30am, 1.25pm and 2.50pm (June to September) and at 9.15am and 1.50pm (October to May).

There are also good views of Rishiri-zan
(p619) from here – especially in winter, when
eagles fly overhead and you can rent snow-
shoes from the visitors centre (¥500) to walk
out over the snow pack.

Fukukō-ichiba   MARKET
(副港市場; ☎0162-29-0829; www.wakkanai-
fukukou.com; 1-6-28 Minato; ☺varies by shop; ℗)
About a 10-minute walk south of JR Wakkanai Station, this complex has restaurants,
souvenir shops and the **Minato-no-yu
Onsen** (港の湯温泉; ☎0162-22-1100; 2nd fl,
Fukukō-ichiba, 1-6-8 Minato; adult/child ¥750/420;
☺10am-10pm; ℗). It's designed to evoke the
Wakkanai of bygone days. Poke around to
see some historical photos and videos of the
town – and also of Sakhalin (when it was
Karafu-tō, and still part of Japan, prior to
1945).

Northern Breakwater Dome   NOTABLE BUILDING
(北防波堤ドーム) Fans of kitsch will want
to walk a few minutes north of the ferry terminal to see Wakkanai's breakwater, built in

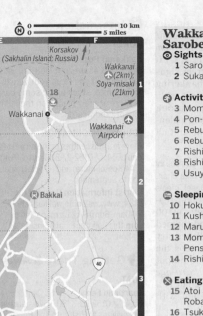

SAPPORO & HOKKAIDŌ WAKKANAI

1936 to look like a straightened version of the Colosseum in Rome.

Sōya-misaki   LANDMARK
(宗谷岬) Thirty kilometres east of Wakkanai, Sōya-misaki is mainland Japan's northernmost point, where walkers and cyclists traversing the full length of Japan either start or finish. Buses depart seven times daily from bus stop 1 at JR Wakkanai Station (one way/round trip ¥1390/2500, 50 minutes).

🛏 Sleeping & Eating

Wakkanai Moshiripa Youth Hostel   HOSTEL ¥
(稚内モシリパユースホステル; ☎0162-24-0180; www.moshiripa.net; 2-9-5 Chūō; dm ¥4500; ☻🛜) Conveniently located a few blocks north of JR Wakkanai Station, this dark-blue, three-storey building offers functional, unfussy dormitories. JYHA card holders can stay for ¥3400; breakfast is ¥750. Check-in is 3pm to 8pm; curfew is 10.30pm.

Tenpoku no Yu Dormy Inn   HOTEL ¥¥
(天北の湯 ドーミーイン稚内; ☎0162-24-5489; www.hotespa.net/hotels/wakkanai/; 2-7-13 Chūō; s/d from ¥7390/11,290; ☻✳@🛜) With an in-house onsen, free laundry machines (dryers extra) and a convenient location, only four minutes' walk from JR Wakkanai Station, this is an easy choice. Rooms are standard issue but clean and not cramped.

ANA Crowne Plaza Wakkanai   HOTEL ¥¥¥
(ANAクラウンプラザホテル稚内; ☎0162-23-8111; www.ana-hotel-wakkanai.co.jp; 1-2-2 Kaiun; s/d incl breakfast from ¥11,900/19,500; ☻✳@🛜) Right on the waterfront and an easy walk to both the ferry and the train station, Wakkanai's only remotely upscale (though a bit weather-worn) option is a good bet – especially if you book an air-ticket package. Ask for an ocean-front room (plus ¥1000) when you book. Bonus: the airport bus stops here.

Pechika RUSSIAN ¥

(ペチカ; ☎0162-23-7070; www.w-kenki.com/pechka; Fukukō-ichiba, 1-6-8 Minato; dishes from ¥400, set meals from ¥1500; ⏰5-11pm; [P] [📖]) If seeing all that Russian on the street signs around Wakkanai has got you hankering for some *pelmeni* (dumplings) or *pirozhki* (stuffed buns), Pechika will help you out. It's not terribly authentic, but there's plenty of Russian beer and vodka to wash it all down.

Take-chan SEAFOOD ¥¥

(竹ちゃん; ☎0162-22-7130; http://take-chan.co.jp; 2-8-7 Chūō; dishes from ¥700, set meals ¥1400-5000; ⏰5-11pm; [📖]) This popular seafood joint does good-value sushi sets (¥1400 to ¥2900) as well as some seafood-themed variations on classic Japanese dishes: try the *tako-shabu* (¥2500), which swaps the pork or beef typically used in the hotpot dish for octopus, or the *tako kara-age* (¥700; deep-fried octopus). Take-chan is a short walk from JR Wakkanai Station, with an illuminated, white vertical sign.

WAKKANAI–RUSSIA FERRY

The **Hokkaidō Sakhalin Line** (北海道サハリン航路; Map p614; ☎0162-22-2550; sahkouro@giga.ocn.ne.jp; one way/round trip ¥18,000/36,000) connects Wakkanai to Korsakov (on the Russian island of Sakhalin). Ferries sail twice weekly from August to mid-September; the trip takes 4½ hours. Many of those who make the journey are Japanese who have family ties to Sakhalin, though there are tourists, too.

You must book through a travel agent, which should also handle the necessary visa preparations. Both **Hokuto Kankō** (北都観光; ☎0162-23-3820; www.hoktokanko.co.jp; 4-5-29 Chūō, Wakkanai; ⏰9am-6pm Mon-Fri, 8am-5pm Sat), in Wakkanai, and **Nomad** (ノマド; Map p578; ☎011-200-8840; www.hokkaido-nomad.co.jp; S2W6 Chūō-ku; ⏰9am-6pm Mon-Fri; [S] Tōzai, Tōhō & Namboku lines to Ōdōri, exit 2), in Sapporo, are set up to do this. Note that this ferry service has been suspended in the past and is currently operating on a trial basis only. If you are not returning to Japan, you may be asked to show an onward ticket at customs in Russia.

ℹ Information

MONEY

Wakkanai Post Office (稚内郵便局; 2-15-2 Chūō; ⏰8.45am-7pm Mon-Fri, 9am-5pm Sat & Sun) If you're on your way to Rishiri-tō or Rebun-tō, stock up on some cash here, as there are few places on the islands that accept credit cards.

TOURIST INFORMATION

There are info centres at the **airport** (稚内空港; Map p614; ☎0162-27-2111; http://wkj-airport.jp; 6744 Koetoi-mura) and ferry terminal, open from May to September.

Tourist Information Counter (☎0162-22-2384; www.welcome.wakkanai.hokkaido.jp/en; ⏰10am-6pm) Pick up maps and bus schedules from this counter located inside JR Wakkanai Station.

ℹ Getting There & Away

BOAT

Heartland Ferry (ハートランドフェリー; Map p614; ☎0162-23-3780; www.heartlandferry.jp) Has sailings to Rishiri-tō and Rebun-tō.

BUS

Buses operate six times daily (including one night bus) between Wakkanai and Sapporo (one way/round trip ¥6200/11,300, six hours), with some going directly to/from the ferry terminal.

CAR & MOTORCYCLE

It's a long, half-day ride to Wakkanai no matter how you do it: straight up Rte 40 from Asahikawa, or along the scenic coastal routes from either Abashiri (the Okhotsk line) or Otaru (the Ororon line).

If you're heading out to Rishiri-tō or Rebun-tō, parking is available at the ferry terminal for ¥1000 per day.

TRAIN

Three daily JR Limited Express Super Sōya/Sarobetsu Liner trains connect Wakkanai to Asahikawa (¥7780, 3¾ hours) and Sapporo (¥9930, five hours).

ℹ Getting Around

Downtown Wakkanai is easy to get around on foot. JR Wakkanai Station is right next to the bus terminal and both downtown and the station are just a 10-minute walk from the ferry port. Ask at the **tourist information counter** about bicycles for rent, which you can use to cycle out to some of the more distant coastal sights.

Rishiri-Rebun-Sarobetsu National Park
利尻礼文サロベツ国立公園

The islands of Rishiri-tō and Rebun-tō are among the remotest in Japan, off the coast of the country's northernmost city, Wakkanai. Part of the Rishiri-Rebun-Sarobetsu National Park, they are largely undeveloped, save for a few scrappy fishing settlements and a small tourism industry. Geographically, they are totally different: Rishiri-tō is dominated by its volcano, Rishiri-zan (p619); Rebun-tō is long and skinny, shaped by shifting plates. Most visitors come in summer, to climb Rishiri-zan, or to hike along the ridges in Rebun-tō, where wild flowers bloom in June and July. Southwest of Wakkanai, the Sarobetsu Wetlands (p614), part of the park, also see impressive blooms.

🛏 Sleeping & Eating

On both Rishiri-tō and Rebun-tō there are campgrounds, hostels, pensions and hotels. The port of Oshidomari on Rishiri-tō is the largest settlement and has the most lodgings and amenities. Note that many accommodation options are seasonal, open roughly from May through October.

Uni (sea urchin) is the islands' speciality. There are two kinds to sample: *kita-murasaki uni* (June to September) and *bafun uni* (July and August). The fresh seafood is delicious but don't expect bargain prices; the going rate for *uni-don* (urchin roe on rice) is ¥3500. There are some restaurants and a Seico Mart in both Oshidomari and Kafuka. Most visitors eat at their accommodation or bring food with them.

Rebun-tō   礼文島

🎵 0163 / POP 2700

Rebun-tō, Japan's northernmost island, gets almost all of its visitors during a two-month span – in June and July when the wild flowers hit peak bloom. However, there is usually something in bloom from May through September (and September can be lovely, too, when the bamboo grass turns golden). Given the island's remoteness, there are some rare and unusual flowers, such as the Rebun Lady's Slipper Orchid. Rebun-tō is primarily a summer destination, as winter is cold and very windy.

⊙ Sights & Activities

Hiking is the main draw on Rebun-tō and there are several trails to suit different levels. You can also rent a scooter or car to visit the capes on the northern end of the island, which offer gorgeous sea views (when the weather cooperates). Year-round you can usually spot harp seals lazing on the rocks in **Funadomari Bay** (船泊湾) and at **Kaneda-misaki** (金田岬).

Sukai-misaki   VIEWPOINT
(澄海岬; Map p614) This is the prettiest of the island's capes, where the waters are an almost tropical blue, framed by craggy rocks and grassy slopes. The Rebun-tō Traverse passes here; it's also accessible by road.

★ Rebun-tō Traverse   HIKING
(8時間コース; Eight-Hour Course; Map p614) This challenging but rewarding hike along the island's west coast starts at **Sukoton-misaki** (スコトン岬), the northernmost point on the island, passes beautiful Sukai-misaki and finishes down by the port in Kafuka. Despite the name, it's best to budget 10 hours. You can also do an abridged version in four hours, returning northward from Sukai-misaki to the bus stop at Hama-naka (浜中).

To do the full hike, you'll need to catch the first bus of the day from the ferry terminal at 6.30am for Sukoton, which means you'll need to sleep in Rebun two nights. Be sure to wear long pants and long sleeves as some of the local flora can cause skin irritation.

Rebun-dake   HIKING
(礼文岳; Map p614) Rebun-dake (礼文岳; 490m) is the highest point on the island. The not-too-challenging 4.5km hike to the top reaps big rewards, with 360-degree views over the island. The trail begins at the Nairo (内路) bus stop, a 20-minute bus ride (¥690) from the ferry terminal. The return hike takes three to four hours.

Momoiwa Course   HIKING
(桃岩コース; Map p614) The easiest and most popular of the island's hikes, and particularly beautiful when the wild flowers bloom, wends from the southernmost point in Shiretoko (知床) across a backbone of highlands to Momoiwa (桃岩; Peach Rock) and across to Kafuka. It takes roughly three hours.

Usuyuki-no-yu Onsen   ONSEN
(うすゆきの湯; Map p614; 🎵0163-86-2345; 961-1 Besshu, Kafuka-mura; ¥600; ⊙noon-10pm) The perfect place to rest after a hike, this

onsen is right on the waterfront, just a couple of minutes' walk from the ferry terminal. From the *rotemburo* (outdoor bath) you can see Rishiri-zan).

🛏 Sleeping & Eating

★ Momoiwa-sō Youth Hostel HOSTEL ¥

(桃岩荘ユースホステル; Map p614; ☑ 0163-86-1421; www.youthhostel.or.jp/n_momoiwaso.htm; dm ¥3600, breakfast/dinner ¥600/1000; ☺ Jun-Sep; 🅿☺) Part *Lost Boys'* hideaway, part loopy summer camp, Momoiwa-sō is a very special place, which you will either love or hate. It has very strict rules, but also a lot of singing and dancing (for example, the 6am wake-up call includes bike horns and retro pop music blasting from loudspeakers). The location, on the remote (though inconvenient) western coast, is stunning.

The wooden building is a 150-year-old former fishery, and the accommodation, in bunks or on tatami mats, is basic. So are the meals, which you'll need unless you've packed food.

Momoiwa-sō organises group hikes along the Rebun-tō Traverse (p617) with shuttle service (¥700) at 5.40am to Sukoton. It also does free shuttle runs to and from the ferry terminal (otherwise it's an hour's walk). The atmosphere is very social; it's near impossible to leave without making friends.

Kushu-kohan Campground CAMPGROUND ¥

(久種湖畔キャンプ場; Map p614; ☑ 0163-87-3110; Funadomari-mura; campsites per person ¥600; ☺ May-Sep; 🅿) Beside Kushu-ko at the northern end of the island, this campground has grassy plots for tents and also some basic cabins that sleep four (¥2000, plus the standard per-person fee). The nearest bus stop is Byōin-mae, a 45-minute (¥960) ride from the ferry terminal.

Pension Uni PENSION ¥¥

(ペンションうーにー; Map p614; ☑ 0163-86-1541; www.p-uni.burari.biz; Tonnai, Kafuka-mura; per person incl/excl 2 meals ¥11,880/8860; 🅿☺@☺) Up the hill from the port, this bright-blue, immaculately clean pension has Western-style twin rooms. Meals include local seafood; rates with board drop when *uni* (sea urchin) season finishes in September. The owners offer free shuttle service to/from anywhere within a 5km radius (including the ferry terminal).

★ Robata Chidori SEAFOOD ¥

(炉ばたちどり; Map p614; ☑ 0163-86-2130; 1115-3 Tonnai; dishes ¥700-1500; ☺ 11am-10pm,

closed irregularly Sep-May) Chidori does real *robata-yaki*, charcoal grilling in a pit built into the table. The speciality of the house is *hokke chanchan-yaki* (ホッケチャンチャン焼; ¥900) – island-caught Okhotsk atka mackerel grilled with miso. The *ika-teppō-yaki* (いか鉄砲焼; stuffed and grilled squid; ¥800) is good, too. The restaurant is along the waterfront in Kafuka, about five minutes' walk from the ferry terminal.

Atoi Shokudō SEAFOOD ¥¥

(あとい食堂; Map p614; ☑ 0163-87-2284; Funadormari-mura; meals ¥1200-3500; ☺ 10am-4pm Apr-Sep; 🅿) Run by the island's fishing collective, Atoi serves generously portioned *kaisen-don* (raw seafood over rice) using locally caught *uni* (sea urchin) and *ebi* (shrimp). There's a picture menu.

❶ Information

Tourist Information Counter (Map p614; ☑ 0163-86-1001; www.rebun-island.jp; ☺ 8am-5pm mid-Apr–Oct) Pick up trail maps and bus schedules in English. The staff, who usually speak some English, can assist with bookings, too. Open until the last ferry departs.

❶ Getting There & Away

Heartland Ferry (p616) operates two to four ferries daily (year-round) between Wakkanai and Kafuka Port (Map p614) (from ¥2260, two hours). Less frequent ferries run in both directions from Kafuka to Oshidomari and Kutsugata ports (from ¥800, 45 minutes) on Rishiri-tō. Tickets are available for purchase at any port.

❶ Getting Around

Five buses daily run along the island's east coast from Kafuka in the south to Sukoton-misaki in the north (¥1220, one hour). There are also five buses daily (three on weekends) to the southern tip at Shiretoko (¥290, 10 minutes). Note that there is a huge gap in the middle of the afternoon; pick up a bus schedule (available in English) at the tourist information counter and plan accordingly – especially if you have a ferry to catch later.

Rental cars (from ¥7000 for three hours), scooters (¥1000 per hour) and electric hybrid bicycles (¥3000 per day) can be picked up just outside the ferry terminal. Note that rates are higher than elsewhere in Hokkaidō.

Rishiri-tō 利尻島

☑ 0163 / POP 5400

Seen from the distance, Rishiri-tō seems to be all mountain, a perfect volcanic cone, topped with snow most of the year, rising from the sea. This is **Rishiri-zan** (1721m), one of Japan's 100 Famous Mountains, and the island's main draw – it's on every Japanese hiker's bucket list. That said, its sheer remoteness means that Rishiri-tō never gets truly crowded. The weather on the island, however, is highly unpredictable: if you're keen on hiking, it's a good idea to stay for three or so nights, in the hope that on at least one of those days the weather will cooperate.

🏃 Activities

Cycling is a great way to see the island: circumnavigating the 60km perimeter on bicycle takes approximately seven to eight hours. There's also a 25km cycling path that runs through woods and coastal plains from Oshidomari to past Kutsugata. Many accommodation places also rent bicycles.

★ Rishiri-zan   HIKING

(利尻山; Map p614) Rishiri-zan is also known as Rishiri-Fuji, as its solitary and perfect cone resembles famous Fuji-san. The hike to the top can be incredibly rewarding, with amazing views of Rebun-tō and even Sakhalin, but requires serious fitness. As the trailhead is at 220m, you've got to scale 1500 vertical metres. On average, the return trip takes 10 to 11 hours.

Unlike Fuji-san, Rishiri-zan is actually a beautiful mountain to climb, with fir, spruce and birch trees on the lower reaches and meadows of alpine flowers higher up. June through September is the best time to attempt an ascent, though even in the best of times the

weather can be highly changeable, especially as the mountain is unshielded from winds. There are actually two peaks, Kita-mine (北峰) and Minami-mine (南峰), though the latter is closed for safety reasons.

There are no facilities on the mountain except for an unstaffed emergency shelter between the eighth and ninth stations. It is recommended to bring a minimum of 2L of water and you'll need to purchase a 'mobile restroom' kit (¥400) to use in designated booths on the mountain.

The main trailhead is 5km from the ferry port at Oshidomari (鴛泊) behind the Hokuroku Campground (p620). There is also a trailhead about 6km from Kutsugata, Rishiri-tō's other port. You can climb one and descend the other. The Kutsugata course is trickier, with a greater possibility of loose and falling rock, and should only be attempted by experienced mountaineers.

Buses, and even taxis, don't start up early enough to get you to the trailhead. As hiking is the most common reason to visit, most lodgings offer free shuttle service to the trailhead at around 5am.

The tourist information office (p620) at the Oshidomari ferry terminal has a pretty good English climbing guide, but the Shobunsha *Yama-to-kōgen Chizu 1 Rishiri; Rausu* (山と高原地図 1 利尻；羅臼) map (in Japanese) is far more detailed.

Pon-yama   HIKING

(ポン山; Map p614) For fantastic views of Rishiri-zan (and a far less challenging climb) you can scale neighbouring Pon-yama

---

SKIING & SURFING ON RISHIRI

Yes, you read that right. There is skiing *and* surfing to be had on Rishiri (for the adventurous and experienced). **Rishiri Nature Guide Service** (利尻自然ガイドサービス; 📞0163-82-2295; www.maruzen.com/tic/guide), run by adventure guide (and Rishiri local) Watanabe Toshiya, offers backcountry tours on Rishiri-zan from late December through May. This is true backcountry stuff (think no lifts) with plenty of hiking up, followed by steep descents down the volcano – which sees few skiers or boarders – all the while taking in the breathtaking ocean views.

The tours (maximum six people; from ¥10,800 per person) are popular and book out fast, especially for peak powder season in January and February (April, Toshiya says, is best for sunny days). You'll need your own gear.

As for surfing, Toshiya swears the waters up this far aren't as cold as you'd think. September and October are the best, after the summer sun has warmed the sea and typhoons from the south drift north to deposit large swells. That said, the appeal of getting to ski or board and surf on the same trip is so strong that some do brave the waters off-season (you'll need a drysuit). Toshiya, who speaks some English, is happy to dispense tips on surf points. You can usually find him in the evenings at his pension, Maruzen Pension Rera Mosir (p620).

(444m) in about two hours, round trip. Start at the Rishiri-zan trailhead; the path to Pon-yama splits off 10 minutes into the hike, to the left.

Rishiri-Fuji Onsen
ONSEN

(利尻富士温泉; Map p614; ☑0163-82-2388; ¥500; ◎11am-9pm Jun-Aug, noon-9pm Sep-May) Could there be a better place to go to recover from climbing Rishiri-zan (p619)? We don't think so. This onsen is conveniently located on the road from Oshidomari to the trailhead. Pick it out on your way to the climb in the morning so you know where to go on the way back. There are a few local buses (¥150, seven minutes) to the onsen from Oshidomari Ferry Terminal.

Sleeping & Eating

Hokuroku Campground
CAMPGROUND ¥

(北麓野営場; Map p614; ☑0163-82-2394; camp-sites per person ¥500, cabins ¥5000; ◎15 May–15 Oct; ℗) Located at the Rishiri-zan (p619) trail-head, this camping ground is a good spot to stay if you want to get an early start to the hike. Cabins, which have blankets and pil-lows, sleep four. It's a 60-minute walk from the ferry terminal, or you can take the local bus as far as Rishiri-Fuji Onsen and walk the remaining 30 minutes.

Rishiri Green Hill Inn
HOSTEL ¥

(利尻ぐりーんひる亭; Map p614; ☑0163-82-2507; http://rishiri-greenhill.net; 35-3 Fujino, Oshidomari; dm from ¥3800; ◎mid-Mar–mid-Oct; ℗ ⊜ @ ☎) An excellent budget option, this hostel has simple Japanese- and Western-style dorm rooms. There's free bread in the morn-ing and a kitchen for cooking, but you'll have to walk 10 minutes to town to pick up sup-plies (or take advantage of the hostel's bicycle rentals). The friendly owners will pick you up from the port and take you to the trailhead for Rishiri-zan (p619).

★ Maruzen Pension Rera Mosir
PENSION ¥¥

(マルゼンペンションレラモシリ; Map p614; ☑0163-82-2295; www.maruzen.com/tic/oyado; 227-5 Sakae-chō, Oshidomari; per person incl/excl 2 meals ¥11,000/7460; ℗ ⊜ ✳ @ ☎) Run by local adventure guide Watanabe Toshiya, Rera Mosir is the best place on the island for active types – whether you're here to climb Rishiri-zan (p619) in summer or ski the backcountry in winter. (It's also one of the few places open year-round.) Though small, it's modern and run like a hotel, and even has an onsen bath.

It does free shuttle runs to/from the port and the trailhead for Rishiri-zan; if you want to explore on your own, its rental cars are the cheapest on the island. The seafood dinners are good, too. Prices drop by ¥2000 to ¥2500 in the winter.

Tsuki Café
CAFE ¥

(月カフェ; Map p614; ☑0163-82-2305; http://tsukirishiri.wix.com/tsuki; 2nd fl, Oshidomari Ferry Terminal; ◎11am-3pm Thu-Tue) A surprising-ly cool little cafe for a ferry terminal, Tsuki serves up coffee, cakes and curries to waiting passengers. The large picture windows look over the port.

It sometimes opens earlier and closes later during busy periods.

ℹ Information

Oshidomari Tourist Information Office (Map p614; ☑0163-82-2201; www.town.rishiri.hok-kaido.jp/kanko; ◎8am-5.30pm 15 Apr–31 Oct) On the ground floor of the new ferry terminal. Pick up English-language climbing guides, maps and bus schedules. English-speaking staff can also help with bookings.

ℹ Getting There & Away

Rishiri-tō Airport, just a few kilometres west of Oshidomari, has flights to/from Sapporo on **ANA** (www.ana.co.jp) and **Hokkaidō Air System** (HAC; www.hac-air.co.jp).

Local buses (¥460, 20 minutes) can get you to the airport to meet departures (check at the tour-ist information office for exact times). A taxi into town costs around ¥1200.

Heartland Ferry (p616) operates two to four ferries daily (year-round) between Wakkanai and **Oshidomari** (Map p614) (from ¥2030, 1¾ hours). Less frequent ferries (¥800, 45 minutes) run in both directions from Oshidomari and **Kutsugata** (Map p614) ports on Rishiri-tō to Kafuka port on Rebun-tō. Tickets are available for purchase at any port.

ℹ Getting Around

Local buses run clockwise (seven times daily) and counter-clockwise (five times daily) around the island. The trip from Oshidomari to Kutsugata (¥750) takes 30 to 45 minutes, depending on whether the bus stops at the airport. You can circumnavigate the island in about two hours (¥2260). The **tourist information office** has a schedule in English.

There are car rental shops in front of the ferry terminal; however, rates are higher than else-where in Hokkaidō, starting at ¥5000 to ¥7000 for three hours. Motorcycles cost ¥3000 to ¥5000 per day.

THE SEA OF OKHOTSK

The Sea of Okhotsk falls between Sakhalin (formerly known as Karafu-tō and part of Japan from 1905 to 1945), a long stretch of eastern Siberia, the Kamchatka Peninsula, the Kuril Islands and Hokkaidō. There are also many, many small, uninhabited islands here that are important breeding grounds for seals and seabirds. The sea, which gets its name from the first Russian settlement in the Far East, is the coldest in East Asia and freezes as far south as Hokkaidō. In February, the coldest month, visitors come to Abashiri and Rausu to ride ice-breakers through the drift ice, hoping to spot seal pups on the ice.

This is just about as remote as it gets in Hokkaidō: the Okhotsk Line, the road that connects Wakkanai to Abashiri, is one long, lonely stretch of mostly nothingness. No towns, no traffic lights, few cars and only wind-battered coastline. For Tokyo drivers this is a dream come true and will shatter any thoughts you had that Japan is a densely populated, crowded country.

EASTERN HOKKAIDŌ 道東

Eastern Hokkaidō (Dō-tō) is a harsh yet hauntingly beautiful landscape that has been shaped by volcanoes and vast temperature extremes. In the winter months, dramatic ice floes in the Sea of Okhotsk can be seen from the decks of ice-breakers off the coast of Abashiri. Both Akan National Park and Shiretoko National Park, the latter a World Heritage Site, are best explored during the mild summers when there are great hiking opportunities. Kushiro Wetlands National Park offers the chance to see the red-crested white crane, the symbol of longevity in Japan.

Abashiri 網走

📞 0152 / POP 37,000

To the Japanese, Abashiri is as synonymous with the word 'prison' as Alcatraz is to Americans – the mere mention can send a chill. Winters here are harsh, too: Abashiri is also known for its frozen seas, which can be explored on ice-breakers. Throughout the warmer months, the town serves as a jumping-off point for both Akan National Park and Shiretoko National Park.

🏃 Activities

★ Aurora CRUISE

(おーろら; 📞 0152-43-6000; http://ms-aurora.com/abashiri/en; adult/child ¥3300/1650; ⊙9am-6pm) From 20 January to 31 March, the ice-breaker *Aurora* departs four to six times a day from Abashiri port for one-hour cruises into the frozen Sea of Okhotsk. Dress warmly.

Buses depart from stop 1 in front of JR Abashiri Station for the Aurora boarding dock.

🎏 Festivals & Events

Okhotsk Drift Ice Festival CULTURAL

(オホーツク流氷まつり; ⊙mid-Feb) An opportunity to celebrate the cold! Ice sculptures and statues, illuminated at night, plus lots of warm sake to keep your blood flowing.

🛏 Sleeping

Business hotels line the road in front of JR Abashiri Station, though most are pretty shabby. There are nicer options near scenic Notoro-ko, if you're not relying on public transport.

Minshuku Lamp MINSHUKU ¥

(民宿ランプ; 📞 0152-43-3928; 3-3-9 Shin-machi; per person ¥2800; 🅿🐾) Minshuku Lamp is a little tatty but the tatami rooms and shared facilities are clean, the owners very friendly and the hallways decorated with photos of old steam locomotives. There's a coin laundry and rental bicycles here, too. Book ahead or ask the tourist information office to call for you.

It's a 10-minute walk from JR Abashiri Station, but can be tricky to find, as you'll have to walk over the train tracks. Ask the information office for directions.

Toyoko Inn Okhotsk Abashiri Eki-mae HOTEL ¥¥

(東横インオホーツク網走駅前; 📞 0152-45-1043; www.toyoko-inn.com/e_hotel/00003/index.html; 1-3-3 Shin-machi; s/d from ¥5180/8450; 🅿🐾❄@🐾) Directly opposite JR Abashiri Station, this is the nicest of Abashiri's business hotels. Simple, but clean and convenient, with free breakfast.

✕ Eating & Drinking

There's a handful of restaurants on the main drag running in front of JR Abashiri Station.

Abashiri Bīru-kan   PUB
(網走ビール館; ☎ 0152-41-0008; www.takahasi. co.jp/beer/yakiniku/index.html; S2W4-1-2; dishes ¥500-1800, beers from ¥400; ⏰ 5-11pm) Traditionalists should put aside all preconceptions when visiting this brewery-restaurant. Abashiri Beer's signature brew is the Ryūhyō (drift ice) Draft, made with melted sea ice and coloured (with algae) acid blue. The *yakiniku* (grilled meat) served here is pretty good.

❶ Information

Tourist Information Office (☎ 0152-44-5849; http://abashiri.jp/tabinavi/en/index.html; ⏰ noon-5pm Mon-Fri, 9am-5pm Sat & Sun) English-language maps and bus schedules. There's usually someone who can speak English and help with booking accommodation and tours. Inside JR Abashiri Station.

❶ Getting There & Around

AIR

Memanbetsu Airport (女満別空港; ☎ 0152-74-3115; http://mmb-airport.co.jp.e.ug. hp.transer.com; 201-3 Memanbetsu, Abashiri), located 15km south of the city centre, is the nearest airport, with flights to/ from Sapporo, Tokyo, Nagoya and Osaka. Airport buses (¥910, 35 minutes) depart from bus stop 3 in front of JR Abashiri Station and are timed to arrive 40 minutes before plane departures.

BUS

Abashiri Bus (網走バス; ☎ 0152-43-4101; www. abashiribus.com) runs nine buses daily (including one night bus) between **Abashiri Bus Terminal** (網走バスターミナル; ☎ 0152-43-2606; S2W1-15; ⏰ 6.40am-6pm) and Sapporo (¥6390, six hours). Reservations required.

From Abashiri, buses run to Shari (¥2100, 1½ hours) and Utoro Onsen (¥3300, two hours).

CAR & MOTORCYCLE

There are several car rental shops around JR Abashiri Station, including **JR Hokkaido Rent-a-car** (JR北海道レンタカー; ☎ 0152-43-6197; www. jrh-rentacar.jp; 2-2 Shin-machi; ⏰ 8am-6pm). There are also counters at Memanbetsu Airport.

TRAIN

JR Limited Express Okhotsk Liner trains run four times daily between Abashiri and Asahikawa (¥7450, four hours), continuing on to Sapporo (¥9390, 5½ hours).

The JR Senmō main line runs between Abashiri and Kushiro (¥3670, 3½ hours, five to seven daily). On the way it passes through Shiretoko-Shari (¥840, 50 minutes), the closest station to Shiretoko National Park, and through Kawayu Onsen (¥1640, two hours) in Akan National Park.

Shari   斜里

☎ 0152 / POP 11,900

The small town of Shari sits on the coast about 40km east of Abashiri and acts as a gateway to Shiretoko National Park. JR Shiretoko-Shari is the closest train station to the World Heritage Site, but you're still about an hour by bus or car from the entrance to the national park.

NORTHERN TERRITORIES DISPUTE

A volcanic archipelago, the Kuril Islands stretch for 1300km from Kamchatka, Russia, towards Hokkaidō, separating the Sea of Okhotsk from the Pacific Ocean. The closest, the Habomai islets, uninhabited apart from a Russian border guard outpost, are barely 10km from Hokkaidō's easternmost point in Nemuro. The Habomai islets, along with three other islands in the southernmost Kurils, are known as the Northern Territories in Japan, and are the subject of a territorial dispute with Russia.

There have been tit-for-tat squabbles over who owned what between Japan and Russia since the early 1800s. Prior to WWII the islands belonged to Japan. At the close of the war, on 15 August 1945, Japan agreed to the terms of surrender in the Potsdam Declaration; however, Russia was not party to that agreement and had only just declared war on Japan on 9 August. Russian military forces started their invasion of the Kuril Islands on 18 August, and have occupied them since.

The ongoing dispute has blighted the Japan–Russia relationship ever since, to the point that the two countries have yet to sign a post-WWII peace treaty. Although sparsely populated, the Kurils have valuable mineral deposits, possibly oil and gas reserves, and are surrounded by rich fishing grounds.

◉ Sights & Activities

Koshimizu Gensei-kaen
PARK

(小清水原生花園; ☑0152-63-4187; ⊙8.30am-5.30pm May-Sep, 9am-5pm Oct) **FREE** This is a spectacular 20km stretch of wildflowers along the coast between Abashiri and Shari. Visit in early summer and catch it at its peak, when more than 40 species of flowers bloom.

Gensei-kaen has its own tiny JR station with an information centre plus short walks through the flora and dunes out to the sea. There are free rental bikes for getting around to other viewing points along the road.

Shari-dake
HIKING

(斜里岳) Shari-dake (1547m), south of town, is a spectacular volcanic cone and one of Japan's 100 Famous Mountains. Allow seven to eight hours for the return hike, which involves plenty of stream crossings plus spots with ropes and chains to help you. The views from the top are superb. Go between June and October, take supplies and use a bear bell.

Either use your own wheels to get to the trailhead (parking ¥500) at the Kiyodake-so (清岳荘) hut at 680m, or hop off the train at JR Kiyosato (清里町) station and take a taxi to the trailhead (¥4000, 30 minutes). If you get stuck, you can stay at the Kiyodake-sō for ¥1000 between June and September but there are no meals.

☎ Sleeping

There's little reason to stay here unless it proves a convenient place to stop over en route to Shiretoko National Park. There is just a handful of options.

Minshuku Yumoto-kan
MINSHUKU ¥

(民宿湯元館; ☑0152-23-3486; www.yumotokan. info; 13-11 Nishi-machi; s/d from ¥4480/7960; Ｐ🛜) This popular spot has a mountain lodge vibe, Japanese-style rooms to accommodate different sized groups and an onsen bath (which nonguests can use for ¥400 between 7am and 8pm). Breakfast (¥390) is excellent. Yumoto-kan is a 20-minute walk from JR Shiretoko-Shari Station.

Hotel Grantia
HOTEL ¥¥

(ホテルグランティア斜里; ☑0152-22-1700; www.hotel-grantia.co.jp/shiretoko; 16-10 Minato-machi; s/tw from ¥8400/17,100; Ｐ❄＊@🛜) This is a convenient place to stay if you're relying on public transport – it's right in front of the train and bus stations in Shari. It's a modern tower hotel with comfortable rooms and an onsen; breakfast is ¥850.

✕ Eating & Drinking

There are some eating options clustered around the train station.

Ekibasha
RAMEN ¥

(えきばしゃ; ☑0152-67-2152; Yamubetsu Station; ramen ¥750-1600; ⊙11am-7.30pm; Ｐ) This cute restaurant – the name means 'stage coach' – inside the old wooden Yamubetsu train station serves up tasty ramen and is naturally a hit with trainspotters.

Yamubetsu is a stop on the JR Senmō line, between Abashiri and Shiretoko Shari, two stops east of Gensei-kaen.

Teishaba
CAFE

(停車場; ☑0152-46-2410; Kita-Hama Station; drinks from ¥480; ⊙11am-5pm Wed-Mon) Inside the 90-year-old Kita-Hama Station, Teishaba is decked out to look like a vintage rail car, with wood and burgundy-velour booths and rotating fans overhead. With views of both the Sea of Okhotsk and the trains coming and going, this is an attractive place for a coffee break.

Kita-Hama is a stop on the JR Senmō line, between Abashiri and Shiretoko Shari, one stop west of Gensei-kaen.

ℹ Information

Tourist Information Centre (☑0152-23-2424; ⊙8.30am-5.30pm Apr-Oct & Feb) Maps, bus timetables and brochures; inside JR Shiretoko-Shari Station.

ℹ Getting There & Away

Infrequent trains run on the JR Senmō main line between Shiretoko-Shari and Abashiri (¥840, 50 minutes), and between Shiretoko-Shari and Kushiro (¥2810, 2½ hours). Between Shari and Kushiro is Kawayu Onsen (¥930, 45 minutes) in Akan National Park.

There are between five and nine buses daily between Shari and Utoro Onsen (¥1650, 50 minutes) in Shiretoko National Park. The bus terminal is right across from the train station.

Shiretoko National Park 知床国立公園

Shiretoko-hantō, the peninsula that makes up Shiretoko National Park, was known in Ainu as 'the end of the world'. This is a magnificent stretch of land, a Unesco

Shiretoko National Park

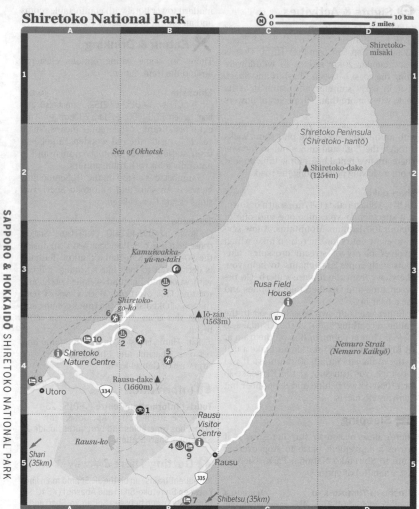

Shiretoko National Park

◎ Sights
1 Shiretoko Pass B4

✪ Activities, Courses & Tours
  Aurora Cruises .... (see 8)
  Godzilla-Iwa Sightseeing .... (see 8)
2 Iwaobetsu Onsen B4
3 Kamuiwakka-yu-no-taki B3
4 Kuma-no-yu B5
  Rausu-dake .... (see 2)
5 Shiretoko Traverse B4
6 Shiretoko-go-ko Nature Trail A4

🛏 Sleeping
7 Marumi B5
8 Oyado Kiraku A4
9 Rausu Dai-Ichi Hotel B5
  Rausu Onsen Campground .... (see 4)
10 Shiretoko Iwaobetsu Youth
    Hostel A4

ℹ Transport
  Utoro Michi-no-eki .... (see 8)
  Utoro Onsen Bus Terminal .... (see 8)

World Heritage Site, and one of Japan's last remaining sections of true wilderness. It's mostly a draw for keen hikers; however, there are also some easier treks around lakes and to waterfalls, nature cruises up the coast and hidden hot springs in the woods. The park has two access points, at Utoro (ウトロ) on the northwestern side of the peninsula, and at Rausu (羅臼) on its southeastern side.

◉ Sights & Activities

Shiretoko Pass   VIEWPOINT
(知床峠; Map p624) Rte 334, where it traverses the Shiretoko Pass, is considered one of Japan's most scenic stretches of road. It winds through the foothills of Rausu-dake and past groves of Erman's birch and Japanese stone pines. There's a lookout point at 740m with parking.

★ Shiretoko Traverse   HIKING
(Map p624) The classic traverse is a two-day hike that stretches for 25km from Iwaobetsu Onsen to Kamuiwakka-yu-no-taki. You'll need to be properly equipped to tackle this route. Starting from the trailhead at Iwaobetsu Onsen, you'll climb Rausu-dake, traverse along the top to Iō-zan (p632), then descend to Kamuiwakka-yu-no-taki, a 'waterfall onsen'.

There are four camping areas along the top that have steel food bins (think bears!). Don't underestimate the difficulty of the terrain. The last bit of this track has recently been reopened. Drop in at the Shiretoko Nature Centre (p627) for the latest on conditions and advise staff there of your intentions. The trail is officially open from mid-June through the September holiday period.

Shiretoko-go-ko Nature Trail   WALKING
(知床五湖; Map p624; www.goko.go.jp/english; ⊙7.30am-6pm late Apr–late Nov) This small area of five lakes (go-ko) is the most accessible part of Shiretoko, and thus the most popular. Around **Ichi-ko** (Lake One), there's an 800m-long (40-minute return) elevated boardwalk protected by an electric fence (to keep bears off, which do appear around here sometimes) on which anyone can stroll.

There's a ground path (adult/child ¥250/100, 1½ hours, 3km) around the other four lakes; however, the number of people that can enter is limited. You'll need to submit an application at the Shiretoko-go-ko Park Service Centre (p627) and, while you're waiting your turn, watch a safety video on bears.

Rausu-dake   HIKING
(羅臼岳; Map p624) One of Japan's 100 Famous Mountains, Rausu-dake (1660m) makes a great day hike, best tackled from the trailhead at Iwaobetsu Onsen. Allow seven to nine hours for the return trip. From the top there are stunning views of one of the Northern Territories/South Kuril Islands (Disputed Territories).

The trailhead is 4km from the closest bus stop at Iwaobetsu, so without your own wheels you'll have to walk (a taxi from Utoro Onsen costs about ¥4000). The trail officially opens 1 July (though there may still be snow then) and closes when snow begins to fall mid-November.

Kuma-no-yu   ONSEN
(熊の湯; Map p624; ⊙7am-5am) **FREE** A few kilometres up and inland from Rausu, this pair of steaming pools on the far side of the river is superb. Park by the road and cross the bridge. Some locals come every day, and the facilities are maintained by a dedicated team of volunteers. The onsen is segregated by sex and has changing facilities.

Kamuiwakka-yu-no-taki   ONSEN
(カムイワッカ湯の滝; Map p624) **FREE** On the west side of the peninsula, literally at the end of the road, this waterfall is warmed by hot springs to 30°C. You can scale the rock bed 100m to a soaking pool (but not any further, as the rest is roped off). Unless by some luck you've got this all to yourself, wear a swimsuit.

🛏 Sleeping

Both Utoro and Rausu have pensions, *minshuku* and hotels. If you're relying on public transport, Utoro makes for a better base, as it's more of a condensed tourist centre; Rausu is a fishing town that sprawls down the coast. There are a few undeveloped campgrounds along the mountain trails, but you will need to be entirely self-sufficient.

Rausu Onsen Campground   CAMPGROUND ¥
(羅臼温泉野営場; Map p624; ☑0153-87-2126; Yunosawa-chō; per person ¥300; ⊙Jun-Oct) This basic campground sits at the base of Rausu-dake, at the trailhead for the very challenging Yunosawa trail up the mountain. It's a short walk from here to the hot waters of Kuma-no-yu and Rausu Onsen.

Shiretoko Iwaobetsu Youth Hostel HOSTEL ¥
(知床岩尾別ユースホステル; Map p624; ☑0152-24-2311; www.youthhostel.or.jp/English/e_iwaobetsu.htm; dm ¥4800; ⊙Jul-Sep; ℗ ⊜) 🖉

At the Iwaobetsu bus stop, 5km north of Utoro, this is a popular base for hikers, open only in summer. It's scruffy and basic, but it's also pretty deep in the park, where you might spot some of the local wildlife. Note that there are only three buses daily here and no amenities nearby. Delicious dinners are ¥2500 per person.

Rausu Dai-Ichi Hotel HOTEL ¥¥
(羅臼第一ホテル; Map p624; ☑0153-87-2259; http://rausu-daiichi-hotel.jp; Yunosawa-chō; s/d ¥5800/10,200, incl 2 meals from ¥9330/17,580; P🐾🌐) This is a cosy place in Rausu Onsen, just a few kilometres inland on the road to Utoro. The Japanese-style rooms with private facilities are spacious, there's a large shared onsen bath with a *rotemburo* and the friendly staff speak a little English.

It's best if you have your own wheels, though the Rausu-Utoro bus stops across the street, at Rausu Onsen.

Oyado Kiraku MINSHUKU ¥¥
(お宿来羅玖; Map p624; ☑0152-24-2550; 133 Utoro-nishi, Shari-chō; s/d ¥4800/9000, incl 2 meals ¥7800/15,500; P🐾🌐) A short walk from the Utoro Michi-no-eki (p627) road stop (and one bus stop before the Utoro Onsen terminal), Kiraku is a good deal with tatami rooms, shared facilities and tasty meals. The staff at the information counter at the Utoro Michi-no-eki will call for you, but it pays to book ahead in summer.

Marumi RYOKAN ¥¥
(羅臼の宿まるみ; Map p624; ☑0153-88-1313; http://www.shiretoko-rausu.com; 24 Yagihama-chō; s/d ¥7560/10,800, incl 2 meals from ¥9060/17,500; P🐾🌐) Marumi prides itself on its gut-busting seafood banquets, making this a good choice if you've worked up a calorie deficit in the mountains. The Japanese-style rooms themselves are simple with shared facilities (you can upgrade for an ocean view and an en-suite bath), but there's an outdoor onsen facing the waters.

The modern, concrete ryokan is 8km southwest of Rausu on Rte 335. Marumi also does cruises to see whales and dolphins and, in winter, to see the drift ice; enquire about packages when you book.

🍴 Eating

There is a handful of small eateries in Utoro and Rausu, mostly serving local seafood (when in doubt, order *kaisen-don*, raw seafood on rice). Most have colourful banners out front so they're easy to spot. *Michi-no-eki* (road stations) are an easy bet, and also good for picking up packaged food. The Rausu Michi-no-eki has a handy cheat sheet of restaurants in town.

ℹ️ Information

Shiretoko National Park has several excellent information centres with knowledgeable staff. Whatever your plans are – from multiday treks to onsen soaks – stop into one of the centres to get the latest information on trail and road conditions, weather warnings and bear sightings. The information will be posted in English or in easy-to-understand images.

Rausu Visitor Centre (羅臼ビジターセンター; Map p624; ☑0153-87-2828; http://rausu-vc. jp; 6-27 Yunosawa-chō; ⊙9am-5pm May-Oct, 10am-4pm Nov-Apr, closed Mon) On the Rausu side of the peninsula, on Rte 334.

Rusa Field House (ルサフィールドハウス; Map p624; ☑0153-89-2722; http://shiretoko-whc. jp/rfh; 8 Kita-hama; ⊙9am-5pm May-Oct, 10am-4pm Feb-Apr, closed Tue) This centre

---

ℹ️ WARNING: BEAR ACTIVITY

Hokkaidō is bear country. The bears up here are different from the small black bears that inhabit Honshū; these are *higuma* (Ussuri brown bear), thought to be the ancestor of the North American grizzly bear, and they're much bigger and more aggressive.

Take all precautions, especially in the early morning and at dusk, and avoid hoofing it alone. Make a lot of noise; like Japanese hikers, tie a *kuma-yoke* (bear bell) to your rucksack. The theory goes that bears want to meet you face to face about as much as you want to meet them face to face and if they hear you coming, they'll avoid you at all costs.

If you're camping, use the steel food bins or tie up your food and do not bury your rubbish. Bear activity picks up noticeably during early autumn when the creatures are actively foraging for food ahead of their winter hibernation. Be especially cautious at this time.

The Shiretoko peninsula is home to the highest concentration of *higuma* on Hokkaidō, but they are also often sighted in Daisetsuzan National Park; really, they could be anywhere there are mountains. Only the remote islands of Rishiri-tō and Rebun-tō are bear-free.

offers support for the truly intrepid and experienced, who plan to trek or kayak out to Shiretoko-misaki. If you have such aspirations, absolutely check in here first. Located on Rte 87, 13km northeast of Rausu, up the coast.

Shiretoko Nature Centre (知床自然センター; Map p624; ☑0152-24-2114; http://center. shiretoko.or.jp/en/; ⊗8am-5.30pm mid-Apr–mid-Oct, 9am-4pm mid-Oct–mid-Apr) Run by the Shiretoko Nature Foundation, this is the largest visitor centre; located 5km past Utoro.

Shiretoko-go-ko Park Service Centre (知床五湖パークサービスセンター; ☑0152-24-3323; ⊗7.30am-6.30pm May-Jul, to 6pm Aug, to 5pm Sep, to 4pm Oct, to 3pm mid-Nov)

ⓘ Getting There & Away

While it's possible to get around by public transport, buses are infrequent, so having your own wheels is better. Pick up a rental in Abashiri or Kushiro, before heading to the park.

AIR

Memanbetsu Airport (p622) is the most convenient for Shiretoko. Between mid-June and mid-October, three 'Shari Airport Liner' buses depart daily from Memanbetsu Airport, via Abashiri Station, for Shari (¥2100, 1½ hours) and Utoro (¥3300, two hours).

BUS

There is a night bus from Sapporo's **Chūō bus terminal** (p588) departing at 11.15pm for **Utoro Onsen Bus Terminal** (ウトロ温泉バスターミナル; Map p624; 107 Utoro-nishi, Shari-chō) (one way/round trip ¥8230/15,430); reservation required. The return bus is at 9.20am. The bus also stops at the **Utoro Michi-no-eki** (ウトロ道の駅; Map p624), one stop before the terminal.

From May to October there are seven buses daily between Shari and Utoro Onsen (¥1650, 50 minutes), continuing to the Shiretoko Nature Centre (¥1800, 10 minutes), Iwaobetsu (¥1960, 15 minutes) and Shiretoko-go-ko (¥2000, 25 minutes); buses are timed to meet trains coming from Abashiri and Kushiro.

Daily buses also run between Rausu and Kushiro (¥4850, 3½ hours), departing from the bus stop behind the Rausu Michi-no-eki.

ⓘ Getting Around

A shuttle bus runs from Utoro Onsen via Shiretoko Nature Centre for Shiretoko-go-ko (¥960) and Kamuiwakka-yu-no-taki (¥1300) from 1 August to 25 August and again over the September holiday period (around the third week of the month).

From June through October, there are four buses daily between Utoro Onsen and Rausu Akan Bus Station (¥1390, 50 minutes) via the dramatic **Shiretoko Pass** (p625).

SHIRETOKO NATURE CRUISES

A number of companies operate cruises up the coasts of the peninsula, to see killer whales, white-tailed sea eagles and possibly even *higuma* (brown bears) prowling along the shoreline. The season for this is May through October. Both **Aurora Cruises** (おーろら; Map p624; ☑0152-24-2147; http://ms-aurora.com/shiretoko/en; 107 Utoro-higashi, Shari-chō) and **Godzilla-Iwa Sightseeing** (ゴジラ岩観光; Map p624; ☑0152-24-3060; http://kamuiwakka.jp; 50 Utoro-higashi, Shari-chō) offer comparable trips, of either 90 minutes (as far as Kamuiwakka-yu-no-taki) or 3½ hours (all the way as far as the end of the cape). Godzilla-Iwa Sightseeing also operates hour-long cruises among the drift ice from Rausu between late January and mid-April. If you're lucky you'll see spotted seals chilling on the ice.

When the summer shuttle bus is in operation, the road from Shiretoko-go-ko (p625) to Kamuiwakka-yu-no-taki (p625) is closed to private traffic. Daily road closures and conditions are posted at the Shiretoko Nature Centre. Come November, beware of early snow-stopping traffic.

Akan National Park 阿寒国立公園

Akan National Park, designated in 1934 and covering 905 sq km, was one of Japan's first national parks. It's home to volcanic peaks, several large caldera lakes, thick forests of Sakhalin spruce, herds of sika deer, rejuvenating onsen and a small Ainu *kotan* (village). While the mountains are obviously a draw for hikers, those less inclined (and travelling by car) can drive out to a number of excellent lookout points around the park.

🛏 Sleeping

There are campgrounds, hostels, *minshuku* and resort-style onsen hotels here. Note that many of the hotels have seen better days – book only if the price is right. Many budget places, such as campgrounds and hostels, are only open in the summer.

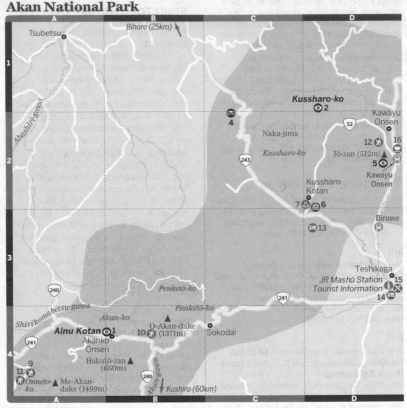

ⓘ Getting There & Around

Kushiro and Abashiri are the main gateways to the park. There are two stations on the JR Senmō line, which runs between Kushiro and Shiretoko-Shari, that are convenient for Kawayu Onsen: Kawayu Station and Mashū Station. For Akanko Onsen, catch a bus from Kushiro, Abashiri or Asahikawa.

From mid-July to mid-October, **Akan Bus** (阿寒バス; ☏ 0154-37-2221; www.akanbus.co.jp) runs a tourist shuttle between Abashiri Station and Kushiro Station, stopping at Bihoro Pass, Kawayu Onsen, Mashū Station and Akanko Onsen. A four-day pass costs ¥4000/2000 per adult/child.

Akan Bus does two daily runs between Mashū Station (for Kawayu Onsen) and Akanko Onsen (¥1500, one hour), stopping at Mashū-ko Viewpoint 1.

While it is possible to get around the park with public transport, you will have to be very mindful of timetables, as buses and trains are infrequent, even during the peak summer season. It is highly recommended that you pick up a rental car in either Kushiro or Abashiri.

Akanko Onsen   阿寒湖温泉

☏ 0154 / POP 6400

The resort town of Akanko Onsen, in the western part of Akan National Park, is on the southern shores of Akan-ko. In addition to lakefront vistas and hot springs, Akanko is known for two things: *marimo*, a rare kind of algae that forms oddly perfect spheres; and its Ainu *kotan* (village), Japan's largest (though it's not big). If you have your own transport, you can use Akanko Onsen as a base for exploring the surrounding mountains.

◉ Sights

A number of hotels open their hot-spring baths to nonguests for a fee (¥500 to ¥1500); the tourist information office has a list.

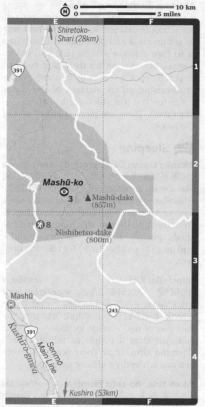

⭐ **Ainu Kotan**   VILLAGE

(アイヌコタン; Map p628) This collection of 36 households is actually the largest Ainu village in Hokkaidō. Residents make a living promoting their culture: dancing on the stage at Ikor, cooking *pochie* (fermented potato dumplings) in restaurants, and selling wood and leather crafts, made with traditional techniques and motifs.

In the evenings (May to November) there's a procession around 8.30pm to light torches around the village.

Ainu Folklore Museum   MUSEUM

(アイヌ文化伝承館, Ainu Bunka Denshō-kan; ☑ 0154-67-2727; www.akanainu.jp/; 4-7-19 Akanko Onsen; ☺ 9am-9pm; P) FREE At the top of the hill in the Ainu *kotan*, this small museum has changing exhibitions of contemporary Ainu artisan work, and sometimes thought-provoking shows (such as 2016's 'Rethinking Retro Ainu Tourist Art').

There are also some traditional dwellings here.

Akan Kohan Eco-Museum Centre   MUSEUM

(阿寒湖畔エコミュージアムセンター; ☑ 0154-67-4100; http://business4.plala.or.jp/akan-eco; 1-1-1 Akanko Onsen, Akan-chō; ☺ 9am-5pm Wed-Mon) FREE At the eastern edge of town, this centre has exhibitions on local flora and fauna, including *marimo* (p630) in aquarium tanks. It also has hiking maps in English and info on trail conditions and bear sightings.

Behind the centre, a trail makes a shaded, breezy loop out to Akan-ko and back through the forest to some volcanic bubbling clay pools (called *bokke*). The walk takes 40 minutes round-trip.

🏃 **Activities**

⭐ **Me-Akan-dake**   HIKING

(雌阿寒岳; Female Mountain; Map p628) The highest mountain in the park, Me-Akan-dake (1499m) is an active volcano that is one of Japan's 100 Famous Mountains. There are three trails up it, though at the time of research the trail nearest Akanko Onsen was closed

MOSSY MARIMO

Akan-ko is legendary throughout Japan for its *marimo* (まりも; *Cladophora aegagropila*), spheres of green algae that are both biologically intriguing – it takes as long as 200 years for them to grow to the size of a baseball – and very, very *kawaii* (cute). *Marimo* became endangered after being designated a national treasure: suddenly, everyone in Japan needed to have one. Members of the Ainu community came to the rescue by starting the **Marimo Matsuri** (まりも祭り), held in mid-October, which ceremonially returns *marimo* to Akan-ko.

There are *marimo* on display at the Akan Kohan Eco-Museum Centre (p629). You can also take a **lake cruise** (p630) out to the Marimo Observation Centre, where a monitor plays live footage of the velvety globes underwater.

because of typhoon damage. We recommend driving around to **Me-Akan Onsen** (720m), from where it's a two-hour hike to the top.

There are some steep bits, over loose volcanic gravel, but the views from the top are spectacular. From the summit, you have the option to descend via the Onneto Nature Trail and loop back to your vehicle at Me-Akan Onsen (total journey four to five hours). Make sure you pick up a map.

Onneto Nature Trail
WALKING

(オンネトーネイチャートレイル; Map p628) The picturesque lake of **Onneto-ko**, emerald green and in the mountains to the west of Me-Akan-dake, can be circumnavigated on foot. There are viewing platforms, toilets, parking, a restaurant and a number of other short nature trails. Allow an hour to circle the lake and less than that for the return trip to **Yu-no-taki** (湯の滝) waterfall.

There is a campsite at the southern end of the lake. There is no public transport to Onneto-ko.

O-Akan-dake
HIKING

(雄阿寒岳; Male Mountain; Map p628) O-Akan-dake is the big volcano (1371m) to the east of Akanko Onsen. The return hike to the top from the Takiguchi trail entrance at 450m takes five to six hours. From the peak there are great views of **Penketō-ko** and **Panketō-ko**, two small lakes formed when O-Akan's eruption separated them from Akan-ko.

Akan-ko Sightseeing Cruise
CRUISE

(☎0154-67-2511; www.akankisen.com; per person ¥2500; ⏱6am-6pm Jun-Sep) The best way to get up close and personal with *marimo* is to hire a motorboat to take you out to a small observation centre where you can hopefully spot a few balls of algae photosynthesising on the surface of the water (or catch the live video feed of them underwater). There are piers at either end of the town.

🛏 Sleeping

Akanko Onsen Campground
CAMPGROUND ¥

(阿寒湖温泉キャンプ場; ☎0154-67-3263; 5-1 Akan Onsen; campsites per adult/child ¥630/315; ⏱Jun-Sep; 🅿) About a five-minute walk west of Akanko Onsen centre, across Rte 241 from the Ainu theatre, this campground has shady pitches, showers, laundry facilities and an *ashi-yu* (foot bath) for relaxing tired feet.

Minshuku Kiri
MINSHUKU ¥

(民宿桐; ☎0154-67-2755; www10.plala.or.jp/kiriminshuku; 4-3-26 Akanko Onsen; r per person ¥3990; 🅿🛜) This *minshuku* has tiny, no-fuss rooms and a great location – above a souvenir shop a couple of minutes' walk from the Ainu kotan. There is a wooden onsen and a friendly welcome here, too.

Akan Yuku-no-sato Tsuruga
RYOKAN ¥¥¥

(あかん遊久の里鶴雅, Lake Akan Tsuruga Resort Spa; ☎0154-67-4000; www.tsuruga.com/en; 4-6-10 Akan Onsen; s/tw incl 2 meals from ¥17,000/30,000; 🅿❄@🛜) This old-style resort is the fanciest spot in town and sprawls over three buildings. The *honkan* (main hall) rooms are the cheapest but don't have lake views; the rooms in the lavish *bekkan* (annexe) have en-suite outdoor onsen baths. Everyone gets to use the two big bathhouses. Look for sculptures from Ainu artists in the lobby.

🍴 Eating & Drinking

★ Poronno
AINU ¥

(ポロンノ; ☎0154-67-2159; www.poronno.com; 4-7-8 Akanko Onsen; dishes ¥400-1500; ⏱noon-3pm & 6-10pm May-Oct; 🅿🍴) Poronno, inside the Ainu kotan (p629), has the most interesting menu of the restaurants in town specialising in Ainu cuisine. You can try *yukku ruibe* (frozen, preserved venison) and dried salmon or pizza with *pochie* (fermented potato dumpling) crust topped with cheese, mountain vegetables and venison salami.

Marukibune Akanko-ten
AINU ¥¥

(丸木舟阿寒湖店; ☎0154-67-230; 4-7-9 Akanko Onsen; meals ¥1100-2100; ⏱11am-8pm) A branch of Kussharo-ko's Ainu restaurant Marukibune (p632), inside Akanko Onsen's Ainu kotan.

Onsen Kōbō Akan
CAFE

(温泉工房あかん; ☎0154-67-2847; 1-4-29 Akanko Onsen; ⏱8am-8pm; 🥄) This is brilliant: a cafe with an *ashi-yu* (foot bath) so you can soak your feet while sipping coffee (¥250). There's food available, too; try the 'zari-bonara' (pasta carbonara with *zarigani* – freshwater crayfish; ¥950). Picture menu.

It's on the main drag running down the hill from the Akan Kohan Eco-Museum Centre towards the Ainu kotan.

☆ Entertainment

Ikor
LIVE PERFORMANCE

(イコロ; ☎0154-67-2727; www.akanainu.jp/; adult/child ¥1080/540) There are several shows daily of traditional singing and dancing at this theatre inside the Ainu kotan. At 9pm nightly, from May through November, performers stage a fire festival, which begins 30 minutes earlier with a procession and the lighting of torches throughout the village.

ⓘ Information

Tourist Information Office (☎0154-67-3200; www.lake-akan.com/en; 2-6-20 Akanko Onsen; ⏱9am-6pm; 🛜) In the middle of the village, with bus and event schedules, hiking maps and info on accommodation and onsen – all in English. Helps with bookings, too.

ⓘ Getting There & Away

Two buses daily run to/from Asahikawa (¥4710, five hours), via Sōunkyō Onsen (¥3350, four hours) in Daisetsuzan National Park. From April to November there are three to four buses daily to/from Kushiro (¥2700, two hours), via Kushiro Airport (¥2110, one hour).

From mid-July through mid-October, two buses daily run to/from Mashū Station (for Kawayu Onsen; one hour, ¥1500), with a stop at Mashū-ko Viewpoint 1.

If you're driving, Akanko Onsen is on Rte 240, which (of course!) has been renamed Marimo Hwy (まりも国道).

ⓘ Getting Around

Between June and October, a free shuttle bus runs around Akanko Onsen, from the bus terminal via the Ainu **kotan** (p629) and **Akan Kohan Eco-Museum Centre** (p629). A few continue to Takiguchi, the trailhead for **O-Akan-dake**. The **tourist office** has rental bikes (¥500 per day), but the town is compact and very walkable.

Kawayu Onsen 川湯温泉

☑ 0154 / POP 7660

Kawayu is a quiet onsen town with a dozen or so hot-spring hotels, but it's in the surrounding area that Akan National Park really comes to life. In the vicinity are two stunning caldera lakes, Kussharo-ko and Mashū-ko, hiking opportunities and plenty of hot springs – including some in-the-rough, free ones.

⊙ Sights

Kawayu Eco-Museum Centre
MUSEUM

(川湯エコミュージアムセンター; ☎0154-83-4100; www6.marimo.or.jp/k_emc; 2-2-6 Kawayu Onsen; ⏱8am-5pm May-Oct, 9am-4pm Nov-Apr, closed Wed) **FREE** Stop by this museum and visitor centre in Kawayu Onsen to see how the surrounding volcanic landscape got its shape and to pick up hiking maps. A number of short **nature trails** start here.

Museum of Ainu Folklore
MUSEUM

(コタンアイヌ民俗資料館; Map p628; ☎0154-84-2128; adult/child ¥420/280; ⏱9am-5pm May-Oct) In the Kussharo *kotan* (Ainu village) on the southern shores of Kussharo-ko, this museum displays traditional Ainu tools and crafts. Ask the staff to play the 25-minute English video, which talks about Ainu history and contemporary Ainu culture.

★ Kussharo-ko
LAKE

(屈斜路湖; Map p628) Japan's largest caldera lake is a rich blue on sunny days. A small volcano peeks out from the centre, creating the island **Naka-jima** – best viewed from the **Bihoro Pass** (美幌峠; Map p628).

The lake is also purportedly the home of a Loch Ness monster-like creature nicknamed Kusshi.

★ Mashū-ko
LAKE

(摩周湖; Map p628) Considered by many to be Japan's most beautiful lake, Mashū-ko once held the world record for water clarity. The island in the middle was known by the Ainu as the Isle of the Gods. A road runs along the western rim. You can't get down to lake level, but there are two official viewing points called Viewpoint 1 and Viewpoint 3; there's no parking fee at the latter.

Iō-zan
VOLCANO

(硫黄山; Map p628) This hissing mountain (512m), a couple of kilometres south of Kawayu Onsen, is stained sunshine-yellow in patches from sulphur. Locals steam eggs in the hot volcanic vapours for a speciality known as *onsen-tamago*. Chances are you'll hear the sellers calling *Tamago! Tamago! Tamago!* (Eggs!) even before you reach the car park.

🏃 Activities

★ Mashū-dake Trail
HIKING

(摩周岳; Map p628) The walk to the top of Mashū-dake (857m) takes you around the lake to its eastern side and back in four to six hours. The pay-off is big: you will be rewarded with amazing volcanic views for much of the hike. The trailhead is at Mashū-ko Viewpoint 1 (400m) at the southern end of the lake; the public bus stops here, though infrequently.

Kotan-yu
ONSEN

(コタン湯; Map p628; ⊙closed 2-3pm) FREE
On the southern shores of Kussharo-ko (p631), in the Ainu *kotan*, this *rotemburo* (outdoor bath) is right on the lake, with unobstructed views over the water. There's also unobstructed views from the road, so bring a swimsuit if that makes you squeamish! The bath is 'divided' into male and female sides by a rock. It's well maintained thanks to devoted volunteers.

Tsutsuji-ga-hara Nature Trail
WALKING

(つつじヶ原ネイチャートレイル; Map p628) This nature trail connects the Kawayu Eco-Museum Centre (p631) and Iō-zan with a very pleasant 2.5km walkway. While climbing Iō-zan is prohibited for safety reasons, the nature trail allows you to get up close to the volcanic activity and smell the sulphur!

🛏 Sleeping

Onsen Minshuku Mako
MINSHUKU ¥

(温泉民宿摩湖; Map p628; ☑0154-82-5124; www.onsenmako.com; 1-2-17 Sakuraoka, Teshikaga-chō; r per person incl/excl 2 meals ¥5000/3500; P😊🛜) The owner of this simple, family-run place is a keen traveller and extends a warm welcome to foreign guests. Rooms are tatami, with shared facilities (including an onsen bath). All-round good value, meals included. Best if you have your own wheels – it's a 20-minute walk from JR Mashū Station.

Kussharo-Genya Youth Guesthouse
HOSTEL ¥

(屈斜路原野ユースゲストハウス; Map p628; ☑0154-84-2609; www.gogogenya.com/intro/e-intro.htm; dm/r per person from ¥3300/5200, breakfast/dinner ¥750/1300; P😊@🛜) On a back road off Rte 243 on the southern shores of Kussharo-ko (p631), this attractive youth hostel has vaulted ceilings, lofty skylights and polished wooden floors, plus an onsen bath. There's a restaurant here (but no private cooking facilities).

As it's a little out of the way, set back from the road among fields, it's better if you've got your own transport, although the English-speaking staff will pick you up from JR Mashū Station, if you request in advance.

★ Marukibune
RYOKAN ¥¥

(丸木舟; Map p628; ☑0154-84-2644; www.sh.rim.or.jp/~moshiri; Kotan, Kussharo-Shigai, Teshikaga-chō; s/tw from ¥8000/14,000; P😊❄🛜) This special spot in the Ainu *kotan* at the southern end of Kussharo-ko (p631) is run by Ainu musician Atuy. It has just a handful of rooms decorated with traditional touches, some with lake views, and an onsen bath. The 'Ainu Room' (single/double ¥17,000/24,000), with wooden walls, carvings and colourful textiles, is a work of art. Meals can be taken in the ground-floor restaurant.

🍴 Eating & Drinking

There are a few eating options in front of Mashū and Kawayu stations, and more scattered around Kussharo-ko (p631). You will greatly increase your options by having a car. Note that outside summer (July and August) many places close.

Poppotei
SHOKUDO ¥

(ぽっぽ亭; Map p628; ☑0154-82-2412; 1-7-18 Asahi, Teshikaga-chō; meals ¥620-1080; ⊙10am-8pm) Right in front of JR Mashū Station this small, cosy restaurant serves up standards such as ramen and *buta-don* (grilled pork on rice), with a generous dash of colourful organic veggies. Bonus: the coffee (¥350 with food) is good. There's a picture menu.

Marukibune Restaurant
AINU ¥¥

(丸木舟レストラン; Map p628; Kotan, Kussharo-Shigai, Teshikaga-chō; meals ¥1100-2100; ⊙11am-7pm; P) OK, the food here isn't dramatically different from what a Japanese diner would serve, but you can get a *donburi* (rice bowl) topped with Hokkaidō venison and *gyōja niniku* (alpine leek), the local aromatic that

AINU: HOKKAIDŌ'S INDIGENOUS PEOPLE

The Ainu draw their ancestry back to the earliest settlers of Hokkaidō, while a distinct Ainu culture is believed to have emerged around 700 years ago. They were hunters, fishers and gatherers, settling along salmon runs and coastal plains. Men wore long, bushy beards and women had distinctive blue tattoos on their hands and faces – especially around the lips, which gave them the appearance of always smiling.

Their gods, called *kamuy*, were found in the natural world, in the rocks and trees and especially in the animals around them. Of all their gods the most important was *kim-un kamuy*, the god of the mountains – known in Japanese as *higuma* (Ussuri brown bear). Ritual ceremonies, called *iyomante*, were held to send spirits – of sacrificed bear cubs but also of plants and broken pots – back to the realm of the gods. Days began with prayer to the deity of fire, *apehuci kamuy*, who resided in the hearth.

While the Japanese and the Ainu had been trading partners for centuries, as the Japanese empire grew in military and economic might, the balance of power gradually shifted in favour of the southern nation. Following the formal annexation of Hokkaidō in 1869, the new Meiji government signed the Hokkaidō Former Aborigines Protection Act in 1899. Though well-meaning in name, it banned traditional practices, such as hunting and tattooing, along with the Ainu language. Ainu were given plots of land (typically small and ill-suited to cultivation) and instructed to take up the lives of sedentary farmers. Those who held out suffered discrimination; many who managed to assimilate feared being 'outed', leading many Ainu to bury their ancestry as deeply as possible.

Today there are roughly 25,000 people in Japan who claim Ainu descent. With the general cultural upheavals of the 1960s, more and more began to speak out against entrenched discrimination and poverty, finding pride and common cause with other indigenous peoples fighting for recognition and justice around the world. A number of community centres were founded; this coincided with a period of increased domestic tourism to Hokkaidō, and many Ainu found work performing their culture for tourists – singing folk songs for tour groups and selling traditional handicrafts. For some members of the community this was a breakthrough, an opportunity to draw positive recognition to their culture and, perhaps more importantly, to make a living. For others, these watered-down cultural displays were at best a distraction from the social justice movement and, at worst, a step backwards.

The way forward for Ainu descendants remains a thorny path. There are still battles being fought on the political front: after decades of lobbying, the Former Aborigines Protection Act was repealed in 1997, and as recently as 2009 activists finally succeeded in winning the passing of a Diet (Japan's national parliamentary body) resolution recognising the Ainu as an indigenous people of Japan.

There is also the question of what it means to be Ainu. There are only a handful of people who can still speak the language (though there are radio programs to learn), and traditional cultural practices can feel frozen in the past, especially to the younger generation who were raised like modern teens. There are, however, artists, musicians and chefs tinkering with the old ways, breathing new life into them. By all means, if you're able to catch acts like Oki Dub Ainu Band (www.tonkori.com) or Marewrew (http://marewrewfes.jimdo.com) live, do!

Akan National Park, which has Ainu *kotan* (villages) in both Akanko Onsen (p628) and Kawayu Onsen (p631), is the best place in Hokkaidō to see Ainu culture in a contemporary context. The villages, with their folklore museums and restaurants serving Ainu dishes, are definitely touristy – though that is the modern reality. Akanko Onsen has a stage, **Ikor** (p631), for traditional folk music performances; Kawayu Onsen is the home base of modern Ainu musician Atuy, who runs the fantastic pension (and occasional performance space) Marukibune (p632).

If you're interested in digging deeper, visit the **Hokkaidō Ainu Center** (p580) in Sapporo. In addition to exhibitions on history and culture, there is a reading room with pretty much every book published in English on the Ainu.

has a long history in Ainu cooking. Also available: *pochie* (ポッチェ), fermented potato dumplings.

Orchard Grass

CAFE

(オーチャードグラス; Map p628; ☑ 0154-83-2906; Kawaya Onsen Station; coffee from ¥370; ⊙10am-6pm May-Oct, 11am-4pm Nov-Apr, closed Tue; ⊜☎) This cafe is inside historic Kawayu Station (1936), which retains much of its original character – in the form of high, wood-panelled ceilings, antique pendant lamps, stained-glass windows and an iron-and-tile stove. Food, such as toast, pizza and ice cream, is available too.

There's a free foot bath on the other side of the station.

ℹ Information

JR Mashū Station Tourist Information (Map p628; ☑ 0154-82-2642; www.masyuko.or.jp; ⊙9am-5pm May-Oct, 10am-4pm Nov-Apr) In JR Mashū Station, with English maps and brochures. Staff can help with accommodation bookings. There's a smaller counter inside JR Kawayu Onsen Station.

ℹ Getting There & Away

Infrequent trains run north on the JR Senmō main line between Kawayu Onsen and Shiretoko-Shari (¥930, 45 minutes), and south between Kawayu Onsen and Kushiro (¥1840, 1¾ hours) via Mashū (¥360, 15 minutes).

Your own wheels will allow you to fully explore the park. On Rte 241, between Mashū Station and Akanko Onsen, there's a particularly scenic stretch with a lookout point at Sokodai where you can see Penketō-ko and Panketō-ko.

ℹ Getting Around

From mid-July to mid-October, **Akan Bus** (p628) has four daily connections between JR Mashū Station and Mashū-ko (25 minutes). There is also a circular route that runs three times daily to/ from Kawayu Station via Mashū-ko, JR Kawayu Onsen Station, Iō-zan (p632), the Ainu Kotan (p629) and Bihoro Pass (p631). This bus usually stops for 15 to 30 minutes so you have time to check stuff out.

Buses, timed to meet trains, make the 10-minute run between Kawayu Onsen Station and Kawayu Onsen town.

All of the above are covered by the **Teshikaga Eco Passport** (弟子屈えこパスポート; pass 2/3/5 days ¥1500/2000/2500) – a must if you are planning to use public transport to get around. The pass also includes free luggage storage and bicycle rental; drop off your bags and pick up wheels at either Mashū or Kawayu Onsen stations.

Kushiro 釧路

☑ 0154 / POP 175,000

The most populous city in eastern Hokkaidō, Kushiro is an industrial port that came to prominence thanks to its harbour, which remains relatively free of ice in winter. For travellers, it is a key transit hub for nearby Kushiro Wetlands National Park and, further north, Akan National Park.

◉ Sights

Washō Market

MARKET

(和商市場, Washō Ichiba; www.washoichiba.com; 13-25 Kurogane-chō; meals ¥1000-2000; ⊙8am-6pm Mon-Sat) This fish market is as much a sightseeing spot as a place to eat. The speciality here is called *katte-don* (勝手丼) – literally 'rice bowl as you like it'. First buy a bowl of rice from one of the vendors on the perimeter then head to a fish monger and have them top it off with your choice of raw fish.

It's a couple of minutes' walk south of JR Kushiro Station.

🛏 Sleeping & Eating

As a transport hub for the region, Kushiro has a good spread of hotels near the train station, mostly national chains.

There are cafes and bakeries in the train station, but few options in the streets nearby.

ℹ Getting There & Away

AIR

Kushiro Airport (釧路空港; ☑ 0154-57-8304; www.kushiro-airport.co.jp; 2 Tsuruoka), located about 10km west of the city, has flights to/from Sapporo and Tokyo. Buses between the airport and JR Kushiro Station (¥940, 45 minutes) are timed for arrivals and departures.

BUS

Two buses daily run between Kushiro and Asahikawa (¥5450, 6½ hours) via Akanko Onsen (¥1530, 1½ hours) and Sōunkyō Onsen (¥4930, five hours). There are also five buses daily (two on weekends) between Rausu and Kushiro (¥4850, 3½ hours). The bus terminal is next to the train station.

TRAIN

There are six daily JR Limited Express Super Ōzora Liner trains between Sapporo and Kushiro (¥9370, 4½ hours), via Obihiro (¥4810, 1½ hours, from Kushiro). The JR Nemuro line runs east to Nemuro (¥2490, 2¼ hours).

Heading north from Kushiro, the JR Senmō line runs between Kushiro and Abashiri (¥3670, 3½ hours) via Kushiro-shitsugen (¥360, 20 minutes), Kawayu Onsen (¥1840, 1½ hours) and Shireto-ko-Shari (¥2810, 2½ hours).

Kushiro-shitsugen National Park
釧路湿原国立公園

☑ 0154

Kushiro-shitsugen National Park, at 269 sq km, is Japan's largest undeveloped wetland. It was designated a national park in 1987 to combat urban sprawl and protect the habitat of numerous species, chiefly the *tanchō-zuru* (red-crested white crane), the traditional symbol of both longevity and Japan.

In the early 20th century, the cranes were thought to be extinct due to overhunting and habitat destruction. In 1926, however, some 20 birds were discovered in the marshes here; with concentrated conservation efforts, they now number over 1000. Cranes can be seen year-round, but the best time to spot them is during winter when they gather at feeding spots.

◉ Sights & Activities

Rte 53 runs up the park's western fringes. If you have your own wheels, you can explore the park at length, including various viewpoints.

Those who travel by train can ride to JR Kushiro-shitsugen Station, then walk uphill for 15 minutes to the **Hosooka Marsh Viewpoint** (細岡展望台).

Japanese Crane Reserve　　　WILDLIFE RESERVE
(丹頂鶴自然公園; 　Tanchō-zuru　Shizen-kōen; ☑ 0154-56-2219; 　http://kushiro-tancho.jp; 112 Tsuruoka; adult/child ¥470/110; ⊙ 9am-6pm Apr-Sep, 9am-4pm Oct-Mar) Run by Kushiro Zoo, this reserve has been instrumental in increasing the crane population. There are currently 14 *tanchō-zuru* (red-crested white cranes) living here, though they are free to leave anytime they like (the fences are for people, not birds).

**Akan International
Crane Centre 'GRUS'**　　　WILDLIFE RESERVE
(阿寒国際ツルセンター"グルス"; 　☑ 0154-66-4011; http://aicc.webcrow.jp; 23-40 Kami-Akan, Akan-chō; adult/child ¥470/240; ⊙ 9am-5pm) You can see a few cranes in breeding pens here but the real attraction is the **Crane Observation Centre** (open 8.30am to 4.30pm November to March), a winter feeding ground that is your

WORTH A TRIP

THE JR SENMŌ LINE

Travellers for whom train travel is part of the journey – rather than just a means to get around – will want to experience the JR Senmō line. It travels from Abashiri to Kushiro, passing some stunning scenery along the way: in summer, the flower fields of Koshimizu Gensei-kaen (p623), the forlorn Sea of Okhotsk and the marshes of Kushiro Wetlands National Park (p635); in winter, plains of glistening white snow and the icy sea.

The line and its stations were constructed in the 1920s and '30s and many original stations remain. Few people actually take the Senmō line because they need to – it's usually only two cars long. Many stations are now unstaffed and have turned their former offices and waiting rooms into charming cafes, such as Teishaba (p623) and Orchard Grass (p634), and restaurants, including Ekibasha (p623).

best chance to see cranes outside of a bird park.

Kushiro-shitsugen Norokko Train　　　RAIL
(釧路湿原ノロッコ号; ⊙ Jul-Sep) This is the best way to see the wetlands without a car: once or twice daily, a vintage train with large picture windows makes a slow journey from Kushiro via Kushiro-shitsugen (¥360) as far as Tōro Station (¥540). It's very popular so be sure to reserve a seat (plus ¥520). The tourist info booth at Kushiro Station can help.

In February, an old steam locomotive, the **Fuyu-shitsugen Norokko Train**, plies the same route; it doesn't run every day though and you'll need to book ahead.

🛏 Sleeping & Eating

There are only a couple of places to eat in the vicinity of the park; better to eat in nearby Kushiro.

**★ Kushiro-shitsugen
Tōro Youth Hostel**　　　HOSTEL ¥
(釧路湿原とうろユースホステル; 　☑ 0154-87-2510; www.tohro.net; 7 Tōro, Shibecha-chō; dm/s/d from ¥4540/5400/9080, breakfast/dinner ¥650/1080; ℗ ⊜ 🛜) ✎ This hostel, run partly on solar power, was designed with birdwatchers in mind. A porch (partly glassed in) looks directly over the marshes and

there are binoculars you can borrow. It's also a peaceful place to spend a few days, with good meals (book ahead, there's not much else around) and comfortable dorm rooms.

From May to November the hostel runs canoe tours and offers a guiding service, while from December to March it offers tours to see the cranes. It's a few minutes' walk from JR Tōro (塘路) Station, two stops north of Kushiro-shitsugen on the JR Senmō line.

ⓘ Getting There & Away

The JR Senmō main line runs from Kushiro to Kushiro-shitsugen (¥360, 20 minutes), on the east side of the park. From Kushiro-shitsugen, trains continue to Kawayu Onsen, Shiretoko-Shari and Abashiri.

The bus from Kushiro Station to Akanko Onsen stops at the Japanese Crane Reserve (¥910, one hour) and Akan International Crane Centre 'GRUS' (¥1450, 1¼ hours). Both are also along Rte 240, which runs between Kushiro and Akanko Onsen.

Tokachi　十勝

Largely rural Tokachi is known throughout Japan for its dairy farms, cattle ranches and vineyards. For travellers this is mostly a place to pass through, en route to Daisetsuzan National Park or eastern Hokkaidō, though there is some lovely countryside here.

It's also a good place to break up a long journey across the island.

🛏 Sleeping & Eating

Obihiro has the most options and the most convenient transport links; however, if you're driving, there are some lovely hostels in the countryside, not too far from the main towns.

Given Tokachi's reputation for agriculture and livestock, you'll see plenty of local beef, pork, dairy products and wine on the menus. Still, outside Obihiro (and outside the summer season), restaurants can be hard to find.

Toipirka Kitaobihiro Youth Hostel HOSTEL ¥ (トイピルカ北帯広ユースホステル; ☑0155-30-4165; http://toipirka.eco.coocan.jp; N4E52-8 Shimo-Shihoro, Otofuke-chō; dm from ¥3450, breakfast/dinner ¥750/1300; P ⊖ @ ☎) A great place to overnight is this attractive log house with a hammock on the porch and sofas around a wood stove on the lounge. The meals, cooked from scratch with no additives, are fantastic. It's near Tokachi-gawa Onsen, a cluster of resort-style onsen and hotels along the Tokachi-gawa, a 15-minute drive east of Obihiro.

ⓘ Getting There & Away

Obihiro, which has **Tokachi Obihiro Airport** (十勝帯広空港; ☑0155-64-5320; www.tokachiobihiro-airport.jp; W9 Chūō 8-41, Izumi-chō) nearby, is the main transit hub for the region.

JR Limited Express Super Tokachi Liner and Super Ōzora Liner trains connect Sapporo and Obihiro (¥6700, 2¾ hours, 11 daily); Super Ōzora Liner trains go from Obihiro to Kushiro (¥4810, 1½ hours, six daily). Obihiro and Ikeda are also stops on the JR Nemuro main line, running between northern Hokkaidō and the eastern tip in Nemuro.

Car rentals from most major companies are available in Obihiro or at Tokachi Obihiro Airport.

HAKODATE　函館

☑0138 / POP 266,600

Built on a narrow strip of land between Hakodate Harbour to the west and the Tsugaru Strait to the east, Hakodate is the southern gateway to the island of Hokkaidō. Under the Kanagawa Treaty of 1854, the city was one of the first ports to open up to international trade, and as such hosted a small foreign community. That influence can still be seen in the **Motomachi district**, a steep hillside that's sprinkled with European buildings and churches; the waterfront lined with red-brick warehouses; and in the nostalgic streetcar that still makes the rounds of the city.

◉ Sights

Hakodate's highlights can easily be done in a day, as they're all time-specific: start early at the morning seafood market; spend the day strolling the attractive flagstone lanes of the Motomachi district; then head up Hakodate-yama (p638) for the famous night view over the bay.

Discounted combination tickets (two/three/four sights ¥500/720/840, half-price for children) are available for the Old British Consulate (p638), the Old Public Hall of Hakodate Ward (p638), the Hakodate Museum of Northern Peoples and the **Hakodate Museum of Literature**.

★**Hakodate Morning Market** MARKET (函館朝市, Hakodate Asa-ichi; Map p637; www.hakodate-asaichi.com; 9-19 Wakamatsu-chō; ⊗5am-noon; ℝ JR Hakodate) FREE With crabs grilling over hot coals, freshly caught squid packed tightly in ice-stuffed styrofoam and the singsong call of vendors, Hakodate Morning Market does a fantastic impression of an old-time seafood market – though the visitors

Central Hakodate

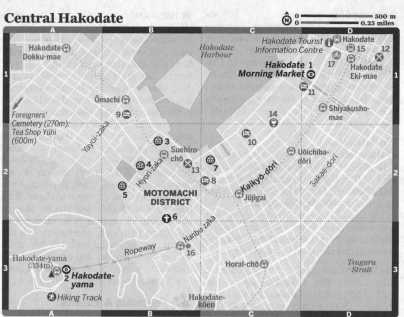

Central Hakodate

today are tourists not wholesale buyers. (The commercial market that was here originally has since moved to a bigger space.)

Red-brick Warehouse District
HISTORIC BUILDING

(赤レンガ倉庫; Map p637) These early-20th-century red-brick warehouses on the waterfront are the legacy of Hakodate's status as a historic, international trade port. They've been restored and turned into a tourist mall (which seems apt). The complex is pretty in the evening, when it's lit up.

Hakodate Museum of Northern Peoples
MUSEUM

(函館市北方民族資料館; Hakodate-shi Hoppō-minzoku Shiryōkan; Map p637; ☏0138-22-4128; www.zaidan-hakodate.com/hoppominzoku/#sisetu; 21-7 Suehiro-chō; ¥300; ⊙9am-7pm Apr-Oct, to 5pm Nov-Mar; ⓕSuehiro-chō) Inside the old Japan Bank building (1926), this museum has interesting exhibitions (labelled in English) about Ainu culture and some other indigenous cultures from Sakhalin (the island north of Hokkaidō, now Russia) and further north.

Orthodox Church
CHURCH

(函館ハリストス正教会, Hakodate Harisutosu Seikyōkai; Map p637; http://orthodox-hakodate.jp; 3-13 Motomachi; donation ¥200; ☺10am-5pm Mon-Fri, 10am-4pm Sat, 1-4pm Sun; 🚊Suehiro-chō) Dating from 1916, this Russian Orthodox church is adorned with distinctive copper domes and spires. It's still in use by the 300 or so (mostly elderly) members of the Japanese Orthodox community.

Old Public Hall of Hakodate Ward
HISTORIC BUILDING

(旧函館区公会堂, Kyū-Hakodate Kūkōkaidō; Map p637; 🖉0138-22-1001; www.zaidan-hakodate.com; 11-13 Motomachi; adult/child ¥300/150; ☺9am-7pm Apr-Oct, to 5pm Nov-Mar; 🚊Suehiro-chō) The Old Public Hall of Hakodate Ward, built in 1910, is an ornate mansion and a well-preserved example of Meiji-era (1868–1912) style. From the verandah there are good views over the bay.

Old British Consulate
HISTORIC BUILDING

(旧イギリス領事館, Kyū-Igirisu Ryōjikan; Map p637; 🖉0138-27-8159; www.hakodate-kankou.com/british/en; 33-14 Motomachi; adult/child ¥300/150; ☺9am-7pm Apr-Oct, to 5pm Nov-Mar; 🚊Suehiro-chō) From 1913 to 1934, this whitewashed mansion served as the British consulate. You can tour the restored interior and have tea (¥540) on the ground floor.

Foreigners' Cemetery
CEMETERY

(外国人墓地, Gaikokujin Bochi; 23 Funami-chō; ☺dawn-dusk; 🚊Hakodate Dokku-mae) Along the bay, on the western fringe of town (where few visitors venture) is the small, grassy cemetery that contains the graves of sailors, clergy and others who died far from their homelands. Many are marked with English, Russian or French inscriptions. It's gated, but you can easily see over the rails.

Goryō-kaku-kōen
PARK

(五稜郭公園; 🚊Goryōkaku-kōen-mae) FREE Japan's first Western-style fort was built in 1864 in the shape of a five-pointed star (goryō-kaku means 'five-sided fort') designed to trap attackers in deadly crossfire. Nothing remains of the actual structure but the footprint – a park encircled by a star-shaped moat. To best appreciate this, visit the observatory atop the 98m Goryō-kaku Tower (五稜郭タワー; 🖉0138-51-4785; www.goryokaku-tower.co.jp; 43-9 Goryōkaku-chō; adult/child ¥840/420; ☺8am-7pm). Exhibitions in the observatory explain the history of the fort; you also get good views over Hakodate. The park itself is a pretty green space, with 1600 cherry trees.

★ Hakodate-yama
MOUNTAIN

(函館山; Map p637) Mention you've been to Hakodate and every Japanese person you know will ask if you took in the night view from atop Hakodate-yama (334m) – it's that famous! Best to get up here for sunset or after dark: what's striking is seeing the lit-up peninsula (which locals say is shaped like Hokkaidō itself) against the pitch-black waters.

There are a few ways to get here: by ropeway (函館山ロープウェイ; Map p637; 🖉0138-23-3105; www.334.co.jp; 19-7 Motomachi; adult/child return ¥1280/640; ☺10am-10pm 25 Apr–15 Oct, 10am-9pm 16 Oct–24 Apr), bus, car or foot. Buses for the ropeway (¥240, 10 minutes) and the summit (¥360, 30 minutes) depart from bus stop 4 at JR Hakodate Station. You can also walk to the ropeway in 10 minutes from the Jūjigai tram stop; alternatively you can hike up one of several trails (all take about an hour) between May and late October. The road to the summit is often closed to private vehicles after sunset as it gets too crowded.

★★ Festivals & Events

For more info on local festivals, see www.hakodate.travel/en/event.

Hakodate Port Festival
CULTURAL

(函館港祭り; Hakodate Minato Matsuri; ☺Aug) Thousands of locals gather to perform traditional dances in the streets, including Hakodate's signature squid dance.

🛏 Sleeping

Most standard budget chains are well represented here, located within a short walk of JR Hakodate Station. Fancier (if a bit overpriced) options overlook the bay. Winter is the low season in Hakodate and rates should drop.

Hakodate Perry House
GUESTHOUSE ¥

(函館ぺりーハウス; Map p637; 🖉0138-83-1457; www.hakodate-perryhouse.com; 3-2 Ōmachi; s/d ¥3500/7500; 🅿🕭🛜; 🚊Ōmachi) Opened 160 years after Perry's American navy ships visited Hakodate, this guesthouse is named after the great naval captain. Rooms are small and the bathroom and toilet facilities are shared, but the price is right and the location is conveniently near the Ōmachi tram stop.

B&B Pension Hakodate-mura
PENSION ¥¥

(B&Bペンションはこだて村; Map p637; 🖉0138-22-8105; www.bb-hakodatemura.com; 16-12 Suehiro-chō; s/d from ¥5940/9500; 🅿🕭@🛜; 🚊Jūjigai) This long-running traveller favourite has a great location near the harbour, and is within walking distance of Motomachi. The owners speak English and are very welcoming. There's a good spread of room options, including family rooms. Filling breakfasts (¥840) are served in the ground-floor lounge.

Tōyoko Inn
Hakodate Eki-mae Asaichi　　　　HOTEL ¥¥
(東横イン函館駅前朝市; Map p637; ☏0138-23-1045; www.toyoko-inn.com/e_hotel/00063/index.html; 22-7 Ōtemachi; s/d from ¥4100/6800; ◉❄ @⬤; ℝJR Hakodate) This budget chain staple is just steps from the morning market (p636) and three minutes from JR Hakodate Station.

La Vista Hakodate Bay Hotel　　　HOTEL ¥¥¥
(ラビスタ函館ベイ; Map p637; ☏0138-23-6111; www.hotespa.net/hotels/lahakodate; 12-6 Toyokawa-chō; s/d from ¥17,500/35,000; ◉❄@⬤; ℝUōichiba-dōri) Rooms here are on the small-ish side but they've been gussied up nicely to evoke an early-20th-century feel (while still being modern). The hotel is right on the waterfront, in the Red-brick Warehouse District (p637), and has a rooftop onsen with outdoor tubs overlooking the bay.

✖ Eating & Drinking

For many visitors, eating is the whole reason to come to Hakodate. Squid, caught in the Tsugaru Strait, is the city's speciality. Hakodate is also known for its *shio-ramen* (塩ラーメン; ramen in a light, salt-flavoured broth).

★Kikuyo Shokudo　　　　　SEAFOOD ¥
(きくよ食堂; Map p637; www.hakodate-kikuyo.com/asaichi; Hakodate Morning Market; meals from ¥1000; ⏱5am-2pm; ℝJR Hakodate) Inside Hakodate Morning Market (p636), Kikuyo Shokudo got its start in the 1950s as a counter joint to feed market workers and is now one of the top reasons to come to Hakodate. The speciality here is the *Hakodate tomoe-don* (函館巴丼; ¥1680), rice topped with raw *uni* (sea urchin), *ikura* (salmon roe) and *hotate* (scallops). There's a picture menu.

You can custom-make *kaisen-don* (raw seafood over rice) from the list of toppings or sample another local speciality: *ika-sōmen* (raw squid sliced very thinly like noodles).

Lucky Pierrot　　　　　　BURGERS ¥
(ラッキーピエロ; Map p637; ☏0138-26-2099; 23-18 Suehiro-chō; burgers ¥270-1100; ⏱10am-12.30am; P◉⬤; ℝSuehiro-chō) Hakodate's iconic burger shop has been voted best in the nation several times – despite its dive image. The house special is the Chinese chicken burger, an oddly addictive combo of twice-

MIZUNASHI KAIHIN ONSEN

A hidden jewel, **Mizunashi Kaihin Onsen** (水無海浜温泉) FREE is an onsen in the sea! You'll need to turn up at the right time as the two main rock pools are covered by the sea when the tide is in; check with the Hakodate Tourist Information Centre (p640) for bathing times. There are changing facilities. While some bathers go naked, others wear bathing suits. You'll need your own wheels to get here: head east from Hakodate on Rte 278 to the Kameda peninsula. When the road heads inland, follow it up and over to the far coast, then turn right on Rte 231 and drive southeast to the end of the road.

cooked chicken, crisp lettuce and mayonnaise on a sesame bun. Much of the menu is similarly fusion; the decor is carnival diner c 1989.

It has several branches around the city, but this is one of the bigger ones.

Daimon Yokochō　　　　STREET FOOD ¥
(大門横丁; Map p637; www.hakodate-yatai.com; 7-5 Matsukaze-chō; ⏱5pm-midnight; ℝJR Hakodate) This is a fun place to gather in the evening, a collection of 25 food vendors in an old-style marketplace, with outdoor seats (when it's not freezing!). You can take your pick from ramen, *donburi* (rice bowl) dishes and typical *izakaya* fare. Most places have picture menus; figure about ¥2000 per person.

Walk straight out of JR Hakodate Station and turn left at the first traffic light.

★Tea Shop Yūhi　　　　　TEAHOUSE
(ティーショップ夕日; 25-20 Funami-chō; tea sets from ¥600; ⏱11am-dusk Fri-Wed mid-Mar–mid-Dec; ⬤; ℝHakodate Dokku-mae) Filling the halls of a wooden building from 1885 (actually the old Hakodate Quarantine Office) is this magical teahouse overlooking the water. It's lit only by natural light so closes after the sun sets. In the meantime, you can while away the afternoon refilling your tiny pot of single-origin green tea, nibbling on the *wagashi* (Japanese sweets) and pickles that accompany it.

The teahouse is a short walk beyond the Foreigners' Cemetery.

Hakodate Beer　　　　　　BREWERY
(はこだてビール; Map p637; ☏0138-23-8000; www.hakodate-factory.com/beer; 5-22 Ōtemachi; pints ¥875, dishes ¥480-1100; ⏱11am-3pm & 5-10pm Thu-Tue; ℝUōichiba-dōri) Hakodate Beer makes

WORTH A TRIP

HISTORIC ESASHI

Esashi (江差; population 8110) was one of Hokkaidō's original boom towns, with a roaring trade in *nishin* (herring) in the 18th and 19th centuries. In the early 20th century the herring schools moved north and the town fell into decline. (Its most recent setback was when its train line, the JR Esashi line, was discontinued with the opening of the Hokkaidō Shin-kansen.) The **Nakamura-ke Residence** (中村家住宅; www.hokkaido-esashi.jp/modules/eng-lish/content0005.html; 22 Nakauta-chō, Esashi-chō; adult/child ¥300/100; ⏰9am-5pm Apr-Oct, closed Mon Nov & Dec, closed Jan-Mar) is the sole legacy of Esashi's glory days. It's a beautiful, sloping wooden house built of cypress and stone (without any nails) by a wealthy merchant.

You can get here by bus from Hakodate (¥1880, 2¼ hours, five daily), but it's better to drive: the Oiwake Sōran Line (追分ソーランライン), which follows the undulating coastline, is a treat. It's built on landfill: the Nakamura-ke Residence originally backed onto the water, so fishing boats could dock. There are some fantastic old photos of the town in the house.

its beer right here on the bay with ground-water from Hakodate-yama (p638). You can buy bottles or sample the brews on tap, served here along with typical Japanese-inflected pub food (like chips and fried squid). Its Ha-kodate Weizen is the tastiest brew.

ℹ Information

Hakodate Tourist Information Centre (函館市観光案内所; Map p637; ☎0138-23-5440; www.hakodate.travel; ⏰9am-7pm Apr-Oct, 9am-5pm Nov-Mar) Inside JR Hakodate Station, with English brochures and maps. Check the website.

ℹ Getting There & Away

AIR

From **Hakodate Airport** (函館空港; ☎0138-57-8881; www.airport.ne.jp/hakodate/en; 511 Takamatsu-chō), just a few kilometres east of the city centre, there are international flights to Seoul and Taipei, and domestic flights to various desti-nations including Sapporo, Tokyo and Kansai.

Frequent buses run direct between Hakodate Airport and JR Hakodate Station (¥410, 20 min-utes), or take a taxi (¥2000 to ¥3000).

BOAT

Tsugaru Kaikyō Ferry (津軽海峡フェリー; www.tsugarukaikyo.co.jp) operates ferries (departing year-round) between Aomori and Hakodate (from ¥3100, 3¾ hours, eight daily), and between Hakodate and Ōma (¥2600, 1¾ hours, two daily) on the Shimokita Peninsula. The ferry terminal, where you also buy your tickets, is on the north-east corner of Hakodate Harbour.

Buses (¥310, 20 minutes) for the ferry terminal depart from bus stop 11 in front of JR Hakodate Station; a taxi should cost about ¥2000.

BUS

Chūō Bus (p592) coaches run eight times daily (including one night departure) between

JR Hakodate Station and JR Sapporo Station (¥4810, 5½ hours); reservations required. The **bus terminal** (函館駅前バスターミナル; Map p637) is in front of JR Hakodate Station; buses also stop at JR Shin-Hakodate-Hokuto Station.

CAR & MOTORCYCLE

If you've just arrived in Hokkaidō, Hakodate is a good place to pick up a rental car and start your road-tripping adventure across the island. Major agencies have offices around JR Hakodate Station and in front of the JR Shin-Hakodate-Hokuto *shinkansen* station.

TRAIN

The JR Hokkaidō Shinkansen travels from Honshū to JR Shin-Hakodate-Hokuto Station, north of Hakodate, via the Seikan Tunnel. There are 10 trains daily to/from Tokyo (¥22,490, four hours). The JR Hakodate Liner connects JR Shin-Hakodate-Hokuto and JR Hakodate sta-tions (¥360, 20 minutes, 16 times daily).

JR Limited Express Hokuto Liner trains run 12 times daily between Hakodate and Sapporo (¥8830, 3½ hours), via JR Shin-Hakodate-Hokuto Station.

A combination of *tokkyū* (limited express) and *kaisoku* (rapid) trains run on the JR Hakodate line between Hakodate and Niseko via Oshamambe (¥5560, about four hours with transfers).

ℹ Getting Around

Single-trip fares on trams and buses generally cost between ¥210 and ¥250. One-day transport passes for bus (¥800), tram (¥600) or combined bus and tram (¥1000) can be purchased at the tourist information centre or on-board.

The Hakodate-yama Ropeway (p638) runs up to the top of Hakodate-yama (p638).

You can rent bikes from **Hakorin** (はこりん; Map p637; per day ¥1600; ⏰9am-6pm), which can be found at the Four Point Bay Sheraton Hotel out-side JR Hakodate Station.

Shikoku

Best Places to Eat

➡ Sanzenkai (p668)

➡ Hirome Ichiba (p665)

➡ Bahati (p654)

➡ YRG Café (p648)

➡ Kappō Yano (p673)

Best Places to Sleep

➡ Shimanto-no-yado Iyashi-no-sato (p668)

➡ Nakahaga Residence Guesthouse (p681)

➡ Chiiori (p658)

➡ Kaiyu Inn (p668)

➡ Sen Guesthouse (p672)

Why Go?

The birthplace of revered ascetic and founder of the Shingon Buddhist sect Kōbō Daishi (774–835), Shikoku (四国) is synonymous with natural beauty and the pursuit of spiritual perfection. It's home to the 88 Sacred Temples of Shikoku, Japan's most famous pilgrimage.

In Japan's feudal past, the island was divided into four regions; hence the name *shi* (four) and *koku* (region). Considered remote and isolated for centuries, Shikoku is now easy to access from Honshū via three impressive bridge systems built in the last three decades.

The island's stunning Iya Valley, rugged Pacific coastline, gorgeous free-flowing rivers and mountain ranges all beckon to be explored with hiking boot, kayak, surfboard and your own earthly vessel. Your physical incarnation will feast upon the remote temples, historic castles and gardens, excellent regional cuisine and modern pleasures of Tokushima, Kōchi, Matsuyama and Takamatsu.

When to Go
Takamatsu

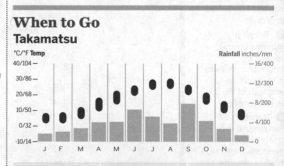

Apr Enlightenment may know no weather, but any pilgrimage is best taken in spring.

Jul–Sep Rivers are running, surf is rolling, and the sun is, well, shining.

Aug Join every man, woman and child for Awa-odori Matsuri, Japan's wildest dance party.

Shikoku Highlights

1 88 Temple pilgrimage (p654) Walking the time-worn route.

2 Muroto-misaki (p655) Finding seclusion, if not enlightenment, like Kōbō Daishi did.

3 Ishizuchi-san (p679) Hiking up the sacred mountain, one of Japan's most gripping ascents.

4 Iya Valley (p656) Picking your way across swaying vine bridges in gorgeous isolation.

5 Dōgo Onsen (p678) Soaking in the venerable waters of the historic onsen in the castle-town metropolis of Matsuyama.

6 Konpira-san (p691) Trekking up 1368 stone steps to pay homage to the god of seafarers.

7 Ritsurin-kōen (p685) Walking off Japan's most famous udon with a stroll through Takamatsu's exquisite Edo-period garden.

8 Tairyū-ji Ropeway (p663) Riding the spectacular ropeway up to mountain-top Temple 21 of the 88 Sacred Temples.

9 Naruto (p649) Marvelling at the vitality of the whirlpools from close up while aboard a sightseeing boat.

10 Ōkinohama (p668) Surfing beautiful swells or relaxing on the beach.

Sleeping

Shikoku has been playing host to 1200 years of walking pilgrims, so there are all kinds of options for places to stay. Major cities and towns have hotels with Western-style rooms, while smaller towns have ryokan (traditional inns), *minshuku* (Japanese guesthouses) and many of the 88 Sacred Temples have *shuku-bō*, pilgrim lodgings. Surfers can stay at beachside pensions, while hikers may like to stay at huts on the island's major mountains.

Getting There & Away

Most visitors to Shikoku over the past 1200 years have been pilgrims who arrived by boat and followed a clockwise route starting near Tokushima. Nowadays, most arrive on the island by train from Okayama via the one rail link over the Seto-Ōhashi bridge, by air to one of the four prefectures' major airports, by highway bus from Honshū, or by a number of ferry routes.

AIR

Air connections are constantly changing, so check for the latest.

On the international front, Takamatsu has direct flights to Taipei, Seoul and Shanghai; Matsuyama has direct flights to Seoul and Shanghai.

Domestically, **All Nippon Airways** (www. ana.co.jp), **Japan Airlines** (www.jal.co.jp) and a growing number of low-cost carriers such as **Peach** (www.flypeach.com) and **Jetstar** (www. jetstar.com/jp/en/home) have services that connect Matsuyama, Kōchi, Takamatsu and Tokushima in Shikoku with Tokyo, Osaka and other major centres.

BUS

There are many buses that use the three bridge systems linking Shikoku with Honshū.
→ In the east, the Akashi Kaikyō-ōhashi (Akashi Kaikyō bridge) connects Tokushima with Kōbe and Osaka via Awaji-shima (Awaji Island).

→ In the middle, Seto-ōhashi (Seto Bridge) runs from Okayama to Sakaide, west of Takamatsu.
→ In the west, the Shimanami Kaidō is an island-hopping series of nine bridges (with bike paths!) leading from Imabari in Ehime Prefecture to Onomichi near Hiroshima.

Local Operators

JR Shikoku Bus (www.jr-shikoku.co.jp/bus) operates between Shikoku's major cities, and to cities on Honshū such as Tokyo, Nagoya, Osaka and Okayama. The route map is available online.

Tokushima Bus (http://tokubus.co.jp) runs long-distance buses to and from Tokushima.

TRAIN

The Seto-ōhashi (Seto Bridge) that links Okayama to Sakaide, west of Takamatsu, is the only one of the bridges to carry trains. JR runs regularly from Okayama to Shikoku.

Getting Around

Trains link all Shikoku's major cities, but do not reach as far as the southern capes of Muroto-misaki and Ashizuri-misaki or into the island's mountainous interior.

Buses link major Shikoku cities and reach points that trains don't get to, but times and connections can be difficult.

TOKUSHIMA & THE ANAN COAST
徳島・阿南海岸

The starting point for 1200 years of pilgrims, Tokushima Prefecture, formerly known as Awa, is home to the first 23 of Shikoku's 88 Sacred Temples. Ryōzen-ji is Temple One as it is the first temple pilgrims came to after visiting Kōya-san

FERRIES TO/FROM SHIKOKU

Numerous ferry routes link Shikoku to destinations in Kansai, Western Honshū, Kyūshū and even Tokyo.

DEPARTING FROM	DESTINATIONS
Matsuyama	Hiroshima (1¼ hours, 12 daily), Kita-Kyūshū (seven hours, daily)
Takamatsu	Kōbe (three hours and 40 minutes, five daily), Naoshima and Uno (in Okayama Prefecture)
Tokushima	Wakayama (two hours, six daily), Kita-Kyūshū (15 hours, once daily) and Tokyo (18 hours, once daily)
Yawatahama (south of Matsuyama)	Beppu (three hours, six daily) and Usuki (2½ hours, six daily) on Kyūshū

in Wakayama Prefecture and asking for Kōbō Daishi's support on their journey. To *henro* (pilgrims), Tokushima is known as Hosshin-no-dōjō, the place to determine to achieve enlightenment. If you haven't got time to walk the 88, the first five temples sit in an east–west line spanning about 15km to the north of the Yoshino River and make a worthy mini-pilgrimage.

These days, notable attractions of the prefecture include the lively Awa-odori Matsuri, which takes place in Tokushima in August; the mighty whirlpools of the Naruto Channel between Shikoku and Awaji-shima; and the surf beaches of the Anan Coast (Anan-kaigan) to the south.

Check out www.topia.ne.jp/english/tourism for information on the area.

Tokushima 徳島

☎0886 / POP 266,000

With Mt Bizan looming in the west, and the Shinmachi-gawa cutting a gentle swath through the middle, bustling Tokushima city is its prefecture's pleasant capital. With a number of nearby temples, the city makes a solid starting point for 88-Temple pilgrims. It's a modern, regional city with plenty going on between JR Tokushima station in the city centre and the Bizan ropeway station.

In the southern part of the city, Bunka-no-mori-kōen is a great option for rainy days, as the complex houses several museums, such as the Tokushima Modern Art Museum, the Tokushima Prefectural Museum and the prefectural library.

Every August, the Awa-odori Matsuri, a traditional dance festival, attracts thousands of Japanese from across the country. Book accommodation well ahead and expect to pay a premium if you're visiting during this time.

Sights

★Bizan MOUNTAIN

(眉山; Map p646) At the foot of Bizan, the 280m-high summit at the southwestern end of Shinmachibashi-dōri, **Awa Odori Kaikan** (阿波おどり会館; Map p646; ☎088-611-1611; www.awaodori-kaikan.jp; 2-20 Shinmachibashi; ¥300; ⏲9am-5pm, closed 2nd & 4th Wed of month) features extensive exhibits relating to the Awa-odori Matsuri and dance. The dance is performed at 2pm, 3pm and 4pm daily (and at 11am on weekends), with a nightly performance at 8pm (afternoon/evening ¥600/800). From the 5th floor, the **Bizan Ropeway** (Map p646; ☎088-652-3617; one way/return ¥610/1020; ⏲9am-5.30pm Nov-Mar, to 9pm Apr-Oct & during special events) whizzes you to the top of Bizan for fine city views. A combined ticket for the museum, cable car and dance show is ¥1620.

LOCAL KNOWLEDGE

SURFING SHIKOKU

It's not the North Shore of O'ahu, but Southern Tokushima is a Japanese surfer's paradise, with great waves and relatively few surfers in the water. Despite the prevalence of concrete on the shoreline, this region has attractive beaches and relaxed, friendly locals – some of whom have been world travellers and can speak English. The area is growing as a destination, with alternative lifestylers moving in, setting up tourism-related lifestyle businesses and catering for a growing number of visiting foreigners.

Shishikui (p653) (宍喰) in Tokushima and the two-street beach-bum town of Ikumi (p655) (生見), just over the border in Kōchi, are prime spots.

Tokushima Modern Art Museum MUSEUM

(徳島県立近代美術館; ☎088-668-1088; www.art.tokushima-ec.ed.jp; Bunka-no-mori-kōen, Hachiman-chō; ¥200, special exhibitions extra ¥600; ⏲9.30am-5pm Tue-Sun) With a permanent collection that includes modern masters, both Japanese and Western, this surprisingly sophisticated prefectural museum houses two- and three-dimensional art by Picasso and Klee as well as Kaburagi and Seishi. It is particularly interesting to compare the more familiar European works to their Japanese counterparts, especially the pieces reflecting Japan's postwar identity; the fusion of traditional and Western-influenced styles embodies the zeitgeist of the period.

Awa Jūrobe Yashiki Puppet Theatre THEATRE

(阿波十郎兵衛屋敷; ☎088-665-2202; http://joruri.info/jurobe; 184 Miyajima Motoura, Kawauchi-chō; ⏲9.30am-5pm, to 6pm Jul & Aug) For hundreds of years, puppet theatre thrived in the farming communities around Tokushima. Performances can still be seen here, in the former residence of Bandō Jūrobe, a samurai who allowed himself to be executed for a crime he didn't

Tokushima

Tokushima

commit in order to preserve the good name of his master. The tale inspired the drama *Keisei Awa no Naruto*, first performed in 1768. Sections from the play are performed at 11am and 2pm daily.

To get to the museum, take a bus for Tomiyoshi Danchi (富吉団地) from bus stop No 7 at Tokushima bus terminal and get off at the Jūrobe Yashiki-mae stop (¥270, 25 minutes). More puppets can be seen at the nearby **Awa Deko Ningyō Kaikan** (阿波木偶人形会館; Awa Puppet Hall; ☎ 088-665-5600; www3.tcn.ne.jp/~awadekon ingyokk/top.html; 1-226 Miyajima Motoura, Ka-wauchi-chō; ¥400; ☉ 9am-5pm, closed 1st & 3rd Mon of month). This small museum displays puppets made by the in-house master, who also gives talks (in Japanese) on the puppet-making process.

Chūō-kōen
PARK

(中央公園; Map p646) Northeast of the train station is Tokushima's central park, Chūō-kōen, a lovely place for a stroll. you'll find the scant ruins of **Tokushima-jō** (Tokushima Castle) and the beautiful **Senshūkaku-teien** (千秋閣庭園; Map p646; ¥50, incl in museum ticket), an intimate 16th-century garden featuring rock bridges and secluded ponds. Get a glimpse into the castle's former grandeur at **Tokushima Castle Museum** (徳島城博物館; Map p646; ☑088-656-2525; www.city.tokushima.tokushima.jp/johaku; 1-8 Jōnai; ¥300; ☺9.30am-5pm Tue-Sun), whose structure is based on the original castle's architecture and location. The museum contains a model of the castle town at its peak as well as artefacts.

☞ Tours

Hyōtan-jima Boats
BOATING

(ひょうたん島周遊船; Map p646; ☑090-3783-2084; tours ¥100) Take the boat cruise around 'gourd-shaped' Hyōtan-jima (Hyōtan Island) in central Tokushima. The tours leave from Ryogoku-bashi (両国橋; Ryōgoku Bridge) on the Shinmachi-gawa every 40 minutes from 1pm to 4pm Monday through Friday from mid-March to mid-October, and daily from 20 July to 31 August. In July and August there are additional departures every 40 minutes from 5pm to 8pm.

✲✲ Festivals & Events

The **Awa-odori Matsuri** (☺12-15 Aug) is the largest and most famous *bon* (Japanese Buddhist custom that honours one's ancestors) dance in Japan, marking the O-Bon holidays. Every night in mid-August, men, women and children don *yukata* (light cotton kimono) and straw hats and take to the streets to dance to the samba-like rhythm of the theme song 'Awa Yoshikono', accompanied by the sounds of *shamisen* (three-stringed guitars), *taiko* (drums) and *fue* (flutes). More than a million people descend on Tokushima for the festival every year, and accommodation is at a premium.

⌷ Sleeping

Most of the top overnight spots are within proximity of JR Tokushima station and range from hotels to *minshuku*.

Sakura-sō
MINSHUKU ¥

(さくら荘; Map p646; ☑088-652-9575; 1-25 Terashima-honchō-higashi; s/d without bathroom ¥3300/6000; ☜) The delightful older lady in charge readily welcomes foreigners to her charming place, which has a dozen large, good-value tatami rooms. There's free wi-fi, laundry facilities, parking and baggage storage at this budget bonanza right opposite the tracks, a few blocks east of the train station, just before the NHK TV tower. Get someone to call and book for you.

No English signage; look for the characters さくら荘.

★ Agnes
Hotel Tokushima
BOUTIQUE HOTEL ¥¥

(アグネスホテル徳島; Map p646; ☑088-626-2222; www.agneshotel.jp; 1-28 Terashima-honchō-nishi; s/d from ¥7500/12,000; P☺✳@☜) Hip little Agnes lies 200m west of the station and offers a more sophisticated aesthetic than the usual business hotel. The rooms are sleek, with stylish interiors, the casual-yet-smart cafe is open all day, and the 'pastry boutique' is a destination in its own right. There's wi-fi in all rooms.

Tokushima Tōkyū REI Hotel
HOTEL ¥¥

(徳島東急ＲＥＩホテル; Map p646; ☑088-626-0109; www.tokyuhotels.co.jp; 1-24 Motomachi; s/d from ¥8000/13,000; P☺✳@☜) A step up in comfort and class from more cramped business hotels, the Tōkyū Inn offers clean, relatively spacious rooms and is conveniently located across the plaza from the JR Tokushima station. Find the hotel entrance on the river side of the Sogō department store building. Book online for more competitive rates.

Hotel Plaza Inn Tokushima
BUSINESS HOTEL ¥¥

(ホテルプラザイン徳島; Map p646; ☑088-626-1771; www.gladonehotels-tokushima.jp; 1-20 Suketobashi; s/d/tw ¥7000/9000/10,000; P☺✳☜) This business hotel has simple but clean rooms, both Japanese- and Western-style, a 15-minute walk from Tokushima Station. There are laundry facilities, free wi-fi, free rental bicycles and parking (¥500) on site and restaurants in the immediate vicinity. It's nothing special, but it's reasonably priced and convenient, especially if you have a rental car.

✕ Eating & Drinking

Options abound in the streets around JR Tokushima station and in the station building itself, both on the upper and the lower

❶ SHIKOKU FREE WI-FI

Shikoku is up with the play in terms of free wi-fi for visitors. The country-wide Japan Connected-free Wi-Fi (www.ntt-bp. net/jcfw/en.html) app works well, plus each of the four prefectures has its own version.

Tokushima Free Wi-fi (http://tokushima-wifi.jp)

Kōchi Free Wi-fi (http://visitkochijapan. com/travelers_kit/wifi)

Ehime Free Wi-fi (www.ehime-wifi.jp/en)

Kagawa Free Wi-fi (www.my-kagawa. jp/wifi)

levels. Head across the Shinmachi-gawa to Akita-machi for more to choose from.

Tokushima's main entertainment district is in Akita-machi across the river, along the streets around the landmark **ACTY 21 building** (Map p646).

⭐ **YRG Café**　　　　　CAFE ¥
(Map p646; ☎ 088-656-7899; http://yrgcafe. html.xdomain.jp; 1-33-4 Terashima Honchō Higashi; meals ¥700-1500; ⊗ 11.30am-8pm Fri-Wed; 🖥) This lovely little cafe down by the train tracks is run by friendly English-speaking Takao. YRG, meaning 'Yellow, Red, Green', serves up nutritious, comforting meals that meet well-balanced diets. Whatever you order, expect it to be healthy. We noted during research that a number of local young women were drooling over the desserts, especially the chocolate pancake stack.

Tokushima Ramen Men Ō　　RAMEN ¥
(徳島ラーメン麺王; Map p646; ☎ 088-623-4116; www.7-men.com; 3-6 Terashima-Honchō-higashi; dishes from ¥500; ⊗ 11am-midnight; 🖥) There are about 20 seats in this Tokushima classic only a couple of minutes' walk from the station. Right outside the front door is a machine with the menu and photos of each dish – pick what looks good, put the appropriate amount of money in and pass over your ticket once inside. Look for the red awning and lantern.

Sawaragi　　　　JAPANESE ¥¥
(さわらぎ; Map p646; ☎ 088-625-2431; 5-3 Ichiban-chō; lunches ¥980; ⊗ 11.30am-2pm & 5-10pm) Its beige facade looks unremarkable, and its atmosphere unassuming, but the traditional Japanese dishes served at this family-run

restaurant are beautifully prepared. Choose from three dinner courses (¥1650 to ¥5500, according to how hungry you are), which feature a variety of seasonal dishes.

⭐ **Izakaya Ikiiki**　　　　IZAKAYA
(活気; Map p646; ☎ 088-635-7130; 1-2-5 Minami-jōsanjima-chō; plates from ¥400; ⊗ noon-2.30pm & 5pm-2am Mon-Sat, to midnight Sun) This slick little *izakaya* is well worth the adventure of having to battle no-English menus. Just past the northeast corner of the park, Ikiiki has friendly, helpful staff, fresh seafood, and best of all, tasting trays of Tokushima-made sake – two different *nomi-kurabe* (compare the taste) trays with three varieties per tray for ¥900 each.

Ingrid's International Lounge　　KARAOKE
(Map p646; ☎ 088-626-0067; https://ingrids international.wordpress.com; 2-7-1 Sakaemachi; ⊗ 6pm-late) Filipina Ingrid is Tokushima's go-to girl for expat gossip and all-night karaoke. The lounge is hard to find, tucked among the hostess clubs in the southwest of Akita-machi, but there's nothing duplicitous about this Tokushima travellers' institution. Head here for live music, karaoke or whatever else is on.

❶ Information

Tourist Information Office (徳島総合観光案内所; Map p646; ☎ 088-622-8556; ⊗ 9am-7pm) In a booth on the plaza outside the station.

Tokushima Prefecture International Exchange Association (徳島県国際交流協会; TOPIA; Map p646; ☎ 088-656-3303; www.topia.ne.jp; 6th fl, Clement Plaza, 1-61 Terashima Honchō-nishi; ⊗ 10am-6pm) On the 6th floor of the Clement Plaza Building, directly above the station, this efficient office has friendly English-speaking staff and is a mine of information for Tokushima Prefecture.

❶ Getting There & Away

AIR

Tokushima Awaodori Airport (徳島阿波おどり空港; ☎ 088-699-2831; www.tokushima-airport. co.jp/en) has flights connecting the prefecture to Tokyo, Fukuoka and Sapporo.

Buses (¥440; 30 minutes) depart from bus stop 1 in front of the station and are timed to coincide with flights.

BOAT

Nankai Ferry (南海フェリー; ☎ 088-636-0750; www.nankai-ferry.co.jp; 5-7-39 Minami-Okinosu) runs daily connections between Tokushima and Wakayama (two hours, six daily).

Ocean Tōkyū Ferry (オーシャン東九フェリー; ☑ 088-662-0489; www.otf.jp; 2-62-2 Higashi-Okinosu; ◷ 9am-5pm) departs once daily to/from Tokyo/Tokushima/Kita-Kyūshū (18 hours to Tokyo, 15 hours to Kita-Kyūshū).

BUS

Highway buses connect Tokushima with Tokyo (nine hours), Nagoya (five hours) and Kyoto (three hours); there are also buses to Osaka (2½ hours) and Kansai airport (2¾ hours). They leave from the **bus terminal** (Map p646) outside the train station.

TRAIN

Tokushima is just over an hour by train from Takamatsu (¥3160 by *tokkyū* – limited express). For the Iya Valley and Kōchi, change trains at Awa-Ikeda (阿波池田; ¥3340, 1¼ hours).

ⓘ Getting Around

To get to Bunka-no-mori-kōen catch a bus (¥210, 20 minutes) from bus stop 3 on the middle island at the Tokushima bus terminal.

Rental bicycles (貸し自転車; Map p646; ☑ 088-652-6661; per half/full day ¥270/450, deposit ¥3000; ◷ 9am-5pm) are available from the underground bike park to the left as you leave the station.

Electric-assist bicycles (ぐるとくサイクル; Map p646; ☑ 088-655-6133; per hour/day/

week ¥100/500/2500; ◷ 9am-7.30pm) are available just opposite the station, down the escalator at SOGO.

Naruto

POP 60,000

Naruto, a sprawling township in the northeast corner of Shikoku, is known all over Japan for whirlpools in the sea underneath **Ōnaruto Bridge** (大鳴門橋), the impressive structure that connects Shikoku with Awaji Island. There's a viewing platform, **Uzu-no-michi** (渦の道; ☑ 088-683-6262; www.uzunomichi.jp; 772-0053 Naruto Park; ¥510; ◷ 9am-6pm, to 5pm Oct-Feb), under the bridge. **Sightseeing boats** (鳴門観光汽船; Naruto Kankō Kisen; ☑ 088-687-0101; www.uzusio.com/en; 264-1 Oge, Tosadomariura; per person from ¥1800; ◷ every 20mins 9am-4.20pm) run out to the pools from the small port next to the Naruto Kankō-kō (鳴門観光港) bus stop. If you're making the effort to do this, check their website to find the best time to head out that particular day. The whirlpools are at their most impressive roughly every six hours.

Nearby you'll find the fascinating **Otsuka Museum of Art** (大塚国際美術館; ☑ 088-687-3737; www.o-museum.or.jp; Naruto Park; adult/child ¥3240/540; ◷ 9.30am-5pm Tue-Sun). One from the 'only in Japan file', this 'ceramic board masterpiece museum'

THE FIRST FIVE TEMPLES: RYŌZEN-JI TO JIZŌ-JI

Naruto is the starting point for Shikoku's 88 Temple pilgrimage. The first five temples are all within easy walking distance of each other, making it possible to get a taste of the *henro* (pilgrim) trail on a day trip from Tokushima.

Ryōzen-ji (霊山寺; ☑ 088-689-1111; www.88shikokuhenro.jp/tokushima/01ryozenji; 126 Bandō, Ōasa-chō) FREE is Temple 1 of the 88 Sacred Temples of Shikoku Pilgrimage. Historically, it was the first temple the pilgrims reached upon arriving on Shikoku by boat, having come from Kōya-san in Wakayama Prefecture to ask Kōbō Daishi for his support on their journey. For pilgrims, everything you need is here – from guidebooks (in English too!) to pilgrimwear to temple stamp books.

To get to Temple 1, take a local train from Tokushima to Bandō (板東; ¥260, 25 minutes). The temple is a 10- to 15-minute walk (about 700m) along the main road; the map at Bandō Station should point you in the right direction. From Ryōzen-ji it's a short walk along the main road from the first temple to the second, **Gokuraku-ji** (極楽寺), and another 2km from here to Temple 3, **Konsen-ji** (金泉寺). There are more-or-less regular signposts (in Japanese) pointing the way. Look for the signs by the roadside marked *henro-michi* (へんろ道 or 遍路道), often decorated with a red picture of a *henro* in silhouette. From here, it's about 5km along an increasingly rural path to Temple 4, **Dainichi-ji** (大日寺), and another 2km to Temple 5, **Jizō-ji** (地蔵寺), where there's an impressive **collection of statues** (¥200) of the 500 Rakan disciples of the Buddha. From the Rakan (羅漢) bus stop on the main road in front of the temple you can catch a bus to Itano Station (板野), where a train will take you back to Tokushima (¥360, 30 minutes).

88 Temples of Shikoku

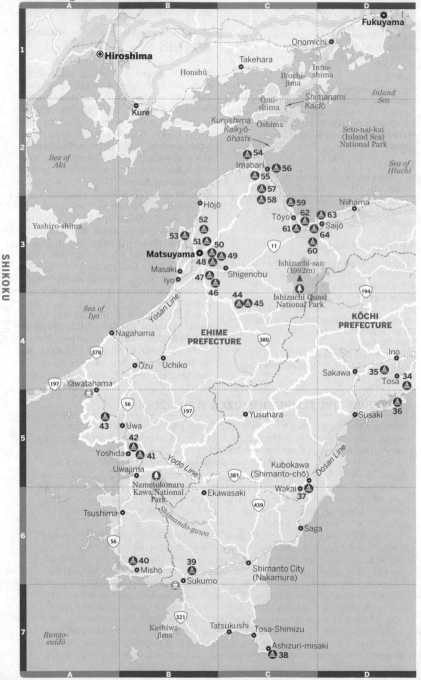

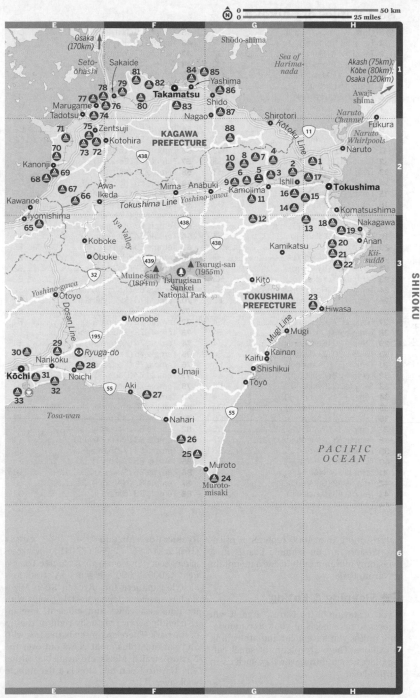

88 Temples of Shikoku

features more than 1000 replicas of priceless Western art on ceramic boards in a five-storey museum built inside a mountain at Naruto Park.

🛏 Sleeping & Eating

If you're staying in the Naruto area, it will be best to take meals at your accommodation, unless you have a car and are willing to explore. There are plenty of small eating places open during the day, such as in Naruto-kōen.

Ryokan Kōen Mizuno　　　　RYOKAN ¥
(旅館公園水野; ☑ 088-687-0411; www.koen-mizuno.com; Tosadomariura, Azafukuike 65; s/d from ¥8000/12,000; P ❄ ⓢ) A traditional-style Japanese inn, Ryokan Kōen Mizuno has spacious Japanese-style rooms with fabulous sea views and efficient, foreigner-friendly service virtually right at the tip of the park. There are onsen baths, free wi-fi and parking, plus great views out over the Naruto straits. Meals are available onsite. The Naruto Kōen bus stop is a five-minute walk away.

ℹ Getting There & Around

JR Naruto station is on the JR Naruto line, 40 minutes north from Tokushima (¥360). Naruto-kōen can be reached by bus from there in 20 minutes.

The Anan Coast 阿南海岸

The highway running south from Tokushima city along the Anan Coast passes through prosperous little agricultural towns fronted by lazy surf beaches. It is flanked by hidden temples and spectacular rocky bluffs. Enjoy the laid-back atmosphere and relaxed attitudes as you get to Surf City, Japan, occupying both sides of the Tokushima–Kōchi prefectural border.

Hiwasa 日和佐

📞 0884 / POP 5500

The main attraction in the small fishing town of Hiwasa is **Yakuō-ji** (薬王寺; 📞 0884-77-0023; http://yakuouji.net Japanese; 285-1 Teramae Okugawachi, Minami-chō) FREE, Temple 23 of the 88. Yakuō-ji dates back to the year 726, and is famous as a *yakuyoke-no-tera* (a temple with special powers to ward off ill fortune during unlucky years). The unluckiest age for men is 42; for women, 33 is the one to watch out for. Kōbō Daishi is said to have visited in 815, the year of his own 42nd birthday. The long set of stone steps leading up to the main temple building comes in two stages: 33 steps for the women, followed by another 42 for the men. The tradition is for pilgrims to put a coin on each step – when it's busy, you may find the steps practically overflowing with one-yen coins.

A *michi-no-eki* (rest stop), on the main road in the middle of town, not far from the entrance gates to Yakuō-ji, provides respite for road-weary pilgrims. In addition to the usual food stalls, immaculate restrooms and small market, this place also has a free footbath.

If you are interested in sea turtles, head out to attractive **Ōhama** (大浜) beach, known as a turtle egg-laying spot from May to August. The **Sea Turtle Museum Caretta** (うみがめ博物館カレッタ; 📞 0884-77-1110; http://caretta-hiwasa.com; 370-4 Hiwasa-ura; ¥600; ⏱ 9am-5pm Tue-Sun) here has a hatchery and baby turtle tanks.

Hiwasa is 54km south of Tokushima city on Route 55. Trains on the JR Mugi line from Tokushima take 1¼ hours (¥1090).

ℹ Getting There & Away

Hiwasa is 54km south of Tokushima city on Route 55. Trains on the JR Mugi line from Tokushima take 1¼ hours (¥1090).

Shishikui 宍喰

📞 0884 / POP 3500

Just north of the Tokushima–Kōchi prefectural border, Shishikui is becoming a hit with visitors, particularly those interested in surfing and other sea activities. Throw in an onsen, some seriously good little eateries and you've got a great place to stay for a couple of days.

🏃 Activities

Pavilion Surf School SURFING, SUP
(📞 0884-76-3277; www.kaorimayaguchi.com; 251-1 Matsubara Azaura; surfing/SUP lesson from ¥5400/6480) Based in Pavilion Surf's shop just east of Shishikui, Kaori Miyaguchi runs surfing and stand-up paddleboard lessons and tours with gear and wetsuits included. Her parents help run the place; the family lived in Honolulu for a number of years and speak English. Surfboard rentals cost ¥3240 per day. It's easy to spot, two doors east of 7-Eleven.

Shishikui Onsen ONSEN
(宍喰温泉; 📞 0884-76-3300; www.hotel-riviera.co.jp; 226-1 Aza Matsubara; adult/child ¥600/300; ⏱ 6.30-9am & 11am-10pm) On the upper floor of the Hotel Riviera complex on the main road in Shishikui, this onsen boasts that its natural water comes from 1000m below the ground. The main baths look out to the sea. There is also a restaurant and a shop onsite.

🛌 Sleeping & Eating

There are some cool little spots to eat in this relaxed surf town.

Pavilion Surf GUESTHOUSE ¥
(📞 0884-76-3277; www.pavilion-surf.com; 251-1 Matsubara Azaura; per person ¥3000; P ⊕ ❄ � 🛜) This place has only basic surfer accommodation, but all are welcome. Rooms are simple, with beds and nothing else; air-con is operated by coin. There are shared male and female bathroom facilities and kitchen in other buildings. That said, this is a great place for budget travellers. The friendly and enthusiastic owners speak English, having lived in Hawai'i.

It's next to the sea a bit north of Shishikui, two doors east of 7-Eleven.

WALKING THE 88 TEMPLE PILGRIMAGE

The *henro* (pilgrim on the 88 Temple walk) is one of the most distinctive sights of any trip to Shikoku. They're everywhere you go, striding along busy city highways, cresting hills in remote mountain valleys – solitary figures in white, trudging purposefully through heat haze and downpour alike on their way from temple to temple. Who are these people and what drives them to make a journey of more than 1400km on foot?

Although the backgrounds and motives of the *henro* may differ widely, they all follow in the legendary footsteps of Kōbō Daishi, the monk who attained enlightenment on Shikoku, established Shingon Buddhism in Japan and made significant contributions to Japanese culture. Whether or not it is true that Kōbō Daishi actually founded or visited all 88 sacred sites, the idea behind making the 88-temple circuit is to do so accompanied by the spirit of Kōbō Daishi himself – hence the inscription on pilgrims' backpacks and other paraphernalia: 同行二人 (*dōgyō ninin*), meaning 'two people on the same journey'.

Regardless of each *henro*'s motivations, the pattern and routine of life on the road is very similar for everyone who undertakes the trail. The dress is uniform, too: *hakue* (white garments) to signify sincerity of purpose and purity of mind; the *sugegasa* (straw hat) that has protected pilgrims against sun and rain since time immemorial; and the *kongōzue* (colourful staff). The routine at each temple is mostly the same, too: a bang on the bell and a chant of the Heart Sutra at the Daishi-dō (one of the two main buildings in each temple compound), before filing off to the *nōkyō-jo* (desk), where the pilgrims' book is inscribed with beautiful characters detailing the name of the temple and the date of the pilgrimage.

If you're eager to become an *aruki henro* (walking pilgrim) yourself, you'll need to budget 40 to 60 days (allowing for an average distance of 25km a day) to complete the circuit. To plan your pilgrimage, the website www.shikokuhenrotrail.com and the guidebook *Shikoku Japan 88 Route Guide* (Buyodo Publishing) are both excellent English-language resources. The book, plus all the *henro* gear you'll need for your walk, can be purchased at Temple 1: Ryōzen-ji (p649).

Travellers who don't have the time or inclination for the whole thing can get a taste of what it's all about by following one of the *henro*-for-a-day minicircuits. Aside from walking the first few temples at Naruto (p649), cities with concentrations of temples within easy reach of each other include Matsuyama (p669; Temples 46 through 53), and Zentsū-ji (p691) in Kagawa Prefecture.

If you're keen to do the pilgrimage, but walking doesn't appeal, take into account that most pilgrims these days travel around the 88 Temples on tour buses, in taxis, cars, on motorbikes and bicycles. It's making an effort that counts!

Pension Shishikui PENSION ¥¥
(ペンションししくい; ☑0884-76-2130; www. p-shishikui.com; 84-18 Akazome; per person incl meals from ¥9250; P ❄ @) Perfect for families or romantic getaways, charming Pension Shishikui occupies a snug cove with a private crescent of beach (protected by a seawall). All rooms, whether in the main house or freestanding log cabins, have ocean views and private bathrooms. The English-speaking owner rents surfboards, kayaks and bikes, and the property includes a tennis court and two communal baths.

Consult the map on the website for the location; it's on the first road just south of Shishikui Bridge.

★**Bahati** INTERNATIONAL ¥
(☑0884-76-2696; 222-1 Shishikui; mains from ¥800; ⏱11.30am-3pm & 6-9pm, from 5pm winter; 🅿) A superb little spot a tad east of Shishikui, Bahati is run by keen surfer Tsuji-san. Serving everything from pasta to *katsu-kareē* (pork cutlet, curry and rice), Bahati has surfboards on the rafters, surf photos on the walls, indoor and outdoor seating, plus a cool and relaxed vibe. If Bahati is late opening, it's because Tsuji is out surfing.

Cafe Hikōsen CAFE ¥
(ひこうせん; ☑0884-76-3488; 82-2 Shishikui-ura; ⏱8.30am-6pm; 🅿) This little roadside cafe is a locals' favourite, particularly for the impressive ¥540 Japanese/Western breakfast that will keep everyone satisfied. Expect

a warm friendly welcome, an English menu (and possibly a speaker), and some gorgeous pottery pieces.

ℹ️ Getting There & Away

Shishikui is 2½ hours (¥1880) from JR Tokushima station by train. If coming from Kōchi via Muroto-misaki, you'll have to use the bus. This is a good area to have your own wheels.

Ikumi 生見

📞 0887 / POP 800

There's not much to Ikumi Beach, on the Kōchi side of the prefectural border with Tokushima. Basically, there is a lovely beach with waves that attract surfers from all over Japan, some good budget accommodation, a few eateries that won't break the bank, and a surf shop or two. That said, if you are into a relaxed day or two looking at a different side of Japan, Ikumi is a great place to hang out. Lie back on the beach and enjoy the sun, catch a few waves, soak in the sea, thumb through surf magazines and enjoy a cool beverage – or two!

🏃 Activities

Surf Shop More   SURFING, BODY-BOARDING

(📞 0887-29-3615; www.surfshopmore.com; 575-1 Ikumi) Head to Surf Shop More for all your surfing needs, be they surf lessons, rentals or shopping. Rentals run board-and-wetsuit/board-only ¥5000/3000; body-board and fins ¥3000. Surfing and body-boarding lessons last two hours for ¥5000. The shop is located in the heart of the action at Ikumi Beach.

🛏️ Sleeping & Eating

Some great options here, though everything is fairly basic. Eat where you stay as there's not a lot open at night. The nearest convenience store is in Shishikui, about 10km away in Tokushima Prefecture.

South Shore   INN ¥

(サウスショア; 📞 0887-29-3211; www.southshore-ikumi.com; 12-10 Ikumi; per person incl/excl meals ¥7250/3800; 🅿️ ❄️ 🛜 ♨️) A sunny, simple inn with shared bathrooms, South Shore sits about a block from the beach in Ikumi and has a relaxed Hawaiian-esque vibe. The cute attached cafe and tiny pool area are convivial spots to hang out après-surf.

Minshuku Ikumi   MINSHUKU ¥

(民宿いくみ; 📞 0887-24-3838; www.ikumiten. com; 7-1 Ikumi; per person with breakfast ¥4100;

🅿️ 🛜) This cosy, family-run *minshuku* (guesthouse) sits right alongside the highway in Ikumi. It's a popular surfer's choice, thanks to the well-presented rooms and the helpful, knowledgable owner, Ten. Check out the website; he often has online specials.

★ Ikumi White Beach Hotel   HOTEL ¥¥

(生見ホワイトビーチホテル; 📞 0887-29-3018; www.wbhotel.net; 575-11 Ikumi; per person from ¥4200; 🅿️ ❄️) This clean, laid-back Ikumi beachfront hotel has Japanese- and Western-style rooms more or less right on the beach. Fall out the door and into the waves. You'll need to bring your own towels. Inexpensive restaurant **Olu-Olu** (オルオル; 📞 0887-29-3018; www.wbhotel.net; meals ¥800-1000; ⊙ 7am-2pm & 5-8pm) is part of the complex and open for breakfast, lunch and dinner. Plenty of parking.

Aunt Dinah   JAPANESE CURRY ¥

(アント・ダイナ; 📞 0887-29-2080; 24-107 Kawauchi, Tōyō-chō; meals ¥800-1500; ⊙ 10am-9pm Wed-Mon) Japanese country music and a range of curries are available at this old-timey spot near the main crossroad in Kannoura. House specialities include a filling Thai coconut curry for ¥1390.

ℹ️ Getting There & Away

Ikumi Beach is on Route 55, just on the Kōchi side of the border with Tokushima. It's about a one-hour drive northeast to Hiwasa and a one-hour drive southwest to Muroto-misaki. You'll want your own wheels (p694) to drop in here.

Muroto-misaki 室戸岬

📞 0887

Muroto-misaki is one of Shikoku's two great capes that jut out into the Pacific. In Japanese literature, Muroto is famed as one of the wildest spots in the nation and as the 'doorway to the land of the dead'. To pilgrims, it is the place where Kōbō Daishi achieved enlightenment and many come to try to do the same. On a calm day, the Pacific is like a millpond; in bad weather Muroto is pounded by huge waves and buffeted by the wind. Visitors can explore Kōbō Daishi's bathing hole among the rock pools, and the cave where he meditated. A *henro* trail leads up through bush to Temple 24, Hotsumisaki-ji, founded by Kōbō Daishi in the early 9th century.

Muroto is a designated Unesco Global Geopark, where sites and landscapes of international geological significance are managed with a holistic concept of protection, education and sustainable development.

◎ Sights

Muroto Unesco
Global Geopark Center   MUSEUM
(室戸ユネスコ世界ジオパーク; ☑0887-22-5161; www.muroto-geo.jp/en; 1810-2 Murotomisaki-cho) FREE The Muroto Geopark was designed to help create a better understanding about how local people have been dealing with ever-changing landforms. The area's geography is fascinating and it possesses a rich heritage of diverse geological formations. The park has walking, cycling and driving courses – head to the Geopark Center to learn more and obtain maps.

Temple 24: Hotsumisaki-ji   BUDDHIST TEMPLE
(最御崎寺; Higashi-dera; ☑0887-23-0024; www.88shikokuhenro.jp/kochi/24hotsumisakiji; 4058-1 Muroto-misaki-chō) FREE This gorgeous hilltop temple is considered one of the most important on the 88 Temple pilgrimage as it is at Muroto that Kōbō Daishi achieved enlightenment. Either walk up on the age-old *henro* trail that starts just northeast of the cape, or drive up the winding road a kilometre to the northwest of the cape. It's easy to feel the sacredness associated with the ancient buildings and statues.

🛏 Sleeping & Eating

If you're overnighting, eat where you stay. There are a few options if you have your own wheels, but you might be driving a while to find something open.

Temple 24:
Hotsumisaki-ji Shukubō   GUESTHOUSE ¥¥
(☑0887-23-0024; Hotsumisaki-ji; per person incl/excl meals ¥6500/4200; P◉❋) Run by Temple 24: Hotsumisaki-ji, this is a great opportunity to stay at a peaceful *shukubō* (pilgrim lodgings) with spotless tatami rooms or bedrooms and a communal bath, and to try traditional vegetarian pilgrim food. Temples on the pilgrimage have been catering to pilgrims for 1200 years and as well as providing a service, they make extra income this way.

Hoshino Resort
Utoco Auberge & Spa   BOUTIQUE HOTEL ¥¥¥
(星野リゾートウトコオーベルジュ＆スパ; ☑0887-22-1811, 050-3786-0022; www.utocods.co.jp; 6969-1 Muroto-misaki-chō; per person incl meals from ¥23,000; P❋🛜🏊) For something completely different, Hoshino Resort Utoco Auberge &

Spa is a remarkable concept hotel founded by the late cosmetics giant Uemura Shū. Pumping water from 1000m below the surface, the spa and resort aim to harness the restorative powers of mineral-rich deep-sea water.

❶ Getting There & Away

Several buses a day run northwest from the cape to Nahari or Aki, where you can change to the JR line for a train to Kōchi.

There are also buses up the northeast coast to Kannoura and Mugi, from where you can change for a train to Tokushima.

Train lines do not reach to the cape. A rental car is very useful here.

IYA VALLEY & AROUND

Venture into the heart of Shikoku for fantastic vistas and mountain hot springs, rafting and hiking opportunities and the chance to get away from it all and experience Japanese rural life in Chiiori (p658).

Iya Valley   祖谷渓

The spectacular Iya Valley is a special place: its staggeringly steep gorges and thick mountain forests lure travellers to seek respite from the hectic 'mainland' lifestyle. Winding your way around narrow cliff-hanging roads as the icy water of the Iya-gawa shoots along the ancient valley floor is a blissful travel experience. Top-notch onsen (hot springs) are well within reach, while evening entertainment is nothing more strenuous than sampling the local Iya soba (buckwheat noodles) and reliving your day's visual feast.

The earliest records of the valley describe a group of shamans fleeing from persecution in Nara in the 9th century. At the end of the 12th century, Iya famously became the last refuge for members of the vanquished Heike clan following their defeat at the hands of the Minamoto in the Gempei Wars. Their descendants are believed to live in the mountain villages to this day.

Despite its remoteness, there are some superb places to stay in the Iya Valley, including onsen hotels, *minshuku* (guesthouses) and even renovated farmhouses.

❶ Getting There & Away

This is one of those places where, if you're going to make the effort to get here, you'll want to have your own wheels (p694).

Iya Valley

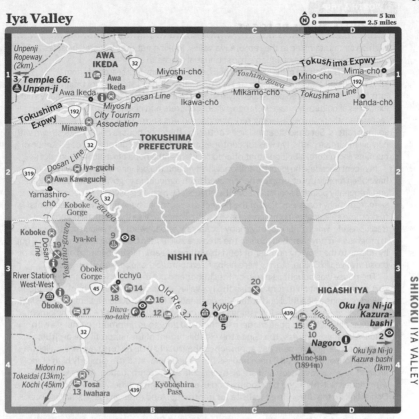

Iya Valley

Public transportation is extremely limited here, with only a few buses per day heading into the valley from Awa-Ikeda Bus Terminal near JR Awa-Ikeda Station. Gather information at the **Miyoshi City Tourism Association** (三好市観光協会; Map p657; ☎0883-76-0877; www.miyoshinavi.jp/english; 1810-18 Sarada, Ikeda-chō; ◷9am-6pm).

CHIIORI: A RURAL RETREAT

High on a mountainside in the remote Iya Valley, looking out over forested hillsides and plunging gorges, is one of Japan's most unusual places to stay.

Chiiori (The Cottage of the Flute; Map p657; www.chiiori.org; high season s/d from ¥34,000/36,000, lower for groups; P) is a once-abandoned 18th-century thatched-roof farmhouse that has been painstakingly restored to its original brilliance. Unlike many such examples of cultural heritage in Japan, where concrete and plastic have wrecked the architectural aesthetic, here glistening red-pine floorboards surround open-floor hearths under soaring rafters. Set amid steep hillsides dotted by thatched houses and forests strewn with narrow mountain paths, Iya was for centuries an example of an untouched coexistence of humans and nature, albeit one that offered residents little hope of wealth and comfort.

In recent decades the locals' traditional lifestyle and the balance with the environment have been rapidly upset; employment moved from agriculture to government-subsidised and frequently pointless construction, the effects of which – eg paved riverbeds – can be seen from many roadsides. Part of the project's mission has been to work with residents to promote sustainable, community-based tourism and realise the financial potential of traditional life, which until recently many locals saw as backward and valueless. It is a work in progress – many thatched roofs in the area are still hidden by corrugated tin sheets – but by adding to the growing number of tourists visiting the area largely because of the work of those involved in Chiiori, staying here helps to encourage those conservation efforts.

The house was bought as a ruin by the author and aesthete Alex Kerr in the early 1970s, and he went on to romanticise the Iya Valley in his award-winning book *Lost Japan*. Chiiori remains a beautiful and authentic destination for sensitive travellers, with its *shōji* (movable screens), antique furnishings and *irori* (traditional hearths) – all complemented by a gleaming, fully equipped modern kitchen and gorgeous bathroom, complete with *hinoki* (Japanese cypress) tub. Since the establishment of the nonprofit Chiiori Trust in 2005, the local government has approached the trust to help restore several smaller traditional houses in the area. These houses have been renovated to a similarly high standard and aesthetic as Chiiori and are also available as accommodation. All are outfitted with modern kitchens and bathrooms, and even washing machines. Follow the Higashi-Iya Ochiai link on the Chiiori Trust website for information and rates on these smaller houses.

To stay in these extraordinary environs, you must reserve in advance; payments must be made in cash. Because of the remote locations of Chiiori and the other houses, the Chiiori Trust strongly recommends that guests bring private vehicles. Hire a rental car and stock up with food at the supermarket before going, because it's very remote.

With your own wheels, the Iya Valley can be accessed from the west, on either Route 32 from Iya-guchi, where the Iya River joins the Yoshino River, or on Route 45 from Ōboke. Both are in the upper Yoshino River valley and both have stations on the JR Dosan line that runs between Takamatsu and Kōchi. The road from Iya-guchi would be the preferred option.

To get to the valley's eastern end (Higashii Iya), use Route 438 to Tsurugi-san from either Tsurugi town to the north or Tokushima city to the east – either way, prepare for a mountainous drive up to Mi-no-koshi (1420m) at the foot of Tsurugi-san and head of the Iya Valley.

Nishi Iya　西祖谷

Nishi-Iya (West Iya) is definitely the more accessible end of the Iya valley, and tour buses stream over Route 45 from Ōboke to fill the monstrous car and bus parking area that casts a huge shadow over **Kazura-bashi** (かずら橋; Map p657; ¥550; 8am-5pm), the vine bridge that people come from far and wide to see. The other attraction is the **Peeing Boy Statue** (小便小僧; Map p657), urinating into the valley far below (as local boys have supposedly been known to do).

For a most pleasurable visit, use old Route 32 from Iya-guchi, enjoy the cliff-hugging, winding road that requires plenty of concentration, and plan to overnight in the valley after the daytrippers have gone home. Nishi-Iya is nice, but we recommend heading east, further up the valley for a more remote and 'away from it all' Iya experience.

🏃 Activities

Iya Onsen
ONSEN

(祖谷温泉; Map p657; ☎0883-75-2311; www.
iyaonsen.co.jp; 367-2 Matsuo Matsumoto; ¥1500;
⊙day-use 7am-6pm) On Old Route 32, this
onsen is a great experience. At Hotel Iya Onsen, a cable car descends a steep cliff-face to
some sulphurous, open-air baths on the riverside. A fantastic place to slow down, enjoy
spectacular views of the forested gorge and,
of course, soak in the onsen, even if you're
not staying there.

🛏️ Sleeping & Eating

Kazura-bashi
Camping Village
CAMPGROUND ¥

(かずら橋キャンプ村; Map p657; ☎090-
1571-5258; campsite ¥1000, plus per person ¥200,
4-5-person bungalow ¥5350; ⊙Wed-Mon Apr-Nov)
This rustic but well-maintained campground
lies 500m upriver from the vine bridge.
Showers are free and rental equipment –
from tents to kitchenware – is available at
reasonable rates. If you don't speak Japanese, have a Japanese speaker call ahead
to reserve, as walk-ins can be problematic.
Check-in between 9am and 5pm.

★ Hotel Iya Onsen
HOTEL ¥¥¥

(ホテル祖谷温泉; Map p657; ☎883-75-2311;
www.iyaonsen.co.jp/english; 367-28 Matsuo Matsumoto, Ikeda-cho; per person incl 2 meals from
¥19,590; P❄🌐) If you've got the funds, this is
the place to stay. Extremely foreigner-friendly
with a multi-language website, a mix of tatami and Western-style rooms, spectacular
meals in a restaurant overlooking the gorge,
plus onsen baths at hotel level and *rotemburo*
(outside baths) down almost at river level that
are reached by a cable car (free for guests).

Hotel Kazura-bashi
RYOKAN ¥¥¥

(ホテルかずら橋; Map p657; ☎0883-87-2171;
www.kazurabashi.co.jp; 33-1 Zentoku; per person incl
2 meals from ¥15,900; P❄🌐) This lovely hotel not far from Kazura-bashi offers spacious,
comfortable Japanese-style rooms with
mountain views. Beautifully prepared traditional meals are served by attentive staff. A
funky cable car ferries guests up to the hotel's highlight: a gorgeous, open-air onsen on
the hill. Non-guests are welcome to use the
onsen (¥1200) between 10am to 4pm.

Iya Bijin
SOBA ¥

(祖谷美人; Map p657; ☎0883-87-2009; www.
iyabijin.jp; 9-3 Zentoku; meals ¥700-3700; ⊙8am-
5pm; 🍴) For a taste of local Iya soba, try Iya
Bijin, in an attractive black-and-white building with lanterns hanging out the front,
overlooking the gorge. Try a simple plate of
zaru soba (cold noodles with dipping sauce),
or a lunch set that includes local dishes such
as *dekomawashi* (grilled skewers of taro,
tofu and *konnyaku* – devil's tongue), boar
and wild vegetables.

Higashi Iya
東祖谷

Also known as Oku-Iya, meaning 'deep Iya',
Higashi-Iya (East Iya) is the area to go to for
an extremely remote Shikoku experience.
The valley narrows, the road climbs and
craggy mountains encroach from both sides.
The spectacular Kazura-bashi here are an absolute pleasure to visit, with minimal visitors
getting this far, and the 'scarecrow village' of
Nagoro is an enthralling eye-opener. Few get
this far as Route 439 is narrow, windy and
requires great care – don't become a road
statistic! If you carry on up to the head of
the valley, you'll be at the foot of Tsurugi-san,
Shikoku's second-highest peak.

👁️ Sights & Activities

★ Oku Iya Ni-jū Kazura-bashi
BRIDGE

(奥祖谷二重かずら橋; Map p657; ¥550; ⊙7am-
5pm) Away from the crowds and tour buses,
the spectacular Oku Iya Ni-jū Kazura-bashi
are two secluded vine bridges hanging side
by side high over the river. Cross one and
come back over the other. A self-propelled,
two-seated wooden cable-cart is another fun
way to cross the river; there's a small public
camping area on the other side. There are
also a couple of spots to get down to the river and enjoy the serenity.

★ Nagoro
PUBLIC ART

(名頃かかしの里; Nagoro Scarecrow Village; Map
p657) If you're travelling along Route 439,
it's not a matter of 'blink and you'll miss it,'
but blink, and blink again, because you may
have a hard time believing your eyes when
you hit Nagoro. Those 'people' – waiting at
the bus stop, gossiping on a porch, toiling in
the fields – are not people at all, but life-sized
scarecrow-type dolls made by resident Ayano
Tsukimi as a way of memorialising former
inhabitants of her hometown. Nagoro is
12km west of Oku Iya Ni-jū Kazura-bashi.

The figures are surprisingly lifelike from
afar and strikingly expressive up close, their
postures and faces each uniquely individual. Equal parts eerie and sweet, the dolls

of Nagoro create a surreal tableau amid the quiet river valley. For a look into the village, check out the beautiful short film *Valley of Dolls* (http://vimeo.com/92453765), created by German filmmaker Fritz Schumann who visited with Ayano-san.

Buke Yashiki
HISTORIC BUILDING

(武家屋敷喜多家; Map p657; ☑ 0883-88-2040; ¥300; ☺ 9am-5pm, closed Tue & Dec-Mar) Several kilometres up a narrow, winding road near Kyōjō, Buke Yashiki is a thatched-roof samurai-house museum commanding spectacular views of the valley. Beside the house is a Shintō shrine that is home to a massive cedar tree dating back more than 800 years.

Higashi Iya History & Folk Museum
MUSEUM

(東祖谷歴史民俗資料館; Map p657; ☑ 0883-88-2286; 14-3 Kyōjō; ¥410; ☺ 8.30am-5pm) This folk museum is in a large red building in Kyōjō, displaying historic artefacts and daily-use tools, as well as items relating to the Heike legend.

Oku-Iya Monorail
RAIL

(奥祖谷モノレール; Map p657; ☑ 0883-88-2975; adult/child ¥2000/1000; ☺ 8.30am-4pm) At Iyashi no Onsen-kyō, this is a cutesy little monorail with two-seater cars that slowly move passengers along a 4.6km

---

DON'T MISS

IYA'S VINE BRIDGES

The wisteria vine bridges (*kazura-bashi*) of the Iya Valley are glorious remnants of a remote and timeless Japan. Crossing the bridges has for centuries been notoriously difficult, which well suited the bandits and humbled warriors who took refuge in the secluded gorges. The bridges are feats of ancient engineering, undertaken roughly a thousand years ago, and were formed by tying together the wild vines that hung on either side of the narrow valley. Only in recent years have the bridges been reinforced with side rails, planks and wire.

Only three *kazura-bashi* survive, one heavily touristed bridge at **Nishi Iya** (p658) and another pair of 'husband and wife' bridges at **Higashi Iya** (p659), which is a further 30km east – the secluded, deep gorge setting is worth the extra effort.

---

course through the mostly untouched forest. Surprisingly, it also climbs nearly 600m in height and takes passengers up to 1400m on a loop track to see different vegetation. The gentle ride takes 70 minutes.

🛏 Sleeping & Eating

Iyashi no Onsen-kyō
HOTEL ¥¥¥

(いやしの温泉郷; Map p657; ☑ 0883-88-2975; http://iyashino-onsenkyo.com; 28 Sugeoi, Higashi Iya; per person incl meals from ¥14,000; ☺ onsen 10am-9pm; P ⊕ ✳ �🛜) Off the main road between Kyōjō and the Higashi Iya vine bridges is this lovely and unpretentious hotel and hot-springs complex, with Japanese- and Western-style rooms, an onsen and a restaurant. A smattering of Japanese-language skills would be helpful here. Nonguests can eat at the attractive restaurant. They also run an intriguing 4.6km monorail up into the mountains.

Soba Dōjō
SOBA ¥

(そば道場; Map p657; ☑ 0883-88-2577; zaru soba ¥800; ☺ 11am-5pm Fri-Wed) At Soba Dōjō on Route 439, you can sample a bowl of *zaru soba* (cold noodles with dipping sauce) and even make your own (¥2500; reservations required). The restaurant has a rusty reddish roof, and a brown curtain hanging over the door. If you're driving, you'll pass within a metre or two of the front door.

Ōboke & Koboke
大歩危・小歩危

Ōboke and Koboke are scenic gorges on the Yoshino-gawa, which fluctuates from languid green waters to Class IV rapids. These are the upper reaches of the same Yoshino River that flows out into the Pacific Ocean near Tokushima city. The area has become a bit of a mecca for outdoors tourism.

Stop by for tourist information, river gear at the Mont Bell shop, and road snacks at the *konbini* (convenience store). Also on hand are excellent Iya soba at the restaurant Momiji-tei and various noodle options at Tokushima Ramen. Unfortunately, it all closes down, except the convenience store, at 5pm.

As well as small tourist boats that ply the quieter waters of the river, there's excellent white-water rafting and canyoning on offer. With plenty of outdoor action, there's a revitalised vibe going on in this remote part of mountainous Shikoku.

◉ Sights & Activities

Lapis Ōboke   MUSEUM
(ラピス大歩危; Map p657; ☑0883-84-1489; 1553-1 Kamimyo; ¥500; ⊙9am-6pm Apr-Nov, to 5pm Dec-Mar) Lapis Ōboke is a geology and local *yōkai* (ghost) museum – interesting rocks, but the reason to stop is to get acquainted with the folkloric apparitions, colourfully represented in a hall of delightful horrors (explained with some English signage).

Happy Raft   RAFTING
(ハッピーラフト; Map p657; ☑0887-75-0500; www.happyraft.com; 221-1 Ikadagi) Around 20 companies run white-water rafting and kayaking trips from mid-March to mid-October. Happy Raft, steps from JR Tosa Iwahara Station, operates sensational rafting trips and canyoning adventures (¥9000) with English-speaking guides (half day ¥5500 to ¥7500, full day ¥10,000 to ¥15,500).

🛏 Sleeping & Eating

Plenty of options in and around the valley, as well as over the hill in the Iya Valley.

Order meals where you are staying. There are eating-out options during the day.

Awa Ikeda Youth Hostel   HOSTEL ¥
(阿波池田ユースホステル; Map p657; ☑0883-72-5277; http://awaikeda-yh.com; 3798 Sako, Nishiyama; dm ¥3900, breakfast/dinner ¥540/1080; ℙ) This isolated hostel with huge communal tatami rooms is run alongside Mitsugon-ji mountain temple high above Awa-Ikeda. Make sure you book ahead if you need to be picked up at JR Awa-Ikeda Station, 5km away, and if you require meals. A good opportunity to stay at a mountain temple.

Ku-Nel-Asob   GUESTHOUSE ¥¥
(空音遊; Map p657; ☑090-9778-7133; www.k-n-a.com; 442 Enoki; per person with dinner/breakfast & dinner ¥9720/10,800; ℙ🛜) Four simple, attractive tatami rooms are available in this near-century-old house, perched on a beautiful bluff overlooking the river. Meals are vegan and served family-style. Since the house doesn't have a bath, the friendly English-speaking owners provide transfers and entry to a local onsen. Reservations must be made at least three days in advance; it's advisable to reserve earlier if you can.

The owners also offer free pick-ups/drop-offs at JR Ōboke Station, 3km away.

Happy Guest House   GUESTHOUSE ¥
(Map p657; ☑0887-75-0500; www.happyraft.com; per person ¥3500; ℙ) Run by the local outfit Happy Raft, these five small guesthouses can each accommodate up to 10 and all come with a kitchen. The original guesthouse is a self-contained and fully restored farmhouse, with a tatami room overlooking the Yoshino Valley. The guesthouses are scattered around the valley – check out the website for details.

★ Iya-soba Momiji-tei   SOBA ¥
(祖谷そば　もみじ亭; Map p657; ☑0883-84-1117; meals ¥900-2000; ⊙10am-5pm Thu-Tue) At the West-West centre, Momiji-tei offers a good opportunity to try Iya soba. It's the lovely old building in the garden at the northern end of the complex. Try the tempura soba set (¥1450), either hot or cold.

ℹ Information

Ōboke Station Tourist Information Office (大歩危駅観光内所; Map p657; ☑0883-76-0877; www.miyoshinavi.jp/english; ⊙8.30am-3.30pm Mon, Tue, Thu & Fri, to 5.30pm Sat & Sun) This extremely efficient office with English-speaking staff on hand and tons of brochures and maps can be found in tiny Ōboke station. Staff can help with organising your trip over the hill and into the Iya Valley.

River Station West-West Information (Map p657; ☑0887-84-1117; www.west-west.com) Information from the River Station West-West tourist complex.

ℹ Getting There & Away

Both JR Ōboke and JR Koboke are stations on the JR Dosan line that connects Takamatsu with Kōchi. JR Ōboke is closer to Kōchi (50 minutes, ¥2980) than to Takamatsu (1½ hours, ¥3510).

You'll be able to do what you want if you arrive by train, but it's much easier to get around mountainous central Shikoku with your own wheels.

Tsurugi-san   剣山

At 1955m, Tsurugi-san is the second-highest mountain in Shikoku and one of Japan's 100 Famous Mountains. Unlike the sharp-edged peak of Shikoku's highest mountain, Ishizuchi-san to the west, which is said to represent a strict father, the summit of Tsurugi-san is gently rounded and frequently likened to a gentle mother.

The summit plain is known as Heike-no-baba and is said to have served as the 12th-century training field for military horses of local Heike warriors. When the Heike clan succumbed to the rival Genji warriors at the Battle of Dan-noura in 1185, legend tells they buried their emperor's sword at the peak of Tsurugi-san; hence the mountain's nickname of *Ken-zan* (sword peak).

🏃 Activities

A **chairlift** (剣山観光登山リフト; ☑0883-62-2772; www.turugirift.com; Mi-no-koshi; return/one way ¥1860/1030; ⏰9am-5pm, last return 4:45pm; mid-Apr–late-Nov) goes most of the way up from the carpark at Mi-no-koshi, after which it is a leisurely 40-minute climb to the top. There are great views from the rounded summit. You can continue on to **Jirōgyū** (1929m) on an easily identifiable trail. Allow 1½ hours for the return hike. There are trails all over these mountains and with careful planning, you can organise a three-day hike from Tsurugi-san west to **Miune-san** (1894m) and a descent into **Kubo** in Higashi Iya.

🛏 Sleeping

Tabi-no-yado Kiri-no-mine MINSHUKU ¥
(旅の宿霧の峰; ☑0883-67-5211; www.kirinomine.jp; Mi-no-koshi; r per person incl/excl 2 meals ¥7000/4000; 🅿) This one-stop shop in the carpark at Mi-no-koshi has the bases covered, with a restaurant, gift shop and *minshuku*, all within a minute's walk of the chairlift station. Rooms are small and facilities shared, but there is a bath for tired hikers and laundry facilities that guests can use.

Tsurugi-san Chōjō Hutte HUT ¥
(剣山頂上ヒュッテ; ☑088-622-0633; http://tsurugisan-hutte.com; Tsurugi-san; incl/excl meals ¥8000/4800) Just below the peak, Tsurugi-san Chōjō Hutte offers basic lodgings. It's fairly simple stuff, as you'd expect at a mountain hut, but the food tastes great at 1955m, the bath is claimed to be the highest *ofuro* in western Japan and you'll sleep well as 'lights out' is at 9pm. Best of all, it's not far to go for a mountaintop sunrise.

ℹ Getting There & Away

The best way to explore the region around Tsurugi-san is with your own wheels (p694); you will thank the Daishi for the freedom and flexibility a car offers here.

Tsurugi-san is at the head of the Iya Valley, so if you've been exploring Iya, carry on up Route 439 to Mi-no-koshi. Alternatively, head up the fascinating Route 438 from the main Yoshino Valley to the north at Sadamitsu. For a long, mountainous approach, take Route 438 from Tokushima city to the east.

It is possible to get to Mi-no-koshi by bus, but it's not easy. Check for the latest at a tourist information office.

KŌCHI & AROUND 高知県

The largest of Shikoku's four prefectures, Kōchi Prefecture spans the Pacific coastline between the two capes of Muroto-misaki and Ashizuri-misaki. Cut off from the rest of Japan by the mountains and sea, the province once known as Tosa was traditionally regarded as one of the wildest and most remote places in the country. To pilgrims, Kōchi is known as Shūgyō-no-dōjō, the place of practice, and has a reputation as 'the testing ground'. Although the trip through Tosa makes up more than a third of the pilgrimage, only 16 of the 88 Temples are located in the province. In fact, it's 84km from the last temple in Tokushima Prefecture at Hiwasa before you get to the first temple in Kōchi Prefecture at Muroto-misaki.

Kōchi Prefecture is a good place for outdoor types; it brims with scenic spots both in and along its rugged mountains and coastlines. Check out http://visitkochijapan.com.

Kōchi 高知

☑0888 / POP 343,000

Kōchi is a smart, compact city with a deserved reputation for enjoying a good time. The castle here is largely undamaged and remains a fine example of Japanese architecture. Excellent access to Muroto-misaki, Ashizuri-misaki and the Iya Valley, and easy day trips to caves, beaches and mountains make Kōchi a perfect base for travels around the island. Also claimed by Kōchi is a samurai of great national significance – during the Meiji Restoration, Sakamoto Ryōma was instrumental in bringing down the feudal government.

The central part of the city is 12km north and inland from the sea and the liveliest part of town is where the tramlines cross near Harimaya-bashi, a tiny red replica of a bridge made famous by song and film in Japan. The main Obiyamachi shopping arcade runs perpendicular to Harimayabashi-dōri. This action is about 1km south of JR Kōchi station.

SHIKOKU KŌCHI

⊙ Sights

★ Kōchi-jō
CASTLE

(高知城; Map p664; 1-2-1 Marunouchi; ¥420; ⊙9am-5pm) Kōchi-jō is one of just a dozen castles in Japan to have survived with its original *tenshu-kaku* (keep) intact. The castle was originally built during the first decade of the 17th century by Yamanouchi Katsutoyo, who was appointed *daimyō* by Tokugawa Ieyasu after he fought on the victorious Tokugawa side in the Battle of Sekigahara in 1600. A major fire destroyed much of the original structure in 1727; the castle was largely rebuilt between 1748 and 1753.

The castle was the product of an age of peace – it never came under attack and for the remainder of the Tokugawa period it was more like a stately home than a military fortress. The fee is for entry to the castle itself; it's free to walk in the surrounding grounds.

★ Sunday Market
MARKET

(日曜市; Map p664; ⊙5am-6pm Sun Apr-Sep, 5.30am-5pm Sun Oct-Mar) Our favourite street market in Shikoku is 300 years old and takes place every Sunday along 1.3km of Ōtc-suji, the main road leading to the castle. Around 430 colourful stalls sell fresh produce, tonics and tinctures, knives, flowers, garden stones, wooden antiques and everything imaginable.

Godaisan
PARK

(五台山) Several kilometres east of the town centre is the mountain of Godaisan, where you can enjoy excellent views of the city from a **lookout point** (展望台). Near the top of the hill is Chikurin-ji (p663), Temple 31 of the 88. By the temple's entrance gates is the **Kōchi Prefectural Makino Botanical Garden** (高知県立牧野植物園; ☑088-882-2601; www.makino.or.jp; 4200-6 Godaisan; ¥720; ⊙9am-5pm), a beautiful network of gardens and parkland. Kōchi's My-Yū tourist bus stops at Godaisan.

Temple 31: Chikurin-ji
BUDDHIST TEMPLE

(竹林寺; ☑088-882-3085; www.chikurinji.com; 3577 Godaisan) FREE At Godaisan in the east of the city, you'll find Chikurin-ji is Temple 31 of the 88. The extensive grounds feature a five-storey **pagoda** and thousands of statues of the Bodhisattva Jizō, guardian deity of children and travellers. The temple's **Treasure House** (¥400) hosts an impressive collection of Buddhist sculpture from the Heian and Kamakura periods; the same ticket gets you into the temple's lovely Kamakura-period **garden** opposite.

WORTH A TRIP

TEMPLE 21: TAIRYŪ-JI

For 1200 years, *henro* have struggled up steep mountain paths to get to the magnificent mountaintop temple, **Tairyū-ji** (太龍寺; ☑0884-62-2021; www.88shikokuhenro.jp/tokushima/21tairyuji; 2 Ryūzan Kamo-chō, Anan-shi) FREE. A 2.7km-long **ropeway** (太龍寺ロープウェイ; ☑0884-62-3100; www.shiko-ku-cable.co.jp/tairyuji/index.htm; 76 Tano, Naka-chō; one way/return ¥1300/2470; ⊙7.20am-5pm), the longest in western Japan, makes easy work of the ascent, giving one and all the opportunity to visit this atmospheric haven. It's worth the effort to get here. Views are magnificent. Getting to the rural ropeway base will be a lot easier with your own wheels, but you can also get here by bus from Tokushima Station in 1½ hours. There's a museum, restaurant and place to stay at the bottom of the ropeway. Make sure to take your passport as there is often a half-price discount to foreign visitors.

Ino Japanese Paper Museum
MUSEUM

(いの町紙の博物館; ☑088-893-0886; http://kamihaku.com/en; 110-1 Saiwai-chō, Ino-chō; ¥500; ⊙9am-5pm Tue-Sun) Discover the history and development of *washi* (Japanese paper) at Ino, about 10km west of downtown Kōchi. There are demonstrations of *nagashizuki* papermaking techniques, and on the first Sunday of each month there's a class (¥400). Check out the excellent English website for details. The museum is a 10-minute walk from both the Ino JR and tram stations.

Katsura-hama
BEACH

(桂浜) Katsura-hama is a popular beach 12km south of central Kōchi at the point where Kōchi's harbour empties out into the bay. Strong currents prohibit swimming, but it's a lovely spot to stroll, with a small **shrine** perched on an oceanside promontory. Just before the beach itself is **Sakamoto Ryōma Memorial Museum** (坂本龍馬記念館; ☑088-841-0001; www.ryoma-kinenkan.jp; 830 Urado-shiroyama; ¥500; ⊙9am-5pm), with exhibits dedicated to the life of a local hero who was instrumental in bringing about the Meiji Restoration in the 1860s.

SHIKOKU KŌCHI

Kōchi

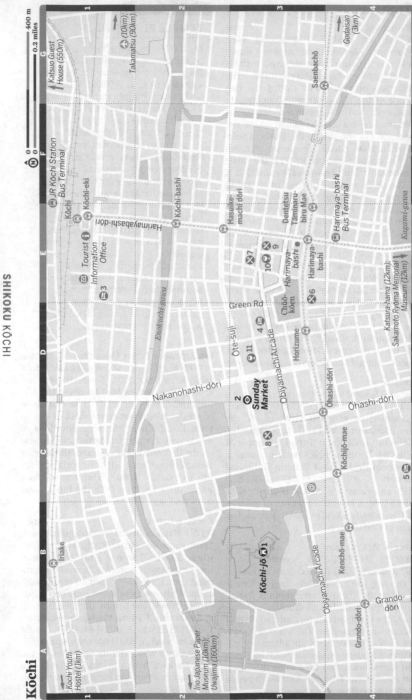

0 0
0 0.2 miles
400 m

Katsuo Guest House (550m)

↑ (10km); Takamatsu (90km)

Godaisan (3km)

Saenbachō

JR Kōchi Station Bus Terminal

Kōchi
Kōchi-eki

Tourist Information Office

Harimayabashi-dōri

Kōchi-bashi

Hasuike-machi-dōri

Dentetsu Taminaru-biru Mae

Harimaya-bashi Bus Terminal

Kagami-gawa

Enokuchi-gawa

Green Rd

Ōte-suji

Chūō-kōen

Harimaya-bashi

Harimaya-bashi

Sunday Market

Obiyamachi Arcade

Horizume

Nakanohashi-dōri

Katsura-hama (12km); Sakamoto Ryōma Memorial Museum (12km)

Ōhashi-dōri

Ōhashi-dōri

Kōchijō-mae

Iriake

Kōchi-jō

Obiyamachi Arcade

Kenchō-mae

Grando-dōri

Grando-dōri

Kōchi Youth Hostel (1km)

Ino Japanese Paper Museum (10km); Uwajima (160km)

7
9
10
11
4
6
8
2
1
3
5

Kōchi

🎊 Festivals & Events

Yosakoi Matsuri   CULTURAL
(よさこい祭り; Yosakoi Festival) Kōchi's lively Yosakoi Matsuri on 10 and 11 August perfectly complements Tokushima's Awa-odori Matsuri (12 to 15 August). There's a night-before event on 9 August and a night-after effort on 12 August, but 10 and 11 August are the big days.

🛏 Sleeping

There are plenty of midrange hotel-type places around JR Kōchi station, Harimaya-bashi and towards the castle. You'll have to head a tad further afield for budget places though.

★ Kochi Youth Hostel   HOSTEL ¥
(高知ユースホステル; ☎088-823-0858; www.kyh-sakenokuni.com; 4-5 Fukuihigashi-machi; dm/s ¥2500/3000; P ⊜ ❄ @ ☎) Sitting along a canal near Engyōjiguchi (円行寺口) Station, this immaculate wood-panelled hostel has simple, comfortable rooms and a welcoming, homely vibe. Spring for the ¥400 breakfast, as it's excellent value. The friendly, English-speaking host Kondo Tomio is a former sake company rep and offers sake sampling courses for ¥500. Find detailed directions on the website in English.

★ Richmond Hotel   HOTEL ¥¥
(リッチモンドホテル高知; Map p664; ☎088-820-1122; http://kochi.richmondhotel.jp; 9-4 Obiyamachi; s/d from ¥6400/8500; P ⊜ ❄ @ ☎) Kōchi's most swish business hotel has the spotless, modern rooms and professional service expected for accommodation of this class, plus it's located just off the main shopping arcade in the heart of the city. Parking (¥700 per day) is a short distance offsite, but the hotel's convenient location puts you in the middle of dining, nightlife and city walkability.

Katsuo Guest House   GUESTHOUSE ¥¥
(かつおゲストハウス; ☎070-5352-1167; http://katuo-gh.com; 4-7-28 Hijima-chō; dm/s/d ¥2800/3800/7600; P ⊜ ☎) Good things come in small packages, as is the case with Katsuo Guest House. In a residential Kōchi neighborhood, this intimate spot (one dorm room and one private) is a haven for those yearning for impromptu jams on the house guitar or djembe, a DIY meal in the communal kitchen and artistic nods to local landmarks adorning the shared bathroom.

It's about a 10-minute walk north of Kōchi station.

Petit Hotel   BUSINESS HOTEL ¥¥
(プチホテル高知; Map p664; ☎088-826-8156; www.phk.jp; 1-8-13 Kitahon-machi; s/d from ¥7000/10,000; P ⊜ ❄ @ ☎) This excellent business hotel near Kōchi Station is an astute alternative to the larger chains. Service is efficient and friendly, and the rooms are reasonably spacious, particularly the sparkling-clean bathrooms. Good breakfast options onsite.

Sansuien   HOTEL ¥¥
(三翠園; Map p664; ☎088-822-0131; www.sansuien.co.jp; 1-3-35 Takajō-machi; r per person with breakfast from ¥7500; P ⊜ ❄ @) Three blocks south of the castle along Kenchō-mae Dōri is this classy multistorey hotel with luxurious onsen baths and a garden incorporating a series of buildings that once formed part of the residence of the *daimyō*. The Japanese tatami rooms far outweigh their Western counterparts for both size and comfort. Nonguests can use the baths from 10am to 4pm (¥900).

🍴 Eating & Drinking

Kōchi's main eating and entertainment district is in the area around the Obiyamachi Arcade and the Harimaya-bashi junction where the tramlines meet, about 1km south of JR Kōchi Station. Local specialities include *katsuo-tataki* (lightly seared bonito fish).

★ Hirome Ichiba   JAPANESE ¥
(ひろめ市場; Map p664; ☎088-822-5287; www.hirome.co.jp; 2-3-1 Obiyamachi; dishes from

¥300; ⊙8am-11pm, from 7am Sun; 🖃) Dozens of mini-restaurants and bars specialising in everything from *gomoku rāmen* (seafood noodles) to *tako-yaki* (octopus balls) surround communal tables; this is the hub of Kōchi's cheap-eats scene. On weekends, it positively heaves with young people drinking hard and happy. It's a full block of mayhem at the end of the main arcade, just before the castle.

Habotan
IZAKAYA ¥
(葉牡丹; Map p664; ☑088-872-1330; http://habotan.jp; 2-21 Sakai-machi; dishes ¥150-1100; ⊙11am-11pm) Red lanterns mark out this locals' *izakaya* opposite Chūō-kōen that opens at the shockingly early hour of 11am. The food is under glass on the counter, so you can point at what you'd like to order. *Sashimi moriawase* (a selection of sashimi) is ¥1050. Local booze includes Tosa-tsuru sake and Dabada Hiburi, a *shōchū* (distilled grain liquor) made from chestnuts.

Hakobe
OKONOMIYAKI ¥
(はこべ; Map p664; ☑088-823-0084; 1-2-5 Obiyamachi; dishes ¥650-1200; ⊙11am-midnight) This is one of the few remaining cook-it-yourself *okonomiyaki* (pancake) joints in Kōchi serving cheap and cheerful Japanese pancakes. The 'mix' of *ika* (squid), *ebi* (shrimp) and *tori* (chicken) is heavenly. Other alternatives include *buta* (pork) and *yasai* (vegetables). They bring it out and you cook it on the hotplate. It's slap bang in the heart of the arcade.

Tosa Ichiba
JAPANESE ¥¥
(土佐市場; Map p664; ☑088-872-0039; www7a.biglobe.ne.jp/~hayakawa_c/tosaichi.htm; 1-3-11 Harimayachō; set meals from ¥1100; ⊙11am-10.30pm) Just back from the start of Obiyamachi Arcade, this is a place to go to try local set meals, especially if you are struggling with Japanese menus. Just about the whole menu is displayed either outside or in the windows in plastic-model form. Pick what looks good and point it out to the friendly staff. Lots of seafood options.

★ Tosa-shu Baru
BAR
(土佐酒バル; Map p664; ☑088-823-2216; 1-9-5 Ōte-suji; ⊙6.30-11.30pm Tue-Sat, to 9.30pm Sun) Without doubt, this is *the* place to go to try Kōchi-made sake. Owner Kōji has a passion for sake and has offerings from all 18 breweries in Kōchi, three daily-changing *nomi-kurabe* (tasting sets), superb small dishes featuring local produce, and an extremely convivial atmosphere. He is a fountain of knowledge on sake, has embraced a nonsmoking environment and plays great jazz.

Amontillado
PUB
(アモンティラード; Map p664; ☑088-875-0599; www.facebook.com/IrishpubAmo; 1-1-17 Obiyamachi; ⊙5pm-1am) When you're *izakaya*'d out and crave fish and chips with a pint of Guinness (¥900), pop into this Irish pub off Obiyamachi Arcade. There's always plenty going on.

EATING IN SHIKOKU

With its long coast and fertile valleys, Shikoku is a fantastic place to eat. In addition to regional specialities, don't miss the vegetarian *shōjin-ryōri* (精進料理; devotion cuisine) that is served to pilgrims at temple lodging houses.

Noodles

Kagawa Prefecture is known throughout Japan for Sanuki-udon, the local noodle dish, with square-shaped, thick, wheat-flour noodles. Tokushima city boasts over 100 shops offering 'Tokushima ramen', while the Iya Valley is known for its soba (buckwheat) noodles.

Seafood

With its long Pacific coastline, Kōchi Prefecture is known for its seafood, particularly *katsuo-tataki*, seared bonito fish that is thinly sliced and eaten with grated ginger. *Sawachi-ryōri* is a huge plate *(sawachi)* of seafood, with various varieties of both sashimi and sushi.

Jakoten, a fishcake made from blended fish paste and then fried, is popular throughout Ehime Prefecture. Uwajima in the south of Ehime is famous for its *tai-meshi*, a snapper and rice dish. In Kagawa Prefecture, *iriko-meshi* is a popular sardine and rice dish, while rice crackers are made from shrimp caught in the Inland Sea.

ℹ Information

Tourist Information Office (高知観光案内所; Map p664; ☎ 088-826-3337; http://visitkochijapan.com; ⏱ 8.30am-5pm, accommodation info to 7.30pm) The helpful tourist information pavilion out front at JR Kōchi Station provides English-language maps, Kōchi mini-guidebooks, accommodation help and more. There's always an enthusiastic English speaker on hand. Also free bicycles are available here from 8.30am-5pm, except on rainy days (bring ID).

Kōchi International Association (高知県国際交流協会; Map p664; ☎ 088-875-0022; www.kochi-kia.or.jp; 2nd fl, 4-1-37 Honmachi; ⏱ 8.30am-5.15pm Mon-Sat, closed Sat Aug) Free internet access, a library and English newspapers.

ℹ Getting There & Away

AIR

Kōchi Ryōma Airport (www.kochiap.co.jp), about 10km east of the city, is accessible by bus (¥720, 40 minutes) from the station. There are daily flights to/from Tokyo, Nagoya, Osaka and Fukuoka.

BUS

The **JR Kōchi Station Bus Terminal** (Map p664) is on the north side of Kōchi Station.

TRAIN

Kōchi is on the JR Dosan line, and is connected to Takamatsu (*tokkyū* ¥5100, 2¼ hours) via Awa-Ikeda (*tokkyū* ¥3340, 70 minutes). Trains also run west to Kubokawa (*tokkyū* ¥3160, 70 minutes), where you can change for Shimanto City (formerly known as Nakamura; *tokkyū* ¥4870, 1¾ hours from Kōchi).

ℹ Getting Around

BICYCLE

Free rental bicycles are available at the Tourist Information Office (p667), out front at JR Kōchi Station. They're available 8.30am to 5pm, except on rainy days (bring ID).

BUS

The **My-Yū bus** (MY遊バス; 1-/2-day pass ¥1000/1600) runs from Kōchi bus station to Godaisan to Katsura-hama and back. Purchase the pass at the tourist information office in front of Kōchi Station; show your foreign passport and you'll get the pass for half price.

Public buses to Katsura-hama leave from Harimaya-bashi Bus Terminal (Map p664).

TRAM

Kōchi's colourful tram service (¥200 per trip) has been running since 1904. There are two

---

OFF THE BEATEN TRACK

SHIMANTO-GAWA SCENIC DRIVE
•••••••••••••••••••••••••••••••••••

Little traffic and stunning scenery make Shikoku one of the best driving destinations in Japan. There's also a lack of regular public transport services in some areas, namely around the two southern capes and the Iya Valley, so your international licence can at last come in handy. Our favourite drive is along the banks of the Shimanto-gawa on Rte 381, which you can organise in Shimanto City (p667). Here you vie with the odd truck for single-lane access to some of the narrowest, bendiest, prettiest roads in the country, boxed in by rocky cliffs on one side and the shimmering Shimanto-gawa on the other. It feels like you're in a rally-driving video game where the animated cars just know how to avoid you.

---

lines: the north–south line from the station intersects with the east–west tram route at the Harimaya-bashi (はりまや橋) junction. Pay when you get off and ask for a *norikae-ken* (transfer ticket) if you have to change lines.

Shimanto City 四万十市

☎ 0880 / POP 37,000

Shimanto City, formerly called Nakamura, is easily confused with Shimanto town, further up the coast – don't worry, even locals get confused! Both Shimanto City and the town further north chose their name as the Shimanto-gawa is known throughout Japan for its beauty and as Japan's last remaining undammed river. Shimanto City claimed the name as this is where the river heads out to the sea. Shimanto town claimed the name as the river's headwaters are within its boundaries.

Shimanto City is a good place to organise trips on and around the beautiful Shimanto-gawa (四万十川) and the surrounding valley. The further up the river you go, the more remote and beautiful it all becomes.

Head to the **Shimanto City Tourist Association** (四万十市観光協会; ☎ 0880-35-4171; www.shimanto-kankou.com; 383-15 Uyama; ⏱ 8.30am-5.30pm) for info on the blossoming number of outdoor activities in the region such as kayaking, canoe trips, and camping.

A number of companies offer **river cruises** on boats called *yakata-bune* (¥2000 for

WORTH A TRIP

ŌKINOHAMA

About 25km south of Shimanto City on the road to Ashizuri-misaki, you'll find Ōkinohama (大岐の浜), Shikoku's most magnificent sandy beach. The only souls to frequent this unspoilt 2km stretch are the pick of the region's surfers, some egg-laying turtles and the odd, grinning clam diver. Facing east means you can watch the sun and moon rise from your beach towel, and warm currents ensure swimming is possible year-round.

For an intriguing contemporary retreat, try the **Kaiyu Inn** (海癒; ☑0880-82-8500; www. kaiyu-inn.jp; 2777-12 Ohki; s ¥7000-23,000, extra person ¥2500; P ⊜ ❋ 🛜 🐾) 🐾. Fluent-English-speaking owner Mitsu has redesigned a concrete 1960s edifice, originally built by his father. Each self-contained apartment has been designed either by Mitsu or a range of emerging Japanese architects. Coupled with Mitsu's keen aesthetic eye and extensive designer-furniture collection, the result are spaces worthy of magazine covers, each with Pacific Ocean views. The on-site, boiler-fired onsen is a simple daily luxury and communal meals are inventive, super-fresh and organic, featuring famed local clams, catch-of-the-day fish, and loads of fruit and vegetables. Meals must be reserved in advance for an additional fee. Many rooms have kitchens and long-stay guests are welcome.

Ōkinohama is on Route 321, about 25km south of Shimanto City (Nakamura) and 15km north of Ashizuri-misaki. To get to Kaiyu Inn, take the bus from Nakamura Station to Ashizuri-misaki and get off at Kaiyu-no-yu-mae (¥1100, 40 minutes).

50 minutes) and kayak rental (half-/full-day from ¥3500/5000).

Bike rental is available here too (per five hours/full-day ¥600/1000), along with information and maps for five suggested cycling routes. Mountain-bike hire is also available.

🛏 Sleeping & Eating

Kawarakko CAMPGROUND ¥
(かわらっこ; ☑0880-31-8400; www.kawarakko. com; campsite from ¥3300) About 12km inland and upriver on Route 441, this is a neatly maintained riverside campground run by an adventure company. Canoes, mountain bikes and even tents are available to hire should you fancy a spontaneous night under the stars.

★ Shimanto-no-yado Iyashi-no-sato SPA HOTEL ¥¥
(四万十の宿　いやしの里; ☑0880-33-1600; www.shimantonoyado.co.jp; 3370 Shimoda; per person from ¥7000; P ⊜ ❋ 🛜) Describing itself as a 'resort-type ecology hotel', this lovely spot out on a hill near Shimoda Port at the mouth of the Shimanto River features beautiful individually designed rooms, superb meals and an onsen that is also open to nonguests (¥680). Iyashi-no-sato is well worth the price; best if you have your own wheels to get here.

★ Sanzenkai JAPANESE ¥¥
(山川海; ☑0880-31-5811; www.shimantonoyado. co.jp; 3370 Shimoda; mains from ¥1500;

⊗11.30am-2pm & 5-9pm) The three kanji characters that make up this classy restaurant's name say it all – mountain, river, sea. Out at the spectacular Iyashi-no-sato eco-hotel, Sanzenkai uses locally sourced seasonal ingredients to tempt the palates of both hotel guests and visitors. If you're not staying here, get the tourist office to call ahead and make a booking. There's also an onsen.

ⓘ Getting There & Away

Shimanto City's station is called Nakamura, and it is 1¾ hours from Kōchi by the fastest train (¥4870). This is it in terms of heading south by train. To get to Ashizuri-misaki, you'll need to use a bus or your own wheels. From Nakamura, the Tosa-Kuroshio Sukumo Line does continue west, however, as far as Sukumo (30 minutes; ¥620).

It is possible to get to Uwajima in Ehime Prefecture by train and carry on around Shikoku. This will involve backtracking north from Nakamura to either Wakai station (若井駅) or Kubokawa station (窪川駅), then taking the JR Yodo Line (予土線) west through the mountains to Uwajima.

Ashizuri-misaki　足摺岬
☑0880

Ashizuri-misaki is a rugged, picturesque promontory that's famous for Kongōfuku-ji, Temple 38 of the 88, its lighthouse and violent weather.

Ashizukuri means 'foot stamping' and the cape got its name from the story of an old monk who stamped his foot in anguish when his young disciple set off looking for the promised land of Fudaraku in a boat. Fudaraku was believed to be the blessed realm of Kannon, goddess of mercy, and many set forth from the cape in their search for paradise in this lifetime, never to be heard from again. Centuries later, Ashizuri is famous for suicides, with stories such as that of a young geisha who danced off the edge onto the beckoning rocks below.

There are enjoyable short walks around the cape, including to an observation platform and the lighthouse.

⊙ Sights

★ **Temple 38: Kongōfuku-ji** BUDDHIST TEMPLE
(金剛福寺; ☑0880-88-0038; www.88shikoku henro.jp/kochi/38kongofukuji; 214-1 Ashizuri-misaki) **FREE** The grounds of Temple 38, set on dramatic Ashizuri-misaki, feel incredibly tropical and consist of a diverse array of small temples, statues, gardens and ponds. Walking pilgrims breathe a sigh of relief on arrival, as they have just survived the longest distance between temples, 94km from Iwamoto-ji in Kubokawa.

🛏 Sleeping & Eating

Eat where you stay as there are not a lot of eating options open in the evening.

Ashizuri Youth Hostel HOSTEL ¥
(足摺ユースホステル; ☑0880-88-0324; www.jyh.or.jp; 1351-3 Ashizuri-misaki; dm from ¥3780; ☎) This hostel is run by a cute older couple who have been providing large, well-cared-for tatami rooms to visitors for years. It's a friendly welcome. With advance notice meals are available – breakfast is ¥650, dinner is ¥1080. It's west of the temple.

Ashizuri Kokusai Hotel HOTEL ¥¥¥
(足摺国際ホテル; ☑0880-88-0201; www.ashizuri.co.jp; 662 Ashizuri-misaki; r per person incl meals from ¥11,500; P ❋) With spacious Japanese-style rooms and onsen baths overlooking the sea, this hotel is one of many located along the main road in town that mainly cater to groups.

❶ Getting There & Away

This is a place to have your own wheels (p694). Alternatively, there are buses to Ashizuri-misaki from Nakamura station (¥1900, 1½ hours).

EHIME PREFECTURE 愛媛県

Occupying the west of Shikoku and formerly known as Iyo, Ehime Prefecture is home to Shikoku's largest city, Matsuyama, and has the largest number of the 88 pilgrimage temples – 27, to be precise. Like Tosa (Kōchi Prefecture), the southern part of the prefecture has always been considered wild and remote; by the time pilgrims arrive in Matsuyama, they know that the hard work has been done and they are well on their way to completing their goal. To pilgrims, Ehime Prefecture is known as Bodai-no-dōjō, the place for attainment of wisdom. There are large clusters of temples around Matsuyama and Imabari, at the southern end of the Shimanami Kaidō bridge system, which links Shikoku with Honshū and makes for a spectacular bike ride.

Prefectural highlights are the immaculately preserved feudal castle and historic Dōgo Onsen in Matsuyama, and the sacred peak of Ishizuchi-san (1982m), the highest mountain in western Japan.

Ehime is known also for its *mikan*, a citrus fruit similar to the mandarin. It is known here as *Iyokan*, using the prefecture's old name of Iyo.

For prefectural information, check http://iyokannet.jp.

Matsuyama 松山

☑089 / POP 515,000

Located in a lush river basin, Shikoku's largest city is handsome and refined, with a hint of 'mainland' hustle. Matsuyama is famed across Japan for Dōgo Onsen Honkan, a luxurious 19th-century public bathhouse built over ancient hot springs. The finest castle on the island towers above the stylish trams criss-crossing the city streets and the harbour glistening in the distance. The city of Matsuyama is also home to eight of the 88 Temples, including Ishite-ji, which is one of the most famous stops on the pilgrimage.

The castle sits on a hill in the middle of the city with JR Matsuyama Station to its west, the city centre to its south and Dōgo Onsen to its east. Trams connect all the areas, including circumnavigating the castle's hill. The ferry port and airport are both west of the city.

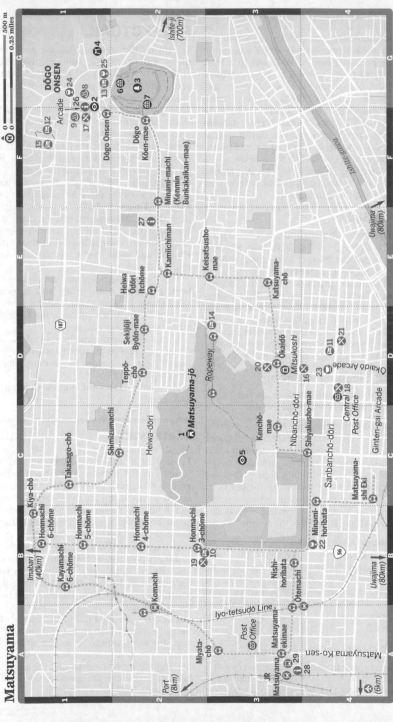

Matsuyama

SHIKOKU MATSUYAMA

Matsuyama

◎ Sights

★ **Matsuyama-jō**   CASTLE
(松山城; Map p670; ☑ 089-921-4873; www.mat-suyamajo.jp; ¥510; ⊙ 9am-5pm, to 5.30pm Aug, to 4.30pm Dec & Jan) Perched on top of Mt Katsuyama in the centre of town, the castle dominates the city, as it has for centuries. Matsuyama-jō is one of Japan's finest surviving castles, and one of the very few with anything interesting to peruse inside: the castle has a treasure trove of artefacts with excellent English-language displays. A rope-way (one way/return ¥270/510) is on hand to whisk you up the hill, though there is a pleasant pathway if you prefer to walk.

It's worth walking down via the back slopes of the castle and stopping off at **Ninomaru Shiseki Tei-en** (二之丸史跡庭園; Map p670; ¥100; ⊙ 9am-5pm, to 5.30pm Aug, to 4.30pm Dec & Jan) in the outer citadel of the fort, consisting of old gardens and modern water features.

★ **Temple 51: Ishite-ji**   BUDDHIST TEMPLE
(石手寺; ☑ 089-977-0870; www.88shikokuhenro.jp/ehime/51ishiteji; 2-9-21 Ishite) **FREE** East of Dōgo Onsen is Ishite-ji, the 51st of the 88 Temples and one of the most impressive in the circuit. *Ishite* means 'stone hand' and comes from a legend associated with Kōbō Daishi in which a baby was born with a stone

in its hand. A statue of Kōbō Daishi overlooks the temple from high on the hillside.

Botchan Karakuri Clock   LANDMARK
(坊ちゃんからくり時計; Map p670) At the start of the arcade at Dōgo Onsen you can check out Botchan Karakuri Clock, which was erected as part of Dōgo Onsen Honkan's centennial in 1994. It features figures based on the main characters from *Botchan*, who emerge to take a turn on the hour from 8am to 10pm. The spectacle is viewed hourly by crowds of excited Japanese visitors.

Shiki Memorial Museum   MUSEUM
(松山市立子規記念博物館; Map p670; ☑ 089-931-5566; http://sikihaku.lesp.co.jp; 1-30 Dōgo-kōen; ¥400; ⊙ 9am-6pm May-Oct, to 5pm Nov-Apr) This memorial museum celebrates the life and work of Matsuyama-born poet Masaoka Shiki (1867–1902), as well as the history of Matsuyama. Shiki initiated the reform of haiku and tanka (two forms of traditional poetry) and influenced a generation of poets after him. The museum has some English-language signage but also offers English-speaking volunteer guides with advance reservations.

Dōgo-kōen   PARK
(道後公園; Map p670; www.dogokouen.jp) **FREE** A small park containing the site of Yuzuki-jō,

CYCLING THE SHIMANAMI KAIDŌ

A fantastic way to travel between Shikoku and Hiroshima Prefecture is via the Shimanami Kaidō (p451), a bicycle route that crosses a series of bridges across six Inland Sea islands.

Sunrise Itoyama (サンライズ糸山; ☎0898-41-3196; www.sunrise-itoyama.jp; 2-8-1 Sunaba-chō, Imabari; bicycle rental per day from ¥1000; ⏰7am-9pm) in Imabari, right at the base of the first bridge, is the most convenient starting point on the Shikoku side. Everything is very well set up here. Rental bicycles (normal, tandem and electric-assist), which you can drop off on the Honshū side, are available; you can stay here (singles/twins ¥4320/6500); and there is a restaurant and information office. Check it all out online. JR Imabari Station is a 15-minute, ¥2000 taxi ride away.

the former residence of the Kōno clan that ruled Iyo province in feudal times. Articles unearthed during recent excavations are on display in **Yuzuki-jō Museum** (湯築城資料館; Map p670; ☎089-941-1480; Dōgo-kōen; ⏰9am-5pm Tue-Sun) FREE, near the west entrance of the park.

Isaniwa-jinja SHINTO SHRINE
(伊佐爾波神社; Map p670; 173 Sakuradani-chō) FREE Designated a National Treasure, this shrine was modelled on Kyoto's Iwashimizu-Hachimangū and was built in 1667. It's located a short walk east of Dōgo Onsen.

Sleeping

There are plenty of options here, both south of the castle in the city centre and to the east at Dōgo Onsen. Business hotels abound in the city centre, while Dōgo caters more to the 'onsen visitor' with large ryokan.

★Sen Guesthouse GUESTHOUSE ¥
(泉ゲストハウス; Map p670; ☎089-961-1513; www.senguesthouse-matsuyama.com; 4-14 Dōgo-takōchō; dm/s/d ¥2800/4600/7200; P ⊜ @ 🛜) This welcoming guesthouse is *the* place in Shikoku to get the lowdown on all things pilgrimage. Run by a super-friendly young American/Japanese couple, Sen has spacious tatami rooms with shared facilities, a roomy and well-equipped kitchen, a small bar and a tidy, homey communal area. The rooftop is a great place to catch the sunset over Matsuyama.

The guesthouse is a five-minute walk from Dōgo Onsen. The owners rent out bicycles and happily share local info on Matsuyama and beyond, as well as advice on undertaking the pilgrimage.

Guest House Matsuyama GUESTHOUSE ¥
(ゲストハウス松山; Map p670; ☎089-934-5296; www.sophia-club.net/guesthouse; 8-3-3 Ōkaidō-chō; s/tw/tr ¥2800/4500/6000, apt ¥10,000; ❄ 🛜) Community-minded Tamanoi-san welcomes foreign guests to her guesthouse and cafe, components of her nonprofit endeavour to foster cultural exchange. Accommodation is no-frills, but it is in a great location, with tidy rooms, free wi-fi and laundry facilities. Email ahead for reservations.

APA Hotel Matsuyamajō-nishi HOTEL ¥¥
(アパホテル松山城西; Map p670; ☎089-943-1011; www.apahotel.com; 2-5-5 Honmachi; s/d from ¥6000/8000; P ⊜ ❄ 🛜) The refurbished APA Hotel is a good option with decent-sized stylish rooms right on the Honmachi 3 tram stop. Very convenient for exploring the city, there are lots of pluses such as free wi-fi, laundry facilities, breakfast buffet (¥950) and on-site parking (¥600). Good deals when booking online.

★Dōgo Yaya HOTEL ¥¥
(道後やや; Map p670; ☎089-907-1181; www.yayahotel.jp; 6-1 Dōgo-takōchō; s/d from ¥7800/11,100; P ❄ @ 🛜) Easy on the eyes and the budget, Dōgo Yaya is aesthetically pleasing as well as a smashing deal. The 68 rooms of various layouts are models of clean, contemporary style infused with traditional Japanese elements: raised tatami platforms for the cushy Western beds, sliding *shōji*-type doors and wood-slat embellishments. No onsen, but guests receive discounted entry to nearby Dōgo Onsen.

Check Inn Matsuyama HOTEL ¥¥
(チェックイン松山; Map p670; ☎089-998-7000; www.checkin.co.jp/matsuyama; 2-7-3 Sanban-chō; s/tw from ¥5120/7920; P ⊜ ❄ @ 🛜) This business hotel is excellent value for money, with well-equipped modern rooms with free wi-fi, a *konbini* (convenience store) in the lobby and an onsen on the roof (the women's onsen is on the 2nd floor). A short walk from the Ōkaidō arcade (大街道), the hotel is super convenient to the city's nightlife and restaurants.

Funaya
RYOKAN ¥¥¥

(ふなや; Map p670; ☎089-947-0278, toll-free 0120-190-278; www.dogo-funaya.co.jp; 1-33 Dō-go-yunomachi; r per person incl meals from ¥22,000; P🅿✳🛜🏊) Natsume Sōseki took refuge here from his writer's block and aching limbs, and so should you if you can afford it. The beauty lies inside, from the central garden and private onsen to the exquisite surrounding tatami rooms fit for Japanese royalty. It's a short walk from the Dōgo Onsen tram station along the road that leads up to Isaniwa-jinja.

✕ Eating

The area around the Ginten-gai and Ōkaidō shopping arcades in central Matsuyama is full of places to eat and drink. There are also plenty of options at Dōgo Onsen.

★ Café Bleu
CAFE ¥

(Map p670; ☎089-907-0402; www.cafe-bleu. net; 4th fl, 2-2-8 Ōkaidō; meals ¥600-900; ⏱11.30am-midnight) This lovely little music cafe serves tasty, simple sustenance with a picture menu and daily specials. The decor includes photos of Andy Warhol and Mick Jagger spying on you in the bathroom, vintage typewriters and shelves of superb art books. Beer (including Guinness on draught) and generous cocktails are also available. Look up to spot the sign; it's on the 4th floor.

Dōgo-no-machiya
CAFE ¥

(道後の町屋; Map p670; ☎089-986-8886; www.dogonomachiya.com; 14-26 Dōgo-yunomachi; meals ¥650-1000; ⏱10am-10pm Wed-Mon, closed every 3rd Wed; 😊🍴) With a traditional shopfront along the Dōgo arcade, this former teahouse now serves as a bakery-cafe offering burgers, sandwiches and soul-satisfying coffee and tea drinks. Its shotgun-style layout leads through beautifully preserved dark-wood rooms to a Japanese garden and tatami room out back.

Tengu no Kakurega
IZAKAYA ¥

(てんぐの隠れ家; Map p670; ☎089-931-1009; http://tengunokakurega.co.jp; 2-5-17 Sanban-chō; dishes ¥400-1200; ⏱noon-midnight, to 1am Fri & Sat) A chic *izakaya* (inn) serving *yakitori* (skewers) and other dishes in a pleasant setting; try the *omakase* (chef's choice) set of grilled, skewered carnivore's delights (¥1260). Paper screens give onto a little garden at the back. Look for the *tengu* (long-nosed goblin) hung above the doorway, on the right-hand side of the second block heading east from the Ōkaidō arcade.

★ Kappō Yano
SEAFOOD ¥¥

(割烹矢野; Map p670; ☎089-931-6346; Matsumae-chō 2-5-8; meals from ¥1500; ⏱11am-3.30pm & 5-10pm Mon-Sat) Yano-san and his family have been running their local's seafood place for over 30 years a block back from APA Hotel in Matsumae-chō. Serving traditional meals, choose from his chef's *omakase* courses from ¥3000, or go for a *teishoku* set meal such as sashimi *teishoku* or *yakizakana teishoku* (grilled fish) for ¥1500. Top seafood at reasonable prices.

SOHSOH
VEGETARIAN ¥¥

(お野菜食堂 S O H S O H; Map p670; ☎089-998-7373; http://greenlabel-group.com; 3-2-10 Ōkaidō; set meal from ¥1050; ⏱11am-11pm; 🌱) This is the first store of what has become a Japan-wide chain for Ehime-based SOHSOH. While meals are not completely vegetarian, they are vegetable and salad heavy with small fish and meat portions (which can be removed when you order). Extremely popular, there are often lines to get in. Another SOHSOH restaurant is underground by Takashimaya at Shi-eki station.

Goshiki Sōmen
NOODLES ¥¥

(五色そうめん; Map p670; ☎089-933-3838; 3-5-4 Sanban-chō; meals ¥780-2000; ⏱11am-10.30pm; 🍴) Next to the central post office is this elegant Matsuyama institution, which specialises in *goshiki sōmen* (thin noodles in five different colours). You'll recognise it by the piles of colourful noodles in the window waiting to be taken home as souvenirs. Set meals are around ¥1500; there is a picture menu with English descriptions of the most popular dishes.

🍷 Drinking & Nightlife

The bulk of drinking establishments are concentrated in Ichiban-chō and Niban-chō amid the network of neon-lit streets either side of the Ōkaidō arcade.

Bokke
CRAFT BEER

(Map p670; ☎089-906-8349; 5-6 Minami-Horibata; ⏱5pm-midnight) This small craft beer bar is developing quite a following in Matsuyama, with a good range of beers from around Japan such as pale ales, IPAs and stouts, and some tasty bar food. With inside and outside seating, friendly staff and stylish design, Bokke is a popular spot, especially on Friday and Saturday nights.

1. Izumo Taisha (p484), Izumo
Huge *shimenawa* (twisted straw ropes)
hang at Izumo Taisha, one of the most
important shrines in Japan.

2. Ibusuki (p758)
Sand baths – in which people are buried
in hot volcanic sand – are popular at this
hot-spring resort.

3. Dōtombori (p365), Osaka
With its glittering neon lights and plenty of
restaurants and theatres, this is Osaka's
liveliest night spot.

1. Sapporo Yuki Matsuri (Sapporo Snow Festival; p582)

The elaborate ice sculptures at this annual event have included full-sized stages, Hello Kitty statues and ice slides.

2. Furano (p605)

This attractive town offers skiing in winter and majestic floral displays in warmer months.

3. Itsukushima-jinja, Miyajima (p446)

Appearing to float at high tide, this much-photographed vermilion *torii* (shrine gate) is considered one of the three best views in Japan.

4. Shiretoko National Park (p623)

A visit to this Unesco World Heritage Site includes dramatic views and the chance to soak tired muscles in steaming onsen.

3

AN INSIDER'S GUIDE TO DŌGO ONSEN

According to legend, Dōgo Onsen (道後温泉) was discovered during the age of the gods when a white heron was found healing itself in the spring. Since then, Dōgo has featured prominently in a number of literary classics and has won itself a reputation for the curative powers of its waters. The mono-alkaline spring contains sulphur, and is believed to be particularly effective at treating rheumatism, neuralgia and hysteria.

Dōgo Onsen Honkan (Map p670; 5-6 Dōgo-yunomachi; ⏰6am-10pm, kami-no-yu to 11pm) was constructed in 1894 and designated an important cultural site in 1994. The three-storey, castle-style building is crowned by a statue of a white heron to commemorate its legendary origins. It is best known for being included in the famous 1906 novel *Botchan* by Natsume Sōseki, the greatest literary figure of Japan's modern age, who based his novel on his time as a schoolteacher in Matsuyama in the early 20th century.

Even if you're well versed in onsen culture, Dōgo can be a bit confusing as there are two separate baths (and four pricing options) from which to choose. The larger and more popular of the two baths is *kami-no-yu* (神の湯; water of the gods), separated by gender and adorned with heron mosaics. A basic bath is ¥410, while a bath followed by tea and *senbei* (rice crackers) in the 2nd-floor tatami room is ¥840 and includes a rental *yukata* (light cotton kimono). A rental towel and soap will set you back a further ¥50. The smaller, more private of the two baths is the *tama-no-yu* (魂の湯; water of the spirit), which is also separated by gender and adorned with simple tiles. A bath followed by tea and *botchan dango* (sweet, skewered rice dumplings) in the 2nd-floor tatami room costs ¥1250, while the top price of ¥1550 allows you to enjoy your snack in a private 3rd-floor tatami room.

There are English-language pamphlets to clarify the correct sequence of steps. After paying your money outside, you should enter the building and leave your shoes in a locker. If you've paid ¥410, go to the *kami-no-yu* changing room (signposted in English), where you can use the free lockers for your clothing. If you've paid ¥840 or ¥1250, first go upstairs to receive your *yukata* and then return to either the *kami-no-yu* or *tama-no-yu* (also signposted in English) changing room. After your bath, you should don your *yukata* and retire to the 2nd-floor tatami room to sip your tea and gaze down on the bath-hoppers clip-clopping by in *geta* (traditional wooden sandals). If you've paid top whack, head directly to the 3rd floor, where you will be escorted to your private tatami room. Here, you can change into your *yukata* before heading to the *tama-no-yu* changing room, and also return after your bath to sip tea in complete privacy.

Regardless of which option you choose, you're allowed to explore the building after taking your bath. On the 2nd floor, there's a small **exhibition room** displaying artefacts relating to the bathhouse, including traditional wooden admission tickets. If you've taken one of the pricier upstairs options, you can also take a guided tour (in Japanese) of the private **imperial baths**, last used by the royal family in 1950. On the 3rd floor, the corner tatami room (the favourite of Natsume Sōseki) has a small **display** (in Japanese) on the writer's life.

Dōgo can get quite crowded, especially on weekends and holidays. To escape the crowds, one minute on foot from the Honkan (through the shopping arcade) is **Tsubaki-no-yu** (椿の湯; Map p670; ¥360; ⏰6.30am-11pm), Dōgo Onsen's hot-spring annex, frequented primarily by locals.

If you don't want a full bath, there are also nine free **ashi-yu** (足湯; foot baths) scattered around Dōgo Onsen where you can take off your shoes and socks and warm your feet.

Wani to Sai   BAR
(ワニとサイ; Map p670; ☎080-3319-2765; www.facebook.com/wanitosai; 1-39 Dōgo-yunomachi; drinks from ¥600; ⏰6pm-late) Easily the funkiest little spot in Matsuyama, Wani to Sai is a 'circus bar' run by a fascinating native son who set off to Florence to study fresco painting and wound up creating marionettes and busking around Europe for eight years instead. Wanting to hang with an artsy crowd? You've come to the right place.

Dōgo Bakushukan   MICROBREWERY
(道後麦酒館; Map p670; ☎089-945-6866; www.dogobeer.co.jp/bakusyukan.html; 20-13 Dōgo-yunomachi; ⏰11am-10pm) Right by Dōgo Onsen Honkan, this brewery is a good spot for

a locally made beer and a bite to eat after a relaxing soak. The names of the brews are allusions to novelist Natsume Sōseki and his famous novel, *Botchan*. There's also a decent range of food available from a picture menu (such as *iwashi no karaage* – fried sardines).

Cafe BC CAFE
(Map p670; ☎089-945-9295; http://bonjour-cafe bc.com; 2-2-20 Ōkaidō; ☺9am-10pm, to 7pm Thu & Sun) The best coffee in Matsuyama. The lady of the house also makes tasty sandwiches, perfect for a light lunch; sandwich lunch sets including a small salad and a hot drink cost ¥680 to ¥780.

ⓘ Information

Ehime Prefectural International Centre (愛媛県国際交流協会; EPIC; Map p670; ☎089-917-5678; www.epic.or.jp; 1-1 Dōgo Ichiman; ☺8.30am-5pm Mon-Sat) The centre provides advice, internet access and bike rental. EPIC is near the Minami-machi (南町; aka Kenmin Bunkakaikan-mae) tram stop. Get off the tram, look towards the castle and you'll see a sign about 200m away above the road pointing to EPIC.

Tourist Information Office (Map p670; ☎089-931-3914; ☺8.30am-8.30pm) The main office is located inside JR Matsuyama Station, while a **branch office** (Map p670; ☎089-943-8342; ☺8am-8pm) is opposite the tram terminus for Dōgo Onsen.

ⓘ Getting There & Away

AIR
Matsuyama Airport (www.matsuyama-airport. co.jp) has direct international flights with Seoul and Shanghai; domestic flights depart to all Japan's major cities.

It's 6km west of the city and easily reached by bus (¥310, 15 minutes, half-hourly) from the front of the JR Matsuyama Station.

BOAT
The superjet hydrofoil, run by the **Setonaikai Kisen** (瀬戸内海汽船; ☎Matsuyama booking office 089-953-1003; www.setonaikaikisen.co.jp; ☺7am-9pm) ferry, has regular hydrofoil connections between Matsuyama and Hiroshima (¥7100, 1¼ hours, 12 daily). The Hiroshima–Matsuyama ferry (¥3600, 2½ hours, 10 daily) is also a popular way of getting to/from Shikoku.

The **Matsuyama Kokura Ferry** (松山・小倉フェリー; ☎089-967-7180; www.matsuyama-kokuraferry.co.jp; 5-2292-1 Takahama-chō) runs between Matsuyama and Kita-Kyūshū (seven hours, daily).

BUS
There are JR Highway buses from the **bus stop** (Map p670) at the train station that run to/from Osaka (5½ hours, five daily) and Tokyo (12 hours). Fares vary considerably depending on the date. There are frequent buses to major cities in Shikoku.

TRAIN
The JR Yosan line connects Matsuyama with Takamatsu (*tokkyū*, or limited express, ¥6190, 2½ hours) and there are also services across the Seto-ōhashi to Okayama (*tokkyū* ¥6830, 2¾ hours) on Honshū.

ⓘ Getting Around

BICYCLE
Rental bikes (Map p670; per day ¥300; ☺9am-6pm Mon-Sat) are available at the large bicycle park to the right as you exit JR Matsuyama Station.

TRAM
Tickets cost a flat ¥160 for each trip (pay when you get off). A day pass costs ¥500. Lines 1 and 2 are loop lines, running clockwise and anticlockwise around Katsuyama (the castle mountain). Line 3 runs from Matsuyama-shi station to Dōgo Onsen; line 5 goes from JR Matsuyama station to Dōgo Onsen; and line 6 from Kiya-chō (木屋町) to Dōgo Onsen.

You can also ride the vintage Botchan Ressha (坊ちゃん列車), small trains that were imported from Germany in 1887. Named for Natsume Sōseki's famous novel, they ran up and down Matsuyama's streets for 67 years, and they're back in occasional use. Combo tickets for the Botchan Ressha plus a one-day tram pass cost ¥500.

Ishizuchi-san 石鎚山

☎0897

At 1982m, Ishizuchi-san is known as 'the roof of Shikoku' and is the highest peak in western Japan. With its name meaning 'stone hammer mountain', Ishizuchi is one of the Hyakumeizan, Japan's 100 Famous Mountains. Long a centre for mountain worship, Ishizuchi attracts pilgrims and climbers alike, particularly during the July and August climbing season. The first 10 days of July are marked with a 'mountain opening festival' attended by white-dressed pilgrims from all over Japan. Views from the peak are spectacular.

With a rental car, Ishizuchi-san can be climbed easily on a day trip from Matsuyama when approached from Tsuchi-goya. A day trip from Matsuyama without your own

SHIKOKU ISHIZUCHI-SAN

wheels will require a fair bit of planning and use of train, bus and cable car via Iyo-Saijo.

🏃 Activities

Skiing and snowboarding is possible using the Ishizuchi Tōzan Ropeway between January and April.

★ Ishizuchi-san
HIKING

There are two good starting points for climbing Ishizuchi-san. For the easier hike, head to Tsuchi-goya at 1500m, to the east of the mountain and allow four hours for the return hike. For a more strenuous day, start at the Ishizuchi cable-car station at Nishi-no-kawa, to the north of Ishizuchi-san. The cable car (石鎚登山ロープウェイ; ☑ 0897-59-0331; www.ishizuchi.com; one way/return ¥1030/1950; ⊙ 8am-6pm Jul & Aug, hours vary Sep-Jun) carries hikers from 455m up to 1300m, followed by a six-hour round-trip hike to the summit.

The two tracks meet before a final climb to the peak of Misen (1974m), where you'll find Ishizuchi-jinja and a mountain hut where you can eat and stay the night.

The last sections before the peak can be climbed using *kusari*, steel chains embedded in the rock that head straight up and are provided to help you test your mettle. If pulling yourself up chains doesn't appeal, there are alternate routes that bypass the chains. From the peak of Misen, there is a final test along a sharp ridge to Tengu-dake (1982m), the highest point.

🛏 Sleeping & Eating

If you are out hiking, there are places to eat at the top of the cable car, at the mountain hut at the peak and at Tsuchi-goya. Take hiking snacks with you.

Ishizuchi-san Summit Hut
HUT ¥¥

(Chōjō-sansō; 石鎚山 頂上山荘; ☑ 0897-55-4168; http://ishizuchisan.jp/sansou/sub02-0.htm; per person incl 2 meals ¥8700) Open from the start of May to the start of November, this is an isolated mountain hut perched on the exposed peak of Ishizuchi-san. It sleeps 50. Nothing luxurious here, but hot meals, a spot with bedding on a tatami mat in a warm shared room, and a solid roof and walls await. A real Japanese mountain experience.

ℹ Getting There & Away

Having your own wheels is the best way to get to Tsuchi-goya. There are buses from Matsuyama, requiring a change of buses at Kuma, but these only operate on weekends and public holidays.

To get to the Ishizuchi cable-car station, Setouchi Bus (せとうちバス; ☑ 0898-23-3450; www.setouchibus.co.jp; one way ¥1000) runs buses between JR Iyo-Saijo station (earliest departure is at 7.47am) and the Shimodani cable-car station (1 hour). The latest departure back is at 5.23pm. There are plenty of parks (¥400) at the bottom cable-car station if you come by car.

Uchiko 内子

☑ 0893 / POP 20,500

Uchiko is undergoing a mini-renaissance, with a growing number of domestic travellers taking interest in this attractive town with its prosperous past. During the late Edo and early Meiji periods Uchiko boomed as a major producer of vegetable wax – the Hon-Haga family established the production of fine wax in Uchiko, winning awards at World Expositions in Chicago (1893) and Paris (1900).

As a result, there are a number of exquisite houses that still stand today along a street called Yōkaichi, these days recognised as a Historic District Preservation Zone. Uchiko is making a determined effort to attract visitors and the town's visitor-centre staff are extremely enthusiastic and helpful.

◉ Sights

★ Yōkaichi Historic District
HISTORIC SITE

(八日市) Uchiko's picturesque and protected main street has a number of interesting buildings, many of which now serve as museums, souvenir stalls, craft shops, accommodation houses and charming teahouses. The old buildings typically have cream-coloured plaster walls and 'wings' under the eaves that serve to prevent fire spreading from house to house. As the street is in the Historic District Preservation Zone, there are strict regulations on how buildings are renovated.

Uchiko-za
THEATRE

(内子座; ☑ 0893-44-2840; 1515 Uchiko; ¥400; ⊙ 9am-4.30pm) About halfway between the station and Yōkaichi is Uchiko-za, a magnificent traditional kabuki theatre. Originally constructed in 1916, the theatre was completely restored in 1985, complete with a revolving stage. Performances are still held at the theatre; call ahead for a schedule.

Ōmori Wa-rōsoku
FACTORY

(大森和ろうそく; ☑ 0893-43-0385; http://o-warousoku.com; ⊙ 9am-5pm, closed Tue & Fri)

Here at Uchiko's last remaining candle manufacturer the candles are still made by hand, according to traditional methods; you can watch the candle makers at work.

🛏 Sleeping & Eating

★ **Nakahaga**
Residence Guesthouse   GUESTHOUSE ¥¥
(中芳我邸ゲストハウス; ☑0893-50-6270; www.we-love-uchiko.jp/stay/581; 2655 Uchiko; s/tw ¥8000/12,000; ☺🛜) Uchiko has some gorgeous traditional places to stay and the Nakahaga Residence on Yōkaichi tops the list. This stylish, remodelled storehouse is a classic and feels like stepping back into the Edo period. They only have the one lodging room with twin beds. No meals on offer, but there are plenty of places to eat nearby.

Takahashi Residence   MINSHUKU ¥¥
(文化交流ヴィラ高橋邸; ☑0893-44-2354; www.we-love-uchiko.jp/stay/562; 2403 Uchiko; s/tw with breakfast ¥5720/10,360; ℗☺🛜) This lovely refurbished two-storey traditional place, just off Yōkaichi, is a registered 'cultural exchange house' and takes only one booking per night. It can sleep up to 10. There are huge stone walls at the entrance, an Edo-period–style gate, and a well-kept Japanese garden. Enjoy a real Japanese experience.

Oyado Tsuki-no-ya   GUESTHOUSE ¥¥
(御宿月乃家; ☑0893-43-1160; http://uchiko-tsukinoya.com; 2646 Uchiko; s/tw ¥6300/10,500; ☺🛜) A brilliant place to stay right on Yōkaichi in the protected area, Tsuki-no-ya is a beautifully restored traditional building with classic tatami rooms and Japanese-style shared bathroom and toilet facilities. Meals are available and lovingly prepared using local produce by the couple who run the place – dinner ¥2310, breakfast ¥1050. Order the meals for the full experience.

Nanze   CAFE ¥
(☑0893-44-6440; 2023 Uchiko; meals from ¥700; ☺10am-5pm Fri-Wed) Nice spot out the back of the visitors centre with tons of parking. Offers interesting options including a seasonal set lunch, French toast, spaghetti and Locomoco (everyone's Hawaiian favorite!). Local products are also for sale.

Uchiko Fresh Park Karari   MARKET ¥
(内子フレッシュパークからり; ☑0893-43-1122; www.karari.jp; 2452 Uchiko; ☺9am-5pm) Above the Oda River, this farmers market offers fresh, locally grown produce, prepared

WORTH A TRIP

TEMPLE 45: IWAYA-JI

Pilgrims will be hoofing it through Shikoku's mountainous interior to get here, but you'll want your own wheels if you're not a *henro* to get to the isolated, but extremely atmospheric Temple 45, the **Iwaya-ji** (岩屋寺; ☑0892-57-0417; www.88shikokuhenro.jp/ehime/45iwayaji; 1468 Nanatori, Kuma-kōgen) FREE. Hanging on a cliffside high above the valley, visitors can almost feel the presence of the holy men of long ago. A trail lined with age-old statues winds up to the temple buildings, then up and over the mountain above. Climb the wooden ladder beside the main hall up to the platform in the indentation in the cliff where pilgrims ascend to pray.

bentō (boxed meals), regional specialities and a **restaurant** (レストランからり; www.karari.jp; 2452 Uchiko; Karari set ¥1200; ☺11am-7.30pm) serving good *teishoku* meals.

ℹ Information

Uchiko Visitor Centre (内子町ビジターセンター; ☑0893-44-3790; www.we-love-uchiko.jp; 2020 Uchiko; ☺9am-5.30pm Apr-Sep, to 4.30pm Oct-Mar, closed Thu) Offers maps, brochures and local information, and can also arrange enthusiastic English-speaking volunteer guides (www.facebook.com/uchiko.locals) with an advance booking. The visitors centre is located in what was formerly the town's police office, a 10-minute walk from JR Uchiko Station. There is free parking out the back and bicycle hire (two hours ¥350).

ℹ Getting There & Around

Uchiko is 25 minutes south of Matsuyama by the fastest train (¥2030) and 55 minutes (¥2790) north of Uwajima.

The visitors centre and Yōkaichi are a 10-minute walk northeast of Uchiko Station and are well signposted in English. It's easy to get around Uchiko on foot. Rental bicycles are available at the station (¥300 for two hours).

Ōzu   大洲

☑0893 / POP 49,500

On the JR Yosan line, the peaceful little town of Ōzu is known for its attractive castle, gardens and cormorant fishing. In season, visitors can watch the cormorants catch and regurgitate their fish from sightseeing boats

DON'T MISS

BEST OUTDOOR ADVENTURES

➡ Rafting Yoshino-gawa (p660)

➡ Hiking Ishizuchi-san (p679)

➡ Surfing the Tokushima coastline (p645)

➡ Hiking Tsurugi-san (p689)

➡ Canyoning in Nametoko Valley (p683)

on the river. These days, most visitors come on a day trip from Matsuyama.

◉ Sights

Ōzu-jō CASTLE
(大洲城; ☎0893-24-1146; www.ozucastle.jp; 903 Ōzu; ¥500; joint ticket with Garyū-sansō ¥800; ⊙9am-5pm) One of Japan's most authentically reconstructed castles, Ōzu-jō and its outlying buildings are original survivors from the Edo period. The castle is an impressive sight above the river, but exploring its interior is particularly fascinating – cross-sections of its roof construction, displays of armour and a scale model of the castle's bones are displayed in pristine condition.

Garyū-sansō GARDENS
(臥龍山荘; ☎0893-24-3759; www.garyusanso.jp; 411-2 Ōzu; ¥500, joint ticket with Ōzu-jō ¥800; ⊙9am-5pm) Across town from Ōzu-jō, Garyū-sansō is an elegant Meiji-period teahouse and garden in an idyllic spot overlooking the river. On Sundays from April to October, you can partake in the tea ceremony (from 9.30am to 3.30pm; ¥400).

☞ Tours

Cormorant Sightseeing Boats BOATING
(☎0893-57-6655; www.kurarinet.jp/ozu-ukai/index.html; per person noon/night tour ¥4000/6000; ⊙noon or 6pm) Traditional *ukai* (鵜飼; cormorant river fishing) takes place on the Hiji-kawa from 1 June to 20 September. Sightseeing boats follow the fishing boats down the river as the cormorants catch fish. Reservations are required.

Cormorant fishing has taken place in Japan for over 1000 years, and though it was formerly a successful industry, its main use today is to entertain tourists. It involves the fisherman tying a snare near the base of the bird's throat so that the bird can swallow smaller fish, but not the larger ones. When a cormorant has caught a large fish, the fisherman brings the bird back to the boat and the cormorant spits the fish out.

🛏 Sleeping & Eating

There are places to eat around the castle.

Ōzu Kyōdokan Youth Hostel HOSTEL ¥
(大洲郷土館ユースホステル; ☎0893-24-2258; http://reiko1932.la.coocan.jp; Sannomaru; dm ¥3200; 🅿⊝🛜) A delightful place to stay right at the foot of Ōzu-jō. Formerly a school building, the tatami rooms are fit for an army and the hostel doubles as a museum, featuring interesting curios and antique ceramics from the town's boom years as a Tokugawa-period castle town. The present owner, a lovely English-speaking octogenarian, is a fine source of local knowledge.

❶ Getting There & Away

JR Iyo-Ōzu station is 40 minutes (¥2220) south of Matsuyama by the fastest train. Ōzu is 45 minutes (¥2220) north of Uwajima, also by the fastest train.

Yawatahama 八幡浜

☎0894 / POP 40,000

Throughout the centuries, pilgrims from Kyūshū traditionally arrived in Yawatahama by ferry and then started and ended their pilgrimage at nearby Temple 43 – Meiseki-ji (明石寺). West of the city is Sada-misaki Peninsula, recognised as Japan's longest peninsula.

The only reason to visit Yawatahama is if you are arriving from, or departing to, Kyūshū by ferry.

If you need to stay overnight, **Super Hotel Yawatahama** (スーパーホテル八幡浜; ☎0894-20-9000; www.superhotel.co.jp; 1460-123 Chiyoda-machi; s/d incl breakfast ¥6150/8200; 🅿⊝❄🛜), just off the main north–south thoroughfare, is the best choice.

❶ Getting There & Around

Take the **Uwajima Unyu Ferry** (宇和島運輸フェリー; ☎0894-23-2536; www.uwajimaunyu.co.jp) from Yawatahama to Beppu (¥3100, three hours, six daily) and Usuki (¥2310, 2½ hours, six or seven daily) on Kyūshū. You can also take your car.

By the fastest train, Yawatahama is 55 minutes from Matsuyama (¥2980) and 30 minutes from Uwajima (¥1930).

From the station, Yawatahama port is a five-minute bus ride (¥150) or taxi ride (around ¥630); because buses are so infrequent, the

20-minute (1.5km) walk from Yawatahama Station is often faster than waiting for a bus.

Uwajima 宇和島

☎ 0895 / POP 87,000

A pleasant unhurried castle town, Uwajima draws a steady trickle of titillated travellers to its Shintō fertility shrine and attached sex museum. Though most travellers bypass Uwajima en route to Matsuyama, the town makes a pleasant stop and retains some noteworthy traditions, such as pearl farming, terraced agriculture and bloodless bullfighting.

◉ Sights & Activities

★ Taga-jinja & Sex Museum SHINTO SHRINE

(多賀神社・凸凹神堂; Map p684; ☎ 0895-22-3444; www.geocities.jp/taga_shrine; 1340 Fujie; ¥800; ⊙ 8am-5pm) Once upon a time, many Shintō shrines had a connection to fertility rites. Of those that remain, Taga-jinja is one of the best known. The grounds of the shrine have a few tree-trunk phalluses and numerous statues and stone carvings. Inside, the somewhat notorious three-storey museum is packed with anthropological erotica from all corners of the procreating world.

Uwajima-jō CASTLE

(宇和島城; Map p684; ☎ 0895-22-2832; 1 Marunouchi; ¥200; ⊙ 9am-4pm Tue-Sun) Dating from 1601, Uwajima-jō is a small three-storey castle on an 80m-high hill in the centre of town. The present structure was rebuilt in 1666 by the *daimyō* (regional lord) Date Munetoshi. The *donjon* (main keep) is one of only 12 originals left in Japan; there is nothing much to see inside. The surrounding park, **Shiroyama-kōen** (城山公園; Map p684; ⊙ sunrise-sunset), is a pleasant place for a stroll.

Municipal Bullfighting Ring NOTABLE BUILDING

(宇和島市営闘牛場; Map p684; www.tougyu.com; ¥3000) *Tōgyū* (闘牛) is probably best described as a type of bovine sumo. In these bloodless 'wrestling' matches, victory is achieved when one animal forces the other to its knees, or when one turns tail and flees from the ring. Fights are held on 2 January, the first Sunday of April, 24 July, 14 August and the fourth Sunday of October. Directions to the bullfighting ring are available at the tourist information office.

★ Forest Canyon ADVENTURE SPORTS

(フォレストキャニオン; ☎ 0895-49-6663; http://nametoko.net; Meguro, Matsuno-chō; canyoning full-/half-day ¥11,000/9000) For an adrenaline rush, try canyoning in the beautiful Nametoko Valley (an easy day trip from Uwajima). Forest Canyon is dedicated to safety, with experienced guides, so guests can freely leap into deep pools, climb up some waterfalls, abseil down others and swoosh down natural slides (including one that's 40m long!) created by the river.

All equipment – including wetsuit, helmet and life jacket – is included in the rate. They also have a river-rafting option.

Temples 41 & 42: Ryūkō-ji & Butsumoku-ji WALKING

(龍光寺・佛木寺; ☎ 0895-58-2186; www.88shikokuhenro.jp/ehime/41ryukoji; 173 Togari, Mima-chō) **FREE** A great way to get a taste of the 88 Temple pilgrimage without having to slog it out along busy main roads is to follow this mini-circuit that starts and ends in Uwajima. This walk between Temple 42 Butsumoku-ji and Temple 41 Ryūkō-ji covers a little over 5km.

Take a bus from Uwajima Station direct to Temple 42, Butsumoku-ji. After admiring the thatched bell-house and the statues of the seven gods of good fortune, follow the clearly marked *henro* (pilgrim) trail back through picturesque farming villages and rice paddies to Temple 41, Ryūkō-ji. Here, a steep stone staircase leads up to a pleasant temple and shrine overlooking the fields. From outside Ryūkō-ji there are signs to Muden Station (務田駅), a 15-minute walk away. From here, you can catch a train or bus back to Uwajima.

🛏 Sleeping & Eating

There's eating and drinking action in the main street outside JR Uwajima Station and in and around the Uwajima Kisaiya Shopping Arcade between the station and the castle.

★ Kiya Ryokan RYOKAN ¥¥¥

(木屋旅館; Map p684; ☎ 0895-22-0101; http://kiyaryokan.com; 2-8-2 Honmachiōte; ryokan rental per night ¥21,600, breakfast per person ¥5400; ❋) A rare opportunity to rent an entire house where literary greats have stayed, Kiya Ryokan offers a compelling reason for an Uwajima stop. Though not a traditional ryokan experience – no in-house staff nor elaborate *kaiseki* (Japanese haute cuisine) dinners – it

SHIKOKU UWAJIMA

Uwajima

Uwajima

is uniquely modern and appealing. Best enjoyed and most economical for groups (house sleeps up to eight).

The house surrounds an inner courtyard garden, and bathing facilities are a beautifully integrated combination of modern and traditional. Even if you don't stay, it's worth a stop to browse its tiny, well-curated boutique and get the lowdown on current happenings around town.

Boulangerie Riz BAKERY ¥
(ブランジュリーリズ; Map p684; ☑ 0895-22-8800; http://boulangerie-riz.com; 1-4-22 Ebisu-machi; pastries ¥50-400; ⊙ 9am-4pm Mon-Sat) Heavenly, light and crisp pastries and breads made with rice flour (50% – not gluten-free) are the house speciality at this bakery along the Kisaiya Road (きさいやロード) shopping arcade. Enjoy a simple breakfast at the counter while watching the bakers expertly turning out handmade treats, such as croissants flecked with local citrus and rolled *matcha* (powdered green tea) cake.

★ Wabisuke SEAFOOD ¥¥
(和日輔; Map p684; ☑ 0895-24-0028; www.sk-wabisuke.com; 1-2-6 Ebisu-machi; dishes ¥1000-1500; ⊙ 11am-10pm Thu-Tue) This restaurant,

just off the arcade, is an elegant spot to try the local *tai* (sea bream) specialities, available here as a *tai-meshi gozen* (sea bream set course; ¥1880). There is a picture menu, plenty of small plates to choose from, and you'll find Wabisuke easy to spot with a red *ushi-oni* (red devil-bull) out front.

ℹ Information

Tourist Information Office (宇和島市観光協会; ☑ 0895-22-3934; ⊙ 9am-6pm) At Kisaiya Hiroba at the port; find a more conveniently located **information booth** (Map p684; ☑ 0895-23-5530; ⊙ 9am-6pm) at the JR station.

ℹ Getting There & Around

If you've come from points south, then from Uwajima you're back in the land of the trains. Uwajima is on the JR Yosan line, and you can head to Matsuyama (*tokkyū* ¥3510, 1½ hours) via Uchiko (*tokkyū* ¥2790, one hour). The JR Yodo line runs east to Kubokawa and Kōchi Prefecture.

You can hire **bicycles** (Map p684; per hour ¥100; ⊙ 9.30am-5pm) at the station, in the corner office on the left after you exit the building.

TAKAMATSU & KAGAWA PREFECTURE

Formerly known as Sanuki, Kagawa Prefecture (香川県) is the smallest of Shikoku's four regions and the smallest of the country's 47 prefectures. The region's hospitable weather and welcoming people have always been a comfort to pilgrims as they come to the end of their journey. To *henro*, Kagawa is known as Nehan-no-dōjō, the Place of Completion, as it has the last 22 of the 88 pilgrimage temples.

Kagawa's attractions include the celebrated shrine of Konpira-san in Kotohira, the lively port city of Takamatsu with its world-renowned Japanese garden, Ritsurin-kōen, and the folk village of Shikoku-mura at Yashima. Today, the prefecture is a major point of arrival for visitors to Shikoku, since the only rail link with Honshū is via the Seto-ōhashi bridge to Okayama. Takamatsu is also only a short ferry ride away from the remarkable Inland Sea islands and their growing art scene. Check out www.my-kagawa.jp for more.

Kagawa is small and most of the places you'll want to visit are within reach of Takamatsu, so it's easy to stay in Takamatsu and visit Kagawa's highlights on day trips.

DON'T MISS

TOP TEMPLES

➜ Temple 45: Iwaya-ji (p681)

➜ Temple 51: Ishite-ji (p671)

➜ Temple 38: Kongōfuku-ji (p669)

➜ Temple 21: Tairyū-ji (p663)

➜ Temple 88: Ōkubo-ji (p687)

➜ Temple 66: Unpen-ji (p694)

Takamatsu   高松

☑ 087 / POP 418,500

The buoyant port city of Takamatsu hums a vibrant, many-part harmony – venerable castle grounds that host contemporary crafts fairs, the small-town-big-city energy of a prefectural capital, regional culinary specialities like Sanuki udon and the heritage of traditional gems like Ritsurin-kōen. It's urban Japan at its most pleasant and pretension-free.

On a practical and pleasurable level, Takamatsu is also a transportation hub. It serves as a jumping-off point for day-trippers to ferry to the snowballing art scene on the islands of the Inland Sea, and good train links mean visitors can consider staying in Takamatsu to visit prefecture hotspots such as Kotohira, Zentsūji, Marugame and Yashima.

◉ Sights

★**Ritsurin-kōen**   PARK
(栗林公園; Map p686; ☑ 087-833-7411; www.my-kagawa.jp/brochure; 1-20-16 Ritsurin-chō; ¥410; ⊙ sunrise-sunset) One of the most beautiful gardens in the country, Ritsurin-kōen dates from the mid-1600s and took more than a century to complete. Designed as a walking garden for the enjoyment of the *daimyō* (regional lord), the park winds around a series of ponds, tearooms, bridges and islands. To the west, **Shiun-zan** (Mt Shiun) forms an impressive backdrop to the garden. The classic view of **Engetsu-kyō bridge** with the mountain in the background is one of the finest in Japan.

Enclosed by the garden are a number of interesting sights, including **Sanuki Folkcraft Museum** (讃岐民芸館; Map p686; ⊙ 8.30am-5pm) FREE, which displays local crafts dating back to the Tokugawa dynasty. There are a number of teahouses in the park, including 17th-century Kikugetsu-tei (p688), where you can sip *matcha* with a traditional sweet and enjoy various

Takamatsu

garden tableaux from the tatami rooms. You can also try the lovely thatched-roof **Higurashi-tei**, which dates from 1898.

The easiest way to reach Ritsurin-kōen is by taking the frequent direct bus (¥230, 15 minutes) from JR Takamatsu Station.

Takamatsu-jō CASTLE
(高松城; Map p686; 2-1 Tamamo-chō; ¥200; ☉ sunrise-sunset) The site of Takamatsu's castle now forms delightful **Tamamo-kōen**, a park where the walls and seawater moat survive, along with several of the original turrets. A swimming race is

held each spring in the moat to honour an age-old chivalrous tradition. The original castle was built in 1588 for Itoma Chikamasa, and was the home of the region's military rulers until the Meiji Restoration, which happened nearly 300 years later. The castle keep has recently been restored and is open to the public.

Takamatsu City Museum of Art MUSEUM
(高松市美術館; Map p686; ☎087-823-1711; www. city.takamatsu.kagawa.jp/museum/takamatsu; 10-4 Konya-machi; ¥200; ☉9.30am-5pm Tue-Sun) This impressive inner-city gallery is testament to Takamatsu's quality art scene. The light and spacious refitting of a former Bank of Japan building is a stroke of curatorial genius, well served by interesting exhibitions on rotation from across Japan and the world. Often open until 7pm during special exhibitions.

🛏 Sleeping

There are some great budget spots in Takamatsu, and midrange hotels here represent great value.

★**Guest House Wakabaya** GUESTHOUSE ¥
(ゲストハウス若葉屋; ☏070-5683-5335;
http://wakabaya.main.jp/en; 603-1 Kankō-chō; dm/s/
tw ¥3000/3800/7000; P☀@☎) Lots of pluses
here at Wakabaya with an English-speaking
owner, reasonable rates, super-clean rooms
and bathroom facilities, living room and
kitchen, a washing machine (¥100), free parking, wi-fi and bicycle rental (¥500 per day);
they'll even keep baggage for you. Best of all,
this is a super-friendly place to stay.

Chottoco-ma GUESTHOUSE ¥
(ちょっとこま; ☏090-6548-8735; chottoco-ma.
com; 3-7-5 Ōgi-machi; dm/d ¥2500/6000; ☀☎)
Spotless, bright and intimate, charming
Chottoco-ma is run by a friendly couple, the
English-speaking former world wanderer
Yutaka and his wife Emi. This tiny guesthouse (reservations essential) has only two
dorm rooms and one private room, all sharing bathroom facilities. Located about 2km
from Takamatsu station, it's in an interesting
neighbourhood with nearby onsen and good
local seafood restaurants.

Find transport details and a map on their
website.

Dormy Inn Takamatsu HOTEL ¥¥
(ドーミーイン高松; Map p686; ☏087-832-
5489; www.hotespa.net/hotels/takamatsu; 1-10-10
Kawaramachi; s/d from ¥7000/10,000; ☀☀@☎)
The Dormy is a little different from the usual
big-hotel fare, with its keen eye for design
and a location at the heart of the entertainment district. The rooms are sleek and
spacious, while service is top notch for the
price. The onsen and *rotemburo* (open-air
bath) on the top floor are welcome additions, as is the wi-fi throughout.

Hotel No 1 Takamatsu BUSINESS HOTEL ¥¥
(ホテルNo.1高松; Map p686; ☏087-812-2222;
www.hotelno1.jp/takamatsu; 2-4-1 Kankō-dōri; s/tw
¥5500/9000; P☀☀@☎) Three blocks east
and three blocks south of Kotoden Kawaramachi Station, this is a sparkling business
hotel with standard rooms and a rooftop
rotemburo (outdoor bath) with sweeping
views of the city. There is free wi-fi throughout the hotel, coin laundry, restaurant and
free rental bicycles.

JR Hotel Clement Takamatsu HOTEL ¥¥¥
(JRホテルクレメント高松; Map p686; ☏087-
811-1111; www.jrclement.co.jp; 1-1 Hamano-chō;
s/d from ¥14,000/23,000; P☀☀@☎) This
eye-catching modern hotel is the top hotel in
town and one of the first buildings you see

as you exit JR Takamatsu Station. The rooms
are spacious, and there's a good selection of
bars and restaurants with sweeping views of
the Inland Sea. Big convenience factor here.

✖ Eating & Drinking

Restaurants and bars are clustered in the
covered arcades and entertainment district to the west side of the tracks between
Kotoden Kataharamachi and Kawaramachi
stations. People in Takamatsu are serious
about their udon and no trip here would be
complete without at least one bowl of Sanuki
udon. Look for the words *te-uchi udon* (手
打ちうどん), meaning 'handmade noodles'.

Kawafuku UDON ¥
(川福; Map p686; ☏087-822-1956; www.
kawafuku.co.jp; 2-1 Daiku-machi; udon lunch set
¥600; ⏰11am-midnight) One of Takamatsu's
best-known udon shops, Kawafuku serves its
silky Sanuki udon in a variety of ways. Choose
from the plastic food models outside. Look for
the red-and-white striped lanterns in front,
along Lion-dōri.

Ofukuro IZAKAYA ¥
(おふくろ; Map p686; ☏087-862-0822; 1-11-12
Kawara-machi; dishes ¥500-1500; ⏰5-11pm Mon-
Sat; 🍴) This fabulous *washofu* (local eating
house) in the heart of the entertainment district offers a well-priced and hearty dining experience. A number of delicious, preprepared
vegetarian and fish dishes sit on the counter,
served with complimentary salad and miso
soup. Find it east of Minami Shinmachi.

★**Bijin-tei** IZAKAYA ¥¥
(美人亭; Map p686; ☏087-861-0275; 2-2-10 Kawara-machi; dishes ¥700-1500; ⏰5-10pm Mon-Sat)

SHIKOKU TAKAMATSU

WORTH A TRIP

TEMPLE 88: ŌKUBO-JI

Ōkubo-ji (大窪寺; ☏0879-56-2278; ww-
w.88shikokuhenro.jp/kagawa/88ookuboji/
index.html; 96 Tawa-kanewari, Sanuki-chō)
FREE, the last of the Shikoku pilgrimage's 88 Temples, sits in the mountains
in the southeast of Kagawa Prefecture
and is well worth a visit.

It's fitting that walking *henro* should
face a stiff climb to get to the final temple,
though if they are doing it properly, they
still have to walk back to Temple 1 to complete the circle – for the search for enlightenment is like a circle, never-ending.

Smiling *mama-san* sees all at this discreet seafood *izakaya*. Point to the menu items already plated – the pickled *tako* (octopus) is a mouthful – or ask for an *osusume* (recommendation). It's on the ground floor of a building containing several snack bars and karaoke joints. Look for the white sign with the shop's name on it in black kanji.

Yakiniku Jinsuke   BARBECUE ¥¥
(焼肉ジンスケ; Map p686; ☑ 087-834-8808; www.yakiniku-jinsuke.jp; 2-9-9 Kawara; course ¥2500; ☺ 5pm-midnight) Loved equally by locals and Japanese celebrities, Yakiniku Jinsuke offers up a solid set menu for meat and beer lovers for just ¥2500. You get pork, chicken, soup, rice and pickles, plus your choice of two drinks. Lots of other course options too.

⭐ **King's Yawd**   BAR
(Map p686; ☑ 087-837-2660; www.facebook.com/ KINGSYAWD; 1-2-2 Tokishin-machi; ☺ 6pm-3am Tue-Sat) Chill out with the diverse crew that hangs out at this Jamaican bar. There's authentic Jamaican food (think jerk chicken and ackee) and generous cocktails, all to a background of reggae and red, gold and green decor. Justifiably popular with both locals and expats.

Kikugetsu-tei   TEAHOUSE
(掬月亭; Map p686; matcha ¥710; ☺ 9am-4pm) Sip *matcha* with a traditional sweet and enjoy various garden tableaux from the tatami rooms in the gorgeous spot at Ritsurin-kōen (p685).

Grandfather's   BAR
(グランドファーザーズ; Map p686; ☑ 087-837-5177; http://grandfather.jp/takamatsu; B1 fl, 1-6-4 Tokiwa-chō; ☺ 7pm-late) The scene here is so smooth you'll fall off your seat as the bookish owner spins vintage '60s and '70s funk and soul records from his enormous collection. Meanwhile, otherworldly waitresses hover through smoke to present your free-poured, icy-cool beverages.

ⓘ NAOSHIMA & SHŌDO-SHIMA

Takamatsu is a great base for exploring the olive groves of Shōdo-shima (p466), the art scene of Naoshima (p460) and islands of the Inland Sea, all less than an hour by boat.

ⓘ Information

Kagawa International Exchange Centre
(アイパル香川国際交流会館; I-PAL Kagawa; Map p686; ☑ 087-837-5908; www.i-pal.or.jp; 1-11-63 Banchō; ☺ 9am-6pm) In the northwest corner of Chūō-kōen, this international exchange association has a small library, satellite TV and internet access.

Tourist Information Office (高松市観光案内所; Map p686; ☑ 087-851-2009; ☺ 9am-8pm) Get everything you need inside JR Takamatsu station. English speakers on hand. They have English brochures and can help you find accommodation.

ⓘ Getting There & Away

AIR

Takamatsu Airport (www.takamatsu-airport. com) has direct international flights to Taipei, Seoul and Shanghai. Domestic flights wing their way to Tokyo, Narita and Naha.

BOAT

Jumbo Ferry (ジャンボフェリー; ☑ 087-811-6688; www.ferry.co.jp; 5-12-1 Asahi-machi) runs between Takamatsu and Kōbe. It also links Takamatsu to Shōdo-shima.

Shikoku Kisen (Map p686; www.shikoku kisen.com; 8-21 Sanpōto) runs ferries between Takamatsu, the art island of Naoshima, and Uno in Okayama Prefecture.

BUS

There are bus services to/from Tokyo (9½ hours), Nagoya (5½ hours), Kyoto (3½ hours) and most major cities from the **bus terminal** (Map p686).

TRAIN

Takamatsu is the only city in Shikoku with regular rail links to Honshū. There are frequent trains to Okayama (¥2030, 55 minutes), where you can connect to *shinkansen* services that will whiz you to any of the major cities in just a few hours.

From Takamatsu, *tokkyū* trains on the JR Kōtoku line run southeast to Tokushima (¥3160, 70 minutes); the JR Yosan line runs west to Matsuyama (¥6190, 2½ hours); and the JR Dosan line runs to Kōchi (¥5100, 2½ hours). The private Kotoden line also runs direct to Kotohira (¥620, one hour).

ⓘ Getting Around

BICYCLE

Takamatsu is flat and excellent for biking. The city offers a great deal on its 'blue bicycles' (¥100 per 24 hours; photo ID is required), which can be picked up at **Takamatsu-shi Rental Cycles** (高松駅前広場地下レンタサイクルポート; Map p686; ☑ 087-821-0400; ☺ 7am-10pm) in the underground bicycle park outside JR Takamatsu Station.

HIKING SHIKOKU

Shikoku is a very mountainous island and there are some great hikes. The island has two of Japan's *Hyakumeizan* – the 100 Famous Mountains – in the form of **Ishizuchi-san** (p680), the highest peak in western Japan at 1982m, and **Tsurugi-san** at 1955m. Both can be climbed as day hikes, with the added possibility of multiday hikes thrown in. Staying at a mountain hut in Japan can be a fun experience!

Of course, the best known walk on Shikoku is around the 88 Sacred Temples of Shikoku pilgrimage (p654). If you don't have 40 to 60 days or the inclination to walk the whole pilgrimage, consider walking part of it. Hiking the first five temples (p649), from Ryōzen-ji to Jizō-ji, will take half a day.

There are *henro-michi* (old pilgrim trails) between many of the temples. The old mountain trail from Temple 11 to Temple 12, both in Tokushima, is considered the hardest climb on the pilgrimage. There are even modern forms of transport such as ropeway and cable car up to some temples. The **Unpenji Ropeway** (p694) whisks pilgrims up to 900m and spectacular Temple 66, **Unpen-ji** (p694). From there it's a 10km downhill walk to Temple 67, Daikō-ji.

TRAIN

Kotoden (ことでん; ☎087-831-6008; www.kotoden.co.jp), a friendly and efficient local train company, runs trains on three lines:

➡ the yellow line runs from Takamatsu-Chikko station, by the castle park in central Takamatsu to Kotohira (stops at Ritsurin-kōen)

➡ the green line runs from Takamatsu-Chikko out to Nagao, where you'll find Temple 87, Nagao-ji

➡ the red line runs from Kawaramachi out east to Shido, stopping at Kotoden-Yashima and Yakuri on the way.

Yashima　　　　　　屋島

About 5km east of Takamatsu and highly visible from the city is the 292m-high tabletop plateau of Yashima, where you'll find Yashima-ji, number 84 of the 88 Temples. Yashima, meaning 'roof island', is a peninsula of lava and is part of Seto-nai-kai National Park. There are great views over the Inland Sea and Takamatsu from various viewing spots.

Just to the east of Yashima and still in Seto-nai-kai National Park is Goken-zan, the mountainous stony peninsula that attracted Isamu Noguchi to live here with a source of stone for his sculptures. Here you'll also find Temple 85, Yakuri-ji.

◉ Sights

★ **Shikoku-mura**　　　　　MUSEUM
(四国村; ☎087-843-3111; www.shikokumura.or.jp; 91 Yashima-nakamachi; ¥1000; ◷8.30am-6pm Apr-Oct, to 5.30pm Nov-Mar) About 500m north of Yashima station, Shikoku-mura is an excellent village museum that houses old buildings transported here from all over Shikoku and neighbouring islands. The village's fine kabuki stage came from Shōdo-shima, which is famous for its traditional farmers' kabuki performances. There's also an excellent restaurant serving, you guessed it, Sanuki udon (from ¥450) in an old farmhouse building as you leave the village.

Temple 85: Yakuri-ji　　　BUDDHIST TEMPLE
(八栗寺; ☎087-845-9603; www.88shikokuhenro.jp/kagawa/85yakuriji; 3416 Mure, Mure-chō) **FREE** Half the fun of visiting Yakuri-ji may be riding the retro **cable car** (八栗ケーブル; ☎087-845-2218; www.shikokucable.co.jp; 3378-3 Mure, Mure-chō; return/one way ¥930/460; ◷every 15 min 7.30am-5.15pm) up and down to the temple, but this is a spectacular place in its own right, sitting in the forest under the high cliffs of Goken-san. Temple 85 of the 88, most pilgrims are excited at Yakuri-ji as they get close to their goal. This is a temple at which to pray for success in business, study and matchmaking!

Take your passport as there's usually a 50% discount for foreigners.

Temple 84: Yashima-ji　　　BUDDHIST TEMPLE
(屋島寺; ☎087-841-9418; www.88shikokuhenro.jp/kagawa/84yashimaji; 1808 Yashima-higashimachi) **FREE** Yashima-ji, number 84 of the 88 Temples, sits atop the tabletop mountain of Yashima. This was the site of a decisive battle between the Genji and Heike clans in the late 12th century, and the temple's **Treasure House** (¥500) exhibits artefacts relating to the battle. Check out the **Pond of Blood**, where victorious Genji warriors washed the blood from their swords. You can either

WORTH A TRIP

UTAZU

For a taste of immersion in a small-town historic district, where nothing caters to tourists, book a night or two in the town of Utazu. Along the old *henro* trail, the local government recently teamed up with the **Chiiori Trust** (p658) to preserve and utilise two historic houses, known as **Co-machi-no-ie** (古街の家; ☑ 0877-85-6941; http://co-machi-no-ie.jp; s/d/tr from ¥14,000/16,000/21,000; ⊕ ⊛).

The Co-machi houses are best for self-caterers looking to connect with the community, who welcome the micro-adventures of interacting with the local shop owners, poking around **Gōshō-ji** (郷照寺; Temple 78) and checking out the landscape paintings housed in the waterfront **Higashiyama Kaii Setouchi Art Museum** (東山魁夷せとうち美術館; ☑ 0877-44-1333; www.pref.kagawa.jp/higashiyama/english/museum; 224-13 Aza Minami-dōri, Shamijima, Sakaide; ¥300; ⊙ 9am-5pm Tue-Sun). Utazu is a good base for self-driving visitors, with easy access to Marugame, Zentsū-ji and Konpira-san.

walk up from Yashima station or drive up the scenic road.

Isamu Noguchi Garden Museum   MUSEUM
(イサムノグチ庭園美術館; ☑ 087-870-1500; www.isamunoguchi.or.jp; 3-5-19 Mure-chō; tours ¥2160; ⊙ tours by appointment 10am, 1pm & 3pm Tue, Thu & Sat) Born in Los Angeles to a Japanese poet and an American writer, Noguchi set up a studio and residence here in 1970. Today the complex is filled with hundreds of Noguchi's works, mostly unfinished. Inspiring sculptures are on display, though, in the beautifully restored buildings and in the surrounding landscape. You can also check out the house in which Noguchi lived. Email ahead for reservations, preferably two weeks or more in advance (see the website for reservations and access details).

🍴 Eating

There are options scattered about and near the train stations of Yashima and Yakuri.

★Udon Honjin Yamada-ya   UDON ¥
(うどん本陣山田家; ☑ 087-845-6522; www.yamada-ya.com; 3186 Mure, Mure-chō; dishes from ¥800; ⊙ 10am-8pm) Something special not too far from the base of the Yakuri Cable Car out east of Takamatsu. This is udon in a lovely setting in the old Yamada residence, a 'Cultural Property of Japan', eating in elegant tatami rooms and gazing out on a perfectly manicured Japanese garden. Tie in lunch here with a visit to Yakuri-ji, Temple 85.

ℹ Getting There & Away

Yashima is six stops from Takamatsu's Kawaramachi station on the private Kotoden line (¥240). It's a very pleasant hour-long hike up the forested back side of the plateau to the temple. If you have your own wheels, the road up Yashima offers great views over Takamatsu and the Inland Sea and runs right up to the temple. At the time of research, the road was free, but it may become a toll road again (¥300).

Yakuri is eight stops from Kawaramachi on the Kotoden line (¥320). The Yakuri Cable Car station is easily reached by car from Takamatsu in 30 minutes.

Marugame   丸亀
☑ 0877 / POP 110,500

Marugame is a bustling city that is only 25 minutes from Takamatsu by train. Home to Marugame-jō, a castle dating from 1597, and the interesting Uchiwa-no-Minato paper fan museum, it makes an interesting day trip. Those wanting an authentic Shikoku experience for a few days might consider staying at one of the Co-machi-no-ie houses in Utazu, next town north.

⊙ Sights

★Marugame-jō   CASTLE
(丸亀城; ☑ 877-24-8816; www.marugame-castle.jp; ¥200; ⊙ 9am-4.30pm) This small castle dates from 1597. It took five years to build and is one of only 12 castles in Japan to have its original wooden *donjon* (keep) intact. It's known for its exquisite stone walls. The entrance fee is to the castle keep; it's free to stroll inside the castle. Marugame Castle is a 10-minute walk southeast from JR Marugame Station.

Uchiwa-no-Minato Museum   MUSEUM
(うちわの港ミュージアム; ☑ 0877-24-7055; www.city.marugame.kagawa.jp/sightseeing/spot/uchiwa_museum; 307-15 Minato-machi; ⊙ 9.30am-5pm Tue-Sun) **FREE** This museum has displays and demonstrations on how *uchiwa* (round paper fans) are made. Around 90% of Japan's *uchiwa* are still made in Marugame.

With prior reservations, you can learn how to make a paper fan in an hour for ¥500. It's a 15-minute walk from the station, near the harbour.

ℹ Information

Marugame Tourist Information Office (丸亀市観光案内所; ☑ 0877-22-0331; www.love-marugame.jp; ⊙ 9.30am-6pm) This office at JR Marugame station has local maps and brochures, including one in English.

ℹ Getting There & Around

Marugame is easily covered as a day trip from Takamatsu (*tokkyū* ¥1070, 25 minutes).

Across from the station, **bike hire** (☑ 0877-25-1127; www.love-marugame.jp/traffic_03-1.html; per day normal/electric ¥200/300; ⊙ 7am-7pm) is available from the bicycle park. By bike, it's five minutes to the castle and less than an hour from Marugame to Zentsuji.

Zentsuji

☑ 0877 / POP 35,000

The small town of Zentsuji is built up around Zentsū-ji, number 75 of the 88 Temples, and the place where Kōbō Daishi was born. The temple came first, then the town. If you're on a bike, there are several other pilgrimage temples within easy reach of this one, including Temple 72, Mandara-ji, and Temple 73, Shusshaka-ji. While these temples were originally sub-temples of Zentsū-ji, they soon became independent and part of the 88 Temple pilgrimage in their own right.

◉ Sights

★ **Temple 75: Zentsū-ji** BUDDHIST TEMPLE
(善通寺; ☑ 0877-62-0111; www.zentsuji.com; 3-3-1 Zentsūji-chō) FREE Zentsū-ji, number 75 of the sacred 88, is the largest of the temples – most of the other 87 could fit in its carpark. This is where Kōbō Daishi was born, and the temple boasts a magnificent five-storey pagoda and giant camphor trees that are said to date back as far as Daishi's childhood. The temple is about 1.5km from the JR Zentsuji Station.

Visitors can venture into the basement of the **Mie-dō** and traverse a 100m-long passageway (戒壇めぐり; ¥500) in pitch darkness. By moving carefully along with your hand pressed to the passageway's wall (painted with mandalas, angels and lotus flowers), you are said to be safely following Buddha's way.

Temple 73: Shusshaka-ji BUDDHIST TEMPLE
(出釈迦寺; ☑ 0877-63-0073; www.88shikokuhenro.jp/kagawa/73shusyakaji; 1091 Yoshiwara-chō) FREE Temple 73 on the 88 Temple Circuit, Shusshaka-ji was moved to the valley 200 years ago to make it more accessible to pilgrims. Before that, it was a steep, precipitous mountain rising 500m above the plain. It is said that at the age of seven, Kōbō Daishi threw himself off this peak crying 'If I am called to save the people, save me Buddha!'. Legend says he was saved by angels who carried him back to the top.

This is one of the places where magical powers are attributed to the mountains.

🛏 Sleeping & Eating

There are a number of well-priced, casual restaurants around JR Zentsuji Station.

Kaze-no-Kuguru HOSTEL ¥
(風のくぐる; ☑ 0877-63-6110; www.kuguru.net; dm ¥3000, s/d from ¥3800/6600; P ❄ ☎) Located on a main road on the *henro* trail, this hostel is an excellent choice: friendly, immaculate and flooded with natural light. There are free laundry facilities and wi-fi. It's a brown building with lots of windows a 15-minute walk from the station; find a map on the website.

ℹ Getting There & Away

Kagawa is a small prefecture. JR Zentsuji Station is only 45 minutes from Takamatsu (*tokkyū* ¥1810) and only five minutes from Kotohira (¥210).

Kotohira 琴平

☑ 0877 / POP 9800

The small village of Kotohira is home to one of Shikoku's most famous tourist attractions, Konpira-san, a Shintō shrine dedicated to the god of seafarers. The 1368 steep stone steps are a rite of passage for many Japanese, with plenty of interesting en-route distractions. Mention to any older Japanese that you've been to Shikoku and one of the first things they'll ask is if you climbed Konpira-san.

◉ Sights & Activities

★ **Konpira-san** SHINTO SHRINE
(金刀比羅宮; Map p692; 892-1 Kotohira-chō; Hōmotsu-kan ¥800, Shoin ¥800; ⊙ Hōmotsu-kan & Shoin 8.30am-4.30pm) Konpira-san or, more formally, Kotohira-gū, was originally a Buddhist and Shintō temple dedicated to the guardian of mariners. It became exclusively a Shintō shrine after the Meiji Restoration.

Kotohira

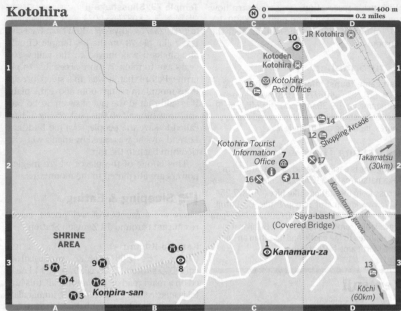

Kotohira

A lot of fuss is made about how strenuous the climb (1368 steps) to the top is, but if you've made it this far in Japan, you've probably completed a few long ascents to shrines already.

The first notable landmark on the long climb is **Ō-mon** (大門; Map p692), a stone gateway that leads to **Hōmotsu-kan** (宝物館; Treasure House; Map p692; ¥800; ⊙8.30am-4.30pm), where the collection of treasures is pretty underwhelming for such a major shrine. Nearby you will find five traditional-sweets vendors at tables shaded by large white parasols. A symbol of ancient times, the vendors (the Gonin Byakushō – Five

Farmers) are descendants of the original families that were permitted to trade within the grounds of the shrine. Further uphill is **Shoin** (書院; Reception Hall; Map p692; ¥800; ⊙8.30am-4.30pm), a designated National Treasure that dates from 1659 and has some interesting screen paintings and a small garden.

Continuing the ascent, you eventually reach large **Asahi-no-Yashiro** (旭社; Shrine of the Rising Sun; Map p692). Built in 1837, this large hall is dedicated to the sun goddess Amaterasu. It's noted for its ornate wood-carving. From here, the short final ascent, which is the most beautiful leg of the walk, brings you to **Gohonsha** (御本社; Gohon Hall; Map p692) and

Ema-dō (絵馬堂; Ema Pavilion; Map p692). The latter is filled with maritime offerings ranging from pictures of ships and models to modern ship engines. From this level, there are spectacular views that extend right down to the coast and over the Inland Sea.

Incurable climbers can continue for another 500 or so steps up to **Oku-sha** (Inner Shrine), which features stone carvings of *tengu* (bird-like demons) on the cliff.

★**Kanamaru-za**   THEATRE
(金丸座; Map p692; ☑0877-73-3846; ¥500; ◐9am-5pm) This is Japan's oldest kabuki playhouse, though it had a lengthy stint as a cinema before falling out of use. The restorations are superb; wander backstage and see the revolving-stage mechanism, basement trapdoors and a tunnel out to the front of the theatre. The playhouse is 200m east of the main approach to Konpira-san. There's a good English leaflet available, and English-speaking volunteer guides are sometimes on hand.

Kinryō-no-Sato   MUSEUM
(金陵の郷; Map p692; ☑0877-73-4133; 623 Kotohira-chō; ◐9am-4pm Mon-Fri, to 6pm Sat & Sun) FREE This sake museum, located along the main approach to the shrine, is in the old premises of a brewery that has owned the building since 1789. There's an English leaflet explaining the sake-making process, but sadly, the sake-tasting component is no longer offered. Look for the sake barrels outside.

Takadōrō   LANDMARK
(Lantern Tower; Map p692) At 27m, this is the highest wooden lantern in Japan, originally built to guide ships sailing on the Inland Sea.

Nakano Udon School   COOKING
(中野うどん学校; Map p692; ☑0877-75-0001; www.nakanoya.net; 796 Kotohira-chō; ¥1500) This is pretty good fun, learning how to make the legendary Sanuki udon in an hour in a shop on the main street leading up to the bottom of the steps to Konpira-san. You get to knead the dough, jump on it, cut it, cook it and finally eat it – and receive a certificate to boot.

🛏 Sleeping & Eating

Kotohira Spa Kotosankaku   RYOKAN ¥¥
(ことひら温泉琴参閣; Map p692; ☑0877-75-1000; www.kotosankaku.jp; 685-11 Kotohira-chō; r incl 2 meals per person from ¥9000; P❉⊛) This large 12-storey place features Japanese-style, Western-style and hybrid rooms, beautiful baths and immaculately

prepared meals only a five-minute walk from the JR and Kotoden stations. The buffet breakfast is superb. Popular with Japanese groups, so reserve early.

Kotohira Kadan   RYOKAN ¥¥
(琴平花壇; Map p692; ☑0877-75-3232; www.kotohira-kadan.jp; 1241-5 Kotohira-chō; r/villa per person from ¥12,000/24,000; P⊖❉⊛@) A luxurious refuge after a climb up Konpira-san, this elegant ryokan is about three minutes' walk from the centre of Kotohira. Most of the rooms are Japanese style; there are three standalone villas as well, all within a garden setting. Soak weary muscles in the house onsen or in your own tub (some of the tubs are open-air).

Beautifully presented meals feature local seafood and specialities of the region, and though staff don't speak much English, they are extremely warm and accommodating.

Kotobuki Ryokan   RYOKAN ¥¥
(ことぶき旅館; Map p692; ☑0877-73-3872; 245-5 Kotohira-chō; per person with breakfast from ¥7000; P❉@) This welcoming ryokan with comfortable tatami rooms and warm hospitality is conveniently situated by the riverside. Umbrellas, internet access and spotless shared bathrooms are all available. The wooden bathtub is gorgeous. Turn left for the arcade and some small restaurants; turn right for the shrine.

Kotohira Riverside Hotel   HOTEL ¥¥
(琴平リバーサイドホテル; Map p692; ☑0877-75-1880; www.hananoyu.co.jp/river; 246-1 Kotohira-chō; s/d with breakfast from ¥7500/13,000; ❝) This well-run business hotel has comfortable Western-style rooms. There's an inhouse bath, but guests also receive discounted rates at its sister property's onsen nearby. The hotel has a comfortable restaurant, coin laundry and wi-fi throughout.

Konpira Udon   UDON ¥
(こんぴらうどん; Map p692; ☑0877-73-5785; www.konpira.co.jp; 810-3 Kotohira-chō; meals ¥500-1200; ◐8am-5pm) Just short of the first set of steps leading up Konpira-san, this is one of dozens of Sanuki udon joints in Kotohira. You can't miss it: the front window shows off the busy udon-makers rolling out dough and slicing noodles by hand. Try the *kake udon* (¥500), a simple dish of hot or cold noodles in broth.

New Green   CAFE ¥
(ニューグリーン; Map p692; ☑0877-73-3451; 722-1 Kotohira-chō; meals ¥850-1600; ◐8.30am-

ROAD TRIPPING SHIKOKU

Renting a car is becoming easier in Japan, and with multilingual navigation systems, Shikoku is perfect for a road trip. Highlights like the Iya Valley, the two southern capes of Muroto-misaki and Ashizuri-misaki and many of the 88 Temples have no train lines and tricky bus connections, so a car makes it a lot easier, especially if you have limited time.

Rent a car and head out on a voyage of exploration. You may consider driving to Shikoku over one of the three bridge systems or travelling on a ferry. If you plan on renting a car, be sure to procure an International Driving Permit before leaving your home country.

A 'Car Pilgrimage' around the 88 Temples is perfectly feasible in 15–20 days. Navigation is easy – just enter the next temple's phone number in your English-speaking car-navi.

Toyota Rent a Car (https://rent.toyota.co.jp/eng) Offices in all four Shikoku prefectures.

Nissan Rent a Car (https://nissan-rentacar.com/english) In Shikoku's four major cities and airports.

8.30pm; 🗐) A cute neighbourhood spot where local ladies meet over coffee, this is also one of the few restaurants in town open for dinner. If the salads, *kaki-furai* (breaded, fried oysters) and *omuraisu* (omelette filled with fried rice) leave you wanting, there's cake as well.

❶ Information

Just before the start of the steps up Konpira-san, the **Kotohira Tourist Information Office** (琴平観光協会; Map p692; ☑0877-75-3500; www.kotohira-rakankou.jp; 811 Kotohira-chō; ◌10am-5.30pm) offers maps and English brochures. There is also a limited number of rental bikes.

❶ Getting There & Away

You can travel to Kotohira on the JR Dosan line from Kōchi (*tokkyū* ¥4450, 1½ hours) and Ōboke (¥2790; 45 minutes). For Takamatsu and other places on the north coast, change trains at Tadotsu. The private Kotoden line also has regular direct trains from Takamatsu (¥620, one hour).

Kanonji 観音寺

☑0875 / POP 64,000

Named after Kannon, Goddess of Mercy, Kanonji makes an interesting stop. In the town itself is Kotohiki-kōen, with an attractive beach and the Zenigata coin-shaped sand sculpture. Nearby are two of the 88 Temples, **Jinne-in and Kanon-ji** (神恵院 • 観音寺; ☑0875-25-3871; www.shikoku88-6869.com; 3875 Yahata-chō) FREE, temples 68 and 69, in one compound. Inland, the 2.6km-long Unpenji Ropeway whisks visitors up to Unpen-ji, Temple 66 of the 88. Take your passport; there is often a half-price discount for foreign visitors.

⊙ Sights

★ **Temple 66: Unpen-ji** BUDDHIST TEMPLE
(雲辺寺; Map p657; ☑0883-74-0066; www.88shikokuhenro.jp/kagawa/66unpenji/index.html; 763-2 Hakuchi, Ikeda-chō) FREE With a name meaning 'Temple of the Surrounding Clouds', Unpen-ji is the highest of the 88 Temples at 900m. Surprisingly, it actually sits in Tokushima Prefecture, although it's more or less right on the Kagawa Prefecture border. While walking pilgrims dreaded the climb for centuries, modern *henro* ride the **cable car** (雲辺寺ロープウェイ; ☑0875-54-4968; www.shikoku-cable.co.jp; 1974-57 Onohara-chō Marui; return ¥2060; ◌every 20 min 7.20am-5pm) up from the Kagawa side. There are 500 marvellous *rakan* statues here – it is said that everyone has a lookalike among the 500 – look for yours.

Zenigata LANDMARK
(銭形; Kotohiki-kōen) Zenigata is a 350m-circumference coin-shaped sculpture in the sand dating from 1633. The coin and its inscription are formed by huge trenches dug in the sand, and are said to have been dug overnight by the local population as a welcome present to their feudal lord. For the best views of the impressive sculpture, drive or climb the hill to the observation point in Kotohiki-kōen, directly behind Temple 68. There is a track up from the back of the temple.

❶ Information

A small **tourist information office** (☑0875-25-3839), over the bridge from the station, has maps.

❶ Getting There & Away

JR Kanonji station is only 45 minutes from Takamatsu by the fastest train (¥2790) and 1¾ hours from Matsuyama (¥4780).

Kyūshū

Best Places to Eat

➡ Tōsenkyō Sōmen Nagashi (p760)

➡ Kawashima Tōfu (p710)

➡ Shippoku Hamakatsu (p724)

➡ Takamori Dengaku-no-Sato (p735)

➡ Gyōza Kogetsu (p744)

Best Places to Sleep

➡ Yōyōkaku (p710)

➡ Hotel Nampuro (p727)

➡ Hostel Akari (p721)

➡ Yufu-no-Oyado Hotaru (p738)

➡ ANA Holiday Inn Resort Miyazaki (p766)

Why Go?

Japan's southern- and westernmost main island is arguably its warmest, friendliest and most beautiful, with active volcanic peaks, rocky, lush and near-tropical coastlines, and great onsen virtually everywhere. Much Japanese history was made in Kyūshū (九州). Jōmon ruins, Shintō's sun goddess, wealthy trading ports, cloistered foreigners, samurai rebels and one of the earth's greatest wartime tragedies all loom large.

Today, burgeoning Fukuoka is a multicultural metropolis. In sweet, picturesque Nagasaki, tragedy contrasts with a colourful trading history. Kumamoto's castle is one of Japan's finest, and the volcanic Aso caldera is the world's largest (note that both were heavily damaged in earthquakes in 2016). Saga Prefecture boasts *three* legendary pottery centres. Steam pours from the earth in Beppu, Miyazaki's Nichinan coast boasts vistas, monkeys and Japan's best surfing, while Kagoshima, heart of the Meiji Restoration, smoulders – literally – with active volcanoes. Peppered throughout are relaxing hot-spring towns, trekking trails and family-friendly fun.

When to Go
Fukuoka

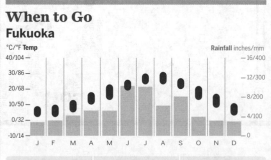

Apr–May Temperate weather and blooming azaleas on the volcanic slopes.

Jul–Aug Beat the night-time heat at delicious *yatai* (food stalls) in Fukuoka.

Oct–Nov Pleasant temperatures bring energetic festivals, such as Nagasaki's Kunchi Matsuri.

Kyūshū Highlights

1 Fukuoka (p704) Joining the night owls for beer and *yakitori* (skewers) at a *yatai* (food stall).

2 Hirado (p711) Being moved – and charmed – by the unique history of this secluded island.

3 Ibusuki (p758) Getting buried in warm volcanic sand in this hot-spring resort.

4 Kurokawa Onsen (p737) Recharging in a tranquil riverside *rotemburo* (outdoor bath).

5 Hashima (p726) Touring the eerie, deserted ghost island' (aka Gunkanjima).

6 Pottery Towns (p715) Marvelling at Japan's unique ceramics traditions in Arita, Imari and Karatsu.

7 Takachiho

Map labels (reading across):

Sea of Iyo · Honshū · Tokuyama · Kudamatsu · Hōfu · Ube · Onoda

YAMAGUCHI PREFECTURE

Kammon Straits · Shimonoseki · Mojikō · Kokura · Kitakyūshū · Yahata · Nakama · Okagaki · Munakata · Fukuma · Koga · Shikanoshima · Nogata · Tagawa

Sea of Genkai · Nokonoshima · Itoshima Peninsula · Maebaru · Karatsu-wan · Genkai Quasi-National Park

Iki · Katsumoto · Ashibe · Indōji · Gonoura · Yobuko

Higashi-Matsuura Peninsula · Hirado · Hirado-shima · Hirado-guchi · Kita-Matsuura Peninsula

Kanda · Yukuhashi · Buzen · Matama · Usa · Nakatsu · Takada · Bungo-Takada · Kunimi · Imi · Futago-san (721m) · Futago-ji · Kunisaki · Kunisaki Peninsula · Furuichi · Ōita Airport · Aki · Kitsuki · Hiji · Beppu-wan · Beppu · Ōita · Saganoseki · Usuki · Saiki · Nobeoka · Maruichibi

Sea of Suō · Kitakyūshū Airport

Fukuoka Airport · Dazaifu · Chikushino · Ono · Kasuga · Nakagawa · Tachiarai · Tosu · Kurume · Yame · Chikugo · Yanagawa · Ōkawa · Ōmuta · Araao · Tamana · Ueki

FUKUOKA PREFECTURE

SAGA PREFECTURE · Saga · Taku · Kashima · Ureshino · Takeo · Oki · Arita · Imari · Takaki

Amagi · Yoshii · Hita · Kusu · Oguni · Senomoto · Yufuin · Yufu · Yufu-dake (1584m) · Yaba-Hita-Hikosan Quasi-National Park · Kumano Magaibutsu

Kurokawa Onsen · Ubuyama · Kujū-san · Ichinomiya · Aso · Aso National Park · Taketa · Mie · Notsu

ŌITA PREFECTURE · JR Nippo Line · JR Hōhi Line

KUMAMOTO PREFECTURE · Yamaga · Yamaga Cycling Route · Kumamoto · Kumamoto Airport · Mashiki · Hakusui · Aso-san · Taka-dake (1592m) · Takamori · Takamori · Kyūshū Chūōsanchi National Park · Kunimi-dake (1739m) · Takachiho

NAGASAKI PREFECTURE · Higashisonogi · Ōmura · Ōmura-wan · Ōmura Airport · Nagayo · Isahaya · Nagasaki · Nagasaki Peninsula · Nomo-zaki

Nishisonogi Peninsula · Saikai · Fukue-jima & Nakadōri-shima (Gotō-rettō Group) (approx 25km) · Sea of Sumō

Tachibana-wan · Obama · Unzen · Unzen-dake (1359m) · Shimabara · Shimabara Peninsula · Shimabara-wan · Fukae · Arie · Kazusa

Ariake Sea · Yabe · Misumi · Uto · Kazusa

Hashima

Scale: 50 km / 25 miles · N

7 Takachiho Gorge
(p748) Rowing the gorge amid waterfalls (and hungry ducks).

8 Kumamoto-jō
(p731) Seeing where the last samurai made their final stand, at this earthquake-damaged, yet still impressive, castle.

9 Nichinan Coast
(p767) Surfing local breaks along the coast.

10 Kagoshima
(p750) Sipping sweet-potato *shōchū* as the Sakurajima volcano billows ash across the bay.

PACIFIC OCEAN

Sea of Hyūga

MIYAZAKI PREFECTURE

Hyūga
Tsuno
10 JR Nippo Line
Takanabe
Saito
Sadowara
Kizaki-hama
Miyazaki
Miyazaki Airport
Aoshima
Udo-jingū
9 Nichinan Coast
Nichinan
220
Nangō
Kōjima
Ishimami-kaigan
Koigaura-hama
Toi-misaki

Ichifusa-yama (1721m)
Saitobaru Burial Mounds
Kyushu

Yunomae
Taragi
Hitoyoshi
Ebino
Kogen
Kobayashi
Karakuni-dake (1700m)
Senriga-taki
Takasaki
Obi
Miyakonojō

Yatsushiro
Ōkuchi
Kurino
Kirishima-Yaku National Park
Kirishima-jingū
Kirishima
Kokubu
Uenohara
10
Ōsumi
Shibushi
Ōsaki
Shibushi-wan

MIYAZAKI PREFECTURE

Hondo
Kami-jima
Matsushima

Ashikita
Minamata
Izumi
Nagashima
Negashima

KAGOSHIMA PREFECTURE
JR Kagoshima Shinkansen Line

Akune
Miyanojō
Hayato
Aira
Kagoshima Airport
Naka-dake (1060m)
Sakurajima
Kirishima-Yaku National Park
Tarumizu
Furue
Kanoya
Ōsumi Peninsula
Nejime
Sata

Amakusa Archipelago
Shimo-jima
Unzen-Amakusa National Park
Ushibuka
Sea of Amakusa

Yatsushiro Sea

Jūin
Sendai
Kushikino
Fukiage
Satsuma Peninsula
225
Chiran
Kaseda
270
Bōnotsu
Makurazaki
JR Makurazaki-Ibusuki Line
Yamakawa
Kaimon-dake (924m)
Kirishima-Yaku National Park
Ibedi-ko
3 Ibusuki
Kiire
Kirkō-wan

Kushima
Ōsumi Peninsula
Kanoya
Sata
Sata Peninsula
Ōsumi Straits

Fukiage-hama
3
Kagoshima 10

Naka-koshiki
Koshiki Islands

EAST CHINA SEA

Tanegashima (40km)
Amami-Ōshima (410km)

History

Excavations dating to around 10,000 BC indicate that southern Kyūshū was the likely entry point of the Jōmon culture, which gradually crept north.

Japan's trade with China and Korea began in Kyūshū, and the arrival of Portuguese ships in 1543 initiated Japan's at-times-thorny relationship with the West and brought on the beginning of its 'Christian Century' (1549–1650). With these, the Portuguese also brought gunpowder weaponry, heralding the ultimate decline of the samurai tradition.

In 1868 rebels from Kyūshū were instrumental in carrying through the Meiji Restoration, which ended the military shogunate's policy of isolation, marking the birth of modern Japan. During the ensuing Meiji era (1868–1912), rapid industrialisation caused profound social, political and environmental change.

Sadly, this historically rich region is best known for one event – the 9 August 1945 atomic bombing of Nagasaki.

ⓘ Getting There & Away

AIR

Fukuoka Airport is Japan's fourth busiest, servicing destinations in Asia and Japan. In addition to domestic connections, Ōita (the closest airport to Beppu), Kagoshima, Kumamoto, Miyazaki and Nagasaki airports all have flights to Seoul, and Kagoshima and Nagasaki airports serve Shanghai directly. Miyazaki serves Taipei, but not always daily. Many airlines offer space-available 'Visit Japan' discount fares for foreign visitors, connecting many Kyūshū airports to Tokyo and Naha (Okinawa).

BOAT

There are sea connections to Kyūshū from Osaka and Okinawa. High-speed ferries shuttle between Fukuoka and Busan, in South Korea.

TRAIN

The *shinkansen* (bullet train) links Shin-Osaka to Kagoshima, via Hakata Station (Fukuoka) and Kumamoto.

ⓘ DISCOUNT BUS PASSES

There are discounted all-you-can-ride passes on JR Kyūshū and Kyūshū buses, from ¥8000/10,000 for three days in northern Kyūshū/all of Kyūshū, or a four-day all-Kyūshū Pass for ¥14,000. For further information visit www.sunqpass.jp.

ⓘ Getting Around

BUS

Kyūshū's extensive highway bus system is often the most efficient and cheapest way around the island. See www.atbus-de.com for routes and reservations.

CAR & MOTORCYCLE

Outside the cities, car rental is the best way to reach many of the best-preserved and least-known landscapes, particularly in rural southern and northeastern Kyūshū and around Aso-san. Car-rental agencies are conveniently located all over Kyūshū.

TRAIN

Kyūshū *shinkansen* lines run north–south through western Kyūshū between Hakata and Kagoshima, and other major Kyūshū cities are connected by *tokkyū* (limited express) train services.

There's even an ultra-luxury **Seven Stars** (www.cruisetrain-sevenstars.jp; s/d 1 night from ¥480,000/600,000, 3 nights ¥950,000/1,260,000) sleeper train, with two-day/one-night or four-day/three-night trips available.

FUKUOKA & AROUND

Fukuoka, on the northwest coast, is Kyūshū at its most urbane – and a rollicking good time. From there, to the west, the land breaks apart into numerous fingers and inlets. Here are the pottery towns of Karatsu, Imari and Arita. All the way to the west is Hirado, a small island that's big on history.

Fukuoka　　福岡

☑ 092 / POP 1,530,000

Fukuoka is Kyūshū's largest city (and Japan's sixth-largest) and still growing. It's made up of two former towns, the Fukuoka castle town on the west bank of the Naka-gawa and Hakata on the east. The two towns merged in 1889 as Fukuoka, though the name Hakata is still widely in use (for instance, it's Fukuoka Airport but Hakata Station).

Hakata traces its trading history back some 2000 years, which continues today with visitors from Seoul and Shanghai. Among Japanese, the city is famed for its SoftBank Hawks baseball team and hearty Hakata ramen (egg noodles).

Fukuoka's warmth and friendliness make it a great gateway to Kyūshū, and warm weather and contemporary attractions – art, architecture, shopping and cuisine – make it a good base for regional excursions.

◎ Sights

For visitors, Fukuoka can be divided into three main districts. Hakata, the old *shitamachi* (downtown), is now dominated by Fukuoka's *shinkansen* stop, the busy JR Hakata Station. Three subway stops away and over the Naka-gawa is Fukuoka's beating heart, the Tenjin district, bursting with department stores, boutiques, eateries and nightlife. Above ground, Tenjin centres on Watanabe-dōri, paralleled underground by Tenjin Chikagai, a long shopping arcade with mood lighting and cast-ironwork ceilings that make it a cool refuge from the summer heat. West of Tenjin is trendy Daimyō, Fukuoka's homage to Tokyo's Harajuku, minus the crowds, heading toward Fukuoka's former castle grounds.

The coastal neighbourhoods, best reached by bus or taxi, have many attractive sights, restaurants and hotels.

◎ Hakata

★ Fukuoka Asian Art Museum   MUSEUM
(福岡アジア美術館; Map p700; ☏092-263-1100; http://faam.city.fukuoka.lg.jp; 7th & 8th fl, Riverain Centre Bldg, 3-1 Shimo-Kawabata-machi; adult/student ¥200/150; ⓘ10am-8pm Thu-Tue; ⓡNakasu-Kawabata) On the upper floors of the Hakata Riverain Centre (博多リバレイ ン), this large museum houses the world-renowned **Asia Gallery**, and additional galleries for special exhibits (admission fee varies) and artists in residence. Changing exhibits cover contemporary works from 23 countries, from East Asia to Pakistan.

★ Hakata Machiya Furusato-kan   MUSEUM
(博多町家ふるさと館; Map p700; ☏092-281-7761; www.hakatamachiya.com; 6-10 Reisen-machi; ¥200; ⓘ10am-6pm; ⓡGion) Spread over three *machiya* (traditional Japanese townhouses), this folk museum re-creates a Hakata *nagare* (neighbourhood unit) from the late Meiji era. The replica buildings house historical photos and displays of traditional Hakata culture, festivals, crafts and performing arts, as well as recordings (more like lessons) of impenetrable Hakata-ben (dialect). Artisans are frequently on hand offering demonstrations.

Kushida-jinja   SHINTO SHRINE
(櫛田神社; Map p700; ☏092-291-2951; 1-41 Kami-kawabata; ⓘ8am-6pm; ⓡGion or Nakasu-Kawabata) **FREE** The intimate Kushida-jinja,

municipal Shintō shrine of Hakata, traces its history to AD 757 and sponsors the Hakata Gion Yamakasa Matsuri (p702), in which storeys-high floats make their way through the streets. The shrine has displays of Hakata festival floats on the grounds, and there's one float visible outside for those just wanting to gawk before moving on. A one-room **local history museum** (博多歴史館; Map p700; ¥300; ⓘ10am-5pm Tue-Sun) covers the festival, plus displays swords, ancient pottery and more.

Shōfuku-ji   BUDDHIST TEMPLE
(聖福寺; Map p700; 6-1 Gokushō-machi; ⓘ24hr; ⓡGion) Shōfuku-ji is a Zen temple founded in 1195 by Eisai, who introduced Zen and tea to Japan; the nation's first tea plants are said to have been planted here. Note: its buildings are closed to the public, but tree-lined stone paths make a nice ramble.

Tōchō-ji   BUDDHIST TEMPLE
(東長寺; Map p700; 2-4 Gokushō-machi; ⓘ24hr; ⓡGion) Tōchō-ji has Japan's largest wooden Buddha (10.8m high, 30 tonnes, created in 1992) and some impressively carved Kannon (goddess of mercy) statues. The temple is said to date from AD 806 and to have been founded by Kūkai, founder of the Shingon school of Buddhism.

◎ Tenjin

Fukuoka-jō & Ōhori-kōen   HISTORIC SITE
(福岡城・大濠公園; ⓡŌhori-kōen) Only the walls of Fukuoka-jō (Fukuoka Castle) remain, but the castle's hilltop site (Maizuru-kōen) provides good panoramas of the city and great views of aircraft landing at nearby Fukuoka airport.

Central Fukuoka

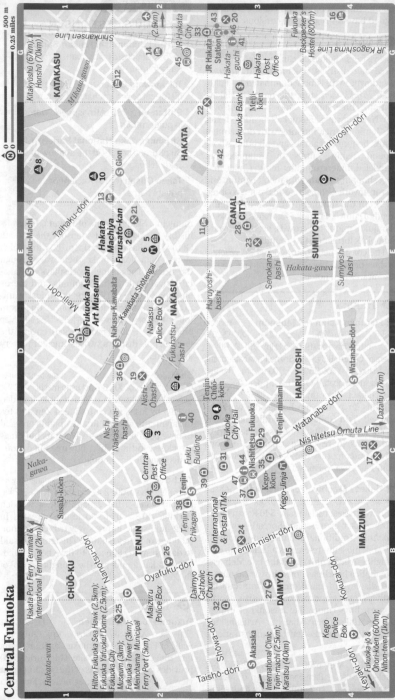

500 m
0.25 miles

Kitakyūshū (67km); Honshū (70km)

Shinkansen Line

KATAKASU

Mikasa-gawa

Fukuoka (800m)
JR Kagoshima Line
Backpacker's Hostel (800m)

16

43
(2.5km)
JR Hakata City
33
20
46
41
45
JR Hakata Station
Hakata-guchi
Hakata Post Office
Meiji-kōen
Fukuoka Bank

14

12

22

HAKATA

42

8
KATAKASU

10
Gion

7
SUMIYOSHI
Sumiyoshi-dōri

Gofuku-Machi

Taihaku-dōri

13

Hakata Machiya Furusato-kan
2
21
5
6
11
CANAL CITY
28
23

Meiji-dōri

Fukuoka Asian Art Museum
30
1

Nakasu-Kawabata
Kawabata Shotengai

Nishi-jima-bashi

Nakasu Police Box

NAKASU

Haruyoshi-bashi

Senokana-bashi

Hakata-gawa

Sumiyoshi-bashi

Watanabe-dōri

Nishi-Ōhashi
36
19

4

Tenjin-Chūō-kōen

HARUYOSHI

Dazaifu (17km)

Nishi

Nakashima-bashi

Central Post Office

3

9
40

Fukuoka City Hall

29
Nishitetsu Fukuoka
Tenjin-minami
Tenjin-minami

Watanabe-dōri

Naka-gawa

Susaki-kōen

CHŪŌ-KU

TENJIN

Fuku Building
Tenjin
31
44
47
35
Kego-kōen
Kego-Jinja
18
17

Nishitetsu Ōmuta Line

Hakata-wan

Hilton Fukuoka Sea Hawk (2.5km); Fukuoka Yahuoka! Dome (2.5km); Fukuoka City Museum (3km); Fukuoka Tower (5km); Meinohama Municipal Ferry Port (5km)

Hakata Port Ferry Terminal & International Terminal (2km)

Nanotsu-dōri

34
38
Tenjin Chikagai
39

International & Postal ATMs
24

15

IMAIZUMI

Maizuru Police Box

Oyafuku-dōri

26

Daimyo Catholic Church

32

27
DAIMYŌ

Kokutai-dōri

Akasaka

International Clinic Tojin-machi (2.5km); Karatsu (40km)

Kego Police Box

Fukuoka-jō & Ōhori-kōen (600m); Nihon-teien (1km)

Keyaki-dōri

Showa-dōri

Taisho-dōri

Tenjin-nishi-dōri

Central Fukuoka

Ōhori-kōen, an expansive park and pond (once part of the castle's moat system), is adjacent to the castle grounds, and has the traditionally styled **Nihon-teien** (日本庭園, Japanese Garden; ☑ 092-741-8377; 1-7 Ōhori-kōen; adult/child ¥240/120; ⏱ 9am-6pm Tue-Sun Jun-Aug, to 5pm Sep-May). It's a more recent construction (1984) around a pond with stone gardens and a teahouse.

Tenjin Chūō-kōen　　　　　　PARK
(天神中央公園; Map p700; ℝ Nakasu-Kawabata or Tenjin) Some attractive historic Western architecture populates this park by City Hall, most notably the French Renaissance–styled **Former Prefectural Hall & Official Guest House** (旧福岡県公会堂貴賓館; Map p700; 6-29 Nishi-nakasu; ¥240; ⏱ 9am-5pm Tue-Sun), dating from 1910 and including a cafe. A couple of blocks north, the copper-turreted **Akarenga Bunka-kan** (福岡市赤煉瓦文化館, Red Brick Cultural Centre; Map p700; ☑ 092-722-4666; 1-15-30 Tenjin; ⏱ 9am-9pm Tue-Sun) FREE

was built in 1909 by the same architect who designed Tokyo Station, and now hosts simple historical exhibits.

◉ Coastal Fukuoka

Fukuoka's northwest coast is a modern mix of corporate headquarters, hotels, large shopping and entertainment venues, and apartment blocks, easiest reached by bus from Tenjin or Hakata.

Several pretty islands are a quick ferry ride from the mainland and offer a nice day-trip diversion for those with extra time.

Fukuoka City Museum　　　　　MUSEUM
(福岡市博物館; http://museum.city.fukuoka.jp; 3-1-1 Momochi-hama; ¥200; ⏱ 9.30am-5.30pm Tue-Sun) This smart museum displays artefacts from local history and culture. The pride of the collection is an ancient 2.3-sq-cm, 108g golden seal with an inscription proving Japan's historic ties to China.

WORTH A TRIP

MOJIKŌ & YAHATA

Kitakyūshū is at the island's far north. Its two enclaves can be a good day trip.

Mojikō (門司港) has been a port since 1889, and its harbour-side 'Retro Town' is a trove of Meiji- and Taishō-period architecture, handsome brick buildings that once housed shipping companies and customs houses, and a drawbridge for pedestrians. Check www.mojiko.info for sightseeing tips. You can walk under the Kanmon Strait via the tunnel to Shimonoseki on Honshū. A row of shops along the waterfront serves Mojikō's signature dish, *yaki-curry* (curry rice broiled with melted cheese on top).

Yahata (八幡) is a one-time industrial town that has cleaned up its act with inspirational results. **Kitakyūshū Kankyō Museum** (北九州市環境ミュージアム, Kitakyūshū Environment Museum; ☎093-663-6751; www.eco-museum.com; 2-2-6 Higashida Yahata; ⏰9am-5pm Tue-Sun; ♿) **FREE** has 'radioramas' (with sound in English) that tell of the environmental degradation of Kyūshū in the early industrial period (including the notorious Minamata disease that struck near Kumamoto in the 1950s, a poisoning caused by mercury released into Minamata Bay by a chemical factory which polluted, knowingly, for more than three decades, according to a 1968 government ruling). Interactive exhibits illustrate the effects of pollution. Steps away, the futuristic **Kitakyūshū Innovation Gallery & Studio** (北九州イノベーションギャラリー; ☎093-663-5411; www.kigs.jp; 2-2-11 Higashida Yahata; ⏰9am-7pm Tue-Fri, to 5pm Sat & Sun; ♿) offers changing special exhibits (entry fees vary, often ¥500) and an excellent chronology of technological innovation. Across the road is a towering **steel foundry** from 1901, now cleaned up and a great place for a *bentō* (boxed meal) picnic.

From Hakata, transfer at Kokura (*shinkansen* ¥3390, 16 minutes; *tokkyū* ¥1320, 40 minutes). From Kokura local trains cost ¥280 to either Mojikō (13 minutes) or Space World Station (for Yahata, 10 minutes).

Fukuoka Tower   OBSERVATORY
(福岡タワー; www.fukuokatower.co.jp; 2-3-26 Momochi-hama; adult/student ¥800/500; ⏰9.30am-10pm) Standing above the Momochi district is the 234m-tall Fukuoka Tower, a symbol of the city and mostly hollow (its main purpose is as a broadcast tower). There's an observation deck at 123m and a cafe for soaking up the views, especially at dusk. Ask for the foreigner discount.

Fukuoka Yafuoku! Dome   STADIUM
(福岡ヤフオク！ドーム; ☎092-847-1006; www.softbankhawks.co.jp/stadium; 2-2-2 Jigyohama) This monolithic, retractable-roof stadium is the home field of Fukuoka's much-loved SoftBank Hawks baseball team. Tours (in Japanese) are offered and there's a museum of the life of Oh Sadaharu, the world's all-time home-run king (best for die-hard fans).

Nokonoshima   ISLAND
(能古島) A 15-minute ferry ride from Fukuoka, pretty Nokonoshima mixes natural and artificial parks. The latter, popular **Island Park** (アイランドパーク; www.nokonoshima.com; adult/child ¥1000/500), has a swimming beach, seasonal wildflower fields, huts selling crafts, and sweeping ocean views. Bicycle rental (¥300/1000 per hour/day) and English maps are available at Noko Market (のこの市) by the ferry dock. Buses 300 and 301 depart frequently from Nishitetsu Tenjin bus terminal (¥360, 20 minutes) for Meinohama Municipal Ferry Port (not to be confused with Meinohama on the subway line).

Shikanoshima   ISLAND
(志賀島) Delightfully rural, this island has fresh seafood restaurants that line the harbour-side streets. Ferries depart hourly (¥670, 33 minutes) from Bayside Place, along with seasonal sightseeing cruises around Hakata Bay. Shikanoshima also has a fishing shrine (志賀海神社), decorated with deer antlers, and a popular beach about 5km east of the shrine. Note that the shrine requests that those in mourning, pregnant, menstruating, or with a baby 100 days old or less refrain from visiting.

✯✯ Festivals & Events

Hakata Gion Yamakasa Matsuri   CULTURAL
(⏰1-15 Jul) The city's main festival is held in July, climaxing at 4.59am on the 15th, when seven groups of men converge at Kushida-jinja to race along a 5km-long course carrying huge portable shrines called *yamakasa*. According to legend,

the festival originated after a 13th-century Buddhist priest was carried aloft, sprinkling holy water over victims of a plague.

Hakata Dontaku Minato Matsuri CULTURAL
(⏰3-4 May) Tracing its roots to the port festival, Fukuoka's Meiji-dōri vibrates to the percussive shock of *shamoji* (wooden serving spoons) being banged together like castanets, with *shamisen* (three-stringed banjo) accompaniment.

🛏 Sleeping

Fukuoka is a destination for both business and pleasure, with plenty of quality accommodation at all budget levels. Stay near JR Hakata Station for convenience if railing around, although Tenjin is a better bet if you plan to spend a few days shopping and bar-hopping.

Hotel New Simple HOTEL ¥
(ホテルニューシンプル; Map p700; ☎092-411-4311; www.hotel-newsimple.jp; 1-23-11 Hakata-ekimae; dm/s/tw from ¥3900/5000/9900; ❄📶; [S]Gion, 🚉Hakata) This boxy, inexpensive yet modern lodging has neat and clean dorms that sleep six people (comfortably) to 12 (tightly), while single and twin rooms have private bath. 'Family' rooms sleep up to five people at ¥3900 per person. Guests in single and twin rooms get a simple Japanese breakfast. Enter from the street across from Family Mart.

Note that the 'dorm'-style rooms are not for strangers, they're for families or groups who already know each other.

Fukuoka Backpacker's Hostel HOSTEL ¥
(☎092-404-6035; www.fukuoka-hostel.com; 11-34 Hiemachi; dm/s/tw from ¥2600/3900/5900; 🚭[@]📶; 🚉Hakata) This 19-room hostel offers bare-bones accommodation and a communal TV and DVDs, plus a roof deck for meeting other travellers. From Hakata Station, head down Chikushi-dōri and turn left at Hotto Motto *bentō* shop.

★Kashima Honkan RYOKAN ¥¥
(鹿島本館; Map p700; ☎092-291-0746; 3-11 Reisen-machi; s/d Sun-Thu ¥3700/7000, Fri & Sat ¥4000/8000; [P]🚭❄📶; 🚉Gion) This charmingly creaky, unpretentious Taishō-era ryokan is a historic landmark, pleasantly faded and focused on a small garden with a stone lantern. Oozing atmosphere, it's a great place to sample traditional Japan. The friendly owners communicate well in English. No private bathrooms, but Japanese/Western breakfasts are available for ¥865. Parking is ¥1000.

Dormy Inn Premium BUSINESS HOTEL ¥¥
(ドーミーインPremium; Map p700; ☎092-272-5489; www.hotespa.net; 9-1 Gionmachi; s/d Sun-Thu from ¥11,990/13,990, Fri & Sat from ¥21,000/22,000; [P]🚭❄[@]📶) Rates are not the cheapest in town and rooms are pretty cramped, but that doesn't tell the whole story. The Dormy Inn has a natural onsen (hot spring) in addition to in-room showers, and rates include nightly bowls of ramen. Plus, the location next to Canal City is hard to beat. Rates rise substantially on weekends.

Plaza Hotel Premier HOTEL ¥¥
(プラザホテルプルミエ; Map p700; ☎092-734-7600; www.plaza-hotel.net; 1-14-13 Daimyō; s/d/tw from ¥8700/14,200/16,150; [P]🚭❄[@]📶; 🚉Tenjin or Akasaka) Location, location and location are the main reasons to stay here in trendy Daimyō, yet business-hotel-size rooms rival far pricier properties. The night vibe on the street outside is ubercool and the ground-floor trattoria, AW Kitchen, looks like it belongs on a fashionable Tokyo side street. Check online for discount coupons.

★With the Style HOTEL ¥¥¥
(ウィズザスタイル福岡; Map p700; ☎092-433-3900; www.withthestyle.com; 1-9-18 Hakataeki-minami; r from ¥45,200; 🚭❄[@]📶; 🚉Hakata) We don't know what the name means, but 'style' is indeed the byword at this sleek designer hotel. You could easily imagine yourself poolside in Hollywood around the fountain courtyard. Each of the 16 rooms exude rock-star cool, all include breakfast, minibar and welcome drinks, and guests can reserve complimentary private use of the rooftop spa or penthouse bar.

Hilton Fukuoka Sea Hawk HOTEL ¥¥¥
(ヒルトン福岡シーホーク; ☎092-844-8111; www.hilton.com; 2-2-3 Jigyohama; s/d from ¥17,000/20,000; [P]🚭❄[@]📶🏊) If you want to make an impression, you can hardly do better anywhere in Japan. The lobby restaurant of this César Pelli–designed hotel soars like its namesake bird, and at 1052 rooms, it's Asia's largest Hilton.

Nishitetsu Hotel Croom Hakata HOTEL ¥¥¥
(西鉄ホテルクルーム博多; Map p700; ☎092-413-5454; www.croomhakata.com; 1-17-6 Hakata-ekimae; s/d/tw from ¥12,000/19,000/24,000; 🚭❄[@]📶; 🚉Hakata) Across from the station, this shiny, spotless 503-room hotel has decent-sized rooms but really scores points for its common baths and sauna (in addition to en-suite facilities). Visit the baths in a spiffy

waffle-pattern *yukata* (light cotton kimono). Female-only floors are available.

🍴 Eating

Fukuokans and non-Fukuokans alike salivate at the mention of Hakata ramen. The distinctive local version of these ubiquitous noodles is called *tonkotsu rāmen*, served in a hearty broth made from pork bones.

And if for some reason Hakata-style ramen doesn't satisfy you, in Canal City there's **Rāmen Stadium** (ラーメンスタジアム; Map p700; ☑092-282-2525; 5th fl, Canal City; ramen ¥550-1290; ⊙11am-11pm), an entire floor of eight ramen vendors imported from the length and breadth of Japan.

★ Ichiran
RAMEN ¥

(一蘭; Map p700; ☑092-262-0433; www.ichiran. co.jp; 5-3-2 Nakasu; ramen ¥790-1200; ⊙24hr; 🅿; 🚊Tenjin) Ichiran has been serving noodles for 39 years. Customers eat at individual cubicles, and fill out forms requesting precisely how they want their noodles prepared. Flavour strength, fat content, noodle tenderness, amount of special sauce and garlic content can all be regulated. An English-language request form is also available.

The corporate office/main location in Nakasu has two storeys: the upper floor has the signature individual booths the chain is known for, the ground floor is more traditional, with sit-down tables and a bar. Look for the bright green and red awning.

Rāmen Jinanbō
RAMEN ¥

(ラーメン二男坊; Map p700; ☑092-473-5558; 2-16-4 Hakata Eki-mae; ramen ¥700-1100; ⊙11am-midnight Mon-Sat, to 9pm Sun; 🚊Hakata) Cosy ramen restaurant-pub that's just a few minutes from Hakata's Higashi-guchi. No

FUKUOKA'S STREET FOOD

The Fukuoka way to eat is at *yatai* (屋台), mobile hawker-style food carts with simple counters and seats; Fukuoka claims about 150 *yatai*, more than in the rest of Japan combined! Let the aromas and chatty conversation lead you to the best cooking and the best companions. For a more local experience, try the *yatai* around Tenjin or Nagahama. Get there early as most seats are soon taken. (Note that if you talk too much without ordering enough you'll be asked to move on.)

frills, just thick, Fukuoka-style broth, noodles and draughts, with most of the seating at the bar. Also has a branch in Rāmen Stadium.

Ippudō
RAMEN ¥

(Map p700; ☑092-413-5088; 10th fl, JR Hakata City, 1-1 Hakata-eki-chūō-gai; ramen ¥700-800; ⊙11am-midnight; 🚊Hakata) This ramen chain has workmanlike and always bustling branches in Tenjin, serving the best-selling Akamaru Modern (with black sesame oil and a fragrant *umami-dama*, or flavour ball), Shiromaru Classic (with thin noodles) and Karaka (spicy ramen). This branch is in the JR Hakata City shopping centre.

Murata
NOODLES ¥

(信州そばむらた; Map p700; ☑092-291-0894; 2-9-1 Reisen-machi; soba ¥650-1100; ⊙11.30am-9pm, closed 2nd Sun of the month; 🖉🅾; 🚊Gion) Down the street from the Hakata Machiya Furusato-kan, this lovely eatery makes homemade soba (buckwheat noodles) from the Shinshū area of central Japan (around Nagano), prepared in a variety of ways including *kake-soba* (in hot broth), *zaru-soba* (cold with dipping sauce) and *oroshi-soba* (cold, topped with grated *daikon*).

★ Zauo
SEAFOOD ¥¥

(ざうお; Map p700; ☑092-716-9988; www.zauo. com; 1-4-15 Nagahama; catch your own fish ¥3600-4000; ⊙5-11pm Mon-Fri, 11.30am-11pm Sat & Sun; 🅿🚹; 🚊Akasaka) Staff equip you with fishing rods, bait and nets to fish your own *tai* (sea bream), *hirame* (flounder) and more, from tanks surrounding tables on boat-shaped platforms. When you catch something, they'll bang drums before taking the fish away to prepare to your taste: sashimi, grilled, fried etc. Kitschy, but fun. There are other *izakaya*-style dishes if fish isn't your thing.

★ Fish Man
IZAKAYA ¥¥

(魚男フィッシュマン, Sakana Otoko; Map p700; ☑092-717-3571; 1-4-23 Imaizumi; set meals ¥680-1500; ⊙11.30am-3pm & 5.30pm-1am; 🚊Tenjin-minami) Fish Man's post-industrial vibe has lacquered plywood and big windows, which show off the unconventional presentations of seafood fresh from the Nagahama market across town: *kaidan-zushi* (sushi served on a wooden spiral staircase), *tsubotai no misoyaki* (miso-grilled snapper) or a *maguro* hamburger served on a steel plate.

There's no English menu here, but the English-speaking staff can help explain. Look for the banner outside reading 'No Fish, No Life'.

Afterwards, stop for dessert at Fish Man's adorable affiliated cake shop **Henry & Cowell** (Map p700; ☎092-741-7888; 1-3-11 Imaizumi; cakes ¥945-1260; ☺11am-9pm), just down the street. It also has a small selection of takeaway foods.

Tenjin Nobunaga   YAKITORI ¥¥
(天神信長; Map p700; ☎092-721-6940; 2-6-21 Tenjin; skewers ¥110-265; ☺5pm-1am Mon-Sun; ᖫTenjin) Nobunaga is raucous and rowdy, and that's just the chefs. There's no English menu, but it's easy to choose from the skewers behind the counter. Another house speciality is *potato-mochiage* (¥420), a fried dumpling of mashed potato, cheese and *mochi* (pounded rice). Look for the red lanterns just to the right of Big Echo karaoke hall.

🍷 Drinking & Nightlife

The weekend starts on Thursday in multicultural, party-friendly Fukuoka. The streets of Tenjin and Daimyō are safe, easy to explore and great for people-watching. The main drag, Oyafuko-dōri, roughly translates to 'street of unruly children' because of the cram schools that once lined it. In a way, the cap still fits. Nakasu Island, while one of Japan's busiest entertainment districts, is often sleazy.

Morris' Black Sheep   BAR
(モーリスブラックシープ; Map p700; ☎092-725-8773; 2-1-20 Daimyō; ☺5pm-1am) This Morris bar is just down the street from its Red Fox cousin. It's often packed, loud and fun, and may open even later on Friday and Saturday nights, depending on numbers.

CC Cafe   BAR
(Map p700; ☎092-791-5444; www.cccafe.jimdo. com; 3-5-15 Tenjin; ☺7pm-3am) This cosy pub hosts a friendly mix of English-interested locals and expats, and doubles in the day as an English-language learning centre, with classes and some international events.

☆ Entertainment

**Kyūshū Bashō
Sumo Tournament**   SPECTATOR SPORT
Held over two weeks at the Fukuoka Kokusai Centre during mid-November. Spectators start lining up at dawn for limited same-day tickets (*tōjitsu-ken;* ¥3400 to ¥15,000).

🔒 Shopping

Fukuoka's department stores occupy a three-block gauntlet of Watanabe-dōri in Tenjin. **Tenjin Core** (天神コア; Map p700; www.tanjincore.com), **Mitsukoshi** (三越; Map

p700; www.m.iwataya-mitsukoshi.co.jp), **Daimaru** (大丸; Map p700; www.daimaru.co.jp), **Solaria Plaza** (ソラリアプラザ; Map p700; www.solariaplaza.com), the **IMS Building** (天神イムズ; Map p700; www.ims.co.jp; Tenjin 1-7-11) and **mina tenjin** (ミーナ天神; Map p700; ☎092-713-3711) are all favourites, as is the subterranean **Tenjin Chikagai** (天神地下街; Map p700; www.mina-tenjin.com; ᖫ).

For contemporary fashion, low-rise boutiques in the Daimyō district show off local designers; lining Keyaki-dōri are intimate shops for antiques, design items and foreign crafts.

Hakata-ori no Sennen Kōbō   CLOTHING
(博多織の千年工房; Map p700; ☎092-283-8111; B1 fl, Hakata Riverain, 3-1 Shimo-Kawabata-machi; ☺10.30am-7.30pm; ᖫNakasu-Kawabata) Hakata is renowned for its weaving tradition, called Hakata-ori, and this elegant shop offers obis, kimonos and accessories from business-card holders to handbags in the distinctive style. None of it is cheap (silk obi start at around ¥10,000), but it's meant to last generations. Hakata-ori is also available at Tenjin's department stores.

Shōgetsudō   ARTS & CRAFTS
(松月堂; Map p700; ☎092-291-4141; 5-1-22 Nakasu; ☺9am-7pm; ᖫNakasu-Kawabata) White-faced clay Hakata *ningyō* (Hakata dolls) depicting women, children, samurai and geisha are a popular Fukuoka craft. This place sells them and also offers painting workshops (¥1575 to ¥3150).

Mandarake   BOOKS
(まんだらけ; Map p700; ☎092-716-7774; 2-9-5 Daimyō; ☺noon-8pm; ᖫTenjin) The Fukuoka branch of Mandarake is Kyūshū's largest manga store, with several storeys of games, comic books and DVDs.

Maruzen   BOOKS
(丸善; Map p700; 8th fl, Hakata Station Bldg, Hakata-eki; ☺10am-9pm; ᖫHakata) Maruzen has

TACHIARAI

From 1919 to 1945, the isolated farm village of Tachiarai (大刀洗) hosted a training school for Japanese fighter pilots, including some on kamikaze suicide missions. Expanded in 2009, **Tachiarai Heiwa Kinenkan** (大刀洗平和記念館, Tachiarai Peace Memorial Museum; ☑0946-23-1227; www.tachiarai-heiwa.jp; ¥500; ⊙9am-5pm) shows the rigorous training these men endured. English signage is basic, but the museum's artefacts are evocative (uniforms, medals, gold-plated sake cups etc). The centrepiece is a jet fighter shot down during the war and recovered from Hakata Bay in 1996. The museum also memorialises kamikaze pilots and townspeople who died during a USAF B-29 bombing on 27 March 1945.

The museum is across from Tachiarai Station. From Fukuoka, take the Nishitetsu line to Nishitetsu Ogōri (¥510, 30 minutes); from Dazaifu (¥340) it takes 25 minutes plus transfer time at Nishitetsu Futsukaichi. Then walk to Ogōri Station on the Amagi Railway for the trip to Tachiarai (¥290, 15 minutes). JR passengers can transfer to the Amagi Railway at Kiyama (¥340, 20 minutes).

a huge selection of Japanese- and English-language books, magazines and DVDs.

Canal City   SHOPPING CENTRE
(キャナルシティ; Map p700; www.canalcity.co.jp; 1-2 Sumiyoshi; ⊙shops 10am-9pm, restaurants 11am-11pm) Canal City shopping centre is Fukuoka's biggest mall, boasting an eponymous artificial canal with illuminated fountain symphony, hotels, a multiplex cinema, a playhouse and about 250 boutiques, bars and bistros. It was designed by Jon Jerde, who later created Tokyo's Roppongi Hills.

ⓘ Information

INTERNET ACCESS

Fukuoka is refreshingly wired, with free public wi-fi available at city hall, major train and subway stations, the airport, tourist information centres and in the Tenjin Chikagai (underground arcade).

MEDICAL SERVICES

International Clinic Tojin-machi (☑092-717-1000; www.internationalclinic.org; 1-4-6 Jigyo; ⊙9am-1pm & 2.20-6pm Mon, Tue, Thu & Fri, 9am-1pm Sat; ⊠Tōjin-machi, Exit 1) Multilingual clinic for general medical services and emergencies. It's two blocks from the station.

TOURIST INFORMATION

Fukuoka City Tourist Information Counters (福岡市観光案内所) at Fukuoka Airport, **Hakata Station** (福岡市観光案内所JR博多駅支店; Map p700; ☑092-431-3003; ⊙8am-9pm) and **Nishitetsu Tenjin Bus Center** (福岡市観光案内所天神支店; Map p700; ☑092-751-6904; ⊙10am-6.30pm) dispense maps, coupons and the helpful *City Visitor's Guide*, and can help with lodging, transport and car rental information. Information centres at **ACROS Fukuoka** (アクロス福岡; Map p700; ☑092-725-9100; www.acros.or.jp/r_facilities/

information.html; Cultural Information Centre, 2nd fl, ACROS Bldg, 1-1-1 Tenjin; ⊙10am-6pm; ⊠Nakasu-Kawabata or Tenjin) and **Rainbow Plaza** (レインボープラザ; Map p700; ☑092-733-2220; www.rainbowfia.or.jp; 8F, IMS Bldg, 1-7-11 Tenjin; ⊙10am-8pm, closed 3rd Tue of the month; ☎) are targeted mostly at foreign residents.

Fukuoka Now (www.fukuoka-now.com) is an indispensable monthly English-language street mag with detailed city maps.

Yokanavi (www.yokanavi.com) is a comprehensive Fukuoka/Hakata tourist information site.

TRAVEL AGENCIES

HIS Travel (Map p700; ☑092-415-6121; www.his-j.com; 4th fl, Yodobashi Hakata Bldg, 6-12 Chūō-gai; ⊙10am-8.30pm; ⊠Hakata) Discount international and domestic arrangements can be made at the Hakata branch of this international chain.

JR Kyūshū Travel Agency (Map p700; ☑092-431-6215; 1-1 Chuo-gai; ⊙10am-8pm Mon-Sat, to 6pm Sun; ⊠Hakata) Provides bookings and advice for travel within Kyūshū and Japan. Located within JR Hakata Station.

ⓘ Getting There & Away

AIR

Fukuoka Airport (p891) is an international hub serving carriers from east and Southeast Asia, as well as many domestic routes including Tokyo (from Haneda/Narita airports), Osaka and Okinawa (Naha).

Cut-rate carrier **Skymark** (☑in Tokyo 0570-051-330; www.skymark.co.jp) flies to Haneda Airport.

BOAT

Ferries from Hakata connect to Okinawa and other islands off Kyūshū. **Beetle** (p892) high-speed hydrofoils connect Fukuoka with Busan in Korea (one way/return ¥13,000/26,000, three hours, twice daily). The **Camellia line** (p892) has a regular ferry service from Fukuoka to Busan (one way/return ¥9000/17,100, 5½ hours, daily at 12.30pm). Both ships dock at Chūō Futō at **Hakata Port International Terminal** (p892) – reach it via bus 88 from JR Hakata Station (¥230) or bus 80 from Tenjin (Solaria Stage-mae; ¥190).

BUS

Long-distance buses (✉ ask operator for English interpreter 0570-00-1010) depart from the **Fukuoka Kōtsū Centre** (福岡交通センター; Map p700) next to JR Hakata Station (Hakata-gate) and also from the **Nishitetsu Tenjin Bus Terminal** (西鉄天神バスセンター; Map p700). Destinations include Tokyo (economy/business ¥8300/12,000, 14½ hours), Osaka (from ¥8800, 10½ hours), Nagoya (¥7500, 11 hours) and many towns in Kyūshū; ask about discounted round-trip fares.

TRAIN

JR Hakata Station (JR博多駅; Map p700; ✆ 092-471-8111, English info line 03-3423-0111) is a hub in northern Kyūshū. *Shinkansen* services operate to/from Tokyo (¥21,810, five hours), Shin-Osaka (¥14,480, 2½ hours), Hiroshima (¥8420, 62 minutes), Kumamoto (¥4610, 37 minutes) and Kagoshima-Chūō (¥9930, 84 minutes).

Within Kyūshū, non-*shinkansen* trains run on the JR Nippō line through Beppu to Miyazaki; the Sasebo line runs from Saga to Sasebo; and the Nagasaki line runs to Nagasaki. You can also travel by subway and JR train to Karatsu and continue to Nagasaki by train.

❶ Getting Around

TO/FROM THE AIRPORT

It's just five minutes on the subway from the airport to JR Hakata Station (¥260) and 11 minutes to Tenjin (¥260). Shuttle buses connect domestic and international terminals.

Taxis from the airport cost around ¥1600 to Tenjin/Hakata.

BUS

City bus services operate from the **Fukuoka Kōtsū Centre** (福岡交通センター; Map p700) adjacent to JR Hakata Station and from the **Nishitetsu Tenjin Bus Terminal** (西鉄天神バスセンター; Map p700). Many stop in front of the station (Hakata-guchi). Specially marked buses have a flat ¥100 rate for city-centre rides, or one-day passes cost ¥900.

SUBWAY

Fukuoka City Subway (http://subway.city.fukuoka.lg.jp; open from 5.30am to 12.25am) has three lines, of which visitors will find the Kūkō (Airport)

line most useful, running from Fukuoka Airport to Meinohama Station via Hakata, Nakasu-Kawabata and Tenjin stations. Fares start at ¥200; a one-day pass costs ¥620/310 per adult/child.

Dazaifu　太宰府

✆ 092 / POP 72,000

Dazaifu, former governmental centre of Kyūshū, has a beautiful cluster of temples, a famous shrine and a striking national museum, making for a popular day trip from Fukuoka.

◎ Sights

★**Kyūshū National Museum**　　MUSEUM
(九州国立博物館; ✆ 092-918-2807; www.kyuhaku.com; 4-7-2 Ishizaka; adult/student ¥430/130; ◷ 9.30am-5pm Tue-Sun) Built into the tranquil hills of Dazaifu and reached through more escalators than the average airport, this striking structure (built in 2005) resembles a massive space station for the arts. One of the best (if not *the* best) and biggest collections of art in Kyūshū, this is a must-see for art aficionados.

Highlights include a fascinating exhibit of the relationship between Japanese arts and culture and those of the rest of Asia, varying special exhibits, pottery, and a wonderful 'please touch' section for the youngest visitors.

★**Tenman-gū**　　SHINTO SHRINE
(太宰府天満宮; www.dazaifutenmangu.or.jp; 4-7-1 Saifu; ◷ 6.30am-7pm) Poet-scholar Sugawara-no-Michizane was a distinguished Kyoto figure until his exile to distant Dazaifu, where he died two years later. He became deified as Tenman Tenjin, god of culture and scholars. Among the countless visitors to the grand, sprawling Tenman-gū, his shrine and burial place, are students hoping to pass college entrance exams. The *hondō* (main hall) was rebuilt in 1591.

Behind the shrine is the **Kankō Historical Museum** (菅公歴史館; ✆ 092-922-8225; ¥200; ◷ 9am-4.30pm Thu-Mon), with dioramas showing Tenjin's life (an English leaflet provides explanations). Across the grounds, the **Daizifu Tenman-gū Museum** (太宰府天満宮宝物殿; ¥400; ◷ 9am-4.30pm Tue-Sun) has artefacts from his life, including some excellent swords. This is a near-mandatory stop on the bus-tour route, so expect to see swarms of people even on weekdays.

DON'T MISS

HIKING HOT SPOTS

Hikers will discover that Kyūshū boasts some of Japan's most awe-inspiring treks. Nearly every prefecture has great getaways. Below are some top spots, several of which follow still-active volcanoes, making for jaw-droppingly awesome vistas...and sometimes requiring special precautions, too. (Note that at the time of writing, Aso-san routes were closed, for volcanic-damage reasons, but may open at any time.) Also look for the *Kyūshū Olle* brochure, available in many tourist booths, for trekking routes through towns and trails.

➜ Kirishima-yaku National Park (p760), Kagoshima

➜ Unzen (p729), Nagasaki

➜ Hirado (p712), Nagasaki

➜ Kaimon-dake (p760), Kagoshima

➜ Kujū-san (p739), Ōita

Kōmyōzen-ji
BUDDHIST TEMPLE

(光明禅寺; ☑092-922-4053; 2-16-1 Saifu; ¥200; ⊙8am-4.30pm) Secreted away on the southern edge of Dazaifu, this small temple has an exquisite jewel of a Zen garden. It's a peaceful contrast to the crowds at the nearby shrine.

Kaidan-in
MONASTERY

(戒壇院) Nestled among rice paddies and reachable by bus (¥100), Kaidan-in dates from 761 and was one of the most important Buddhist ordination monasteries in Japan.

Kanzeon-ji
BUDDHIST TEMPLE

(観世音寺; ☑092-921-2121) FREE Adjacent to Kaidan-in, this temple dates from 746, but only the great bell (said to be Japan's oldest) remains from the original construction. Its **Exhibition Hall** (宝蔵; ☑092-922-1811; ¥500; ⊙9am-5pm) has an impressive collection of statuary, most of it wood, dating from the 10th to 12th centuries. Many of the items show Indian or Tibetan influence.

Dazaifu Exhibition Hall
MUSEUM

(大宰府展示館; ☑092-922-7811; ⊙9am-4.30pm Tue-Sun) FREE Dazaifu Exhibition Hall displays finds from local archaeological excavations. Nearby are the **Tofurō ruins** (都府楼) of ancient government buildings.

✕ Eating

The main street between the station and the temple has over 40 stores all selling the local *meibutsu* (speciality) – in this case, it's *umegaemochi*, a sweet-bean-paste-filled cake with toasted *mochi* rice on the outside. The products bear a plum-branch insignia, symbolising the branch of blossoms given to distinguished poet-scholar Sugawara-no-Michizane to 'cheer him up' during his Dazaifu exile.

★ Saifu Udon
NOODLES ¥

(さいふうどん; ☑092-922-0573; 3-4-31 Saifu; ⊙11am-4pm Wed-Mon) Handmade udon noodles are so sought-after here that this tiny eight-seat shop closes whenever it runs out. Plan on arriving early and you may need to wait for your turn at the table. The reward is a bowl of broth and noodles that are as fresh and tasty as handmade food can be. If it's warm, additional outdoor seating is opened up.

Kasanoya
CAFE ¥

(かさの家; ☑092-222-1010; www.kasanoya.com; 2-7-24 Zaifu; meals ¥750-1080; ⊙9am-5.30pm; ⛽Nishi-tetsu Dazaifu) The best reason to come here is to grab some of the best *umegaemochi* this street has to offer (five for ¥600), assuming you're willing to wait in line. You can eat here, too – either set menus or items à la carte. From the station, it's on your right as you head toward the temple, just after you pass the second *torii* (shrine gate).

ⓘ Information

Tourist Information Office (太宰府市観光案内所; ☑092-925-1880; ⊙9am-5pm) Inside Nishitetsu Dazaifu Station; has helpful staff and an English-language map.

ⓘ Getting There & Around

The private Nishitetsu train line connects Nishitetsu Fukuoka (in Tenjin) with Dazaifu (¥400, 30 minutes). Change trains at Nishitetsu Futsukaichi Station. A bus to Dazaifu leaves from JR Hakata station (¥600, 40 minutes) and the Fukuoka Airport (¥500, 25 minutes).

Bicycles can be rented for ¥500 per day at Nishitetsu Dazaifu Station (9am to 6pm). Electric bikes cost ¥800 per day.

Karatsu
唐津

☑0955 / POP 125,200

Karatsu is at the base of the picturesque Higashi-Matsuura Peninsula, an ideal location for its historic pottery trade. Korean influences elevated the town's craft from useful ceramics to art.

In Karatsu, pottery fanatics will be in their element, viewing earth-toned vases and tea bowls that sell for more than a luxury car. For everyone else, there's a hilltop castle, historic buildings, a simple Shōwa-era town centre and a pretty seaside cycling trail. Outside of town, the coastline, pounded into shape by the roiling Sea of Genkai, makes for dramatic vistas and pleasant day hikes.

The Nakamachi shopping area, a five-minute walk from Karatsu Station, offers good restaurants and souvenir shops, all within an easy stroll.

◉ Sights

It's about a 25-minute walk from JR Karatsu Station to the sea. Ceramic shops are dotted around town, along with **kilns** and **studios** where you can see local potters at work.

A walking and cycling path cuts through the pine trees planted behind the 5km-long Niji-no Matsubara Beach.

★ Karatsu-jō   CASTLE
(唐津城; 8-1 Higashi-jōnai; adult/child ¥410/200; ☺9am-6pm Jul & Aug, to 5pm Sep-Jun) This 1608 castle (rebuilt 1966) is picturesquely perched on a hill overlooking the sea, and houses antique ceramics, samurai armour and archaeological displays. It's a formidable sight even from the outside. To avoid the climb through the park, Maizuru-kōen, take the outdoor elevator (¥100/50 per adult/child).

Even if you opt to not go inside, the views from the castle grounds are breathtaking: Meinohama Bay and the town of Karatsu lie below, making it easy to see why the location was such prime real estate for the shogun centuries ago.

Kyū-Takatori-tei   HISTORIC BUILDING
(旧高取邸; 5-40 Kita-jōnai; adult/child ¥510/260; ☺9.30am-5pm Tue-Sun) This fabulously restored late Meiji Period villa of a local trader is built in a mix of Japanese and Western styles, with lantern-filled gardens, a Buddhist altar room, a wealth of paintings on cedar boards and an indoor *nō* stage. English audioguide available (¥300).

Nakazato Tarōemon   MUSEUM
(中里太郎右衛門; ☎095-572-8171; www. nakazato-tarouemon.com; 3-6-29 Chōda; ☺9am-5.30pm Thu-Tue) **FREE** This kiln-gallery is dedicated to the life and work of potter Nakazato Tarōemon (1923–2009), who was responsible for the revival of Karatsu ware. His work is in the inner gallery.

Hikiyama Festival
Float Exhibition Hall   MUSEUM
(曳山展示場; ☎0955-72-8278; 6-33 Nishi-jōnai; ¥300; ☺9am-5pm) This museum contains the 14 amazing floats used in the annual Karatsu Kunchi Matsuri. Floats include the Aka-jishi (Red Lion, constructed 1819), samurai helmets, and the auspicious phoenix and sea bream. There's good signage in English and a video shows festival scenes. It's near scenic Karatsu-jinja, the shrine that sponsors the festival.

Karatsu Ware
Federation Exhibition Hall   GALLERY
(唐津焼総合展示場; ☎0955-73-4888; 2nd fl, Arpino Bldg; ☺9am-6pm) **FREE** Adjacent to Karatsu Station, this exhibition hall displays and sells local potters' works, with prices ranging from ¥500 to I-can't-believe-someone-would-pay-THAT-much-for-THAT! Potters have a display area and many have (Japanese only) info.

Karatsu-jinja   SHINTO SHRINE
(唐津神社; 3-13 Minami-jōnai) Scenic shrine that sponsors the Karatsu Kunchi Matsuri festival.

★☆ Festivals & Events

Karatsu Kunchi Matsuri   CULTURAL
(唐津くんち祭り; ☺2-4 Nov) Karatsu comes to life with this spectacular festival, dating from 1592 and designated a festival of national cultural importance. The highlight is a parade of massive, exquisitely decorated *hikiyama* (floats).

Doyō-yoichi   FOOD & DRINK
(土曜夜市; ☎095-572-9114; ☺late Jul-early Aug) This food festival and market is held in the town centre over four consecutive Saturdays from late July into early August, ending when Obon starts.

🛏 Sleeping & Eating

Quiet Karatsu's sleeping options are limited mainly to business hotels and high-end ryokan that cater to ceramics buyers here to drop hundreds (or thousands!) on pottery.

Karatsu Dai-Ichi Hotel   HOTEL ¥¥
(唐津第一ホテル; ☎0955-74-1000; www.kugi moto.co.jp; 488-1 Nishi-Teramachi; s/d/tw from ¥7000/11,000/12,000; P🅿❀✿@🖥) Seven minutes on foot from Karatsu Station, this hotel doesn't win style points, but has clean

rooms and friendly, accommodating staff. Some singles are nonsmoking. Rates include a decent breakfast buffet with both Western and Japanese options.

Karatsu Dai Ichi Hotel Riviere HOTEL ¥¥
(唐津第一ホテルリベール; ☑ 0955-75-2000; www.kugimoto.co.jp; 1-9 Higashi-machi; s/d/tw ¥7000/11,000/13,000; 🅿 ❄ ✴ @ 🛜) Sister to the Karatsu Dai Ichi, the Dai Ichi Riviere lives up to its name: situated on the banks of the Matsuura-gawa, the hotel has lovely views of the water and castle, a nice onsen bath (with great views as well), and the same ample breakfast catering to both Western and Japanese diners.

⭐ **Yōyōkaku** RYOKAN ¥¥¥
(洋々閣; ☑ 0955-72-7181; www.yoyokaku.com; 2-4-40 Higashi-Karatsu; r per person incl 2 meals from ¥18,360; 🅿 ✴ @ 🛜) In a word: gorgeous. Also: rambling and minimalist, with 100-year-old woodwork, a pine garden and Karatsu-yaki pottery for your in-room seafood meals. Koi swim lazily in the immaculate 200-year-old garden. This property is a real getaway, yet it's less than a 10-minute walk from the castle. If you can't stump up to stay here, visit the on-site gallery of Nakazato family pottery.

Karatsu Bāgā BURGERS ¥
(からつバーガー; ☑ 090-6299-0141; burgers ¥310-490; ⏱ 9am-8pm) In the middle of nowhere (in a parking lot) in Niji no Matsubara is a brown-and-white Toyota serving burgers so famous people line up to buy them, and have for decades. The 'Special' is the most popular: a steaming cheeseburger topped with a fried egg and a ham slice. There's also an alternate branch in **Nakamachi** (からつバーガー; ☑ 080-9101-6912; 1513-18 Nakamachi; burgers ¥340-460), near Karatsu station.

⭐ **Kawashima Tōfu** TOFU ¥¥¥
(川島豆腐店; ☑ 0955-72-2423; www.zarudoufu.co.jp; Kyōmachi 1775; set meals lunch ¥1500-3500, dinner ¥7000-13,000; ⏱ 8am-10pm, meal seatings 8am, 10am, noon, 2pm & 5.30pm) On the shopping street near the station, this renowned tofu shop has been in business since the Edo period and serves set meals starring tofu, plus other seasonal specialities, around the 10-seat counter in a jewel box of a back room. Soft, warm, fresh – this is tofu as good as it gets. There's also frozen tofu 'soft cream' for ¥300. Reservations are necessary.

Indeed, reservations are essential – don't be surprised by a curt response if you turn up without a booking.

ℹ️ Information

Tourist Information Office (☑ 0955-72-4963; 2935-1 Shinmachi; ⏱ 9am-6pm) Inside JR Karatsu Station; has a selection of English-language tourist maps and brochures, and some enthusiastic English-speaking staff who can book accommodation or show points of interest on the map. It's well worth stopping here before heading into the town.

ℹ️ Getting There & Around

From Fukuoka, take the Kūkō (Airport) subway line from Hakata or Tenjin to the end of the line at Meinohama. Many trains continue directly (or you may need to switch) to the JR Chikuhi line to reach Karatsu (¥1140, 70 minutes). From Karatsu to Nagasaki (¥3710, three hours) take the JR Karatsu line to Saga, and the Kamome *tokkyū* on the JR Nagasaki line from there.

From Karatsu's **Ōteguchi Bus Centre** (大手口バスセンター; ☑ 0955-73-7511), highway buses depart for Fukuoka (¥1030, 70 minutes) and Yobuko (¥750, 30 minutes).

At the **Arpino** (アルピノ; ☑ 0955-75-5155; www.karatsu-arpino.com; 2881-1 Shinmachi) building, next to the station, you can rent bicycles (free) with your passport on the 1st floor; the station no longer rents bicycles.

Imari 伊万里

☑ 0955 / POP 55,300
You can tell you're getting close to Imari by the blue and white tiles that start appearing everywhere: street signs, bridge totems, even crushed gravel has shards of Imari's signature blue and white. The town proper lies near the border of Nagasaki Prefecture.

Imari is best enjoyed as a day trip from Karatsu.

⦿ Sights

⭐ **Ōkawachiyama** VILLAGE
(大川内山) The area's renowned pottery kilns are concentrated in photogenic Ōkawachiyama, a 15-minute bus ride from the station. Around 30 workshops and public galleries make for a lovely ramble uphill alongside streams, cafes and a stunning bridge covered with local Imari-ware shards. Arrive by noon to allow for exploring and shopping.

Imari City Ceramic Merchant's Museum MUSEUM
(伊万里市陶器商家資料館; ☑ 0955-22-7934; ⏱ 10am-5pm Tue-Sun) **FREE** In Imari town near the river, this museum houses some

priceless pieces of Koimari (as old Imari ware is known) from the 18th and 19th centuries, inside the handsomely preserved home of a merchant family.

🛏 Sleeping & Eating

There are a few local eateries near the station.

Central Hotel Imari   HOTEL ¥
(セントラルホテル伊万里; ☑ 095-522-0880; www.central-imari.jp; 549-17 Hamanoura; s/d incl breakfast from ¥5900/9600; ⊜ ✳ ☏) Clean and convenient hotel just a minute's walk from Imari JR Station. The hotel has rental bikes available and some nonsmoking rooms.

Kippō   TEMPURA ¥¥
(天ぷらの吉峰; ☑ 0955-23-3563; 196 Tatemachi; lunch set menus ¥1000-2000; ⊙ 11am-2pm & 5-9pm Thu-Tue) A few hundred metres from the Imari Station area, this family-run place serves up super-fresh tempura, some on Imari-ware dishes. No English is spoken, so just say *'setto o kudasai'* (set menu please).

ℹ Information

Imari City Information (伊万里市観光協会; ☑ 0955-23-3479; ⊙ 9am-6pm) Tourist brochures are available from this outlet on the regional Matsūra Railway, across the street from JR Imari Station.

ℹ Getting There & Around

Imari is connected to Karatsu (¥650, 50 minutes) by the JR Chikuhi line or bus (¥1030, 60 minutes), and also to Arita by the private Matsūra-tetsudō line (¥460, 25 minutes).

Five to six buses per day (¥170) make the trip to Ōkawachiyama. Alternatively, the taxi fare is approximately ¥1800 each way.

Hirado   平戸

☑ 0950 / POP 32,000

The tragic irony of sweet, off-the-beaten-path Hirado is that it was once *the* spot where foreigners visited Japan before *sakoku* (isolationism) and Dejima island. As trains, then planes, surpassed ships as the main entry to Japan, Hirado has been all but forgotten, especially since the town lies off a private, non-JR rail line.

This secluded yet lovely little island has many reminders of early Western involvement, particularly of Kakure Kirishitan (hidden Christians) who populated this region. It's also a popular beach getaway and has a lovely old-style shopping street, great seafood, a castle and wonderful museums.

◎ Sights

★ **Oranda Shōkan**   HISTORIC BUILDING
(オランダ商館; ☑ 0950-26-0636; 2477 Ōkubo; ¥300; ⊙ 8.30am-5.30pm, closed 3rd Tue, Wed & Thu of Jun) Across from the waterfront, this building was the trading house of the Dutch East India Company. Shogunal authorities took the Gregorian date on the front of the building (1639) as proof of forbidden Christianity, ordered it destroyed and used it to justify confining Dutch traders to Dejima (p717). It has been rebuilt according to the original plans and now houses displays of the textiles, pewter ware, gin and pottery once traded.

★ **Ji-in to Kyōkai no Mieru Michi**   AREA
(寺院と教会の見える道, Street for Viewing Temples & a Church) This street, rising up a steep hill from town, is one of the most photogenic vantage points in all of Kyūshū. The Buddhist temples and large Christian church are testimony to the island's history.

Matsūra Historical Museum   MUSEUM
(松浦史料博物館; ☑ 0950-22-2236; www.matsura.or.jp; 12 Kagamigawa-chō; ¥510; ⊙ 8.30am-5.30pm) Across the bay from the tourist centre, this museum is housed in the stunning residence of the Matsūra clan, who ruled the island from the 11th to the 19th centuries. You'll find armour that you can don to pose for photos; *byōbu* (folding screen) paintings; and the thatched-roof **Kanun-tei**, a *chanoyu* (tea ceremony) house for the unusual Chinshin-ryū warrior-style tea ceremony (¥500) that is still practised on the island.

If you can get here on a sunny day, be sure to participate in the tea ceremony offered between 9.30am and 5pm. Clothed in a traditional kimono, you'll partake in a tea service very similar to those served when this custom was first brought to Japan from China centuries ago. Along with the tea, old-style Hirado sweets are also provided.

Hirado Christian Museum   MUSEUM
(平戸切支丹資料館; ☑ 0950-28-0176; Ōnowaki-machi 1502-1; ¥200; ⊙ 9am-5.30pm Thu-Tue) Across the middle of the island, this small museum displays items including a Maria-Kannon statue that the hidden Christians used in place of the Virgin Mary.

Hirado-jō
CASTLE

(平戸城; ☎0950-22-2201; 1458 Iwanoue-chō; ¥510; ◷8.30am-5.30pm) Hirado-jō presides over the town, with an enormous number of rebuilt structures. Inside you'll see traditional armour and clothing, and photos and models of old Hirado.

🏃 Activities

Kawachi Pass
HIKING

(川内峠) West of central Hirado, this series of grassy hilltops offers views of both sides of the island – east toward the Japanese mainland and west toward the East China Sea – and above the tiny islands that populate the waters. Paths are lined with eulalia and azaleas, and the occasional condor flies overhead.

Cape Shijiki
BEACH

(🚗) From Hirado, it's about a 40km (one-hour) drive to the island's southern tip at Cape Shijiki, from where there are views of the Gotō-rettō archipelago. Hotel Ranpū is en route for those needing to overnight.

Long **Neshiko Beach** on Hirado's lovely west coast is popular for swimming. Jellyfish are common, so heed warnings.

🎎 Festivals & Events

Jangara Matsuri
CULTURAL

(ジャンガラ祭り; ◷18 Aug) Hirado's famous Jangara Matsuri folk festival is particularly colourful, reminiscent of Okinawa or Korea. Arrive in Hirado by late morning for the afternoon events.

Okunchi Matsuri
CULTURAL

(平戸おくんち祭り; ◷24-27 Oct) The Okunchi Matsuri has dragon and lion dancing at Kameoka-jinja.

🛏 Sleeping & Eating

Inomoto Ryokan
MINSHUKU ¥¥

(井元旅館; ☎095-022-2719; 873 Sakigata-chō; s/d ¥3900/7000; ❄) Spartan but clean and cheap, Inomoto Ryokan is also in a perfect location for seeing Hirado's sights and historic waterfront. Note that it is cash only, and there are no nonsmoking rooms.

Hotel Ranpū
HOTEL ¥¥

(ホテル蘭風; ☎0950-23-2111; www.hotel-ranpu.com; 55 Kawauchi-chō; s/tw incl 2 meals ¥8500/10,800; P❄❅❆) About a 30km (one-hour) drive from Cape Shijiki, this hotel has expansive indoor and outdoor onsen baths, a beach and restaurants. It's also your only option if you're doing sightseeing around here.

Samson Hotel
RESORT ¥¥

(サムソンホテル; ☎0950-57-1110; www.samson-hotel.jp; 210-6 Nodamen, Tabira-chō; capsule ¥3390, r per person incl 2 meals from ¥9720; P❄❅❆@) This 10-storey hot-spring hotel on the mainland was renovated in 2012. Public baths are like lookouts over the water, and pricey giant suites contain multiple rooms, some with balconies. By contrast, capsule hotel beds are as simple as you can get (meals not included), and there's a summertime beer garden. Rates listed are for the old building.

Shunsenkan
SEAFOOD ¥

(旬鮮館; ☎0950-22-4857; 655-13 Miyano-chō; sashimi set meal ¥700; ◷10am-4pm Wed-Mon) Across from the tourist information office and operated by local fishing families, this cooperative is basically a market with picnic tables, where staff will prepare meals. Look for the red building and ask for *sashimi moriawase* (assorted sashimi; ¥400), *kaisendon* (seafood over rice) or just point.

Ichiyama
STEAK ¥¥

(市山; ☎0950-22-2439; 529 Tsukiji-machi; set meals ¥3800; ◷11.30am-2pm & 5-10pm Wed-Mon) Hirado beef compares well in taste with other *wagyū* varieties. Try it at this spacious and comfy spot for *yakiniku* (Korean-style grilled beef). Multicourse set menus are a good deal.

ℹ Information

Tourist Information Centre (平戸観光案内所; ☎0950-22-2015; 776-6 Sakigata; ◷8am-6pm; 🛜) Located near the ferry terminal and has lots of English materials, free computers/wi-fi and helpful staff to assist with booking accommodation.

ℹ Getting There & Away

Hirado is closer to Saga-ken than to Nagasaki city, joined to Kyūshū by a mini Golden Gate–lookalike bridge from Hirado-guchi. The closest train station, Tabira-Hirado-guchi on the private Matsūra-tetsudō line (to Imari ¥1230, 72 minutes; Sasebo ¥1340, 90 minutes), is Japan's westernmost; and local buses cross the bridge to the island (¥260, 10 minutes). From Nagasaki, journey to Sasebo by JR/express bus (¥1600/1450, both 1½ hours) and continue to Hirado by bus (¥1500, 1½ hours).

ℹ Getting Around

Hirado township is small enough to navigate on foot, but you'll need your own transport for points elsewhere on the island.

Rental bikes are available at the **tourist information centre** for ¥500 per four hours. Rental cars, starting at ¥5300 per day, are well worth it if you plan to see the furthest sights or beaches.

Arita 有田

📱 0955 / POP 20,170

Kaolin clay was discovered in Arita in 1615 by Ri Sampei, a naturalised Korean potter, enabling the manufacture of fine porcelain in Japan for the first time. By the mid-17th century, the porcelain was being exported to Europe.

Between the station and Kyūshū Ceramic Museum is the **Yakimono Sanpo-michi** (Pottery Promenade) of around 16 galleries. The tourist office has a map that's in Japanese but is easy enough to follow. Arita's streets fill with vendors for the annual **pottery market**, held from 29 April to 5 May.

Out of the town centre, two of Arita-yaki's prime practitioners have been at it for 14 generations. The Imaemon Gallery and Kakiemon Kiln both have museums in addition to sales shops. Genemon Kiln makes and sells more contemporary styles.

◉ Sights

★ Kouraku Kiln　　　　　FACTORY
(幸楽窯; 📱0955-42-4121; www.kouraku.jp.net; Marunohei 2512; ⊙9am-8pm) This fascinating pottery factory has something for everyone: you can try making simple pottery on the throwing wheel (which can be fired and mailed to you within Japan); you can stay here longer in a residency to learn the craft (¥49,000/200,000 per week/month); or shoppers can go 'Treasure Hunting' in the vast seconds warehouse and spend as much time filling a box (¥5000) with whatever fits.

Headed by a genial Brazilian, this kiln has opted – at some risk of criticism – to offer reasonably priced pieces for tourists who aren't deep-pocketed art collectors. As such, you'll find it far less manicured, but the chance to have as much Arita-yaki as you can take home for ¥5000 is unique and fun. The residency includes up to 40kg of porcelain clay and you live and work with potters, learning the Arita ceramic craft.

★ Kyūshū Ceramic Museum　　MUSEUM
(九州陶磁文化館; 📱095-543-3681; ⊙9am-5pm Tue-Sun) FREE Five minutes on foot from Arita Station, this large, hilltop operation

is the best ceramics museum in the region. The Shibata Collection comprehensively showcases the development and styles of Kyūshū's many ceramic arts, with excellent English signage. An entrance fee may be charged for some special exhibits.

Imaemon Gallery　　　　GALLERY
(今石衛門ギャラリー; 📱0955-42-5550; ¥300; ⊙9.30am-4.30pm Tue-Sun) Stunning works of art are on display in the gallery of one of Japan's living national treasures. The adjoining shop is open daily, even when the gallery is closed.

Kakiemon Kiln　　　　　FACTORY
(柿右衛門窯; 📱0955-43-2267; ⊙9am-5pm) FREE This kiln is one of Arita's don't-miss sights. The wood-fired kiln produces a particular kind of porcelain, known (not surprisingly!) as Kakiemon-ware.

🏃 Activities

Takeo Onsen　　　　　　ONSEN
(武雄温泉; 📱095-423-2001; ¥400; ⊙6.30am-midnight) The original Takeo Onsen has a 1300-year history and is said to have refreshed the armies of Toyotomi Hideyoshi. Its impressive lacquered Chinese-style entrance gate was built without nails, and the oldest existing bathing building (Moto-yu) is a wooden hall from 1870. It's a 15-minute walk west of the Takeo Station's north exit.

The complex even has *rotemburo* (outdoor baths) and *kashikiri* (private reservable baths for families or couples), making it a good spot for people uncomfortable bathing nude among others.

🛏 Sleeping & Eating

There are a few nondescript hotels. Takeo Onsen would be a better spot to overnight.

Takeo Onsen Youth Hostel　　HOSTEL ¥
(武雄温泉ユースホステル; 📱0954-22-2490; www.e-yh.net/takeo; 16060-1 Nagashima; dm HI member/nonmember ¥3400/4000; 🅿 😊 ❄ @ 🤖) You can stay among hot-spring baths at the 14-room Takeo Onsen Youth Hostel, with a green and orange paint job so bright it's likely visible from space. The friendly owners can pick you up from the station if you ring ahead saying you'll be later than the 4pm check-in. A few loaner bikes are available. Rates include a simple breakfast.

Because neither lunch nor dinner is served, you'll need to bring provisions if you won't be dining in town.

Gallery Arita
CAFE ¥¥

(☑095-542-2952; Honmachi Ōtsu 3057; godōfu set menu ¥1350, coffee from ¥450; ☺9am-7pm) Choose from over 2000 cup and saucer sets from hundreds of different Arita-yaki potters. The waitstaff seem to know each one personally, too. Coffee is brewed filter style and the godōfu set meal is an excellent lunch. Don't miss the Arita-yaki-style Mini Cooper in the driveway.

🛍 Shopping

Genemon Kiln
CERAMICS

(源右衛門窯; ☑0955-42-4164; www.gen-emon.co.jp; ☺8am-8pm Mon-Sat) Potters work in a large studio crafting stunning examples of Arita-ware.

ⓘ Information

Tourist Information Desk (☑0955-42-4052; www.arita.jp; ☺9am-5pm) The staff at this tiny info desk inside Arita Station can assist with maps in English, timetables and accommodation, predominantly small private *minshuku* (guesthouses). Be sure to grab a *hama* (ceramic disk used in firing) as a free souvenir.

ⓘ Getting There & Away

The private Matsūra-tetsudō line connects Arita with Imari (¥460, 24 minutes). JR *tokkyū* trains between Hakata (¥2750, 80 minutes) and Sasebo (¥760, 31 minutes) stop at Arita and Takeo Onsen. Takeo Onsen is also connected to Arita by local trains (¥280, 20 minutes).

Infrequent community buses (¥200) cover most sights, but you'll save time by taking taxis (about ¥1000 to most sights). Arita Station rents out bicycles (¥500 to ¥1000 per day).

NAGASAKI & AROUND

Nagasaki sits high on the list of Kyūshū's must-sees, and not just for the tragedy most often associated with it – the atomic bombing by the United States at the end of WWII. The city has a colourful cosmopolitan history, and a dynamic cuisine to match. Travelling east, there's more history (and volcanic landscapes) to explore on the Shimabara Peninsula.

Nagasaki 長崎

☑095 / POP 430,000

It's both unfortunate – and important – that the name Nagasaki is synonymous with the dropping of the second atomic bomb.

Unquestionably, this history overshadows everything else, yet today Nagasaki is a vibrant, charming and totally unique gem that begs to be explored far beyond the bomb museums, monuments and memorials. Not that the WWII history can be overlooked or denied: it's as much a part of the city's fabric as the hilly landscape and cobblestones, and a visit to the scenes of atomic devastation is a must. You'll find, however, that this welcoming, peaceful city also boasts a colourful trading history, alluring churches, shrines and temples, and an East-meets-West culinary scene, all set prettily around a gracious harbour. A few days will only let you scratch the surface, so plan for a week or more if you have the extra time.

◉ Sights

Nagasaki's sights are scattered over a broad area, but once you're in a district it's easy to walk from one location to the next. The atomic bomb hypocentre is in the suburb of Urakami, about 2.5km north of JR Nagasaki Station. Central and southern Nagasaki are where you'll find sights related to its history of trade and foreign influence. Main enclaves are around JR Nagasaki Station and about 2km south: Shinchi Chinatown, the Dutch Slopes and Glover Garden. Near Shinchi Chinatown, Shianbashi is the main nightlife and shopping district.

Parts of Nagasaki are quite hilly, so bring good walking shoes. Because of the hills, people rarely cycle, and even driving can be challenging.

◉ Urakami (Northern Nagasaki)

Urakami, the hypocentre of the atomic explosion, is today a prosperous, peaceful suburb. While nuclear ruin seems comfortably far away seven decades later, many sights here keep the memory alive.

★Nagasaki
Atomic Bomb Museum
MUSEUM

(長崎原爆資料館; Map p716; ☑095-844-1231; www.nagasakipeace.jp; 7-8 Hirano-machi; ¥200, audioguide ¥154; ☺8.30am-6.30pm May-Aug, to 5.30pm Sep-Apr; 🚋Matsuyama-machi) An essential Nagasaki experience, this sombre place recounts the city's destruction and loss of life through photos and artefacts, including mangled rocks, trees, furniture, pottery and clothing, a clock stopped at 11.02 (the hour of the bombing), firsthand accounts from survivors, and stories of heroic relief efforts.

KYŪSHŪ POTTERY TOWNS

In mountainous Kyūshū, many villages had difficulty growing rice and looked toward other industries to survive. Access to good clay, forests and streams made pottery-making a natural choice, and a number of superb styles can be found here.

Karatsu, Arita and Imari are the major pottery towns of Saga-ken. From the early 17th century, pottery was produced in this area by captive Korean potters, experts who were zealously guarded so that neither artist nor the secrets of their craft could escape. When trade routes opened up to the West, potters in Japan began imitating the highly decorative Chinese-style wares popular in Europe. Pottery styles are often known by the town name with the suffix -yaki (pottery) added.

Arita (p713) Highly decorated porcelain, often with squares of blue, red, green or gold.

Imari (p710) Fine porcelain, originally blue and white, bursting into vibrant colours in the mid-Edo period.

Karatsu (p708) Marked by subtle earthy tones, prized for its use in the tea ceremony.

In southern Kyūshū, Kagoshima Prefecture is known for Satsuma-yaki (Satsuma is the feudal name for that region). Styles vary from crackled glazes to porcelains painted with gleaming gold, and rougher, more ponderous 'black Satsuma' ware.

Exhibits also include the postbombing struggle for nuclear disarmament, and conclude with a chilling illustration of which nations bear nuclear arms.

★ Nagasaki National Peace Memorial Hall for the Atomic Bomb Victims MEMORIAL

(国立長崎原爆死没者追悼平和祈念館; Map p716; www.peace-nagasaki.go.jp; 7-8 Hirano-machi; ☺8.30am-6.30pm May-Aug, to 5.30pm Sep-Apr; ☒Matsuyama-machi) FREE Adjacent to the Atomic Bomb Museum and completed in 2003, this minimalist memorial by Kuryū Akira is a profoundly moving place. It is best approached by quietly reading the carved inscriptions and walking around the sculpted water basin. In the hall below, 12 glass pillars, containing shelves of books of the names of the deceased, reach skyward.

★ Peace Park PARK

(平和公園, Heiwa-kōen; Map p716; ☒Ōhashi) North of the hypocentre, the Peace Park is presided over by the 10-tonne bronze **Nagasaki Peace Statue** (平和祈念像; Map p716), designed in 1955 by Kitamura Seibō. It also includes the dove-shaped Fountain of Peace (1969), and the Peace Symbol Zone, a sculpture garden with contributions on the theme of peace from around the world. On 9 August, a rowdy antinuclear protest is held within earshot of the more respectful official memorial ceremony for those lost to the bomb.

Atomic Bomb Hypocentre Park PARK

(長崎爆心地公園; Map p716; ☒Matsuyama-machi) One of the must-see sites for anyone coming to the city for its historic value. The park has a smooth, black-stone column marking the point above which the bomb exploded. Nearby are bomb-blasted relics, including a section of the wall of the Urakami Cathedral.

Urakami Cathedral CHURCH

(浦上天主堂; Map p716; 1-79 Motō-machi; ☺9am-5pm; ☒Matsuyama-machi) Once the largest church in Asia (1914), the cathedral took three decades to complete and three seconds to flatten. This smaller replacement cathedral was completed in 1959 on the ruins of the original. Walk around the side of the hill to see a belfry lying in state where the original building fell after the atomic blast.

Nagai Takashi Memorial Museum MUSEUM

(永井隆記念館; Map p716; 22-6 Ueno-machi; ¥100; ☺9am-5pm; ☒Ōhashi) This small but quietly moving museum celebrates the courage and faith of one man in the face of overwhelming adversity. Already suffering from leukaemia, Dr Nagai survived the atomic explosion but lost his wife to it. He immediately devoted himself to the treatment of bomb victims until his death in 1951. In his final days, he continued to write prolifically and secure donations for survivors and orphans, earning the nickname 'Saint of Nagasaki'. Ask to watch the video in English.

Next door is **Nyokodō** (如己堂), the simple hut from which Dr Nagai worked – its name comes from the biblical commandment 'love thy neighbour as thyself'.

Nagasaki

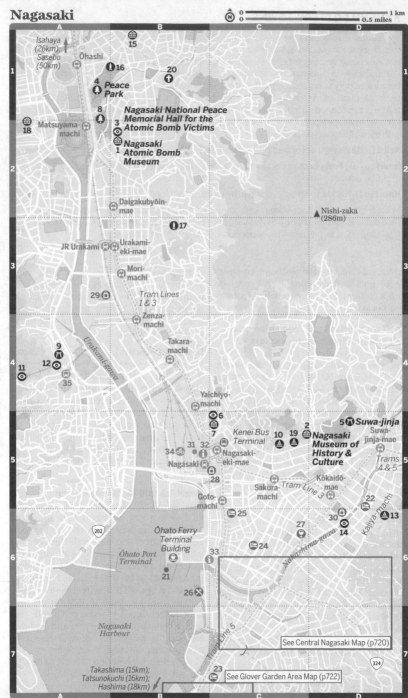

0 1 km
0 0.5 miles

Isahaya (26km);
Sasebo (50km)

Ōhashi

15

16

20

4 Peace Park

8

3 Nagasaki National Peace Memorial Hall for the Atomic Bomb Victims

Matsuyama-machi

18

1 Nagasaki Atomic Bomb Museum

Daigakubyōin-mae

Nishi-zaka (286m)

17

JR Urakami

Urakami-eki-mae

Mori-machi

29

Tram Lines 1 & 3

Zenza-machi

Takara-machi

9

12

11

35

Urakami-gawa

Yaichiyo-machi

6

7

Kenei Bus Terminal

10 **19** **2** Nagasaki Museum of History & Culture

5 Suwa-jinja

Suwa-jinja-mae

Trams 4 & 5

34 **31** **32**

Nagasaki-eki-mae

Nagasaki

28

Goto-machi

Sakura-machi

Tram Line 3

Kōkaidō-mae

22

30

14

Kajiya-machi

13

25

27

Ōhato Ferry Terminal Building

Ōhato Port Terminal

33

21

24

Nawashima-gawa

202

26

Nagasaki Harbour

Tram Line 5

See Central Nagasaki Map (p720)

324

Takashima (15km);
Tatsunokuchi (16km);
Hashima (18km)

23

See Glover Garden Area Map (p722)

A B C D

Nagasaki

KYŪSHŪ NAGASAKI

Shiroyama
Elementary School   HISTORIC BUILDING
(城山小学校; Map p716; ☑095-861-0057; 23-1 Shiroyama-chō; ◉8.30am-4.30pm Mon-Fri; 🚇Matsuyama-machi) This was the closest school to the nuclear blast, up a hill a mere 500m away, where 1400 children perished. It's hard not to be moved by the very ordinariness that exists here today. Except for one building that still stands as it did following the bombing (to the right at the top of the stairs), this functioning school looks much like any other, albeit with the addition of sculptures, monuments and memorials commemorating the loss of life.

The last of these is laden with strands of 1000 origami cranes, the traditional children's prayer for peace.

One-Pillar Torii   MONUMENT
(一本柱鳥居; Map p716; 🚇Daigakubyōin-mae or Urakami-eki-mae) The atomic blast knocked down half of the stone entrance arch to the Sanno-jinja shrine, 800m southeast of the hypocentre, but the other pillar remains, a quiet testimony to the power of human strength and resilience.

◉ Central Nagasaki

★Dejima   HISTORIC SITE
(出島; Map p720; 🚇Dejima) In 1641, the Tokugawa shogunate banished all foreigners from Japan, with one exception: Dejima, a fan-shaped, artificial island 560m in circumference (15,000 sq metres) in Nagasaki harbour. From then until the 1850s, this tiny Dutch trading post was the sole sanctioned foreign presence in Japan. Today the city has filled in around the island and you might miss it. Don't. Seventeen buildings, walls and structures (plus a miniature Dejima) have been painstakingly reconstructed into the **Dejima Museum** (出島資料館; Map p720; ☑095-829-1194; www.nagasakidejima.jp; 6-1 Dejima-machi; ¥510; ◉8am-7pm mid-Jul–mid-Oct, to 6pm mid-Oct–mid-Jul).

Restored and reopened in 2006 and constantly being upgraded, the buildings in the museum are as instructive inside as they are good-looking outside, with exhibits covering the spread of trade, Western learning and culture, archaeological digs, and rooms combining Japanese tatami (tightly woven floor matting) with Western wallpaper. There's

THE ATOMIC EXPLOSION OVER NAGASAKI

••

When USAF B-29 bomber *Bock's Car* set off from the Marianas on 9 August 1945 to drop a second atomic bomb on Japan, the target was Kokura on Kyūshū's northeastern coast. Due to poor visibility, the crew diverted to the secondary target, Nagasaki.

The B-29 arrived over Nagasaki at 10.58am amid heavy cloud. When a momentary gap appeared and the Mitsubishi Arms Factory was sighted, the 4.57-tonne 'Fat Man' bomb, with an explosive power equivalent to 21.3 kilotonnes of TNT (almost twice that of Hiroshima's 'Little Boy'), was released over Nagasaki.

The bomb missed the arms factory, its intended target, and exploded at 11.02am, at an altitude of 500m almost directly above the largest Catholic church in Asia (Urakami Cathedral). In an instant, it annihilated the suburb of Urakami and 74,000 of Nagasaki's 240,000 people. Ground temperatures at the hypocentre were estimated at between 3000°C and 4000°C, and as high as 600°C 1.5km away. Everything within a 1km radius of the explosion was destroyed, and searing winds up to 170km/h (typhoons generally top out at 150km/h) swept down the valley of the Urakami-gawa towards the city centre. With able-bodied men at work or at war, most victims were women, children and senior citizens, as well as 13,000 conscripted Korean labourers and 200 Allied POWs. Another 75,000 people were horribly injured (and it is estimated that as many people died due to the after-effects). After the resulting fires burned out, a third of the city was gone.

Yet the damage might have been even worse had the targeted arms factory been hit. Unlike in the flatlands of Hiroshima or the Nagasaki port itself, the hills around the river valley protected outlying suburbs from greater damage.

excellent English signage. Allow at least two hours. There's even a kimono rental shop (¥2000/6000 per hour/day) for those who want to feel even more in character.

Shinchi Chinatown
AREA

(新地中華街; Map p720; 📷 Tsuki-machi) During Japan's long period of seclusion, Chinese traders were theoretically just as restricted as the Dutch, but in practice they were relatively free. Only a couple of buildings remain from the old area, but Nagasaki still has an energetic Chinese community, evident in the city's culture, architecture, festivals and cuisine. Visitors come from far and wide to eat here and shop for Chinese crafts and trinkets.

Nakashima-gawa Bridges
BRIDGE

(中島川; 📷 Kōkaidō-mae or Nigiwai-bashi) Parallel to Teramachi, the Nakashima-gawa is crossed by a picturesque collection of 17th-century stone bridges. At one time, each bridge was the distinct entranceway to a separate temple. Best known is the double-arched **Megane-bashi** (めがね橋, Spectacles Bridge; Map p716), originally built in 1634 and so-called because the reflection of the arches in the water looks like a pair of Meiji-era spectacles. Six of the 10 bridges, including Megane-bashi, were washed away by flooding in 1982, but restored using the recovered stones.

Sōfuku-ji
BUDDHIST TEMPLE

(崇福寺; Map p720; 7-5 Kajiya-machi; ¥300; ⊙8am-5pm; 📷 Shōkakuji-shita) In Teramachi, this Ōbaku temple (Ōbaku is the third-largest Zen sect after Rinzai and Sōtō) was built in 1629 by Chinese monk Chaonian. Its red entrance gate (*Daiippo-mon*) exemplifies Ming dynasty architecture. Inside the temple you can admire a huge cauldron that was used to prepare food for famine victims in 1681, and a statue of Maso, goddess of the sea, worshipped by early Chinese seafarers.

Kōfuku-ji
BUDDHIST TEMPLE

(興福寺; Map p716; 4-32 Tera-machi; ¥300; ⊙8am-5pm; 📷 Kōkaidō-mae) This temple in Teramachi dates from the 1620s and is noted for the Ming architecture of the main hall. Like Sōfuku-ji, it is an Ōbaku Zen temple – and the oldest in Japan.

★Nagasaki Museum of History & Culture
MUSEUM

(長崎歴史文化博物館; Map p716; 📞095-818-8366; www.nmhc.jp; 1-1-1 Tateyama; ¥600; ⊙8.30am-7pm, closed 3rd Tue of the month; 📷 Sakura-machi) This large museum with attractive displays opened in 2005 to focus on Nagasaki's proud history of international exchange. The main gallery is a fabulous reconstruction of a section of the Edo-period Nagasaki Magistrate's Office, which controlled

KYŪSHŪ NAGASAKI

trade and diplomacy. At the time of writing, detailed English-language explanations were in the works.

★ Suwa-jinja SHINTO SHRINE
(諏訪神社; Map p716; 18-15 Kaminishiyama-machi; ⊙24hr; 🚃Suwa-jinja-mae) **FREE** Situated on a forested hilltop and reached via multiple staircases, this enormous shrine was established in 1625. Around the grounds are statues of *komainu* (protective dogs), including the *kappa-komainu* (water-sprite dogs), which you pray to by dribbling water onto the plates on their heads. The *gankake komainu* (turntable dog) was often called on by prostitutes, who prayed that storms would arrive, forcing the sailors to stay at the port another day.

Fukusai-ji Kannon BUDDHIST TEMPLE
(福済寺·長崎観音, Nagasaki Universal Kannon Temple; Map p716; 2-56 Chikugo-machi; ¥200; ⊙8am-4pm; 🚃Sakura-machi) This temple takes the form of a huge turtle carrying an 18m-high figure of the goddess Kannon on its back. Inside, a Foucault pendulum (demonstrating the rotation of the earth on its axis) hangs from near the top of the hollow statue. Only St Petersburg and Paris have larger examples.

The original temple, Chinese in origin, was built in 1628, but was completely burnt by the A-bomb fire. The replacement was built in 1976. The temple bell tolls at 11:02 daily, the exact time of the explosion of the atomic bomb.

26 Martyrs Memorial MEMORIAL
(日本二十六聖人殉教地; Map p716) This memorial wall has reliefs of the 26 Christians crucified in 1597, commemorating a harsh crackdown when six Spanish friars and 20 Japanese were killed. The youngest killed were boys aged 12 and 13. Behind the memorial is a simple **museum** (二十六聖人記念館; Map p716; ☎095-822-6000; www.26martyrs.com; 7-8 Nishizaka-machi; ¥500; ⊙9am-5pm) with Christianity-related displays. The memorial is a 10-minute walk from JR Nagasaki Station.

Inasa-yama MOUNTAIN
(稲佐山; Map p716) West of the harbour, a **cable car** (長崎ロープウェイ; Map p716; www.nagasaki-ropeway.jp; Takara-machi; return ¥1230; ⊙9am-10pm; 🚃) ascends every 20 minutes to the top of 333m-high Inasa-yama, offering superb views over Nagasaki, particularly at night. From 7am to 10pm there's a free shuttle from five Nagasaki hotels (reserve at the front desk) and from JR Nagasaki Station

going towards Shimo-Ōhashi; get off at the Ropeway-mae bus stop and walk up the steps through the grounds of **Fuchi-jinja** (淵神社; Map p716).

⊙ Southern Nagasaki

Glover Garden GARDENS
(グラバー園; Map p722; ☎095-822-8223; www.glover-garden.jp; 8-1 Minami-yamate-machi; adult/student ¥610/300; ⊙8am-9.30pm May–mid-Jul, to 6pm mid-Jul–Apr; 🚃Ōura Tenshudō-shita) Some former homes of the city's Meiji-period European residents have been reassembled in this hillside garden. Glover Garden is named after Thomas Glover (1838–1911), the Scottish merchant who built Japan's first railway, helped establish the shipbuilding industry and whose arms-importing operations influenced the course of the Meiji Restoration. It's a lovely spot to stroll around.

The best way to explore the garden is to take the moving walkways to the top of the hill then walk back down. The **Mitsubishi No 2 Dock building** (旧三菱第2ドックハウス) is highest, with panoramic views of the city and harbour from the 2nd floor. Next highest is **Walker House** (旧ウォーカー住宅; Map p722), filled with artefacts donated by the families, followed by **Ringer House** (旧リンガー住宅; Map p722), **Alt House** (旧オルト住宅; Map p722) and finally **Glover House** (旧グラバー住宅). Halfway down is the **Madame Butterfly Statue** (Map p722) of Japanese opera singer Tamaki Miura, who performed as Cio-Cio-san in Puccini's famous opera (the story took place here in Nagasaki). Exit the garden through the **Nagasaki Traditional Performing Arts Museum** (長崎伝統芸能館), which has a display of dragons and floats used in Nagasaki's colourful Kunchi Matsuri (p721).

Ōura Catholic Church CHURCH
(大浦天主堂; Map p722; ☎095-823-2628; 5-3 Yamate-machi; ¥300; ⊙8am-6pm; 🚃Ōura Tenshudō-shita) This hilltop church, Japan's oldest (1865), is dedicated to the 26 Christians who were crucified in Nagasaki in 1597. It's more like a museum than a place of worship, with an ornate Gothic altar and bishop's chair, and an oil painting of the 26 martyrs. To pray for free, use the regular church across the street.

Dutch Slopes AREA
(オランダ坂; Map p722; Oranda-zaka; 🚃Ishibashi) The gently inclined flagstone streets

Central Nagasaki

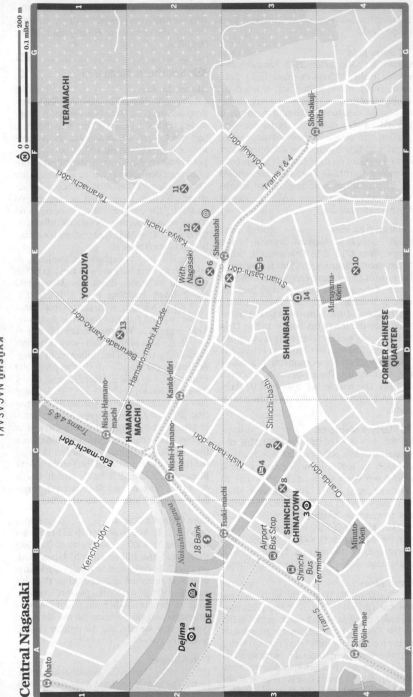

KYŪSHŪ NAGASAKI

TERAMACHI

Shōkakuji-shita

Teramachi-dōri

Sōfukuji-dōri

Trams 1 & 4

YOROZUYA

Kaiya-machi

11 ✗

12 ✗

@

Shianbashi

With Nagasaki

6 ✗

7 ✗

5 🏨

Shian-bashi-dōri

10 ✗

Maruyama-kōen

14 🏨

SHIANBASHI

FORMER CHINESE QUARTER

Berunade-Kankō-dōri

13 ✗

Hamano-machi Arcade

Kankō-dōri

Shinchi-bashi

Shinchi-bashi

Olanda-dōri

Nishi-Hamano-machi

HAMANO-MACHI

Trams 4 & 5

Edo-machi-dōri

Kenchō-dōri

Nishi-Hamano-machi1

Nishi-hama-dōri

Tsuki-machi

9 ✗

4 🍴

8 ✗

SHINCHI CHINATOWN

3 ◎

Minato-kōen

Nakashima-gawa

18 Bank 💲

Airport Bus Stop 🚌

Shinchi Bus Terminal

Tram 5

Shimin-Byōin-mae

Dejima

1 ◎

2 🏛

DEJIMA

Ōhato

200 m

0.1 miles

0 0

Central Nagasaki

known as the Dutch Slopes were once lined with wooden **Dutch houses**. Several buildings here have been beautifully restored and offer glimpses of Japan's early interest in the Western world. The quiet **Ko-shashin-shiryōkan** (古写真資料館, Museum of Old Photographs; Map p722; 6-25 Higashi-yamatemachi; combined admission ¥100; ⏰9am-5pm Tue-Sun) and **Maizō-shiryōkan** (埋蔵資料館, Museum of Unearthed Artefacts; Map p722; 6-25 Higashi-yamatemachi; combined admission ¥100; ⏰9am-5pm Tue-Sun) showcase the area's history (note that most signage is in Japanese).

Kōshi-byō & Historical Museum of China
CONFUCIAN SHRINE

(孔子廟・中国歴代博物館; Map p722; ☎095-824-4022; 10-36 Ōuramachi; shrine & museum ¥600; ⏰8.30am-5.30pm; 🚋Ishibashi) The jauntily painted Kōshi-byō shrine claims to be the only Confucian shrine built by and for Chinese outside of China, and the statues of sages in its courtyard certainly make you feel like you've journeyed across the sea. The original 1893 building was destroyed by fire following the A-bomb explosion.

Behind the shrine, a glossy museum of Chinese art spans jade artefacts, Neolithic archaeological finds, terracotta warriors and Qing-dynasty porcelain. There's also a large gift shop with Chinese trinkets, from classy to kitschy.

🚌 Tours

One-hour **Nagasaki Harbour Cruises** (長崎港めぐりクルーズ; Map p716; ☎095-822-5002; Nagasaki Harbour Terminal Bldg; adult/child ¥2000/1000; ⏰noon & 4pm Thu-Mon) are a great way to glimpse picturesque Nagasaki. Check at the ferry terminal for up-to-date schedules.

🎭 Festivals & Events

Kunchi Matsuri CULTURAL
(⏰7-9 Oct) This energetic festival features Chinese dragons dancing all around the city, but especially at Suwa-jinja. The festival is marked by elaborate costumes, fireworks, cymbals and giant dragon puppets.

Peiron Dragon-Boat Races CULTURAL
(⏰late Jul) Colourful boat races were introduced by the Chinese in the mid-1600s, and held to appease the god of the sea. They still take place in Nagasaki harbour.

Shōrō-nagashi CULTURAL
(⏰15 Aug) During this festival, lantern-lit boats are floated on the harbour to honour ancestors. The boats are of various sizes and hand-crafted from a variety of materials (bamboo, wood, rice stems etc). Eventually they are carried out to sea and destroyed by the waves. The best viewpoint for the procession is at the Ōhato ferry terminal.

🛏 Sleeping

For ease of transport and access to restaurants and nightlife, we recommend staying near JR Nagasaki Station or Shianbashi.

⭐ **Hostel Akari** HOSTEL ¥
(ホステルあかり; Map p716; ☎095-801-7900; www.nagasaki-hostel.com; 2-2 Kōjiya-machi; dm/s from ¥2700/3300, d & tw from ¥6800, tr ¥9900; ⏰reception 9am-1pm & 3-8pm; ❄✳@🛜; 🚋Kōkaidō-mae) This commendably friendly 28-bed hostel sets the standard, with bright, clean Japanese-style rooms with Western-style bedding and bathrooms, uberhelpful staff, an open kitchen, and a dedicated crew of local volunteers who lead free walking tours around the city. It's by the lovely Nakashima-gawa. Towel rental is ¥100. Check-in or even bag dropping can be tough between 1pm and 3pm.

Glover Garden Area

Glover Garden Area

**ANA Crowne Plaza
Hotel Nagasaki Gloverhill**   HOTEL ¥¥
(ANAクラウンプラザホテル長崎グラバ
ーヒル; Map p722; ☎095-818-6601; www.ana-
crowneplaza-nagasaki.jp; 1-18 Minami-yamate-
machi; s/d/tw from ¥9060/13,800/16,800; P⊜

✳@🛜; ⛴Ōura-Tenshudō-shita) Near Glover
Garden, Ōura Catholic Church and the
Dutch Slopes, this sprawling hotel has three
types of room: Standard, which are relatively plain; then Superior and Deluxe, which
are both quite stylish on account of recent

renovations. About the only downside: no view to speak of.

Hotel Dormy Inn Nagasaki BUSINESS HOTEL ¥¥

(ドーミーイン長崎; Map p720; ☑095-820-5489; www.hotespa.net; 7-24 Dōza-machi; s/d/tw from ¥6790/7790/9790; P ❷ ❄ @ 🛜; 🚇 Tsuki-machi) Adjacent to Chinatown, this hotel would be worth it just for the location. Rooms are crisp and neat as a pin, with quality mattresses, and there are large gender-separated common baths and saunas in addition to in-room facilities. The breakfast buffet (¥1200) has Western/Japanese/Chinese options including *sara-udon,* and there's free soba served from 9.30pm to 11pm. Prices vary widely based on season and online discounts.

S-Peria Hotel Nagasaki BUSINESS HOTEL ¥¥

(エスペリアホテル長崎; Map p716; ☑095-826-1211; www.s-peria.com; 5-35 Goto-machi; s/d/tw ¥6500/9000/10,000; P ❷ ❄ @ 🛜; 🚇 Goto-machi) On the main drag, look for this hotel with 153 sleek rooms that come with dark wood panelling and a separate shower, tub and vanity. Staff are used to foreign guests and there's a coin laundry. Discounted rates on the website. Parking costs ¥1000 per night.

★ Sakamoto-ya RYOKAN ¥¥¥

(料亭御宿坂本屋; Map p716; ☑095-826-8211; www.sakamotoya.co.jp; 2-13 Kanaya-machi; r per person incl 2 meals from ¥16,200; P ❷ ❄ @ 🛜; 🚇 Goto-machi) This magnificent old-school ryokan has been in business since 1894. Look for art-filled rooms, hallways lined with Arita-yaki pottery, postage-stamp-sized gardens off 1st-floor rooms, *shippo-ku-ryōri* (Nagasaki haute cuisine), and only 11 rooms for personal service, each with a *hinoki-buro* (cypress wood bath). From Goto-machi tram stop, walk past S-Peria Hotel and turn left. It's diagonally across from the TV broadcast tower.

Richmond Hotel
Nagasaki Shianbashi HOTEL ¥¥¥

(リッチモンドホテル長崎思案橋; Map p720; ☑095-832-2525; http://nagasaki.richmond-hotel.jp; 6-38 Motoshikkui-machi; s/d/tw from ¥20,000/20,000/25,000; P ❷ ❄ @ 🛜; 🚇 Shianbashi) You can't be closer to the heart of Shianbashi than this travellers' favourite. Deluxe rooms are large by Japanese standards. There's cheerful, English-speaking staff and a terrific breakfast buffet (¥1200) including Nagasaki specialities.

Hotel Monterey Nagasaki HOTEL ¥¥¥

(ホテルモントレ長崎; Map p716; ☑095-827-7111; www.hotelmonterey.co.jp/nagasaki; 1-22 Ōura-machi; d/tw from ¥20,000/25,000; P ❷ ❄ @ 🛜; 🚇 Ōura-Tenshudōshita) At this Portuguese-themed hotel near the Dutch Slopes and Glover Garden, rooms are spacious and light-filled, beds are comfy, and staff are courteous and used to the vagaries of foreign guests. Look for online discounts.

✕ Eating

The **Mirai Nagasaki Cocowalk** (みらい長崎ココウォーク; Map p716; ☑095-848-5509; www.cocowalk.jp; 1-55 Morimachi; ⊙10am-9pm; 🚇 Mori-machi, 🚉 JR Urakami) shopping mall features some 20 restaurants on its 4th and 5th floors. **AlettA** (アレッタ; Map p716; ☑095-801-5245; lunch/dinner ¥1650/2070; ⊙11am-3.30pm & 5-11pm; 🚇 Mori-machi) is an airy buffet restaurant on the 4th floor, with a different national theme each month.

Other good places for restaurant browsing include the restaurant floors of the shopping mall **Amu Plaza** (アミュプラザ長崎; Map p716), and **Dejima Wharf** (出島ワーフ; Map p716; 🚇 Dejima), a picturesque, harbour-side collection of open-air restaurants (from seafood to Italian) at a variety of price points, plus bars and galleries, just west of Dejima.

Hōuntei IZAKAYA ¥

(宝雲亭; Map p720; ☑095-821-9333; 1-8 Motoshikkui-machi; dishes ¥360-520; ⊙5-11pm; 🚇 Shianbashi) Patrons have been ordering the *hito-kuchi gyōza* (one-bite *gyōza;* ¥380 for 10) at this rustic hole-in-the-wall since the 1970s. Also try *butaniratoji* (pork and shallots cooked omelette style; ¥540). There's a picture menu. Look for the lantern and brown *noren* (door curtain) across from With Nagasaki.

Shikairō CHINESE ¥

(四海楼; Map p722; ☑095-822-1296; 4-5 Matsugae-machi; champon ¥970; ⊙11.30am-3pm & 5-8pm; ❷ 🈂; 🚇 Oura-Tenshudō-shita) This huge, free-standing Chinese restaurant (look for the giant red pillars) near Glover Garden is credited as the creator of *champon* and has been in operation since 1899. There are dead-on harbour views and a small *champon* museum. At peak times you should expect to wait. And wait. And wait.

★ Organic Restaurant Tia JAPANESE ¥¥

(ティア; Map p720; ☑095-828-2984; www.tia-nagasaki.com; 7-18 Ginza-chō; set meals

NAGASAKI'S POWERFUL HISTORY

Nagasaki Prefecture's multilayered role in Japanese history started when an off-course Chinese ship landed in Kagoshima Prefecture in 1543, carrying guns and Portuguese adventurers. Catholic missionaries arrived soon thereafter, ushering in Japan's 'Christian Century' (1549–1650), centred in Nagasaki, Hirado and other local communities.

By 1570 Nagasaki was a wealthy, fashionable port, as Portuguese traders shuttled between Japan, China and Korea and missionaries converted Japanese. In 1580 the *daimyō* (domain lord) briefly ceded Nagasaki to the Society of Jesuits.

The shogun then reclaimed Nagasaki, expelled the Jesuits and, in 1597, crucified 26 European and Japanese Christians. Christianity was officially banned altogether in 1613, yet some 'hidden Christians' continued to practise.

After a peasant uprising at Shimabara in 1637–38, the shogunate forbade all foreigners from Japan and Japanese from travelling overseas, beginning a period called *sakoku* (national seclusion), which lasted over two centuries. The single exception was Dejima, an artificial island in Nagasaki harbour where Dutch traders lived under close scrutiny.

When Japan reopened its doors to the West in the 1850s, Nagasaki was uniquely positioned to become a major economic force, particularly in shipbuilding, the industry that ultimately led to its tragic bombing on 9 August 1945.

from ¥1500; ⊙11am-2.30pm & 6-10pm Tue-Sun; ⍟Tsuki-machi) In a new location, Tia serves mouth-watering home-style Japanese cooking made with local, organic products. It's on the 2nd floor, with an entry that's easy to miss on the corner of the Links Ginza Bldg.

★ **Shippoku Hamakatsu** KAISEKI ¥¥
(卓袱浜勝; Map p720; ☑095-826-8321; www.
sippoku.jp; 6-50 Kajiya-machi; lunch/dinner from ¥1500/3500; ⊙11.30am-10pm; ⍟; ⍟Shianbashi) Come here if you would like to experience *shippoku-ryōri* and still afford your airfare home. Course menus are filling and varied (the Otakusa Shippoku is served on a dramatic round tray). In addition, there is a choice of either Japanese- or Western-style seating.

Higashi-yamate Chikyū-kan INTERNATIONAL ¥¥
(東山手「地球館」; Map p722; ☑095-822-7966; www.h3.dion.ne.jp/~chikyu; 6-25 Higashiyamate-machi; varies week by week; ⊙cafe 10am-5pm Thu-Mon, restaurant noon-3pm Sat & Sun; ⍟Ishibashi) In the Dutch Slopes, this quirky 'World Foods Restaurant' operates most weekends; each week a different chef comes to prepare inexpensive meals from their home country – some 70 nations and counting. This little gem is what cultural exchange is all about. Chess and language exchange are also reasons to stop by.

Tsuru-chan CAFE ¥¥
(ツル茶ん; Map p720; ☑095-824-2679; 2-47 Aburaya-machi; Toruko rice ¥1180; ⊙9am-10pm; ⍟; ⍟Shianbashi) Despite the name Toruko (Turkish) rice, there's nothing much Turkish

about the hearty Nagasaki signature dish served here: pork cutlets in a curry-flavoured gravy over pasta and rice. This retro *kissaten* (coffee shop) claims to have invented it. Creative preparations include chicken and beef, and even cream sauce. For dessert, try the 'Nagasaki Milkshake' – so thick it must be eaten with a spoon.

Yosso JAPANESE ¥¥
(吉宗; Map p720; ☑095-821-0001; www.
yossou.co.jp; 8-9 Hama-machi; set meals from ¥1350; ⊙11am-8pm; ⍟Shianbashi) People have been coming here to eat *chawanmushi* (savoury egg custard) since 1866. Look for the traditional shop front festooned with red lanterns. The Yosso *teishoku* (¥2380) adds fish, *soboro* (sweetened, minced chicken over rice), *kakuni* (braised pork belly), dessert and more. There's no English menu, but a display case makes ordering easy.

Kairaku-en CHINESE ¥¥
(会楽園; Map p720; ☑095-822-4261; www.
kairakuen.tv; 10-16 Shinchi-chō; dishes ¥800-1600; ⊙11am-4pm & 5-9.30pm; ⍟; ⍟Tsuki-machi) At this Shinchi Chinatown standby, the cheerful staff dressed in black with white aprons have been serving southern Chinese cuisine since the Shōwa era. The ¥800 lunch set meals (noodle dishes, sweet and sour pork etc) are a good deal or, for a splurge, try the Peking duck (¥5000).

Ryōtei Kagetsu KAISEKI ¥¥¥
(史跡料亭花月; Map p720; ☑095-822-0191; www.
ryoutei-kagetsu.co.jp; 2-1 Maruyama-machi; lunch/

dinner set meals from ¥10,370/14,260; ⊙noon-3pm & 6-10pm Wed-Mon; Shianbashi) A sky-high *shippoku* restaurant dating to 1642, when it was a high-class brothel. If you have Japanese skills or a chaperone, dining companions and a love of food, you might not flinch at the price. There's an English sign with the building's history and beautiful gardens as you walk in, complementing the movie-set ambience. Reservations essential.

★Butaman Momotaro   CHINESE ¥
(ぶたまん 桃太呂; Map p720; ⊇0120-23-7542; www.butaman.co.jp; 10-19 Hamanomachi; dumplings ¥80; ⊙10am-3am) These small, mouthwatering dumplings are a Nagasaki standard, and family-run Butaman Momotaro has been making them since 1960. Grab a couple of these tasty treats for breakfast, lunch, a snack, dinner, or after a late night out. This branch is just opposite Bar IWI in Shianbashi. Note that it may close early if the dumplings sell out.

🍷 Drinking & Nightlife

Bar IWI   BAR
(イーウィ; Map p720; 1-7 Motoshikkui-machi; ⊙8pm-3am Mon-Sat) Owned by Brynn, a friendly Kiwi, this cosy one-coin bar has ¥500 drinks and stays open to the wee hours, with an ever-changing mix of foreigners and primarily English-speaking locals. It's steps away from the Shianbashi tram stop, marked with a large yellow and red sign over the door.

Inokuchiya   WINE BAR
(猪ノ口屋; Map p716; ⊇095-821-0454; 4-11 Sakae-machi; ⊙5.30-11pm Mon-Sat; Nigiwaibashi) Away from Shianbashi but worth the trip, this cool spot has a wine store fronting a warren of rooms for sampling wines, *shōchū* (a strong distilled liquor) and Nagasaki sake, alongside delectable small plates of pâté, carpaccio and salads. Not much English on the menu, but you can usually make yourself understood.

ⓘ Information

INTERNET ACCESS
Nagasaki offers free wi-fi in many public places including JR Nagasaki Station, Dejima Wharf and Shinchi Chinatown. Visit www.ninjin-area.net/ sites/map to find locations, and look for ninjin. net in your browser to sign on (there's an option in English).
Cybac Café (サイバックカフェ; Map p720; ⊇095-818-8050; 3rd & 4th fl, Hashimoto Bldg, 2-46 Aburaya-chō; registration fee ¥320, 1st 30min/extra 15min ¥320/110; Shianbashi)

This enormous internet cafe has showers, darts, drinks and more.

MONEY
In addition to postal and 7-Eleven ATMs, several branches of 18 Bank handle foreign-currency exchange, including a convenient **branch** (十八銀行; Map p720; ⊇095-824-1818; 1-11 Douza-machi; ⊙9am-3pm Mon-Fri, ATM 8am-9pm daily) in the Dejima area.

TOURIST INFORMATION
In addition to tourist brochures available at locations following, look for the free English-language magazine *Nagazasshi*, published by local expats, containing events, sightseeing tips and features. A new multilingual **call centre** (⊇095-825-5175) caters to English-speaking visitors, and is being heavily pushed by the info desks, unfortunately, as speaking with a real person is often 10 times more effective than a phone call. It leads to a less-than-optimal tourist experience, but at the moment, if your questions run beyond which train to catch or if there's a map available you'll likely be directed to call the number. It may be that your most frustrating moments will be there at the info desks – luckily, people are far friendlier and eager to help once you're outside.
Nagasaki City Tourist Information Centre (長崎市総合観光案内所; Map p716; ⊇095-823-3631; www.at-nagasaki.jp/foreign/english;

NAGASAKI CUISINE

Nagasaki cuisine reflects its rich international history. *Champon* is a local take on ramen featuring squid, pork and vegetables in a milky, salt-based broth. *Sara-udon* nests the same toppings in a sauce over fried noodles. Chinese and Portuguese influences converge in *shippoku-ryōri*, Nagasaki-style *kaiseki* (Japanese haute cuisine). *Kakuni-manju* is pork belly in a sweet sauce, a Chinese dish often found at street stalls. And *chirin-chirin*, flavoured shaved ice, is sold from tiny carts in warmer months.

The yellow, brick-shaped castella cake remains a must-have Nagasaki sweet. Two of the finer shops are **Fukusaya** (福砂屋; Map p720; ⊇095-821-2938; www.fukusaya.co.jp; 3-1 Funadaiku-machi; ⊙8.30am-8pm; Shianbashi), making the cakes since 1624, and **Shōkandō** (匠寛堂; Map p716; ⊇095-826-1123; www. shokando.jp; 7-24 Uo-no-machi; ⊙9am-7pm; Nigiwaibashi), across from Megane-bashi, supplier to the Japanese imperial family.

GHOST ISLAND HASHIMA

From afar, the island of **Hashima** (端島), an eerie cluster of buildings rising out of the bay, resembles a battleship, hence its alternative name – Gunkan-jima (軍艦島; 'battleship island'). Much of the island is unsafe and several structures have collapsed or been damaged; however, guided tours operate several times a day, allowing visitors to ramble on safe walkways among the disused skyscrapers. Three-hour cruises from Nagasaki run twice daily from April to October (conditions permitting), with fewer departures November to March. Contact **Gunkanjima Concierge** (軍艦島コンシェルジュ; Map p722; ☑ 095-895-9300; www.gunkanjima-concierge.com; Tokiwa town, 1-60 Tokiwa terminal Bldg 102; tour ¥4300) for reservations. Bring sunscreen and make sure you've gone to the bathroom prior to exiting the boat: there are no facilities on the island.

Once the world's most densely populated area, Hashima became a ghost island when its coal mines, in operation since the 1890s, were closed in 1974. Left to the elements, the island looks like it comes straight out of an apocalyptic manga, so much so that it was the backdrop for the villain's lair in the 2012 James Bond film *Skyfall*. Thanks, however, to the tireless work of some concerned Nagasaki citizens the island was protected and is now in the process of being designated of world cultural interest by Unesco.

Some of the architecture (such as the iconic 'X' stairways, alas, not visible on the tour) is considered remarkable for its time, as engineers tackled the challenges of designing for such cramped living.

While most of the spoken guiding is in Japanese, English info is available.

1st fl, JR Nagasaki Station; ☺ 8am-8pm) This often-busy office can assist with basic needs such as finding accommodation, and has brochures and maps in English. The English spoken is minimal though, and they emphatically push English-speakers toward a telephone help line rather than help face-to-face.

Nagasaki Prefectural Tourism Association & Visitors Bureau (Map p716; ☑ 095-828-9407; www.visit-nagasaki.com; 8th fl, 14-10 Motofuna-machi; ☺ 9am-5.30pm; ᗡ Ōhato) Check the website for info on tourism and activities.

TRAVEL AGENCIES

JR Kyūshū Travel Agency (Map p716; ☑ 095-822-4813; JR Nagasaki Station; ☺ 10.30am-7pm Mon-Fri, 10am-6pm Sat & Sun) Handles domestic travel and hotel arrangements.

ⓘ Getting There & Away

AIR

Nagasaki's **airport** (☑ 0957-52-5555; www.nabic. co.jp; 593 Mishima-machi, Ōmura-shi) is about 40km from the city. There are flights between Nagasaki and Tokyo (Haneda), Osaka (Itami), Okinawa and Nagoya, as well as Seoul and Shanghai. In addition, Skymark flies to Kobe, and Peach has a flight to Kansai International. Oriental Air Bridge (an ANA codeshare) flies to Nagasaki's island towns such as Iki, Tsushima and Goto-Fukue.

BOAT

Ferries sail from a few places around Nagasaki, including **Ōhato terminal** (Map p716), south of JR Nagasaki Station.

BUS

From the Kenei bus station opposite JR Nagasaki Station, buses depart for Unzen (¥1800, 1¾ hours), Sasebo (¥1500, 1½ hours), Fukuoka (¥2570, three hours), Kumamoto (¥3700, 3¼ hours) and Beppu (¥4630, 3½ hours). Night buses for Osaka (¥10,900, 10 hours) leave from both the **Kenei bus terminal** (県営バスターミナル; Map p716) and the **Shinchi bus terminal** (新地バスターミナル; Map p720).

TRAIN

JR lines from Nagasaki head for Sasebo (¥1650, 2¼ hours), Hirado (¥2990, four hours) and Fukuoka (Hakata Station; *tokkyū* ¥4500, two hours). Most other destinations require a change of train. Nagasaki is not currently served by *shinkansen*.

ⓘ Getting Around

Nagasaki is easy to navigate, with most sights easily accessible by foot or tram.

TO/FROM THE AIRPORT

Airport buses (¥900, 45 minutes) operate from stand 4 of the Kenei bus terminal opposite JR Nagasaki Station and from outside the **Shinchi bus terminal** (新地バスターミナル; Map p720). A taxi to the airport costs about ¥10,000.

BICYCLE

Bicycles can be rented from JR Nagasaki Station at the **Eki Rent-a-Car** (Map p716; ☑ 095-826-0480; 1-89 Onoemachi; per 2hr/day ¥500/1500; ☺ 8am-8pm). They are electric powered; however, due to the hilly nature of the terrain, bikes are not the ideal way to get around. JR Pass holders receive a 20% discount.

TRAM

The best way of getting around Nagasaki is by tram. There are four colour-coded routes numbered 1, 3, 4 and 5 (route 2 is for special events) and stops are signposted in English. It costs ¥120 to travel anywhere in town, but you can transfer for free at the Tsuki-machi (築町) stop only (ask for a *noritsugi*, or transfer pass), unless you have a ¥500 all-day pass for unlimited travel, available from tourist information centres and many hotels. Most trams stop running around 11.30pm.

Shimbara Peninsula
島原半島

The hilly Shimabara Peninsula along the calm Ariake Sea is a popular route between Nagasaki and Kumamoto, via ferry from Shimabara.

The 1637–38 Shimabara Uprising led to the suppression of Christianity in Japan and the country's subsequent two centuries of seclusion from the West. Peasant rebels made their final stand against overwhelming odds (37,000 versus 120,000) and held out for 80 days before being slaughtered.

More history was made on 3 June 1991, when the 1359m peak of **Unzen-dake** erupted after lying dormant for 199 years, taking the lives of 43 journalists and scientists. Over 12,000 people were evacuated from nearby villages before the lava flow reached the outskirts of Shimabara.

A car is ideal for touring the peninsula freely, but it's accessible by train and bus as well.

Shimabara　　　　　　　　島原

📞 0957 / POP 45,000

This relaxed castle town (and ferry gateway to Kumamoto) flows with springs so clear that koi-filled waterways line the streets. The springs first appeared following the 1792 eruption of nearby Unzen-dake, and the town still vividly recalls the deadly 1991 eruption, commemorated with a harrowing museum. Other attractions to note include the reconstructed Shimabara-jō, a samurai street and a reclining Buddha.

⊙ Sights

★ **Samurai Houses**　　　　HISTORIC SITE
(武家屋敷; Map p728; FREE) In the Teppō-machi area, northwest of the castle, are *buke yashiki* (samurai houses) set along a pretty, 450m-long gravel road with a stream

down the middle. Most of the houses are currently inhabited, but several are open to the public.

★ **Shimabara-jō**　　　　　　CASTLE
(島原城; Map p728; 📞 0957-62-4766; www.shimabarajou.com; combined admission incl museums adult/child ¥540/260; ⊗ 9am-5.30pm) This hilltop castle was ruled mostly by the Matsudaira clan from the 1660s, played a part in the Shimabara Rebellion, and was rebuilt in 1964. As well as lotus ponds, tangled gardens, almost 4km of mossy walls, and staff dressed in period costume, the castle grounds house four museums. Most notable is the main castle, displaying arms, armour and items relating to the Christian uprising, with English explanations, and **Seibō Kinenkan** (西望記念館; Map p728), which is dedicated to the work of native son Kitamura Seibō, sculptor of the Nagasaki Peace Statue.

**Gamadas Dome Mt Unzen
Disaster Memorial Hall**　　　　MUSEUM
(がまだすドーム雲仙岳災害記念館; 📞 0957-65-5555; www.udmh.or.jp; 1-1 Heisei-machi; ¥1000; ⊗ 9am-6pm) About 4km south of the town centre, this excellent high-tech museum is larger than many a good-sized city's city hall. It focuses on the 1991 eruption and vulcanology in general, and is plonked eerily at the base of the lava flow. Get the free English audioguide, and visit the disturbingly lifelike simulation theatre.

Nehan-zō　　　　　　　　　STATUE
(ねはん像; Map p728) In the cemetery of Kōtō-ji Buddhist temple (江東寺) is this tranquil Nirvana statue, dating from 1957. At 8.6m, it's the longest reclining Buddha in Japan.

🛏 Sleeping & Eating

★ **Hotel Nampuro**　　　　　HOTEL ¥¥
(ホテル南風楼; 📞 0957-62-5111; www.nampuro.com; 2-7331-1 Bentenmachi; s from ¥9000, d with/without 2 meals ¥17,600/11,600; 🅿🚬❄@🛜🚻) Stop at Hotel Nampuro if you're ready for a splurge – or a splash, if you're into onsen bathing: its multiple (day-use OK) *rotemburo* offer stunning ocean views. Staff take time to make you feel at home and there's a large family-friendly play area for young kids, as well as inflatable toys and even a cage with *kabuto* beetles. Pool in summer only.

As a new hotel, the Nampuro is trying to (really!) have something for everyone: they've got a free beverage and ice-cream

Shimabara

Samurai Houses
Ninomaru-dōri
Nishi Horibata-dōri
Higashi Horibata-dōri
Shimabara
Shimabara-jō
Minami Horibata-dōri
Shimabara-wan
Sunshine Chūō-gai
Shimabara Ichiban-gai
Shimatetsu Honsha-mae
Tourist Information Office (1.2km);
Kyusho Ferry Co (1.2km);
Ocean Arrow Ferries (1.2km);
Shimabara-gaikō (2km);
Gamadas Dome
Mt Unzen Disaster
Memorial Hall (4km)
Shirachi-ko

Shimabara

bar, table-tennis tables, lawn games, even their own fairy-floss machine.

Hotel & Spa Hanamizuki   BUSINESS HOTEL ¥¥
(花みずき; Map p728; ☑ 0957-62-1000; www.hanamizuki-shimabara.com; 548 Nakamachi; s/tw ¥5300/9500; ⓟ❄✳🛜) Near Shimabara Station, this kindly 42-room tower has communal baths with wooden tubs (in addition to in-room baths), a sauna and Japanese-style breakfast (¥800). Parking is ¥500 extra.

★**Inohara**   CAFE ¥
(猪原金物店; Map p728; ☑ 0957-62-3117; www.inohara.jp; 912 Ueno-machi; shave ice ¥400, curry ¥1000, sōmen ¥680; ⊙ 11am-6pm Thu-Tue, closed 3rd Thu of the month) This busy blade and sharpening store is filled with incredible knives, hatchets, swords, and even ninja *shuriken* (throwing stars), but it is also a lovely cafe, offering good Japanese curry, *sōmen*, *dango* and shave ice. All made with fresh Shimabara water and using hand-sharpened blades.

Himematsu-ya   JAPANESE ¥
(姫松屋; Map p728; ☑ 0957-63-7272; 1-1208 Jōnai; dishes ¥500-1000, set meals ¥750-2100; ⊙ 11am-7pm, closed 2nd Tue of month; 📷) This venerable restaurant across from the castle serves Shimabara's best-known dish, *guzōni*, a clear broth with *mochi* (pounded rice dumplings), seafood and vegetables. There's more standard Japanese fare, too, and Unzen-raised *wagyū* beef goes for ¥1600.

ⓘ Information

Tourist Information Office (島原温泉観光協会; ☑ 0957-62-3986; 7-5 Shimokawashiri-machi; ⊙ 8.30am-5.30pm) Inside the ferry-terminal bus station (note: not in the train station!).

ⓘ Getting There & Around

JR trains from Nagasaki to Isahaya (*futsū/tokkyū* ¥460/760, 34/17 minutes) connect with hourly private Shimabara-tetsudō line trains to Shimabara/Shimabara-gaikō Stations (¥1430/1510, 1/1¼ hours) by the castle/port respectively.

Ferries to Kumamoto Port depart frequently from Shimabara Port (7am to 7pm), including **Ocean Arrow Ferries** (オーシャンアロー; ☑ 0957-63-8008; www.kumamotoferry.co.jp; adult/child ¥1000/500, driver with economy-size car ¥3100; ⊙ 7.30am-5.30pm), which take 30 minutes, and slower (one hour) **Kyusho Ferry Co** (九商フェリー; ☑ Kumamoto 096-329-6111, Shimabara 0957-65-0456; www.kyusho-ferry.co.jp; 7-5 Shimokawashirimachi; adult/child ¥780/390, driver with economy-size car ¥2310; ⊙ office 9am-7pm Mon-Fri, ticket office 6am-7.30pm daily) ferries. From Kumamoto Port, buses take you to the city (¥480, 30 minutes).

Local buses shuttle between Shimabara Station and the port (¥170) or train station (¥150). Bikes can also be rented at the castle or at Shimabara Gaikō Station (¥150 per hour).

Unzen   雲仙

☑ 0957 / POP 900

In Unzen-Amakusa National Park, said to be Japan's first, Unzen is another gem that's off the beaten path but spectacularly worth a visit. It boasts dozens of onsen and woodsy trekking through volcanic landscapes. Unzen village is easily explored in an afternoon, and once the day-trippers clear out you can enjoy a peaceful night's stay in some great hot-spring accommodation. The village also has the honour of being perhaps the last place in all of Japan without a convenience store.

A path just outside the village winds through the bubbling *jigoku* (meaning 'hells'; boiling mineral hot springs). Unlike the touristy *jigoku* of Beppu, these natural wonders are broken up only by stands selling *onsen tamago* (onsen-steamed hard-cooked eggs). A few centuries ago, these *jigoku* lived up to their infernal name, when some 30 Christian martyrs were plunged alive into Oito Jigoku.

🏃 Activities

Onsen

Check at Unzen Tourist Association for which lodgings accept visitors during your stay. A number of public facilities are open regularly, and several of the hotels offer *higueri* (day-use) entry.

One favourite is **Kojigoku** (小地獄温泉館; ☑ 0957-73-2351; 462 Unzen; ¥420; ⊙ 9am-9pm), a super-rustic wooden public bath, a few minutes' drive or about 15 minutes on foot from the village centre. **Shinyu** (雲仙新湯温泉館; ☑ 0957-73-3233; 320 Unzen; ¥100; ⊙ 9am-11pm Thu-Tue) is a simple *sentō* (public bath) with lots of local colour; **Yunosato Kyōdō Yokujō** (湯の里共同浴場; ☑ 080-5286-2576; 303 Unzen; ¥200; ⊙ 9am-11pm, closed 10th & 20th of the month) is known for its distinctive round stone bathtubs.

Hiking

From the town, there are popular walks to Kinugasa, Takaiwa-san and Yadake, all situated within the national park. The **Mt Unzen Visitors Centre** (雲仙お山の情報館; ☑ 0957-73-3636; www.unzenvc.com; ⊙ 9am-6pm Fri-Wed mid-Jul–Aug, to 5pm Sep–mid-Jul) has displays on volcanoes, flora and fauna, and information in English.

Nearby, via Nita Pass, is **Fugen-dake** (1359m), part of the Unzen-dake range. Its hiking trail has incredible views of the lava flow from the summit. A shared Heisei Taxi (p730) takes you to the Nita-tōge parking area (¥430), which is the starting point for the Fugen-dake walk. A **cable car** (雲仙ロープウェイ; ☑ 0957-73-3572; one-way ¥630; ⊙ 8.50am-

5.20pm) gets you close to a shrine and the summit of **Myōken-dake** (1333m), from where the hike via **Kunimi-wakare** takes just under two hours return. Walk 3.5km back from the shrine to Nita via the village and valley of Azami-dani.

For a longer excursion (three hours), detour to **Kunimi-dake** (1347m) for a good glimpse of Japan's newest mountain, the smoking lava dome of **Heisei Shinzan** (1483m), created in November 1990 when Fugen-dake blew its stack.

🛏 Sleeping & Eating

Nearly all dining is done in the hotels themselves, so eating options are limited and nearly all close early.

Shirakumo-no-Ike Camping Ground CAMPGROUND ¥
(白雲の池キャンプ場; ☑ 0957-73-2543; www.unzenvc.com/camp.html; campsites per person from ¥1000; ⊙ 29 Apr-7 May & 23 Jul-30 Aug) This picturesque summertime campsite next to Shirakumo Pond is about a 600m walk downhill from the post office, then a few hundred metres from the road. Tent hire is available (¥3000) or you may pitch your own. The dates change slightly each year based on school vacations, so check first before making plans.

★ **Unzen Sky Hotel** HOTEL ¥¥
(雲仙スカイホテル; ☑ 0957-73-3345; www.unzen-skyhotel.com; r per person with/without 2 meals from ¥11,150/6630; P ❀ 🛜) The lobby is kitschy, but the well-maintained rooms (mostly Japanese-style) are a great deal. The *rotemburo* is in an attractive garden, and the boat-shaped indoor bath is the largest in Unzen. Families will appreciate the baby seats for the bath. Day-use bathing (¥800/700 with/without towel) is also fine. Unlike many hotels, this one can prepare vegetarian meals on request.

What makes a stay here special is the chance to experience the kind of 'classic' onsen-hotel experience at a fraction of the cost. The welcome tea service, the family-friendly atmosphere, and the polite, courteous staff are all big pluses.

Fukudaya HOTEL ¥¥
(福田屋; ☑ 0957-73-2151; www.fukudaya.co.jp; Unzen Kokuritsu Koen; r from ¥12,000; P ❀ 🛜) Fukudaya is a hip, stylish onsen hotel that mixes Western and Japanese decor. The rooms with private outdoor baths are gorgeous, with

DON'T MISS

SHIMABARA'S TEAHOUSES

With all the clear water flowing through town, Shimabara is known for its teahouses. For a quick break, the city-owned former villa **Shimeisō** (四明荘; Map p728; ☑ 095-763-1121; 2-125 Shinmachi; ☺ 9am-6pm) sits on stilts over a spring-fed pond and serves tea for free (you can see the sand literally bubbling). Off Shimabara's central arcade, the delightful, Meiji-era **Shimabara Mizuyashiki** (しまばら水屋敷; Map p728; ☑ 0957-62-8555; www.mizuyashiki.com; 513 Yorozumachi; tea & sweets ¥325-700; ☺ 11am-5pm) features a lovely garden, a spring-fed pond and an obsessive collection of *maneki-neko* (lucky cat) figurines from all over Japan, some for sale. The enthusiastic owner has created a detailed walking map of sights and restaurants in town.

milky water and decks that overlook a small creek running below. A cafe-lounge in the lobby serves steaks sizzling on heated lava stones. The bar has an expansive collection of vinyl ranging from classic to eclectic. There's even a disco ball.

Unzen Kankō Hotel　　　HOTEL ¥¥¥
(雲仙観光ホテル; ☑ 0957-73-3263; www.unzenkankohotel.com; s from ¥18,000, d & tw from ¥26,000; ⓟ🅮✳🅢) The designers of this 1935 luxury hotel clearly had a Swiss chalet in mind. A destination in itself, with lots of history on the walls, it has a charming library, woody billiard room, decadent onsen baths (available for day use with lunch for ¥1080 per person) and large, ornate but not overdone rooms with claw-foot tubs.

The cafe is tasty; dinners start at ¥10,600.

Kyūshū Hotel　　　HOTEL ¥¥¥
(九州ホテル; ☑ 0957-73-3234; www.kyushu-htl.co.jp; r per person incl 2 meals from ¥16,430; ⓟ🅮✳@🅢) Unzen's *jigoku* make a dramatic backdrop for this five-storey, mid-century property updated with a stylish lobby, a variety of tempting room types (Japanese and Western, some with open-air baths), lovely indoor–outdoor common baths, Japanese and fusion meals, and lots of photos on the walls. If you'll be hiking, reserve a box lunch to eat on the trail.

ℹ Information

Unzen Tourist Association (雲仙観光協会; ☑ 0957-73-3434; 320 Unzen; ☺ 9am-5pm) Town maps and accommodation bookings.

ℹ Getting There & Away

Three buses run daily between Nagasaki and Unzen (¥1800, one hour and 40 minutes). Unzen is also a stop on the more frequent bus route from Shimabara (¥830, 54 minutes) to Isahaya (¥1350, one hour and 24 minutes), with train connections to Nagasaki (¥460, 34 minutes).

Unzen is so small you can walk to most of the major hotels. If you want to get to the cable car or other hiking spots you'll need a **taxi** (☑ 0957-73-2010).

CENTRAL KYŪSHŪ

This beautiful region is firmly placed on the tourist map for its historic towns, towering mountains, active volcanoes, grassland plateaus, river-cut chasms and, above all, its bubbling hot springs. Beppu, Yufuin and Kurokawa Onsen are among the most famous springs in the country. Takachiho, meanwhile, is the mythical home of the sun goddess Amaterasu. (Note that it's not Takachiho-no-mine – Mt Takachiho – in nearby Kagoshima; the two are often confused.)

The city of Kumamoto, known for its castle, is the main hub for central Kyūshū. In 2016 the Kumamoto region experienced several severe earthquakes that killed many people and destroyed thousands of homes. In October, Aso-san (Mt Aso) erupted, further damaging the area. At the time of writing, some sites and roads were still closed pending repair.

Kumamoto　　　熊本

☑ 096 / POP 731,000

Kumamoto is deeply proud of its greatest landmark, Kumamoto-jō, the castle around which the city radiates. There's a tempting collection of restaurants, bars and shops in the busy arcades east of the castle. Kumamoto City is also the gateway to the popular Aso-san region, known for its cooler summer temperatures and for its impressive volcano. Kumamoto Prefecture also has its own rampantly popular mascot, Kumamon, soon to take its place alongside Kitty-chan and Pikachu in the *kawaii* culture hall of fame.

The Kumamoto area was hit by strong earthquakes on 14 and 16 April 2016, resulting in several deaths and causing severe damage to roads and buildings, including Kumamoto-jō. Full restoration of the castle is estimated to take decades.

◉ Sights

★ Kumamoto-jō   CASTLE
(熊本城; Map p732; ☑096-322-5900; ¥500; ☺8.30am-6pm Mar-Nov, to 5pm Dec-Feb) Dominating the skyline, Kumamoto's robust castle is one of Japan's best, built in 1601–07 by *daimyō* Katō Kiyomasa, whose likeness is inescapable around the castle (look for the distinctive tall pointed hat). From 1632 it was the seat of the powerful Hosokawa clan. Unfortunately, the castle and its buildings is closed indefinitely due to earthquake damage, but is still worth seeing from the street.

★ Suizenji-jōjuen   GARDENS
(水前寺成趣園; Suizenji Park; www.suizenji.or.jp; 8-1 Suizenji-kōen; ¥400; ☺7.30am-6pm Mar Oct, 8.30am-5pm Nov-Feb) Southeast of the city centre, this photogenic lakeside garden represents the 53 stations of the Tōkaidō (the old road that linked Tokyo and Kyoto). The miniature Mt Fuji is instantly recognisable, though much of the rest of the analogy is often lost in translation. The pond drained during the quake and groundskeepers hand-carried the many carp to safety tanks, replacing them after the pond refilled.

A *'yukata* experience' offers visitors the chance to dress in period costume and take a photo for ¥2160.

Honmyō-ji   BUDDHIST TEMPLE
(本妙寺) On the grounds of this sprawling hillside temple complex northwest of the castle, 176 steps lined with hundreds of lanterns lead to the mausoleum of Katō Kiyomasa (加藤清正公の墓; 1562–1611), *daimyō* and architect of Kumamoto-jō. The mausoleum was designed at the same height as the castle's *tenshūkaku* (central tower). A **treasure house** exhibits Kiyomasa's crown and other personal items.

Shimada Museum of Art   MUSEUM
(島田美術館; ☑096-352-4597; 4-5-28 Shimazaki; ¥700; ☺10am-5pm Wed-Mon) Through the winding backstreets south of Honmyō-ji (about 20 minutes on foot), this quiet museum displays the calligraphy and scrolls of Miyamoto Musashi (1584–1645), samurai, artist and strategist. Current artists' work is on display in adjoining galleries. There's also a cafe at the museum if you're feeling peckish.

Kumamoto Prefectural
Traditional Crafts Centre   GALLERY
(熊本県伝統工芸館; Map p732; 3-35 Chibajō-machi; ¥210; ☺9am-5pm Tue-Sun) Near the prefectural art museum annexe, this large facility displays local Higo inlay, Yamaga lanterns, porcelain and woodcarvings, many for sale in the excellent museum shop (free entry). **Sakuranobaba Johsaien** (桜の馬場城彩苑; Map p732; ☺9am-5pm) and the Kumamoto Prefectural Products Centre also sell craft items (plus food and *shōchū* liquor).

Chibajo Annexe   GALLERY
(熊本県立美術館 分館; Map p732; ☑096-351-8411; 2-18 Chibajō-machi; ☺9.30am-6.30pm Tue-Fri, to 5.15pm Sat & Sun) FREE The Kumamoto Prefectural Museum of Art's postmodern Chibajo Annexe was built in 1992 by the Spanish architects Elias Torres and José Antonio Martínez-Lapeña as part of the Artpolis urban reconstruction project, and is recognised by architects worldwide.

✦ Festivals & Events

Autumn Festival   CULTURAL
From mid-October to early November, Kumamoto-jō stages its grand festival, including *taiko* drumming and cultural events.

⊨ Sleeping

Wasuki   HOTEL ¥¥
(和数奇; Map p732; ☑096-352-5101; www.wasuki.jp; 7-35 Kamitōri-machi; d/tw ¥8900/11,000, incl 2 meals ¥14,400/16,500; P ➤ ✽ 🛜) Designed very much in the style of Kumamoto-jō, with a charcoal exterior, white plaster and dark beams, and brooding *tansu*-style furniture in the generously sized rooms (most combining tatami, hardwood floors and Western-style bedding). It's well located for eating and nightlife, and there are common baths on the top floor (plus in-room facilities). Staff are friendly, but there's little English signage to aid in getting around.

Maruko Hotel   RYOKAN ¥¥
(丸小ホテル; Map p732; ☑096-353-1241; www.maruko-hotel.jp; 11-10 Kamitōri-machi; r per person with/without 2 meals from ¥12,960/7560; P ✽ 🛜) Kindly, old-school Japanese-style rooms, a top-storey *o-furo* (traditional Japanese bath) and tiny ceramic *rotemburo*, and some English-speaking staff, just outside the covered arcade. Parking costs ¥1000.

Central Kumamoto

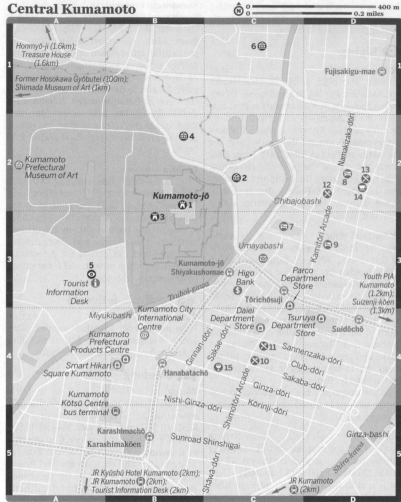

Central Kumamoto

◉ Top Sights
1 Kumamoto-jō B2

◉ Sights
2 Chibajo Annexe C2
3 Honmaru Palace B3
4 Kumamoto Prefectural Traditional
   Crafts Centre B2
5 Sakuranobaba Johsaien A3
6 Sōseki Memorial Hall C1

🛏 Sleeping
7 Kumamoto Hotel Castle C3

8 Maruko Hotel D2
9 Wasuki D3

🍴 Eating
10 Kome no Kura C4
11 Kōran-tei C4
12 Ramen Komurasaki D2
13 Yokobachi D2

🍸 Drinking & Nightlife
14 Andcoffeeroasters D2
15 Good Time Charlie C4

★**Kumamoto Hotel Castle**   HOTEL ¥¥¥
(熊本ホテルキャッスル; Map p732; ☑096-326-3311; www.hotel-castle.co.jp; 4-2 Jōtō-machi; s/d/tw from ¥10,100/17,820/19,000, r Japanese-style ¥35,640; ℙ✿✳︎🛜) Overlooking the castle, this upmarket hotel has professional, friendly service (staff normally wear Hawaiian shirts in Kumamoto's hot summers, though due to the earthquake, the perceived 'frivolity' has been on indefinite hold), a beamed ceiling inspired by its namesake, and rooms with slick renovations in muted browns and whites. Request a castle-view room.

JR Kyūshū
Hotel Kumamoto   BUSINESS HOTEL ¥¥¥
(JR九州ホテル熊本; ☑096-354-8000; www.jrhotelgroup.com; 3-15-15 Kasuga; s/tw from ¥8700/16,200; ℙ✿✳︎@🛜) The best stay among the hotels around JR Kumamoto Station, this 150-room tower has a comfortably contemporary design, some staff who speak English and larger-than-usual rooms for a business hotel. Thick-paned glass minimises train noise, but request a room away from the tracks if sensitive. Discounts and promotions may drop the price at times.

✖ Eating

The Kamitōri and Shimotōri Arcades and vicinity are happy grazing grounds for Japanese and foreign cuisines. Kumamoto is famous for *kurashi-renkon* (fried lotus root with mustard) and *Higo-gyū* (Higo beef) and the Chinese-inspired *taipien* (bean vermicelli soup with seafood and vegetables). However, the most popular dish seems to be *basashi* (raw horsemeat). Note that some menus include whale meat (*kujira*; 鯨).

To sample many foods in one place, visit Sakuranobaba Johsaien (p731), a tourist complex near the castle, with lots of stalls and restaurants serving local specialities.

Ramen Komurasaki   RAMEN ¥
(熊本ラーメンこむらさき; Map p732; ☑096-325-8972; 8-16 Kamitōri; ramen ¥580-1030; ⏱10am-4pm & 6-10pm; 🍴) This ramen joint is next to Yoshinoya at the north end of the Kamitōri Arcade. The signature 'king ramen' is garlicky, cloudy Kumamoto-style *tonkotsu* (pork) broth with bamboo shoots, julienned mushrooms and *chāshū* (roast pork) so lean you'd think it had been working out.

★**Kome no Kura**   IZAKAYA ¥¥
(米乃蔵; Map p732; ☑096-212-5551; 2nd fl, 1-6-27 Shimotōri; dishes ¥250-950; ⏱5pm-midnight; 🍴) This black-walled, quietly chic *izakaya* (Japanese pub-eatery), with cosy private booths and *hori-kotatsu* (well in the floor for your feet) seating, has a whole menu of Kumamoto specialities along with standard fare. *Tsukune* (chicken meatballs) are served pressed around a bamboo skewer. Look for the red 'dynamic kitchen' on its square, black and white sign.

If you're having trouble finding it, look for Docomo: it's next door.

★**Yokobachi**   IZAKAYA ¥¥
(Map p732; ☑096-351-4581; 11-40 Kaminoura; small plates ¥480-1800; ⏱5pm-midnight; 🍴) Yokobachi's leafy courtyard and open kitchen are distinctive. Stand-out small plates include spicy *tebasaki* (chicken wings), an inventive Caesar salad with sweet potato and lotus root chips, delicately fried *mābō-doufu* (tofu in spicy meat sauce) and, if you dare, *basashi* (¥880). There are 13 *shōchū* liquors to choose from. Reservations are wise.

Kōran-tei   CHINESE ¥¥
(紅蘭亭; Map p732; ☑096-352-7177; www.kouran-tei.com; 5-26 Ansei-machi; mains from ¥810; ⏱11am-9pm; ✿🍴🍺) Next to a Swiss pastry shop on the Shimotōri Arcade, this glossy restaurant has an endless menu. Enjoy the action on the arcade as you tuck into *taipien* ('bean thread noodle with veggies' on the English menu; ¥750), daily lunch specials (¥810) or a six-course feast for a mere ¥1620.

🍷 Drinking & Nightlife

The laneways off Shimotōri Arcade and the hip Namikizaka-dōri area at the north end of Kamitōri Arcade are lively after dark.

★**Good Time Charlie**   BAR
(Map p732; ☑096-324-1619; 5th fl, 1-7-24 Shimotōri; ⏱8pm-2am Thu-Tue) Charlie Nagatani is a living legend, the 'Johnny Cash of Japan', *the* founding figure behind the country's entire country music scene, and an accomplished musician and songwriter. He earned the rank of Kentucky Colonel for his contributions to the world of country music (he runs the Country Gold Festival near Aso-san), and this bar is his home base.

Look for live music, a tiny dance floor and thousands of pictures on the walls. He is now in his 80s, but still plays nightly and tours regularly and is always happy to chat with visitors. Even if you don't care much for

ⓘ KUMAMOTO AFTER THE EARTHQUAKE

In addition to **Kumamoto-jō** (p731), a number of sights in Kumamoto remained closed at the time of research. These include the **Honmaru Palace** (本丸御殿, Honmaru Goten; Map p732); the **Former Hosokawa Gyōbutei** (旧細川刑部邸; 3-1 Furukyō-machi), a villa built for the Hosokawa clan; **Sōseki Memorial Hall** (夏目漱石内坪井旧居; Map p732; 4-22 Tsuboi-machi), the 1870s home of the novelist Natsume Sōseki; and the **treasure house** (p731) at **Honmyō-ji** (p731). Enquire at one of the tourist information centres for the latest on-the-ground update.

country music, a beer at Good Time Charlie's is an experience well worth detouring for.

★ **Andcoffeeroasters**   CAFE
(Map p732; ☑ 096-273-6178; www.andcoffeeroasters.com; 11-22 Kamitōri-machi; ⊙ 8am-8pm) Delightful boutique coffee shop with freshly roasted beans and a 'tart of the day', such as persimmon or Earl Grey. Coffee nerds will feel right at home with the rich lattes, creamy cappuccinos and other speciality espresso drinks. It's outside the north end of the arcade.

ⓘ Information

There is a tourist information desk at both **JR Kumamoto Station** (熊本駅総合観光案内所; ☑ 096-352-3743; ⊙ 8.30am-8pm) and **Sakuranobaba Johsaien** (桜の馬場城彩苑総合観光案内所; Map p732; ☑ 096-322-5060; ⊙ 9am-5.30pm). Both have English-speaking assistants and accommodation listings.

Kumamoto City International Centre (熊本市国際交流会館; Map p732; ☑ 096-359-2020; 4-18 Hanabata-chō; ⊙ 9am-10pm, closed 2nd & 4th Mon of the month; 🛜) has free wi-fi on the 1st and 2nd floors, plus BBC News and English-language magazines. Note the reception desk closes at 7pm.

Visit www.kumamoto-icb.or.jp for information about the city.

ⓘ Getting There & Away

Flights connect **Aso-Kumamoto Airport** (www.kmj-ab.co.jp) with Tokyo and Osaka. Buses to and from the airport (¥800, 50 minutes) stop at **Kumamoto Kōtsū Centre bus terminal** (熊本交通センター; Map p732; ☑ 096-325-0100;

7-20 Sakura-machi; ⊙ 7am-9.30pm) and JR Kumamoto Station.

JR Kumamoto Station is an inconvenient few kilometres southwest of the centre (though an easy tram ride). It's a stop on the Kyūshū *shinkansen* with destinations including Kagoshima-Chūō (¥6740, 45 minutes), Fukuoka (Hakata Station; ¥4930, 35 minutes), Hiroshima (¥13,340, 1¾ hours) and Shin-Osaka (¥18,340, 3¼ hours), as well as Beppu (¥4610, three hours) via the JR Hōhi line.

Highway buses depart from the Kumamoto Kōtsū Centre bus terminal. Routes include Fukuoka (¥2060, two hours), Kagoshima (¥3700, 3½ hours), Nagasaki (¥3700, 3¼ hours) and Miyazaki (¥4630, three hours).

ⓘ Getting Around

Kumamoto's tram service (Shiden) reaches the major sights for ¥170 per ride. One-day passes (¥500) can be bought on board, offer discounted admission to sights and can be used on city buses.

City buses are generally hard to manage without Japanese skills, with one exception: the Castle Loop Bus (¥150/400 per ride/day pass) connecting the bus terminal with most sights in the castle area at least every half-hour, between 9am and 5pm daily.

Renting a car is recommended for trips to Aso and beyond (from about ¥5250 per 12 hours). Rental services line the street across from JR Kumamoto Station.

Aso-san & Around   阿蘇山

☑ 0967 / POP 27,000

Halfway between Kumamoto and Beppu lies the Aso-san volcanic caldera. It's among the world's largest (128km in circumference), so big that it's hard at first to understand its scale, and strikingly beautiful. Formed through a series of eruptions over the past 300,000 years, the current outer crater is about 90,000 years old and now accommodates towns, villages and train lines. Aso is the main town, but Takamori, to the south, is more intimate and charming.

Aso-san is still active, and the summit is frequently off-limits due to toxic gas emissions or wind conditions. In October 2016 the volcano had a major eruption, resulting in severe damage to surrounding areas. Some access roads were also still inaccessible from the earthquakes earlier in 2016, so be sure to check with the tourist information centre or at www.aso.ne.jp/~volcano/eng for updates before planning a trip.

Best explored by car, the Aso-san region offers fabulous drives, diverse scenery and peaceful retreats. Routes 57, 265 and 325 encircle the outer caldera, and the JR Hōhi line runs across the northern section from Kumamoto, but is currently cut, so there is no through train service.

◉ Sights & Activities

If you're driving, **Daikanbō Lookout** (大観峰; Map p736) is one of the best places to view the region from on high, but it's often crowded with tour buses. **Shiroyama Tembōdai** (城山展望所; Map p736; Yamanami Hwy) is a nice alternative.

★ Aso-gogaku   MOUNTAIN
(阿蘇五岳) The **Five Mountains of Aso** are the smaller mountains within the outer rim: Eboshi-dake (1337m); Kijima-dake (1321m); Naka-dake (1506m); Neko-dake (1408m), furthest east; and the highest, Taka-dake (1592m). Access roads were damaged in the 2016 earthquakes, and at the time of writing this area was closed.

Aso Volcano Museum   MUSEUM
(阿蘇火山博物館; Map p736; ☑0967-34-2111; www.asomuse.jp; 1930-1 Akamizu; admission ¥840, parking ¥410; ⊙9am-5pm) This unique museum has a real-time video feed from inside the active crater, informative English-language brochures and audioguides (free), and a video presentation of Aso locals showing off.

🛏 Sleeping & Eating

Aso Base Backpackers   HOSTEL ¥
(阿蘇ベースバックパッカーズ; Map p736; ☑0967-34-0408; www.aso-backpackers.com; 1498 Kurokawa; dm/s/tw/d without bathroom ¥2800/5500/6000/6600; ⊙closed mid-Jan–mid-Feb; P🐾@🔊) A quick walk from JR Aso Station, this clean, 30-bed hostel has English signage, a balcony with mountain views, the aroma of cedar in the bedrooms, a coin laundry, warm staff, and an excellent local guide to transport and sights. There are showers on-site, and many guests like to bathe in the nearby onsen.

Shukubō Aso   RYOKAN ¥¥
(宿坊あそ; Map p736; ☑0967-34-0194; 1076 Kurokawa; r per person incl 2 meals from ¥12,000; P🔊) This lovely, rustic ryokan in a reconstructed 300-year-old samurai house has modern touches and a tree-lined setting, less than 500m from Aso Station. Its 12 rooms have private toilet and shared bath,

and dinner of local meats and fish is served around an *irori* (hearth). It's near pretty Saiganden-ji temple, which dates from AD 726. (Note that it's *not* nonsmoking.)

★ Takamori Dengaku-no-Sato   GRILL ¥¥
(高森田楽の里; Map p736; ☑0967-62-1899; 2685-2 Ōaza-Takamori; set meals ¥1890-2850; ⊙10am-7.30pm; 🗐) A fantastic thatch-roofed ex-farmhouse, where around your own *irori* embedded in the floor the staff use oven mitts to grill *dengaku* (skewers of vegetables, meat, fish and tofu covered in the namesake sweet miso paste). It's a few minutes by car or taxi (about ¥600) from Takamori Station. Cash only.

ℹ Information

Tourist Information Centre (道の駅阿蘇施設案内所; Map p736; ☑0967-35-5077; 1440-1 Kurokawa; ⊙9am-6pm; 🔊) Next to JR Aso Station, this helpful centre offers free road and hiking maps, and local information in English, as well as coin lockers.

ℹ Getting There & Around

Aso lies on the (now suspended) JR Hōhi line between Kumamoto and Ōita. Currently trains from Beppu end in Aso (¥3050, 1¾ hours) and trains

---

ℹ NAKA-DAKE ERUPTION

Naka-dake, part of Aso-san, is very much an active volcano. With pale green waters bubbling and steaming below, the 100m-deep crater is the region's most popular attraction. At the time of research, following a significant eruption in 2016, the area was closed to visitors. Should it reopen, access is via a **cable car** (Ropeway; Map p736; one-way/round-trip ¥750/1200; ⊙8.30am-6pm mid-Mar–Oct, 8.30am-5pm Nov, 9am-5pm Dec–mid-Mar); alternatively, it's a 30-minute walk from the parking lot.

Several trails, such as the one to **Sensui Gorge** (仙酔峡, Sensui-kyō; Map p736), which blooms with azaleas in mid-May, wend through the area from the summit. These too were off-limits at the time of research. **Aso-jinja** (阿蘇神社; Map p736), dedicated to the 12 gods of the mountain, also suffered damage and was closed.

The vistas here are awe-inspiring and should Naka-dake reopen it's well worth a visit. For the latest, enquire at the tourist information office here or in Kumamoto.

Aso-San Area

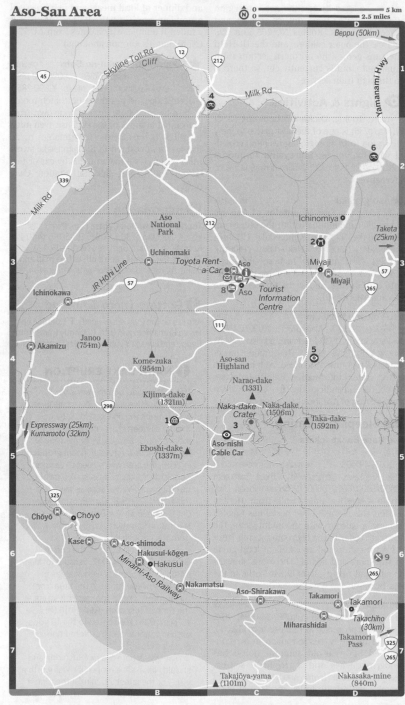

Aso-San Area

from Kumamoto end in Higo-Ōtsu (¥2980, 3¼ hours). The line will eventually be repaired, but at the time of writing the connection was indefinitely suspended and no through pricing was available.

There is currently no Aso–Takamori train service. Buses from Takamori continue southeast to Takachiho (¥1320, 80 minutes, two daily).

Buses usually operate approximately hourly from JR Aso Station via the volcano museum to Aso-nishi cable-car station (¥650, 40 minutes), stopping at Kusasenri (¥570). At the time of writing, it was only possible to ride the bus as far as Kusasenri.

Rent electric bikes at JR Aso Station (¥400 for two hours), or cars at **Toyota Rent-a-Car** (Map p736; ☑ 096-735-5511; per day from ¥5600; ⊙ 8am-6pm), adjacent to the train station (reserve in advance).

Kurokawa Onsen 黒川温泉

☑ 0967 / POP 1700

Nestled on either side of a steep gorge about one hour northeast of Aso town, tranquil Kurokawa Onsen is one of Japan's prettiest hot-spring villages and has won top onsen honours several years in a row. Safely secluded from the rest of the world, it's the perfect spot to experience what an onsen ryokan getaway is all about.

For day trippers, a *nyūtō tegata* (onsen passport; ¥1300) allows access to three baths from Kurokawa's 24 ryokan (open 8.30am to 9pm). Buy one at the **tourist information desk** (旅館組合, Ryokan Association; ☑ 0967-44-0076; www.kurokawaonsen.or.jp; Kurokawa-sakura-dōri; ⊙ 9am-6pm) and ask which locations are open during your visit. The office even has an official onsen sommelier!

Favourite baths include Yamamizuki, Kurokawa-sō and Shimmei-kan, with cave baths and riverside *rotemburo* (Kurokawa is especially famous for its *rotemburo*). Many places offer *konyoku* (mixed bathing).

🛏 Sleeping

Kurokawa's onsen ryokan aren't cheap, but this isn't an experience you'll have every

day. English is spoken to varying degrees, and some ryokan can arrange pick-up from Kurokawa Onsen bus stop.

If you're staying overnight, plan on eating ryokan meals. If you're just a day visitor, know that there are few lunch places and they often close promptly.

Chaya-no-Hara Campground CAMPGROUND ¥ (茶屋の原キャンプ場; ☑ 0967-44-0220; 6323 Manganji; campsites per person from ¥600, plus per tent/car ¥600/600, bungalows ¥6000; ℗) This campground, about 5km before Kurokawa Onsen, is essentially a sloping lush green field with inspirational views. Rustic bungalows are also available.

Sanga Ryokan RYOKAN ¥¥¥ (山河旅館; ☑ 0967-44-0906; www.sanga-ryokan. com; r per person incl 2 meals from ¥16,000; ℗ ✳) Deep in the gorge, about 1.5km from the town centre, this romantic ryokan has 16 deluxe rooms, all but one of which have private onsen attached. Exquisite *kaiseki* (Japanese haute cuisine) meals, attention to detail and heartfelt service make this a place to experience the Japanese art of hospitality.

Okyakuya Ryokan RYOKAN ¥¥¥ (御客屋旅館; ☑ 0967-44-0454; www.okyakuya. jp; r per person incl 2 meals from ¥15,270; ℗ ✳ 🛜) At Kurokawa Onsen's oldest ryokan (in its seventh generation of the same family) all 10 rooms have river views, plus sink and toilet, and share common onsen baths; the riverside *rotemburo* is worth it by itself.

ⓘ Getting There & Away

Experiencing this area is most enjoyable by car, but several daily buses connect Kurokawa Onsen with Aso (¥990, one hour) and Kumamoto (¥2060, 2½ hours). A couple also travel to Beppu (¥2980, 2½ hours) via Yufuin (¥2370). Check timetables if you intend to make this a day trip. These durations currently reflect route changes due to earthquake damage.

You can also take a three-hour express bus from Hakata Station (and the airport, too) for ¥3090;

there are two departures in the morning and two from Kurokawa Onsen in the afternoon.

Yufuin　由布院

☑ 0977 / POP 34,000

About 25km inland from Beppu, delightful Yufuin sits in a ring of mountains, with the twin peaks of Yufu-dake especially notable. The town lives for tourism and is a good place to see contemporary Japanese crafts, including ceramics, clothing and woodworking, and interesting foods. It gets crowded on holidays and weekends. If staying overnight, arrive before dusk, when the day-trippers leave and wealthier Japanese retreat to their ryokan.

🏃 Activities

As in Beppu, making a pilgrimage from one onsen to another is a popular activity. Alternatively, work up a sweat on double-peaked **Yufu-dake** (1584m) volcano, which overlooks Yufuin and takes about 90 minutes to climb.

Shitan-yu　　　　　　　　ONSEN
(下ん湯; ☑ 097-784-3111; ¥200; ⊙10am-9pm) An atmospheric one-room thatched bathhouse with mixed bathing only, on the northern shore of **Kinrin-ko** (Lake of Golden Fish Scales, named by a Meiji-era philosopher). Note that you should deposit your payment in the slot outside.

Nurukawa Onsen　　　　　ONSEN
(ぬるかわ温泉; ☑ 0977-84-2869; 1490-1 Kawakami Takemoto; ¥430; ⊙8am-8pm) Separated by gender, this cluster of small bathing rooms boasts character and lovely mountain views.

🛏 Sleeping

This is an onsen town and not surprisingly, most of the hotels, ryokan and even hostels have onsen baths.

Yufuin Country Road Youth Hostel　HOSTEL ¥
(湯布院カントリーロードユースホステル; ☑ 0977-84-3734; www.countryroadyh.com; 441-29 Kawakami; dm HI member/nonmember ¥3300/3900; P ⊜ @ ☎) John Denver fans will love staying here on a forested hillside overlooking the town. Especially pretty at night, this first-rate 25-bed hostel has its own onsen and hospitable English-speaking owners who've clearly made the singer a major part of their lives. Infrequent buses (¥200, Monday to Friday only) service the area, or you can arrange for pick-up, but call ahead first.

Two meals are available for an extra ¥1750.

Makiba-no-ie　　　　　　RYOKAN ¥¥
(牧場の家; ☑ 0977-84-2138; 2870-1 Kawakami; r per person incl 2 meals from ¥14,190; P ❃ ☎) There's atmosphere aplenty in these thatched-roof huts with sink and toilet surrounding a beautiful *rotemburo*. The antique-filled garden restaurant offers *jidori* (local chicken) and *Bungō-gyū teishoku* (local beef set meals) from ¥1600. Visitors can use the *rotemburo* for ¥600, and there are seven family (private) baths as well.

★Yufu-no-Oyado Hotaru　　RYOKAN ¥¥¥
(由布のお宿ほたる; ☑ 0977-84-5151; www. yufuin-hotaru.com; 1791-1 Kawakita; r per person from ¥16,500; ⊙reception 7am-9pm; P ❃ ☎) This lovely, family-run traditional ryokan is nestled among cypress and bamboo. A variety of onsen baths make it a lovely spot for dippers, and one of the owners speaks excellent English.

Kamenoi Bessō　　　　　　RYOKAN ¥¥¥
(亀の井別荘; ☑ 0977-84-3166; www.kamenoi-bessou.jp; 2633-1 Kawakami; r per person incl 2 meals from ¥44,000; P @ ☎) For the no-holds-barred Yufuin splurge, look no further. From Kinrin-ko, enter the *kayabuki* (thatched-roof) gate to this campus of craftsman-style wooden buildings encircling stone baths with peaked wooden roofs. Meals contain local specialities, and staff seem never to have heard of the concept 'no'. Choose from Japanese, Western and combination-style guestrooms.

🍴 Eating

Most patrons have their meals while relaxing in their inn, but there's a handful of eateries by the station.

Hidamari　　　　　　　　JAPANESE ¥
(陽だまり食堂; ☑ 0977-84-2270; 2914 Kawakami; mains ¥750-1620; ⊙lunch 11am-3pm, shop 8.30am-5.30pm; P ⊜) Operated by a local agriculture cooperative, this informal restaurant and produce market nails the local standards such as *toriten* (chicken tempura), *dangojiru* (miso soup with thick-cut noodles) and local beef in *teishoku* (set meals); order from the picture menu. Outside of lunchtime you can buy *bentōs*, local yoghurt and ice cream. It's about 150m from the station, at the intersection with the large stone *torii*.

Izumi Soba　　　　　　　NOODLES ¥¥
(泉そば; ☑ 0977-85-2283; 1599-1 Kawakami; soba ¥1295-2160; ⊙11am-5pm) There are less expensive soba shops in town, but at this

KUJŪ-SAN & TAKETA

Tucked in Ōita Prefecture's southwest corner lies its biggest mountain range, collectively known as Kujū-san, a favourite for hikers and mountaineering clubs. Accessed by car either from Ōita or Kumamoto (via Aso National Park) it offers more than 20 peaks, including the island's highest, Naka-dake (1791m). Because of this, the range is known as the 'rooftop of Kyūshū'. One of the most popular climbs is from Makinotoi-tōge, which is an easy day hike thanks to access via a circuitous yet lovely road that goes most of the way. It's more peopled than other peak ascents. From there you can hike all the way to Naka-dake if you want. The **Aso Kujū-Kōgen Youth Hostel** (阿蘇くじゅう高原ユースホステル; ☑0967-44-0157; www.asokujuuyh.sakura.ne.jp; 6332 Senomoto; dm HI member/nonmember from ¥2000/2600, with 2 meals ¥5000; P❄❀@) in Kurokawa Onsen is a good base camp for excursions.

Hiding at the edges of the Kujū-san is the lovely town of Taketa (竹田). As the '竹' character implies, the area is known for its impressive bamboo craftwork, and there is even a workshop for tourists in this attractive art. The town is also known for its award-winning *shōchū* (a strong distilled liquor) – well worth picking up a bottle or two!

Beautiful walls are all that remain of Taketa's castle (Oka-jō), but strolling amid the cherry trees past moss-covered stonework harkens back to a simpler Japan.

A recently discovered cave was used by 'hidden Christians' to worship; interestingly, the rock-hewn chapel was located just behind a well-known samurai residence. Current theory surmises that the warrior – or someone in the household – must have been aware of it, or been a member.

Taketa is best reached by car from Yufuin (70 minutes) or Beppu (75 minutes), as the sights are spread out and not easily accessible by bus.

classy place with a view of Kinrin-ko you can watch the noodles being made in the window before you sit down. The standard is *seirō-soba* (on a bamboo mat); *oroshi-soba* comes topped with grated *daikon* (radish).

❶ Information

Tourist Information Office (由布院温泉観光案内所; ☑0977-84-2446; ☺9am-5.30pm) Inside the train station, this office has some information in English, including a detailed walking map showing galleries, museums and onsen.

❶ Getting There & Away

Trains connect Beppu with Yufuin (*futsū/tokkyū* ¥1110/1410, 1¼ hours/100 minutes) via Ōita.

Buses connect JR Beppu Station with Yufuin throughout the day (¥900, 57 minutes). Express buses serve Fukuoka (¥2880, two hours), Aso (¥2370, 2½ hours) and Kumamoto (¥3550, 4½ hours).

❶ Getting Around

Some buses from Yufuin stop at the base of Yufu-dake at Yufu-tozanguchi (由布登山口; ¥360, 15 minutes, about hourly).

Electric bikes can be rented at the JR station (two hours with/without JR pass ¥400/500). Normal bicycles are also available for rent (¥250 per hour) from 9am to 5pm.

Beppu 別府

☑0977 / POP 123,000

You don't have to look far in Beppu, in Ōita Prefecture, to see the reason for its popularity: steam rising from vents in the earth means there are onsen bathing opportunities galore. Beppu is at turns quaint, touristy, modern, traditional, solid and rickety, but the charm of this hilly, hospitable city grows on visitors as sure as the waters are warm. Winter visitors get the seasonal treat of seeing the entire town filled with warm, escaping steam.

◉ Sights

Beppu has two types of hot springs, collectively pumping out more than 100 million litres of hot water every day. *Jigoku* (boiling hot springs; literally 'hells') are for looking at; onsen are for bathing.

★**Beppu Traditional Bamboo Crafts Centre** MUSEUM
(別府市竹細工伝統産業会館; Map p740; ☑0977-23-1072; 8-3 Higashi-sōen; ¥300; ☺8.30am-5pm Tue-Sun) This hands-on crafts centre displays a range of refined works from Edo-period masters as well as current examples of uses for this versatile material, which grows copiously in the region. If you'd like to try your hand at crafting bamboo

Beppu

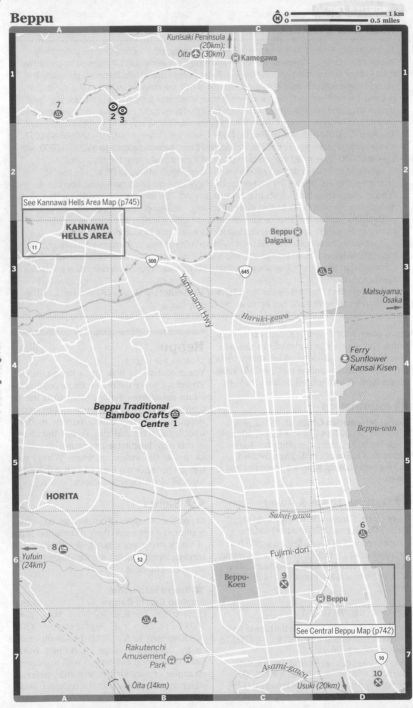

See Kannawa Hells Area Map (p745)

KANNAWA
HELLS AREA

Kunisaki Peninsula
(20km);
Ōita (30km)

Kamegawa

Beppu
Daigaku

Matsuyama;
Ōsaka

Yamanami Hwy

Haruki-gawa

Ferry
Sunflower
Kansai Kisen

Beppu-wan

**Beppu Traditional
Bamboo Crafts
Centre** 1

HORITA

Sakai-gawa

Yufuin
(24km)

Fujimi-dori

Beppu-
Koen

Beppu

See Central Beppu Map (p742)

Rakutenchi
Amusement
Park

Asami-gawa

Ōita (14km)

Usuki (20km)

Beppu

(¥400/1000, depending on the complexity of the item), request a reservation at least one week ahead. From Beppu Station, take bus 22 or 25 to Takezaiku-densankan-mae or bus 1 to Minami-baru (about 200m away).

Hells HOT SPRINGS
(single/combination ticket ¥400/2000; ⊙ 8am-5pm) Beppu's most hyped attraction is the **jigoku meguri** (hell circuit), where waters bubble forth from underground with unusual results. Unlike Unzen, where the geothermal wonders are unadorned, the circuit's eight stops have become mini amusement parks, each with a theme and some loaded with tourist kitsch; consider yourself warned. Note: the combo ticket no longer includes Mountain Hell (Yama Jigoku).

The hells are in two groups, six at **Kannawa**, over 4km northwest of Beppu Station, and two about 2.5km further north. In the Kannawa group are steaming blue **Umi Jigoku** (海地獄, Sea Hell; Map p745; ¥400; ⊙8am-5pm); **Oniishibōzu Jigoku** (鬼石坊主地獄, Demon Monk Hell; Map p745; ¥400; ⊙8am-5pm), where bubbling mud looks like a monk's shaved head; **Shira-ike Jigoku** (白池地獄, White Pond Hell; Map p745; ¥400; ⊙8am-5pm); and **Kamado Jigoku** (かまど地獄; Map p745; ¥400; ⊙8am-5pm), named because it was once used for cooking. At **Oni-yama Jigoku** (鬼山地獄, Devil's Mountain Hell; Map p745; ¥400; ⊙8am-5pm) and **Yama Jigoku** (山地獄, Mountain Hell; Map p745; ¥400; ⊙8am-5pm), a variety of animals are kept in enclosures that look uncomfortably small. Take a

bus from Beppu Station to Umi-Jigoku-mae (¥330) to start.

The smaller group of hells has **Chi-no-ike Jigoku** (血の池地獄; Blood Pool Hell; Map p740; ¥400; ⊙8am-5pm), with its photogenic red water, and **Tatsumaki Jigoku** (龍巻地獄, Tornado Hell; Map p740; ¥400; ⊙8am-5pm), where a geyser shoots off about every 35 minutes.

🏃 Activities

Beppu has eight onsen districts, **Beppu Hattō** (www.city.beppu.oita.jp/01onsen/english/index.html). Onsen aficionados spend their time in Beppu moving from one bath to another and consider at least three baths a day de rigueur; bathing costs from ¥100 to ¥1000. Bring your own soap, cloth and towel, as some places don't rent them.

★ **Takegawara Onsen** ONSEN
(竹瓦温泉; Map p742; ☎097-723-1585; 16-23 Moto-machi; ¥100, sand bath ¥1030; ⊙6.30am-10.30pm, sand bath 8am-9.30pm, sand bath closed 3rd Wed of the month) Near JR Beppu Station, this classic onsen dates from the Meiji era. Its bath is very simple and very hot; simply scoop out water with a bucket, pour it over yourself, and jump in! It also has a relaxing sand bath where a *yukata* is provided.

The sand bath involves lying down in a shallow trench and being buried up to your neck in heated sand, followed by an onsen dip and shower. The entire affair takes about 40 minutes.

Kaihin Sand Bath ONSEN
(海浜砂湯; Map p740; ☎097-766-5737; ¥1030; ⊙8.30am-6pm Apr-Oct, 9am-5pm Nov-Mar) Between JR Beppu Station and the Kamegawa onsen area, this sand bath is at the very popular Shōnin-ga-hama beach; it has a great location and English is spoken. It closes early if the wait gets too long, so go early to make sure you don't miss out.

Kannawa Mushi-yu ONSEN
(鉄輪蒸し湯; Map p745; ☎097-767-3880; 1-gumi Kannawa-kami; ¥510; ⊙6.30am-8pm) Downhill from Kannawa bus stop is Kannawa Mushi-yu, where wrapped in a *yukata* you steam at 65°C (ow!) on top of Japanese rush leaves. Eight to 10 minutes here is said to have the detoxifying power of up to 30 minutes in a sauna.

Shibaseki Onsen ONSEN
(柴石温泉; Map p740; ☎097-767-4100; 4-kumi Noda; ¥210; ⊙7am-8pm, closed 2nd Wed of the month) This onsen is en route to the smaller

Central Beppu

pair of hells. You can rent a private *kazoku-buro* (family bath) for ¥1620 per hour.

Ichinoide Kaikan　ONSEN
(いちのいで会館; Map p740; ☑097-721-4728; 14-2 Uehara-machi; ☺11am-5pm) The owner of Ichinoide Kaikan is an onsen fanatic, so much so that he built three pool-sized *rotemburo* in his backyard. The view, overlooking Beppu and the bay, is the city's finest. Bathing is free when you order a set menu (*teishoku;* around ¥1500), and the chefs prepare it while you swim. To get there by bus and foot, enquire at the Foreign Tourist Information Office.

A shared taxi (from Beppu, around ¥900) might be a good investment.

Kitahama Termas Onsen　ONSEN
(北浜温泉テルマス; Map p740; ☑0977-24-4126; ¥510; ☺10am-10pm Fri-Wed) For an onsen experience next to the beach, head to Kitahama. There are separate baths for men and women; the outside *rotemburo* mixes it up, but you'll need a bathing suit.

Onsen Hoyōland　ONSEN
(温泉保養ランド; ☑097-766-2221; 5-1 Myōban; ¥1100; ☺9am-8pm) Boasts wonderful giant mud baths, as well as mixed-gender and open-air bathing.

🛏 Sleeping

Beppu is a dense town with a large variety of accommodation options. Several youth hostels and numerous *minshuku* cater to budget travellers, and then things go up to the posh and fancy. Be aware that rooms facing even the side streets can be noisy at times, as the city's nightlife can be boisterous, and doesn't end until the wee hours.

Cabosu House Beppu　HOSTEL ¥
(かぼすハウス別府; Map p742; ☑097-785-8087; www.facebook.com/cabosuhouse; 3-3-10 Kitahama; dm/s ¥2000/3000; P🅿❋@🛜) There's new-wave decor at this new hostel, which is spread over two buildings about a two-minute walk from each other. There's a well-stocked bar on the ground floor and some nice common areas for making friends. Doors are locked after 9pm, but you can enter with a code. The older building also has its own hot-spring bath.

Beppu Guest House　HOSTEL ¥
(別府ゲストハウス; Map p742; ☑0977-76-7811; http://beppu.cloud-line.com; 1-12 Ekimae-chō; dm/s/d ¥1700/2700/5000; ❋@🛜) The big kitchen and living rooms are great places to hang out with fellow travellers at this arty, funky and welcoming hostel. Other positives:

Central Beppu

¥200 loaner bikes, washing machines and English-speaking staff with local knowledge. There's no bath on-site, but a ¥100 public bath is nearby. Cash only.

★ Yamada Bessou
RYOKAN ¥¥

(山田別荘; Map p742; ☎0977-24-2121; www.yamadabessou.jp; 3-2-18 Kitahama; r per person with/without breakfast from ¥7500/6500; 🅿🌀❄📶) You could be stepping back in time at this sprawling family-run 1930s inn with wonderfully well-preserved rooms and fabulous art deco features and furnishings. The onsen and private *rotemburo* (day use ¥500 to ¥700, 10am to 3pm) are so lovely you'll hardly mind that only a couple of its eight rooms have full bath and toilet.

Kokage International Minshuku
MINSHUKU ¥¥

(国際民宿こかげ; Map p742; ☎0977-23-1753; ww6.tiki.ne.jp/~kokage; 8-9 Ekimae-chō; s/d ¥4350/7650; 🅿❄@📶) Off an alley near Ekimae-dōri, this cosy nine-room inn is old and friendly, chock-full of atmospheric woodwork, antiques and curios. There's a lovely stone onsen, and toast and coffee for breakfast. Rooms over the entrance are quietest.

Hotel Seawave Beppu
BUSINESS HOTEL ¥¥

(ホテルシーウェーブ別府; Map p742; ☎0977-27-1311; www.beppuonsen.com; 12-8 Ekimae-chō; s/d/tw/ste from ¥6000/7500/8600/18,000; 🅿🌀❄📶) For late arrivals or early getaways this hotel with small rooms is right across from the station. There are in-room baths and

a recently opened in-house onsen. It even has a restaurant.

★ Beppu Hotel Umine
HOTEL ¥¥¥

(別府ホテルうみね; Map p742; ☎0977-26-0002; www.umine.jp; 3-8-3 Kitahama; r per person incl breakfast from ¥17,280; 🅿❄❄📶) In-room onsen baths with water views, gorgeous common baths, savvy contemporary design, excellent restaurants and oodles of personal service make this Beppu's top stay. Rates are expensive but include snacks in the library lounge. Wi-fi rental is available.

Suginoi Hotel
HOTEL ¥¥¥

(杉乃井ホテル; Map p740; ☎0977-24-1141; www.suginoi-hotel.com; 1 Kankaiji; r per person incl 2 meals from ¥10,000; 🅿❄❄@📶🏊) On a hillside above town, Suginoi offers the tiered rooftop Tanayu *rotemburo*, the Aqua Garden onsen swimming pool (combined day-use ¥1300, bathing suit required), and high standards indoors. Japanese-style rooms are more alluring than Western ones, but the 15 Ceada Floor rooms are slick and special. Note that rates vary widely with the season.

Eating

Beppu is renowned for *toriten* (chicken tempura), freshwater fish, *Bungō-gyū* (local beef), *fugu* (pufferfish), wild mountain vegetables and *dangojiru* (miso soup with thick-cut noodles). On the 1st floor of the **You Me Town**

KYŪSHŪ BEPPU

DON'T MISS

ONSEN COOKING EXPERIENCE

Ingenious! Amid the hells of Kannawa, **Jigoku Mushi Kōbō** (地獄蒸し工房, Hell Steaming Workshop; Map p745; ☑0977-66-3775; 5-kumi Furomoto; egg ¥150, dishes ¥600-1300, steamers per 30min ¥510, seafood set ¥2500; ⊙9am-9pm, closed 3rd Wed of the month) offers the opportunity for you to cook your own meal in onsen steam. Purchase ingredients on the spot (or bring your own), and steam them in *kama* (vats) roiling from the onsen below. It shares a building with the Foreign Tourist Information Office, so there's usually an English speaker on hand to help until 5pm. It can be crowded at peak times, such as weekend lunch.

shopping mall (ゆめタウン別府; Map p742; ☑097-726-3333; 382-7 Kusunoki-machi; ⊙9.30am-10.30pm), English-friendly spots include conveyor-belt sushi, noodles and a buffet.

★ **Gyōza Kogetsu**   GYOZA ¥
(餃子湖月; Map p742; ☑0977-21-0226; 1-9-4 Kitahama; gyōza ¥600; ⊙2-9pm Wed-Mon; ☞) This seven-seat counter shop with a manic local following has only two things on the menu, both ¥600 – generous plates of *gyōza* (dumpling) perfection fried to a delicate crunch, and bottles of beer. It's in the tiny alley behind the covered arcade; look for the display case filled with cat figurines. It's also nonsmoking.

★ **Shinanoya**   CAFE ¥
(信濃屋; Map p740; ☑0977-25-8728; 6-32 Nishi-noguchi; mains ¥600-1300; ⊙9am-9pm Thu-Mon, to 6pm Tue & Wed) A few minutes from the station's west exit and dating back to 1926, this kindly *kissaten* also serves a renowned *dangojiru* loaded with veggies and best enjoyed while viewing the piney garden or sitting at the giant common table in a plush, green-velvet armchair. It's the traditional building just before Family Mart.

Tomonaga Panya   BAKERY ¥
(友永パン屋; Map p740; ☑0977-23-0969; Chiyo-machi 2-29; pastries from ¥100; ⊙8.30am-5.30pm Mon-Sat) This charming but busy historic bakery has been in business since 1916, and people still queue for its ever-changing selection of oven-fresh breads and pastries. The *wanchan* (doggie) bun (¥110) is filled with custard cream and uses raisins for the eyes and nose. The shop closes when sold out.

Note that staff are too busy to assist or answer questions; best to get your goodies and go.

Jin Robata & Beer Pub   IZAKAYA ¥
(ろばた仁; Map p742; ☑0977-21-1768; 1-15-7 Kitahama; dishes ¥400-1400; ⊙5pm-midnight) A neon fish sign directs you to this welcoming international pub. To go with your booze, pick from the rows of fresh fish on display (get it sashimi or cooked) or sample *toriten*, local beef and more. Or try the ever-popular fried chicken if you're hungry for a taste of home.

Toyotsune   JAPANESE ¥¥
(とよ常; Map p742; ☑0977-22-3274; 2-13-11 Kitahama; mains ¥750-1650; ⊙11am-2pm & 5-10pm Thu-Tue) Toyotsune nails the Beppu specialities: *toriten*, *Bungō-gyū* and lots of fresh fish, plus tempura. This main branch is on the corner behind Jolly Pasta; a **second branch** (Map p742; ☑0977-23-7487; 3-7 Ekimae-honmachi; ⊙11am-2pm & 5-10pm Fri-Wed; 🖰) is across from Beppu Station. Plan to wait at peak times.

Fugu Matsu   SEAFOOD ¥¥¥
(ふぐ松; Map p742; ☑0977-21-1717; www.fugu matsu.jp; 3-6-14 Kitahama; fugu set meals from ¥8640; ⊙11am-9pm; 🖰) This friendly shop has been serving simple *fugu* since 1958. Sit on *hori-kotatsu* seating and chow on sashimi, *karaage* (fried *fugu*) and *hirezake* (sake boiled with a grilled *fugu* fin). Reservations are required.

🍷 Drinking & Nightlife

Beppu has a vibrant scene after dark and certainly knows how to party. While most of the clubs and bars cater to a Japanese clientele, there are a number of fun spots for tourists to meet fellow travellers or hang out with English-speaking locals.

★ **Real Point**   CAFE
(リアルポイント; Map p742; ☑080-5255-1141; 1-2-24 Kitahama; ⊙noon-10pm Thu-Tue; 🛜) If a tepee in the middle of Beppu's urban sprawl doesn't pique your curiosity, nothing will. This eclectic cafe has hand-brewed coffees, soy lattes, teas, occasional barbecue parties, and even ukulele lessons. This is certainly one of the more unique coffee experiences you'll encounter in Japan. Finding it is nearly impossible: from Kitahama-dōri, look for the blue-and-white sign down a narrow alleyway beside Taniguchi Dental Clinic.

Kissa Natsume   CAFE
(喫茶なつめ; Map p742; ☑097-721-5713; 1-4-23 Kitahama; ⊙10am-8pm Thu-Tue) This retro snack

Kannawa Hells Area

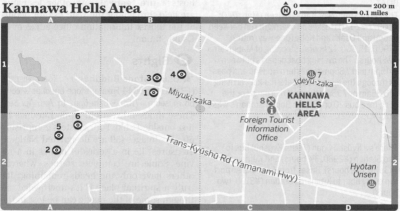

Kannawa Hells Area

and dessert spot in the covered arcade is best known for its own *onsen kōhī* (¥550), coffee made with hot-spring water. Look for the wooden barrel above the door. The pet soft-shelled turtle has been raised since it was the size of a ¥500 coin.

Beppu Social Bar　BAR
(BSB; Map p742; ☑ 080-4367-4850; www.face book.com/aurabsb; 1-4-24 Kitahama; ⏰ 8pm-3am) BSB has a good drink selection and a fun, youthful vibe, with a dance floor, tables, and even a hookah. The crowd here varies, but you'll find it easy to make friends and perhaps even lose a few games of Four Square if you're lucky. It's also one of the few local venues that's wheelchair accessible.

Shopping

Oita Made Shop　GIFTS & SOUVENIRS
(Map p742; ☑ 097-775-8413; www.oitamade.asia; 6-21 Moto-machi; ⏰ 11am-6pm Wed-Mon) This lovely shop features special products, foods,

liquors and crafts from Ōita Prefecture, most with explanations, in Japanese, English and Korean, describing the artistry, region and history of the item. Find it at the far end of the Ginza Arcade.

Information

MONEY

International ATMs can be found at Beppu Station, **Kitahama post office** (別府北浜郵便局; Map p742; 2-9-1 Kitahama; ⏰ 9am-5pm Mon-Fri; ATM 8am-8pm Mon-Fri, 9am-8pm Sat, 9am-7pm Sun) as well as the nearby Cosmopia shopping centre. **Ōita Bank** (大分銀行; Map p742; ☑ 097-723-3111; 2-9-1 Kitahama; ⏰ 9am-3pm Mon-Fri) handles foreign-exchange services.

TOURIST INFORMATION

Foreign Tourist Information Branches are at **Beppu International Plaza** (Map p742; ☑ 0977-21-6220; 12-13 Ekimae-machi; ⏰ 8.30am-5pm), **Beppu Station** (Map p742; ☑ 0977-23-1119; cnr Ekimae-dōri & Ginza Arcade; ⏰ 10am-4pm; 🐾) and **Kannawa** (Map p745; ☑ 0977-66-3855; 5-kumi Furomoto; ⏰ 9am-5pm; 🐾). Well equipped with helpful bilingual volunteers and an arsenal of local information and advice.

Getting There & Away

AIR

Flights go to nearby **Ōita Airport** (☑ 0978-67-1174; www.oita-airport.jp) from Tokyo Haneda and Osaka. Flights also operate to Seoul.

Beppu Airport buses (¥1500) from Ōita Airport stop outside Tokiwa department store (48 minutes) and Beppu Station (51 minutes).

BOAT

The **Ferry Sunflower Kansai Kisen** (Map p740; ☑ 0977-22-1311) makes an overnight run between Beppu and Osaka and Kōbe (one-way/return ¥7900/15,500, 12 hours), stopping at Matsuyama (4½ hours). The evening boat departs between 6.45pm and 7.35pm to western Honshū and passes through the Inland Sea (Seto-nai-kai), arriving at 6.35am or 7.35am the next morning. For the port, take bus 20 or 26 from Beppu Station's **west exit** (Map p742).

BUS

There's a Kyūshū Odan (Trans-Kyūshū) bus to Aso Station (¥2980, 3¼ hours) and Kumamoto (¥3960, five hours). Buses from Fukuoka Airport run every hour to Kitahama Station (¥3190, two hours).

TRAIN

The Kyūshū *shinkansen* from Hakata (Fukuoka) connects with the JR Nippō line at Kokura (*shinkansen* and *tokkyū* ¥5740, 100 minutes) to Beppu. The JR Nippō line continues to Miyazaki via Ōita (*tokkyū* ¥5480, 3¼ hours). Trains also run to Kagoshima-Chūō (¥14,610, 194 minutes) via Kokura.

An express train runs from Beppu to Hakata Station (¥5050, 120 minutes), and is convenient and cheap.

ⓘ Getting Around

Much of Beppu centre is walkable, but buses are a good way to reach the Hells and outskirts.

Kamenoi is the main bus company. An unlimited 'My Beppu Free' pass comes in two varieties: 'mini' (adult/student ¥900/700), which covers Beppu city (and offers discounts); and 'wide' (one/two days ¥1600/2400), which extends to Yufuin. Passes are available from foreign tourist information offices, the train station and ferry terminal, and some lodgings. From JR Beppu Station, buses 2, 5, 7, 9, 20, 24, 25 and 41 go to Kannawa (15 to 25 minutes), and buses 26 and 26A serve Chi-no-ike and Tatsumaki *jigoku*. Kannawa-bound buses also leave from a **bus stop** (Map p742) near Route 10.

If you really need to get away, **Eki Rent-a-Car** (Map p742; ☑ 097-724-4428; www.ekiren.co.jp; 12-13 Ekimae-chō) is inside Beppu Station, with cars that start at about ¥5400 per day.

Usuki 臼杵

☑ 0972 / POP 39,000

Usuki is best known for its astounding thousand-year-old stone Buddhas, but the town also has several temples and well-preserved traditional houses, and a pretty downtown of historic wood and stucco homes and shops. On the last Saturday in August, the town hosts a **fire festival**, and other festivities are held throughout the year; ask for details at the tourist information office adjacent to Usuki Station.

◉ Sights

★ Usuki Stone Buddhas   BUDDHIST SITE

(臼杵石仏; 804-1 Fukata; stone buddhas & combo museum ¥710; ⊙ 6am-6pm, to 7pm Apr-Sep) These thousand-year-old stone Buddhas lie just outside Usuki. Four clusters comprising 60-plus images (59 are designated National Treasures) lie in a series of niches in a ravine. Some are complete statues, whereas others have only the heads remaining. It's truly a spiritual place if it's uncrowded, although some of the magic can be lost in the touristy ambience just outside. The museum has Edo-period and other artefacts from nearby excavations. Free coin lockers.

Nearby is a lovely lotus pond (free).

🛏 Sleeping & Eating

The options for staying in Usuki are limited, consisting mainly of inns offering packages to bus tours. Beppu or Yufuin have better overnight options.

About a dozen local restaurants boast some of the best *fugu* (pufferfish) in Japan; expect to pay from about ¥5000/8000 for a lunch/dinner set, including sake.

Credo Hotel Usuki   HOTEL ¥¥

(クレドホテル臼杵; ☑ 0972-63-5666; www.credo-hotel.com; 2573-10 Kaizoe; s/d/tr ¥6400/13,000/15,900; 🅿 ❄ ✳ 🛜) This convenient option is just a minute's walk from the train station. It has a selection of Western and Japanese rooms, and some floors are entirely nonsmoking.

Chikuba   FUGU ¥¥¥

(竹馬; ☑ 0972-62-5073; 3-Kumi Hamamachi; fugu set meals from ¥10,000; ⊙ 4.30-10.30pm) If you're going to sample *fugu*, this is a renowned place to try it: with just three tables, it better be good! There's also non-*fugu* options, as well as a good variety of beers, sakes and hard liquors.

ⓘ Information

Tourist Information Office (臼杵市観光情報協会; ☑ 0972-63-2366; Usuki JR Station; ⊙ 9am-3pm) Inside the JR Station.

Usuki City Tourism & Community Plaza (臼杵市観光交流プラザ; ☑ 097-263-1715; 100-2 Ōaza; ⊙ 9am-6pm; 🛜) This sparkling new tourist plaza is set inconveniently far from the

KUNISAKI PENINSULA

It would be easy to overlook the Kunisaki Peninsula (国東半島), a remote corner of Kyūshū north of Beppu, under-served as it is by public transport, but you'd be missing some of the most undisturbed *pawā spotto* (power spots, Japanese slang for spiritual places) in the nation. Buses circle the peninsula, but getting to the temples using public transport is inconvenient and time-consuming. **Oita Kōtsū Bus** (大分交通バス; Map p742; ☎ 097-536-3655; www.oitakotsu.co.jp; Kunisaki Peninsula tour ¥5050; ◷ 9am-5pm) runs daily bus tours from Beppu to view the main temples, but the best way to view this area is by car.

The sprawling, wooded and water-crossed **Usa-jingū** (宇佐神宮; www.usajinguu.com; 2859 Minami Usa) FREE, the original of which dates back some 1200 years, is the chief shrine among some 40,000 in Japan dedicated to the warrior-god Hachiman. It's a 4km bus or taxi ride from Usa Station (get off at Usa-Hachiman-mae), on the JR Nippō line from Beppu. Parking costs ¥400. A monorail helps the mobility impaired.

The town of Bungo-takada is nicknamed 'Buddha's Village' and the region is noted for its early Buddhist influence, including some rock-carved images linked to the more famous ones at Usuki. Located on the outskirts of Bungo-takada, **Fuki-ji** (富貴寺; ¥300; ◷ 8.30am-4.30pm), a national treasure made of fragrant nutmeg wood, is the oldest wooden structure in Kyūshū and one of the oldest wooden temples in Japan. Its overgrown grounds and moss-covered stupas complement the 11th-century structure beautifully. Ōita Kōtsū buses from Usa Station go to Bungo-takada (¥810, 20 minutes); from there, it's a 10-minute taxi ride (around ¥1000).

In the centre of the Kunisaki Peninsula, near the summit of Futago-san (721m), the temple **Futago-ji** (両子寺; www.futago.jp; 1548 Futago, Akimachi; ¥300; ◷ 8am-5pm Apr-Nov, 8.30am-4.30pm Dec-Mar) was founded in 718 and dedicated to Fudō-Myō-o, the fire-enshrouded, sword-wielding deity. It's a lovely climb, especially in spring or autumn, and there are plenty of subtemples to explore around the mountain's forested gorges. There's a lovely mossy stream and detours for hiking.

Nearby **Taizō-ji** (胎蔵寺; ◷ 9am-5pm) FREE is known for its famously uneven stone stairs. Local legend says that they are so random and haphazard that the Oni (devils) must have created them in a single night. Monks will give you stickers to put on the statue of your Chinese birth year.

Deep in a forest along a mossy riverbed, are two Heian-period Buddha images carved into a cliff: a 6m figure of the Dainichi Buddha; and an 8m figure of Fudō-Myō-o. Known as **Kumano Magaibutsu** (熊野磨崖仏; ¥300; ◷ 8am-5pm Apr-Oct, 8.30am-4.30pm Nov-Mar), these are the largest Buddhist images of this type in Japan. If you thought the few hundred steps to the carvings were tough, wait until the next few hundred to the shrine at the top.

Timed right, **Soba Cafe Yuuhi** (Soba Cafe ゆうひ; ☎ 0978-25-8533; www.facebook.com/sobacafeyuuhi; 5125 Usuno; soba dishes ¥650-1000; ◷ 11am-sunset Wed-Mon) might be the most spectacular view you see your entire trip: the glowing setting sun sinking into the ocean or behind mud flats that seem to go right out to the horizon. On Kunisaki's north-west coast, this humble soba shop in a roadside turnout sells handmade soba and rents stand-up paddle boards (SUP; ¥2000 per hour) for use at high tide.

station. It has maps, pamphlets and life-sized figures of Usuki's mascot, 'Hotto-san', a cute stone Buddha cartoon character.

ⓘ Getting There & Around

Usuki is 40km southeast of Beppu. Take the JR Nippō line to Usuki Station (*tokkyū/futsū* ¥2070/940, 45/60 minutes), usually with a change in Ōita.

From the station, infrequent buses take 20 minutes to the Buddha images, or it's about ¥2020 in a taxi, or 35 minutes by bike. You can rent normal bikes (free!) or electric bikes (¥300 per hour) at the station from 9am to 3pm, or from the **Tourism & Community Plaza** until 6pm.

Takachiho 高千穂

☎ 0982 / POP 12,650

In far northern Miyazaki Prefecture, the pretty mountain town of Takachiho is a remote but rewarding destination. Legend has it that this is the site where Japan's sun

Takachiho

KYŪSHŪ TAKACHIHO

goddess brought light back to the world and, as if that weren't reason enough to visit, there's a deep and dramatic gorge through the town centre.

◎ Sights

★ Takachiho Gorge
GORGE

(高千穂峡, Takachiho-kyō; Map p748) Takachiho's magnificent gorge, with its waterfall, overhanging rocks and sheer walls, was formed over 120,000 years ago by a double volcanic eruption. There's a 1km-long nature trail above the gorge. Alternatively, view it up close from a **row boat** (Map p748; ☑ 0982-73-1213; per 30 min ¥2000, up to 3 adults per boat; ⏰ 7.30am-6pm), though during high season it can be as busy as rush hour. In season, rowers will be mobbed by throngs of hungry ducks.

Ama-no-Iwato-jinja
SHINTO SHRINE

(天岩戸神社; Map p748; 1073-1 Iwato; ⏰ 24hr, office 8.30am-5pm) One of Shintō's loveliest shrines honours the cave where the goddess Amaterasu hid. The cave itself is off-limits, but Nishi Hongū (the shrine's main building) sits right across the Iwato-gawa (Iwato River). If you're with a Japanese speaker, ask a staff member to show you the viewpoint behind the *honden* (main hall). Buses leave approximately hourly (¥300, 20 minutes) from Takachihō's Miyakō bus centre.

A seven-minute walk beside a picturesque stream takes you to **Ama-no-Yasukawara**, a deep cave where tradition says that thousands of other deities discussed how to lure Amaterasu from the cave. Modern-day visitors have left innumerable stacks of stones in tribute, imparting a sort of Indiana Jones feeling.

Takachiho-jinja
SHINTO SHRINE

(高千穂神社; Map p748) About 10 minutes' walk from the bus centre, Takachiho-jinja is dramatically set in a grove of Cryptomeria pines, including one that's over 800 years old. Some of the buildings here look like they could almost be the same age.

🛏 Sleeping & Eating

Takachiho has about 30 hotels, ryokan, *minshuku* and pensions, which all typically book out during the autumn foliage season.

There are only a few eating options in this small town, as most visitors prefer to have meals at their hotels.

Takachiho Youth Hostel HOSTEL ¥

(高千穂ユースホステル; Map p748; ☑ 0982-72-3021; http://ww6.tiki.ne.jp/~takachiho-yh; 5899-2 Mitai; dm HI member/nonmember ¥2800/3400; P❄✳@) This large hostel is far from the sights, but it's clean, efficient and deep in the woods. Rooms are Japanese-style, with breakfast available (¥500), as are laundry machines and pick-up from the bus centre (call ahead).

Hotel Takachiho HOTEL ¥¥

(ホテル高千穂; Map p748; ☑ 098-272-3255; 1037-4 Mitari; s/d ¥6600/11,600, incl 2 meals ¥12,600/24,600; P❄✳🤝) This reasonably priced luxury hotel is a 15-minute walk (steeply downhill) from the gorge. The bath is not real onsen water, but is refreshing nonetheless. A restaurant on the premises serves *shabu-shabu* (thinly sliced beef cooked with vegetables in boiling water and then dipped in sauce), *yakiniku* (grilled meat) and other Japanese specialities.

Chiho-no-ie NOODLES ¥

(千穂の家; Map p748; ☑ 0982-72-2115; 62-1 Mukoyama; sōmen ¥500, set meals from ¥1300; ⊗ 9am-5pm; 📖) At the base of the gorge (though, sadly, with no water views), this simple building serves *nagashi-sōmen* (flowing noodles; ¥500) – have fun catching tasty noodles with your chopsticks as they float by in halved bamboo shafts. Note there are three buildings, all with the same name. You want the one with the large fish pools in front.

Gamadase Ichiba MARKET ¥¥

(がまだせ市場; Map p748; ☑ Nagomi 0982-73 1109; 1099-1 Mitai; Nagomi set menus lunch ¥1700-3000, dinner ¥2600-6000; ⊗ markets & Nagomi 11am-2.30pm & 5-9pm, closed 2nd Wed of the month) Operated by the local agricultural collaborative, this facility has markets for local produce and the **Nagomi** (和) restaurant for local beef set menus. Be sure to say 'hi' to the full-size replicas of beloved now-departed bovines that stand outside.

ℹ️ Information

Michi-no-Eki Tourist Information Booth (道の駅観光案内所; Map p748; ☑ 098-272-4680; www.takachiho-kanko.jp; 1296-5 Mitai; ⊗ 8.30am-5.30pm) A well-stocked tourist-info counter with friendly staff who can assist with making day plans or reservations.

Town Centre Information Office (町中案内所; Map p748; ☑ 0982-72-3031; 1296-5 Mitai; ⊗ 8.30am-5.30pm) Helpful staff and a variety of maps, brochures, info, postcards, and souvenirs.

ℹ️ Getting There & Around

Takachiho is most easily reached by car from the Aso-san area in Kumamoto Prefecture. Two buses daily serve Takachiho's **Miyakō bus centre** (高千穂宮交バスセンター; Map p748; ☑ 0982-72-4133) from Kumamoto (¥2370, 3½ hours) usually via Takamori (¥1320, 1¼ hours). Note that as of November 2016, the route has been diverted due to earthquake damage; without this diversion it normally takes under three hours via Takamori.

From the bus centre the gorge and Takachiho-jinja are within walking distance, but you'll need transport to reach other sights. The town centre information office has wi-fi and rents out electric bicycles for ¥300 per hour or ¥1500 per day.

SOUTHERN KYŪSHŪ

Including the prefectures of Kagoshima (鹿児島) to the west and Miyazaki (宮崎) to the east, with Kagoshima Bay in the middle,

---

TAKACHIHO'S SACRED DANCES

Takachiho's artistic claim to fame is **kagura** (sacred dance). In May, September and November (the dates change annually), performances are held at Ama-no-Iwato-jinja from 10am to 10pm, while hour-long performances of **yokagura** (night-time kagura; tickets ¥700; ⊗ 8pm) take place nightly at Takachiho-jinja. Arrive up to an hour early for front-row seating.

There are also all-night performances (*satokagura*) in farmhouses on 19 nights from November to February. In all, 33 dances are performed from 6pm until 9am the next morning. If you brave the cold until morning, you'll be caught up in a wave of excitement. Contact the tourist information office for details.

According to Shintō legend, the sun goddess Amaterasu, angered by the misbehaviour of her brother, exiled herself into a cave sealed by a boulder, plunging the world into darkness. Alarmed, other gods gathered at another nearby cave to discuss how to get her to re-emerge. Eventually the goddess Ame-no-Uzume performed a bawdy dance that aroused Amaterasu's curiosity, and she emerged from the cave and light was restored to earth. *Iwato kagura* dances performed in Takachiho today re-enact this story.

southern Kyūshū is the furthest south you can get in Japan without boarding a ferry.

Kagoshima pops up in the annals of history again and again: from ancient Jōmon-era dwellings to the beginnings of the Meiji Restoration and, more recently, to the departure point for thousands of WWII pilots. The prefecture also boasts the smouldering Kirishima mountain range – popular for bird- and wildlife-watchers, and for James Bond fans, who will enjoy the views of Sakurajima that were filmed here for *Live and Let Die*.

Miyazaki is Kagoshima's 'hippie sibling' – relaxed and quiet, with a renowned coastline that draws surfers from all over Japan. Coastal drives here may remind you of California or the Italian Riviera until, of course, you detour inland and meet the resident bands of wild monkeys.

Kagoshima 鹿児島

🖉099 / POP 600,000

Sunny Kagoshima has a personality to match its climate, and has been voted Japan's friendliest city nationwide. Its backdrop/deity is Sakurajima, a very active volcano *just* across the bay. Locals raise their umbrellas against the mountain's recurrent eruptions, when fine ash coats the landscape like snow and obscures the sun like fog – mystical and captivating. The entire prefecture even has a special 'Ash Forecast' as part of the weather report. Once ash starts falling you'll understand why: it stings, coats your teeth with grit, dirties futons and laundry, and makes anyone who has just washed their car burst into tears.

History

Once called Satsuma, Kagoshima was ruled by the Shimazu clan for a remarkable 700 years. The location helped it grow wealthy through trade, particularly with China. Contact was also made with Korea, whose pottery methods were influential in the creation of Satsuma-yaki.

When Japan opened to the world in the mid-19th century, Satsuma's government competed with the shogunate, engaging in war with Britain and hosting a Satsuma pavilion – independent from the Japanese pavilion – at the 1867 Paris Expo. Satsuma's best known samurai, the complicated and (literally) towering figure of Saigō Takamori, played a key role in the Meiji Restoration.

There's a **statue of Saigō Takamori** (Map p752) in central Kagoshima.

◉ Sights

★ Museum of the Meiji Restoration
MUSEUM

(維新ふるさと館; Map p752; 🖉099-239-7700; 23-1 Kajiya-chō; ¥300; ⊗9am-5pm; 🚉JR Kagoshima-Chūō) This museum offers insights into the unique social system of education, samurai loyalty and sword techniques that made Satsuma one of Japan's leading provinces, with a good smartphone app in English. There are hourly audiovisual presentations about the ground-breaking visits of Satsuma students to the West and the Satsuma Rebellion told by animatronic Meiji-era reformers, including Saigō Takamori and Sakamoto Ryōma.

Sengan-en (Iso-teien)
GARDENS

(仙巌園・磯庭園; 🖉099-247-1551; 9700-1 Yoshino-chō; admission with/without guided villa tour & tea ceremony ¥1600/1000; ⊗8.30am-5.30pm) In 1658, the 19th Shimazu lord laid out this hilly, rambling bayside property of groves, gardens, hillside trails and one of Japan's most impressive pieces of 'borrowed scenery': the fuming peak of Sakurajima. It was a place of pleasure and a strategically important lookout for ships entering Kinkō-wan.

Allow at least 30 minutes for a leisurely stroll, and 20 minutes more to tour the 25-room Goten, a former villa of the Shimazu clan (traditional tea and sweets provided).

Reimeikan
MUSEUM

(黎明館, Kagoshima Prefectural Museum of Culture; Map p752; 7-2 Shiroyama-chō; ¥310; ⊗9am-6pm Tue-Sun, closed 25th of the month; 🚉Shiyakushō-mae) The Reimeikan has extensive displays on Satsuma history and ancient sword-making. It's inside the site of Kagoshima's castle, **Tsurumaru-jō** (1602); the walls and moat are all that remain, and bullet holes in the stones are still visible. It's behind Kagoshima's City Hall and government buildings.

🏃 Activities

Kagoshima boasts some 50 bathhouses, most meant for locals and recalling the humble, everyday *sentō* (public bath) of old. They include local favourite **Nishida Onsen** (西田温泉; Map p752; 1-2-17 Takashi; ¥390; ⊗5.30am-10.30pm, closed 2nd Mon of the month), just a few minutes' walk from JR Kagoshima-Chūō Station, and **Kagomma Onsen**

(かごっま温泉; Map p752; 3-28 Yasui-chō; ¥390; ⊘8am-midnight, closed 15th of the month), near City Hall. A great onsen brochure is available from most tourist info desks and in many hotel lobbies.

👉 Tours

Kagoshima Fish Market Tour　　TOURS
(鹿児島市中央卸売市場; ☎099-226-8188; www.gyokago.com; adult/child ¥1500/800; ⊘6.45am Sat Mar-Nov; 🚃Shinyashiki) Get up early, don rubber boots and tour Kagoshima's central fish market, like a miniature (and much more accessible) version of Tokyo's Tsukiji Market. Pick-up is offered from many hotels in town. Reserve well in advance if you'll need English translation. After the tour (about 8am), the guides can introduce you to restaurants in the market for a sushi breakfast (from about ¥1000).

Note that children younger than 'school age' are not allowed.

🎉 Festivals & Events

Sogadon-no-Kasayaki　　CULTURAL
(⊘late Jul) One of Kagoshima's more unusual events is the Umbrella Burning Festival. Boys burn umbrellas on the banks of Kōtsuki-gawa in honour of two brothers who used umbrellas as torches in one of Japan's oldest revenge stories.

🛌 Sleeping

Kagoshima has plenty of good-value places to sleep. The station is a bit far from the action, so aim to stay toward Tenmonkan.

Green Guest House　　HOSTEL ¥
(グリーンゲストハウス;Mapp752;☎0998-02-4301; www.green-guesthouse.com; 5-7 Sumiyoshi-chō; dm/tw/private room ¥1800/2300/2800; 😀❄@🛜; 🚃Izuro-dōri) Clean and compact, this hostel is very convenient to the ferry docks and great if you're going to (or coming from) Sakurajima. Separate gender dorms and private rooms are available. Some English is spoken at the front desk, and all important signage is in English and Japanese.

Sun Days Inn Kagoshima　　BUSINESS HOTEL ¥¥
(サンデイズイン鹿児島; Map p752; ☎099-227-5151; www.sundaysinn.com; 9-8 Yamanokuchi-chō; s/d/tw ¥5550/7600/9200; P😀❄@🛜; 🚃Tenmonkan-dōri) The Sun Days provides good value in the heart of Tenmonkan, with a wall of *shōchū* bottles in the lobby. Rooms are compact, but the beds, showers and warm

decor make up for it, and the city hot spots are steps away. Rates are cheaper booked online (in Japanese). The breakfast buffet (some 30 choices including local specialities) is a bargain at ¥540.

Hotel Gasthof　　HOTEL ¥¥
(ホテルガストフ; Map p752; ☎099-252-1401; www.gasthof.jp; 7-1 Chūō-chō; s/d/tr ¥5700/9200/13,200; P❄✳@🛜; 🚃JR Kagoshima-Chūō) Old-world Europe meets urban Japan at this unusual 48-room hotel, with good-sized rooms, hardwood panelling and stone- and brick-wall motifs. Near the station and with triple and interconnecting rooms, it's a good choice for families.

⭐**Onsen Hotel Nakahara Bessō**　HOTEL ¥¥¥
(温泉ホテル中原別荘; Map p752; ☎099-225-2800; www.nakahara-bessou.co.jp; 15-19 Terukuni-chō; r per person with/without 2 meals from ¥12,960/8640; P❄✳@🛜; 🚃Tenmonkan-dōri) Just outside Tenmonkan and across from a park, this family-owned inn traces its history to 1904. Ignore its boxy exterior; inside is a modern *rotemburo*, spacious Japanese-style rooms with private bath, traditional artwork and a good *Satsuma-ryōri* restaurant. Non-smokers will appreciate the strict policy, and wi-fi is available as well.

Remm Kagoshima　　HOTEL ¥¥¥
(レム鹿児島; Map p752; ☎099-224-0606; http://kagoshima-remm.hh-hotels.jp; 1-32 Higashi-sengoku-chō; s/d/tw from ¥10,800/15,120/19,980; P😀❄@🛜; 🚃Tenmonkan-dōri) At this hotel in Tenmonkan, rooms are business-hotel-sized, but futuristic in style and amenities, with custom-designed beds, fluffy white duvets, massage chairs, rain showers, and glass windows in the bathrooms for natural light (and, thoughtfully, curtains). The ageless design in the public spaces incorporates ancient stones and hardwoods, and it's worth springing for

Central Kagoshima

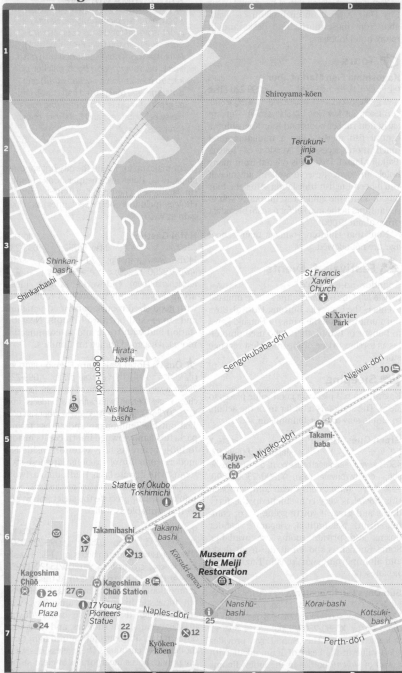

Shiroyama-kōen

Terukuni-jinja

Shinkan-bashi

Shinkanbashi

St Francis Xavier Church

St Xavier Park

Ōgon-dōri

Hirata-bashi

Sengokubaba-dōri

Nigiwai-dōri 10

Nishida-bashi

5

Miyako-dōri

Takami-baba

Kajiya-chō

Statue of Ōkubo Toshimichi

21

Takamibashi

Takami-bashi

Kōtsuki-gawa

Museum of the Meiji Restoration 1

Takamibashi
17

13

Kagoshima Chūō

26

27 Kagoshima Chūō Station 8

Amu Plaza

17 Young Pioneers Statue

Naples-dōri

Nanshū-bashi

25

Kōrai-bashi

Kōtsuki-bashi

24

22

12

Kyōken-kōen

Perth-dōri

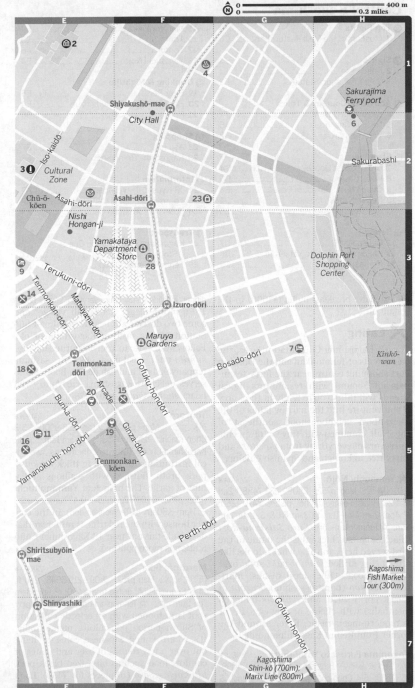

KYŪSHŪ KAGOSHIMA

Central Kagoshima

the extensive breakfast buffet (¥1000) in the restaurant.

✕ Eating

The JR Kagoshima-Chūō Station area, the backstreets of Tenmonkan and the Dolphin Port shopping centre near the ferry terminals all abound with restaurants. Local friends will think you're really in the know if you venture into the narrow lanes of the Meizanbori neighbourhood southeast of City Hall, crammed with tiny yet often chic purveyors of everything from *yakitori* and curry rice to French and Spanish cuisine.

★ Yamauchi Nōjō   IZAKAYA ¥
(山内農場; Map p752; ☑099-223-7488; 2nd fl, 1-26 Higashi-sengoku-chō; dishes ¥410-1250; ⊙4pm-2am Mon-Thu, to 3am Fri & Sat, to 1am Sun; ◙Tenmonkan-dōri) *Kuro Satsuma-dori* (black Satsuma chicken) is the name of the bird served here, and also what it looks like after being grilled *sumibi-yaki*-style over open charcoal. Other local dishes: marinated *katsuo* (bonito) sashimi, *kurobuta* (black pork) salad, and *tsukune* (chicken meatballs) with cheese or raw egg. Decor is modern-meets-rustic. Enter around the corner from Remm Kagoshima hotel.

Kagomma Furusato Yatai-mura   JAPANESE ¥
(かごつまふるさと屋台村; Map p752; ☑099-255-1588; 6-4 Chūō-chō; prices vary; ⊙lunch &

dinner, individual stall hours vary; ◙Takami-bashi) *Yatai-mura* means 'food stall village', and some two dozen stalls near Kagoshima-Chūō Station offer a taste of Kagoshima of old. Follow your nose to your favourite stalls for *sumibi-yaki* (coal-fired chicken), sashimi, teppanyaki beef and fish dishes. Booth No 16 serves delicious Kagoshima *kurobuta* (wild boar), *shabu-shabu* style (¥1280).

Tontoro   RAMEN ¥
(豚とろ; Map p752; ☑099-258-9900; 3-3 Chūō-machi; ramen ¥750; ⊙11am-1am; ◙JR Kagoshima-Chūō) Tontoro's locations are local institutions for ramen in thick *tonkotsu* pork broth, finished with scallions and a hint of garlic. The branch at **Yamanokuchi** (Map p752; ☑099-222-5857; 9-41 Yamanokuchi; ⊙11am-3.30am; ◙Tenmonkan-dōri), in the corner house with the red trim, is rather workaday, while this one near JR Kagoshima-Chūō Station is more polished.

Marutora Ikka   IZAKAYA ¥
(○虎一家; Map p752; ☑099-219-3948; 2nd fl, 14-17 Sennichi-chō; dishes from ¥400; ⊙6pm-3am Tue-Sun; ◙; ◙Tenmonkan-dōri) This happy spot is festooned with an eclectic collection of Shōwa-period pop-culture memorabilia. It's where young Japanese come to hang out over a few rounds of beer and plates of comfort food such as bite-sized black pork *hitokuchi-gyōza* (10 pieces for ¥450). Look for the dark wooden street frontage and

staircase leading upstairs, down the block from the 7-Eleven.

★ **Cafe Lakan** FUSION ¥¥
(カフェラカン; Map p752; ☏0992-10-5572; 3-1 Uenosono-chō; set meals from ¥1200; ◑11am-4pm; ☺▣; ▣JR Kagoshima-Chūō) This lovely little cafe has delicious daily specials that mix Japanese, Italian and other Western cuisines. Decor is dark wood with a bar; it's the kind of place you'll see groups of office ladies out for lunch, salarymen there for a glass of wine after work, or someone in the back with a book. It's nonsmoking, too.

★ **Kumasotei** JAPANESE ¥¥
(熊襲亭; Map p752; ☏099-222-6356; 6-10 Higashi-Sengoku-chō; set meals lunch/dinner from ¥1500/3000; ◑11am-2pm & 5-10pm; ▣; ▣Tenmonkan-dōri) This atmospheric multistorey restaurant near central Tenmonkan covers all your *Satsuma-ryōri* needs: *Satsuma-age*, *tonkotsu*, *kurobutu shabu-shabu*, and lots of fresh fish and seafood. Look for the vertical sign with red lettering and large wooden kanji above the entryway.

▼ Drinking & Nightlife

Tenmonkan is where most of the action happens – shot bars, clubs and karaoke boxes. Most dance clubs don't get going until around 11pm and many bars charge admission (¥500 to ¥1000 on average). Many also charge a 'table fee' or 'service' for the snacks or bar nuts they'll serve, whether you eat them or not.

★ **Honkaku Shōchū Bar Ishizue** BAR
(本格焼酎Bar 礎; Map p752; ☏099-227-0125; www.honkakushochu-bar-ishizue.com; 6-1 Sengoku-chō, 4th fl, Flower Bldg; ¥2000; ◑8pm-3am) This chic, amber-and-wood *shōchū* (potato vodka) bar has everything going for it, and is considered one of the finest places to drink Kagoshima's prefectural liquor, with over 500 different bottles available, each with its own story, which the owner can discuss personally (if time permits). Reservations required.

Recife BAR
(レシフェ; Map p752; ☏099-213-9787; 1-3 Kajiya-chō; ◑noon-11pm Sun, Mon, Wed & Thu, to midnight Fri & Sat; ▣Kajiya-chō) This arty, mellow three-floor shop-bar-restaurant also has DJ decks and hosts occasional parties. It's popular with expat groovers and Japanese English-speaking locals, and it offers Latin-American eats before turning into a bar for the wee hours. It's along

Miyako-dōri halfway between Kajiya-chō and Takamibashi tram stops. No smoking except on the roof.

Beer Reise BAR
(ビアライゼ; Map p752; ☏099-227-0088; Hirata Bldg, 9-10 Sennichi-chō; ◑5pm-2am; ▣Tenmonkan-dōri) This cheery, narrow bar has Guinness and Nagano's own YonaYona, plus a variety of German and Belgian beers, and a ¥100-off happy hour from 5pm to 7pm. Enter from the side door to the left of the tobacco shop.

🛍 Shopping

Regional specialities include Satsuma Kiriko cut glass, Tsumugi silk, bamboo and wood products, and Satsuma-yaki pottery (most typically in austere black and white). Some are for sale at Sengan-en (p751) and the **Kagoshima Brand Shop** (鹿児島ブランドショップ; Map p752; ☏099-225-6120; 1st fl, Sangyo Kaikan Bldg, 9-1 Meizan-chō; ◑9am-6pm; ▣Asahi-dōri) near Tenmonkan. Pick up the free English-language *A Guide to Kagoshima Products*.

Fun shopping experiences include the **Asa-ichi** (朝市, Morning Market; Map p752; ◑4.30am-1pm Mon-Sat) just south of JR Kagoshima-Chūō Station.

ℹ Information

TOURIST INFORMATION

Tourist information is available on the prefectural site, www.kagoshima-kankou.com. The city

---

SHŌCHŪ

Reviled for ages, Kagoshima's prefectural drink has of late become one of its many prides. *Shōchū*, a strong distilled liquor (sometimes nicknamed Japanese vodka), is now drunk in high-end bars all across Japan. Kagoshima Prefecture claims the highest consumption in Japan, which may well explain why everyone's so friendly! Each prefecture is known for its own particular variety. In Kumamoto, *shōchū* is usually made from rice; in Ōita, it's barley; and here it's *imojōchū* from sweet potatoes. Drink it straight, with soda or over ice, but the most traditional way is *oyuwari*, with water heated in a stone pot over glowing coals. Drink until you yourself begin to glow.

ℹ KAGOSHIMA TRANSIT PASS

Visitors can take advantage of the Cute transit card (one/two days ¥1200/1800) covering city buses (including the City View and Sakurajima Island View buses), trams, Sakurajima ferries and the Yorimichi Cruise. Cardholders can also get discounted admission to many attractions. Pick it up at tourist information offices.

website (www.city.kagoshima.lg.jp) has detailed info on transport, sights and living in town. For sightseeing info, and arts and entertainment listings, see www.kic-update.com.

Tourist Information Centre (鹿児島中央駅総合観光案内所; Map p752; ☑ 099-253-2500; JR Kagoshima-Chūō Station; ⊙ 8am-8pm) Has plenty of information in English and the handy *Kagoshima* visitor's guide.

Tourism Exchange Centre (観光交流センター; Map p752; ☑ 099-298-5111; 1-1 Uenosono-chō; ⊙ 9am-7pm) Near the Museum of the Meiji Restoration, has pamphlets and can make hotel reservations.

TRAVEL AGENCIES

JR Kyūshū Travel Agency (JR九州旅行鹿児島支店; Map p752; ☑ 099-253-2201; 2nd fl, JR Kagoshima-Chūō Station; ⊙ 11am-7pm Mon-Fri, 10.30am-6pm Sat & Sun) Can assist with domestic travel bookings.

ℹ Getting There & Away

AIR

Kagoshima Airport (www.koj-ab.co.jp) has connections to Shanghai, Hong Kong, Taipei and Seoul, and convenient domestic flights, including to Tokyo, Osaka and Okinawa (Naha).

BOAT

Ferries depart from Minami-futō pier to Yakushima (jet foil ¥8300, one hour and 40 minutes; regular ferry ¥4900, four hours). From Kagoshima Shin-kō (Kagoshima New Port), **Marix Line** (☑ 099-225-1551) has ferries to Naha (Okinawa) via the Amami archipelago (¥14,610, 25 hours).

Frequent passenger and car ferries shuttle around the clock between Kagoshima and Sakurajima (¥160, 15 minutes). Reach the **ferry terminal** (Map p752), near the aquarium, on the City View Bus or other buses headed for Suizokukan-mae, or by tram to Suizokukan-guchi.

The **Yorimichi Cruise** (よりみちクルーズ船; Map p752; ☑ 099-223-7271; adult/child ¥500/250; ⊙ 11.05am) takes one of six circui-

tous sightseeing routes from Kagoshima Port to Sakurajima Port in about 50 minutes.

BUS

Long-distance buses depart from the express bus stops at the **Kagoshima Chūō Station bus stops** (Map p752), near the station's east exit, and from streetside stops at Takashima Plaza (aka 'Takapura') in **Tenmonkan** (Map p752).

Routes include Miyazaki (¥2780, three hours), Fukuoka (¥5450, 4½ hours), Ōita (¥5660, 7½ hours) and Nagasaki (¥6690, 5½ hours).

TRAIN

JR Kagoshima-Chūō Station is the terminus of the Kyūshū *shinkansen*, with stops including Kumamoto (¥6420, 52 minutes), Hakata (¥9930, 90 minutes), Hiroshima (¥17,150, 2½ hours) and Shin-Osaka (¥21,380, 3¾ hours). Also stopping at Kagoshima Station, the JR Nippō line goes to Miyazaki (*tokkyū* ¥3710, two hours) and Beppu (¥9090, five hours).

ℹ Getting Around

TO/FROM THE AIRPORT

Express buses depart every five to 20 minutes to and from JR Kagoshima-Chūō Station/Tenmon-kan (¥1250, 45/60 minutes).

BICYCLE

Bikes can be rented (¥500/1500 per two hours/day, with a 20% discount for JR users) at JR Kagoshima-Chūō Station.

BUS

Hop-on, hop-off City View Buses (¥190, every 30 minutes, 9am to 6.20pm) loop around the major sights in two routes. A one-day pass (¥600) is also valid on trams and city bus lines and offers discounted admission to many attractions. Otherwise, local buses tend to be inconvenient, particularly if you don't speak Japanese (you're better off with trams).

CAR & MOTORCYCLE

Many outlets around JR Kagoshima-Chūō Station rent cars for trips around the region.

TRAM

If you're doing only a limited amount of sightseeing, trams are the easiest way around town. Route 1 starts from Kagoshima Station and goes through the centre into the suburbs. Route 2 diverges at Takami-baba (高見馬場) to JR Kagoshima-Chūō Station and terminates at Kōrimoto. Either pay the flat fare (¥170) or buy a one-day travel pass (¥600) from the tourist information centre or on board. A third line, Chokko-bin, runs from Kagoshima Station only at peak commuting times, bypassing Kōrimoto and ending in Taniyama.

Sakurajima

♪ 099 / POP 4880

Kagoshima's iconic symbol Sakurajima has been spewing an almost continuous stream of smoke and ash since 1955, and it's not uncommon to have over 1000 mostly small 'burps' per year. In 1914 over three billion tonnes of lava swallowed numerous island villages – over 1000 homes – and joined Sakurajima to the mainland to the southeast.

Despite its volatility, Sakurajima is currently friendly enough to get fairly close. Among the volcano's three peaks, only Minami-dake (South Peak; 1040m) is active. Climbing is prohibited, but there are some lookout points.

On the mainland, Kagoshima residents speak proudly of Sakurajima. It is said to have *nanairo* (seven colours) visible from across Kinkō-wan, as the light shifts throughout the day on the surface of the mountain.

◉ Sights

Karasujima Observation Point　　VIEWPOINT
(烏島展望台) South of the visitors centre is this observation point, where the 1914 lava flow engulfed a small island that had once been 500m offshore. There's now an *ashi-yu* (foot bath), Japan's second-longest.

Arimura Lava Observatory　　VIEWPOINT
(有村溶岩展望所; ☑ 099-298-5111; 952 Arimura; ⊙24hr) FREE Don't be confused by the name 'Observatory', as there's no building here. It's a shaded picnic area with some lava escape tunnels and walking trails that let you get up close to recent lava, much of it covered now with small pine trees. Smoky Minami-dake, the southern-most peak of Sakurajima, smoulders above you.

Buried Torii　　LANDMARK
(黒神埋没鳥居) On the east coast, the top of a once-3m-high *torii* gate emerges from the volcanic ash at Kurokami; the rest was buried in the 1914 eruption.

Yunohira Lookout　　VIEWPOINT
(湯之平展望所) A drive along the tranquil north coast and then inland will lead you to Yunohira Lookout, for views of the mountain and back across the bay to central Kagoshima.

✦ Festivals & Events

Isle of Fire Festival　　CULTURAL
(⊙late Jul) The summer festival of Sakurajima, with dancing and fireworks.

🛏 Sleeping & Eating

Options for staying here are limited, with just a couple of properties; otherwise take the ferry to Kagoshima or circle north to Kirishima.

With great eats only a short ferry ride away, Kagoshima is your best option for dining, though there are some convenience stores and ferry food near the terminal.

Rainbow Sakurajima Hotel　　RYOKAN ¥¥
(レインボー桜島; ☑ 099-293-2323; www.rainbow-sakurajima.com; 1722-16 Yokoyama-chō; r per person incl 2 meals from ¥9700; 🅿 ⊝ ❋ 🛜) Adjacent to the ferry terminal, this light-filled property faces the puffing volcano in one direction and central Kagoshima across the bay in the other. Most rooms are Japanese style, but seven are Western style. There's an onsen open to the public (¥390) from 10am to 10pm, and a bayside beer garden over summer. Rooms increase by about ¥1000 on weekends.

ℹ Information

Sakurajima Visitors Centre (☑ 099-293-2443; www.sakurajima.gr.jp/svc; ⊙9am-5pm) Nearish the ferry terminal, with exhibits about the volcano including a model showing its growth, with helpful English-speaking staff.

ℹ Getting There & Away

Frequent passenger and car ferries shuttle around the clock between Kagoshima and Sakurajima (¥160, 15 minutes).

The **Yorimichi Cruise** (よりみちクルーズ船; Map p752; ☑ 099-223-7271; adult/child ¥500/250; ⊙11.05am) takes one of six circuitous sightseeing routes from Kagoshima Port to Sakurajima Port in about 50 minutes, then purchase a regular ferry ticket back from Sakurajima to Kagoshima.

ℹ Getting Around

Sakurajima Island View Buses (one-way ¥120-440, day pass ¥500; ⊙8 per day 9am-4.30pm) loop around Sakurajima. Alternatively, try **Sakurajima Rentacar** (☑ 099-293-2162; 2hr/day from ¥4800/11,000), which also rents out bicycles (¥300 per hour), though biking is not recommended since, if the volcano erupts during your ride, you may find yourself unprotected from breathing the ash.

Though there are buses, this volcanic island is best enjoyed by car; the drive around takes an hour, more depending on stops.

Satsuma Peninsula
薩摩半島

The Satsuma Peninsula south of Kagoshima city has fine rural scenery, samurai houses, a haunting kamikaze museum and spectacular sand baths. While buses operate to Chiran and trains to Ibusuki, renting a car from Kagoshima will save time and hassles. You'll also find wonderful views along Ibusuki Skyline Rd of Kinkō-wan and the main islands' southernmost mountains. Time permitting, zip all the way to the tip for great glimpses of Kaimon-dake, this area's 'Mt Fuji'.

Chiran 知覧

☑ 0993 / POP 13,250

A river runs through Chiran, 34km south of Kagoshima, parallel to a collection of restored samurai houses, surrounded by placid green tea and sweet potato fields. On the town's edge is a fascinating memorial to WWII's kamikaze pilots.

👁 Sights

★ Chiran Peace Museum   MUSEUM
(知覧特攻平和会館; ☑ 0993-83-2525; www.chiran-tokkou.jp; 17881 Chiran-chō; ¥500; ⊙ 9am-5pm) Around 2km west of town, Chiran's air base was the point of departure for 1036 WWII kamikaze pilots (Tokkō), the largest percentage in the Japanese military. On its former site, the large, thought-provoking Kamikaze Peace Museum presents aircraft, mementoes and photographs of the fresh-faced young men selected for the Special Attack Corps. It's worth renting the English-language tablets (rental ¥200), which harrowingly tells individual pilots' stories.

Samurai Houses   HISTORIC BUILDING
(武家屋敷; 6198 Chiran-chō; combined admission to all houses ¥500; ⊙ 9am-5pm) Seven of the mid-Edo period residences along Chiran's 700m street of samurai houses have gardens open to the public, in which water is usually symbolised by sand, *shirasu* (volcanic ash) or gravel. Allow one to one leisurely hour to view them all.

🍴 Eating & Drinking

Taki-An   NOODLES ¥
(高城庵; ☑ 0993-83-3186; 6329 Chiran-chō; soba ¥650, set meals from ¥2100; ⊙ 10.30am-3pm) Just off the samurai street, Taki-An is a lovely restaurant in another traditional house where you can sit on tatami and admire the garden over a bowl of hot soba (¥650) or Satsuma specialities such as *tonkotsu teishoku* (pork set meal, ¥1620) and Chiran's famous green tea. Picture menu available.

Satsuma Eikoku-kan   TEAHOUSE
(知覧英国館, Tea World; ☑ 0993-83-3963; 13746-4 Chiran-chō; ⊙ 10am-6pm Wed-Mon) Chiran Eikoku-kan is across the main road from the samurai houses and marked by a slightly dented double-decker British-style bus. It offers tea (from ¥540), a cup of which entitles you to take the tour of the tiny one-room collection of newspaper accounts, photos and memorabilia of the **Anglo-Satsuma Museum**.

It commemorates the 1862 war between Britain and Satsuma, which started when British visitors refused to bow to a samurai of the Shimazu clan. Eikoku-kan's Yumefuki loose tea, made with Chiran leaves, has won Britain's Great Taste Award for several years.

ℹ Information

Chiran Samurai Residence & Garden Preservation Association (知覧武家屋敷庭園事務所; ☑ 0993-58-7878; www.chiran-bukeyashiki.jp; 13731-1 Chiran-chō; ⊙ 9am-5pm) This tourist info office details everything you'll need to know about the samurai houses. There's even a helmet you can try on for size.

ℹ Getting There & Away

Kagoshima Kōtsū (鹿児島交通) buses to Chiran (samurai houses/Peace Museum, ¥890/930, 80/85 minutes, hourly) run from the Kagoshima bus stops in Tenmonkan and JR Kagoshima-Chūō Station. From Chiran, buses run five times daily to Ibusuki (¥940, 69 minutes).

Ibusuki 指宿

☑ 0993 / POP 41,850

In southeastern Satsuma Peninsula, around 50km from Kagoshima, the hot-spring resort of Ibusuki is quiet, particularly in the low season, and more especially after dark. Ibusuki Station is located about 1km from the beachfront and most accommodation, but the few eateries are near the station.

👁 Sights & Activities

Ibusuki's biggest attraction is its sand baths, in which onsen steam rises through natural sand, reputedly with blood-cleansing properties. Most visitors spend time at the baths, but there are a few other options and some nice scenic detours if you can get away.

Chiringashima   ISLAND
(知林ヶ島) Lovely Chiringashima is connected to the mainland by a thin land bridge that appears only at low tide, when hikers, beachcombers and tide-pool explorers can walk the coral and shell-strewn connector and visit a small shrine on the island itself. Hours vary with the tides, which you may have to race if you walk too slowly. A taxi from Ibusuki Station takes 10 minutes; the over-sand hike, one-way, takes about half an hour, more if you stop along the way.

Satsuma Denshōkan   MUSEUM
(薩摩伝承館; www.satsuma-denshokan.com; 12131-4 Higashikata; ¥1500; ◉8.30am-7pm) This striking museum offers a history of Satsuma plus displays of Chinese ceramics and gleaming Satsuma-yaki in a temple-style building that seems to float on its own lake. There are English-language audioguides. It's about 3.5km from Ibusuki Station (taxi ¥1220, 10 minutes), at the Hakusuikan onsen hotel.

★Ibusuki Sunamushi
Kaikan Saraku   ONSEN
(いぶすき砂むし会館　砂楽; ☑0993-23-3900; 5-25-18 Yunohama; sand bath & onsen ¥1080, onsen only ¥610; ◉8.30am-9pm, closed noon-1pm Mon-Fri) Pay at the entrance, change into the provided *yukata* and wander down to the beach where, under a canopy of bamboo slat blinds, women with shovels bury you in hot volcanic sand. Reactions range from panic to euphoria. It's said that 10 minutes will get rid of impurities, but many stay longer. When you're through, head back up to soak in the onsen bath.

Yaji-ga-yu   ONSEN
(弥次ヶ湯; 1068 Jūcchō; ¥300; ◉7am-9pm, closed 2nd & 4th Thu of the month;) There's loads of atmosphere in this historic wooden *sentō* (1892) away from the town centre, so old it has no showers; you wash by dipping buckets in the tub. A crib in the ladies' bath makes bathing easier for families with toddlers.

Yoshi-no-yu   ONSEN
(吉乃湯; 4-2-41 Yunohama; ¥300; ◉2-9.30pm Fri-Wed) Up-to-date *sentō* with a pretty *rotemburo* in a garden.

🛏 Sleeping & Eating

Ibusuki offers a variety of sleeping options, most of them with onsen baths. Rather than staying near the station, you may prefer locations closer to the water and the sand baths.

Eating options are limited and your tastiest options may be the meals at your hotel.

Minshuku Takayoshi   MINSHUKU ¥
(民宿たかよし; ☑0993-22-5982; 5-1-1 Yunohama; r with/without 2 meals ¥6630/3880; ▣❄☎) No frills, clean *minshuku* just seven minutes' walk from the sand baths. Home-grown produce is used in the meals.

Tsukimi-sō   RYOKAN ¥¥
(月見荘; ☑0993-22-4221; www.tsukimi.jp; 5-24-8 Yunohama; r per person incl 2 meals from ¥13,110; ▣❄☎) Rooms at this spotless seven-room ryokan across from the sand baths have private facilities, in addition to pretty indoor and outdoor baths and meals featuring *Satsuma-ryōri* such as *tonkotsu* and sashimi. There's not much English spoken, but amenable staff make it work. Wi-fi is in the lobby only (along with a giant Totoro doll and other curios).

Ryokan Ginshō   RYOKAN ¥¥¥
(旅館吟松; ☑0993-22-3231; www.ginsyou.co.jp; 5-26-27 Yunohama; r per person incl 2 meals from ¥16,200; ▣◐❄☎) The exquisite 2nd- and 9th-floor *rotemburo* of this upmarket beachfront ryokan have broad views and a lovely relaxation garden. Ocean-facing rooms start from ¥17,280 and rooms with baths on the balcony are available. There's an onsen vent right in your dinner table, as genteel servers cook *Satsuma-age* before your eyes. Day use of the bath (¥1000) is from 6pm to 9pm.

Hakusuikan   HOTEL ¥¥¥
(白水館; ☑0993-22-3131; www.hakusuikan.co.jp; 12126-12 Higashi-kata; r per person incl 2 meals from ¥18,510; ▣◐❄@☎⛲) Visiting dignitaries might stay in one of the stratospheric-priced rooms in the sumptuous, 40-room Rikyū wing, but those of more modest means can splurge on the less expensive of its 164 rooms. The opulent onsen/*rotemburo*/sand baths are worth the stay by themselves. The Fenice restaurant in the Denshōkan building is as tasty as it is attractive.

Aoba   IZAKAYA ¥
(青葉; ☑0993-22-3356; 1-2-11 Minato; dishes from ¥480; ◉11am-3pm & 5.30-10pm Thu-Tue;) Behind the yellow or green *noren* (door curtain) a minute's walk left of the station, this cheery shop serves satisfying *kurobuta rōsukatsu* (black pork cutlet) *teishoku* (¥1420) or, if you dare, *Kurosatsuma dori*

sashimi (raw sliced chicken, ¥850). Picture menu available.

ⓘ Information

Ibusuki City Tourist Information Centre (指宿市観光協会; ☏ 0993-22-3252; 2-5-33 Minato; ◷ 9am-5pm; 🛜) A 15-minute walk from the station, this large centre has a variety of brochures, maps and information. Staff are helpful and friendly, though English may be hit or miss.

Station Information Desk (指宿駅総合観光案内所; ☏ 0993-22-4114; ◷ 9am-6pm; 🛜) Has wi-fi and basic maps, and can assist with directions and accommodation.

ⓘ Getting There & Around

Ibusuki Station is about 1½ hours from Kagoshima by bus (¥950) or 51 minutes by train from Kagoshima-chūō (*tokkyū* ¥2130). Train geeks and sightseers will love the special wood-panelled Ibutama *tokkyū* with specially angled seats for breathtaking bay views.

The Mawari bus MyPlan pass (¥1100 per day) offers unlimited hop-on/hop-off service around the city. Rent bikes (¥500 for two hours) from the station. Car rental offices are steps away.

Ibusuki to Makurazaki

Ikeda-kō is a volcanic caldera lake west of Ibusuki, inhabited by giant eels kept in tanks by the parking lot. South of the lake is **Cape Nagasaki-bana**, from where you can see offshore islands on a clear day.

The beautifully symmetrical 924m cone of **Kaimon-dake**, nicknamed 'Satsuma Fuji', dominates the southern skyline and can be climbed in two hours. An early start may reward you with views of Sakurajima, the Sata Peninsula, and Yakushima and Tanegashima islands.

In a gorge near Ikeda-kō, **Tōsenkyō Sōmen Nagashi** (唐船峡そうめん流し; ☏ 0993-32-2143; 5967 Jūchō; sōmen ¥570; ◷ 10am-8pm Aug, to 7pm Jul & Sep, to 5pm Mar-Jun & Oct, to 3pm Nov-Feb) is a pilgrimage site for many Japanese (an estimated 200,000 annual visitors!) as the 1967 birthplace of *nagashi-sōmen* (flowing noodles). *Sōmen* (thin wheat-flour noodles) spin around tyre-shaped table-top tanks of swiftly flowing 13°C water; catch the noodles with your chopsticks and dip in sauce to eat. Lots of fun and ultra-refreshing on hot days.

Midway between Ibusuki and Makurazki is **Seahorse House** (タツノオトシゴハウス; ☏ 0993-38-1883; www.seahorseways.com; 5202-2 Beppu, Ei-chō; ◷ 10am-4.30pm Wed-Mon) FREE,

offering close-up looks at thousands of hatchling seahorses, plus information, videos, souvenirs and a small cafe. There are also great walking trails, some tide pools, beaches perfect for shell collecting, and stunning views of Kaimon-dake on a clear day.

At the southwestern end of the peninsula, about one hour from Ibusuki, is **Makurazaki**, a port famous for *katsuo* (bonito). Fish fans should head to humble **Daitoku** (だいとく; ☏ 0993-72-0357; 17 Origuchi-chō; donburi ¥880; ◷ 11am-3.30pm & 5.30-8.30pm, closed irregularly) on Makurazaki's main drag for award-winning *katsuo funado meshi*, a *donburi* (dish served over rice) with fresh bonito, bonito flakes, green onion, *nori* strips and rice crisps in *katsuo* broth. At the **Makurazaki O-Sakana Centre** (枕崎お魚センター; ☏ 0993-73-2311; www.makurazaki-osakana.com; 33-1 Matsunō-chō; ◷ 9am-5pm), about 20 vendors sell fish and related products in a market-like setting. There are lots of free samples and interesting demos, such as *katsuo-bushi* (bonito flakes) being made.

Kirishima-yaku National Park 霧島屋久国立公園

This mountainous park straddling northern Kagoshima and western Miyazaki Prefectures has excellent hikes of many lengths, although ash eruptions, toxic gases and other volcanic activity sometimes changes accessibility. The area is known for its wild azaleas, hot springs and the 75m waterfall, **Senriga-taki**. It is also famous in Japanese mythology as being the place where the gods first descended to earth and began the imperial dynasty, unbroken to this day.

Hikers should monitor the weather closely before setting out. Thunderstorms and fog are common during the rainy season (mid-May to June) and winters can be bitter; otherwise, the vistas are superb.

◎ Sights

Kirishima-jingū　　　　SHINTO SHRINE
(霧島神宮; 2608-5 Kirishima-Taguchi; ◷ 24hr) FREE Picturesque, tangerine Kirishima-jingū has a good vantage point. Though the original dates from the 6th century, the present shrine was built in 1715. It is dedicated to Ninigi-no-mikoto, who, according to *Kojiki* (a book compiled in 712), led the gods from the heavens to the Takachiho-no-mine summit. The shrine is accessible by bus

ARCHAEOLOGICAL FINDS IN SOUTHERN KYŪSHŪ

Uenohara Jōmon-no-Mori

Archaeology enthusiasts will want to detour to this **museum** (上野原縄文の森; ☑0995-48-5701; 1-1 Uenohara Jōmon-no-mori, Kokubu; ¥310; ⏱9am-5pm Tue-Sun), on the site where the oldest authenticated Jōmon-era pottery shards were discovered during excavations for nearby office parks. Based on these findings, anthropologists began to conclude that the first humans may have come to Japan from the south rather than the north, via canoes or rafts along the Ryūkyū island chain. Look also for a re-created village of Jōmon-era dwellings, demonstrations, tools and artefacts. The museum can be reached by train from Kagoshima to Kokubu, from where it's about 8km (20 minutes) by taxi or private car.

Saitobaru

North of Miyazaki, the **Saitobaru Burial Mounds Park** looks like a golf course at first glance, but the hillocks dotting the several square kilometres of fields and forests are actually more than 300 *kofun* (tumuli, or burial mounds). These mostly keyhole-shaped mounds, dating from AD 300 to 600, served much the same function as Egyptian pyramids for early Japanese nobility. Bike rental is free.

The **Saitobaru Archaeological Museum** (西都原考古博物館; ☑0983-41-0041; ⏱10am-6pm Tue-Sun) **FREE** displays excavated items such as Jōmon pottery, ancient swords and *haniwa* (earthenware figures found in Kōfun-period tombs). Rent the English audioguide (¥400); signage is in Japanese. A hall nearby is built around an excavation site.

Buses run twice a day to Saitobaru from Miyakō City bus terminal (¥1140, 70 minutes) in Miyazaki, but you'll need your own transport if you want to explore the tomb-strewn countryside. Saitobaru is not on the Visit Miyazaki Bus Card.

(¥240, 15 minutes) from JR Kirishima-jingū Station.

There's a small village with inns and restaurants at the foot of the shrine.

🏃 Activities

Onsen

This area has numerous onsen, both 'wild' ones (just hot spots in rivers!) to expansive onsen hotels. You'll see steam rising up from numerous places as you travel around. All of the hotels in this area have baths, and a number of them offer them to day-only visitors. Some include mixed-gender bathing pools as well as segregated male and female baths.

Hiking

The **Ebino-kōgen circuit** is a relaxed 4km stroll around a series of volcanic lakes – **Rokkannon Mi-ike** is a stunning, intensely cyan lake. Across the road from the lake, **Fudō-ike**, at the base of Karakuni-dake, is a steaming *jigoku*. The stiffer climb to the 1700m summit of **Karakuni-dake** skirts the edge of the volcano's deep crater before arriving at the high point on the eastern side. The panoramic view southwards is outstanding, taking in the perfectly circular caldera lake of Ōnami-ike,

Shinmoe-dake (the volcano that erupted in January 2011; parts remain inaccessible) and the perfect cone of **Takachiho-no-mine**. On a clear day, you can see Kagoshima and the smoking molar of Sakurajima. Friendly wild deer roam freely through the town of **Ebino-kōgen** and are happy to be photographed. Several of the rivers here have pools hot enough for bathing, and you'll find the routes leading up here thick with *higaeri* (day-use) onsen lodges.

🛏 Sleeping & Eating

Lodgings are clustered near Kirishima-jingū or in Ebino-kōgen village.

Eating options are limited; most visitors opt for meals provided by their hotels. Most village shops close by 5pm.

Minshuku Kirishima-ji　MINSHUKU ¥
(民宿きりしま路; ☑0995-57-0272; 2459 Kirishima-Taguchi; r per person with/without 2 meals ¥7080/4500; ℗) This spartan but friendly six-room inn, just across the gorge from the shrine, has forest views and shared onsen baths. Day visitors can stop here for a lunch of house-made soba dishes (¥480 to ¥880) including a house-special *champon*. Day use of the bath is possible for ¥300.

ℹ️ SHINMOE-DAKE ERUPTION

On 26 January 2011, the massive eruption of Shinmoe-dake, in the centre of the mountainous Kirishima-yaku National Park, shut down roads and air travel and blanketed much of the region in a thick layer of ash. It also left impassable a popular 15km hiking route along the summit of the park's other volcanic peaks: Karakuni-dake (1700m) via Shishiko-dake, Naka-dake and Takachiho-gawara to the summit of Takachiho-no-mine (1574m). Check with local authorities in case of a change in conditions. Daily updates are available at the visitors centres.

Kirishima Jingū-mae Youth Hostel HOSTEL¥ (霧島神宮前ユースホステル; ☑ 0995-57-1188; 2459-83 Kirishima-Taguchi; dm HI member/non-member ¥3390/3990, minshuku per person incl 2 meals ¥7710; P@🛜) A few minutes from Kirishima-jingū, this neat, comfy youth hostel has Japanese rooms and mountain views from its onsen baths. Breakfast/dinner costs ¥540/1080. It operates as a more expensive *minshuku*, with better meals and amenities.

Ebino-Kōgen

Campground & Lodge CAMPGROUND¥ (えびの高原キャンプ村; ☑ 0984-33-0800; 1470 Ōaza Suenaga; campsites/tent rental/lodge cabins per person from ¥830/1440/1640; P) A pretty stream runs through the middle of this delightful campground with onsen baths (open 5pm to 8pm), 500m from the Eco Museum Centre. Rates rise in July and August, and midwinter closing dates vary.

⭐ **Ebino-Kōgen Sō** HOTEL¥¥¥ (えびの高原荘; ☑ 0984-33-0161; www.ebino kogenso.com; 1489 Ōaza Suenaga; r per person incl 2 meals with/without bathroom from ¥10,500/9500; P😊❄️🛜) This friendly onsen hotel boasts some excellent facilities including mountain-view rooms and coin laundry. The lovely *rotemburo* (¥520) is open to the public from 11.30am to 8pm, and there's a family-style bath deep in the forest (¥1030 per hour). The location, near Ebino-Kōgen village, is superb and the restaurant makes tasty meals. Rates may be lower depending on the meal calibre; ask when you reserve.

There's a shuttle bus to JR Kirishima-Jingū and JR Kobayashi Stations; ring ahead to get one.

ℹ️ Information

Nature centres at each end of the volcano walk have bilingual maps and hiking information, and exhibits on local wildlife.

Ebino-kōgen Eco Museum Centre (えびのエコミュージアムセンター; ☑ 0984-33-3002; ⊙ 9am-5pm) This lodge-like tourist centre has information, maps, some dioramas of the area's wildlife and nature, and helpful staff. There's also info about daily volcanic eruptions for hikers.

Kirishima City Tourist Information (霧島市観光案内所; ☑ 0995-57-1588; 2459-6 Taguchi; ⊙ 9am-6pm Apr-Sep, to 5pm Oct-Mar) Right near the giant *torii* gate at the entrance to Kirishima-jingū. There's a foot onsen steps from the entrance. Rental bikes are available, but not cheap (¥1000 per two hours).

Takachiho-gawara Visitors Centre (高千穂河原ビジターセンター; ☑ 0995-57-2505; ⊙ 9am-5pm) A small centre at the base of Takachiho with hiking info, maps and safety suggestions.

ℹ️ Getting There & Around

The main train junctions are JR Kobayashi Station, northeast of Ebino Plateau, and Kirishima-jingū Station to the south.

Two buses per day connect the Kirishima-jingū area with Ebino-kōgen (¥990), but this area is vastly more accessible by car.

Miyazaki 宮崎

☑ 0985 / POP 401,000

The prefectural capital of Miyazaki makes a convenient base for forays around the region, with a friendly, low-key vibe and fun, unique restaurants and night spots in the Nishitachi nightlife district, about 700m from the station.

⊙ Sights

Heiwadai-kōen PARK (平和台公園, Peace Park; ☑ 098-535-3181; www. heiwadai-bunkakoen.info; ⊙ 24hr) The park's centrepiece is the 37m-high **Peace Tower** monument constructed in 1940, a time when peace in Japan was about to disappear. Its timeless design may remind you of ancient Inca or Khmer monuments, and it's made of stones from all over the world. The **Haniwa Garden** is dotted with reproductions of clay *haniwa* (earthenware figures found in Kōfun-period tombs) excavated from the Saitobaru burial mounds (p761), set among mossy hillocks.

Heiwadai-kōen is about 1km north of Miyazaki-jingū. Buses from Miyazaki Station stop along Tachibana-dōri (¥290, 20 minutes, at least two per hour).

Miyazaki

Miyazaki

◎ Sights
1 Miyazaki Science Centre D2

🛏 Sleeping
2 Hotel Route Inn B1
3 Miyazaki Kankō Hotel........................ B4
4 Youth Hostel Sunflower
    Miyazaki B3

✖ Eating
5 Bon Belta Department Store B1
6 Kitchen Hiro Nee.................................. B1
7 Maruman Honten.................................. A2

8 Miyachiku B4
9 Ogura Honten B1
10 Ogura Segashira................................. C4
11 Okashi no Hidaka................................ A2
12 Togakushi.. A2
13 Yamakataya Department Store B1

🍷 Drinking & Nightlife
14 Igokochiya Anbai................................. A2
15 The Bar B2

🛍 Shopping
16 Miyazaki Products Shop Konne B3

Miyazaki Science Centre MUSEUM
(宮崎科学技術館; Map p763; ☎0985-23-2700;
1-2-2 Miyazaki-eki Higashi; with/without sky show
¥750/540; ⊙9am-4.30pm Tue-Sun) Steps away
from Miyazaki Station, this family-friendly
interactive science museum boasts one of the
world's largest planetariums; some exhibits
include English translations. Look for the
life-size rocket replica outside the entrance.
Inside, see robots and a spaceship lander.

Miyazaki-jingū SHINTO SHRINE
(宮崎神宮; 2-4-1 Jingū) This shrine honours
the Emperor Jimmu, the semi-mythical first

KYŪSHŪ MIYAZAKI

emperor of Japan and founder of the Yamato court. Spectacular centuries-old wisteria vines cover the thickly forested grounds and bloom in April. It's a 500m walk from Miyazaki-jingū Station, one stop (¥160, three minutes) north of Miyazaki Station.

**Miyazaki Prefectural
Museum of Nature & History** MUSEUM
(宮崎県総合博物館; ☑ 098-524-2071; 2-4-4 Jingū; ☺ 9am-5pm Wed-Mon) FREE Just north of Miyazaki-jingū, this museum exhibits items on local history, archaeology, festival artefacts and folk crafts. Behind it, **Minka-en** (民家園) FREE features four traditional-style Miyazaki farmhouses and other outbuildings.

✸ Festivals & Events

Miyazaki-jingū Grand Festival CULTURAL
(☺ late Oct) This festival rings in autumn with horses and *mikoshi* (portable shrines) being carried through the streets.

Fireworks FIREWORKS
(☺ early Aug) This large fireworks shows lights up the summer sky over the Ōyodo-gawa.

⛵ Sleeping

Youth Hostel Sunflower Miyazaki HOSTEL ¥
(ユースホステルサンフラワー宮崎; Map p763; ☑ 0985-24-5785; 1-3-10 Asahi; dm HI member/nonmember ¥3240/3888; P ☺ ☎) Near the prefectural office, this institutional-style, 20-bed hostel has Japanese and Western-style rooms and doubles as a community centre during the day. There's a giant kitchen, loaner bikes (free for guests), a coin laundry, a restaurant and a nominal 10pm curfew.

Hotel Route Inn BUSINESS HOTEL ¥¥
(ホテルルートイン宮崎; Map p763; ☑ 0985-61-1488; www.route-inn.co.jp; 4-1-27 Tachibana-dōri-nishi; s/d/tw incl breakfast ¥6550/11,800/12,300; P ☺ ✳ @ ☎) Across from the Nishitachi district, this hotel is excellent value, with a great breakfast buffet, spacious, decently appointed rooms, free coffee in the lobby and common baths (in addition to private bathrooms).

Miyazaki Kankō Hotel HOTEL ¥¥¥
(宮崎観光ホテル; Map p763; ☑ 0985-27-1212; www.miyakan-h.com; 1-1-1 Matsuyama; s/tw from ¥9870/19,740; P ☺ ✳ @ ☎) This towering hotel has two buildings: the west wing, and the recently remodelled east wing (with room prices around ¥3000 more per person). All rooms are relatively spacious. There's an on-site onsen with *rotemburo* (day use ¥1150). The hotel is next to the river, which means some nice strolls in the evening, but it's quite far from the station and nightlife district.

🍴 Eating

The Nishitachi neighbourhood is great for restaurant browsing, although don't expect many English menus. For takeaway food, try the basement marketplaces at **Bon Belta** (ボンベルタ橘; Map p763; ☑ 098-578-2983; 3-10-32 Tachibana-dōri-nishi; ☺ 10am-10pm) and **Yamakataya** (山形屋; Map p763; 3-4-12 Tachibana-dōri-higashi; ☺ 10am-8pm or later) department stores, or pick up a *shiitake ekiben* (mushroom boxed lunch) at Miyazaki Station.

★ **Okashi no Hidaka** SWEETS ¥
(お菓子の日高; Map p763; ☑ 0985-25-5300; 2-7-25 Tachibana-dōri-nishi; sweets from ¥120; ☺ 9.30am-9pm) This is a 67-year-old family-run legend. Take a look at the refrigerator case of luscious-looking Japanese and Western pastries, but order the giant *nanjakō-daifuku* (dumpling of sweet bean paste, strawberry, chestnut and cream cheese in a wrapper of airy *mochi*; ¥360). Cheese *manju* (dumplings; ¥168) are another signature taste of Miyazaki. If time permits staff will serve your sweet with tea right there in the store.

★ **Togakushi** NOODLES ¥
(戸隠; Map p763; ☑ 0985-24-6864; www.miyazaki-togakushi.com; 7-10 Chūō-dōri; noodles ¥650-950; ☺ 7pm-2am) Workmanlike Togakushi has no English menu, but come for the delicate, thin *kama-age udon* for dipping in tangy sauce of *negi* (green onion), *tempura-ko* (tempura crispies) and refreshing *yuzu* (Japanese citron); pour the water from the noodles into the sauce to make soup. This is what locals crave after a bender. Look for the giant red lantern.

Kitchen Hiro Nee JAPANESE ¥
(Map p763; ☑ 098-527-1233; 3-4-25 Tachibana-dōri Higashi; lunch/dinner ¥700/1000; ☺ 11.30am-3pm & 6-9pm) This cosy one-man, one-waitress cafe serves the chef's selections of typical Japanese mains: ginger pork, rice omelettes, braised chicken and veggies. College kids come for home-cooked meals and the friendly conversation. Only Japanese is spoken, though some of the students may speak English.

Maruman Honten YAKITORI ¥¥
(丸万本店; Map p763; ☑ 0985-22-6068; 3-6-7 Tachibana-dōri-nishi; grilled chicken ¥1100; ☺ 5-11pm)

Mon-Sat) This homely shop serves *jidori* (local chicken), full of flavour but tougher and cooked rarer than you may be used to. The standard is *momoyaki* (grilled chicken leg), but *tataki* (seared; ¥600) and *sashimi* (what you think it is; ¥650) are also popular, and meals come with a light and delicious chicken broth. For more thorough cooking, say '*yoku yaite kudasai*'. Basic English spoken. Look for the red marble facade.

Ogura Honten　　　　　　　　JAPANESE ¥¥
(おぐら本店; Map p763; ☑0985-22-2296; 3-4-24 Tachibana-higashi; chikin nanban ¥1010; ☺11am-3pm & 5-8.30pm Wed-Mon) *Chikin nanban* was invented here over half a century ago, and crowds still flock to Ogura's red-and-white awning in the narrow alley just behind Yamakataya department store. For shorter queues, try the larger, kitsch-filled cross-town **Ogura Segashira** (おぐら瀬頭店; Map p763; ☑0985-23-5301; 2-2-23 Segashira; chikin nanban ¥1010; ☺11am-10pm; ☻).

★ Miyachiku　　　　　　　　STEAK ¥¥¥
(みやちく; Map p763; ☑0985-62-1129; 2nd fl, Miyazaki Kankō Hotel, 1-1-1 Matsuyama; set menu lunch/dinner from ¥2500/5750; ☺11am-3pm & 5-10pm) If you're going to splurge on *Miyazaki-gyū*, do it at this gracious *yakiniku* (Korean-style barbecue) and steak house with river views. Lunch set menus are a nice deal with appetiser, salad, beef, vegetables, dessert and coffee.

🍷 **Drinking & Nightlife**

Miyazaki plays to the wee hours, especially in summer, with hundreds of tiny bars. Most of the action is in Nishitachi. Be advised that many of the bars here will add a 'service' charge of ¥300 to ¥500 to any tab.

Igokochiya Anbai　　　　　　　　BAR
(いごこち屋　あんばい; Map p763; 1st fl, 7-30 Chūō-dōri; ☺6pm-1am Mon-Sat) Tucked away on Chūō-dōri, Anbai is a sophisticated *izakaya* with more than 350 varieties of *shōchū*, well-chosen local dishes and cool background music. It's across the street from the Onishi Clinic. The '*mama-san*' (hostess) is extremely kind, and if you order alcohol staff will bring the bottle so you can study the label as you sip.

The Bar　　　　　　　　BAR
(ザ・バー; Map p763; www.thebarmiyazaki.com; 3rd fl, Paul Smith Bldg, 3-7-15 Tachibana-dōri-higashi; ☺8pm-3am; ☻) This hub of the expat community and its local friends draws a cheery mixed crowd who are proud of the city and keen to welcome visitors over a few cold beers. There's

---

MIYAZAKI CUISINE

Miyazaki is famous for *chikin nanban* (sweet fried chicken with tartar sauce), *hiya-jiru* (cold summer soup made from baked tofu, fish, miso paste and cucumbers, served over rice), *jidori* (local chicken) and *kama-age udon* (wheat noodles boiled in a cauldron). *Miyazaki gyū* (beef) has won national competitions. Snack foods include *nikumaki onigiri* (rice balls wrapped in marinated pork) and *chiizu manjū* (cream-cheese-filled dumplings). Local produce includes mango and *yuzu* (citron), sometimes mixed with pepper for spicy *yuzu-kōshō* paste.

even a well-used, full-sized billiard table. Astonishingly, it's nonsmoking, a rarity in Japan.

🛍 **Shopping**

Miyazaki Products Shop Konne　　ARTS & CRAFTS
(みやざき物産館; Map p763; ☑098-522-7389; 1-6 Miyata-chō; ☺9am-7pm Mon-Fri, 9.30am-6.30pm Sat & Sun) This place sells local wood crafts, clay *haniwa* (earthenware figures), lots of snacks and a wall of *shōchū* liquors.

ℹ **Information**

Miyazaki Prefectural International Plaza
(宮崎県国際交流協会; Map p763; ☑0985-32-8457; 9th fl, Carino Bldg; ☺10am-7pm Tue-Sat) Information good for longer-term visitors who need to make connections, find services or job hunt; walk to the back of the building to find this office on the 9th floor.

Tourist Information Centre (宮崎市観光案内所; Map p763; ☑0985-22-6469; ☺9am-6pm) Helpful centre inside JR Miyazaki Station; has maps of the city and its surroundings.

ℹ **Getting There & Away**

AIR

Miyazaki is served by a variety of airlines that fly to Tokyo, Osaka, Nagoya, Fukuoka, Okinawa, Seoul, Taipei and Hong Kong. **Miyazaki Airport** (www.miyazaki-airport.co.jp) is connected to the city centre by bus (¥440, 26 minutes) or train (¥350, 10 minutes) from JR Miyazaki Station.

BOAT

Miyazaki Car Ferry (宮崎カーフェリー; ☑0985-29-5566; www.miyazakicarferry.com; 2nd-class from ¥9050) Links to Kōbe (12 hours).

ℹ️ VISIT MIYAZAKI BUS CARD

For budget travellers not in a hurry, this bus pass (¥1000 per day) is a fabulous deal, covering *most* Miyazaki buses including to Aoshima and Nichinan Coast; however, it does not include buses that go to Takachiho or Nobeoka. Buy the pass at tourist counters and some hotels. There's also a 'One Coin' ¥500 pass on weekends.

BUS

Routes include Kagoshima (¥2780, three hours), Kumamoto (¥4630, 3½ hours), Nagasaki (¥6690, 5½ hours) and Fukuoka (¥4630, 4½ hours). Phone the **Miyazaki Eki Bus Centre** (宮崎駅バスセンター一; Map p763; ☑ 0985-23-0106) for more info.

TRAIN

The JR Nippō line runs down to Kagoshima (*tokkyū* ¥4020, two hours) and up to Beppu (*tokkyū* ¥5790, 3¼ hours).

ℹ️ Getting Around

Most city bus services use the Miyazaki Eki Bus Centre diagonally opposite the station.

Car rental (12 hours from about ¥5500) is the most convenient way to explore the coastal region outside the city. There are many agencies outside the station's west exit.

Aoshima 青島

☑ 0985 / POP 3810

Aoshima is a tiny palm-covered island (1.5km in circumference), and also the name of the adjacent mainland town, one of Japan's more relaxed, alternative communities. Surfers and sunbathers come for its lovely beaches, which are strewn with sand-dollars after rough storms. A quiet alternative to Miyazaki.

◉ Sights

Aoshima Island   ISLAND

The first thing you'll notice as you cross the water to the island of Aoshima is the unique geological feature surrounding it. Called the **devil's washboard** (*oni no sentaku-ita;* 鬼の洗濯板), it looks just like a washboard of centuries ago. On the island, the photogenic Shintō shrine **Aoshima-jinja** (青島神社) is reputedly good for matchmaking, and the **Legend of Hyūga Hall** (日向神話館; ☑ 098-565-1262; ¥600; ⊙8am-6pm Jul & Aug, to 5pm Sep-Jun) tells the story of Amaterasu, Emperor Jimmu

and the founding of Japan in wax-museum-style dioramas with English explanations.

An estimated 200 species of plants and animals can be found within the island's small circumference.

On the second Monday in January, loincloth-clad locals dive ceremoniously into the ocean at Aoshima-jinja. At the end of July there's more splashing as *mikoshi* are carried through the shallows to the shrine.

Kaeda Gorge   GORGE

(加江田渓谷) West of town, an 8km-long, well-maintained hiking path winds through Kaeda Gorge (加江田渓谷) following the Kaeda-gawa, a refreshingly clear stream filled with boulders and excellent swimming holes. Lush foliage includes banana palms and mountain cedars.

Your own transport is helpful to get here; turn off Rte 220 onto prefectural road 339.

🛌 Sleeping & Eating

The famous dish here in Aoshima is *ise-ebi* (spiny lobster).

★ **Minshuku Misakisō**   MINSHUKU ¥¥
(民宿みさき荘; ☑ 0985-65-0038; www.misakisou.com; 1 chōme 5-4; s/d with shared bath ¥5000/8000; 🅿 ✳ 🛜) Gracious and friendly, the Misakisō is a one-stop-shop: it's a place to stay, a bar (guests only), a cafe and a surf-rental outlet (boards from ¥2500; cafe and rental closed Wednesday). Rooms are mainly Japanese-style, but there's one Western option, and all are clean and very convenient for anyone planning to surf or sunbathe: just cross the street and you're at the beach.

No English is spoken, but foreigners are welcomed just the same.

★ **ANA Holiday Inn Resort Miyazaki**   HOTEL ¥¥
(ANAホリデイインリゾート宮崎; ☑ 0985-65-1555; www.anahirmiyazaki.com; 1-16-1 Aoshima; s/tw from ¥8200/12,200; 🅿 ➡ ✳ @ 🛜 🐾) This shiny white, semi-cylindrical, beachfront tower with glass elevators has ocean-view rooms and onsen baths (day use ¥1050). In the low season, rooms are surprisingly reasonable given the quality of the stay; however, in high season rates can rise by ¥5000 or more. There's a large fountain and pool (mid-July to August), some kiddie attractions and the beach couldn't be closer.

Nearly all of the 200-plus rooms have ocean views, but a few don't. Those may be cheaper, so ask if you're trying to stretch the yen.

Minato Aoshima
SEAFOOD ¥¥

(港あおしま; ☑ 0985-65-1044; 3-5-1 Aoshima; set menus ¥1100-1700; ⊙ 11am-2.30pm Tue-Sun) Overlooking the port, owned and run by the local fisherman's collective, this take-your-shoes-off spot offers some of the finest and freshest seafood that Aoshima has to offer. Most meals are sets, including several side dishes and miso soup.

ⓘ Getting There & Away

Aoshima is on the JR Nichinan line from Miyazaki (¥360, 30 minutes). Buses from Miyazaki Station stop at Aoshima (¥720, 48 minutes, hourly) en route to Udo-jingū (¥1480). It's about 800m to the island from the station.

Nichinan-kaigan & Cape Toi 日南海岸・都井岬

The palm-lined stretch of coastal road from Aoshima to Toi-misaki (Cape Toi) via the town of Nichinan is a rewarding drive, with seaside cliffs and views of the islands reminiscent of gumdrops and camels. On a sunny day the light pierces the water and turns it an electric blue colour, making for lovely photos at nearly every turn. Cape Toi and Kō-jima are popular destinations. En route is **Koigaura-hama** (Koigaura Beach) where the *surf-zoku* (surf tribe) hang out.

If you turn inland please drive slowly: several bands of wild monkeys inhabit the mountains and it's often possible to see them. Earthworms the size of garter snakes are another curious denizen.

⊙ Sights

Udo-jingū
SHINTO SHRINE

(鵜戸神宮; ☑ 0987-29-1001; 3232 Ōaza Miyaura) Reached via a coastal path, this brightly painted Shintō shrine occupies an open cavern overlooking unusual rock formations in the cove below. It's protocol to buy five *undama* (luck stones; ¥100), make a wish, and try to hit the shallow depression on top of the turtle-shaped rock.

Men use their left hand, women their right when making the throw. Wishes are usually related to marriage, childbirth and lactation, because the boulders in front of the cavern are said to represent Emperor Jimmu's grandmother's breasts (no, really!).

Hourly buses from Aoshima (¥1010, 36 minutes) and Miyazaki (¥1480, 1½ hours) stop on the highway. From the bus stop, it's about a 700m walk to the shrine past rock formations and picturesque fishing boats.

Kō-jima
ISLAND

(幸島; ☑ 098-772-0479; ⊙ varies due to tide & weather) Just off the coast from Ishinami-kaigan, the tiny island of Kō-jima is home to a group of monkeys that apparently rinse their food in the ocean before eating, but they're a fickle bunch, and hard to spot. Boats can be hired at the beach near the bus stop (¥1000 per person or ¥3000 per boat). Ask a fisherman if you don't see any near the seawall.

ⓘ Getting There & Around

Far and away the best transport option for this area is a rental car, as you'll want to stop at nearly every corner to take photographs. You can be dropped off by bus at Cape Toi, but the park is vast and driving is perhaps the best – or only – realistic way to get around.

Obi 飫肥
☑ 0987

In the quaint town of Obi, nicknamed 'Little Kyoto', the wealthy Ito clan ruled from Obi castle for 14 generations from 1587, somehow surviving the 'one kingdom, one castle' ruling in 1615. The castle ruins are now the main tourist attraction.

The rest of the town has photogenic streetscapes, shrines and a historic shopping street; your admission ticket has a simple map.

Only the walls of the original **Obi-jō** (飫肥城; ☑ 0987-25-4411; ¥610; ⊙ 9am-4.30pm) are intact, but the grounds have six important buildings, including the impressive, painstakingly reconstructed **Ōte-mon gate**, and **Matsuo-no-maru**, the lord's private residence. The museum has a collection relating to the Itō clan's long rule over Obi. **Yōshōkan**, formerly the residence of the clan's chief retainer, stands just outside the castle entrance and has a large garden with Atago-san (Mt Atago) as 'borrowed scenery'.

By Obi-jō, **Obiten** (おび天; ☑ 0987-25-5717; 9-1-8 Obi; mains ¥850-1150; ⊙ 9am-5pm) serves a local version of *Satsuma-age* (fried cakes of fish paste and vegetables, here called *tempura*). The signature Obiten with udon is ¥850.

The JR Nichinan line connects Obi with Miyazaki (*kaisoku* ¥940, 65 minutes) via Aoshima. From Obi Station, it's a 10-minute walk to the castle. Buses from Miyazaki (¥2080, 2¼ hours, last return bus 4pm) stop below the castle entrance. Rent bikes (¥500 per day) from the castle parking lot.

Okinawa & the Southwest Islands

Best Places to Eat

➡ Nanraku (p801)

➡ Pōcha Tatsuya (p801)

➡ Yūnangi (p790)

➡ Nuchigafu (p790)

Best Places to Sleep

➡ Sōyōtei (p775)

➡ Sankara Hotel & Spa (p775)

➡ Minshuku Sango Beach (p779)

➡ Minshuku Gettō (p789)

➡ Soraniwa (p802)

Why Go?

The Southwest Islands (南西諸島; Nansei-shotō) reveal a Japan you may not know exists: a chain of semitropical, coral-fringed islands evocative of Hawaii or Southeast Asia.

They're a nature-lover's paradise: in the northern Kagoshima Prefecture, lush primeval forests hide among the craggy peaks of Yakushima, and the starfish-shaped Amami-Ōshima has fine beaches on its convoluted coastline. Heading south, Okinawa-hontō is the bustling main island of Okinawa Prefecture and jumping-off point for the nearby Keramas, tiny gems with white-sand beaches and crystal-clear waters. Miyako-jima boasts killer beaches and laid-back, retro appeal. And furthest south, the Yaeyama Islands boast Japan's best coral reefs, subtropical jungles and mangrove swamps.

But spectacular nature is only part of it – the Southwest Islands exude a peculiarly 'un-Japanese' culture. Indeed, they made up a separate country for most of their history, and the Ryūkyū cultural heart still beats strongly here.

When to Go
Naha

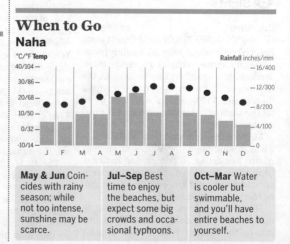

May & Jun Coincides with rainy season; while not too intense, sunshine may be scarce.

Jul–Sep Best time to enjoy the beaches, but expect some big crowds and occasional typhoons.

Oct–Mar Water is cooler but swimmable, and you'll have entire beaches to yourself.

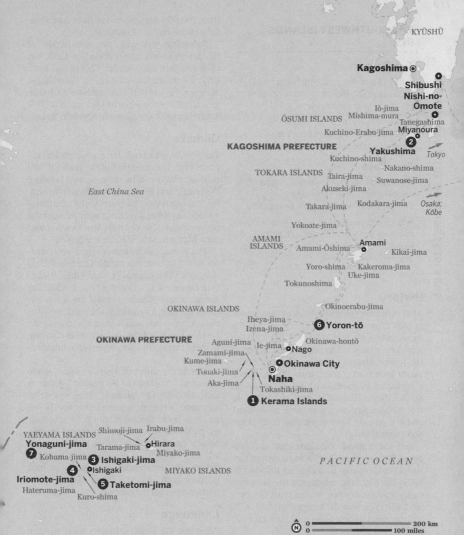

KYŪSHŪ

Kagoshima ◉

Shibushi
Nishi-no-
Omote

Iō-jima
Mishima-mura
ŌSUMI ISLANDS   Tanegashima
Kuchino-Erabu-jima   Miyanoura

KAGOSHIMA PREFECTURE   Yakushima
Kuchino-shima   *Tokyo*
                                    Nakano-shima
TOKARA ISLANDS   Taira-jima
                  Akuseki-jima   Suwanose-jima

Takara-jima   Kodakara-jima   *Osaka;
                                Kōbe*

Yokoate-jima

East China Sea

AMAMI
ISLANDS   Amami-Ōshima   Amami
                                      Kikai-jima
Yoro-shima   Kakeroma-jima
                  Uke-jima
Tokunoshima

OKINAWA ISLANDS   Okinoerabu-jima

Iheya-jima   ❻ Yoron-tō
Izena-jima

OKINAWA PREFECTURE   Aguni-jima Ie-jima   Okinawa-hontō
                  Zamami-jima,   ⦿Nago
                  Kume-jima   Okinawa City
                  Tonaki-jima   ⦿
                  Aka-jima   Naha
                        Tokashiki-jima
                  ❶ Kerama Islands

                                    PACIFIC OCEAN
YAEYAMA ISLANDS Shimoji-jima Irabu-jima
Yonaguni-jima   *Hirara
❼ Kohama-jima ❸ Ishigaki-jima   Miyako-jima
❹ *Ishigaki
Iriomote-jima   ❺ Taketomi-jima   MIYAKO ISLANDS
Hateruma-jima
        Kuro-shima

Ⓝ 0 |————————————| 200 km
    0 |————————————| 100 miles

Okinawa & the Southwest Islands Highlights

❶ **Kerama Islands** (p794)
Soaking up the sun on one
of the islands' white-sand
beaches.

❷ **Yakushima** (p771) Hiking
into the mountainous heart
to commune with ancient
yakusugi trees.

❸ **Ishigaki-jima** (p802)
Diving with playful manta rays.

❹ **Iriomote-jima** (p808)
Exploring the mangrove
swamps, jungles and coral
reefs of Japan's last frontier.

❺ **Taketomi-jima** (p811)
Taking a ferry to a simpler time
on this 'living museum' island.

❻ **Yoron-tō** (p784) Chilling
out in peace, against a blissful

scenic backdrop of beaches
and sugar cane.

❼ **Yonaguni-jima** (p813)
Searching the horizon
for Taiwan from Japan's
westernmost island, and diving
its mysterious underwater
rock formations.

THE SOUTHWEST ISLANDS IN...

Two Days

➡ Spend one day exploring Naha and the next beach-lounging and snorkelling on Aka-jima or Zamami-jima.

➡ Alternatively, fly directly to Miyako-jima and rent a car to explore the beaches of these bridge-linked islands.

Four Days

➡ Enjoy epic hikes and seaside onsen on Yakushima, then ferry over to Tanegashima for surfing and beach time.

➡ Bookend two days of hiking and kayaking on Iriomote-jima with a day exploring Ishigaki-jima and a day cycling around Taketomi-jima.

History

After centuries ruled by *aji* (local chieftains), in 1429 Okinawa and the Southwest Islands were united by Sho Hashi of the Chūzan kingdom, which led to the establishment of the Ryūkyū dynasty. During this period Sho Hashi increased contact with China, which contributed to the flourishing of Okinawan music, dance, literature and ceramics. In this 'Golden Era' weapons were prohibited, and the islands were rewarded with peace and tranquillity.

But the Ryūkyū kingdom was not prepared for war when the Shimazu clan of Satsuma (modern-day Kagoshima) invaded in 1609. The Shimazu conquered the kingdom easily and established severe controls over its trade. The islands were controlled with an iron fist, and taxed and exploited greedily for the next 250 years.

With the restoration of the Meiji emperor, the Ryūkyūs were annexed to Japan as Okinawa Prefecture in 1879. However, life hardly changed for the islanders as they were treated as foreign subjects by the Japanese government. Furthermore, the Meiji government stamped out local culture by outlawing the teaching of Ryūkyū history in schools, and establishing Japanese as the official language.

In the closing days of WWII, the Japanese military made a decision to use the islands of Okinawa as a shield against Allied forces. Sacrificing it cost the islanders dearly: more than 100,000 Okinawan civilians lost their lives in the Battle of Okinawa.

Following the war, the occupation of the Japanese mainland ended in 1952, but Okinawa remained under US control until 1972. Its return was contingent upon Japan agreeing to allow the Americans to maintain bases on the islands; and some 30,000 American military personnel remain today.

Climate

The Southwest Islands have a subtropical climate. With the exception of the peaks of Yakushima, which can be snow-capped between December and February, there's no real winter. You can comfortably travel the Southwest Islands any time of year, but swimming might be uncomfortable between late October and early May, unless you're the hardy sort.

The average daily temperature on Okinawa-hontō in December is 20°C, while in July it is 30°C. The islands of Kagoshima Prefecture average a few degrees cooler, while the Yaeyama and Miyako Islands are a few degrees warmer. The islands are most crowded during June, July and August and during the Golden Week holiday in early May. Outside of these times, the islands are often blissfully quiet.

The main thing to keep in mind when planning a trip to the Southwest Islands is the possibility of typhoons, which can strike any time between June and October. If you go then, build flexibility into your schedule, as typhoons often cause transport delays. Ideally purchase tickets that allow changes without incurring a fee. The website of the Japan Meteorological Agency (www.jma. go.jp/en/typh) has the latest details on typhoons approaching Japan.

Language

Although the Ryūkyū islands used to have their own distinctive language and dialects, by and large these have disappeared. Standard Japanese is spoken by almost every resident of the islands. That said, travellers who speak some standard Japanese might find the local dialects and accent a little hard to catch.

ℹ Getting There & Away

AIR

There are flights between major cities in mainland Japan and Amami-Ōshima, Okinawa-hontō (Naha), Miyako-jima and Ishigaki-jima. Kagoshima has flights to/from all these islands and many of the smaller islands as well. Other islands such as Yonaguni-jima and Kume-jima can be reached from Naha or Ishigaki.

Peach Airlines (www.flypeach.com) is a new low-cost carrier that offers cheap deals to Naha and Ishigaki from major cities in mainland Japan.

BOAT

Ferries run between Osaka/Kōbe and Kagoshima to the Amami Islands and Okinawa-hontō, and are plentiful between Kagoshima and Yakushima and Tanegashima. Once you arrive in a port such as Naze on Amami-Ōshima or Naha on Okinawa-hontō, there are local ferry services to nearby islands. However, you cannot reach the Miyako Islands or Yaeyama Islands by ferry from mainland Japan or Okinawa-hontō; it's necessary to fly to these destinations.

ⓘ Getting Around

Aside from the regular ferry services and hydrofoils between island groups, there are also excellent air networks throughout the islands. While most islands have public bus systems, there are usually not more than a few buses per day on each route. We recommend bringing an International Driving Permit and renting a car or scooter, particularly on Yakushima, Ishigaki, Iriomote and Okinawa-hontō.

ŌSUMI ISLANDS 大隈諸島

The Ōsumi Islands comprise the two main islands of Yakushima and Tanegashima and the seldom-visited triumvirate of islands known as Mishima-mura. The all-star attraction in the group is Yakushima, a virtual paradise for nature lovers that attracts large numbers of both domestic and international Tanegashima, famous as the hom space program, sees few foreig though it is a popular surfing Japanese. Finally, the most con ed island in the Mishima-mura group is Iō-jima, a gem of a volcanic island with excellent onsen (hot springs).

Yakushima 屋久島

☑ 0997 / POP 12,915

Designated a Unesco World Heritage Site in 1993, Yakushima is one of the most rewarding islands in the Southwest Islands. The craggy mountain peaks of the island's interior are home to the world-famous *yakusugi* (屋久杉; *Cryptomeria japonica*), ancient cedar trees that are said to have been the inspiration for some of the scenes in Miyazaki Hayao's animation classic *Princess Mononoke*.

Keep in mind that Yakushima is a place of extremes: the mountains wring every last drop of moisture from the passing clouds and the interior of the island is one of the wettest places in Japan. In the winter the peaks may be covered in snow, while the coast is still relatively balmy. Whatever you do, come prepared and don't set off on a hike without a good map and the proper gear.

◎ Sights

Hiking among the high peaks and mossy forests is the main activity on Yakushima, but the island is also home to some excellent coastal onsen and a few sandy beaches.

YAKUSHIMA: KNOW BEFORE YOU GO

Read Up

The yakumonkey.com website is a super-handy planning resource for visitors to Yakushima. If you're going to do some serious hiking on the island, it's worth purchasing the excellent Yakumonkey guide to Yakushima before you arrive, as it's near impossible to find on the ground. Full of useful information on Yakushima, it includes detailed descriptions of hikes and trails. It's available in both print and e-book formats.

Another valuable resource for hikers is the Japanese-language trail map, *Yama to Kougen-no-Chizu-Yakushima* (山と高原の地図屋久島; ¥1080), available at major bookshops in Japan.

Stay Dry

With Yakushima being one of the wettest places on Earth, it rains *a lot* in the island's interior. Be sure to prepare adequately for hiking rainforests in which you may find yourself slogging through torrential rain for a whole day. **Nakagawa Sports** (ナカガワスポーツ; ☑ 0997-42-0341; http://yakushima-sp.com; 421-6 Miyanoura; rainwear rentals ¥1200-2400; ⓣ 9am-7pm, closed every other Wed) in Miyanoura rents out everything from rainwear and waterproof hiking boots (also in large sizes) to tents and baby carriers.

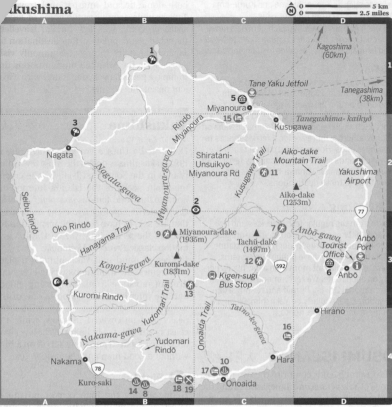

Yakushima

Yakushima's main port is **Miyanoura** (宮之浦), on the island's northeast coast. This is the most convenient place to be based, as most buses originate from here. From Miyanoura, a road runs around the perimeter of the island, passing through the secondary port of **Anbō** (安房), on the east coast, and then through the hot-springs town of **Onoaida** (尾之間) in the south. Heading north from Miyanoura, the road takes you to the town of **Nagata** (永田), which has a brilliant stretch of white-sand beach.

Jōmon-sugi
LANDMARK

(縄文杉; Map p772) **FREE** This enormous *yakusugi* tree is estimated to be between 3000 and 7000 years old, and though no longer living, it remains a majestic sight. Most hikers reach the tree via the 19.5km, eight-to-10-hour round trip from the **Arakawa-tozanguchi** (Arakawa trailhead; 荒川登山口; Map p772).

Yakusugi Museum
MUSEUM

(屋久杉自然館; Map p772; ☑ 0997-46-3113; 273 9343 Anbō; ☺ 9am-5pm, closed 1st Tue of the month) In a forested spot with sea views, the Yakusugi Museum has informative, beautifully designed exhibits about *yakusugi* and the history of the islanders' relationship to these magnificent trees. The museum offers an excellent audio guide in English. It's conveniently located on the road leading up to Yakusugi Land (p774). Two daily buses run to and from Miyanoura (¥960, 80 minutes, March to November).

Ōko-no-taki
WATERFALL

(大川の滝; Map p772) On the west coast is Yakushima's highest waterfall, at 88m. It's a five-minute walk from Ōko-no-taki bus stop, which is the last stop for some of the buses running south and west from Miyanoura and Anbō (note that only two buses a day run all the way out here).

Umigame-kan
MUSEUM

(うみがめ館; Map p772; ☑ 0997-49-6550; 489-8 Nagata; ¥300; ☺ 9am-5pm Wed-Mon) This non-profit organisation has displays and information about turtles, mostly in Japanese. During nesting (June and July) and hatching (August) seasons, they arrange night tours on the beach. In order to protect the nesting turtles, eggs and hatchlings, it is imperative that visitors go with a sanctioned tour.

Yakushima Environmental & Cultural Village Center
MUSEUM

(屋久島環境文化村センター; Map p772; ☑ 0997-42-2900; admission & film ¥520; ☺ 9am-5pm, closed 3rd Tue of the month) In Miyanoura at the corner of the ferry-terminal road, it has exhibits about the island's natural environment and history, with limited English signs. It screens a large-format 25-minute film (sparsely subtitled in English) at 20 minutes past the hour.

Issō-kaisuiyokujō
BEACH

(一湊海水浴場; Map p772) This small, coarse-sand beach is located on the north coast of the island, about midway between Miyanoura and Nagata. It's a short walk from the Ya-hazu bus stop (served by any Nagata-bound bus from Miyanoura).

Nagata Inaka-hama
BEACH

(永田いなか浜; Map p772) On the island's northwest coast, Nagata Inaka-hama is a beautiful beach for sunsets, and it's where sea turtles lay their eggs from May to July. It's beside the Inaka-hama bus stop, served by Nagata-bound buses from Miyanoura.

🏃 Activities

Hiking

Hiking is the best way to experience Yakushima's beauty. The most popular hike is the long, one-day trip up to Jōmon-sugi and back, but there are other attractive alternatives. Yakusugi Land is designed for casual hikers.

Even though trails can be very crowded during holidays, be sure to alert someone at your accommodation of your intended route and fill in a *tōzan todokede* (route plan) at the trailhead.

★ Shiratani-unsuikyō-tozanguchi
HIKING

(白谷雲水峡登山口; Map p772; ¥300) Although the long day trek to Jōmon-sugi is the most famous in Yakushima, the shorter Shiratani-unsuikyō hike is arguably more beautiful, passing waterfalls, moss-lined rocks and towering *yakusugi* to the overlook at **Taiko-iwa**. The trailhead (622m) is served by up to 10 daily buses to and from Miyanoura (¥550, 40 minutes, March to November). Allow three or four hours for this hike.

Miyanoura-dake
HIKING

(Map p772) The granddaddy of hikes here is the day-long outing to the 1935m summit of Miyanoura-dake, the highest point in southern Japan. Fit climbers should allow about seven hours return from **Yodogawa-tozanguchi** (Yodogawa trailhead; 淀川登山口; Map p772).

It's also possible to traverse Miyanoura-dake with a stop at Jōmon-sugi en route. Do not attempt this in a day; you'll have to spend the night in one of the *yama-goya* (mountain huts) above Jōmon-sugi. Typical routes are between Yodogawa and Arakawa or Yodogawa and Shiratani-unsuikyō.

The Yodogawa trailhead is about 1.5km (about 30 minutes) beyond the **Kigen-sugi bus stop** (Map p772), served by two buses a day to/from Anbō (¥940, one hour). The

YAKUSHIMA'S SEA TURTLES

Loggerhead sea turtles and green sea turtles come ashore on the beaches of Yakushima to lay their eggs. Unfortunately, human activity can significantly interfere with the egg-laying process. Thus we recommend that you keep the following rules in mind when visiting the beaches of Yakushima (particularly those on the northwest coast):

➡ Never approach a sea turtle that has come ashore.

➡ Don't start fires on the beach; the light will confuse the hatchlings (who use moonlight to orient themselves). Likewise, don't shine torches (flashlights) or car headlights at or near the beach.

➡ Do not walk on the beach at night.

➡ Be extremely careful when you walk on the beach, as you might inadvertently step on a newly hatched turtle.

➡ If you want to observe the turtles, enquire at **Umigame-kan** (p773).

buses do not give you sufficient time to complete the round trip in a day – an early-morning taxi from Miyanoura (around ¥11,000) gives you time to make the second bus back to Anbō. Of course, renting a car gives you maximum flexibility on timing your hike.

Yakusugi Land
HIKING

(ヤクスギランド; Map p772; ☎0997-42-3508; http://y-rekumori.com; ¥300; ◷9am-5pm) A great way to see some *yakusugi* without a long trek into the forest, Yakusugi Land offers shorter hiking courses over wooden boardwalks, and longer hikes deep into the ancient cedar forest. There are four buses a day to and from Anbō (¥740, 40 minutes).

Onsen

Yakushima has several onsen, from beautifully desolate seaside pools to upmarket hotel facilities. Seaside onsen here are typically *konyoku* onsen (mixed sex baths) where swimsuits are not allowed; women traditionally wrap themselves in a thin towel for modesty.

Hirauchi Kaichū Onsen
ONSEN

(平内海中温泉; Map p772; ¥100; ◷24hr) Onsen lovers will be in heaven here. The outdoor baths are in the rocks by the sea

and can only be entered at or close to low tide. You can walk to the baths from the Kaichū Onsen bus stop, but the next stop, Nishikaikon, is actually closer. From Nishikaikon, walk downhill towards the sea for about 200m and take a right at the bottom of the hill.

Yudomari Onsen
ONSEN

(湯泊温泉; Map p772; ¥100; ◷24hr) This blissfully serene onsen can be entered at any tide. Get off at the Yudomari bus stop and take the road opposite the post office in the direction of the sea. Once you enter the village, the way is marked. It's a 300m walk and you pass a great banyan tree en route.

Onoaida Onsen
ONSEN

(尾之間温泉; Map p772; ☎0997-47-2872; 136-2 Onoaida; ¥200; ◷7am-9.30pm May-Oct, to 9pm Nov-Apr, from noon Mon) In the village of Onoaida, about 350m uphill from the Onoaida Onsen bus stop, rub shoulders with the village elders at this rustic indoor bathhouse. BYO everything and ease slowly into the divine, naturally hot water.

🛏 Sleeping

The most convenient place to be based is Miyanoura. You'll also find lodgings in larger villages and several bare-bones *yama-goya* (mountain huts) in the mountains. In July and August and the spring Golden Week holiday, it's best to try to reserve ahead since places fill up early.

★ Yakushima South Village
HOSTEL ¥

(屋久島サウスビレッジ; Map p772; ☎0997-47-3751; www.yakushima-yh.net; 258-24 Hirauchi; dm/s/d ¥3500/4500/6500; P✻@🖲) This well-run youth hostel is about 3km west of Onoaida, nestled into the forest. Accommodation is in either Japanese- or Western-style dorms, and the shared kitchen and bathroom facilities are spotless. Get off any southbound buses from Miyanoura at the Hirauchi-iriguchi bus stop and take the road towards the sea for about 200m.

Yakushima Youth Hostel
HOSTEL ¥

(屋久島ユースホステル; ☎0997-49-1316; www.yakushima-yh.net; 278-2 Miyanoura; dm/d ¥3800/4400; P✻@🖲) This simple and clean hostel doesn't offer meals, but there are several good restaurants close by. It's a 10-minute walk from Miyanoura port – turn left off the main port road and veer left after passing the portside park; it's about 100m further.

Minshuku Kaisei 1 MINSHUKU ¥¥
(民宿海星; ☎0997-42-2145; 378-3 Miyanoura; per person with breakfast from ¥5000; P❀⊛) Homey and comfortable, this family-run *minshuku* (Japanese guesthouse) is conveniently situated on Miyanoura's main drag. Breakfasts are served in a cosy dining room, and though not much English is spoken here, the Yakushima hospitality shines through. Coming from the port, look for the star on the signage and cars parked out the front; the entrance is on the side not facing the street.

Lodge Yaedake-sansō LODGE ¥¥
(ロッジ八重岳山荘; Map p772; ☎0997 42 1551; http://yaedake.jp; Miyanoura; r per person with meals ¥8100; P♲❀⊛) This secluded accommodation features Japanese- and Western-style rooms in rustic riverside cabins connected by wooden walkways. Soak up the beauty of your surroundings in the communal baths; children will enjoy splashing in the river. Meals served in the tatami dining room are balanced and exquisite. The lodge is located inland on the Miyanoura-gawa; staff can pick you up in Miyanoura.

The lodge also runs the **Minshuku Yaedake Honkan** (民宿八重岳本館; ☎0997-42-2552; 208 Miyanoura; r per person incl meals ¥6800; P❀) in town.

★**Sankara Hotel & Spa** HOTEL ¥¥¥
(Map p772; ☎0997-47-3488, toll-free 0800-800-6007; www.sankarahotel-spa.com; 553 Haginoue, Mugio; r per person incl breakfast from ¥36,000; P❀@⊛≋) 🍃 Overlooking Yakushima's southeast coast, this stunning collection of luxury villas blends ocean views with Balinese design elements. Sustainable practices at Sankara include all water used on the property being sourced from mountain run-off, and the restaurant utilising as much local and organic produce as possible, much of which is grown expressly for the hotel. Guests 15 years and older only.

The main restaurant's French fusion cuisine is created by Chef Takei Chiharu, who trained at several three-Michelin-star establishments in France. Staff can pick you up, but if you have transport, look for the green signs in English along the road between Hirano and Hara.

★**Sōyōtei** RYOKAN ¥¥
(送陽邸; Map p772; ☎0997-45-2819; per person incl meals ¥13,650; P❀) On the northwest coast near Nagata Inaka-hama, this gorgeous, family-run guesthouse has a collection of semidetached units that boast private verandas and ocean views. The traditional structures feature rooftops unique to Yakushima, with stones anchoring the roof tiles – you'll recognise the place immediately. There are several baths for private use, including an outdoor bath overlooking the crashing waves.

Lovely seafood-focused meals are served in a communal, open-air dining room that looks out over Inaka-hama and the sea.

Yakushima Iwasaki Hotel HOTEL ¥¥¥
(屋久島いわさきホテル; Map p772; ☎0997-47-3888; http://yakushima.iwasakihotels.com; 1306 Onoaida; d from ¥26,140; P❀@⊛≋) Though a bit dated, the higher-end Iwasaki commands impressive views from its hilltop location above Onoaida, and encloses a huge tree within the lobby. Spacious Western- and Japanese-style rooms have either ocean or mountain views. The hotel has its own onsen and meals are available in two restaurants. Southbound buses from Miyanoura stop right out the front.

🍴 Eating

There are a few restaurants in each of the island's villages, with the best selection in Miyanoura. If you're staying anywhere but Miyanoura, ask for the set two-meal plan at your lodgings. If you're going hiking, you can ask your lodging to prepare a *bentō* (boxed meal) the night before you set out.

Naa Yuu Cafe CAFE ¥
(なーゆーカフェ; Map p772; ☎0997-49-3195; http://charu.air-nifty.com/naayuu/naa-yuu-cafe. html; 349-109 Hirauchi; lunch sets ¥850-1250; ☺11.30am-7pm Wed-Sun; 🚭) Down a dirt road and facing a field of wild reeds, this cute cafe feels vaguely Hawaiian. The menu, however, leans more toward Thailand. Lunch sets range from red curry to Kagoshima black pork–sausage pizza, and the fresh, homemade breads are dreamy. Look for a green sign in English, about 3km west of Onoaida.

Restaurant Yakushima JAPANESE ¥
(レストラン屋久島; ☎0997-42-0091; 2nd fl, Yakushima Kankō Centre; meals ¥1000; ☺9am-4pm; P⊛🚭) This simple restaurant serves a ¥520 breakfast set with eggs, toast and coffee and a tasty *tobi uo sashimi teishoku* (flying fish sashimi set meal; ¥980) for lunch. Look for the green, two-storey building on the main road, near the road to the pier.

Yakuden SUPERMARKET ¥
(ヤクデン; ◉9am-10pm) Stock up on provisions for camping or hiking, on the main street in Miyanoura, just north of the entrance to the pier area.

Shiosai SEAFOOD ¥¥
(潮騒; ◐0997-42-2721; 305-3 Miyanoura; dishes ¥1200; ◉11.30am-2pm & 5.30-9.30pm Fri-Wed) Find a full range of Japanese standards such as *sashimi teishoku* (sashimi set; ¥1700) or *ebi-furai teishoku* (fried shrimp set; ¥1400). Look for the blue and whitish building with automatic glass doors along the main road through Miyanoura.

❶ Information

Miyanoura's helpful **tourist information centre** (◐0997-42-1019; 823-1 Miyanoura; ◉8.30am-5pm) is on the road leading away from the port; you can't miss its dramatic architecture. Staff here can help you find lodgings and answer all questions about the island.

In Anbō there's a smaller **tourist office** (Map p772; ◐0997-46-2333; ◉9am-5.30pm) in the first alley off the main road just north of the river.

The best place to get money on Yakushima is at one of the island's post offices, the most convenient of which is in Miyanoura.

❶ Getting There & Away

AIR

Japan Air Commuter (JAC) flies to Yakushima from Osaka, Fukuoka and Kagoshima, offering several flights a day to and from Kagoshima.

Yakushima's **airport** (屋久島空港; Map p772; ◐0997-42-1200) is on the northeastern coast between Miyanoura and Anbō. Hourly buses stop at the airport, though you may be able to arrange pickup in advance from your accommodation.

> ## ❶ INTER-ISLAND FLIGHT PASS
>
> If you are arriving in Japan by air, it's worth noting that Japan Transocean Air (JTA) offers the Okinawa Island Pass for up to five inter-island flights (between Okinawa-hontō, Miyako-jima, Ishigaki-jima and Kume-jima only). The pass must be purchased outside of Japan and with proof of onward travel – sorry, expats. The pass represents substantial savings from standard domestic airfares bought within the country.

BOAT

Hydrofoil services operate between Kagoshima and Yakushima, some of which stop at Tanegashima en route. **Tane Yaku Jetfoil** (Map p772; ◗ in Kagoshima 099-226-0128, in Miyanoura 0997-42-2003; ◉8.30am-5.30pm Mon-Fri, to 7pm Sat & Sun) runs six Toppy and Rocket hydrofoils per day between Kagoshima (leaving from the high-speed ferry terminal just to the south of Minamifutō pier) and Miyanoura (¥8300, one hour 50 minutes for direct sailings, two hours 40 minutes with a stop in Tanegashima). There are also two hydrofoils per day between Kagoshima and Anbō Port (2½ hours) on Yakushima. Booking ahead is wise.

The normal ferry *Yakushima 2* sails from Kagoshima's Minamifutō pier for Yakushima's Miyanoura port (one way/return ¥4900/8900). It leaves at 8.30am and takes four hours.

The **Hibiscus** (フェリーはいびすかす; ◗099-261-7000) also sails between Kagoshima and Yakushima, leaving at 6pm, stopping overnight in Tanegashima, and arriving at Miyanoura at 7am the following day (one way/return ¥3600/7200). Reservations aren't usually necessary for this ferry; it normally leaves from Kagoshima's Taniyama pier.

❶ Getting Around

Local buses travel the coastal road part way around Yakushima roughly every hour or two, though only a few head up into the interior. You'll save a lot of money by purchasing a Yakushima Kotsu Free Pass, which is good for unlimited travel on Yakushima Kotsu buses. One-/two-day passes cost ¥2000/3000 and are available at the airport, the **Anbō port** (Map p772) and the tourist information centre in Miyanoura.

Hikers should note that from March through November, in order to limit traffic congestion and environmental impact, all hikers must transfer to an **Arakawa Mountain Bus** (round trip ¥1740) from the Yakusugi Museum parking lot to get to the Arakawa-tozanguchi. You must buy a ticket at least a day in advance; also note that this fare is not covered by the one- or two-day bus passes.

Hitching is also possible, but an International Driving Permit will vastly increase your enjoyment here, as buses are few and far between. **Toyota Rent-a-Car** (◗0997-42-2000; https://rent.toyota.co.jp; up to 12hr from ¥5250; ◉8am-8pm) is north of the port in Miyanoura.

Tanegashima 種子島

◗0997 / POP 29,839

A long, narrow island about 20km northeast of Yakushima, Tanegashima is a laid-back destination popular with Japanese surfers and beach lovers. Home to Japan's Space Centre, Tanegashima was where firearms were first introduced to Japan by shipwrecked Portuguese in 1543. Good ferry connections make this island easy to pair with a trip to Yakushima.

The island's main port of **Nishi-no-Omote** (西之表) is on the northwest coast of the island, while the airport is about halfway down the island near the west coast. The best beaches and most of the surfing breaks are on the east coast of the island, which is also home to an onsen.

◉ Sights

Space Science & Technology Museum   MUSEUM

(宇宙科学技術館; ☎0997-26-9244; Kukinaga, Minamitane-chō; ◷9.30am-5.30pm Tue-Sun, closed on launch days) FREE Tanegashima's Space Centre, on the island's spectacular southeastern coast, is a large parklike complex with rocket-launch facilities. Its Space Science & Technology Museum details the history of Japan's space program, with models of Japan's rockets and some of the satellites it has launched (with some English interpretive signage).

Buses running from Nishi-no-Omote all the way to Tanegashima Space Centre take two hours.

Takezaki-kaigan   BEACH

(竹崎海岸) Nearby to the Space Centre, this coastline is home to a beautiful stretch of white sand popular with surfers. The best spot to enjoy it is the beach in front of the Iwasaki Hotel (closest bus stop: Iwasaki Hotel), which has some impressive rock formations.

Nagahama-kaigan   BEACH

(長浜海岸) The west coast of Tanegashima is also home to a 12km stretch of beach that is equally popular with surfers and egg-laying sea turtles.

Tanegashima Development Centre – Gun Museum   MUSEUM

(種子島開発総合センター・鉄砲館; ☎0997-23-3215; 7585 Nishi-no-Omote; admission ¥420, combo ticket ¥550; ◷8.30am-5pm, closed 25th of the month) Though one focus is on the history of guns in Tanegashima, with an excellent collection of antique firearms, this is actually a cultural and natural-history museum. The combined ticket includes admission to the interesting Gessōtei samurai house about 50m away. Make as straight a beeline as possible uphill from the port;

IŌ-JIMA & TOKARA-RETTŌ

Depending on when you go, the more remote Southwest Islands can be havens of tranquillity with few other travellers. But if you really want to escape, it's just a question of hopping on the right ferry. In Kagoshima Prefecture, **Iō-jima** (硫黄島) is a tiny bamboo-covered island with a smouldering volcano and two brilliant seaside onsen. **Ferry Mishima** (フェリーみしま; ☎099-222-3141) sails there from Kagoshima. The city is also home to **Ferry Toshima** (フェリーとしま; ☎099-222-2101), which plies the **Tokara-rettō** (トカラ列島), a chain of seven inhabited and five uninhabited islands between Yakushima and Amami-Ōshima, which offer plenty of hiking, fishing and onsen. Even for the Japanese, they seem like the end of the world.

the building resembles the stern of an old galleon.

Gessōtei   HISTORIC BUILDING

(月窓亭; ☎0997-22-2101; http://gessoutei.blogspot.com; 7528 Nishi-no-Omote; ¥200; ◷9am-5pm, closed 25th of the month) At the southern border of the Akaogi Castle ruins, this preserved samurai house and garden contains a few cultural artefacts. A short informational video is available in English, narrated by local students, and accompanied by tea and a small snack.

🏃 Activities

Akaogi-no-Yu   ONSEN

(赤尾木の湯; ☎0997-22-1555; http://araki-hotel.co.jp; 78 Nishimachi, Nishi-no-Omote; single entry/all-day access ¥800/1000; ◷6am-11pm) Just a five-minute walk from the Nishi-no-Omote port, this sparkling new onsen offers a soothing end to a day of surfing or sunning – BYO towel. Or simply soak your feet in the free footbath before or after a ferry ride.

Nakatane-chō Onsen Center   ONSEN

(中種子町温泉保養センター; ☎0997-27-9211; 5542 Sakai, Nakatane; ¥300; ◷11am-8pm Fri-Wed) Bring your own bathing supplies to this ocean-view hot spring at Kumano-kaigan. Floor-to-ceiling one-way glass allows you to soak while enjoying the views of rock formations offshore. The closest bus stop is Kumano-kaisuiyokujō; if driving, follow the signs to Kumano Onsen.

Sleeping & Eating

Most travellers base themselves in the port town of Nishi-no-Omote. Unless you're staying in Nishi-no-Omote, it's a good idea to book meals with your accommodation.

Nagareboshi MINSHUKU ¥
(流れ星; ☎0997-23-0034; www.t-shootingstar. com; 7603-10 Nishi-no-Omote; r with shared bathroom & breakfast from ¥3500; P ✳ @ ☎) Run by a friendly, English-speaking woman, charming Nagareboshi has spotless, spacious rooms and a very laid-back vibe. From the pier road in Nishi-no-Omote, walk to the traffic light and jog around the right side of the post office, then walk uphill, bearing right at the top of the steps. Look for the sign, and veer right towards the temple.

Miharu-sō RYOKAN ¥¥
(美春荘; ☎0997-22-1393; 7486-6 Nishi-no-Omote; r per person incl breakfast ¥5500; P ⊜ ✳ ☎) Tidy Japanese-style rooms in this family-run ryokan in Nishi-no-Omote are homey and full of natural light. If you speak Japanese, you can hit up the owner for local info on surf spots. If not, he's likely to point you in the right direction anyway.

East Coast BUNGALOW ¥¥
(イーストコースト; ☎0997-25-0763; www.east coast.jp; 140-2 Anjo; s/d/tr from ¥2700/5400/8100, large cabin ¥13,000; P) With two homey, fully equipped bungalows near the local break, this place is (as you might guess) on the east coast of Tanegashima. Reservations are essential. The owner is an English-speaking Japanese surfer who also runs a great onsite cafe serving simple favourites like curry and fried shrimp with rice (open from 11am to 6pm, Thursday to Tuesday).

Koryōri Shirō IZAKAYA ¥¥
(小料理しろう; ☎0997-23-2117; 24-6 Higashi-chō; dishes from ¥500; ⊙5-11pm; ✳) Head to this friendly little *izakaya* (Japanese pub-eatery) in Nishi-no-Omote to sample tasty dishes such as the *sashimi teishoku* (sashimi set; ¥1200). There are plants out the front and blue-and-white *noren* (doorway curtains). It's along the main road east of the post office.

ⓘ Information

There is a helpful **information office** (種子島観光案内所; ☎0997-23-0111; ⊙9am-5pm) at the pier in Nishi-no-Omote, inside the ferry office/waiting room.

The road from the Nishi-no-Omote pier dead-ends at a post office with an international ATM.

ⓘ Getting There & Away

Tanegashima has six flights to and from Kagoshima (about 30 minutes) on Japan Air Commuter (JAC).

Depending on the season, **Tane Yaku Jetfoil** (p776) runs at least five daily high-speed ferries (¥7100, 1½ hours) between Kagoshima and Tanegashima. The **Ferry Hibiscus** (p776) travels each evening between Kagoshima and Tanegashima (¥3500, three hours and 40 minutes).

ⓘ Getting Around

Unfortunately, the relative lack of buses makes it difficult to enjoy this island without a rental car or scooter, or, at least, a good touring bicycle.

There's a rental-car counter in the arrivals hall of the airport, and a couple of rental agencies outside Nishi-no-Omote port.

AMAMI ISLANDS 奄美諸島

The islands of the Amami group are the southernmost in Kagoshima Prefecture. Amami-Ōshima, the largest and most popular island, lies at the northern end of the group. It serves as the main transport hub and boasts excellent beaches, as well as dense jungle. The other islands in the chain are dominated by sugar cane cultivation but have their low-key charms aside from pretty, quiet beaches and uncrowded dive spots. Tokunoshima is famous for its *tōgyū* (bovine sumo), while Okinoerabu-jima has intriguing caves and giant banyans, and tiny Yoron-tō holds fast to its unique culture and dialect.

Amami-Ōshima 奄美大島

☎0997 / POP 61,291

Amami-Ōshima (奄美大島) is Japan's third-largest offshore island after Okinawa-hontō and Sado-ga-shima. With a mild subtropical climate year-round, the island is home to some unusual flora and fauna, including the endemic Amami black rabbit (奄美野黒兎), tree ferns and mangroves. The coastline of the island is incredibly convoluted – a succession of bays, points and inlets, punctuated by the occasional white-sand beach – all ascending into dense forest, making the island a more complex, interesting alternative to islands further south.

DIVING IN THE SOUTHWEST ISLANDS

Stunning both above and below the water's surface, the Southwest Islands set the scene for some excellent diving with an impressive variety of species such as whale sharks, manta rays, sea snakes, turtles and corals. Keeping it even more interesting are underwater wrecks, cavern systems and even some mysterious ruins (...or very unusual rock formations).

Costs for diving in the Southwest Islands are higher than you might pay in Southeast Asia, but standards of equipment and guiding are fairly high. If you are not in possession of a valid diving certification, many operators offer introductory diving courses for novices. To rent equipment, you should know your weight in kilograms, your height in metres and your shoe size in centimetres.

Here are some English-speaking operators who welcome foreigners:

Penguin Divers (p799), Miyako-jima

Piranha Divers (p793), Okinawa-hontō

Umicoza (p803), Ishigaki-jima

Yonaguni Diving Service (p814), Yonaguni-jima

To keep things confusing, the main city and port on the north coast is called both Amami-shi and Naze (名瀬).

Sights

Amami-Ōshima is great to explore by touring bike or rental car. The coastal route to **Uken** (宇検) on the west coast has some lovely stretches. Another option is Rte 58 south to **Koniya** (古仁屋), from where you can continue southeast to the **Honohoshi-kaigan** (ホノホシ海岸), a rocky beach with incredible coastal formations, or catch a ferry to **Kakeroma-jima** (加計呂麻島), a small island with a few shallow beaches. The best beaches are at the northeast end.

Ōhama-kaihin-kōen BEACH
(大浜海浜公園; Map p780) With forest rolling down to white sand and turquoise water, the gorgeous Ōhama-kaihin-kōen is popular for swimming, snorkelling, sea kayaking and fishing. As it's the closest beach to Naze, it can get crowded during the summer, but it's convenient and spacious. Take an Ōhama-bound bus from Amami and get off at the Ōhama stop (¥400).

Sakibaru-kaigan BEACH
(崎原海岸; Map p780) This stunner of a beach lies about 4.5km down a point of land just north of Kise (about 20km northeast of Naze). Take a Sani-bound bus from Amami and get off at Kiseura (¥950), and then walk. If you're driving, it's marked in English off the main road (be prepared for *narrow* roads).

Tomori-kaigan BEACH
(土盛海岸; Map p780) It's easy to get to this beach, which offers brilliant white sand and some great snorkelling with a channel leading outside the reef. It's about 3km north of the airport. Take a Sani-bound bus from Naze and get off at Tomori (¥1210).

Amami-no-Sato MUSEUM
(奄美の郷; Map p780; ☑0997-55-2333; www.amamipark.com; 1834 Setta, Kasari-chō; ¥620; ☺9am-6pm, to 7pm Jul & Aug, closed 1st & 3rd Wed of the month) Though most displays are in Japanese, there's enough multimedia here to make this cultural and natural-history museum engaging, even if finer details are lost. Short films documenting island traditions, musical exhibits and dioramas bring Amami traditions to life. This cultural centre, plus an art museum showcasing the work of Tanaka Isson, form part of Amami Park, five minutes by bus from the airport.

Sleeping

⭐**Minshuku Sango Beach** MINSHUKU ¥¥
(民宿さんごビーチ; Map p780; ☑0997-57-2580; sangobeach0315@gmail.com; 68 Kuninao; per person incl 2 meals from ¥6800; ▣☀@) Overlooking a lovely sandy beach, this laid-back *minshuku* offers peace in abundance. Guests sleep in six semidetached units and meals are taken overlooking the sea. Call ahead for a pick-up from the ferry port or Naze. From the airport, take a bus to Naze and get off at the West Court–mae stop to await pick-up.

Amami-Ōshima

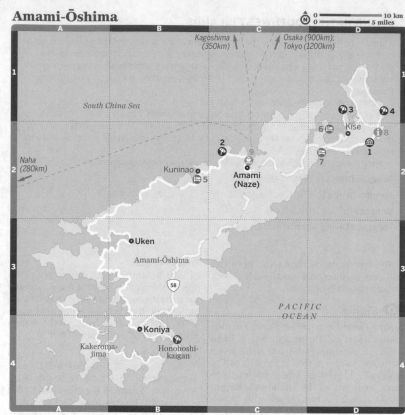

Amami-Ōshima

◎ Sights
1 Amami-no-Sato	D2
2 Ōhama-kaihin-kōen	C2
3 Sakibaru-kaigan	D1
4 Tomori-kaigan	D1

🛏 Sleeping
5 Minshuku Sango Beach	B2
6 Native Sea Amami	D2
7 Pension Green Hill	D2

🍴 Eating
Surf x Cafe Green Hill	(see 7)

ℹ Information
8 Tourist Information Counter	D2

🚌 Transport
9 A Line Ferry	C2
Marix Line	(see 9)
Times Car Rental	(see 8)

Pension Green Hill   GUESTHOUSE ¥¥
(ペンショングリーンヒル; Map p780; ☎ 0997-62-5180; www.greenhill-amami.com; 1728-2 Akaogi, Tatsugō-chō; s/d incl 2 meals ¥9720/17,280; P❄@🛜) A favourite among Japanese surfers, convivial Green Hill has ocean views (including the local surf spot, Tebiro Point), and Japanese- and Western-style rooms, some with lofts. It's about 30 minutes from the airport and a few minutes' walk to the beach. They will pick you up if you've made a request in advance.

Amami Sun Plaza Hotel   BUSINESS HOTEL ¥¥
(奄美サンプラザホテル; ☎ 0997-53-5151; www.amami-sunplaza.co.jp; 2-1 Minato-machi; s/d incl breakfast from ¥6500/9500; P♨❄@🛜) This squeaky-clean, comfortable, accommodating business hotel is the best in its class, right in downtown Naze, with easy access

to local restaurants. It's a 10-minute walk to the port, making it very convenient if you're leaving town on an early ferry.

Native Sea Amami   HOTEL ¥¥¥
(ネイティブシー奄美; Map p780; ☑0997-62-2385; www.native-sea.com; 835 Ashitoku, Tatsugō-chō; per person incl 2 meals from ¥16,200; P✳@�) This dive centre/resort has comfortable wood-floored, Western-style accommodation perched on a promontory over a lovely bay. Guest rooms have gorgeous, sweeping views of the bay and access to a nice, shallow beach below. For a more romantic stay, opt for one of their spacious beachfront rooms at their annex, the Petit Resort (プチリソート) about 100m down the road.

Native Sea is about 28km east of Naze (or 3km from the Akaogi bus stop).

✕ Eating

Your best option is to book meals at your accommodation. Consider also picking up groceries in Naze for lunches and picnics if you haven't rented a car, as shops outside of town are few and far between.

Okonomiyaki Mangetsu   OKONOMIYAKI ¥
(お好み焼き満月; ☑0997-53-2052; 2-2 Irifune-chō; dishes ¥1000; ☺noon-2am; 🅟) Locals pile in for the excellent *okonomiyaki* (batter and cabbage cakes cooked on a griddle) at this excellent Naze eatery. For carnivores, we recommend the *kurobuta* mix (pork-shrimp-squid mix; ¥1260), and for veggies, the *isobecchi* (*mochi* rice and *nori*; ¥750). There's a picture menu.

Surf x Cafe Green Hill   CAFE ¥
(Map p780; ☑0997-62-3131; http://green-hill-amami.com/cafe; 1728-2 Akaogi, Tatsugō-chō; meals ¥900-1200; ☺10am-10pm) Spacious and relaxed, the cafe run by Pension Green Hill has reggae setting the mood (of course) and Japanese-style surf grub like green curry and tom yum ramen. It's pretty much the only dining choice if you're staying in the area sans vehicle, and has a great terrace for beers after a beach day.

Hokorashi-ya   IZAKAYA ¥¥
(誇羅司屋; ☑0997-52-1158; 13-6 Irifune-chō; meals ¥3000; ☺5.30pm-midnight; 🅟) An atmospheric *izakaya* in downtown Naze, Hokorashi-ya dishes up toothsome Amami specialities such as *aosa-no-tempura* (fish-and-shellfish cakes fried in a freshwater seaweed batter; ¥600) and a regional *chāhan* (fried rice flecked with bonito and egg;

¥800), as well as beautifully plated sushi and sashimi specials. There's a picture menu.

ℹ️ Information

There's a basic **tourist information counter** (Map p780; ☑0997-63-2295; ☺8am-5.30pm) in the airport arrivals hall.

ℹ️ Getting There & Away

Amami-Ōshima has flights to/from Tokyo, Osaka, Fukuoka and Kagoshima with Japan Airlines (JAL) or JAC.

Ryukyu Air Commuter (RAC) operates a daily flight between Naha and Amami-Ōshima. There are also flights between Amami-Ōshima and the other islands in the Amami group.

Travelling by sea, Marix and A Line run their own ferries along the same routes for the same rates, but on alternating days. If you find that one does not offer a route on the day you wish to travel, simply book with the other company.

Marix (マリックスライン; Map p780; ☑in Amami 0997-53-3112, in Kagoshima 099-225-1551; www.marix-line.co.jp) and **A Line** (Map p780; ☑in Amami 099-222-2338, in Kagoshima 099-226-4141; www.aline-ferry.com) run four or five ferries a month from Osaka/Kobe (¥15,120, 29 hours), as well as daily ferries to and from Kagoshima (¥9050, 11 hours) and Naha (¥9570, 13 hours).

ℹ️ Getting Around

Amami-Ōshima has a good bus system, but you will definitely appreciate a rental car if you have an International Driving Permit. **Times Car Rental** (タイムズレンタカー; Map p780; ☑0997-63-0240; 467 Kasari-chō; ☺8am-7pm) has subcompacts from ¥5500, with a branch in Amami and another across from the airport.

The island's tiny airport is on the northeast end of the island; 55 minutes from Naze by bus (¥1100, almost hourly) with buses timed to meet flights.

Tokunoshima   徳之島

☑0997 / POP 23,513

Tokunoshima (徳之島), the second-largest island of the Amami Islands, has some interesting coastal rock formations and a few good beaches. The island is famous for **tōgyū** (闘牛, bovine sumo), which has been practised on the island for more than 500 years. Attractions include decent diving and snorkelling, and views that occasionally call to mind parts of Hawaii.

On the island's east coast is the main port of **Kametoku-kō** (亀徳港) and the main town of **Kametsu** (亀津). Tokunoshima's airport is on its west coast, not far from the secondary port of **Hetono** (平土野).

◉ Sights

If the spectacle of bulls locking horns interests you, there are 13 official *tōgyū* venues on the island that stage tournaments. In *tōgyū*, the animals are goaded by human handlers, and the bloodless match ends when one bull retreats; it's more like eight-legged sumo than anything remotely resembling European bullfighting. The three biggest tournaments are held in January, May and October – call the tourist office to confirm details.

Several appealing beaches are dotted around the coast.

Mushiroze   BEACH
(ムシロ瀬) About 9km north of the airport at the northwestern tip of the island, Mushiroze is an interesting collection of wave-smoothed rocks that makes a great picnic spot. On stormy days, tread carefully, as the incoming waves can crash powerfully close.

Innojō-futa   VIEWPOINT
(犬の門蓋) On a point on the northwest coast of the island, this collection of bizarrely eroded upthrust coral includes a formation that resembles a giant pair of spectacles. Blink and you'll miss the sign on the main road about 10km south of the airport. From the turn-off into the maze of sugar-cane fields, it's a bit poorly signed in kanji.

Aze Prince Beach   BEACH
(畦プリンスビーチ) Near the Aze/Fruits Garden bus stop on the northeast coast, this excellent beach is backed by a simple park area.

🛏 Sleeping & Eating

Stay in Kametoku if you want to be near the port and have options for dining. If you rent your own wheels, opt for Kanami-sō for a more peaceful and rustic beachside stay.

Tokunoshima doesn't stand out for its dining, but you'll find the most options in Kametsu.

Aze Campground   CAMPGROUND
(畦キャンプ場; P) FREE This fine little campground at Aze Prince Beach has showers, nice grassy campsites and a trail down to its own private beach.

★**Pension Shichifukujin**   MINSHUKU ¥
(ペンション七福人; ☑0997-82-1126; 1637-3 Kametoku; s/d ¥3500/4500; P❋🅪) Run by

the effusive Shikasa-san, this hillside *min-shuku* has spacious, comfortable Japanese- and Western-style rooms. There's a cheery kitchen area, and discounts are available for long-term stays. Add ¥1600 per person to include two meals. They'll pick you up from the port for free with advance notice; if you're arriving independently, the turquoise-painted wall signals that you've found the right place.

Kanami-sō   MINSHUKU ¥¥
(金見荘; ☑0997-84-9027; www.kanamiso. com; r per person incl 2 meals with/without bath ¥9180/7560; P❋@🅪) In the village of Kanami, at the very northeast tip of the island, this friendly, homely divers' lodge has a great location overlooking a good snorkelling beach. Some of the upstairs rooms have sweeping views; cheaper rooms with shared bath are also available. The place specialises in *ise ebi ryōri* (Japanese lobster cuisine).

ⓘ Information

A small **tourist information office** (徳之島観光協会; ☑0997-82-0575; ⊙9am-5.30pm Mon-Sat) at the ferry building has a detailed Japanese pamphlet and a simple English one about the island. It can help with accommodation, but you're best off booking ahead.

ⓘ Getting There & Around

Tokunoshima has flights to/from Kagoshima and Amami-Ōshima (JAC).

The island is served by **Marix** (p781) and **A Line** (p781) ferries, which run between Kagoshima (some originating in Honshū) and Naha, and Amami Kaiun ferries, which run between Kagoshima and Okinoerabu-jima.

There are bus stations at both Hetono and Kametoku ports, and a decent bus system to all parts of the island, but you'll definitely appreciate the convenience of a car, scooter or touring bicycle. **Toyota Rentacar** (トヨタレンタカー; ☑0997-82-0900; ⊙9am-6pm) is right outside Kametoku Port pier. There are also car-rental places near the airport.

Okinoerabu-jima   沖永良部島

☑0997 / POP 13,008
About 33km southwest of Tokunoshima, Okinoerabu is a sugar cane–covered island edged with excellent beaches, interesting coastal formations and a brilliant limestone cave.

Wadomari (和泊), the island's main town, is decidedly retro. The airport is at the eastern tip of the island, with **Wadomari Port** (和泊港) in Wadomari, 6km away on the east coast.

⊙ Sights

Excellent, mostly empty beaches await all around the island, many boasting interesting geological features. You'll also find Japan's biggest banyan tree and several 'secret' little beaches off the coastal road between the Fūcha blowhole and the airport.

Tamina-misaki   VIEWPOINT
(田皆岬) This cape, at the northwest tip of the island, has ancient coral that has been upthrust to form a 40m cliff.

Fūcha   VIEWPOINT
(フーチャ) At the island's northeast tip, this blowhole in the limestone rock shoots water 10m into the air on windy days. Otherwise, it's a dramatic spot to watch waves crash and swirl through the rock formations below.

Shōryū-dō   CAVE
(昇竜洞; ☑ 0997-93-4536; 1520 Yoshino; ¥1100; ☺ 9am-5pm) On the southwest slopes of Ōyama (the mountain at the west end of the island), you will find this brilliant limestone cave with 600m of walkways, disco-era illumination and narration in Japanese. It's a few kilometres inland from the southwest coastal road.

🛏 Sleeping & Eating

Though not the most inspiring little town, Wadomari is the most convenient place to base yourself, as it's where most facilities are located.

Many local eateries are open only for dinner or keep limited lunch hours, so plan accordingly.

Okidomari Campground   CAMPGROUND
(沖泊キャンプ場; P) FREE This excellent beachside campground at Okidomari Kaihin-kōen has showers and large grassy areas with trees for shade. The area is next to a small harbour and has some interesting mushroomlike coral formations on the beach.

Azuma Hotel   HOTEL ¥¥
(観光ホテル東; ☑ 0997-92-1283; 568 Wadomari; tw incl/excl meals ¥14,000/9000; P ❖) Offering free pick-up from the port or airport, this downtown Wadomari hotel has rooms in a quiet building set back from the street. Don't be put off by the ageing lobby:

it's friendly and the rooms are simple and comfortable.

Mōri Mōri   IZAKAYA ¥¥
(もおりもおり; ☑ 0997-92-0538; 582 Wadomari; meals from ¥1500; ☺ 5pm-midnight Mon-Sat) This super-friendly *izakaya* in Wadomari offers small dishes such as *gōyā champurū* (bitter melon stir-fry; ¥500). See if you can break the local beer-chugging record, which stands at under three seconds. It's a little hard to spot: from the Menshiori Shopping St (when coming from port), take the first right, then the first left, and look for the dark-wood shopfront.

Sō   IZAKAYA ¥¥
(草; ☑ 0997-92-1202; 512-7 Tedechina; meals from ¥1800; ☺ 5pm-midnight) Head towards the port from town, and on the main road after the bridge you'll spy an ersatz waterwheel in front of a corner restaurant. Step inside and you'll find a friendly *izakaya* serving interesting local specialities like *yagi-jiru* (goat soup; ¥800) and *yachimochi* (rice cake made with black sugar; ¥650), as well as more typical *izakaya* items.

❶ Information

There is a small **tourist information booth** (☑ 0997-92-2901; ☺ 8.30am-5pm) at Wadomari port on the 2nd floor of the terminal building, which has maps of the island (the office is next to the ferry ticket window).

❶ Getting There & Around

Okinoerabu has flights to and from Kagoshima, Amami-Ōshima and Yoron-tō on JAC.

Okinoerabu-jima is also served by **Marix** (p781) and **A Line Ferry** (p781), which run between Kagoshima (some originating in Honshū) and Naha.

The island has a decent bus system, but you'll welcome the convenience of a car, scooter or touring bicycle. You'll find **Toyota Rentacar** (トヨタレンタカー; ☑ 0997-92-2100; ☺ 9am-6pm) right across the street from the airport.

DON'T MISS

BEST DIVING SPOTS

➡ Yonaguni-jima (p813)

➡ Kerama Islands (p794)

➡ Ishigaki-jima (p802)

➡ Iriomote-jima (p808)

Yoron-tō 与論島

☑ 0997 / POP 5190

Fringed with white, star-sand-speckled beaches and extensive coral reefs, Yoron-tō is one of the most appealing islands in the Southwest Islands chain. A mere 5km across, it is the southernmost island in Kagoshima Prefecture. On a good day, Okinawa-hontō's northernmost point of Hedo-misaki is visible 23km to the southwest.

The harbour is next to the airport on the western tip of the island, while the main town of **Chabana** (茶花) is 1km to the east.

◉ Sights

Lovely beaches border the island, with the best dive spots clustered off the northwest and southwest coasts.

★**Yoron Minzoku-mura** MUSEUM
(与論民族村; ☑ 0997-97-2934; http://minzoku-mura.jp; 693 Higashi-ku; ¥400; ⊙9am-6pm) At the island's southeastern tip, the excellent Yoron Minzoku-mura is a collection of traditional thatch-roof island dwellings and storehouses that contain exhibits on the island's culture and history. If at all possible, come with a Japanese speaker, as the owner is an incredible source of information on the island's heritage and dialect.

Southern Cross Center MUSEUM
(サザンクロスセンター; ☑ 0997-97-3396; 3313 Ritchō; ¥400; ⊙9am-6pm) A short walk from the Ishini (石仁) bus stop, 3km southeast of Chabana, is a lookout that serves as a museum of Yoron-tō and Amami history and culture. Offering good views south to Okinawa, it celebrates the fact that Yoron-tō is the northernmost island in Japan from where the Southern Cross constellation can be seen.

Terasaki-kaigan BEACH
(寺崎海岸) Located on the northeast coast, Terasaki-kaigan represents the archetypical Amami beach, with its white sand, rocky outcrops and aquamarine water.

Oganeku-kaigan BEACH
(大金久海岸) The popular Oganeku-kaigan is Yoron-tō's best beach, located on the eastern side of the island. About 500m offshore from here lies **Yurigahama** (百合ヶ浜), a stunning stretch of white sand that disappears completely at high tide and is rich with star sand. Boats (¥2000 return) ferry visitors between the two beaches.

🛏 Sleeping

Chabana is the most convenient base for exploring the island, as it's Yoron-tō's big city.

Shiomi-sō MINSHUKU ¥
(汐見荘; ☑ 0997-97-3582, 0997-97-2167; 2229-3 Chabana; r per person without bathroom, incl 2 meals ¥5940; P❋@) This friendly and casual *minshuku* is popular with young people. Both Western- and Japanese-style rooms are available, and all share bathrooms. Starting from Chabana harbour, take the main road north (uphill) out of town and look for the cute little white house on the left after the turn. Staff will pick you up if you phone ahead.

★**Pricia Resort** HOTEL ¥¥¥
(プリシアリゾート; ☑ 0997-97-5060; www.pricia.co.jp; 358-1 Ricchō; r per person incl breakfast from ¥10,800; P❋@🛜🏊) These relaxing whitewashed cottages by the airport evoke Yoron-tō's sister island, Mykonos, in Greece. The best cottages are the beachside 'B type' units. Breezy Western-style rooms and Jacuzzi baths are popular with Japanese divers and holidaying US servicemembers from Okinawa. The hotel offers an entire menu of activities, including windsurfing, snorkelling and banana-boat rides. They also rent out bicycles and cars.

🍴 Eating & Drinking

There's a large supermarket and two minimarkets in the centre of Chabana.

Umi Café CAFE ¥
(海カフェ; ☑ 0997-97-4621; 2309 Chabana; meals from ¥800; ⊙11am-6pm Sun-Wed & Fri, 1-6pm Sat, closed Thu; 📶) This delightful terraced gallery-cafe with ocean views is something you'd expect to find perched on a Greek cliff; it's no surprise to find chicken gyros (¥700) on the menu. Go to the village office at the top of the main drag, turn left and then right at the end of the street. Look for small signs pointing uphill.

The owner also runs a small hostel (dorm beds ¥1500).

Bar Natural Reef BAR

(ナチュラルリーフ; ☎0997-97-3661; 16-1 Chabana; snacks from ¥600; ⊙9pm-1am) This tiki bar on Chabana's main drag is the best watering hole on the island, with plenty of *yū sen*, a local *shōchū* (strong distilled alcohol) made from sugar cane, to keep everyone happy. Owner Kowaguchi-san has lots of tips about the best spots on Yoron-tō.

ⓘ Information

Beside the city office in Chabana is the friendly **tourist information office** (ヨロン島観光協会; ☎0997-97-5151; 32-1 Chabana; ⊙8.30am-5.30pm), which provides a basic English-language map of the island and can make accommodation bookings.

There is an international ATM at the post office in Chabana.

ⓘ Getting There & Away

Yoron-tō has direct flights to/from Kagoshima, Amami-Ōshima (JAC) and Naha (RAC).

It's also served by **Marix** (マリックスライン; Map p780; ☎in Amami 0997-53-3112, in Kagoshima 099-225-1551; www.marix-line. co.jp) and **A Line** (Map p780; ☎in Amami 099-222-2338, in Kagoshima 099-226-4141; www. aline-ferry.com), which run between Kagoshima (some originating in Honshū) and Naha.

ⓘ Getting Around

Yoron-tō has a bus system, but you'll definitely appreciate the convenience of a car, scooter or touring bicycle. **Yoron Rentacar** (ヨロンレンタカー; ☎0997-97-3633; 48-7 Chabana; ⊙8am-6pm), in Chabana, will meet car- or scooter-rental clients at the airport, and may even offer you an energy drink when sending you on your way. If you don't opt for a pick-up, find Yoron Rentacar on the road just east of the post office, off Chabana's main drag.

OKINAWA-HONTŌ
沖縄本島

Okinawa-hontō is the largest island in the Southwest Islands, and the historical seat of power of the Ryūkyū dynasty. Although its cultural differences with mainland Japan were once evident in its architecture, almost all traces were completely obliterated in WWII. Fortunately Allied bombing wasn't powerful enough to completely stamp out other remnants of Okinawan culture, and today the island is home to a unique culinary, artistic and musical tradition.

The island is also home to some excellent beaches, delicious food and friendly people, many of whom speak a little more English than their mainland counterparts.

OKINAWA'S LIVING LANGUAGES

If you spend a little time in Okinawa, you might hear bits of the Okinawan language: *mensōre* ('welcome') instead of the standard Japanese *yokoso* or *nifei dēbiru* instead of *arigatō*. What you may not realise is that besides Okinawa, there exists a colourful diversity of distinct dialects throughout the island chain – all considered Ryūkyūan languages. Sadly many of these dialects are dying out with older generations.

According to Unesco, of the existing 7000 or so languages spoken in the world, around 2500 are considered endangered. When Kiku Hidenori, owner of Yoron Minzoku-mura on Yoron-tō, heard this statistic several years ago, he was dismayed to find the Amami, Okinawa and Yoron dialects included among the endangered tongues. As someone who actively preserves traditional Yoron culture and grew up speaking Yoron-hōgen (Yoron dialect), he decided that he needed to help save his island's language from extinction.

Kiku notes that while he and peers of his generation can still speak Yoron-hōgen, nowadays fewer children grow up in the same homes as their grandparents, so they don't hear Yoron-hōgen spoken regularly, contributing to its decline in younger generations.

For his part, Kiku has begun teaching Yoron-hōgen in the local primary schools, and bringing junior high school students to Yoron Minzoku-mura to give older kids a sense of pride in their unique heritage and dialect. His independent work has attracted the attention of Japanese language academics. He is actively liaising with other dialect preservationists elsewhere in Japan to find the best strategies and methods for keeping these tongues alive. With any luck, such grass-roots efforts by him and others can bring these island dialects back from the brink.

Okinawa-hontō

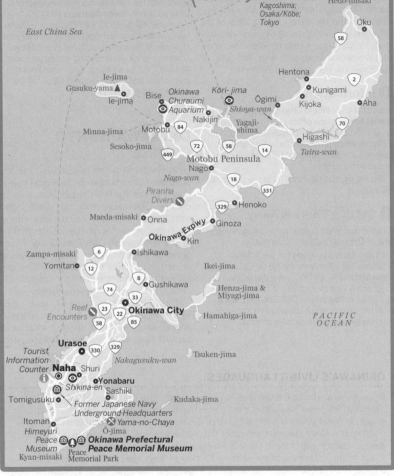

Of course, with US Air Force jets flying overhead from time to time, it's hard to forget the reality of the continuing American military presence on the island and the history behind that presence.

Prefectural capital Naha is a transport hub for the other islands.

War memorials are clustered in the south of the island, while there are some good beaches and other attractions on the Motobu Peninsula. The north is relatively undeveloped.

It's worth noting that Okinawa-hontō has been somewhat overdeveloped for domestic

tourism. If you seek Southeast Asian–style beaches and fewer big resorts, the majority of your time will be best spent on Okinawa Prefecture's smaller islands.

Naha 那覇

☑ 098 / POP 319,449

Flattened during WWII, the prefectural capital of Naha is now a thriving urban centre. The city sports a convenient elevated monorail and a rapidly expanding skyline of modern high-rise apartments, as well as the inevitable traffic jams.

The city plays host to an interesting mix of young Japanese holidaymakers, American GIs looking for off-base fun and a growing number of foreign tourists. The action centres on Kokusai-dōri (International Blvd), and overlooking it all from a safe distance to the east is Shuri-jō, a wonderfully restored castle that was once the home of Ryūkyū royalty.

◎ Sights

Naha is fairly easy to navigate, especially since the main sights and attractions are located in the city centre. The city's main artery is **Kokusai-dōri** (国際通り), a riot of neon, noise, souvenir shops, bustling restaurants and Japanese young things out strutting their stuff. It's a festival of tat and tackiness, but it's a good time if you're in the mood for it.

Many people prefer the atmosphere of the three covered shopping arcades that run south off Kokusai-dōri: **Ichibahon-dōri** (市場本通り), **Mutsumibashi-dōri** (むつみ橋通り) and **Heiwa-dōri** (平和通り).

The Shuri district is about 3km to the east of the city centre.

Daichi Makishi Kōsetsu Ichiba   MARKET
(第一牧志公設市場; Map p788; 2-10-1 Matsuo; ⊙8am-8pm, restaurants 10am-7pm) Our favourite stop in the arcade area is the covered food market just off Ichibahon-dōri, about 200m south of Kokusai-dōri. The colourful variety of fish and produce on offer here is amazing, and don't miss the wonderful local restaurants upstairs.

★Tsuboya Pottery Street   AREA
(壺屋やちむん道り; Tsuboya Yachimun-dōri; Map p788) One of the best parts of Naha is this neighbourhood, a centre of ceramic production from 1682, when Ryūkyū kilns were consolidated here by royal decree. Most shops along this old-timey street sell all the popular Okinawan ceramics, including *shisā* (lion-dog roof guardians) and containers for serving *awamori* (Okinawan liquor distilled from rice), the local firewater. The lanes off the main street here contain some classic crumbling old Okinawan houses. To get here from Kokusai-dōri, walk south through the entirety of Heiwa-dōri arcade (about 350m).

Tsuboya Pottery Museum   MUSEUM
(壺屋焼物博物館; Map p788; ☎098-862-3761; www.edu.city.naha.okinawa.jp/tsuboya; 1-9-32 Tsuboya; ¥350; ⊙10am-6pm Tue-Sun) The ex-cellent Tsuboya Pottery Museum houses some fine examples of traditional Okinawan pottery. Here you can also inspect potters' wheels and *arayachi* (unglazed) and *jōyachi* (glazed) pieces. There's even a cross-section of a *nobori-gama* (kiln built on a slope) set in its original location, where crushed pieces of pottery that date back to the 17th century lay suspended in earth.

★Okinawa Prefectural Museum & Art Museum   MUSEUM
(沖縄県立博物館・美術館; Map p788; ☎098-941-8200; www.museums.pref.okinawa.jp; Omoromachi 3-1-1; prefectural/art museum ¥410/310; ⊙9am-6pm Tue-Thu & Sun, to 8pm Fri & Sat) Opened in 2007, this museum of Okinawa's history, culture and natural history is easily one of the best museums in Japan. Displays are well laid-out, attractively presented and easy to understand, with excellent bilingual interpretive signage. The art museum section holds interesting special exhibits (admission prices vary) with an emphasis on local artists. It's about 15 minutes' walk northwest of the Omoromachi monorail station.

Shikina-en   GARDENS
(識名園; Map p786; ☎098-855-5936; 421-7 Aza Māji; ¥400; ⊙9am-6pm Thu-Tue Apr-Sep, to 5.30pm Oct-Mar) Around 4km east of the city centre is a Chinese-style garden containing stone bridges, a viewing pavilion and a villa that belonged to the Ryūkyū royal family. Despite its flawless appearance, everything here was painstakingly rebuilt after WWII. To reach the garden, take bus 2, 3 or 5 to the Shikinaen-mae stop (¥230, 20 minutes).

Fukushū-en   GARDENS
(福州園; Map p788; ☎098-869-5384; 2-29 Kume; ⊙9am-6pm Thu-Tue) **FREE** Garden fans should take a stroll through Chinese-style Fukushū-en. All materials were brought from Fuzhou, Naha's sister city in China, including the pagoda that sits atop a small waterfall.

Naha City Traditional Arts & Crafts Center   GALLERY
(那覇市伝統工芸館; Map p788; ☎098-868-7866; 2nd fl, 3-2-10 Makishi; ¥310; ⊙9am-6pm) Right on Kokusai-dōri, this gallery houses a notable collection of traditional Okinawan crafts by masters of the media. You can also try your hand at Ryūkyūan glassblowing, weaving, *bingata* (painting on fabric) and pottery-making in workshops (¥1500 to ¥3000), and make your own souvenir from Okinawa.

Naha

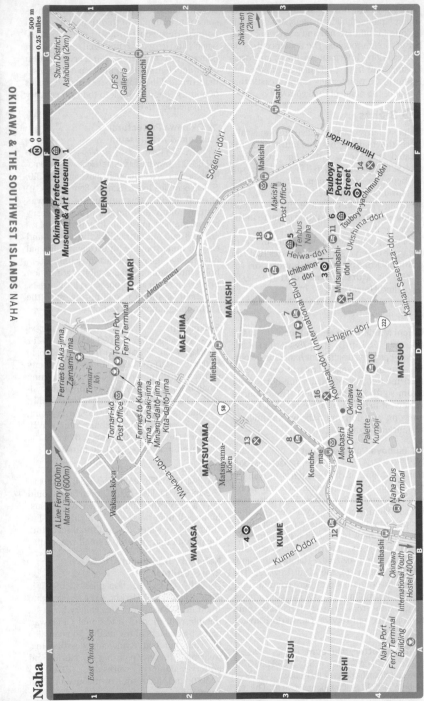

East China Sea

A Line Ferry (600m);
Marix Line (600m)

Ferries to Aka-jima,
Zamami-jima

Tomari-kō

Tomari Port
Ferry Terminal

Tomari-kō
Post Office

Ferries to Kume-
jima, Tonaki-jima,
Minami-daitō-jima,
Kita-daitō-jima

Shuri District;
Ashibiunā (2km)

DFS
Galleria

Omoromachi

Shikina-en
(2km)

Asato

Sōgenji-dōri

Makishi

Makishi
Post Office

Himeyuri-dōri

Tsuboya
Pottery
Street

Tenbus
Naha

Tsuboya-yachimun-dōri

Ukishima-dōri

Okinawa Prefectural
Museum & Art Museum 1

UENOYA

DAIDŌ

TOMARI

MAKISHI

MAEJIMA

Miebashi

Asato-gawa

Heiwa-dōri

Ichibahon-
dōri

Mutsumibashi-
dōri

Kaihan Seseraza-dōri

Ichigin-dōri

Kokusai-dōri (International Blvd)

Okinawa
Tourist

Palette
Kumoji

MATSUO

MATSUYAMA

Matsuyama-
kōen

Wakasa-dōri

Wakasa-kōen

WAKASA

KUME

Kume-Ōdōri

Kenchō-
mae

Miebashi
Post Office

Naha Bus
Terminal

KUMOJI

Asahibashi

Okinawa
International Youth
Hostel (400m)

Naha Port
Ferry Terminal
Building

TSUJI

NISHI

58

222

500 m
0.25 miles

Naha

◉ Shuri District

The original capital of Okinawa, Shuri's temples, shrines, tombs and castle were all destroyed in WWII, but the castle and surrounding structures were rebuilt in 1992.

★ Shuri-jō   CASTLE
(首里城; ☎098-886-2020; http://oki-park.jp/shurijo; 1-2 Kinjō-chō, Shuri; ¥820, with 1- or 2-day monorail pass discounted to ¥660; ⊙8.30am-7pm Apr-Jun, Oct & Nov, to 8pm Jul-Sep, to 6pm Dec-Mar, closed 1st Wed & Thu Jul) This reconstructed castle was originally built in the 14th century and served as the administrative centre and royal residence of the Ryūkyū kingdom until the 19th century. Enter through the **Kankaimon** (歓会門) and go up to the **Hōshin-mon** (奉神門), which forms the entryway to the inner sanctum of the castle. Visitors can enter the impressive **Seiden** (正殿), which has exhibits on the castle and the Okinawan royals.

About 200m west of the Seiden, the observation terrace **Iri-no-Azana** (西のアザナ) affords great views over Naha and the Kerama Islands. There is also a small collection of displays in the nearby **Hokuden** (北殿).

To reach the complex, which sits atop a hill overlooking Naha's urban sprawl, take the Yui-rail monorail to Shuri Station. Exit to the west, go down the steps, walk straight ahead, cross one big street, then a smaller one and go right on the opposite side, then walk about 350m and look for the signs on the left.

✿ Festivals & Events

Dragon-Boat Races   CULTURAL
(⊙May) Held in early May, particularly in Itoman and Naha. These *hari* (races) are thought to bring luck and prosperity to fishers.

Naha Ōzunahiki   SPORTS
(⊙Oct) Takes place in Naha on Sunday around the national Sports Day Holiday in October, and features large teams that compete in the world's biggest tug of war, using a gigantic 1m-thick rope weighing over 40 tonnes.

Ryūkyū-no-Saiten   CULTURAL
(⊙Oct) Brings together more than a dozen festivals and special events celebrating Okinawan culture for three days at the end of October.

⌂ Sleeping

★ Minshuku Gettō   MINSHUKU ¥
(民宿月桃; Map p788; ☎098-861-7555; 1-16-24 Matsuo; s with/without shared bath from ¥3500/3000; P✿@⬡) Tucked into a quiet little neighbourhood just a couple of minutes' walk to Kokusai-dōri, this spotless little *minshuku* offers secure, stand-alone apartments, some with private bathrooms and kitchenettes. Reserve well in advance for a coveted spot, as it's a steal.

Stella Resort   GUESTHOUSE ¥
(ステラリゾート; Map p788; ☎098-863-1330; www.stella-cg.com; 3-6-41 Makishi; dm/s/d ¥1400/3000/4200; P✿@⬡) Between Heiwa-dōri arcade and the Tsuboya pottery area, this tropical-themed guesthouse has small, basic rooms with shared bathrooms, a pool table, a zone-out room and some English-speaking staff. Look for the turquoise building at the end of the covered section of Heiwa-dōri and climb the stairs to the lobby.

Its sister guesthouse, **Lohas Villa** (ロハスヴィラ; Map p788; ☎098-867-7757; www.lohas-cg.com; 3rd fl, Breath Bldg, 2-1-6 Makishi; dm/s/d ¥1600/3600/5200; @ 📶), is on the other side of Kokusai-dōri.

★Hotel Sun Palace Kyūyōkan HOTEL ¥¥
(ホテルサンパレス球陽館; Map p788; ☎098-863-4181; www.palace-okinawa.com/sunpalace; 2-5-1 Kumoji; s/d incl breakfast from ¥7000/14,700; P ⊖ ❄ 📶) About three minutes' walk from Kokusai-dōri, the Sun Palace is a giant step up in warmth and quality from a standard business hotel. Staff are friendly, the fairly spacious rooms include small potted plants and a welcoming Okinawan feel, and there's even a rooftop terrace, a refreshing bit of outdoor space laced with greenery.

Tōyoko Inn HOTEL ¥¥
(東横イン; Map p788; ☎098-951-1045; www.toyoko-inn.com/e_hotel/00076/; 2-1-20 Kume; s/d incl breakfast from ¥6050/8200; P ⊖ ❄ @ 📶) Just a short walk north of Kokusai-dōri, the Tōyoko is a good-value business hotel with small but serviceable rooms and useful features such as free internet and breakfast. It's one of the better options in this price range.

Hotel JAL City Naha HOTEL ¥¥¥
(ホテルJALシティ那覇; Map p788; ☎098-866-2580; http://naha.jalcity.co.jp; 1-3-70 Makishi; s/d from ¥13,300/16,500; P ⊖ ❄ @ 📶) In the middle of the action on Kokusai-dōri, JAL City has 304 swish, modern rooms, in which even the single beds are wide enough to serve as snug doubles. Though staff here speak limited English, the service is excellent and the accommodation an elegant refuge from the noise of Kokusai-dōri.

Eating

In Naha, a great place to sample everyday Okinawan eats is at one of the 2nd-floor eateries at Daichi Makishi Kōsetsu Ichiba (p787); roam around for a look at what others are eating and grab a seat.

Ashibiunā OKINAWAN ¥
(あしびうなぁ; ☎098-884-0035; 2-13 Shuri Tonokura-chō; lunch sets ¥800-1250; ⏲11.30am-3pm & 5.30pm-midnight; 📖) Perfect for lunch after touring Shuri-jō (p789), Ashibiunā has a traditional ambience and picturesque garden. Set meals feature local specialities such as *gōyā champurū* (bitter melon stir-fry), *okinawa-soba* (thick white noodles in a pork broth) and *ikasumi yakisoba* (stir-fried squid-ink noodles). On the road leading away from Shuri-jō, Ashibiunā is on the right, just before the intersection to the main road.

Mikasa OKINAWAN ¥
(三笠; Map p788; ☎098-868-7469; 1-3-17 Matsuyama; dishes from ¥500; ⏲24hr) Come to Mikasa hungry, and at any hour, for cheap, no-nonsense grub with the locals. All the Okinawan favourites are whipped up here – *gōyā champuru* and *champon* (sautéed meat, onion and egg over rice) – and served with a smile. You'll find it on a nondescript block on busy Rte 58, just a few blocks from Kokusai-dōri.

★Nuchigafu OKINAWAN ¥¥
(ぬちがふ; Map p788; ☎098-861-2952; 1-28-3 Tsuboya; set dinner from ¥3000; ⏲11.30am-5pm & 5.30-10pm Wed-Mon) For a memorable, elegant meal in Naha, don't pass up dinner at the hilltop Nuchigafu, off the southern end of Tsuboya Pottery Street (p787). Formerly a lovely Okinawan teahouse, and long before that a historic Ryūkyūan residence, Nuchigafu serves lunch and frothy *buku-buku* tea during the day and beautifully plated, multi-course Okinawan dinners by night. Children 11 and older are welcome.

★Yūnangi OKINAWAN ¥¥
(ゆうなんぎい; Map p788; ☎098-867-3765; 3-3-3 Kumoji; dishes ¥1200; ⏲noon-3pm & 5.30-10.30pm Mon-Sat; 📖) You'll be lucky to get a seat here, but if you do, you'll be treated to some of the best Okinawan food around, served in traditional but bustling surroundings. Try the *okinawa-soba* set (¥1400), or choose from among the appealing options on the picture menu. It's on a side street off Kokusai-dōri – look for the wooden sign with white lettering above the doorway.

Ukishima Garden VEGETARIAN ¥¥
(浮島ガーデン; Map p788; ☎098-943-2100; www.ukishima-garden.com/okinawa; 2-12-3 Matsuo; lunch/dinner from ¥1250/3800; ⏲11.30am-3pm & 6-11pm; 🌱 📖) With pork featuring prominently in traditional Okinawan cuisine, Ukishima Garden is a refreshing, cleansing change. Here vegetarian and vegan creations utilise as much organic and locally grown produce as possible, resulting in balanced and complex renditions of dishes from taco rice to spaghetti carbonara. Pair your meal with organic wine; end with an *amazake* (fermented rice milk) smoothie.

🍸 Drinking & Nightlife

Naha is the biggest and rowdiest city for hundreds of miles around, most of its nightlife centring on Kokusai-dōri.

Rehab
BAR

(Map p788; ☑ 098-988-1198; 3rd fl, 2-4-14 Makishi; ⊗7pm-late) This 3rd-floor international bar on Kokusai-dōri attracts a friendly, mixed crowd and has cosy nook seating, imported beer and two-for-one drinks on Tuesdays. The cool bartenders here speak English.

Helios Pub
PUB

(ヘリオスパブ; Map p788; ☑ 098-863-7227; 1-2-25 Makishi; ⊗11.30am 11pm Sun-Thu, to midnight Fri & Sat) Craft-beer lovers who tire of Orion can perk up bored palates with a sample flight of four house brews (¥900) and pints for ¥525. Edibles cover the pub-menu gamut, all very reasonably priced.

❶ Information

At Naha airport's helpful **Tourist Information Counter** (Map p786; ☑ 098-857-6884; 1F Arrivals Terminal, Naha International Airport; ⊗9am-9pm), pick up a copy of the *Naha Guide Map* before heading into town, and an *Okinawa Guide Map* if you plan to explore outside Naha.

The city **Tourist Information Office** (那覇市観光案内所; Map p788; ☑ 098-868-4887; 3-2-10 Makishi; ⊗9am-8pm), located in the Tenbus Building, gives out free maps and information.

On Kokusai-dōri, **Okinawa Tourist** (沖縄ツーリスト; OTS; Map p788; ☑ 098-862-1111; 1-2-3 Matsuo; ⊗9.30am-6pm Mon-Fri, to 3.30pm Sat) is a competent travel agency with English speakers who can help with all manner of ferry and flight bookings.

❶ Getting There & Away

AIR

Naha International Airport (OKA) has connections with Seoul, Taipei, Hong Kong and Shanghai.

Connections with mainland Japan include Fukuoka, Osaka, Nagoya and Tokyo; significant discounts (*tabiwari* on All Nippon Airways and *sakitoku* on JAL) can sometimes be had if you purchase tickets a month in advance. Note that this is only a partial list; most large Japanese cities have flights. Low-cost carrier Peach Airlines flies to Naha from Fukuoka, Tokyo's Haneda and Narita, and Osaka's Kansai airports.

A FOOD LOVER'S GUIDE TO OKINAWA

Reflecting the islands' geographic and historical isolation, Okinawa's food shares little in common with that of mainland Japan. The cuisine originated in the splendour of the Ryūkyū court and from the humble lives of the impoverished islanders. Healthy eating is considered to be extremely important; indeed, islanders have long held that medicine and food are essentially the same. And it must be noted that Okinawans are among the longest-lived people in the world.

Today one of the island's staple foods is pork, which is acidic and rich in protein. Every part of the pig is eaten. *Mimigā* (ミミガー) is thinly sliced pig's ears marinated in vinegar, perfect with a cold glass of local Orion beer (オリオンビール). *Rafutē* (ラフテー) is pork stewed with ginger, brown sugar, rice wine and soy sauce until it falls apart. If you need some stamina, try some *ikasumi-jiru* (イカスミ汁), which is stewed pork in black squid ink.

While stewing is common, Okinawans prefer stir-frying, and refer to the technique as *champurū* (チャンプルー). Perhaps the best-known stir-fry is *gōyā champurū* (ゴーヤーチャンプルー), a mix of pork, bitter melon and the island's uniquely sturdy tofu, *shima-dōfu* (島豆腐). Occasionally you'll come across an unusual tofu variant known as *tōfuyō* (豆腐瑤), a type of *shima-dōfu* whose strong flavour is due to fermentation in *awamori* (Okinawan liquor distilled from rice).

The ubiquitous *okinawa-soba* (沖縄そば) is udon (thick white noodles) served in a pork broth. The most common variants are *sōki-soba* (ソーキそば), topped with pork spare ribs; and *Yaeyama-soba* (八重山そば), which contains soba topped with tiny pieces of tender pork, bean sprouts and scallions.

Aside from *gōyā champuru*, bitter melon appears in all kinds of dishes, delivering a dose of antioxidants and holding promise for its potential to combat diabetes.

Finally there's nothing quite like Blue Seal (ブルーシール) brand ice cream, an American favourite introduced here after WWII. It's best savoured at a shop rather than in prepacked containers.

AWAMORI

While travelling through the Southwest Islands, be sure to sample the local firewater, *awamori* (泡盛), which is distilled from rice and has an alcohol content of 30% to 60%. Although it's usually served *mizu-wari* (水割; diluted with water), this is seriously lethal stuff, especially the *habushu* (ハブ酒), which comes with a small snake in the bottle. If you're hitting the *awamori* hard, take our advice and cancel your plans for the next day (or two).

Naha also has air connections with Ishigaki-jima, Kume-jima, Miyako-jima and Yoron-tō, among other Southwest Islands.

BOAT

Naha has regular ferry connections with ports in Honshū (Tokyo and Osaka/Kōbe) and Kyūshū (Kagoshima).

Marix (☑ in Kagoshima 099-225-1551; www.marix-line.co.jp) and **A Line** (☑ in Naha 098-861-1886, in Tokyo 03-5643-6170; www.aline-ferry.com) operate four to six ferries a month to/from Tokyo (¥27,230, 47 hours) and Osaka/Kōbe (¥19,330, 42 hours), as well as daily ferries to/from Kagoshima (¥14,610, 25 hours).

There are three ports in Naha, and this can be confusing: Amami Islands ferries operate from **Naha Port** (Naha-kō; Map p788); Tokyo/Osaka/Kōbe/Kagoshima ferries operate from **Naha Shin Port** (Naha Shin-kō); and Kume-jima and Kerama Islands ferries operate from **Tomari Port** (Tomari-kō; Map p788).

Note that there is no ferry service to the Miyako or Yaeyama Islands from Naha.

ⓘ Getting Around

The Yui-rail monorail conveniently runs from Naha International Airport in the south to Shuri in the north. Prices range from ¥200 to ¥290; one- and two-day passes cost ¥700 and ¥1200, respectively. Kenchō-mae Station sits at the western end of Kokusai-dōri, while Makishi Station is at its eastern end.

Naha Port is a 10-minute walk southwest from Asahibashi Station, while Tomari Port is a similar distance north from Miebashi Station. Bus 101 from **Naha bus terminal** (那覇バスターミナル; Map p788) heads further north to Naha Shin Port (20 minutes, hourly).

When riding on local town buses, simply dump ¥200 into the slot next to the driver as you enter. For longer trips, take a ticket showing your starting point as you board and pay the appropriate fare as you disembark. Buses run from Naha to destinations all over the island.

A rental car makes everything easier when exploring Okinawa-hontō. The rental-car counter in the arrivals hall of Naha International Airport offers information on the dozen or so rental companies in Naha, allowing you to comparison shop.

Southern Okinawa-hontō
沖縄本島の南部

During the closing days of the Battle of Okinawa, the southern part of Okinawa-hontō served as one of the last holdouts of the Japanese military and an evacuation point for wounded Japanese soldiers. A visit to the area, a day or half-day trip from Naha, is highly recommended for those with an interest in wartime history or deeper understanding of the modern Okinawan identity.

Okinawa's most important war memorials are clustered in the Peace Memorial Park, located in the city of Itoman on the southern coast of the island.

Southern Okinawa-hontō is conveniently served by regular buses from Naha.

⊙ Sights

★ Okinawa Prefectural Peace Memorial Museum   MUSEUM
(沖縄県平和祈念資料館; Map p786; ☑098-997-3844; www.peace-museum.pref.okinawa.jp; 614-1 Aza Mabuni, Itoman; ¥300; ⊙9am-5pm) The centrepiece of the Peace Memorial Park is the Okinawa Prefectural Peace Memorial Museum, which focuses on the suffering of the Okinawan people during the invasion of the island and under the subsequent American occupation. While some material may stir debate, the museum's mission is to serve as a reminder of the horrors of war, so that such suffering is not repeated. There is a free English-language audio guide available, providing great detail on the 2nd-floor exhibit.

➡ Peace Memorial Park
(平和祈念公園; Map p786; ⊙dawn-dusk) Housing Okinawa's most important war memorials, the Peace Memorial Park occupies an appropriately peaceful coastal location in the southern city of Itoman.

To reach the park, take bus 89 from Naha bus terminal to the Itoman bus terminal (¥580, one hour, every 20 minutes), then transfer to bus 82, and get off at Heiwa Kinen-dō Iriguchi (¥470, 30 minutes, hourly).

→ **Cornerstone of Peace** MONUMENT
(平和の礎; ⊙dawn-dusk) **FREE** Outside the Okinawa Prefectural Peace Memorial Museum is the Cornerstone of Peace, inscribed with the names of everyone who died in the Battle of Okinawa.

Himeyuri Peace Museum MUSEUM
(ひめゆり平和祈念資料館; Map p786; ☑098-997-2100; www.himeyuri.or.jp; 671-1 Ihara, Itoman; ¥310; ⊙9am-5.30pm) Located above a cave that served as an emergency field hospital during the closing days of the Battle of Okinawa, the Himeyuri Peace Museum is a haunting monument whose mission is to promote peace, driven by survivors and alumnae of the school. Here 240 female high-school students were pressed into service as nurses for Japanese military wounded. As American forces closed in, the students were summarily dismissed and, thus abandoned, most perished. Excellent, comprehensive interpretive signage is provided in English. Bus 82 stops outside.

Former Japanese Navy Underground Headquarters MUSEUM
(旧海軍司令部壕; Kyūkaigun Shireibu-gō; Map p786; ☑098-850-4055; 236 Tomishiro, Tomigusuku; ¥440; ⊙8.30am-5pm Oct-Jun, to 5.30pm Jul-Sep) Directly south of Naha in Kaigungo-kōen is the Former Japanese Navy Underground Headquarters, where 4000 men committed suicide or were killed as the battle for Okinawa drew to its bloody conclusion. Only 250m of the tunnels are open, but you can wander through the maze of corridors, see the commander's final words on the wall of his room, and inspect the holes and scars in other walls from the grenade blasts that killed many of the men.

To reach the site, take bus 55 or 98 from Naha bus terminal to the Uebaru Danchi-mae stop (¥220, 10 minutes, several hourly). From there it's a five-minute walk – follow the English signs (the entrance is near the top of the hill).

🏃 Activities

Reef Encounters DIVING
(Map p786; ☑098-995-9414, 090-1940-3528; www.reefencounters.org; 1-493 Miyagi, Chatan-chō; 2-dive boat trips from ¥14,040, equipment rental ¥5000) Experienced, safety-oriented dive guides at this organised outfit can, between the lot of them, speak fluent English, Spanish, Portuguese, Japanese, Mandarin and Cantonese.

Piranha Divers DIVING
(Map p786; ☑098-967-8487, 080-4277-1155; www.piranha-divers.jp; 2288-532 Aza-Nakama, Nago; 2-dive boat trips from ¥14,000, equipment rental ¥5000) In Onna Village in the Nago area, this family operation caters to individuals and small groups. Dive guides speak fluent English, German and Japanese.

🍴 Eating

Most points of interest in this area either have restaurants on site, or have many eateries nearby catering to tourist traffic.

Yama-no-Chaya OKINAWAN ¥¥
(山の茶屋; Map p786; ☑098-948-1227; http://yama.hamabenochaya.com; 19-1 Tamagusuku, Nanjō-shi; meals ¥800-1350; ⊙11am-6pm Fri-Wed; 🅿🐕) If you're exploring southern Okinawa-hontō, seek out this serene, ocean-view cafe nestled in the forest. This is a lovely place for refreshing vegetarian fare made with organic and local ingredients. It's a 10-minute walk from the Mibaru Beach stop on bus 39 from Naha.

Motobu Peninsula 本部半島

Jutting out to the northwest of Nago, the hilly peninsula of Motobu (Motobu-hantō) is home to some scenic vistas, islets and decent beaches, as well as an incredibly popular aquarium.

◎ Sights

Okinawa Churaumi Aquarium AQUARIUM
(沖縄美ら海水族館; Map p786; ☑0980-48-3748, for GPS navigation systems 0980-48-2741; https://churaumi.okinawa; 424 Ishikawa, Motobu-chō; adult/child ¥1850/610; ⊙8.30am-6.30pm Oct-Feb, to 8pm Mar-Sep) The centrepiece of Motobu's **Ocean Expo Park** (海洋博公園) is the Okinawa Churaumi Aquarium, which features the world's largest aquarium tank. The aquarium houses a wide variety of marine life, including whale sharks. Dolphins are also kept here, a practice widely acknowledged as harmful to the animals' health.

Unfortunately it's on every visitor's checklist, so it's usually packed. From Nago, buses 65, 66 and 70 run directly to the park (¥860, 50 minutes).

Kōri-jima ISLAND
(古宇利島; Map p786) Aquariums and crowds not your cup of tea? If you've got your own wheels, drive out to Kōri-jima

via **Yagaji-jima** (屋我地島). The bridge between the two islands is surrounded by picturesque turquoise water, and there's a decent beach on either side of the road as you reach Kōri-jima. The bridge to Yagaji-jima starts just north of the Motobu Peninsula off Rte 58.

Bise   VILLAGE
(備瀬) At the northwestern tip of the peninsula is the quaintly preserved village of Bise, a leafy beachside community of traditional Okinawan houses. Stroll along **Fukugi-namiki-dōri** (フクギ並木通り), an atmospheric lane lined with old garcinia trees, taking a peek at the local beach on the northern end. Near the lane's southern end, find refreshment at beachside cafe **Ca-haya Bulan** (チャハヤブラン; ☎098-051-7272; 429-1 Bise; ajian-soba ¥800; ⊙noon-sunset Thu-Tue, winter Fri-Tue; 🅿😊🐾📶🛜).

❶ Getting There & Away
Motobu Peninsula is served by frequent loop lines from Nago – buses 66 and 65 respectively run anticlockwise and clockwise around the peninsula.

By car, the drive from Naha takes about 1½ hours.

Northern Okinawa-hontō
沖縄本島の北部
The northern part of Okinawa-hontō is largely undeveloped and comparatively wild and rugged. Rte 58 hugs the west coast all the way up to **Hedo-misaki** (辺土岬; Hedo Cape), which marks the northern end of Okinawa. The point is an incredibly scenic spot backed by hills, with rocks rising from the dense greenery. On a good day, Yoron-tō, the southernmost island in the Amami Islands, is easily seen, only 23km to the northeast.

KERAMA ISLANDS
慶良間諸島
The islands of the Kerama archipelago are truly a world away from the buzz of Okinawa-hontō, although due to their easy accessibility, they do get crowded during the summer holiday season. Declared a national park (Kerama Shotō Kokuritsu Kōen, 慶良間諸島国立公園) in 2014, the Keramas are not only surrounded by reefs of diverse corals, but their clear, blue waters also provide sanctuary for breeding humpback whales and grazing sea turtles.

Each of the three main islands – Zamami-jima, Aka-jima and Tokashiki-jima – can be visited as day trips from Naha. But to really savour the slow-paced pleasures, stay a night or two in one of the islands' *minshuku*.

Aka-jima   阿嘉島
🎵 098 / POP 300
A mere 2km in diameter, tiny Aka-jima makes up for in beauty what it lacks in size. Some of the best beaches in the Keramas and an extremely peaceful atmosphere mean it's easy to get stuck here for several days. There's also some great snorkelling and diving offshore.

If you keep your eyes open around dusk you might spot a **Kerama deer** (慶良間シカ), descendants of deer that were brought by the Satsuma from Kagoshima when they conquered the Ryūkyūs in 1609. The deer are smaller and darker than their mainland cousins, and have been designated a National Treasure.

⊙ Sights & Activities
Lovely beaches fringe every side of the island, although **Nishibama Beach** (北浜ビーチ) is the clear favourite and can get crowded in summer. If you want privacy, there are quieter beaches on the other sides of the island.

Both Marine House Seasir and Kawai Diving double as dive shops and *minshuku*. Both have English-speaking dive guides and friendly vibes.

🛏 Sleeping & Eating
Though the island is small, accommodation is surprisingly plentiful. But book ahead, as it is also finite.

Be sure to book meals with your lodgings, as pickings are slim, restaurant-wise. You'll find the handful of cafes and markets on the island open only during the day.

Hanamuro
Inter-Islander's Hotel   MINSHUKU ¥¥
(ハナムロインターアイランダーズホテル; ☎098-987-2301; http://hanamuroint.wixsite.com/keramablue; 179 Aka; per person incl 2 meals from ¥9100; 😊❄📶) Since the building that houses it is also a marine biology research facility, this *minshuku* may look a little industrial from the outside. But the rooms are quiet,

spacious and comfortable, with private terraces affording excellent sunrise views. Hire snorkelling equipment here (¥1000) and hop on the free shuttle to Nishibama Beach before returning for a creatively delicious dinner. Rates are reduced for stays longer than one night.

Hanamuro Inn GUESTHOUSE ¥¥
(ハナムロ・イン; ☑ 098-98-2301; www.geocities.jp/hanamuroint; 52 Aka; per person incl 2 meals ¥7500; ⊝❄☎) All six rooms at this cosy inn share bathrooms and a terrace with one-person tubs. It's a one-minute walk to the beach if you dawdle. It closes completely after high season, but the innkeepers also run the Hanamuro Inter-Islander's Hotel at the back of the village, year-round.

Kawai Diving MINSHUKU ¥¥
(☑ 098-987-2219; http://oki-zamami.jp/~kawai/; 153 Aka; s/d incl meals from ¥7780/15,550;

P❄@☎) Perched just above Maehama Beach on the south coast, this inn has simple rooms, a family atmosphere and a relaxed beachside location. English-speaking staff are happy to tell guests about the island and take them diving (one/two dives ¥6480/10,840, including equipment rental).

Marine House Seasir MINSHUKU ¥¥
(マリンハウスシーサー; ☑ 090-8668-6544, in English 098-869-4022; www.seasir.com; s/d incl 3 meals from ¥9280/16,360; P❄☎) At the west end of the main village, this diver-focused *minshuku* has good, clean Western- and Japanese-style rooms just a minute's amble from the beach.

ℹ Getting There & Around

Zamami Sonei Ferry (☑ 098-868-4567) has two fast ferries a day (¥3140, 70 minutes) and one regular ferry (¥2120, 1½ hours) to/from Naha's Tomari Port. The Mitsu Shima

AMERICAN BASES IN OKINAWA

The US officially returned Okinawa to Japanese administration in 1972, but it negotiated a Status of Forces Agreement that guaranteed the Americans the right to use large tracts of Okinawan land for military bases, most of which are on Okinawa-hontō. These bases are home to approximately 27,000 American servicemembers.

Although the bases have supported Okinawa's economic growth in the past, they now contribute to about 5% the Okinawan economy. The bases are a sore spot for islanders due in part to occasional crimes committed by American servicemen. Antibase feelings peaked in 1995, after three American servicemen abducted and raped a 12-year-old Okinawan girl. Similar incidents in recent years have perpetuated animosity, including the death of a 20-year-old Okinawan woman in 2016 – a former Marine working at a US base has been charged with her rape and murder.

Plans to relocate the base from Futenma to the less-densely populated Henoko district were officially approved by both the US and Japan in 1996, but have continually met with vocal opposition from Okinawan residents, the majority of whom would like to see the US military presence take leave of the island entirely.

In April 2010, 90,000 protesters gathered to call for an end to the bases, the biggest such demonstrations in 15 years. That year, then Prime Minister Hatoyama Yukio fell on his sword after breaking a promise to move Futenma air base off the island; he finally admitted it would stay.

Though the USA formally agreed in early 2012 to move 9000 Marines (amounting to around half of the Marines on Okinawa) to bases on Guam, Hawaii and elsewhere in the Pacific, this plan will not begin manifesting until the mid-2020s.

As of December 2016 Okinawa's governor, Onaga Takeshi, was battling the Japanese government in court over his revocation of a landfill permit issued by his predecessor – this delay in construction represents Okinawan residents' wishes to see a significant reduction in the US military presence on the island.

During the same month, the US returned 4000 hectares of land to Okinawa – a move that, on the surface, appears to be a positive development. However, the return of land was made on the condition that helipad construction for controversial Osprey aircraft be completed. Many Okinawans oppose the presence of Osprey aircraft flying near residential areas, as the aircraft have had a string of accidents over the last several years, including a crash-landing in Nago as recently as mid-December 2016.

motorboat also makes four trips a day between Aka-jima and Zamami-jima (¥300, 15 minutes).

Due to its small size, the best way to get around the island is on foot.

Zamami-jima 座間味島

📻 098 / POP 870

A stone's throw from Aka-jima, Zamami-jima is *slightly* more developed, with its own lovely beaches. It's got some brilliant offshore islands and great diving and snorkelling in the surrounding waters.

⊙ Sights & Activities

Approximately 1km southeast from the port (over the hill) is **Furuzamami Beach** (古座間味ビーチ), a stunning 700m stretch of white sand, fronted by clear, shallow water and a bit of coral. The beach is well developed for day trippers, with toilets, showers and food stalls. You can also rent snorkelling gear here (¥1000).

If you fancy a little solitude, you'll find picturesque empty beaches in the coves on the other sides of the island, away from the village.

The best beaches, however, are on the islets of **Gahi-jima** (嘉比島) and **Agenashiku-jima** (安慶名敷島), about a kilometre south of the port. Ringed by delightful white-sand beaches, they are perfect for a half-day Robinson Crusoe experience. **Zamami Tour Operation** (📞 080-1766-6745) can take you to the islands and can arrange snorkelling trips. The tourist information office can help arrange boat tours (¥1500 per person round trip).

Diving is one of the main draws of the gorgeous Keramas; if you haven't booked ahead, stop by Joy Joy, which usually has guides on staff who speak limited English, though it's adequate for dives.

Whale-watching is possible between the months of December and April. For more information, either enquire at the Tourist Information Centre (p797) or call the **Zamami-mura Whale-Watching Association** (座間味村ホエールウォッチング協会; 📞 098-896-4141; www.vill.zamami.okinawa.jp/whale; adult/child ¥5400/2700), which has one to two tours daily (two hours).

🛏 Sleeping & Eating

The village is *packed* with guesthouses and *minshuku,* ranging in size from modest to teeny. In the busy summer months it's best to book ahead.

Local restaurants tend to keep limited hours, so plan to eat lunch between around 11.30am and 2pm, or pick up a *bentō* box earlier in the day. An exception is Zamamia International Guesthouse, which slings Western-style burgers all afternoon.

Zamamia International Guesthouse HOSTEL ¥
(📞 098-987-3626; www.zamamia-guesthouse.com; dm/s/d from ¥2000/5000/6000; ❄ 🛜) The convivial Zamamia International Guesthouse is run by a super-friendly Canadian expat who often organises barbecue dinners for guests. Dorm beds here are spacious and outfitted with privacy curtains; bathrooms are shared.

Joy Joy PENSION ¥
(ジョイジョイ; 📞 0120-10-2445, 098-987-2445; http://keramajoyjoy.com; 434-2 Zamami; r per person without bathroom incl breakfast from ¥5400; ❄ 🛜) This pension in the northwest corner of the village has Western- and Japanese-style rooms that surround a small garden area. It

---

THREE-STRING HARMONY

Stroll through any Okinawan town and before long you'll likely hear the tinkly sound of the *sanshin*, a banjolike precursor to the ubiquitous *shamisen* that is played on Japan's main islands. Typically constructed of a wooden frame covered with python skin, the *sanshin* has a long lacquered neck, a bamboo bridge and three strings that are struck with a plectrum, often carved from the horn of a water buffalo.

Introduced from China in the 16th century, the *sanshin* was used for court music during the Ryūkyū kingdom and later prized by commoners for its soothing sound; in the devastation that followed WWII, *sanshin* made of tin cans and nylon string cheered the exhausted survivors. Today you can hear folk songs featuring *sanshin* all over Japan. Musicians such as Takashi Hirayasu and Yoriko Ganeko have helped popularise the sound in and out of Japan; so you can even find *sanshin* groups overseas.

also runs a dive shop, with two-dive boat tours that include all equipment from ¥11,700.

Cha Villa
GUESTHOUSE ¥¥

(チャーヴィラ; ☎098-987-3737; www.miniyon3737.sakura.ne.jp; 90 Zamami; s/d ¥8000/12,000; 🅿❄🀄) Anchored by a shady tree in the garden out the front, the homey Cha Villa also runs a cosy attached cafe that serves breakfast. This is ideal should you crave toast and eggs rather than the usual Japanese spread. Both Japanese- and Western-style rooms are available here, all with private bath and kitchenette. Look out for the sign pointing you down its narrow alley.

Marumiya
OKINAWAN ¥¥

(まるみや; ☎098-987-3166; 432-2 Zamami; lunch special ¥750; ⊙11am-2.30pm & 6-10.30pm Thu-Tue; ❄📶) Cheap, delicious and friendly – therefore popular – the busy Marumiya offers a variety of Okinawan and Japanese dishes. Their inexpensive lunch specials are a great deal.

ℹ Information

Pick up a map and excellent English-language information at Zamami Village **Tourist Information Center** (☎098-987-2277; https://zamamitouristinfo.wordpress.com; ⊙9am-5pm; 📶).

ℹ Getting There & Around

Zamami Sonei (☎098-868-4567) has two or three fast ferries a day (¥3140, 50 minutes) and one regular ferry (¥2120, two hours) to/from Naha's Tomari Port. The ferries usually stop at Aka-jima en route from Naha to Zamami. The Mitsu Shima motorboat also makes four trips a day between Aka-jima and Zamami-jima (¥300, 15 minutes).

Rental cars, scooters and bicycles are available near the pier.

KUME-JIMA 久米島

📶 098 / POP 8133

The furthest flung of the outer islands, Kume-jima is a quiet island that sees fewer visitors than the Keramas. It's mostly flat and covered with sugar cane, with a few good beaches, and the mother of all sandbars off its east coast.

The airport is at the western extreme of the island, with the main port of **Kanegusuku** (兼城) just a few kilometres south.

⦿ Sights

Hate-no-hama
BEACH

(はての浜) Kume-jima's most famous attraction is this 7km sandbar that extends from the eastern point of the island, pointing back towards Okinawa-hontō. If you arrive by air, you can't miss this coral-fringed strip of white framed by the turquoise waters of the sea. **Hatenohama Kankō Service** (はての浜観光サービス; ☎090-8292-8854; ⊙9am-5pm) runs three-hour snorkelling tours to the sandbar for ¥4500. Have your hotel make a reservation for you, and staff members can pick you up from your accommodation.

Eef Beach
BEACH

(イーフビーチ) On the east coast is the most popular beach on the island. *Iifu (Eef)* means 'white' in the local Kume dialect, and not surprisingly, the beach is known for its powdery white sand.

Tatami-ishi
BEACH

(畳石) On tiny **Ōjima (**奥武島**)**, which is connected to Kume-jima's east coast by a causeway, you'll find the intriguing Tatami-ishi, a natural formation of flat pentagonal rocks that covers the seashore.

Shinri-hama
BEACH

(シンリ浜) As any local will tell you, this attractive beach is the best place on the island for watching the sunset over the East China Sea. Find it on the west coast near the airport.

🛏 Sleeping & Eating

Eef Beach is the place to stay and eat, with plenty of options to choose from along the 1.5km waterfront.

Minshuku Nankurunaisā
MINSHUKU ¥

(民宿なんくるないさぁ; ☎098-985-7973; 160-68 Higa; r per person from ¥5000; 🅿@📶) Clean, safe and family-run, this simple *minshuku* is a solid option on Eef Beach.

Kumejima Eef Beach Hotel
HOTEL ¥¥¥

(久米島イーフビーチホテル; ☎098-985-7111; www.courthotels.co.jp/kumejima; 548 Janadō; s/d incl breakfast from ¥7200/18,900; 🅿⊖❄@📶🀄) If you've come this far, the slightly retro Eef Beach Hotel is the best place to base yourself, with the beach steps away. Conveniently, the airport bus stops right in front of the hotel lobby.

Yangwa Soba
OKINAWAN ¥

(そば やん小〜; ☎080-3150-2720; 509 Nakadomari; dishes ¥550-800; ⊙noon-2pm or until sold out Mon-Sat; P 📷) Kume-jima's most famous *soba* shop is open for lunch only and is worth the trip. Serving handmade noodles out of his own home, the hospitable Nakasone-san cultivates a warm and nurturing island vibe. Enjoy your Kume-jima soba (with barbecued pork rib), or miso and bean sprout soba, in the open-air tatami dining room or at the table in the front garden.

ℹ️ Information

There is a **tourist information office** (☎098-985-7115) at the airport that opens to meet incoming flights in summer.

ℹ️ Getting There & Around

JTA and RAC operate five to six flights a day between Naha and Kume-jima.

Kume Shōsen (久米商船; ☎098-868-2686) runs one or two daily ferries from Naha's Tomari Port to/from Kume-jima (¥3390, three hours).

The island has an efficient bus system, and there are several rental-car companies at the port and airport.

MIYAKO ISLANDS
宮古諸島

Just north of the Tropic of Cancer, the Miyako Islands are an open secret that more visitors have lately been discovering. The islands' appeal is not at all surprising, as they happen to have some of the most beautiful white-sand beaches in the Southwest Islands, with good diving, snorkelling and kiteboarding to boot. Comprising the island group are the main island of Miyako-jima, along with Ikema-jima, Irabu-jima, Shimoji-jima and Kurima-jima, plus a scattering of tiny islets.

In 2015, nine years of construction culminated in the opening of the 3540m **Irabu Bridge** (伊良部大橋), rendering the ferry obsolete and making Irabu-jima and Shimoji-jima much more easily accessible from Miyako-jima. Despite the increased ease of getting here, these islands retain a stuck-in-time feel and unhurried pace, enhanced by abiding island congeniality.

Miyako-jima 宮古島

☎0980 / POP 51,196

Miyako-jima, the main island in the Miyako group, is a mostly flat expanse of sugar cane edged with excellent beaches, and

long fingers of land pointing out into the sea. Lying just offshore are four smaller islands, all of which are connected to the main island by bridges.

You can happily spend your days here hopping from one great beach to the next, with a spot of snorkelling or stand-up paddleboarding here and there if you're so inclined. If you tire of that, a seaside drive to the various capes and wetlands is a great way to spend a few hours.

◉ Sights

Miyako-jima's white-sand beaches and their super-clear, turquoise waters are the driving (diving?) reason to come to the island. You'll find dreamy beaches on the southwest corner of the island, the southwest side just below the main town of Hirara, then a few kilometres north of Hirara and on the outlying islands.

Renting a car is probably the best way to get around the island and find your new favourite beach.

Yonaha-Maehama   BEACH
(与那覇前浜ビーチ; Map p799) On the southwest coast, beautiful Yonaha-Maehama is a 6km stretch of white sand that attracts a lot of families and young folk due to its shallow waters. It's a lovely beach, but it can get crowded and the presence of the occasional jet ski is a drawback. It's just before the Kurima-Ōhashi bridge, on the north side.

Nagamahama   BEACH
(長間浜; Map p799) If you've had a look at the crowds at Yoneha-Maehama and decided you want something quieter, head across the Kurima Bridge and drive to the northwest coast of **Kurima-jima** (来間島), where you will find the brilliant (and usually uncrowded) Nagamahama.

★**Sunayama Beach**   BEACH
(砂山ビーチ; Map p799) Just 4km north of Hirara you will find this little, archetypically tropical-Japan beach, which lies at the bottom of a large sand dune (hence the name 'Sand Mountain Beach'). If you've only got one beach day to spend, or are getting around via bus, park yourself here. Find showers and toilets here, too.

Ikema-jima   ISLAND
(池間島; Map p799) Head north to drive across **Ikema-Ōhashi** (池間大橋) to the little island of Ikema-jima. The shallow aquamarine water on either side of this 1.4km

Miyako Islands

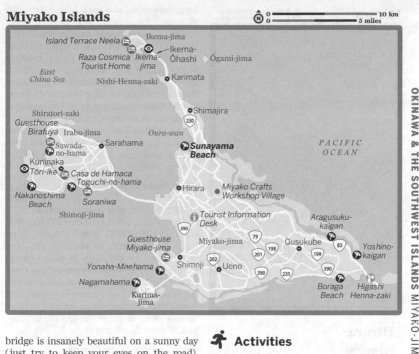

bridge is insanely beautiful on a sunny day (just try to keep your eyes on the road). You'll find several secluded pocket beaches around the coast of Ikema-jima.

Aragusuku-kaigan BEACH
(新城海岸; Aragusuku Coast; Map p799) On the north side of the island's southeast end, this popular beach is great for shallow-water snorkelling and has showers and toilets.

Yoshino-kaigan BEACH
(吉野海岸; Yoshino Coast; Map p799) On the north side of Miyako-jima's southeastern cape, this long, shallow beach has a park featuring showers and toilets.

Higashi Henna-zaki LIGHTHOUSE
(東平安名崎; Map p799) If you've got a car, we recommend taking a drive out to the southeastern tip of the island, a narrow finger of land that extends 2km into the Pacific Ocean. There are picnic tables, walking trails and a lighthouse at the point to explore.

Boraga Beach BEACH
(保良泉ビーチ; Map p799) On the southeast end of the island, this is a popular spot for snorkelling and kayaking (with a hair-raisingly steep access road).

🏃 Activities

Penguin Divers DIVING
(ペンギンダイバーズ; ☑0980-79-5433; www.diving-penguin.com; 40 Shimozato, Hirara; 2 boat dives ¥13,000) Run by a fluent English-speaking Fijian-Japanese couple, this dive shop is based in Hirara.

🐾 Courses

Miyako Crafts Workshop Village COURSE
(宮古島市体験工芸村; Map p799; ☑090-2961-4111, 0980-73-4111; www.miyakotaiken.com; 1166-286 Higashi-nakasone, Hirara; workshops from ¥1500; ⏰10am-6pm) At this crafts village adjoining the Miyako Botanical Garden, you can learn about Miyako-jima's traditional handicrafts with some hands-on creativity. Course offerings, most of which are suitable for kids, include making *shiisā* (lion-dog roof guardians) from clay, cooking Miyako specialities, and *Miyako-jōfu* (traditional weaving). Though some workshops accommodate walk-ins, it's best to make reservations beforehand.

🛏 Sleeping

Most of the accommodation is located in the town of Hirara, but you'll also find places to stay closer to the beaches. There are

Hirara

free camping grounds at many beach parks, including Yonaha-Maehama (p798), Boraga (p799) and Aragusuku-kaigan (p799).

Hiraraya GUESTHOUSE ¥
(ひららや; Map p800; ☎0980-75-3221; www.miyako-net.ne.jp/~hiraraya; 282-1 Higashi-nakasone, Hirara; dm per night/week ¥2500/15,000, s/d ¥3500/6000; [P][❄][☎]) The genial, English-speaking Hiro presides over this laid-back spot where young neighbours and friends cruise in to hang out. Accommodation is available in a dorm with huge curtained bunk beds, or a Japanese-style private room. All guests share the facilities, which include a big kitchen. Look for the doorway curtain that says 'Hiraraya' down this quiet alley.

Guesthouse Miyako-jima GUESTHOUSE ¥
(ゲストハウス宮古島; Map p799; ☎0980-76-2330; www2.miyako-ma.jp/yonaha/test-top.html; 233 Yoneha; dm/s/d with shared bathroom ¥1800/3500/5000, s/d with private bathroom ¥4500/7000; [P][❄][☎]) This bright and cheery guesthouse run by kiteboarding enthusiasts has a scenic location near Yoneha-Maehama beach. Accommodation is in Western-style dorms and small private rooms, with special rates available for long-term stays. Guests can also borrow bicycles, scooters and snorkelling equipment. Book ahead for airport pick-up (¥500).

Hotel Peace Island Miyakojima HOTEL ¥¥
(ホテルピースアイランド宮古島; Map p800; ☎0980-74-1717; http://peace-k.jp/miyako; 310 Nishizato, Hirara; s/d incl breakfast ¥7800/13,000, annex s/d ¥7800/9500; [P][❄][☎]) Peace Island has a bright, clean, welcoming vibe, even if the rooms are decidedly average – except for the luxury of washer-dryer units in every room. The hotel's brand-new annex across the street (the 'Hotel Peacely In Miyakojima Nexus') has the best rooms, set up like mini-condos with wood flooring, tiny kitchenettes and in-room laundry units.

Raza Cosmica Tourist Home HOTEL ¥¥
(ラザ・コスミカツーリストホーム; Map p799; ☎0980-75-2020; www.raza-cosmica.com; 309-1 Hirara-maezato; r per person without bathroom ¥7000; [P][❄][☎]) This serene South Asian–themed inn sits above a lovely secluded beach on Ikema-jima. Wood-floored, Western-style rooms offer peace and quiet – especially as children under 12 are not permitted. Spotless bathroom facilities are shared. Because of its somewhat isolated location, it's best to rent a car. Reservations must be made in advance via email.

Island Terrace Neela BOUTIQUE HOTEL ¥¥¥
(アイランドテラス・ニーラ; Map p799; ☎0980-74-4678; www.neela.jp; 317-1 Hirara-maezato; s/d incl breakfast from ¥38,500/70,000; [P][❄][☎][⊠]) Overlooking a serene white-sand beach on Ikema-jima, this intimate high-end resort looks like a whitewashed Mediterranean retreat airlifted to Japan. The private villas would make a decadent honeymoon destination. Rates are moderately less expensive during slower seasons.

✕ Eating & Drinking

The downtown alleys of Hirara come alive at night and offer the best variety of options.

One of Miyako-jima's local specialities worthy of a taste is the seaweed known as *umibudō* (literally 'sea grapes'), with a softly crunchy texture and sweet seawater flavour. It doesn't travel well, so it's almost exclusively a delicacy here and in the Yaeyama Islands.

Mojapan
BAKERY ¥

(モジャパン; Map p800; ☑ 090-3977-6778; 20 Higashi-Nakasone, Hirara; bread ¥160-180, coffee ¥250-400; ☐ 11am-3pm or until sold out Tue-Sat) If you weren't looking for it, you'd smell it – but you still might miss Mojapan, this hole-in-the-wall bakery unique for its owner's commitment to selling fresh bread throughout its opening hours. This means you'll find fresh rolls – plain (which are nothing but), black sesame, walnut and a variety of other flavours – hot out of the oven from opening time until closing.

Kuusu
SOUTHEAST ASIAN ¥

(Map p800; ☑ 0980-75-5963; 553-3 Shimozato, Hirara; dishes ¥500-800; ☐ 6pm-2am Fri-Wed; ☐) Fresh spring rolls, green curry, *gōyā champurū* and nasi goreng all feature on the menu here. A young crowd keeps it lively if you're just here for a Singha beer or a sip of *awamori*.

★ Nanraku
IZAKAYA ¥¥

(南楽; ☑ 0980-73-1855; 568 Nishizato, Hirara; meals ¥2500; ☐ 6pm-midnight, closed irregularly) Nanraku is Miyako-jima embodied in an *izakaya* – an earthy, convivial atmosphere, with ingredients sourced from local bounty. Chef Nanraku-san is a local boy, and his celebration of the island's cuisine and its provenance shines through in what he plates. He's famous for the *nekomanma* (*donburi* with bonito and *umibudō*). Splurge on Miyako beef sashimi (¥3500 for a small dish for two).

This is an excellent place for *osusume* (recommendation) – name your budget and food preferences. Note that the business may change location in 2018, so ask around if you don't find it initially.

★ Pōcha Tatsuya
IZAKAYA ¥¥

(ぽうちゃたつや; Map p800; ☑ 0980-73-3931; 275 Nishizato, Hirara; meals ¥3000-4000; ☐ 6.30-11pm Wed-Mon) This hospitable *izakaya* is a warm, efficient bastion of Miyako-jima quality, serving fresh, thoughtfully prepared local fare such as *kobushime-yawaraka-ni* (steamed cuttlefish; ¥730) and *sūchiki* (vinegared pork with bitter melon; ¥630). Its justified popularity necessitates reserving

ahead. Some Japanese skills are helpful here, as the specials change often, but requesting *omakase* (chef's choice) will result in a succession of regional delights.

Bar Pulse
BAR

(バーパルス; Map p800; ☑ 0980-73-6441; 299-7 Nishizato; drinks ¥700; ☐ 8pm-4am) Run by the English-speaking P-Boo, who spins tunes from his extensive and eclectic collection, this bar is a welcome aural refuge from Okinawa's ubiquitous soft-samba covers of Beatles ditties. The interior is pretty bare-bones, but there's no cover and the company is interesting. Look for the pink neon sign outside.

ℹ Information

At the **Tourist Information Desk** (Map p799; ☑ 0980-72-0899; ☐ 9am-6pm) in the arrivals hall of the airport, you can pick up a copy of the *Miyakojima Sightseeing Guide*. Travellers who can read Japanese should also pick up a copy of the detailed *Guide Map Miyako*.

The centrally located **Hirara-Nishizato Post Office** (平良西里郵便局; Map p800; 142 Nishizato, Hirara; ☐ 9am-5pm Mon-Fri, ATM to 7pm) has an international ATM.

ℹ Getting There & Away

Miyako-jima has direct flights to/from Tokyo's Haneda Airport (JTA/ANA), Osaka's Kansai Airport (ANA), Naha (JTA/RAC/ANA) and Ishigaki (RAC/ANA).

ℹ Getting Around

Miyako-jima has a limited bus network that operates from two bus stands in Hirara. Buses run between the airport and Hirara (¥210, 10 minutes). Buses also depart from Yachiyo bus terminal for Ikema-jima (¥500, 35 minutes), and from the Miyako Kyōei bus terminal, 700m east of town, to Yoshino-kaigan/Boraga Beach (¥500, 50 minutes). Yet another line runs between Hirara and Yoneha-Maehama/Kurima-jima (¥390, 30 minutes).

The island's flat terrain is perfectly suited to biking; hire bicycles at the guesthouse Hiraraya in Hirara.

If you want to move faster, there are rental-car counters at the airport and offices in Hirara.

Irabu-jima & Shimoji-jima
伊良部島・下地島

Not much goes on in Irabu-jima and Shimoji-jima aside from sugar-cane cultivation and the 'touch-and-go' (landing and immediate take-off) exercises by ANA pilots. These islands are blessed with uncrowded beaches and a snail-paced vibe – well worth a day trip from Miyako-jima.

👁 Sights

Nakanoshima Beach
BEACH

(中の島ビーチ; Map p799) Easily the best snorkelling beach, Nakanoshima Beach is protected by a high-walled bay on the west coast of Shimoji-jima. You'll greatly enhance your experience by making your visit early in the morning, around lunchtime or in lower seasons, when buses and boats aren't descending on the beach all at once. Look for the sign reading 'Nakano Island The Beach'.

Tōri-ike
CAVE

(通り池; Map p799) An intriguing site for a stroll or dive is this pair of seawater pools on the west coast of Shimoji-jima, known by locals as 'dragon's eyes' – these are actually sinkholes in the coral that formed the island.

Toguchi-no-hama
BEACH

(渡口の浜; Map p799) On Irabu-jima's west coast, this is the island's best swimming beach, with showers, toilets and a small cafe (open in high season).

🛏 Sleeping & Eating

As the new bridge has opened up these sleepy isles, more eating options have begun to sprout, but a reliably lovely standby is the cafe at Soraniwa.

Guesthouse Birafuya
GUESTHOUSE ¥

(ゲストハウスびらふやー; Map p799; ☑0980-78-3380; 1436-1 Irabu; dm/s/d ¥2000/3000/5000, breakfast ¥300) A few blocks inland from the beach, this tiny guesthouse is run by welcoming, clued-in couple Aya and Raita, who have made it a social hub for local musicians and artists. They offer inexpensive bike rental, snorkelling tours, sunset beers on the rooftop patio and an all-around serene vibe. Stay a week and you'll get one night free.

Casa de Hamaca
GUESTHOUSE ¥

(カサ・デ・アマカ; Map p799; ☑080-3277-8941; 621-3 Kuninaka; s/d without bathroom ¥3000/5400; ⊗closed Jan-Mar; [P][❄][🤶]) If you're seeking something out of the ordinary, opt to stay at the singular, utterly delightful Casa de Hamaca. Run by Japanese runner and world traveller Sekiyama Tadashi, this is likely the only accommodation in Japan outfitted solely with hammocks *and* with a Spanish-speaking proprietor. He also rents out bicycles for exploring the islands by the best means (¥500 per day for guests).

⭐ Soraniwa
BOUTIQUE HOTEL ¥¥

(そらにわ; Map p799; ☑0980-74-5528; www.soraniwa.org; 721-1 Irabu-azairabu; s incl breakfast/2 meals from ¥12,500/17,000, lunch ¥950-1400; [P][❄][@]) For a secluded and romantic experience, head to Soraniwa on the south coast. This small, stylish cafe-hotel is run by a young couple transplanted from the 'mainland'. The restaurant (open 11.30am to 6pm Friday to Tuesday) uses local, organic ingredients, while the intimate, modern hotel features sumptuous beds, shelves made from repurposed wood and a rooftop Jacuzzi looking on to the sea.

ℹ Getting There & Around

Irabu-jima and Shimoji-jima are connected to each other and Miyako-jima via a bridge; and can be accessed by bus or car.

YAEYAMA ISLANDS
八重山諸島

At the far southwestern end of the Southwest Islands are the gorgeous Yaeyama Islands, which include the main islands of Ishigaki-jima and Iriomote-jima as well as a spread of 17 isles. Located near the Tropic of Cancer, they are renowned for their lovely beaches, superb diving and lush landscapes.

The Yaeyama Islands are arguably the top destination in the Southwest Islands. They offer Japan's best snorkelling and diving, and some of the country's last intact subtropical jungles and mangrove swamps (both on Iriomote-jima). Perhaps the best feature of the Yaeyamas is their variety and the ease with which you can explore them: plentiful ferry services run between Ishigaki City and nearby islands such as Iriomote-jima and Taketomi-jima, and you can easily explore three or four islands in one trip.

Ishigaki-jima
石垣島

☑0980 / POP 47,660

Blessed with excellent beaches and brilliant dive sites, Ishigaki-jima also possesses an attractive, low-lying geography that invites long drives and day hikes. Located 100km southwest of Miyako-jima, Ishigaki is the most populated and developed island in the

Yaeyama group and embodies tropical Japan through and through.

◉ Sights

Ishigaki City (石垣市) occupies the southwestern corner of the island. You'll find most of the action in the two shopping arcades known as **Euglena Mall** (ユーグレナモール), which run parallel to the main street, Shiyakusho-dōri. The city is easily walkable; while it can be explored in an hour or two, it's worth spending a half-day here to get a sense of the local identity.

The sea around Ishigaki-jima is famous among the Japanese diving community for its large schools of manta rays, particularly from June to October. Some of the best beaches on the island are found on the west coast.

A series of roads branch out from Ishigaki City and head along the coastline and into the interior. There are several settlements near the coast, while most of the interior is mountains and farmland.

Ishigaki City Yaeyama Museum　MUSEUM
(石垣市立八重山博物館; Map p807; ☏ 0980-82-4712; 4-1 Tonoshiro; ¥200; ◷9am-5pm Tue-Sun) This modest museum has exhibits on the culture and history of the island, which are quite well presented with English explanations. Notable among the more typical cultural artefacts: a few informational pages about some of Japan's oldest human remains (estimated, using carbon dating, to be 24,000 years old), discovered on Ishigaki in 2011 during construction of the new airport.

Miyara Dōnchi　HISTORIC BUILDING
(宮良殿内; Map p807; 178 Ōkawa; ¥200; ◷9am-5pm Wed-Mon) The unique home of a Ryūkyū kingdom official dates from 1819; walk north along Sanbashi-dōri until you see signs in English. The house is still an actual residence, so you can only peer into the open rooms from the outside and enjoy the small garden.

Yonehara Beach　BEACH
(米原海岸; Map p804) On the north coast along Rte 79, Yonehara Beach is a decent sand beach with a good bit of reef offshore. Hire snorkel gear (¥1000) at any of the shops along the main road, where you'll also find plentiful cafes. Be aware that the currents can be strong, so it's not a great choice for children or weak swimmers.

★**Kabira-wan**　BEACH
(川平湾; Map p804) Kabira-wan is a sheltered bay with white-sand shores and a couple of interesting clumplike islets offshore. Swimming is not allowed in the bay, as pearls are cultivated here, but there's no shortage of glass-bottomed boats offering up a look at the reef life below.

★**Sunset Beach**　BEACH
(サンセットビーチ; Map p804) At the north end of the island, on the west coast, you will find this long strip of sand with a bit of offshore reef. As the name implies, this is one of the island's best spots to watch the sun set into the East China Sea. Shower and toilet facilities are also located here.

🏃 Activities

Umicoza　DIVING
(海講座; Map p804; ☏0980-88-2434; www.umicoza.com; 1287 97 Kabira; 1/2 dives with equipment rental ¥9450/12,600; ◷8am-6pm) At Kabira-based Umicoza, all the dive guides speak English, and the shop itself has a long-running reputation for professionalism and reliability.

Manta Scramble　DIVING
(Map p804) The most popular dive spot on Ishigaki-jima is Manta Scramble, off the coast of Kabira Ishizaki. Although you'll likely be sharing with a fair number of dive boats, you're almost guaranteed to see a manta (or four) in season. There are a number of dive shops on Ishigaki.

🛏 Sleeping

Ishigaki City has several inexpensive guesthouses as well as a swankier beach resort, plus everything in between. The northern end of the island is less developed and has some lovely retreats.

★**Iriwa**　GUESTHOUSE ¥
(イリワ; Map p804; ☏0980-88-2563; http://iriwa.org; 599 Kabira; dm ¥2700, s/d from ¥4800/8200; P✸@🛜) Just above Kabira-wan on the north coast, Iriwa is a comfortable guesthouse with dorm beds, two large private rooms, a small self-contained cottage and two converted trailers, all warmly decorated with a Hawaiian aesthetic. All but one trailer share bathroom facilities. It's run by a super-chilled, friendly young Korean/Japanese couple who like to share meals and snorkelling expeditions with guests.

Yaeyama Islands

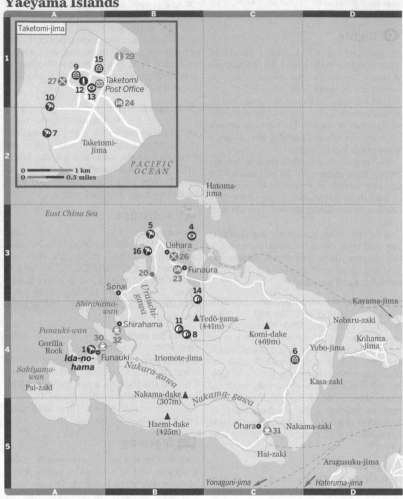

Yaeyama Islands

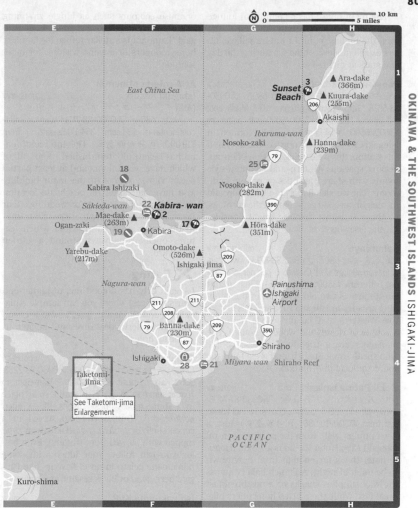

The main house has a communal lounge room and spacious, sunny kitchen – the roof, the highest point in Kabira village, offers excellent views of the sea during the day and stars at night.

Pension Yaima-biyōri
GUESTHOUSE ¥

(ペンションやいま日和; Map p807; ☎0980-88-5578; http://yaimabiyori.com; 10-7 Miaski-chō; s/d without bathroom ¥3200/5600, with bathroom ¥3600/6600; P❄@🛜) Centrally located in Ishigaki City two blocks north of the ferry and bus station, this welcoming pension offers appealing, spacious Western- and Japanese-style rooms with shared facilities or private bathrooms. The wooden floors are a bit creaky and the neighbourhood gets going in the evenings, so those sensitive to noise might consider staying elsewhere.

Rakutenya
GUESTHOUSE ¥

(楽天屋; Map p807; ☎0980-83-8713; www3.big.or.jp/~erm8p3gi; 291 Ōkawa; r per person without bathroom ¥3500; P❄@🛜) This quaint guesthouse is two blocks north of the shopping arcades in Ishigaki City, and has attractive Western- and Japanese-style rooms in a couple of rickety old wooden houses. The managers are a friendly Japanese couple who speak some English, and are a fantastic source of local information.

Hotel Patina Ishigaki-jima
HOTEL ¥¥

(ホテルパティーナ石垣島; ☎0980-87-7400; www.patina.in; 1-8-5 Yashima-chō; s/tw incl breakfast from ¥7300/10,500; P🐶❄@🛜) Just a few minutes' walk from the port and central Ishigaki City, Hotel Patina is a small, friendly hotel that's far enough from downtown to be quiet at night. A French bakery across the way supplies snacks or a postbreakfast breakfast, while the relaxed hotel offers bike and scooter rentals as well as free laundry (dryers are coin operated).

★Tsundara Beach Retreat
APARTMENT ¥¥¥

(つんだらビーチ・リトリート; Map p804; ☎090-7587-2029, 0980-89-2765; http://tsundarabeach.com; 895-2 Nosoko; d/tr/q incl breakfast ¥40,000/50,000/60,000; P❄🛜) Truly a retreat, this spacious, fully equipped beach house affords privacy and peace in beautiful abundance. On Ishigaki's sparsely populated northern peninsula, the house sits on a 1-hectare grassy property with a vegetable garden, trails to the gorgeous private beach and an enormous tepee.

The pacifist American owners (who speak fluent Japanese and live on the premises) can organise ecotours such as jungle zip-lining and are extremely knowledgable about Ishigaki. Tsundara is a stellar refuge for families, honeymooners or anyone wishing for quiet solitude.

ANA Intercontinental Ishigaki Resort
HOTEL ¥¥¥

(ANAインターコンチネンタル石垣リゾート; Map p804; ☎0980-88-7111; www.anaintercontinental-ishigaki.com; 354-1 Maezato; r from ¥19,000; P🐶❄@🛜🏊) The Intercontinental has beautifully refurbished rooms, all of which have wood floors and at least partial ocean views; rooms in the main building also have balconies. Its beachside location makes it a popular spot for weddings. Our favourite rooms are the more spacious ones in the lower-scale Coral Wing, which features open-air hallways around a garden courtyard.

✖ Eating

Ishigaki City has a good mix of higher-end touristy places, where you can sample Ishigaki beef and Okinawan fare, as well as cheap and atmospheric local dives and boisterous watering holes.

Oishiisā-gu
NOODLES ¥

(おいシーサー遇; Map p804; ☎0980-88-2233; 906-1 Kabira; meals ¥600-1000; ⏱11am-5pm, to 7pm in summer; P📷) This sunlit *soba* place in Kabira serves local dishes like chilled *yomogi-soba* (mugwort *soba*) served in a conch shell, or *tebichi soba* (Okinawan *soba* topped with stewed pork trotters). Even better, you can follow your lunch with some homemade gelato in novel flavours like Ishigaki beer, *gōyā* or black sesame and soybean.

Ishigaki-jima Kids
SOBA ¥

(石垣島キッズ; Map p807; ☎0980-83-8671; 203-1 Ōkawa; meals ¥850; ⏱noon-2pm & 6-9pm Thu-Tue) Tucked into a tiny, tidy space in Euglena Mall, Ishigaki-jima Kids serves good Yaeyama-style cafe fare – *sōki-soba,* taco rice and the like – all detailed in a picture menu. There's usually a great lunch set of taco rice or *Yaeyama soba* (soba topped with tiny pieces of tender pork, bean sprouts and scallions) with a glass of Orion beer for ¥1250.

★Paikaji
IZAKAYA ¥¥

(南風; Map p807; ☎0980-82-6027; 219 Ōkawa; dishes ¥700; ⏱5pm-midnight) This Ishigaki City favourite serves all the Okinawan and Yaeyama standards. The boisterous

Ishigaki City

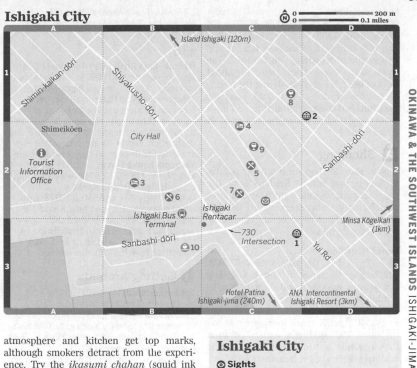

atmosphere and kitchen get top marks, although smokers detract from the experience. Try the *ikasumi chahan* (squid ink fried rice; ¥700), *gōyā champurū* (¥750) or *sashimi moriawase* (sashimi assortment; ¥750/1300/1800 depending on size). Look for the traditional front, with coral around the entryway and a red-and-white sign.

Ishigakijima Village   JAPANESE ¥¥
(石垣島ヴィレッジ; Map p807; ☑0980-87-0708; 8-9 Misaki-chō; meals around ¥2000; ⊙11am-10pm, individual shop hours vary) A contemporary version of the old-school dining *yokochō* (alleys) ferreted away in Japanese cities, this new restaurant complex is the perfect place to dine when feeling indecisive. Tiny eateries, each with some culinary speciality – be it Ishigaki beef, *izakaya* eats or Italian food – all vie for your attention here. Friendly restaurateurs and locals are the icing on the cake.

🍷 Drinking & Nightlife

Cafe Taniwha   BAR
(カフェたにふぁ; Map p807; ☑0980-88-6352; 188 Ōkawa; ⊙11am-11pm Tue-Sat) You can't do better than Cafe Taniwha as a first stop in Ishigaki. Owners and citizens of the world Kuri and Fusa have created a snug,

Ishigaki City

welcoming space for local eccentrics and international travellers. They sometimes host live music, and it's a great place to start your evening or park yourself for the duration.

Mori-no-Kokage
IZAKAYA

(森のこかげ; Map p807; ☑0980-83-7933; 199 Ōkawa; dishes ¥800; ⏱5pm-midnight Fri-Wed) This little Ishigaki City *izakaya* is a friendly refuge true to its name, which means 'the shade of the forest'. Local treats are sliced steak of Ishigaki beef (¥1280) and the microbrew *ishigaki-jima-zake* (¥500). Look for the plants and tree trunks outside, and meet some friendly locals under the canopy of an ersatz forest.

🛍 Shopping

A good place to shop for *o-miyage* (souvenirs) is in and around Euglena Mall, the main shopping arcade, which also houses a public market. Shopkeepers start slashing prices in the hour or so before closing up shop in the early evening.

Minsā Kōgeikan
ART

(みんさー工芸館; Map p804; ☑0980-82-3473; 909 Tonoshiro; ⏱9am-6pm) Minsā Kōgeikan is a weaving workshop and showroom with exhibits on Yaeyama Islands textiles. You can also try your hand at weaving a coaster (¥1500); you'll need to reserve ahead by phone. The building is located between the city centre and the airport, and can be reached via the airport bus (there's a Minsā Kōgeikan stop).

ℹ Information

There's a small but helpful **information counter** (☑0980-87-0468; ⏱7.30am-9pm) in the arrivals hall of the airport.

Ishigaki City's **Tourist Information Office** (石垣市観光協会; Map p807; ☑0980-82-2809; 1st fl, Ishigaki-shi Shōkō Kaikan; ⏱8.30am-5.30pm Mon-Fri) sometimes has English-speaking staff available and always has an English-language *Yaeyama Islands* brochure. Japanese readers should pick up the *Ishigaki Town Guide* and the *Yaeyama Navi*. All of the above publications can also be found at the ferry terminal downtown.

In downtown Ishigaki City, **Yaeyama Post Office** (八重山郵便局; Map p807; ☑0980-82-3742; 12 Ōkawa; ⏱lobby 9am-7pm Mon-Fri, to 3pm Sat, ATM 8am-9pm) has international ATMs.

ℹ Getting There & Away

AIR

Ishigaki-jima's **Painushima Ishigaki Airport** (南ぬ島石垣空港; Map p804; ☑0980-87-0468; www.ishigaki-airport.co.jp; ⏱7.30am-9pm) has direct flights to/from Tokyo's Narita Airport (Vanilla Air) and Haneda Airport (JTA/ANA), Osaka's Kansai International Airport (JTA/ANA/Peach Airlines), Naha (JTA/ANA), Miyako-jima (RAC/ANA) and Yonaguni-jima (RAC).

BOAT

Ishigaki-jima Rittō Ferry Terminal (石垣港離島ターミナル; Map p807) serves islands including Iriomote-jima, Kohama-jima, Taketomi-jima and Hateruma-jima. Departures are frequent enough that you can usually just turn up in the morning and hop on the next ferry departing for your intended destination (except during the summer high season). The three main ferry operators are **Yaeyama Kankō Ferry** (八重山観光フェリー; Map p807; ☑0980-82-5010; www.yaeyama.co.jp), **Ishigaki Dream Kankō** (石垣島ドリーム観光; Map p807; ☑0980-84-3178; www.ishigaki-dream.co.jp) and **Anei Kankō** (安栄観光; Map p807; ☑0980-83-0055; www.aneikankou.co.jp; ⏱6am-10pm). To get to the ferry terminal, head southwest along the waterfront from the 730 Intersection.

ℹ Getting Around

The **bus terminal** (Map p807) is across the road from the ferry terminal in Ishigaki City. Several buses an hour go to the airport (¥540, 45 minutes). A few daily buses go to Kabira-wan (¥680, 50 minutes) and Yonehara Beach (¥820, one hour). One-/five-day (¥1000/2000) bus passes are available for purchase directly from the driver.

Rental cars, scooters and bicycles are readily available at shops throughout the city centre. If you're comfortable on a scooter, it's a scenic four- to five-hour cruise around the island, though you should plan for longer if you want to spend some time relaxing on the island's beaches. **Ishigaki Rentacar** (石垣島レンタカー; Map p807; ☑0980-82-8840; 25 Ōkawa; ⏱8am-7pm) is located in the city centre and has reasonable rates.

Iriomote-jima 西表島

☑0980 / POP 2402

Although it's only 20km west of Ishigaki-jima, Iriomote-jima could easily qualify as Japan's last frontier. Dense jungles and mangrove swamp blanket more than 90% of the island, and it's fringed by some of the most beautiful coral reefs in all Japan. If you're super-lucky, you may even spot one of the island's rare *yamaneko*, a nocturnal and rarely seen wildcat (they are most often seen crossing the road at night, so drive carefully after dark).

Several rivers penetrate far into the lush interior of the island and these can be explored by riverboat or kayak. Add to the mix sun-drenched beaches and spectacular diving and snorkelling, and it's easy to see why Iriomote-jima is one of the best destinations in Japan for nature lovers.

◉ Sights

Iriomote-jima's best sights are its natural features – beaches speckled with star sand, year-round waterfalls and green rivers snaking through mangroves. The majority of the island's beaches are shallow due to the extensive coral reef that surrounds the island.

★ Ida-no-hama   BEACH
(イダの浜; Map p804) From **Shirahama** (白浜港; Map p804), at the western end of the north coast road, there are four daily boats (¥500) to the isolated settlement of **Funauki** (船浦港; Map p804). Once there, it's a mere 10-minute walk on to the absolutely gorgeous Ida-no-hama.

Hoshisuna-no-hama   BEACH
(星砂の浜; Star Sand Beach; Map p804) If you're looking to do a bit of snorkelling, head to this beach on the northwestern tip of the island. The beach is named after its star sand, which actually consists of the dried skeletons of marine protozoa. If you are a competent swimmer and the sea is calm, make your way with mask and snorkel to the outside of the reef – the coral and tropical fish here are spectacular.

Iriomote Wildlife
Conservation Center   MUSEUM
(西表野生生物保護センター; Map p804; ☑ 0980-85-5581; Komi Taketomi; ⊘ 10am-4pm Tue-Sun, closed noon-1pm) **FREE** If you are at all intrigued by the *yamaneko* (Iriomote's endemic wildcat), whose critically endangered population hovers around 100, it's worth stopping by this small natural-history centre. Exhibits include English signage, and they also screen a short documentary film in Japanese about the *yamaneko* and its population decline, due to hazards like human refuse and fast cars. A basic pamphlet in English is available for ¥100.

Pinaisāra-no-taki   WATERFALL
(ピナイサーラの滝; Map p804) At the back of a mangrove-lined bay called **Funaura-wan**, a few kilometres east of Uehara, you can make out the lovely Pinaisāra-no-taki, Okinawa's highest waterfall at 55m. When the tide is right, you can paddle a kayak across the shallow lagoon and then follow

the Hinai-gawa (on the left) to the base of the falls.

The short Māre-gawa (on the right) meets a trail where it narrows. This climbs to the top of the falls, from where there are superb views down to the coast. From the river, walk inland until you come to a pumping station, then turn around and take the right fork in the path. The walk takes less than two hours, and the river is great for a cooling dip.

Unfortunately, it is difficult to find a tour company that will rent you a kayak without requiring you to join a guided tour (half-/full days cost about ¥6000/10,000).

Tsuki-ga-hama   BEACH
(月ヶ浜; Moon Beach; Map p804) The best swimming beach on the island is Tsuki-ga-hama, a crescent-shaped yellow-sand beach at the mouth of the Urauchi-gawa on the north coast.

🏃 Activities

Fully immerse yourself in Iriomote's beauty by trekking in the jungle, kayaking between banks of mangroves or snorkelling around its accessible reefs.

Hiking

Iriomote has some great hikes, but do not head off into the jungle interior without registering with the police: the trails in the interior are hard to follow – many people have become lost and required rescue. We strongly suggest that you stick to well-marked tracks like the ones along the Urauchi-gawa, or arrange for a guide through your accommodation (from ¥10,000).

Diving

Much of the brilliant coral fringing Iriomote's shores is accessible to proficient snorkellers. Most of the offshore dive sites around Iriomote are served by dive operators based on Ishigaki.

One spot worth noting is the unusual **Barasu-tō** (バラス島; Map p804) – an islet formed entirely of bits of broken coral – located between Iriomote-jima and Hatoma-jima; the reefs nearby are good for calm days.

👉 Tours

Iriomote's number-one attraction is a boat trip up the **Urauchi-gawa** (浦内川), a winding brown river reminiscent of a tiny stretch of the Amazon. This is a great, accessible way to get a feel for Iriomote's inner-island wildness.

Iriomote Osanpo Kibun
KAYAKING

(西表おさんぽ気分; ☑0980-84-8178; www.iriomote-osanpo.com; full-/half-day kayaking & trekking tours from ¥10,000/6000) Choose from trekking, kayaking and snorkelling tours with this reliable outfit, all with an English-speaking guide who will illuminate your experience with local knowledge. This is the easiest way to check out Pinaisāra-no-taki (p809) and Iriomote's other natural attractions on land and water. Tour prices normally include lunch and transfers.

Urauchi-gawa Kankō
TOURS

(浦内川観光; Map p804; ☑0980-85-6154; www.urauchigawa.com; adult/child river tours ¥1800/900, full-day trekking & kayak tours ¥8400) From the river's mouth, Urauchi-gawa Kankō runs boat tours 8km up the river (round trip ¥1800, 30 minutes each way, multiple departures daily between 9.30am and 3.30pm). At the 8km point, the boat docks and you can walk a further 2km to the scenic waterfalls of **Mariyudō-no-taki** (マリユドゥの滝; Map p804), from where another 200m brings you to another waterfall, **Kanpire-no-taki** (カンピレーの滝; Map p804).

The return walk from the dock back to Kanpire-no-taki takes around two hours. You can also opt to just take the boat trip to the dock and back. The **pier** (浦内川遊覧船乗場) is about 6km west of Uehara; river trips don't require reservations, but the full-day kayaking trips do.

🛏 Sleeping

Iriomote-jima's accommodation is spread out around the island. Most places will send a car to pick you up from the ferry terminal if you let them know what time you will be arriving.

Kanpira-sō
MINSHUKU ¥

(カンピラ荘; ☑0980-85-6508; www.kanpira.com; 545 Uehara; r per person with/without bathroom from ¥4700/3700; P✳🛱) Two minutes' walk from the ferry landing in Uehara, this hospitable *minshuku* has basic Japanese-style rooms and an informative manager who produces extraordinarily good bilingual maps of the island (although little English is spoken here). Rates include breakfast. From Uehara Port, turn right on the main road; you'll soon see it on the right.

Irumote-sō
HOSTEL ¥

(いるもて荘; Map p804; ☑0980-85-6255; 870-95 Uehara; dm incl/excl dinner from ¥5300/4000, r per person incl/excl dinner ¥7250/5900; P✳@🛱) Between Uehara Port (上原港) and Funaura Port (船浦港), this peaceful hillside hostel has comfortable dorms and simple Japanese-style private rooms. Meals are served in the large communal dining room. We recommend calling for a pick-up before you arrive as it's hard to find. Discounts available for Hostelling International members.

Coral Garden
PENSION ¥¥

(コーラルガーデン; Map p804; ☑0980-85-6027; www.e-iriomote.com; 289-17 Uehara; s/d incl breakfast from ¥8500/13,000; ⏰closed Dec-Feb; P✳@🛱) A five-minute drive from Uehara, this beachside pension has simple Japanese- and Western-style rooms overlooking Hoshisuna-no-hama (p809). There's a small pool, and a path leading down to the beach, which is a great spot for snorkelling. Call ahead for pick-up from the port.

🍴 Eating

With few restaurants on the island, most travellers prefer to take meals at their accommodation (or self-cater). But Iriomote also has some good options for a meal out.

Densā Shokudō
OKINAWAN ¥

(デンサー食堂; Map p804; ☑0980-85-6453; 558 Uehara; meals ¥850; ⏰11.30am-6pm Thu-Mon, to 4pm Tue) This comfy daytime eatery serves up Okinawan favourites, like *gōyā champurū teishoku* (¥850) and *Yaeyama soba* (¥500), in a homey dining room with an outdoor terrace. Browse a selection of manga (comics) while you wait. It's directly across the road once you head out of the Uehara Port.

Laugh La Garden
OKINAWAN ¥

(ラフラガーデン; ☑0980-85-7088; 2nd fl, 550-1 Uehara; dishes ¥900; ⏰11.30am-2pm & 6-9pm Fri-Wed) Near the road from Uehara Port and beside the petrol station, this relaxed cafe-restaurant has sets such as *ishigakib-uta-no-misokatsu teishoku* (miso-seasoned Ishigaki pork cutlets; ¥950) and Iriomote delicacies such as *inoshishi-sashimi* (wild boar sashimi; ¥600).

Kitchen Inaba
OKINAWAN ¥¥

(Map p804; ☑0980-84-8164; http://kitchen-inaba.com; 742-6 Uehara; dishes ¥400-1800; ⏰11.30am-2.30pm & 6-8.30pm; P✳📶) In the

Tsuki-ga-hama area, the relatively upmarket Kitchen Inaba serves the usual local specialities in a spot where no other dining options exist. It's a lovely place for a meal if you're spending a day at the beach and are reliant on public transport; consider making reservations for the sometimes crowded dinner hours.

❶ Getting There & Away

Yaeyama Kankō Ferry (八重山観光フェリー; ☑ 0980-82-5010; www.yaeyama.co.jp; to Uehara/Ōhara ¥2060/1570), **Ishigaki Dream Kankō** (石垣島ドリーム観光; ☑ 0980-84-3178; www.ishigaki-dream.co.jp; to Uehara/Ōhara ¥1420/1570) and **Anei Kankō** (安栄観光; ☑ 0980-83-0055; www.aneikankou.co.jp; to Uehara/Ōhara ¥2060/1570) operate ferries between Ishigaki City (on Ishigaki-jima) and Iriomote-jima. Ferries from Ishigaki sail to/from two main ports on Iriomote: **Uehara Port** (上原港; Map p804), one hour, up to 20 daily, convenient for most destinations; and **Ōhara Port** (大原港; Map p804), 40 minutes, up to 27 daily. Strong north winds will require Uehara-bound ferries to travel the safer route to Ōhara; in these cases, buses at the port will shuttle passengers to Uehara for free.

❶ Getting Around

Iriomote-jima has a 58km-long perimeter road that runs about halfway around the coast. No roads run into the unspoiled interior.

Six to nine buses daily run between Ōhara Port and Shirahama (¥1240, 1½ hours); raise your hand to get on anywhere. There's a 'free pass' for buses (one-/three-day passes ¥1030/1540) that also gives you 10% off attractions such as the Urauchi-gawa cruise.

If you have an International Driving Permit, try **Yamaneko Rentacar** (やまねこレンタカー; Map p804; ☑ 0980-85-6111; 984-57 Uehara; ⏰ 8am-6pm).

Most of the island accommodation also rent out bicycles to guests.

Taketomi-jima 竹富島

☑ 0980 / POP 361

A mere 15-minute boat ride from Ishigaki-jima, the tiny island of Taketomi-jima is a living museum of Ryūkyū culture. Centred on a flower-decorated village of traditional houses complete with red *kawara* (tiled) roofs, coral walls and *shiisā* statues, Taketomi is a breath of fresh air if you're suffering from an overdose of modern Japan.

In order to preserve the island's historical ambience, residents have joined together to ban some signs of modernism. The island is criss-crossed by crushed-coral roads bedecked with bougainvillea and is free of chain convenience stores.

While Taketomi is besieged by Japanese day trippers in the busy summer months, the island remains blissfully quiet at night. This is true even in summer, as the island offers little in the way of after-dark entertainment. If you have the chance, it's worth spending a night here as Taketomi truly weaves its spell after the sun dips below the horizon.

Ferries arrive at the small port on the northeast corner of the island, while Taketomi village is located in the centre of the island.

⊙ Sights

There are a number of modest sights in Taketomi village, though it's best to simply wandering around and soaking up the surrounds. Hiring a bicycle is the ideal way to do this, as you pedal along crushed-coral roads, ceding right of way to placidly plodding ox-carts and admiring the variety of *shiisā* adorning local homes and walls.

Nagomi-no-tō   MONUMENT
(なごみの塔; Map p804; ⏰ 24hr) **FREE** Roughly in the centre of the village, this modest lookout tower has good views over the red-tiled roofs of the pancake-flat island.

Nishitō Utaki   SHRINE
(西塘御嶽; Map p804) This shrine is dedicated to a 16th-century ruler of the Yaeyama Islands who was born on Taketomi-jima, and whose tomb lies behind the shrine.

Kihōin Shūshūkan   MUSEUM
(喜宝院蒐集館; Map p804; ☑ 0980-85-2202; ¥300; ⏰ 9am-5pm) At the west of the village, this private museum houses a diverse collection of local folk artefacts.

Taketomi Mingei-kan   GALLERY
(竹富民芸館; Map p804; ☑ 0980-85-2302; 381-4 Taketomi; ⏰ 9am-5pm) **FREE** This is the workshop where the island's woven *minsā* belts and other textiles are produced.

Kaiji-hama   BEACH
(カイジ浜; 皆治浜; Map p804) On the southwest coast is Kaiji-hama, this lovely stretch of beach also happens to be the main *hoshi-suna* (star sand) hunting ground. If you don't arrive here bearing some kind of container for the miniscule treasures,

there's usually a stall selling small vials of star sand.

Kondoi Beach   BEACH
(コンドイビーチ; Map p804) Kondoi Beach, on the west coast, offers the best swimming on the island, after you've negotiated your way through the gamut of the Kondoi's resident feral cats. At the entrance to the beach you'll find bike parking, picnic tables and toilets.

🛏 Sleeping & Eating

Many of the traditional houses around the island are Japanese-style ryokan. Note that Taketomi fills up quickly in the summer, so be sure to book ahead if you plan to stay overnight.

One of the ubiquitous menu items on Taketomi is *Yaeyama soba* – similar to Okinawan *sōki-soba,* soba topped with tiny pieces of tender pork, bean sprouts and scallions.

Takana Ryokan   RYOKAN ¥
(高那旅館; Map p804; ☑ 0980-85-2151; www.kit.hi-ho.ne.jp/hayasaka-my; 499 Taketomi; dm incl/excl meals ¥5000/3500, r per person incl meals from ¥8800; ❀) Opposite the tiny post office, Takana consists of a basic youth hostel and an attached upmarket ryokan. Basic Western-style dorms in the youth hostel are a great option if you're on a budget, though the Japanese-style tatami rooms in the ryokan are a bit more comfortable.

Soba-dokoro Takenoko   NOODLES ¥
(そば処竹の子; Map p804; ☑ 0980-85-2251; 101-1 Taketomi; dishes ¥800; ⏰ 10.30am-4pm & 7-9pm; ▣) This tiny restaurant on the northwest side of the village (look for the blue banner and the umbrellas) serves up *sōki-soba* (¥800) and *Yaeyama soba* (¥600) in amazing broth.

ℹ Information

There's a basic **information desk** (Map p804; ☑ 0980-84-5633; ⏰ 7.30am-6pm) in the port building.

An international ATM is in the **post office** (竹富郵便局; Map p804; ☑ 0980-85-2342; 500 Taketomi; ⏰ 9am-5pm Mon-Fri) in Taketomi village.

ℹ Getting There & Away

Yaeyama Kankō Ferry (八重山観光フェリー; Map p804; ☑ 0980-82-5010), **Ishigaki Dream Kankō** (石垣島ドリーム観光; Map p804;

☑ 0980-84-3178) and **Anei Kankō** (安栄観光; Map p804; ☑ 0980-83-0055) operate ferries between Ishigaki City (on Ishigaki-jima) and Taketomi-jima (¥600, 10 minutes, up to 45 daily).

ℹ Getting Around

Since the island is only 3km long and 2km wide, it is easily explored on foot or by bicycle. An assortment of bike-rental outfits meet arriving ferries at the port and run free shuttles between their shops and the port. The going rate for bike rentals is ¥300 per hour or ¥1500 for the day.

Another way to see the island is by taking a tour in a water-buffalo cart. Two operators in the village offer 30-minute rides (hosted in Japanese) for ¥1200 per person.

Hateruma-jima   波照間島
☑ 0980 / POP 528

Forty-five kilometres south of Iriomote-jima is the tiny islet of Hateruma-jima, Japan's southernmost inhabited island. Just 15km around, Hateruma-jima has a couple of beauteous beaches and a seriously laid-back vibe.

Ferries arrive at the small port on the northwest corner of the island, while Hateruma village is in the centre.

⊚ Sights

Simple, rural island relaxation is the reason to come to Hateruma – encountering goats on the road, snorkelling impossibly clear water and taking a selfie at the southernmost point in Japan are probably the pinnacle of excitement here.

Nishihama   BEACH
(ニシ浜) Just to the west of the port is this perfect beach of snow-white sand with some good coral offshore. Here you will find free public showers, toilets and a camping ground.

Japan's Southernmost Point   LANDMARK
(日本最南端の碑) Cycling along roads criss-crossing fields of sugar cane and tracing kilometres of unspoiled coastline – the southernmost point in Japan feels appropriately far-flung once you've arrived. There's also a monument marking the spot, a popular locale for photo ops.

Takanazaki   BEACH
(高那崎) At the southeast corner of the island is this impressive 1km-long cliff of Ryūkyū limestone, pounded by the Pacific Ocean. There's a small **observatory** here,

and at the western end of the cliffs is a small monument marking Japan's southernmost point, an extremely popular photo spot for Japanese visitors and a must-do if you've come all this way.

🛏 Sleeping & Eating

You can book meals at most *minshuku;* self-caterers will find a few small shops in town.

House Minami MINSHUKU ¥
(ハウス美波; ☑ 0980-85-8050, 080-5885-5050; 3138 Hateruma; s/d from ¥3000/5000; P ✳ 🐾) East of the town centre, these fully equipped, detached quarters are arranged around a cosy courtyard close to sugar-cane fields. Though the proprietors don't speak English, they are very foreigner-friendly.

Pension Sainantan PENSION ¥¥
(ペンション最南端; ☑ 0980-85-8686; http://pensionsainantan.wixsite.com/hateruma/contact; 886-1 Hateruma; r per person incl 2 meals from ¥8800; P ✳ @) This airy pension offers Japanese-style rooms with small terraces downstairs and Western-style rooms with balconies upstairs. There's also a rooftop terrace with spectacular views of the beach and sea, and it's all three minutes' walk from Nishihama.

ℹ Getting There & Around

Anei Kankō (安栄観光; ☑ 0980-83-0055; www.aneikankou.co.jp) has three to four ferries a day to Hateruma-jima from Ishigaki (¥3090, one hour).

There is no public transport on the island. Rental bicycles and scooters are readily available for hire near the port and from the local *minshuku.*

Yonaguni-jima 与那国島

☑ 0980 / POP 1843

About 125km west of Ishigaki and 110km east of Taiwan is the island of Yonaguni-jima, Japan's westernmost inhabited island. Renowned for its strong sake, small horses and marlin fishing, the island is also home to the jumbo-sized Yonaguni atlas moth, the largest moth in the world.

However, most visitors come to see what lies beneath the waves. In 1985 a local diver discovered what appeared to be human-made 'ruins' off the south coast of the island. Adding to the underwater allure are the large schools of hammerhead sharks

that frequent the waters off the west coast, making Yonaguni perhaps the most famous single diving destination in Japan.

The ferry port of **Kubura** (久部良) is at the island's western extreme. The main settlement is around the secondary port of **Sonai** (祖納) on the north coast. In between, on the northwest coast, you'll find the airport.

◉ Sights

Yonaguni has an extremely rugged, wind- and sea-battered landscape, and the coastline is marked with dramatic rock formations, much like those on the east coast of Taiwan. The island's most notable examples are off the southeast coast.

Tachigami-iwa (立神岩), literally 'Standing-God Rock' (although another name might come to mind), is the most famous. This offshore obelisk can be viewed from several spots on the bluffs above. **Sanninu-dai** (サンニヌ台) and the aptly named **Gunkan-iwa** (軍艦岩; Battleship Rock) are two others to look for.

At the eastern tip of the island, wild Yonaguni horses graze in the pastures leading out to the lighthouse at **Agarizaki** (東崎). On the south coast of the island is the pleasant little village of Higawa, which has a wide, sandy crescent of beach, **Higawa-hama** (比川浜). The water here is clear and shallow, and a seawall makes it a calm spot for swimming and snorkelling.

Just as Hateruma-jima has a monument to mark Japan's southernmost point, the island of Yonaguni-jima has one to mark the country's westernmost point (日本最西端の碑) at **Irizaki** (西崎). If the weather is perfect, the mountains of Taiwan are visible far over the sea (this happens only about twice a year – don't be disappointed if you can't see them).

🏃 Activities

Local divers have long known about the thrill of swimming with schools of hammerhead sharks in the winter months at **Irizaki Point** (西崎ポイント).

In addition to diving, the seas off Yonaguni are also renowned for marlin, and the All-Japan Billfish Tournament is held here each year in June or July. Boats in Kubura can be chartered from ¥55,000 a day – call the **Yonaguni Fishing Co-operative** (与那国町漁協; ☑ in Japanese 0980-87-2803) for information.

★ **Kaitei Iseki**   DIVING

(海底遺跡, Underwater Ruins) The Kaitei Iseki were discovered by chance in 1985 by marine explorer Aratake Kihachirō. Some claim that these ruins, which look like giant blocks or the steps of a sunken pyramid, are the remains of a Pacific Atlantis, although there are equally compelling arguments that they are just the random result of geological processes.

Yonaguni Diving Service   DIVING

(与那国ダイビングサービス;   ☑0980-87-2658; 3984-3 Yonaguni; 2-dive boat trips ¥12,500, equipment rental ¥4600) The most reliable diving outfit on Yonaguni also runs the diver-friendly Minshuku Yoshimaru-sō in Kubura.

Mosura no Tamago   BOATING

(もすらのたまご; ☑0980-87-2112; 4022-380 Yonaguni; per person ¥3700) Offers glass-bottomed boat tours of Kaitei Iseki for nondivers.

🛏 Sleeping & Eating

It's wise to book accommodation ahead of your visit; Yonaguni is quite a distance to travel without a reservation.

There's a decent camping ground on the south coast near the village of Higawa, next to a nice beach called Kataburu-hama.

Your best bet is to book meals at your accommodation; self-caterers will find simple supermarkets in both Sonai and Kubura.

Minshuku Yoshimaru-sō   MINSHUKU ¥

(民宿よしまる荘; ☑0980-87-2658; www.yonaguniyds.com; 3984-3 Yonaguni; dm/r per person incl 2 meals ¥6000/7050; P🅿❄🛜) Up the hill from the port in Kubura, Yoshimaru-sō is ideal for divers, as the friendly owners also operate the on-site and long-standing Yonaguni Diving Service. Simple Japanese- and Western-style rooms have nice views of the nearby port and spacious communal bathing facilities.

The real appeal of this *minshuku* is the owners' local diving expertise. Book ahead to get picked up at the airport or ferry terminal.

Villa Eden no Sachi   RYOKAN ¥¥

(Villa エデンの幸旅館; ☑0980-87-2450; 4022-253 Yonaguni; per person incl 2 meals ¥9000; P❄🛜) Uphill to the north of Kubura's port,

this clean, bright ryokan offers a convenient and restful base for exploring Yonaguni.

Island Cuisine Isun   IZAKAYA ¥¥

(島料理; ☑0980-87-2158; 4022 Yonaguni; meals around ¥2500; ⊙11.30am-2pm & 6-11pm Thu-Tue) In Kubura, this cosy *izakaya* is a local favourite. Though the menu is in Japanese only, we recommend the *kajiki* (locally caught swordfish) sashimi and the *sansai* (locally gathered wild mountain vegetables) salad. Ask a Japanese speaker to make reservations for you, as it's a small and popular spot that fills up quickly.

Dōurai   IZAKAYA ¥¥

(どうーらい; ☑0980-87-2909; 62 Yonaguni; dishes ¥800; ⊙5pm-midnight Mon-Sat) In the centre of Sonai is this delightful little Okinawan *izakaya* that serves local specialities such as *Ishigakigyū-sutēki* (Ishigaki-style steak; ¥1300) and *rafutē* (gingered, stewed pork; ¥700). It's about 100m southeast of the post office in Sonai. Look for the small blue sign by the door.

ℹ Information

There is an **information counter** (☑0980-87-2402; ⊙8.30am-noon, phone after) in the airport, which can help you find accommodation. You can also pick up the Japanese-language *Yonaguni-jima* map, and an English-language version that includes set locations of the erstwhile TV drama *Dr Koto's Clinic,* which was set on Yonaguni.

Each post office in Kubura and Sonai has an international ATM.

ℹ Getting There & Around

RAC flies once daily between Yonaguni and Naha, and operates three flights a day between Yonaguni and Ishigaki-jima.

Fukuyama Kaiun (福山海運; ☑in Ishigaki 0980-82-4962, in Yonaguni 0980-87-2555) operates two ferries a week between Ishigaki-jima and Kubura Port on Yonaguni (¥3550, four hours). Be warned: these are not for the faint of stomach.

There are public buses here, but they make only four trips around the island per day, so the best transport is rental car or scooter. **Yonehama Rentacar** (米浜レンタカー; ☑0980-87-2148; www.yonehama.com; ⊙open for flight arrivals) offers very reasonable rates and has a counter inside the airport terminal.

Understand
Japan

Japan Today

The stubbornly stagnant economy and a shrinking population (projected to decline by one-third in the next half-century) have been a near constant backdrop for political discussion in Japan for decades. Was the post-WWII miracle growth a fluke, or could Japan pull it off again – ideally in time for the 2020 Olympics? There have been glimmers of hope on the economic front, but no one is popping champagne. Meanwhile, the 2011 earthquake has had the unexpected legacy of increased civic engagement.

Best on Film

Osaka Elegy (Mizoguchi Kenji; 1936) A modern girl makes her way in Osaka.
Tokyo Story (Ozu Yasujirō; 1953) Portrait of a family in rapidly changing, post-WWII Japan.
Lost in Translation (Sofia Coppola; 2003) Disorienting, captivating Tokyo through the eyes of two Americans.
Adrift in Tokyo (Satoshi Miki; 2008) Two luckless antiheroes on a long walk through the city.

Best in Print

A Different Kind of Luxury (Andy Couturier; 2010) Life lessons from Japanese who choose time and freedom over wealth.
The Wages of Guilt: Memories of War in Germany and Japan (Ian Buruma; 1994) A comparison of the postwar psyche in Japan and Germany.
The Book of Tokyo: A City in Short Fiction (Edited by Michael Emmerich, Jim Hinks and Masashi Matsuie; 2015) Ten stories by contemporary Japanese writers set in the capital.
Sazae-san (Hasegawa Machiko; 1946–74) Long-running manga (Japanese comic) of manners starring a plucky postwar housewife.

The Olympics

When the International Olympic Committee announced in 2013 that Tokyo would host the 2020 Summer Olympics, it felt like the first good news Japan had heard in ages. Now the media could talk about fun things again – like new stadium designs! The enthusiasm didn't last long though: with construction costs for the Zaha Hadid–designed stadium spiralling out of control, the government scrapped it in favour of a cheaper-to-make design by Kuma Kengo. While many locals disliked the Hadid stadium – saying it looked like a giant bicycle helmet – nobody is terribly excited about Kuma's either (which has been compared to a hamburger). With costs still snowballing, firm-fisted Tokyo governor Koike Yuriko has sent more plans back to the discussion table – and possibly the chopping block.

On a darker note, victims of the 2011 earthquake, who lost homes (and even whole communities) in the tsunami or to radiation have grown increasingly resentful, still living in temporary housing while public funds are spent on showpiece projects. Statistics from the Reconstruction Bureau report that as of 2016, there were still more than 100,000 (the majority of whom are from Fukushima) who are still living in temporary housing.

The Nuclear Power Dilemma

More than five years after the meltdown at the Fukushima nuclear power plant, nuclear power is still a hot topic. Before 2011, 30% of Japan's power was nuclear; by 2013, due to a combination of scheduled maintenance and revamped safety inspections, all reactors were offline. Carbon emissions rose 14% as Japan resorted to burning more oil. The government wants Japan back on the nuclear grid; in 2015, two reactors in Kyūshū went live, with more scheduled to follow.

Citizens and local governments, however, have been unusually proactive, some taking legal action to prevent nearby reactors from restarting in a David vs Goliath scenario that pits them against the central government and the national nuclear regulating body. Local residents in Fukui Prefecture petitioned (and succeeded in court) to keep their reactors offline, while Niigata Prefecture elected a governor running as an independent purely on a no-nukes platform in 2016.

Article 9

Article 9 of Japan's post-WWII constitution prohibits Japan from using military force in international conflict; however, the country maintains a Self Defense Force (SDF) that participates in UN peacekeeping missions abroad. In 2014 the Liberal Democratic Party (LDP) coalition government decided to reinterpret Article 9 to allow the SDF (a force of about 200,000) to come to the aid of allies.

In 2016, Prime Minister Shinzo Abe's cabinet approved the use of weapons in situations not limited to self-defence for soldiers participating in a mission in Sudan. This has led some to ask: could this escalate into more involvement in international armed conflicts?

Abe has suggested that his ultimate aim is to amend the constitution; however, a majority of the public is against a change; 2016 polls from Japan's leading newspaper show more than half the population to be against constitutional revision. The country's seniors – typically supporters of the LDP, but for whom memories of WWII and its aftermath remain potent – are particularly opposed; retirees have been hitting the streets for regular (and peaceful) protests for the first time in decades.

The Tourists Are Here!

Japan has long hoped to boost its underdeveloped inbound tourism industry. Then, it got real, by relaxing visa regulations for visitors from its Asian neighbours, which, along with the periodically weak yen, has resulted in a dramatic uptick of foreign visitors. Inbound numbers have more than doubled since 2010; in 2015 the country logged 19.7 million visitors, just shy of the 20 million target set for 2020.

There is hand-wringing, of course: How do we please them? Where are we going to park all these tour buses? And will we ever be able to visit Kyoto in peace again? But there is also intense fascination: What, exactly, do they find interesting about Japan? There has been an explosion of TV shows trying to figure that out, interviewing tourists (even sending TV personalities to check out places listed in the Lonely Planet guide). The popular show, 'You! ha nani shini nihon e?' ('Why did you come to Japan?') sends cameras to Narita Airport to look for interesting subjects and then follows them around (you've been warned!).

After decades of stagnation-bred doldrums, Japan is looking to the outside world for a pick-me-up: if people are willing to spend money to come here, it can't be so bad, right?

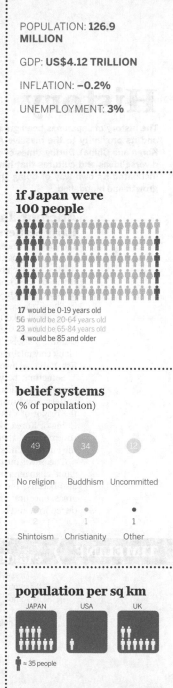

POPULATION: **126.9 MILLION**

GDP: **US$4.12 TRILLION**

INFLATION: **−0.2%**

UNEMPLOYMENT: **3%**

if Japan were 100 people

17 would be 0-19 years old
56 would be 20-64 years old
23 would be 65-84 years old
4 would be 85 and older

belief systems
(% of population)

49 No religion
34 Buddhism
12 Uncommitted

2 Shintoism
1 Christianity
1 Other

population per sq km

JAPAN   USA   UK

❚ ≈ 35 people

History

The history of Japan has been greatly shaped by both its isolation, as an island nation, and its proximity to the massive Asian continent (and particularly by its neighbours, Korea and China). During times of openness it has been a fascinating percolator of the diverse ideas and cultures that have appeared on its shores; in times of retreat it has incubated its own way of doing things. Like most histories, it is also one of conflict, growth and bloodshed.

Ancient Japan

Early Settlers

The earliest traces of human life in Japan date to around 30,000 years ago, but it is possible that people were here much earlier. Until the end of the last ice age about 15,000 years ago, a number of land bridges linked Japan to the continent – Siberia to the north, Korea to the west and probably present-day Taiwan to the south – so access was not difficult.

The first recognisable culture to emerge was the neolithic Jōmon, from about 13,000 BC. They were named by scholars after the 'rope-mark' pottery they made, by imprinting twisted cords on hand-formed ceramic vessels. The Jōmon lived a quasi-nomadic life in settlements along coastal areas, particularly in northeastern Japan, where they could fish, gather seaweed and wild mushrooms, and also hunt deer and bear.

Sometime between 800 and 300 BC a new culture began to take shape, that which is referred to as Yayoi (again after a distinctive form of pottery, now created on a wheel). There remains much debate regarding the origin of this shift, whether it was brought about by settlers from China or Korea (or both); the earliest known Yayoi settlements were discovered in northern Kyūshū, which is close to the Korean Peninsula, and the cultural shifts spread from there.

The Yayoi introduced wet rice farming techniques. This was a huge game-changer, not just because it demanded more stable settlement but also because the labour-intensive practice was better suited to lowland areas, encouraging population growth in fertile basins. They also introduced iron and bronze.

TIMELINE	c 13,000 BC	c 400 BC	3rd century AD
	First evidence of the hunter-gatherer Jōmon, neolithic peoples, who migrated from mainland Asia.	Yayoi people appear in southwest Japan (probably via Korea), practising wet rice cultivation and using metal tools. They also promote a sense of territoriality.	Queen Himiko reigns over a region called Yamatai and is recognised by Chinese visitors as 'over-queen' of Japan's more than 100 kingdoms.

By the 1st century AD, the Yayoi had spread to the middle of Honshū; northern Honshū could still be considered Jōmon territory until at least the 8th century (Hokkaidō and Okinawa were not even in the picture at this point).

Rise of the Yamato Clan

Agriculture-based settlement led to territories and boundaries being established. According to Chinese sources, by the end of the 3rd century AD there were more than a hundred kingdoms in Japan, some of which were ruled by a queen named Himiko. Where exactly her realm was located is disputed, with some scholars favouring northwest Kyūshū, but most favouring the Nara region. Her territory was known as Yamatai (possibly the origin for the later name Yamato); the Chinese also called this nascent state Wa, and referred to Himiko as its sovereign. Through tributes, she acknowledged her allegiance to the Chinese emperor.

Concurrently, a practice was spreading of burying tribal leaders in mounded tombs (called *kofun*), whose shape and size corresponded to status – evidence of a burgeoning material culture and increasing societal stratification. (After her death in 248, Himiko is said to have been buried in a massive tomb, along with 100 sacrificed slaves). This development ushered in the start of what scholars call the Kofun, or Yamato, period, during which administrative and military power began to coalesce around the Yamato clan in the Kansai basin.

FEATURE: MYTHIC ORIGINS

Once upon a time, the male and female deities Izanagi and Izanami came down to a watery world from Takamagahara (the Plains of High Heaven), to create land. Droplets from Izanagi's 'spear' solidified into the land now known as Japan, and Izanami and Izanagi then populated it with gods. One of these was Japan's supreme deity, the Sun Goddess Amaterasu (Light of Heaven), whose great-great-grandson Jimmu became the first emperor of Japan, reputedly in 660 BC.

This is the seminal creation myth of Japan, as it is laid out in Japan's first historical record books, the *Kojiki* (*Record of Old Things*; 712) and *Nihon Shoki* (*Record of Japan*; 720). The imperial family had these works compiled in the late 7th and early 8th centuries – to legitimise its power by tracing its lineage back to the divine.

Scholars are sceptical of the existence of the earliest emperors. Some believe the 10th emperor, Sujin, was the first to really exist, and was perhaps the founder of the Yamato dynasty (some also think he led a clan of horsemen into Japan from the Korean Peninsula). Different accounts place his reign anywhere from the 1st century BC to the 4th century AD.

Emperor Kinmei (509–71 AD), who reigned 539–71 AD, is the first emperor of verifiable historical record. According to the lineage of legend, he would have been the 29th emperor.

mid-5th century	mid-6th century	700s	710
Writing – and thus record-keeping – is introduced into Japan by scholars from the Korean kingdom of Baekje (though based on the Chinese system of characters).	Baekje scholars introduce Buddhism. Its texts can be read by a now-literate elite, who use it as a unifying tool.	The classical age of Japanese religious sculpture, in which some of Japan's greatest works of Buddhist art are produced (some still visible in and around Nara).	Japan's first capital is established at Nara, based on Chinese models. By now, Japan, with its estimated five million people, has many characteristics of a nation-state.

Starting under the reign of Empress Suiko (592–628) – and her powerful regent Prince Shōtoku (573–620) – a series of administrative reforms were enacted, inspired by Tang-dynasty China, to consolidate power through taxes, regulated land distribution and official ranks.

Prince Shōtoku was also instrumental in the early spread of Buddhism (which also entered Japan through Korean influence), founding several temples in the Kansai area.

The Age of Courtiers

Establishing a Capital

Prior to 694, the Yamato court had a habit of moving and building a new palace every time it got a new emperor or empress (and remember, we're up to 30 or 40 now, depending on how you're counting). Empress Jito was the first to order the construction of a more permanent capital, based on the Chinese model of a neat grid. It only lasted 16 years, but the idea stuck and in 710 a new capital was established at Nara (Heijō-kyō).

By now Buddhism was flourishing, as evinced by the construction of the temple Tōdai-ji (745); it still stands today, housing a huge bronze Buddha, and is the world's largest wooden building (and one of the oldest). *Kofun* had fallen out of fashion in the capital (though they were still erected in outer territories) and funereal tombs were decorated with Buddhist motifs.

Emperor Kammu (r 781–806) decided to relocate the capital in 784, likely prompted by a series of disasters following the move to Nara, including a massive smallpox epidemic that killed up to one-third of the population in 735–37. In 794 the capital was transferred to nearby Kyoto (Heian-kyō), which remained Japan's capital for more than a thousand years (even if it wasn't always the centre of actual power).

The Rise & Fall of the Heian Court

In Kyoto over the next few centuries courtly life reached a pinnacle of refined artistic pursuits and etiquette, captured famously in the novel *The Tale of Genji*, written by the court-lady Murasaki Shikibu in about 1004. It showed courtiers indulging in diversions such as guessing flowers by their scent, building extravagant follies and sparing no expense for the latest luxury. On the positive side, it was a world that encouraged aesthetic sensibilities, such as of *mono no aware* (the bittersweetness of things) and *okashisa* (pleasantly surprising incongruity), which have endured to the present day. But it was also a world increasingly estranged from the real one. Manipulated over centuries by the politically powerful Fujiwara family, the imperial throne was losing its authority.

While the nobles immersed themselves in courtly pleasures and intrigues, out in the provinces powerful military forces were developing.

The Yamato dynasty is the longest unbroken monarchy in the world, and Hirohito's reign from 1926 to 1989 the longest of any Japanese monarch.

The official written language of the Heian court was Chinese characters; women, who were often shut out of formal education, employed a shorthand that would come to be known as hiragana. Courtesan Murasaki Shikibu used this script to write *The Tale of Genji* (1004).

712 & 720	740	794	804
The compilation of two major historical works, *Kojiki* (712) and *Nihon Shoki* (720), allows the imperial family to trace its 'divine' origins and, in this way, legitimise its right to rule.	Construction begins on the vast Tōdai-ji temple complex in Nara. It is thought the complex was built to provide a focus for the nation and to ward off smallpox.	The imperial capital moves to Heian-kyō, renamed Kyoto in the 11th century. It is laid out in a grid in accordance with Chinese geomancy principles.	After travelling to China to study Buddhism, Kūkai (also known as Kōbō Daishi) founds Shingon (Esoteric) Buddhism in Japan and establishes the famous Kōya-san religious centre.

They were typically led by minor nobles, often sent on behalf of court-based major nobles to carry out tedious local duties. Some were distant imperial family members, barred from succession claims – they were given new names and farmed out to provincial clans – and hostile to the court. Their retainers included skilled warriors known as samurai (literally 'retainer').

The two main clans of disenfranchised lesser nobles, the Minamoto (also known as Genji) and Taira (Heike), were enemies. In 1156 they were employed to help rival claimants to the Fujiwara family leadership, but these figures soon faded into the background when an all-out feud developed between the Minamoto and the Taira.

The Taira prevailed, under their leader Kiyomori (1118–81), who based himself in the capital and, over the next 20 years, fell prey to many of the vices that lurked there. In 1180 he enthroned his two-year-old grandson, Antoku. When a rival claimant requested the help of the Minamoto family, who had regrouped, their leader, Yoritomo (1147–99), was more than ready to agree.

Both Kiyomori and the claimant died shortly afterwards, but Yoritomo and his younger half-brother Yoshitsune (1159–89) continued the campaign against the Taira. By 1185 Kyoto had fallen and the Taira had been pursued to the western tip of Honshū. A naval battle ensued, won by the Minamoto. In a well-known tragic tale, Kiyomori's widow leapt into the sea with her grandson Antoku (now aged seven), rather than have him surrender. Minamoto Yoritomo, now the most powerful man in Japan, was to usher in a martial age.

Shintō is one of the few religions in the world with a female solar deity. Amaterasu (Light of Heaven), the Sun Goddess, is enshrined at Ise-jinja, the most important shrine in the country, where members of the imperial family serve as chief priest or priestess.

The Age of Warriors
The First Shogun

Yoritomo did not seek to become emperor, but wanted the new emperor to give him legitimacy by conferring the title of shogun (generalissimo), which was granted in 1192. He left many existing offices and institutions in place and set up a base in his home territory of Kamakura (not far from present-day Tokyo) rather than Kyoto. His 'shogunate' was known in Japanese as the *bakufu*, meaning the tent headquarters of a field general. While in theory Yoritomo represented the military arm of the emperor's government, in practice he was in charge of government. The Kamakura *bakufu* established a feudal system – which would last almost 700 years as an institution – centred on a loyalty-based lord-vassal system.

When Yoritomo died in 1199 (after falling from his horse in suspicious circumstances) his son succeeded him to the title of shogun. However his widow, Masako (1157–1225), was a member of the Hōjō clan and a formidable figure, holding significant power for much of her remaining

In 1191 the Zen monk Eisai is said to have brought tea leaves from China, starting Japan's tradition of tea drinking.

early 1000s	1100s	1156	1185–92
Lady of the court, Murasaki Shikibu, writes *The Tale of Genji*, considered to be the world's first novel.	The Northern Fujiwara clan, largely independent of the court, wrests control of northeastern Honshū (present-day Tohoku), pushing the native peoples (possible Jōmon descendants) north to Hokkaidō.	The major provincial clans Taira and Minamoto are employed by rival court factions and engage in bitter warfare, with the Taira prevailing under its warrior-leader Kiyomori.	Minamoto Yoritomo topples the Taira and fights to secure his authority by eliminating rivals (including his own half-brother). By defeating the Northern Fujiwara in 1189 he adds northeast Japan to his territory.

JAPANESE HISTORICAL PERIODS

PERIOD	DATE	KEY EVENTS
Jōmon	c 13,000 BC– c 400 BC	Japan is populated by neolithic peoples, who migrated from mainland Asia
Yayoi	c 400 BC– c AD 250	Technologically advanced immigrants arrive by boat from the Korean Peninsula, introducing wet-rice farming and bronze tool-making
Kofun	250–538	Burial mounds codified according to status indicate a society with increasing stratification
Asuka	538–710	Buddhism takes hold; civil codes over a burgeoning empire are established by the ruling Yamato clan
Nara	710–94	The first permanent capital of Japan is established in the city of Nara
Heian	794–1185	A period of peace and cultural refinement ensues under the imperial court in its new capital, Kyoto
Kamakura	1185–1333	Feudalism is imposed by a new military regime in Kamakura led by a shogun, who is granted power from the (now largely powerless) emperor
Muromachi	1333–1568	The shogunate, under new leadership, is removed to Kyoto; though a period of instability, culture influenced by Zen Buddhism flourishes
Azuchi-Momoyama	1568–1603	A time of near constant civil war until Tokugawa Ieyasu establishes a new shogunate in Edo (Tokyo)
Edo	1603–1868	The Tokugawa shogunate closes the country and ushers in a period of significant peace and prosperity
Meiji	1868–1912	The shogunate is abolished and the emperor is reinstated as the supreme power; Japan, now open to the world, begins a wholesale importation of Western ideas
Taishō	1912–26	Western-style democracy takes hold briefly, before giving way to militarisation
Shōwa	1926–89	The first half of the era is marked by imperial aggression and war; the latter half sees remarkable postwar growth and the emergence of a solid middle class
Heisei	1989–present	Growth screeches to a halt and inequality widens; the country considers its role in the world

life (despite shaving her head and taking religious vows on her husband's death). Her father acted as regent – a title the Hōjō would continue to hold until suspicion and infighting killed the last Minamoto heir and the Hōjō claimed the shogunate outright.

1192	1199	1200–50	1223
Yoritomo takes the title shogun (generalissimo) from a largely powerless emperor and establishes the *bakufu* (shogunate) in his home territory at Kamakura, heralding the start of feudalism in Japan.	After Yoritomo's suspicious death, his formidable wife Masako (nicknamed the 'nun shogun') lays the groundwork for establishing her family, the Hōjō, as shoguns.	Hōnen and Shinran promote the 'Pure Land' schools of Buddhism, which remain the country's most popular Buddhist sects.	The monk Dōgen studies Chang Buddhism in China and later returns to found the Sōtō school of Zen Buddhism. Zen proves popular with the warrior class and goes on to influence Japanese aesthetics.

Mongol Invasions

It was during the Hōjō shogunate that the Mongols twice tried to invade, in 1274 and 1281. Under Kublai Khan (r 1260–94), the Mongol empire was close to its peak and after conquering Korea in 1259 he sent requests to Japan to submit to him, but these were ignored.

Kublai Khan's expected first attack came in November 1274, allegedly with about 900 vessels carrying 40,000 men, though these figures may be exaggerated. They landed near Hakata in northwest Kyūshū and, despite spirited Japanese resistance, made progress inland. However, for unclear reasons, they retreated to their ships and shortly afterwards a violent storm blew up, damaging about a third of the fleet. The remainder returned to Korea.

A more determined attempt was made from China seven years later. Kublai had a fleet of 4400 warships built to carry a force of 140,000 men – again, these are questionable figures. In August 1281 they landed once more in northwest Kyūshū and again met spirited resistance and had to retire to their vessels. Once more, the weather intervened – this time a typhoon – and half their vessels were destroyed. The survivors went back to China, and there was no further Mongol attempt to invade Japan.

The typhoon of 1281 prompted the idea of divine intervention to save Japan, with the coining of the term kamikaze (literally 'divine wind'). Later this term was used to describe Pacific War suicide pilots who, said to be infused with divine spirit, gave their lives to protect Japan from invasion.

KAMIKAZE

The kamikaze ('divine wind') of 1281 is said to have drowned 70,000 Mongol troops. If true, it would be the world's worst maritime disaster.

The Fall of Kamakura

Despite its successful defence of Japan, the Hōjō shogunate suffered. Its inability to make promised payments to the warriors involved in repelling the Mongols caused considerable discontent, while the payments it did make severely depleted its finances.

Dissatisfaction towards the shogunate came to a head under the unusually assertive emperor Go-Daigo (1288–1339). After escaping from exile imposed by the Hōjō, he started to muster anti-shogunal support in western Honshū. In 1333 the shogunate dispatched troops to counter this threat, under one of its most promising generals, the young Ashikaga Takauji (1305–58). However, recognising the resentment towards the Hōjō and that together he and Go-Daigo would have considerable military strength, Takauji threw in his lot with the emperor and attacked the shogunal offices in Kyoto. Others also soon rebelled against the shogunate itself in Kamakura.

This was the end for the Hōjō shogunate, but not for the institution. Takauji wanted the title of shogun, but his ally Go-Daigo feared that conferring it would weaken his own imperial power. A rift developed,

1274 & 1281	1333	1338–92	late 1300s
Under Kublai Khan, the Mongols twice attempt to invade Japan, but fail due to poor planning, spirited Japanese resistance and, especially, the destruction of their fleets by typhoons.	General Ashikaga Takauji, allied with Emperor Go-Daigo, topples the unpopular Hōjō shogunate. Takauji requests the title of shogun, but Go-Daigo declines and a rift develops.	Takauji installs a new puppet emperor who names him shogun, establishing the Ashikaga shogunate in Kyoto's Muromachi district. Two rival emperors exist till Go-Daigo's line is betrayed by Takauji's grandson in 1392.	Kyoto's Kinkaku-ji (Golden Temple) is designed as a retreat for the shogun; in accordance with his will, it is transformed into a Zen temple on his death.

and Go-Daigo sent forces to attack Takauji. However, Takauji emerged victorious and turned on Kyoto, forcing Go-Daigo to flee into the hills of Yoshino about 100km south of the city, where he set up a court in exile. In Kyoto, Takauji installed a puppet emperor from a rival line, who returned the favour by declaring him shogun in 1338. The two courts coexisted until 1392 when the 'southern court' (at Yoshino) was betrayed by Ashikaga Yoshimitsu (1358–1408), Takauji's grandson and the third Ashikaga shogun.

Warring States

Takauji set up his shogunal base in Kyoto, at Muromachi. With a few exceptions such as Takauji and his grandson Yoshimitsu (who had Kyoto's famous Kinkaku-ji built and once declared himself 'King of Japan'), the Ashikaga shoguns were relatively ineffective. Without strong, centralised government and control, the country slipped into civil war as regional warlords – who came to be known as *daimyō* (domain lords) – engaged in seemingly interminable feuds and power struggles. Starting with the Ōnin War of 1467–77 and for the next hundred years, the country was almost constantly in civil war. This time was known as the Sengoku (Warring States) era.

During this time, the warrior class succeeded in siphoning land and cultural sway from the landed nobility and it was their tastes that set the fashions of the time. The austerity and self-discipline of Zen Buddhism, which had entered Japan from China in the 13th century, appealed greatly to the warrior class. It also influenced their aesthetic values, such as *sabi* (elegant simplicity), *yūgen* (elegant and tranquil otherworldliness, as seen in *nō*), *wabi* (rustic) and *kare* (severe and unadorned).

And thus it happened that during this time of near constant war and instability there came a flourishing of the arts, such as in the refined *nō* (stylised dance-drama performed on a bare stage), ikebana (flower arranging) and *chanoyu* (tea ceremony).

Reunification

Nobunaga Seizes Power

The first Europeans arrived in 1543 – three Portuguese traders blown ashore on the island of Tanegashima south of Kyūshū. Soon other Europeans arrived, bringing with them Christianity and firearms. They found a land torn apart by warfare, ripe for conversion to Christianity – at least in the eyes of missionaries such as Francis Xavier, who arrived in 1549. The Japanese warlords, however, were more interested in the worldly matter of guns.

One of the most successful of the warlords to take advantage of firearms was Oda Nobunaga (1534–82). Starting from a relatively minor

Top Historic Sites

Ishibutai-kofun, Asuka

Izumo Taisha, Shimane

Tōdai-ji, Nara

Tō-ji, Kyoto

Hiraizumi, Iwate

Daibutsu, Kamakura

Dejima, Nagasaki

Shimoda, Shizuoka

Imperial Palace, Tokyo

1400s	1543	1568	1582
The Ōnin War (1467–77), ignited by succession claims, kicks off a near constant era of civil war, referred to as the Sengoku (Warring States) period, that lasts through the 16th century.	Portuguese, the first Westerners, arrive by chance in Japan, bringing firearms and Christianity. Firearms prove popular among warlords; Christianity gets a mixed reception.	The warlord Oda Nobunaga seizes Kyoto and becomes the supreme power, though he does not take the title of shogun. He is noted for his massive ego and brutality.	Nobunaga is betrayed and forced to commit suicide. Power transfers to one of his loyal generals, Toyotomi Hideyoshi, who takes the title of regent.

power base (in what is now Aichi Prefecture), his skilled and ruthless generalship produced a series of victories over rivals. In 1568 he seized Kyoto and installed one of the Ashikaga clan (Yoshiaki) as shogun, only to drive him out in 1573 and make his own base at Azuchi. Although he did not take the title of shogun, Nobunaga held de-facto power.

Noted for his brutality, Nobunaga was not a man to cross. He hated Buddhist priests, and tolerated Christianity as a counterbalance to them. His stated aim was 'Tenka Fubu' (A Unified Realm under Military Rule) and he went some way to achieving this by redistributing territories

SAMURAI: JAPAN'S LEGENDARY WARRIORS

The prime duty of a samurai – a member of the warrior class from about the 12th century onwards – was to give faithful service to his lord. In fact, the origin of the term 'samurai' is closely linked to a word meaning 'to serve'. The samurai's best-known weapon was the *katana* sword. They were among the world's finest swordsmen and formidable opponents in single combat.

Over the centuries, the samurai established a code of conduct that came to be known as *bushidō* (the way of the warrior), drawn from Confucianism, Shintō and Buddhism. Confucianism required a samurai to show absolute loyalty to his lord. Towards the oppressed, a samurai was expected to show benevolence and exercise justice. Subterfuge was to be despised, as were all commercial and financial transactions. A real samurai had endless endurance and total self-control, spoke only the truth and displayed no emotion. Since his honour was his life, disgrace and shame were to be avoided above all else, and all insults were to be avenged.

From Buddhism, the samurai learnt the lesson that life is impermanent – a handy reason to face death with serenity. Shintō provided the samurai with patriotic beliefs in the divine status both of the emperor and of Japan (promulgated to be the abode of the gods).

Seppuku (ritual suicide), also known as hara-kiri, was an accepted means of avoiding dishonour. Seppuku required the samurai to ritually disembowel himself, watched by an aide, who then drew his own sword and lopped off the samurai's head. One reason for this ritual was the requirement that a samurai should never surrender but always go down fighting.

Of course not all (and probably very few) samurai lived up to these strict standards. Some were professional mercenaries who were unreliable and often defected. Samurai indulging in double-crossing or subterfuge, or displaying outright cowardice, were popular themes in Japanese theatre. Those who became lordless were known as *rōnin* (wanderers or masterless samurai); they acted more like brigands and were a serious social problem.

During modernisation in the late 19th century, the government – itself comprising samurai – realised that a conscript army was more efficient as a unified fighting force and disestablished the samurai class. However, samurai ideals such as endurance and fighting to the death were revived through propaganda prior to the Pacific War, and underlay the determination of many Japanese soldiers.

late 1500s	1592 & 1597–98	1600	1603
Sen-no-Rikyū lays down the form of the tea ceremony, the ritualised drinking of tea originally practised by nobility and later spreading to wealthy commoners.	Hideyoshi twice tries to conquer Korea as part of a plan to control Asia, the second attempt ending after his death in 1598. The invasions seriously damage relations between Japan and Korea.	The warlord Tokugawa Ieyasu breaks an earlier promise to the dying Hideyoshi to protect his young son and heir Hideyori, and seizes power at the Battle of Sekigahara.	Ieyasu becomes shogun, establishing a new shogunate in the small castle town Edo (now Tokyo), beginning 250 years of relative peace under Tokugawa rule.

among the *daimyō,* having land surveyed and standardising weights and measures. What sort of ruler he might have made, however, was never to be discovered: before he could complete his mission, he was betrayed by one of his generals and killed in 1582.

The Ambitions of Hideyoshi

Another of Nobunaga's generals, Toyotomi Hideyoshi (1536–98), took up the torch of unification. He, too, was an extraordinary figure, a foot soldier who had risen through the ranks to become Nobunaga's favourite. Small

HIDDEN CHRISTIANS

Japan's so-called 'Christian Century' began in 1549 with the arrival of Portuguese missionaries on the island of Kyūshū. Within decades, hundreds of thousands of Japanese, from peasants to *daimyō* (domain lords), were converted.

The rapid rise of Christian belief, as well as its association with trade, Western weaponry and possibly territory grabbing, came to be viewed as a threat by the *bakufu* (shogunate) under Toyotomi Hideyoshi. In 1597 Hideyoshi ordered the crucifixion of 26 Japanese and Spanish Franciscans in Nagasaki. Despite his death in 1598, an era of suppression of Christians had begun and, with the expulsion of missionaries ordered in 1614 by Tokugawa Hidetada, thousands of Christians were persecuted over the following six decades. Many thousands of Christian peasants resisted in the 1637–38 Shimabara Rebellion, after which Christianity was outlawed completely.

Other persecution took the form of *fumi-e,* in which suspected Christians were forced to walk on images of Jesus. The Gregorian date on the Dutch trading house on the island of Hirado was taken as proof of the Dutch traders' Christianity and used to justify their exile to Nagasaki's Dejima. This ushered in more than two centuries of *sakoku* (closure to the outside world).

Japanese Christians reacted by going undercover as *kakure Kirishitan* (hidden Christians). Without priests, they worshipped in services held in secret rooms inside private homes. On the surface, worship resembled other Japanese religions, including using *kamidana* (Shintō altars) and *butsudan* (Buddhist ancestor-worship chests) in homes, and ceremonial rice and sake. But *kakure Kirishitan* also kept hanging scrolls of Jesus, Mary and saints, as well as statues like the Maria-Kannon, depicting Mary in the form of the Buddhist deity of mercy holding an infant symbolising Jesus. The sounds of worship, too, mimicked Buddhist incantations. Scholars estimate there were about 150,000 hidden Christians.

It was not until 1865 – 12 years after the arrival of the American expedition led by Commodore Matthew Perry, who eventually forced Japan to reopen to the West – that Japan had its first large-scale church again, Ōura Cathedral in Nagasaki. The Meiji government officially declared freedom of religion in 1871. Today, there are estimated to be between one and two million Japanese Christians (about 1% of the population).

1606	1638	1689–91	1800s
Matsumae castle is erected in southern Hokkaidō giving Japan a toehold on the northern island, then called Ezo and populated by a people called Ainu.	The *sakoku* policy of national isolation is enacted; shogunal forces massacre Japanese Christians in the Christian-led Shimabara Rebellion.	Matsuo Bashō, the greatest name in haiku poetry, completes a journey around Japan that inspires his most famous collection of poems, *The Narrow Road to the Deep North.*	The vivacious entertainment districts bubbling up in tight-laced Tokugawa Japan are chronicled in *ukiyo-e* (woodblock prints).

and with simian features, he was nicknamed 'Saru-chan' (Little Monkey) by Nobunaga, but his huge will for power belied his physical size.

He disposed of potential rivals among Nobunaga's sons, took the title of regent, continued Nobunaga's policy of territorial redistribution and insisted that *daimyō* should surrender their families to him as hostages to be kept in Kyoto. He also banned weapons for all classes except samurai.

In his later years, Hideyoshi became increasingly paranoid, cruel and megalomaniacal. He would saw in half messengers who gave him bad news, and had young members of his own family executed for suspected plotting. He also issued the first expulsion order of Christians (1587), whom he suspected were an advance guard for an invasion. His grand scheme for power included a pan-Asian conquest, and as a first step he attempted an invasion of Korea in 1592, which failed amid much bloodshed. He tried again in 1597, but the campaign was abandoned when Hideyoshi died of illness in 1598.

Ieyasu Takes Over

Hideyoshi's power had been briefly contested by Tokugawa Ieyasu (1542–1616), son of a minor lord allied to Nobunaga. After a brief struggle for power, Ieyasu agreed to a truce with Hideyoshi; in return, Hideyoshi granted him eight provinces in eastern Japan. While Hideyoshi intended this to weaken Ieyasu by separating him from his ancestral homeland Chūbu (now Aichi Prefecture), the upstart looked upon the gift as an opportunity to strengthen his power. He set up his base in a small castle town called Edo (which would one day become Tokyo).

On his deathbed, Hideyoshi entrusted Ieyasu, who had proven to be one of his ablest generals, with safeguarding the country and the succession of his young son Hideyori (1593–1615). Ieyasu, however, had bigger ambitions and soon went to war against those loyal to Hideyori. Ieyasu's forces finally defeated Hideyori and his supporters at the legendary Battle of Sekigahara in 1600, moving him into a position of supreme power. He chose Edo as his permanent base and ushered in two and a half centuries of Tokugawa rule.

Through these three men – Nobunaga, Hideyoshi and Ieyasu – by fair means, or more commonly, foul, the country was reunified within three decades.

A Time of Stability

Tokugawa Rule

Having secured power for the Tokugawa, Ieyasu and his successors were determined to retain it. Their basic strategy was extreme micro-management. They kept tight control over the provincial *daimyō*, who ruled as vassals for the Tokugawa regime, requiring authorisation for

NINJAS

Besides loyal samurai, Tokugawa Ieyasu stocked his capital with ninja. Their commander was Hattori Hanzō, renowned for his cunning, deadly tactics that helped Ieyasu at key moments in his career. The ninja master's legacy was enshrined in Hanzōmon, a gate that still exists today at the Imperial Palace.

early to mid-19th century	1853–54	1859	1854–67
The nation's isolation is threatened by increasing numbers of foreign whalers and other vessels entering Japanese waters. Treatment of those attempting to land is harsh.	US commodore Matthew Perry's 'black ships' arrive off the coast of Shimoda, forcing Japan to open up for trade and reprovisioning.	Five international ports are established in Yokohama, Hakodate, Kōbe, Niigata and Nagasaki, opening the way for foreign settlements.	Opposition to the shogunate grows, led by samurai from the Satsuma and Chōshū domains, resulting in civil war; the last shogun retires in 1867.

The Tokugawa regime promoted a brand of neo-Confucianism that emphasised hierarchical order and had the (perhaps unintended) positive effect of promoting literacy: by the end of the period of Tokugawa rule, up to a third of the 30 million Japanese were literate – far ahead of Western populations of the time.

castle-building and marriages. They continued to redistribute (or confiscate) territory and, importantly, required *daimyō* and their retainers to spend every second year in Edo, where their families were kept permanently as hostages – an edict known as *sankin kōtai*. This dislocating policy made it hard for ambitious *daimyō* to usurp the Tokugawas.

The shogunate also directly controlled ports, mines, major towns and other strategic areas. Movement was severely restricted by checkpoints; written authority was required for travel and wheel transport was outlawed.

Society was made rigidly hierarchical, comprising (in descending order of importance): *shi* (samurai), *nō* (farmers), *kō* (artisans) and *shō* (merchants). Class dress, living quarters and even manner of speech were all strictly codified, and interclass movement was prohibited. Village and neighbourhood heads were enlisted to enforce rules at the local level, creating an atmosphere of surveillance. Punishments could be harsh, cruel and even deadly for minor offences.

Retreat from the World

Early on, the Tokugawa shogunate adopted a policy of *sakoku* (closure to the outside world), which was to last for more than two centuries. The regime was leery of Christianity's potential influence and expelled missionaries in 1614. Following the Christian-led Shimabara Rebellion, Christianity was banned and several hundred thousand Japanese Christians were forced into hiding. All Westerners except the Protestant Dutch were expelled by 1638.

The shogunate found Protestantism less threatening than Catholicism (knowing that the Vatican could muster one of the biggest military forces in the world) and would have let the British stay on if the Dutch had not convinced it that Britain was a Catholic country. Nevertheless, the Dutch were just a few dozen men confined to a tiny trading base on the artificial island of Dejima near Nagasaki.

David Mitchell's *Thousand Autumns of Jacob de Zoet: A Novel* (2010) tells about the Dutch living on the island of Dejima during the period of *sakoku*. Mitchell (who also wrote the award-winning novel *Cloud Atlas*) spent most of the 1990s teaching in Western Honshū, an early inspiration for the book.

Overseas travel for Japanese was banned (as well as the return of those already overseas). And yet, the country did not remain completely cut off: trade with Asia and the West continued through the Dutch and Ryūkyū empire (now Okinawa) – it was just tightly controlled and, along with the exchange of ideas, funnelled exclusively to the shogunate.

Rise of the Merchant Class

For all its constraints, the Tokugawa period had a considerable dynamism. Japan's cities grew enormously during this period: Edo's population topped one million in the early 1700s, dwarfing much older London and Paris. Kyoto, which evolved into a production centre for luxury goods, and Osaka, a centre for trade, each hovered around 400,000 for much of the period.

1867–68 >	1869 >	1879 >	1870s– early 1890s >
The Meiji Restoration reinstates imperial authority, installing 15-year-old emperor Mutsuhito as head of state (though real power is wielded by oligarchs). Japan's capital is moved to Edo, renamed Tokyo.	Japan formally annexes Hokkaidō; in 1889 laws enforcing assimilation of the indigenous Ainu people are enacted.	Japan annexes the Ryūkyū Kingdom (then a tributary of China) and renames it Okinawa; assimilation policies are also carried out against native Okinawans.	The Meiji government introduces policies of modernisation and Westernisation, such as creating a conscript army (1873), disestablishing the samurai (1876) and adopting a constitution (1889).

Despite the best efforts of rulers to limit the growing merchant class, it prospered greatly from the services and goods required for *daimyō* processions to and from Edo. And so costly were these processions that *daimyō* had to convert much of their domain's produce into cash. This boosted the economy in general.

A new culture that thumbed its nose at social hardships and the strictures of the shogunate began to flourish. Increasingly wealthy merchants patronised the kabuki theatre, sumo tournaments and the pleasure quarters – generally enjoying a *joie de vivre* that the dour lords of Edo castle frowned upon. Central to this pleasure-oriented culture was the concept of *ukiyo* – 'floating world' – a term derived (or perhaps corrupted) from a Buddhist metaphor for life's fleeting joys. Today, the best glimpses we have into that time come from *ukiyo-e* (woodblock prints).

THE REAL LAST SAMURAI

Saigō Takamori (1828–77) was born into a samurai family in Kagoshima, Kyūshū (then called Satsuma Province, in the southwestern corner of the main islands). He was an ardent supporter of the emperor Meiji and field commander of the imperial army against the forces of the Tokugawa shogunate. It was he who led the army to quash a rebellion of Tokugawa loyalists in Ueno (now a district in Tokyo) in 1868, which cemented the Meiji Restoration.

But things did not turn out as Saigō had hoped. The samurai system was abolished once Meiji ascended the throne, and by 1872 this system of professional warriors had given way to a Western model of military conscription. Saigō was a member of the new government and lobbied for investment in the military (instead of railroads) and for an invasion of Korea. His ideas, however, found little support. In 1873 he resigned and returned to Satsuma.

Saigō was by no means the only disaffected former samurai, but he was the most prominent. Others rallied around him, urging him to lead a rebellion against the imperial forces. The resulting 1877 siege of Kumamoto Castle lasted 54 days, with a reported force of 40,000 samurai and armed peasants arrayed against the imperial army. When the castle was incinerated and defeat became inevitable, it is said that Saigō retreated to Kagoshima and committed seppuku (ritual suicide).

The Satsuma Rebellion, as it came to be called, soon gained legend status among common Japanese. Capitalising on this fame, the Meiji government posthumously pardoned Saigō and granted him full honours, and today he remains an exemplar of the samurai spirit. Statues of his image can be found most prominently in Kagoshima and, walking his faithful dog, in Tokyo's Ueno-kōen. His most famous maxim, *keiten aijin*, translates to 'revere heaven, love humankind'.

Fans of the 2003 movie *The Last Samurai* may recognise elements of this story in Katsumoto, the character played by Watanabe Ken (though the character played by Tom Cruise has no historical basis).

1895	1902	1904–05	1910
Defeating China in the Sino-Japanese War, Japan, who initiated the conflict in 1894, gains Taiwan and its territorial expansion begins.	Japan signs the Anglo-Japanese Alliance, the first-ever equal alliance between a Western and non-Western nation and an indicator of Japan's growing power.	Japan wins the Russo-Japanese War. Antipathy towards Russia had developed after the Sino-Japanese War, when Russia pressured Japan to renounce Chinese territory that it then occupied.	Free of any Russian threat, Japan formally annexes Korea, in which it had been increasingly interested since the 1870s. The international community makes no real protest.

The samurai, meanwhile, had no major military engagements. Well educated, most ended up fighting paper wars as administrators and managers.

Modernisation

Arrival of the Black Ships

It is questionable how much longer the Tokugawa shogunate and its secluded world might have continued, but as it happened, external forces were to hasten its demise. A number of Western vessels – which the Japanese called *kurofune* (black ships), because they were cloaked in pitch – had begun appearing in Japanese waters since the start of the 19th century. However, any Westerners who landed, even through shipwreck, were almost always expelled or even executed.

America in particular was keen to expand its interests across the Pacific, with its numerous whaling vessels in the northwest needing regular provisioning. In 1853 and again the following year, US commodore Matthew Perry steamed into Edo-wan (now Tokyo Bay) with a show of gunships and demanded Japan open up to trade and provisioning. The shogunate was no match for Perry's firepower and had to agree to his demands. Soon an American consul arrived, and other Western powers followed suit. Japan was obliged to sign what came to be called the 'unequal treaties', opening ports and giving Western nations control over tariffs.

> The disorienting collapse of the regimented Tokugawa world produced a form of mass hysteria called *ee ja nai ka* (who cares?), with traumatised people dancing naked and giving away possessions.

Meiji Restoration

Despite last ditch efforts by the Tokugawa regime to reassert their power, anti-shogunal sentiment was high, particularly in the outer domains of Satsuma (southern Kyūshū) and Chōshū (western Honshū). A movement arose to 'revere the emperor and expel the barbarians' *(sonnō jōi)*; in other words, to restore the emperor to a position of real power (rather than titular authority) and to kick the Westerners out.

After unsuccessfully skirmishing with the Western powers, however, the reformers realised that expelling the foreigners was not feasible. Restoring the emperor, however, was: following a series of military clashes between the shogun's armies and the rebels – which showed the rebels to have the upper hand – the last shogun, Yoshinobu (1837–1913), agreed to retire in 1867. He lived out his remaining years peacefully in Shizuoka.

In 1868, the new teenage emperor Mutsuhito (1852–1912; later known as Meiji) was named the supreme leader of the land, commencing the Meiji period (1868–1912; Enlightened Rule). The institution of the shogun was abolished and the shogunal base at Edo was refashioned into the imperial capital and given the new name, Tokyo (Eastern Capital). Which is not to say Tokugawa loyalists went quietly into the night; fighting continued, especially in the north, through 1868–69, in what is known as the Boshin War.

1912	1914–15	1923	1931
Emperor Meiji (Mutsuhito) dies, after seeing Japan rise from a remote pre-industrial nation to a world power in half a century. His mentally disabled son, Yoshihito, succeeds him.	Japan sides with the Entente in WWI in 1914; in 1915 it presents China with 'Twenty-One Demands' for more control in China, earning rebuke from its new allies.	The Great Kantō Earthquake strikes Japan near Tokyo, killing an estimated 100,000 to 140,000 people. Much of the destruction is caused by fires sweeping through Tokyo and Yokohama after the quake.	Increasingly defiant of the West, Japan invades Manchuria and then dramatically withdraws from the League of Nations in response to criticism.

In truth, the emperor still wielded little actual power. A new government was formed, primarily of leading Satsuma or Chōshū samurai aged in their early 30s. Though they claimed that everything was done on behalf of the emperor and with his sanction, they were driven as much by personal ambition as genuine concern for the nation.

Westernisation

Above all, the new leaders of Japan – keen observers of what was happening throughout Asia – feared colonisation by the West. They moved quickly to modernise, as defined by the Western powers, to prove they could stand on an equal footing with the colonisers.

The government embarked on a grand project of industrialisation and militarisation. A great exchange began between Japan and the West: Japanese scholars were dispatched to Europe to study everything from literature and engineering to nation building and modern warfare. Western scholars were invited to teach in Japan's nascent universities.

The new Japanese establishment learned quickly: in 1872 the first railroad opened, connecting Tokyo with the new port of Yokohama, south along Tokyo Bay. By 1889 the country had a constitution, modelled after the government frameworks of England and Prussia. Banking systems, a new legal code and political parties were established. *Daimyō* were 'persuaded' to give their domain land to the government in return for governorships or other compensation, enabling a prefectural system to be set up.

Democracy was, of course, not an overnight process and cronyism persisted. The government took responsibility for establishing major industries and then selling them off at bargain rates to chosen government-friendly industrial entrepreneurs – a factor in the formation of huge industrial conglomerates known as *zaibatsu*, many of which still exist today (such as Mitsubishi, Sumitomo and Mitsui).

In the early years, Japan's main industry was textiles and its main export silk, but later in the Meiji period it moved into manufacturing and heavy industry, becoming a major world shipbuilder.

New Ideologies

The Meiji Restoration also heralded far-reaching social changes. The four-tier class system was scrapped; after centuries of having everything prescribed for them, citizens were now free to choose their occupation and place of residence. The new intellectual elite, well-travelled and well-read, encouraged citizens to make a success of themselves and become strong, and in so doing show the world what a successful and powerful nation Japan was. Improvement in agricultural technology freed up farming labour, and many moved to the cities to join the growing workforce in manufacturing sectors.

The feat of the 47 *rōnin* (masterless samurai), who plotted for over a year (1701–03) to avenge their master's death, is among Japan's most storied historical events. While sentenced to death, so great was the outpouring of respect, that the loyal samurai were allowed to keep their honour and commit seppuku (ritual suicide).

1937	1941	1942	1945
During an attempted occupation of China, Japan commits grave atrocities in Nanjing, killing many thousands of people, mostly civilians.	Japan enters WWII by striking Pearl Harbor without warning on 7 December, destroying much of the USA's Pacific fleet and drawing America into the war.	After early military successes, Japan's expansion is thwarted at the Battle of Midway in June, with significant losses. From this time, Japan is largely in retreat.	Following intensive firebombing of Tokyo in March, Hiroshima and Nagasaki become victims of an atomic bombing on 6 and 9 August, leading Japan's leader, Hirohito, to surrender on 15 August.

Buddhism, which had strong ties to the shogunate, suffered under the new government. Shintō – and particularly rituals of emperor worship – were promoted in its place, as a pure (read: nativist) system of beliefs. Elements of new-Confucianism were retained, however, for the orderliness they encouraged; new laws codified a patriarchal family system wherein women were subordinate to their husbands. The ban on Christianity was lifted (though few took advantage of it).

The World Stage

Imperialist Japan

A key element of Japan's aim to become a world power was military might. Following Prussian (army) and British (navy) models, Japan built up a formidable armed force. Using the same 'gunboat diplomacy' on Korea that Perry had used on the Japanese, in 1876 Japan was able to force on Korea an unequal treaty of its own, and increasingly meddled in Korean politics.

Using Chinese 'interference' in Korea as a justification, in 1894 Japan manufactured a war with China, a weak nation at this stage despite its massive size, and easily emerged victorious. As a result, it gained Taiwan and the Liaotung Peninsula. Russia pressured Japan into renouncing the peninsula and then promptly occupied it, leading to the Russo-Japanese War of 1904–05, won by Japan. When Japan officially annexed Korea in 1910, there was little international protest.

By the time of Mutsuhito's death in 1912, Japan was recognised as a world power. In addition to its military victories and territorial acquisitions, in 1902 it had signed the Anglo-Japanese Alliance, the first-ever equal alliance between a Western and non-Western nation. The unequal treaties had also been rectified.

Mutsuhito was succeeded by his son Yoshihito (known as the Taishō emperor), though his mental deterioration led to his son Hirohito (1901–89) becoming regent in 1921. While it was not without challenges, the short-lived Taishō period (1912–26; Great Righteousness) was generally a time of optimism. Old feudal-era loyalties finally buckled and party politics flourished for the first time, giving rise to the term Taishō Democracy.

Japan entered WWI on the side of the Allies, and was rewarded with a council seat in the newly formed League of Nations. It also acquired German possessions in East Asia and the Pacific. The war had been a boon for industry, creating a new stratum of wealth (though the vast majority of the population was left out).

Militarisation

As the 1920s rolled around, a sense of unfair treatment by Western powers once again took hold in Japan. The Washington Conference of 1921–22 set naval ratios of three capital ships for Japan to five American

Until Japan was occupied by the USA and other Allies following WWII, the nation had never been conquered or occupied by a foreign power.

1945–52	1955	1960s	1964
Japan undergoes USA-led occupation and a rapid economic recovery follows. Hirohito is spared from prosecution as a war criminal, angering many American allies.	The Liberal Democratic Party is formed; excepting the periods of 1993–94 and 2009–12, it will hold continuous power.	Protests against the signing of the 'Treaty of Mutual Cooperation and Security between the United States and Japan' (known as ANPO) erupt in 1960, ushering in a decade of social agitation.	Tokyo hosts the Summer Olympics, an event that for many Japanese marked Japan's full re-entry into the international community and the completion of its recovery from WWII.

and five British, which upset the Japanese (despite being well ahead of France's 1.75). Around the same time, a racial-equality clause Japan proposed to the League of Nations was rejected. And in 1924 America introduced race-based immigration policies that effectively targeted Japanese.

This dissatisfaction intensified in the Shōwa period (1926–89; Illustrious Peace), which commenced with the death of Yoshihito and the formal accession of Hirohito. The rural populace decried what they saw as an elite under the sway of Western decadence. The Great Depression that began in the late 1920s created a new class of urban poor who now recoiled at what had been deemed progress; leftist networks, inspired by developments in Russia, began agitating for workers' rights.

The armed forces, meanwhile, bristled at the humiliation of yet another round of capitulations. Japan needed to look after its own interests, they believed, which meant a resource-rich, Japan-controlled Greater East Asian Co-Prosperity Sphere. Prime Minister Hamaguchi Osachi who favoured economic austerity over increased military spending was shot in 1931 (dying some months later). By then, the military was acting on its own accord.

Aggression in China

In the fall of 1931, members of the Japanese army stationed in Manchuria, who were there to guard rail lines leased by China to Japan, detonated explosives along the track and blamed the act on Chinese dissidents. This ruse, which gave the Japanese army an excuse for armed retaliation, became known as the Manchurian Incident. The Japanese easily overpowered Chinese forces and within months had taken control of Manchuria (present-day Heilongjiang, Jilin and Liaoning provinces) and installed a puppet government. The League of Nations refused to acknowledge the new Manchurian government; in 1933 Japan left the league.

Skirmishes continued between the Chinese and Japanese armies, leading to full-blown war in 1937. Following a hard-fought victory in Shanghai, Japanese troops advanced south to capture Nanjing. Over several months somewhere between 40,000 and 300,000 Chinese were killed in what has become known as the Nanjing Massacre or Rape of Nanjing. To this day, the number of deaths and the prevalence of rape, torture and looting by Japanese soldiers is hotly debated among historians (and government nationalists) on both sides. Japanese attempts to downplay this and other massacres in Asia remain to this day a stumbling block in Japan's relations with many Asian nations.

WWII

Encouraged by Germany's early WWII victories, Japan signed a pact with Germany and Italy in 1940 (though these European allies offered little actual cooperation). With France and the Netherlands distracted and weak-

Historical Reads

Unbeaten Tracks in Japan (Isabella Bird; 1881)

The Coming of the Barbarians (Pat Barr; 1967)

Embracing Defeat (John Dower; 2000)

Samurai William (Giles Milton; 2003)

Inventing Japan (Ian Buruma; 2004)

1972	1990	1995	2005
The USA returns administrative control of Okinawa to Japan, but keeps many bases in place, which is a continuing source of tension.	The so-called 'Bubble Economy', based on overinflated land and stock prices, finally bursts in Japan. By the end of the year, the stockmarket has lost 48% of its value.	The Great Hanshin Earthquake (magnitude 6.9) strikes Kōbe, killing over 6000; two months later a cult releases sarin gas on the Tokyo Metro, killing 12.	Japan's population declines for the first year since WWII, a trend that will continue.

ened by the war in Europe, Japan quickly moved on their colonial territories – French Indo-China and the Dutch West Indies – in Southeast Asia.

Tensions between Japan and the USA intensified, as the Americans, alarmed by Japan's aggression, demanded Japan back down in China. When diplomacy failed, the USA barred oil exports to Japan – a crucial blow. Japanese forces struck at Pearl Harbor on 7 December 1941, damaging much of the USA's Pacific fleet and apparently catching the USA by surprise (though some scholars believe Roosevelt and others deliberately allowed the attack, to overcome isolationist sentiment and to bring the USA into the war against Germany; many also believe Japan never expected to beat the USA, but hoped to bring it to the negotiating table and emerge better off).

Japan advanced swiftly across the Pacific; however, the tide started to turn in the Battle of Midway in June 1942, when much of its carrier fleet was destroyed. Japan had overextended itself, and over the next three years was subjected to an island-hopping counter-attack. By mid-1945, Japan, ignoring the Potsdam Declaration calling for unconditional surrender, was preparing for a final Allied assault on its homeland. On 6 August the world's first atomic bomb was dropped on Hiroshima, killing 90,000 civilians. Russia, which Japan had hoped might mediate, declared war on 8 August. And on 9 August another atomic bomb was dropped, this time on Nagasaki, with another 50,000 deaths. The emperor formally surrendered on 15 August.

> When NHK, Japan's national broadcaster, played a message prerecorded by Emperor Hirohito declaring Japan's surrender to the Allies in WWII, it was the first time the people of Japan had heard their emperor speak.

The Modern Period

The terms of Japan's surrender to the Allies allowed the country to hold on to the emperor as the ceremonial head of state, but he no longer had authority – nor was he thought of as divine – and Japan was forced to give up its territorial claims in Korea and China. In addition, America occupied the country under General Douglas MacArthur, a situation that would last until 1952. Defeat was a bitter pill to swallow, but the population was largely starving and food from the Americans was better than nothing.

Then in the 1950s Japan took off on a trajectory of phenomenal growth that has been described as miraculous. (Though many historians, both Japanese and American, say Japan's role as a forward base for the USA in the Korean War reignited the Japanese economy.) It wasn't until 1990, with the bursting of the 'Bubble Economy', that it finally came down to earth.

> Based on the price paid for the most expensive real estate in the late 1980s, the land value of Tokyo exceeded that of the entire US.

The following decades were marked by protracted economic stagnation that was only worsened by the 2008 Global Financial Crisis. Three years later, Japan was devastated by the Great East Japan Earthquake and subsequent tsunami, in which more than 15,000 people perished. The 21st century has so far been an era of soul-searching for Japan, as it grapples with the legacy of the previous centuries highs and lows while trying to find its niche in a rapidly changing world.

2010	2011	2013	2013
China surpasses Japan as the world's second-largest economy after the USA.	On 11 March, the Great East Japan Earthquake strikes off the coast of northeast Japan (Tōhoku), generating a tsunami that kills many thousands and setting off a crisis at a nuclear power plant in Fukushima Prefecture.	The Japanese government approves the Special Secrecy Law, raising fears of censorship and threats to freedom of speech.	The International Olympic Committee awards Tokyo the right to host the 2020 Summer Olympics.

The People of Japan

The people of Japan are often depicted as inscrutable. Or reticent. Or shy. They are often these things, but they are often not. Japan is typically thought of as a homogeneous nation, and it largely is, ethnically (though there are minority cultures), but there are also deep divides between the urban and rural, stubbornly persistent gendered spheres and growing social stratification. Increasingly, the people of Japan are a people grappling with the same problems as developed nations the world over.

Population

The population of Japan is approximately 127 million. That alone makes Japan a densely populated nation; to make things worse, 91% of people live in areas classified as urban. Roughly a quarter of the population (about 36 million) lives within the Greater Tokyo Metropolitan Area, which encompasses the cities of Tokyo, Kawasaki and Yokohama plus the commuter towns stretching deep into the suburbs; it's the most heavily populated metropolitan area in the world. Another nearly 20 million live in the Kyoto–Osaka–Kōbe conurbation (often called Keihanshin).

Besides density, the most notable feature of Japan's population is the fact that it is shrinking. Japan's astonishingly low birth rate of 1.4 births per woman is among the lowest in the developed world and over a quarter of the population is already over 65. The population peaked at 128 million in 2007 and has been in decline since; it's predicted to reach 100 million in 2050 and 67 million in 2100. Needless to say, such demographic change will have a major influence on the economy in coming decades.

Diversity

One notable feature of Japan's population is its relative ethnic and cultural homogeneity. This is particularly striking for visitors from the USA, Australia and other multicultural nations. The Japanese census does not ask questions pertaining to race, only nationality. As a result, discussions of diversity in Japan tend to fall on divisions of national identity – who is Japanese and who is not.

The 2015 census revealed 2.23 million foreigners living in Japan – an uptick of 5% from the year before; the count includes those holding permanent residence status as well as students and temporary workers. The largest non-Japanese group in the country is the Chinese, who number roughly 666,000, or almost 30% of Japan's foreign population; next are the Koreans, who number 458,000 (20%) and the Filipinos (229,600; 10%). Despite declining population numbers, Japan has shown a reluctance to let immigrants make up the difference.

Minority Cultures

Buried within the population stats are Japan's invisible minorities – those who are native-born Japanese, who appear no different from other native-born Japanese but who can trace their ancestry to historically disenfranchised peoples. Chief among these are the descendants of the Ainu, the native people of Hokkaidō, and Okinawans.

WE JAPANESE

It's common to hear Japanese begin explanations of their culture by saying, *ware ware nihonjin*, which means, 'we Japanese'. There's a strong sense of national cohesion, reinforced by the media which plays up images of Japan as a unique cultural Galapagos; TV programs featuring foreign visitors being awed and wowed by the curious Japanese way of doing things are popular with viewers. The Japanese in turn are often fascinated (and intimidated) by what they perceive as the otherness of outside cultures.

Prior to being annexed by Japan in the 19th century, Hokkaidō and Okinawa (formerly the Ryūkyū Empire) were independent territories. Following annexation, the Japanese government imposed assimilation policies that forbade many traditional customs and even the teaching of native languages.

The number of Japanese who identify as Ainu is estimated to be around 20,000, though it is likely that there are many more descendants of Hokkaido's indigenous people out there – some who may not know it, perhaps because their ancestors buried their identity so deep (for fear of discrimination) that it became hidden forever. There are maybe 10 native speakers of Ainu left; however, in recent decades movements have emerged among the younger generation to learn the language and other aspects of their culture.

Today's Okinawans have a strong regional identity, though it is less about their ties to the former Ryūkyū Empire and more about their shared recent history since WWII. The Okinawans shouldered an unequal burden, both of casualties and of occupation.

Oya-koko is the Japanese expression for filial piety, though it more literally means something like 'making your parents happy'. This can mean taking care of them when they're older but also calling them up, taking them out to lunch or popping around to do some odd chores.

Another group is the *burakumin*. Racially no different from other Japanese, they were the disenfranchised of the feudal era social hierarchy, whose work included tanning, butchering, the handling of corpses and other occupations that carried the taint of death. Shunned, they lived in isolated settlements (called *buraku*). When the old caste system was abolished and the country modernised, the stigma should have faded, but it didn't: official household registries (often required as proof of residence when applying for a job) tied the ancestors of the *burakumin* to towns known to be former *buraku* settlements.

Discrimination in work and marriage was once common, though negative feelings towards *buraku* descendants appear to be diminishing with each generation.

Though English is slim, the Liberty Museum in Osaka has exhibits on Japan's minority cultures and their fights for social justice.

Lifestyle

Until the beginning of last century, the majority of Japanese lived in close-knit rural farming communities. Today, only one in 10 Japanese lives in the small farming and fishing villages that dot the mountains and cling to the rugged coasts. Mass postwar emigration from these rural enclaves has doubtless changed the weave of Japanese social fabric, as has the dizzying onslaught of Western material and pop culture. These days, the average young Tokyoite has more in common with her peers in Melbourne or London than she does with her grandmother back in the country.

In the City

Japan's urbanites live famously hectic lives dominated by often gruelling work schedules and punctuated by lengthy commutes from more affordable outlying neighbourhoods and suburbs to city centres.

Until fairly recently, the nexus of all this activity was the Japanese corporation, which provided lifetime employment to the legions of blue-suited, white-collar workers, almost all of them men, who lived, worked, drank, ate and slept in the service of the companies for which they toiled. Families typically consisted of a salaryman father, a housewife mother, kids who studied dutifully in order to earn a place at one of Japan's elite universities and an elderly in-law who had moved in.

These days, as the Japanese economy makes the transition from a manufacturing economy to a service economy, the old certainties are vanishing. On the way out are Japan's famous 'cradle to grave' employment and age-based promotion system. In their place are the legions of *furitaa* (part-time workers); for some, this is a conscientious rejection of their parents' lifestyles, but for most it is because they find themselves shut out of the full-time workforce. As in most developed countries, *tomobataraki* (both spouses working) is now increasingly common.

The kids in the family probably still study like mad. If they are not yet in high school, they will be working towards gaining admission to a select high school by attending an evening cram school, known as *juku*. If they are already in high school, they will be attending a *juku* in the hopes of passing university admission exams. With the number of full-time jobs up for grabs shrinking, getting into a top university is all the more vital.

Which isn't to say it's all glum in the cities; Japan's urbanites have a work hard, play hard ethos that fuels the famous nightlife of the major cities.

For decades Japan has prided itself on being a nation made up almost exclusively of the middle class. However, in recent years, the numbers haven't been adding up: a combination of economic stagnation and liberalisation policies has resulted in an increasing income gap, especially for single-parent households.

THE PEOPLE OF JAPAN LIFESTYLE

In the Country

Japan's rural population makes a living doing a variety of work, often seasonally – farming or fishing for part of the year and picking up other work, such as construction, in the off-season. As of 2015, Japan had 2.1 million full-time commercial farmers, and nearly two-thirds of them were over 65. Many more manage small, subsistence plots, getting up at dawn to weed and prune before heading in to town for work.

ZAINICHI KOREANS

There are just under half a million Koreans living in Japan today. For those that trace their origin to Japan's colonial empire, their history is a complicated one. When Japan annexed Korea in 1910 many migrants came to Japan for work; during WWII hundreds of thousands were brought over by the Japanese government to work in wartime factories or stand on the front lines. When the war ended and Korea regained its independence most Koreans returned home, but quite a few stayed. Some had established lives in Japan; others couldn't afford the trip home; and still others were wary of instability on the peninsula.

Under the colonial empire Koreans were subjects of the Japanese emperor; however after the war, the Japanese government did not automatically grant those Koreans who stayed citizenship. Instead they became Zainichi (temporary residents) and were effectively stateless. Up until the 1980s, Zainichi Koreans who wished to become naturalised citizens were required to adopt Japanese-sounding names.

Zainichi Koreans who did not naturalise faced discrimination in the workplace and in marriage. Those who did were often accused of betrayal by those who hadn't; if outed, they would face discrimination anyway.

When Japan resumed diplomatic relations with South Korea in 1965, the latter allowed Zainichi Koreans to claim South Korean nationality, which would now be recognised in Japan. Those who chose not to, perhaps because their allegiance or family ties lay with North Korea, and had not become naturalised Japanese citizens, remain stateless. According to the 2015 census, there are 34,000 of them.

While some Zainichi Koreans are now fourth or fifth generation residents of Japan many do still report episodes of discrimination or hate speech.

Children who would have followed in the footsteps of their parents now head to the cities for university, often never looking back. However some, after putting in a couple of decades at a corporation, feel a pull to return to their *jika* (hometown). Often it's to take care of aging parents, but sometimes, too, there is a sense of weariness of city life or a desire to give back to their communities.

Meanwhile, there is now a generation of urban Japanese who are so removed from rural life as to think it all sounds very romantic. They dream of finding an old *minka* (country house), fixing it up and starting an organic farm, selling their wares online to their former urban peers. Some actually follow through. Whether this is enough to save Japan's rural communities from steep population decline remains to be seen.

Religion

Shintō and Buddhism are the main religions in Japan. For much of history they were intertwined. Only about one-third of Japanese today identify as Buddhist and the figure for Shintō is just 3%; however most Japanese participate in annual rituals rooted in both, which they see as integral parts of their culture and community ties. New Year's visits to shrines and temples are just one example. Generally in Japan, Shintō is concerned with this life: births and marriages for example are celebrated at shrines. Meanwhile, Buddhism deals with the afterlife: funerals and memorials take place at temples.

Shintō

Shintō, or 'the way of the gods' is the indigenous religion of Japan. It locates divinity in the natural world. Its *kami* (gods) inhabit trees, rocks, waterfalls and mountains; they can be summoned through rituals of dance and music into the shrines the Japanese have built for them, where they are beseeched with prayers for a good harvest, fertility and the like. The pantheon of deities includes thousands, from the celebrated sun goddess Amaterasu to the humble hearth *kami*.

Shintō has no central scripture, so it is hard to pin down, but one central tenet is purity. Visitors to shrines first wash their hands and mouth at a font at the gate; many rituals involve fire or water, prized for their cleansing powers. Over time, shrines have accrued specialisations – this one is good for business; that one for matchmaking. While very few Japanese say they believe in Shintō, it is still common to visit a shrine for luck. At the very least, people think, it can't hurt.

VISITING A SHINTŌ SHRINE

A visit to a shrine is a prescribed ritual. Upon entering a *torii* gate, it's the custom to bow, hands pressed together, and then proceed to the *temizuya* (font). Use the dipper to collect water from the spigot, pour it over your left hand and then your right (careful not to let the water drip back into the font). Fill your left hand with water and rinse out your mouth; then rinse your left hand a final time with the remaining water.

Next, head to the *haiden* (hall of worship), which sits in front of the *honden* (main hall) enshrining the *kami* (god of the shrine). Here you'll find a thick rope hanging from a gong, with an offerings box in front. Toss a coin – a ¥5 coin is considered lucky – into the box and ring the gong by pulling on the rope (to summon the deity). Then pray, clap your hands twice, bow and then back away from the shrine. Be sure to bow again at the gate on your way out.

Buddhism

When Buddhism entered Japan via Korea in the 6th century it didn't so much displace Shintō as envelop it; now there were *kami* and bodhitsattvas (people who put off entry into nirvana in order to save the rest of us stuck in the corrupt world of time).

Several waves of Buddhist teachings arrived on Japanese shores; notably meditative Zen, Shingon (an esoteric sect related to Tantric Buddhism), and Pure Land, which preached of the salvation of heaven (the Pure Land). It was the latter that most struck a chord with common Japanese and Pure Land (called Jōdo-shū) remains the most popular form of Buddhism today. Kannon (the bodhitsattva of mercy and an important Pure Land figure) is the most worshiped deity in Japan.

Women in Japan

Women have traditionally been viewed as keepers of the home, responsible for overseeing the household budget, monitoring the children's education and taking care of the day-to-day tasks of cooking and cleaning. Of course this ideal was rarely matched by reality: labour shortfalls often resulted in women taking on factory work and, even before that, women often worked side by side with men in the fields.

As might be expected, the contemporary situation is complex. There are women who prefer the traditionally neat division of labour. They tend to opt for shorter college courses, often at women's colleges. They may work for several years, enjoying a period of freedom before settling down, leaving the role of breadwinner to the husband and becoming full-time mums.

This is often seen as the path of least resistance. While gender discrimination in the workforce is illegal, it remains pernicious. And while there is less societal resistance to women working, they still face enormous pressure to be doting mothers. Most women see the long hours that Japanese companies demand as incompatible with child-rearing, especially in the early years; few fathers are willing or, given their own work commitments, able to pick up the slack. Attempts at work-life balance, such as working from home, can result in guilt trips from colleagues or bosses. Working women have coined the phrase 'maternity harassment' to describe the remarks they hear in the office after announcing a pregnancy, the subtle suggestions that she quit so as not to cause trouble.

Women do in fact make up over 40% of the workforce; however, over half of them are working part-time and often menial, low-paying jobs.

In the face of Japan's declining birth rate, the central government has acknowledged the untapped labour potential of its female population (while still encouraging women to have more babies, naturally). In 2003 the government set a target of having women make up 30% of managerial positions by 2020; it has since scaled back its expectations to 15%. The current rate is 12% in the private sector; it's similarly low in the Diet.

Japan has the third largest pay-gap among developed countries: in 2015 Bloomberg reported that women who are in full-time employment make roughly 30% less than their male counterparts. Taking all of this into account, the World Economic Forum has given Japan the damning rating of 111 out of 144 countries in its Global Gender Gap Report for 2016.

On the upside: Japanese women have the longest life expectancy on earth, at 86.83 years of age.

Additional Reading

Contemporary Japan: History, Politics and Social Change Since the 1980s (Jeff Kingston; 2010)

Zen and Japanese Culture (Daisetz T Suzuki; 2010)

Ametora: How Japan Saved American Style (W David Marx; 2016)

Handbook of Japanese Mythology (Michael Ashkenazi; 2008)

Japanese Cuisine

At its best, Japanese food is highly seasonal, drawing on fresh local ingredients coaxed into goodness with a light touch. In 2013 *washoku* (Japanese cuisine) was added to Unesco's Intangible Cultural Heritage list. There are classic dishes, like tempura, that can be found all over and regional specialities that may be local to just one small town. Larger cities, meanwhile, have vibrant, cosmopolitan dining scenes.

The Japanese Restaurant Experience

When you enter a restaurant in Japan, you'll be greeted with a hearty *irasshaimase* (Welcome!). In all but the most casual places, the waiter will next ask you *nan-mei sama* (How many people?). Indicate the answer with your fingers, which is what the Japanese do. You may also be asked if you would like to sit at a *zashiki* (low table on the tatami), at a *tēburu* (table) or the *kauntā* (counter). Once seated you will be given an *o-shibori* (hot towel), a cup of tea or water (this is free) and a menu.

Ordering: more and more restaurants these days (especially in touristy areas) have English menus. If they don't and you can't work out what to order, there are two phrases that may help: *o-susume wa nan desu ka* (What do you recommend?) and *omakase shimasu* (Please decide for me).

Often the bill will be placed discreetly on your table. If not, you can ask for it by catching the server's eye and making a cross in the air (to form a kind of 'x') with your index fingers. You can also say *o-kanjō kudasai*.

There's no tipping, though higher-end restaurants usually tack on a 10% service fee. During dinner service, some restaurants (especially *izakaya*) may instead levy a kind of cover charge (usually a few hundred yen); this will be the case if you are served a small appetiser (called *o-tsumami*, or 'charm') when you sit down.

Payment is usually settled at the register near the entrance. Keep in mind that many smaller restaurants, especially those in the countryside, may not accept credit cards.

MAGIC WORDS FOR DINING IN JAPAN

If you're generally an adventurous (or curious) eater, don't let the absence of an English menu put you off. Instead, tell the staff (or ideally the chef), *omakase de onegaishimasu* (I'll leave it up to you).

This works especially well when you're sitting at the counter of a smaller restaurant or *izakaya*, where a rapport naturally develops between the diners and the cooks. It's best said with enthusiasm and a disarming smile, to reassure everyone that you really are game.

This isn't just a tourist hack: Japanese diners do this all the time. Menus might not reflect seasonal dishes and odds are the chef is working on something new that he or she is keen to test out on the willing.

It's probably a good idea to set a price cap, like: *hitori de san-zen-en* (one person for ¥3000).

Eating Etiquette

All but the most extreme type-A chefs will say they'd rather have foreign visitors enjoy their meal than agonise over getting the etiquette right. Still, a few points to note if you want to make a good impression:

Chopsticks This is really the only big deal: do not stick your chopsticks upright in a bowl of rice or pass food from one pair of chopsticks to another – both are reminiscent of Japanese funereal rites. When serving yourself from a shared dish, it's polite to use the back end of your chopsticks (ie not the end that goes into your mouth) to place the food on your own small dish.

Lunchtime Lunch is one of Japan's great bargains; however, restaurants can only offer cheap lunch deals because they anticipate high turnover. Spending too long sipping coffee after finishing your meal might earn you dagger eyes from the kitchen.

Polite Expressions Before digging in, it is customary in Japan to say *itadakimasu* (literally 'I will receive' but closer to 'bon appétit' in meaning). Similarly, at the end of the meal, thanks is given to the host or cook with the phrase, *gochisō-sama deshita,* which means 'It was a real feast'.

Soy Sauce There's nothing that makes a Japanese chef grimace more than out-of-towners who over-season their food – a little soy sauce and wasabi goes a long way (and heaven forbid, don't pour soy sauce all over your rice; it makes it much harder to eat with chopsticks).

Kampai It's considered bad form to fill your own glass. Instead, fill the drained glasses around you and someone will quickly reciprocate; when they do, raise your glass slightly with two hands – a graceful way to receive anything. Once everyone's glass has been filled, the usual starting signal is a chorus of *kampai,* which means 'Cheers!'.

Slurp In Japan, it's perfectly OK, even expected, to slurp your noodles. They should be eaten at whip speed, before they go soggy (letting them do so would be an affront to the chef); that's why you'll hear diners slurping, sucking in air to cool their mouths.

Where & What to Eat

The Japanese dining scene is distinguished by (at the very minimum) two things: the sheer number of restaurants and the fact that most of them are rather small, often specialising in just one or two things. Sushi shops make sushi; tempura shops make tempura. A restaurant that does too much might be suspect: how can it compare to a speciality shop that has been honing its craft for three generations?

An unintended benefit of this is that it simplifies ordering. Restaurants with broader menus, especially franchises, will often have picture menus. High-end restaurants often have no menu at all – just a set course decided that day by the chef depending on what happened to look good at the market that morning.

Shokudō

Dining trends may come and go but *shokudō* (食堂; inexpensive, all-round eateries) are forever. You'll find them in and around train stations and in tourist areas.

They serve classic comfort foods like rice bowls with various toppings (*donburi*; どんぶり or 丼) and *katsu* (breaded and fried) dishes. Office workers love *shokudō* because they're quick and cheap (a meal often costs less than ¥1000); families love them because there's a good variety of things kids will likely eat.

At lunch, and sometimes dinner, the easiest meal to order at a *shokudō* is a *teishoku* (set-course meal), which is sometimes also called *ranchi setto* (lunch set). This generally includes a main dish of meat or fish, a

Rice has been the staple food in Japan since the country's first recorded history. Today, the average Japanese person consumes 57kg of rice per year. That's half as much as 50 years ago – a reflection of rapidly changing diet trends.

JAPANESE CUISINE WHERE & WHAT TO EAT

Cullinary Reading

Kitcho: Japan's Ultimate Dining Experience (Kunio Tokuoka & Nobuko Sugimoto; 2010)

Food, Sake, Tokyo (Yukari Sakamoto; 2010)

What's What in Japanese Restaurants: A Guide to Ordering, Eating & Enjoying (Robb Satterwhite; 2011)

bowl of rice, *miso-shiru* (bean-paste soup), shredded cabbage and some *tsukemono* (Japanese pickles).

Many *shokudō* have plastic food displays in the windows, which of course makes ordering simple. If it's a smaller place, odds are they will have a daily lunch special (*kyō-no-ranchi*; 今日のランチ).

ebi-katsu	海老カツ	breaded and fried prawns
katsu-don	かつ丼	rice topped with a fried pork cutlet
katsu-karē	カツカレー	rice topped with a fried pork cutlet and curry
omu-raisu	オムライス	omelet and fried rice, with ketchup
oyako-don	親子丼	rice topped with egg and chicken
shōga-yaki	生姜焼き	stir-fried pork and ginger
ten-don	天丼	rice topped with tempura prawns and vegetables

Izakaya

Izakaya (居酒屋) translates as 'drinking house' – the Japanese equivalent of a pub – and you'll find them all over Japan. Visiting one is a great way to dig into Japanese culture.

An evening at an *izakaya* is dinner and drinks all in one: food is ordered for the table a few dishes at a time along with rounds of beer, sake or *shōchū* (a strong distilled alcohol often made from potatoes). While the vibe is lively and social, it's perfectly acceptable to go by yourself and sit at the counter. If you don't want alcohol, it's fine to order a soft drink instead (but it would be strange to not order at least one drink).

There are orthodox, family run *izakaya*, often with rustic interiors, that serve sashimi and grilled fish to go with sake; large, cheap chains, popular with students, that often have a healthy (er, unhealthy) dose of Western pub-style dishes (like chips); and there are also stylish chef-driven ones with creative menus.

A night out at an average *izakaya* should run ¥2500 to ¥5000 per person, depending on how much you drink. Chains often have deals where you can pay a set price for a certain amount of dishes and free drinks.

The highly prized Japanese *matsutake* mushroom can sell for up to US$2000 per kilogram. They are usually enjoyed in the autumn, sometimes in the form of a tea, at other times grilled or with rice.

agedashi-tōfu	揚げだし豆腐	deep-fried tofu in a *dashi* (fish) broth
edamame	枝豆	salted and boiled fresh soy beans
hiyayakko	冷奴	a cold block of tofu with soy sauce and spring onions
jaga-batā	ジャガバター	baked potatoes with butter
karaage	唐揚げ	fried chicken
moro-kyū	もろきゅう	sliced cucumbers and chunky barley miso
niku-jaga	肉ジャガ	beef and potato stew
sashimi mori-awase	刺身盛り合わせ	a selection of sliced sashimi
shio-yaki-zaka-na	塩焼魚	a whole fish grilled with salt
yaki-onigiri	焼きおにぎり	a triangle of grilled rice with *yakitori* sauce

Yakitori

Putting away skewers of *yakitori* (charcoal-grilled chicken and vegetables), along with beer, is a popular after-work ritual. Most *yakitori-ya* (*yakitori* restaurants) are convivial counter joints where the food is grilled over hot coals in front of you. It's typical to order a few skewers at a time. They're usually priced between ¥100 and ¥300 a piece; one order may mean two skewers (and thus may mean double the price). The chef will ask if you want your skewers seasoned with *shio* (salt) or *tare* (sauce). *Yakitori* restaurants are often located near train stations and are best identified by a red lantern outside (and the smell of grilled chicken).

hasami/negima	はさみ/ねぎま	pieces of white meat alternating with leek
kawa	皮	chicken skin
piiman	ピーマン	small green capsicums (peppers)
rebā	レバー	chicken livers
sasami	ささみ	skinless chicken-breast pieces
shiitake	しいたけ	Japanese mushrooms
tama-negi	玉ねぎ	round white onions
tebasaki	手羽先	chicken wings
tsukune	つくね	chicken meatballs
yaki-onigiri	焼きおにぎり	a triangle of grilled rice with *yakitori* sauce

Sushi & Sashimi

Sushi (寿司 or 鮨) is raw fish and rice seasoned with vinegar and it comes in many forms. The most common kind is *nigiri-zushi*, the bite-sized slivers of seafood hand-pressed onto pedestals of rice. This style originated in Tokyo but is now served all over. It can be very high-end, served piece by piece at exclusive *sushi-ya* (sushi restaurants) where a meal of seasonal delicacies could run over ¥20,000 per person.

It can also be very cheap, at *kaiten-zushi* (回転寿司), for example, where ready-made plates of sushi (about ¥200 each) are sent around the restaurant on a conveyor belt. Here there's no need to order: just grab whatever looks good.

At an average *sushi-ya*, a meal should run between ¥2000 and ¥5000 per person. You can order à la carte – often by just pointing to the fish in the refrigerated glass case on the counter – or *mori-awase*, as an assortment plate; the latter is a better deal (unless you are set on eating only your favourites). These usually come in three grades: *futsū* or *nami* (regular), *jō* (special) and *toku-jō* (extra-special). The price difference is determined more by the value of the ingredients than by volume.

Unless otherwise instructed by the chef (who may have preseasoned some pieces), you can dip each piece lightly in *shōyu* (soy sauce), which you pour from a small decanter into a low dish specially provided for the purpose. *Nigiri-sushi* is usually made with wasabi, so if you'd prefer it without, order *wasabi-nuki*.

Sushi is one of the few foods in Japan that is perfectly acceptable to eat with your hands (even at high-end places!). Slices of *gari* (pickled ginger) are served to refresh the palate.

Sushi restaurants usually serve *chirashi-zushi*, bite-sized pieces of seafood scattered on a bowl of rice; this too tends to be offered at different grades (using the same terms) and makes for a great lunch. You can also order seafood without rice, called sashimi or *o-tsukuri*, or rolled in rice and seaweed (*maki-zushi*).

One of the most popular Shintō deities is Inari, traditionally the god of the rice harvest. Reflecting the changing nature of the Japanese economy, Inari is now the god of all sorts of commerce. At last count there were 2970 shrines to Inari around Japan.

Though much is made of the freshness of the ingredients in modern sushi, the dish originated as a way to make fish last longer: the vinegar in the rice was a preserving agent. An older form of sushi, called *hako-zushi* or *oshi-zushi* ('box' or 'pressed' sushi) and more common in western Japan, is made of fish pressed onto a bed of heavily vinegared rice in a wooden mould with a weighted top. Left to rest, it acquires a slight tang of fermentation.

ama-ebi	甘海老	sweet shrimp
awabi	あわび	abalone
ebi	海老	prawn or shrimp
hamachi	はまち	yellowtail
ika	いか	squid
ikura	イクラ	salmon roe
kai-bashira	貝柱	scallop
kani	かに	crab
katsuo	かつお	bonito
maguro	まぐろ	tuna
tai	鯛	sea bream
tamago	たまご	sweetened egg
toro	とろ	the choice cut of fatty tuna belly
unagi	うなぎ	eel with a sweet sauce
uni	うに	sea-urchin roe

Sukiyaki & Shabu-shabu

Both sukiyaki and *shabu-shabu* are hotpot dishes, cooked by diners at the table, and the same restaurant usually serves both (but may be known for one or the other). For sukiyaki, thin slices of beef are briefly simmered in a broth of *shōyu* (soy sauce), sugar and sake and then dipped in raw egg (you can skip the last part, though it makes the marbled beef taste even creamier).

For *shabu-shabu*, thin slices of pork and/or beef are swished around in boiling broth, then dipped in either a sesame sauce *(goma-dare)* or *ponzu* (citrus and soy sauce).

In either case, a healthy mix of veggies and tofu are added to the pot a little bit at a time followed by noodles at the end. So while sukiyaki and *shabu-shabu* can seem expensive (from around ¥3000 per person to upwards of ¥10,000 for premium beef), it is an all-inclusive meal.

One party shares the pot and the minimum order is usually two (though some places do lunch deals for solo diners); so unless there are four or more of you, you'll all have to choose one or the other, sukiyaki or *shabu-shabu*. The waitstaff will set everything up for you and most likely mime instructions.

Tabelog (https://tabelog.com/en) is Japan's most popular customer-review website for restaurants. While it's not un-impeachable, it's pretty reliable.

Tempura

Tempura is seafood (fish, eel or prawns) and vegetables (like pumpkin, green pepper, sweet potato or onion) lightly battered and deep-fried in sesame oil. Season by dipping each piece lightly in salt or a bowl of *tentsuyu* (broth for tempura) mixed with grated *daikon* (Japanese radish).

Tempura is usually served as a set (all at once, with rice and soup) or as a course, with pieces delivered one at a time freshly cooked; a tempura meal can cost between ¥2000 and ¥10,000, with a course being the most expensive.

kaki age	かき揚げ	tempura with shredded vegetables or fish
shōjin age	精進揚げ	vegetarian tempura
tempura moriawase	天ぷら盛り合わせ	a selection of tempura

Ramen

Ramen originated in China, but its popularity in Japan is epic. If a town has only one restaurant, odds are it's a ramen shop.

Your basic ramen is a big bowl of crinkly egg noodles in broth, served with toppings such as *chāshū* (sliced roast pork), *moyashi* (bean sprouts) and *negi* (leeks). The broth can be made from pork or chicken bones or dried seafood; usually it's a top-secret combination of some or all of the above, falling somewhere on the spectrum between *kotteri* (thick and fatty – a signature of pork bone ramen) or *assari* (thin and light).

It's typically seasoned with *shio* (salt), *shōyu* (soy sauce) or hearty miso – though at less orthodox places, anything goes. Most shops will specialise in one or two broths and offer a variety of seasonings and toppings. Another popular style is *tsukemen*, noodles that come with a dipping sauce (like a really condensed broth) on the side.

Given the option, most diners get their noodles *katame* (literally 'hard' but more like al dente). If you're really hungry, ask for *kaedama* (another serving of noodles), usually only a couple of hundred yen more.

Top Ramen Towns

Fukuoka, Kyūshū

Sapporo, Hokkaidō

Onomichi, Hiroshima

Asahikawa, Hokkaidō

Tokyo

DINING MADE EASY

Some tips for when the options seem overwhelming and you just want to grab a bite.

Department Stores

Department stores always have restaurant floors on their upper levels; often the restaurants are branches of famous ones, the food quality rather high and the price point not bad. These restaurants also tend to be family- and wheelchair-friendly and have English menus. Takeaway and deli dishes can be purchased in the food halls in the basement; go just before closing to get discounted items.

Chain Restaurants

Fast food is plenty big in Japan and there are several domestic chains that have loyal followings. Bonus: many have English menus.

Curry House CoCo Ichibanya 'Coco Ichi' does big plates of Japanese-style curry and rice.

MOS Burger Swap your standard patty for a shrimp croquette or the bun for one made of rice. Has veggie burgers, too.

Ootoya (大戸屋) *Shokudō*-style standby for healthy set meals of rice, fish, vegetables and soup.

Yoshinoya (吉野家) *Gyūdon* (sukiyaki-style beef served over a bowl of rice) is the speciality here; it's filling and super cheap.

Convenience Stores

Always good in a pinch – and virtually everywhere – *konbini* (コンビニ; convenience stores) sell *bentō* (boxed meals, which you can ask to have microwaved), sandwiches and *onigiri* (stuffed rice balls) packaged to go. Next to the register, look for *niku-man* (肉まん), which are steamed buns filled with pork, curry and more; and, in winter, *oden*, a dish of fish cakes, hard-boiled egg and vegetables in *dashi* (fish stock) broth.

Well-executed ramen is a complex, layered dish – though it rarely costs more than ¥1000 a bowl. Costs are minimised by fast-food-style service: often you order from a vending machine (you'll get a paper ticket, which you hand to the chef); water is self-serve. Many *ramen-ya* (ramen restaurants) also serve *chāhan* (fried rice) and *gyōza* (dumplings).

Japan's Famous Markets

Tsukiji (p79), Tokyo

Nishiki (p304), Kyoto

Kuromon (p367), Osaka

Ōmi-chō (p249), Kanazawa

Makishi (p787), Naha

chāshū-men	チャーシュー麺	ramen topped with slices of roasted pork
miso ramen	みそラーメン	ramen with miso-flavoured broth
ramen	ラーメン	soup and egg noodles topped with meat and vegetables
tsuke-men	つけ麺	ramen noodles with soup on the side

Soba & Udon

Soba (thin brown buckwheat noodles, often cut with wheat) and udon (thick white wheat noodles) are Japan's traditional noodles. Restaurants usually serve both, though eastern Japan tends to favour soba while western Japan leans towards udon.

Cheap noodle shops, where a meal costs less than ¥1000, are everywhere. There are also nicer ones, with tasteful, often rustic interiors, that specialise in handcut noodles made from premium flours and mountain spring water. Here, a meal might cost two or three times more.

Noodles can be ordered in a hot broth lightly flavoured with bonito and soy sauce with various toppings. They can also be ordered cooled, with dipping sauce (a more condensed broth) on the side. The weather may be a deciding factor but so is personal preference: cooled noodles won't go mushy like those in hot broth so can be savoured (rather than scoffed).

At a good soba shop, one dish to try is *zaru soba* (ざるそば), cooled soba served on a bamboo mat with a cup of broth on the side. Season the broth to taste with wasabi and sliced spring onions and scoop up

JAPANESE BEEF

Wagyū (Japanese beef) has cult status both in Japan and abroad. The meat is incredibly tender, largely so because it is heavily marbled in soft, melty fat – a result of careful breeding techniques. Most *wagyū* comes from a breed of cattle known as Japanese Black. Some cows are hand-fed or drink mountain spring water.

Within the world of *wagyū* are a few premium brands that hew to strict quality control and are prized as top-grade meat. These include Kōbe, Matsusaka and Ōmi. Kōbe, the most well-known brand, is strictly limited to beef from cows raised in Hyōgō-ken (the prefecture in which the city of Kōbe is located) and who are descendants of Tajiri-go, a famed (and prolific) bull from the 1930s.

Kōbe, Matsusaka and Ōmi are all named for places, which have naturally become pilgrimage spots for keen carnivores, though high-grade *wagyū* can be enjoyed in any major Japanese city. Brand-name beef comes with pedigree but it doesn't come cheap (prices start around ¥5000 for a small lunch portion and rise steadily from there). Two things to keep in mind: as the meat is very rich, often a small portion will do. Also, any non-brand *wagyū* with a rating of A4 or, even better, A5 is going to be top-notch (and probably cheaper).

Often the meat is seared at high temperature on a *teppan* (steel hotplate), diced and served with rice and miso soup. You can also grill strips of *wagyū* over coals at Korean-style barbecue restaurants (called *yakiniku*); eat it sukiyaki or *shabu-shabu* style; or order it at steakhouses paired with wine.

All mention of premium Japanese beef comes with the following disclaimer: eat this, and you'll be spoiled for life.

one mouthful of noodles at a time with your chopsticks, sinking them in the broth before slurping them up. When you finish the noodles, staff will bring you a kettle of hot *soba-yu* (the water in which the noodles were cooked), which you can add to the remaining broth to drink like hot soup.

kake soba/udon	かけそば/うどん	soba/udon noodles in broth
kitsune soba/udon	きつねそば/うどん	soba/udon noodles with fried tofu
tempura soba/udon	天ぷらそば/うどん	soba/udon noodles with tempura prawns
tsukimi soba/udon	月見そば/うどん	soba/udon noodles with raw egg
te-uchi	手打ち	handmade
to-wari soba	十割そば	soba made with 100% buckwheat (not cut with wheat)

Tonkatsu

Tonkatsu is a deep-fried breaded pork cutlet, almost always served as a set meal that includes rice, miso soup and a heaping mound of shredded cabbage. At around ¥1500 to ¥2500 a meal, it's perfect for when you want something hearty and filling. When ordering at a speciality shop, you can choose between *rōsu* (a fatter cut of pork) and *hire* (a leaner cut). Season with *tonkatsu* sauce, a curious (and highly addictive) ketchup-y Worcestershire-like condiment.

hire katsu	ヒレかつ	tonkatsu fillet
tonkatsu teishoku	とんかつ定食	a set meal of tonkatsu, rice, miso-shiru (bean-paste soup) and shredded cabbage
rōsu katsu	ロースかつ	tonkatsu pork loin

Okonomiyaki

Okonomiyaki is a dish that flies in the face of the prevailing image of Japanese food being subtle. It's a thick, savoury pancake, stuffed with pork, squid, cabbage, cheese, *mochi* (pounded rice cake) – anything really (*okonomi* means 'as you like'; *yaki* means fry). Once cooked, it's seasoned with *katsuo-bushi* (bonito flakes), *shōyu* (soy sauce), *ao-nori* (an ingredient similar to parsley), a tonkatsu sauce and mayonnaise.

Restaurants specialising in *okonomiyaki* have hotplates built into the tables or counter. Some places do the cooking for you; others give you a bowl of batter and fillings and leave you to it. (Don't panic: the staff will mime instructions and probably keep an eye on you to make sure no real disasters occur.)

Lonely Planet's *From the Source, Japan* (2016) explores the country's regional cuisine through interviews with chefs, homecooks and fishing cooperatives, recipes in their words and gorgeous full-colour photos.

gyū okonomiyaki	牛お好み焼き	beef okonomiyaki
ika okonomiyaki	いかお好み焼き	squid okonomiyaki
mikkusu	ミックスお好み焼き	okonomiyaki with a mix of fillings, including seafood, meat and vegetables
modan-yaki	モダン焼き	okonomiyaki with yaki-soba and a fried egg
negi okonomiyaki	ネギお好み焼き	thin okonomiyaki with spring onions

Kaiseki

Kaiseki is the pinnacle of Japanese cuisine, where ingredients, preparation, setting and presentation come together to create a highly ritualised, aesthetically sophisticated dining experience. It was born in Kyoto as an adjunct to the tea ceremony; though fish is often served, meat never appears in traditional *kaiseki*.

The meal is served in several small courses, giving the diner an opportunity to admire the plates and bowls, which are carefully chosen to complement the food and season. It usually includes sashimi (raw fish), something steamed, something grilled, soup and finishes with rice and then a simple dessert (though there may be many more courses).

At its best, it's eaten in the private room of a *ryōtei* (an especially elegant style of traditional restaurant), often overlooking a private, tranquil garden. This is about as pricey as dining can get in Japan, upwards of ¥20,000 per person, with advance reservations required. There are cheaper places though, and lunch can be a good deal as some restaurants do boxed lunches containing a small sampling of their dinner fare for around ¥2500.

bentō	弁当	boxed meal with rice and several side dishes
kaiseki	懐石	traditional Japanese haute cuisine
matsu	松	extra-special course
take	竹	special course
ume	梅	regular course

Best Cookbooks

Izakaya: The Japanese Pub Cookbook (Mark Robinson; 2012)

Japanese Farm Food (Nancy Singleton Hachisu; 2012)

Kansha (Elizabeth Andoh; 2010)

Japanese Soul Cooking (Tadashi Ono & Harris Salat; 2013)

Sweets

Dessert isn't really a thing in Japanese cuisine, though some restaurants serve sliced fruit or ice cream at the end of a meal; instead, sweets are generally an accompaniment for tea.

Japanese confections are known generically as *wagashi* (as opposed to *yōgashi*, Western-style sweets like cake and cookies). The basic ingredients are just rice and a sweetened paste of red *azuki* beans (called *anko*). Flavour (usually subtle) and design (often exquisite) are influenced by the seasons. In spring they may be shaped like cherry blossoms or wrapped in cherry leaves; in autumn they might be golden coloured, like the leaves, or flavoured with chestnut.

Okashi-ya (sweet shops) are easy to spot: they usually have open fronts with their wares laid out in wooden trays to entice passers-by. Buying sweets is simple – just point at what you want and indicate with your fingers how many you'd like.

Cooking Courses

Buddha Bellies (p114), Tokyo

A Taste of Culture (www.tasteofculture.com), Tokyo

Green Cooking School (p237), Takayama

Tokyo Cooking Studio (p114), Tokyo

Uzuki (p330), Kyoto

Haru Cooking Class (p331), Kyoto

anko	あんこ	sweet paste or jam made from *azuki* beans
kashiwa-mochi	柏餅	pounded glutinous rice with a sweet filling, wrapped in an aromatic oak leaf
mochi	餅	pounded rice cakes made of glutinous rice
wagashi	和菓子	Japanese-style sweets
yōkan	ようかん	sweet red-bean jelly

Special Diets

Vegetarian & Vegan

On the surface, Japan would appear to be an easy place for veggies and vegans, but the devil is in the details: many dishes (including miso soup) are seasoned with *dashi*, a broth made from fish.

Many cities in Japan do have restaurants that specifically offer vegetarian and vegan dishes. **Happy Cow** (www.happycow.net/asia/japan) is a good resource. In the countryside, you'll need to work a little bit harder and be prepared to explain what you can and cannot eat. If you're staying in a ryokan, make sure to put in a request for a vegetarian meal when you book; places that regularly get foreign travellers can usually accommodate this.

You might want to seek out *shōjin-ryōri*, the traditionally vegetarian cuisine of Buddhist monks; Kōya-san in Kansai is a good place for this.

Gluten Free & Allergies

Many chain restaurants and deli counters label their dishes with icons indicating potential allergens (such as dairy, eggs, peanuts, wheat and shellfish). Gluten free is hard: many kitchen staples, like soy sauce, contain wheat and even restaurant staff may not be aware of this. The Gluten Free Expats Japan Facebook group is a good resource.

Halal

Japan now has more halal options than it used to have. See Halal Gourmet Japan (www.halalgourmet.jp) for a list of restaurants that can accommodate halal (and vegetarian) diners.

Drinks

Visitors to Japan will have numerous opportunities to get better acquainted with the country's signature beverages, sake and green tea. In the last few years, craft-beer pubs and indie coffee shops have taken off in larger cities.

Where to Drink

Alcohol is largely considered an accompaniment for food (or often the other way around) so places to eat, like *izakaya* (Japanese pubs) and *yakitori-ya* (restaurants specialising in charcoal-grilled skewers), double as nightspots. Rather than tucking into a full meal, a succession of small plates, often to share, are ordered bit by bit along with drinks. Larger cities have a huge variety of bars, including many that specialise in craft beer, and a growing coffeehouse scene. In summer, look for beer gardens that pop up on the rooftops of department stores.

Japan has lots of farmers markets, especially in the big cities. For info on upcoming ones (and some musing on seasonal produce), see the English-language blog Japan Farmers Markets (www.japanfarmersmarkets.com).

THE WATER TRADE

The murkier side of Japan's nightlife culture is what is euphemistically called 'the water trade' *(mizu-shōbai)*. Here customers pay more for the charm factor (and sex appeal) of the cocktail waitresses (and sometimes waiters) than for the drinks, and a night in a 'hostess' or 'host' bar can wind up costing an unholy sum. Such establishments are often obvious, with photos of attractive young women or men plastered outside; others – usually the more expensive ones – can be more discreet.

Most typically decline entry to visitors who can't speak Japanese, but in some nightlife districts touts sometimes target foreign male travellers (knowing that by not understanding how things work, the tourists might end up spending big bucks in their establishment).

A 'snack' (スナック; *sunakku*) is a more low-key, less expensive version of a hostess bar where the relationship between the waitresses and their customers (usually older men) is more friendly than charged. These bars typically have covered windows and loud karaoke.

Oft-maligned 'gaijin bars' – bars frequented by expats that are often a bit grotty – can be good sources of local intel, as bartenders usually speak good English.

Nightlife Districts

Any Japanese city of reasonable size will have a *hankagai* (繁華街), a lively commercial and entertainment district. Famous ones include: Tokyo's Kabukichō, Osaka's Dōtombori and Sapporo's Susukino. Such districts are stocked, often several storeys high, with a medley of drinking options that include *izakaya* (traditional pubs), cocktail bars, Western-style pubs, jazz cafes, karaoke parlours, nightclubs and more – all awash in the neon lights that form Japan's urban signature.

What to Drink

Alcohol

The legal drinking age in Japan is 20. Bars generally don't require photo ID as proof of age, but nightclubs are required to check ID cards (of everyone, no matter how far past 20 you look).

Check out the Japan Beer Times website (http://japanbeertimes.com) and app for more info on the craft beer scene in Japan, and keep an eye out for its magazine at brewhouses around the country.

Beer

First brewed in Japan at the end of the 1800s, *biiru* (beer) is now the country's favourite tipple. Many a night out at an *izakaya* (Japanese pub-eatery) begins with the phrase, *toriaezu biiru!* ('first off, beer!').

In 2015, 425 million cases were sold (and beer consumption stats are closely watched by economic pundits; the latest figures, a slight uptick, were welcomed with enthusiasm).

Beer in Japan has long been ruled by what are known as the big five: Kirin, Asahi, Sapporo, Suntory and Orion (the latter is Okinawa's signature beer). Kirin Lager, which you'll often see served in 633mL 'big bottles' (大瓶; *ō-bin*) for the table at old-school *izakaya* has long been synonymous with beer. The younger generation prefers Asahi's Super Dry (also a lager), by the can or from the tap.

The average mug of lager at a bar or restaurant costs around ¥500. Vending machines and convenience stores sell beer for around ¥200 a can.

biiru	ビール	beer
bin-biiru	瓶ビール	bottled beer
nama biiru	生ビール	draught beer

KARAOKE

Karaoke (カラオケ; pronounced kah-rah-oh-kay) isn't just about singing: it's an excuse to let loose, a bonding ritual, a reason to keep the party going past the last train and a way to kill time until the first one starts in the morning. When words fail, it's a way to express yourself – are you the type to sing the latest J-pop hit (dance moves included) or do you go in for an Okinawan folk ballad? It doesn't matter if you're a good singer or not (though the tone-deaf might sign up for singing lessons – such is the important social function of karaoke), as long as you've got heart.

In Japan, karaoke is sung in a private room among friends. Admission is usually charged per person by the half-hour. Food and drinks (ordered by phone) will be brought to the door. To choose a song, use the touch-screen device to search by artist or title; most have an English function and plenty of English songs to choose from. Then let your inner diva shine!

All major cities will have karaoke parlours, usually in well-marked tower buildings with dozens of private rooms.

Sake

What much of the world calls 'sake' the Japanese call *nihonshu* ('the drink of Japan'). It's made from rice, water and *kōji*, a mould that helps to convert the starch in the rice into fermentable sugars.

Sake has existed for as long as history has been recorded in Japan (and odds are a lot longer). It plays an important part in a variety of Shintō rituals, including wedding ceremonies, and many Shintō shrines display huge barrels of sake in front of their halls (most of them are empty). Naturally, sake is the best pairing for traditional Japanese cuisine.

Sake is always brewed during the winter, in the cold months that follow the rice harvest in September. Fresh, young sake is ready by late autumn.

Shōchū

Shōchū is a distilled spirit that can be made from a variety of raw materials, including potato (in which case it's called *imo-jōchū*), barley (*mugi-jōchū*) and black sugar (*kokutō-shōchū*). It's quite strong, with an alcohol content of about 25% (but can be as much as 45%).

The beverage is strongly associated with Kagoshima, in southern Kyūshū, where it was likely first introduced from Okinawa (Okinawa has its own signature distilled spirit called *awamori*, actually made of long-grain rice). Like any spirit, *shōchū* can be harsh – it's long had a rough image to match – or deliciously complex and balanced. The growing presence of the latter over the last two decades has done much to raise *shōchū*'s esteem.

The good stuff can be drunk on the rocks *(rokku de)*. Go down a notch and have it *oyu-wari* (with hot water) or mixed in a *chūhai* (a highball with soda and lemon). *Chūhai* in fruity, seasonal flavours is also a convenience-store staple.

chūhai	チューハイ	shōchū with soda and lemon
oyu-wari	お湯割り	shōchū with hot water
shōchū	焼酎	strong distilled liquor

Tea & Coffee

Coffee

Japan's first-wave coffee shops are called *kissaten* and they tend to serve small cups of dark roast (for around ¥500) accompanied by tiny, adorable single-serving pitchers of cream. Many are quite charming, with vintage mid-20th-century interiors, though they're known to get quite smokey. Until around 11am they often serve a *mōningu setto* (morning set) of tea or coffee, toast and eggs for about the same price as they usually charge for coffee.

The coffee third wave is still cresting in Japan's cities, bringing with it all sorts of indie shops that specialise in hand-poured, single-origin brews or ever more elaborate latte art. Many serve truly excellent coffee.

Filling the need for mediocre on-the-go brews are a number of chains, which charge about ¥300 a cup and can be found all over any city. Staff will usually ask if you want it *hotto* (hot) or *aisu* (cold). If you just want coffee (and not a place to rest), Japan's convenience stores sell coffee that is no better or worse for about ¥100.

There's also the Japanese phenomenon of canned coffee, which can be bought hot or cold from vending machines or convenience stores. It's often very sweet and tastes more like a coffee-flavoured beverage, but it does have the necessary kick.

The online magazine *Sake Today* (www.sake-today.com) has articles on regional sake styles and emerging trends. Managing editor John Gaunter is also the author of the book *Sake Confidential: A Beyond-the-Basics Guide to Understanding, Tasting, Selection and Enjoyment* (2014).

With the exception of the indie speciality shops, cafes in Japan also serve black tea and soft drinks like juice.

American kōhii	アメリカンコーヒー	weak coffee
burendo kōhii	ブレンドコーヒー	blended coffee, fairly strong
kafe ore	カフェオレ	*café au lait*, hot or cold
kōcha	紅茶	black English tea
kōhii	コーヒー	regular coffee
orenji jūsu	オレンジジュース	orange juice

Japanese Tea

Japan is a treat for tea lovers. Here *o-cha* (tea) means green tea and broadly speaking there are two kinds: *ryokucha* (steeped with leaves) and *matcha*, which is made by whisking dried and milled leaves with water until a cappuccino level of frothiness is achieved. It's *matcha* that is served in the tea ceremony; it is quite bitter, so it is accompanied by a traditional sweet.

When you order *o-cha* in a Japanese restaurant (it's usually free, like water), you'll most likely be served *bancha*, ordinary tea. (In summer, you might get cold *mugicha*, roasted barley tea, instead.) So if you want to try out the more rarefied stuff, you'll have to seek out a teahouse or speciality shop. After a course meal, restaurants often serve *hōjicha*, roasted green tea, which is weaker and less caffeinated.

A plethora of hot and cold bottled teas can be purchased from vending machines and convenience stores; department store food halls are a good spot for buying higher-grade loose-leaf tea.

bancha	番茶	ordinary-grade green tea, with a brownish colour
matcha	抹茶	powdered green tea used in the tea ceremony
mugicha	麦茶	roasted barley tea
o-cha	お茶	green tea
sencha	煎茶	medium-grade green tea
hōjicha	ほうじ茶	roasted green tea
genmaicha	玄米茶	green tea mixed with roasted brown rice
gyokuro	玉露	the highest grade of green tea, shaded from the sun and picked early in the season

Soft Drinks

While drinking plays a big role in Japanese society, you needn't drink alcohol to participate. The most common nonalcoholic *izakaya* order is oolong tea (烏龍茶; *ūron-cha*), a Chinese tea that can be ordered hot or cold; bars also serve soft drinks and juices. You just need to order something, for the first round at least, so you have a glass to raise.

At shrines, teahouses and winter festivals, you can sometimes find a sweet, nonalcoholic fermented rice drink called *amazake* (甘酒), served hot.

Tea served at a teahouse in Tokyo

Arts

Japan has a sublime artistic tradition that transcends gallery walls, the pages of books and the kabuki stage to seep into everyday life. It animates the tea cups used in the tea ceremony and the sculptural assemblage of flowers in ikebana (among other things). It is a tradition that has been influenced by the cultures of continental Asia and later the West while being shaped by a tendency to refine techniques and materials to an almost maniacal degree.

Traditional Visual Art

Painting

The screen paintings of Hasegawa Tohaku, created almost 400 years ago, are said to be the first examples of Impressionist art.

Japan has a rich history of painting, albeit one routinely influenced by China and then, from the 19th century, by the West (which was influenced by Japan in return). Traditionally, paintings consisted of black ink or mineral pigments on *washi* (Japanese handmade paper) and were sometimes decorated with gold leaf. These works adorned folding screens, sliding doors and hanging scrolls; never behind glass, they were a part of daily life.

Paintings of the Heian era (794–1185) depicted episodes of court life, like those narrated in the novel *Genji Monogatari (The Tale of Genji)*, or seasonal motifs, often on scrolls. Works such as these were later called *yamato-e* (Yamato referring to the imperial clan), as they distinguished themselves thematically from those that were mere copies of Chinese paintings. Gradually a series of style conventions evolved to further distinguish *yamato-e;* one of the most striking is the use of a not-quite-bird's-eye perspective peering into palace rooms without their roofs (the better to see the intrigue!).

With the rise of Zen Buddhism in the 14th century, minimalist monochrome ink paintings came into vogue; the painters themselves were priests and the quick, spontaneous brush strokes of this painting style were in harmony with their guiding philosophies.

It was during the Muromachi period (1333–1573) that the ruling class became great patrons of Japanese painters, giving them the space and the means to develop their own styles. Two styles emerged at this time; the Tosa school and the Kano school.

Pottery Towns

Arita

Bizen

Hagi

Kanazawa

Mashiko

The Tosa clan of artists worked for the imperial house, and were torch-bearers for the now classic *yamato-e* style, using fine brushwork to create highly stylised figures and elegant scenes from history and of the four seasons; sometimes the scenes were half-cloaked in washes of wispy gold clouds.

The Kano painters were under the patronage of the Ashikaga shogunate and employed to decorate their castles and villas. It was they who created the kind of works most associated with Japanese painting: decorative polychromatic depictions of mythical Chinese creatures and scenes from nature, boldly outlined on large folding screens and sliding doors.

One of the most famous ukiyo-e is The Great Wave by Hokusai (1760–1849), one of his series Thirty-Six Views of Mt Fuji. Visit the Hokusai Museum in Obuse, where the artist spent his final years, and the new Sumida Hokusai Museum in Tokyo.

The Kano school came to dominate Japanese painting, reaching a near hegemony that lasted through the Tokugawa years, when the lords favoured ever more showy works caked with gold leaf. Meanwhile in

Kansai, another school emerged in the Edo period, Rimpa, which took the shimmering gold of Kano and married it with the more delicate line work of Tosa.

With the Meiji Restoration (1868), when artists and ideas were sent back and forth between Europe and Japan, painting necessarily became either a rejection or an embracing of Western influence. Two terms were coined: *yōga* for Western-style works and *nihonga* for works in the traditional Japanese style. In reality though, many *nihonga* artists incorporated shading and perspective into their works, while using techniques from all the major traditional Japanese painting schools. There are many artists today who continue to create and redefine *nihonga*.

Shodō (Calligraphy)

Shodō (the way of writing) is one of Japan's most valued arts, cultivated by nobles, priests and samurai alike, and is still studied by Japanese school children today as *shūji*. Like the characters of the Japanese kanji script, the art of *shodō* was imported from China. In the Heian period, a fluid, cursive, distinctly Japanese style of *shodō* called *wayō* evolved, though the Chinese style remained popular in Japan among Zen priests and the literati for some time.

In both Chinese and Japanese *shodō* there are three important types. Most common is *kaisho* (block-style script). Due to its clarity, this style is favoured when readability is key. *Gyōsho* (running hand) is semi-cursive and is often used in informal correspondence. *Sōsho* (grass hand) is a truly cursive style. *Sōsho* abbreviates and links the characters together to create a flowing, graceful effect.

Ukiyo-e (Woodblock Prints)

The term *ukiyo-e* means 'pictures of the floating world' and derives from a Buddhist metaphor for the transient world of fleeting pleasures. This 'floating world' was the topsy-turvy kingdom of the pleasure quarters in cities such as Edo (present-day Tokyo), Kyoto and Osaka. Here, the social hierarchies dictated by the Tokugawa shogunate were inverted: money meant more than rank, actors were the arbitrators of style and courtesans were the most accomplished of artists. *Ukiyo-e* were often rather bawdy; there were also those that functioned more like travel postcards – for a populace that wasn't allowed to travel.

The vivid colours, novel composition and flowing lines of *ukiyo-e* caused great excitement in the West, sparking a vogue that one French art critic dubbed *japonisme*. *Ukiyo-e* became a key influence on Impressionists (for example, Toulouse-Lautrec, Manet and Degas) and post-Impressionists. Among the Japanese, the prints were hardly given more than passing consideration – millions were produced annually in Edo. They were often thrown away or used as wrapping paper for pottery. For many years, the Japanese continued to be perplexed by the keen interest foreigners took in this art form, which they considered of ephemeral value.

HIGHLIGHTS OF JAPANESE CINEMA

1950s

The golden age of Japanese film. **Watch** Kurosawa Akira's *Rashōmon* (1950); Mizoguchi's *Ugetsu Monogatari* (1953).

1960s

Colour and prosperity arrive. **Watch** Ozu's *Sanma no Aji* (*An Autumn Afternoon;* 1962).

1970s

Ōshima Nagisa brings new-wave visual techniques and raw sex. **Watch** *Ai no Korīda* (*In the Realm of the Senses;* 1976).

1980s

Imamura Shōhei and Itami Jūzō earn critical success for a new generation. **Watch** Imamura's *Naruyama Bushiko* (*The Ballad of Naruyama;* 1983); Itami's *Tampopo* (1986).

1990s

Actor and comedian Takeshi Kitano emerges as director of merit and vision. **Watch** *Hana-bi* (*Fireworks;* 1997).

2000s

Anime and horror flicks are international hits. **Watch** Miyazaki Hayao's *Sen to Chihiro no Kamikakushi* (*Spirited Away;* 2001) and Fukasaku Kinji's *Battle Royale* (2000).

2010s

New voices and visions. **Watch** Shion Sono's *Love & Peace* (2015) and Hirokazu Koreeda's *Soshite Chichi ni Naru* (*Like Father Like Son;* 2013), which won the Jury Prize at Cannes.

Shikki (Lacquerware)

Known in Japan as *shikki* or *nurimono*, lacquerware is made using the sap from the lacquer tree *(urushi)*, a close relative of poison oak. Raw lacquer is actually toxic and causes severe skin irritation in those who have not developed immunity. Multiple layers of lacquer are painstakingly applied and left to dry, and finally polished to a luxurious shine; once hardened, it becomes extraordinarily durable.

Lacquer is naturally clear; pigments such as iron oxide (which produces vermillion) are added for colour. People in Japan have been using lacquer to protect and enhance the beauty of wood since at least 5000 BC. During the Heian period, black lacquerware decorated with gold and silver powder (called *maki-e*) became popular with court nobles. More sophisticated techniques that developed include inlay (such as mother-of-pearl) and layering different colours and then sanding away the top coat, to create a worn appearance (*negoro* style).

Famous laquer-ware-producing areas include Wajima in Ishikawa Prefecture, where it takes over 100 steps to create pieces that are known for their sturdy elegance, and Okinawa, where the style known as Ryūkyū-shikki incorporates designs of flowers and dragons more common to Chinese art.

Ikebana (Flower Arranging)

The Japanese art of flower arranging known as ikebana is thought to date back to the 6th century when Buddhism entered the country, bringing with it the tradition of leaving flowers as offerings for the spirits of the dead. However, given the older Shintō religion's deification of nature, it's possible that the roots of the art go back even further.

What sets Japanese ikebana (literally 'living flowers') apart from Western forms of flower arranging is the suggestion of space and the symbolism inherent in the choice and placement of the flowers and, in some cases, bare branches. It's not as esoteric as it sounds. It's hard to pinpoint when it emerged (being the most ephemeral of Japanese arts), but it reached its artistic zenith in the 16th century with its incorporation into the rituals and tradition of the tea ceremony.

There are several distinct styles of ikebana. The main contemporary schools are the Kyoto-based Ikenobo (www.ikenobo.jp), and the Tokyo-based Ohara (www.ikebanahq.org/ohara.php) and Sōgetsu (www.sogetsu.or.jp); all hold exhibitions and the Tokyo-based ones conduct classes in English.

Arts in Print

KIE (http://int.kateigaho.com)

Performing Arts Network (www.performingarts.jp)

WABI-SABI

Wabi-sabi is an aesthetic that embraces the notion of ephemerality and imperfection and is Japan's most distinct – though hard to pin down – and profound contribution to the arts. *Wabi* roughly means 'rustic' and connotes the loneliness of the wilderness, while *sabi* can be interpreted as 'weathered', 'waning' or 'altered with age'. Together the two words signify an object's natural imperfections, arising in its inception, and the acquired beauty that comes with the patina of time.

It is most often evoked in descriptions of the tea ceremony, a kind of participatory performance art surrounding the ritual of drinking tea that came into vogue in the 16th century. Ceramics made for the tea ceremony – and this is where Japanese ceramics finally came into their own – often appeared dented or misshapen or had a rough texture, with drips of glaze running down the side. They were prized all the more for their imperfections. The most famous styles associated with the tea ceremony are *raku*, *shigaraki* and *bizen*.

The teahouses too, small, exceedingly humble and somewhat forlorn (compared to the manors they were attached to) also reflected *wabi-sabi* motifs, as did the *ikebana* (flower arrangements) and calligraphy scrolls that would be placed in the teahouse's alcove.

Contemporary Art Scene

The '90s was a big decade for Japanese contemporary art: love him or hate him, Murakami Takashi brought Japan back into an international spotlight it hadn't enjoyed since 19th-century collectors went wild for *ukiyo-e*. His work makes fantastic use of the flat planes, clear lines and decorative techniques associated with *nihonga*, while lifting motifs from the lowbrow subculture of manga (Japanese comics); his spirited, prankish images and installations have become emblematic of the Japanese aesthetic known as *poku* – a concept that combines pop art with an *otaku* (manga and anime super-fan) sensibility.

As much an artist as a clever theorist, Murakami proclaimed in his 'Superflat' manifesto that his work picked up where Japanese artists left off after the Meiji Restoration – and this might just be the future of painting, given that most of us now view the world through the portals of two-dimensional screens. Murakami inspired a whole generation of artists who worked in his 'factory', Kaikai Kiki, and presented their works at his Geisai art fairs.

Naturally, younger artists have had trouble defining themselves in the wake of 'Tokyo Pop', as the highly exportable art of the '90s came to be known. Some artists making a mark include: Tenmyouya Hisashi, who coined the term 'neo-nihonga' to describe his works, which echo the flat surfaces and deep impressions of woodblock prints, while singing a song of the street; conceptual artist Tanaka Koki (named Deutsche Bank's Artist of the Year in 2015); and the collection of irreverent pranksters known as ChimPom, who run a gallery space in Tokyo.

Tokyo is the centre of Japan's contemporary art world, though Kyoto has a thriving gallery scene as well. Travellers with a keen interest in contemporary art will want to make a trip to Naoshima.

Traditional Theatre & Dance

Nō

Sometimes transliterated as noh, this is the oldest of Japan's traditional performing arts, with its roots in Shintō rites. *Nō* is not drama in the usual sense; it seeks to express a poetic moment by symbolic and almost abstract means: glorious movements, sonorous chorus and music, and subtle expression. The stage is furnished with only a single pine tree.

There are two principal characters: the *shite,* who is sometimes a living person but more often a demon or a ghost whose soul cannot rest; and the *waki,* who leads the main character towards the play's climactic moment. The haunting masks of *nō* theatre always depict female or nonhuman characters; adult male characters are played without masks.

Providing light relief to the sometimes heavy drama of *nō* are the comic vignettes known as *kyōgen,* some of which reference the main play, others of which stand alone. Colloquial language is used, so they are easier to understand for a contemporary audience than the esoteric chanting of *nō*.

The National Nō Theatre is located in Tokyo and there are many active schools that occasionally host performances. In summer and fall, outdoor, firelit performances called *takagi-nō* take place at shrines; Sado-ga-shima is famous for these.

Kabuki

Around the year 1600, a charismatic shrine priestess in Kyoto led a troupe of female performers in a new type of dance people dubbed kabuki – a slang expression that meant 'cool' or 'in vogue' at the time. The dancing – rather ribald and performed on a dry riverbed for gathering crowds – was also a gateway to prostitution. A series of crackdowns by

Art Festivals

Echigo-Tsumari Art Triennale (www. echigo-tsumari.jp)

Fukuoka Asian Art Triennale (http:// fukuokatriennale. ajibi.jp)

Sapporo International Arts Festival (http://siaf.jp)

Setouchi Triennale (www.setouchi-art-fest.jp)

Yokohama Triennale (www. yokohamatriennale.jp)

Suggested Reading

From Postwar to Postmodern, Art in Japan 1945–1989 (Dorun Chung; 2013)

Hundred Years of Japanese Film (Donald Richie; 2012)

The Columbia Anthology of Modern Japanese Drama (Eds J Thomas Rimer, Mitsuya Mori & M Cody Poulton; 2014)

the Tokugawa establishment (first on female performers, then on adolescent male performers) gave rise to one of the most fascinating elements of kabuki, the *onnagata* (adult male actors who specialise in portraying women).

As kabuki spread to Edo (Tokyo), it developed hand in hand with the increasingly affluent merchant class, whose decadent tastes translated into the breathtaking costumes, dramatic music and elaborate stagecraft that have come to characterise the art form. It is this intensely visual nature that makes kabuki accessible to foreign audiences – you don't really have to know the story to enjoy the spectacle. (Tip: if you opt for the cheap seats, bring binoculars).

Over the course of several centuries, kabuki has developed a repertoire that draws on popular themes, such as famous historical accounts and stories of love-suicide, while also borrowing copiously from *nō*, *kyōgen* (comic drama) and bunraku (classical puppet theatre).

Formalised beauty and stylisation are the central aesthetic principles of kabuki; highlights for many fans are the dramatic poses (called *mie*) that actors strike at pivotal moments. Kabuki actors are born into the art form and training begins in childhood; they prepare for a role by studying and emulating the style perfected by their predecessors. A few actors today enjoy such social prestige that their activities on and off the stage are chronicled in the tabloids.

Bunraku

In bunraku, Japan's traditional puppet theatre, sophisticated and large – nearly two-thirds life-sized – puppets are manipulated by up to three black-robed puppeteers. The puppeteers do not speak; the story is provided by a narrator performing *jōruri* (narrative chanting) to the accompaniment of a *shamisen* (a three-stringed instrument resembling a lute or banjo). The syncronisation required to pull all this off is incredible.

Bunraku developed alongside kabuki; in fact, many famous plays in the kabuki repertoire were originally written for puppet theatre. Osakans were particularly fond of the puppet theatre, and the best place to see it is at Osaka's National Bunraku Theatre.

Rakugo

A traditional Japanese style of comic monologue, *rakugo* (literally 'dropped word') dates to the Edo period. The performer, usually in kimono, sits on a square cushion on a stage. Props are limited to a fan and hand towel. The monologue begins with a *makura* (prologue), which is followed by the story itself and, finally, the *ochi* (punch line or 'drop', which is another pronunciation of the Chinese character for *raku* in *rakugo*). Some comedians specialise in classic monologues, which date to the Edo and Meiji periods; others pen new ones that address issues relevant to contemporary life. A number of famous comedians, including movie director Kitano Takeshi, have studied *rakugo* as part of their development.

Today, *rakugo* is most often performed at *yose* (vaudeville theatres) as part of a line-up of jugglers, magicians and more. While some Japanese ability is certainly helpful, it can also be fun just to pop into one of these old halls for the experience; there are a few in Tokyo, such as Asakusa Engei Hall.

Contemporary Theatre & Dance

The *angura* (underground) theatre movement of the 1960s saw productions take place in any space available: tents, basements, open spaces and street corners. This was no doubt influenced by concurrent

For kabuki tickets in Tokyo and Kyoto, try http://www.kabuki-bito.jp/eng/contents/theatre/kabukiza.html. For tickets to traditional performances (*nō*, bunraku) at Japan's national theatres, head to Japan Arts Council (www.ntj.jac.go.jp/english.html).

Tokyo has long claimed to be Japan's centre for contemporary theatre with its international festival F/T (www.festival-tokyo.jp/en); however, when it comes to critical merit, Kyoto is drawing focus with its edgier festival, Kyoto Experiment (http://kyoto-ex.jp). To learn more about Japan's contemporary theatre scene, see the blog *Tokyo Stages* (https://tokyostages.wordpress.com).

movements abroad, such as that of the situationists; however it also entailed a reconsideration and re-evaluation of just what a Japanese aesthetic should – and could – mean after a century of cultural influence from the West. For influential avant-garde playwright and director Kara Jūrō, taking the stage outside was evocative of kabuki's formative years along the riverbed. The *angura* also gave rise to *shōgeki* (literally 'small theatre', but more like 'fringe theatre').

Contemporary dramatists to look for include Okada Toshiki and his troupe chelfitsch, which earned critical acclaim for *Five Days in March* (*Sangatsu no Itsukukan;* 2004), a hyper-realistic portrayal of two *furītā* (part-time workers) holed up in a Shibuya love hotel at the start of the second Iraq War. Chelfitsch rely heavily on disjointed, hyper-colloquial language. More accessible to visitors with little or no Japanese ability are the physical and often risqué works of Miura Daisuke and his troupe Potudo-ru. He recently adapted his award-winning *Love's Whirlpool (Ai no Uzu;* 2005), set at a Roppongi swingers' party, into a film of the same name (2014).

Tokyo Art Beat (www.tokyoart-beat.com) and its sister site Kansai Art Beat (www.kansaiartbeat.com) are bilingual art-and-design guides, with regularly updated lists of events and art-world happenings.

Butō

Butō is Japan's unique and fascinating contribution to contemporary dance. It was born out of a rejection of the excessive formalisation that characterises traditional forms of Japanese dance and of an intention to return to more ancient roots. Hijikata Tatsumi (1928–86) is credited with giving the first *butō* performance in 1959; Ōno Kazuo (1906–2010) was also a key figure.

During a performance, one or more dancers use their naked or seminaked bodies to express the most elemental and intense human emotions. Nothing is forbidden in *butō* and performances often deal with taboo topics such as sexuality and death. For this reason, critics often describe *butō* as scandalous, and *butō* dancers delight in pushing the boundaries of what can be considered beautiful in artistic performance. It's also entirely visual, meaning both Japanese and non-Japanese spectators are on a level footing.

Butō has been a largely underground scene and performances often take place in unconventional locations outdoors. However, in 2016 the Kyoto Butoh-kan (www.butohkan.jp), opened as a dedicated performance space. Top Tokyo-based troupes who perform in the capital (and beyond) include Sankai Juku (www.sankaijuku.com) and Dairakudakan Kochūten (www.dairakudakan.com).

Some of the earliest examples of Japanese literature were penned by women who, with no access to education in Chinese, used the simplified phonetic script *hiragana*. Their male counterparts at the time were busy copying and perfecting the imported Chinese characters known as *kanji*.

Literature

Japan has a literary history that stretches back over a millennium.

Tales of the Heian Court

Japan's first major literary works were penned by women of the Heian court. Murasaki Shikibu's *Genji Monogatari* (*The Tale of Genji;* 1008) is credited as the world's first novel; the lengthy and complex serial, starring the lesser noble and playboy Genji, documents the intrigues and romances of court life. An easier (and quicker!) read is Sei Shōnagon's *Makura no Sōshi* (*The Pillow Book*; 1002), which reads curiously like the blog of a lady-in-waiting.

Haiku

Japan has a rich poetic tradition, and one that was historically social in nature. Poetry groups would come together to collaborate on long *renga* (linked verse), with each new verse playing off some word or association in the one that came before. *Renga* were composed in a game-like atmosphere and were more about witty repartee than about creating works to be preserved and read. Sometime in the 17th century, however, the opening stanza of a *renga* became accepted as a standalone poem – and the haiku was born. Today, the haiku is Japan's most widely known form of poetry; at just 17 sparse syllables, it is also the shortest.

Matsuo Bashō (1644–94) is considered the master of the form and is Japan's most famous poet. He's also the origin of the popular image of the haiku artist as a Zen-like ascetic figure. In 1689 Bashō left his home in Edo (Tokyo) to embark on a five-month, 2400km walk around northern Japan – then considered the ends of the earth. He returned to write his most famous work, *Oku no Hosomichi* (*The Narrow Road to the Deep North*; 1702), a poetic account of his journey.

Edo-Era Excess

Ihara Saikaku (1642–93), a contemporary of Bashō and also active in poetry circles (in his hometown, Osaka) was a famous chronicler of the *ukiyo* – the 'floating world' of the pleasure districts (which are also captured in *ukiyo-e*, woodblock prints). His first novel, *Koshoku Ichidai Otoko* (*The Life of an Amorous Man;* 1682), reads like an updated (and funnier) *Tale of Genji*, with the wealthy son of a 17th-century Osakan merchant as its antihero. The book was a contemporary bestseller.

The Modern Period

Most of Japan's important modern literature has been penned by authors who live in and write about cities. Though these works are sometimes celebratory, many lament the loss of a traditional rural lifestyle that has given way to the pressures of a modern, industrialised society. *Kokoro* (1914), the modern classic by Sōseki Natsume (1867–1916), outlines these rural–urban tensions, as does *Yukiguni* (*Snow Country;* 1935–37), by Nobel laureate Kawabata Yasunari (1899–1972). These works touch upon the conflict between Japan's nostalgia for the past and its rush towards the future, between its rural heartland and its burgeoning metropolises.

Contemporary Literature

Among contemporary novelists, Murakami Haruki (b 1949) is the biggest star, both at home and internationally. His 2013 novel, *Colorless Tsukuru Tazaki and His Years of Pilgrimage*, moved a million copies in a week. The English translation topped the US bestsellers list when it was released the following year. (His latest collection of short stories, *Men Without Women*, is due out in English in 2017). Of all his books, the one most Japanese people are likely to mention as their favourite is the one that established his reputation, *Norwegian Wood* (1987). It's a wistful story of students in 1960s Tokyo trying to find themselves and each other.

The other literary Murakami, Murakami Ryū, is known for darker, edgier works that look at Japan's urban underbelly. His signature work is *Coin Locker Babies* (1980), a coming-of-age tale of two boys left to die in coin lockers. Both survive, though the Tokyo they live to face is literally toxic. His most recent work in English translation is the short story collection *Tokyo Decadence: 15 Stories* (2016).

Literature in Japan is not, entirely, a boys' club. Banana Yoshimoto (b 1964) – who picked her pen name because it sounded androgynous – had an international hit with *Kitchen* (1988). In 2003, the prestigious Akutagawa Prize for emerging writers was awarded to two young women: Wataya Risa (b 1984) for the novel *The Back You Want to Kick* (just published in English in 2015) and Kanehara Hitomi (b 1983) for the novel *Snakes and*

The plots of most modern Japanese horror films can be traced back to the popular *kaidan* (traditional horror or ghost stories) of the Edo and Meiji periods.

All Studio Ghibli fans will want to make a pilgrimage to the delightful Ghibli Museum in the Tokyo suburb of Mitaka.

Check out the annual anthology of new Japanese writing *Monkey Business* (http://monkeybusinessmag.tumblr.com). For news and reviews of Japanese works translated in English, see the blog *Contemporary Japanese Literature* (https://japaneselit.net), edited by academic Kathryn Hemmann.

Earrings. Wataya has gone on to have further success, winning the Kenzoburo Oe prize in 2012 for her latest work *Isn't It a Pity?*

Manga & Anime
Manga

Walk into any convenience store in Japan and you can pick up several phone-directory-sized weekly manga anthologies. Inside you'll find about 25 comic narratives spanning everything from gangster sagas and teen romance to bicycle racing and *shōgi* (Japanese chess), often with generous helpings of sex and violence. The more successful series are collected in volumes *(tankōbon)*, which occupy major sections of bookshops. No surprise then that manga accounts for roughly a quarter of all sales of Japan's US$15 billion book and magazine publishing industry.

You can trace manga's roots to the graphic art of Edo-era *kibyōshi* woodblock print publications and in the comic books that entered the country with the American occupation, but manga is fully its own art, often conveying the kind of complex themes and character development you'd expect from a novel. Popular series like *One Piece*, by Oda Eiichirō, have been going on for 20 years now, meaning many devoted readers are now well into middle age.

An excellent introduction to the art of manga is the Kyoto International Manga Museum.

> Beloved TV anime *Astro Boy* and *Kimba the White Lion* are based on hit manga by Tezuka Osamu (1928–89), an artist frequently referred to as *manga no kamis-ama* – the 'god of manga'.

MIYAZAKI HAYAO – THE KING OF ANIME

Miyazaki Hayao, who together with Takahata Isao founded Studio Ghibli, is largely responsible for anime gaining widespread, mainstream appeal abroad. His 2001 *Spirited Away* earned the Academy Award for best animated film and he was given an Academy Honorary Award in 2014.

Miyazaki was born in 1941 in wartime Tokyo and his father was the director of a firm that manufactured parts for the famous Japanese Zero fighter plane. This early exposure to artificial flight had a deep impression on Miyazaki, and one of the hallmarks of his films is skies filled with whimsical flying machines; *The Wind Rises* (2013) is a fictionalised biopic about Zero designer Hirokoshi Jirō. The studio's name Ghibli (pronounced zhibli) comes from an Italian scouting plane used in WWII.

In high school, Miyazaki saw Japan's first feature-length anime, *Hakujaden* (known overseas as *Panda and the Magic Serpent*; 1958) and resolved to become an animator himself. After graduating from university in 1963, he joined Tōei and worked on some of the studio's most famous releases, including *Little Norse Prince* (1968), where he first teamed up with Takahata. His debut as a movie director was in 1979 on *Lupin III: Castle of Cagliostro.*

In 1984, Miyazaki directed an anime version of his manga *Nausicaa of the Valley of the Winds*. The movie provides a brilliant taste of many of the themes that run through Miyazaki's subsequent work, including environmental concerns and the central role of strong female characters. The film's critical and commercial success established Miyazaki as a major force in the world of Japanese anime and led to the creation of the animation studio, Studio Ghibli, through which he has produced all his later works.

In 1988 Studio Ghibli released *My Neighbor Totoro*. Much simpler and less dense than many Miyazaki films, *Totoro* is the tale of two young girls who move with their family to the Japanese countryside while their mother recuperates from an illness. There they befriend Totoro, a magical creature who lives in the base of a giant camphor tree. For anyone wishing to make an acquaintance with the world of Miyazaki, this is the perfect introduction.

Anime

Anime can mean anything from the highly polished hand-drawn output of Studio Ghibli to the low-budget series churned out each season for Japanese TV. It is created for all ages and social groups, encompassing genres from science fiction and action adventure to romance and historical drama.

The medium includes deep explorations of philosophical questions and social issues, humorous entertainment aimed at kids and bizarre fantasies. Many popular manga are later serialised as anime. Some works offer breathtakingly realistic visuals, exquisite attention to detail, complex and expressive characters, and elaborate plots. Leading directors and voice actors are accorded fame and respect, while characters become popular idols.

Among the best-known anime is *Akira* (1988), Ōtomo Katsuhiro's psychedelic fantasy set in a future Tokyo inhabited by speed-popping biker gangs and psychic children. *Ghost in the Shell* (1995) is an Ōishii Mamoru film with a sci-fi plot worthy of Philip K Dick involving cyborgs, hackers and the mother of all computer networks. The works of Kon Satoshi (1963–2010), including the Hitchcockian *Perfect Blue* (1997), the charming *Tokyo Godfathers* (2003) and the sci-fi thriller *Paprika* (2006), are also classics.

One new director to watch is Shinkai Makoto: his 2016 *Kimi no Na wa* (Your Name) was both a critical and box-office smash – the second highest-grossing domestic film ever, after *Spirited Away*. It's scheduled for world release in 2017.

Comiket (www. comiket.co.jp; short for 'Comic Market') is a massive twice-yearly convention in Tokyo for fan-produced amateur manga known as *dōjinshi*. To the untrained eye, *dōjinshi* looks like 'official' manga, but most are parodies (sometimes of a sexual nature) of famous manga titles.

Traditional Music

Japan's classical music is *gagaku*, the music played in the court from the 7th century onward, on the *koto* (zither) and *biwa* (short-neck lute), among other instruments, brought over from China. Haunting and ancient sounding, it is occasionally performed for the public in national theatres or at Shintō shrines.

More accessible (and admittedly way more fun), *min'yo* (folk music) is usually played on a *shamisen* (similar to a lute or a banjo). Different regions have different styles (even different structures) and in some areas of Japan (particularly Aomori and Okinawa) you can find bars and restaurants with spirited live performances. Another crowd pleaser are the energetic (an understatement, really) performances of the Sado-ga-shima–based *taiko* (drum) troupe Kodo (www.kodo.or.jp).

Music also plays a big part in Japan's traditional performing arts: *nō* is punctuated by *taiko* and flute music; kabuki and bunraku are accompanied by *shamisen*.

Architecture

Japan's traditional design aesthetic of clean lines, natural materials, heightened spatial awareness and subtle enhancement has long been an inspiration to creators around the world. You'll see it in the country's centuries-old shrines, temples, teahouses and gardens, but also in modern works that riff on the old while striving for the new. Japan's contemporary architects are among the most internationally acclaimed today; seeing their creations, in the cities and countryside, is one of the highlights of any visit.

Traditional Architecture

Traditional Japanese architecture is almost exclusively constructed of wood. Japanese carpenters were true masters, employing a complex system of joinery techniques to build large-scale wooden structures entirely without nails – some of which are still standing hundreds of years later (and if they're not, it's most likely due to fire).

Early architectural styles and techniques were greatly influenced by Korea and China, and well into the modern era (and possibly still today) building projects would begin by consulting a geomancer practised in the art of feng shui. Over the centuries, the tastes of various ruling classes have left their own mark, from the austere elegance favoured by the medieval warrior class to the more ostentatious styles that were in vogue during the Edo period. Even in the showiest buildings, however, the function of ornamentation was to draw out the beauty of the structure itself and that of the materials employed.

Throughout Japan's civilised history and until the Meiji era, building was heavily regulated according to status, down to the width of a gate. The grandest structures were the temples and shrines and the villas of the ruling classes – and of course the castles.

Traditional wooden structures were very vulnerable to fire and few truly old, original structures remain – though many reconstructions follow the old patterns.

Foreign Influences

When Japan opened its doors to Western influence following the Meiji Restoration (1868), the city's urban planners sought to remake downtown Tokyo in the image of a European city. A century-long push and pull ensued, between enthusiasts and detractors: architects who embraced the new styles and materials and those who rejected them. Tokyo Station, with its brick facade and domes looking very much like a European terminus, went up in 1914. Meanwhile, the Tokyo National Museum (1938) was done in what was called the Imperial Style, a sturdy, modern rendering of traditional design.

The new port cities, like Yokohama, Kōbe and Hakodate, with their foreign settlements and influence, acquired many new Western-style buildings including churches with their signature steeples and domes. These new buildings were often made of brick or stone. What is most striking about the architecture of this time is the incongruity of it all: a Russian Orthodox church next to a Victorian-style manor, around the corner from

Hōryū-ji (607) is commonly believed to have the two oldest wooden structures in the world, including a 32m-high pagoda. Tōdai-ji's main hall is among the world's biggest wooden buildings; the current structure (1709) is actually only two-thirds of its original 8th-century size.

a Buddhist temple and maybe across the street from a neo-Baroque bank. Hakodate in particular preserves this sense of perhaps rather muddled cosmopolitanism. At the time, it was also the vogue for the wealthy elite to build hybrid homes, with Japanese- and European-style wings.

In 1917 Frank Lloyd Wright, a noted Japanophile, visited Japan, bequeathing it six structures and a bevy of disciplines schooled in the principles of modernism. Many Meiji-era structures, including part of Wright's original design for the Imperial Hotel (rebuilt in 1967), can be seen at Meiji-mura, outside Nagoya.

Modern Icons

Modern Japanese architecture really came into its own in the 1960s. The best known of Japan's 20th-century builders was Tange Kenzō (1913–2005), who was influenced by traditional Japanese forms as well as the aggressively sculptural works of French architect Le Corbusier. One of his early commissions was the Hiroshima Peace Center and Memorial Park (1955). He also designed the National Gymnasium built for the 1964 Tokyo Olympics – a structure that looks vaguely like a samurai helmet and uses suspension-bridge technology – and later the Tokyo Metropolitan Government Offices (1991), a looming complex with the silhouette of a Gothic cathedral.

Concurrent with Tange were the 'metabolists', Shinohara Kazuo, Kurokawa Kishō, Maki Fumihiko and Kikutake Kiyonori. The Metabolism movement promoted flexible spaces and functions at the expense of fixed forms in building. Design-wise, they were a radical bunch who produced a number of fascinating sketches and plans, the majority of which went unbuilt. One that did go up is Kurokawa's Nakagin Capsule Tower (1972), an apartment complex in Tokyo, with apartments designed as pods that could be removed whole from a central core and replaced. Maki, the most realistic of the bunch, went on to have a celebrated career, winning the prestigious Pritzker Architecture Prize in 1993 (Tange won it earlier in 1987); his buildings, which make use of new and varied materials, have a geometric, uncentred composition. Tokyo's Spiral Building is a great example.

Standing 634m tall, Tokyo Sky Tree (2012) is the world's tallest free-standing tower. It employs an ancient construction technique used in pagodas: a *shimbashira* column (made of contemporary, reinforced concrete), structurally separate from the exterior truss. It acts as a counterweight when the tower sways, cutting vibrations by 50%.

GLOSSARY OF TRADITIONAL JAPANESE ARCHITECTURE

fusama	papered sliding screens used to divide space into rooms
gasshō-zukuri	a distinct style of thatch-roof farmhouse, so named for the shape of the rafters, which resemble a pair of palms pressed together in prayer
hinoki	Japanese cypress; the preferred material for monumental structures
kawara	slate roof tile
machiya	traditional Japanese townhouse, made of wood and usually of two storeys, with a shop on the ground floor and living quarters upstairs
mon	main entrance gate of a temple or castle constructed of several pillars or casements, joined at the top by a multitiered roof; a Chinese-style entrance gate is called *karamon*
shoin-zukuri	style of elegant and refined architecture for the ascendant warrior class; originated in the 14th century with the spread of Zen Buddhism
sukiya-zukuri	humbler than, though similar to, *shoin-zukuri*; shabby-chic style that developed in accordance with the tea ceremony in the 16th century
shōji	movable wooden screens, covered with mulberry paper, used as doors
tatami	mats of woven reeds that cover the floors in traditional Japanese buildings; the size is codified and area is often measured by the number of mats
torii	Shintō shrine gate composed of two upright pillars, joined at the top by two horizontal crossbars, the upper of which is normally slightly curved; often painted a bright vermilion

TRADITIONAL JAPANESE GARDENS

Gardening is one of Japan's finest art forms. You'll encounter four major types of gardens during your horticultural explorations.

Funa asobi Meaning 'pleasure boat' and popular in the Heian period, such gardens feature a large pond for boating and were often built around nobles' mansions. The garden that surrounds Byōdō-in in Uji is a vestige of this style.

Shūyū These 'stroll' gardens are intended to be viewed from a winding path, allowing the design to unfold and reveal itself in stages and from different vantages. Popular during the Heian, Kamakura and Muromachi periods, a celebrated example is the garden at Ginkaku-ji in Kyoto.

Kanshō Zen rock gardens (also known as *kare-sansui* gardens) are an example of this type of 'contemplative' garden intended to be viewed from one vantage point and designed to aid meditation. Kyoto's Ryōan-ji is perhaps the most famous example.

Kaiyū The 'varied pleasures' garden features many small gardens with one or more teahouses surrounding a central pond. Like the stroll garden, it is meant to be explored on foot and provides the visitor with a variety of changing scenes, many with literary allusions. The imperial villa of Katsura Rikyū in Kyoto is the classic example.

Contemporary Architecture

Since the 1980s a new generation of Japanese architects have emerged who continue to explore both modernism and postmodernism, while incorporating a renewed interest in Japan's architectural heritage. Among the most esteemed are Itō Toyō and Andō Tadao, both winners of the Pritzker Prize.

Andō's works are heavy, grounded and monumental; his favourite medium is concrete. Many of his structures can be found in Tokyo and on Naoshima. Itō's designs are lighter and more conceptual. Among his signature works is the Sendai Mediatheque.

Sejima Kazuyo and Nishizawa Ryue who helm the SANAA firm (also a Pritzker winner) are noted for their luminous form-follows-function spaces. They have dozens of impressive projects under their belt, including the 21st Century Museum of Contemporary Art in Kanazawa, and the other-worldly Teshima Art Museum.

Japan's most recent Pritzker winner, in 2014, is Ban Shigeru. He marches to his own drum entirely, purposefully using low-cost and recycled materials, building pre-fab houses and disaster shelters in addition to prestigious projects. Among his more storied works is a temporary cathedral built of cardboard tubes in Kōbe following the 1995 Hanshin earthquake; when a more permanent structure was finally rebuilt, Ban's structure was packed up and shipped to Taiwan, which had recently had a quake of its own.

Japan's feudal palaces and castles incorporated a straightforward security system known as *uguisubari* (nightingale floors). The creaking floors of Kyoto's Nijō-jō are an excellent example of this melodic security technique designed to catch out stealthy ninja assassins.

Traditional Japanese Accommodation

A hotel is a hotel wherever you go. And while some of Japan's hotels are very nice indeed, staying in traditional-style accommodation offers an added cultural experience. Sleeping on futons (quilt-like mattresses), soaking in an o-furo (Japanese-style bath, often communal) or starting your day with grilled fish and rice are all opportunities to connect a little deeper with Japan. Options include ryokan (traditional inns), *minshuku* (traditional guesthouses) and *shukubō* (temple lodgings).

The Basics

Slippers

Best Ryokan

....

Tawaraya, Kyoto

....

Arai Ryokan, Shuzen-ji Onsen

....

Hōshi Onsen Chō-jūkan, Minakami

....

Lamp no Yado, Aoni Onsen

....

Iwasō Ryokan, Miyajima

At any traditional lodging you should leave your shoes at the door and put on the slippers set out for you. At smaller, casual places, there will be a shelf or cupboard for you to stash your shoes (or barring that just leave them neatly to the side). At fancier places, you can just step out of your shoes and staff will whisk them away. Separate slippers will be set out for use just in the toilet; don't forget to slip back into your regular slippers on the way out! There will also be outdoor slippers (either wooden-soled *geta*, traditional sandals, or clunky plastic ones) in the entrance way, if you need to pop outside. Given all this sharing of slippers, most guests prefer to wear socks.

Yukata

All lodgings in Japan (save hostels) supply sleepwear and at a traditional accommodation this will be a *yukata*, a light, cotton kimono-like robe. Don't be insulted if you're given one marked extra large – they're sized by length not by girth! Put it on over your underwear, left over right; women might want to wear a camisole, as the robes tend to creep open on top. Men typically tie the *obi* (sash) low on their hips while women tend to secure it snugly at the waist. You can wear the *yukata* anywhere around the inn: to and from the baths and during meals (though of course this is optional). At some onsen resort towns, guests wear them around town as well, while going from bathhouse to bathhouse.

Check-in

For Japanese guests, a ryokan is a destination in and of itself and as a result most will check-in as early as possible (usually 3pm). Most places (ryokan, *minshuku* and *shukubō*) expect you to check in by 6pm, unless you have arranged otherwise. After signing in (yes, by hand), you'll be escorted to your room and perhaps given a basic tour of the inn on the way – to show you where the baths and dining rooms are located. Staff will most likely enter the room with you, to show you where the robes and towels are stashed. If you've reserved meals, the staff may then ask what time you would like them. Dinner is typically early, at 6 or 7pm; breakfast is usually sometime between 7am and 8.30am. You can make yourself a pot of tea – the supplies should be on the low table, along with some traditional sweets or snacks – and relax.

Baths

The vast majority of traditional inns, regardless of whether they have en suite facilities, will have communal baths separated by gender. Inns that see a significant number of overseas guests may be an exception, having instead several small baths that can be used privately. The same etiquette rules apply as at public baths: wash yourself first in the shower area and then soak in the tub.

Many Japanese guests will head right to the bath upon check-in. Soaking in the hot tubs can be uncomfortable after a big meal and especially after alcohol (be warned that this might have a dizzying effect), so it's best to wait a bit if you go after dinner. And by all means, if you're staying in an *onsen ryokan*, go several times!

Ryokan

Simply put, ryokan are traditional Japanese inns; they are where Japanese travellers stayed long before they heard the word *hoteru* (hotel). Usually this means rooms with tatami mats and futons (instead of beds). Most inns also serve meals.

From there, ryokan can differ greatly. Some are famous for their onsen baths, which may be indoors or outdoors – located along riverbeds, overlooking mountains or perhaps even on your own private verandah; others are famous for their food, serving *kaiseki ryōri* (Japanese haute cuisine) that rival the meals served in the best restaurants. The most exclusive are famous for both. Some *onsen ryokan* offer *kashikiri-buro* (baths, either indoors or outdoors) which you can rent for private use

ACCOMMODATION TIPS

➡ It's always best to have a reservation, even if it's just a quick call a few hours before arriving. One easy way to do this is to have your present accommodation call ahead and reserve your next night's lodging. Tourist information centres can often suggest places to stay and call ahead for you.

➡ Email is the best means of communication; most Japanese tend to be more comfortable with written than spoken English.

➡ If you have any dietary restrictions (or foods you wish to avoid) be upfront about this at the time of booking. Places that regularly welcome foreign guests may be able to accommodate certain requests, but others may not.

➡ If you'd prefer to forgo meals entirely, most inns offer *sudomari* (staying only) rates.

➡ Old buildings (with no elevators) can be tricky with large luggage. If you plan to stay in many such inns, it's best to pack as light as possible. If you are just making an overnight excursion to one, consider asking your previous night's accommodation if they'd be willing to store your suitcase (and just travel with a day pack).

➡ You could also take advantage of Japan's new 'hands-free' travel service to send larger bags onward to your next stop. For details see, www.jnto.go.jp/hands-free-travel.

Etiquette

➡ Sound carries in older buildings, so it's considerate to be quiet after dinner hours.

➡ Don't put your luggage in the *tokonoma* (sacred alcove); it's usually decorated with a scroll.

➡ Slippers should never be worn on tatami mats.

(alone, as a couple or as a family) for 40 minutes to an hour; the cost is usually between ¥2000 and ¥4000.

Ryokan can be rambling old wooden buildings that look like they're straight out of a *ukiyo-e* (woodblock) print or they can be modern concrete structures. The latter are more likely to have an elevator, en suite bathrooms and a few rooms with beds (including a wheelchair-accessible room). Older inns may be drafty, with thin walls and shared toilets, but the atmosphere more than makes up for it: often made entirely of natural materials, such as wood, earth, paper, grass, bamboo and stone, they can feel like an extension of the natural world. Many, too, have beautiful traditional gardens.

Ryokan staff (often clad in kimono) tend to be very doting. During meals they'll serve you course by course – and at some fancier inns you can take your meals in your room; during or after dinner, the staff will come to lay out the bedding for you. After check-out, you'll be seen off with deep bows.

There are ryokan at both ends of the price spectrum. Simpler ones (where the distinction between ryokan and *minshuku* becomes murky) may cost only ¥5000 to ¥7000 per person (including meals). A night in a high-end ryokan could literally cost 10 times that. For a very nice experience, expect to pay between ¥12,000 and ¥20,000 per person.

Minshuku

A *minshuku* is usually a family-run private lodging, rather like a B&B in Europe or the USA. In some very simple *minshuku* you're really just staying with a Japanese family that has turned a few of the rooms in their house into guest rooms. Other places are purpose-built to serve as accommodation. In either case, the rooms will be Japanese style, with tatami mats and futons. Bathroom facilities are usually shared; meals are much simpler than what you'd get in a ryokan – more like home cooking – and are usually eaten in a common dining room. Unlike at a ryokan, in a *minshuku* you are usually expected to lay out and put away your own bedding.

The average price per person per night, including two meals, is around ¥5500. *Minshuku* are a little hard to find on your own if you don't speak and read Japanese. Many are still rather analogue and don't do online bookings; few have English-speaking owners. The best way to find a *minshuku* is to ask at a local tourist information office, where they will usually call ahead and make all arrangements for you.

Shukubō

A *shukubō* is lodging offered at Buddhist temples, traditionally for pilgrims or official visitors to the temple, but these days just as often for casual travellers.

Shukubō vary tremendously in style and amenities: some are downright luxurious (rivalling high-end ryokan), while others are merely spartan rooms that resemble those found at a cheap hostel or guesthouse. Most are somewhere in between. Rooms are almost always traditionally Japanese, meaning tatami mats on the floor and a futon for sleeping. Occasionally, sexes will be segregated, but most places allow couples to stay together. Sometimes you are simply allocated a room in the temple precincts and left to your own devices. At other places, you may also be allowed (or even required) to participate in prayers, services or meditation. If you're lucky, you might find an English-speaking monk on hand who will be willing to give you a tour of the temple and explain the treasures and history of the place.

According to government statistics there are roughly 40,000 ryokan in Japan; however the number decreases each year. Many young Japanese prefer the anonymous convenience of hotels; costly maintenance expenses for older buildings and inheritance taxes are also a factor.

Ryokan Booking Services

Japanese Inn Group (http://japaneseinngroup.com)

Ryokan Collection (www.ryokancollection.com)

Selected Onsen Ryokan (http://selected-ryokan.com)

You can find *shukubō* all across Japan, including at temples in Kyoto and Nara. Many provide meals. Expect to pay between ¥6000 to ¥14,000 per person, depending on meals and facilities offered.

The most popular spot to try a *shukubō* is at the mountain monastery complex of Kōya-san in Wakayama Prefecture (Kansai), about two hours by train south of Osaka. Almost all temples here offer lodging and some of them are truly spectacular, with beautiful gardens and well-appointed rooms (though there are modest ones, too). The speciality of Kōya-san is shōjin-ryōri (Buddhist vegetarian cuisine) and some temples here offer truly memorable fare. For a list of temple accommodations in Kōya-san, visit Koyasan Shukubo Association (http://eng.shukubo.net).

Sport

Sumo, steeped in ancient ritual, is Japan's national sport. While it has its devout followers, it's baseball that is the clear fan favourite; soccer is popular, too. Martial arts have a following among both spectators and participants and gets a boost every four years during the Olympics, as Japan excels at judo. In 2019 the country will host the Rugby World Cup, which will be but a prelude to the hoopla surrounding the 2020 Summer Olympics in Tokyo.

Sumo

The national sport is a ritualistic form of wrestling that developed out of ancient Shintō rites for a good harvest. Two overweight, amply muscled men, clothed only in *mawashi* (loin cloths) with their hair slicked back into a topknot, battle it out in a packed earth *dōyo* (ring) over which hangs a roof that resembles that of a shrine. Before bouts, which typically last only seconds, the *rikishi* (wrestlers) rinse their mouths with water and toss salt into the ring – both purification rituals. They also perform the *shiko* movement, where they squat, clap their hands and alternately raise each leg as high as it can go before stamping it down – all shows of strength and agility.

Bashō (grand tournaments) are held over a 15-day period, six times a year (January, May and September in Tokyo, March in Osaka, July in Nagoya and November in Fukuoka) and they are well worth a visit. It's the pageantry as much as the actual wrestling of a *bashō* that is so memorable, including spectacles such as the ceremonial entrance of *maku-uchi* (top division) wrestlers in their decorative *keshō-mawashi* aprons and the bow-twirling moves of the *yokozuna*, sumo's supreme champions.

SUMO

Nihon Sumo Kyokai (www. sumo.or.jp) offers online ticket sales. Sumo Fan Magazine (www. sumofanmag. com) is a multilingual online fanzine. Sumotalk (www.sumotalk. com) will give you the skinny on all things sumo.

Baseball

The Japanese call it *yakyū*; it was introduced in 1873 by Horace Wilson, an American teacher in Tokyo. Games are played between April and October across the country in two pro leagues (Central and Pacific; www. npb.or.jp), each with six teams sponsored by big businesses. The victors in each league then duke it out in the end-of-season, seven-match Japan Series. The most successful team by a wide margin is Tokyo-based Yomiuri Giants, who have 35 Central League and 22 Japan Series titles to their name. In Kansai, the Hanshin Tigers are the hometown favourite. Regardless of your interest in baseball, it's worth catching a game just to watch the fans who engage in elaborately choreographed cheering.

Martial Arts

Although they have roots in historical combat techniques honed by samurai and other warriors, the martial arts most closely associated with Japan today developed in the modern era. These *gendai budō* (Japanese martial arts) aim for self-improvement and self-protection rather than aggression.

Aikido

Developed in the early 20th century, this form of self-defence combines elements of judo, karate and kendō so that the practitioner uses, rather than opposes, an adversary's attack through techniques such as throws and controls. Tokyo's Hombu-dōjō is the headquarters of the International Aikido Federation (www.aikikai.or.jp) and you can sign up for classes there.

Kendō

An evolution of *kenjutsu* (the art of sword fighting), kendō is a sport whose practitioners use *shinai* (blunt bamboo swords) and *bōgu* (light body armour). The sport is governed by the All-Japan Kendo Federation (www.kendo-fik.org) based at Tokyo's Nippon Buddōkan, where many of the championship matches are held.

Judo

An Olympic sport since 1964, judo (literally meaning 'the gentle way') is a wrestling style of martial art that developed at the end of the 19th century from the more harmful jujitsu fighting school. The controlling body is the Tokyo-based All-Japan Judo Federation (www.judo.or.jp); check their website for information on tournaments. The Kodokan Judo Institute has training centres in Tokyo and Osaka; the former has a hostel at which recommended students can stay.

Karate

Meaning 'empty hand', karate came to mainland Japan from Okinawa and is a fusion of an Okinawan martial art known as *ke* and Chinese martial arts. Today there are various styles of karate, with the Japan Karate Association (www.jka.or.jp) representing the most popular Shokotan tradition. The association's *dōjō* (practice hall) in Tokyo welcomes visitors who wish to join a training session.

Five new sports have been approved by the IOC for inclusion in the 2020 Tokyo Summer Games: karate, skateboarding, surfing, climbing and – back for the first time since 2008 – baseball and softball.

Soccer

The beautiful game has a 150-year-old pedigree in Japan, but it was only with the creation of the professional J-League (www.j-league.or.jp) in 1993 that it began to gain wider spectator popularity. There are 18 clubs in the premier J1 division and 22 in the J2 division; the season runs March to October with top teams competing for the J-League Cup. Meanwhile all teams – down to high-school teams – can compete in the Emperor's Cup, with play from September until the final match, held on New Year's Day.

SUMO MOVES

Size is important in sumo, but woe betide any *rikishi* who relies solely on bulk as, more often than not, it's *kimari-te* (wrestling techniques) that win the day. There are 82 official *kimari-te* a *rikishi* may legitimately employ, including:

Abisetaoshi Using body weight to push an opponent backwards to the ground.

Oshidashi Pushing an opponent's arms underneath or in the chest to force him out of the ring.

Oshitaoshi Pushing an opponent to the ground either inside or outside the ring.

Shitatenage Tackling an opponent by grabbing inside his arms.

Tsukiotoshi Grabbing an opponent underneath the arm or on his side and forcing him down at an angle.

Uwatenage Grabbing an opponent's *mawashi* from outside the opponent's arms and throwing him to the ground.

Uwatedashinage As above but also dragging an opponent.

Yorikiri Lifting an opponent out of the ring by his *mawashi*.

Moves that will get a wrestler disqualified include punching with a closed fist, boxing ears, choking, grabbing an opponent in the crotch area and pulling hair.

Living Art of the Geisha

The word geisha literally means 'arts person'; in Kyoto the term used is *geiko* – 'child of the arts'. Though dressed in the finest silks and often astonishingly beautiful, geisha are first and foremost accomplished musicians and dancers. On top of that, they are charming, skilled conversationalists. These now-rare creatures – who seem lifted from another world – still continue to entertain. Kyoto is particularly known for its geisha districts, where elaborately costumed *maiko* (apprentice *geiko*) can be spotted on the streets.

Life of a Geisha, Then & Now

Geisha now live a dramatically different life to their predecessors. Prior to the mid-20th century, a girl might arrive at an *okiya* (geisha living quarters) still a young child, and indeed some were sold into service by desperate families, to work as a maid. Should she show promise, the owner of the *okiya* would send her to begin training at the *kaburenjo* (school for geisha arts) at around age six. She would continue maid duty, waiting on the senior geisha of the house, while honing her skills and eventually specialising in one of the arts, such as playing the *shamisen* (three-stringed instrument resembling a lute or a banjo) or dance.

Training typically lasted about six years; those who passed exams would begin work as an apprentice under the wing of a senior geisha and eventually graduate to full-fledged geisha themselves.

Geisha were often indebted to the *okiya* who covered their board and training. Given the lack of bargaining chips that have been afforded women in history, there is no doubt that many geisha of the past, at some point in their careers, engaged in compensated relationships; this would be with a *danna* (a patron) with whom the geisha would enter a contractual relationship not unlike a marriage (and one that could be terminated). A wealthy *danna* could help a woman fulfil her debt to the *okiya* or help her start her own.

Other geisha married, which required them to leave the profession; some were adopted by the *okiya* and inherited the role of house mother; still others worked until old age.

Today's geisha begin their training no earlier than in their teens – perhaps after being inspired by a school trip to Kyoto – while completing their compulsory education (in Japan, until age 15). Then they'll leave home for an *okiya* (they do still exist) and start work as an apprentice. While in the past, a *maiko* would never be seen out and about in anything but finery, today's apprentices act much like ordinary teens in their downtime. For some, the magic is in the *maiko* stage and they never proceed to become geisha; those that do live largely normal lives, free to live where they choose, date as they like and change professions when they please.

Mizoguchi Kenji's 1936 black-and-white film *Sisters of Gion* is a riveting portrayal of two very different sisters working in the famous Kyoto geisha district. The actress Yamada Isuzu, who plays one of the sisters, was herself the daughter of a geisha.

GEISHA MANNERS

No doubt spotting a *maiko* dressed to the hilt on the street in Kyoto is a wondrous experience, and a photo is a much-coveted souvenir of a visit to Japan. However, please keep in mind that these are young women – many of whom are minors – trying to get to work. In Kyoto the sport of geisha-spotting has gotten out of hand, with tourists sometimes blocking the women's paths in popular districts like Gion in order to get photos. Let them through; *maiko* and geisha are professionals – if you want to get close to them, support their art and go to see them perform. You can also find plenty of tourists dressed as geisha on the streets of Higashiyama during the daytime; many are happy to be photographed if asked.

Geisha Dress

In Kyoto, the *maiko* are easily distinguished by their ornate dress, long trailing obi and towering wooden clogs; the *maiko* also wears her own hair in a dramatic fashion, accentuated with opulent (and extremely expensive) ornaments, called *kanzashi*. Geisha, or *geiko*, in contrast wear more subdued robes and a simpler chignon (or a wig). Every stage of a geisha's career is marked by a change in dress. The most pronounced is the promotion from trainee to full-fledged geisha, which is marked with a ceremonial changing of the collar of the under-kimono from red to white, a ritual called *erikae*.

Maiko and young geisha paint their faces with thick white make-up, leaving only a suggestive forked tongue of bare flesh on the nape of the neck. Eyebrows are painted and the lower lip is coloured red, traditionally charcoal was used for the brows and safflower for the lips. As geisha grow older their make-up becomes increasingly natural; by then their artistic accomplishments need no fine-casing.

The novel *Geisha in Rivalry* (1918), by Nagai Kafu, chronicles the love lives of two Tokyo geisha with a penchant for drama. Kafu, a notorious dandy, did plenty of on-the-ground research for this one.

Experience Geisha Culture

Modern *maiko* and geisha entertain their clients in exclusive restaurants, banquet halls and traditional *ochaya* much like they did a century ago. This world is largely off limits to travellers, as a personal connection is required to get a foot in the door, though some tour operators can act as mediator. Of course, these experiences can cost hundreds of dollars (if not more).

The best way to experience geisha culture is to see one of Kyoto's annual public dance performances (known as *odori*), a city tradition for over a century. Three of the geisha districts perform their dance in April, to coincide with the cherry blossoms; one performs in May, and the final one performs in November, to coincide with the autumn foliage.

Historical Kyoto geisha districts such as Gion and Pontochō preserve well the atmosphere of a *hanamachi*. Though it's one of the smallest of Tokyo's entertainment districts, Kagurazaka, with its cobblestone lanes, is lovely. Kanazawa has some well preserved *hanamachi*, too, with many old *ochaya* that have been beautifully restored and are open to the public, either as museums or bars.

In an effort to save their art, some geisha are working with local tourism boards to create experiences for visitors; if you're visiting Kyoto, Tokyo or Kanazawa, it's worth doing a quick internet search or inquiring at a tourist information centre for events that might be happening.

Environment

Stretching from the tropics to the Sea of Okhotsk, the Japanese archipelago is a fantastically diverse place. Few countries enjoy such a variety of climates and ecosystems, with everything from coral-reefed islands to snow-capped mountains. Unfortunately, this wonderful landscape is also one of the world's most crowded, and almost every inch of the Japanese mainland bears the imprint of human activity.

The Land

Japan's four main islands – Honshū (slightly larger than Britain), Hokkaidō, Kyūshū and Shikoku – make up 95% of the country's landmass. A further 6848 smaller islands make up the archipelago, which stretches from the Ryūkyū Islands (of which Okinawa is the largest) at around 25°N to the northern end of Hokkaidō at 45°N. Cities at comparable latitudes are Miami (south) and Montreal (north). Japan's total land area is 377,435 sq km, of which mountains comprise around 80% and as a result population is largely concentrated in dense areas along the coasts.

Situated along the 'Ring of Fire', Japan occupies one of earth's most seismically active regions, which has deeply shaped both its geography and culture and continues to impact on these today. Before the last Ice Age, Japan was connected by a land bridge to the East Asian continent.

CO_2

In 2005 the Japanese Ministry of the Environment launched the 'Cool Biz' campaign to cut CO_2 emissions. The program encouraged offices to hold 'casual Fridays' and raise thermostats in summer (to use less air-con). After a year it was estimated that annual CO_2 emissions were reduced by over 1 million tonnes.

Seismic Activity

It's estimated that 1500 or so earthquakes happen annually in Japan. Most go unfelt, though gentle rocks that can be felt are not uncommon. The last truly devastating earthquake to occur was the 9.0-magnitude Great East Japan Earthquake in 2011, the fourth largest earthquake recorded in modern history. Earthquakes can frequently trigger tsunamis. The scale of the 2011 tsunami caught experts by surprise; they are usually not nearly that big. Regardless, after a major jolt, the prevailing wisdom is to get away from the coast and up to high ground.

Volcanoes

Japan has 10% of the world's active volcanoes, including majestic Mt Fuji (which last erupted 300 years ago). Of these, Kyūshū's are the most active: spectacular Sakura-jima in Kagoshima frequently puts on a show. While the country's volcanoes are actively monitored and fatalities rare, an unexpected eruption of Ontake-san in Nagano killed 56 hikers in 2014.

Japan's Construction Addiction

As traditional Japanese culture makes much of nature and the changing seasons, many visitors to Japan are shocked to see a countryside marred significantly by concrete. It's fair to say that Japan's public works programs started out in earnest as an infrastructure overhaul – paving rural roads and shoring up eroding hillsides against landslides, for example, were sorely needed projects in the postwar period. Along the way, however, construction went from being a source of jobs for rural populations to becoming one of the *only* sources of jobs for declining rural populations.

Rural areas yield enormous power in Japanese politics, as representation is determined more by area than by population. In order to ensure the support of their constituencies, rural politicians have little choice but to lobby for government spending on public-work projects – to keep jobs in their areas. As a result, Japan is number four in the world in dam construction; state-of-the-art bridges loom over villages that have little use for them; and small cities can boast of sophisticated cultural facilities (though they're often largely devoid of content).

In 2009, the opposition Democratic Party of Japan came into power, running on a platform to curb Japan's construction addiction (the Liberal Democratic Party, or LDP, had been in power since 1955); however they faced resistance in rural communities when they cancelled pending projects. In 2012, the LDP were voted back in.

Alex Kerr writes extensively on this phenomenon in his 2001 book *Dogs and Demons*.

Wildlife

The latitudinal spread of Japan's islands makes for a wide diversity of flora and fauna. The Nansei and Ogasawara archipelagos in the far south are subtropical, and flora and fauna in this region are related to those found on the Malay peninsula. Mainland Japan (Honshū, Kyūshū and Shikoku) shows more similarities with Korea and China, while Hokkaidō shares many features with Russia's nearby Sakhalin Island. For more information on wildlife in Japan, visit the website of the Biodiversity Center of Japan at www.biodic.go.jp.

Animals

Land bridges to the Asian continent allowed the migration of animals from Korea and China (and in Hokkaidō from Sakhalin). There are also species that are unique to Japan, such as the Japanese giant salamander and the Japanese macaque. In addition, the Nansei archipelago, which has been separated from the mainland for longer than the rest of Japan, has a few examples of fauna that are classified by experts as 'living fossils', such as the Iriomote cat.

Japan's largest carnivorous mammals are its bears. Two species are found in Japan: the *higuma* (brown bear) of Hokkaidō, and the *tsukinowaguma* (Asiatic brown bear or 'moon bear' because of the white crescent on its chest) of Honshū, Shikoku and Kyūshū.

The International Union for Conservation of Nature and Natural Resources (IUCN) 'Red List' currently tallies 123 endangered fauna species in Japan, including Blakiston's fish eagle, the widely consumed Japanese eel and the red-crowned crane (an imperial emblem and symbol of longevity in Japan). The Iriomote cat, along with 28 other species, is listed as 'critically endangered' and the Japanese river otter went extinct in 2012. The majority of the critically endangered species

---

ENVIRONMENT WILDLIFE

HONSHŪ BLOSSOM & FOLIAGE SEASONS

January
Hot-pink camellias add colour to winter.

Early February– mid-March
Whether white or pink, plum blossoms signal winter is loosening its grip.

Mid-March– mid-April
Sakura season. Wherever you are, in a really good cherry-blossom year it can seem like Mother Nature has decided to put on her best party dress and go mad; crowds gather everywhere for *hanami* (cherry-blossom viewing).

April & May
Hikers delight in the many varieties of wild azaleas that festoon the highlands.

Late April–May
In Japanese, a word exists to describe the luminous green that typifies the trees of Japan for the first few weeks after budding: *shinryoku*. Photographers use the word 'oversaturation'.

May
Divine purple blossoms of draping wisteria decorate temple gardens and mountainsides.

June
Irises add jolts of purple and yellow to gardens and temple grounds.

July & August
Wildflowers bloom on alpine plains.

are located in the Ogasawara Islands, a remote island chain in the Pacific that's something like Japan's own Galapagos.

Plants

The flora of Japan today is, for the most part, not what the Japanese saw hundreds of years ago. The cool-to-temperate zones of central and northern Honshū and southern Hokkaidō were once home to broad-leaf mixed deciduous forests. While roughly two-thirds of the country remains forested, natural forests make up only about half of that; the rest is planted forest, mainly of cedar and cypress. It is also thought that 200 to 500 plant species have been introduced to Japan since the Meiji period, mainly from Europe, but also from North America.

Japan is the fifth leading contributor of carbon emissions globally. It ratified the Paris climate accord in 2016.

The subtropical islands of Yakushima and Iriomote are part of the Nansei archipelago, that extends southwest from Kyūshū. The islands stand out for their largely untouched landscapes; Iriomote in particular is a mostly unexplored primordial jungle, home to numerous endemic plants not found elsewhere. At the other end of the country, at the north-eastern tip of Hokkaidō, Shiretoko National Park is home to old-growth temperate and sub-alpine forests of Erman's birch, Sakhalin fir and Mongolian oak. The sheer inaccessibility of some alpine regions in central Honshū has preserved some areas of great natural beauty there, too.

National Parks

In 1931 Japan laid the groundwork for its national park system and today has 32 national parks, ranging from the far south (Iriomote National Park) to the northern tip of Hokkaidō (Rishiri-Rebun-Sarobetsu National Park), plus 57 awkwardly titled quasi-national parks. National parks cover 5.5% of Japan's landmass and are administered by the Ministry of the Environment. Including quasi-national parks and prefectural national parks, the total amount of protected land extends to 14.3%.

Unlike national parks in some other countries, the ones in Japan are not entirely government-owned land – the system was far too late for that. Shintō shrines, in particular, laid claim to many of Japan's mountains long ago. National parks also contain towns, farmland, on-sen resorts, industry – anything really. Much of the land that is government-owned land is forested and instead overseen by the Forestry

---

SUSTAINABLE TRAVEL IN JAPAN

As a traveller, you can minimise your impact on the Japanese environment in several simple ways.

Refuse packaging At the cash register, you can say: *Fukuro wa irimasen* (I don't need a bag), or just hold up a reusable shopping bag to show you've already got one.

Carry your own chopsticks Buy a pair of *hashi* (washable chopsticks with a carrying case) from a convenience store, to avoid relying on the disposable ones many restaurants use.

Less tuna and eel, please Limit your consumption of seafood threatened by over-fishing, such as *unagi* (eel) and *maguro* (tuna) – including *toro* (fatty tuna belly). We know, this one hurts!

Use public transport Japan's public transport system is among the best in the world; there's little reason not to use it.

Hop on a bike Many guesthouses and even some tourist information centres offer bike rentals (often for free).

Skip vending machines While ubiquitous vending machines are part of Japan's urban identity, they eat up a considerable amount of energy.

Agency (rather than the Ministry of the Environment). A convoluted multi-tier system is used to regulate development in such a way as to minimise environmental impact to varying degrees.

All of this amounts to a curious atmosphere, where you're more likely to be greeted by a *torii* gate on entering a national park, or to find a noodle shop on top of a mountain, than to come across a ranger station (though the number of the latter are increasing). For descriptions of Japan's parks, see www.env.go.jp/en/np.

Environmental Issues

Environmentalism in Japan is largely a consumer movement; people here have been eager adopters of hybrid cars, tank-less toilets and the like, produced by the country's own leading manufacturers. Environmental activism (and, well, any kind of activism) is largely viewed in Japan as a fringe activity. However, groups such as Japan for Sustainability (japanfs.org), Green Action (www.greenaction-japan.org) and Greenpeace Japan (www.greenpeace.org/japan) each lobby for concerns such as denuclearisation, research and development of renewable energy technologies, and the reduction of carbon emissions.

Whaling

Commercial whaling was banned by the International Whaling Commission (IWC) in the 1980s; however, the Japanese government continues to fund the Japan Institute of Cetacean Research (JICR), which kills several hundred whales each year in the name of scientific research. Critics have long questioned the actual scientific aims of the program; in 30 years the research has led to no notable discoveries. Moreover, after the whales have been purportedly studied, meat is sold on the commercial market. The Japanese counter these claims by saying that they don't want the meat to be wasted and that, furthermore, whaling has long been an important part of Japanese culture.

The cultural claim is dubious: whales have been hunted over time in some coastal communities; however, the scientific whaling program takes place in deep waters near Antarctica aboard a factory ship. Whale meat was eaten with frequency during WWII and its aftermath, when food was seriously scarce. For this reason, some elderly Japanese feel fondly towards it. But consumption levels today are so low that much of the whale meat presented at auction goes unsold. Stockpiles continue to rise, leading the JICR to begin selling it at bargain rates to schools, which serve it in the cafeteria (despite whale meat being known to contain significant amounts of mercury).

The issue over whaling became international news in 2010 when the anti-whaling organisation Sea Shepherd's vessel *Ady Gil* was rammed and sunk by Japanese whalers. The following year, it was revealed that US$29 million of funds earmarked for tsunami recovery efforts had gone to shore up the whaling industry. Critics say it's hard to understand why Japan would continue to hold out, given the huge amount of negative publicity these developments have brought. A 2012 survey by the Nippon Research Center showed the public is ambivalent towards whale meat and has little to no interest in continuing to fund the whaling program.

In 2014 the International Court of Justice ruled that Japan's whaling program was not scientific and ordered Japan to cease whaling; in the 2015–16 season, 333 minke whales were killed by Japanese whalers in Antarctica. Japan has since said it would review its program in 2017.

Late October–early December

The brilliant spectacle of *kōyō* (autumn foliage season) sees *momiji* (maples), ginkgos and other broad-leaved trees cycle through yellow, crimson, orange and flaming red.

CHOPSTICKS

Twenty-five billion pairs of *waribashi* (disposable wooden chopsticks) are used in Japan annually – equivalent to the timber needed to build 17,000 houses.

FUKUSHIMA NUCLEAR INCIDENT

The 2011 Great East Japan Earthquake unleashed a tsunami that overwhelmed the seaside six-reactor Fukushima Dai-ichi nuclear power plant. The flooding knocked out backup generators which resulted in a catastrophic loss of essential cooling capacity, causing a core meltdown in three reactors.

While it is thought that much of the deadly radioactive material remains contained on-site, a significant amount of radiation was dispersed in a plume to the northwest. Radioactive water continues to leak or be released into the Pacific Ocean (and may for years). Hundreds of makeshift tanks have been filled with contaminated water used to cool spent fuel.

The real scope of the environmental and public health impact is largely unknown. The central government has maintained that the situation is under control and decontamination is proceeding at a measured pace; however the pro-nuclear LDP administration has not been forthcoming with much detailed information and has imposed policies to limit the freedom of the media.

Scientists have largely reinforced the government's claims, though there is little precedent to go on. There has been only one other nuclear disaster of this magnitude to date – Chernobyl – and the two unfolded very differently (Chernobyl is believed to have released significantly more radiation into the air).

The 20km exclusion zone instated shortly after the disaster remains largely in place, though some communities have been permitted to return (if they want; many don't). Few researchers have been allowed on site.

A study released in 2015 by researchers at Nagoya University, who used highly sophisticated radiograph technology to spy on the reactors' cores, revealed that one of the reactors appeared to have little to no fuel in its containment vessel (while in others it was clearly visible). These results encouraged speculation that the vessels had been breached and the ground below contaminated.

Even optimistic government forecasts set the target for decommissioning the plant at 2051.

Taiji Dolphin Hunt

In 2009, the documentary *The Cove* brought to light a hitherto little-known practice in the small town of Taiji (in southern Kansai) of herding pods of dolphins into a cove and slaughtering them. Condemnation from international wildlife organisations was swift; the film won the Academy Award for best documentary feature. Only six cinemas in Japan screened the film. The Taiji fishermen claim that the filmmakers lied to them and misrepresented them.

Taiji (pop 3500) was one of those coastal communities that had long hunted whales – a commercial activity now banned by the IWC. Local residents do in fact eat dolphin and whale meat; a 2010 study by the National Institute for Minamata Disease showed that Taiji residents have higher mercury levels than average in Japan.

The annual cull continues, drawing protesters from around the globe. Hundreds of dolphins are killed and sold for meat; others are captured and sold to aquariums. Activists have had one recent victory: in 2015 the Japan Association of Zoos and Aquariums ordered its member aquariums not to purchase dolphins from Taiji.

Survival Guide

Directory A–Z

Accommodation

Japan offers a wide range of accommodation, from cheap guesthouses to first-class hotels, and distinctive Japanese-style ryokan (traditional inns) and *minshuku* (guesthouses). Advance booking is highly recommended, especially in major tourist destinations. For more on traditional Japanese accommodation, see p866.

Reservations

➡ Bookings can mostly be made online in English, through booking sites or directly from the lodging's homepage, except for some older, traditional inns.

➡ Many smaller, independent inns and hostels offer slightly better rates if you book directly (rather than through a booking site).

➡ For hotels of all classes, rates can vary tremendously, and discounts significantly below rack rates can be found online. Many hotels offer cheaper rates if you book two weeks or a month in advance.

➡ Not all tourist information centres can make bookings, but the ones in smaller towns and cities, where finding accommodation might be challenging, usually can. Note that these can close as early as 5pm in rural areas.

➡ Providing you speak clearly and simply, making phone reservations in English is usually possible at larger hotels and foreigner-friendly ryokan.

BOOKING SERVICES

Jalan (www.jalan.net) Popular Japanese discount accommodation site, searchable in English.

Japanese Inn Group (www.japaneseinngroup.com) Bookings for ryokan and other small, family-run inns.

Japanican (www.japanican.com) Accommodation site for foreign travellers run by JTB, Japan's largest travel agency.

Lonely Planet (lonelyplanet.com/japan/tokyo/hotels) Reviews, recommendations and bookings.

Camping

Japan has a huge number of campgrounds (キャンプ場; *kyampu-jō*), which are popular with students and families during the summer holidays; as such, many campgrounds are only open July through September. They're typically well maintained with showers and barbecue facilities. JNTO has a list of recommended campgrounds: www.jnto.go.jp/eng/location/rtg/pdf/pg-804.pdf.

Camping is also possible year-round (when conditions permit) at campgrounds – often more basic – in the mountains or around certain mountain huts. 'Guerrilla' or unofficial camping is also possible in many parts of rural Japan, but we recommend asking a local person about acceptable areas before setting up your tent.

Hostels

Japan has an extensive network of hostels. These include official Japan Youth Hostel (JYH; www.jyh.or.jp/e/index.php) properties as well as a growing number of independent, often quite stylish, hostels.

JYH lodgings are usually tightly run ships: hostellers are expected to check in between 3pm and 8pm to 9pm and there may be a curfew of 10pm or 11pm. Check-out is usually before 10am and dormitories may be closed between 10am and 3pm. Bath time is usually between 5pm and 9pm, dinner is between 6pm and 7.30pm, and breakfast is between 7am and 8am.

The price for members is usually around ¥3000 for a dorm room (around ¥3600 for nonmembers); a one-year membership costs ¥2500. Most of these hostels serve meals that are usually quite good and excellent value (about ¥1000 for dinner and ¥500 for breakfast); however, as meals are prepared in-house, kitchens are usually closed to guests. See the website for a list of properties and information on membership.

Independent hostels tend to have a more laid-back atmosphere, with more flexible check-in times and no curfew (though less quality control). Staff, often travellers themselves, usually speak good English and are good sources of local information. These hostels usually don't provide meals so will have an open kitchen. Prices are similar to those charged by official hostels, sometimes even a bit cheaper. Among the more popular are the K's House (https://kshouse.jp/index_e.html) and J-Hoppers (http://j-hoppers.com) groups.

Hostels supply bedding, which you may need to make up yourself. Most are dorm-style but some have tatami rooms with futons. There will usually be some private and family rooms, too (costing about ¥1000 extra per person). Towels can be hired for about ¥100; basic toiletries (soap and shampoo) may or may not be supplied.

Hotels

You'll find a range of Western-style hotels in most Japanese cities and resort areas. Even budget hotels are generally clean and well serviced (though older ones might have smoky rooms). In the top-end bracket, you can expect to find the amenities of deluxe hotels anywhere in the world.

Boutique hotels don't have much of a presence in Japan. This is perhaps because the concept – intimate and with memorable decor – is too

SLEEPING PRICE RANGES

The following price ranges refer to a double room for hotels, and per person without meals for ryokan. Unless otherwise stated, the national 8% consumption tax is included in the price, but note that some hotels quote exclusive of taxes.

¥ less than ¥6000 (less than ¥8000 in Tokyo)

¥¥ ¥6000 to ¥15,000 (¥8000 to ¥25,000 in Tokyo)

¥¥¥ more than ¥15,000 (more than ¥25,000 in Tokyo)

similar in the minds of some to that of a hotel with unsavoury repute: the love hotel.

BUSINESS HOTELS

Functional and economical, 'business hotels' (ビジネスホテル; *bijinesu hoteru*) are geared to the lone traveller on business, but they're great for any kind of traveller – so long as you don't need a lot of space. The compact rooms usually have semidouble beds (140cm across; roomy for one, a bit of a squeeze for two) and tiny en suite bathrooms. Business hotels are famous for being deeply unfashionable, though many chains have updated their rooms in recent years. Expect to pay from ¥8000/12,000 for single/double occupancy (more in big cities like Tokyo).

Business hotels are usually clustered around train stations. Some reliable chains with huge networks include Toyoko Inn (www.toyoko-inn.com/eng) and **Dormy Inn** (www.hotespa.net/dormyinn/en).

CAPSULE HOTELS

Capsule hotels (カプセルホテル; *kapuseru hoteru*) offer rooms the size of a single bed, with just enough headroom for you to sit up. Think of it like a bunk bed with more privacy (and a reading light, TV and alarm clock). Prices range from ¥3500 to ¥5000, which usually includes access to a large shared bath and sauna. Personal belongings are kept in a locker room. Most

only accept cash and do not permit guests with visible tattoos.

Capsule hotels are common in major cities and often cater to workers who have partied too hard to make it home or have missed the last train. Most are men-only, though some have floors for women, too; there is also a growing number of stylish ones aimed at foreign tourists.

LOVE HOTELS

At these hotels for amorous encounters – known in Japanese as *rabu hoteru* (ラブホテル; or *rabuho* for short) – you can stop for a short afternoon 'rest' (from ¥3000) or an overnight 'stay' (from ¥6500); you can't stay consecutive nights, though. Some have flamboyant facades or kitschy interiors (and amenities that range from costumes to videogame consoles).

Love hotels are designed for maximum privacy: entrances and exits are kept separate; keys are provided through a small opening without contact between desk clerk and guest; and photos of the rooms are displayed to make the choice easy for the customer.

They can be found in entertainment districts in cities; if you're driving, you can also spot them off highways (these ones tend to be the most over-the-top looking). Most love hotels are comfortable with foreign guests, but travellers have reported being turned away at some places. Same-sex couples may have more trouble than heterosexual couples.

Kokumin-shukusha

Kokumin-shukusha (people's lodges) are government-supported institutions offering affordable accommodation in scenic areas. Private Japanese-style rooms are the norm, though some places offer Western-style rooms. Prices average ¥5500 to ¥6500 per person per night, including two meals.

Mountain Huts

Mountain huts (*yama-goya*) are common in many of Japan's hiking and mountain-climbing areas. While you'll occasionally find free emergency shelters, most huts are privately run and charge for accommodation. These places offer bed and board (two meals) at around ¥5000 to ¥8000 per person (¥3000 to ¥5000 if you prepare your own meals); sleeping is in a common room on either bunks or the floor. On well-trafficked mountains like Mt Fuji, reservations are essential; in general it's best to call ahead, though if there's space you won't usually be turned away.

Rental Accommodation

Short-term rental and apartment share sites currently operate in a grey zone in Japan. According to law, a unit may be rented for a minimum of 30 days. Tokyo's Ota-ku (where Haneda Airport is located) and Osaka (the city, not the prefecture) are exceptions; in these places the minimum stay is seven nights. This may change, as the government has been reviewing legislation pertaining to vacation rentals (called *min-paku* in Japanese).

Rider Houses

Rider houses (ライダーハウス; *raidā hausu*) are bare-bones budget accommodation options reserved for travellers on two wheels, usually on the outskirts of town. Nicer ones are similar to youth hostels; at the most basic, you might get a spare futon in a shed. Prices vary, but ¥1500 per person per night is about average. It's a good idea to have a sleeping bag, though you can ask to rent bedding from the owner. For bathing facilities, you will often be directed to the local *sentō* (public bath).

Many have been running for decades and have a devoted following. They can be a little tricky to find at first, as there's little information out there in English; but stay in one and you can tap into the local network of motorcyclists and cyclists, who can help you work out where to stay next.

Rider houses are most common in Hokkaidō, but there are some all over. Though it's in Japanese, the website Hatinosu (www. hatinosu.net/house) has info and a map of rider houses around Japan.

As they're small they can fill up fast, so it's wise to call ahead during summer. Not all are open year-round, especially those in Hokkaidō.

Customs Regulations

➡ Japan has typical customs allowances for duty-free items; see Visit Japan Customs (www. customs.go.jp) for more information.

➡ To bring a sword out of the country, you will need to apply for a permit; reputable dealers will do this for you.

➡ Pornography that clearly shows genitalia is illegal in Japan.

Electricity

Tokyo and eastern Japan are on 50Hz, and western Japan, including Nagoya, Kyoto and Osaka, is on 60Hz.

100V/50hz/60hz

Embassies & Consulates

Australian Embassy (☎03-5232-4111; www.australia.or.jp/en; 2-1-14 Mita, Minato-ku; ⓢNambuku line to Azabu-Jūban, exit 2)

Australian Consulate (☎06-6941-9271; http://japan.embassy.gov.au; 16th fl, Twin 21 MID Tower, 2-1-61 Shiromi, Chūō-ku, Osaka; ⓢNagahori Tsurumi-ryokuchi line to Osaka Business Park, exit 4)

Canadian Embassy (カナダ大使館; ☎03-5412-6200; www.canadainternational.gc.ca/japan-japon/index.aspx-?lang=eng; 7-3-38 Akasaka, Minato-ku; ⓢGinza line to Aoyama-itchōme, exit 4)

Chinese Embassy (☎03-3403-3388; www.china-embassy.or.jp/jpn; 3-4-33 Moto-Azabu, Minato-ku; ⓢHibya line to Hiro-o, exit 3)

Chinese Consulate (中華人民共和国駐大阪総領事館; ☎06-6445-9481; http://osaka.china-consulate.org/jpn; 3-9-2 Utsubo-Honmachi, Nishi-ku, Osaka; ⓢChūō line to Awaza, exit 9)

French Embassy (☎03-5798-6000; www.ambafrance-jp.org;

4-11-44 Minami-Azabu, Mina-to-ku; S Hibiya line to Hiro-o, exit 1)

German Embassy (☏03-5791-7700; www.japan.diplo.de; 4-5-10 Minami-Azabu, Minato-ku; S Hibiya line to Hiro-o, exit 1)

German Consulate (☏06-6440-5070; www.japan.diplo.de; 35th fl, Umeda Sky Bldg Tower East, 1-1-88-3501 Ōyo-do-naka, Kita-ku, Osaka; R JR Osaka, north central exit)

Irish Embassy (☏03-3263-0695; www.irishembassy.jp; Ireland House, 2-10-7 Kōji-machi, Chiyoda-ku; S Hanzōmon line to Hanzōmon, exit 4)

Netherlands Embassy (☏03-5776-5400; http://japan.nlembassy.org; 3-6-3 Shiba-kōen, Minato-ku; S Hibiya line to Kamiyachō, exit 1)

Netherlands Consulate (☏06-6484 6000; http://japan.nlembassy.org; 8b, Kitahama Itchōme Heiwa Bldg, 1-1-14 Kitahama, Chūō-ku, Osaka; S Sakai-suji line to Kitahama, exit 29)

New Zealand Embassy (☏03-3467-2271; www.nzembassy.com/japan; 20-40 Kamiyama-chō, Shibuya-ku, Tokyo; ◷9am-5.30pm; R JR Yamanote line to Shibuya, Hachikō exit)

Russian Embassy (☏03-3583-4445; www.rusconsul.jp; 2-1-1 Azabudai, Minato-ku; S Hibiya line to Roppongi, exit 3)

South Korean Embassy (☏03-3452-7611, emergency 090-1693-5773; http://jpn-tokyo.mofa.go.kr/worldlanguage/asia/jpn-tokyo/main/; 1-2-5 Minami-Azabu, Minato-ku; S Namboku line to Aza-bu-Jūban, exit 1)

South Korean Consulate (駐大阪大韓民国総領事館;☏06-6213-1401; http://jpn-osaka.mofa.go.kr; 2-3-4 Shinsaibashi, Chūō-ku, Osaka; S Midō-suji line to Namba, exit 14)

UK Embassy (☏03-5211-1100; www.gov.uk/government/world/organisations/british-embassy-tokyo; 1 Ichiban-chō, Chiyoda-ku; S Hanzōmon line to Hanzōmon, exit 3A)

UK Consulate (☏06-6120-5600; www.gov.uk/government/world/organisations; 19th fl, Epson Osaka Bldg, 3-5-1 Bakurō-machi, Chūō-ku, Osaka; R Midō-suji line to Honmachi, exit 14)

US Embassy (米国大使館; ☏03-3224-5000; http://japan.usembassy.gov; 1-10-5 Akasaka, Minato-ku; S Ginza line to Tameike-sannō, exits 9, 12 or 13)

US Consulate (☏06-6315-5900; http://osaka.usconsulate.gov; 2-11-5 Nishi-Tenma, Kita-ku, Osaka; R JR Tōzai line to Kita-Shinchi, exit 1)

Food

For information on eating in Japan see Eat & Drink Like a Local (p54) and Japanese Cuisine (p840).

LGBTI Travellers

Gay and lesbian travellers are unlikely to encounter problems in Japan. There are no legal restraints on same-sex sexual activities in Japan apart from the usual age restrictions.

Some travellers have reported being turned away or grossly overcharged when checking into love hotels with a partner of the same sex. Otherwise discrimination is unusual (though you'll likely be given a hotel room with twin beds). One note: Japanese people, regardless of their sexual orientation, do not typically engage in public displays of affection.

Tokyo has the largest and most welcoming gay scene, followed by Osaka. Most cities have at least a few gay bars, though the scene may not be as open to foreign travellers as that of Tokyo and Osaka. In rural areas, if there is a meeting spot, it's likely very underground. Utopia Asia (www.utopia-asia.com) has good recommendations for Japan.

Health

Before You Go
HEALTH INSURANCE

The only insurance accepted at Japanese hospitals is Japanese insurance. For any medical treatment you'll have to pay up front and apply for a reimbursement when you get home.

MEDICATIONS

➡ Pharmacies in Japan do not carry foreign medications, so it's a good idea to bring your own. In a pinch, reasonable substitutes can be found, but the dosage may be lower than what you're used to.

➡ Though no prescription is necessary, thrush pessaries are only stocked behind the counter (you'll have to ask) and many pharmacies don't carry them.

➡ Stimulant drugs, which include the ADHD medication Adderall, are strictly prohibited in Japan.

➡ To bring in certain narcotics (such as the painkiller codeine), you need

---

EATING PRICE RANGES

The following price ranges refer to a standard main meal.

¥ less than ¥1000 (less than ¥2000 in Tokyo and Kyoto)

¥¥ ¥1000 to ¥4000 (¥2000 to ¥5000 in Tokyo and Kyoto)

¥¥¥ more than ¥4000 (more than ¥5000 in Tokyo and Kyoto)

to prepare a *yakkan shōmei* – an import certificate for pharmaceuticals. See the Ministry of Health, Labour & Welfare's website (www.mhlw.go.jp/english/policy/health-medical/pharmaceuticals/01.html) for more details about which medications are classified and how to prepare the form.

VACCINATIONS

No vaccines are required for travel to Japan.

In Japan

AVAILABILITY & COST OF HEALTH CARE

Japan enjoys a high level of medical services, though unfortunately most hospitals and clinics do not have doctors and nurses who speak English. Even for those that do, getting through reception can still be challenging.

University hospitals should be your first choice; doctors are most likely to speak English and the level of care is usually highest. Larger cities, especially Tokyo, are likely to have clinics that specialise in caring for the foreign community; these will have doctors who speak English but they will be pricey. Most hospitals and clinics will accept walk-in patients in the mornings (usually 8.30am to 11am); be prepared to wait.

Expect to pay about ¥3000 for a simple visit to an outpatient clinic and from around ¥20,000 and upwards for emergency care.

TAP WATER

Tap water is fine to drink in Japan; in some rural areas, locals swear by its health benefits.

Insurance

A travel-insurance policy to cover theft, loss and medical problems is essential. Worldwide travel insurance is available at www.lonelyplanet.com/travel-insurance. You can buy, extend and claim online anytime – even if you're already on the road.

Internet Access

Many cities in Japan (including Tokyo, Osaka and Kyoto) and even some regions (like Shikoku) have free wi-fi networks for travellers, though the system is still clunky in areas. To avoid frustration, heavy users might consider hiring a pocket internet device.

Most accommodation now has wi-fi. Hostels and business chain hotels are the most reliable for this; other places might only have a solid connection in the lobby.

Wi-fi Hot Spots These include train and subway platforms, tourist sites and convenience stores – though signals are often weak. Look for the sticker that says 'Japan Wi-Fi'. Download the Japan Connected (www.ntt-bp.net/jcfw/en.html) app to avoid having to log in to individual networks; if you are unable to connect, try clearing your cache.

Pocket Wi-fi If you want the confidence that comes with a steady signal, portable wi-fi hubs that can connect to multiple devices are a good choice (especially for group travellers). Japan Wireless (http://japan-wireless.com) and Rentafone Japan (www.rentafonejapan.com) rent them out for around ¥5000/12,000 per week/month and can deliver to your hotel.

Boingo Subscribers to Boingo's global plan (www.boingo.com) can use BB Mobilepoint wi-fi at McDonald's restaurants, some convenience stores and some restaurants; coverage in urban Japan is good.

Internet Cafes Ubiquitous *manga kissa* (cafes for reading comic books) double as internet cafes; prices range from ¥200 to ¥700 per hour.

Starbucks All (1000-plus!) Starbucks stores in Japan offer free wi-fi to customers. You must register online to use the service (go to http://starbucks.wi2.co.jp).

Legal Matters

Japanese police have extraordinary powers. They can detain a suspect for up to three days without charging them; after this time a prosecutor can decide to extend this period for another 20 days. Police can also choose whether to allow a suspect to phone their embassy or lawyer, though if you find yourself in police custody you should insist that you will not cooperate in any way until allowed to make such a call. Your embassy is the first place you should call if given the chance.

Police will speak almost no English; insist that a *tsūyakusha* (interpreter) be summoned (police are legally bound to provide one before proceeding with any questioning). Even if you do speak Japanese, it's best to deny it and stay with your native language.

Note that it is a legal requirement to have your

GOVERNMENT TRAVEL ADVICE

The following government websites offer travel advisories and information on current hot spots.

➡ **Australian Department of Foreign Affairs** (www.smarttraveller.gov.au)

➡ **British Foreign Office** (www.gov.uk/foreign-travel-advice)

➡ **US State Department** (http://travel.state.gov/content/passports/english/country.html)

passport (or, if you are staying longer than 90 days, your resident card) on you at all times. Though checks are not common, if you are stopped by police and caught without it, you could be hauled off to a police station to wait until someone fetches it for you.

Japan takes a hard-line approach to narcotics possession, with long sentences and fines even for first-time offenders.

Media

Newspapers are sold at convenience stores, train-station kiosks and some hotels in major cities. Look for free mags at airports and hotels; and bars and restaurants popular with expats; many cities have expat-run online magazines, too. Bilingual DJs on Tokyo's InterFM (76.1FM; www.intertm.co.jp) do news broadcasts and public service announcements in English; in Kansai, tune into multilingual FM Cocolo (76.5FM; www.cocolo.jp).

Japan Times (www.japantimes. co.jp) Long-running English-language daily.

Japan News (http://the-japan-news.com) English version of Japan's most popular (and right-of-centre) daily, *Yomiuri Shimbun*.

Asahi Shimbun (www.asahi. com/ajw) Japan's left-of-centre daily has English articles online.

Time Out Tokyo (www.timeout. com/tokyo) Quarterly magazine on pop culture and events; look for its excellent mini city guides at TICs around Japan.

Metropolis (http://metropolis japan.com) Tokyo's not-quite-as-relevant-as-it-used-to-be free expat rag.

Kansai Scene (www.kansais-cene.com) Free paper for Kansai's expat community.

Kyoto Journal (www.kyoto journal.org) In-depth articles on arts and culture from Japan and Asia.

Money
ATMs

Most Japanese bank ATMs do not accept foreign-issued cards. Even if they display Visa and MasterCard logos, most accept only Japan-issued versions of these cards.

The following have ATMs that routinely work with most cards (including Visa, MasterCard, American Express, Plus, Cirrus and Maestro; some MasterCard and Maestro with IC chips may not work). Be aware that many banks place a limit on the amount of cash you can withdraw in one day.

7-Eleven (セブン・イレブン; www.sevenbank.co.jp/english) The Seven Bank ATMs at 7-Eleven convenience stores have English instructions and are available 24 hours a day. 7-Eleven convenience stores are ubiquitous, so this is the easiest option for getting quick cash. Withdrawal limit of ¥100,000 per transaction.

Japan Post Bank (ゆうちょ銀行; www.jp-bank.japanpost.jp/en/ias/en_ias_index.html) Post offices have Japan Post Bank ATMs with English instructions; opening hours vary depending on the size of the post office, but are usually longer than regular post-office hours. Withdrawal limit of ¥50,000 per transaction.

Credit & Debit Cards

More places in Japan accept credit cards than they used to, and now many bookings can be paid for online. Businesses that do take credit cards will often display the logo for the cards they accept. Visa is the most widely accepted, followed by Master-Card, American Express and Diners Club. Foreign-issued cards should work fine.

Currency

The currency in Japan is the yen (¥). The Japanese pronounce yen as 'en', with no 'y' sound. The kanji for yen is 円.
Yen denominations:

¥1 coin; lightweight, silver colour

¥5 coin; bronze colour, hole in the middle, value in Chinese character only

¥10 coin; copper colour

¥50 coin; silver colour, hole in the middle

¥100 coin; silver colour

¥500 coin; large, silver colour

¥1000 banknote

¥2000 banknote (rare)

¥5000 banknote

¥10,000 banknote

International Transfers

Western Union (http://wu-japan.com/find-locations/en) has counters in most major cities. For sending money out of Japan, Shinsei Bank's GoRemit service (www.shinseibank. com/goremit/en) is convenient.

Moneychangers

With a passport, you can change cash or travellers cheques at any Authorised Foreign Exchange Bank (signs are displayed in English), major post offices, some large hotels and most big department stores.

For currency other than US dollars, larger banks, such as Sumitomo Mitsui (SMBC), are a better bet. They can usually change at least US, Canadian and

PRACTICALITIES

→ **Smoking** Japan has a curious policy: in many cities (including Tokyo, Osaka and Kyoto) smoking is banned in public spaces but allowed inside bars and restaurants. Designated smoking areas are set up around train stations. The number of smokers is declining every year; in Tokyo especially, an increasing number of restaurants and bars are banning smoking.

→ **Weights & Measures** Japan uses the metric system.

Australian dollars, pounds sterling, euros and Swiss francs.

Tokyo-Mitsubishi UFJ (MUFG) operates World Currency Shop (www.tokyo-card.co.jp/wcs/wcs-shop-e.php) foreign-exchange counters near major shopping centres in Tokyo, Nagoya, Kyoto, Osaka and Fukuoka. They will exchange a broader range of currencies, including Chinese yuan, Korean won, and Taiwan, Hong Kong, Singapore and New Zealand dollars.

Note that you receive a better exchange rate when withdrawing cash from ATMs than when exchanging cash or travellers cheques in Japan. Rates for the US dollar and euro are generally reasonable in Japan; other currencies, including the Australian dollar and the currencies of nearby countries, often fetch poor exchange rates.

Taxes & Refunds

Japan's consumption tax is 8% (with an increase to 10% planned for October 2019). A growing number of shops offer tax-free shopping (noted by a sticker in English on the window) if you spend more than ¥5000. Passport required.

Since the tax is not charged at point of sale, there is no need to collect a refund when leaving the country; however, you should hand in a form affixed to your passport to customs officials when you depart. For details see http://enjoy.taxfree.jp.

Opening Hours

Note that some outdoor attractions (such as gardens) may close earlier in the winter. Standard opening hours:

Banks 9am to 3pm (some to 5pm) Monday to Friday

Bars from around 6pm to late

Department stores 10am to 8pm

Museums 9am to 5pm, last entry by 4.30pm; often closed Monday (if Monday is a national holiday then the museum will close on Tuesday instead)

Post offices 9am to 5pm Monday to Friday; larger ones have longer hours and open Saturday

Restaurants lunch 11.30am to 2pm; dinner 6pm to 10pm; last orders taken about half an hour before closing

Post

→ The Japanese postal system is extremely reliable, efficient and, for regular postcards and airmail letters, not markedly more expensive than in other developed countries.

→ The airmail rate for postcards is ¥70 to any overseas destination; aerograms cost ¥90. Letters weighing less than 25g are ¥90 to other countries within Asia, ¥110 to North America, Europe or Oceania (including Australia and New Zealand), and ¥130 to Africa and South America.

→ If you want to ship purchases back, boxes are available for purchase at post offices.

→ One peculiarity of the Japanese postal system is that you will be charged extra if your writing runs over onto the address side (the right side) of a postcard.

→ The symbol for post offices is a red T with a bar across the top on a white background (〒).

→ Mail can be sent to, from or within Japan when addressed in English (Roman script).

Public Holidays

When a public holiday falls on a Sunday, the following Monday is taken as a holiday. If that Monday is already a holiday, the following day becomes a holiday as well.

Ganjitsu (New Year's Day) 1 January

Seijin-no-hi (Coming-of-Age Day) Second Monday in January

Kenkoku Kinem-bi (National Foundation Day) 11 February

Shumbun-no-hi (spring equinox) 20 or 21 March

Shōwa-no-hi (Shōwa Emperor's Day) 29 April

Kempō Kinem-bi (Constitution Day) 3 May

Midori-no-hi (Green Day) 4 May

Kodomo-no-hi (Children's Day) 5 May

Umi-no-hi (Marine Day) Third Monday in July

Yama-no-hi (Mountain Day) 11 August

Keirō-no-hi (Respect-for-the-Aged Day) Third Monday in September

Shūbun-no-hi (autumn equinox) 22 or 23 September

Taiiku-no-hi (Health-Sports Day) Second Monday in October

Bunka-no-hi (Culture Day) 3 November

Kinrō Kansha-no-hi (Labour Thanksgiving Day) 23 November

Tennō Tanjōbi (Emperor's Birthday) 23 December

Safe Travel

Japan is prone to natural disasters: earthquakes, tsunamis, volcanic eruptions, typhoons and landslides. Sophisticated early warning systems and strict building codes do much to mitigate impact (but they are not foolproof – a devastating lesson from the 2011 earthquake and tsunami). Smartphone app Safety Tips sends notifications regarding weather alerts, tsunami warnings and impending seismic activity and also lists key phrases to help you get information in the event of an emergency.

Otherwise, the biggest threat to travellers is Japan's general aura of safety. It's wise to keep up the same level of caution and common sense that you would back home.

Telephone

Mobile Phones

Japan operates on the 3G network, so overseas phones with 3G technology should work.

Pre-paid SIM cards that allow you to make voice calls are not available in Japan. You must sign a contract for a monthly plan (minimum six months commitment with cancellation fees).

Iijmio Japan Travel SIM (https://t.iijmio.jp/en) cards work around this by partnering with telecom company Brastel (www.brastel.com/pages/eng/home), whose dedicated app will allow you to make and receive phone calls through your own 050 telephone number. Included with the SIM is a Brastel card that you can top up to pay for calls. Packages are good for 30 days or three months.

For short-term visitors (who think all of the above sounds awfully complicated), Rentafone Japan (www.rentafonejapan.com; email@rentafonejapan.com) offers straightforward phone rentals

for ¥3900 a week (plus ¥300 for each additional day); domestic calls cost a reasonable ¥35 per minute (overseas calls start at ¥45 per minute).

Good for heavy users, JCR (http://jcrcorp.com) rents smartphones with plans that include voice calls, large amounts of data and tethering (meaning it can work as a portable wi-fi hub for other devices) from US$30 per week.

Both Rentafone Japan and JCR have good customer service in English.

Data-only SIM cards for unlocked smartphones are available at kiosks at Narita, Haneda and Kansai airports and at large electronics stores (like Bic Camera, Yodobashi Camera etc) in major cities. You'll need to download and install an APN profile; ask staff to help you if you are unsure how to do this (they usually speak some English).

There is a wide range of options, depending on your data and speed needs (many cards will continue to work after data usage has been exceeded but the speed will be very slow).

B-Mobile's Visitor SIM (www.bmobile.ne.jp/english/index.html), which offers 14 days of unlimited data (the speed will be reduced for heavy users) for ¥2380, is a good choice.

Local Calls

Japanese telephone numbers consist of an area code plus the number. You do not dial the area code when making a call in that area from a landline. When dialling Japan from abroad, dial the country code (⌨81), followed by the area code (drop the '0') and the number. The most common toll-free prefixes are ⌨0120, ⌨0070, ⌨0077, ⌨0088 and ⌨0800. Directory-assistance numbers:

Local directory assistance ⌨104 (¥60 to ¥150 per call)

Local directory assistance in English ⌨0120-36-4463 (9am to 5pm Monday to Friday)

International Calls

For international operator-assisted calls dial ⌨0051 (KDDI; operators speak English).

There's very little difference in the rates of direct-dial international numbers. Dial one of the numbers, then the international country code, the local code and the number.

➡ KDDI ⌨001-010

➡ NTT ⌨0033-010

➡ SoftBank Telecom ⌨0041-010

Pay Phones

Public phones do still exist and they work almost 100% of the time; look for them around train stations. Ordinary public phones are green; those that allow you to call abroad are grey and are usually marked 'International & Domestic Card/Coin Phone'.

Local calls cost ¥10 per minute; note that you won't

HIGH SEASON
. . . .
Peak travel periods include cherry-blossom season (late March to early April); Golden Week (late April to early May); O-Bon (mid-August); autumn-foliage season (October to early December, depending on the region); and the New Year period (late December to early January). During these times, accommodation can be hard to come by, especially in Kyoto and resort towns, and will likely be pricier (sometimes significantly so). If you plan to be in Japan then, it's wise to make reservations as far in advance as possible.

JAPAN HELPLINE

Japan Helpline (☎0570-000-911) is an emergency English-language hotline that operates 24 hours a day, seven days a week; you can also make contact online at http://jhelp.com/english/index.html. Staff can help you negotiate tricky situations – such as dealing with a police station – or simpler ones, like recovering a bag you left on the subway.

get change on a ¥100 coin. If you anticipate using pay phones regularly, you can purchase a telephone card (terefon kādo), sold in ¥500 and ¥1000 denominations at convenience stores.

The minimum charge for international calls is ¥100, which buys you a fraction of a minute – good for a quick check-in but not economical for much more.

Phonecards

Prepaid international phonecards can be used with any push-button phones, including regular pay phones. Look for the KDDI Super-world Card or the SoftBank Telecom Comica Card at convenience stores.

Time

All of Japan is in the same time zone: nine hours ahead of Greenwich Mean Time (GMT). Sydney and Wellington are ahead of Japan (by one and three hours, respectively), and most of the world's other big cities are behind: (New York by 14 hours, Los Angeles by 17 and London by nine). Japan does not have daylight-savings (summer) time.

Toilets

➡ You will come across both Western-style toilets and traditional squat toilets in Japan. When you are compelled to squat, the correct position is facing the hood, away from the door.

➡ Public toilets are free. The katakana for 'toilet' is トイレ, and the kanji is お手洗い. Also good to know: the kanji for female (女) and male (男).

➡ Toilet paper is usually provided, but it is still a good idea to carry tissues with you. You may also be given small packets of tissues on the street – a common form of advertising.

➡ In many bathrooms, separate toilet slippers are provided – usually located just inside the toilet door. These are for use in the toilet only, so remember to change out of them when you leave.

Tourist Information

Even the smallest towns have tourist information offices (kankō annai-sho; 観光案内所), located inside or in front of the main train station. Outside of major cities, staff may or may not speak English (there is no consistency); however, there are usually English-language materials and staff are accustomed to the usual concerns of travellers (food, lodging and transport schedules). Many Tourist Information Centers (TICs) have free wi-fi.

Japan National Tourism Organization (JNTO; www.jnto.go.jp) is Japan's government tourist bureau. It produces a great deal of useful literature in English, which is available from its overseas offices as well as its TIC in **Tokyo** (☎03-3201-3331; www.jnto.

go.jp; 1st fl, Shin-Tokyo Bldg, 3-3-1 Marunouchi, Chiyoda-ku; ⏰9am-5pm; ☎; Ⓢ Chiyoda line to Nijūbashimae, exit 1). JNTO's website, with content available in many languages, is a useful planning tool.

JNTO has overseas offices in Australia, Canada, France, Germany, the UK and the USA (see the website for details).

Travellers with Disabilities

Japan gets mixed marks in terms of ease of travel for those with disabilities. On the plus side, many new buildings have access ramps, major train stations have lifts, traffic lights have speakers playing melodies when it is safe to cross, and train platforms have raised dots and lines to provide guidance for the visually impaired. You'll find most service staff will go out of their way to be helpful, even if they don't speak much English.

On the negative side, many of Japan's cities are still rather difficult to negotiate, with many narrow streets lacking pavements.

Major sights take great pains to be wheelchair friendly and many have wheelchairs you can borrow for free. Note, however, that 'accessible' at traditional sights (like castles and temples) might still mean steep slopes or long gravel paths. Often the accessible routes aren't obvious; tell staff (such as those at the ticket counter) that someone in your party is travelling in a wheelchair (車椅子; kuruma-isu) and you may be led around to some secret back corridors.

Train cars on most lines have areas set aside for people in wheelchairs. Those with other physical disabilities can use the priority seats near the train doors. You will also find these seats near the front of buses; usually they're a different colour from the other seats.

A fair number of hotels, from the higher end of midrange and above, offer a 'barrier-free' (バリアフリー; *bariafurii*) room or two (book well in advance). Larger attractions and train stations, department stores and shopping malls should have wheelchair-accessible bathrooms (which will have Western-style toilets).

Japan Accessible Tourism Center (www.japan-accessible.com/city/tokyo.htm) is a cheat-sheet for accessible sights and hotels in Tokyo.

Download Lonely Planet's free Accessible Travel guide from http://lptravel.to/AccessibleTravel.

Visas

Visitor Visa

Citizens of 67 countries, including Australia, Canada, Hong Kong, Korea, New Zealand, Singapore, USA, UK and almost all European nations will be automatically issued a *tanki-taizai* (temporary visitor visa) on arrival. Typically this visa is good for 90 days. For a complete list of visa-exempt countries, consult www.mofa.go.jp/j_info/visit/visa/short/novisa.html#list.

Japanese law requires that visitors entering on a temporary-visitor visa possess an ongoing air or sea ticket or evidence thereof. In practice, few travellers are asked to produce such documents, but it pays to be on the safe side.

For additional information on visas and regulations, contact your nearest Japanese embassy or consulate, or visit the website of the Ministry of Foreign Affairs of Japan (www.mofa.go.jp).

On entering Japan, all short-term foreign visitors are photographed and finger-printed.

VISA EXTENSIONS

Citizens of Austria, Germany, Ireland, Lichtenstein, Mexico, Switzerland and the UK are able to extend the temporary visitor visa once, for another 90 days. To do so, you need to apply at the nearest immigration bureau before the initial visa expires; there is a processing fee of ¥4000. For a list of immigration bureaus, see www.immi-moj.go.jp/english/soshiki/index.html.

For other nationalities, extending a temporary visa is difficult unless you have family or business contacts in Japan who can act as a guarantor on your behalf.

Work Visa

Holders of student or cultural visas who have filed for permission to work or holders of working-holiday visas can work legally in Japan under certain restrictions. A full-time job requires a working visa. There are legal employment categories for foreigners that specify standards of experience and qualifications.

Arriving in Japan and finding a job that offers visa sponsorship is quite a tough proposition these days; though some do accomplish this, you will need sufficient funds to support yourself during the process.

Once you find an employer in Japan who is willing to sponsor you, it is necessary to obtain a Certificate of Eligibility from your nearest Japanese immigration office. The same office can then issue your work visa, which is valid for either one or three years. This procedure can take two to three months.

The JET (Japan Exchange and Teaching) program as well as some large English conversation school chains sponsor qualified applicants. Such jobs are best applied for before leaving home.

RESIDENCE CARD

Anyone entering Japan on a visa for longer than the standard 90 days for tourists will be issued a resident card, which must be carried at all times.

Working Holiday Scheme

Citizens of Australia, Austria, Canada, Denmark, France, Germany, Ireland, Korea, New Zealand, Norway, Poland, Portugal, Slovakia, Taiwan and the UK, and residents of Hong Kong between the ages of 18 and 30 (or 18 and 25 for Australians, Canadians and Koreans) can apply for a working-holiday visa.

This visa allows an initial six-month stay and two six-month extensions. It is designed to enable young people to travel extensively during their visit and there are legal restrictions about how long and where you can work. If you are considering moving to Japan and are eligible, a working-holiday visa is a good strategy: it allows you to work while looking for a full-time position that will sponsor a work visa.

To apply, single applicants must have the equivalent of US$1800 in funds (US$3000 for a married couple), plus an onward ticket from Japan. The working-holiday visa must be obtained from a Japanese embassy or consulate abroad. For more details visit www.mofa.go.jp/j_info/visit/w_holiday.

Volunteering

Most meaningful volunteer work in Japan requires Japanese language ability; however, there are a few organisations that accept short-term, English-speaking volunteers.

World Wide Opportunities on Organic Farms Japan (www.wwoofjapan.com) Popular with travellers, this organisation places volunteers on organic farms around the country and provides participants with a good look at Japanese rural life and the running of an organic farm. It's also a great chance to improve your Japanese-language skills.

OGA for Aid (www.ogaforaid.org) This bilingual (Japanese and English) group does community work in the coastal regions affected by the 2011 tsunami.

Women Travellers

Japan is a relatively safe country for women travellers, though perhaps not quite as safe as some might think. Crimes against women are generally believed to be widely under-reported, especially by Japanese women. Foreign women are occasionally subjected to some forms of verbal harassment or prying questions. Physical attacks are very rare, but have occurred.

The best advice is to avoid being lulled into a false sense of security by Japan's image as one of the world's safest countries and to take the normal precautions you would in your home country. If a neighbourhood or establishment looks unsafe, then treat it that way. As long as you use your common sense, you will most likely find that Japan is a pleasant and rewarding place to travel as a woman.

Several train companies have introduced women-only cars to protect female passengers from *chikan* (men who grope women and girls on packed trains). These cars are usually available during rush-hour periods on weekdays on busy urban lines. There are signs (usually in pink) on the platform indicating where you can board these cars, and the cars themselves are usually labelled in both Japanese and English (again, often in pink).

While it's a little old, Caroline Pover's *Being A Broad in Japan* (2001) is still a good resource for any woman setting up in Japan.

Work

Japan is an interesting place to live and work for a year or two and you'll find expats in all the major cities doing just that. Teaching English is still the most common job for Westerners, but bartending, hostessing, modelling and various writing/editorial jobs are also possible. Outside of these fields, Japanese language ability or local connections are vital.

Note that it is illegal for non-Japanese to work in Japan without a proper visa. To qualify for most work visas you need a four-year university degree (even for the same jobs that hire working-holiday visa holders, who are not required to have a four-year degree). An exception is modelling, acting or entertainment work; however, most agencies have their own recruitment channels and landing a contract on arrival is near impossible without connections and a portfolio.

The key to landing English teaching jobs is presentation. While an English teaching certificate helps, a polished appearance and an eager, upbeat attitude go a long way.

Transport

GETTING THERE & AWAY

Flights, tours and rail tickets can be booked online at lonelyplanet.com/bookings.

Entering the Country

For most travellers, entering Japan is simple and straightforward. Visas (p889) are given on arrival for many nationalities. Foreigners are fingerprinted and photographed on arrival.

Air

Airports & Airlines

Narita Airport (NRT; 成田空港; ☑0476-34-8000; www.narita-airport.jp), near Tokyo, is the main point of entry for international travellers; Tokyo has another smaller international airport, **Haneda** (HND; 羽田空港; ☑international terminal 03-6428-0888; www.tokyo-airport-bldg.co.jp/en), which is closer to the city centre. For travel to a specific region outside Tokyo, international airports in **Kansai** (KIX; 関西空港; Map p410; www.kansai-airport.or.jp) (for Osaka and Kyoto), **Hokkaidō** (新千歳空港; CTS;☑0123-23-0111; www.new-chitose-airport.jp/en), **Kyūshū** (☑domestic terminal 092-621-6059, international terminal 092-621-0303; ⊙domestic 6.20am-10.20pm, international 7am-9.30pm; ☒Fukuoka Airport) and Naha (for Okinawa) might be more time and cost effective.

Chubu Centrair International Airport (www.centrair.jp) Nagoya's airport has direct flights to countries in East Asia and Southeast Asia.

Fukuoka International Airport (www.fuk-ab.co.jp) At the northern end of Kyūshū, and the main arrival point for destinations in western Japan. The airport is conveniently located near the city and has connections with several countries, mostly in Asia.

Haneda Airport (www.tokyo-airport-bldg.co.jp) Tokyo's more convenient airport – about 30 minutes by train or monorail to the city centre – Haneda, also known as Tokyo International Airport, is getting an increasing number of international arrivals; domestic flights to/from Tokyo usually arrive/depart here.

Kagoshima Airport (www.koj-ab.co.jp) At the southern end of Kyūshū, with flights to/from Hong Kong, Shanghai, Seoul and Taipei.

Kansai International Airport (www.kansai-airport.or.jp) Serves the key Kansai cities of Kyoto, Osaka, Nara and Kōbe. Not as many direct international services as the Tokyo airports, but useful if you want to zero in on the Kansai area (or fly in from one and out of the other).

Kumamoto Airport (www.kmj-ab.co.jp) In central Kyūshū, with flights to/from Seoul and Kaohsiung.

CLIMATE CHANGE & TRAVEL

Every form of transport that relies on carbon-based fuel generates CO_2, the main cause of human-induced climate change. Modern travel is dependent on aeroplanes, which might use less fuel per kilometre per person than most cars but travel much greater distances. The altitude at which aircraft emit gases (including CO_2) and particles also contributes to their climate change impact. Many websites offer 'carbon calculators' that allow people to estimate the carbon emissions generated by their journey and, for those who wish to do so, to offset the impact of the greenhouse gases emitted with contributions to portfolios of climate-friendly initiatives throughout the world. Lonely Planet offsets the carbon footprint of all staff and author travel.

DEPARTURE TAX

Departure tax is included in the price of a ticket.

Nagasaki Airport (http://nagasaki-airport.jp) On the west coast of Kyūshū, with flights to/from Shanghai and Seoul.

Naha Airport (www.naha-airport.co.jp) On Okinawa-hontō (the main island of Okinawa), with flights to/from Beijing, Hong Kong, Pusan, Seoul, Shanghai, Taichung and Taipei.

Narita International Airport (www.narita-airport.jp) About 75 minutes east of Tokyo by express train, Narita gets the bulk of international flights to Japan; most budget carriers flying to Tokyo arrive here.

New Chitose Airport (www.new-chitose-airport.jp) In central Hokkaidō, south of Sapporo, with flights to many countries, mostly in Asia.

Niigata Airport (www.niigata-airport.gr.jp) In Honshū, on the Sea of Japan coast, with flights to/from Harbin, Khabarovsk, Seoul, Shanghai, Taipei and Vladivostok.

Two major international carriers with extensive domestic networks in Japan are **Japan Airlines** (JAL; ☎0570-025-121, 03-6733-3062; www.jal.co.jp/en) and **All Nippon Airways** (ANA; ☎0570-029-709, in Osaka 06-7637-6679, in Tokyo 03-6741-1120; www.ana.co.jp).

Sea

South Korea

Ferries connect Japan to its nearest neighbours, China and South Korea, and during summer, Russia. There are several ferry routes to Busan, South Korea. The following run from **Hakata Port International Terminal** (博多港国際ターミナル; ☎092-282-4871; www.hakata-port.com):

Beetle (☎in Japan 092-281-2315, in Korea 051-469-0778; www.jrbeetle.co.jp) ¥13,000, three hours, twice daily.

Camellia Line (☎in Japan 092-262-2323, in Korea 051-466-7799; www.camellia-line.co.jp) From ¥9000, 5½ hours from Fukuoka to Busan, six to 10 hours from Busan to Fukuoka, daily at 12.30pm.

From **Shimonoseki International Ferry Terminal** (下関港国際ターミナル; Map p498; ☎083-235-6052; www.shimonoseki-port.com):

Kampu Ferry (関釜フェリー; Map p498; ☎083-224-3000; www.kampuferry.co.jp) From ¥9000 (plus ¥300 fuel surcharge and ¥610 terminal fee), 12 hours, daily.

From **Osaka Port International Ferry Terminal** (大阪港国際フェリーターミナル; Osaka-kō Kokusai Ferry Terminal; ☎06-6243-6345; 1-20-52 Nan-kō-kita, Suminoe-ku; [S]Chūō line to Cosmo Square, 🚆Nankō Port Town Line to Cosmo Square):

Panstar Ferry (パンスターフェリー; ☎06-6614-2516; www.panstar.jp) One-way 2nd-class fares from ¥13,000, 19 hours, Mondays, Wednesdays and Fridays.

China

The following ferries depart from **Osaka Port International Ferry Terminal** (大阪港国際フェリーターミナル; Osaka-kō Kokusai Ferry Terminal; ☎06-6243-6345; 1-20-52 Nan-kō-kita, Suminoe-ku; [S]Chūō line to Cosmo Square, 🚆Nankō Port Town Line to Cosmo Square) for Shanghai, China:

Japan China International Ferry (日中国際フェリー; ☎06-6536-6541; www.shinganjin.com) Every other Tuesday (alternating with Kōbe).

Shanghai Ferry Company (上海フェリー; www.shanghai-ferry.co.jp) On Fridays.

One-way 2nd-class fares start at ¥20,000; the journey takes approximately 48 hours.

Russia

Hokkaidō Sakhalin Line (北海道サハリン航路; Map p614; ☎0162-22-2550; sahkouro@giga.ocn.ne.jp; one way/round trip ¥18,000/36,000) connects Wakkanai (p613) to Korsakov (on the Russian island of Sakhalin). Ferries sail twice weekly from August to mid-September; the trip takes 4½ hours. Many of those who make the journey are Japanese who have family ties to Sakhalin, though there are tourists, too.

You must book through a travel agent, which should also handle the necessary visa preparations. Note that this ferry service has been suspended in the past and is currently operating on a trial basis only.

GETTING AROUND

Air

Air services in Japan are extensive, reliable and safe. Flying is often faster and cheaper than *shinkansen* (bullet trains) and good for covering long distances or hopping islands.

All local carriers have websites in English on which you can check prices and book tickets.

Airlines in Japan

All Nippon Airways (ANA; ☎0570-029-709, in Osaka 06-7637-6679, in Tokyo 03-6741-1120; www.ana.co.jp) Major international carrier with an extensive domestic network.

Hokkaidō Air System (HAC; www.hac-air.co.jp) Flies from Sapporo's domestic airport, Okadama, to points in Hokkaidō.

Japan Airlines (JAL; ☎0570-025-121, 03-6733-3062; www.jal.co.jp/en) Major international carrier with an extensive domestic network.

Japan Transocean Air (☎0570-025-121, 03-6733-3062; www.jal.co.jp/jta) Small plane carrier, part of the JAL group, that mostly services routes in the Southwest Islands. Website in Japanese only; book in English through the JAL site.

New Central Air Service (NCA; Shinchūō Kōkū; ☑0422-31-4191; www.central-air.co.jp) Light-plane flights between Chōfu Airport, outside Tokyo, and the islands of the Izu Archipelago.

BUDGET AIRLINES

Japan has opened up its skies to low-cost carriers and the result is a proliferation of affordable airlines flying to various parts of the archipelago. This has brought previously expensive and distant destinations like Hokkaidō and Okinawa within the reach of budget travellers.

Air Do (www.airdo.jp) Connects Hokkaidō's **New Chitose Airport** (新千歳空港; CTS; ☑0123-23-0111; www.new-chitose-airport.jp/en) with major destinations around Japan.

Jetstar (www.jetstar.com) Cheap flights from Tokyo's **Narita Airport** (NRT; 成田空港; ☑0476-34-8000; www.narita-airport.jp) and Osaka's **Kansai International Airport** (KIX; 関西空港; Map p410; www.kansai-airport.or.jp) to Okinawa (Naha) and Sapporo (New Chitose).

Peach (www.flypeach.com) Good for flights out of Kansai.

Skymark Airlines (www.skymark.co.jp) Connects many regional airports; Tokyo routes fly in/out of **Haneda** (HND; 羽田空港; ☑international terminal 03-6428-0888; www.tokyo-airport-bldg.co.jp/en).

Vanilla Air (www.vanilla-air.com) Cheap flights from Tokyo (Narita) to Okinawa (Naha) and Sapporo (New Chitose).

Tickets & Discounts

➡ Both **All Nippon Airways** (ANA; ☑0570-029-709, in Osaka 06-7637-6679, in Tokyo 03-6741-1120; www.ana.co.jp) (ANA) and **Japan Airlines** (JAL; ☑0570-025-121, 03-6733-3062; www.jal.co.jp/en) (JAL) offer discounts of up to 50% if you purchase your ticket a month or more in advance, with smaller discounts for purchases made one to three weeks in advance.

➡ Foreign travellers can purchase **ANA Experience Japan Fare** one-way domestic tickets for the flat rate of ¥10,800. For details, see www.ana.co.jp/wws/th/e/wws_common/promotions/share/experience_jp.

➡ JAL's **Visit Japan Fare** offers a similar ¥10,800 flat-rate ticket for domestic routes to foreign travellers flying inbound on any Oneworld carriers. For details, see www.jal.co.jp/yokosojapan.

➡ ANA Mileage Club members over 65 can purchase **Senior Sorawari** domestic tickets from ¥8000 to ¥16,000 per sector. See www.ana.co.jp/wws/japan/e/local/book-plan/fare/domestic/senior-sorawari.

➡ JAL's **Okinawa Island Pass** (www.churashima.net/jta/company/islandpass_en.html) is good for affordable island hopping; it's only available for foreign visitors and must be purchased abroad.

➡ Early morning and late-night flights are usually the cheapest.

Bicycle

Japan is a good country for bicycle touring, and several thousand cyclists, both Japanese and foreign, traverse the country every year. Favourite bike-touring areas include Kyūshū, Shikoku, the Japan Alps (if you like steep hills!), the Noto Peninsula and Hokkaidō.

There's no point in fighting your way out of big cities by bicycle. Put your bike on the train or bus and get out to the country before you start pedalling. To take a bicycle on a train you need to use a bicycle-carrying bag, available from good bicycle shops.

A useful series of maps is *Touring Mapple* (Shōbunsha), which is aimed at motorcyclists, but is also very useful for cyclists.

Both KANcycling (www.kancycling.com) and Japan Cycling Navigator (www.

BAGGAGE FORWARDING

Baggage courier services (called *takkyūbin*) are popular in Japan and many domestic tourists use them to forward their bags, golf clubs, surfboards etc ahead to their destination, to avoid having to bring them on public transport. The tourism bureau has been working to open this service up to foreign travellers; see its guide, Hands-Free Travel Japan (www.jnto.go.jp/hands-free-travel), for a list of luggage forwarding counters, mostly at airports, train stations and shopping centres, set up for travellers.

This is a great service except for one caveat: in most cases, your bags won't get there until the following day. (So, for example, if you want to ship your luggage to or from the airport, you'll need a day pack with one night's worth of supplies.) On the other hand, this can free you from large luggage for a one-night detour to an onsen – just send your bags to the following night's destination.

Hotels can also often arrange this service for you (and the couriers will pick up the luggage from the lobby). Costs vary depending on the size and weight of the bag and where it's going, but is typically around ¥2000.

japancycling.org) have tutorials on cycling Japan and trip reports.

Hire

Many tourist areas have bicycles for hire. They may be free, as part of a local tourism initiative; otherwise private businesses, usually in the vicinity of train stations, rent them out for about ¥1000 per day. Check with the local tourist information centre for info. Many youth hostels also have bicycles to rent or borrow.

Note that the bicycles for rent are almost always what the Japanese call *mama chari* (literally 'mama's bicycles'): one- or three-speed shopping bikes that are often too small for anyone more than 180cm in height.

Buying a Bike

Prices for used bicycles range from a few thousand yen for an old shopping bike to several tens of thousands of yen for good mountain and road bikes. Prices for new bikes will likely be more than what you'd pay at home,

starting at around ¥10,000 for a shopping bike and easily rising above ¥100,000 for a flash mountain or road bike.

There's a fairly large turnover of bicycles within the expat community – especially good for tall riders. The odds are you'll find one listed in the classifieds section of magazines like Tokyo's *Metropolis* (http://metropolisjapan.com) or *Kansai Scene* (www.kansai-cene.com), or on the bulletin board of the Kyoto International Community House (www.kcif.or.jp).

Boat

Ferries are pretty much never the cheapest way to get anywhere, and are always the least time-efficient, but the boat rides themselves can be fun: long-haul ferries in Japan have communal bathhouses, dining halls and even karaoke rooms.

On overnight ferries, 2nd-class travel means sleeping in common tatami-mat

rooms on plastic mats; however, you can pay a little extra to upgrade to a dorm room (or a lot extra for a suite).

Most major ferry companies have English websites for booking tickets; otherwise book through a travel agency like JTB (www.jtb.co.jp).

Bus

Japan has a comprehensive network of long-distance buses. They're nowhere near as fast as the *shinkansen*, but a lot cheaper. Buses also travel routes that trains don't.

Japan Railways (JR) operates the largest network of highway buses in Japan; it tends to be a little pricier than other operators, but is reliable and buses tend to depart and arrive at train stations rather than bus stops elsewhere in the city. You can purchase these tickets from JR train stations.

Cheaper operators with large networks include **Willer Express** (☑from outside

SAMPLE FERRY FARES & DURATIONS

Ferry fares fluctuate by season and also by oil price and are updated every three months.

ROUTE	2ND-CLASS FARE (¥)	DURATION (HRS)
HOKKAIDŌ–HONSHŪ		
Otaru–Maizuru	9570-16,350	20
Otaru–Niigata	6480-10,180	18
Tomakomai–Hachinohe	5000	7-9
Tomakomai–Ōarai	8740-14,910	17
FROM TOKYO		
Shinmoji (Kitakyūshū)	16,110	35
Tokushima (Shikoku)	11,690	18-19½
FROM OSAKA/KŌBE		
Beppu (Kyūshū)	11,200-12,000	12
Miyazaki (Kyūshū)	9460-10,700	12½
Naha (Okinawa)	19,330	40
Shibushi (Kyūshū)	12,880-13,400	15
Shinmoji (Kitakyūshū)	6170-6480	12½
KYŪSHŪ–OKINAWA		
Kagoshima–Naha	14,610	25

Japan 050-5805-0383; http://willerexpress.com), which offers three-/four-/five-day bus passes. You can book seats on Willer and other buses through the company's Japan Bus Lines service (http://japanbuslines.com).

There are some truly bargain bus deals out there, but note that, while the government has been cracking down, cheaper operators have been known to skirt safety regulations (by overworking their drivers).

Night Services

Night buses are a good option for those on a tight budget without a Japan Rail Pass. They are relatively cheap and spacious – depending on how much you are willing to pay – and they also save on a night's accommodation. They typically leave at around 10pm or 11pm and arrive the following day at around 6am or 7am.

Car & Motorcycle

Driving in Japan is quite feasible, even for just the mildly adventurous. Most roads are signposted in English and major rental agencies offer cars with English-language navigation systems; roads are in excellent condition; road rules are generally adhered to; and petrol, while expensive, is not prohibitively so. Indeed, in some areas of the country it can prove much more convenient than other forms of travel and, between a group of people, it can also prove quite economical.

In some parts of Japan (most notably Hokkaidō, the Noto Peninsula, some parts of Kyūshū and the Southwest Islands), driving is really the only efficient way to get around unless you have a good touring bicycle or the patience for long waits for buses each time you need to make a move.

On the other hand, it makes little sense to have a car in the big cities, like Tokyo and Osaka, where traffic is thick, a preponderance of one-way streets makes navigation a challenge and parking is expensive.

Crash helmets are compulsory for motorcyclists in Japan.

Automobile Associations

If you're a member of an automobile association in your home country, you're eligible for reciprocal rights with the Japan Automobile Federation, which has an office in **Tokyo** (JAF; Map p72; ☎03-6833-9100, emergency roadside help 0570-00-8139; www.jaf.or.jp; 2-2-17 Shiba, Minato-ku; ⏰9am-5.30pm Mon-Fri; [S]Mita line to Shiba-kōen, exit A1).

Driving Licences

Travellers from most nations are able to drive (both cars and motorcycles) in Japan with an International Driving Permit backed up by their own regular licence. The International Driving Permit is issued by your national automobile association. Make sure it is endorsed for cars and motorcycles if you're licensed for both.

Travellers from Switzerland, France and Germany (and others whose countries are not signatories to the Geneva Convention of 1949 concerning international driving licences) are not allowed to drive in Japan on a regular International Driving Permit. Rather, travellers from these countries must have their own licence backed by an authorised translation of the same licence. These translations can be made by their embassy or consulate in Japan or by the JAF. If you are unsure which category your country falls into, contact the nearest JNTO office for more information.

Foreign licences and International Driving Permits are only valid in Japan for six months. If you are staying longer, you will have to get a Japanese licence from the local department of motor vehicles.

SAMPLE BUS FARES

Typical long-distance one-way fares and travel times out of Tokyo include the following. Early booking often offers discounts; prices usually rise on weekends.

DESTINATION	FARE (¥)	DURATION (HR)
Aomori	9000	9½
Hakata	9000	14½
Hiroshima	10,230	11½
Kōbe	5000	10
Kyoto	5000	8
Nagano	3200	4
Nagoya	5250	5½
Nara	5000	8½
Osaka	5000	8½

Expressways

The expressway system is fast, efficient and growing all the time, though it is not cheap.

➡ Tolls are calculated at ¥24.60 per kilometre (plus surcharges for some tunnels). Tokyo to Kyoto, for example, will cost about ¥10,500 in tolls.

➡ If you can cut and paste the characters for your starting point and destination, you can calculate fares at www. driveplaza.com. Nexco West (http://global.w-nexco. co.jp), which operates the highways in Western Honshū and Kyūshū, has fare charts in English posted online for its regions.

➡ Exits are well signposted in English, but make sure you know the name of your exit as it may not necessarily be the same as the city you're heading towards.

➡ Staffed toll booths will be marked in green with the characters 一般 (ippan) for drivers without ETC cards; automated ETC booths are marked ETC.

➡ National highway toll booths accept credit cards; others will take only cash.

ETC CARDS

With an ETC card (www.go-etc.jp/english/guidebook/index.html) you can pass through the automated toll booths at 20km/h without stopping. The cards also save money: tolls for ETC users can be up to 30% less than standard tolls (depending on the time of day and distance travelled).

Rental cars have ETC card readers and major agencies will rent the cards for a small fee; you'll be presented with a bill for your tolls when you return the car.

PASSES

Several regions offer fixed-fare expressway passes for foreign tourists. These can save money if you plan to cover a lot of ground in a short time by relying on expressways to get around; they're less useful if you prefer to take more scenic roads.

Central Nippon Expressway Pass (http://hayatabi.c-nexco. co.jp/cep)

Hokkaidō Expressway Pass (www.driveplaza.com/trip/drawari/hokkaido_expass)

Kyūshū Expressway Pass (http://global.w-nexco.co.jp/en/kep)

Tōhoku Expressway Pass (www. driveplaza.com/trip/drawari/tep2015)

Fuel

You'll find gasoreen sutando (petrol stations) in almost every town and in service stations along the express-ways. Petrol usually costs around ¥130 per litre for regular grade. Credit cards are accepted everywhere.

While self-serve petrol stations are increasing in number, full-service stations are still the most common. To say 'fill 'er up' in Japanese, it's mantan (full tank). You will likely be asked how you intend to pay: Oshiharai ha dono yō ni saremasu ka? (How would you like to pay?) The two possible answers are genkin (cash) or kaado (credit card). Full service costs slightly more, but the service is excellent: staff will empty your ashtray, take any garbage you have, wipe your windshield inside and out and then wave you back into the traffic.

Hire

➡ Typical rates for a small car are ¥5000 to ¥7000 per day, with reductions for rentals of more than one day. On top of the rental charge, there's about a ¥1000-per-day insurance cost. Prices among major agencies are comparable.

➡ Car rental agencies are clustered around transit hubs: airports, major train stations and ferry piers. Those at the major international airports (**Narita** (NRT; 成田空港; ☑0476-34-8000; www.narita-airport.jp), **Haneda** (HND; 羽田空港; ☑international terminal 03-6428-0888; www.tokyo-airport-bldg.co.jp/en), **Kansai** (KIX; 関西空港; Map p410; www.kansai-airport.or.jp) and **New Chitose** (新千歳空港; CTS; ☑0123-23-0111; www.new-chitose-airport.jp/en)) are most likely to have English-speaking staff.

➡ Toyota Rent-a-Car (https://rent.toyota.co.jp) and Nippon Rent-a-Car (www.nrgroup-global.com) have large rental networks and cars with English navigation systems. Booking in English is possible online.

➡ Japanese law requires children under the age of six to ride in a car seat; rental car agencies provide them for a small extra fee.

➡ Hiring a motorcycle for long-distance touring is not as easy as hiring a car. Rental 819 (www.rental819.com) is one of the few agencies that makes it possible to book in English.

USING CAR NAVIGATION SYSTEMS

Rental cars come equipped with satellite navigation systems that are generally very reliable; major agencies offer ones that have an English function. As Japanese addresses can be confusing, the best way to set your destination is by inputting the phone number. Many tourist organisations now also provide pamphlets with 'map codes' for major destinations, which you can input into car navigation systems.

➔ Scooter rentals are common on smaller islands; you'll still need an international licence (though not a motorcycle licence) to rent one of these.

➔ If you walk into a rental shop where the staff don't speak English, the best thing to do is first show them your international licence, as whether or not you have a valid licence will be the shop's primary concern.

Maps & Navigation

➔ Kodansha's *Japan Atlas: A Bilingual Guide* has maps labelled in English and kanji, though the road maps are not terribly detailed.

➔ The best Japanese road atlases are the *Super Mapple* series (Shōbunsha), which are available in bookshops and some convenience stores. Though lacking English, they have a high level of detail (and many routes do have numbers).

Parking

In larger cities (like Tokyo, Osaka and Kyoto) parking is expensive and largely confined to car parks where you might pay anywhere from ¥300 to ¥600 per hour; metered street parking is rare in Japan. Car parks are easy to spot, as signs sport a big 'P' on them. Most urban hotels have car parks, which can cost anywhere from ¥500 to ¥1500 per night (the larger the city, the higher the cost).

In smaller cities and in the countryside, where locals rely on cars, parking is generally plentiful and free.

Rest Stops

There are regular service areas (SA) and parking areas (PA) along national expressways; the former usually have more amenities, including restaurants, cafes and souvenir shops. Only some are open 24 hours, but even those that aren't will always have a

clean, well-lit restroom open for travellers.

Country roads have their own rest stops, called *michi-no-eki* (道の駅; road stations), which have toilets and coffee (and sometimes even local farm stands), but no petrol.

Road Rules

Driving is on the left. There are no unusual rules or interpretations of them and most signposts follow international conventions. JAF publishes a *Rules of the Road* guide (digital/print ¥864/1404) in English, which is handy.

Speed limits tend to be low, though many local drivers ignore them (at their peril: patrol cars are often lurking).

Safe Driving

Japanese drivers are generally safe and courteous, but there are a few quirks to be aware of:

Turn signals Drivers may use turn signals only after stopping at a light, entering an intersection or initiating a lane change.

Headlights Drivers can be slow to turn their lights on at dusk or in inclement weather, an issue mainly because the vast majority of cars in Japan are white, grey or black.

Hitching

Hitching is never entirely safe, and we don't recommend it. Travellers who decide to hitch should understand that they are taking a

small but potentially serious risk.

In particular, Japan can be a dangerous place for solitary female hitchhikers; there have been cases of lone female hitchers being attacked, molested and raped. People who do choose to hitch will be safer if they travel in pairs and let someone know where they are planning to go.

Provided you understand the risks and take appropriate precautions, Japan is known as a good country for hitchhiking. Many hitchhikers have tales of extraordinary kindness from motorists who have picked them up.

The rules for hitchhiking are similar to those anywhere else in the world. Dress neatly and look for a good place to hitch – expressway on-ramps and expressway service areas are probably your best bets.

Truck drivers are particularly good for long-distance travel as they often head out on the expressways at night. If a driver is exiting before your intended destination, try to get dropped off at one of the expressway service areas. The *Service Area Parking Area* (SAPA) guide maps are excellent for hitchhikers. They're available free from expressway service areas and show full details of each interchange (IC) and rest stop. These are important orientation points if you have a limited knowledge of Japanese.

IC CARDS

IC cards are prepaid travel cards with chips that work on subways, trams and buses in the Tokyo, Kansai, Sapporo, Niigata, Nagoya, Okayama, Hiroshima and Fukuoka metro areas. Each region has its own card, but they can be used interchangeably in any region where IC cards are used; however, they cannot be used for intercity travel.

The two most frequently used IC cards are Suica (www.jreast.co.jp/e/pass/suica.html) from JR East and Icoca (www.westjr.co.jp/global/en/ticket/icoca-haruka) from JR West; purchase them at JR travel counters at Narita and Haneda or Kansai airports, respectively. Cards can also be purchased and topped up from ticket vending machines in any of the cities that support them.

To use the card, simply swipe it over the reader at the ticket gates or near the doors on trams and buses.

Local Transport

Japan's larger cities are serviced by subways or trams, buses and taxis; indeed, many locals rely entirely on public transport.

Bus

Almost every Japanese city has a bus network, although, with the exception of heavily touristed areas like Tokyo and Kyoto, the stops are often announced only in Japanese. City buses often have a flat fare.

Buses can be confusing: in Tokyo you board from the front door and pay the driver upfront, either by scanning an IC card (p898) or depositing coins in the fare box, and disembark from the rear door; in Kyoto, it's the opposite.

Buses that head out of cities or traverse rural areas calculate fares based on distance. When you board (from the rear door most likely), pick up a paper ticket marked with a zone number from the dispenser; when you get off, match your zone number to the electric signboard in the front of the bus and put the posted fare and ticket into the fare box. (Or show the driver your ticket and a handful of coins and have him or her pick out the required fare; they're used to this.)

All buses have change machines near the front door that can exchange ¥100 and ¥500 coins and ¥1000 notes.

Taxi

→ Taxis are ubiquitous in big cities; they can be found in smaller cities and even on tiny islands, too, though usually just at transport hubs (train and bus stations and ferry ports) – otherwise you'll need to get someone to call one for you.

→ Transit stations and hotels have taxi stands where you are expected to queue. In the absence of a stand, you can hail a cab from the street, by standing on the curb and sticking your arm out.

→ Fares are fairly uniform throughout the country and all cabs run by the meter.

→ Flagfall (posted on the taxi windows) is around ¥600 to ¥710 for the first 2km, after which it's around ¥100 for each 350m (approximately). There's also a time charge if the speed drops below 10km/h and a 20% surcharge between 10pm and 5am.

→ A red light means the taxi is free and a green light means it's taken.

→ The driver opens and closes the doors remotely – full service indeed!

→ Drivers rarely speak English, though fortunately most taxis now have navigation systems. It's a good idea to have your destination written down in Japanese, or better yet, a business card with an address.

Subway, Train & Tram

Subway systems operate in Fukuoka, Kōbe, Kyoto, Nagoya, Osaka, Sapporo, Tokyo and Yokohama. They are usually the fastest and most convenient way to get around the city. The Tokyo metro area and Kansai metro area are further linked by a network of JR and private rail lines. Stops and line names are posted in English.

If you plan to zip around a city in a day, an unlimited-travel day ticket (called *ichi-nichi-jōsha-ken*) is a good deal; most cities offer them and they can be purchased at station windows. If you plan to spend more than a day or two, then getting a prepaid IC card is highly recommended.

Smaller cities have tram lines. These include Nagasaki, Kumamoto and Kagoshima on Kyūshū; Hiroshima on Honshū; Kōchi and Matsuyama on Shikoku; and Hakodate on Hokkaidō. These usually offer unlimited-travel day tickets.

Train

Japanese rail services are among the best in the world: they are fast, frequent, clean and comfortable.

The predominant operator is Japan Railways, commonly known as 'JR', which is actually a number of distinct rail systems providing one linked service throughout the country. JR runs the *shinkansen* (bullet train) routes. A variety of rail pass schemes make the network very affordable.

In addition to JR services, there is a huge network of private railways. Each large city usually has at least one private train line that services that city and the surrounding area, or connects that city to nearby cities. These are often a bit cheaper than equivalent JR services.

Types of Trains

Most long-haul routes run local (called *futsū* or *kaku-eki-teisha*), express (called *kyūkō* or *kaisoku*) and limited express trains (called *tokkyū*). Limited express trains have reserved seats, with comfortable reclining chairs, and toilets. All trains, save for a few *shinkansen* cars, are nonsmoking. Many different trains run on the same platforms, so be mindful of the signboards that note the schedule of departures.

Many long-haul trains have 'green car' carriages, which are akin to business class. Seats are a little more spacious and the carriages tend to be quieter and less crowded; they're also usually the last to sell out.

SHINKANSEN

Japan's *shinkansen* ('bullet trains'), which run at a maximum speed of 320km/h, operate on separate tracks from regular trains. In some places, the *shinkansen* station is a fair distance from the main JR station (as is the case in Osaka), and a transfer is required to get into the city centre.

Even the bullet train has local and express routes; however, there is no difference in fare. Luggage storage is limited to an overhead shelf, which can hold a bag similar in size to what would fit in the overhead bin on an airplane.

OVERNIGHT TRAINS

Japan used to have a number of overnight services, but these have been retired as the *shinkansen* network grows and cheap buses and flights have become more popular. As of 2016 only one remained, Sunrise Seto/ Izumo, which runs between Tokyo and Okayama before splitting in two directions – one for Takamatsu on Shikoku (Sunrise Seto; from ¥15,750) and one for Izumo (Sunrise Izumo; from ¥15,070). Trains have private

compartments and 'nobi nobi' berths (partitioned person-sized patches of carpet); the latter are free of charge for Japan Rail Pass (p901) holders, while the former require a surcharge.

Tickets can be purchased one month in advance at 10am from JR *midori-no-madoguchi* ticket counters; the 'nobi nobi' berths, in particular, sell out fast.

Ticketing

Tickets can be purchased from touch-screen vending machines in major train stations; most have an English function and those for *shinkansen* journeys often accept credit cards.

If you are booking a series of journeys, have questions or just want the reassurance of buying a ticket from a person, major JR stations have what are called *midori-no-madoguchi*, which function as JR's inhouse travel agency; these days most staff speak enough English to answer basic questions. Private line trains will have their own ticket windows.

Tickets can also be purchased from travel agencies

TRAIN LINGO

PRONUNCIATION	SCRIPT	ENGLISH
futsū	普通	local
green-sha	グリーン車	1st-class car
jiyū-seki	自由席	unreserved seat
kaisoku	快速	JR rapid or express
kaku-eki-teisha	各駅停車	local
katamichi	片道	one way
kin'en-sha	禁煙車	nonsmoking car
kitsuen-sha	喫煙車	smoking car
kyūkō	急行	ordinary express
ōfuku	往復	round trip
shin-kaisoku	新快速	JR special rapid train
shinkansen	新幹線	bullet train
shitei-seki	指定席	reserved seat
tokkyū	特急	limited express
wanman-kā	ワンマンカー	conductorless train (driver only)

in Japan, which can also often be found within train stations. Japan Travel Bureau (JTB; www.jtb.co.jp) has branches everywhere.

Reservations can only be made for limited express (*tokkyū*) liners and *shinkansen* services. There are also unreserved *shinkansen* seats; the policy on limited express trains varies by route and operator (some are all-reserved; others are not).

It is generally not necessary to make reservations in advance except on weekends and national holidays and during peak travel seasons – such as Golden Week (late April to early May), Obon (mid-August) and the New Year period.

Reserved-seat tickets can be bought any time from a month in advance to the day of departure.

ADVANCE RESERVATIONS

➜ There isn't really a system in place for making train reservations from abroad. JR East allows travellers (with or without rail passes) to make some reservations online via its website (www.jreast.co.jp/e/index.html), though many useful lines are ineligible for this service.

➜ There are online travel agencies that will buy tickets for you, but at a heavy mark-up.

➜ Note that if you have a Japan Rail Pass (p901), you will not be able to reserve through a travel agent outside Japan, as you must activate the pass in Japan and show the pass when you make reservations.

➜ If you have a firm itinerary, you can reserve all your long-haul train tickets at once

immediately upon arrrival at the nearest major JR train station.

➜ Reservations can be changed once free of charge up to the time of departure.

DISCOUNT TICKETS

Platt Kodama (www.jrtours.co.jp/kodama) This is a discounted ticket (around 20% off) for the *shinkansen* journey between Tokyo and Osaka (via Nagoya and Kyoto) on Kodama trains. These are the slowest trains on the line, which make many stops. Tickets must be purchased at least one day before departure and are nonrefundable.

Discount shops Called *kakuyasu-kippu-uriba* (格安切符売り場) or *kinken shoppu* (金券ショップ) in Japanese, these shops deal in discounted tickets for trains, buses, domestic flights, ferries and a host of other things such as cut-rate stamps and phonecards. Savings aren't dramatic, maybe 5% (or at best 10%) on *shinkansen* tickets. They're usually small kiosks plastered in signs located in the vicinity of train stations; your lodgings might know where to find one.

STUDENT DISCOUNTS

Students enrolled in Japanese universities (including foreign exchange students with a student ID issued by a Japanese university) are eligible for 20% discount vouchers for *shinkansen* and JR limited express trains and some ferries; unfortunately students enrolled in universities abroad are not able to obtain the vouchers.

Rail Passes
JR EAST RAIL PASS

JR East (www.jreast.co.jp) offers a few different rail passes that cover travel in different areas within eastern Honshū – a region that encompasses the Tokyo metro area, the Izu Peninsula, Nagano and the Japan Alps, and Tōhoku (Northern Honshū).

In addition to the routes outlined below, all of the

SAMPLE TRAIN FARES

JR fares are calculated on the basis of *futsū-unchin* (basic fare), *tokkyū-ryōkin* (an express surcharge levied only on express services) and *shinkansen-ryōkin* (a special charge for *shinkansen* services). Note that if you buy a return ticket for a trip that is more than 600km each way, you qualify for a 10% discount on the return leg (within a limited period of time).

Fares for reserved seats cost, on average, ¥520 more than unreserved seats. The rate is calculated by the distance of the journey and the time of year (more for high season, less for low season). JR Rail pass holders can reserve seats at no extra charge; however, they must pay extra for a private berth in a sleeper car.

The following are some typical fares from Tokyo (prices given for *shinkansen* are the total price of the ticket).

DESTINATION	BASIC (¥)	SHINKANSEN (¥)
Hakata	13,820	22,950
Hiroshima	11,660	19,080
Kanazawa	7340	14,120
Kyoto	8210	13,910
Morioka	8420	14,740
Nagoya	6260	10,880
Niigata	5620	10,570
Okayama	10,480	17,340
Shin-Hakodate-Hokuto	11,560	22,690
Shin-Osaka	8750	14,450
Shin-Shimonoseki	13,180	21,470

following passes cover travel on JR limited express trains between Tokyo, Nikkō, Kofu (near Mt Fuji), Shimoda (at the tip of the Izu Peninsula) and **Narita Airport** (NRT; 成田空港; ☑0476-34-8000; www.narita-airport.jp).

The Tokyo Wide Pass is the only rail pass that can be used by foreign passport holders who are not on a tourist visa (foreign residents of Japan, for example).

➡ **Nagano & Niigata Area Pass** (adult/child

JAPAN RAIL PASS

The Japan Rail Pass (www.japanrailpass.net) is a must for anyone planning to do extensive train travel within Japan; it's perfect for first-time visitors who want to zip around to see the highlights.

It covers travel on all *shinkansen* trains except for the very fastest ones: the Nozomi and Mizuho trains on the Tokaidō, San-yō and Kyūshū lines. A 'green' pass is good for rides in 1st-class 'green' train cars.

A one-way reserved-seat Tokyo–Kyoto *shinkansen* ticket costs ¥13,910, so you only need make one round trip between Tokyo and Kyoto on the *shinkansen* to make a seven-day pass come close to paying off (add a round trip between Narita Airport and Tokyo and you're already saving money).

The Japan Rail Pass *must* be purchased outside Japan. In order to get a pass, you must first purchase an 'exchange order' outside Japan at a JAL or ANA office or a major travel agency. Once you arrive in Japan, you must bring this order to a JR Travel Service Centre (in most major JR stations and at **Narita** (NRT; 成田空港; ☑0476-34-8000; www.narita-airport.jp), **Haneda** (HND; 羽田空港; ☑international terminal 03-6428-0888; www.tokyo-airport-bldg.co.jp/en) and **Kansai** (KIX; 関西空港; www.kansai-airport.or.jp) international airports. When you validate your pass, you'll have to show your passport in addition to the exchange order.

When you validate the pass, you select the date on which you want the pass to become valid. You can choose to make it valid immediately or on a later date. So, if you just plan to spend a few days in Kyoto or Tokyo before setting out to explore the country by rail, set the validity date to the day you start your journey outside the city.

Once you've validated your pass, you can make seat reservations from any *midori-no-madoguchi* ('green window' ticket counters) at JR train stations. You can also just show your pass at the ticket gates and hop on any unreserved train car (though you'd be wise to book ahead during peak travel times).

For more information on the pass and overseas purchase locations, visit the Japan Rail Pass website.

Prices

DURATION	REGULAR (ADULT/ CHILD)	GREEN (ADULT/ CHILD)
7 days	¥29,110/14,550	¥38,880/19,440
14 days	¥46,390/23,190	¥62,950/31,470
21 days	¥59,350/29,670	¥81,870/40,930

¥18,000/9000) Flexible use for five days within 14 days; covers travel on the Jōetsu Shinkansen between Tokyo and Niigata and the Hokuriku Shinkansen between Tokyo and Jōetsu-Myōkō. As these are mountain areas, this pass is good for skiers and hikers.

➡ **South Hokkaidō Rail Pass** (adult/child ¥26,000/13,000) Flexible use for six days within 14 days; covers travel on the Tōhoku and Hokkaidō *shinkansen* between Tokyo and Hakodate. While only slightly cheaper than the country-wide JR pass, the flexibility here is a bonus.

➡ **Tōhoku Area Pass** (adult/child ¥22,000/11,000) Flexible use for five days within 14 days; covers travel on the Tōhoku Shinkansen between Tokyo and Aomori (on the northern tip of Honshū) and on the Jōetsu Shinkansen between Tokyo and ski resort **Gala Yuzawa** (ガーラ湯沢; www.galaresort.jp/winter/english; day lift tickets ¥4600; ◷Dec-Apr). Good for a tour of the rustic north (and some skiing).

➡ **Tokyo Wide Pass** (adult/child ¥10,000/5000) Valid for three consecutive days for travel on the Jōetsu Shinkansen between Tokyo, Gala Yuzawa and Karuizawa. Good for sightseers with limited time.

JR CENTRAL RAIL PASSES
JR Central (http://english.jr-central.co.jp/shinkansen/value/index.html) has a few passes, the most useful of which is the **Takayama-Hokuriku Area Pass** (adult/child ¥14,000/7000). Valid for five consecutive days, it covers travel on limited express trains that link **Kansai International Airport** (KIX; 関西空港; Map p410; www.kansai-airport.or.jp), Osaka, Kyoto, Kanazawa, Takayama, Gero Onsen and Nagoya – a loop that takes in many major sights plus mountain towns and onsen.

JR WEST RAIL PASSES

JR West (www.westjr.co.jp) offers several different rail passes that cover travel in different areas within Western Honshū – a region that encompasses the Kansai metro area (Kyoto, Osaka, Kōbe and Nara), the Hokuriku area (Kanazawa and the Sea of Japan coast), the Okayama area (for Himeji and Kurashiki) and the Hiroshima area. Some also include Takamatsu (the northern gateway for Shikoku) and Hakata (the northern gateway for Kyūshū).

In addition to the routes outlined following, all Kansai area passes cover transport on JR lines to/from **Kansai International Airport** (KIX; 関西空港; Map p410; www.kansai-airport.or.jp) to Kyoto and Osaka.

Kansai Area Pass (one-/two-/three-/four-day pass ¥2200/4300/5300/6300, children half-price) Unlimited travel on all JR lines – except *shinkansen* lines – between major Kansai cities, including Himeji, Kōbe, Osaka, Kyoto and Nara. Perfect for exploring the Kansai region in depth. See www.westjr.co.jp/global/en/travel-information/pass/kansai/ for more.

Kansai Wide Area Pass (adult/child ¥8500/4250) Valid for five consecutive days; covers the same destinations as the Kansai Area Pass plus travel on the San-yō Shinkansen between Osaka and Okayama and JR limited express trains going as far as Kinosaki in the north and Shingū in the south. Good for Kansai and detours to Himeji (en route to Okayama) and the onsen of Kinosaki.

Kansai–Hiroshima Area Pass (adult/child ¥13,000/6500) Valid for five consecutive days; covers all JR limited express trains in Kansai, as well as the San-yō Shinkansen between Osaka and Hiroshima (via the castle town Himeji). Perfect for covering the highlights of Kansai and Western Honshū.

Kansai–Hokuriku Area Pass (adult/child ¥15,000/7500) Valid for seven consecutive days; covers all JR limited express trains in Kansai and Kanazawa (on the Sea of Japan coast), as well as the San-yō Shinkansen between Osaka and Okayama and the Hokuriku Shinkansen between Kanazawa and Jōetsu-Myōkō (in Niigata; good for skiing). The pass covers a good spread of well-travelled and less-travelled destinations.

Hiroshima–Yamaguchi Area Pass (adult/child ¥11,000/5500) Valid for five consecutive days; covers travel on the San-yō Shinkansen between Mihara (east of Hiroshima) and Hakata (Kyūshū), via Miyajima. Good for an in-depth journey through the

RAIL PASSES

JR Kyūshū Rail Passes

JR Kyūshū (www.jrkyushu.co.jp) offers two passes, which are good for a deep dive into this often overlooked region.

The **Northern Kyūshū Area Pass** covers travel on the Kyūshū *shinkansen* between Hakata and Kumamoto and on JR limited express trains between Nagasaki, Aso, Beppu and Yufuin. The **All Kyūshū Area Pass** covers the same area as the Northern Kyūshū Area Pass plus travel on the Kyūshū *shinkansen* all the way to Kagoshima (via Kumamoto) and limited express trains to Miyazaki and Ibusuki.

DURATION	ALL KYŪSHŪ AREA (ADULT/CHILD)	NORTHERN KYŪSHŪ AREA (ADULT/CHILD)
3 days	¥15,000/7500	¥8500/4250
5 days	¥18,000/9000	¥10,000/5000

Shikoku Rail Pass

Largely untouristed Shikoku doesn't have *shinkansen* lines, but the reasonably priced **All Shikoku Pass** (http://shiko-ku-railwaytrip.com/railpass.html) allows unlimited travel on the island's express train network, including non-JR lines and scenic trains.

DURATION	REGULAR (ADULT/CHILD)
2 days	¥7400/3700
3 days	¥8500/4250
4 days	¥9400/4700
5 days	¥10,000/5000

JR Hokkaidō Rail Pass

The **Hokkaidō Rail Pass** (www2.jrhokkaido.co.jp/global/english/railpass/rail.html) covers all JR limited express trains on Hokkaidō (but not travel on the Hokkaidō *shinkansen*). As pass holders are entitled to 30% off car rentals through JR's Ekiren agency, if you're strategic and want to cover a lot of Hokkaidō, this pass is good value.

DURATION	REGULAR (ADULT/CHILD)
3 days	¥16,500/8250
4 days flexible	¥22,000/11,000
5 days	¥22,000/11,000
7 days	¥24,000/12,000

less-explored areas of Western Honshū, and then onward travel to Kyūshū.

Hokuriku Area Pass (adult/ child ¥5000/2500) Valid for four consecutive days; covers JR limited express trains running along the Sea of Japan coast in the Hokuriku region of Central Honshū, as well as the Hokuriku Shinkansen between Kanazawa and Kurobe-Unazuki Onsen. This pass can be combined with the Kansai Area Pass for slight savings and more flexible travel times.

San-yō-San'in Area Pass (adult/ child ¥19,000/9500) Valid for seven consecutive days; covers all JR limited express trains in and around Kansai and to Takamatsu (Shikoku), as well as the San-yō Shinkansen between Osaka and Hakata in Kyushu, via Okayama and Hiroshima. If you're skipping Tokyo and points east, this pass covers a good spread for significantly less than the classic JR Pass.

KANSAI THRU PASS

The **Kansai Thru Pass** (www.surutto.com/tickets/ kansai_thru_english.html) is not a JR pass and is a good alternative to the Kansai Area Pass (p902). Good for two (adult/child ¥4000/2000) or three (adult/child ¥5200/2600) days, it covers city subways and buses and private railways that connect Kyoto, Nara, Osaka, Kōbe, Himeji and Wakayama (including Kōya-san). It also entitles you to discounts at many attractions in the Kansai area.

Purchase it at **Kansai International Airport** (KIX; 関西空港; Map p410; www. kansai-airport.or.jp) or at any tourist information centres in the Kansai area.

SEISHUN JŪHACHI KIPPU

With time, a sense of adventure and an affinity for slow travel, the **Seishun Jūhachi Kippu** (www.jreast.co.jp/e/pass/ seishun18.html) is the best deal around and can be a really fun way to see the country. It literally means 'Youth 18 Ticket' and is designed for students to travel cheaply, but there are no actual age restrictions.

For ¥11,850 you get five one-day tickets valid for travel anywhere in Japan on JR lines. The only catches are that you can't travel on *tokkyū* (limited express) or *shinkansen* trains and each ticket must be used within 24 hours.

Purchase tickets at any JR ticket counter (*midori-no-madoguchi*). As they're geared for students, travel time is limited to school holiday periods. Sale and validity periods are outlined in the following table:

SEASON	SALES PERIOD	VALIDITY PERIOD
Summer	1 Jul–31 Aug	20 Jul–10 Sep
Winter	1 Dec–31 Dec	10 Dec–10 Jan

HOKURIKU ARCH PASS

Slightly cheaper than the Japan Rail Pass (p901), the **Hokuriku Arch Pass** (adult/ child ¥24,000/12,000) is valid for seven consecutive days and covers travel on the Hokuriku Shinkansen, which connects Tokyo to Kanazawa (via Nagano) and the Sea of Japan coast, and JR limited express trains that run from Kanazawa to and around the Kansai metro area (for Kyoto, Osaka, Nara and Kōbe). Express train travel to and from **Narita** (NRT; 成田空港; ☎0476-34 8000; www. narita-airport.jp) and **Kansai** (KIX; 関西空港; Map p410; www.kansai-airport.or.jp) airports is also included (but not direct *shinkansen* travel between Tokyo and Kansai), so this pass works well if you are flying into one airport and out the other and want to do a classic itinerary in a fixed amount of time. The four-day flexible pass is valid for 10 days.

Note that these periods are subject to change, so check online for the latest information.

Schedules & Information

Japan's extensive rail network is run by multiple operators (with their own websites), which makes searching timetables a chore. Train stations will have them posted for the lines running in and out of that particular station. You can also use the website HyperDia (www.hyperdia.com) to search routes and times in English.

For enquiries relating to JR, such as schedules, fares, fastest routes, lost baggage, discounts on rail travel, hotels and car hire, contact the **JR East Infoline** (☎from inside Japan 050-2016-1603, from overseas 81-50-2016-1603; www.jreast.co.jp/e/customer_support/infoline.html; ◷10am-6pm). Information is available in English, Korean and Chinese.

Language

Japanese is spoken by more than 125 million people. While it bears some resemblance to Altaic languages such as Mongolian and Turkish and has grammatical similarities to Korean, its origins are unclear. Chinese is responsible for the existence of many Sino-Japanese words in Japanese, and for the originally Chinese kanji characters which the Japanese use in combination with the home-grown hiragana and katakana scripts.

Japanese pronunciation is easy to master for English speakers, as most of its sounds are also found in English – if you read our coloured pronunciation guides as if they were English, you'll be understood. Note though that in Japanese, it's important to make the distinction between short and long vowels, as vowel length can change the meaning of a word. The long vowels, shown in our pronunciation guides with a horizontal line on top of them (ā, ē, ī, ō, ū), should be held twice as long as the short ones. It's also important to make the distinction between single and double consonants, as this can produce a difference in meaning. Pronounce the double consonants with a slight pause between them, eg sak·ka (writer).

Note also that the vowel sound ai is pronounced as in 'aisle', air as in 'pair' and ow as in 'how'. As for the consonants, ts is pronounced as in 'hats', f sounds almost like 'fw' (with rounded lips), and r is halfway between 'r' and 'l'. All syllables in a word are pronounced fairly evenly in Japanese.

WANT MORE?

For in-depth language information and handy phrases, check out Lonely Planet's *Japanese Phrasebook*. You'll find it at **shop.lonelyplanet.com**, or you can buy Lonely Planet's iPhone phrasebooks at the Apple App Store.

BASICS

Japanese uses an array of registers of speech to reflect social and contextual hierarchy, but these can be simplified to the form most appropriate for the situation, which is what we've done in this language guide too.

Hello.	こんにちは。	kon·ni·chi·wa
Goodbye.	さようなら。	sa·yō·na·ra
Yes.	はい。	hai
No.	いいえ。	ī·e
Please. (when asking)	ください。	ku·da·sai
Please. (when offering)	どうぞ。	dō·zo
Thank you.	ありがとう。	a·ri·ga·tō
Excuse me. (to get attention)	すみません。	su·mi·ma·sen
Sorry.	ごめんなさい。	go·men·na·sai

You're welcome.
どういたしまして。　dō i·ta·shi·mash·te

How are you?
お元気ですか？　o·gen·ki des ka

Fine. And you?
はい、元気です。　hai, gen·ki des
あなたは？　a·na·ta wa

What's your name?
お名前は何ですか？　o·na·ma·e wa nan des ka

My name is ...
私の名前は　wa·ta·shi no na·ma·e wa
…です。　... des

Do you speak English?
英語が話せますか？　ē·go ga ha·na·se·mas ka

I don't understand.
わかりません。　wa·ka·ri·ma·sen

Does anyone speak English?
どなたか英語を　do·na·ta ka ē·go o
話せますか？　ha·na·se·mas ka

ACCOMMODATION

Where's a ...? …が ありますか? ... ga a·ri·mas ka

campsite	キャンプ場	kyam·pu·jō
guesthouse	民宿	min·shu·ku
hotel	ホテル	ho·te·ru
inn	旅館	ryo·kan
youth hostel	ユース ホステル	yū·su· ho·su·te·ru

Do you have a ... room? …ルームは ありますか? ...rū·mu wa a·ri·mas ka

single	シングル	shin·gu·ru
double	ダブル	da·bu·ru

How much is it per ...? …いくら ですか? ... i·ku·ra des ka

night	1泊	ip·pa·ku
person	1人	hi·to·ri

air-con	エアコン	air·kon
bathroom	風呂場	fu·ro·ba
window	窓	ma·do

DIRECTIONS

Where's the ...?
…はどこですか? ... wa do·ko des ka

Can you show me (on the map)?
(地図で)教えて くれませんか? (chi·zu de) o·shi·e·te ku·re·ma·sen ka

What's the address?
住所は何ですか? jū·sho wa nan des ka

Could you please write it down?
書いてくれませんか? kai·te ku·re·ma·sen ka

behind ...	…の後ろ	... no u·shi·ro
in front of ...	…の前	... no ma·e
near ...	…の近く	... no chi·ka·ku

next to ...	…のとなり	... no to·na·ri
opposite ...	…の 向かい側	... no mu·kai·ga·wa
straight ahead	この先	ko·no sa·ki

Turn ... …まがって ください。 ... ma·gat·te ku·da·sai

at the corner	その角を	so·no ka·do o
at the traffic lights	その信号を	so·no shin·gō o
left	左へ	hi·da·ri e
right	右へ	mi·gi e

EATING & DRINKING

I'd like to reserve a table for (two people).
(2人)の予約を お願いします。 (fu·ta·ri) no yo·ya·ku o o·ne·gai shi·mas

What would you recommend?
なにが おすすめですか? na·ni ga o·su·su·me des ka

What's in that dish?
あの料理に何 が入っていますか? a·no ryō·ri ni na·ni ga hait·te i·mas ka

Do you have any vegetarian dishes?
ベジタリアン料理 がありますか? be·ji·ta·ri·an ryō·ri ga a·ri·mas ka

I'm a vegetarian.
私は ベジタリアンです。 wa·ta·shi wa be·ji·ta·ri·an des

I'm a vegan.
私は厳格な 菜食主義者 です。 wa·ta·shi wa gen·ka·ku na sai·sho·ku·shu·gi·sha des

I don't eat ... …は 食べません。 ... wa ta·be·ma·sen

dairy products	乳製品	nyū·sē·hin
(red) meat	(赤身の) 肉	(a·ka·mi no) ni·ku
meat or dairy products	肉や 乳製品は	ni·ku ya nyū·sē·hin
pork	豚肉	bu·ta·ni·ku
seafood	シーフード 海産物	shī·fū·do/ kai·sam·bu·tsu

Is it cooked with pork lard or chicken stock?
これはラードか鶏の だしを使って いますか? ko·re wa rā·do ka to·ri no da·shi o tsu·kat·te i·mas ka

I'm allergic to (peanuts).
私は (ピーナッツ)に アレルギーが あります。 wa·ta·shi wa (pī·nat·tsu) ni a·re·ru·gī ga a·ri·mas

That was delicious!
おいしかった。 oy·shi·kat·ta

Cheers!
乾杯! kam·pai

Please bring the bill.
お勘定をください。 o·kan·jō o ku·da·sai

Key Words

appetisers	前菜	zen·sai
bottle	ビン	bin
bowl	ボール	bō·ru
breakfast	朝食	chō·sho·ku
cold	冷たい	tsu·me·ta·i
dinner	夕食	yū·sho·ku
fork	フォーク	fō·ku
glass	グラス	gu·ra·su
grocery	食料品	sho·ku·ryō·hin
hot (warm)	熱い	a·tsu·i
knife	ナイフ	nai·fu
lunch	昼食	chū·sho·ku
market	市場	i·chi·ba
menu	メニュー	me·nyū
plate	皿	sa·ra
spicy	スパイシー	spai·shī
spoon	スプーン	spūn
vegetarian	ベジタリアン	be·ji·ta·ri·an
with	いっしょに	is·sho ni
without	なしで	na·shi de

Meat & Fish

beef	牛肉	gyū·ni·ku
chicken	鶏肉	to·ri·ni·ku
duck	アヒル	a·hi·ru
eel	うなぎ	u·na·gi
fish	魚	sa·ka·na
lamb	子羊	ko·hi·tsu·ji
lobster	ロブスター	ro·bus·tā
meat	肉	ni·ku
pork	豚肉	bu·ta·ni·ku
prawn	エビ	e·bi
salmon	サケ	sa·ke
seafood	シーフード/海産物	shī·fū·do/kai·sam·bu·tsu
shrimp	小エビ	ko·e·bi
tuna	マグロ	ma·gu·ro
turkey	七面鳥	shi·chi·men·chō
veal	子牛	ko·u·shi

KEY PATTERNS

To get by in Japanese, mix and match these simple patterns with words of your choice:

When's (the next bus)?
(次のバスは) (tsu·gi no bas wa)
何時ですか? nan·ji des ka

Where's (the station)?
(駅は)どこですか? (e·ki wa) do·ko des ka

Do you have (a map)?
(地図) (chi·zu)
がありますか? ga a·ri·mas ka

Is there (a toilet)?
(トイレ) (toy·re)
がありますか? ga a·ri·mas ka

I'd like (the menu).
(メニュー) (me·nyū)
をお願いします。 o o·ne·gai shi·mas

Can I (sit here)?
(ここに座って) (ko·ko ni su·wat·te)
もいいですか? mo ī des ka

I need (a can opener).
(缶切り) (kan·ki·ri)
が必要です。 ga hi·tsu·yō des

Do I need (a visa)?
(ビザ) (bi·za)
が必要ですか? ga hi·tsu·yō des ka

I have (a reservation).
(予約)があります。 (yo·ya·ku) ga a·ri·mas

I'm (a teacher).
私は(教師) wa·ta·shi wa (kyō·shi)
です。 des

Fruit & Vegetables

apple	りんご	rin·go
banana	バナナ	ba·na·na
beans	豆	ma·me
capsicum	ピーマン	pī·man
carrot	ニンジン	nin·jin
cherry	さくらんぼ	sa·ku·ram·bo
cucumber	キュウリ	kyū·ri
fruit	果物	ku·da·mo·no
grapes	ブドウ	bu·dō
lettuce	レタス	re·tas
nut	ナッツ	nat·tsu
orange	オレンジ	o·ren·ji
peach	桃	mo·mo
peas	豆	ma·me
pineapple	パイナップル	pai·nap·pu·ru
potato	ジャガイモ	ja·ga·i·mo

QUESTION WORDS

How?	どのように？	do·no yō ni
What?	なに？	na·ni
When?	いつ？	i·tsu
Where?	どこ？	do·ko
Which?	どちら？	do·chi·ra
Who?	だれ？	da·re
Why?	なぜ？	na·ze

pumpkin	カボチャ	ka·bo·cha
spinach	ホウレンソウ	hō·ren·sō
strawberry	イチゴ	i·chi·go
tomato	トマト	to·ma·to
vegetables	野菜	ya·sai
watermelon	スイカ	su·i·ka

Other

bread	パン	pan
butter	バター	ba·tā
cheese	チーズ	chi·zu
chilli	唐辛子	tō·ga·ra·shi
egg	卵	ta·ma·go
honey	蜂蜜	ha·chi·mi·tsu
horseradish	わさび	wa·sa·bi
jam	ジャム	ja·mu
noodles	麺	men
pepper	コショウ	ko·shō
rice (cooked)	ごはん	go·han
salt	塩	shi·o
seaweed	のり	no·ri
soy sauce	しょう油	shō·yu
sugar	砂糖	sa·tō

Drinks

beer	ビール	bī·ru
coffee	コーヒー	kō·hī
(orange) juice	（オレンジ）ジュース	(o·ren·ji·)jū·su
lemonade	レモネード	re·mo·nē·do
milk	ミルク	mi·ru·ku
mineral water	ミネラルウォーター	mi·ne·ra·ru·wō·tā
red wine	赤ワイン	a·ka wain
sake	酒	sa·ke

tea	紅茶	kō·cha
water	水	mi·zu
white wine	白ワイン	shi·ro wain
yogurt	ヨーグルト	yō·gu·ru·to

EMERGENCIES

Help!
たすけて！ tas·ke·te

Go away!
離れろ！ ha·na·re·ro

I'm lost.
迷いました。 ma·yoy·mash·ta

Call the police.
警察を呼んで。 kē·sa·tsu o yon·de

Call a doctor.
医者を呼んで。 i·sha o yon·de

Where are the toilets?
トイレはどこですか？ toy·re wa do·ko des ka

I'm ill.
私は病気です。 wa·ta·shi wa byō·ki des

It hurts here.
ここが痛いです。 ko·ko ga i·tai des

I'm allergic to ...
私は…
アレルギーです。 wa·ta·shi wa ... a·re·ru·gī des

SHOPPING & SERVICES

I'd like to buy ...
…をください。 ... o ku·da·sai

I'm just looking.
見ているだけです。 mi·te i·ru da·ke des

Can I look at it?
それを見ても
いいですか？ so·re o mi·te mo ī des ka

How much is it?
いくらですか？ i·ku·ra des ka

That's too expensive.
高すぎます。 ta·ka·su·gi·mas

Can you give me a discount?
ディスカウント
できますか？ dis·kown·to de·ki·mas ka

There's a mistake in the bill.
請求書に間違いが
あります。 sē·kyū·sho ni ma·chi·gai ga a·ri·mas

ATM	ATM	ē·tī·e·mu
credit card	クレジットカード	ku·re·jit·to·kā·do
post office	郵便局	yū·bin·kyo·ku
public phone	公衆電話	kō·shū·den·wa
tourist office	観光案内所	kan·kō·an·nai·jo

TIME & DATES

What time is it?
何時ですか？ nan·ji des ka

It's (10) o'clock.
(10)時です。 (jū)·ji des

Half past (10).
(10)時半です。 (jū)·ji han des

am	午前	go·zen
pm	午後	go·go

Monday	月曜日	ge·tsu·yō·bi
Tuesday	火曜日	ka·yō·bi
Wednesday	水曜日	su·i·yō·bi
Thursday	木曜日	mo·ku·yō·bi
Friday	金曜日	kin·yō·bi
Saturday	土曜日	do·yō·bi
Sunday	日曜日	ni·chi·yō·bi

January	1月	i·chi·ga·tsu
February	2月	ni·ga·tsu
March	3月	san·ga·tsu
April	4月	shi·ga·tsu
May	5月	go·ga·tsu
June	6月	ro·ku·ga·tsu
July	7月	shi·chi·ga·tsu
August	8月	ha·chi·ga·tsu
September	9月	ku·ga·tsu
October	10月	jū·ga·tsu
November	11月	jū·i·chi·ga·tsu
December	12月	jū·ni·ga·tsu

TRANSPORT

boat	船	fu·ne
bus	バス	bas
metro	地下鉄	chi·ka·te·tsu
plane	飛行機	hi·kō·ki
train	電車	den·sha
tram	市電	shi·den

What time does it leave?
これは何時に ko·re wa nan·ji ni
出ますか？ de·mas ka

Does it stop at (...)?
(…)に (...) ni
停まりますか？ to·ma·ri·mas ka

Please tell me when we get to (...).
(…)に着いたら (...) ni tsu·i·ta·ra
教えてください。 o·shi·e·te ku·da·sai

A one-way/return ticket (to ...).
(...行きの) (...·yu·ki no)
片道/往復 ka·ta·mi·chi/ō·fu·ku
切符。 kip·pu

bus stop	バス停	bas·tē
first	始発の	shi·ha·tsu no
last	最終の	sai·shū no
ticket window	窓口	ma·do·gu·chi
timetable	時刻表	ji·ko·ku·hyō
train station	駅	e·ki

I'd like to …を借りたい ... o ka·ri·tai
hire a ... のですが。 no des ga

4WD	四駆	yon·ku
bicycle	自転車	ji·ten·sha
car	自動車	ji·dō·sha
motorbike	オートバイ	ō·to·bai

Is this the road to ...?
この道は … ko·no mi·chi wa ...
まで行きますか？ ma·de i·ki·mas ka

(How long) Can I park here?
(どのくらい)ここに (do·no·ku·rai) ko·ko ni
駐車できますか？ chū·sha de·ki·mas ka

NUMBERS

1	一	i·chi
2	二	ni
3	三	san
4	四	shi/yon
5	五	go
6	六	ro·ku
7	七	shi·chi/na·na
8	八	ha·chi
9	九	ku/kyū
10	十	jū
20	二十	ni·jū
30	三十	san·jū
40	四十	yon·jū
50	五十	go·jū
60	六十	ro·ku·jū
70	七十	na·na·jū
80	八十	ha·chi·jū
90	九十	kyū·jū
100	百	hya·ku
1000	千	sen

GLOSSARY

For lists of culinary terms, see p787; for useful words when visiting an onsen, see the box, p817; and for train terminology, see p847.

Ainu – indigenous people of Hokkaidō and parts of Northern Honshū

Amaterasu – sun goddess and link to the imperial throne

ANA – All Nippon Airways

annai-sho – information office

asa-ichi – morning market

bama – beach; see also *hama*

bashō – *sumō* tournament

bonsai – the art of growing miniature trees by careful pruning of branches and roots

bugaku – dance piece played by court orchestra in ancient Japan

buke yashiki – *samurai* residence

bunraku – classical puppet theatre which uses huge puppets to portray dramas similar to *kabuki*

Burakumin – traditionally outcasts associated with lowly occupations such as leatherwork; literally 'village people'

bushidō – a set of values followed by the *samurai*; literally 'the way of the warrior'

butsudan – Buddhist altar in Japanese homes

chō – city area (in large cities) between a *ku* and a *chōme* in size; also a street

chōchin – paper lantern

chōme – city area of a few blocks

Daibutsu – Great Buddha

daimyō – regional lord under the *shōgun*

daira – plain; see also *taira*

dake – peak; see also *take*

dani – valley; see also *tani*

danjiri – festival float

dera – temple; see also *tera*

dō – temple or hall of a temple

eki – train station

fu – prefecture; see also *ken*

fusuma – sliding screen door

futsū – local train; literally 'ordinary'

gaijin – foreigner; literally 'outside people'

gasoreen sutando – petrol station

gasshō-zukuri – an architectural style (usually thatch-roofed); literally 'hands in prayer'

gawa – river; see also *kawa*

geiko – the Kyoto word for *geisha*

geisha – woman versed in arts and drama who entertains guests; *not* a prostitute

gekijō – theatre

genkan – foyer area where shoes are removed or replaced when entering or leaving a building

geta – traditional wooden sandals

gū – shrine

gun – county

habu – a venomous snake found in Okinawa

haiku – 17-syllable poem

hama – beach; see also *bama*

hanami – blossom viewing (usually cherry blossoms)

haniwa – earthenware figure found in tombs of the Kōfun period

hantō – peninsula

hara – uncultivated field or plain

hari – dragon-boat race

hatsu-mōde – first shrine visit of the new year

henro – pilgrim on the Shikoku 88 Temple Circuit

Hikari – the second-fastest type of *shinkansen*

hiragana – phonetic syllabary used to write Japanese words

hondō – main route or main hall

honsen – main rail line

ichi-nichi-jōsha-ken – day pass for unlimited travel on bus, tram or subway systems

ikebana – art of flower arrangement

irezumi – a tattoo or the art of tattooing

irori – hearth or fireplace

izakaya – pub-style eatery

JAF – Japan Automobile Federation

JAL – Japan Airlines

ji – temple

jigoku – boiling mineral hot spring, which is definitely not for bathing in; literally 'hells'

jikokuhyō – timetable or book of timetables

jima – island; see also *shima*

jingū – shrine

jinja – shrine

jizō – small stone statue of the Buddhist protector of travellers and children

JNTO – Japan National Tourism Organization

jō – castle

JR – Japan Railways

JTB – Japan Travel Bureau

juku – after-school 'cram' school

JYHA – Japan Youth Hostel Association

kabuki – a form of Japanese theatre based on popular legends, characterised by elaborate costumes, stylised acting and the use of male actors for all roles

kaikan – hall or building

kaikyō – channel/strait

kaisoku – rapid train

kaisū-ken – a book of transport tickets

kami – Shintō gods; spirits of natural phenomena

kamikaze – typhoon that sunk Kublai Khan's 13th-century invasion fleet and the name adopted by suicide pilots in the waning days of WWII; literally 'divine wind'

kana – the two phonetic syllabaries, *hiragana* and *katakana*

kanji – Chinese ideographic script used for writing Japanese; literally 'Chinese script'

Kannon – Bodhisattva of Compassion (commonly referred to as the Buddhist Goddess of Mercy)

karaoke – bar where you sing along with taped music; literally 'empty orchestra'

katakana – phonetic syllabary used to write foreign words

katamichi – one-way transport ticket

katana – Japanese sword

kawa – river; see also *gawa*

ken – prefecture; see also *fu*

kendo – oldest martial art; literally 'the way of the sword'

ki – life force, will

kimono – brightly coloured, robe-like traditional outer garment

kin'en-sha – nonsmoking train carriage

kippu – ticket

kissaten – coffee shop

ko – lake

kō – port

kōban – police box

kōen – park

kōgen – high plain (in the mountains); plateau

kokumin-shukusha – people's lodge; an inexpensive form of accommodation

kokuritsu kōen – national park

kotatsu – heated table with a quilt or cover over it to keep the legs and lower body warm

koto – 13-stringed instrument derived from a Chinese zither that is played flat on the floor

ku – ward

kūkō – airport

kura – earth-walled storehouse

kyō – gorge

kyūkō – ordinary express train (faster than a *futsū*, only stopping at certain stations)

machi – city area (in large cities) between a *ku* and *chōme* in size; also street

machiya – traditional Japanese townhouse or merchant house

maiko – apprentice *geisha*

mama-san – woman who manages a bar or club

maneki-neko – beckoning or welcoming cat figure frequently seen in restaurants and bars; it's supposed to attract customers and trade

manga – Japanese comics

matsuri – festival

meishi – business card

midori-no-madoguchi – ticket counter in large Japan Rail stations, where you can make more complicated bookings (look for the green band across the glass)

mikoshi – portable shrine carried during festivals

minato – harbour

minshuku – the Japanese equivalent of a B&B; family-run budget accommodation

misaki – cape; see also *saki*

mon – gate

mura – village

N'EX – Narita Express

NHK – Nihon Hōsō Kyōkai (Japan Broadcasting Corporation)

Nihon – Japanese word for 'Japan'; literally 'source of the sun'; also *Nippon*

ningyō – Japanese doll

Nippon – see *Nihon*

nō – classical Japanese drama performed on a bare stage

noren – cloth hung as a sunshade, typically carrying the name of the shop or premises; indicates that a restaurant is open for business

norikae-ken – transfer ticket (trams and buses)

NTT – Nippon Telegraph & Telephone Corporation

o- – prefix used to show respect to anything it is applied to

ōfuku – return ticket

o-furo – traditional Japanese bath

OL – 'office lady'; female clerical worker; pronounced 'ō-eru'

onnagata – male actor playing a woman's role (usually in *kabuki*)

onsen – hot spring; mineral-spa area, usually with accommodation

oshibori – hot towel provided in restaurants

pachinko – popular vertical pinball game, played in *pachinko* parlours

rakugo – Japanese raconteur, stand-up comic

rettō – island group; see also *shotō*

Rinzai – school of Zen Buddhism which places an emphasis on *kōan* (riddles)

romaji – Japanese roman script

rōnin – student who must resit university entrance exam; literally 'masterless *samurai*', sometimes referred to as 'wanderer'

ropeway – Japanese word for a cable car, tramway or funicular railway

rotemburo – open-air or outdoor bath

ryokan – traditional Japanese inn

saki – cape; see also *misaki*

sakoku – Japan's period of national seclusion prior to the Meiji Restoration

sakura – cherry blossom

salaryman – male white-collar worker, usually in a large firm

sama – even more respectful suffix than *san*; used in instances such as *o-kyaku-sama* – the 'honoured guest'

samurai – warrior class

san – mountain; also suffix which shows respect to the person it is applied to

san-sō – mountain hut or cottage

sentō – public bath

seppuku – ritual suicide by disembowelment

shamisen – a three-stringed traditional Japanese instrument that resembles a banjo or lute

shi – city (used to distinguish cities from prefectures of the same name, eg Kyoto-shi)

shikki – lacquerware

shima – island; see also *jima*

shinkaisoku – express train or special rapid train (usually on JR lines)

shinkansen – super-express train, known in the West as 'bullet train'

Shintō – the indigenous religion of Japan; literally 'the way of the gods'

shirabyōshi – traditional dancer

shitamachi – traditionally the low-lying, less affluent parts of Tokyo

shodō – Japanese calligraphy; literally the 'way of writing'

shōgekijō – small theatre

shōgi – a version of chess in which each player has 20 pieces and the object is to capture the opponent's king

shōgun – former military ruler of Japan

shōgunate – military government

shōji – sliding rice-paper screen

shōjin ryōri – Buddhist vegetarian meal (served at temple lodgings etc)

shokudō – all-round restaurant

shotō – archipelago or island group; see also *rettō*

Shugendō – offbeat Buddhist school, which incorporates ancient shamanistic rites, *Shintō* beliefs and ascetic Buddhist traditions

shūji – a lesser form of *shodō*; literally 'the practice of letters'

shukubō – temple lodging

soapland – Japanese euphemism for a bathhouse offering sexual services, eg massage parlour

Sōtō – a school of Zen Buddhism which places emphasis on *zazen*

sumi-e – black-ink brush painting

sumō – Japanese wrestling

tabi – split-toed Japanese socks used when wearing *geta*

taiko – drum

taira – plain; see also *daira*

taisha – great shrine

take – peak; see also *dake*

taki – waterfall

tani – valley; see also *dani*

tanuki – racoon or dog-like folklore character frequently represented in ceramic figures

tatami – tightly woven floor matting on which shoes are never worn; traditionally, room size is defined by the number of tatami mats

teien – garden

tera – temple; see also *dera*

to – metropolis, eg Tokyo-to

tō – island

tokkyū – limited express train; faster than a *kyūkō*

tokonoma – sacred alcove in a house in which flowers may be displayed or a scroll hung

torii – entrance gate to a Shintō shrine

tōsu – lavatory

uchiwa – paper fan

ukiyo-e – woodblock print; literally 'pictures of the floating world'

wa – harmony, team spirit; also the old *kanji* used to denote Japan, and still used in Chinese and Japanese as a prefix to indicate things of Japanese origin, eg *wafuku* (Japanese-style clothing)

wabi – enjoyment of peace and tranquillity

wan – bay

washi – Japanese handmade paper

yabusame – samurai-style horseback archery

yakimono – pottery or ceramic ware

yakuza – Japanese mafia

yama – mountain; see also *zan*

yamabushi – mountain priest (Shugendō Buddhism practitioner)

yama-goya – mountain hut

yamato – a term of much debated origins that refers to the Japanese world

yamato-e – traditional Japanese painting

yatai – festival float; hawker stall

yukata – light cotton summer *kimono*, worn for lounging or casual use; standard issue when staying at a *ryokan*

zaibatsu – industrial conglomerate; the term arose pre-WWII but the Japanese economy is still dominated by huge firms such as Mitsui, Marubeni and Mitsubishi, which are involved in many different industries

zaki – cape

zan – mountain; see also *yama*

zazen – seated meditation emphasised in the Sōtō school of Zen Buddhism

Zen – an offshoot of Buddhism, introduced to Japan in the 12th century from China, that emphasises a direct, intuitive approach to enlightenment rather than rational analysis

Behind the Scenes

SEND US YOUR FEEDBACK

We love to hear from travellers – your comments keep us on our toes and help make our books better. Our well-travelled team reads every word on what you loved or loathed about this book. Although we cannot reply individually to your submissions, we always guarantee that your feedback goes straight to the appropriate authors, in time for the next edition. Each person who sends us information is thanked in the next edition – the most useful submissions are rewarded with a selection of digital PDF chapters.

Visit **lonelyplanet.com/contact** to submit your updates and suggestions or to ask for help. Our award-winning website also features inspirational travel stories, news and discussions.

Note: We may edit, reproduce and incorporate your comments in Lonely Planet products such as guidebooks, websites and digital products, so let us know if you don't want your comments reproduced or your name acknowledged. For a copy of our privacy policy visit lonelyplanet.com/privacy.

OUR READERS

Many thanks to the travellers who used the last edition and wrote to us with helpful hints, useful advice and interesting anecdotes:

Alberto Escribano, Alvin Hudec, Amandine Favier, Carlos Mendez, Christoph Ris, Connie Nakamura, Damping Wang, David Lee, Emma Dhesi, Eric Lauryn, Florence Petrie , Gertjan Martens, Harumi Murata, Jade Johnston, James Martin, John Osman, Kaomi Goetz , Kevin Bruce, Kirsten Kinkead, Lisa Nolan, Lucy & Stuart Stirland, Madoka Aoyama, Marie Armstrong, Marina Ramos, Marjolein Stegeman, Mark Chesney, Megumi Takamori, Michael Jahn, Miriam Vázquez, Niall Christie, Robin Kish, Sarah Dhesi, Tim Glover, Tristram Wyatt, Yasutaka Hori, Yuko Kobayashi

WRITER THANKS

Rebecca Milner

Thank you to everyone on the Japan team. Laura, thank you for giving me so many opportunities. Simon and Craig, thank you for your advice. Thank you to Ross, Tomoko, Roberto, Nara-san, Kokubu-san, Watanabe-san, Will, Max, Jon, Andy and Shannon for your time, tips, conversation and company. Thank you to my husband and family for always encouraging me, even if it means long absences.

Ray Bartlett

No-one deserves thanks more than my family, who dealt with me disappearing and supported every aspect of this project. You're amazing. Thanks also to my editor, Laura C, and other great folks at Lonely Planet. Shouts to James T, Mia Y, Adeline R, Toru-san, Deea, Jamie, Miki H, Memory-san, Noriko-san, Satoko-san, and countless others who went the extra mile to make sure I could represent this amazing part of Japan in the best possible way.

Andrew Bender

Special thanks to Yohko Scott, Matsuura Kei, Rose Tanasugarn, Urakami Masahiro, Taniguchi Takehiro, Noro Randria, Colin Fukai, Hiraoka Hiroko, Hayashi Minako, Akagi Hideki, Hattori Katsuhiko, Brad Towle, Tabata Kumiko and every innkeeper, restaurant owner and tourist information office staffer who put up with my niggling questions. You are the essence of *omotenashi*.

Craig McLachlan

A hearty thanks to all those who helped out on the road, but most of all, to my living kanji dictionary and exceptionally beautiful wife, Yuriko. Gratitude also to Nezia, who let her husband and my buddy, Paul, come along for his Shikoku pilgrimage. And of course, thanks to Kōbō Daishi, who looked over us on our journey.

Kate Morgan

A huge thank you to Destination Editor Laura, for giving me the opportunity to work on a dream gig and for all of your assistance throughout. A big *arigatou gozaimasu* to Kengo Nakao from the Kyoto Tourist Information office for all of your help, also to

Keiji Shimizu for your assistance and Motoki Ito for some great local tips. And finally, to my partner, Trent, who I missed travelling with on this trip, thanks for all of your support.

Simon Richmond

My thanks to Hollie Mantle, Will Andrews, Yoshizawa Tomoko, Toshiko, Kenichi, Chris, Giles, Steve and Emiko, and my co-author Rebecca.

Tom Spurling

To the *yamasbushi* who walk the mountains of Tohoku, for carrying on. To every fellow onsen bather, for the bum flash in the woods. To every ryokan operator, for sweeping those tatamis clean. To the shinkansen, for the green car. To the not-so-shinkansen, for winding me through gorgeous valleys. To the *tachinomi*, for letting me stand up and drink to this wonderful country. Oh, and to Mum, Lucy, Oliver, Poppy, Anna, Tez, Mia, Evie, Lex, Fred. And to Dad for not coming.

Phillip Tang

Massive thanks to Xavier 邹嘉 for sky-high views, rainbows, weddings, and luggage offloading. Thanks 郝成义 for making Fukuyama and Miyajima come alive. Thank you Eric Mikuski, Ayako Noguchi and Nic Williamson for soul-enrichment, and Dale Stein for Okayama tips. I'm ever-grateful to the tourism-office angels, and to Laura Crawford for sharing Western Honshū again.

Benedict Walker

This is for Aunty Bonnie, who gave me my first LP guide (Japan) when I was just a boy, and who waited until I returned from this research, for one last goodbye. Thanks to her oncologist, Dr. Sanjiv Gupta and to Mum, Collywolly and Meg, for your unfaltering care; to Michelle and Saralinda (my editors), for your patience and to Laura Crawford, whose kindness and trust allowed me to always be in the right place at the right time. Finally, thanks to my friends on the road: Grahame Roth, Kaori and Takashi Shimizu, Taku Yamada and Yuko Yasuoka. Love all round.

Wendy Yanagihara

Many thanks to those who offered me insight, context and companionship, especially Tsuchiya Keiko, Yokoyama Ikuyo and Shin in Shimoda, Karina and Oscar in Toi, Ezaki Sachiyo and Junta in Amami, Endo Satoko in Nikkō, Utsumi Shino in Matsuzaki, Michael and Doug in Fuji-Yoshida, Toita Yoshiyuki and Yun Yongdu in Ishigaki and Ogata-san in Yokohama. Thank you Laura, Rebecca, and Imogen for being such delights to work with. Love to my incredible support system: Sanchita, Whitney, Victoria, Jason and Jasper.

ACKNOWLEDGEMENTS

Climate map data adapted from Peel MC, Finlayson BL & McMahon TA (2007) 'Updated World Map of the Köppen-Geiger Climate Classification', Hydrology and Earth System Sciences, 11, 163344.

Illustrations pp98-9 and pp396-7 by Michael Weldon.

Cover photograph: Red-blossomed plum tree, Kyoto, Masanori Shimizu/500px ©

THIS BOOK

This 15th edition of Lonely Planet's *Japan* guidebook was researched and written by Rebecca Milner, Ray Bartlett, Andrew Bender, Craig McLachlan, Kate Morgan, Simon Richmond, Tom Spurling, Phillip Tang, Benedict Walker and Wendy Yanagihara. This guidebook was produced by the following:

Destination Editor Laura Crawford
Product Editor Sandie Kestell
Senior Cartographer Diana von Holdt
Assisting Cartographers Julie Dodkins, Rachel Imeson, Gabe Lindquist, Alison Lyall
Book Designer Gwen Cotter
Assisting Editors Imogen Bannister, Michelle Bennett, Pete Cruttenden, Gabrielle Innes, Helen Koehne, Kristin Odijk, Monique Perrin, Gabrielle Stefanos, Saralinda Turner, Maja Vatrić, Simon Williamson
Cover Researcher Naomi Parker
Thanks to Naoko Akamatsu, Heather Champion, Kate Chapman, Katie Connelly, Joel Cotterell, Victoria Harrison, Liz Heynes, Indra Kilfoyle, Genna Patterson, Kathryn Rowan, Jessica Ryan, Dianne Schallmeiner, Angela Tinson

BEHIND THE SCENES

Index

Map Pages **000**
Photo Pages **000**

Map Legend

Sights
- Beach
- Bird Sanctuary
- Buddhist
- Castle/Palace
- Christian
- Confucian
- Hindu
- Islamic
- Jain
- Jewish
- Monument
- Museum/Gallery/Historic Building
- Ruin
- Shinto
- Sikh
- Taoist
- Winery/Vineyard
- Zoo/Wildlife Sanctuary
- Other Sight

Activities, Courses & Tours
- Bodysurfing
- Diving
- Canoeing/Kayaking
- Course/Tour
- Sento Hot Baths/Onsen
- Skiing
- Snorkelling
- Surfing
- Swimming/Pool
- Walking
- Windsurfing
- Other Activity

Sleeping
- Sleeping
- Camping

Eating
- Eating

Drinking & Nightlife
- Drinking & Nightlife
- Cafe

Entertainment
- Entertainment

Shopping
- Shopping

Information
- Bank
- Embassy/Consulate
- Hospital/Medical
- Internet
- Police
- Post Office
- Telephone
- Toilet
- Tourist Information
- Other Information

Geographic
- Beach
- Gate
- Hut/Shelter
- Lighthouse
- Lookout
- Mountain/Volcano
- Oasis
- Park
- Pass
- Picnic Area
- Waterfall

Population
- Capital (National)
- Capital (State/Province)
- City/Large Town
- Town/Village

Transport
- Airport
- Border crossing
- Bus
- Cable car/Funicular
- Cycling
- Ferry
- Metro/MTR/MRT station
- Monorail
- Parking
- Petrol station
- Skytrain/Subway station
- Taxi
- Train station/Railway
- Tram
- Underground station
- Other Transport

Note: Not all symbols displayed above appear on the maps in this book

Routes
- Tollway
- Freeway
- Primary
- Secondary
- Tertiary
- Lane
- Unsealed road
- Road under construction
- Plaza/Mall
- Steps
- Tunnel
- Pedestrian overpass
- Walking Tour
- Walking Tour detour
- Path/Walking Trail

Boundaries
- International
- State/Province
- Disputed
- Regional/Suburb
- Marine Park
- Cliff
- Wall

Hydrography
- River, Creek
- Intermittent River
- Canal
- Water
- Dry/Salt/Intermittent Lake
- Reef

Areas
- Airport/Runway
- Beach/Desert
- Cemetery (Christian)
- Cemetery (Other)
- Glacier
- Mudflat
- Park/Forest
- Sight (Building)
- Sportsground
- Swamp/Mangrove

Kate Morgan

Kyoto Having worked for Lonely Planet for over a decade now, Kate has been fortunate enough to cover plenty of ground working as a travel writer on destinations such as Shanghai, Japan, India, Zimbabwe, the Philippines and Phuket. She has done stints living in London, Paris and Osaka but these days is based in one of her favourite regions in the world – Victoria, Australia. In between travelling the world and writing about it, Kate enjoys spending time at home working as a freelance editor.

Simon Richmond

Tokyo Journalist and photographer Simon Richmond has specialised as a travel writer since the early 1990s and first worked for Lonely Planet in 1999 on their *Central Asia* guide. He's long since stopped counting the number of guidebooks he's researched and written for the company, but countries covered including Australia, China, India, Iran, Japan, Korea, Malaysia, Mongolia, Myanmar (Burma), Russia, Singapore, South Africa and Turkey. For Lonely Planet's website he's penned features on topics from the world's best swimming pools to the joys of Urban Sketching - follow him on Instagram to see some of his photos and sketches.

Tom Spurling

Northern Honshū Tom Spurling is an Australian travel writer and high school teacher who has worked on 13 travel guides for Lonely Planet. His titles include *Australia, Turkey, Central America, China, India* and *South Africa*. On his second Japan guide he covered the mythical northeast where the wild things roam but the shinkansen Green Car still runs. He is looking forward to returning in winter to attempt to ski where he once trod.

Phillip Tang

Hiroshima & Around, Okayama & Around Phillip Tang grew up on typically Australian pho and fish'n'chips. A degree in Chinese- and Latin-American cultures launched him into travel and writing about it for Lonely Planet's *Canada, China, Japan, Korea, Mexico, Peru* and *Vietnam* guides. More pics and words: philliptang.co.uk. Phillip has made his home in Sydney, Melbourne, London and Mexico City. His travels include most countries in Europe, much of Asia and Latin America, as well as the greatest hits of North America.

Benedict Walker

The Japan Alps & Central Honshū, Matsue & Around, Tottori & Around, Yamaguchi & Around Born in Newcastle, Australia, notions of the beach are core to Ben's idea of self, having travelled hundreds of thousands of kilometres from the sandy shores of home. Ben was given his first Lonely Planet guide (*Japan*) when he was 12. Two decades later, he'd write chapters for the same publication: a dream come true. A communications graduate and travel agent by trade, Ben whittled away his twenties gallivanting around the globe. He speaks fluent Japanese and has contributed to LP's Japan guide, twice. Ben thinks the best thing about travel isn't as much about where you go as who you meet: living vicariously through the stories of kind strangers enriches one's own experience. Ben has also written and directed a play, toured Australia managing the travel logistics for top-billing music festivals and is experimenting with a return to his original craft of photography and film-making.

Wendy Yanagihara

Around Tokyo, Okinawa & the Southwest Islands Wendy serendipitously landed her dream job of writing for Lonely Planet in 2003, and has since spent the intervening years contributing to titles including *Southeast Asia on a Shoestring, Vietnam, Japan, Mexico, Costa Rica, Indonesia,* and *Grand Canyon National Park*. In the name of research, she has hiked remote valleys of West Papua, explored the tiny nooks and alleys of Tokyo sprawl, trekked on a Patagonian glacier, and rafted Colorado River whitewater. Wendy has also written for BBC Travel, the *Guardian, Lonely Planet Magazine*, lonelyplanet.com, and intermittently freelances as a graphic designer, illustrator, and visual artist. Instagram: @wendyyanagihara

OUR STORY

A beat-up old car, a few dollars in the pocket and a sense of adventure. In 1972 that's all Tony and Maureen Wheeler needed for the trip of a lifetime – across Europe and Asia overland to Australia. It took several months, and at the end – broke but inspired – they sat at their kitchen table writing and stapling together their first travel guide, *Across Asia on the Cheap*. Within a week they'd sold 1500 copies. Lonely Planet was born.

Today, Lonely Planet has offices in Franklin, London, Melbourne, Oakland, Dublin, Beijing and Delhi, with more than 600 staff and writers. We share Tony's belief that 'a great guidebook should do three things: inform, educate and amuse'.

OUR WRITERS

Rebecca Milner

Curator, Tokyo, Hokkaido, Osaka California born. Longtime Tokyo resident (14 years and counting!). Co-author of Lonely Planet guides to Tokyo, Japan, Korea and China. Freelance writer covering travel, food & culture. Published in the *Guardian*, the *Independent*, the *Sunday Times Travel Magazine*, the *Japan Times* and more. After spending the better part of my twenties working to travel – doing odd jobs in Tokyo to make money so I could spend months at a time backpacking around Asia – I was fortunate enough to turn the tables in 2010, joining the Lonely Planet team of freelance authors.

Ray Bartlett

Kyushu Ray Bartlett has been travel writing for nearly two decades, bringing Japan, Korea, Mexico and many parts of the United States to life in rich detail for top-industry publishers, newspapers and magazines. His acclaimed debut novel, *Sunsets of Tulum*, was a *Midwest Book Review 2016* Fiction pick. Among other pursuits, he surfs regularly and is an accomplished Argentine tango dancer. Follow him on Facebook, Twitter, Instagram, or contact him for questions or motivational speaking opportunities via www.kaisora.com, his website. Ray Bartlett currently divides his time between homes in the USA, Japan and Mexico.

Andrew Bender

Kansai Andrew is a native New Englander who worked in the financial industry in Tokyo and the film industry in Los Angeles before setting out to pursue his dream of travelling and writing about it. He has since authored more than three dozen LP titles as varied as Japan, Korea, Taiwan, Norway, Amsterdam, Germany and his current home of Southern California. He also writes the Seat 1A travel site for Forbes.com, and contributes to the *Los Angeles Times* and airline magazines. Catch his work at www.wheres-andy-now.com.

Craig McLachlan

Hiking in Japan, Skiing in Japan, Shikoku Craig has covered destinations all over the globe for Lonely Planet for two decades. Based in Queenstown, New Zealand, for half the year, he runs an outdoor activities company and a sake brewery, then moonlights overseas for the other half, leading tours and writing for Lonely Planet. Describing himself as a 'freelance anything', Craig has an MBA from the University of Hawai'i and is also a Japanese interpreter, pilot, photographer, hiking guide, tour leader, karate instructor and budding novelist. Check out www.craigmclachlan.com.

OVER PAGE | MORE WRITERS

Published by Lonely Planet Global Limited

CRN 554153
15th edition – Aug 2017
ISBN 978 1 78657 035 2
© Lonely Planet 2017   Photographs © as indicated 2017
10 9 8 7 6 5 4 3 2 1
Printed in Singapore